VISUAL QUICKPRO GUIDE

DVD Studio Pro 3

FOR MAC OS X

Martin Sitter

Peachpit Press

Visual QuickPro Guide

DVD Studio Pro 3 for Mac OS X

Martin Sitter

Peachpit Press

1249 Eighth Street
Berkeley, CA 94710
510/524-2178
800/283-9444
510/524-2221 (fax)
Find us on the World Wide Web at: http://www.peachpit.com
To report errors, please send a note to errata@peachpit.com
Peachpit Press is a division of Pearson Education

Editor: Judy Ziajka
Production Coordinator: Andrei Pasternak
Compositor: Jerry Ballew
Indexer: James Minkin
Cover Design: The Visual Group
Cover Production: George Mattingly/GMD

Photo Credits

All photos featuring chairs are courtesy of Sli-fi Media, Inc., which can be found online at www.sli-fi.com. The chairs themselves come from Microsphere, available on the Web at www.microsphere.com.

ISBN 0-321-26789-3

9 8 7 6 5 4 3 2 1

Printed and bound in the United States of America

Dedication

This book is dedicated to all the people who go forth and review it on Amazon.com! Good or bad, POST YOUR REVIEW!

The Amazon.com customer review is open to everyone, not just Amazon.com purchasers. It is there to let all book buyers know how you feel about a book, so tell them! It's also there to let the *author* know how you feel about the book, so tell *me*.

Acknowledgments

First and foremost, thank you Marjorie Baer for endless patience and perfect guidance.

I'd also like to thank my friends on the Apple DVD Studio Pro Discussion forum for their tireless support of the newcomers to our community. In particular, I'd like to thank Chris Vargas, Hal MacLean, Bob Hudson, and jAY-R…my heroes!

Thanks also to Patty Montesion, Brian Schmidt, Don Steele, Margaret Tinsley, Phil Jackson, Jessica Steigerwald, Bill Forester, Vidas Neverauskas, David Dvorin, Victor Alexander, and all of my other friends at Apple.

Last, but not least, my deepest thanks goes to all of my readers for continuing to support my books. They are a labor of love.

TABLE OF CONTENTS

Introduction xi

PART I: GETTING READY 1

Chapter 1: Before You Begin 3
Choosing a Platform 4
Expanding Your System 7
Optimizing Your Hard Disk 12
Installing DVD Studio Pro 14
Exploring Software Extras 15

Chapter 2: DVD 101 19
DVD versus CD 20
About DVD Formats 24
Editing in DVD Studio Pro 27
About DVD Studio Pro Workflow 30
About the DVD-Video Data Structure 31

Chapter 3: Preparing Graphics 33
Preparing Source Video 34
Preparing Still Graphics 40

Chapter 4: The QuickTime MPEG-2 Exporter 53
About MPEG Video 54
About MPEG-2 Compression 55
About the QuickTime MPEG-2 Exporter 60
Opening the QuickTime MPEG-2 Exporter 62
Choosing a Video System 65
About Timecode 66
Choosing an Aspect Ratio 69
Setting the Field Order 70
Saving the Audio Track 71
Creating a Log File 72
Creating Parse Files 73
Setting Encoding Quality 74

Setting Motion Estimation 77
About the Progress Window 78
Exporting MPEG-2 Streams from Final Cut Pro . . 79

Chapter 5: Using Compressor 81
Encoding a File 82
Creating Presets 92
Previewing Compression 96
Creating a Droplet 98

Chapter 6: Using A.Pack 101
About Source Audio Streams 102
Converting Audio Formats 104
About AC-3 Audio 107
About A.Pack 108
Launching A.Pack 110
Encoding AC-3 Audio 111
Using Audio Coding Modes 114
Assigning Input Channels 117
Choosing a Bit Rate 119
Using Dialog Normalization 120
Determining an Audio Stream's DNV 121
About Dynamic Range Control 123
Using Compression Profiles 124
About Downmixing 125
About Other AC-3 Settings 127
Auditioning AC-3 Files 131
Using a Third-Party Audio Interface 133
About Batch Lists 134

PART II: DVD STUDIO PRO 137

Chapter 7: Touring the Workspace 141
Launching DVD Studio Pro 142
Exploring the DVD Studio Pro Workspace 145
Using Window Configurations 148
Using the Toolbar 156
Using the Inspector 159
Using the Palette 160

Chapter 8: Viewing Your Project 167
About the Outline and Graphical Views 168
Exploring the Outline View 169
Exploring the Graphical View 171
Zooming the Graphical View 172

Flagging an Item 174
Using the Macro View 175
Laying Out Tiles 177
Setting a First Play Item 178

Chapter 9: Exploring the Assets Tab 179
About the Assets Tab 180
About Assets 181
Managing Assets 183
Working with Columns 186
Relinking Assets 189
Previewing Assets 190

Chapter 10: Importing Assets 193
Importing Assets 194
Importing QuickTime Movies 198

Chapter 11: Using Tracks 209
About the Track Editor 210
Creating Tracks 212
Changing Track Order in the Outline View 219
Setting Jump Actions 221
Adding Clips to Streams 223
Using Timecode in the Track Editor 227
Positioning the Playhead 231
Zooming in the Timeline 233
Working with Streams in the Track Editor 237
Editing Video and Audio Clips 241
Viewing Tracks 247

Chapter 12: Enhancing Tracks 251
About Markers 252
Using Markers and I-frames 253
Using Marker Snapping 256
Fixing Invalid Markers 257
Viewing Markers 258
Naming Markers 259
Moving Markers 262
Specifying the Marker Type 265
Setting a Marker's End Jump 269
Using Marker Playback Settings 270
Adding Markers with Final Cut Pro 272
Importing Markers into DVD Studio Pro 276
About Stories 280
About Alternate Angles 287
Multi-Angle versus Mixed-Angle Tracks 290

Chapter 13: The Menu Editor 295

Creating Menus ... 296
Exploring the Menu Editor ... 301
Adding Backgrounds ... 302
Adding Menu Buttons ... 307
Setting Button Targets ... 313
Setting a Menu Timeout Action ... 316
About Menus and the Remote Control ... 318
Using Rulers and Guides ... 322
Using Dynamic Guides ... 327
Using Alignment Modes ... 328
Using Distribution Modes ... 329

Chapter 14: Layered Menus 331

Designing Layered Menus ... 332
Working with Layers in Photoshop ... 333
Using Layered Menus in DVD Studio Pro ... 337
Previewing Button States ... 343

Chapter 15: Overlay Menus 345

Creating Overlay Menus ... 346
Creating a Simple Overlay Menu ... 354
Creating an Advanced Overlay Menu ... 359
Choosing Highlight Sets ... 365
Adding Audio to Menus ... 367
Using the At End Setting ... 369
Using Button Highlight Markers ... 373
Working with Text ... 377
Styling Text ... 381
Creating Drop Shadows ... 385

Chapter 16: Using Transitions 387

Using Transitions ... 388
Adding Track Transitions ... 390
Adding Slideshow Transitions ... 392
Adding Menu Transitions ... 395
Using a Video Clip as a Transition ... 397

Chapter 17: Templates, Styles, and Shapes 399

About Templates ... 400
Using Templates ... 403
Creating Custom Templates ... 408
Importing iDVD Themes ... 413
About Styles ... 415
Using Styles ... 416
Creating Custom Styles ... 420
Linking Styles to Templates ... 423

About Shapes 426
Using Shapes 427
Creating Custom Shapes 429
Importing Custom Shapes 440
Updating Custom Shapes 443

Chapter 18: Slideshows 445
About Slideshows 446
Setting Slideshow Preferences 449
Using the Slideshow Editor 451
Adding Audio Streams 455
Converting Slideshows to Tracks 458
Setting Slideshow End Jumps 459
Previewing Slideshows 460

Chapter 19: Finishing the DVD 461
Setting the First Play Action 462
Assigning Remote-Control Buttons 464
Using the Connections Tab 469
Creating Hybrid DVDs 479
Protecting Your Content 481
Simulating the Project 486
About Item Description Files 491
Embedding Text 493
Using Jacket Pictures 494

Chapter 20: Outputting the Project 495
Exporting the Project 496
Building the Project 497
Using Apple's DVD Player 502
Building and Formatting 503
Making Multiple Copies 512
Using Toast 6 Titanium 515
Outputting to DLT 521
Creating DVD-9 Projects 524
Reading a DLT Tape 527

PART III: ADVANCED DVD AUTHORING 529

Chapter 21: DVD@ccess 531
About DVD@ccess 532
Installing DVD@ccess on Windows PCs 534
Enabling DVD@ccess on the Macintosh 536
Using DVD@ccess 537
Linking to Buttons 541
Linking to the Disc 548
Simulating DVD@ccess 549

Chapter 22: Widescreen: 16:9 551
About Widescreen Video ... 552
Using DVD Studio Pro's Embedded Encoder ... 553
Using the QuickTime MPEG-2 Exporter ... 555
About Anamorphic Video ... 558
Playing Widescreen Tracks on 4:3 TVs ... 560
Creating 16:9 Menus ... 565
Simulating 16:9 Projects ... 568

Chapter 23: Working with Languages 569
About Multilingual DVDs ... 570
Working with Multiple-Language Menus ... 572
Working with Multilingual Tracks ... 578
Previewing Multiple-Language Projects ... 583

Chapter 24: Subtitles 587
About the Subtitle Editor ... 588
Setting Subtitle Text Preferences ... 589
Creating Subtitles ... 592
Editing Subtitles ... 594
Formatting Subtitle Text ... 596
Positioning Subtitles ... 597
Changing Subtitle Duration ... 600
Using Fades ... 603
Using Color ... 605
Forcing Subtitle Display ... 611
Simulating Subtitles ... 612
Creating Text Subtitles ... 615
Importing Text Subtitles ... 618
Using Subtitle Graphics ... 620
Adding Closed Captions ... 623

Chapter 25: Scripting 627
Creating a Script ... 628
Using the Script Editor ... 630
Using Prescripts ... 633
Programming Commands ... 635
Using Parameter Registers ... 639
Using a Compare Command ... 646
Troubleshooting Scripts ... 647

Appendix A: Surviving on a Bit Budget 649
Making a Bit Budget ... 650

Appendix B: Online Resources 657

Index 659

INTRODUCTION

In 1996, desktop audio experienced a revolution powered by three key events. Computer processors sped past the 100 MHz mark, making real-time multitrack recording possible for the first time. Stock hard disks expanded to hold gigabytes instead of megabytes, providing room enough to store huge digital audio files. And most important, with the introduction of the CD-R, it finally become possible to economically mix, master, and *deliver* audio recordings produced entirely on the humble desktop computer.

Eight years later, the same revolution that swept desktop audio has hit desktop video. With processors surpassing the 2.5 GHz mark, real-time video is at long last a reality. Sporting vastly expanded storage capacities, hard disks can hold hours of high-bandwidth DV footage on a single drive. And like the CD-R, the DVD-R provides a reliable and inexpensive means of delivery. As consumer DV cameras continue to drop in price, the filmmaking industry is teetering on the brink of changing how it does business—forever.

The CD-R let us share music with anyone who had a CD player, and in a similar fashion, the DVD-R now lets us share video with anyone who has a television and a DVD-Video player. But producing a DVD is not quite as easy as creating a song. Unlike DVD-Video, audio recordings aren't interactive. To create an interactive video, you need a program that takes separate bits of media (menu graphics, video, audio, and subtitle streams) and assembles them into an intuitive, interactive project that can be played on a TV. Regardless of platform, the program that does this best, without a doubt, is DVD Studio Pro 3.

About the Author

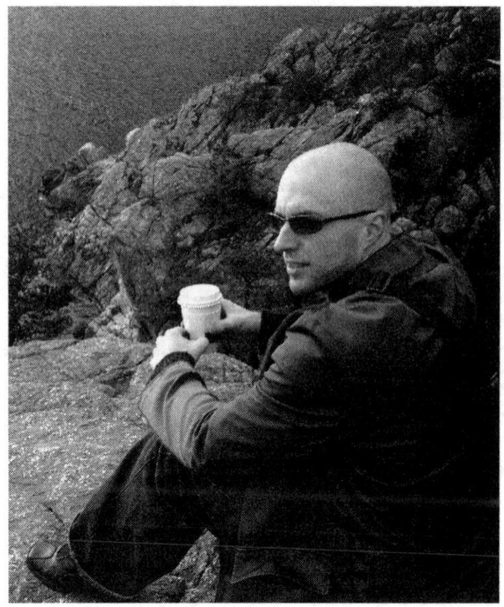

Figure i.1 Martin contemplates DVD authoring while enjoying a coffee near his home in Vancouver.

Martin Sitter (**Figure i.1**) is the director of the online video training site, macProVideo.com and an experienced Peachpit Press author who has written or contributed to over eight books on digital audio/video design.

After producing electronic music albums (house/tech house) for record labels including Peng Records UK and Phatt Phunk Records LA, Martin went on to embrace interactive video design. His first book was about an at-the-time little-known interactive QuickTime authoring tool named LiveStage Professional (for Peachpit Press's Visual QuickStart series). Since then, Martin has written the previous and current versions of the book you're holding. He is also the author of *Apple Pro Training Series: DVD Studio Pro 3* and *Apple Pro Training Series: Logic 6* and a contributing author to *Apple Pro Training Series: Advanced Editing and Finishing Techniques in Final Cut Pro 4*.

When not writing or producing DVD-Videos, Martin is a lead instructor for Apple, teaching DVD Studio Pro and Logic Platinum to audio/video educators and enthusiasts across North America. To learn more about the Apple Pro training and certification program, visit `www.apple.com/software/pro/training/`.

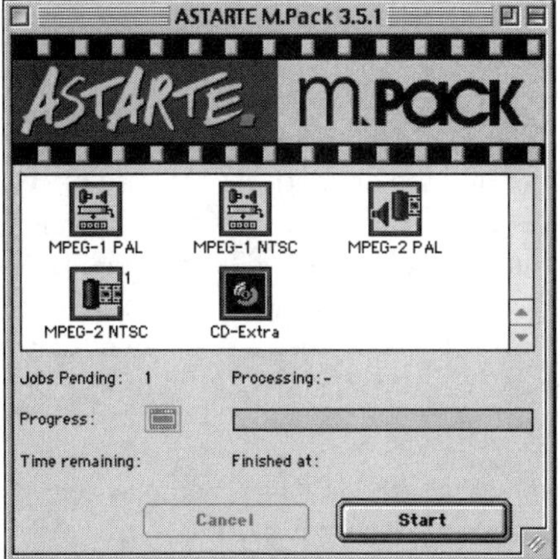

Figure i.2 Astarte's M.Pack—a great MPEG-2 encoding program, and one of the few software-only encoders that works on a G3 Macintosh.

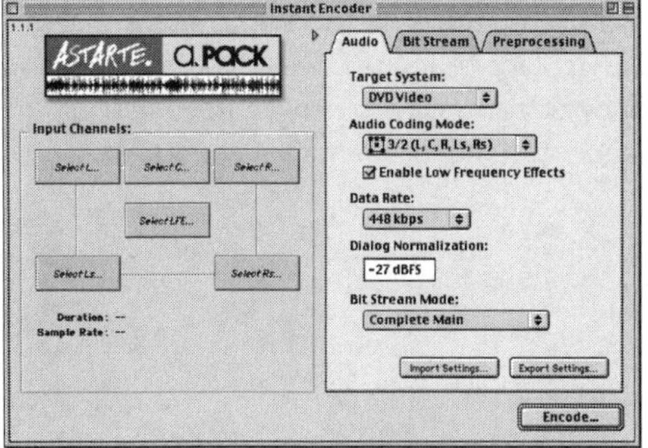

Figure i.3 Astarte's A.Pack—look familiar?

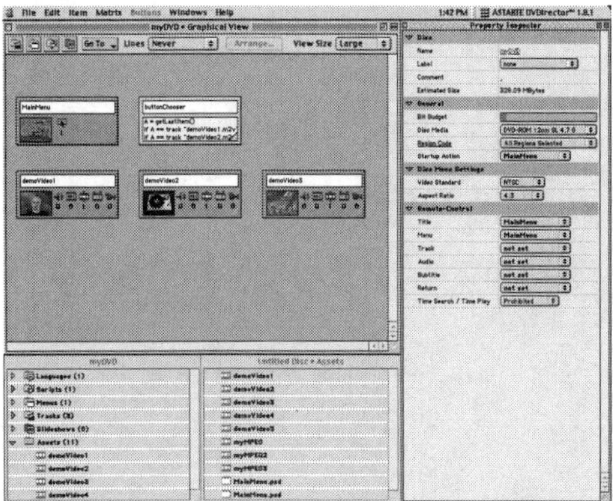

Figure i.4 Astarte's DVDirector—although the interface was tweaked and extra features have been added, DVD Studio Pro 1.*x* worked much the same as DVDirector did in 1999 (albeit at a fraction of the cost!).

About DVD Studio Pro

DVD Studio Pro was born in 1999 as part of a suite of DVD authoring tools produced by a small software company called Astarte. This suite included M.Pack, an MPEG-2 encoding application (**Figure i.2**); A.Pack, an AC-3 audio encoder (**Figure i.3**); and DVDirector, a DVD-Video authoring application (**Figure i.4**).

When DVDirector first hit the market, it wasn't cheap. Wearing a $5,400 price tag, the program was priced out of reach for the average consumer. In April 2000, Apple purchased Astarte and began transforming DVDirector into DVD Studio Pro. It would take close to a year, however, before Apple released DVD Studio Pro 1.0, in March 2001, at a reasonably priced $1,000.

Although Mac OS X was already available when DVD Studio Pro was first released, it would take another year and two upgrades before DVD Studio Pro 1.5 for Mac OS X was shipped, in April 2002. At that time, Adobe Photoshop 7.0 had just made it to market, and Apple's Final Cut Pro 3.0 was already taking advantage of Mac OS X's increased performance to offer real-time video editing. With the inclusion of a killer audio-editing application—Bias Peak DV 3.0—on the DVD Studio Pro installation DVD-ROM, all of the tools needed to make DVD-Video were in place, and all of them worked on Mac OS X.

For over a year, the professional DVD authoring community reveled in the power that DVD Studio Pro 1.5 offered. It was a great program, but there were a few questions about the product's "professional" abilities. For example, the MPEG encoder that came with DVD Studio Pro 1.*x* was incredibly quick at encoding MPEG-2 streams, though unfortunately the streams it produced...well, they looked like they were encoded incredibly quickly. Many users found version 1.*x* hard to learn, and indeed, with all of its small "gotchas," this version took some getting used to.

Instead of fixing the small problems in DVD Studio Pro 1.*x*, Apple scrapped it and began anew. In July 2001, Apple purchased Spruce, a company that produced advanced—and expensive—DVD authoring tools, including their flagship application, DVDMaestro. Much of the technology from that acquisition made its way into DVD Studio Pro 3—but the $25,000 price tag stayed behind.

When Apple released DVD Studio Pro 2 on August 18, 2003, many people were shocked to see its expanded functionality in comparison to version 1.*x*, its far superior MPEG-2 encoder, and the dramatically reduced price: $499! This was the moment that professional DVD authoring houses had been dreading: finally, a professional-caliber DVD authoring environment had reached a price point that put it squarely in the hands of most consumers and video enthusiasts.

And now that version 3 has been released, this awesome program has come of age. With the reintroduction of version 1's Graphical view and the introduction of new transition features that let you quickly and professionally create engaging transitions that blend menus into other project items, all the pieces are in place to make DVD-Video production not just a fun way to deliver video, but a mandatory one—Hollywood, beware!

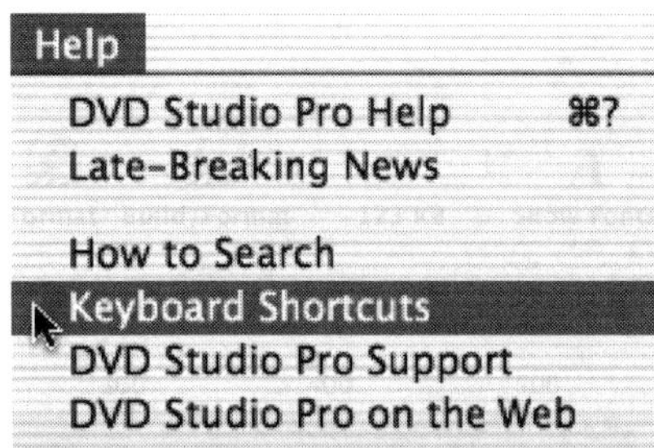

Figure i.5 In DVD Studio Pro, choose Help > Keyboard Shortcuts to launch a PDF listing all of the keyboard shortcuts available to DVD Studio Pro.

How to Use This Book

This is a *task-based reference book*. All aspects of DVD Studio Pro are broken down into simple, easy-to-follow steps packed with pictures so you can see exactly how things work. Each section builds in theory and complexity on the last, so if you're new to DVD Studio Pro, you may want to read this book from beginning to end, following all of the steps and figures. If you're using this book as a reference, just turn to the index when you have a problem, flip to the page you need, and find your solution.

Keyboard Shortcuts

To get the most out of any software application, you have to become a keyboard commander. Keyboard shortcuts take a while to remember, but once you have them, they speed up your workflow tremendously. While the mouse is a necessary tool that you'll continuously use to arrange and edit project items, over time you'll find DVD Studio Pro's extensive keyboard shortcuts to be huge time-savers.

To speed you on your way, this book lists all keyboard shortcuts when their corresponding functions are discussed. For a full list of the keyboard shortcuts available in DVD Studio Pro, open DVD Studio Pro and choose Help > Keyboard Shortcuts (**Figure i.5**) to launch a PDF document detailing all available keyboard shortcuts.

Getting Help

You'll find the Internet to be a valuable source of information on using DVD Studio Pro. There are several Web sites devoted to DVD Studio Pro issues and many forums where you can post questions and get answers. Appendix B, "Online Resources," contains a list of Web sites that you can turn to when the going gets tough.

Part I: Getting Ready

Chapter 1 Before You Begin 3

Chapter 2 DVD 101 19

Chapter 3 Preparing Graphics 33

Chapter 4 The QuickTime MPEG-2 Exporter 53

Chapter 5 Using Compressor 81

Chapter 6 Using A.Pack 101

Part I: Getting Ready

1. **Before You Begin**
   Choosing a Platform
   Expanding Your System
   Optimizing Your Hard Disk
   Installing DVD Studio Pro
   Exploring Software Extras

2. **DVD 101**
   DVD versus CD
   About DVD Formats
   Editing in DVD Studio Pro
   About DVD Studio Pro Workflow
   About the DVD-Video Data Structure

3. **Preparing Graphics**
   Preparing Source Video
   Preparing Still Graphics

4. **The QuickTime MPEG-2 Exporter**
   About MPEG Video
   About MPEG-2 Compression
   About the QuickTime MPEG-2 Exporter
   Opening the QuickTime MPEG-2 Exporter
   Choosing a Video System
   About Timecode
   Choosing an Aspect Ratio
   Setting the Field Order
   Saving the Audio Track
   Creating a Log File
   Creating Parse Files
   Setting Encoding Quality
   Setting Motion Estimation
   About the Progress Window
   Exporting MPEG-2 Streams from Final Cut Pro

5. **Using Compressor**
   Encoding a File
   Creating Presets
   Previewing Compression
   Creating a Droplet

6. **Using A.Pack**
   About Source Audio Streams
   Converting Audio Formats
   About AC-3 Audio
   About A.Pack
   Launching A.Pack
   Encoding AC-3 Audio
   Using Audio Coding Modes
   Assigning Input Channels
   Choosing a Bit Rate
   Using Dialog Normalization
   Determining an Audio Stream's DNV
   About Dynamic Range Control
   Using Compression Profiles
   About Downmixing
   About Other AC-3 Settings
   Auditioning AC-3 Files
   Using a Third-Party Audio Interface
   About Batch Lists

Before You Begin

Is my computer fast enough?

How do I know if my computer has a SuperDrive?

Do I need an extra hard disk?

What other applications do I need to use DVD Studio Pro 3?

If you're new to DVD authoring with DVD Studio Pro, these are important questions, and this chapter is designed to help you answer them. We'll start by examining the four main platforms available for DVD authoring (as this book was written): the G5 tower, the PowerBook G4, the iMac G4, and the eMac. All of these computers are capable DVD authoring workstations, but some platforms enjoy advantages that others don't. So to help you get over these hardware hurdles, the first third of this chapter looks at the computers that are currently available and helps you determine exactly how much power you need.

Your computer is like a thoroughbred racehorse: the better you care for it, the better it performs. DVD Studio Pro uses (and produces) files that are often measured in gigabytes. With all this data racing around your computer, proper hard-disk maintenance becomes very important. The second third of this chapter offers tips on keeping your disks optimized and in prime working condition for DVD Studio Pro.

The rest of this chapter shows you how to install DVD Studio Pro and discusses some of the problems that you may encounter along the way. If everything goes smoothly with your installation, read on to learn about other software applications that work in tandem with DVD Studio Pro to produce the video streams, audio streams, and menu graphics that snap together to produce a complete DVD-Video.

Choosing a Platform

In the video world, it's generally safe to assume that the more powerful your computer, the better. More power reduces render times. More power means that you can run more programs simultaneously. More is better, especially when you're working in DVD Studio Pro 3. With its compositing features, an MPEG-2 encoder under the hood, and the ability to directly import unrendered LiveType and Motion project files, DVD Studio Pro 3 needs a lot of horsepower.

Do you need a brand-new G5? Well, no. In fact, even a 1 GHz, single-processor PowerBook is competent enough to handle DVD Studio Pro 3's processor demands. It will, however, take longer to encode MPEG-2 video, and you will find that your computer slows down if you try to multitask by running Apple's Final Cut Pro, DVD Studio Pro, and/or Logic, along with Adobe Photoshop all at once. But if you have more time than money, a G4 is terrific.

A G3 processor, however, is not capable of running DVD Studio Pro 3. DVD Studio Pro 3 will install only on computers with processors that use Velocity Engine technology, which means that you actually must have a G4/G5 to even install the program.

As of this writing, Apple offers four product lines that are compatible with DVD Studio Pro 3: the Power Mac G5 tower, the iMac G4/eMac G4, the PowerBook G4, and the iBook G4. Each has its own set of advantages for you to consider.

Power Mac G5

On June 23, 2003, Steve Jobs introduced the Power Mac G5 to an anticipatory crowd at the Worldwide Developers Conference (WWDC), and the video world as a whole breathed a collective "Ahhhhh..." Finally, a computer had been unleashed that offered a tangible promise of real-time video editing.

DVD authoring is a processor-intensive process. A typical session involves multiple programs—Final Cut Pro, Photoshop, Logic, and DVD Studio Pro—all open and working together in tandem. Only the heartiest of computers can pull this off satisfactorily. A G5 will not flinch under the strain.

Advantages of a Power Mac G5:

- **Up to a 1.25 GHz system bus.** The system bus ships data around the computer, so the faster the system bus, the faster information moves from RAM to the processor and back. Almost six times the speed of the G4's system bus, this bus is as fast as it gets on a desktop computer. Period.
- **Room for extra RAM.** Add up to 8 GB SDRAM to run multiple processor-intensive programs simultaneously.
- **Three PCI-X slots.** Expand your system with SCSI cards to attach DLT tape recorders. (DLT tapes are the preferred medium for transporting finished projects to a replicator for mass replication.)

Disadvantages of a Power Mac G5:

- **Low portability.** Once embedded in its snake nest of cables and power cords, this puppy won't often be accompanying you into the field.

iMac and eMac

Apple's iMac G4 and eMac G4 (with SuperDrive) are both great platforms for DVD-Video authoring. Although these computers come with relatively small hard disks, you can safely increase storage capacity by adding external FireWire hard disks to your setup.

If you're using DVD-Video as a means of artistic exploration, or if you intend only to build one-off projects for events such as family reunions and piano recitals, the iMac and eMac are great little computers—you'll find them well suited for use with DVD Studio Pro 3.

Advantages of an iMac/eMac:

- **Two FireWire ports.** You'll find them invaluable for connecting external hard disks and DVD recorders.
- **Attractive design and price.** They look cool, they're inexpensive, and they're Macs. Enough said.

Disadvantages of an iMac/eMac:

- **No expandability.** Need 1,000 copy-protected copies of your project? Better buy a Power Mac, because you need a DLT drive and, by association, a SCSI card; see "Digital linear tape (DLT) drives" later in this chapter.

✔ Tip

- Yes, it's true that increasing numbers of replicators are bowing to the unrelenting forces of technology, and most now accept DVD-R (General) media or even a hard disk formatted with a finished build of your DVD-Video. But if you need to copy-protect or region-code your DVD-Video, a DLT tape is necessary. Before sending anything to a replicator, check to see if the replicator will accept your intended delivery format (DLT, DVD-R, hard disk, and so on).

PowerBook G4 and iBook G4

A gaggle of Unix developers could sing the G5's praises until the cows come home, but the Power Mac G5, by virtue of its power cord, is anchored to a wall. If you want to work in the field, nothing beats a PowerBook or iBook. A PowerBook does not match a G5 in brute processing power, but with an internal DVD burner and over four hours of battery life, a PowerBook's elegance and portability make it one of the best computers currently available for DVD authoring.

However, PowerBooks and iBooks do suffer from the same lack of expandability as iMacs and eMacs, so if replicating projects is important to your work, you need a Power Mac (as well?).

Advantages of a PowerBook/iBook:

- **Portability.** Use it in a plane, use it on a train. Author in a car, author at a bar. It makes no difference; the PowerBook goes anywhere and everywhere.
- **Style points.** Nothing says "Coooooool" better than a PowerBook.

Disadvantages of a PowerBook/iBook:

- **No expandability.** As with the iMac, if you need to replicate a copy-protected project, you're up the creek without a SCSI card.

Additional requirements

If you're using a Power Mac G4 or G5, your system includes all the base hardware you need to author DVD-Video titles. Nonetheless, take a moment to ensure that your system has each of the following Apple-recommended components:

- Macintosh computer with a 733 MHz or faster PowerPC processor (G4 minimum) and AGP graphics card
- 8 MB of video memory (32 MB recommended)
- Mac OS X v10.3.2
- QuickTime 6.5
- 256 MB of RAM (512 MB recommended)
- 4.4 GB of available disk space
- DVD drive (required for installation)

✔ Tip

- For more information, visit the Apple Web site: `www.apple.com/dvdstudiopro/specs.html`.

Expanding Your System

A few other pieces of hardware will make your life easier as you continue to experiment with DVD Studio Pro 3. This section describes these devices, telling you what they are and why you need them.

Apple SuperDrive

The SuperDrive is essential to DVD-Video creation because it enables you to record DVD-Video projects onto DVD-R discs, which is probably why all Power Mac G5s ship with a built-in 8*x* SuperDrive. Used with DVD Studio Pro 3, a SuperDrive writes DVD-Videos to DVD-R (General) optical discs that can be read by a DVD-Video player and viewed on a TV.

The SuperDrive is versatile. It not only reads most CD and DVD formats (excluding DVD-RAM), but it also records data to DVD-R, DVD-RW, CD-R, and CD-RW discs.

If you're unsure about whether your Mac contains a SuperDrive, you can check the Apple System Profiler to find out.

External DVD Recorders

An external FireWire DVD recorder is simply a standard internal ATAPI-IDE DVD recorder like the one in a G5, but it's in an enclosure that connects to your computer via a FireWire cable. If you're planning to purchase a new DVD recorder, consider the high degree of flexibility that a FireWire DVD recorder offers. For example, you can move a FireWire DVD recorder among several computers, lend it to your little sister, and so on. (An external FireWire DVD recorder will even work on a FireWire-enabled Windows PC!)

To determine the type of optical disc drive in your Mac:

1. Open the Apple System Profiler by choosing your startup disk and then the Applications/Utilities/Apple System Profiler.

   The Apple System Profiler opens (**Figure 1.1**).

2. On the left side, choose the ATA option (**Figure 1.2**).

   The ATA device tree appears. In this tree, you will find your internal DVD drive. If you have a SuperDrive in your system, a CD-RW/DVD-R device will be listed here. If CD-RW/DVD-ROM appears (note the *DVD-ROM* part), your system is not equipped with a SuperDrive and cannot record DVD-R discs.

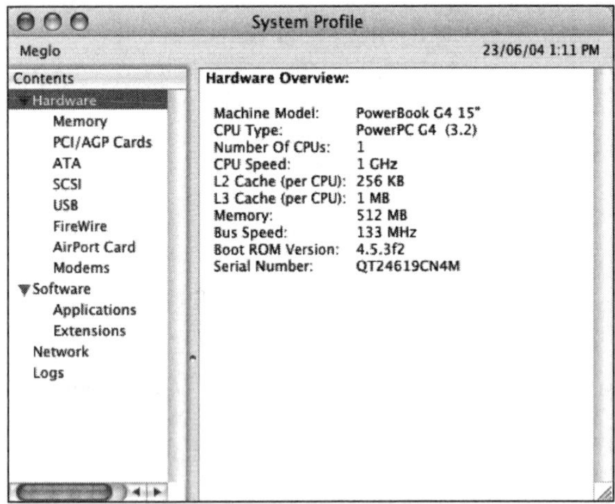

Figure 1.1 The Apple System Profiler is buried deep inside your startup disk's Applications/Utilities folder.

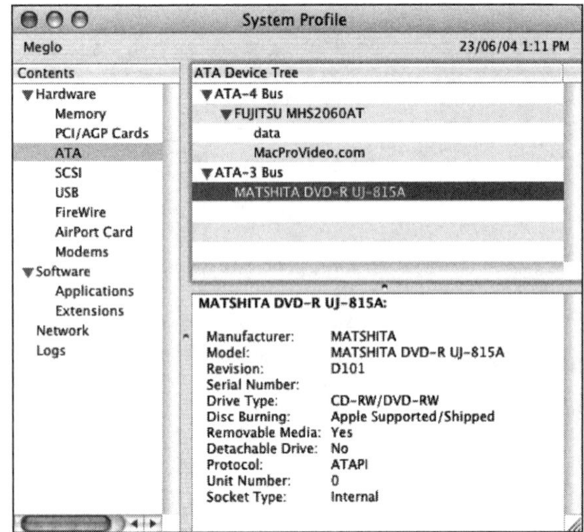

Figure 1.2 Select the ATA option to see what type of optical drive your computer has.

Set-top DVD-Video player

A set-top DVD-Video player connects to your TV and lets you view any DVD-Video in your collection, including the ones you create with DVD Studio Pro 3. A set-top DVD-Video player is a necessary part of your production chain. You'll need it when testing your finished DVDs to see how they perform in a real-world environment—in other words, on a television.

✔ Tips

- Before you purchase a new DVD-Video player, write a DVD Studio Pro project to both a DVD-R and a DVD-RW disc. When you go to the showroom, take these discs with you and try out a few different DVD-Video players. If the player doesn't read your discs, don't buy it! If you're not yet comfortable authoring your own project, you can open the finished tutorial project that comes with DVD Studio Pro 3 and burn that. Presto! Instant DVD-Video.
- To maximize the readability of your DVD-R discs, write them only at 1*x*. This slows down the writing process and allows the laser to burn more defined marks onto the DVD-R, which in turn makes it easier for DVD-Video players to read the disc.
- For a list of Apple-recommended DVD-Video players, check the following Web site: `www.apple.com/dvd/compatibility`.

Why Won't My DVD-R Disc Run on My Set-Top Player?

Think back to the mid 1990s, and you'll probably recall that awkward stage when some CD players couldn't play CD-R discs. Mixed CDs were just starting to replace mixed tapes, and getting CD-Rs to play on the average living room stereo soon became of vital international importance. Now, of course, all new CD players can read CD-R discs, and burning audio CDs has become so popular it's practically illegal.

Today's DVD-Video players suffer from similar growing pains. While all DVD-Video players can read replicated DVD discs, some DVD-Video players have a problem reading recorded DVD-R discs. Although each new generation of player becomes more tolerant of the medium, it will be a while before all DVD players read DVD-R discs 100 percent of the time. As a result, there are bound to be a few players out there that won't read your recorded DVD-R discs.

Should you run into this problem, there's not necessarily something wrong with your project. In fact, if your project works correctly in some DVD-Video players but not in others, the problem is very likely an incompatibility between the DVD-Video player and DVD-R or DVD-RW media.

Extra hard disks

Digital video takes up a lot of storage space. (Okay, that might be the biggest understatement in this book, because video files are huge!) This problem particularly plagues the DVD-Video author. You'll be using large video files along with their associated audio tracks, menu graphics, subtitle files, and so on. Even the process of creating a DVD-Video involves the creation a lot of extra media, such as motion-menu experiments or audio loops for background music. There's a lot of media to juggle, and having at least one extra hard disk makes the process easier.

Ideally, you should have at least two hard disks for DVD-Video authoring (see "Optimizing Your Hard Disk" later in this chapter). When buying a new hard disk, however, remember that speed is king. While 5,400-rpm hard disks are inexpensive, they are not fast enough to read several streams of DV video simultaneously. Stick with hard disks of at least 7,200 rpm.

Building External Hard Disks

An external hard disc is just a normal ATAPI-IDE hard disk, similar to the one inside your computer. Sure, you can buy ready-made external hard drives, but those tend to be expensive—an external hard disk is cheap and easy to build on your own.

Many computer stores sell empty external FireWire enclosures that come without an installed device. You can stock these external cases with any ATAPI-IDE device that will fit, including DVD recorders and hard disks.

Building your own external FireWire drive has other advantages. For example, you can switch out the internal device in mere minutes (or seconds), thus enabling you to quickly swap hard disks in and out of your system.

Digital linear tape (DLT) drives

Currently, the SuperDrive can record only to single-layer DVD-R or DVD-RW discs, which hold 4.7 billion bytes of data. (To learn more about single-layer and dual-layer DVD disks, see Chapter 2, "DVD 101.") Dual-layer DVDs can store more data, but to produce one, you must send your project to a DVD replication facility.

Some DVD replicators will accept an external FireWire hard disk, or even copy a DVD-R disc, that contains your finished DVD-Video. While most replicators are beginning to offer these services, you may occasionally find one that accepts *only* DLT tapes. This may seem like a senseless limitation, and you're right—it is. Nonetheless, if you want to produce a dual-layer DVD-Video project, you should purchase a DLT drive. (For details on writing your project to DLT tape, see Chapter 20, "Outputting the Project.")

The internal mechanisms of all DLT drives are made by Quantum, but there are several types of DLT drives on the market. Of them all, the DLT 4000 is perhaps the most popular choice for DVD authoring. Used DLT 4000s are cheap and plentiful at online auction sites such as eBay, and since there's not much to break on these devices, used units usually work well. To learn more about DLT drives, go to the Quantum Web site: `www.quantum.com/`.

✔ Tip

- Several manufacturers are currently working on dual-layer DVD-R burners. Expect these to hit the market by the end of 2004.

DLT Things to Remember

If you plan to purchase a DLT drive, keep two things in mind. First, all DLT drives use SCSI, so you'll need to install a SCSI card in your computer. Second, DLT tapes are not cheap. You need one DLT tape per layer of your project, so to produce one dual-layer DVD, you need two DLT tapes. Retail prices range from around $30 (USD) for one DLT III tape to over $60 (USD) for one DLT IV tape.

If your DLT drive supports DLT III tapes, these are the best to use for DVD authoring. They're cheaper than the other varieties, and they have more than enough storage capacity to hold a DVD-Video project. But, as always, be sure to verify that your replicator accepts the type of DLT tape that you plan to use before submitting project.

Optimizing Your Hard Disk

DVD-Video uses huge files, which can be murder on your hard disk. This section outlines a few simple rules and maintenance techniques that you can use to keep your hard disks running smoothly and efficiently.

Using multiple hard disks

Ideally, you should have at least three hard disks to use DVD Studio Pro: one for audio files, one for video and graphics files, and one for the final, multiplexed DVD Studio Pro project (**Figure 1.3**). If you have only two hard disks, use one to hold your source files and the second for the multiplexed project (**Figure 1.4**).

iMac, eMac, and PowerBook users have only one internal hard disk at their disposal. Fortunately, external FireWire hard disks are fast enough for use with DVD Studio Pro. Using your computer's FireWire ports, you can expand your system to include as much hard disk storage space as you need.

If external FireWire hard disks are a bit beyond your budget, then consider partitioning your current hard disk. While a partitioned hard disk is not as good as three separate hard disks, it is easier to maintain and preferable to keeping all of your files lumped together.

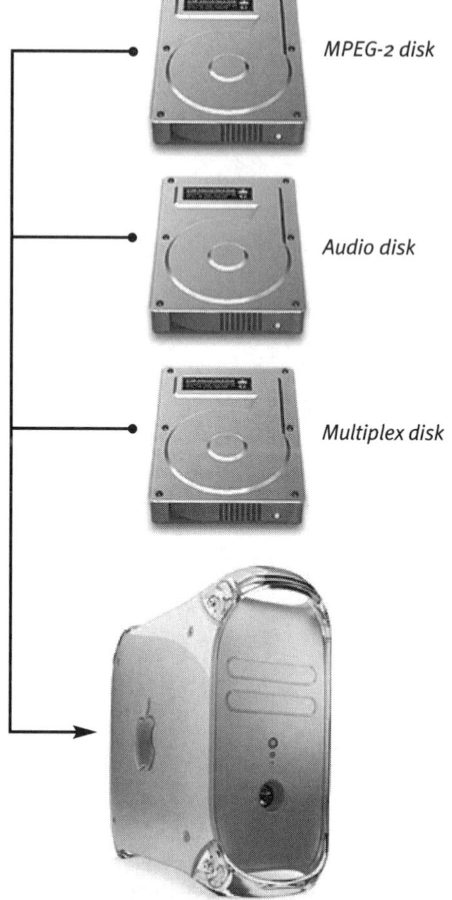

Figure 1.3 The ideal DVD-Video authoring station uses three hard disks: one for MPEG-2 assets, one for audio assets, and one for the finished, multiplexed DVD-Video project (these can be a mixture of internal and external FireWire hard disks).

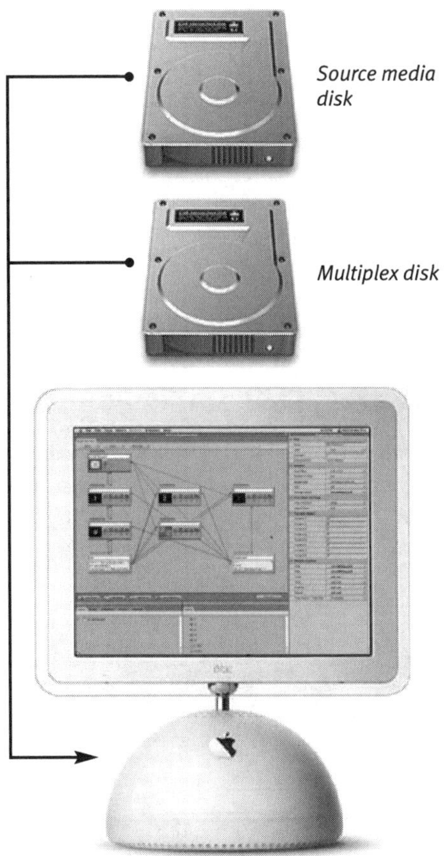

Figure 1.4 A common DVD-Video authoring setup has only two hard disks. Use one for the source files and the second for the finished, multiplexed DVD-Video project (a mixture of internal and external FireWire hard disks is acceptable).

✔ Tip

- To partition a hard disk, use the OS X Disk Utility that came with your Macintosh (**Figure 1.5**). When you partition a hard disk, you erase all of the content currently stored on that disk, including files stored in other partitions on the same disk—so be careful!

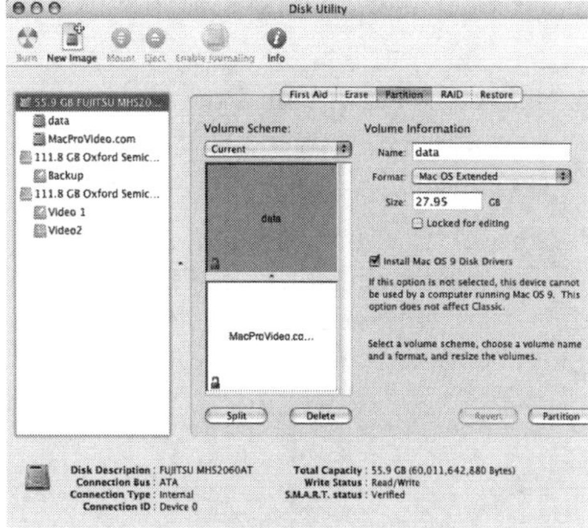

Figure 1.5 To partition a hard disk, use Disk Utility, which comes with Mac OS X.

Installing DVD Studio Pro

Installation of DVD Studio Pro is a fast process that produces no surprises. Simply insert the DVD Studio Pro DVD-ROM, launch the DVD Studio Pro installer, and follow the directions that appear on your screen (**Figure 1.6**).

The DVD Studio Pro installer places four important pieces of software on your computer:

- **DVD Studio Pro 3.** The main event and the application that's discussed throughout this book.
- **A.Pack.** A helper application used to convert AIFF, WAV, and SDII files into compressed Dolby Digital AC-3 files.
- **QuickTime MPEG Encoder.** One- and two-pass variable-bit-rate (VBR) MPEG-2 encoder. Constant-bit-rate (CBR) encoding is also available.
- **Compressor.** Apple's batch list for encoding multiple media files at once. Compressor is a valuable time-saver when you have lots of video files that need to be encoded to MPEG-2. It also lets you add chapter markers and filters to video before encoding.

Figure 1.6 The DVD Studio Pro installer guides you through the installation procedure.

Once you've installed DVD Studio Pro, you must register it before you can use it. Registering DVD Studio Pro also enables the QuickTime MPEG Encoder and A.Pack.

Registering DVD Studio Pro

The first time you launch DVD Studio Pro, a dialog opens asking for your registration information. After you correctly enter this information, DVD Studio Pro opens.

To register DVD Studio Pro:

1. From the Finder, double-click the DVD Studio Pro application icon.

   DVD Studio Pro begins to launch but is interrupted by the Licensing dialog (**Figure 1.7**).

2. Enter your registration information in the dialog.

3. Click OK.

   The dialog closes, and DVD Studio Pro opens. Congratulations! You are ready to start making DVDs.

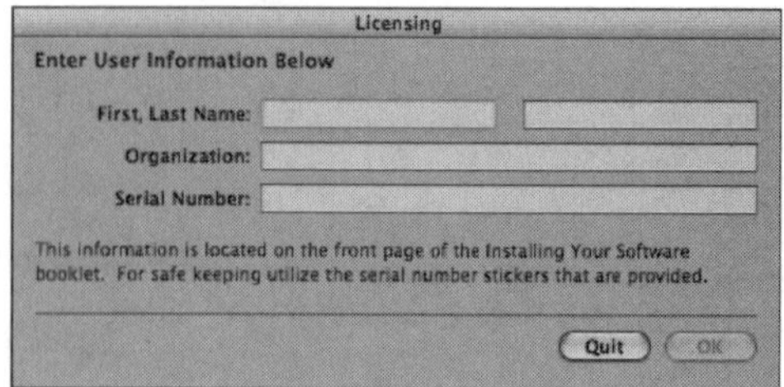

Figure 1.7 To authorize DVD Studio Pro, A.Pack, and the QuickTime MPEG-2 Encoder, enter your registration information in the Licensing dialog.

Exploring Software Extras

DVD Studio Pro is not a content-creation program—it's a content-assembly program. Before you can produce a DVD-Video project, you must prepare source material, such as edited video, menu graphics, audio, and subtitles. To create this content, you'll use programs such as Photoshop, A.Pack, and Final Cut Pro.

Adobe Photoshop

You'll use Photoshop to create the interactive parts—including menus, buttons, and highlight overlays—of your DVD Studio Pro projects. You can also use Photoshop to create still images for DVD-Video slideshows. Chapter 3, "Preparing Graphics," contains detailed information on how to use Photoshop to create still graphics for use with DVD Studio Pro.

Apple A.Pack

A.Pack compresses digital audio into small, efficient Dolby AC-3 audio streams optimized for DVD-Video playback (**Figure 1.8**). A.Pack can compress stereo audio streams as well as multichannel surround streams, which enables you to bring the ambiance of the big screen into the living room or create experimental surround soundscapes. To learn more about using A.Pack, see Chapter 6, "Using A.Pack."

When you install DVD Studio Pro, A.Pack is automatically installed on your hard disk in the same folder as DVD Studio Pro.

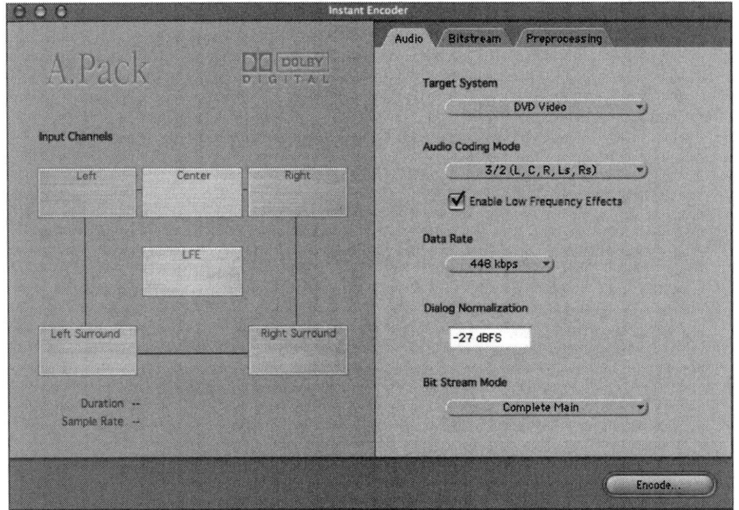

Figure 1.8 A.Pack is an AC-3 encoding utility that lets you encode mono, stereo, and multichannel surround audio streams (including 5.1 surround) for use with DVD Studio Pro.

Apple Compressor

Compressor is Apple's batch list for media encoding, and it comes free with DVD Studio Pro 3 (**Figure 1.9**). You can use Compressor to turn DV video into MPEG-2 streams, add chapter markers to video streams, and even create open—as well as closed—GOP MPEG-2 streams. (The QuickTime MPEG-2 Exporter is not capable of creating open GOPs by itself.)

Apple Final Cut Pro 4

Final Cut Pro 4 is such an awesome non-linear video editor that its release scared its nearest competitor (Adobe Premiere) right off the Mac. Indeed, Adobe has decided not to compete with Final Cut Pro's impressive feature set, so if you're editing video on the Mac, Final Cut Pro is the way to go.

Final Cut Pro 4 is particularly appealing to DVD authors because of the two helper applications that come bundled with it: Soundtrack and LiveType. Soundtrack lets you quickly produce customized, royalty-free music, while LiveType is a titling and motion-graphics application. Together, they create fierce and unique motion menus that can really put some zing into your project.

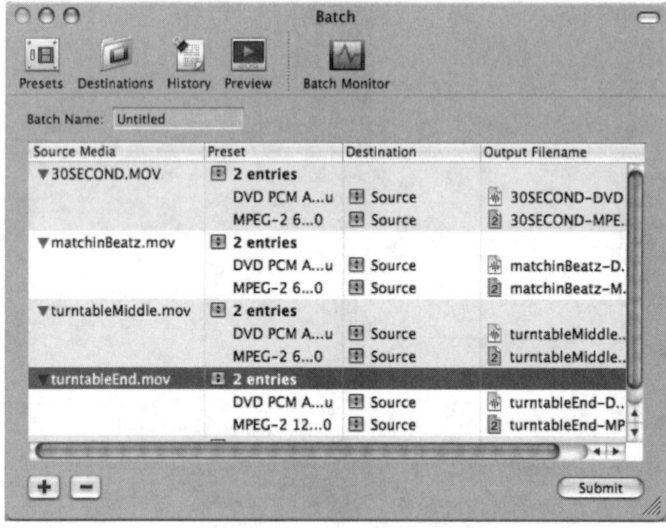

Figure 1.9 Apple's batch compression utility, Compressor.

Emagic Logic Pro

Logic Pro is undeniably the hot audio editor of the moment (**Figure 1.10**). Long understood and appreciated by only top audio producers, Logic leapt out of obscurity and moved into the mainstream when Apple purchased it from Emagic in 2002.

Logic Pro is the perfect tool for designing and mastering audio for DVD-Video. It offers surround-sound mixing, integrated video display, and a suite of software instruments that give you access to any sound you could ever desire. And at less than $800 (USD), Logic Pro is one of the most affordable audio editors on the market. For more information, go to the Apple Web site, or visit Emagic's Web site: `www.emagic.de`.

✔ Tip

- If you intend to mix 5.1 surround audio, you need a hardware audio interface with at least six outputs (five full-frequency channels and a single .1 low-frequency effects channel). With two inputs and six outputs, the Emagic A26 is a perfect audio interface for 5.1 surround mixing.

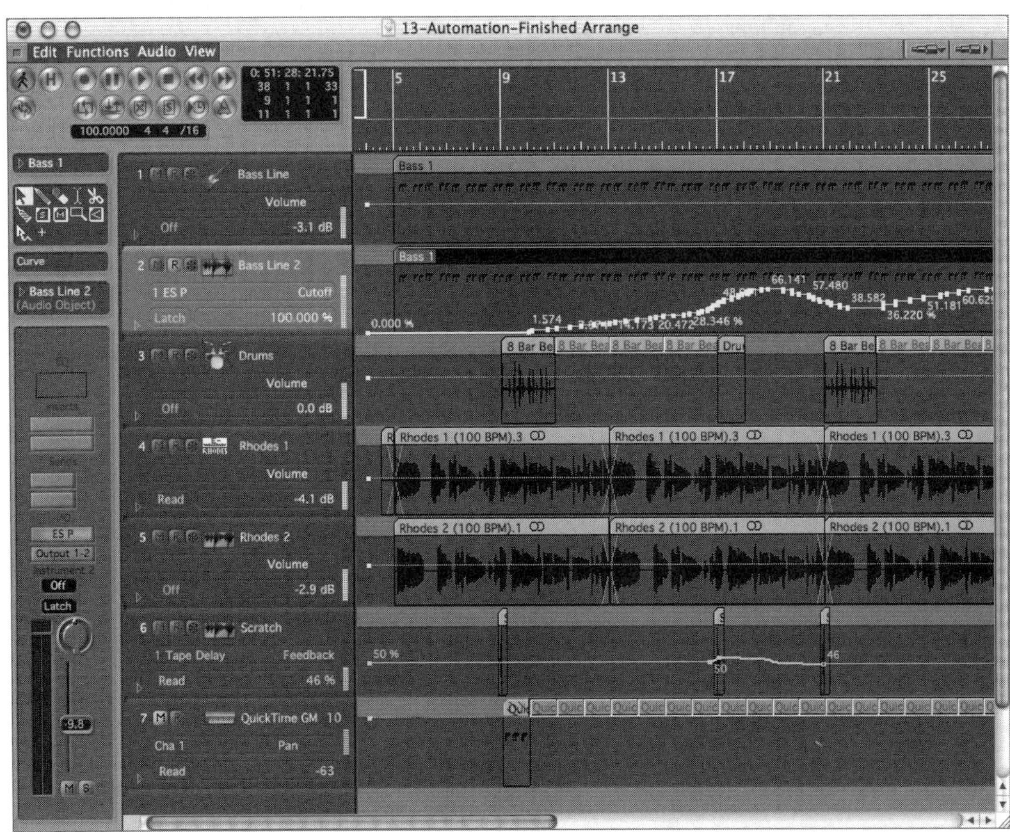

Figure 1.10 Logic Pro is a great tool for creating, or even just cleaning up, audio files for your DVDs.

Innobits BitVice

With support for dual-processor Macs, two-pass variable-bit-rate encoding, and batch processing, BitVice is a workhorse that fits snugly into any serious DVD production workflow (**Figure 1.11**). On a dual-processor G5, BitVice is capable of encoding at faster than real time, which is impressive for an encoder of this quality.

Time lost to a hung or frozen encoder is time you'll never get back. In this area, BitVice demonstrates its true value: it rarely crashes. Have no fear; when you come back in the morning, your MPEGs will be ready.

As for quality, well, that's all in the eye of the beholder. To see for yourself, download the demo from Innobits: `www.innobits.com`.

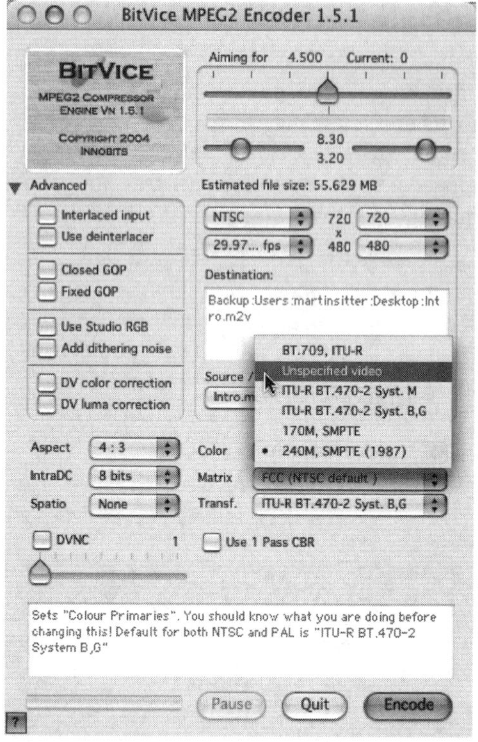

Figure 1.11 Innobits BitVice is a high-quality MPEG-2 encoder that is extremely reliable.

Digigami Mpressionist.X

If you need to analyze MPEG-2 video streams, Digigami Mpressionist.X is the application for you (**Figure 1.12**). Mpressionist.X let's you open MPEG streams and check things like motion vectors and bit rates (see Chapter 4, "The QuickTime MPEG-2 Exporter," for more information). An invaluable educational tool, Mpressionist.X should be an arrow in the quiver of any serious DVD-Video author.

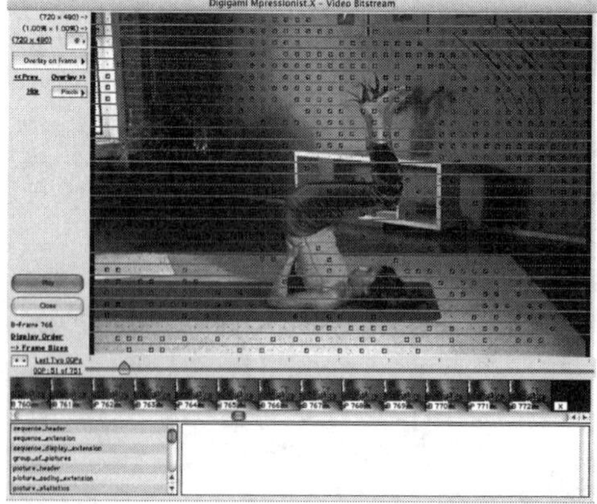

Figure 1.12 Digigami Mpressionist.X lets you analyze motion vectors and bit rates in already encoded MPEG-2 video streams.

2

DVD 101

Authoring a DVD-Video is like building a house: no matter how elaborate the structure, you must start with a strong foundation. For the purpose of DVD-Video authoring, the foundation you build upon is the DVD disc itself, so it pays to know how that disc is made. In this chapter, you'll learn exactly how a DVD disc works—how much data a DVD stores, the types of discs available, how DVD-Video is structured and why.

DVD versus CD

If you physically compare a DVD to a CD, you won't see many differences. A DVD's edges may feel slightly smoother and even look a bit rounder, but other than that, a standard DVD is indistinguishable from a standard CD (**Figure 2.1**).

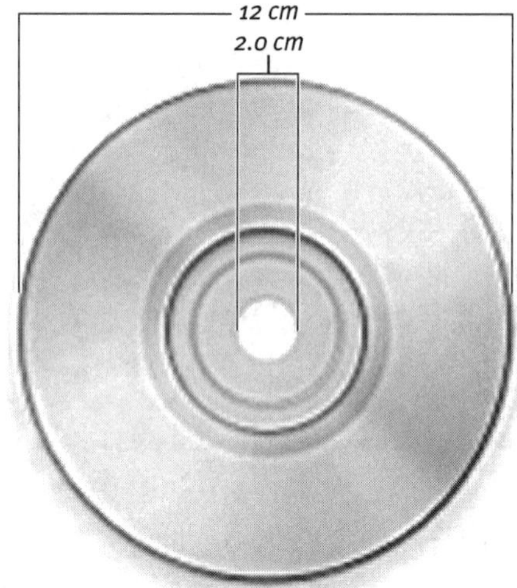

Figure 2.1 CDs and DVDs share the same physical dimensions: a diameter of 12 cm and a thickness of 0.12 cm, with a 2.0-cm hole in the middle.

Though they appear identical on the surface, a DVD can store much more data than a CD. In fact, you can cram up to 4.37 computer gigabytes of data on a DVD. That's over six times more data than a standard 700 MB CD-ROM disc will hold. So what's the difference? How do DVDs pack so much more information onto that little optical disc?

Pits and tracks

The CDs and DVDs you buy from a store come in two varieties: ROM discs and recordable discs.

- *ROM discs* include any disc that can't be recorded, such as DVD-Videos rented from Blockbuster or the DVD Studio Pro Installation DVD-ROM. ROM discs are replicated in huge quantities by specialized facilities that stamp the data directly onto the disc.
- For *recordable discs,* a tightly focused, high-powered laser etches marks into an organic dye recording layer that's sandwiched between two (or more) layers of molded plastic.

Out of the Blue

Several companies are working on a new breed of DVD-R recording devices that use a blue (or violet) laser with a wavelength of about 405 nanometers. With this more focused laser, these devices can record over 27 GB of data on a single layer of a 12-centimeter-diameter optical disc. That's more than six times the storage capacity of today's DVDs.

Like current DVDs, these next-generation discs will also come in dual-sided and/or dual-layered varieties, which means they may potentially store a staggering 100+ GB of information. Sony, Toshiba, and a few other manufacturers have unveiled working prototypes of these machines. Stay tuned!

If you use a microscope to inspect a stamped or recorded disc, you'll see that the data is represented by very small pits arranged in a tiny track that spirals out from the center of the disc toward its edge. When you place the disc into a DVD drive, the laser follows the disc's track, reading the track's pits in much the same way that a record needle follows the groove on a vinyl record, reading the bumps in the vinyl.

In the case of a CD-ROM drive, the infrared laser's wavelength (about 780 nanometers) is relatively long and not terribly accurate by DVD standards. A DVD-ROM drive, on the other hand, uses a more advanced red laser (that's *red*, not *infrared*) with a shorter wavelength (635 or 650 nanometers) and a narrower focus. As a result, it can precisely follow a DVD's densely spun data tracks, reading the smaller pits.

✔ Tips

- DVD-R (General) and DVD-RW discs use a recording wavelength of 650 nanometers, while DVD-R (Authoring) discs use a wavelength of 635 nanometers. This difference in recording wavelengths makes it physically impossible to record a DVD-R (Authoring) disc in a DVD-R (General) recorder, such as the SuperDrive in your computer. The differences between DVD-R (General) and DVD-R (Authoring) discs are discussed later in this chapter in the section "About DVD Formats."
- Pioneer has a great online DVD technical guide at `www.pioneer.co.jp/crdl/tech/index-e.html`.

Labeling DVDs

Most people label their CD-Rs and DVD-Rs with a black felt-tip Sharpie. Some people prefer to print a label and stick it on the disc. With CD-Rs, this works fine, but attaching a stick-on label to a DVD-R is a no-no. If the label is even minutely off-center, the DVD will wobble as it spins. This makes it hard for the reading laser to lock onto the DVD's microscopic track, which in turn makes it hard for the laser to read those tiny pits.

For a truly professional touch, check out the new generation of CD/DVD printers. These printers print in color directly on the surface of any *inkjet-printable* DVD-R. Inkjet-printable DVD-Rs have a special ink-absorption layer that allows the ink to set. If the DVD does not have an inkjet-printable surface, don't print on it! Doing so causes the ink to puddle and slide off the disc, which may damage the disc and your printer.

Storage capacity

Today, the standard CD-ROM disc holds up to 700 MB of data in one layer, on one side of the disc only. A similarly configured DVD-ROM disc, with one layer and one side, can hold up to 4.37 GB of data. (Did you think DVDs held 4.7 GB of data? See the sidebar "Billions of Bytes versus Gigabytes" for a detailed look at the math.)

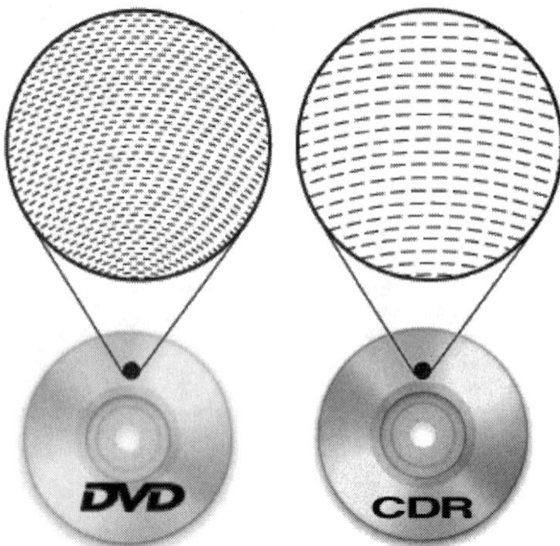

Figure 2.2 Data pits on a DVD (left) are smaller and packed much more closely together than data pits on a CD (right).

So why, you may ask, do DVDs have such a vastly increased storage capacity? CDs and DVDs are physically the same size. Both contain pits and tracks. What's the difference? The answer is simple: on a DVD, the pits are smaller and closer together and the track is wound much more tightly than the pits and track on a CD (**Figure 2.2**). These two differences together allow DVDs to fit significantly more data on the surface area of the disc.

But DVD-ROM discs do not stop at 4.37 GB of storage space. Unlike CD-ROM discs, DVD-ROM discs can contain up to two data layers, or 7.95 GB of data, per side. If that's not enough storage space, there are also double-sided DVD-ROM discs that double the disc's capacity by pressing data onto both the bottom and top surfaces of the disc. **Table 2.1** lists the four most common types of DVD-ROM discs and their corresponding storage capacities.

Table 2.1

CD-ROM and DVD-ROM Storage Capacity

Media Type	Capacity (Computer GB)	Capacity (DVD GB)	Data Sides	Data Layers per Side
CD-ROM	0.68 GB	0.75 GB	1	1
DVD-5	4.37 GB	4.7 GB	1	1
DVD-9	7.95 GB	8.54 GB	1	2
DVD-10	8.75 GB	9.4 GB	2	1
DVD-18	15.9 GB	17.08 GB	2	2

✔ Tip

- A dual-layer DVD contains an extra data layer that the reading laser must penetrate as it harvests information from the disc. Just as putting a pane of glass between you and a mirror makes your reflection a bit blurry, this extra data layer reduces the disc's reflectivity, making it harder for the reading laser to focus. Consequently, data cannot be stamped onto a dual-layer DVD disc as densely as it can be stamped onto a single-layer disc, which in turn means that dual-layer DVDs store slightly less than double the data of a single-layer disc.

Billions of Bytes Versus Gigabytes

You may have read that DVDs hold up to 4.7 GB of data. In fact, that number is printed on the top of every DVD-R disc you buy. This number is misleading. DVDs store up to 4.7 *billion bytes* of data, which is not the same as *computer gigabytes.* Confused? Here's how it works: A DVD holds 4.7 billion bytes of information. But, in computer terms, 1 kilobyte is equal to 1,024 bytes, 1 megabyte is equal to 1,024 kilobytes, and 1 gigabyte is equal to 1,024 megabytes. There's a lot of extra "24s" hanging around, and indeed, if you do the math, 4.7 billion bytes actually equals approximately 4.37 computer gigabytes. The difference in perceived data storage is over 300 MB!

For those who want to do the math, here's the equation:

- 4.7 billion bytes = 4,700,000,000 bytes
- 4,700,000,000 bytes/1,024 = 4,589,844 Kbytes
- 4,589,844 Kbytes/1,024 = 4,482.269 MB
- 4,482.269 MB/1,024 = 4.377216 GB

Because you're using a computer to make your DVDs, this book uses the computer storage numbers (unless otherwise stated). You can use Table 2.1 as a quick reference to help you convert between computer and DVD storage capacities.

About DVD Formats

DVD formats fall into two categories: physical and logical. This section explores the differences between the two types.

DVD physical formats

A disc's *physical format* determines how the DVD is physically configured, including how the pits are stamped or recorded and other low-level characteristics that you, as a DVD-Video author, seldom need to worry about. Just be sure to use the appropriate disc for your purpose, and everything will work fine. If you want to record a DVD using your SuperDrive, for example, you must use a DVD-R (General) and *not* a DVD-R (Authoring), DVD+R, or DVD-RAM disc.

- **DVD-ROM.** DVD-ROM is a read-only format similar to a CD-ROM disc, but it stores much more information. A DVD-ROM disc can hold games, a series of QuickTime movies, MPEG-2 video, text files, or any other type of data.
- **DVD-R.** Using a SuperDrive and DVD Studio Pro (or a third-party application like Roxio's Toast Titanium), you can write data to a DVD-R disc and retrieve that data later.

  There are two types of DVD-R media: General and Authoring. If you're using a SuperDrive, you can write to only DVD-R (General) media. The second variety, DVD-R (Authoring), is used with professional DVD-recordable drives, including Pioneer's DVR-S201.
- **DVD-RW.** DVD-RW provides all the benefits of DVD-R, but discs can be erased and rewritten up to 1,000 times or more.

  Most new DVD-Video players can read DVD-RW discs, which can dramatically decrease your materials costs. You can build your DVD-Video project on a DVD-RW disc, for example, and then test that project in a set-top DVD-Video player. If there's a problem with the project, simply fix it and rerecord the disc without wasting a DVD-R—or any extra cash.
- **DVD-RAM.** DVD-RAM lets you write to the disc in multiple sessions, similar to the way a floppy or Iomega Zip disk works. DVD-R and DVD-RW, on the other hand, use "disc at once" recording, which means that the whole disc must be recorded in a single session.

  DVD-RAM disks will not play in most DVD-Video players and, consequently, are not recommended for testing DVD-Video projects. A DVD-RAM drive is a fine storage medium for backing up projects, but to utilize DVD Studio Pro to its full potential, you must also have a DVD-R recorder such as the Apple SuperDrive.

Disc versus *Disk*

Same word, different spelling. How confusing. Actually, the spelling is meant to help you *avoid* confusion. *Disc*, with a *c*, is always used to refer to optical discs such as CDs and DVDs, while *disk*, with a *k*, refers to magnetic disks, such as hard disks and floppy disks.

- **DVD+R and DVD+RW.** DVD+R does more or less the same thing as DVD-R: it lets you record up to 4.37 GB of data onto a DVD disc. However, DVD+R uses a different recording process than DVD-R. Consequently, DVD+R discs *cannot* be recorded with a SuperDrive. This incompatibility, however, affects only the *recording* process—any DVD drive, including the SuperDrive, will *read* DVD+R discs. DVD+R drives will also read DVD-R discs, so playback of these different formats is rarely a problem.

✔ Tips

- If you have a SuperDrive in your computer, you can record only DVD-R (General) or DVD-RW blank discs. DVD-R (Authoring) discs will not work, nor will DVD+R, DVD+RW, or DVD-RAM discs.
- **IMPORTANT:** On the topic of formats and compatibility, if you have an older SuperDrive that records at 1*x* or 2*x* only, don't buy 4*x* DVD-R discs! At least, don't buy them unless you update your SuperDrive's firmware, or the 4*x* discs will literally fry the laser on your 2*x* drive. (After updating your firmware, you can record 4*x* discs with no physical trauma to your SuperDrive.) To update your 2*x* SuperDrive's firmware, visit `www.apple.com/hardware/superdrive/`.

DVD-R: General versus Authoring

In the beginning, there were only DVD-R (Authoring) discs. As DVDs made inroads into the general consumer market, DVD-R (General) discs were created. There are several differences between DVD-R (General) and DVD-R (Authoring) discs:

- DVD-R (General) uses a recording wavelength of 650 nanometers, and DVD-R (Authoring) uses a recording wavelength of 635 nanometers. Consequently, you cannot record to a DVD-R (Authoring) disc in a DVD-R (General) drive, or vice versa.
- DVD-R (Authoring) discs are capable of storing Cutting Master Format (CMF) information on the disc. This allows DVD-R (Authoring) discs to store copy-protection information, making it possible to use a DVD-R (Authoring) disc as a master for DVD replication.

Here's how it works: DVD-R (Authoring) discs let you write data to an area where it's physically impossible to write data on a DVD-R (General) disc. This is called the burst area, and it sits right at the center of the disc. On a replicated DVD, the Content Scrambling System (CSS) encryption keys are stored in this burst area, but on a DVD-R (General) disc, this burst area is preembossed and impossible to record to. DVD-R (Authoring) discs, on the other hand, use this burst area to store the CMF data that a replicator can use to copy-protect the title.

DVD logical formats

Each DVD has a *logical format* reflecting the type of data held on the disc. A blank DVD-R, for example, is an empty slate that contains no data and consequently has no logical format. If you record a DVD-Video project onto the disc, you give it a logical format—DVD-Video, of course. If you record computer files onto the disc (HTML, QuickTime movies, and so on), it becomes a DVD-ROM disc with a corresponding logical format. Put both DVD-Video and computer data onto the disc, and you create a hybrid DVD.

- **DVD-ROM.** A DVD-ROM disc holds any type of file you would normally find on your computer's hard disks (**Figure 2.3**).
- **DVD-Video.** A DVD-Video disc contains DVD-Video that can be read only by DVD-Video players. The video data is stored inside a VIDEO_TS folder at the disc's root level (**Figure 2.4**).
- **Hybrid DVDs.** A hybrid DVD contains VIDEO_TS and AUDIO_TS folders at the disc's root level, but also has other data files and/or folders housing data files. These other files and/or folders may include HTML pages, QuickTime movies, Word documents, or any type of file you would normally find on your computer's hard disk.
- **DVD-Audio.** DVD-Audio discs are designed to replace the audio CD format. Due to the increased storage space available on a DVD, DVD-Audio discs deliver higher-quality audio than that found on a standard stereo, 16-bit, 44.1 kHz audio CD. In fact, a DVD-Audio disc can hold multichannel, 24-bit surround audio at sample rates of up to 192 kHz. DVD Studio Pro does not create DVD-Audio discs.

✔ Tip

- The AUDIO_TS folder located at the root level of all DVD-Video discs is meant to contain DVD-Audio files only! Because DVD Studio Pro creates DVD-Video files, the AUDIO_TS folder will always be empty for projects multiplexed by DVD Studio Pro.

Figure 2.3 If you open the DVD-ROM disc and look at its file structure, you'll see that it contains only data files and no VIDEO_TS or AUDIO_TS folders.

Figure 2.4 If you open a DVD-Video disc and look at its file structure, you'll see a VIDEO_TS and an AUDIO_TS folder. The VIDEO_TS folder contains all the files that make a DVD-Video. The AUDIO_TS folder is always empty—it's designed to hold files that only a DVD-Audio player can read.

Editing in DVD Studio Pro

Until DVD-Video came along, VHS video was the most common full-motion video format that could play on television sets. VHS video is a linear format with many limitations, including a lack of interactivity, no random-access capabilities, and audio/video streams of an often-questionable quality. For a generation raised on video games and the Internet, a Fast Forward button is just not good enough. Let's face it: VHS video is boring.

DVD-Video significantly enhances the video experience by adding support for interactivity, multiple video streams, high-quality surround audio, dynamic alternate language streams, and scripting capabilities that allow DVD-Video authors to create immersive video environments and games. Unlike VHS video, DVD-Video is loaded with possibilities, and DVD Studio Pro is designed to help you make the most of them. Here's a quick look at what you can do:

- **Tracks.** In DVD Studio Pro, a track is a container that holds video, audio, and subtitles. Each track must hold at least one video stream (or still image), and you can use a maximum of 99 tracks in any DVD Studio Pro project.
- **Multiple angles.** Each track can have up to eight alternate camera angles along with the main video stream (for a total of nine different camera angles). These camera angles can supply anything from an alternate view of a sports event to a wireframe composite that lets you get under the skin of a 3D animation.
- **Menus.** A menu provides a visual backdrop for buttons. A menu can use a still image as a background (still menu) or a video stream (motion menu). Each project can have up to 1 GB of menus (the combined file size of all encoded assets that comprise all of your project's menus must be less than 1 GB).
- **Buttons.** Buttons allow viewers to interact with the DVD-Video project. Each 4:3 menu can have up to 36 buttons, while 16:9 menus can have 18 buttons per menu.
- **Slideshows.** A slideshow is a series of still images and/or MPEG video segments that play sequentially from beginning to end. Each slide can advance automatically after a certain pause interval has passed or can be programmed to advance when the viewer presses the Next button on the DVD player's remote control.
- **Audio streams.** Uncompressed PCM (AIFF, WAV, SDII), MPEG-1 Layer 2, digitally compressed AC3 audio, and DTS streams are accepted by DVD Studio Pro 3. These audio streams can be mono, stereo, or (format allowing) multichannel surround. Each track can have up to eight audio streams; menus are limited to only one audio stream per menu.
- **Subtitles.** Subtitles are used for text translations of your movie in alternate languages. DVD Studio Pro supports up to 32 subtitle streams per track. Each subtitle is synchronized to the track's main video stream, and each can use a maximum of four colors (2 bits per pixel).

continues on next page

- **Scripting.** Scripting programs your DVD-Video to make its own decisions. Through scripting, you can tell a menu to highlight the button corresponding to the last track played, program a track to loop a set number of times, create a Random button that randomly plays all of the tracks in the project, passcode-protect certain tracks and/or menus, and much more.
- **Region coding.** Region coding lets you, as a DVD-Video author, decide where in the world your DVD-Video disc can play (**Table 2.2**). All DVD-Video players are hardwired with a certain region code at the time they are manufactured. When you place a DVD-Video disc into a DVD-Video player, the player checks the DVD's region code against its own. If the codes match, the DVD player allows you to view the disc. If the codes are different, the disc won't work.

✔ Tip

- You cannot region-protect a DVD-R (General) disc.

Table 2.2

DVD Region Coding Compatibility

Region	Geographic Area
Region 1	Canada, USA
Region 2	Europe, Japan, the Near East, Egypt, South Africa
Region 3	East Asia, Hong Kong, South Asia
Region 4	Australia, the Caribbean, Central and South America, New Zealand
Region 5	Africa, India, Mongolia, Pakistan, North Korea, the states of the former USSR
Region 6	China
Region 7	Reserved
Region 8	Special purpose (for in-flight DVD-Video players installed in airplanes)

Figure 2.5 If you try to drag the contents of a copy-protected DVD-Video onto your hard disk, this alert dialog appears.

Using Macrovision

To use Macrovision copy protection, you must enter into a usage agreement with Macrovision Corporation. For more information, contact Macrovision:

- Telephone: (408) 743-8600
- Fax: (408) 743-8610
- E-mail: acp-info@macrovision.com
- Web site: www.macrovision.com

- **Copy protection.** Copy protection prevents viewers from dragging your DVD-Video's media files onto their computers (**Figure 2.5**) or copying them to an analog recording device such as a VHS tape recorder. Two forms of copy protection are available to DVD Studio Pro: the Content Scrambling System (CSS) and Macrovision.

  CSS uses an encryption system to scramble each sector of the DVD-Video disc. DVD Studio Pro provides an option that lets you copy-protect your DVD-Video disc using CSS, but to do so you must build your DVD-Video on a DLT tape and send it to a qualified replication house, where the appropriate encryption keys are inserted. DVD-R (Authoring) discs recorded using CMF can also be used as masters for CSS copy-protected projects—if you have a DVD-R (Authoring) drive. The SuperDrive that comes with your computer will not record a DVD-R (Authoring) disc.

  Macrovision copy protection (also known as the Analog Protection System, or APS) is used to prevent consumer DVD users from recording a DVD-Video disc to a VHS tape. If a Macrovision-protected DVD is recorded to VHS, the signal appears to fluctuate between very bright and very dark, and the colors are distorted. In other words, Macrovision degrades the signal to a point where most consumers will not enjoy watching the production.

✔ Tip

- DVD-R (General) discs do not allow you to protect your projects using CSS.

About DVD Studio Pro Workflow

Although there's no set way to produce a DVD-Video project, in general you'll find yourself following a similar routine almost every time:

1. Plan the project. The planning stage involves determining how many menus you need, what tracks they will link to, and where you need to use alternate angles or audio streams and where you don't. This is perhaps the most important part of the whole process, because careful planning will make your project flow smoothly from start to finish.
2. Use programs such as Apple Final Cut Pro, Adobe Photoshop, and Logic Platinum to create your source files, which include audio and video streams as well as menu and slideshow graphics.
3. Encode video and audio, respectively, to MPEG-2 and AC3 streams and import the encoded assets into DVD Studio Pro. (DVD Studio Pro 3 includes an MPEG-2 encoder under the hood, so you can import QuickTime movies straight into DVD Studio Pro and start authoring without the need to visit the QuickTime MPEG-2 Exporter or Compressor first.)
4. Create menus and buttons to allow the viewer to interact with and navigate your DVD-Video.
5. Create one or more tracks, including alternate angles, subtitles, markers, and stories.
6. Link the project together by connecting its menus and tracks.
7. Enhance the DVD-Video by adding scripts, slideshows, and Web links.
8. Build the project on your hard disk.
9. Test the built project using the Apple DVD Player.
10. Record the project to a DVD-R, DVD-RW, or DVD-RAM disc (or a DLT tape if you intend to send the project to a replication house).

✔ Tip

- At each applicable step of the process, you should also use DVD Studio Pro's Simulator to preview your project, ensuring that everything works correctly. (The Simulator is covered in Chapter 19, "Finishing the DVD.")

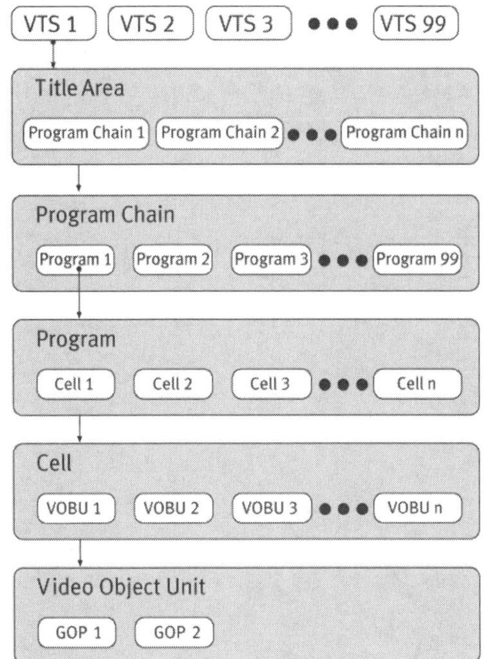

Figure 2.6 The DVD-Video data structure.

About the DVD-Video Data Structure

This section provides an overview of the DVD-Video data structure and how it relates to DVD Studio Pro (**Figure 2.6**).

Groups of pictures

The MPEG group of pictures (GOP) is the smallest random-access unit available to DVD Studio Pro. As you jump from chapter to chapter in a DVD-Video, you jump to the beginning of a GOP. (All markers lock onto a special frame in the GOP, called an I-frame—this will mean more to you after you read about markers in Chapter 12, "Enhancing Tracks.") A single GOP represents 15 frames of NTSC video or 12 frames of PAL video. To learn more about GOPs, see Chapter 4, "The QuickTime MPEG-2 Exporter."

Video object units

A video object unit (VOBU) contains one or more MPEG GOPs. A VOBU can be between 0.4 and 1.2 seconds long, which means that a VOBU typically holds two full GOPs. Occasionally, you may experience build errors when one or more of the VOBUs in your MPEG stream is less than 0.4 second long. To learn more about these errors, see Chapter 20, "Outputting the Project."

Cells

A cell is a collection of VOBUs and their corresponding audio packets.

Programs

A program is analogous to a single chapter in a track. A chapter represents the segment of an MPEG video as defined by chapter markers set in the Track editor's timeline (see Chapter 12). By default, every track has one chapter and, consequently, one program. As you fill the track with more chapter markers, you create more chapters and thus more programs, creating a *program chain.*

DVD Studio Pro allows you to create up to 99 individual programs, or chapters, per track.

Program chains

A program chain is a sequential group of programs. In DVD Studio Pro, a story is equivalent to a program chain. For more information on stories, see Chapter 12.

Title area

The title area is a collection of program chains in one track.

Video title set

The DVD-Video format allows each DVD-Video disc to have up to 99 video title sets (VTSs). In DVD Studio Pro, each track and slideshow is a VTS. If your project has 66 tracks, for example, you have room left for only 33 slideshows.

3 Preparing Graphics

All graphics used in DVD Studio Pro fall into one of two categories—moving or still—and you can't use DVD Studio Pro to create either. Moving graphics, which are used in tracks and motion menus, always contain a video component created in a video-editing program such as Apple's Final Cut Pro, Final Cut Express, Motion, or iMovie. Still graphics—used in still menus and slideshows—are usually fashioned with design programs such as Adobe Photoshop, Adobe Illustrator, Macromedia FreeHand, or even Apple iPhoto.

Although moving and still graphics share what seem to be similar traits, they're like identical twins: they may look the same, but they don't act the same, and it's best to recognize their differences and learn how to deal with them early. For example, still images created in Photoshop use a different resolution than video edited in Final Cut Pro. They also use a different RGB color space than what's used for NTSC video. You'll need to keep these differences in mind when creating your still and moving graphics for use in DVD Studio Pro. Armed with the right knowledge, you'll have little problem creating perfect video and still-image files for your projects.

Preparing Source Video

The entire reason you're learning DVD Studio Pro is to get video off your computer and onto an optical disc that can be played on a TV. Your computer and your TV, however, display video very differently. For example, your computer can display far more colors than a standard CRT (cathode-ray tube) television set, and TVs often crop the edges off a video, while computers don't. This section explains these (and other) differences and shows you how to work around them.

NTSC versus PAL

Broadcast video works under two major competing standards: NTSC (National Television Standards Committee) and PAL (Phase Alternation Line). DVD Studio Pro lets you work with either standard, but each project must be either NTSC or PAL, not both.

- NTSC video uses a screen resolution of 720 × 480 pixels per frame and a frame rate of 29.97 frames per second. If you live in North America, this is your standard.
- PAL video uses a screen resolution of 720 × 576 pixels per frame and a frame rate of 25 frames per second. If you live in Europe (including the United Kingdom), this is your standard.

Tables 3.1 and **3.2** categorize many (but not all) countries by their broadcast standard. As you develop your project, keep your target market in mind and be sure to use the correct standard for your source video streams.

✔ Tips

- NTSC reigns as the dominant video standard; consequently, most PAL DVD-Video players also play NTSC DVDs (provided that the DVD's region coding allows it). On the flip side, very few NTSC DVD-Video players also play PAL DVDs.
- Playing an NTSC DVD-Video on a PAL player can lead to problems, including poorly reproduced color and stuttering playback. If your DVD is to be distributed in both Europe and North America, you should consider making two completely separate discs: one PAL and one NTSC.

Table 3.1

NTSC Countries		
Antigua	Ecuador	Peru
Bahamas	El Salvador	Philippines
Barbados	Greenland	Puerto Rico
Belize	Guam	Saint Kitts
Bermuda	Guatemala	Samoa
Bolivia	Guyana	South Korea
Burma	Honduras	Taiwan
Canada	Jamaica	Tobago
Chile	Japan	Trinidad
Colombia	Mexico	USA
Costa Rica	Nicaragua	Venezuela
Cuba	Panama	Virgin Islands

Table 3.2

PAL Countries		
Afghanistan	Cyprus	Pakistan
Africa	Europe	Paraguay
Argentina	Hong Kong	Qatar
Australia	India	Saudi Arabia
Bahrain	Indonesia	Singapore
Bangladesh	Israel	Sri Lanka
Brunei	Jordan	Thailand
Cameroon	Kuwait	Turkey
Canary Islands	New Zealand	Uruguay
China	Oman	Yemen

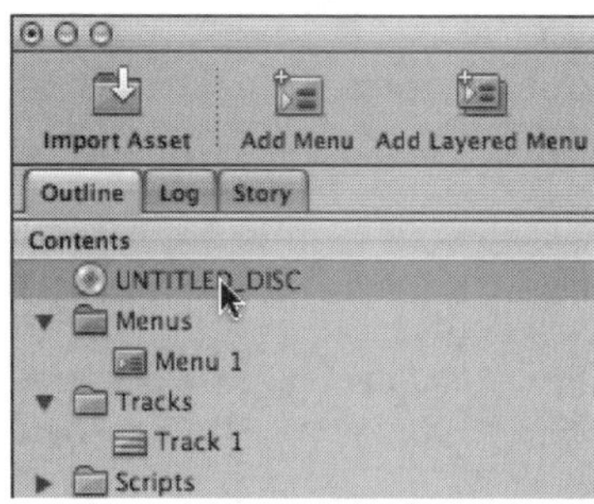

Figure 3.1 To set the project's video standard (NTSC or PAL), first select the disc itself on the Outline tab.

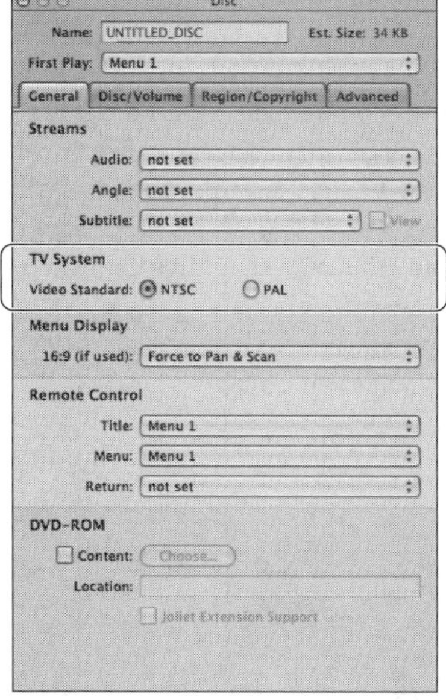

Figure 3.2 The Inspector updates to show the disc's (or the project's) properties. Here, there's a TV System area, which you'll use to set the project's video standard.

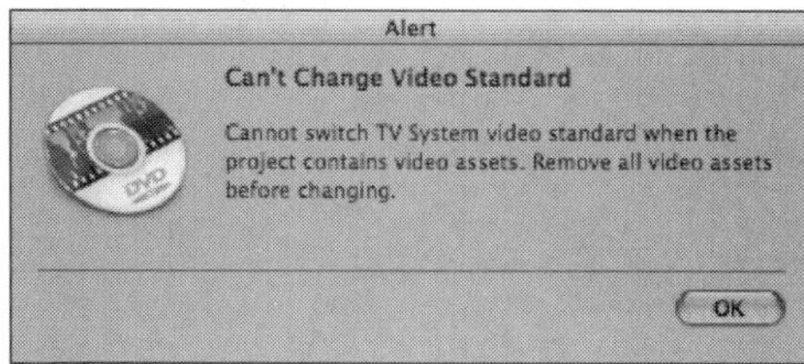

Figure 3.3 Trying to change a project's video standard after assets have been added on the Assets tab results in this dialog.

To set DVD Studio Pro's video standard:

1. At the upper left of the workspace, select the Outline tab.
2. At the top of the Outline tab, select the disc (**Figure 3.1**).

   Because a DVD-Video must be either NTSC or PAL, you set your project's video standard for the entire disc—not for individual items in the project. Consequently, you must first choose the disc itself on the Outline tab, which causes the Inspector to display the disc's properties. In these properties lies the project's video standard setting.
3. In the Inspector's TV System area, choose either NTSC or PAL by selecting the appropriate Video Standard radio button (**Figure 3.2**).

✔ Tip

- Setting the disc's video standard should always be done at the very beginning, prior to adding assets on the Assets tab. If you try to switch the video standard after adding assets on the Assets tab, a dialog appears (**Figure 3.3**). If you see this dialog, you'll have to remove all assets and start over.

About safe zones

Televisions blast electron beams at the surface of the picture tube, causing phosphors on the face of the tube to emit red, green, and blue light. As you move toward the edges of the screen, the electron beams become less accurate, and visual distortion occurs. Televisions hide this distortion "in the wings," or past the visible edges of the screen, using a process called *overscanning*.

Overscanning causes your video's displayed resolution to be less than that defined by the NTSC and PAL standards. For example, you will have created your NTSC video streams at a resolution of 720 × 480 pixels per frame, but some televisions may display only 640 × 430 (or fewer) of those pixels. The video is not resized to fit within these shrunken dimensions; in fact, all those extra pixels are hidden past the visible boundary of the screen. On televisions, the edges of your video are *always* cut off (this problem affects only CRT televisions, not digital televisions, plasma displays, or computer monitors).

To compensate for this, there are two safe zones that you can use to ensure that your viewers see everything they are supposed to see:

- The *action safe zone* is represented by a rectangular border set 5 percent in from the edges of your video (**Figure 3.4**). For NTSC video, that's 36 pixels from the left and right edges, and 24 pixels from the top and bottom edges. You should always assume that viewers watching your DVD-Video on a TV will not see everything outside the action safe zone.
- The *title safe zone* is represented by a rectangular border set 10 percent in from the edges of your video (refer to Figure 3.4). For NTSC video, that's 72 pixels from the left and right edges, and 48 pixels from the top and bottom edges. Older televisions overscan more than newer ones, so you must be sure to set all text (including closed captions and subtitles) and very important imagery inside the title safe zone.

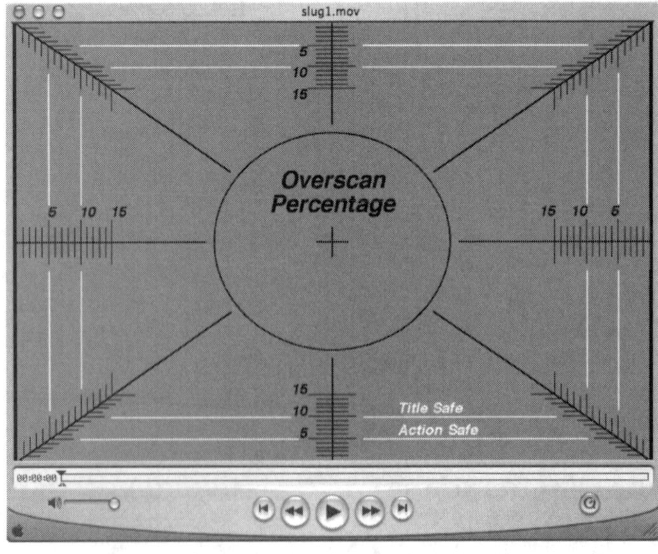

Figure 3.4 The title safe and action safe zones for NTSC video.

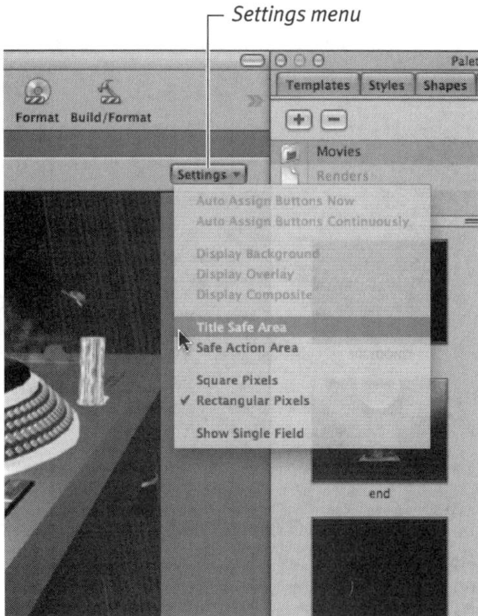

Figure 3.5 From DVD Studio Pro's Menu or Viewer tab, you can use the Settings menu to enable title and/or action safe overlays.

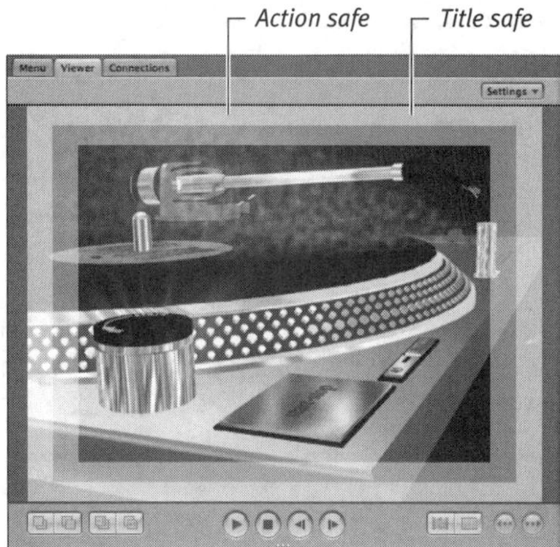

Figure 3.6 The action safe and title safe overlays on DVD Studio Pro's Viewer tab.

All video-editing programs, including DVD Studio Pro and Final Cut Pro, provide overlays that define the action and title safe zones. As you prepare your video, you should occasionally turn on these overlays and check that important visual content falls within the safe zones.

✔ Tips

- For menus, make sure all buttons are placed inside the title safe zone, or they may get sliced from view, cut in half, or otherwise truncated.
- Computers display video at its full dimensions, so nothing gets cut off. If your DVD-Video is destined only for computer playback, you do not need to design with the safe zones in mind.

To enable/disable the title or action safe overlay in DVD Studio Pro:

1. At the upper right of the workspace, click either the Menu or Viewer tab.
2. From the Settings menu in the upper-right corner of these tabs, choose Title Safe Area and/or Safe Action Area (**Figure 3.5**).

   The title safe and action safe areas appear as semitransparent white overlays on top of the menu or video (**Figure 3.6**).

To enable the title safe overlay in Final Cut Pro:

1. In the Final Cut Pro Viewer or Canvas window, click and hold the View pop-up menu.
2. Make sure Show Overlays and Show Title Safe are both selected (**Figure 3.7**).

   The action safe and title safe zones are drawn on top of the video (**Figure 3.8**). As you edit your video, make sure that no important action falls outside of these safe zones.

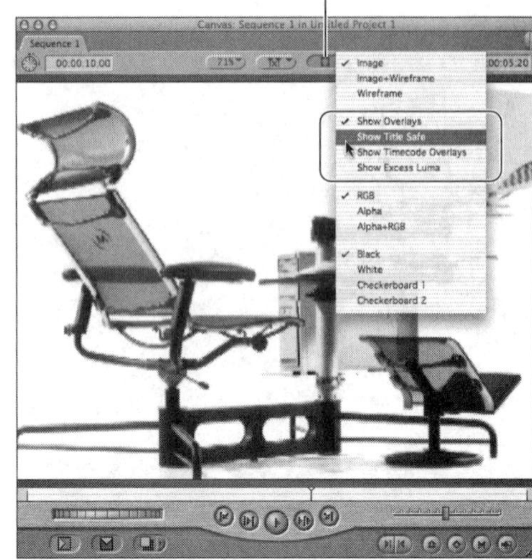

Figure 3.7 To show the title safe overlay in Final Cut Pro, from the View pop-up menu, select both Show Overlays and Show Title Safe.

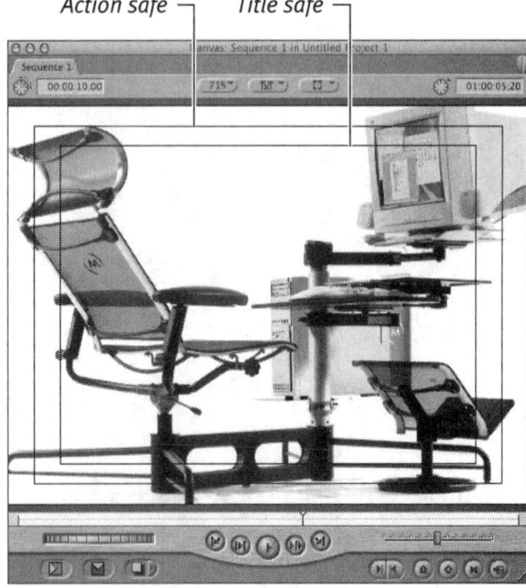

Figure 3.8 The action safe and title safe zone overlays in Final Cut Pro.

Figure 3.9 To ensure that your video conforms to the Broadcast Safe color space, first select the clips you want to filter in Final Cut Pro's timeline.

Figure 3.10 Then apply the Broadcast Safe filter. The Broadcast Safe filter is located deep in Final Cut Pro's Effects menu.

Table 3.3

Broadcast Safe Colors		
Color Value	**Standard RGB Value**	**Broadcast Safe RGB**
Red	255, 0, 0	204, 0, 0
Green	0, 255, 0	0, 204, 0
Yellow	255, 255, 0	153, 153, 0
Black	0, 0, 0	15, 15, 15
White	255, 255, 255	235, 235, 235

About color depth

Televisions cannot display as many colors as computers. In particular, TVs struggle to display bright red, green, yellow, and white, and even deep black (**Table 3.3**). If you don't filter these colors out of your video, they will appear to *bleed* into surrounding areas, making the overall image look mushy. In extreme situations, pure white (also known as *super-white*) can even cause distortion in your video's audio that sounds like buzzes and crackles. To avoid this problem, use the Broadcast Safe color filter that comes with your video-editing application. (This filter is sometimes called Broadcast Colors or NTSC Colors; see "Creating video-safe colors" later in this chapter.) On the computer screen, your bright yellows turn a bit brown, reds deepen, and pure white becomes noticeably gray, but on a television set, everything will look—and sound—perfect.

To apply the Broadcast Safe filter in Final Cut Pro:

1. In the Final Cut Pro timeline, select the clips to which you want to apply the Broadcast Safe colors filter (**Figure 3.9**).
2. Choose Effects > Video Filters > Color Correction > Broadcast Safe (**Figure 3.10**).

   The Broadcast Safe filter is applied to the selected video clips. This filter dulls all colors that are too hot, or bright, for NTSC video broadcast.

Preparing Still Graphics

When you create a still graphic for use with DVD Studio Pro, you are essentially creating a single frame of still video. Just like video, the still graphic ends up playing on a TV. And just as for video, you must follow certain rules when creating still graphics. In fact, most of the rules that apply to the creation of video—including color saturation limitations and the need for title and action safe zones—also apply to the creation of still graphics.

But there *is* one big difference between still graphics and video frames: still-image programs such as Photoshop use square pixels to represent images on the computer screen, whereas the pixels in a video frame are slightly taller than they are wide. In other words, Photoshop uses square pixels, whereas pixels in video are nonsquare (rectangular). There's a big difference between the two, and if you fail to compensate for this difference, stills from Photoshop will look thin on a television (unless you are using Photoshop CS's New Document presets—more on that in the section "About pixel aspect ratio and Photoshop CS " later in this chapter).

Following are the still-image formats for DVD Studio Pro:

- Photoshop
- PICT files
- BMP files
- JPEG files
- GIF files
- PNG files
- QuickTime image files
- Targa (TGA) files
- TIFF (TIF) files

✔ Tips

- When DVD Studio Pro compiles, or multiplexes, your project into a finished DVD-Video, all still graphics are converted into MPEG-2 stills. MPEG-2 stills are encoded as I-frames. This means that a certain amount of spatial compression is always applied to the still image when DVD Studio Pro builds the project and converts the still images to MPEG-2. To learn more, see Chapter 4, "The QuickTime MPEG-2 Exporter."
- Slideshows in DVD Studio Pro 2 do not use multilayered Photoshop files the same way that menus do. While you can use a multilayered Photoshop file as a slide, you cannot choose which layers are visible. In fact, DVD Studio Pro chooses for you by displaying only the layers that were visible the last time the Photoshop file was saved.

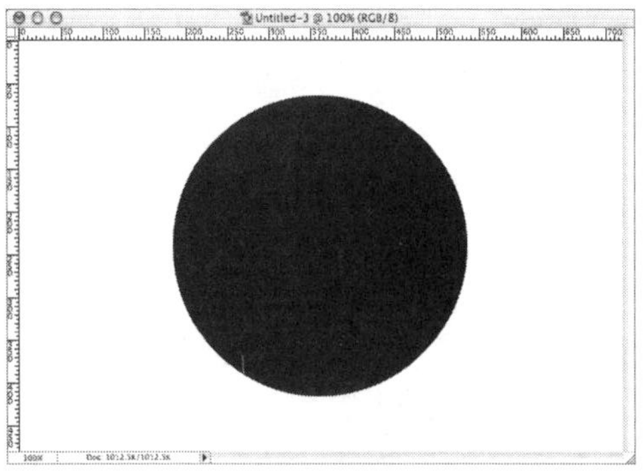

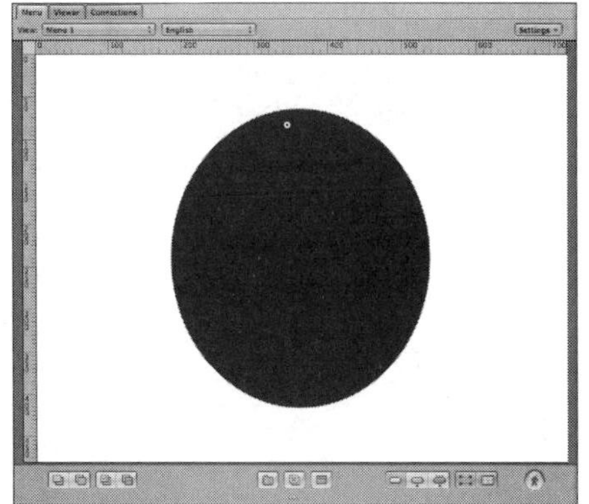

Figure 3.11 The top screen shows a Photoshop document designed with 720 x 480 square pixels. The bottom shows the graphic after it has been imported into DVD Studio Pro. As you can see, the circle in Photoshop becomes an oval in DVD Studio Pro.

About pixel aspect ratios

To display images, computers use perfectly square pixels (with an aspect ratio of 1:1), while televisions use nonsquare pixels (with an aspect ratio of 0.9:1 for NTSC and 1.07:1 for PAL). If you don't compensate for this difference between the way computers and TVs display pixels, the TV squeezes the square pixels, making the images appear taller than they are wide. As a result, graphics designed in Photoshop seem a little bent out of shape when displayed on a TV (**Figure 3.11**)—but they don't have to. There is a cure.

The difference between the aspect ratio of square and nonsquare pixels remains constant, so you can compensate by designing still graphics larger and then resizing them to the dimensions of the video standard that you're using (NTSC or PAL). The images look squeezed in your graphics program, but when played on a television, they stretch back to their original proportions.

continues on next page

D1 versus DV NTSC

As if all the different dimensions, resolutions, and aspect ratios aren't enough, there are also two forms of NTSC video, each using different dimensions. The one most applicable to you is DV NTSC. DV NTSC's dimensions are 720 × 480 pixels (you guessed it—this is the NTSC format used for DVD-Video). The other type of NTSC video is D1 NTSC. D1 NTSC's dimensions are 720 × 486 pixels—an extra six pixels taller. If you're working with D1 NTSC, create your Photoshop documents at 720 × 540 and then resize to 720 × 486. And before you bring the document into DVD Studio Pro, crop six lines off to make the document 720 × 480.

For those of you who like math and are wondering what the difference is, think of it this way: NTSC televisions use pixels with an aspect ratio of 0.9:1. When you multiply 540 by 0.9, you get 486—that's D1 NTSC. Multiply 534 by 0.9, however, and your total equals 480, which is DV NTSC. (Well, the total is actually 480.6, but what's a few tenths among friends?)

In your graphics program, design your menus as follows:

- For NTSC, create the still graphic at 720 × 534.
- For PAL, create the still graphic at 768 × 576.

DVD Studio Pro will actually resize your still image documents to 720 × 480 before it displays or multiplexes your project. In other words, all of the heavy lifting is done for you, and you can directly import a 720 × 534 document right into DVD Studio Pro without resizing it to DV resolution first. Now that's a big bonus, isn't it!

✔ Tips

- Computer DVD players, including the Apple DVD Player, compensate for rectangular TV pixels by resizing the 720 × 480 NTSC frame down to 640 × 480.
- Many people create their Photoshop documents at 720 × 540. While this works well enough, it's not the recommended practice. The correct square-pixel ratio for D1 NTSC video is 720 × 540, but DVD-Video uses DV NTSC video, and there's a bit of a difference between the frame size of the two. To learn more, see the sidebar "D1 versus DV NTSC" earlier in this chapter.
- If you do directly import a 720 × 540 document, there will be four-pixel-wide bars on the left and right edges of your menus. That's probably not the effect you were after, so stick to 720 × 534.

What about 640 x 480?

Some DVD authors prefer to create their source stills at 640 × 480 and then resize to 720 × 480 before importing them into DVD Studio Pro. Mathematically, 640 × 480 can be represented by the aspect ratio 4:3—four units across for every three units tall. Televisions also use an aspect ratio of 4:3, so when displayed on a TV, 640 × 480 graphics look correct.

The decision regarding document size comes down to the image's contents. If the image is a menu that relies on thin horizontal lines, for example, it's better to create the document at 640 × 480, because when you resize the document, the thin lines will be stretched horizontally but not resized vertically. On the other hand, when you resize a document from 720 × 534 to 720 × 480, the document will be vertically compressed, so those thin horizontal lines will become even thinner. At best, this can add to interlacing issues that make your graphic flicker onscreen. At worst, the thin lines may disappear altogether from the resized graphic. To learn more about interlacing issues, see "Preventing menu flicker" later in this chapter.

If the image does not rely on thin horizontal lines, then always begin the document at 720 × 534 (see the sidebar "D1 versus DV NTSC"). The reason is simple: When resizing a large document to make it smaller, Photoshop interpolates the data in the image and throws out what it doesn't need. When resizing a smaller document to make it bigger, Photoshop must actually create new picture data to fill these greater dimensions. This can introduce artifacts and other unwanted problems into your document. As a general rule, Photoshop is much better at throwing away data than at creating it, so if possible, you should start with a larger document and then downsize the dimensions.

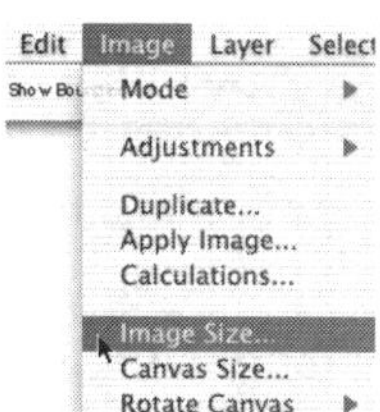

Figure 3.12 To resize a Photoshop document, choose Image > Image Size.

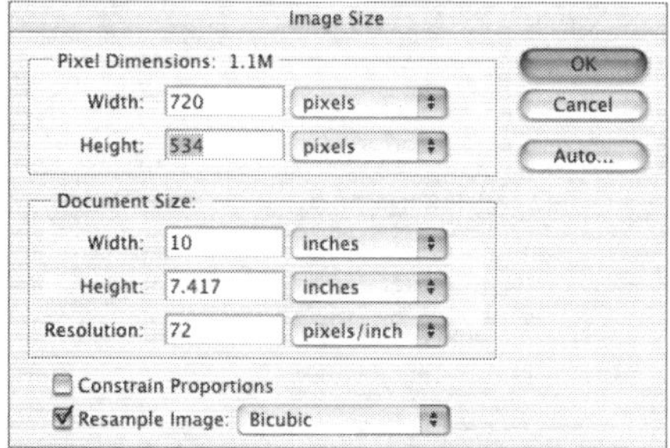

Figure 3.13 The Image Size dialog.

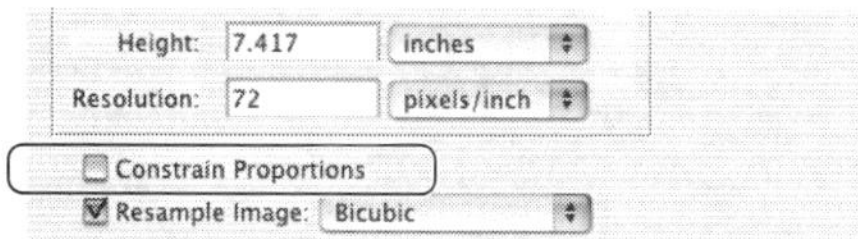

Figure 3.14 Always deselect the Constrain Proportions check box when resizing graphics that you plan to import into DVD Studio Pro.

To resize a Photoshop file:

1. Create a 720 × 534–pixel Photoshop document.
2. Choose Image > Image Size (**Figure 3.12**).

   The Image Size dialog opens (**Figure 3.13**).
3. At the bottom of the Image Size dialog, deselect the Constrain Proportions check box (**Figure 3.14**).

   This is an important step, because if you don't deselect the Constrain Proportions check box, Photoshop will resize both the height and width of the document.
4. At the top of the dialog, enter `480` in the Height text box.
5. Click OK.

   The Photoshop document is resized to 720 × 480.

To Resize or Not to Resize—Should It Even Be a Question?

DVD Studio Pro handles still pictures quite intelligently, and you don't need to resize graphics before importing them. In fact, you can directly import still images of any dimension, and DVD Studio Pro will automatically resize them to 720 × 480 pixels (NTSC) or 720 × 576 (PAL).

However, you should keep two points in mind:

- Photoshop is far better at interpolating images than is DVD Studio Pro. If you let DVD Studio Pro resize your images, you may notice artifacts, particularly in diagonal lines. For example, if a diagonal line looks like a staircase after you import an image into DVD Studio Pro, use Photoshop to resize the image to 720 × 480.
- To ensure that circles are circles and squares are squares in the final DVD-Video, however, you should still be sure to design Photoshop documents using a 4:3 aspect ratio. For example, a 1,200 × 900–pixel Photoshop document uses a 4:3 aspect ratio, as does a document that's 400 × 300, 640 × 480, or 900 × 675. When documents of these sizes are added to your project, DVD Studio Pro resizes them so they look correct in the final DVD-Video.

About pixel aspect ratio and Photoshop CS

If all this business of designing Photoshop files at 720 × 534 before converting them to 720 × 480 in DVD Studio Pro seems confusing and unnecessary, it is—but only if you're using Adobe Photoshop CS, the newest version of Photoshop.

With each Photoshop release, Adobe makes the program even more video friendly. Photoshop 7, for example, introduced several video presets to the New dialog's Presets menu. In Photoshop CS, those video presets automatically compensate for video aspect ratios. In fact, at the bottom of the New dialog is a Pixel Aspect Ratio menu. By choosing the DV video aspect ratio from this menu, you can create and work directly in a 720 × 480-pixel document—Photoshop will automatically resize your work on the fly so it conforms to the correct video pixel aspect ratio.

To create a new document in Photoshop CS:

1. Choose File > New, or press Command-N (**Figure 3.15**).

   The New dialog opens (**Figure 3.16**).

2. To name your document, type a name in the Name field.

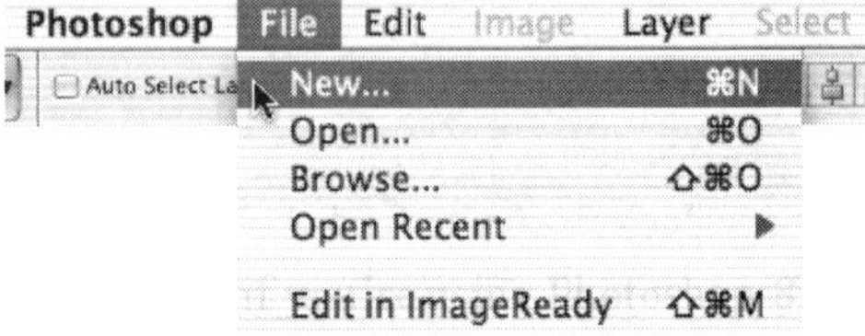

Figure 3.15 To create a new document in Photoshop CS, choose File > New.

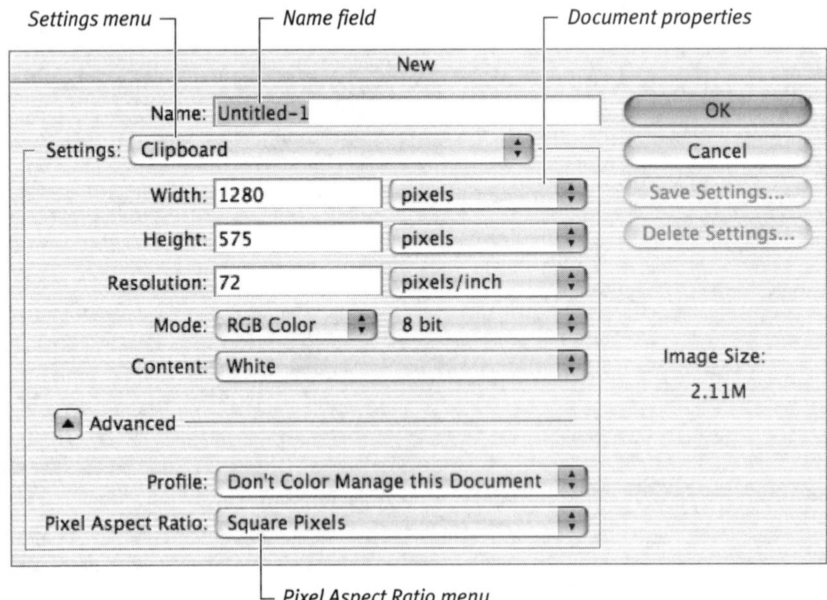

Figure 3.16 Photoshop CS's New dialog.

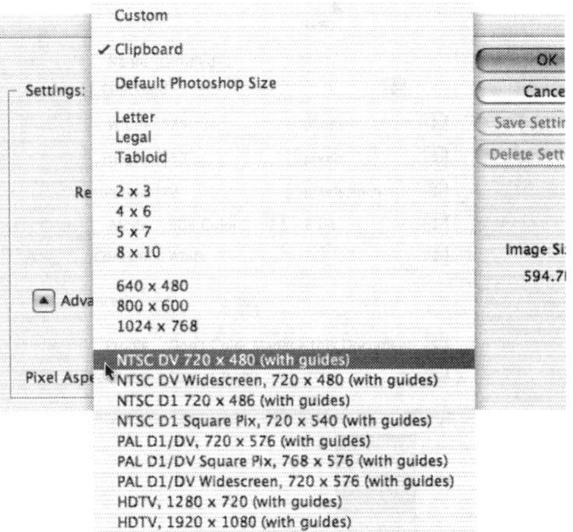

Figure 3.17 Photoshop CS's New dialog contains a range of video presets. The NTSC DV 720 x 480 (with Guides) preset is perfect for still images destined for use in DVD Studio Pro.

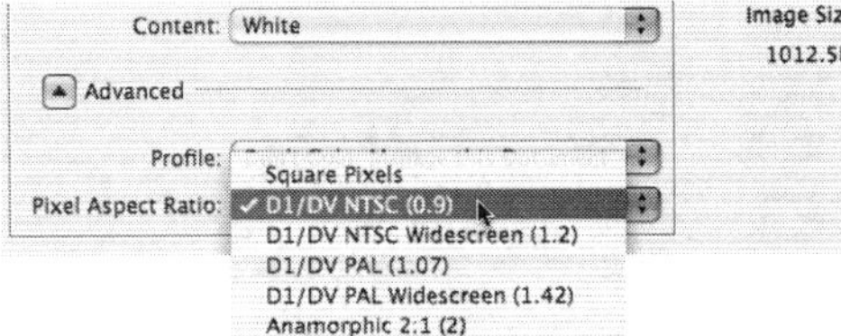

Figure 3.18 The Pixel Aspect Ratio menu can be used to switch between square and nonsquare NTSC pixels.

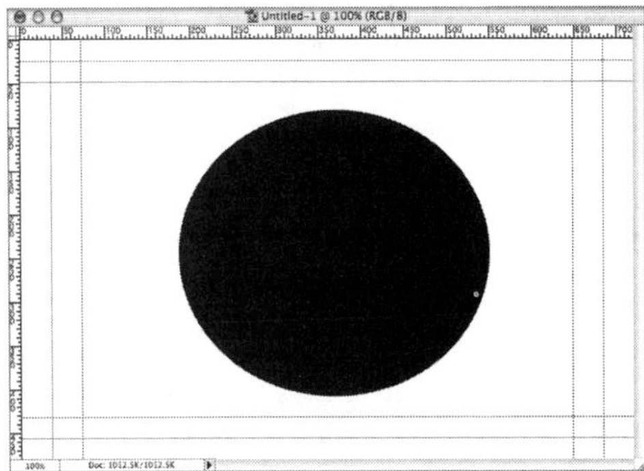

Figure 3.19 Photoshop CS automatically compensates for the difference between square computer pixels and nonsquare NTSC pixels. Notice how this circle looks slightly oval.

3. From the Settings menu, choose NTSC DV 720×480 (with Guides) (**Figure 3.17**).

   The New dialog's width and height settings update to 720 and 480, respectively. At the bottom of the New dialog, the Pixel Aspect Ratio menu should also now read D1/DV NTSC (0.9). If it doesn't, change it now (**Figure 3.18**).

4. Click OK.

   A new Photoshop document is created. Photoshop also adds title and action safe guides to the document, so you can tell at a glance which parts of the new image will always be seen and which parts may get cut off by the edge of a TV screen.

5. Draw a perfect circle in the new document (**Figure 3.19**).

   Photoshop CS automatically compensates for the difference between square computer pixels and nonsquare NTSC pixels. (To learn why a circle is used, see the "Why Circles?" sidebar later in this chapter.)

Why Circles?

When you're experimenting with pixel aspect ratio, circles make great test graphics because you can easily see if the shape appears round or oval.

To draw a perfect circle in Photoshop, use the Elliptical Marquee tool. By default, this tool is hidden behind the Square Marquee tool in the upper-left corner of Photoshop's tool palette. To access the Elliptical Marquee tool, click and hold the Square Marquee tool and then select the Elliptical Marquee tool from the menu that appears (**Figure 3.20**). To create a circle, hold down the Shift key as you drag out a circle selection. Then fill the selection with color.

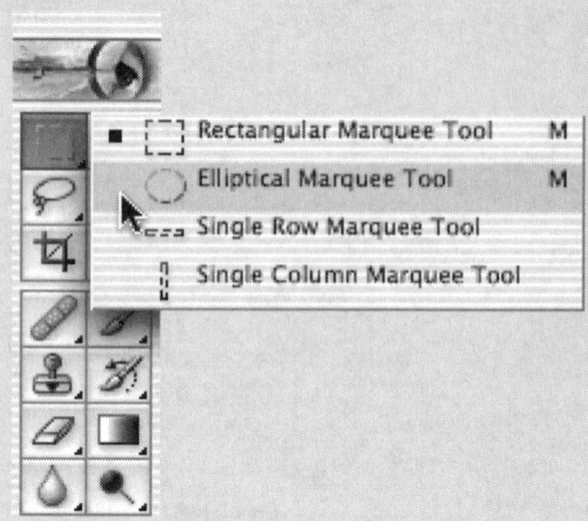

Figure 3.20 The Elliptical Marquee tool is tucked away under the Square Marquee tool. Click and hold the Square Marquee tool to open a menu that lets you select the Elliptical Marquee tool.

Working with Pixel Aspect Ratio in DVD Studio Pro

Should the need arise, you can set DVD Studio Pro to display either square or non-square pixels. Typically, you will want to leave DVD Studio Pro set to display rectangular pixels, which shows you how your graphics will look on a TV.

To change DVD Studio Pro's pixel aspect ratio display, from the Menu or Viewer tab's Settings menu, choose either Square Pixels or Rectangular Pixels (**Figure 3.21**). In the Menu editor, you can also press Option-P to toggle back and forth between square and nonsquare pixels.

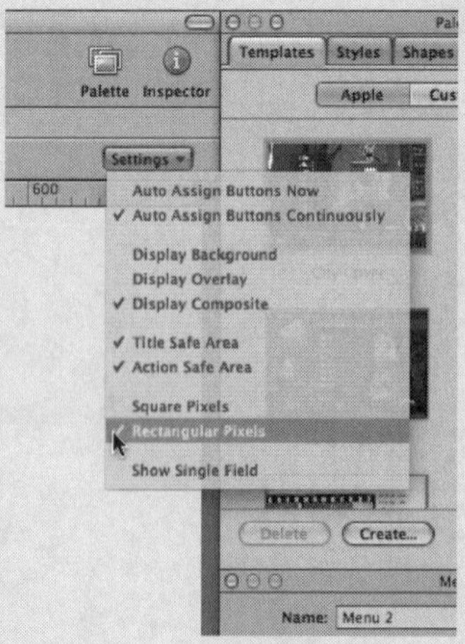

Figure 3.21 The Menu and Viewer tabs' Settings menus let you decide whether DVD Studio Pro displays pixels as square or rectangular.

About still-image resolution

If you're coming to DVD Studio Pro from a print background, you're used to designing still images at 300 pixels per inch (ppi) or perhaps even higher. If you're from a video or Web background, you're probably more comfortable designing at 72 ppi. Either way, DVD Studio Pro caters to you. DVD Studio Pro will import Photoshop files of any resolution, so your Photoshop documents can be 72 ppi, 300 ppi, or whatever resolution you feel is needed for your designs. Just keep this in mind: once imported into DVD Studio Pro, all images are scaled to 72 ppi, so it's debatable whether designing at higher pixel resolutions really offers any advantage in image quality.

To choose the pixel density of your Photoshop document:

- When creating a new document using Photoshop's New dialog, adjust the Resolution setting until it displays the pixel density that you want to use (**Figure 3.22**).

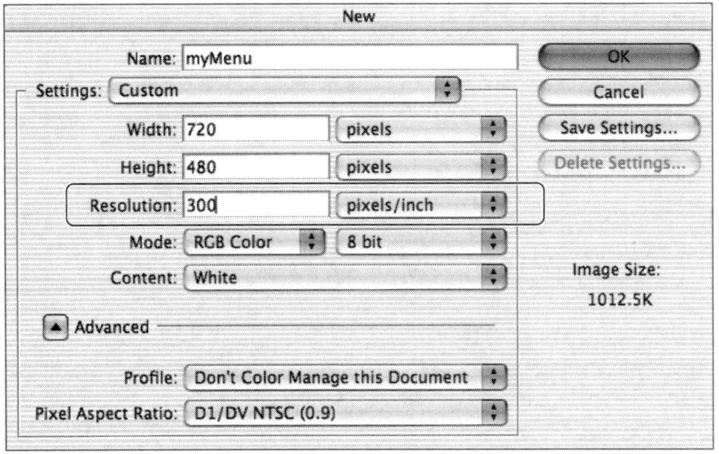

Figure 3.22 Photoshop's New dialog has a Resolution setting for specifying the document's pixel density. While 72 ppi is typically used for all documents destined for DVD Studio Pro, you can use higher ppi settings if desired.

Using layer styles

You can use Photoshop layer styles—bevels, embosses, glows, drop shadows, and so on—to add depth and dimension to otherwise flat Photoshop documents. It's always a good idea, for example, to apply a drop shadow to text, because this makes the text easier to read on TV. But Photoshop layer styles are not represented as permanent pixels on a Photoshop layer; Photoshop actually generates the layer styles each and every time the document is opened.

DVD Studio Pro cannot generate layer styles, so all Photoshop layer styles must be flattened into actual pixels on a layer before they are brought into DVD Studio Pro. Flattening a layer style is not the same as flattening the document. When you flatten a Photoshop document, all layers are collapsed into the document's background. Flattening a layer style, on the other hand, merges the layer style into the layer it is applied to—the rest of the document's layers remain just as they were.

To flatten a Photoshop layer style:

1. In Photoshop 7 or CS, if the Layers palette isn't already open, choose Windows > Layers.

   At the bottom of the Layers palette (**Figure 3.23**) is a strip of icons. Pay particular attention to the folded page icon beside the Trash can. This is the New Layer icon.

2. Click the New Layer icon to create a new layer in the Layers palette.

3. Drag the new layer underneath the layer containing the layer style (**Figure 3.24**).

   The new layer must be the one on the bottom. For layer styles to flatten, they need to merge down into the layer below.

4. Select the layer with the layer style.

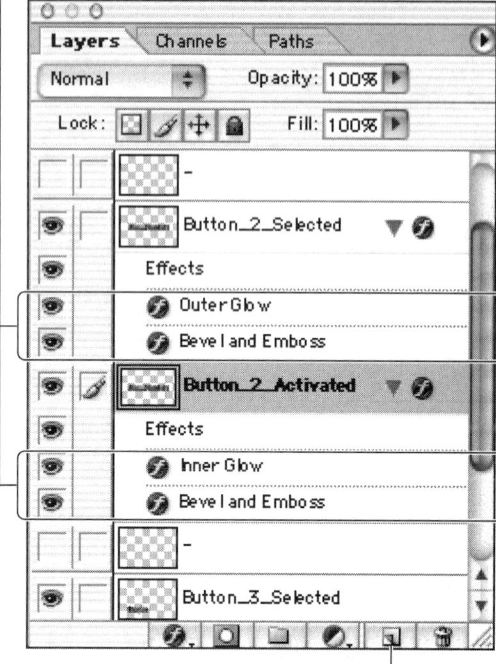

Figure 3.23 Photoshop's Layers palette, displaying a few layers that use layer styles such as glows and embossing.

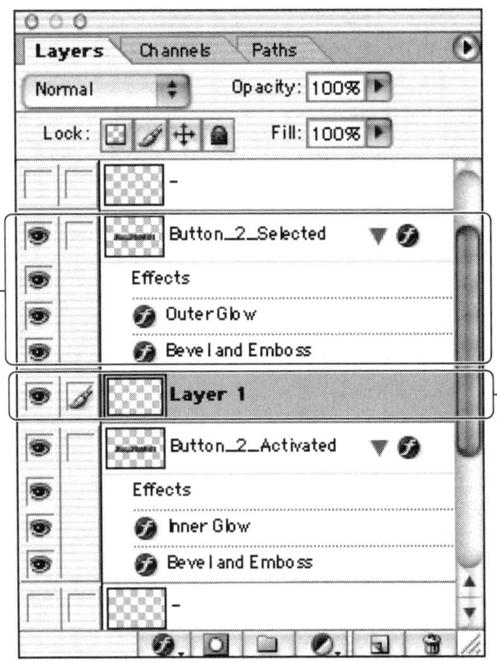

Figure 3.24 Create a new layer and drag it under the layer that you want to flatten.

Figure 3.25 To flatten the layer, click the Layers palette menu button and choose Merge Down.

5. From the Layers palette menu, choose Merge Down (**Figure 3.25**).

   The layer style is flattened, along with its layer, into the new layer below. When you bring this Photoshop document into DVD Studio Pro, the layer's drop shadows, embossing, glows, and other layer styles will be visible.

✔ Tip

- When you flatten a layer, it assumes the name of the layer it merges into, so be sure to rename the new layer.

Preventing menu flicker

Televisions display interlaced images, in which each video frame is divided into two sets of alternating one-pixel horizontal lines. As the picture flicks by on the television, one set of lines is displayed, then the second, and so on. The result is that at any one time, only half of the lines in your video frame are visible. This has an unfortunate side effect: if any of the horizontal lines in your Photoshop file are one-pixel high, they'll flicker on and off 30 times per second. Compensate for this by making all horizontal lines a minimum of three pixels high—then at least a portion of the line will always be onscreen, preventing menu flicker.

✔ Tips

- If your still image depends on thin horizontal lines, instead of designing the image at 720 × 534 pixels, use 640 × 480 and resize it to 720 × 480 before importing it into DVD Studio Pro. (To learn more, see the sidebar "What about 640 × 480?" earlier in this chapter.)
- Flicker can also creep into small text. In general, serif fonts are more prone to flicker than sans-serif fonts. Applying a drop shadow or stroke helps to reduce flicker. For more information, see the sidebar "What's a Serif Font?"

What's a Serif Font?

In medieval angelology, the seraphim are angels (and by the way, they are angels so enraptured by their love for God that they literally burn with flames of passion!). Like other angels, the seraphim have wings (actually, three pairs of wings, but who's counting?).

A serif font has small strokes at the top and bottom of the letters that are said metaphorically to look like an angel's wings—hence the term. When it comes to video, the tiny wings on serif fonts can be very thin and thus are prone to interlacing issues that make them flicker on televisions (**Figure 3.26**). Sans-serif fonts, on the other hand, do not have these wings, and thus do not flicker (in French, *sans* means "without," so *sans-serif* means "without wings").

Serif font

M

Sans-serif font

Figure 3.26 Serif fonts have small strokes—or wings—at the top and bottom of some letters, while sans-serif fonts do not.

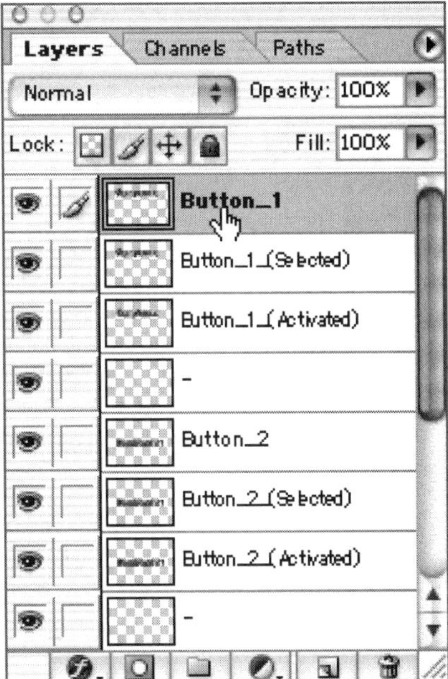

Figure 3.27 Photoshop's filters work on only one layer at a time, so you have to apply the NTSC Colors filter to each layer in your document. To ensure that you don't miss a layer, start at the top and work your way down.

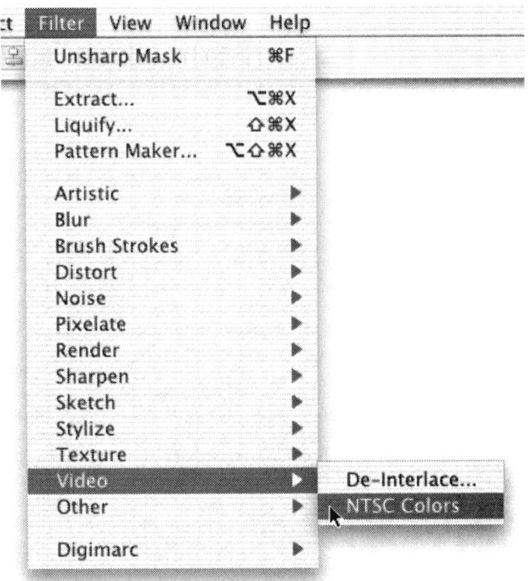

Figure 3.28 Use Photoshop's NTSC Colors filter to ensure that the colors in your Photoshop document are not too saturated for display on a television.

Creating video safe colors

In the video section earlier in this chapter, you learned about the NTSC color space (also called color depth) and saw that it is rather limited. Photoshop can display far more colors than a television can. Fortunately, Photoshop contains a filter—the NTSC Colors filter—that automatically adjusts colors to fit within the range that can be safely displayed on televisions. After you finish designing your still graphics, apply the NTSC Colors filter to each layer in your Photoshop document, and you can rest safe in the knowledge that your DVD-Video will look great on all TVs.

To apply the Photoshop NTSC Colors filter:

1. From the Layers palette, choose the top layer in your Photoshop document (**Figure 3.27**).
2. Choose Select > All, or press Command-A, to select the Photoshop layer.
3. Choose Filter > Video > NTSC Colors (**Figure 3.28**).

   The colors in the selected layer become noticeably less saturated.

continues on next page

4. Working down the Layers palette, select each layer in turn and apply the NTSC Colors filter as demonstrated in steps 2 and 3.

   The NTSC Colors filter works on one layer at a time, so you must apply it to all the layers individually.

✔ Tip

- Photoshop's NTSC Colors filter does not adjust the document's black and white areas, so you must do so by hand. White should have RGB values no higher than 235, 235, 235, and black should have RGB values no lower than 15, 15, 15. (For more information, see the sidebar "Filtering NTSC Colors Using the Levels Dialog.")

Filtering NTSC Colors Using the Levels Dialog

The RGB colors used in Photoshop span a range from 0 to 255 in each color channel, where 0 is black and 255 is 100 percent saturated, full color. Here's an old video designer's trick: All NTSC safe colors fall in a range between 15 and 235. Consequently, you can use Photoshop's Levels dialog to filter your *output color range* so that all colors sit snugly inside this range (**Figure 3.29**). The benefit of using this technique is that, unlike Photoshop's NTSC Colors filter, the Levels dialog will also filter superwhite and superblack out of your image.

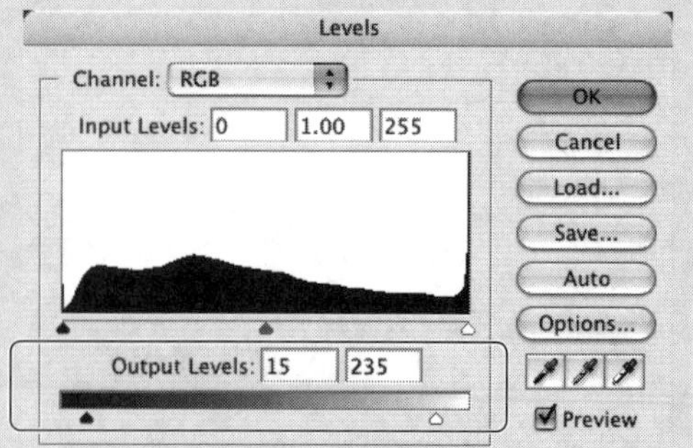

Figure 3.29 Use Photoshop's Levels dialog to filter your output colors between 15 and 235—the safe range for all NTSC colors, including white and black.

4 The QuickTime MPEG-2 Exporter

The QuickTime MPEG-2 Exporter is installed on your computer along with DVD Studio Pro. This is Apple's MPEG-2 encoder, and it alone is responsible for converting your source video into MPEG-2 streams. Whether you encode your video using QuickTime Pro Player, Final Cut Pro's QuickTime Export, Compressor, or DVD Studio Pro itself, the QuickTime MPEG-2 Exporter is always there working behind the scenes or doing the encoding.

With the release of DVD Studio Pro 2, the QuickTime MPEG-2 Exporter came of age. While its predecessor offered only basic control over the way MPEG video was encoded, the QuickTime MPEG-2 Exporter gives you access to many more choices and options—including constant-bit-rate (CBR), one-pass variable-bit-rate (VBR), and two-pass VBR encoding, along with three qualities of motion tracking (called *motion estimation* in DVD Studio Pro). All of these features combine to create one important piece of the DVD Studio Pro puzzle: professional-level MPEG-2 video with quality that's equal to, or better than, that of most other MPEG-2 encoders on the Mac. The QuickTime MPEG-2 Exporter comes free with DVD Studio Pro, but the quality of MPEG-2 video it produces is difficult to beat at any price!

This chapter covers video encoding using the QuickTime MPEG-2 Exporter, beginning with an overview of how MPEG video works. You'll look at important concepts related to MPEG streams, such as how video frames are divided for encoding and what a "group of pictures" is. Once you have a solid grasp on how MPEG video works, you'll open the QuickTime MPEG-2 Exporter and examine the fine control it gives you over the way you encode your MPEG streams. The QuickTime MPEG-2 Exporter is extremely easy to use, so once you understand its many settings, you can confidently encode MPEG video from QuickTime Pro Player, Final Cut Pro, DVD Studio Pro, or Compressor.

About MPEG Video

Although the typical DVD-R disc's 4.37 GB storage capacity might seem like a lot, in digital video terms it's but a drop in the bucket. Digital video that's compressed using the DV codec (*codec* is short for compression/decompression algorithm) uses approximately 216 MB of storage space per minute of footage. That's over one gigabyte every five minutes! Without some more efficient form of compression, you'd be able to store only 20 minutes of DV on a single-layer 4.37 GB DVD-R disc.

Happily, the good people of the Moving Picture Experts Group invented MPEG video compression, which dramatically reduces digital video file size while maintaining the full motion, resolution, and visual quality of the source video file.

MPEG video comes in two flavors: MPEG-1 and MPEG-2.

MPEG-1 video

MPEG-1 is the preferred format for video compact discs (VCDs). But due to its relatively low bit rate (typically 1.4 Mbps, with a maximum of 1.8 Mbps), for the purpose of DVD-Video, MPEG-1 is restricted to a maximum resolution of 352 × 240 pixels (NTSC) or 352 × 288 (PAL)—less than a quarter of the resolution of broadcast-quality video (**Figure 4.1**). In North America, MPEG-1 is more commonly seen on the Internet than on video-store shelves. Nonetheless, MPEG-1 is a legal format for a DVD-Video title, and DVD Studio Pro lets you use MPEG-1 video streams in your projects.

✔ Tips

- MPEG-1 video is great if you need to back up a series of videos that have been recorded to VHS. VHS is an inherently low-quality format, so you won't notice much loss in picture quality when you transfer VHS to MPEG-1.
- Using MPEG-1, you can get up to eight hours of video on a DVD-R.

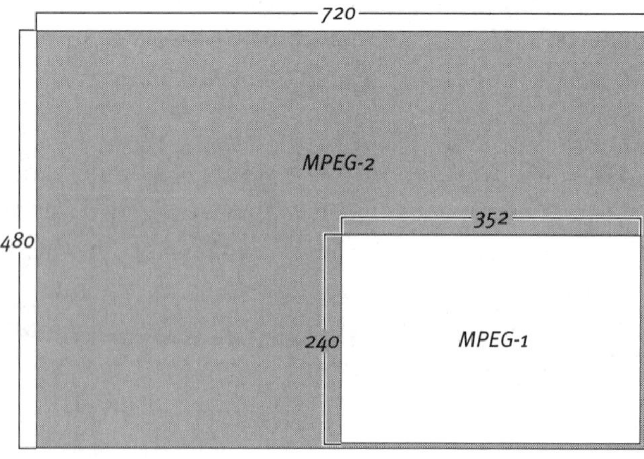

Figure 4.1 At 352 x 240 pixels, MPEG-1 offers only a quarter of the resolution of MPEG-2 video.

MPEG-2 video

MPEG-2 video is the preferred format for DVD-Video titles, and it is the format you will typically use while authoring in DVD Studio Pro. MPEG-2 video provides a resolution of 720 × 480 at 29.97 frames per second (NTSC) or 720 × 576 at 25 frames per second (PAL), with a maximum bit rate of 9.8 Mbps. In other words, MPEG-2 video provides full-motion, full-resolution, broadcast-quality video at a data rate that most computers and all DVD-ROM drives can handle.

✔ Tip

- The "sweet spot" for MPEG-2 encoding—or the data rate that most often balances file size against quality—is 6 Mbps. With the QuickTime MPEG-2 Exporter's two-pass VBR option, however, 4.5 Mbps is a high enough data rate to provide excellent quality in all but the most demanding source footage. To learn more, see "Choosing a bit rate" later in this chapter.

About MPEG-2 Compression

Video is a progression of still images that flick by in rapid succession. If you stop a video, you see a single image, called a *frame*. The frame itself is made of a grid of colored dots, called *pixels*. On a micro level, the effect of motion in a video is actually caused by color changes in these tiny pixels, frame after frame, over time. Consequently, a video encoder has a daunting task ahead of it; to be truly efficient, it must compress the data that represents each frame's pixels, both spatially (within the video frame) and temporally (over time, or across several video frames).

MPEG encoders start by breaking the video into several small segments called *groups of pictures (GOPs)*. The first frame in a typical GOP (technically, the I-frame, but more on that in a moment) is spatially compressed using a process similar to JPEG compression for still images. With the first frame completely compressed, the encoder moves on to the next frame and checks to see if blocks of color have shifted or changed. Where blocks of color have shifted, the encoder creates a *motion vector* to represent this change.

Motion vectors

MPEG encoders divide the video frame into 16 × 16–pixel blocks (called *macroblocks*) and then search through surrounding frames looking for similar blocks of color. If the encoder finds a similar block, it creates a motion vector to describe how far the block has moved. This approach is a major boon to compression because instead of reencoding each pixel in each color block for each frame of video in the stream, the MPEG encoder need record only a small number representing the amount that the color block has moved from one frame to the next.

For example, take a video of a zeppelin floating through the sky. The macroblocks composing the zeppelin don't change in color as the zeppelin floats along, and there is no need to spatially re-encode those blocks frame after frame after frame. Instead, a motion vector is used to describe the movement of the zeppelin (or rather, the movement of the macroblocks composing the zeppelin).

✔ Tips

- In the QuickTime MPEG Exporter, the amount of detail applied in determining motion vectors is controlled by the motion estimation setting, which you'll explore later in this chapter.
- Motion vectors work well wherever large blocks of color move together. Panning shots (where the whole frame moves sideways) compress well; zooms (where the camera focuses on a particular object, causing it to grow larger in relation to other objects in the frame) do not.

GOPs

As mentioned earlier, MPEG encoding utilities begin the compression process by breaking the source video into GOPs (**Figure 4.2**). According to the DVD-Video format, a GOP must be no larger than 18 pictures, or frames of sequential video. However, it's more common to use a GOP size of 15 for NTSC video and 12 for PAL video (roughly equivalent to two GOPs per second of video).

A GOP is composed of one intra frame (*I-frame*) followed by several predicted frames (*P-frames*) and bidirectional predicted frames (*B-frames*). Of the three frame types, I- and P-frames are considered *reference frames*. A reference frame can be used as the basis for mathematically deriving other frames in the GOP.

- **I-frames.** Each GOP created with the QuickTime MPEG Exporter begins with an I-frame. An I-frame contains all of the data needed to fully re-create the source video frame and is spatially compressed in a process similar to JPEG still-image compression. I-frames represent complete pictures and are equivalent to keyframes in other forms of digital video compression.
- **P-frames.** Using motion vectors, a P-frame calculates the difference between itself and the preceding reference frame. Areas not accounted for by motion vectors are instead encoded with the same process used to compress I-frames. Consequently, P-frames contain only data that has changed.
- **B-frames.** B-frames are encoded similarly to P-frames except all motion vectors are bidirectional, or mathematically derived from both the previous and following reference frames.

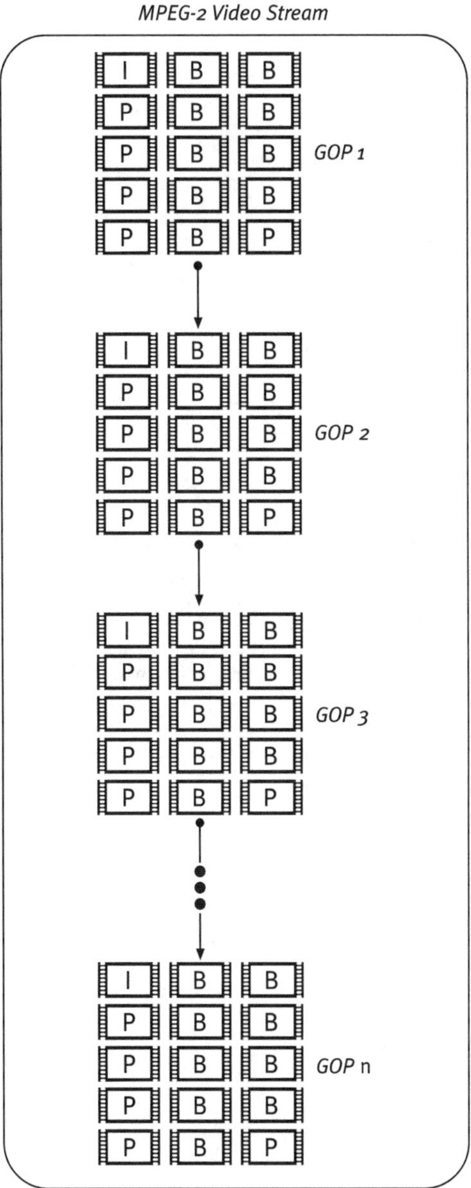

Figure 4.2 An MPEG-2 video stream is divided into many groups of pictures (GOPs).

✔ Tips

- The QuickTime MPEG-2 Exporter GOP size is fixed at 15 pictures. Although some compression utilities (including Apple's Compressor) will let you set your own GOP size, stick with a GOP size of 15. Playing with GOP size can lead to higher-quality MPEG-2 streams, but you may not be able to use them in alternate-angle tracks. In general, it's best to avoid adjusting the GOP size unless you know exactly what you're doing.
- Because only I-frames contain all of the data needed to completely re-create the source frame, the thumbnails that appear on MPEG-2 clips in DVD Studio Pro's Track Editor are all I-frames. Similarly, markers can be placed only on I-frames (to learn more, see Chapter 12, "Enhancing Tracks").

Open versus closed GOPs

The QuickTime MPEG-2 Exporter creates only closed GOPs. DVD Studio Pro, however, comes with a compression utility called Compressor, which allows you to create both open and closed GOPs. While open GOP MPEG-2 streams generally have smaller file sizes, they cannot be used in multi-angle tracks. Because the savings in actual file size is quite small, it's usually best to follow the QuickTime MPEG-2 Exporter's lead and just use closed GOPs.

So what's the technical difference between open and closed GOPs? Well, it all comes down to the order of I-, P-, and B-frames in the GOP. A closed GOP begins with an I-frame and ends with a P-frame (**Figure 4.3**). An open GOP, however, typically begins with a B-frame and ends with a P-frame (**Figure 4.4**). With an I-frame at the front and a P frame at the end, a GOP becomes self-contained—or closed—because all of the data needed to reproduce the GOP is contained within the GOP itself. An open GOP, on the other hand, may start with a B-frame, which means the GOP must get information from the last frame of the previous GOP in order to properly display that first B-frame.

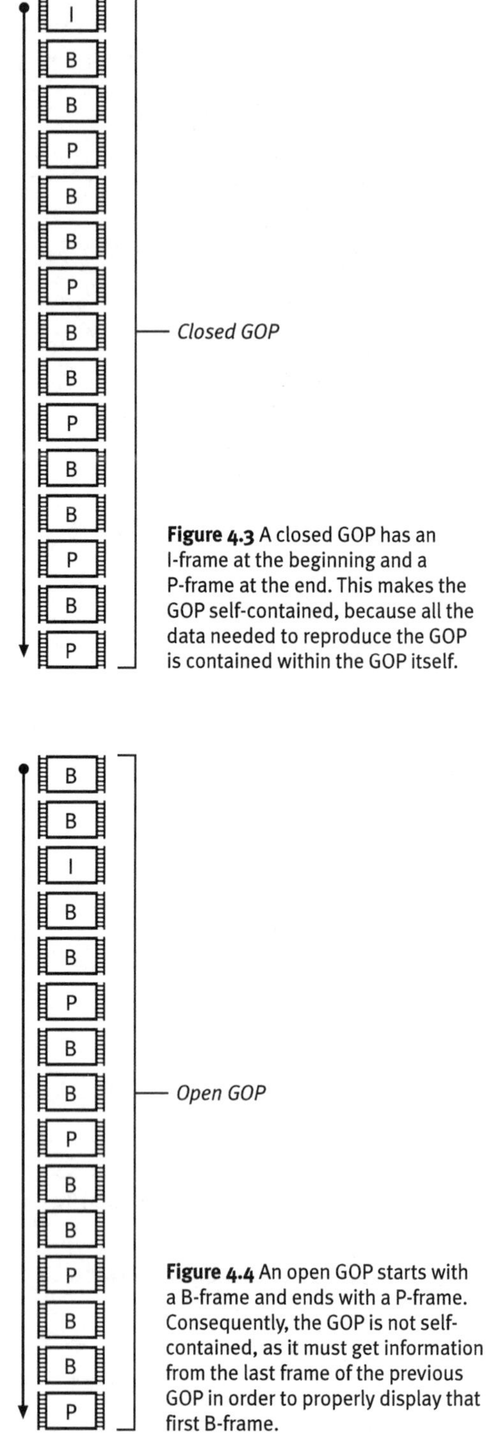

Figure 4.3 A closed GOP has an I-frame at the beginning and a P-frame at the end. This makes the GOP self-contained, because all the data needed to reproduce the GOP is contained within the GOP itself.

Figure 4.4 An open GOP starts with a B-frame and ends with a P-frame. Consequently, the GOP is not self-contained, as it must get information from the last frame of the previous GOP in order to properly display that first B-frame.

Shooting Video for Optimum Compression

MPEG encoders compress video temporally, over time. This feature produces very small, high-quality MPEG files, but only if macroblocks within the video remain constant from frame to frame. While shooting the source video for your DVD project, you can do a few things to make sure your video compresses at the best possible quality:

- **Use a tripod.** No matter how steady your hand, if you "shoot from the hip," or hold the camera, there will inevitably be some twitches and shakes in your footage. However slight, these twitches cause pixels to jiggle around the frame, and jiggling pixels increase the bit rate needed for high-quality compression. Use a tripod to eliminate these unwanted and hard-to-compress twitches.
- **Shoot against a solid background.** Solid blocks of color compress better than noisy backgrounds. If at all possible, set up your shot against a backdrop of uniform color.

Nooooooo Noise!

Noise is undeniably the bane of all DVD authors. Although a bit of noise in a video stream is barely noticeable when you're *watching* video on TV—or even on a computer—it can be a big problem when encoding MPEG-2 video.

MPEG compression works best when pixels do not change color over time, but in a noisy signal, all pixels change color all the time. Even though the colors shift only slightly, it's still a mess of changing hues and tones, and this mess inevitably gets encoded into the video.

The QuickTime MPEG-2 Exporter does not have a noise filter, but other third-party MPEG encoders do. Innobits BitVice, for example, comes with a great noise filter (**Figure 4.5**). For more information, check out the Innobits Web site: `www.innobits.com/`.

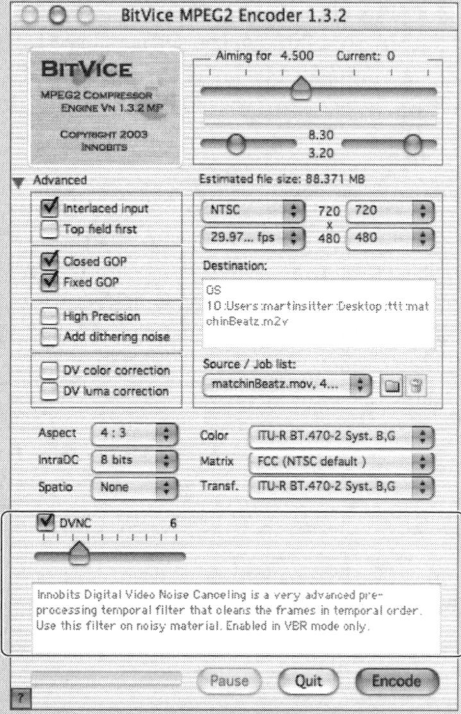

Figure 4.5 The Innobits Digital Video Noise Canceling (DVNC) filter removes noise from video streams before encoding the MPEG-2 stream. This can result in higher-quality MPEG video with smaller file sizes.

About the QuickTime MPEG-2 Exporter

Before version 2, one major criticism of DVD Studio Pro was that the QuickTime MPEG-2 Exporter was not capable of producing professional-quality MPEG-2 streams. That complaint is a thing of the past—DVD Studio Pro now ships with a professional-quality MPEG-2 encoder that provides CBR, one-pass VBR, and two-pass VBR encoding with quality comparable to—or better than—most other MPEG encoders offered on the Macintosh.

If you've diligently read the beginning of this chapter, you're armed with all the theory you need to compress great-looking MPEG-2 video streams. You're about to put that theory into action, because the following sections go step by step through the settings used to encode MPEG-2 video using the QuickTime MPEG-2 Exporter.

✔ Tip

- If your source video's resolution is different from the standard resolution for NTSC video (or PAL video, if you're compressing a PAL MPEG stream), the QuickTime MPEG-2 Exporter automatically adjusts the encoded stream to the correct dimensions.

When do I encode the video?

Typically, you will finish your video edits in Final Cut Pro, Final Cut Express, or iMovie and then encode the video to MPEG-2 before bringing it into DVD Studio Pro. The key word here is *typically*, because DVD Studio Pro will let you directly import unencoded QuickTime movies. You can then start editing your DVD-Video using these unencoded movies, and DVD Studio Pro will work behind the scenes to encode them for you either as you author or when the finished project is multiplexed.

This feature is called background encoding. It works great, but it sucks up your computer's CPU power, which in turn makes your computer seem to run slowly. Unless you have a cutting-edge Mac, it's still best to encode your video to MPEG-2 before bringing it into DVD Studio Pro.

✔ Tip

- Using the QuickTime MPEG Encoder, you must encode each QuickTime movie individually, one by one. Apple's Compressor, on the other hand, has a batch list that lets you encode several QuickTime movies with the click of a button. Using Compressor, you can set up several movies with unique encoding parameters and then set them all to encode while you go make a cup of tea, create menu graphics in Photoshop, get a good night's sleep, or whatever. When you come back to your computer, all of your video will be encoded and ready for import into DVD Studio Pro. The bottom line is, get to know Compressor—it's a real time-saver.

Figure 4.6 In QuickTime, high-quality playback is enabled in the Movie Properties window. To open the Movie Properties window, choose Movie > Get Movie Properties.

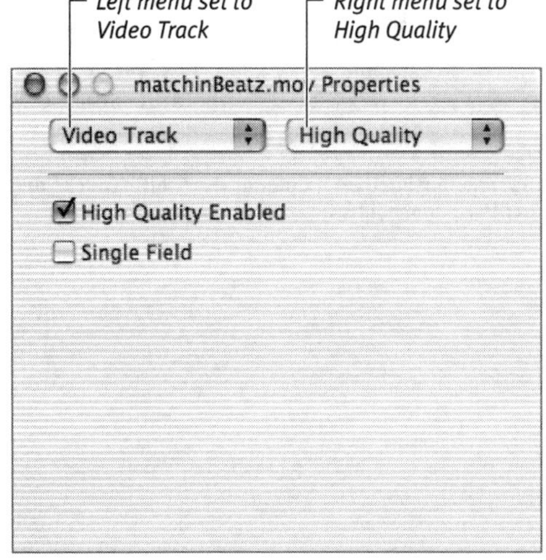

Figure 4.7 The Movie Properties window lets you select the movie's video track (left menu) and then enable high-quality display (right menu).

Blurry video in QuickTime?

Have you ever opened a DV video in QuickTime and noticed that it looked a bit blurry, not quite as sharp as it should be? You'll be pleased to hear that the problem is not your DV video stream. It's QuickTime—or rather, the way QuickTime displays DV video.

The problem is this: QuickTime automatically uses a low-quality display setting for DV video. This is a vestigial organ of QuickTime, left over from the days when computers simply couldn't read data off a hard disk fast enough to display DV video at its full frame rate and resolution. With modern Macs, this isn't an issue, but low-quality display remains a confusing QuickTime "feature." Happily, you can set QuickTime to use high-quality playback, which displays your DV video exactly as it was meant to be seen. In fact, high-quality playback is not at all high quality—it's normal!

Although you can easily enable high-quality playback, it's important to note that the blurriness you see with QuickTime's automatic setting will not affect your video in any way; the final, encoded MPEG streams will look sharp and accurate regardless of whether QuickTime is set to high-quality playback.

To set high-quality playback in QuickTime:

1. Open a DV video in QuickTime.
2. Open the Movie Properties window by choosing Movie > Get Movie Properties (**Figure 4.6**), or pressing Command-J.
3. From the Movie Properties window's left pop-up menu (the Track menu), choose Video Track, and from the right pop-up menu (the Properties menu), choose High Quality (**Figure 4.7**).
4. Select the High Quality Enabled check box.

   The movie snaps into focus.

Opening the QuickTime MPEG-2 Exporter

The QuickTime MPEG-2 Exporter is a QuickTime component that is installed by the DVD Studio Pro installer (**Figure 4.8**). As a piece of QuickTime's component architecture, the QuickTime MPEG-2 Exporter's major advantage is that it's available to most Macintosh video programs. For example, you can use the QuickTime MPEG-2 Exporter to encode MPEG-2 video streams directly from Final Cut Pro or Compressor.

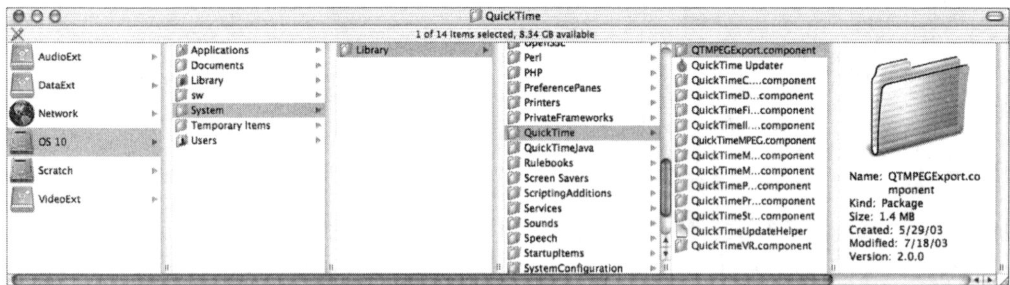

Figure 4.8 The path to the QuickTime MPEG Export component as traced using OS X's Column view. If the QuickTime MPEG-2 Export component is not in this exact location on your hard disk, you will not be able to export MPEG-2 video from QuickTime.

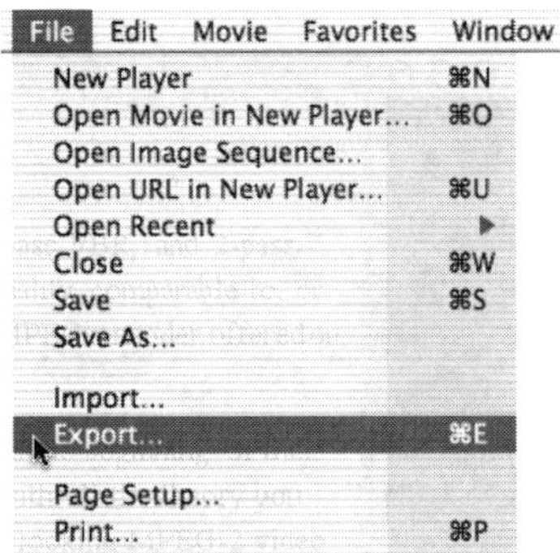

Figure 4.9 The first step in encoding an MPEG-2 video stream is to open a movie in QuickTime and choose File > Export.

To open the QuickTime MPEG-2 Exporter:

1. Open a digital video in QuickTime.
2. Choose File > Export (**Figure 4.9**), or press Command-E, to open the Save Exported File As dialog (**Figure 4.10**).
3. Navigate to the directory where you want to save your exported MPEG file and enter a name for it in the Save As text box.
4. From the Export pop-up menu, select Movie to MPEG2 (**Figure 4.11**).

   In the Save As text box, a .m2v file extension is added to your movie's name. This is the QuickTime MPEG-2 file extension.

continues on next page

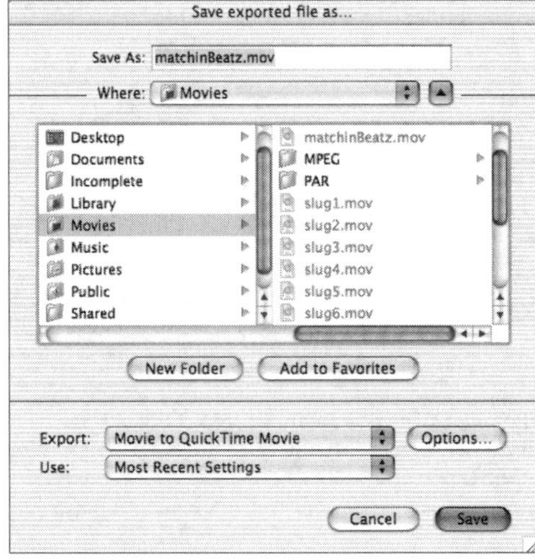

Figure 4.10 QuickTime's Export dialog.

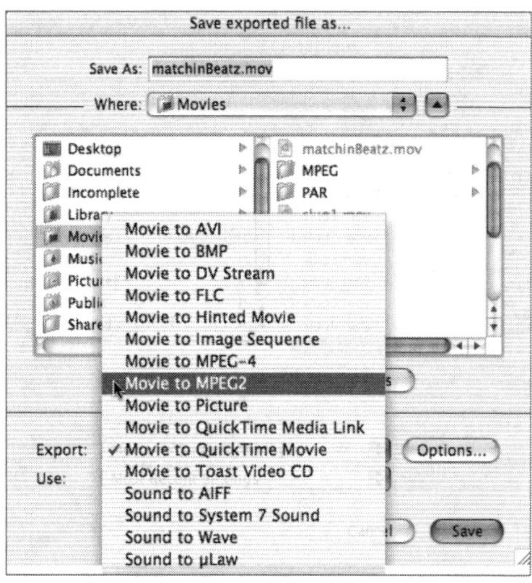

Figure 4.11 The Export menu determines the format to which the QuickTime movie will be converted. There are several options to choose from, but Movie to MPEG2 is the one you'll choose to create MEPG-2 video streams for use with DVD Studio Pro.

5. At the right of the Export menu, click the Options button (**Figure 4.12**).

   The QuickTime MPEG-2 Exporter window opens (**Figure 4.13**).

✔ Tip

- If you're in a hurry, the Use menu at the very bottom of the QuickTime Save Exported File As dialog holds several presets you can use to encode your video streams (**Figure 4.14**).

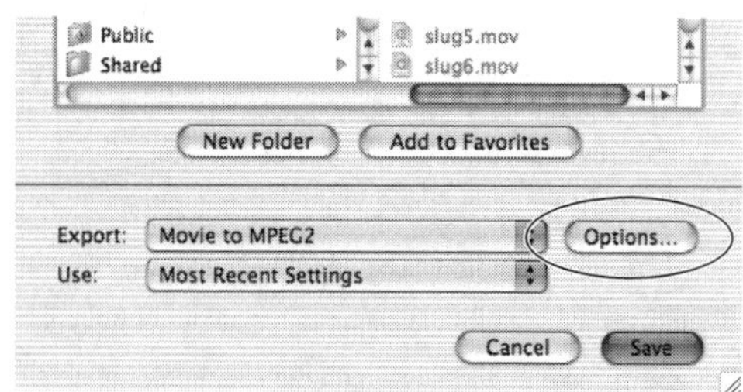

Figure 4.12 With Movie to MPEG2 selected in the Export menu, click Options to open the QuickTime MPEG-2 Exporter.

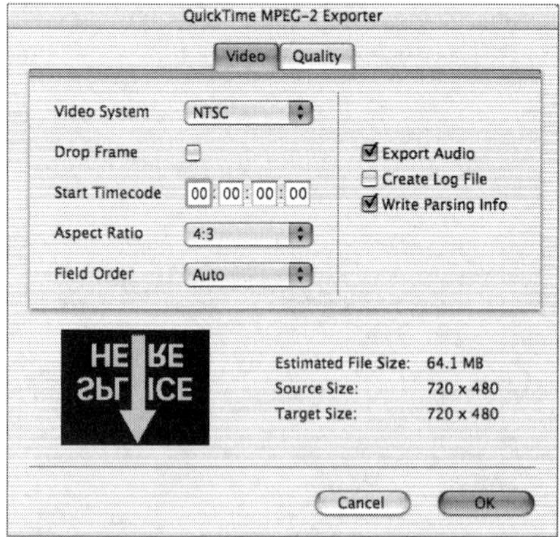

Figure 4.13 The QuickTime MPEG-2 Exporter.

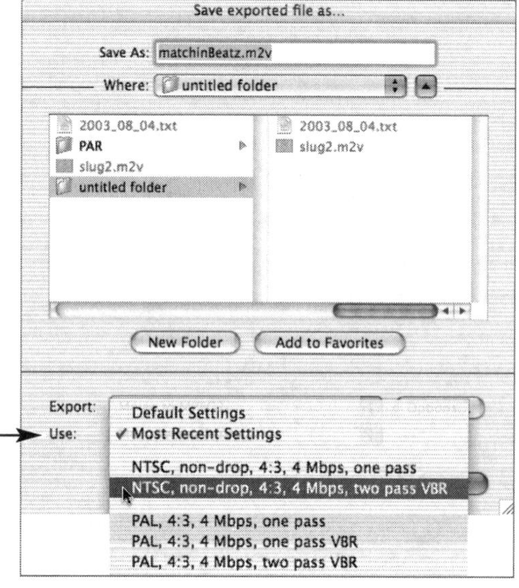

Figure 4.14 The Use menu, located at the bottom of QuickTime's Export dialog, contains several MPEG-2 presets.

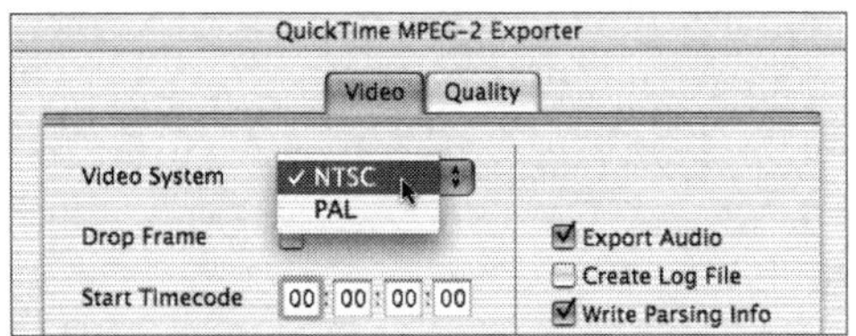

Figure 4.15 Choose your video standard from the QuickTime MPEG-2 Exporter's Video System menu.

Choosing a Video System

Your choice of video system depends upon the area of the world where your DVD-Video will be distributed and viewed. For video destined for playback in North America, select NTSC. For video destined for playback in Europe, select PAL. To learn more about video standards, see Chapter 3, "Preparing Graphics."

To choose a video system:

1. Open the QuickTime MPEG-2 Exporter.
2. Click the Video tab.
3. From the Video System menu, choose NTSC or PAL (**Figure 4.15**).

About Timecode

Timecode is a system used to number the frames in a video stream. The timecode is sort of like the address given to every house on a street, and it helps you and your video-editing program locate specific frames of video when needed. Timecode is also used to synchronize different parts of a video, such as the audio and video streams. Timecode is displayed in hours, minutes, seconds, and frames, with each number separated by a colon. For example, the timecode 01:05:04:15 represents the frame at 1 hour, 5 minutes, 4 seconds, frame 14.

Using drop- versus non-drop-frame timecode

NTSC video can be either drop or non-drop frame, and your choice depends entirely upon the way the video stream was created. To learn more about drop-frame versus non-drop-frame video, see the sidebar "To Drop or Not to Drop?"

To select drop- or non-drop-frame video:

1. Open the QuickTime MPEG-2 Exporter.
2. Click the Video tab.
3. Select or deselect the Drop Frame check box (**Figure 4.16**).

Figure 4.16 The Drop Frame check box should be set to reflect timecode settings used as you edited your video in Final Cut Pro, Final Cut Express, or iMovie.

To Drop or Not to Drop?

The issue of drop- versus non-drop-frame timecode is complicated. Drop-frame timecode ensures that the timing of an NTSC video stream matches the actual ticking of a clock. This is important only for situations that demand exact timing, such as when your NTSC video is intended for broadcast.

Here's the explanation. NTSC video uses a frame rate of 29.97 frames per second. That's 0.03 second slower than the nearest whole-number frame rate of 30 frames per second. Timecode, however, can be represented only by whole numbers—you can't have 0.97 of a frame. Consequently, drop-frame timecode actually counts 30 frames per second, but in its numbering scheme it drops frames 0 and 1 from the first second of every minute, except for minute numbers that are exactly divisible by 10.

It is important to note that *no video frames are actually dropped!* Drop-frame timecode simply specifies the way each frame is numbered, and not whether the frame is displayed. To avoid confusion, unless your video is intended for broadcast, it's best to use non-drop-frame timecode.

In any video-editing program, including DVD Studio Pro and Final Cut Pro, to determine if a timecode is drop or non-drop frame, just look at the divider between the timecode's seconds and frames fields. Drop frame timecode always has a semicolon, as shown in **Figure 4.17**, while non-drop-frame timecode always has a colon, as shown in **Figure 4.18**. In Final Cut Pro, you can change a sequence's timecode by Control-clicking the timecode field at the top left of the timeline (**Figure 4.19**).

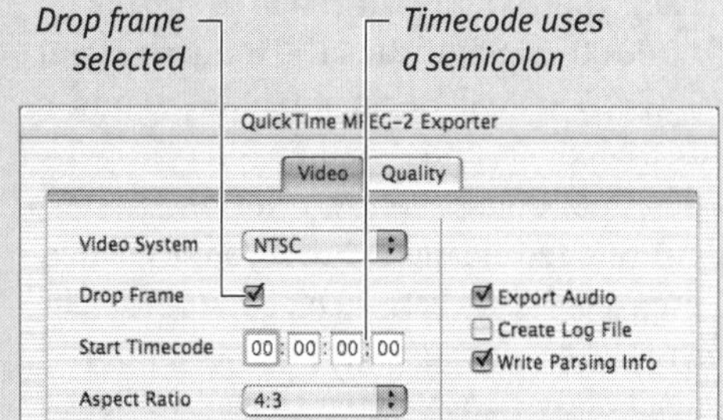

Figure 4.17 Drop-frame timecode always has a semicolon between the seconds and frames fields.

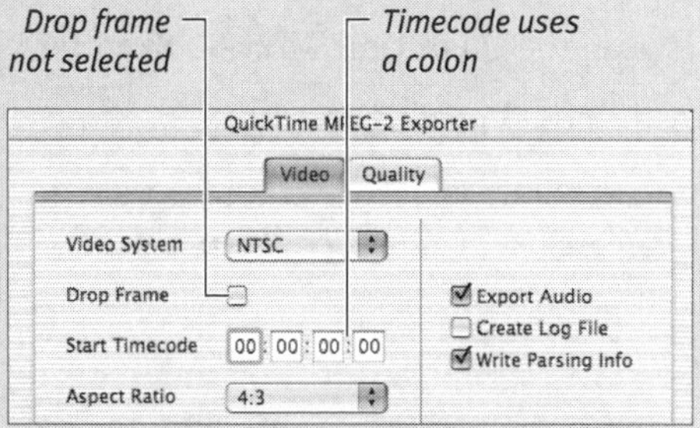

Figure 4.18 Non-drop-frame timecode always has a colon between the seconds and frames fields.

Figure 4.19 In Final Cut Pro, change your sequence from drop to non-drop frame by Control-clicking the timecode field at the top left of the timeline.

Setting a start timecode value

Usually, you want all timecode to start at 00:00:00:00, which means the frames in your MPEG stream will begin at 0 hours, 0 minutes, 0 seconds, and 0 frames—in other words, at 0. Consequently, you won't need to adjust this setting often. But if you've created a timecode-based list, such as a subtitle file where the timecode begins at, say, 1 hour instead of 0 hours, you may have to adjust the MPEG stream's start timecode to ensure that everything lines up in DVD Studio Pro.

To set the start timecode value:

1. Open the QuickTime MPEG-2 Exporter.
2. Click the Video tab.
3. In the Start Timecode text boxes, set the stream's start timecode (**Figure 4.20**).

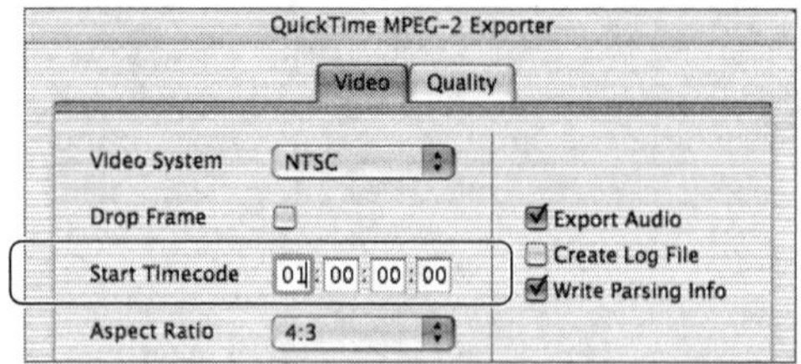

Figure 4.20 Use the QuickTime MPEG-2 Exporter's Start Timecode field to offset the start timecode used in the encoded MPEG stream.

Figure 4.21 A 4:3 aspect ratio is used for normal video streams (PAL or NTSC), while 16:9 is used for widescreen video.

Choosing an Aspect Ratio

Aspect ratio is measured in generic units, and it reflects the width of a video compared to its height. There are two different aspect ratios used for DVD-Video: 4:3 and 16:9. A 4:3 video is 4 units across by 3 units tall, while a 16:9 video is 16 units across by 9 units tall. The 4:3 aspect ratio matches most televisions that are currently on the market (NTSC or PAL), so you'll usually use this instead of 16:9 when encoding MPEG streams for use in DVD Studio Pro. The 16:9 aspect ratio is used for widescreen video. To learn more about 16:9 (widescreen) video, see Chapter 22, "Widescreen: 16:9."

To set the aspect ratio:

1. Open the QuickTime MPEG-2 Exporter.
2. Click the Video tab.
3. From the Aspect Ratio menu, choose either 4:3 or 16:9 (**Figure 4.21**).

Setting the Field Order

Televisions display video as an alternating series of odd and even lines, called *fields,* that flick by at double the perceived frame rate to create smoother video playback. But the video looks smooth only if you encode your MPEG-2 streams using the correct field order. If you don't, your video will look choppy and disturbed. Consequently, it's important to select the correct field order when you encode your video streams.

When you edit video on a computer, however, these two sets of alternating lines are *interlaced* to create one frame. This makes the editing process easier but causes frames from high-motion scenes to exhibit a comb-like effect on a computer monitor. If you notice this as you edit with DVD Studio Pro, don't worry; everything will look fine when the completed project is played back on a television.

To select the field order:

1. Open the QuickTime MPEG-2 Exporter.
2. Click the Video tab.
3. Set the Field Order pop-up menu to match the field order (also called field dominance) of your source video (**Figure 4.22**).

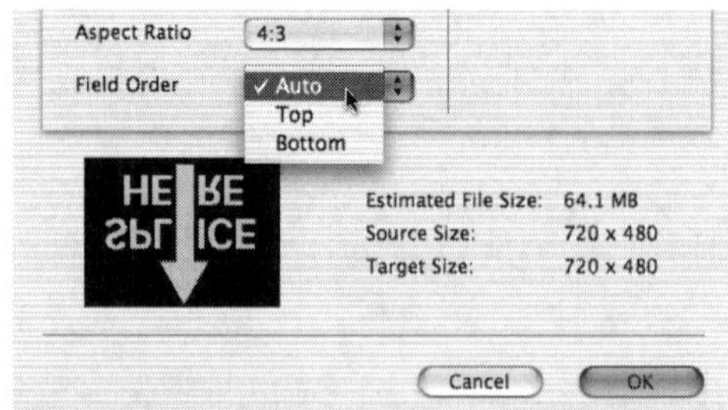

Figure 4.22 For most source video streams, the Auto setting will determine the field order correctly. Choose Top or Bottom only if you are absolutely sure of your source video's field order.

✔ Tips

- For most source video streams, choose Auto as the field order. The QuickTime MPEG-2 Exporter will look at the field order of your video stream and choose Top or Bottom as needed.
- DV video always starts with the lower, or bottom field.
- If you chose the Auto setting and want to see which field order the QuickTime MPEG-2 Exporter selected, you can check the log file (see "Creating a Log File" later in this chapter).

Figure 4.23 With the Export Audio check box selected, the QuickTime MPEG-2 Exporter strips all audio streams out of the source file and encodes them as a 48 kHz, 16-bit AIFF file.

Saving the Audio Track

If your source video has one or more audio tracks, the QuickTime MPEG-2 Exporter strips out those audio tracks and encodes them separately once it has finished encoding the MPEG-2 video stream. The audio from your source video may be in any format that QuickTime understands and at any bit depth and sample rate.

QuickTime takes this source audio and converts it to a single 48 kHz, 16-bit stereo AIFF file ready for import into DVD Studio Pro or A.Pack. The AIFF file itself is saved in the same folder as the newly created MPEG-2 video stream, with the same name but a different file extension (.aif). To learn more about encoding audio for DVD Studio Pro, see Chapter 6, "Using A.Pack."

To save an audio stream:

1. Open the QuickTime MPEG-2 Exporter.
2. Click the Video tab.
3. If your source video has audio, select the Export Audio check box (**Figure 4.23**).

Elementary versus Program MPEG Streams

Elementary files contain only single data streams: either video or audio. Program streams, on the other hand, contain both video and audio—all of the content needed to reproduce the program. A program stream is the product of the multiplexing of two or more elementary streams. If you've ever downloaded MPEG-1 video from the Internet, for example, you've seen that these files have both audio and video combined. These are program streams.

The QuickTime MPEG-2 Exporter produces elementary streams that DVD Studio Pro multiplexes into program streams.

Creating a Log File

A log file stores information—including the file name, bit rate, and aspect ratio and a list of all encoded chapter markers—about an encoded MPEG-2 video stream (**Figure 4.24**).

If you select the QuickTime MPEG-2 Exporter's Create Log File check box, QuickTime creates a text file that holds all encoding information and saves that file in the same destination folder as the MPEG-2 video stream. Over the course of a day, you may continue to encode MPEG streams to the same folder, and QuickTime will update the original log file. QuickTime writes one log file per folder per day; as soon as the clock strikes midnight, QuickTime creates a new log file. In fact, the QuickTime MPEG-2 Exporter automatically names each log file with the date it was created.

To create a log file:

1. Open the QuickTime MPEG-2 Exporter.
2. Click the Video tab.
3. Select the Create Log File check box (**Figure 4.25**).

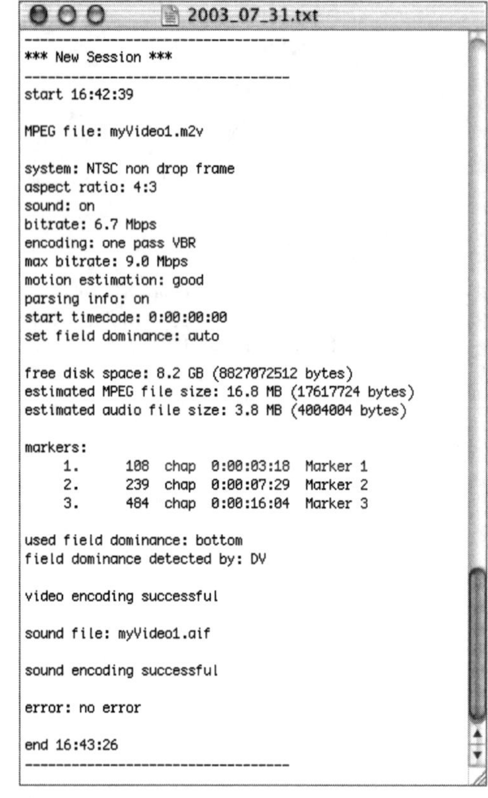

```
2003_07_31.txt
-----------------------------------
*** New Session ***
-----------------------------------
start 16:42:39

MPEG file: myVideo1.m2v

system: NTSC non drop frame
aspect ratio: 4:3
sound: on
bitrate: 6.7 Mbps
encoding: one pass VBR
max bitrate: 9.0 Mbps
motion estimation: good
parsing info: on
start timecode: 0:00:00:00
set field dominance: auto

free disk space: 8.2 GB (8827072512 bytes)
estimated MPEG file size: 16.8 MB (17617724 bytes)
estimated audio file size: 3.8 MB (4004004 bytes)

markers:
    1.      108  chap  0:00:03:18  Marker 1
    2.      239  chap  0:00:07:29  Marker 2
    3.      484  chap  0:00:16:04  Marker 3

used field dominance: bottom
field dominance detected by: DV

video encoding successful

sound file: myVideo1.aif

sound encoding successful

error: no error

end 16:43:26
-----------------------------------
```

Figure 4.24 Log files—like this one, for example—store information about the settings used to encode an MPEG stream.

Figure 4.25 Select the Create Log File check box to have the QuickTime MPEG-2 Exporter create a text file that stores the settings used to encode the MPEG stream.

Figure 4.26 DVD Studio Pro needs to know certain information (such as the type and length) about an MPEG stream before it can import the stream. This is called parse information, and creating this parse information during encoding speeds up the process of importing the MPEG stream into DVD Studio Pro.

Creating Parse Files

To use a file, DVD Studio Pro needs to know some information about it, such as its length and what type of file it is. The QuickTime MPEG-2 Exporter will create this information, but only if you select the Create Parsing Info check box.

If you do not select this check box, the QuickTime MPEG-2 Exporter does not create parsing information for the MPEG stream. Consequently, DVD Studio Pro must create a parse file as soon as the MPEG stream is imported into a project. This takes time–depending on the MPEG stream's duration, it could take several minutes or longer. To import MPEG files more quickly, create the parsing information during encoding.

✔ Tip

- All parsing information, whether saved by the QuickTime MPEG-2 Exporter or by DVD Studio Pro (upon importing an MPEG file), is saved in a subfolder called Par, which is placed in the same folder on your hard disk as the MPEG stream.

To create parse information:

1. Open the QuickTime MPEG-2 Exporter.
2. Click the Video tab.
3. Select the Write Parsing Info check box (**Figure 4.26**).

Setting Encoding Quality

Three types of MPEG-2 video streams can be created using the QuickTime MPEG-2 Exporter: constant-bit-rate (CBR, or one-pass, encoding), one-pass variable-bit-rate (VBR) encoding, and two-pass VBR encoding.

- **CBR encoding.** In CBR encoding, picture quality fluctuates while the data rate remains constant. In general, areas of an MPEG-2 stream with a low degree of motion (such as a person sitting in front of a still backdrop) need fewer bits to look good than do more visually complex areas of the video stream (high-motion parts, such as a car chase). CBR encoding ignores this fact and simply applies the same number of bits to all parts of the MPEG stream, whether they need it or not. Consequently, you won't often choose to use CBR encoding for MPEG-2 compression. But CBR encoding is the fastest encoding option, so if time is of the essence and quality doesn't matter, rest safe in the knowledge that CBR encoding is available.
- **One-pass VBR encoding.** In one-pass VBR encoding, the picture quality stays constant while the data rate fluctuates. A VBR encoder allocates only as many bits as needed to low-motion scenes, while high-motion scenes are given more bits to avoid digital artifacts. Consequently, the data rate of a VBR-encoded MPEG stream tends to teeter-totter around the target data rate—sometimes higher, sometimes lower.
- **Two-pass VBR encoding.** Two-pass VBR encoding is similar to one-pass VBR encoding, except the encoder first analyzes the source video to figure out which sections can use fewer bits and which need more (pass one). After determining more or less where the bits should be allocated, the encoder then does a second pass to refine its calculations and encode the video. Although two-pass VBR encoding creates the highest-quality video, it also takes longer to encode the MPEG-2 stream because of that extra pass.

To choose an MPEG encoding type:

1. Open the QuickTime MPEG-2 Exporter.
2. Click the Quality tab.
3. From the Encoding menu, choose One Pass, One Pass VBR, or Two Pass VBR (**Figure 4.27**).

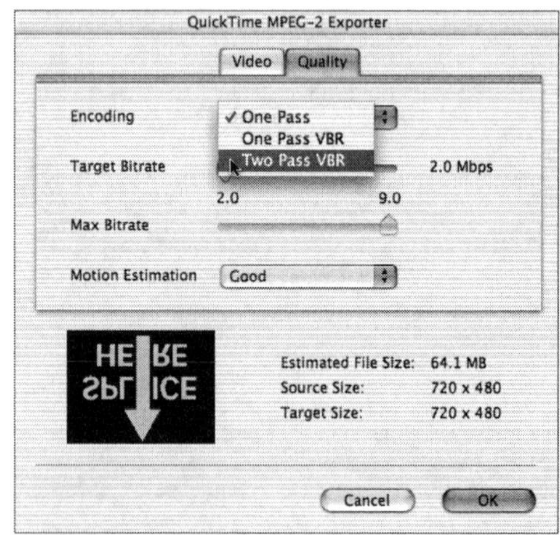

Figure 4.27 The Quality tab's Encoding menu sets the encoder to use one-pass (CBR), one-pass VBR, or two-pass VBR encoding.

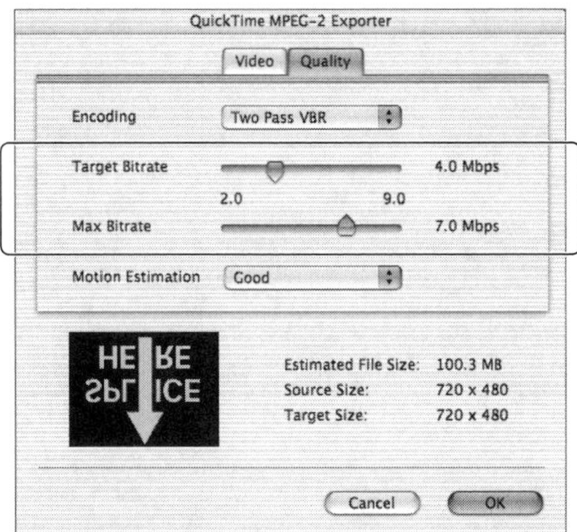

Figure 4.28 The Target Bitrate and Max Bitrate sliders determine the data rate and file size of the encoded MPEG-2 stream.

Testing Bit Rates

The trick to video compression is selecting a bit rate that's low enough to provide the smallest possible file size but high enough to maintain your source content's visual quality. Low bit rates produce files that take up less space on the DVD, and they also make it easier for the DVD-Video player to play the disc. But if you use too low a bit rate, you'll see compression artifacts in your video.

If you're not sure what bit rate to use, run a few tests before compressing the entire source video file. Open the file in QuickTime Pro Player and slice out a couple of 10-second chunks. Choose sections that have quite a bit of motion, such as panning shots, transitions, or other areas of high visual complexity. Encode these sections at several bit rates, and see which setting gives you the best quality at the lowest bit rate. Once you've determined the appropriate bit rate, go back and encode the entire source video using that setting.

Choosing a bit rate

Using the QuickTime MPEG-2 Exporter, you can encode your MPEG-2 streams at bit rates ranging from 1 to 9.0 Mbps. As a rule of thumb, the higher the bit rate, the better the output video quality. Scenes that include a high degree of motion (transitions, cuts, zooms, and so on) need a higher bit rate to achieve the same quality as scenes with a lower degree of motion (a newscaster seated in front of a backdrop).

The QuickTime MPEG-2 Exporter has two bit-rate settings: Target Bitrate and Max Bitrate (**Figure 4.28**).

- **Target Bitrate.** The Target Bitrate slider tells the QuickTime MPEG Exporter at which bit rate it should attempt to encode. For CBR encoding, the QuickTime MPEG Exporter encodes the video at the target bit rate and never fluctuates. For VBR encoding, the target bit rate is the bit rate the QuickTime MPEG-2 Exporter aims for as it encodes the video, though the bit rate may vary above and below the target if needed.
- **Max Bitrate.** The Max Bitrate slider is disabled for CBR encoding. For VBR encoding, the Max Bitrate setting controls the maximum allowable bit rate for the MPEG stream. This setting is most useful for ensuring that you have enough available headroom to include multiple audio or subtitle streams in a single DVD Studio Pro track, as you'll see in Chapter 11, "Using Tracks."

To choose a bit rate:

1. Open the QuickTime MPEG-2 Exporter.
2. Click the Quality tab.
3. On the Target Bitrate slider, choose a target bit rate.
4. If you are encoding a VBR stream, on the Max Bitrate slider, choose a maximum bit rate.

✔ Tips

- For VBR encoding, when in doubt, start with a target bit rate of 4.5 Mbps and a maximum bit rate of 7 Mbps.
- If your DVD uses a lot of video, be sure to create a bit budget. In many cases, the bit budget will tell you exactly what bit rate is needed to squeeze all of your video onto the DVD disc. To learn more about bit budgets, see Appendix A, "Surviving on a Bit Budget."

Know Your Limits

For most applications, 9 Mbps is a much higher bit rate than needed to preserve the quality of your source content. Unless a scene has a lot of motion, a bit rate between 3.5 and 6 Mbps is often enough to maintain quality.

There are other limitations you must respect when encoding your video streams:

- **The upper limit.** MPEG-2 video allows a maximum bit rate of 9.8 Mbps, which falls just within the maximum DVD-Video data rate of 10.08 Mbps (the QuickTime MPEG-2 Exporter allows a maximum bit rate of 9.0 Mbps). While it may be tempting to set the MPEG encoder to the maximum, don't do it. In fact, you should never use a bit rate higher than 8 Mbps; go beyond that and you leave little room for audio and subtitle streams. Plus some DVD-Video players will not smoothly play MPEG-2 video encoded at bit rates higher than 8 Mbps.
- **Know your audience.** Set-top DVD-Video players contain dedicated hardware for decoding MPEG video streams. In general, set-top DVD-Video players have no problem handling MPEG-2 streams encoded at 8 Mbps.

  This is not the case with some computers, which typically use software MPEG-2 decoders that rely on the computer's CPU for their processing power. While newer computers are fast enough to decode MPEG-2 video streams at any bit rate up to 9.8 Mbps, slower computers (especially old laptops) have a hard time keeping up with data rates higher than 6 or 7 Mbps.

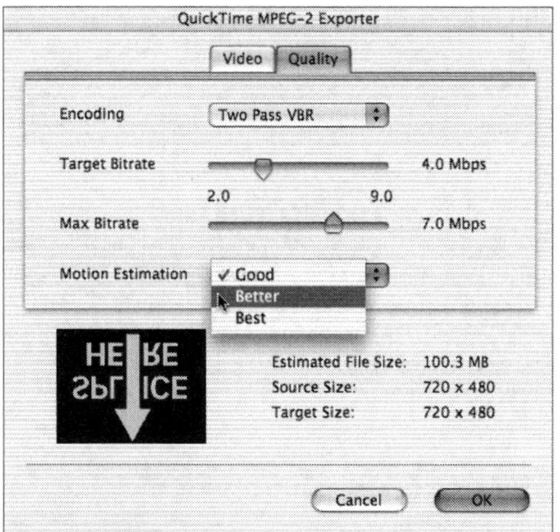

Figure 4.29 Use motion estimation to determine the accuracy of an MPEG stream's motion vectors.

Setting Motion Estimation

As mentioned earlier in this chapter, a motion vector is used to determine how far a block of color has moved from one frame to the next. The process of creating a motion vector is called *motion estimation*. The QuickTime MPEG-2 Exporter lets you choose between three levels of motion estimation: Good, Better, and Best.

It's tempting to set motion estimation to Best and be done with it, but usually this is not the best way to encode your video—mainly because it takes longer. In some cases, you don't really need the Best setting anyway. After all, you're dealing with motion estimation here—if your video has very little motion, there isn't much to estimate. For low-action video, Good or Better motion estimation is often good enough. If you're shooting an action flick, or if visual quality is of paramount importance, Best would be a more appropriate choice.

Can the untrained eye see the difference between these settings? Well, yes—but only if you're comparing file size, because the Best motion estimation setting creates smaller MPEG-2 files. If you have the time, choose Best motion estimation. But be prepared for *long* encode times.

To choose a motion estimation type:

1. Open the QuickTime MPEG-2 Exporter.
2. Click the Quality tab.
3. From the Motion Estimation menu, choose Good, Better, or Best (**Figure 4.29**).

✔ Tip

- To determine which type of motion estimation to use, try encoding a few short sections of your source video with all three settings and see which provides the most acceptable results given the amount of time it takes to encode versus the final file size.

About the Progress Window

As the QuickTime MPEG-2 Exporter encodes your video stream, the Progress window opens to let you keep track of the action. When it first appears, the Progress window has a progress bar and an information section that show you—both graphically and numerically—how long the encoding will take. You get to track the percentage of video already encoded and the estimated time remaining in the encoding process (**Figure 4.30**).

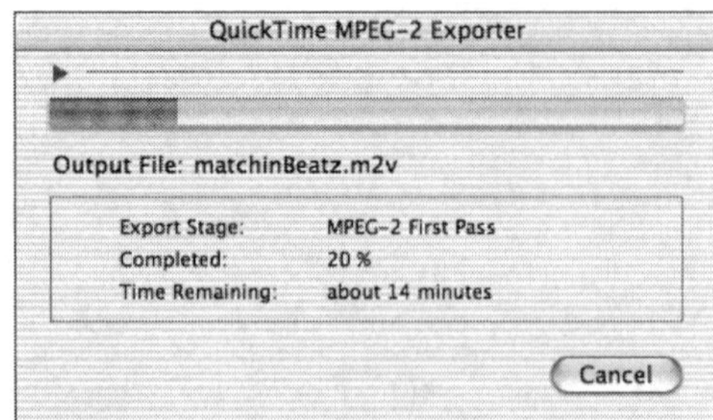

Figure 4.30 The QuickTime MPEG-2 Exporter's Progress window.

Watching while encoding

To watch your video as it encodes, click the disclosure triangle at the top left of the progress bar, and your video will appear (**Figure 4.31**). While it's entertaining to watch the video as it compresses, you should be warned that previewing during encoding slows down the process. If time is money, collapse the preview area and take the opportunity to make yourself a cup of tea.

Figure 4.31 The Progress window lets you watch as your MPEG stream is encoded. Just remember: compression takes longer if you watch while encoding.

✔ Tip

- While previewing the video, you may notice that the picture lurches, or jumps. Don't worry; this is normal behavior. In fact, if you look at the progress bar, you'll see that it jumps in unison with the picture. If you read the earlier section on GOPs, you know that only I-frames contain all the information needed to completely reconstruct the source video frame. The lurches you see reflect the preview picture jumping from I-frame to I-frame through the video stream.

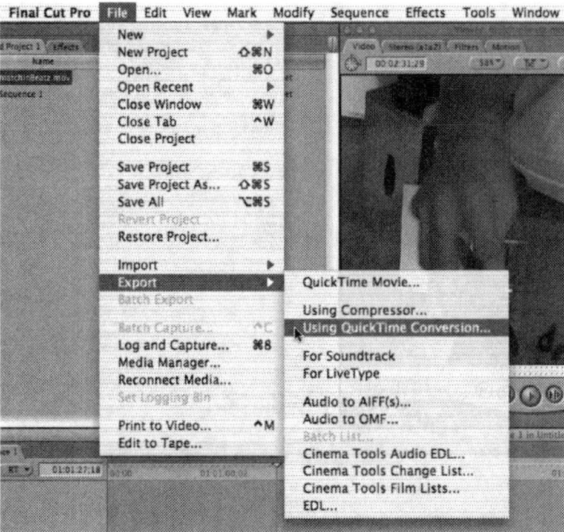

Figure 4.32 To export MPEG-2 video straight from Final Cut Pro, choose File > Export > Using QuickTime Conversion.

Exporting MPEG-2 Streams from Final Cut Pro

The similarities between the look and feel of Final Cut Pro (FCP) and DVD Studio Pro should be enough to convince you that Apple has designed these two applications to work together. At first glance, you'll notice that both applications use a Grayspace color scheme (dark gray colors ease eyestrain as you spend hours upon hours squinting at the screen). With closer scrutiny, you'll notice that DVD Studio Pro's Track editor works much the same way as the timeline in Final Cut Pro. There's no denying it—these applications were made to work together, and Final Cut Pro includes features that not only integrate with DVD Studio Pro but also speed up the process of creating a DVD-Video.

One dramatic time-saving feature is Final Cut Pro's ability to directly export MPEG-2 video streams. The advantages of using this option are huge, because exporting MPEG-2 streams directly from Final Cut Pro lets you avoid exporting a finished version of your sequence to open in QuickTime. This saves you not only time but hard disk space.

To export MPEG streams from Final Cut Pro:

1. From within Final Cut Pro, choose File > Export > Using QuickTime Conversion (**Figure 4.32**).

   A Save dialog opens.

2. Name your MPEG stream and navigate to the folder that you want to save it in.

continues on next page

3. From the Format pop-up menu, choose MPEG2 (**Figure 4.33**).
4. Click Options.
   The QuickTime MPEG-2 Exporter opens.
5. Use the information you learned in earlier sections of this chapter to encode your MPEG-2 stream.

✔ Tips

- Final Cut Pro sequences must be rendered before the QuickTime MPEG-2 Exporter will encode them (**Figure 4.34**).
- DV uses approximately 1 GB of storage space for every five minutes of video. For a one-and-a-half-hour video, you need over 18 GB of free storage space. Avoid rendering this huge DV file by encoding your MPEG-2 video streams directly from Final Cut Pro.
- Final Cut Pro also supports MPEG-2 export using Compressor. To open your Final Cut Pro sequence in Compressor, choose File > Export > Using Compressor.

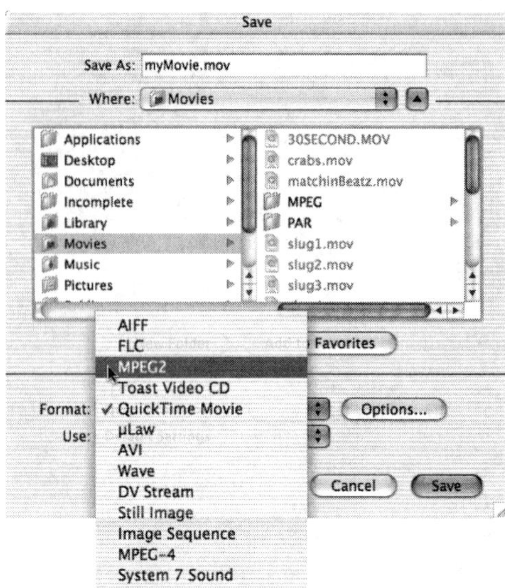

Figure 4.33 From the Export dialog's Format menu, choose MPEG2.

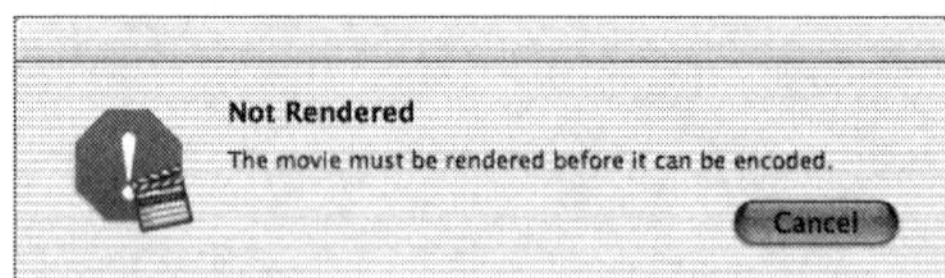

Figure 4.34 All Final Cut Pro sequences must be rendered before they're exported using the QuickTime MPEG-2 Exporter.

5

USING COMPRESSOR

Compressor is a media encoder—its job is to convert digital files such as AIFF, DV Video, and QuickTime Movie files from one format to another, usually while reducing the file size (hence the name *Compressor*). For DVD-Video authors, Compressor's biggest virtue is its ability to create high-quality MPEG-2 files—in fact, Compressor can actually produce better-looking files than QuickTime can alone. While Compressor uses the same MPEG Encoder as QuickTime, it expands upon QuickTime's encode settings, giving you access to several features that QuickTime doesn't, including higher quality settings and open GOPs.

But most useful of all, Compressor's Batch window lets you specify settings for several different files before encoding those files, all in one shot. From a workflow perspective, Compressor's Batch window is a real time saver. This alone makes learning Compressor worthwhile.

Encoding a File

Encoding a file in Compressor follows this set of tasks:

1. Import a file into Compressor's Batch window.
2. Assign the file a compression preset.
3. Choose a destination for the compressed file.
4. Submit the file for compression.

This section steps you through each of these tasks while introducing you to Compressor's main editing window, the Batch window.

When you open Compressor, the Batch window appears on your screen. You can add media files to be compressed to this window, and these files will appear as a list—a *batch list*. Each file can be assigned customized encode settings. When all the files are ready to go, with all encode settings properly assigned, just click the Submit button at the bottom right of the Batch window, and Compressor will process the whole list of files, from top to bottom, while you do other things. Barring any encoding errors, when you come back to your computer, your files will all be encoded and ready for import into DVD Studio Pro.

To import a file:

1. If Compressor's Batch window isn't already open, choose Window > Batch (**Figure 5.1**), or press Command-1.
2. *Do one of the following:*
   - ▲ Drag a file from the Finder into Compressor's Batch window (**Figure 5.2**).

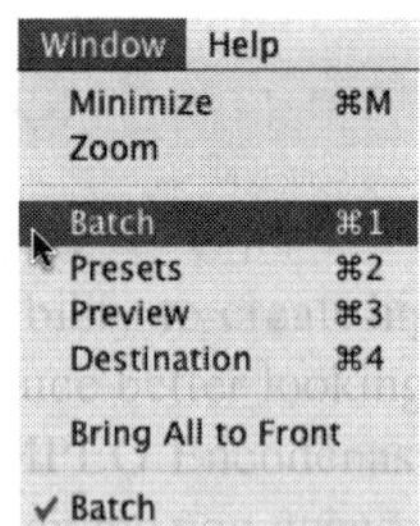

Figure 5.1 Use Compressor's Batch window to import files before encoding.

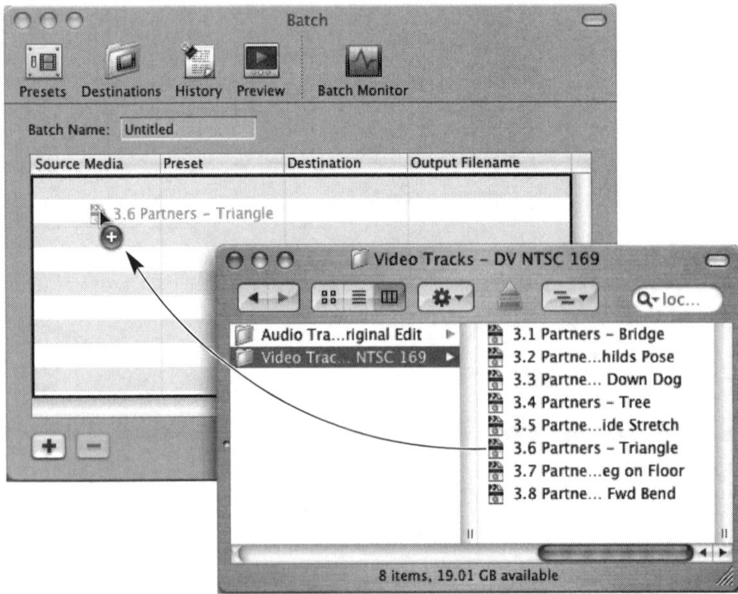

Figure 5.2 Drag a file from the Finder directly into Compressor's Batch window, or...

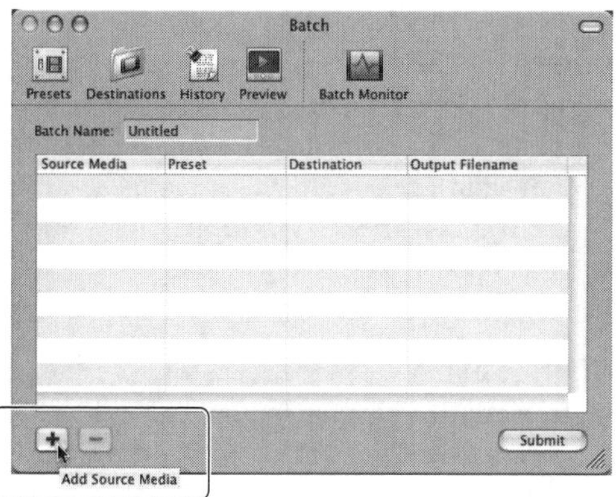

Figure 5.3 ...click the Batch window's Add Source Media button to import a file.

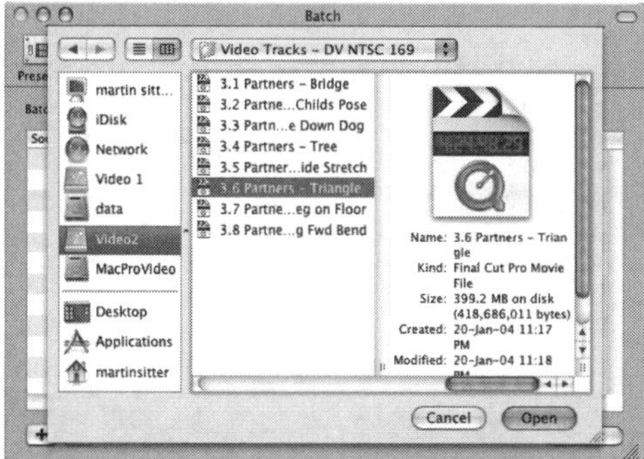

Figure 5.4 Clicking the Add Source Media button causes an Open dialog to drop down from Compressor's title bar. Use this dialog to locate the file you want to compress.

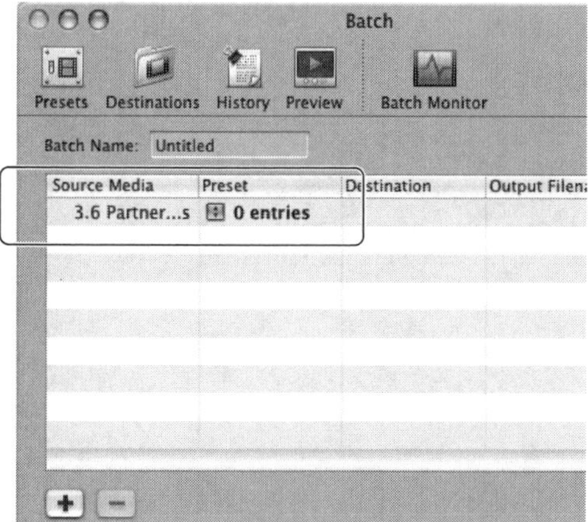

Figure 5.5 A media file in Compressor's Batch window.

- At the bottom left of Compressor's Batch window, click the Add Source Media button (**Figure 5.3**).

An Open dialog drops down from Compressor's title bar (**Figure 5.4**).

3. Choose the media file you want to compress and click the Open button.

   The file is added to Compressor's Batch window (**Figure 5.5**).

continues on next page

✔ **Tip**

- To import multiple files into Compressor's Batch window, select the files in the Finder and drag them directly into Compressor's Batch window (**Figure 5.6**).

Choosing a preset

In Compressor, you don't specify encode settings on a file-by-file basis. Instead, you create presets, and these presets are assigned to media files.

A preset is simply a group of encode settings. It can be used once, twice, or as many times as you want. For example, if you've created a bit budget that says you should encode your project's MPEG streams at 4.8 Mbps, you can create a 4.8 Mbps preset and then use that preset to encode all your project's media files.

We'll look at how to create custom presets a little later in this chapter, in the section "Creating Presets." For now, we'll examine the process for assigning one of Compressor's default MPEG-2 compression presets.

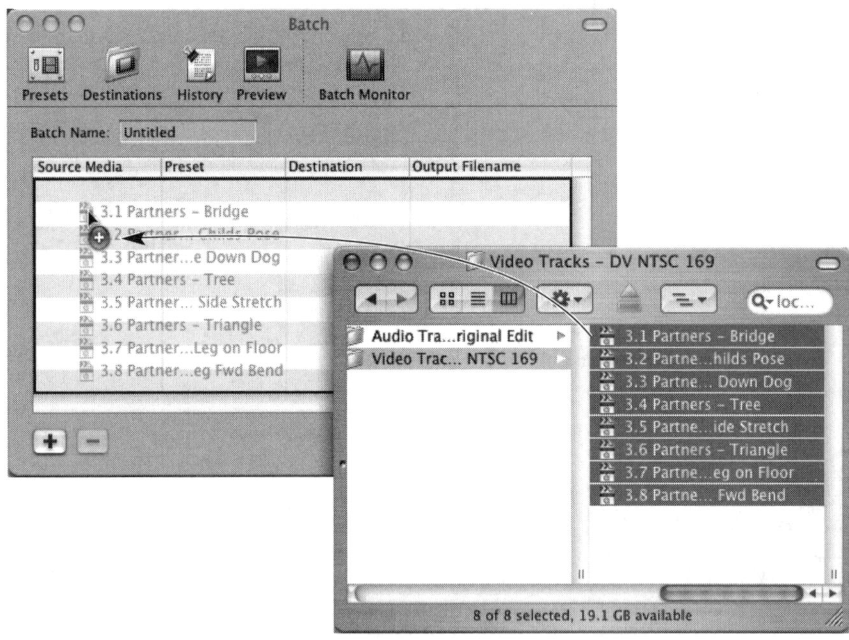

Figure 5.6 Drag multiple media files directly from the Finder into Compressor's Batch window.

To assign a preset to a media file:

1. In Compressor's Batch window, select the file you want to assign a preset to (**Figure 5.7**).
2. *Do one of the following:*
   - ▲ From the Preset menu, choose a compression preset (**Figure 5.8**).

continues on next page

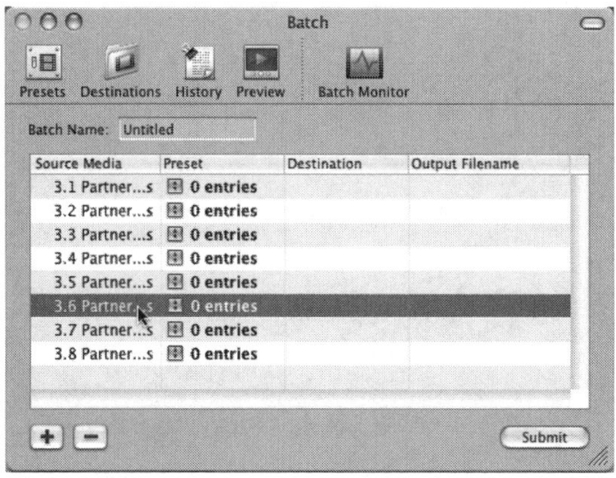

Figure 5.7 To assign a preset to a media file in Compressor's Batch list, first select the media file.

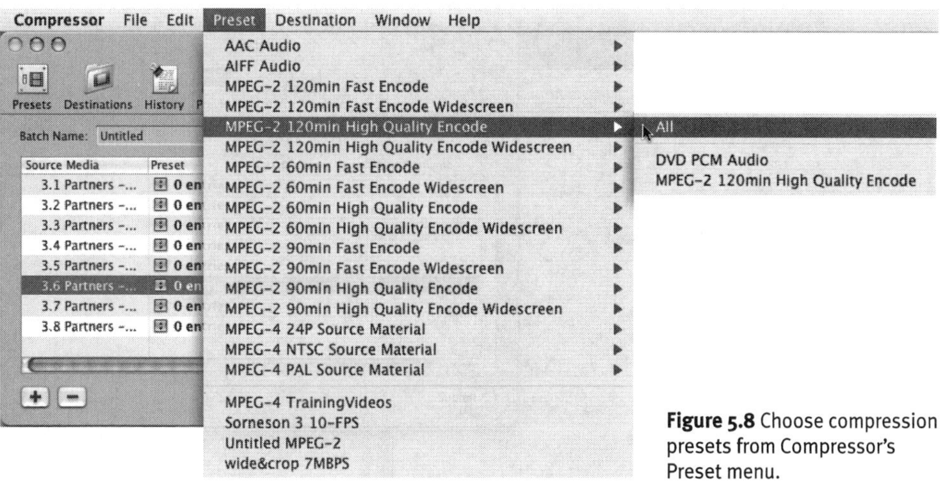

Figure 5.8 Choose compression presets from Compressor's Preset menu.

▲ From the Preset shortcut menus in the Batch window's Preset column, choose a compression preset (**Figure 5.9**).

The compression preset is assigned to the selected media file (**Figure 5.10**).

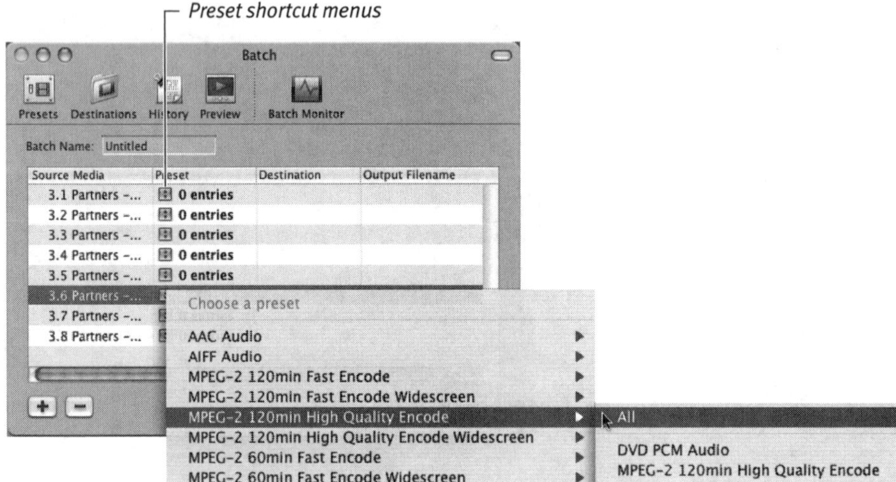

Figure 5.9 The Preset shortcut menus located in the Batch window's Preset column also let you assign presets to media files.

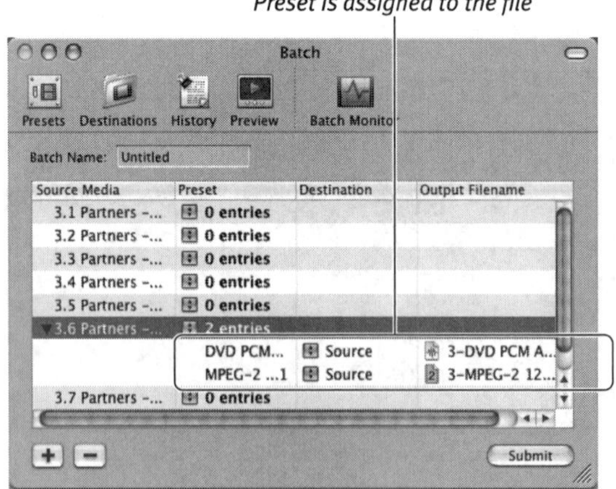

Figure 5.10 A preset assigned to a file.

Setting a destination

By default, Compressor places the encoded file in the same folder as the source file (**Figure 5.11**), but you can change this behavior by assigning a new destination, or even creating a custom destination template that is available from any of Compressor's Destination menus.

To set an encoded file's destination:

1. In Compressor's Batch window, choose the stream for which you want to adjust the destination.

   Be careful to select the stream and not the media file itself. The stream is located under the media file, as shown in **Figure 5.12**.

continues on next page

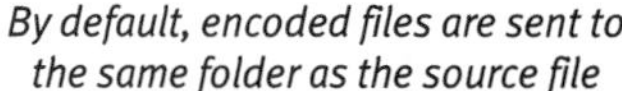

By default, encoded files are sent to the same folder as the source file

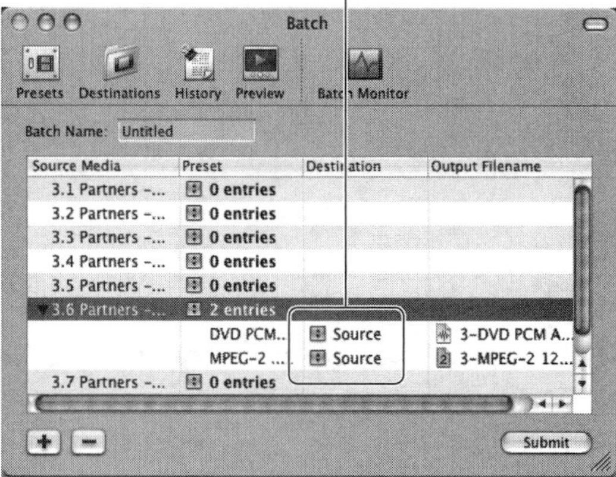

Figure 5.11 The Batch window's Destination column displays the target folder for encoded files.

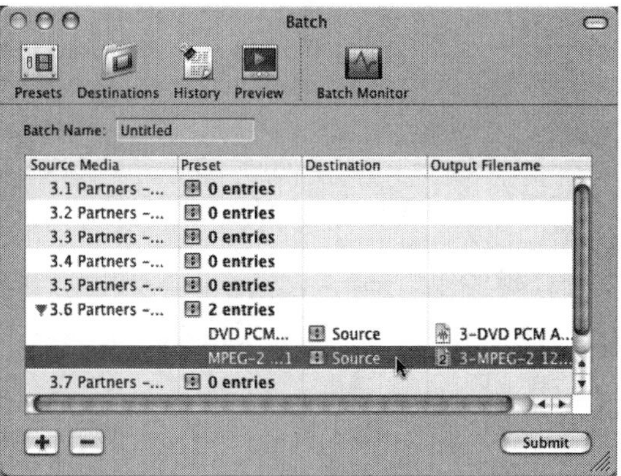

Figure 5.12 To adjust the target destination for an encoded file, first select it in the Batch window.

2. *Do one of the following:*
   - ▲ Choose Destination and select a destination (**Figure 5.13**).
   - ▲ From the shortcut menu in the Batch window's Destination column, choose a destination (**Figure 5.14**).

✔ Tips

- To set the destination for multiple streams, hold down the Command key and select all of the streams; then choose a destination from the Destinations menu in the top menu bar.
- If you're encoding directly to Compressor from Final Cut Pro, don't choose Source as your destination. If you do, your encoded files will all be placed at the root of your startup disk—and that's probably not where you expect them to go.

To choose a different folder for encoded files:

1. Choose Destination > Other (**Figure 5.15**).

   An Open dialog drops down from the Batch window's title bar (**Figure 5.16**).
2. In the Open dialog, select a folder for your encoded files and then click Open.

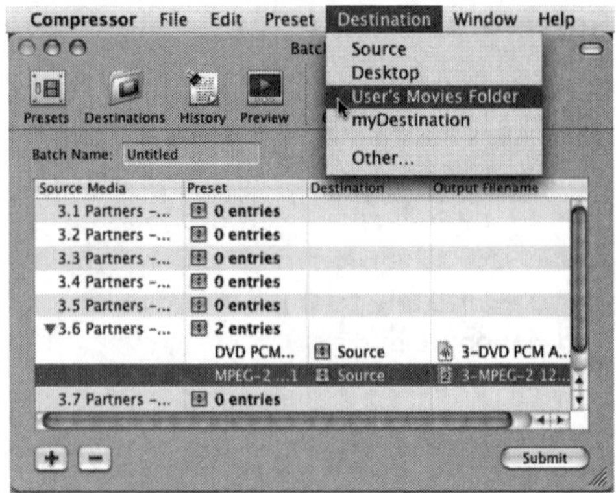

Figure 5.13 Next, choose Destination and select a destination.

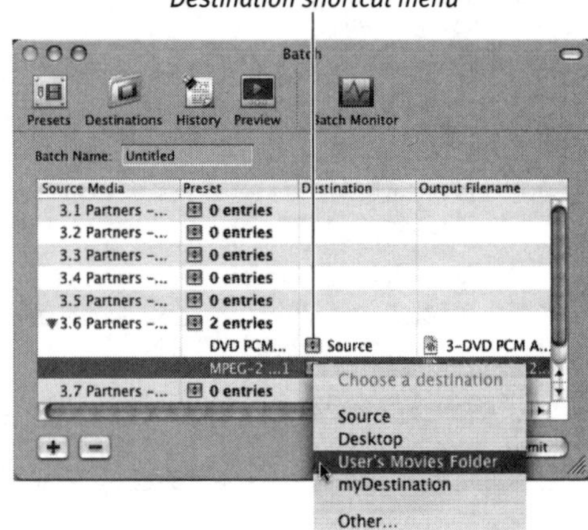

Figure 5.14 The Batch window's Destination column has a shortcut menu you can use to set destinations.

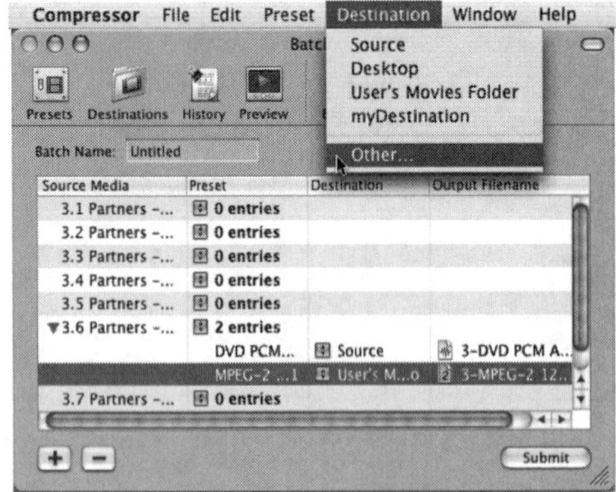

Figure 5.15 To set a custom destination, choose Destination > Other.

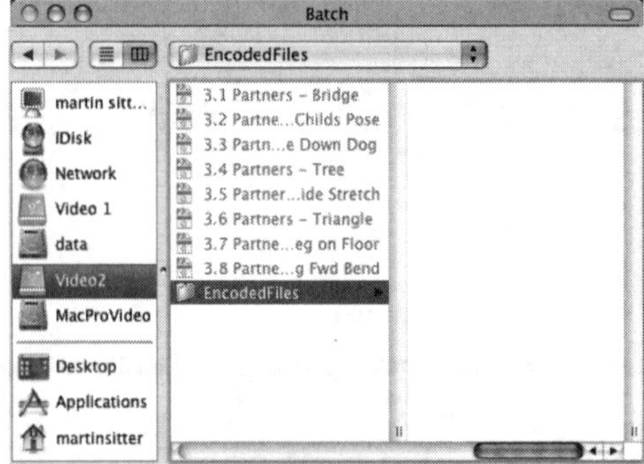

Figure 5.16 An Open dialog drops down from the Batch window's title bar. Use this dialog to select the folder the encoded file will be sent to.

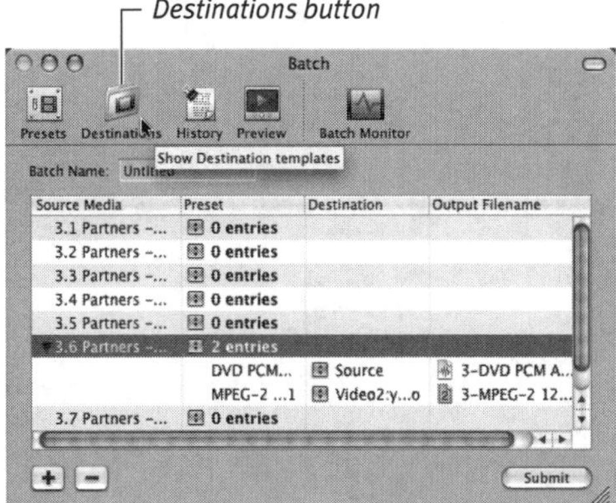

Figure 5.17 Click the Destinations button to open the Destinations window.

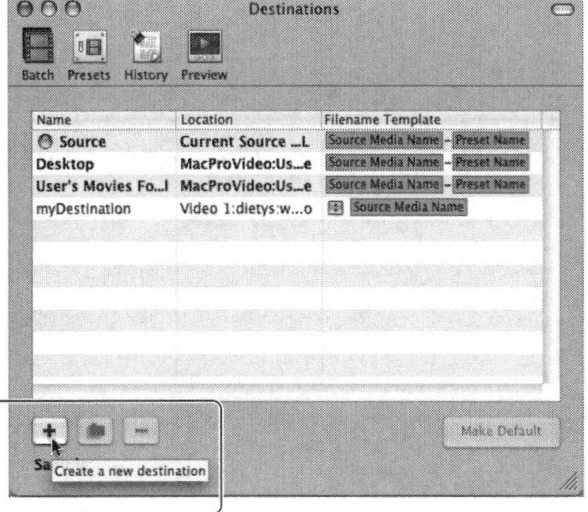

Figure 5.18 Click the Create a New Destination button to add a custom destination template.

Figure 5.19 Choose Local from the Create a New Destination button's drop-down menu.

To create a custom destination template:

1. In the Batch window's toolbar, click the Destinations button (**Figure 5.17**).

   The Destinations window opens.

2. At the bottom left of the Destinations window, click and hold the Create a New Destination button (the button with the + on it; **Figure 5.18**).

3. From the drop-down menu, choose Local (**Figure 5.19**).

   An Open dialog drops down from the Destinations window's title bar (**Figure 5.20**).

continues on next page

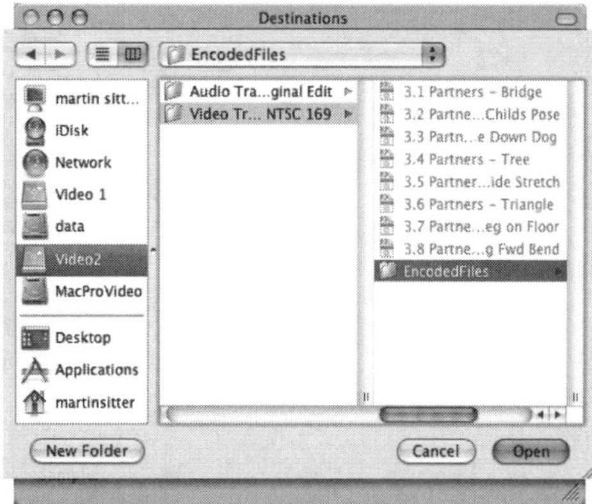

Figure 5.20 Use the Open dialog to select a folder to use as a new destination template.

4. Use the Open dialog to choose a new destination.

   The new destination is added to your destination templates and is now available from any Destination menu (**Figure 5.21**).

To name a destination template:

1. In the Destinations window's Name column, double-click the destination template's name (**Figure 5.22**).
2. Type a new name and press Return.

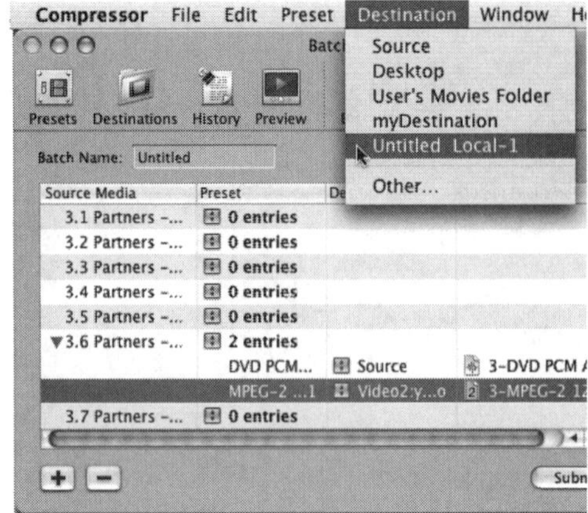

Figure 5.21 The new destination template is now available from any Destination menu inside Compressor.

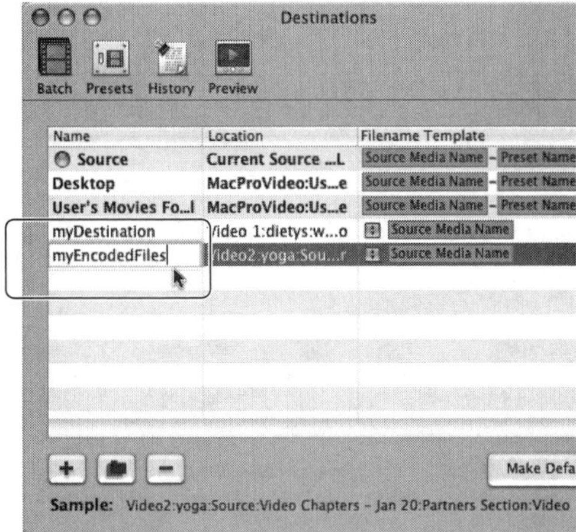

Figure 5.22 To rename a destination template, type a new name in the Destinations window's Name column.

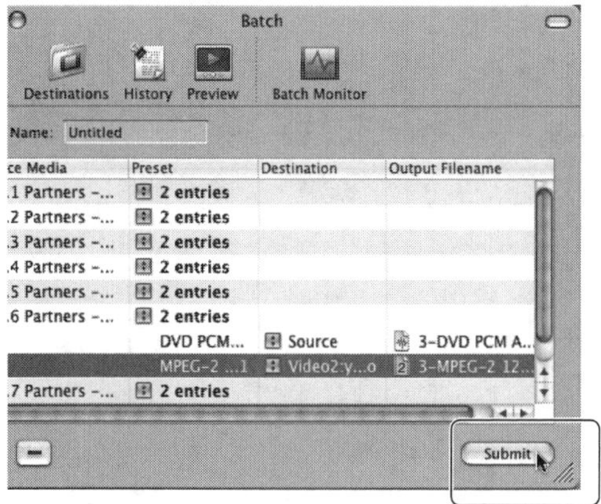

Figure 5.23 After you've assigned an encoding preset and destination to each file in the Batch window, click the Submit button to encode the files.

Submitting the files for encoding

With the presets and destinations assigned, encoding the final video streams is all that remains. To do this, just click the Batch window's Submit button.

To submit the Batch window's files for encoding:

- At the bottom right of the Batch window, click the Submit button (**Figure 5.23**).

  Compressor submits the batch (**Figure 5.24**), and the Batch Monitor opens to let you follow the progress of your batch while it is encoded (**Figure 5.25**).

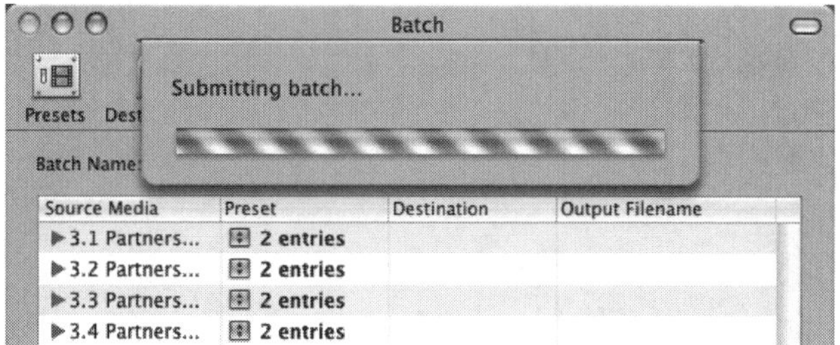

Figure 5.24 Clicking the Submit button causes Compressor to submit the batch.

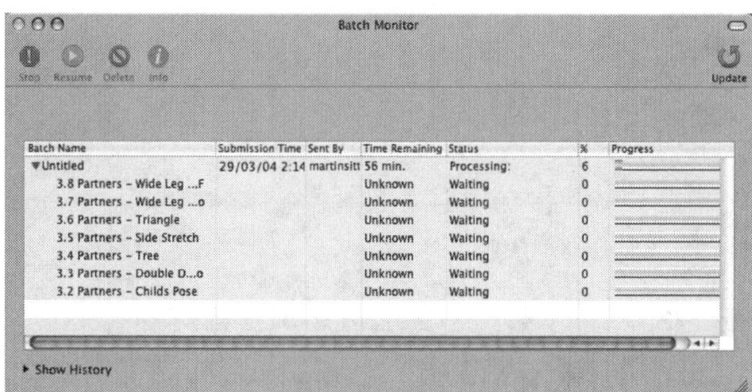

Figure 5.25 Next, the Batch Monitor opens. Use the Batch Monitor window to follow the progress as the media files are encoded.

Creating Presets

As you've seen, encode settings are stored in Compressor presets, and these presets are then assigned to media files in the Batch window. Compressor comes stocked with many default MPEG-2 presets, but there will be times when you need to create your own customized presets. For example, you may want to create an MPEG stream using open instead of closed GOPs, or you may want to use Compressor's Best quality settings. In these situations, you need to create a custom preset and then assign this custom preset to media files in the Batch window.

To create a preset:

1. In the Batch window's toolbar, click the Presets button (**Figure 5.26**).
   The Presets window opens.
2. In the Presets window, click and hold the Create a New Preset button (**Figure 5.27**).
3. From the drop-down menu, choose MPEG-2 (**Figure 5.28**).

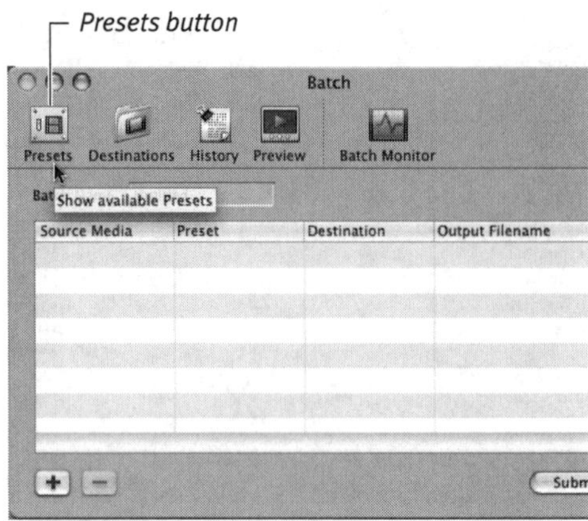

Figure 5.26 Click the Batch window's Presets button to open the Presets window.

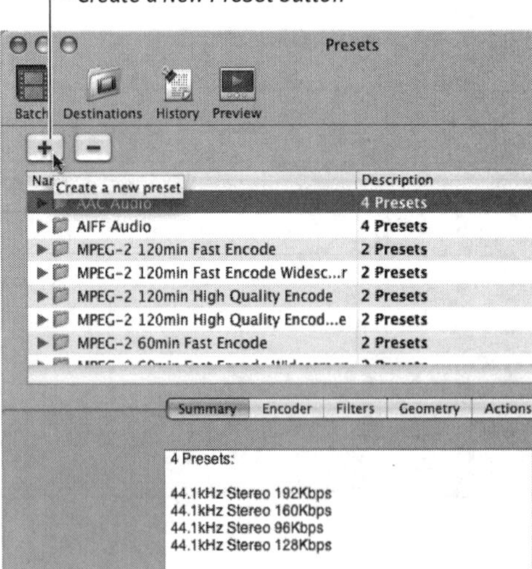

Figure 5.27 Click the Create a New Preset button to add a customized preset to Compressor's list of preset encoding templates.

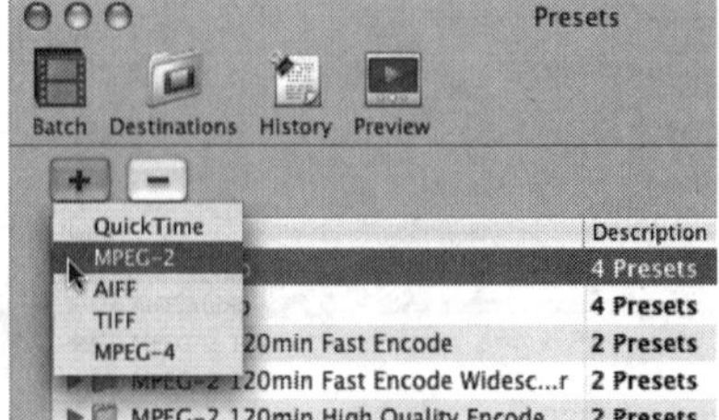

Figure 5.28 Choose MPEG-2 as the preset format.

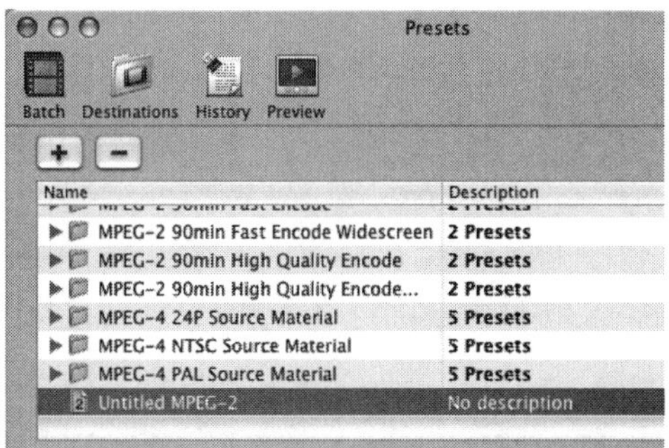

Figure 5.29 A new, untitled MPEG-2 preset appears at the bottom of the Presets list.

A new, untitled MPEG-2 preset appears at the bottom of the Presets list (**Figure 5.29**).

4. Use the Settings section at the bottom of the Presets window to configure your preset (**Figure 5.30**).

   This new preset will now be available from any Preset menu inside Compressor.

✔ Tip

- The MPEG-2 settings you can configure in the Settings section of the Presets window are all discussed in Chapter 4, "The QuickTime MPEG Exporter."

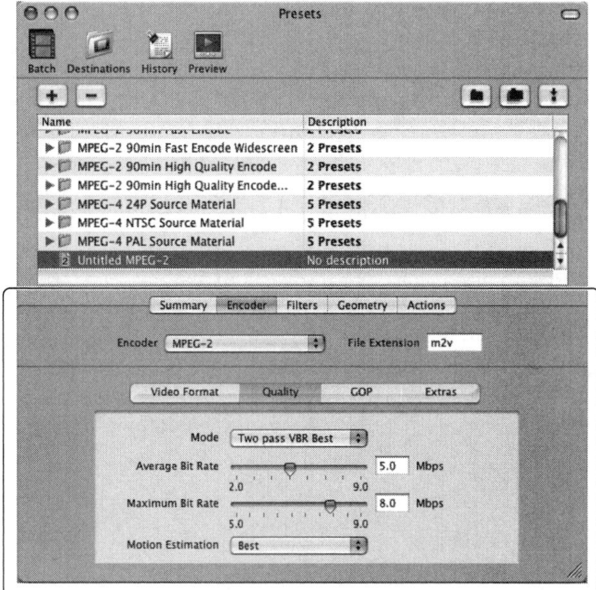

Figure 5.30 You can use the Settings section of the Presets window to configure the encode settings of any preset selected in the Presets window.

Creating multi-angle or mixed-angle presets

As you will see in Chapter 12, "Enhancing Tracks," mixed- and multi-angle tracks must use exactly the same GOP structure across all alternate-angle video streams. The reason for this requirement is that the I-frames in these streams act as the bridges that let the DVD player jump from one steam to the next. Consequently, these I-frames must align across all alternate-angle streams (for more detailed information on alternate-angle video streams, see Chapter 12).

However, if you are encoding from Final Cut Pro using Compressor, Final Cut Pro will automatically place a compression marker (an I-frame) at each scene cut in the sequence you are encoding. For example, any hard cut between clips in your Final Cut Pro sequence will be automatically assigned an I-frame. This leads to great looking compression, because an I-frame (and, hence, a new GOP) will automatically be assigned to these sudden changes in picture content. However, if you are trying to create mixed- or multi-angle tracks, all these unexpected I-frames create a bit of a nightmare, because they make it very difficult to ensure that the I-frames align across your alternate-angle streams. Fortunately, Compressor has a setting that overrides this, ...er, feature.

Additionally, you must not use open GOPs in mixed- or multi-angle streams, so make sure that you set the encode parameters discussed here in any Compressor preset that will be used to encode video for alternate-angle tracks.

To create a preset for mixed- or multi-angle tracks:

1. In Compressor's Presets window, choose the preset you want to use to encode a mixed- or multi-angle track.
2. On the Settings section's GOP tab, click the Closed GOP button (**Figure 5.31**).
3. On the Extras tab, select the Include Chapter Markers Only check box (**Figure 5.32**).

If this check box is selected, Compressor ignores scene transitions and does not place an I-frame at every cut in your Final Cut Pro sequence. Chapter markers from the Final Cut Pro sequence, however, *will* still be included in the final MPEG-2 stream.

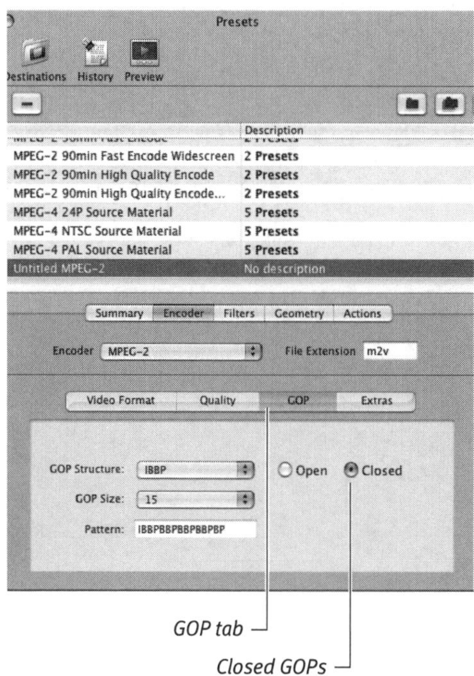

Figure 5.31 In presets that will be used for multi- or mixed-angle tracks, ensure that you use closed GOPs.

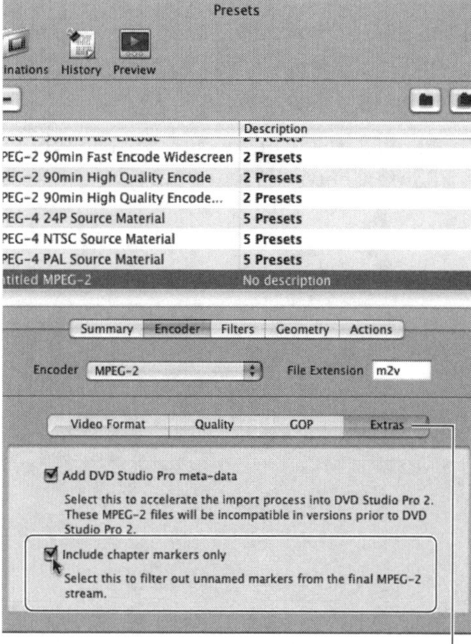

Figure 5.32 On the Extras tab, also ensure that the Include Chapter Markers Only check box is selected.

Previewing Compression

Compressor can simulate the look of your final, encoded video stream. This is a handy feature for previewing compression before you click that Submit button.

But keep this in mind: when it comes to MPEG encoding, the proof is in the pudding. In other words, you don't really know what your encoded files will look like until you encode the files. While Compressor's Preview window provides a reasonable simulation of the final output file, it is only a simulation.

To preview a file's encode settings:

1. In the Batch window, select the encode settings for the file you want to preview (**Figure 5.33**).
2. In the Batch window's toolbar, click the Preview button (**Figure 5.34**).

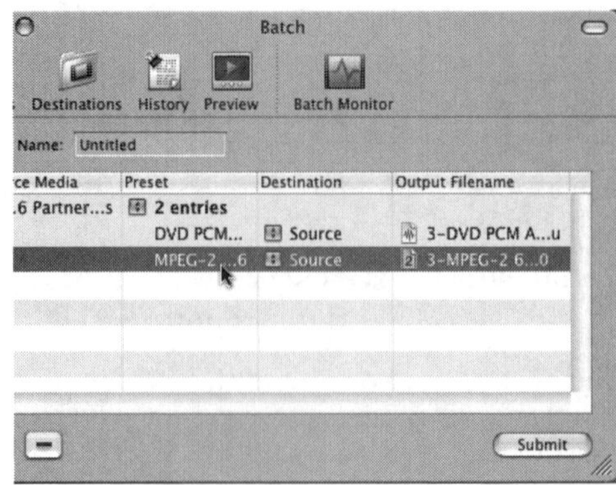

Figure 5.33 To preview a file's encode settings, first select the encode settings in Compressor's Batch window.

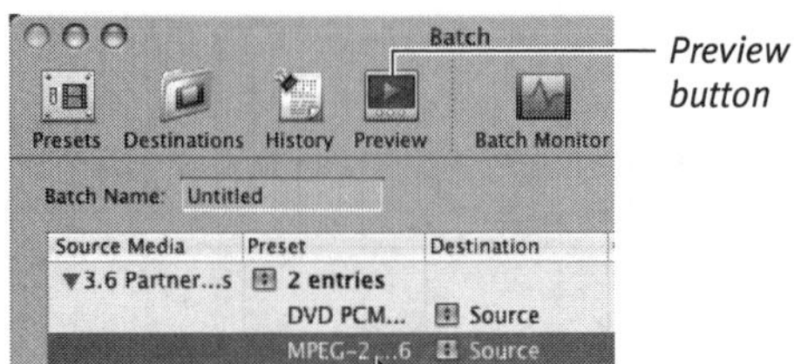

Figure 5.34 Click the Batch window's Preview button to preview your encode settings.

The Preview window opens (**Figure 5.35**). Along the top of the preview area is a slider, and a vertical line stretches down from the slider, across the preview area.

3. Move the slider left or right to preview your encode settings.

   The area to the left of the slider displays the source file, while the area to the right of the slider shows a simulation of the output file, or the final MPEG-2 stream. As you move the slider left and right, you can do quick comparisons to see if the encoded file will be of acceptable quality.

✔ Tip

- Make sure you select the encode settings and not the media file itself; otherwise, you will simply preview the media file and not the encode settings assigned to the media file. You reveal the encode settings by clicking the disclosure triangle to the left of the media file's name in the Batch list.

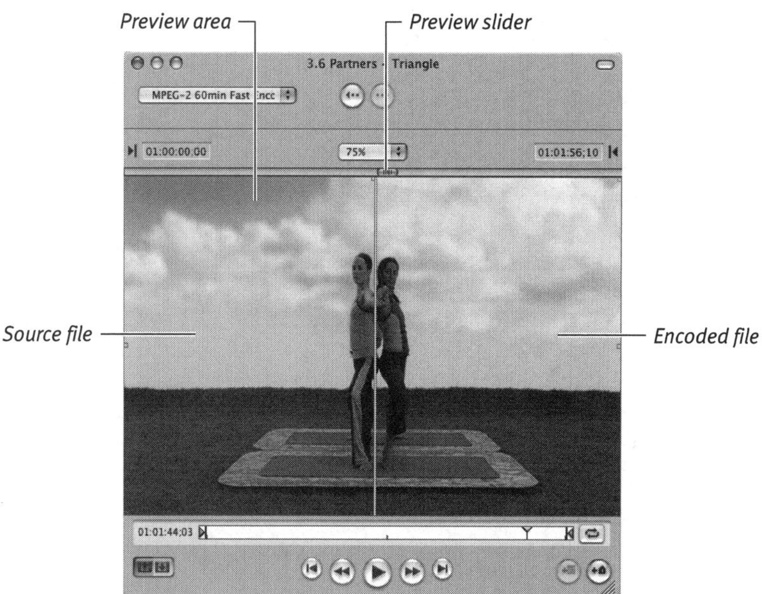

Figure 5.35 The Preview window lets you see how a media file looks before and after encoding.

Creating a Droplet

A droplet is a Compressor shortcut that appears as an icon on your desktop or inside a folder. You can turn any Compressor preset into a droplet, including custom presets you've made yourself. Once you've created a droplet, you can simply drag and drop a media file onto it, and Compressor will automatically start encoding the file.

To create a droplet:

1. In Compressor's Presets window, select the preset you want to turn into a droplet.
2. Click the Save Selection as Droplet button (**Figure 5.36**).

   A Save dialog appears (**Figure 5.37**).

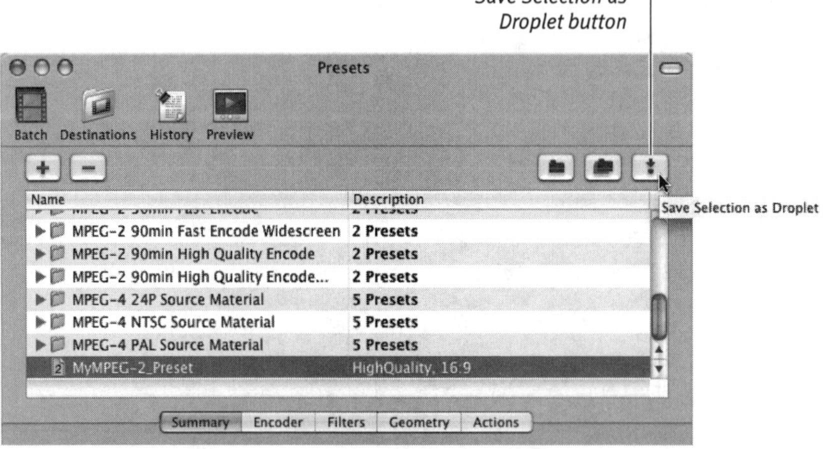

Figure 5.36 To create a droplet from a Compressor preset, select a preset and then click the Preset window's Save Selection as Droplet button.

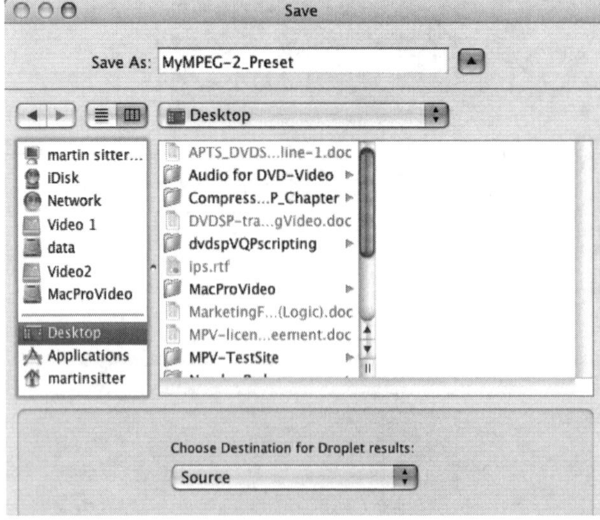

Figure 5.37 Compressor lets you name your droplet and choose where on your computer you want the droplet saved.

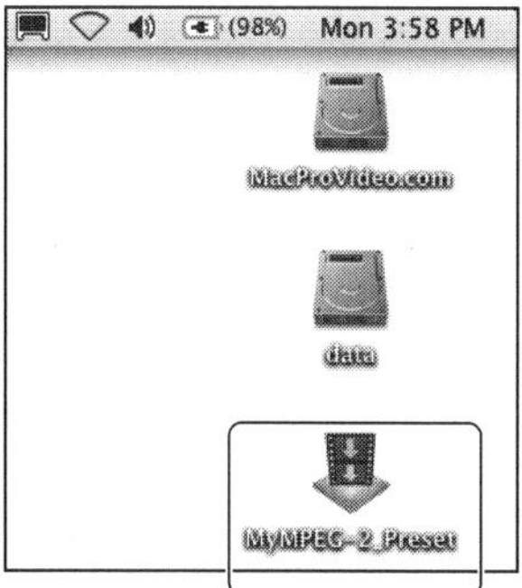

Figure 5.38 A droplet saved on the desktop for easy access.

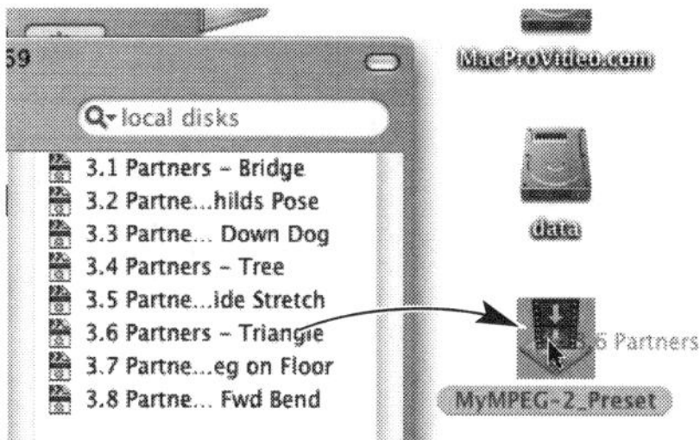

Figure 5.39 To expedite compression, drag media files directly onto a droplet.

3. Name the droplet and save it either on the desktop or in a different directory on your computer.

   The droplet is saved and ready for use (**Figure 5.38**).

To use a droplet to encode a media file:

1. Drag a media file from the Finder directly onto the droplet (**Figure 5.39**).

   The Droplet window opens (**Figure 5.40**).

2. Check the Droplet window to ensure that the correct encode settings will be used to encode your file.

3. In the Droplet window, click the Submit button (**Figure 5.41**).

   Compressor's Batch Monitor window opens, and Compressor begins encoding the file.

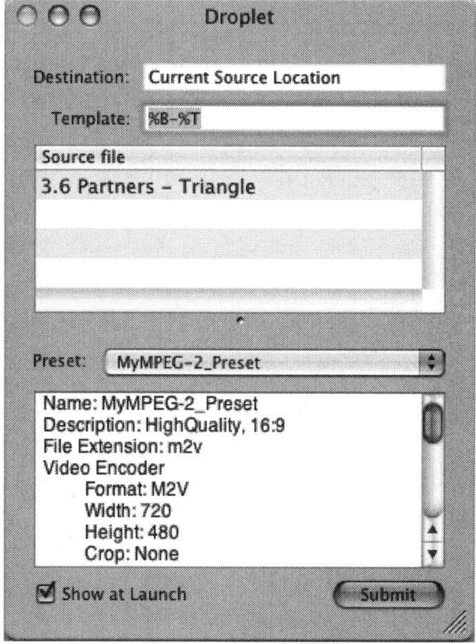

Figure 5.40 The Droplet window lets you quickly check to make sure that the droplet's encode settings are the ones you want to use.

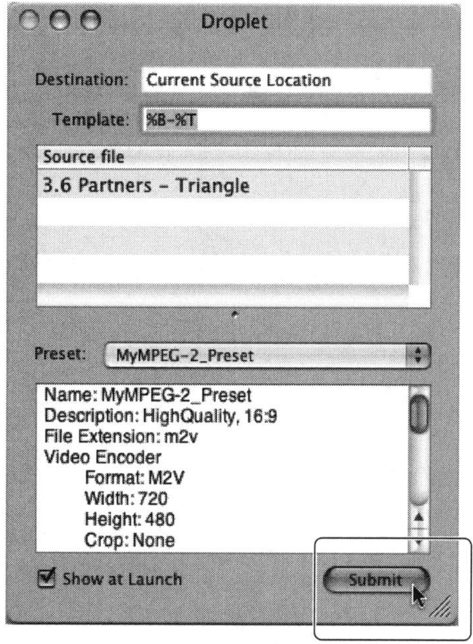

Figure 5.41 If the settings look correct, click the Droplet window's Submit button to encode the file.

USING A.PACK

DVD Studio Pro can directly import and use several audio formats, including MPEG-1 Layer 2, AIFF, WAV, SDII, and Digital Theatre Systems (DTS) sound. Of all these formats, by far the most commonly used in DVD-Video is Dolby Digital AC-3. The reason is simple: all DVD-Video players in the world must support AC-3 playback. While you'd be hard pressed to find a DVD-Video player that doesn't also support the other formats, only AC-3 files are guaranteed to work on every player, everywhere.

In addition to being the most compatible of all audio formats, the AC-3 format is one of the most compact. By converting your audio to AC-3, you reduce the audio stream's file size by a factor of up to 12:1. For example, a 16-bit stereo AIFF file at 48 kHz has a bit rate of 1.5 Mbps (or 187.5 kilobytes/second)—about 15 percent of the 10.08 Mbps data rate available to your DVD-Video. This doesn't leave much room for alternate audio streams, subtitles, or even a high-data-rate MPEG-2 video stream. Because AC-3 streams are up to 12 times smaller than uncompressed audio, converting audio streams to AC-3 provides more space for your project's video.

Apple acknowledges the benefits of AC-3 audio compression by including A.Pack with DVD Studio Pro. A.Pack is a Dolby Digital AC-3 encoder that you can use to turn AIFF, WAV, and SDII files into AC-3 audio streams ready for import into DVD Studio Pro. AC-3 encoding, however, takes a while to master. Although seasoned sound designers will appreciate the control that the encoder offers, audio newcomers face a daunting array of choices. If you're ready to face the music, let's dive in.

About Source Audio Streams

As you'll see in Chapter 10, "Importing Assets," DVD Studio Pro will import and use any audio format that QuickTime recognizes. A.Pack, however, is not as accommodating. A.Pack will accept only AIFF, WAV, and SDII files at a sampling rate of 48 kHz and a bit depth of either 16- or 24-bit (for more information on sampling rates and bit depths, see the sidebar "Sampling Rate versus Bit Depth"). While the DVD-Video spec itself allows for 96 kHz audio files, currently A.Pack won't accept a 96 kHz file—trying to use such a file results in the dialog pictured in **Figure 6.1.** In most situations, however, this isn't a problem. DV video typically uses 48 kHz, 16-bit audio, so 99 percent of the time your audio streams will already be in a format that A.Pack understands.

Figure 6.1 A.Pack accepts only 48 kHz audio files. If you attempt to import an audio file with a different sampling rate, this dialog stops you in your tracks.

What's PCM Audio?

There's no mystery to PCM (pulse code modulated) audio—it's simply uncompressed digital audio in AIFF, WAV, or SoundDesigner II (SDII) format. Audio editing tools, such as Logic Platinum and Propellerheads Reason, produce PCM audio. When you render your Final Cut Pro movies, the audio is recorded in PCM format (AIFF). In other words, all digital audio always begins life as a linear PCM file.

Sampling Rate versus Bit Depth

When it comes to digital audio, there are two important concepts to understand: sampling rate and bit depth.

- **Sampling rate.** When you record a sound on your computer, the sound must be *digitized*, or changed from an analog wave into a series of digital numbers that the computer understands. Computers sample sound by capturing the voltage level of an analog sound a certain number of times per second. When played back in rapid succession, this series of samples can be reconverted into a voltage level that is amplified and drives a speaker—in other words, the fluctuating voltage levels recorded by a digital audio file's samples are turned back into sound that we can hear.

  The file's *sampling rate* reflects the number of times per second its voltage is sampled, or recorded (**Figure 6.2**). A file sampled 48,000 times per second, for example, has a sampling rate of 48 kHz, while a file sampled 96,000 times per second has a sampling rate of 96 kHz.

- **Bit depth.** Bit depth is the amplitude portion of the sampling process, and it represents a sample's *sound*. Often called quantization, bit depth defines the number of discreet voltage steps used in the sampling process. A 16-bit audio file, for example, uses 65,536 discrete voltage steps to represent the sound at each particular sample. A 24-bit audio file uses 16,777,216 discrete voltage steps. With all those millions of extra voltage steps, a 24-bit file usually represents the source audio much more realistically than does a 16-bit file. Think of a staircase: a staircase with a lot of steps looks smoother than one with few steps. In a similar fashion, an audio wave with a higher bit depth sounds smoother, or more natural, than one with a lower bit depth.

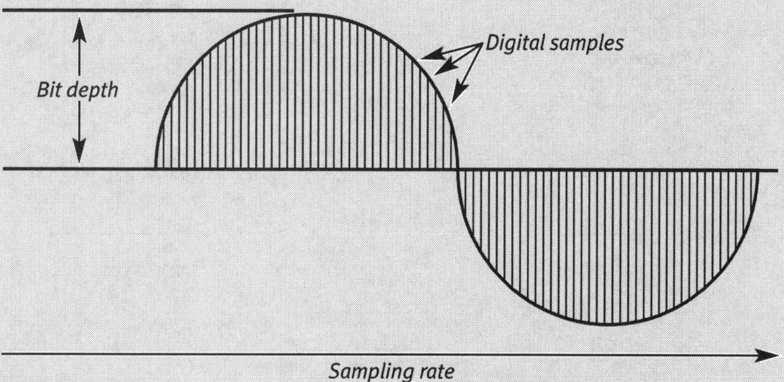

Figure 6.2 Where each line intersects with the waveform, a single sample is recorded. For 48 kHz audio, the waveform is sampled 48,000 times per second.

Converting Audio Formats

In the past, CDs were a major source of audio for DVD-Video projects. These days, the Internet is a common place to locate copyright-free background music to use in DVD Studio Pro. Both sources are good sonic orchards from which to harvest audio—as long as you keep the following in mind: CD-Audio uses a sampling rate of 44.1 kHz, and audio obtained online often uses the MP3 or AAC codec, neither of which A.Pack understands. If your source audio files are not exactly 48 kHz, 16- or 24-bit PCM files, you'll need to convert them before you can import them into A.Pack.

To convert audio to 48 kHz:

1. Open the digital audio file in QuickTime Pro Player.
2. Choose File > Export (**Figure 6.3**), or press Command-E.

   The Save Exported File As dialog opens.
3. Name your file and choose a folder to save it in.
4. From the Export pop-up menu, choose Sound to AIFF (**Figure 6.4**).
5. Click the Options button.

   The Sound Settings dialog opens (**Figure 6.5**).

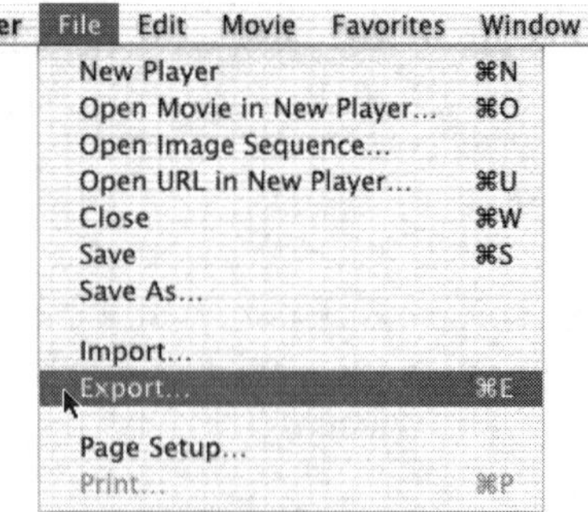

Figure 6.3 To convert an audio file to a format that A.Pack understands, open it in QuickTime Pro Player and choose File > Export.

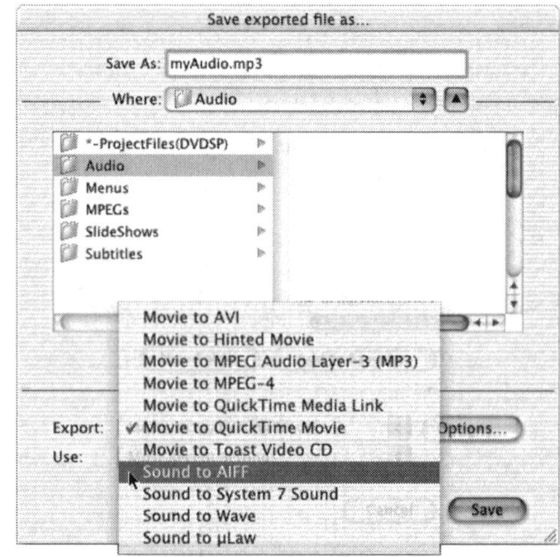

Figure 6.4 A.Pack prefers AIFF linear PCM files, so choose Sound to AIFF from the Export pop-up menu.

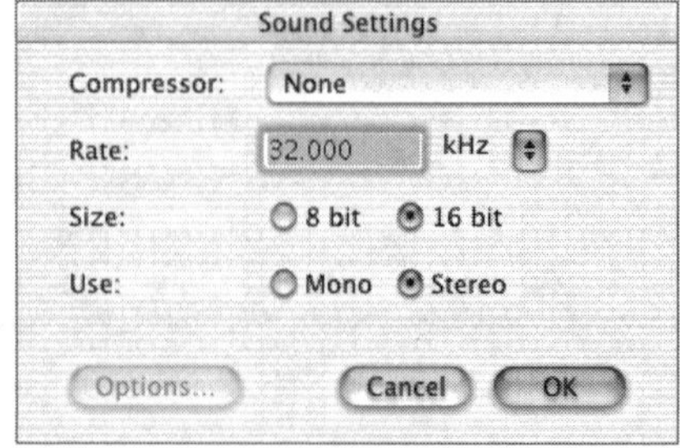

Figure 6.5 Use the Sound Settings dialog to make your audio file stereo and to set its bit rate to 16-bit.

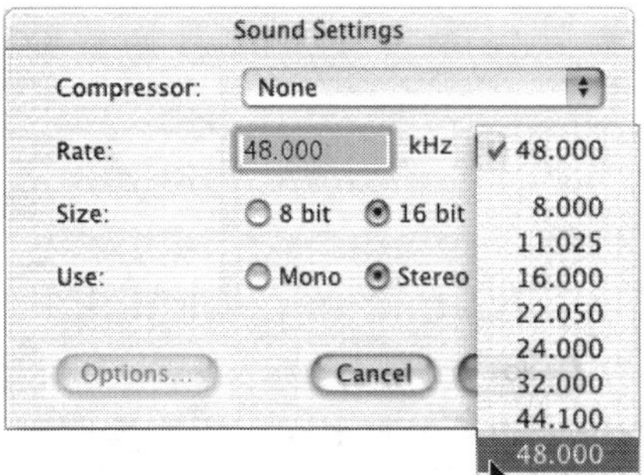

Figure 6.6 Choose 48 kHz from the Rate pop-up menu.

6. From the Rate pop-up menu, choose 48.000 (**Figure 6.6**).
7. In the center of the Sound Settings dialog, choose 16 Bit as the Size setting and Stereo as the Use setting.
8. In the lower-right corner of the Sound Settings dialog, click OK.

   The Sound Settings dialog closes, leaving the Save Exported File As dialog on your screen.
9. In the Save Exported File As dialog, click Save.

   QuickTime converts the audio file into a 48-kHz AIFF file that can be imported directly into DVD Studio Pro or encoded to AC-3 using A.Pack.

✓ Tip

- DVD Studio Pro can also convert digital audio files to 48 kHz AIFFs. Start by importing the file into DVD Studio Pro. If background encoding is enabled, the program will automatically convert the file to a 48 kHz AIFF file. Next, Control-click the audio file in DVD Studio Pro's Assets container and choose Show in Finder. A Finder window will pop open, and your encoded file will be in it. Now you can easily and quickly drag the encoded file into A.Pack.

To check sample rate and bit depth:

1. Open the digital audio file in QuickTime Pro Player.
2. Choose Movie > Get Movie Properties (**Figure 6.7**), or press Command-J.

   The Properties window opens.
3. From the left pop-up menu, choose Sound Track, and from the right pop-up menu, choose Format (**Figure 6.8**).

   The Properties window displays the audio file's format, including its sample rate, number of channels, sample size (bit depth), and method of compression. If the sampling rate does not say 48 kHz, you must convert the audio file as demonstrated earlier in the task "To convert audio to 48 kHz."

✔ Tip

- You can also look at a file's properties by opening the file in QuickTime Player and pressing Command-I. The Movie Info dialog opens to display the file's properties (**Figure 6.9**).

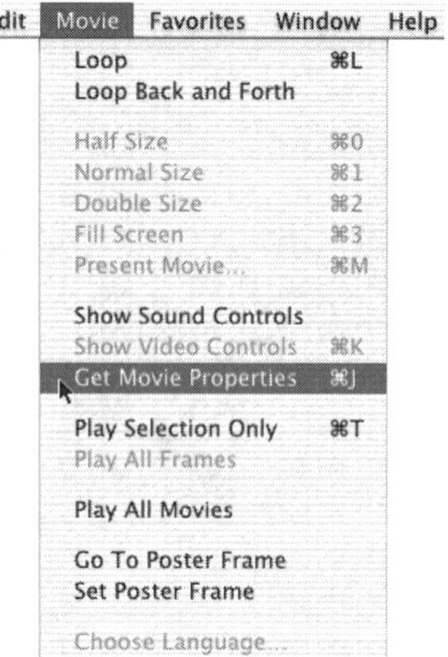

Figure 6.7 To check an audio file's sample rate, use QuickTime Pro Player. Open the file in QuickTime and choose Movie > Get Movie Properties.

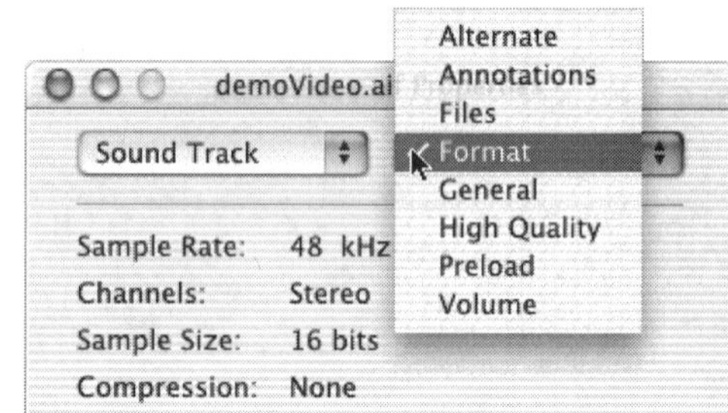

Figure 6.8 The Properties window displaying the sound track's format information.

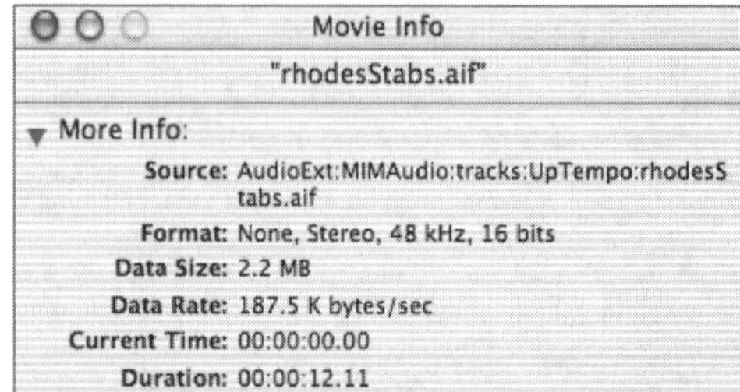

Figure 6.9 If you open a file in QuickTime 6 or higher and then press Command-I, the Movie Info window opens to show you the file's properties.

About AC-3 Audio

AC-3 is a perceptual audio coding system that analyzes an audio signal and throws away the parts we can't hear. As it turns out, we can't hear a lot, which allows AC-3 encoders to produce audio streams with compression ratios of up to 12:1 over PCM audio.

AC-3 encoders use a process called *frequency masking* to determine which sounds are audible to the human ear. Frequency masking (herein referred to as just *masking*) occurs when high-volume frequencies drown out their low-volume neighbors, making the low-volume frequency bands less noticeable or even completely inaudible. Before encoding an audio file, an AC-3 encoder divides it into many narrow-frequency bands. It searches through those frequency bands to determine which ones are the loudest. It then looks at neighboring frequency bands to see if they contain enough sound to be heard. Frequency bands that are too low in volume are *masked* by the louder ones. AC-3 encoders largely ignore masked frequencies, assigning fewer bits to masked frequencies than to their more audible counterparts.

✔ Tip

- AC-3 encoding is a lossy compression system. Because some of the original data gets thrown away, the AC-3 stream is only a close approximation, not an exact re-creation of the original digital audio file.

Control parameters

Control parameters are hints sent with the encoded AC-3 file that tell the decoder how to play the AC-3 stream. Control parameters include the dialog normalization setting, dynamic range profile, and downmix options, all of which are explained later in this chapter.

Control parameters do not alter the AC-3 stream itself. You set control parameters when you encode the AC-3 file, but it's up to the playback device to interpret and apply them. Most (if not all) DVD-Video players are capable of decoding control parameters.

✔ Tip

- Some AC-3 decoders allow the viewer to determine how control parameters are applied. Most viewers don't mess with these settings, so rest assured that the majority of AC-3 decoders available should correctly interpret all control parameters.

Real-Life Masking

Here's how masking works: Imagine that you and a friend are sitting in your car at a stoplight, with the windows rolled up, listening to an AM radio station. A lowrider pulls up beside you with R&B pumping loud enough that your car shakes in rhythm with the subpulses. You can no longer hear the subfrequencies coming from your AM radio, because the bass from the other car overpowers, or *masks,* them. You can, however, still hear the complaints from your friend in the passenger seat. Why? Well, your friend's voice is loud and in a frequency range far enough from the bass range that it is not masked (but try opening the window...).

About A.Pack

Apple's A.Pack is an AC-3 encoder that converts 48 kHz PCM audio files into Dolby Digital AC-3 audio streams. (Currently, A.Pack does not support 96 kHz PCM files.) A.Pack is composed of three parts: the Instant Encoder (**Figure 6.10**), the Batch Encoder (**Figure 6.11**), and the AC-3 Monitor (**Figure 6.12**).

The Instant Encoder is the main encoding window, which you use when encoding audio files one at a time in a single encode job. The left side of this window contains an Input Channels matrix, which is used to assign audio files to the AC-3 stream's left, right, and surround channels; the right side contains tabs that define encoding settings such as the file's encoded bit rate and dialog normalization value.

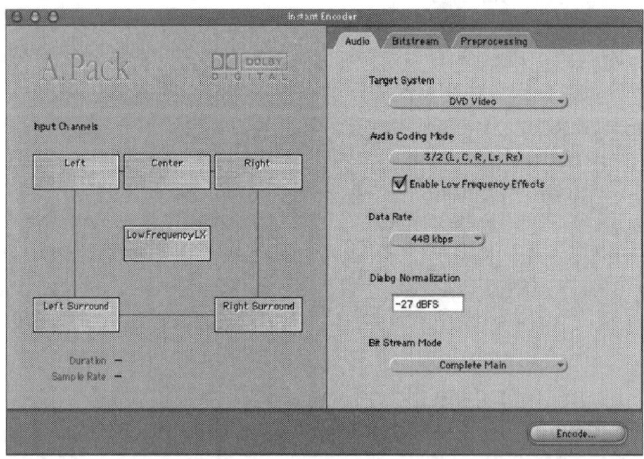

Figure 6.10 The Instant Encoder allows you to encode AC-3 files one at a time.

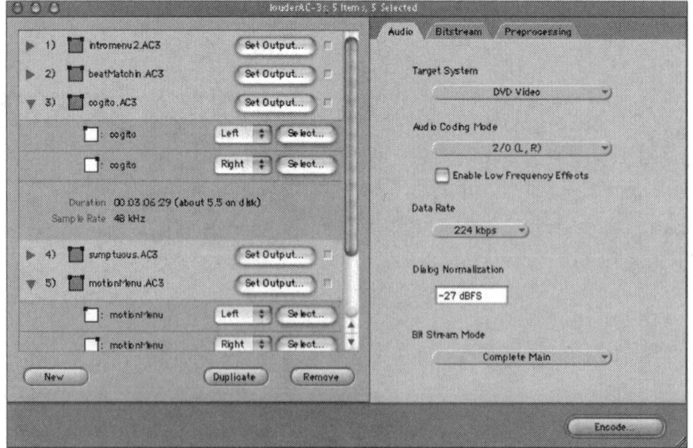

Figure 6.11 The Batch Encoder lets you set up several AC-3 encoding jobs at the same time. The Batch Encoder looks similar to the Instant Encoder, but instead of an Input Channels matrix occupying the left side, there's a batch list that holds multiple audio files.

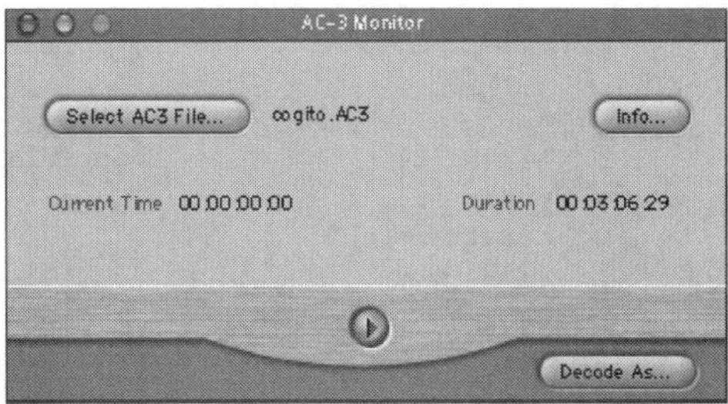

Figure 6.12 The AC-3 Monitor plays your encoded AC-3 streams. You'll use the AC-3 Monitor to make sure that dialog normalization and dynamic range compression are correctly applied, and that all surround streams sound good when downmixed into stereo.

Figure 6.13 If you can't see the encoding settings, click the window's expansion box to reveal them.

The Batch Encoder offers the same functions as the Instant Encoder, but as a bonus the Batch Encoder groups multiple encode jobs together so you can compress them all at once.

The AC-3 Monitor is a playback utility that lets you preview your encoded AC-3 files to ensure that they were encoded correctly. It also lets you decode AC-3 files back into PCM audio streams, which can be a lifesaver if you need to alter the AC-3 stream's sound but no longer have the source files.

✔ Tip

- If you can't see the Instant Encoder's encoding settings, click the green button at the top left of the Input Channels section (**Figure 6.13**). This button expands or hides the encoding settings section.

Launching A.Pack

The DVD Studio Pro installation utility places A.Pack in the same folder as DVD Studio Pro.

To launch A.Pack:

1. Double-click the A.Pack application icon (**Figure 6.14**).

   The A.Pack splash screen appears (**Figure 6.15**).

2. Click the splash screen.

   A.Pack launches, and the Instant Encoder window opens. You don't have to click the splash screen, but doing so opens A.Pack more quickly. Otherwise, the splash screen stays visible for up to 10 seconds—that's a long time to stare at the A.Pack logo.

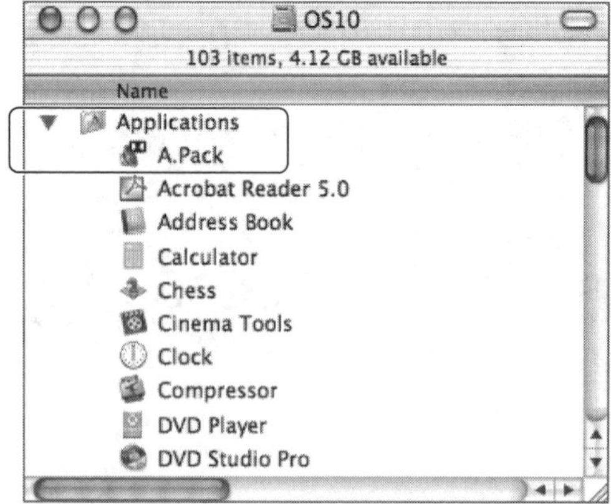

Figure 6.14 The A.Pack application icon is located in the same folder as DVD Studio Pro.

Figure 6.15 Click the A.Pack splash screen to dismiss it instantly.

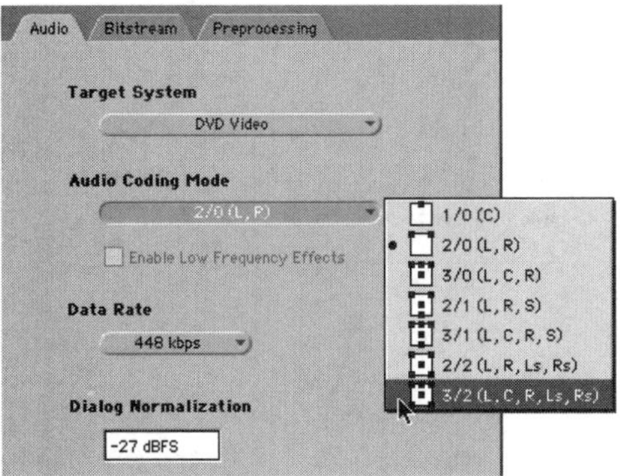

Figure 6.16 The Audio Coding Mode menu defines the channel configuration for your AC-3 file.

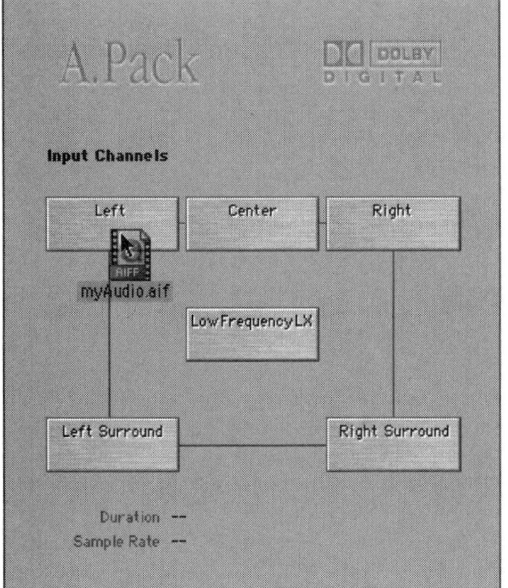

Figure 6.17 The Input Channels matrix reflects the selected audio coding mode. Assign PCM files to A.Pack input channels by dragging them from the Finder onto the channel buttons.

Encoding AC-3 Audio

Converting PCM audio into an AC-3 file is called an *encoding job.* And it *is* a job. There are no shortcuts or set formulas to help you bluff your way through it—you need to know how all of A.Pack's settings work to encode an audio stream. (Well, okay, there actually are some quick settings you can use in a pinch, but these are not guaranteed to give you great-sounding audio if you use them; see the sidebar "A.Pack Quick Settings" later in this chapter.)

Although the number of settings you have to configure varies with every project, you'll always have to determine an audio stream's volume and bit rate as well as the number and configuration of its channels to set A.Pack correctly. Once these settings are specified, everything else falls into place.

In general, you'll perform the following steps when encoding an AC-3 stream in A.Pack:

- **Choose an audio coding mode.** The audio coding mode determines the number of channels your final AC-3 audio stream contains and sets their configuration within the surround-sound field (**Figure 6.16**).
- **Assign audio files to input channels.** Assign audio streams to channels by dragging and dropping PCM files onto channel buttons in the Input Channels matrix (**Figure 6.17**).

continues on next page

- **Set the bit rate.** The bit rate (measured in kilobits per second, or kbps) sets the combined data rate of all channels within the AC-3 file (**Figure 6.18**). Higher bit rates increase the AC-3 file's fidelity but also create large file sizes.
- **Set dynamic range controls.** You control your AC-3 stream's volume level using several settings, including dialog normalization, dynamic range compression, and RF overmodulation (**Figure 6.19**). Setting these controls is perhaps the most confusing aspect of AC-3 encoding, so to help you through it, all of the necessary settings are described in separate sections in this chapter.
- **Downmix surround sound.** Surround AC-3 files contain hints that tell the decoder in a DVD-Video player how to turn multichannel sound into a stereo signal for playback on systems that have only stereo outputs (**Figure 6.20**). Specifying the downmix settings incorrectly can cause parts of the downmixed audio to play back at the wrong volume, creating unpleasant spikes in your sound.

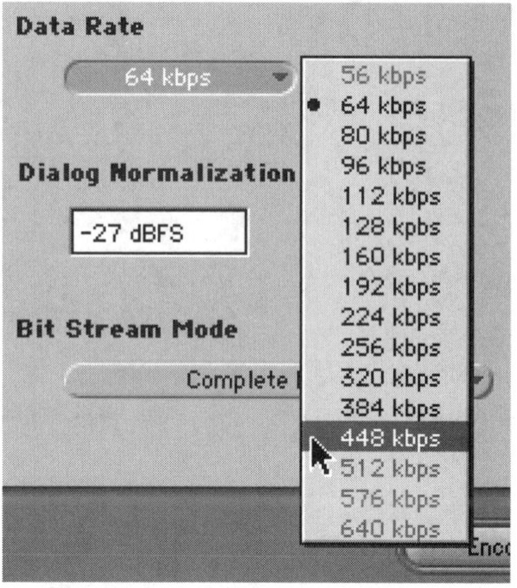

Figure 6.18 A.Pack compresses audio files at bit rates ranging from 64 kbps for a mono stream to 448 kbps for a 5.1 surround stream.

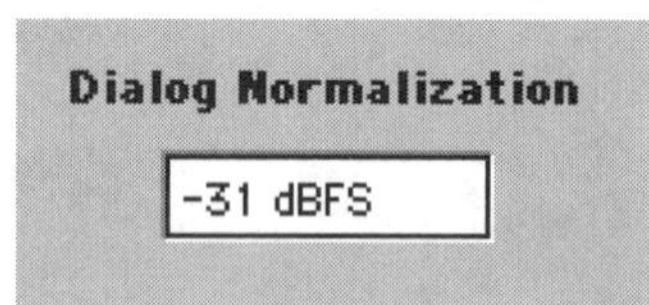

Figure 6.19 The dialog normalization setting is critical to the proper playback of your AC-3 file. This number also controls all other dynamic range settings (compression profile, RF overmodulation, and so on), so make sure you set it right!

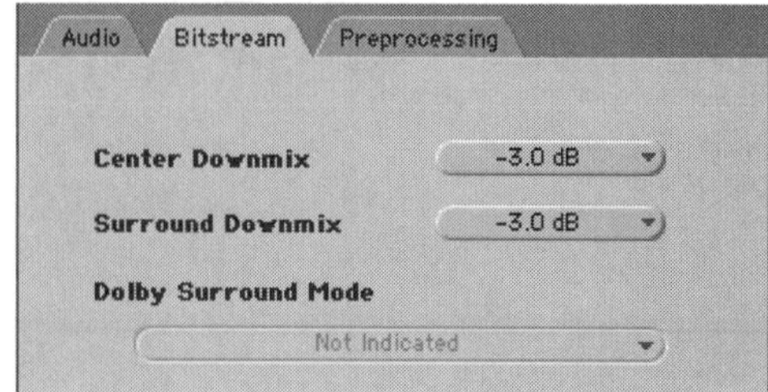

Figure 6.20 Downmix settings determine how the AC-3 file will sound when decoded by DVD-Video players sending sound to fewer channels than the AC-3 audio stream.

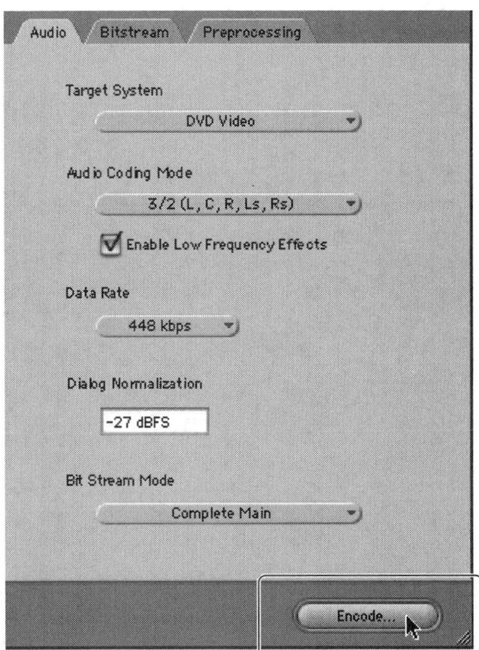

Figure 6.21 After you've defined your encoding settings, click the Encode button to begin compressing an AC-3 file.

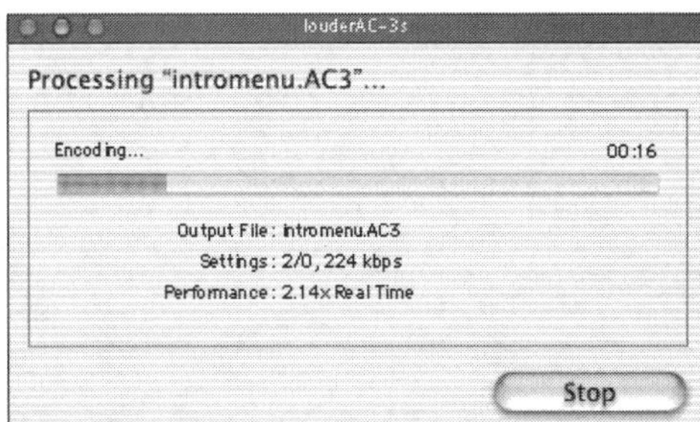

Figure 6.22 The Progress window follows the encoder's progress.

- **Encode your audio.** The Encode button sits in the lower-right corner of the Instant Encoder (**Figure 6.21**). Clicking this button launches the Instant Encoder Progress window. Use the Progress window to monitor A.Pack's progress while encoding (**Figure 6.22**).

A.Pack Quick Settings

For rush jobs, start with the default A.Pack settings, enter an audio coding mode to give the file the correct number of channels, and then use these encoding settings (leave all the rest at their default values):

- **Bit rate:** Stereo: 196 kbps; 5.1: 448 kbps
- **Dialog normalization:** –31
- **Compression preset:** None
- **RF overmodulation protection:** Off

Using Audio Coding Modes

The audio coding mode determines the speaker configuration for your AC-3 file. Each audio coding mode is defined by two numbers separated by a slash (**Figure 6.23**). The first number represents the number of speakers across the front of the audio field; the second defines the number of speakers across the back. For example, 1/0 is a single mono signal with sound coming only from the center channel, 2/0 represents stereo audio, and any other combination yields some form of multichannel or surround sound. (To learn more about surround sound, see the sidebar "AC-3 and 5.1 Surround Files" later in this chapter.)

To select an audio coding mode:

1. On the Instant Encoder's Audio tab, click the Audio Coding Mode drop-down menu (refer to Figure 6.23).

   The menu lists several audio coding modes, from 1/0 (mono) up to 3/2 (5.1 surround sound).

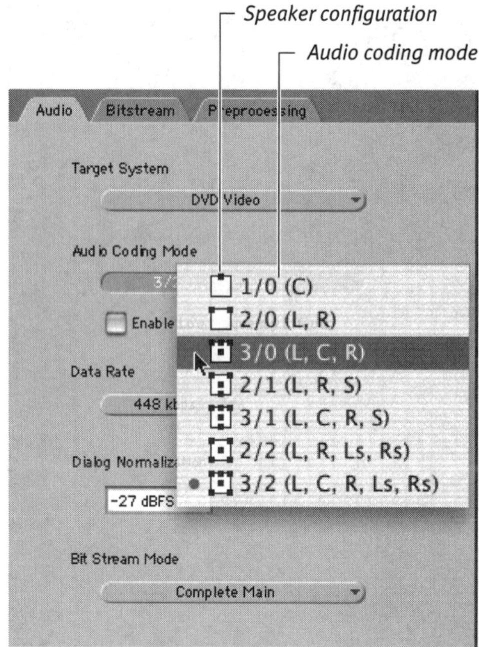

Figure 6.23 To help you visualize the target speaker configuration, the left side of the Audio Coding Mode menu provides icons that show how channels will be arranged within the audio field.

2. Choose an audio coding mode (**Figure 6.24**).

   The Input Channels matrix updates to show the configuration that you chose.

3. If your audio has a low-frequency effects channel (a subwoofer channel), select the Enable Low Frequency Effects check box (**Figure 6.25**), found directly under the Audio tab's Audio Coding Mode menu.

   In the Input Channels matrix, the low-frequency effects channel is enabled.

✔ Tip

- If you've assigned a full-spectrum audio file to the low-frequency effects channel, on the Instant Encoder's Preprocessing tab, in the LFE Channel section, select Apply Low-Pass Filter. This filter removes all sound above 120 Hz from the LFE channel.

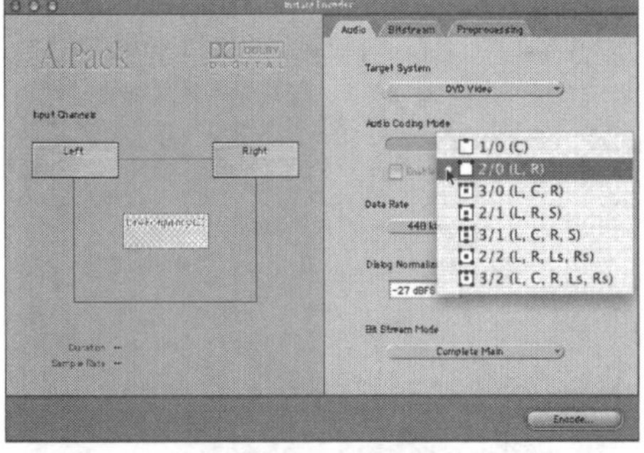

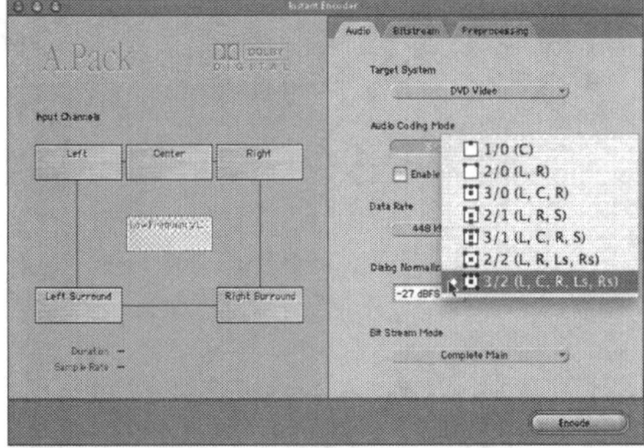

Figure 6.24 The audio coding mode sets the number of channels available to the Input Channels matrix. In the top image, a stereo audio coding mode is selected, and the Input Channels matrix has two channels available. The bottom image uses a five-channel surround audio coding mode, so five channels are available in the Input Channels matrix.

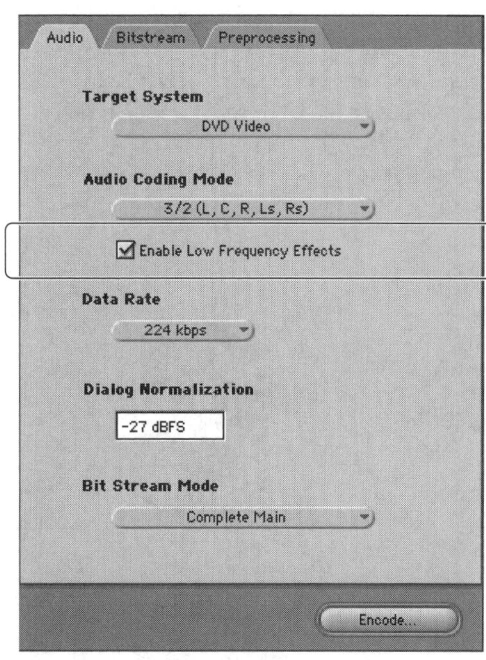

Figure 6.25 The Enable Low Frequency Effects check box turns on the .1 channel (subwoofer channel) that you'll use to store all low-frequency effects such as explosions or jet-plane rumble.

AC-3 and 5.1 Surround Files

An AC-3 file can have up to six channels, allowing for fully supported 5.1 surround sound. 5.1 surround sound uses six discrete channels to feed speakers arranged in a matrix around a central point (**Figure 6.26**). A 5.1 surround field has three full-spectrum speakers in the front and two in the back, and one subwoofer for reproducing low-frequency effects (the subwoofer may be placed anywhere in the room).

AC-3 decoders deal with 5.1 surround streams in a very clever way. When faced with a surround signal, the decoder directs each channel in the AC-3 file to the appropriate speaker. If there are fewer than 5.1 channels available to the decoder, it downmixes the surround stream into a configuration that works with the available speakers. As a result, if the viewer has a two-speaker stereo system, the center, left-surround, and right-surround channels are *downmixed*, or blended, into the left and right speakers. The viewer still hears everything, just not exactly as the audio engineer intended.

By the way, have you ever wondered about the ".1" in "5.1" surround sound? Subwoofers reproduce frequencies of only up to 120 Hz, while all other speakers are full range (up to 20 kHz). The limited frequency range of the subwoofer is said to represent only 10 percent, or 0.1, of a full channel—hence, 5.1 surround sound.

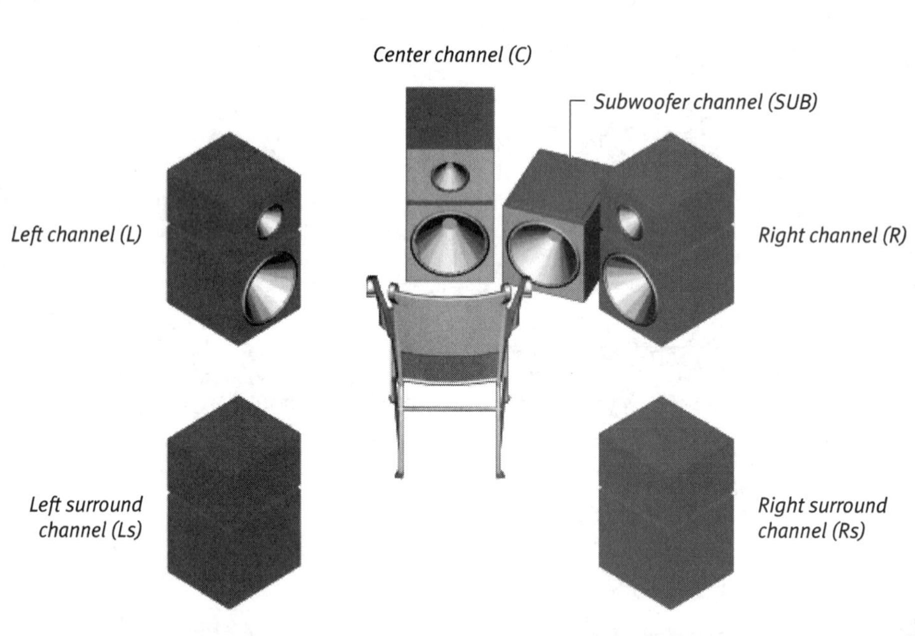

Figure 6.26 A typical 5.1 surround mix includes a stereo signal fed to both the left (L) and right (R) speakers, a dialog track in the center (C) channel, surround effects in the left surround (Ls) and right surround (Rs) channels, and low-frequency effects in the subwoofer channel (SUB). The result is a three-dimensional sound field surrounding the listener.

Assigning Input Channels

In A.Pack, you assign PCM audio files to input channels by dragging the files from the Finder onto the appropriate input channel buttons. Unlike DVD Studio Pro, which accepts almost any type of digital audio file, A.Pack accepts only 48 kHz audio files. If your audio uses any other sampling rate, you'll need to convert it before assigning it to an input channel. (To learn how to convert your audio files to 48 kHz, see "Converting Audio Formats" earlier in this chapter.)

To assign an audio file to a channel:

1. From the Finder, select an audio file.
2. In A.Pack's Instant Encoder window, drag the audio file onto an input channel button (**Figure 6.27**), or click the input channel button and select an audio file from the Select File dialog.

   If the audio file has more than one channel, the Select Input Channel dialog opens (**Figure 6.28**).

continues on next page

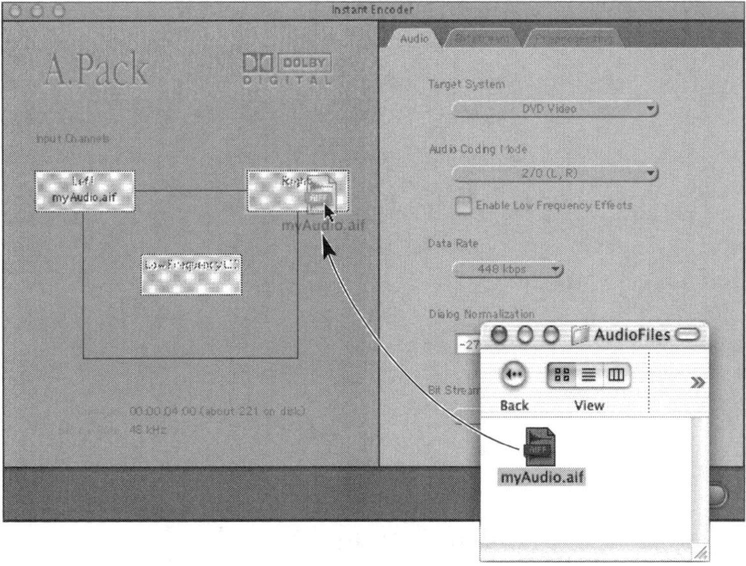

Figure 6.27 To assign audio files to A.Pack input channels, drag the audio files from the Finder directly onto the correct input channel buttons.

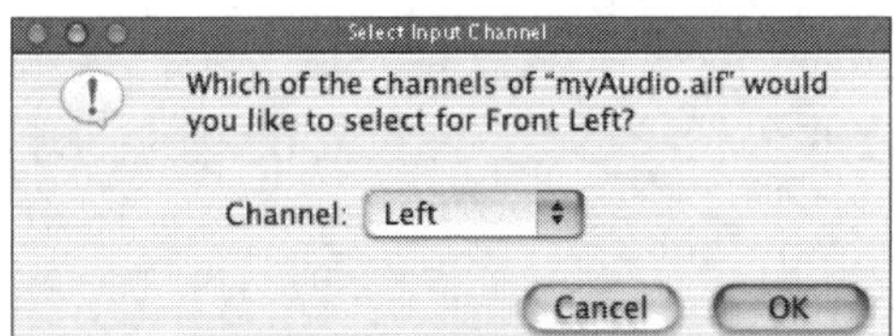

Figure 6.28 If the source file has more than one channel, the Select Input Channel dialog lets you assign each one to an A.Pack input channel button.

3. From the Channel menu in the Select Input Channel dialog, choose the correct audio track for the input channel.

   If your source audio file is stereo, the Channel menu lists both the left and right audio tracks (**Figure 6.29**).

4. Repeat steps 1 through 3 until all input channels have been assigned a source audio track.

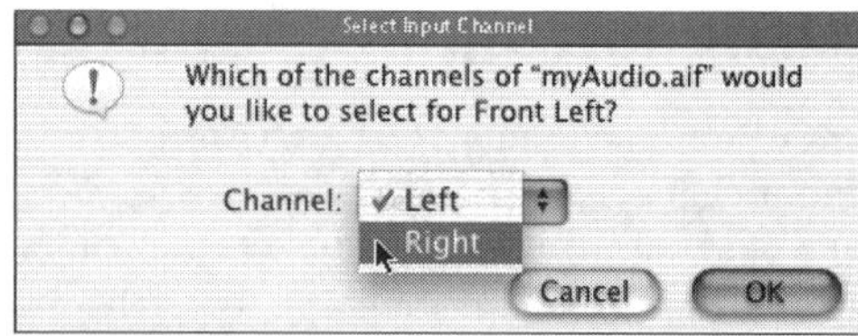

Figure 6.29 When you add a stereo PCM file, such as an interleaved AIFF file, to an A.Pack input channel button, A.Pack lets you choose either the left or right channel.

✔ Tip

- If you have a QuickTime movie that contains video as well as audio, you can still drop it into A.Pack. A.Pack ignores everything but the audio tracks. (You can even drop a Final Cut Pro reference movie directly into A.Pack.)

Faking Surround Sound

A.Pack allows you to combine audio tracks from different files in one encoding job. You can use this technique to fake a surround audio mix, for example, by assigning a stereo song to the front-left and front-right speakers, a narration track to the center channel, and stereo ambient sound (crowd noise, blowing wind, and so on) to the rear-left and rear-right speakers. When you combine audio from different files in one encoding job, the files you use should be the same length. If your source files vary in length, A.Pack equalizes them by adding silence to the end of the shorter audio streams.

While 5.1 surround systems are slowly working their way into living rooms everywhere, most DVD-Video players are still hooked up to stereo playback devices. If you're faking a surround mix, be sure to test the AC-3 file to ensure that it sounds good when the surround channels are downmixed into stereo.

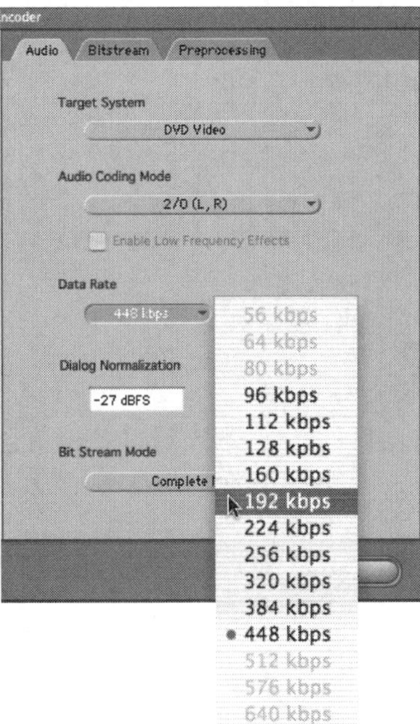

Figure 6.30 The Data Rate drop-down menu lists possible bit rates for your AC-3 file. If you've selected DVD Video from the Target System drop-down menu, only DVD-Video-compatible data rates are selectable.

Choosing a Bit Rate

The bit rate you choose depends on how many channels your AC-3 file needs and how much storage space you have available on your DVD disc. The ear is more critical than the eye, and viewers are more likely to enjoy a DVD-Video with poor visual and high audio quality than vice versa. Consequently, you should give audio streams the highest possible setting given your DVD disc's storage capacity.

Here are some guidelines to help you select the correct bit rate:

- **Mono:** 64 to 128 kbps
- **Stereo:** 192 to 224 kbps
- **5.1 surround:** 224 to 448 kbps

To choose a bit rate:

1. In A.Pack, select the Audio tab.
2. From the Audio tab's Data Rate menu, choose a bit rate (**Figure 6.30**).

   The AC-3 stream is set to be encoded at the selected bit rate.

✔ Tips

- 192 kbps provides high-quality stereo streams.
- 448 kbps is recommended for 5.1 streams.
- Still not sure if there's enough space on your DVD disc to encode that 5.1 track at a full 448 kbps? Check out Appendix A, "Surviving on a Bit Budget," to learn how to determine the appropriate bit rate for your audio (and video) streams.

Using Dialog Normalization

In audio terms, *normalization* is a process in which the volume level of one (or several) audio programs is altered to a set (normalized) level. Using the same principle, *dialog normalization* raises or lowers the volume of an audio program to ensure that all dialog reaches the listener at the same average volume level.

For all dialog to play back at consistent levels, you must determine the dialog normalization value (DNV) for your audio stream and key that value into A.Pack. When the decoder processes the AC-3 stream, it reads the file's DNV and alters the stream's volume accordingly. **Table 6.1** shows typical DNVs that are needed to match several different source audio streams to the standard volume level of a DVD-Video.

Table 6.1

Dialog Normalization Values

Source Audio	Dialog Normalization
DV camera	–31
Dance music	–8
Television broadcast	–12
Orchestra	–25
Movie sound track	–31

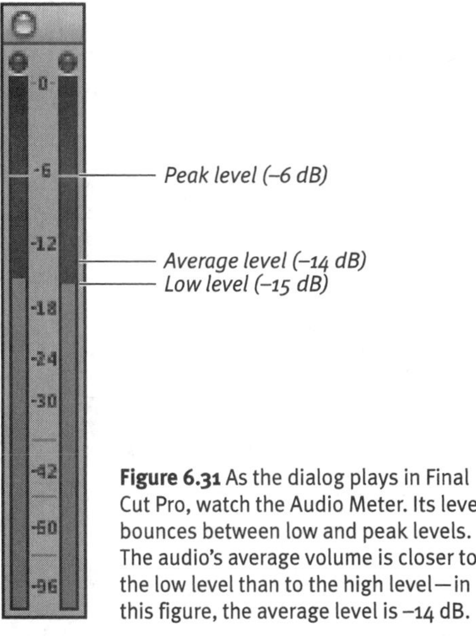

Figure 6.31 As the dialog plays in Final Cut Pro, watch the Audio Meter. Its level bounces between low and peak levels. The audio's average volume is closer to the low level than to the high level—in this figure, the average level is –14 dB.

Determining an Audio Stream's DNV

To determine an audio stream's DNV, you need to look at the audio stream in a program that has an audio-level meter, such as Final Cut Pro or Logic Pro. Because most video—and its corresponding audio—begin life in Final Cut Pro, the following steps show you how to find an audio stream's DNV in Final Cut Pro. The concept is the same regardless of the program you are using and can easily be applied to Logic, Cubase, Pro Tools, or whatever application you're using to create your DVD-Video's audio.

To determine the DNV in Final Cut Pro:

1. Open the audio file in Final Cut Pro.

   If the audio comes from a video sequence, that's fine—just open the original video sequence in Final Cut Pro.

2. Find a section of the audio file that's dialog only.

3. Play the dialog part of the file and look at Final Cut Pro's Audio Meter (**Figure 6.31**).

   Watch the audio levels as the dialog plays. You'll notice that they bounce between low and peak levels.

4. Determine the average volume level of the file's dialog; this is your audio file's DNV.

   It takes a bit of practice to determine your audio file's average volume level. As you watch the level meter bounce between its high and low values, at first you'll be tempted to choose a number right in the middle. In fact, the average volume level of dialog is often much closer to the lowest volume level.

DNV and Reference Tone Level

There is another advantage to using Final Cut Pro to determine an audio stream's DNV. If you've mixed your audio correctly in Final Cut Pro, the dialog's average volume should be around –12 dB on Final Cut Pro's digital volume meter. This number (–12 dB) is *exactly* the DNV of the audio stream, and this is the number you enter into A.Pack to properly normalize the stream's audio level.

While this concept may seem esoteric to new video editors, it's extremely important to understand. An essential description of how to use reference tones to define dialog levels is contained in *Apple Pro Training Series: Advanced Editing and Finishing Techniques in Final Cut Pro 4*, published by Peachpit Press.

To enter a dialog normalization value into A.Pack:

1. In A.Pack, choose the Instant Encoder's Audio tab.
2. In the Dialog Normalization text box, enter the DNV for your audio stream (**Figure 6.32**) and press Return.

   Make sure you press Return because A.Pack will not lock in the changed DNV unless you do so.

✔ Tips

- How do you determine the DNV of an instrumental source audio track that doesn't have any dialog? Here's a trick. Open the file in a multitrack audio editor such as Logic Pro or Final Cut Pro; then import a dialog track and run it on top of the instrumental (go on—fire up that microphone). Adjust the dialog track so that it fits well into the mix and then play the dialog track by itself (solo the dialog track). Use this dialog track's average volume level as the DNV for your instrumental AC-3 file.
- When you're trying to determine a file's DNV, it often helps to set up a batch and encode multiple versions of the same AC-3 file, each with a different DNV (see "About Batch Lists" later in this chapter). You can then audition these files with A.Pack's AC-3 monitor to see which one sounds the best (see "Auditioning AC-3 Files" later in this chapter).
- Dialog normalization is generally measured in dBFS LAeq, which is a slightly different volume scale than that found in Logic Pro or Final Cut Pro. LAeq measures an audio stream's long-term average sound-pressure level and typically yields readings lower than the dB reading on the volume-level meters in most audio-editing programs.

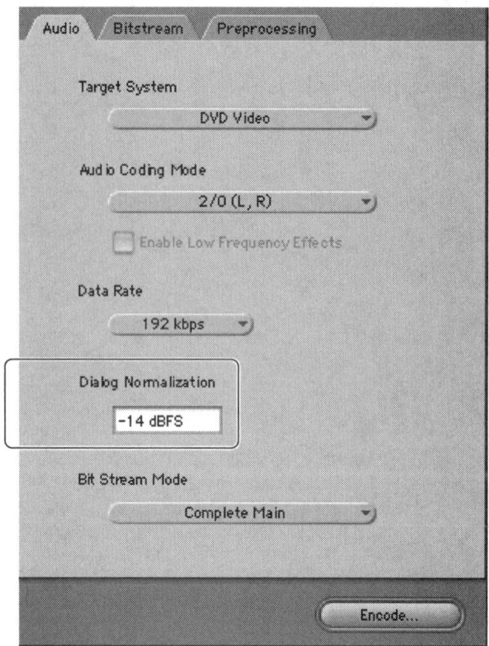

Figure 6.32 Type your audio stream's dialog normalization value into A.Pack's Dialog Normalization text box.

How Dialog Normalization Works

In audio terms, when you *attenuate* a track, you lower its volume. Dialog normalization heals discrepancies in volume levels by attenuating *every* AC-3 audio stream by 31 + DNV dB. If the AC-3 file is a movie sound track, you assign it a DNV of –31. Consequently, the track is attenuated 31 + (–31) dB. That's 0 dB, which means that the track's volume doesn't change at all. A dance track has a DNV of around –8; at playback, the track is attenuated 31 + (–8) dB, or 23 dB. This may seem like a lot of volume to cut off, but now that dance track doesn't overpower the love scene, so everyone is happy.

About Dynamic Range Control

Dynamic range compression works by shaving off an audio track's loudest peaks while boosting its lower volume sections, resulting in quieter loud sections, louder quiet sections, and a more unified volume level for the entire AC-3 file—that is, if you don't foul it up. Miscalculating dynamic range compression can result in *gain pumping*, which causes the track's audio to sound like it's pumping rapidly up and down in volume. In truth, the sound track plays at a fairly constant volume, but because the volume peaks are being noticeably lowered while the lows are noticeably accentuated, the overall impression is that the volume is jumping back and forth erratically.

With AC-3 files encoded using A.Pack, this problem most often occurs when the dialog normalization number is set incorrectly. If your DVD-Video uses loud techno background music, for example, but you've left A.Pack's DNV at the factory default position of –27 with the compression profile set to Film Standard, the sound will appear to increase in volume any time the beat stops pounding. When the beat returns, the sound will become quieter. This is called *gain pumping*. To fix the problem, either raise the dialog normalization number to around –8 or turn off compression on the Preprocessing tab's Compression menu.

✔ Tip

- A.Pack's RF overmodulation setting can also cause gain pumping. To learn more, see "RF Overmodulation Protection" later in this chapter.

Using Compression Profiles

AC-3 dynamic range compression (DRC) is divided into three distinct bands. Inside the middle band, called the null band, audio is neither boosted nor attenuated. When audio levels drift outside the null band, they are boosted (increased in volume) or attenuated (lowered in volume) according to a *compression profile.*

Compression profiles come preset by Dolby; you can't change their characteristics. A.Pack lets you choose from a selection of five DRC profiles, all found on the Preprocessing tab's Compression Preset menu (**Figure 6.33**). The characteristics of each profile are listed in **Table 6.2**.

To choose a compression profile:

1. In A.Pack's Instant Encoder, choose the Preprocessing tab.
2. From the Compression Preset menu, choose a DRC profile (refer to Figure 6.33).

   This DRC profile will be applied to your AC-3 stream as it's decoded.

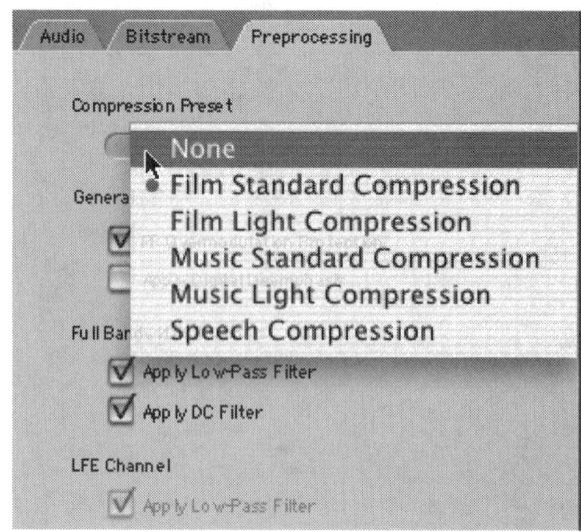

Figure 6.33 The Compression Preset menu lists five preset compression profiles you can use to tame errant volume spikes in your audio programs.

When in Doubt, Don't!

If you don't have time to test your AC-3 streams to make sure that the compression profile is correct, choose None from the Preprocessing tab's Compression Preset menu. No compression always sounds better than poorly applied compression, which can lead to gain pumping or *transient distortion* (when the volume level of low-volume sounds, such as the offscreen movement of a chair or the cameraman's breathing, is increased).

Table 6.2

Comparing Dynamic Range-Compression Profiles

Profile Quality	Film Standard	Film Light	Music Standard	Music Light	Speech
Null Band Width	10 dB	20 dB	10 dB	20 dB	10 dB
Null Band Range(dB)	(–31 to –21)	(–41 to –21)	(–31 to –21)	(–41 to –21)	(-31 to -21)
Max Boost (dB)	6	6	12	12	15
Boost Ratio	2:1	2:1	2:1	2:1	5:1
Max Cut (dB)	24	24	24	15	24
Cut Ratio	20:1	20:1	20:1	2:1	20:1

About Downmixing

When a 5.1 audio program is played on a 5.1 surround system, the result is nothing short of spectacular. Crowds thunder behind you, and bombs explode in the back-right corner of the room as all of the video's sounds conspire to make you feel like you're smack in the center of a larger-than-life movie moment.

When that same surround signal plays back on a stereo with just two front speakers—well, what happened to the crowd noise? Without the two back speakers, there's nothing to reproduce the sound. *Surround downmixing* solves this problem by adding audio from the surround speakers into the stereo channels.

The missing center channel poses a similar problem. Many 5.1 mixes include dialog only in the center channel, with music and effects (dialog reverb, chorusing, and so on) in the left and right channels. This gives a voice tremendous presence, but only if there's a center channel: if you remove the center channel from the mix, the dialog disappears. On a stereo system, the AC-3 decoder downmixes the center channel into both the left and right channels so that all of the dialog can still be heard.

Downmixing leads to an increase in the program's overall volume (see the sidebar "Why Attenuate the Downmix?"). You counter this volume increase by reducing the level of the downmixed channels using DVD Studio Pro's Center Downmix and Surround Downmix menus, found on the Bitstream tab in the Instant Encoder.

Why Attenuate the Downmix?

When you combine audio signals, certain parts of the new signal sound much louder than either of the source signals when they're played separately. The following paragraph provides a simple test that demonstrates this fact.

Open a mono audio file in a multitrack audio editor. Give it a quick listen. Then duplicate the mono file so two versions of it are playing at the same time. Create a stereo signal by panning one version hard left and the other hard right. If you listen closely, you'll notice that this new stereo signal is louder—typically about 6 dB, which is double the volume of the original mono signal.

Downmix attenuation counters this volume increase, allowing stereo decoders to play the signal at the correct volume.

To attenuate the downmix:

1. In A.Pack's Instant Encoder, choose the Bitstream tab.
2. *Do one of the following:*
   - ▲ To attenuate a center channel downmix, select a value from the Center Downmix menu.
   - ▲ To attenuate a surround downmix, select a value from the Surround Downmix menu (**Figure 6.34**).

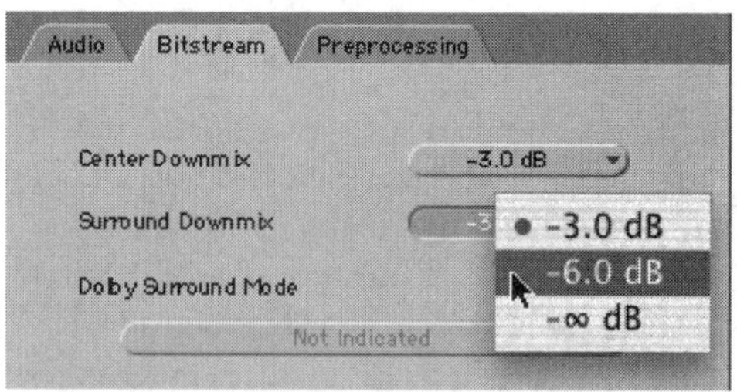

Figure 6.34 To ensure that your multichannel AC-3 files downmix properly, choose a downmix attenuation value from both the Center Downmix and Surround Downmix options (typically, the default value of –3.0 works just fine).

✔ Tips

- The low-frequency effects (LFE) channel is not downmixed into other channels. If the viewer's AC-3 decoder lacks an LFE channel, no LFE content is heard. To guard against this, mix a bit of the LFE channel into the audio stream's left and right channels when producing the source audio files.
- If you don't want the surround channels to be downmixed into the main stereo stream, set the Surround Downmix menu to –∞ dB (refer to Figure 6.34).
- After creating a 5.1 stream, open it in the AC-3 monitor and check out your downmix settings. If you hear any unwanted volume spikes, re-encode the stream using a lower downmix setting.

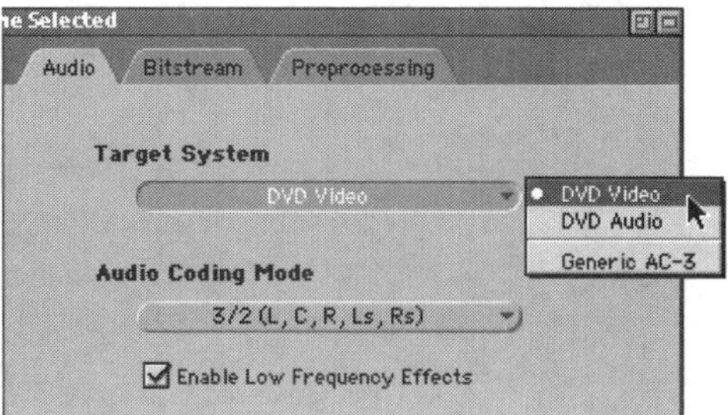

Figure 6.35 DVD Studio Pro is used to make DVD-Videos, so always choose DVD Video from A.Pack's Target System menu.

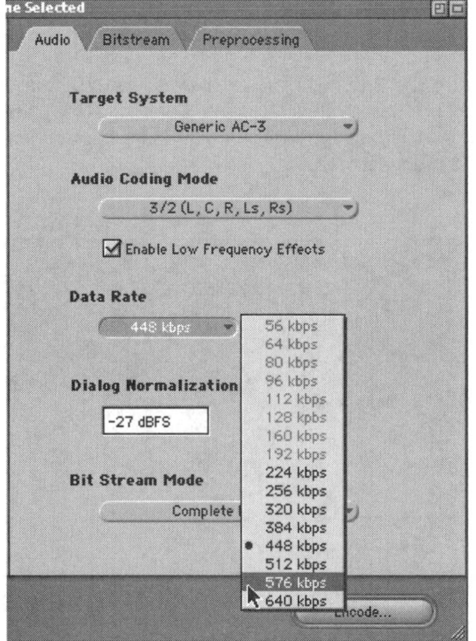

Figure 6.36 If you choose another setting from the Target System menu, your AC-3 files may not be compatible with DVD-Video specifications. For example, choosing Generic AC-3 lets you encode your files at bit rates higher than 448 kbps. These settings are too high for DVD-Video.

About Other AC-3 Settings

There are still a few AC-3 encoding settings that we haven't covered. All of the remaining settings can be left at their default values, and your AC-3 file will turn out just fine. If you're curious about what they do, read on.

Target System

The Target System drop-down menu on the Instant Encoder's Audio tab has three settings: DVD Video, DVD Audio, and Generic AC-3 (**Figure 6.35**). You're authoring DVD-Video, so select DVD Video. The other options make extra settings available, but these settings may make your AC-3 stream incompatible with the DVD-Video specification (**Figure 6.36**). A.Pack's DVD Audio setting, for example, is used to gain more Data Rate settings, which come in handy if you're making a DVD-Audio disc. However, since DVD Studio Pro does not make DVD-Audio discs, do not choose this setting.

Bit Stream Mode

The Bit Stream Mode menu assigns each AC-3 stream information that a select number of DVD-Video players can use to mix multiple AC-3 files together while the DVD-Video plays. For example, you could provide one AC-3 file of just audio and effects, with up to seven other AC-3 files of dialog in different languages. At run time, the DVD-Video player would check the bit-stream mode of each AC-3 file and then mix the correct language into the music and effects file, playing them both simultaneously.

Because very few DVD-Video players understand bit-stream modes, you will probably never have to deal with this setting and can leave it at its default of Complete Main (**Figure 6.37**).

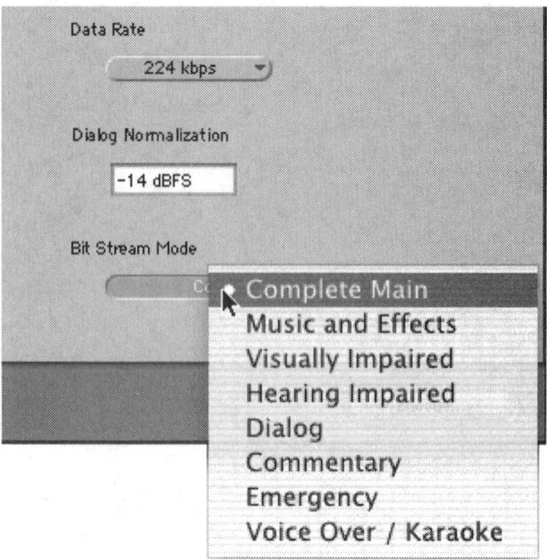

Figure 6.37 Bit-stream modes allow some DVD-Video players to mix multiple AC-3 files together as the DVD-Video plays back. You will normally leave this option set to Complete Main.

✔ Tip

- If you want to learn more about bit-stream modes, go straight to the source. Visit Dolby's Web site, download the Dolby Digital Professional Encoding Guidelines, and then click to page 107: `www.dolby.com/tvaudio`.

Copyright Exists and Content Is Original

If you (or your client) produced the audio and own the copyright to your material, leave the Copyright Exists and Content Is Original check boxes on the Bitstream tab selected (**Figure 6.38**). If you're using someone else's audio (with permission, of course), deselect these check boxes.

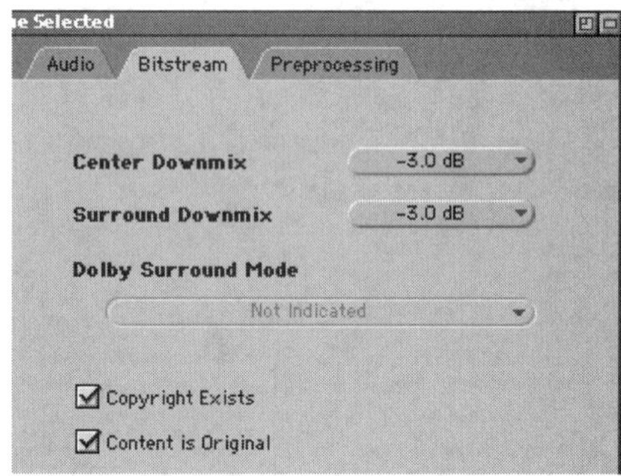

Figure 6.38 If you're using audio created by someone else (other than you or your client), deselect the Copyright Exists and Content Is Original check boxes.

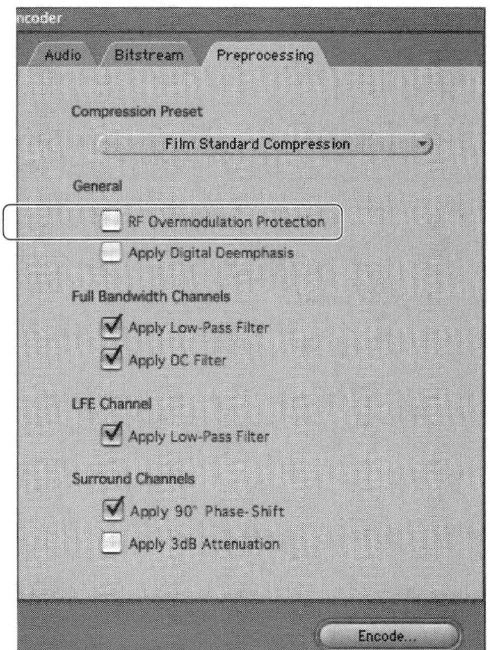

Figure 6.39 Leave RF Overmodulation Protection deselected, or you may experience gain pumping in your AC-3 streams.

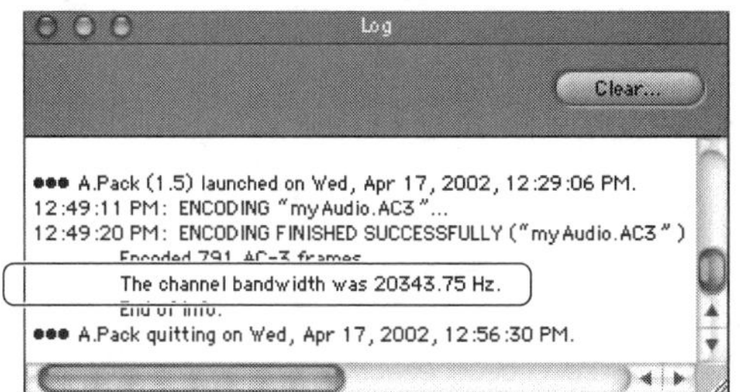

Figure 6.40 A.Pack automatically determines the audio stream's frequency range and applies its Full Bandwidth low-pass filter accordingly.

RF Overmodulation Protection

Some DVD-Video players downmix multichannel AC-3 files into a signal that's transmitted to the radio frequency (RF), or antenna, input of a television set. Signals sent to the television's RF input are boosted in volume by 11 dB. This can cause the RF signal to become *overmodulated,* or distorted.

On the Instant Encoder's Preprocessing tab, leave RF Overmodulation Protection deselected (**Figure 6.39**). The reason? Sometimes selecting the RF Overmodulation Protection check box causes gain pumping. This certainly should not be the case, but it does happen. However, one thing is certain: very few DVD players transmit signals to the television through the antenna input, so deselecting this option is not going to cause any problems and may even solve a few.

Apply Low-Pass Filter

Leave the Preprocessing tab's Apply Low-Pass Filter check box selected.

A low-pass filter removes all frequencies above a certain *cutoff* frequency, allowing all sounds below that cutoff frequency to pass through unhindered. Selecting Apply Low-Pass Filter removes all audio frequencies above the range allowed for AC-3 encoding. A normal 48 kHz digital audio file is already safely within this range, but leaving this check box selected acts as a safeguard (A.Pack automatically determines the correct cutoff frequency, as shown in **Figure 6.40**).

Apply DC Filter

Leave the Preprocessing tab's Apply DC Filter check box selected.

Poorly calibrated analog-to-digital converters can introduce DC offset into your recordings (**Figure 6.41**). DC offset can't be heard, but it takes up space in the audio file and consequently consumes encoding bits (particularly in quiet sections of your audio program). For files of the highest fidelity, you don't want to waste bits on something the viewer won't hear, so leave the Apply DC Filter check box selected.

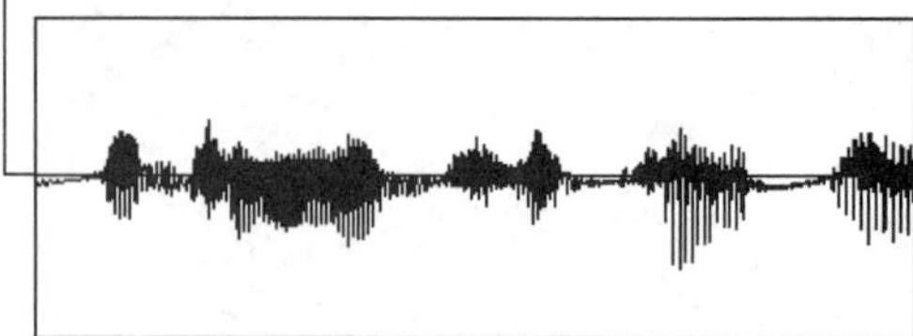

Figure 6.41 This file exhibits DC offset. Notice how it's off-center and doesn't fluctuate around the waveform's zero axis.

Apply 90° Phase-Shift

The Preprocessing tab's Apply 90° Phase-Shift option produces multichannel bit streams that certain decoders can translate into two-channel Dolby Surround audio streams. Selecting this check box doesn't hurt anything, so leave it checked. This option is available only to files that contain surround channels.

Apply 3dB Attenuation

When big studios create a blockbuster soundtrack for playback in a movie theater, surround channels are mixed at 3 dB relative to the front channels. If your AC-3 file didn't originate as the soundtrack from a Hollywood blockbuster, you should *not* select the Preprocessing tab's Apply 3dB Attenuation check box. This option is available only to files that contain surround channels.

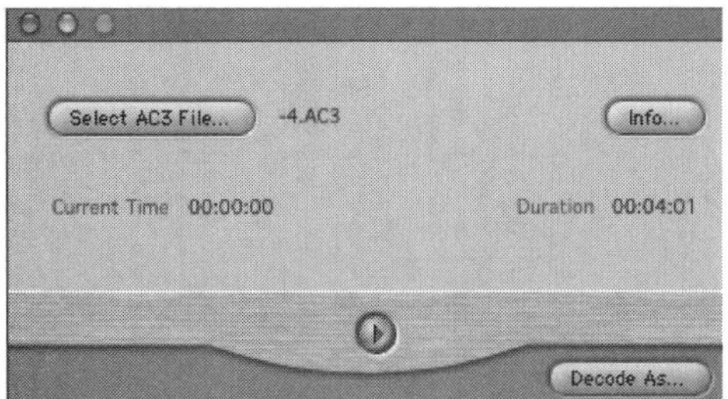

Figure 6.42 The AC-3 Monitor plays AC-3 files. Use it to audition your encoded files to verify dialog normalization and dynamic range compression settings.

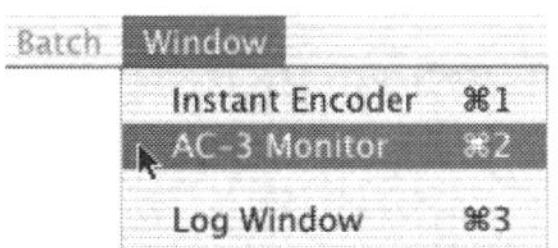

Figure 6.43 To open the AC-3 Monitor, choose Window > AC-3 Monitor.

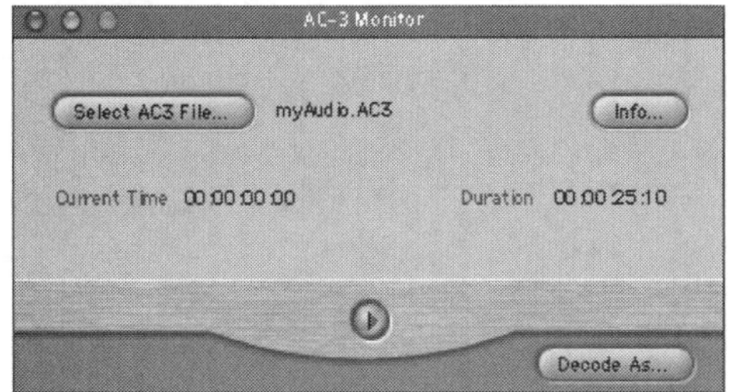

Figure 6.44 After loading an AC-3 file into the AC-3 Monitor, click the Play button to hear what it sounds like.

Auditioning AC-3 Files

In audio terms, when you're *auditioning* an audio file, you're listening to it with a critical ear. You might audition an audio file if, for example, you want to check the results of a dialog normalization setting or perhaps to verify that the file's compression profile sounds okay. To audition encoded AC-3 audio streams in A.Pack, you use the program's built-in AC-3 Monitor (**Figure 6.42**).

✔ Tip

- Currently, the AC-3 monitor downmixes multichannel audio files to stereo before playback. Will future versions allow you to monitor 5.1 files? Well, with the new digital outputs on the G5, things certainly seem to be heading in that direction. However, if you have a multichannel audio interface such as Emagic's EMI 2|6, you can monitor surround files today. See "Using a Third-Party Audio Interface" later in this chapter.

To audition an AC-3 file:

1. From within A.Pack, choose Window > AC-3 Monitor (**Figure 6.43**), or press Command-2.

   The AC-3 Monitor opens.
2. Click the Select AC-3 File button to open the Select AC-3 File dialog.
3. Select the file that you want to audition.
4. Click the AC-3 Monitor's Play button (**Figure 6.44**).

   The AC-3 Monitor plays the AC-3 file.

continues on next page

✔ Tips

- The secret to good sound is systematically auditioning all of your AC-3 streams. Open every newly encoded file in the AC-3 Monitor and compare it to your DVD-Video's other AC-3 files. For safety's sake, play a DVD-Video from a major studio and compare its volume level to that of your AC-3 files. If everything has about the same volume, you know you've encoded your files correctly.
- To peek at an AC-3 file's encoding settings, open the file in the AC-3 Monitor and click the Info button. The AC-3 Stream Information window opens, displaying the file's duration, data rate, dialog normalization number, and several other settings (**Figure 6.45**).

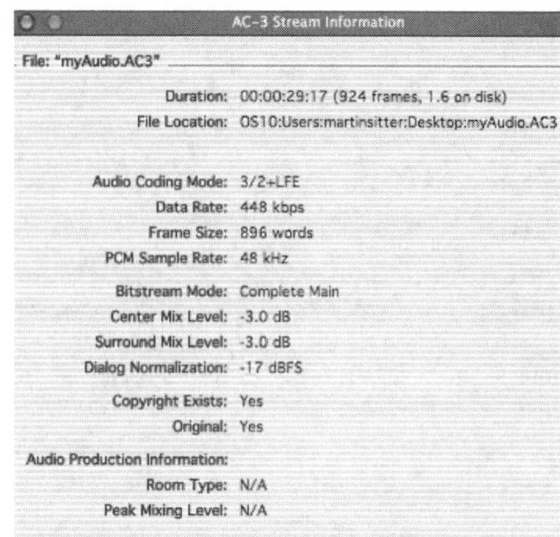

Figure 6.45 Clicking the AC-3 Monitor's Info button launches this AC-3 Stream Information window and reveals the file's encoding settings.

Decoding an AC-3 File

The AC-3 Monitor has a Decode As button (**Figure 6.46**). If you load an AC-3 file into the AC-3 Monitor and click the Decode As button, the AC-3 file is transformed into PCM files that you can open and manipulate in an audio-editing program such as Logic Pro.

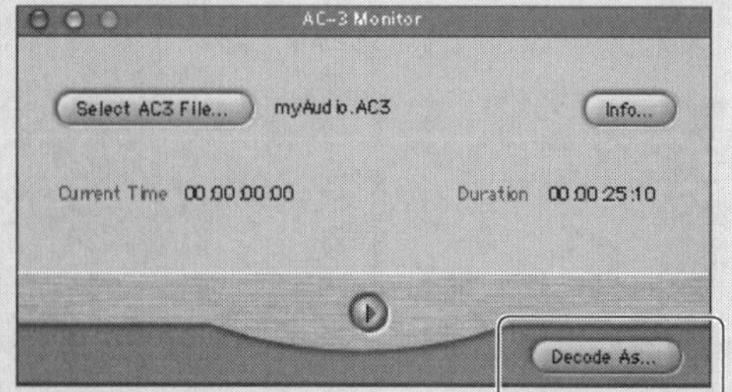

Figure 6.46 To decode an AC-3 file into linear PCM files that you can edit in Logic Pro (or any other digital audio editor), open the AC-3 file in A.Pack's AC-3 Monitor and click the Decode As button.

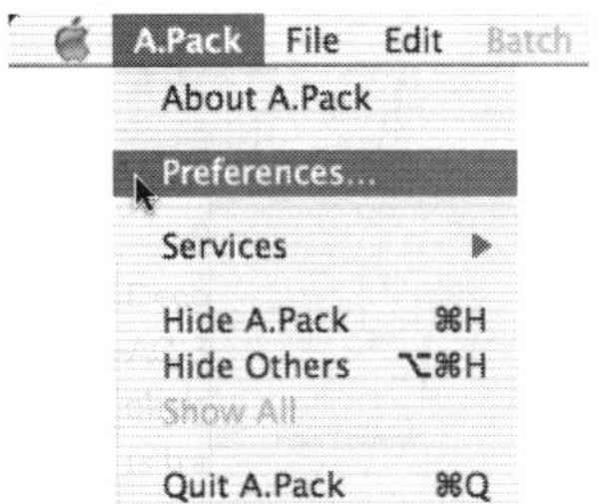

Figure 6.47 Choose A.Pack > Preferences to open A.Pack's Preferences window.

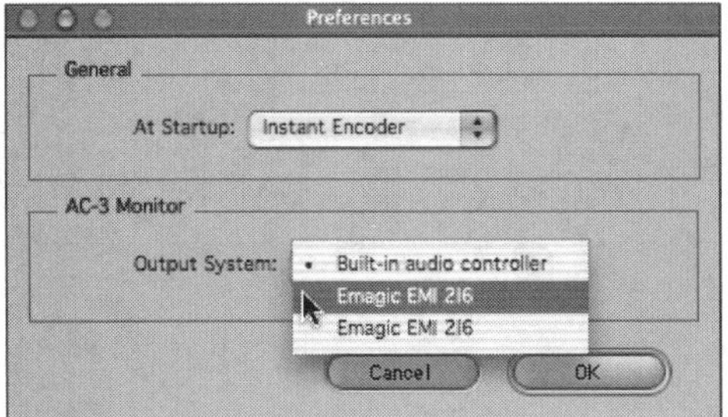

Figure 6.48 The AC-3 Monitor area has a menu for specifying the audio interface used when you listen to sound from the AC-3 Monitor.

Using a Third-Party Audio Interface

If you're using a third-party audio interface (sound card), such as an Emagic EMI 2|6, you need to select that audio interface from A.Pack's preferences or you will not hear audio auditioned with the AC-3 Monitor.

A.Pack is designed to create surround audio streams, and if you're using a supported audio interface, you can use the AC-3 Monitor to audition your 5.1 encodes in surround sound. However, you must have an audio interface with multiple outputs, such as the EMI 2|6, and you also must configure A.Pack to see your audio interface. To do so, follow these steps.

To select a third-party audio interface:

1. Choose A.Pack > Preferences (**Figure 6.47**).

   A.Pack's Preferences window opens.

2. In the AC-3 Monitor area, choose your audio interface (**Figure 6.48**).

   All sound is now sent to the selected audio interface.

About Batch Lists

Batch lists are used to set up multiple encode jobs that you can *batch render* (automatically encode in sequential order). If you've ever batch rendered video files using a program such as Final Cut Pro or Compressor, the A.Pack batch list should feel familiar. If you're new to batch rendering, prepare to meet a great labor-saving tool.

To create a new batch list:

- Choose File > New Batch List (**Figure 6.49**), or press Command-N.

  A new batch list opens (**Figure 6.50**).

To create a new encode job:

- At the bottom of the batch list, click the New button (**Figure 6.51**), or press Command-K.

  A new encode job appears at the bottom of the batch list (**Figure 6.52**).

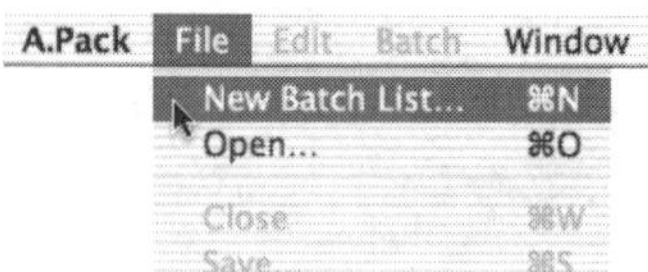

Figure 6.49 To create a new batch list, choose File > New Batch List.

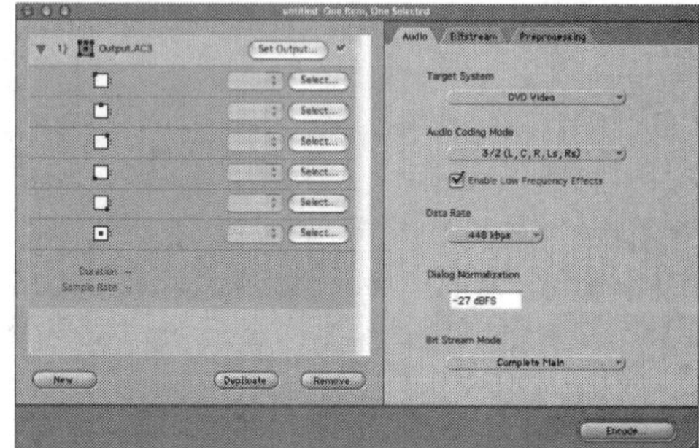

Figure 6.50 A batch list.

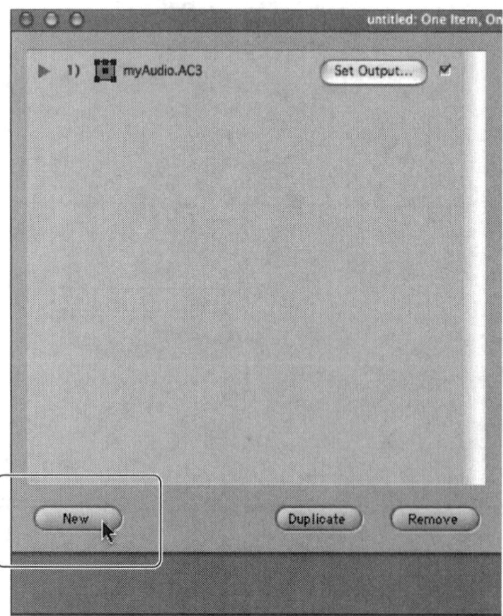

Figure 6.51 To add a new encode job to a batch, click the batch list's New button.

Figure 6.52 New encode jobs are added to the bottom of the batch list.

Figure 6.53 Clicking the batch list's Remove button deletes the currently selected encode job.

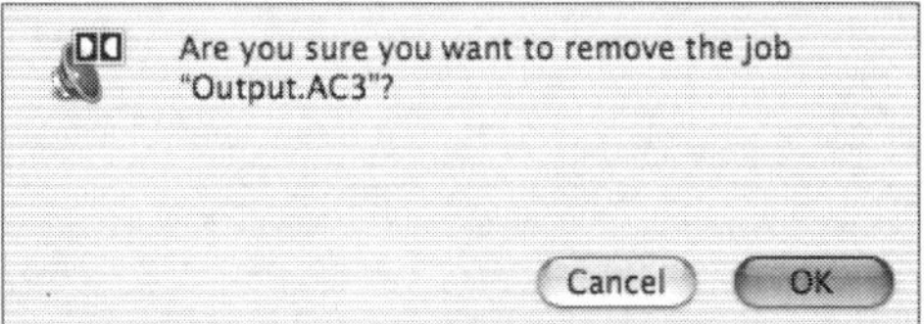

Figure 6.54 A.Pack gives you a second chance to make sure you want to remove the encode job. If you do, click OK.

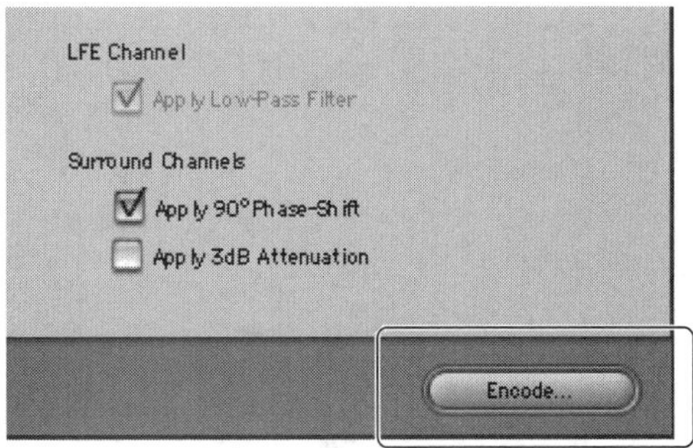

Figure 6.55 When your batch is all set up and ready to go, click the Encode button in A.Pack's lower-right corner. A.Pack encodes all the files in the batch list, starting at the top and working its way down to the bottom.

To delete an encode job:

1. In the batch list, select the encode job that you want to delete.
   The encode job is highlighted.
2. At the bottom of the batch list, click the Remove button (**Figure 6.53**), or press the Delete key.
   A dialog appears asking if you are sure that you want to remove the encoding job (**Figure 6.54**).
3. Click OK.
   The encode job is removed from the batch list.

To encode a batch list:

◆ Click the Encode button in the lower-right corner of the batch list (**Figure 6.55**).
  A.Pack encodes the batch, working progressively through files from the top of the batch list to the bottom.

Testing AC-3 Encoding Settings

Batch lists are particularly useful if you're not sure which dialog normalization, compression profile, and/or downmix settings to use with an AC-3 file. Instead of encoding your files one at a time, you can use a batch list to set up several encode jobs, each with different settings. After A.Pack finishes encoding the batch, open the finished AC-3 files in the AC-3 Monitor and check to see which one sounds best.

Part II: DVD Studio Pro

Chapter 7 Touring the Workspace 141

Chapter 8 Viewing Your Project 167

Chapter 9 Exploring the Assets Tab 179

Chapter 10 Importing Assets 193

Chapter 11 Using Tracks 209

Chapter 12 Enhancing Tracks...........................251

Chapter 13 The Menu Editor............................295

Chapter 14 Layered Menus..............................331

Chapter 15 Overlay Menus 345

Chapter 16 Using Transitions 387

Chapter 17 Templates, Styles, and Shapes 399

Chapter 18 Slideshows 445

Chapter 19 Finishing the DVD 461

Chapter 20 Outputting the Project...................495

Part II: DVD Studio Pro

7. Touring the Workspace
Launching DVD Studio Pro
Exploring the DVD Studio Pro Workspace
Using Window Configurations
Using the Toolbar
Using the Inspector
Using the Palette

8. Viewing Your Project
About the Outline and Graphical Views
Exploring the Outline View
Exploring the Graphical View
Zooming the Graphical View
Flagging an Item
Using the Macro View
Laying Out Tiles
Setting a First Play Item

9. Exploring the Assets Tab
About the Assets Tab
About Assets
Managing Assets
Working with Columns
Relinking Assets
Previewing Assets

10. Importing Assets
Importing Assets
Importing QuickTime Movies

11. Using Tracks
About the Track Editor
Creating Tracks
Changing Track Order in the Outline View
Setting Jump Actions
Adding Clips to Streams
Using Timecode in the Track Editor
Positioning the Playhead
Zooming in the Timeline
Working with Streams in the Track Editor
Editing Video and Audio Clips
Viewing Tracks

12. Enhancing Tracks
About Markers
Using Markers and I-frames
Using Marker Snapping
Fixing Invalid Markers
Viewing Markers
Naming Markers
Moving Markers
Specifying the Marker Type
Setting a Marker's End Jump
Using Marker Playback Settings
Adding Markers with Final Cut Pro
Importing Markers into DVD Studio Pro
About Stories
About Alternate Angles
Multi-Angle versus Mixed-Angle Tracks

13. The Menu Editor
Creating Menus
Exploring the Menu Editor
Adding Backgrounds
Adding Menu Buttons
Setting Button Targets
Setting a Menu Timeout Action
About Menus and the Remote Control
Using Rulers and Guides
Using Dynamic Guides
Using Alignment Modes
Using Distribution Modes

14. Layered Menus

Designing Layered Menus
Working with Layers in Photoshop
Using Layered Menus in DVD Studio Pro
Previewing Button States

15. Overlay Menus

Creating Overlay Menus
Creating a Simple Overlay Menu
Creating an Advanced Overlay Menu
Choosing Highlight Sets
Adding Audio to Menus
Using the At End Setting
Using Button Highlight Markers
Working with Text
Styling Text
Creating Drop Shadows

16. Using Transitions

Using Transitions
Adding Track Transitions
Adding Slideshow Transitions
Adding Menu Transitions
Using a Video Clip as a Transition

17. Templates, Styles, and Shapes

About Templates
Using Templates
Creating Custom Templates
Importing iDVD Themes
About Styles
Using Styles
Creating Custom Styles
Linking Styles to Templates
About Shapes
Using Shapes
Creating Custom Shapes
Importing Custom Shapes
Updating Custom Shapes

18. Slideshows

About Slideshows
Setting Slideshow Preferences
Using the Slideshow Editor
Adding Audio Streams
Converting Slideshows to Tracks
Setting Slideshow End Jumps
Previewing Slideshows

19. Finishing the DVD

Setting the First Play Action
Assigning Remote-Control Buttons
Using the Connections Tab
Creating Hybrid DVDs
Protecting Your Content
Simulating the Project
About Item Description Files
Embedding Text
Using Jacket Pictures

20. Outputting the Project

Exporting the Project
Building the Project
Using Apple's DVD Player
Building and Formatting
Making Multiple Copies
Using Toast 6 Titanium
Outputting to DLT
Creating DVD-9 Projects
Reading a DLT Tape

7 Touring the Workspace

No serious racer would ever launch down a course without taking a tour of it first—if you don't know the twists and turns ahead, it's more difficult to navigate through them. If you've never used DVD Studio Pro 3 before, make your race to the finish line easier by reading this tour.

In the following pages, you'll be introduced to the windows that work together to help you create DVD-Videos. Collectively, these windows are called *the workspace.* Along the tour, you'll learn how to customize DVD Studio Pro's default workspace to create your own custom window configurations. You'll also see just how easy it is to save this custom workspace for later use. After that, you'll race deeper into DVD Studio Pro's main editing windows, the Graphical view, Menu and Track editors, Palette, and Inspector. Racers ready ... On your marks ... GO!

Launching DVD Studio Pro

If you haven't used DVD Studio Pro before, you must be excited! Excited and perhaps a little intimidated, because DVD authoring is a deep subject—especially if you come from an audio or video background where interactivity is not the central aim. Don't worry. DVD-Video is really nothing more complex than buttons over video. It's how you place the buttons over the video that's the key.

As you'll come to see through reading this book, DVD Studio Pro 3 is incredibly easy to use. It just takes a little time to learn how the pieces snap together. With that in mind, you're ready to open DVD Studio Pro.

To launch DVD Studio Pro:

1. In the Finder, locate the DVD Studio Pro application icon (**Figure 7.1**).
2. Double-click the application icon.

   DVD Studio Pro begins opening but is stopped by the Choose Application Configuration dialog (**Figure 7.2**).

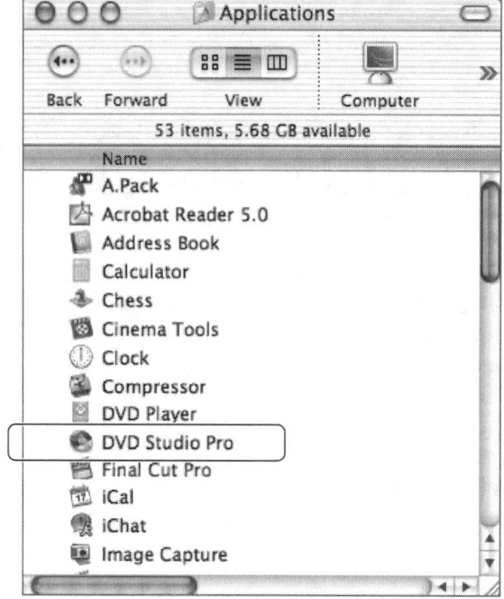

Figure 7.1 By default, the DVD Studio Pro application is placed at the root level of your startup disk in Disk/Applications/DVD Studio Pro.

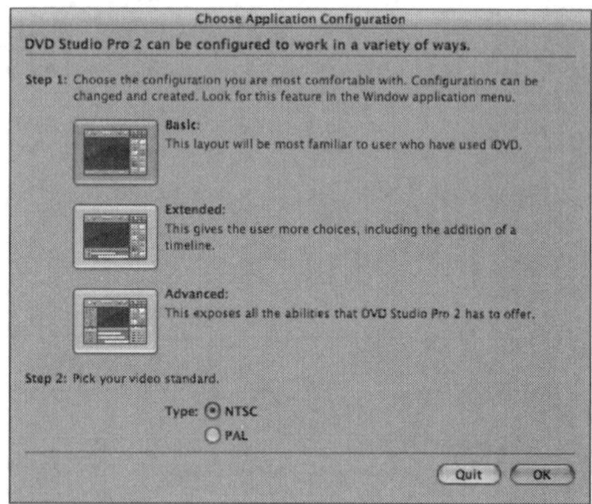

Figure 7.2 The first time you open DVD Studio Pro, the Choose Application Configuration dialog appears.

Using the Choose Application Configuration dialog

The Choose Application Configuration dialog is used to set DVD Studio Pro's video standard and window configuration.

The *video standard* determines several important characteristics—such as frame rate and frame dimensions (resolution)—of the video you're working with. For information about video standards, see Chapter 4, "The QuickTime MPEG-2 Exporter."

The *window configuration* that you choose determines your workspace window layout. There are three default window configurations: Basic, Extended, and Advanced (for more information, see the sidebar "Window Configuration Overview").

If this is the first time you've opened the application, you may not know which window configuration is the correct one for you. Don't worry—you can easily change the default window configuration once DVD Studio Pro opens. All the window configurations are discussed in the section "Using Window Configurations" later in this chapter.

However, because this is a Visual QuickPro Guide, the purpose of this book is to show you *all* of DVD Studio Pro's features, not just basic or extended features. Consequently, the figures in this book use the Advanced window configuration. To keep your screen looking the same as the figures in this book, just follow the steps presented here to choose the Advanced configuration.

Window Configuration Overview

DVD Studio Pro provides three default window configurations: Basic, Extended, and Advanced.

- **Basic.** With a layout and functionality mimicking iDVD's, the Basic configuration offers only a limited subset of authoring options. This configuration is good for new DVD Studio Pro users making the transition from iDVD.
- **Extended.** The Extended window configuration provides access to all of DVD Studio Pro's main editors as tabbed windows in DVD Studio Pro's workspace. DVD Studio Pro's timeline-based Track editor is the central focus of the extended configuration. In this configuration, the Track editor stretches across the entire width at the bottom of the workspace—it is an extended Track editor, providing lots of space for you to arrange video clips along its timeline.
- **Advanced.** Containing all the same tabbed editors as the Extended window configuration, the Advanced configuration places the Assets tab in the lower-left corner of the screen. This configuration makes it easy to drag assets into any of the other editing windows and is a good configuration to choose for everyday authoring.

To configure DVD Studio Pro:

1. In the Choose Application Configuration dialog, choose the Advanced window configuration (**Figure 7.3**).
2. At the bottom of the Choose Application Configuration dialog, choose a video standard (**Figure 7.4**).

   If you're in North America, choose NTSC. In Europe, choose PAL. All other users should refer to the discussion of video standards in Chapter 3, "Preparing Graphics."
3. In the lower-right corner of the Choose Application Configuration dialog, click the OK button to open DVD Studio Pro.

✔ Tip

- If you've set the default window configuration but DVD Studio Pro's windows stretch past the right edge of your screen, choose Windows > Configurations > Advanced. DVD. Studio Pro will check your monitor's resolution and then reorganize the windows so they are displayed correctly.

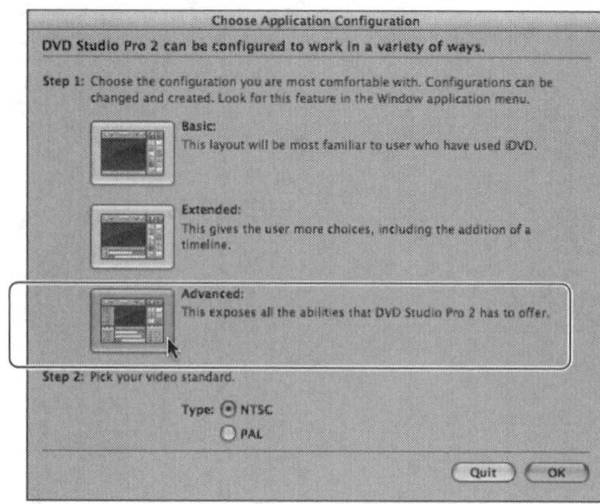

Figure 7.3 To ensure that your screen looks like the figures in this book, choose the Advanced window configuration.

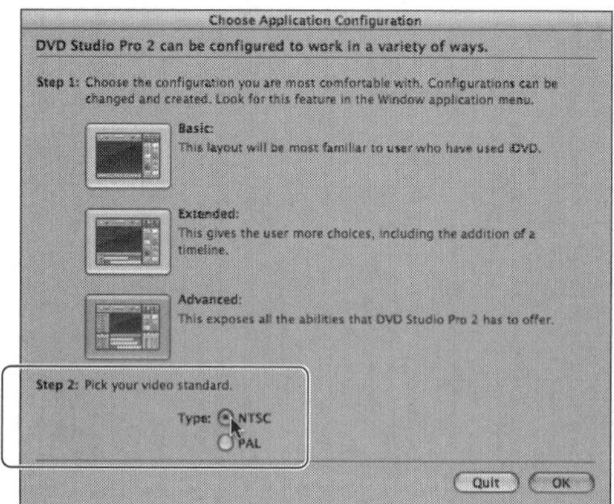

Figure 7.4 In North America, choose NTSC as the video standard; in Europe, choose PAL.

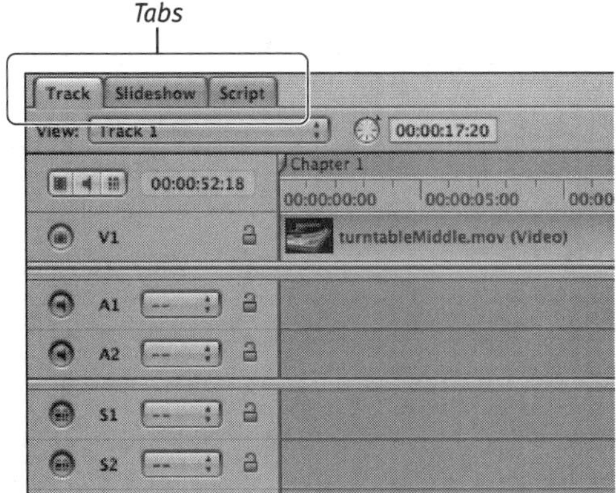

Figure 7.5 Each DVD Studio Pro editor appears as a tab in the workspace.

Exploring the DVD Studio Pro Workspace

The DVD Studio Pro *workspace* is composed of the windows and tabs you see on your screen—it's the space you work in as you create DVD-Videos. The workspace itself is divided into *tabbed editors* that are grouped in *quadrants*. Along the right edge of the screen are two particularly important windows: the Inspector, and the Palette.

- **Tabbed editors** (**Figure 7.5**). Each tab in the workspace is a discrete editor used for a certain aspect of DVD authoring. For example, the Track tab contains DVD Studio Pro's timeline-based Track editor, which is used to organize video and audio assets into tracks for your finished DVD-Video. The Assets tab is your project's library, and all of the individual pieces of media (assets) used in your project are stored here.

continues on next page

- **Quadrants** (**Figure 7.6**). Quadrant's are customizable areas of the workspace that are used to group certain tabs together. The DVD Studio Pro workspace can contain between one and four quadrants, depending on your authoring needs and the window layout that makes the most sense to you. You can also tear tabs out of one quadrant and drop them into another, and this flexibility in window layout makes DVD Studio Pro's workspace completely user customizable.

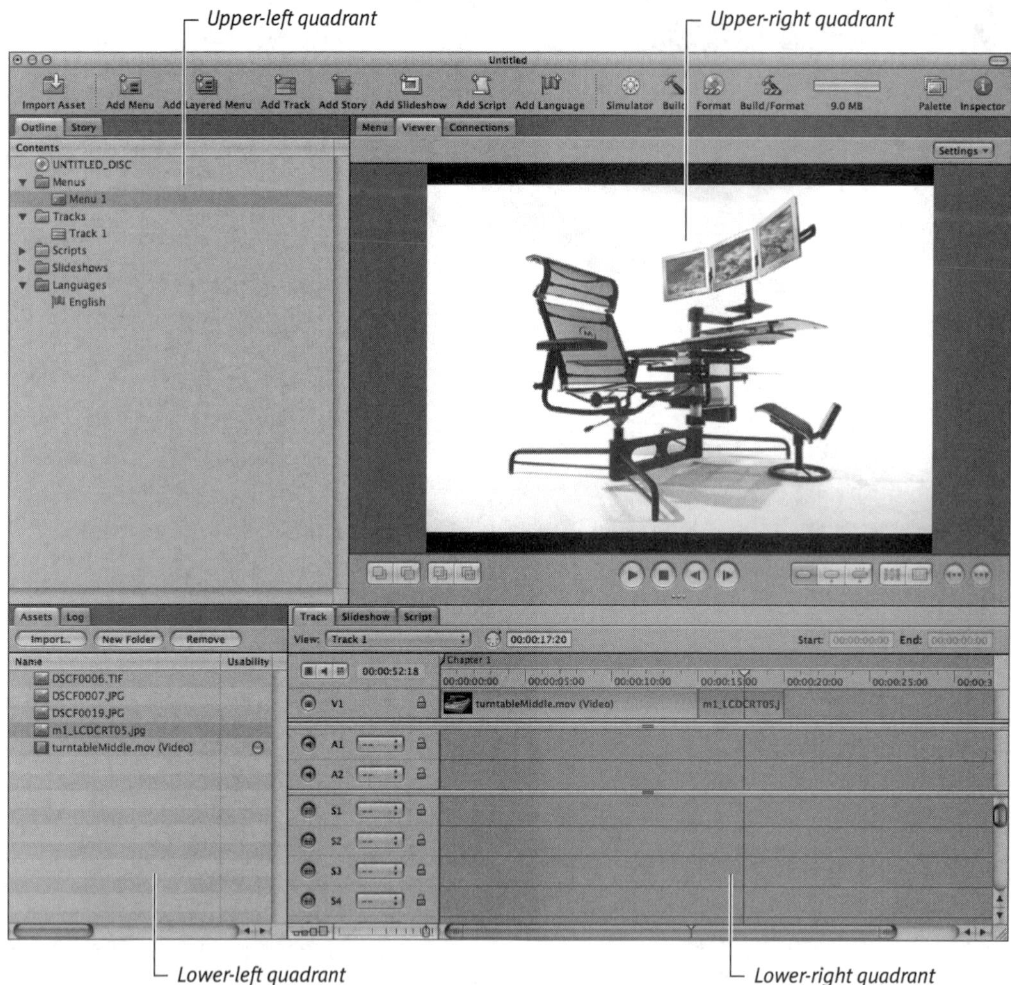

Figure 7.6 For easy access, similar tabs are arranged into quadrants.

- **The Inspector** (**Figure 7.7**). The Inspector is a context-sensitive window that updates to show the unique properties of any item selected in the workspace. For example, if you select an asset on the Assets tab, the Inspector changes to show you the asset's properties, such as file type, length, and dimensions. (The Inspector is explored in detail later in this chapter, in the section "Using the Inspector.")

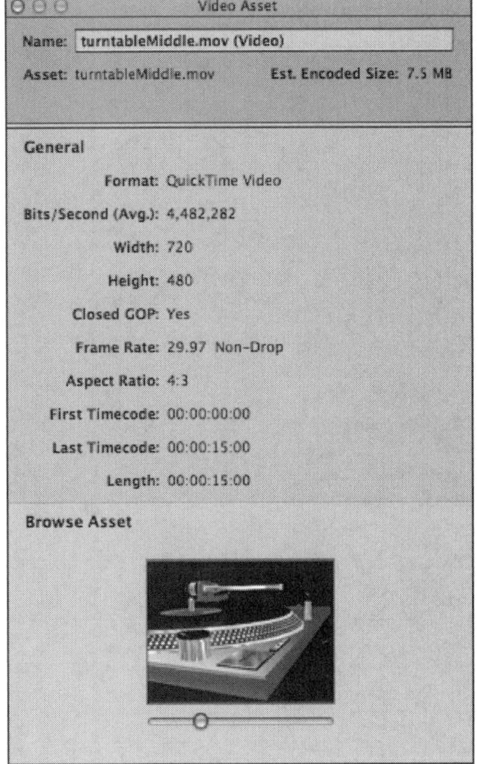

Figure 7.7 The Inspector shows you the properties of any item selected in DVD Studio Pro's workspace.

- **The Palette** (**Figure 7.8**). The Palette provides a shortcut to media files on your hard disks. To gain quick access to media files you use frequently, you can add folders from your hard disks to the Palette, and any media in those folders will always be available for your projects. The Palette is a handy tool, because it saves you from having to open a Finder window to locate files or to use DVD Studio Pro's Import function to get files into your projects—just drag them into the workspace, directly from the Palette. Note that media files from your User Movies folder, iTunes library, and iPhoto library are always available in the Palette. (For more about the Palette, see "Using the Palette" later in this chapter.)

Figure 7.8 The Palette provides direct access to media files—including your iPhoto and iTunes libraries and your User Movies folder—on your hard disks.

Using Window Configurations

DVD Studio Pro gives you access to three default window configurations, which allows you to tailor the workspace to your authoring situation and experience level. The Advanced window configuration (**Figure 7.9**) provides four windows, referred to here as quadrants, that display every tabbed editor available to DVD Studio Pro's workspace. The Extended window configuration (**Figure 7.10**) contains all the same tabbed editors as the Advanced configuration, but it displays only one lower quadrant, and the Timeline-based Track editor is stretched across this quadrant to fill the bottom half of the workspace. The Basic window configuration (**Figure 7.11**) limits authoring to a subset of the editors available in the Advanced and Extended configurations and is meant to smooth the transition for users switching to DVD Studio Pro from iDVD.

✔ Tips

- While most of the figures in this book use the Advanced window configuration, by no means are you restricted to this configuration. If the Basic or Extended window configuration offers what you need for day-to-day DVD authoring, feel free to use that configuration instead.
- The main advantage of the Advanced window configuration is that the Assets tab is located in the lower-left quadrant. This is a pivotal position, because from there you can drag assets straight into the Outline or Graphical view, Menu editor or Viewer, or Track or Slideshow editor to quickly create project elements.

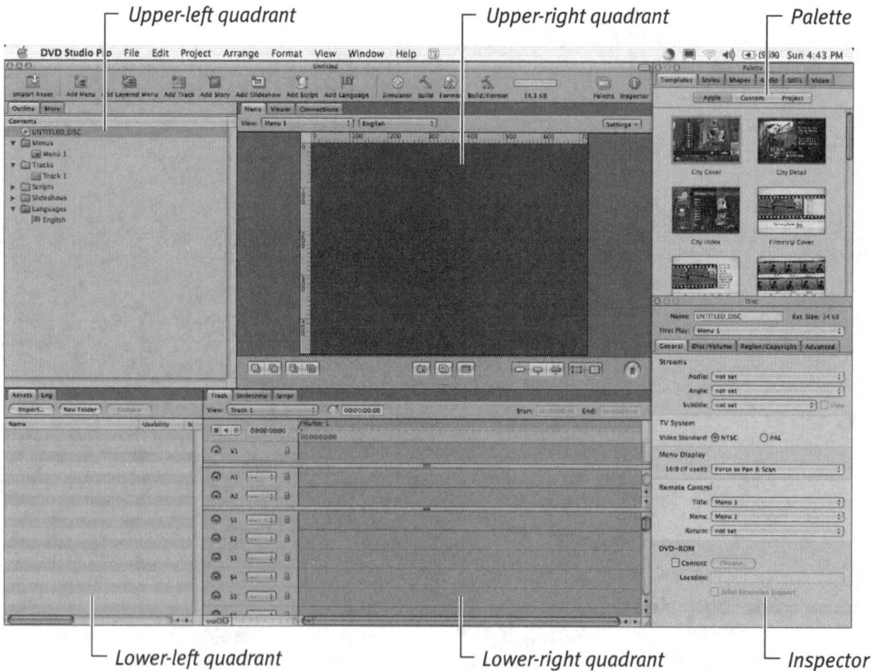

Figure 7.9 The Advanced DVD Studio Pro window configuration is divided into quadrants, with the Palette and the Inspector occupying the right edge of the screen. Every editor available to DVD Studio Pro is displayed or available as a tab in the workspace.

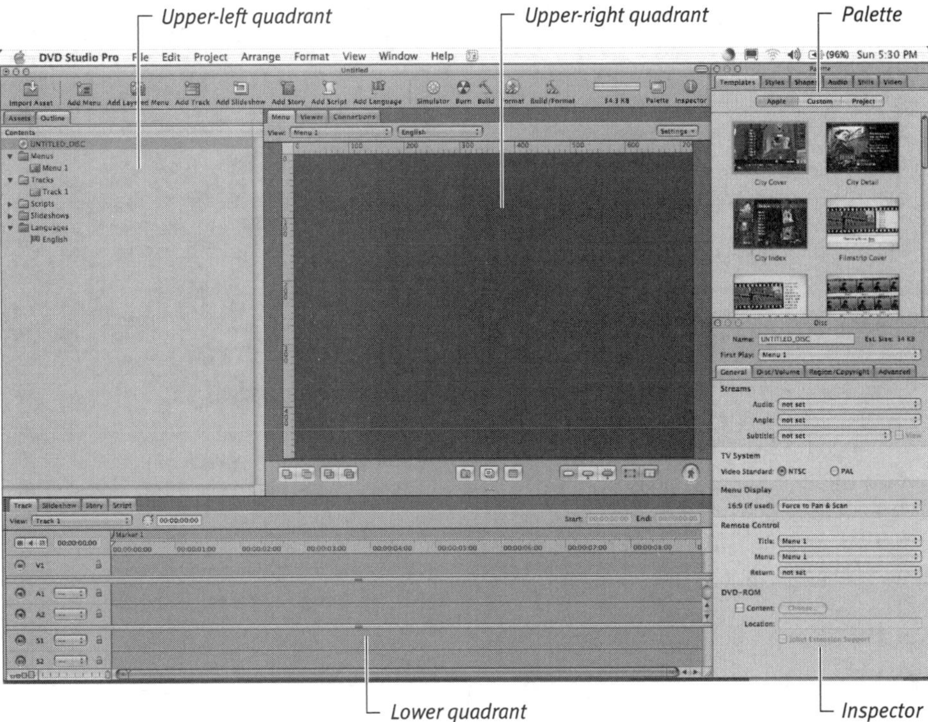

Figure 7.10 The Extended window configuration has a long, or extended, quadrant that fills the bottom of the workspace, providing extra horizontal space for editing long tracks and scripts. This layout does not have a Log tab.

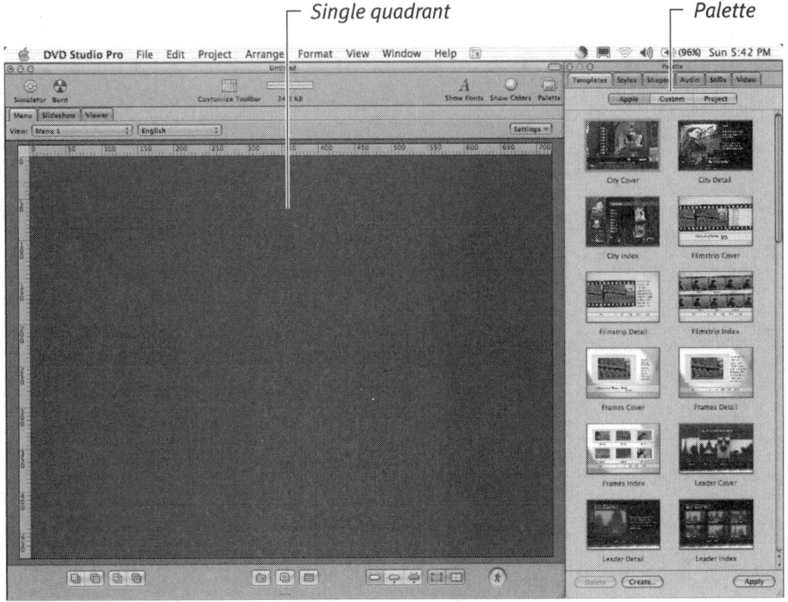

Figure 7.11 The Basic configuration has only a single quadrant and the Palette. Similar to iDVD, this layout provides a good starting point for users switching from iDVD to DVD Studio Pro.

To choose a window configuration:

1. With DVD Studio Pro open, choose Window > Configurations.

   A hierarchical menu appears (**Figure 7.12**) with several choices: Basic, Extended, Advanced, and Advanced (Cinema).

2. From the menu, choose a window configuration.

   Your window configuration updates to reflect the selected setting.

   Notice the key command beside each configuration in the Window > Configurations menu (F1, F2, F3, and F4). Press F1 to open the Basic, F2 to open the Extended, F3 to open the Advanced, or F4 to open the Advanced (Cinema) window configuration.

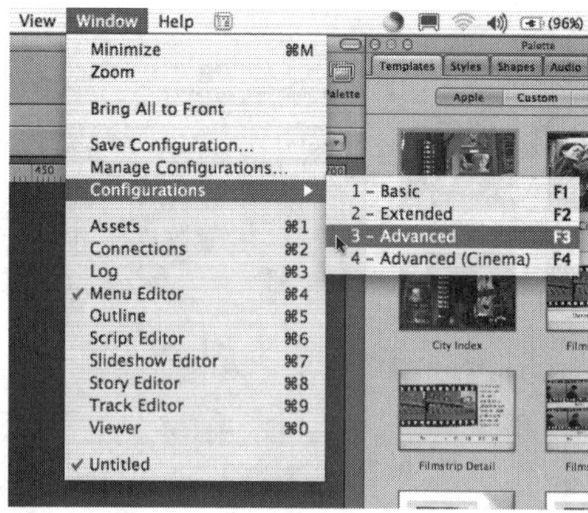

Figure 7.12 The Window menu's Configurations option controls the layout of editing windows in the workspace.

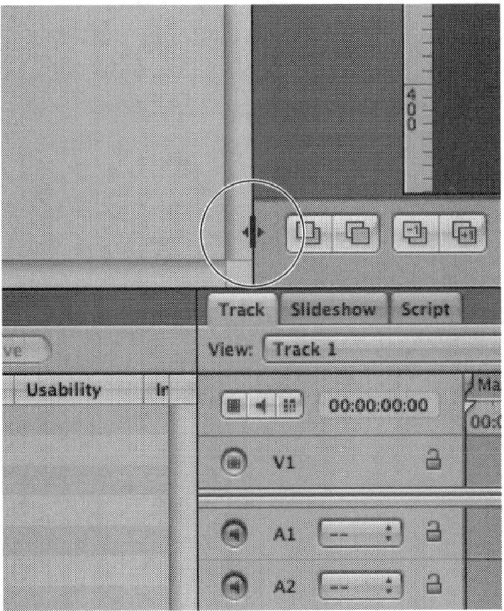

Figure 7.13 Moving the pointer over the line that separates two quadrants turns the pointer into the Resize tool, which you use to change the size of the workspace's quadrants.

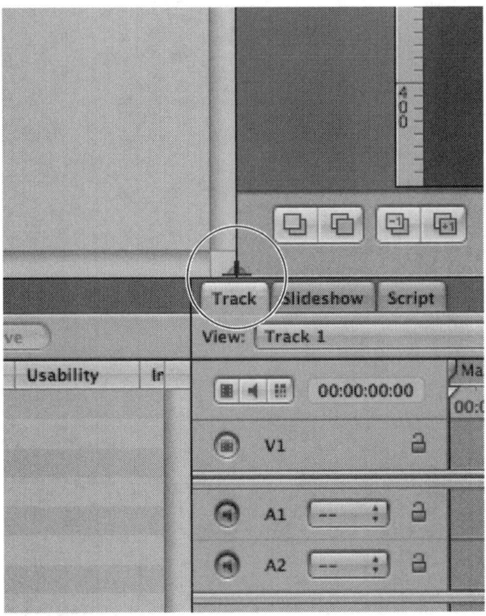

Figure 7.14 With the pointer over the intersection of two divider lines, you can resize quadrants vertically and horizontally at the same time.

Customizing the workspace

DVD Studio Pro's workspace is completely customizable. For example, you can resize quadrants or tear tabs from one quadrant and drop them into another. This high degree of flexibility lets you streamline your workflow by grouping certain tabs into specific quadrants. (Of course, how you group the tabs is up to you and your particular authoring situation.) Once the workspace is organized to your satisfaction, you can (and should!) save your customized window configuration for later use, as demonstrated at the end of this section.

To resize window quadrants:

1. Place the pointer over the line that separates two quadrants.

   The pointer turns into the Resize tool (**Figure 7.13**).

2. Drag to resize the quadrants.

✔ Tips

- Move the pointer over the intersection of two divider lines to resize quadrants both horizontally and vertically at the same time (**Figure 7.14**).
- To resize quadrants in only a horizontal or vertical direction, hold down Option as you drag the edge or intersection of the quadrants.

To move a tab from one quadrant to another:

1. In the lower-left quadrant, select a tab and drag it out of the quadrant (**Figure 7.15**).
2. Drag the tab to another quadrant and move the pointer until it's directly over the empty area to the right of the other tabs (**Figure 7.16**).

   The tabs are outlined in light blue, indicating that the quadrant is ready to accept the new tab.
3. Drop the tab into the quadrant.

   The tab becomes part of the quadrant (**Figure 7.17**).

✔ Tip

- If you're using multiple monitors, it's sometimes helpful to tear tabs out of the workspace and move them to a second monitor. For example, you might choose to tear the Menu and Viewer tabs out of the workspace and move them to a second monitor, which in turn gives you more space to see these editors as you author your project. Depending on your setup, you can even move them to an NTSC monitor (PowerBook users take note: you have an SVHS output right on the back of your computer).

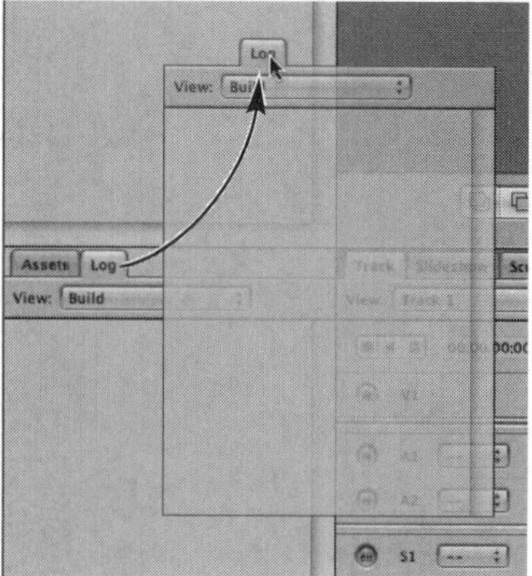

Figure 7.15 You can tear tabs out of quadrants to open them in their own windows or transfer them to different quadrants.

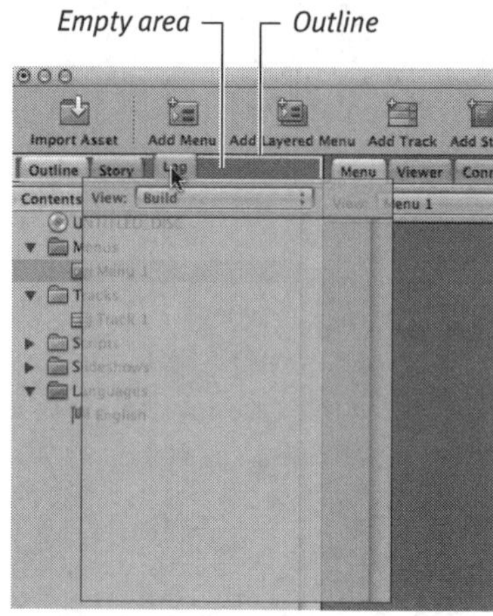

Figure 7.16 To drop a tab into another quadrant, you must drag the tab over the empty area to the right of the quadrant's other tabs.

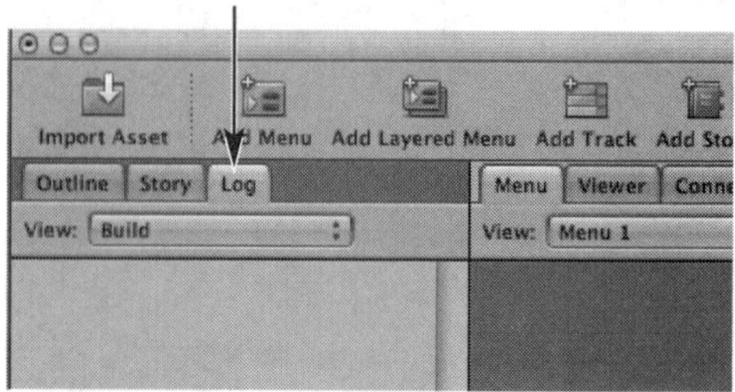

Figure 7.17 The Log tab after it's dropped into a new quadrant.

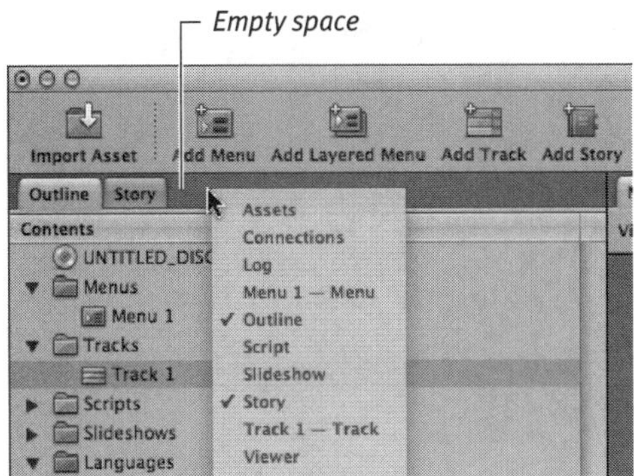

Figure 7.18 To quickly move a tab into a new quadrant (or open it), Control-click the empty space to the right of the quadrant's other tabs.

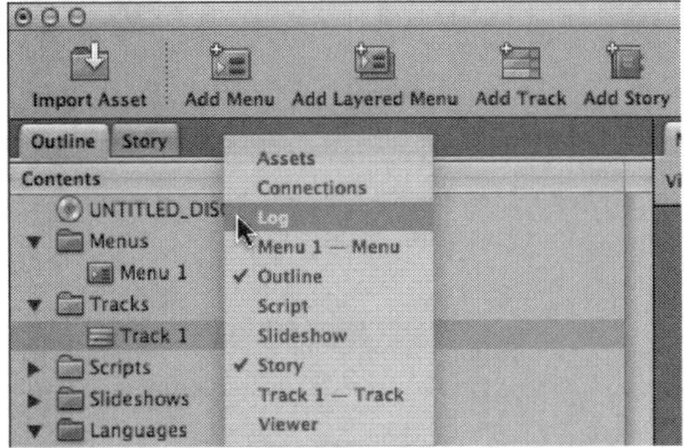

Figure 7.19 Then, from the shortcut menu, choose the tab that you want to open in the quadrant.

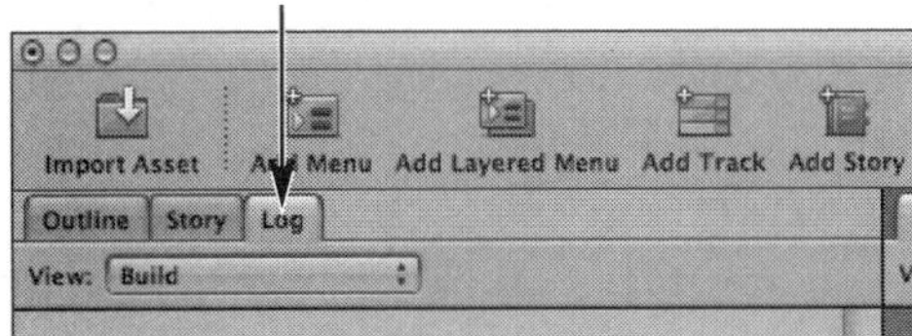

Figure 7.20 The selected tab jumps to the new quadrant.

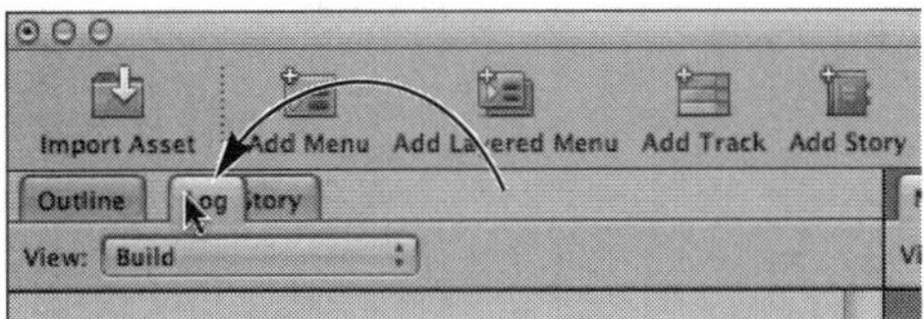

Figure 7.21 To reorder tabs in the same quadrant, select a tab and move it left or right. The other tabs jump out of the way to make room for the moved tab.

To move a tab using a shortcut menu:

1. In the destination quadrant, hold down Control while clicking the empty space to the right of the quadrant's current tabs.

   A shortcut menu appears (**Figure 7.18**).
2. Choose the tab that you want to move to the quadrant (**Figure 7.19**).

   The selected tab jumps into the new quadrant (**Figure 7.20**).

To reorder tabs in the same quadrant:

1. Select the tab that you want to move.
2. Drag the tab left or right (**Figure 7.21**).

   The other tabs in the quadrant jump out of the way to make room for the moved tab.
3. Drop the tab where you want it.

To save a custom window configuration:

1. Create a custom window configuration by resizing quadrants or dragging tabs from one quadrant to another.
2. Choose Window > Save Configuration (**Figure 7.22**).

   A dialog opens at the top of the workspace (**Figure 7.23**).
3. In the dialog, type a name for your custom window configuration and click Save (**Figure 7.24**).

   The custom window configuration is saved and is now available to all your DVD Studio Pro projects directly from the Window > Configurations menu (**Figure 7.25**).

To assign a custom configuration to a function key:

1. Choose Window > Manage Configurations (**Figure 7.26**).

   A dialog drops down from DVD Studio Pro's Title bar (**Figure 7.27**). This dialog has two columns: Configurations and Key. The menus in the Key column are used to assign custom configurations to function keys.
2. In the Key column to the left of your custom window configuration, use the menu to choose a function key.

   Each time you press this function key, the screen will update with your custom window configuration.

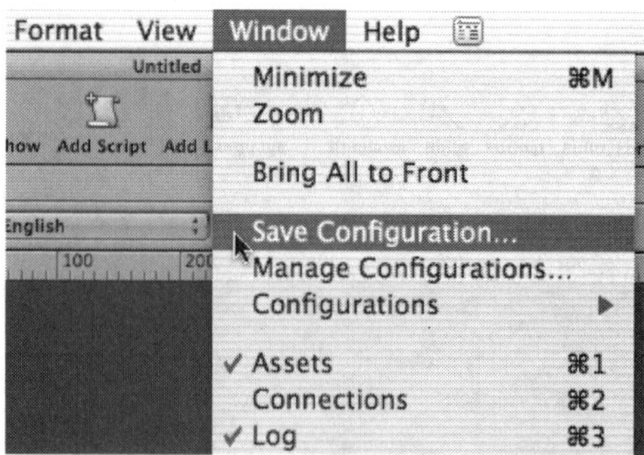

Figure 7.22 The Window menu's Save Configuration option lets you save customized window layouts for later use.

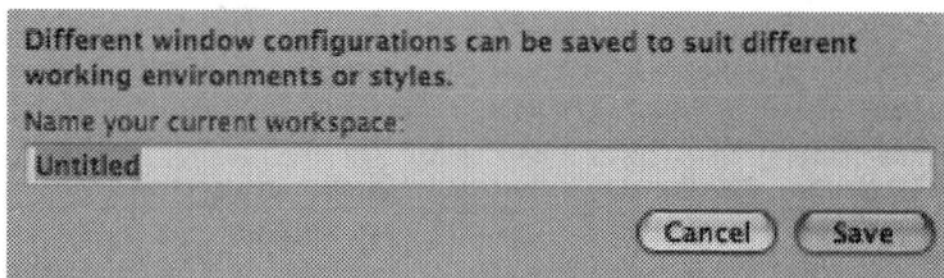

Figure 7.23 This dialog allows you to name your custom window configuration.

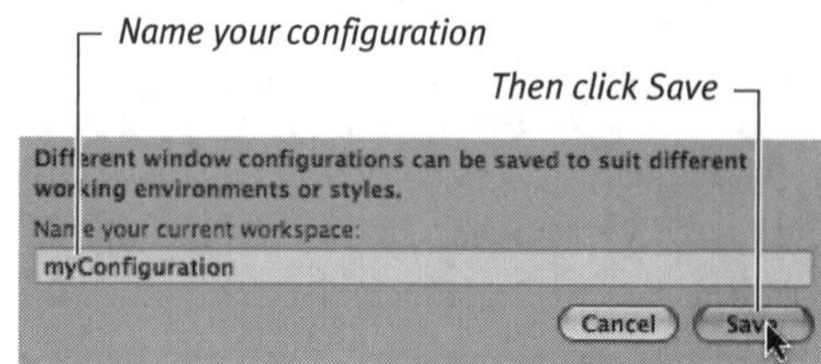

Figure 7.24 Type a name and click Save.

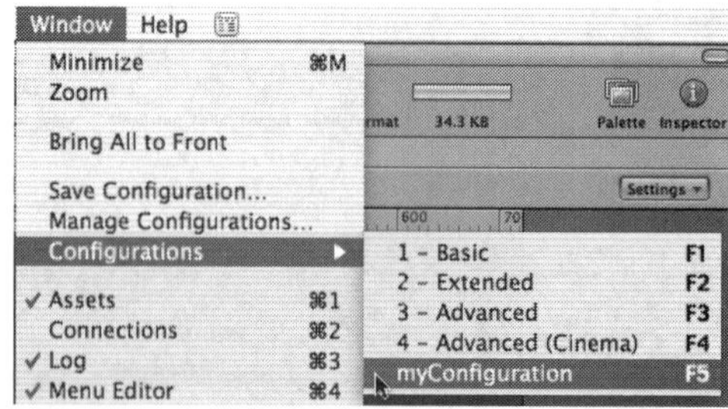

Figure 7.25 Saved window configurations appear on the Window > Configurations menu.

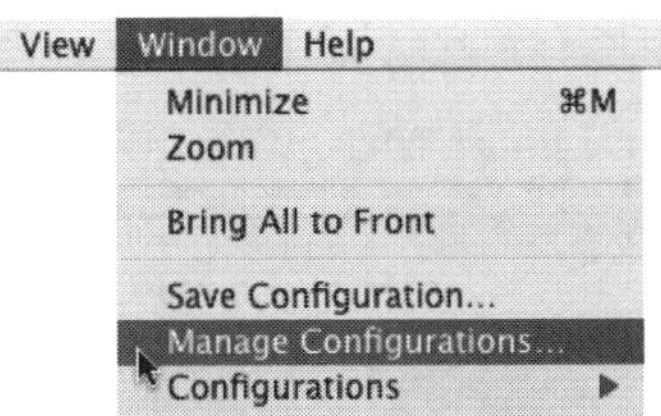

Figure 7.26 To assign a function key to a window configuration, first choose Window > Manage Configurations.

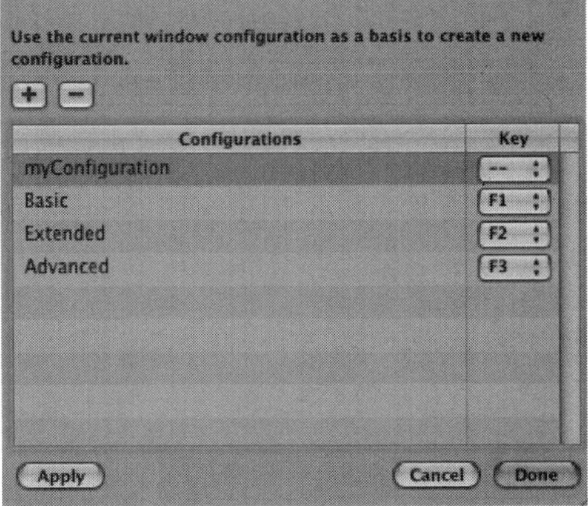

Figure 7.27 Then use the Manage Configurations dialog to assign a function key to particular configurations.

✔ Tips

- Panther's Expose feature uses the F9, F10, and F11 keys. Unless you turn Expose off (or map Expose's functions to other keys), you will not be able to use the F9, F10, and F11 keys for custom window configurations.
- Use the Manage Configurations dialog's plus and minus buttons to add or delete custom window configurations.

Where's My Custom Configuration?

While the activity is probably not as popular as trading baseball cards, if you want to, you can trade your custom window configurations with friends. When you save a custom window configuration, it is stored in your User/Library/Application Support/DVD Studio Pro/ Configurations folder with a .dspconfig extension (**Figure 7.28**). Now apply Stuff-It and e-mail it to all of your friends.

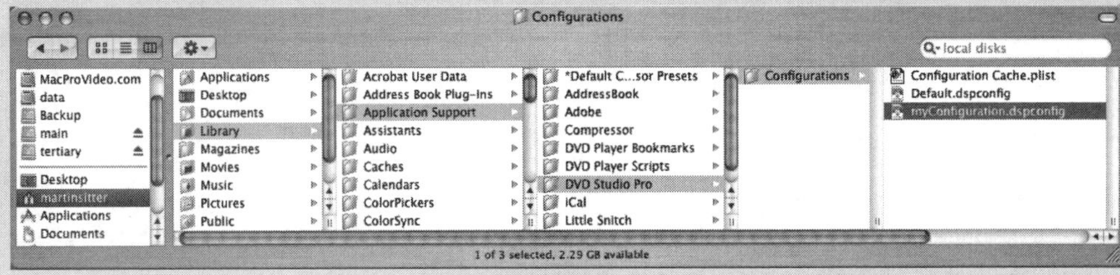

Figure 7.28 Custom window configurations are stored in the User/Library/Application Support/DVD Studio Pro/ Configurations folder.

Using the Toolbar

Across the top of DVD Studio Pro's workspace is a toolbar (**Figure 7.29**) that gives you one-click access to several important capabilities, such as functions to import assets, create new tracks and menus, and build the finished project. If the toolbar's default tool set doesn't offer the tools you need, you can customize it by adding—or subtracting—specific tools.

✔ Tip

- The toolbar's tool configuration is saved along with the window configuration.

To show or hide the toolbar:

- Choose View > Show Toolbar (**Figure 7.30**).

  The toolbar appears at the top of the workspace.

To show/hide icons and/or text in the toolbar:

1. Hold down the Control key while clicking the toolbar.

   A shortcut menu appears at the pointer's position (**Figure 7.31**). At the top of this menu are three display options: Icon & Text, Icon Only, and Text Only.

2. Choose one of the three display options.

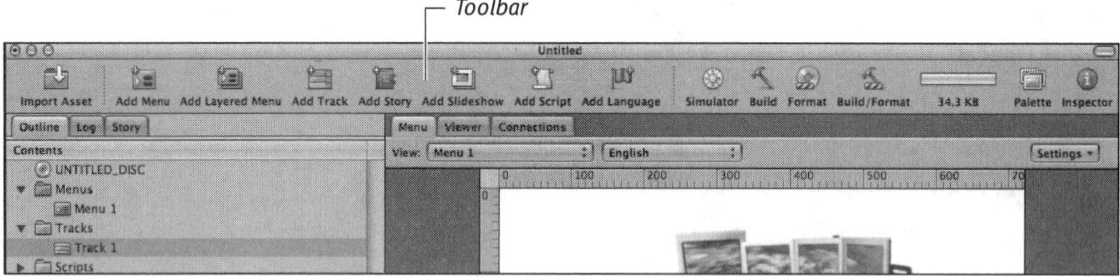

Figure 7.29 The toolbar provides one-click access to tools that you use regularly.

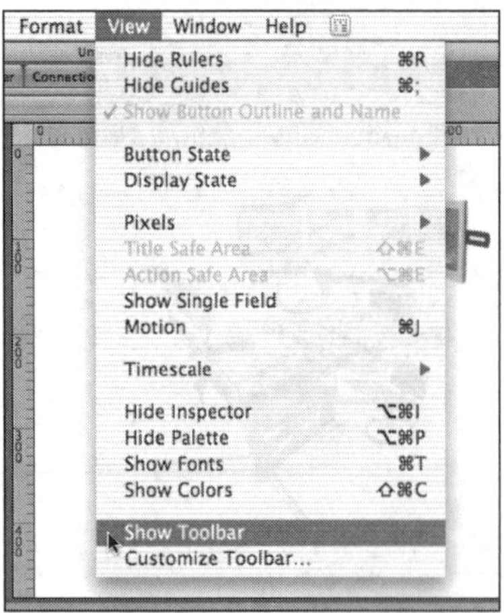

Figure 7.30 To show the toolbar, choose View > Show Toolbar.

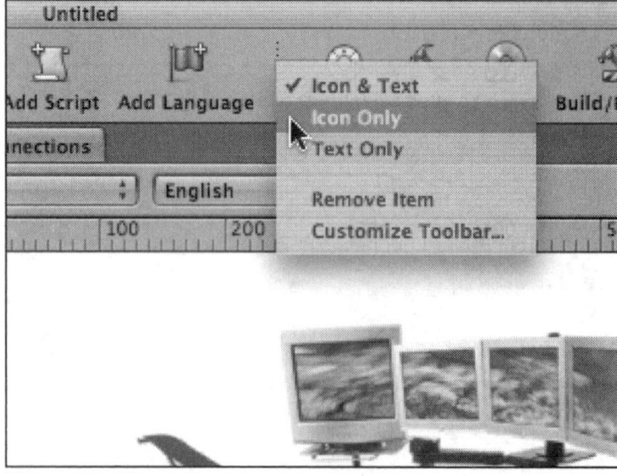

Figure 7.31 To customize the toolbar's appearance, Control-click anywhere in the toolbar. A shortcut menu appears that lets you choose whether the toolbar should show icons, text, or both.

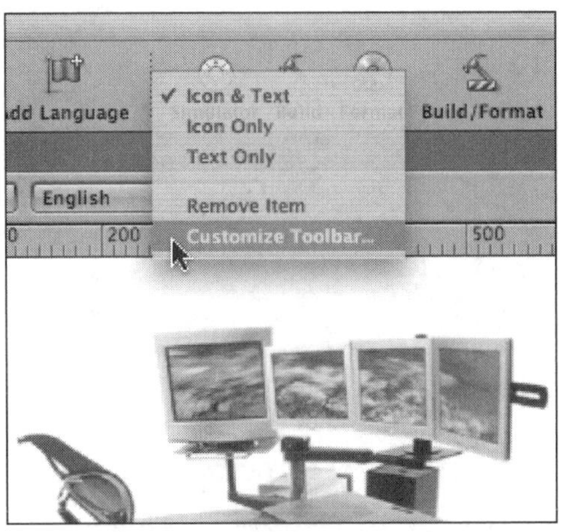

Figure 7.32 To customize the toolbar, Control-click the toolbar and choose Customize Toolbar.

To add tools to the toolbar:

1. Choose View > Customize Toolbar, or press the Control key while clicking the toolbar.

   A shortcut menu appears.

2. From the menu, choose Customize Toolbar (**Figure 7.32**).

   The Toolbar palette drops down from the toolbar. This palette contains all of the tools you can add to the toolbar (**Figure 7.33**).

continues on next page

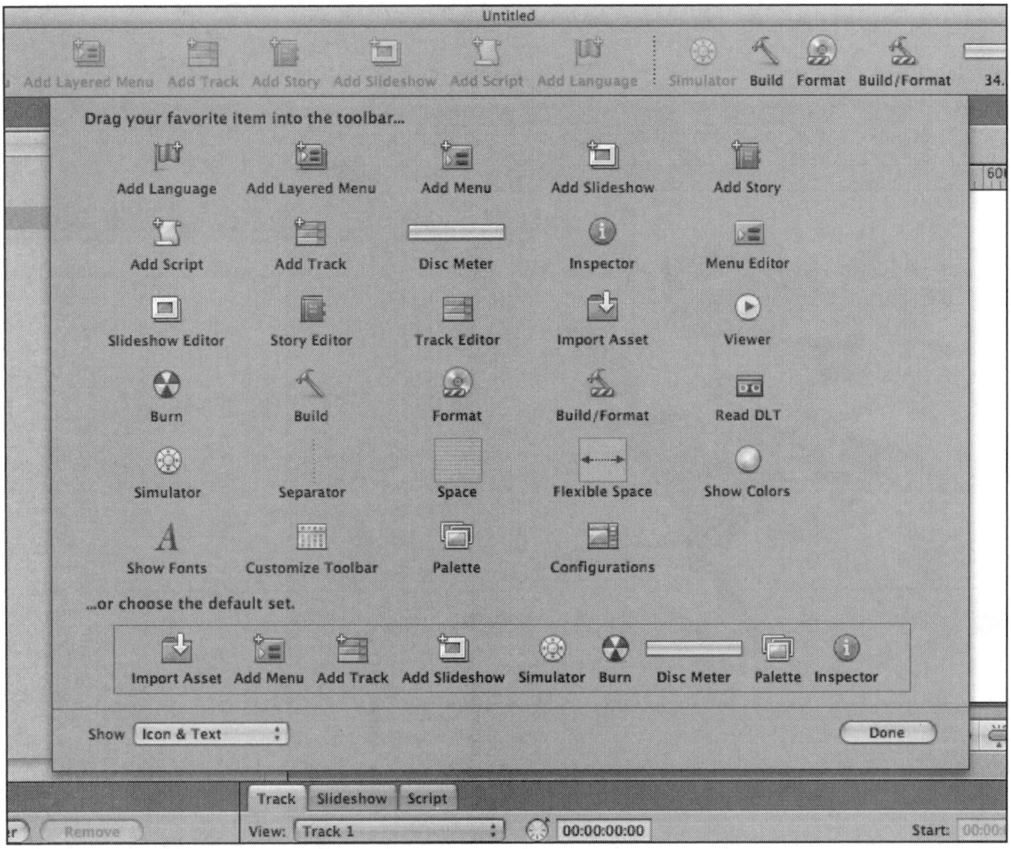

Figure 7.33 The Toolbar palette, which shows all of the tools that you can add to the toolbar, drops down from the toolbar.

3. Drag tools from the Toolbar palette and drop them into the toolbar (**Figure 7.34**).
4. Continue adding icons to the toolbar until you've stocked it with the tools you need.
5. Click the Done button to close the Toolbar palette.

To remove a tool from the toolbar:

1. Press the Control key while clicking the tool that you want to remove from the toolbar.

   A menu appears under the pointer.
2. Choose Remove Item (**Figure 7.35**).

   The tool is removed from the toolbar.

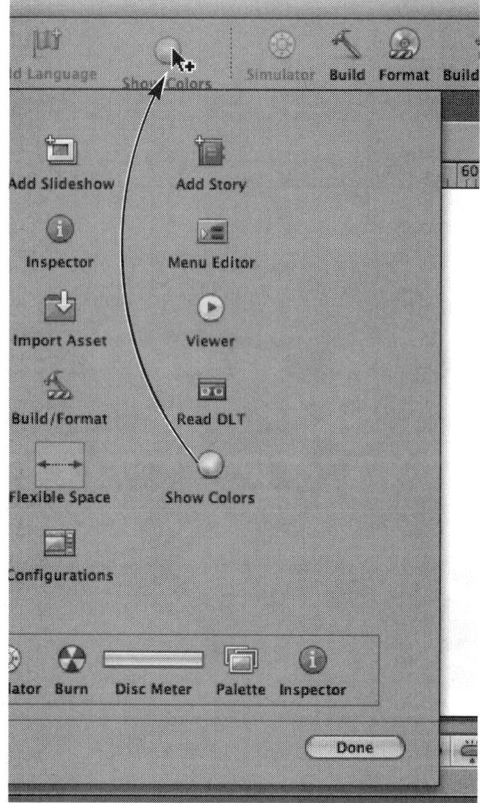

Figure 7.34 Drag icons from the Toolbar palette to the toolbar.

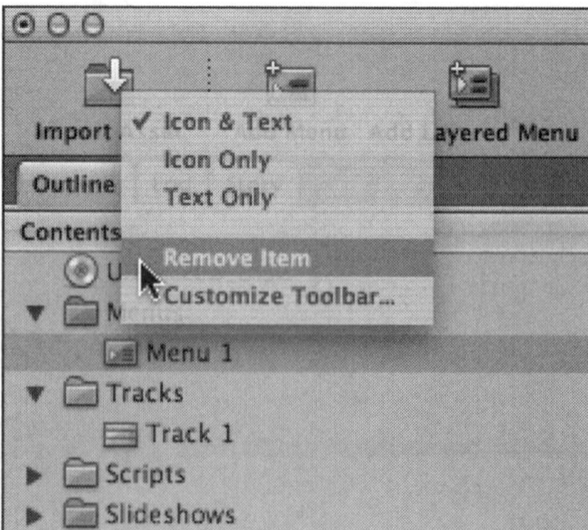

Figure 7.35 To remove a tool from the toolbar, Control-click the tool and choose Remove Item from the menu that appears.

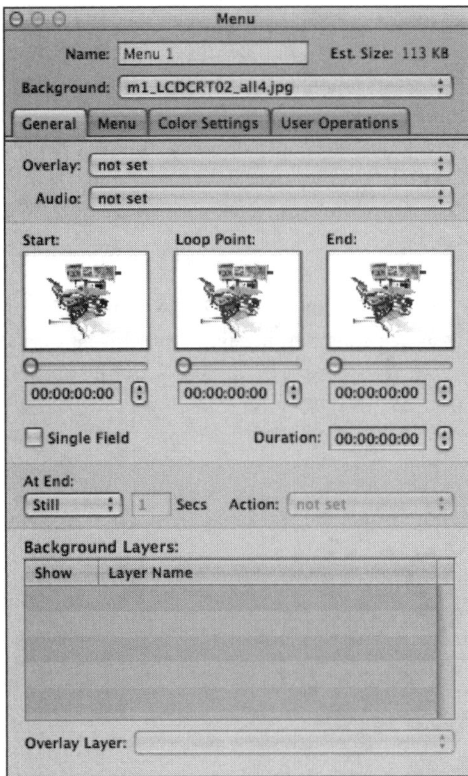

Figure 7.36 As you select items in DVD Studio Pro's workspace, the Inspector updates to show you the unique properties of each selected item.

Figure 7.37 To show or hide the Inspector, choose View > Show Inspector, or...

Using the Inspector

The Inspector is like a digital Sherlock Holmes that holds its magnifying glass over any item you select in the workspace. If you select an item—from audio/video assets on the Assets tab (also called the Assets container) to tracks or menus on the Outline tab (also called the Outline view)—in DVD Studio Pro's workspace, the Inspector instantly updates to display the selected item's properties (**Figure 7.36**).

To show or hide the Inspector:

- *Do one of the following:*
  - Depending on whether the Inspector is showing or not, choose View > Show/Hide Inspector (**Figure 7.37**).
  - Press Option-Command-I.
  - On the toolbar, click the Inspector icon (**Figure 7.38**).

Figure 7.38 ...click the Inspector tool on the toolbar.

Using the Palette

Just as a painter's palette holds the variously hued paints that the artist uses to create a picture, DVD Studio Pro's Palette displays items—such as audio files, movies, and menu templates—that you use to create your DVD-Video.

The Palette has six tabs (**Figure 7.39**). The first three tabs (Templates, Styles, and Shapes) hold preassembled items that you can use to format menu text, create buttons, or even create complete menus from DVD Studio Pro's included menu templates. The next three tabs (Audio, Stills, and Video) provide direct access to media—including songs from your iTunes library, pictures in your iPhoto albums, movies from your User Movies folder, or any other media that DVD Studio Pro recognizes as a usable file—that's stored on your hard disk.

✔ Tip

- Palette items are not actually part of your project. You still must add the items to your project by dragging them from the Palette into DVD Studio Pro.

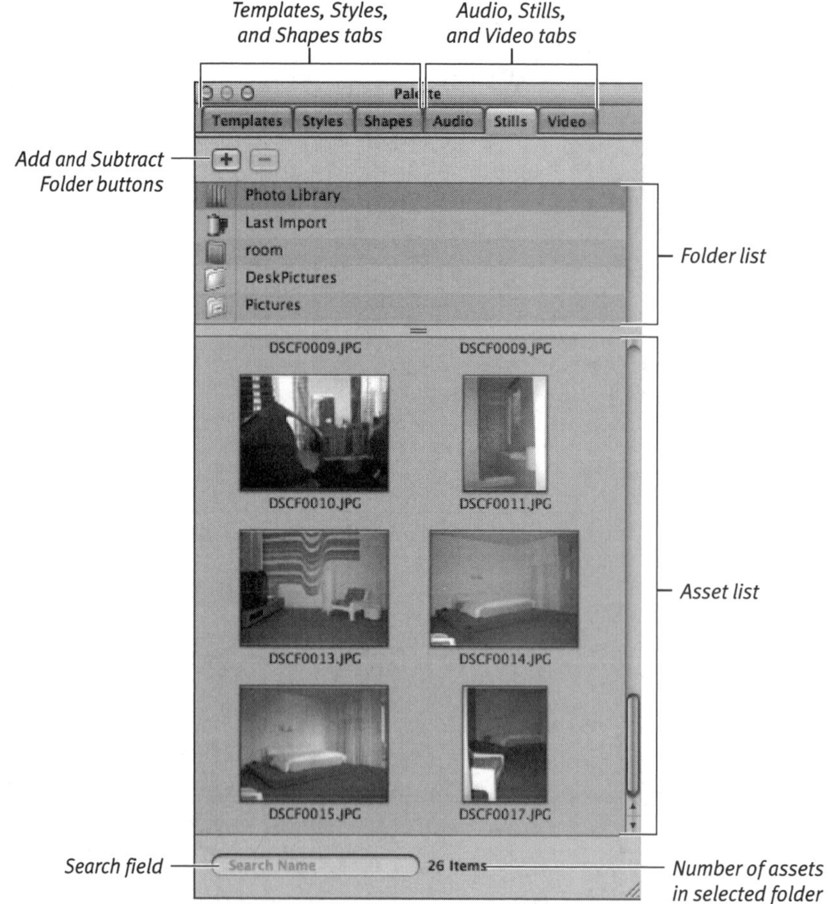

Figure 7.39 The Palette gives you direct access to items you can use in your projects.

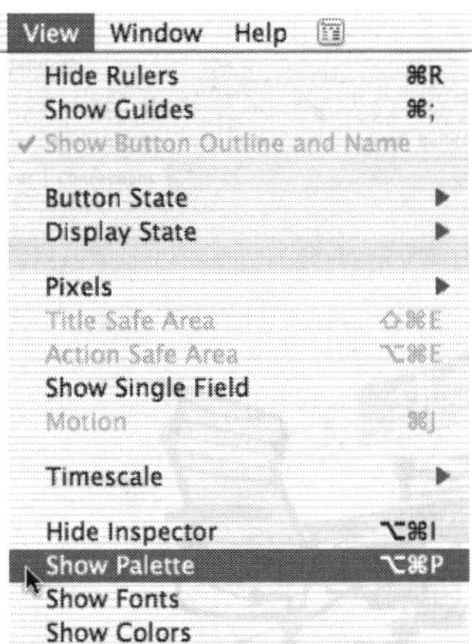

Figure 7.40 To show or hide the Palette, choose View > Show Palette, or...

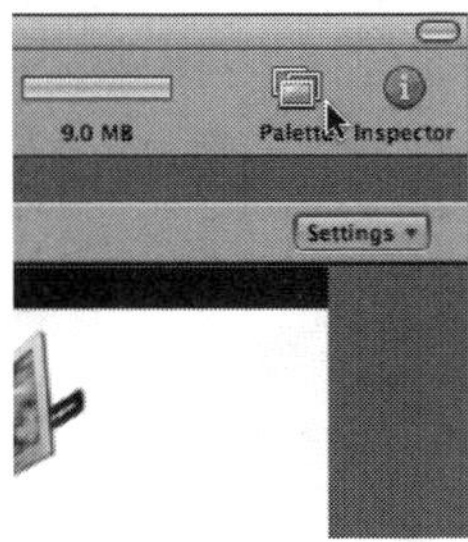

Figure 7.41 ...click the Palette tool on the toolbar.

To hide or show the Palette:

◆ *Do one of the following:*

▲ Depending on whether the Palette is showing or not, choose View > Show/Hide Palette (**Figure 7.40**).

▲ Press Option-Command-P.

▲ On the toolbar, select the Palette icon (**Figure 7.41**).

Opening Palette Media Files in an External Editor

Here's a great trick for quickly opening media files from the Palette in an external editor like Adobe Photoshop or QuickTime Pro Player. First, add the external editor's application icon to your computer's dock. With the application icon in the dock, you can drag media files from DVD Studio Pro's Palette and drop them on the external editor's icon in the dock. The external editor will now open to display the file, allowing you to make quick edits or changes to the media file itself.

Using folders in the Palette

The Palette actually acts like a specialized Finder window that you can use for quick access to oft-used items, such as background music loops, and video files. Like the Finder, the three tabs on the right side of the Palette hold folders, which in turn link to actual folders on your hard disks. You can add folders to these tabs, as well as delete them, in much the same way as you add and delete folders in a Finder window. This section shows you the way.

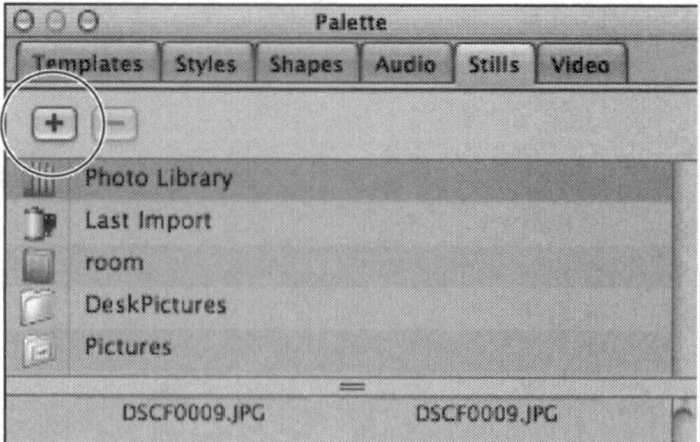

Figure 7.42 To add a folder to the Palette, click the Add Folder (+) button.

To add a folder to the Palette:

1. Select the Audio, Stills, or Video tab.

   These are the only tabs with Folder lists, which means that these are the only tabs that can have folders added to them.

2. At the top-left corner of the Palette, click the Add Folder (+) button (**Figure 7.42**).

   A folder selection dialog drops down from the top of the Palette (**Figure 7.43**).

3. Navigate to the folder that you want to add to the Palette and click the Add button.

   DVD Studio Pro adds the folder to the Palette's Folder list. All usable media files inside that folder are now displayed whenever you select the folder in the Folder list.

   Note that subfolders nested inside the selected folder will *not* appear in the Palette's Folder list.

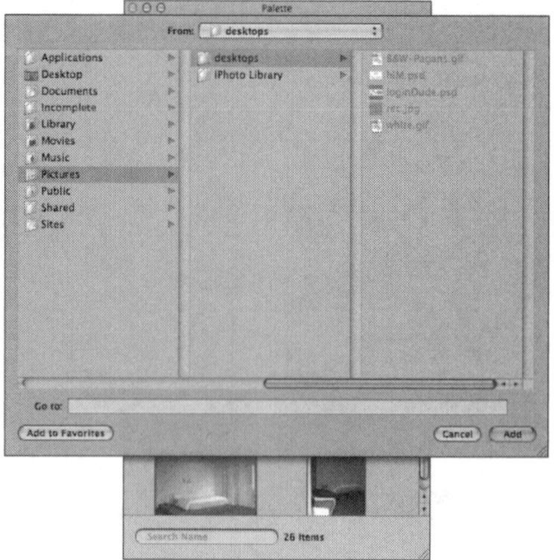

Figure 7.43 The Palette's folder selection dialog lets you choose folders to add to the Palette's Folder list.

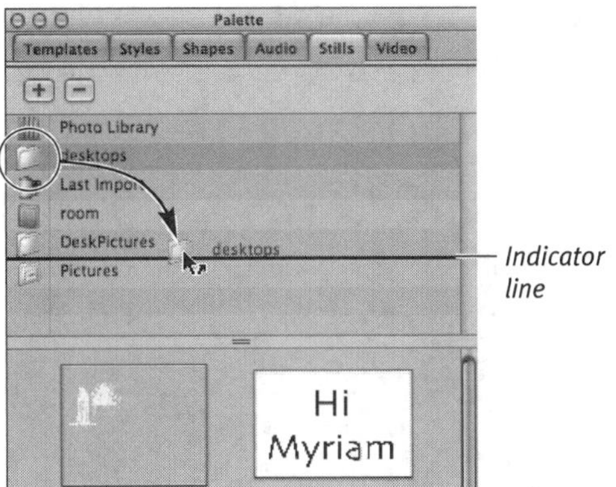

Figure 7.44 To reorder folders in the Palette's Folder list, select the folder and drag it to a new position. As you drag, a black indicator line shows you where the folder will drop when you release the mouse button.

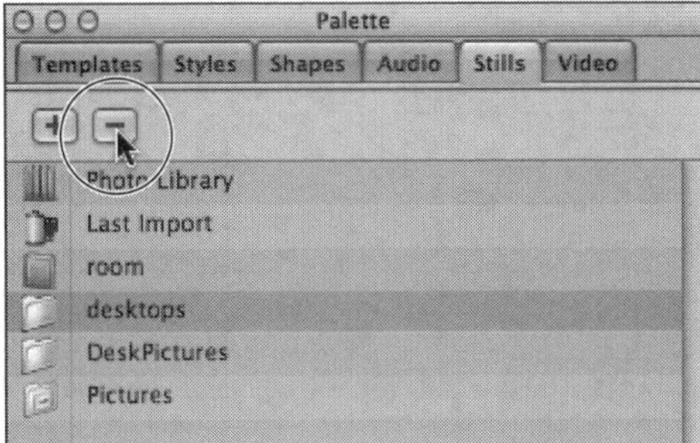

Figure 7.45 The Remove Folder button (–) deletes any folder currently selected in the Palette's Folder list.

Figure 7.46 The quickest way to remove folders from the Palette is to Control-click the folder and choose Remove Selected Folder from the shortcut menu that appears.

To change the order of folders:

1. In the Folder list, select a folder and drag it up or down the list.

   As you drag the folder, a black indicator line shows you where the folder will drop when you release the mouse button (**Figure 7.44**).

2. When the folder is in the correct position, release the mouse button.

   The folder drops into its new position.

✔ Tip

- To move a folder, you must select the folder's icon—not its name—in the Folder list. (Clicking the name selects the folder but does not allow you to move it.)

To delete a folder from the Folder list:

1. In the Palette's Folder list, select a folder.
2. *Do one of the following:*
   - Press the Delete key.
   - In the top-left corner of the Palette, click the Remove Folder (–) button (**Figure 7.45**).
   - Control-click the Folder list and choose Remove Selected Folder from the menu that appears (**Figure 7.46**).

   The folder is removed from the Palette but is not deleted from your hard disks.

✔ Tip

- The Remove Folder button is disabled until you select a folder in the Folder list.

USING THE PALETTE

Previewing media files

If you need a quick reminder of what you have tucked away in a specific media file, you can preview the file using the Palette's Play button. But previewing with the Play button works only for files that have a time component—in other words, audio and video files. Still-picture files, such as TIFFs and JPEGs, don't change over time; consequently, the Play button is unavailable to the Stills tab. But that's fine, because you can see at a glance what these files contain by looking at the Palette's Asset list.

However, audio and video files are not as accommodating. The Palette's Asset list, for example, displays the first frame of a video file by default. Because most video files fade in from a black frame, the Video tab's Asset list often shows only a series of black frames, which don't really tell you much about what the files contain. Thank goodness for the Play button!

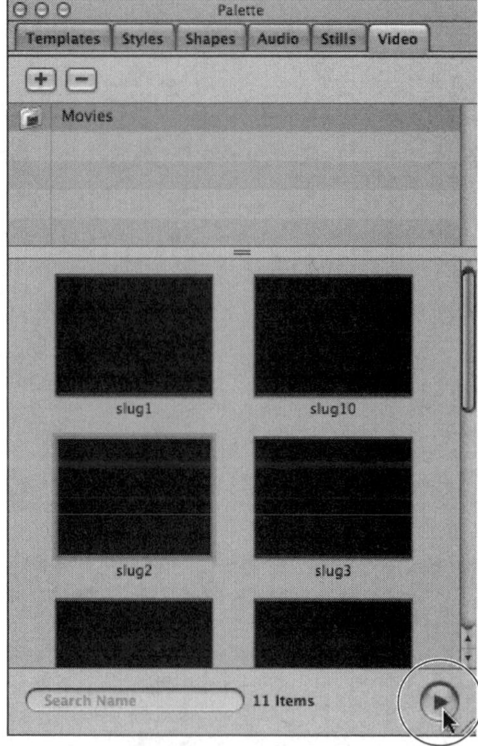

Figure 7.47 Click the Palette's Play button to preview selected media files right inside the Palette. The Play button is available only to the Audio and Video tabs.

To preview media files in the Palette:

1. In the Palette's Asset list, select an audio or video file.
2. In the bottom-right corner of the Palette, click the Play button (**Figure 7.47**).

   In the Asset list, the selected asset plays.
3. To stop previewing the media file, click the Play button a second time.

✔ Tip

- By default, the Palette thumbnails display the first frame of video files. However, you can change this default so the Palette thumbnails show any frame within the first five seconds of the video (well, any I-frame actually; see Chapter 4). Here's how to do it: Choose DVD Studio Pro > Preferences to open the Preferences window. Then click the Track icon to open the Track preferences pane. In this section of the Preferences window, use the Thumbnail Offset setting (**Figure 7.48**) to adjust the offset of all video thumbnail images, including the thumbnails in the Palette, used in DVD Studio Pro.

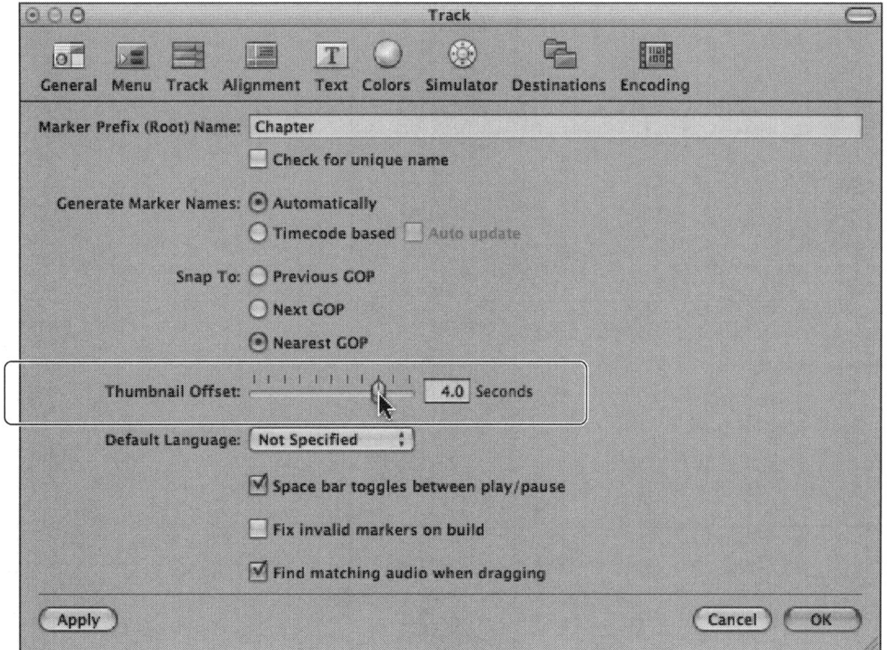

Figure 7.48 Use the Thumbnail Offset setting in the Preferences window's Track pane to adjust the frame of video displayed in the thumbnail image for videos in the Palette.

8

VIEWING YOUR PROJECT

A DVD-Video is a composite of many smaller items—menus, tracks, slideshows, and scripts. Even simple DVD-Video projects often use dozens of items that you, the DVD author, need to organize and keep track of. DVD Studio Pro 3 provides two windows for just this purpose: the Outline and Graphical views.

About the Outline and Graphical Views

Located in the top-left quadrant of the Advanced window configuration, the Outline view displays a series of folders that contain project items (**Figure 8.1**). The Graphical view, also at the top left of the Advanced window configuration, organizes items into tiles arranged in a flowchart (**Figure 8.2**). Both windows let you *view* your project at a glance (hence the names Outline *view* and Graphical *view*).

These windows are central to your projects, because it is from here that you create items and select items for editing, so we'll explore them in detail.

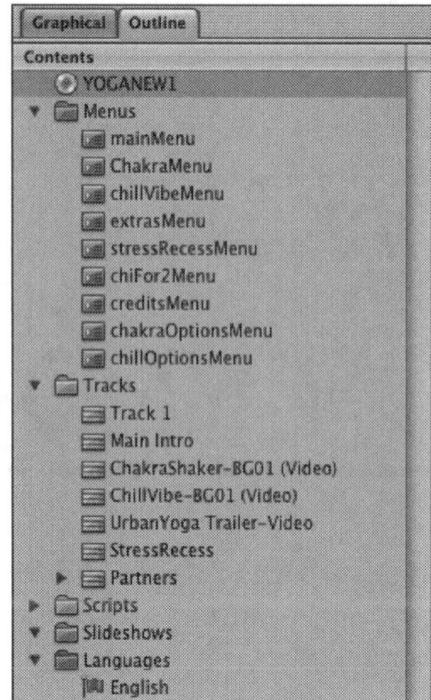

Figure 8.1 The Outline view lists project items as files in folders.

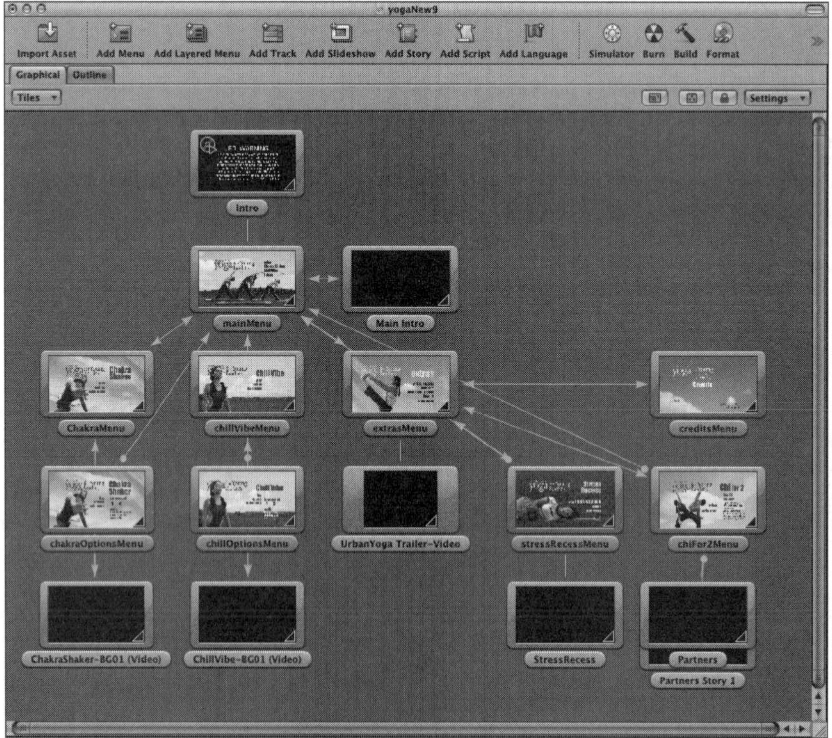

Figure 8.2 The Graphical view displays project items as tiles in a flowchart.

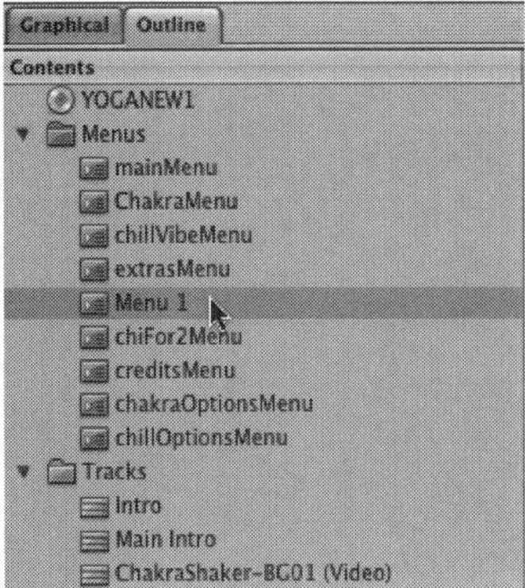

Figure 8.3 To name an item, click once to select the item.

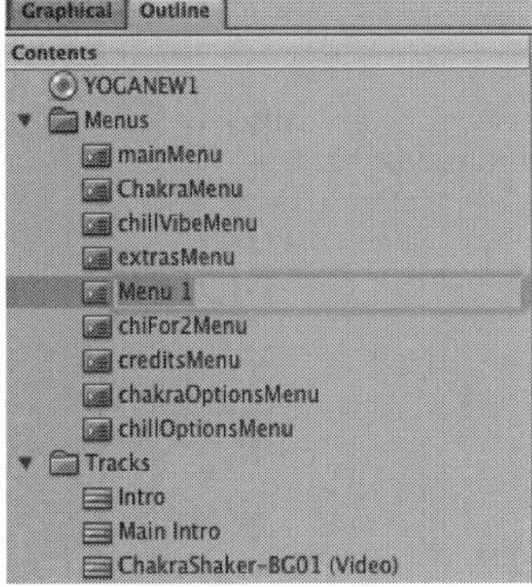

Figure 8.4 Then click a second time to open a text box.

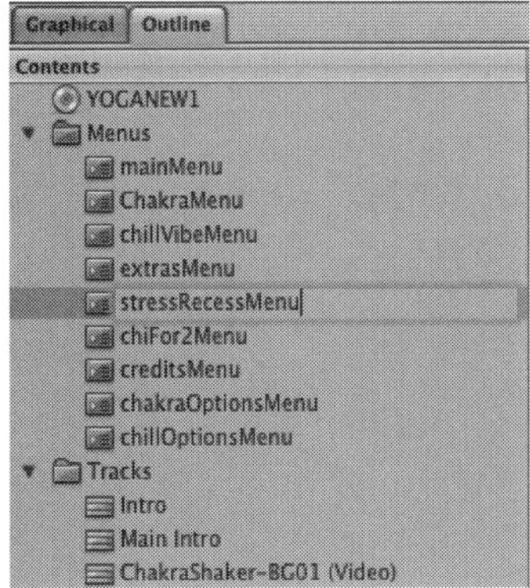

Figure 8.5 Type a name in the text box.

Exploring the Outline View

The Outline view shows all your project items as a list of files organized in folders. Notice that the items are not arranged in alphabetical order. Instead, items in the Outline view are arranged in the order they will be burnt on the final DVD-Video disc. For example, the track at the top of the track folder will be burnt first, then the next track, and so on. Keep this in mind when it comes time to burn your final DVD.

To create a project item:

- Control-click the background of the Outline view and choose Add and then the item you want to add.

To name/rename an item:

1. Click an item once (**Figure 8.3**).
   The item is selected
2. Click the item a second time.
   A text box opens (**Figure 8.4**).
3. Use the text box to name or rename the item (**Figure 8.5**).

continues on next page

To edit an item's properties:

1. In the Outline view, click an item once.

   The Inspector updates to display the item's properties.

2. Use the Inspector to update the item's properties as necessary.

To open an item in an editor:

- In the Outline view, double-click an item.

  The item opens in the appropriate editor.

To change item order:

1. In the Outline view, select an item in the list.

2. Drag the item up or down the list (**Figure 8.6**).

   A thin, horizontal black line shows where the item will drop when you release the mouse button.

3. When the item is in the right position in the list, release the mouse button.

   The item is inserted in the selected position.

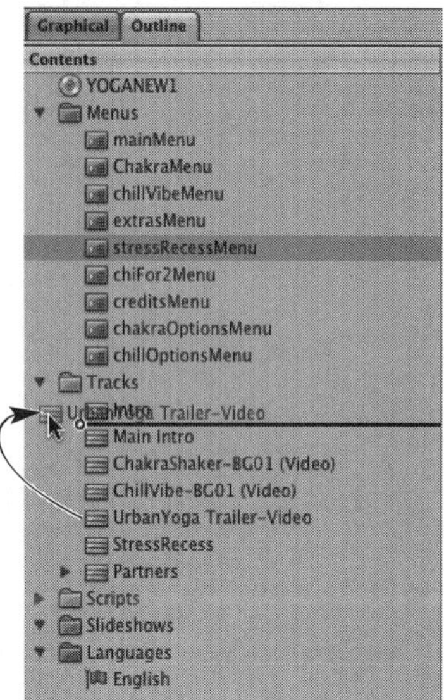

Figure 8.6 Items are recorded to disc in the order they appear in the Outline view. Change the item order by dragging items up or down the list.

Exploring the Graphical View

DVD Studio Pro 3 reintroduces the Graphical view, a central window in version 1 of this product that disappeared when the product went to version 2. But it's back now, with some great new features to boot!

The Graphical view itself acts as a flowchart for your project. Items, including menus, tracks, stories, slideshows, and scripts, are organized into tiles. Arrows between the tiles graphically show you how the items are connected.

To create a project item:

- Control-click the background of the Outline view and choose Add and then the item that you want to add.

To name/rename an item:

1. In the graphical view, double-click the tiles name (**Figure 8.7**).

   A text box appears.

2. Use the text box to name/rename the item (**Figure 8.8**).

To edit an item's properties:

1. In the Outline view, click an item once.

   The Inspector updates to display the item's properties.

2. Use the Inspector to update the item's properties as necessary.

To lock/unlock the Graphical view:

- *Do one of the following:*
  - Choose Arrange > Lock all Tiles (**Figure 8.9**).
  - At the top right of the Graphical view, click the lock icon (**Figure 8.10**).
  - Press L.

  All tiles in the Graphical view are locked into position and cannot be moved. You can, of course, still select and click tiles to modify their properties and open them in editors.

Figure 8.7 To name an item in the Graphical view, double-click its name at the bottom of the tile.

Figure 8.8 Type a new name into the tile's text box.

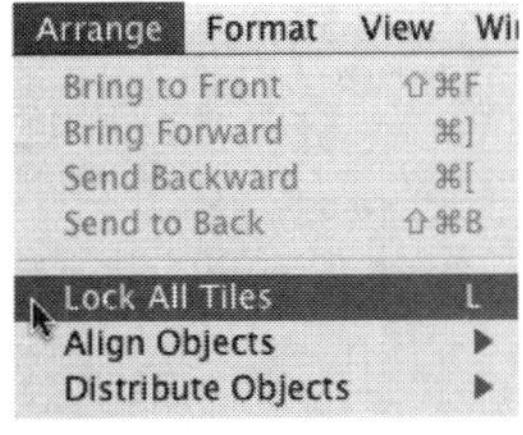

Figure 8.9 To lock the Graphical view, choose Arrange > Lock All Tiles...

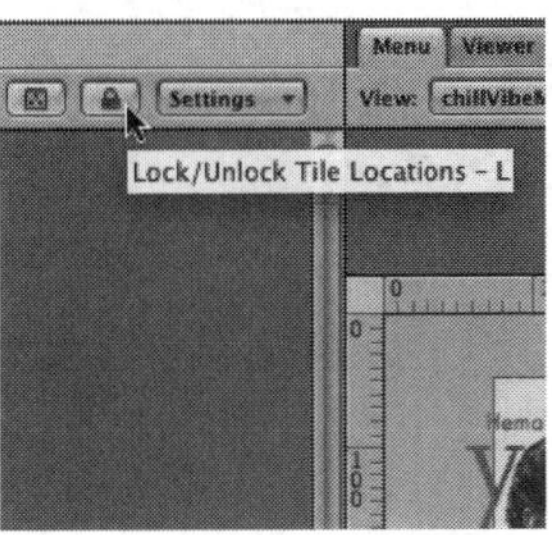

Figure 8.10 ...or click the lock icon at the top right of the Graphical view.

Zooming the Graphical View

Complex projects may use dozens of tiles. If you're working with only one monitor, it can be hard to increase the Graphical view to a size where all the tiles are immediately visible. Consequently, to locate and edit tiles, you'll have to zoom in and out as you work in the Graphical view.

As in Final Cut Pro, you can drag the ends of the Graphical view's scroll bars to zoom the window in and out. You can also use the Zoom tool (also called the magnifying glass) to zoom in on particular tiles. To quickly resize the display so that all tiles are visible in the Graphical view, you can use DVD Studio Pro's Zoom to Fit feature.

To zoom with the scroll bars:

- Grab the end of a scroll bar and drag (**Figure 8.11**).

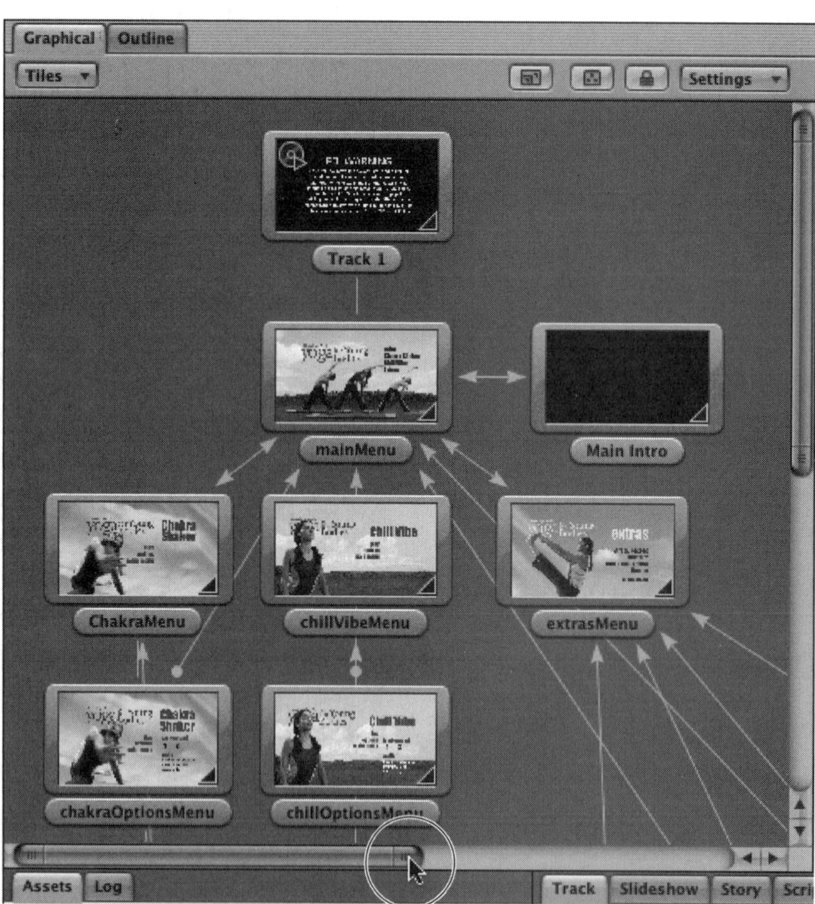

Figure 8.11 To zoom the Graphical view, grab the end of a scroll bar and drag.

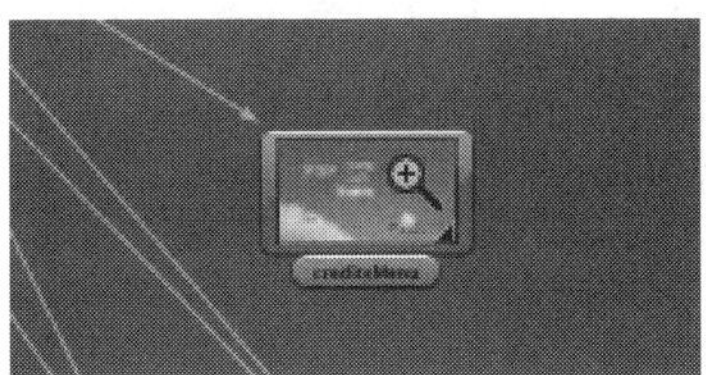

Figure 8.12 To zoom in on a particular tile, press the Z key and click the tile.

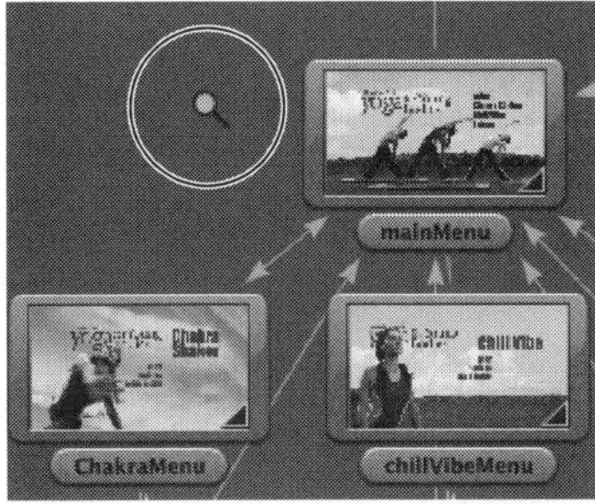

Figure 8.13 When the plus sign disappears from the center of the Zoom tool, you are zoomed in as far as possible.

To zoom in on an individual tile:

- In the Graphical view, press the Z key and click a tile (**Figure 8.12**).

  The pointer turns into a magnifying glass, and the Graphical view zooms in on the clicked tile.

✔ Tip

- When the plus sign disappears from the center of the Zoom tool, you are zoomed in as far as possible (**Figure 8.13**).

To zoom in on a selection of tiles:

- Press the Z key and drag a selection marquee around several tiles (**Figure 8.14**).

  The pointer turns into a magnifying glass, and the Graphical view zooms in on the selected tiles.

To zoom to fit:

- *Do one of the following:*
  - ▲ Click anywhere in the Graphical view to ensure that the Graphical view has the focus and then press Shift-Z.
  - ▲ At the top of the Graphical view, click the Zoom to Fit button (**Figure 8.15**).

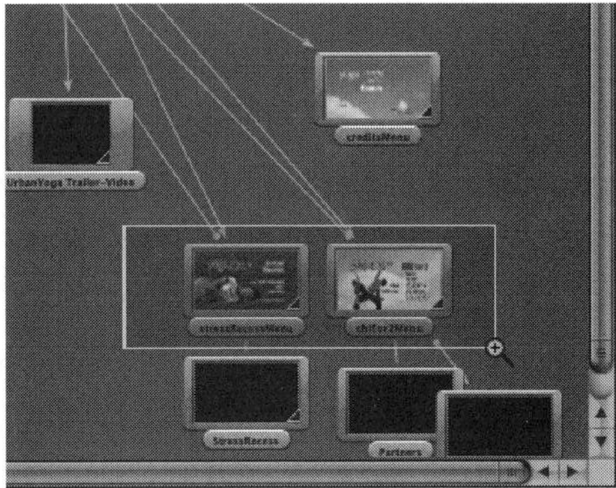

Figure 8.14 To zoom in on multiple tiles, press Z and drag a selection marquee around the tiles.

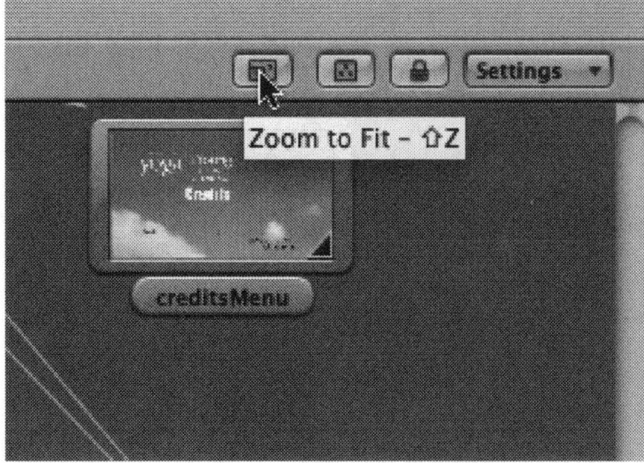

Figure 8.15 Click the Zoom to Fit button to zoom out so that all tiles are displayed in the Graphical view.

Flagging an Item

In the Graphical view, you can label tiles that need further attention by flagging them. A flagged tile displays a little flag that is easy to spot among the multitude of tiles in the Graphical view. You can flag tiles one by one, or you can select multiple tiles and flag them all at once.

To flag a tile:

- *Do one of the following:*
  - ▲ Control-click a tile and choose Flag Tile (**Figure 8.16**).
  - ▲ Hover the pointer over a tile and press F.
  - ▲ Select one or more tiles and choose Edit > Flag Tile.

  The tile is flagged (**Figure 8.17**)

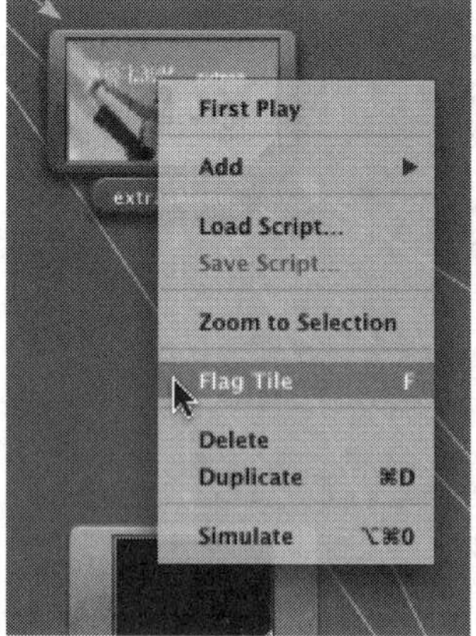

Figure 8.16 To flag a tile, control-click it and choose Flag Tile.

Figure 8.17 A flagged tile.

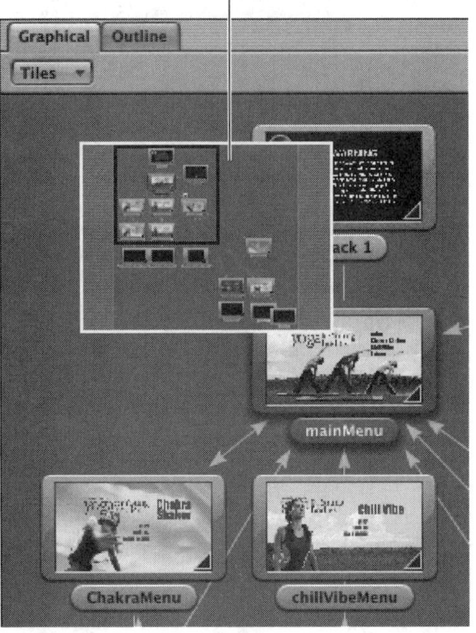

Figure 8.18 The Macro view shows an overview of all the tiles in your project and indicates the Graphical view's current display area with a red outline.

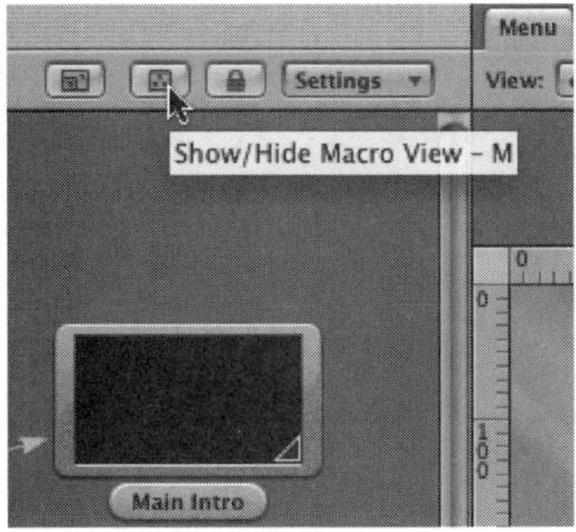

Figure 8.19 Click the Show/Hide Macro View button (or press M) to toggle the Macro view on and off.

Using the Macro View

The Macro view is a small subwindow in the Graphical view that shows all project tiles at a glance. A red box inside the Macro view indicates the current display area in the Graphical view (**Figure 8.18**).

To show/hide the Macro view:

- *Do one of the following:*
  - At the top of the Graphical view, click the Show/Hide Macro View button (**Figure 8.19**).
  - Press the M key.

  If the Macro view was hidden, it is now displayed. If the macro view was displayed, it is now hidden.

To increase the Macro view's size:

1. Position the pointer over the Macro view.

   Depending on where you position the pointer, a title bar appears at the top or bottom of the Macro view. At the edge of the title bar there is a triangle (**Figure 8.20**).
2. Drag the triangle to resize the Macro view.

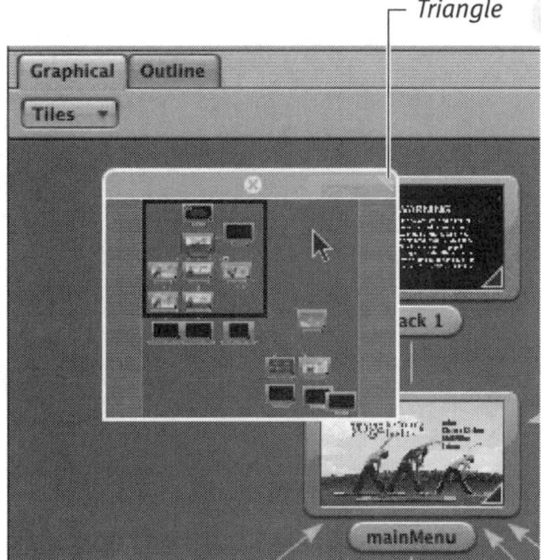

Figure 8.20 Drag the title bar's triangle to resize the Macro view.

To change the Graphical view's display area:

- In the Macro view, click the red outline and drag it to a new position.

  The Graphical view updates to display the area indicated by the Macro view's red outline.

To use the Macro view to zoom the Graphical view:

- In the Macro view, grab a corner of the red outline and drag inward or outward (**Figure 8.21**).

  The outline becomes bigger or smaller, and the Graphical view updates to display the area indicated by the Macro view's red outline.

Figure 8.21 To zoom the Graphical view, grab the corner of the Macro view's red outline and drag.

Figure 8.22 To align tiles, select them and then choose Arrange > Align Objects and an alignment option.

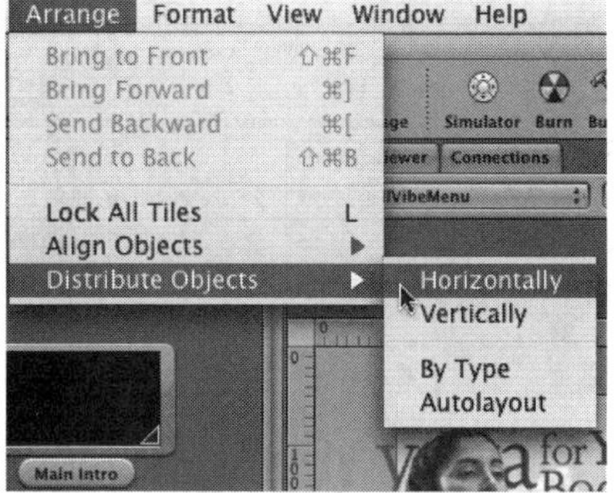

Figure 8.23 To distribute tiles, select them and then choose Arrange > Distribute Objects and a distribution option.

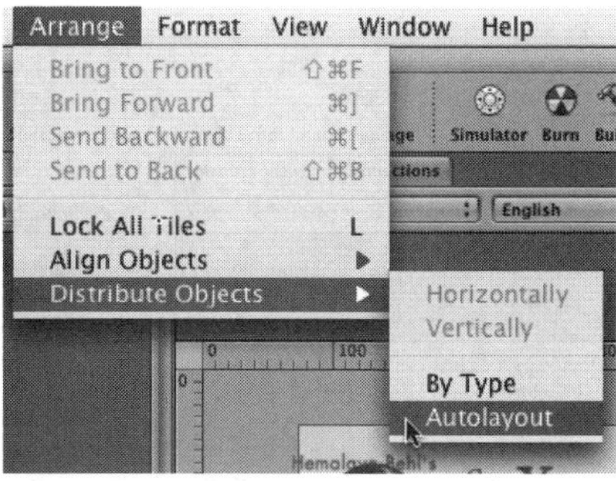

Figure 8.24 To have DVD Studio Pro automatically lay out Graphical view tiles and show their connections, choose Arrange > Distribute Objects > Autolayout.

Laying Out Tiles

The Graphical view includes several features to help you quickly and aesthetically organize tiles, including alignment and distribution options and an autolayout feature that organizes the Graphical view for you.

To align tiles:

1. In the Graphical view, select the tiles you want to align.
2. Choose Arrange > Align Objects and choose an alignment option (**Figure 8.22**).

To distribute tiles:

1. In the Graphical view, select the tiles you want to distribute.
2. Choose Arrange > Distribute Objects and choose a distribution option (**Figure 8.23**).

To create an autolayout:

◆ Choose Arrange > Distribute Objects > Auto Layout (**Figure 8.24**).

DVD Studio Pro automatically distributes the Graphical view tiles to show how items are connected (**Figure 8.25**).

✔ Tip

■ In the Distribute Objects menu, the By Type option distributes tiles across the Graphical view by type.

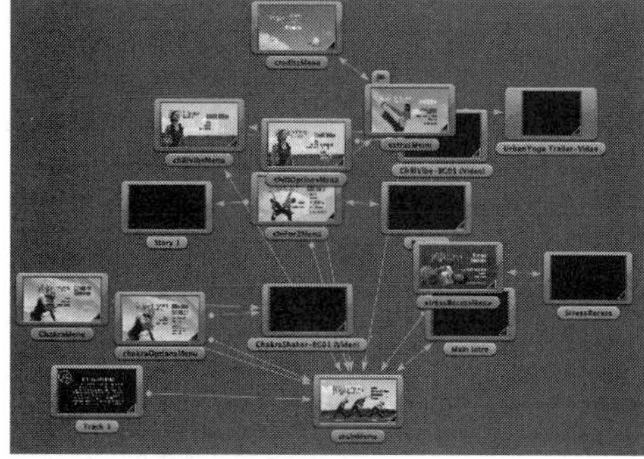

Figure 8.25 An example of tiles distributed using DVD Studio Pro's autolayout feature.

Setting a First Play Item

When you insert a DVD-Video into a player, one project item must play first. It's up to you to choose the item, and you'll often do so right in the Graphical view. In fact, the First Play item is graphically differentiated from all others by the First Play icon (a disc with an arrow) prominently displayed in the tile's top-left corner (**Figure 8.26**).

Figure 8.26 The First Play item is tagged with an icon in the top-left corner of the Graphical view tile.

The First Play item is an important setting. For starters, the First Play item is always the first item displayed when you click the toolbar's Simulator icon—if no First Play item is selected, the Simulator will not open. Even more important, many DVD-Video players won't play a disc that does not have the First Play item set. To learn more, see Chapter 19, "Finishing the DVD."

To set a First Play item:

- In the Graphical view, control-click a tile and choose First Play (**Figure 8.27**).

  The tile is tagged as the First Play item.

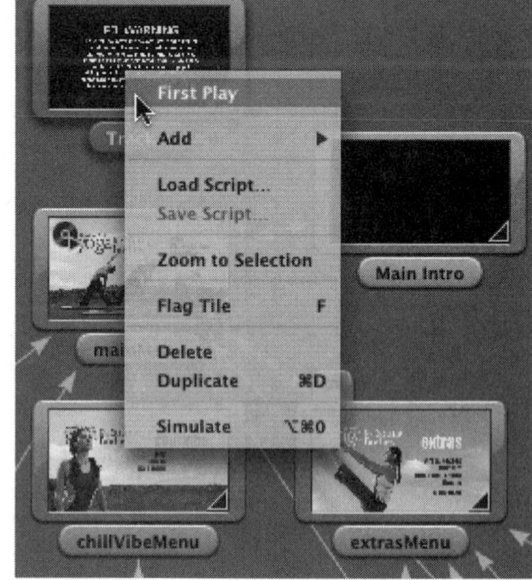

Figure 8.27 To set a tile as the First Play item, Control-click it and choose First Play.

9

Exploring the Assets Tab

Make no mistake about it: DVD Studio Pro is not a content-creation program—it's a content-assembly program. Its sole function is to "snap together" a final presentation out of separate pieces of media that you create in other applications such as Final Cut Pro, Photoshop, Logic, and A.Pack. DVD Studio Pro simply creates the final presentation, and the media that are combined to create that presentation are collectively called *assets*.

In earlier chapters, you learned about the concepts important to the creation of assets—pixel aspect ratio, video color space, frame rate, frame dimensions, and so on. Now it's time to import these assets into DVD Studio Pro and get them ready for assembly into that final DVD-Video. In this chapter, you'll learn how to work with assets on the Assets tab (also often called the Assets container).

About the Assets Tab

DVD Studio Pro stores all assets on the Assets tab (**Figure 9.1**). The Assets tab serves as your project's library, and all the individual media files that you intend to use in your project are stored here, ready for quick access when you need them. Note that the last sentence says, "all the individual media files that you intend to use"; assets on the Assets tab are not automatically part of your project, and they do not add to the file size of your final DVD-Video. To make an asset part of your project, you must add it to a menu, track, or slideshow.

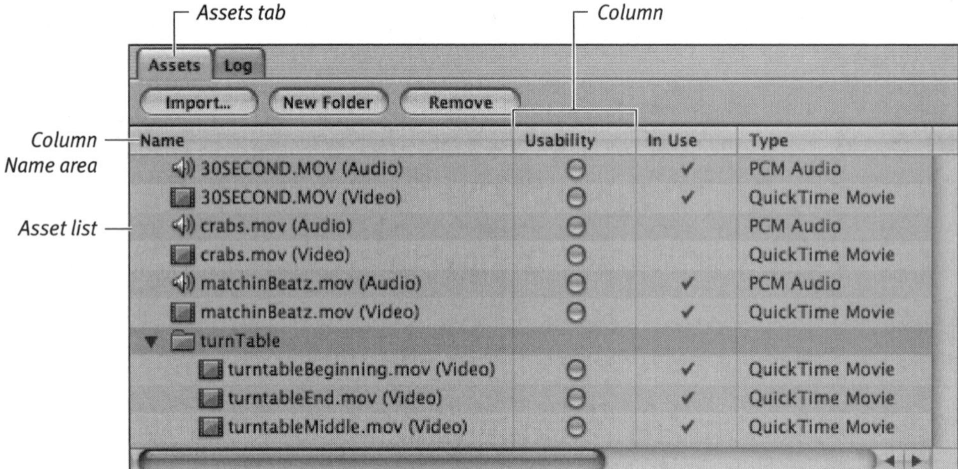

Figure 9.1 The Assets tab is your project's media library. It functions much the same way as the Finder and is used to organize the media that makes up your project.

About Assets

So what exactly is an asset? An asset can be a video file, an audio file, a subtitle file—any individual piece of media used in your project. When you import an asset into DVD Studio Pro, a link (or pointer) is created that shows DVD Studio Pro where that asset is located on your computer's hard disks. DVD Studio Pro never alters assets in any way during the process of authoring a DVD-Video; it simply references the assets when needed, leaving all source media files safely on your hard disks, ready for use at any time.

This approach to media management is common in digital video- and audio-editing programs. It's called *nondestructive editing,* because regardless of how you edit or affect the project's assets in DVD Studio Pro, the source files are never changed. There are many advantages to nondestructive editing. For one, because the source media is never altered by DVD Studio Pro, several different projects can safely use the exact same source media files.

But that's not the best part. If you update or otherwise change the source media file, DVD Studio Pro will automatically refresh the asset, and the change will ripple into your project. If you're working on a still menu, for example, and you notice that a button crosses into the action safe area, you can open the source menu file in Photoshop, move the button, and resave the file. Back in DVD Studio Pro, the button automatically moves to its new position!

Locating source media files

As just noted, if you change an Asset's source media file on your hard disks, your project updates to reflect the change. This feature is especially helpful when, for one reason or another, one of your assets isn't working as you want it to. For example, you may discover compression artifacts in an MPEG-2 video stream, a button graphic that you've accidentally placed in the action safe zone, or an audio stream that's too quiet in comparison to the project's other audio streams.

To fix these problems, you must fix the source media file. To fix the source media file, you first need to find it. After you've tracked down the errant file, you can open it in an external editor—such as the QuickTime MPEG-2 Exporter, Adobe Photoshop, or A.Pack—and make the appropriate edits. To make the entire process easier, you can use DVD Studio Pro's Reveal in Finder function to help with the detective work.

To reveal an asset in the Finder:

1. In the Asset list, Control-click an asset.

   A shortcut menu appears under the pointer (**Figure 9.2**).

2. From the shortcut menu, choose Reveal in Finder.

   A Finder window opens with the asset selected (**Figure 9.3**). You can now easily open the asset in an external editor, such as the MPEG-2 Exporter, Photoshop or A.Pack.

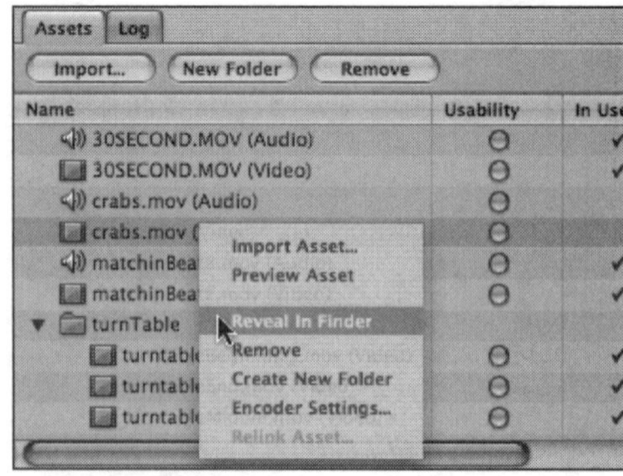

Figure 9.2 To quickly locate an asset on your hard disks, Control-click the asset in the Asset list and then choose Reveal in Finder.

Figure 9.3 A Finder window opens with the asset selected.

Figure 9.4 To add a folder to the Assets tab, Control-click the Asset list and choose Create New Folder, or...

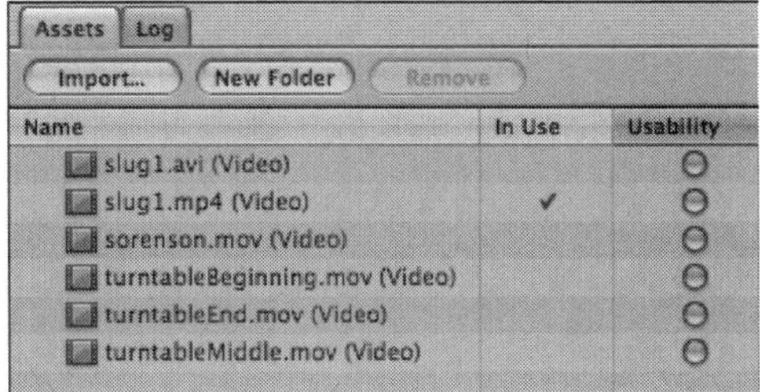

Figure 9.5 ...click the New Folder button, or...

Figure 9.6 ...choose Project > New Asset Folder.

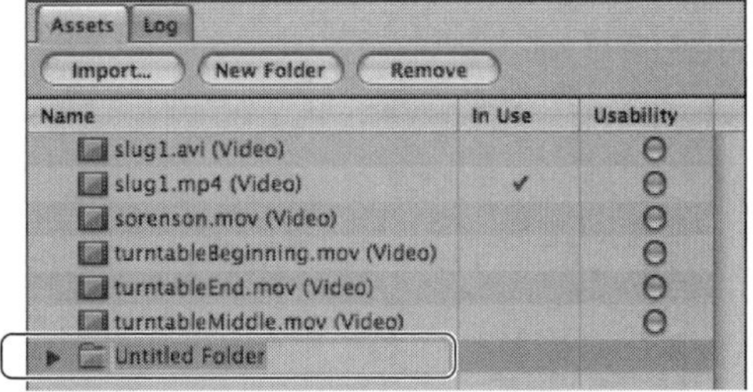

Figure 9.7 Type a name for your new folder in the highlighted text box.

Managing Assets

A DVD project can be huge, and depending upon its complexity, it may have dozens—or even hundreds—of assets. That's a lot of media to manage. Thankfully, DVD Studio Pro 3 offers several essential media management functions directly on the Assets tab.

DVD Studio Pro 3's Assets tab works more or less exactly the same way as a Finder window. You can create folders and subfolders, rename assets, delete assets, and drag assets in and out of folders in the Asset list. It's important to note, however, that the way you organize your assets in DVD Studio Pro has no effect on the way the assets are stored on your computer's hard disks. The Assets tab simply organizes media inside DVD Studio Pro; your source media are never moved, deleted, transferred from folder to folder, or otherwise altered on your computer's hard disks.

To add folders to the Assets tab:

1. *Do one of the following:*
   - ▲ Control-click the Asset list and choose Create New Folder from the shortcut menu (**Figure 9.4**).
   - ▲ At the top of the Assets tab, click the New Folder button (**Figure 9.5**).
   - ▲ Choose Project > New Asset Folder (**Figure 9.6**), or press Option-Command-B.

   A new, untitled folder is added to the Assets tab, and the text box is automatically selected so you can type a name (**Figure 9.7**).
2. Type a name for your folder in the text box.

To rename assets and folders on the Assets tab:

1. Click the asset or folder's name once to select it.
2. *Do one of the following:*
   - ▲ Press Return.
   - ▲ Click the name a second time.

   The text box opens (**Figure 9.8**).
3. Type a new name in the text box and press Return.

✔ Tip

- If you want to rename a folder, don't double-click it! Doing so opens the Import Assets dialog.

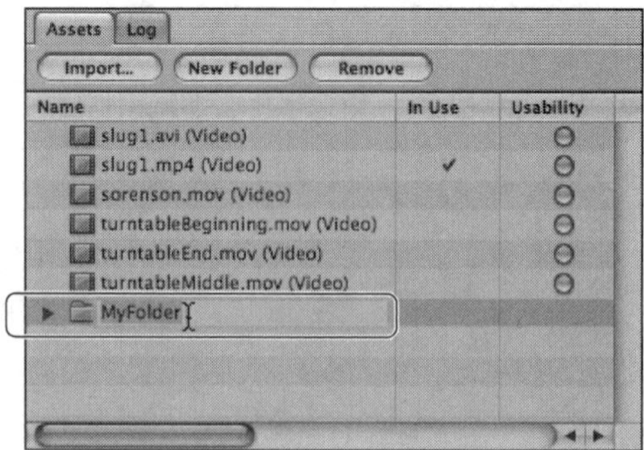

Figure 9.8 To rename a folder, click it once to select it; then press the Return key to open a text box in which you can type a name.

To reorder assets and folders on the Assets tab:

1. On the Assets tab, select an asset or folder and drag it up or down (**Figure 9.9**).

   A black indicator line shows you where the asset or folder will drop.
2. When the asset or folder is in the position you want, release the mouse button to drop it into place.

✔ Tip

- You can also follow the steps in this task to move assets into folders, folders into folders, and so on.

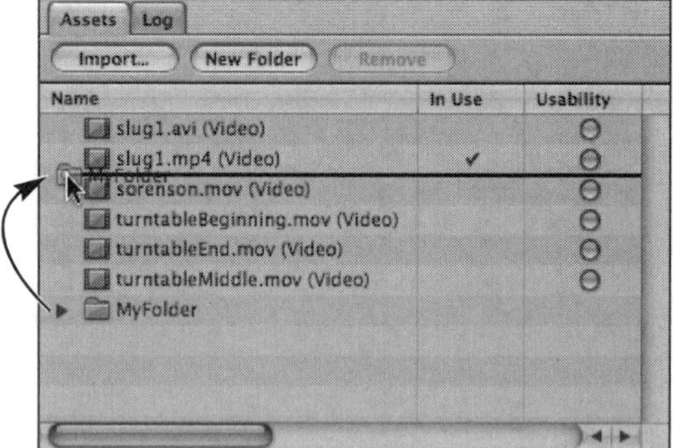

Figure 9.9 To change the position of an asset or folder on the Assets tab, select the item and drag it to its new home in the Asset list.

Column head   Sort arrow

	Size	Rate	Location
00	138.15 MB	30.00	/Users/martinsitter/
15	60.61 MB	30.00	/Users/martinsitter/
00	212.95 MB	29.97	/Users/martinsitter/
29	1.02 MB	29.97	/Users/martinsitter/
29	165.80 KB	29.97	/Users/martinsitter/
00	210.79 KB	14.99	/Users/martinsitter/

Figure 9.10 To sort assets on the Assets tab, click the column head representing the property by which you want to sort. A triangle appears at the right edge of the column to indicate that the column is controlling the way the assets are sorted.

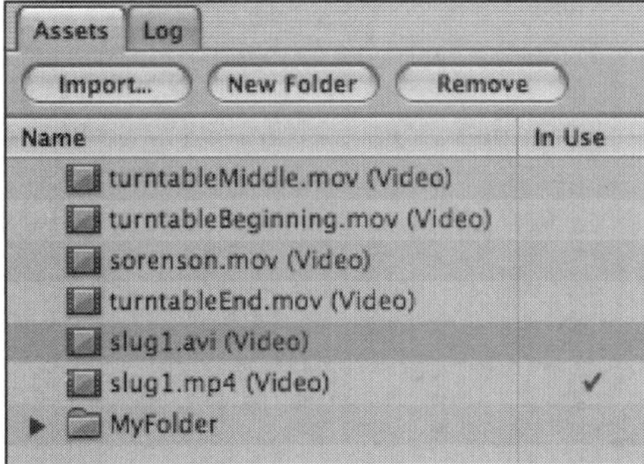

Figure 9.11 To remove an asset from the Assets tab, select the item in the Asset list and click the Remove button, or...

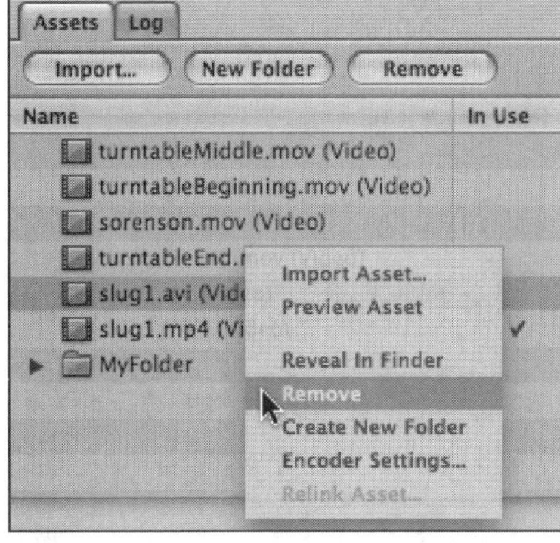

Figure 9.12 ...Control-click the asset and choose Remove.

To sort assets on the Assets tab:

1. In the Assets tab's Column Name area, click a column head to select the column on which you want to sort (**Figure 9.10**). (To learn more about columns, see the section "Working with Columns" later in this chapter.)

   A triangle appears at the right edge of the column you selected, and the assets are sorted. The way the assets are sorted depends on the column that you selected. If you click the Name column, for example, the assets are sorted alphabetically by name. Clicking the Size column sorts assets from smallest to largest, as determined by their file size.

2. To reverse the sort order, click the column head a second time.

✔ Tip

- The Assets tab's In Use column displays the assets that are currently used in your project. By clicking the In Use column header, you can quickly sort assets by those that are used and those that are not used in the project, which makes it easy to select and delete assets you don't need.

To remove an asset from the Assets tab:

1. In the Asset list, select an asset.
2. *Do one of the following:*
   - ▲ At the top of the Assets tab, click the Remove button (**Figure 9.11**).
   - ▲ Control-click the asset and choose Remove from the shortcut menu (**Figure 9.12**).
   - ▲ Press the Delete key.

Working with Columns

In all of DVD Studio Pro's default window configurations, the Assets tab is thin, and only a few columns are visible. You may be surprised to discover that the Assets tab is actually very wide, with up to 15 columns available. Each column provides information, such as asset type, bit depth, and whether or not the asset is currently used in the project. To see more than just a few of these informative columns, you can stretch the Assets tab, to make it wider.

To widen the Assets tab:

1. Position the pointer over the right edge of the Assets tab (**Figure 9.13**).

   The pointer turns into a double arrow.

2. Click the right edge of the Assets tab and drag it toward the right edge of the workspace.

   The Assets tab becomes wider, and several more columns come into view (**Figure 9.14**).

✔ Tip

- Don't forget: you can tear the Assets tab out of the workspace to view it in its own window. This really helps when you need to compare the properties of many assets at once, because you can make the Assets tab as large as necessary without changing the size of the workspace's other quadrants. If you're using more than one monitor, tearout tabs are a very cool feature, because you can expand DVD Studio Pro's workspace over multiple monitors.

Figure 9.13 To widen the Assets tab, select the right edge of the tab and drag it out.

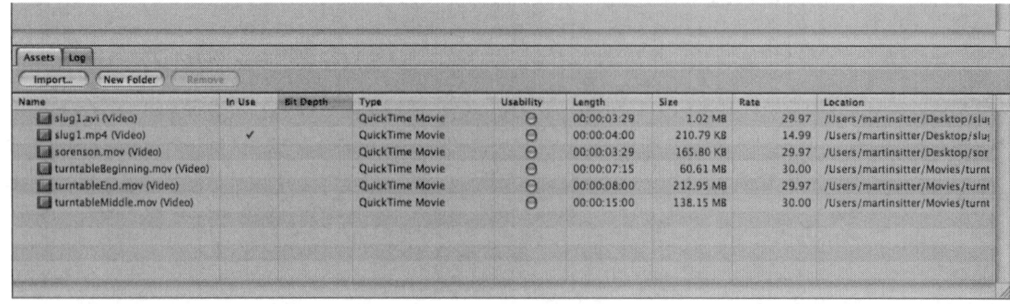

Figure 9.14 A wider Assets tab displays more columns and, thus, more information about the assets it contains. This view is particularly useful when you need to compare the properties of several assets at the same time.

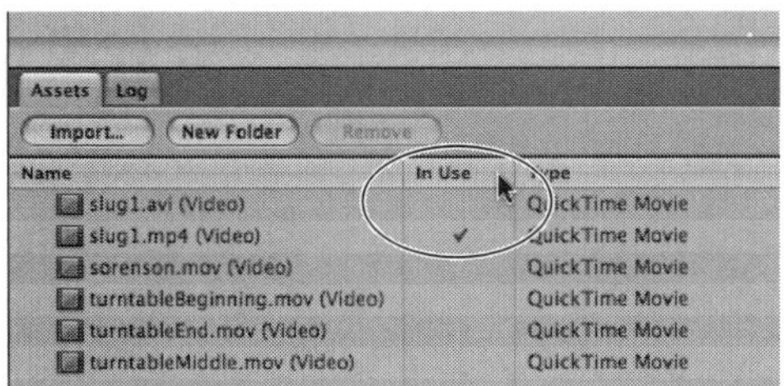

Figure 9.15 To display a new column on the Assets tab, begin by Control-clicking the Assets tab's Column Name area to the left of where you want the new column to appear.

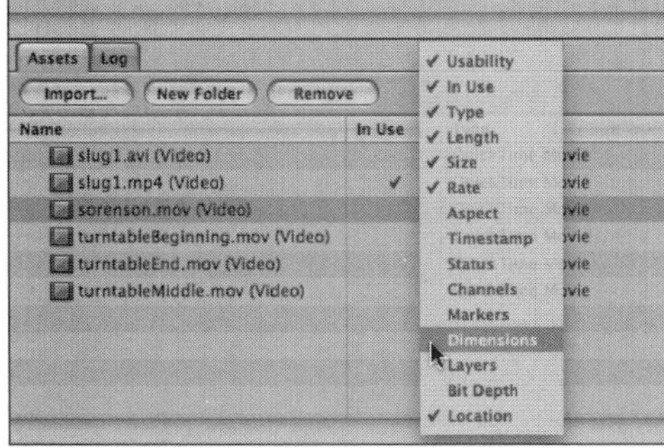

Figure 9.16 Control-clicking the Column Name area opens a menu listing the names of columns that you can add to the Assets tab.

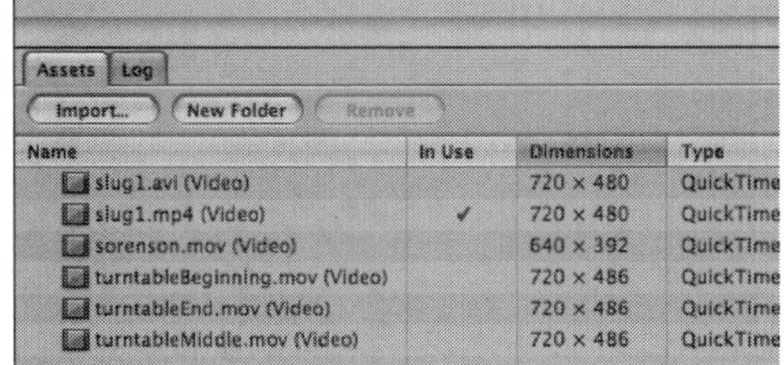

Figure 9.17 The added column appears on the Assets tab.

To display a hidden column:

1. In the Assets tab's Column Name area, position the pointer over the column to the left of where you want the new column to appear (**Figure 9.15**).

   New columns are always added to the right of the clicked column, so this is an important step.

2. Control-click the Column Name area.

   A shortcut menu appears (**Figure 9.16**). This menu lists the names of all columns available to the Assets tab. Checked columns are currently displayed on the Assets tab; unchecked columns are not.

3. Choose the name of the column that you want to see on the Assets tab.

   The column appears (**Figure 9.17**).

To reorder columns:

1. In the Assets tab's Column Name area, position the pointer over the name of the column that you want to reorder.

2. Drag the column left or right (**Figure 9.18**).

   As you drag, the other columns shift left or right to make room for the moved column.

3. When the column is in the correct position, release the mouse to drop the column into place.

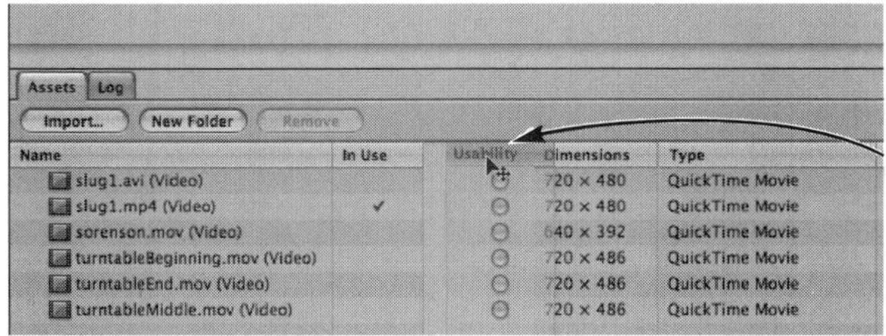

Figure 9.18 To reposition a column on the Assets tab, select the column head and drag it left or right.

To change the width of a column:

1. In the Asset tab's Column Name area, position the pointer at the column's right edge (**Figure 9.19**).

   The pointer turns into a double-arrow.

2. Select the column edge and drag it to the right or left to make the column wider or narrower.

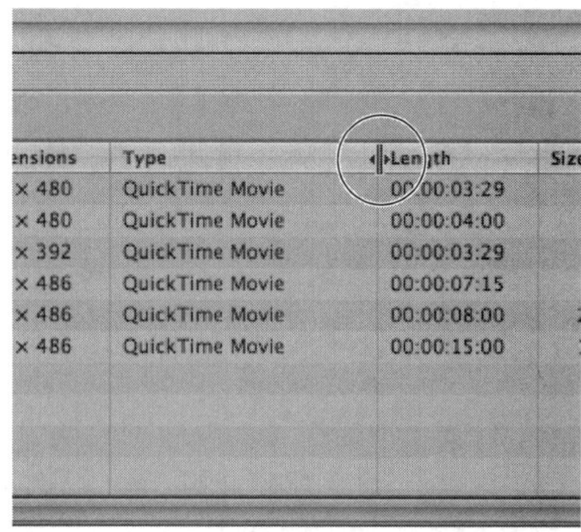

Figure 9.19 To change the width of a column, in the Column Name area, grab the column's right edge and drag it either left or right.

Tricks with Asset Container Columns

There are a few things to keep in mind when working with Assets tab columns:

- The order of columns on the Assets tab is stored with the window configuration.
- Often, Assets tab columns are much wider than they need to be. To conserve screen real estate on the Assets tab, drag the right edge of each column to the left to make the column thinner. For example, in the Status column, you're interested in seeing only the status indicator, so make the column thin (**Figure 9.20**). Similarly, you can condense the In Use column until the name in the column head just says "In."

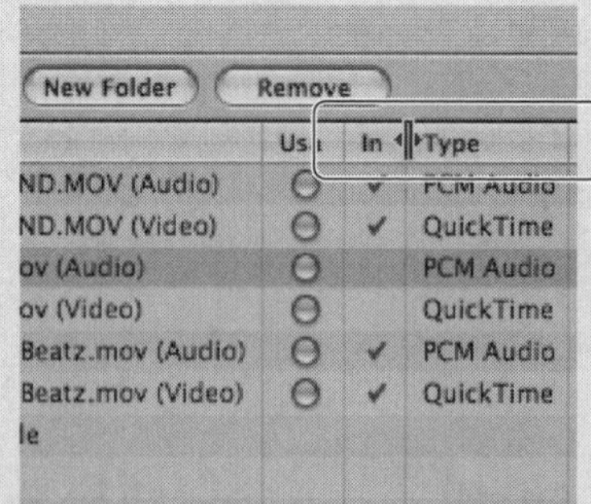

Figure 9.20 To conserve screen real estate on the Assets tab, make its columns as thin as possible.

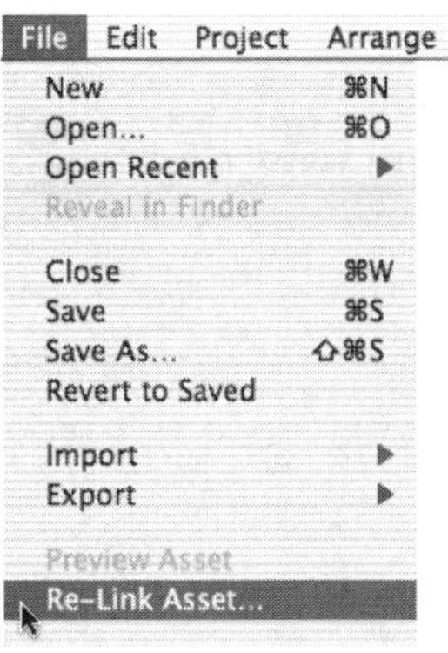

Figure 9.21 To relink an asset to its source media file, select the asset on the Assets tab and then choose File > Re-Link Asset, or...

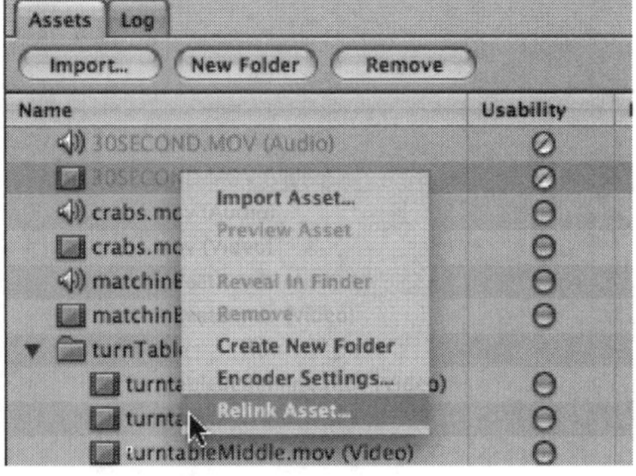

Figure 9.22 ...on the Assets tab, Control-click the asset and choose Relink Asset.

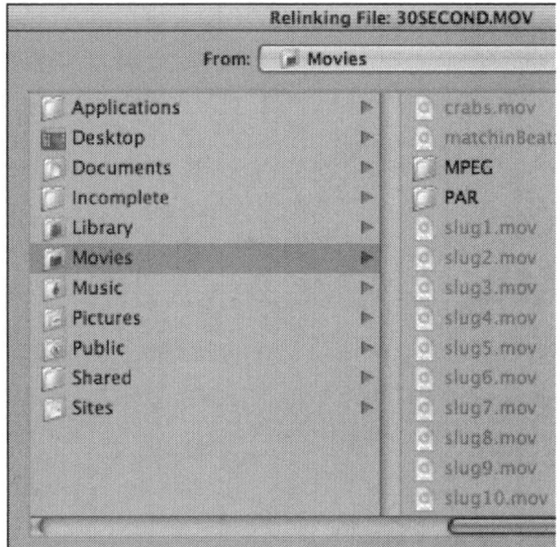

Figure 9.23 The Relinking File dialog takes you to the missing asset.

Relinking Assets

As mentioned earlier, DVD Studio Pro locates assets by following a link or pointer that shows DVD Studio Pro where the asset is on your hard disks. If you add an asset to your project but later move or rename that asset on the hard disks, this link is broken, and DVD Studio Pro will not be able to locate the asset. In this situation, the asset's name appears in red in the Asset list to indicate that DVD Studio Pro can't locate the asset's source media file. You'll have to relink the asset before you can use it in your project.

To relink an asset:

1. On the Assets tab, select the asset that you need to relink (the asset's name will appear in red to indicate that DVD Studio Pro can't locate the asset's source media file).
2. *Do one of the following:*
   - ▲ Choose File > Re-Link Asset (**Figure 9.21**).
   - ▲ Control-click the asset and choose Relink Asset (**Figure 9.22**).

   The Relinking File dialog opens (**Figure 9.23**).
3. In the Relinking File dialog, locate the missing asset.
4. Click the Relink button.

   DVD Studio Pro relinks the asset to its source media file.

Previewing Assets

DVD Studio Pro projects can be complex, using dozens of assets that are combined to create the final DVD-Video. With all this media to manage, you'll be forgiven if you occasionally forget what type of content some of those assets contain. This problem is made worse if you haven't named your assets to reflect their content. So from time to time, you may need to preview an asset to see exactly what it is.

Previewing in the Inspector

In Chapter 7, "Touring the Workspace," you saw that the Inspector updates to show you the unique properties of any item selected in the workspace. As you might expect, if you select an asset on the Assets tab, the Inspector updates to show you the asset's properties.

Using the Inspector, you can check such details as the asset's format, frame rate, and length. There's even a small preview area (called the Browse Asset area) at the bottom of the Inspector that lets you see graphically what the asset contains.

✔ Tip

- The Browse Asset area displays only graphical assets such as images and video; audio assets must be previewed in a different way, as you'll see in the next section, "Previewing in the Viewer."

To preview assets in the Inspector:

1. On the Assets tab, select an asset.

   The Inspector updates to show the selected asset's properties (**Figure 9.24**). For graphical assets such as images and video, a Browse Asset area appears at the bottom of the Inspector.

2. Use the Browse Asset area to preview the asset.

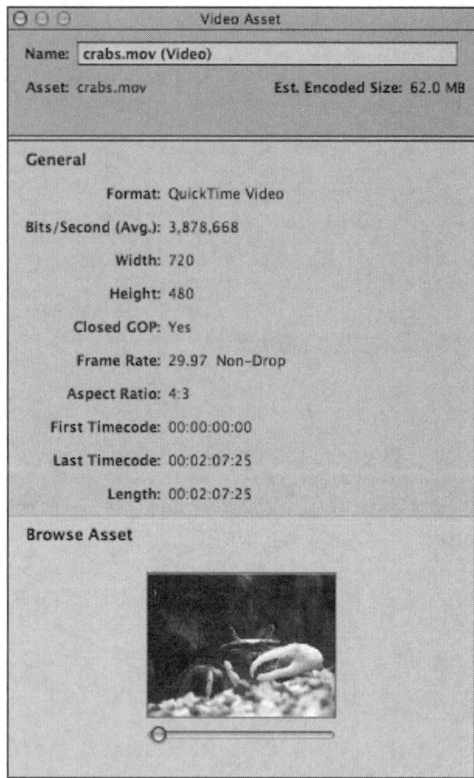

Figure 9.24 If you select an asset on the Assets tab, the Inspector updates to show the asset's properties. At the bottom of the Inspector is a Browse Asset area that you can use to preview the asset's content.

Figure 9.25 For video files, a slider appears in the Browse Asset area. Use this slider to scroll through the video.

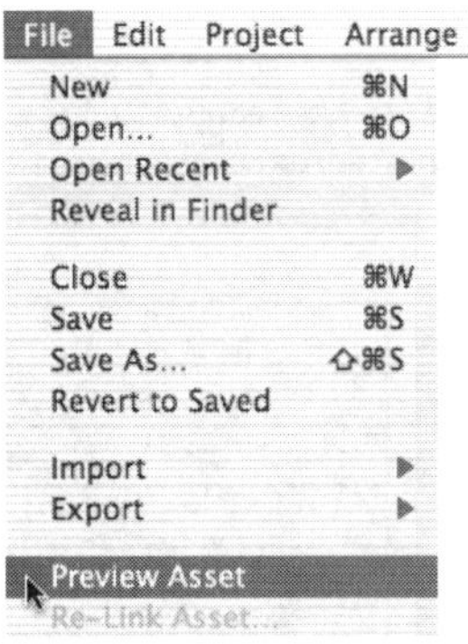

Figure 9.26 To preview an asset, select it in the Asset list and then choose File > Preview Asset, or...

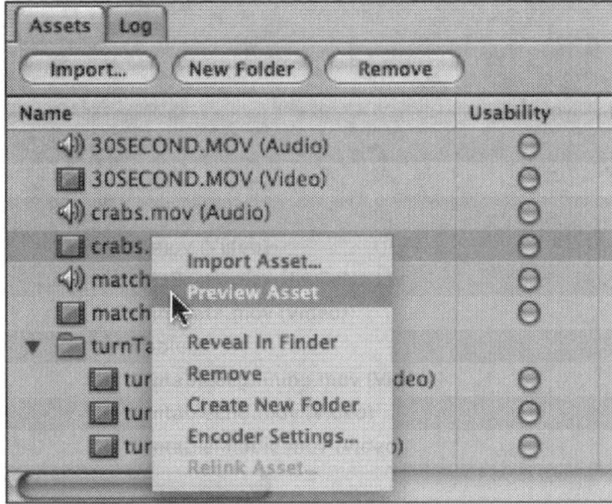

Figure 9.27 ...Control-click the asset and choose Preview Asset.

If you are previewing a video asset, a slider appears in the Browse Asset area (**Figure 9.25**). Use this slider to scroll through the video.

Previewing in the Viewer

The Inspector provides a good quick preview of an asset. But if you want to play a video asset or audition an audio asset, you need to preview it in the Viewer.

To preview assets in the Viewer:

1. On the Assets tab, select an asset.
2. *Do one of the following:*
   - ▲ Choose File > Preview Asset (**Figure 9.26**).
   - ▲ Control-click the asset and choose Preview Asset from the resulting menu (**Figure 9.27**).
   - ▲ On the Assets tab, double-click the selected asset.
   - ▲ Press the spacebar.

continues on next page

The Viewer jumps to the surface of its quadrant and begins playing the asset. For video assets, the video plays in the Viewer (**Figure 9.28**), but if the video has an associated audio file, that audio file *does not* play. To hear the audio asset, you must preview it separately (**Figure 9.29**).

3. At the bottom of the Viewer, use the playback buttons to start and stop previewing.

✔ Tip

- QuickTime assets preview in their native format in the Viewer. If you want to see the MPEG-encoded version of the asset (for example, to see the quality of compression applied by DVD Studio Pro's background MPEG encoding), you must add the asset to a track first and then preview the track.

Figure 9.28 When you preview an asset, the asset plays in the Viewer. Use the playback controls at the bottom of the Viewer to start and stop playback.

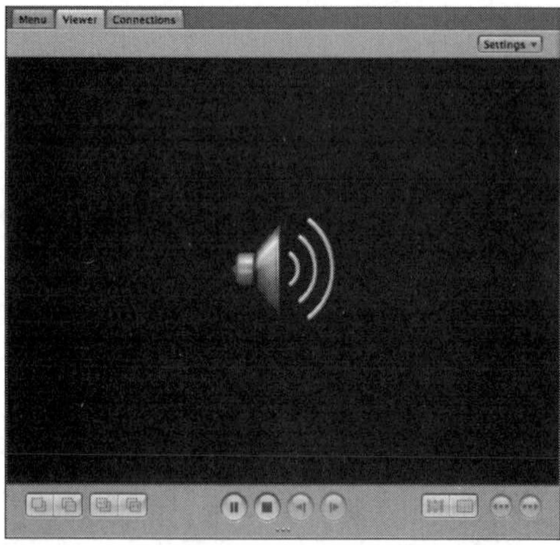

Figure 9.29 An audio asset preview in the Viewer.

10

Importing Assets

Assets for DVD Studio Pro fall into two categories: DVD-compliant, and non–DVD-compliant. DVD-compliant assets include MPEG-1 and MPEG-2 video streams, Dolby Digital AC-3 files, MPEG 1 Layer-2 audio streams, and any other file format that is part of the DVD-Video specification and can be used directly in a DVD-Video without needing to be encoded first. Everything else—including QuickTime movies, MP3 audio, TIFFS, JPEGs, and more or less any other type of media that QuickTime understands—can be considered non–DVD-compliant. The key words here are "media that QuickTime understands," because with DVD Studio Pro 3, if QuickTime can recognize the file, you can import it into your project. DVD Studio Pro will need to encode the file to a usable format before building the final DVD, but even so, there are very few limitations on the types of media files you can use with DVD Studio Pro 3.

This ability to directly import QuickTime movies is a great workflow feature because you can skip the step of encoding your assets before authoring—when you import a QuickTime movie into your project, DVD Studio Pro converts the movie for you. The process isn't entirely hands-off—there are a few tricks you'll need to master, such as setting the background encoding options and telling DVD Studio Pro where it should store the converted files on your hard disk.

Importing Assets

Before you can use an asset, you must import it to DVD Studio Pro's Assets tab, also called the Assets container. There are many ways to do this, such as using DVD Studio Pro's File > Import > Asset function and even just dragging a file (or a folder filled with usable media files) directly from the Finder onto the Assets tab. To speed you on your way, this section provides an overview of the import process.

To import individual assets to the Assets tab:

1. Open the Import Asset window by *doing one of the following:*
   - ▲ Choose File > Import > Asset (**Figure 10.1**).
   - ▲ On the Assets tab, click the Import button (**Figure 10.2**).
   - ▲ Control-click anywhere on the Assets tab to open a shortcut menu; then choose Import Asset (**Figure 10.3**).
2. In the Import Asset window, navigate to and select the asset you want to import (**Figure 10.4**).

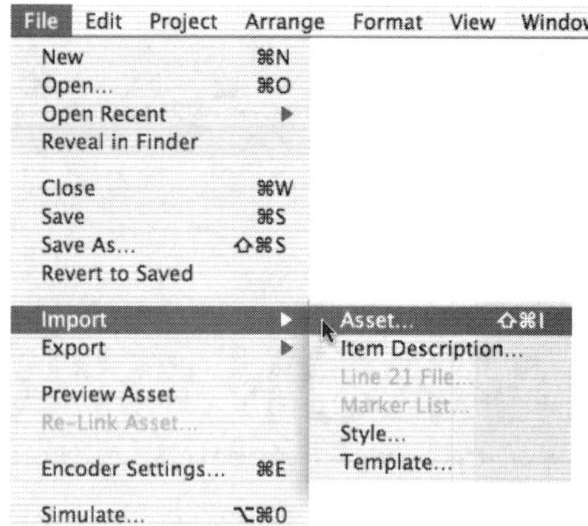

Figure 10.1 To import assets into DVD Studio Pro, choose File > Import > Asset, or...

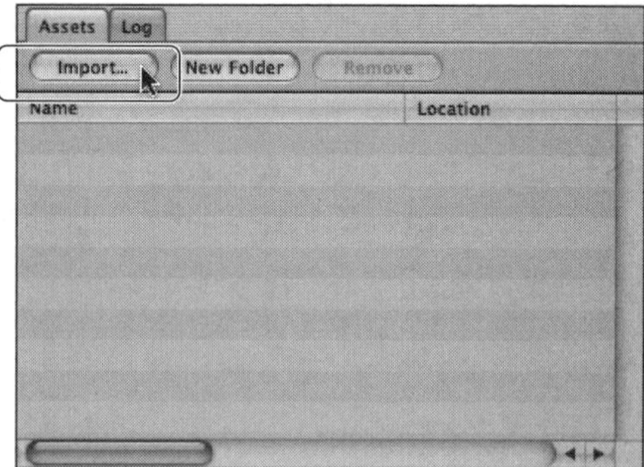

Figure 10.2 ...click the Assets tab's Import button, or...

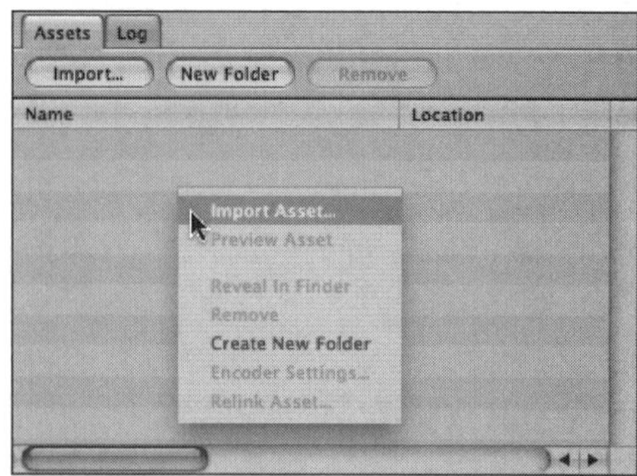

Figure 10.3 ...Control-click anywhere on the Assets tab; then, in the shortcut menu that opens, choose Import Asset to add media files to your project.

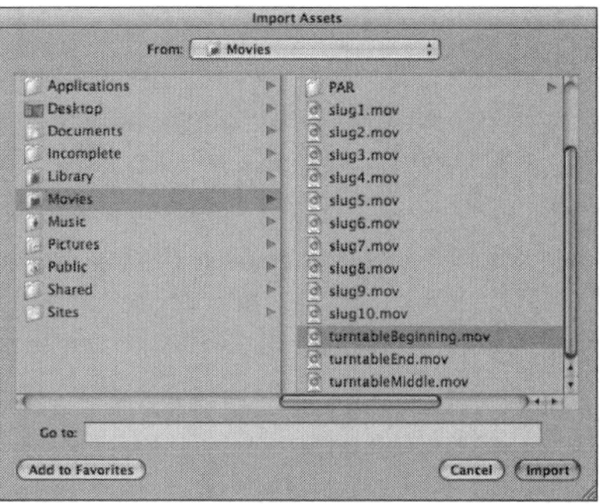

Figure 10.4 Use the Import Assets dialog to locate and import assets from your hard disk.

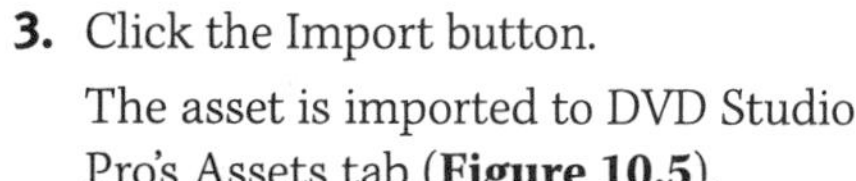

3. Click the Import button.

   The asset is imported to DVD Studio Pro's Assets tab (**Figure 10.5**).

✔ Tips

- To import an asset directly into a folder on the Assets tab, select the folder before initiating the preceding steps. If you don't select a folder, the asset will be imported to the root level of the Assets tab.
- If you double-click a folder on the Assets tab, the Import Asset dialog will open to let you import an asset directly into the folder.
- You can use the Import Assets dialog to import multiple assets at once. To import noncontiguous assets (not side by side in the folder hierarchy), hold down the Command key and select more than one asset in the Import Assets dialog. To import contiguous assets (all in a row), hold down the Shift key as you select assets (**Figure 10.6**).

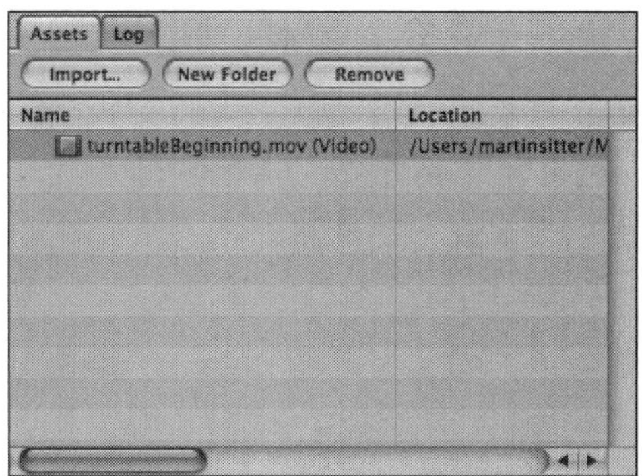

Figure 10.5 All assets are imported to DVD Studio Pro's Assets tab.

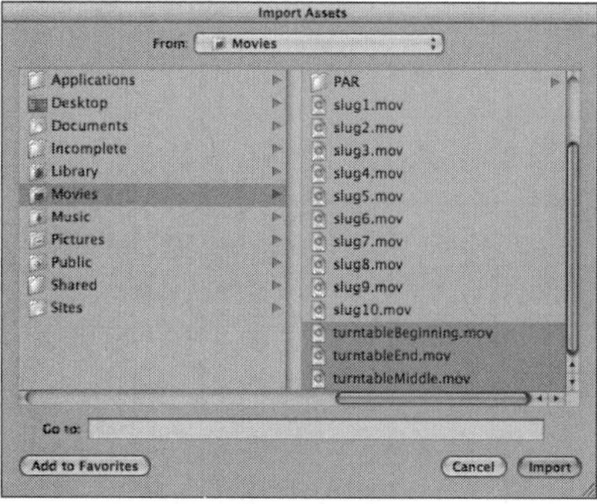

Figure 10.6 Hold down the Shift or Command key to select multiple assets in the Import Assets dialog. Holding down Shift allows you to import contiguous, or sequential, assets; holding down Command lets you choose assets that are noncontiguous, or not side by side.

Importing Folders into DVD Studio Pro

DVD Studio Pro 3 lets you import folders directly to the Assets tab, which means that instead of importing each asset individually, you can simply select a folder that contains many assets and import the entire folder all at once.

If the folder has subfolders inside, DVD Studio Pro will maintain the folder hierarchy on the Assets tab. For example, if you have a master folder named MyProject that contains subfolders holding MPEG-2, AC-3, and menu files, each subfolder will show up on the Assets tab, leaving your folder structure intact, as shown in **Figure 10.7**.

To import a folder, follow exactly the same process as when you import an individual asset, except select a folder instead of a media file. DVD Studio Pro will import the entire folder, along with any assets in the folder that DVD Studio Pro can use. If the folder contains files that DVD Studio Pro cannot recognize, such as log files for MPEG encoding, the dialog in **Figure 10.8** appears, letting you know that some of the files will not be imported.

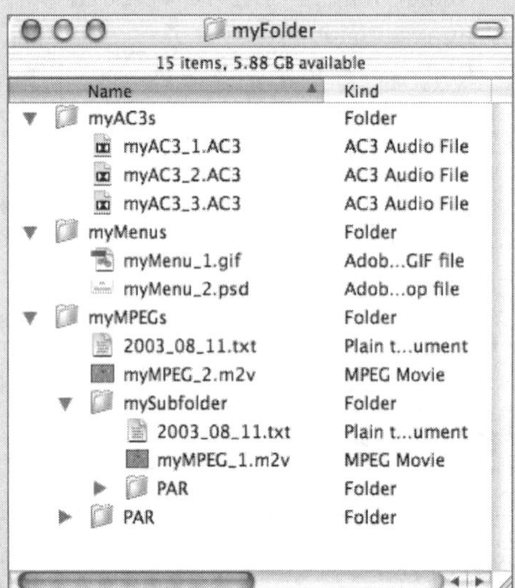

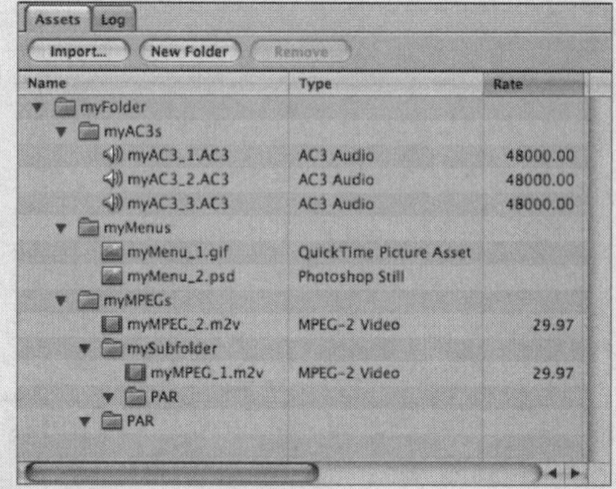

Figure 10.7 The Finder window on the left side of this figure shows a folder (named myFolder) that contains several subfolders storing assets for a DVD-Video project. The window on the right side of this figure shows the same folder after it has been imported to DVD Studio Pro's Assets tab.

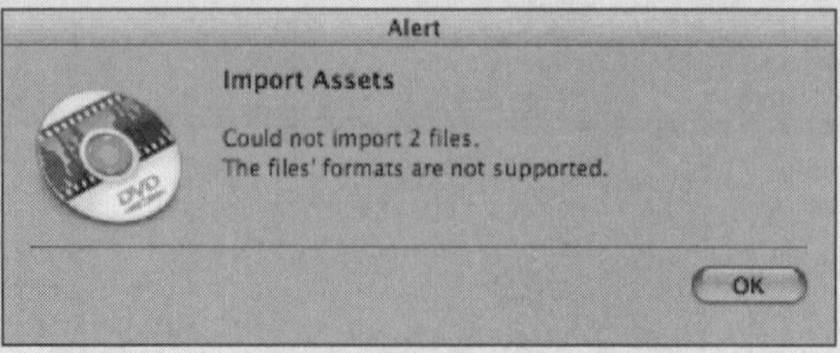

Figure 10.8 If a folder contains files that DVD Studio Pro does not understand, this dialog appears.

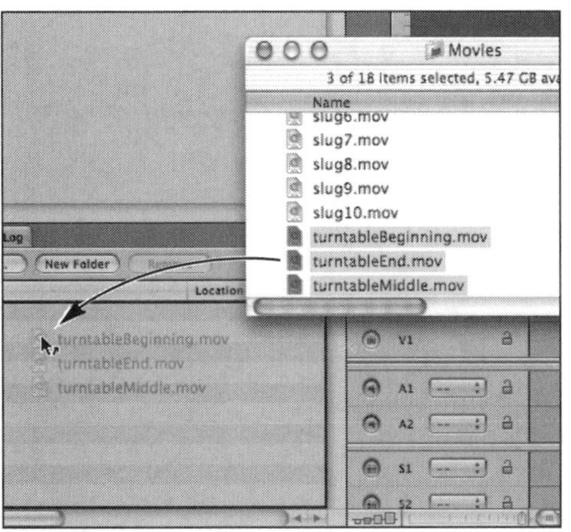

Figure 10.9 Dragging assets from a Finder window directly onto DVD Studio Pro's Assets tab is a quick way to add assets to your project.

To drag assets onto the Assets tab:

1. In the Finder, select one or more source media files. (If you want to add more than one source file, hold down the Command key while selecting multiple files in the Finder window.)
2. Drag the files directly onto the Assets tab and then release the mouse (**Figure 10.9**).

✔ Tip

- You can also drag folders directly from the Finder onto the Assets tab.

Asset File Management

DVD-Video projects can get very complex and may use several dozen—or even several hundred—source files. Before you begin authoring, gather all of your source files in one folder, with each file placed in an appropriately named subdirectory, as shown in **Figure 10.10**. This keeps all source media organized and in a place where you can easily find them. Additionally, keeping source media organized saves innumerable headaches when it comes time to archive your project, and makes it easy to delete all of the source files when you've finished authoring and want to clean up your hard disks.

And here's a great feature: you can just drag the root folder directly onto the Assets tab to quickly import all of the media needed to create the project!

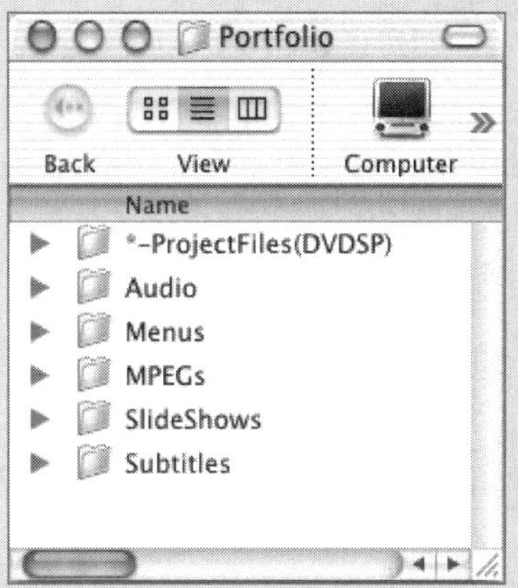

Figure 10.10 Keep all of your source media well organized! This figure shows a folder hierarchy that has one separate folder for each type of source file used in a DVD-Video project (including a folder for the project files themselves).

Importing QuickTime Movies

DVD Studio Pro 3 uses the QuickTime MPEG-2 Encoder to encode standard QuickTime Movies—you don't need to visit Compressor or QuickTime Pro Player first. For example, you can import QuickTime movies directly into DVD Studio Pro, and the QuickTime MPEG-2 Exporter will activate automatically to encode the video while you author the DVD. As a bonus, DVD Studio Pro lets you import any video format QuickTime understands, including AVI, Sorenson 3, and even MPEG-4.

Setting internal encoding options

DVD Studio Pro uses the QuickTime MPEG-2 Exporter to encode QuickTime movies, and all of the options available to the QuickTime MPEG-2 Exporter are available to internal encoding in DVD Studio Pro. If you are not familiar with these options, see Chapter 4, "The QuickTime MPEG-2 Exporter," to learn everything you need to know.

If you're ready to proceed, then it's time to open DVD Studio Pro's Preferences window. The reason? All MPEG-2 encoding options are contained there. Let's take a look around.

Encoding icon

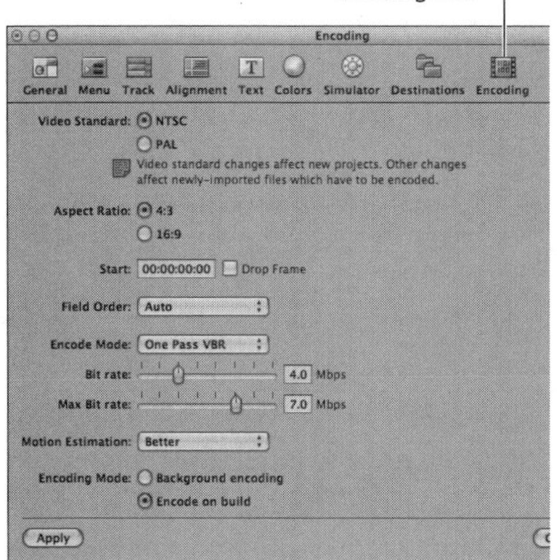

Figure 10.11 The Encoding section of the Preferences window contains all of the settings DVD Studio Pro uses to internally encode MPEG-2 video streams.

To set DVD Studio Pro's internal MPEG-2 encoding options:

1. Choose DVD Studio Pro > Preferences, or press Command-, (comma), to open the Preferences window.

   Along the top of the Preferences window is a bar that lists icons representing groups of preferences.

2. At the upper right of the Preferences window, click the Encoding icon, which displays the Encoding section of the Preferences window (**Figure 10.11**).

   DVD Studio Pro's internal encoding options are displayed in the Encoding section of the Preferences window.

3. Set the encoding preferences.

   The settings contained in the Encoding section of the Preferences window are exactly the same as the settings available to the QuickTime MPEG-2 Exporter. For a detailed explanation of these settings, refer to Chapter 4.

4. At the bottom right of the Encoding section of the Preferences window, click the OK button.

   The Preferences window closes. All QuickTime movies imported into DVD Studio Pro 3 will be encoded using the settings you've just specified.

Setting encoding options for individual movies

The encoding options assigned in DVD Studio Pro's Preferences window are global, which means they are automatically applied to each QuickTime movie imported into your project. From time to time, however, you may have a movie that needs some special attention and does not look right using the global settings applied in the Preferences window. For example, you may have a movie with a lot of motion which thus requires a higher bit rate than your project's other movies to maintain its visual quality. You can set the encoding options for individual QuickTime movies using the following trick.

To set the encoding options for individual QuickTime movies:

1. On the Assets tab, Control-click the movie whose encoding settings you want to change.

   A shortcut menu appears.

2. From the shortcut menu, choose Encoder Settings (**Figure 10.12**).

   The Encoder Settings window appears (**Figure 10.13**).

3. In the Encoder Settings window, set the encoding options required for the movie.

4. Click the OK button.

   The Encoder Settings window closes, and the movie is now encoded with the new encoder settings.

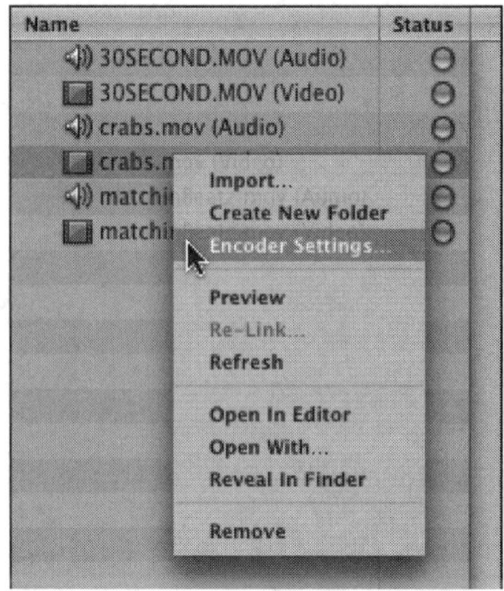

Figure 10.12 To set the encoding options for an individual QuickTime movie, Control-click it on the Assets tab and choose Encoder Settings from the shortcut menu that appears.

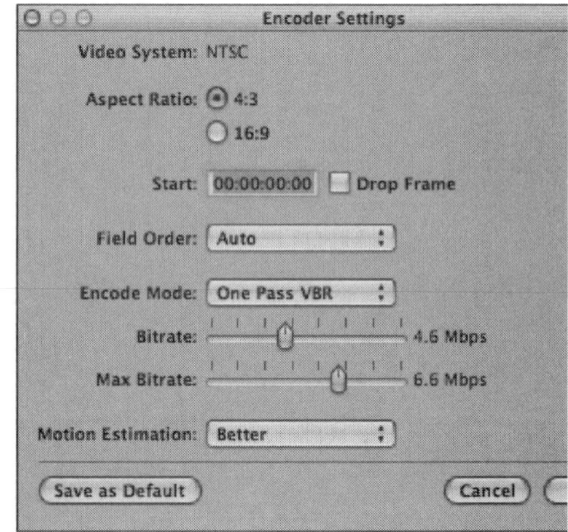

Figure 10.13 The Encoder Settings window lets you set the encoding options for individual QuickTime movies on the Assets tab.

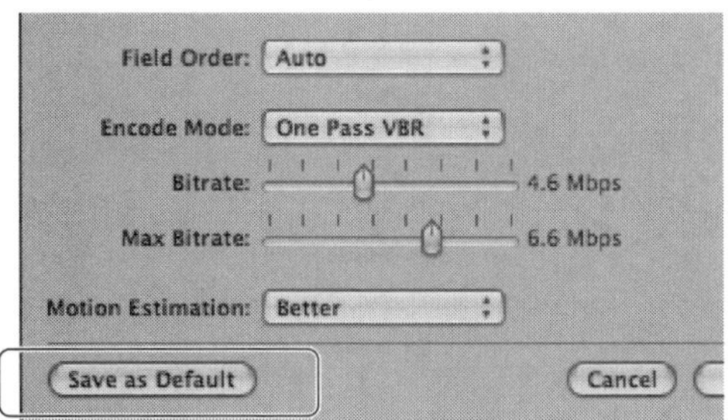

Figure 10.14 Click the Encoder Settings window's Save as Default button to update DVD Studio Pro's preferences with the new encoder settings. All new QuickTime movies will then be encoded with these new encoder settings.

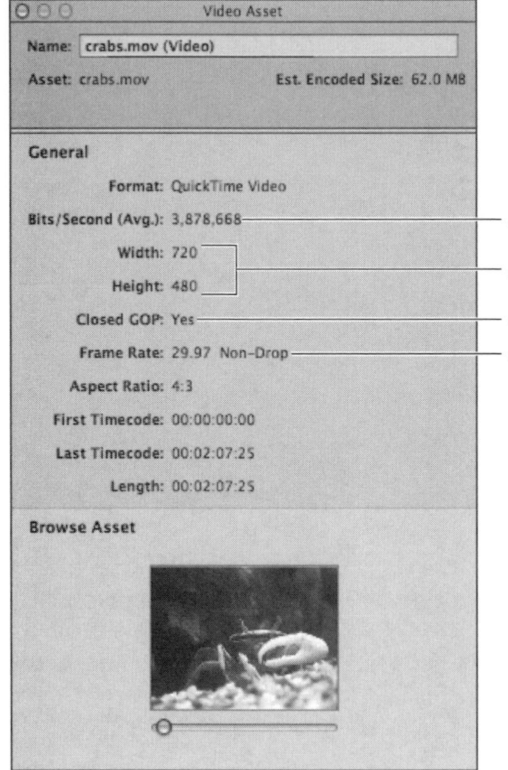

Figure 10.15 If you select an MPEG-2 steam on the Assets tab, the Inspector updates to show you information about how that stream was encoded.

✔ Tips

- If you want to apply the new settings to all new QuickTime movies imported into your project, click the Encoder Settings window's Save as Default button (**Figure 10.14**). This button updates DVD Studio Pro's Preferences window with the new encoder settings.
- To see how an individual MPEG-2 video was encoded, select the movie on the Assets tab and look at the Inspector (**Figure 10.15**). There you'll find information about how the video was encoded, including the movie's bit rate, frame rate, dimensions, and whether or not it uses open or closed groups of pictures (GOPs).
- You can also open the Encoder Settings window by selecting an asset on the Assets tab and choosing File > Encoder Settings.

Background encoding versus encoding on build

At the bottom of the Encoding section of the Preferences window is a setting called Encoding Mode (**Figure 10.16**). This setting lets you choose whether DVD Studio Pro encodes QuickTime movies in the background as you author or when you build the project. There are advantages to both settings.

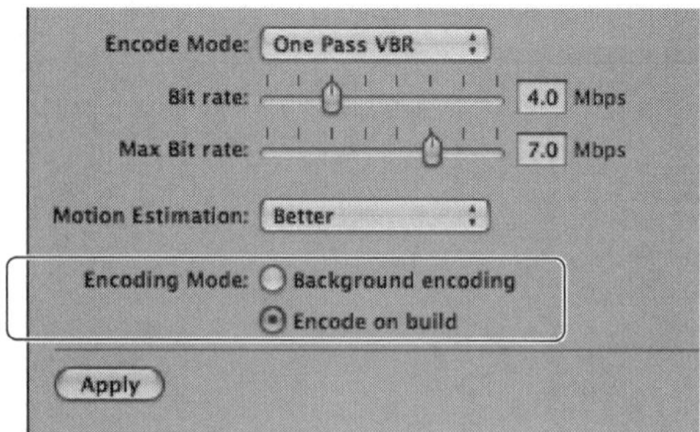

Figure 10.16 The Encoding Mode preferences tell DVD Studio Pro either to encode video in the background as you author the DVD or to wait until you build the project to encode the MPEG-2 streams.

- **Background Encoding.** Use the Background Encoding option when you're working on a small project with short video streams. Background encoding uses as much CPU power as is currently available, so it's *not* recommended if you're using Final Cut Pro, Photoshop, or Logic Pro while authoring in DVD Studio Pro. Also, if your MPEG streams are long (say, half an hour or more) and you've set DVD Studio Pro's background encoder to the highest possible settings, background encoding becomes inefficient. The reason? Often, it takes hours for the QuickTime MPEG-2 Exporter to encode long video streams, but will you spend hours authoring the DVD-Video? Probably not, which means that you'd finish authoring before the encoder finishes encoding.
- **Encode on Build.** The Encode on Build option is best used for long MPEG streams or for projects in which you're using multiple applications at the same time. For example, it's quite common to composite motion menus at the same time as you author the DVD-Video. In this case, you want to reserve as much CPU power as possible for Final Cut Pro and Photoshop, so it makes sense to turn off background encoding. The disadvantage to using the Encode on Build option is that it takes a *long* time to build your project. DVD Studio Pro must first encode all video used in the project and

Monitoring CPU Load

Mac OS X has a great utility for monitoring how hard your central processing unit (CPU) is working: the Activity Monitor. If you're using DVD Studio Pro's internal encoding, it's a good idea to open the Activity Monitor so you can watch your CPU work. The Activity Monitor is located on your Startup disk: choose Applications/Utilities/Activity Monitor.

then build the project. Depending on the encoding settings used, an hour or more of video can take five or six hours to encode! That's a long build.

✔ Tip

- In general, it's best to use QuickTime or even Compressor to encode your video streams before bringing them into DVD Studio Pro. This makes the authoring process more efficient and much quicker.

To set the encoding mode:

- ◆ In the Encoding Mode area of the Encoding section of the Preferences window, choose either Background Encoding or Encode on Build (refer to Figure 10.16).

Understanding the Assets Tab's Status Column

The Assets tab's Status column indicates an asset's encoding status inside DVD Studio Pro (**Figure 10.17**). If background encoding is enabled in DVD Studio Pro's Preferences window, all video (except for MPEG-2 streams) and audio assets will have a colored-dot indicator in the Status column. This indicator will be one of two colors:

- ◆ **Yellow.** The asset has been parsed but has not been encoded in a DVD-compliant format. Nonetheless, now you can add the asset to the project.
- ◆ **Green.** The asset has been parsed and encoded in a DVD-compliant format. This light also serves as a visual cue to remind you that the asset was originally a QuickTime movie and can be re-encoded if needed (imported MPEG-2 streams do not have a status indicator, because they are always usable, right from the start).

Figure 10.17 The Assets tab's Status column displays a yellow indicator for assets that are parsed but not yet encoded and a green indicator for assets that are parsed and encoded.

Setting the encoding location

DVD Studio Pro needs to know where to place encoded MPEG-2 files; specify this location in the Preferences window's Destinations section (**Figure 10.18**). You can instruct DVD Studio Pro to store your files in three places: in the same folder as the asset, in the project bundle, or in a specified location or fallback folder.

Same Folder as the Asset. This is the default setting, and it places the encoded MPEG file in a subfolder called MPEG within the same folder as the original file on your hard disk. If the original files are on a volume that can't be written to, such as a CD-ROM or a mounted disc image, DVD Studio Pro automatically writes the encoded file to the specified folder or fallback folder location.

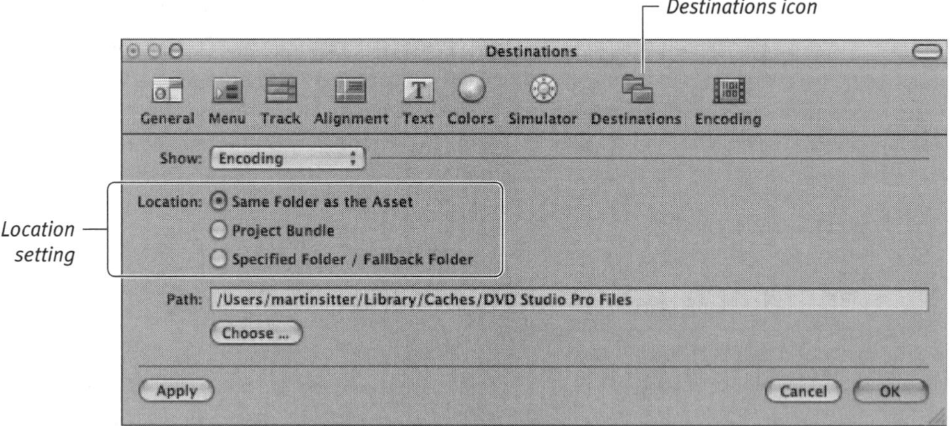

Figure 10.18 The Destinations section of the Preferences window lets you specify where encoded assets are stored.

Importing Audio Assets

DVD Studio Pro 3 enables you to import any audio file that QuickTime understands, including 44.1 kHz audio ripped from a CD-Audio disc, MP3s downloaded from the Internet, and AppleLoops (the native file format for Apple's Soundtrack loop utility). When you import a non-DVD-compliant audio file into DVD Studio Pro, the QuickTime MPEG-2 Exporter automatically fires up in the background and converts the audio file to a 48 kHz (sampling rate), 16-bit (bit depth) AIFF file that's ready for use in your project. (To learn more about sampling rate and bit depth, see Chapter 6, "Using A.Pack.")

By default, DVD Studio Pro 3 automatically places all converted audio files in a sub-folder named MPEG, located in the same folder as the source audio asset. You can, however, change this default location by visiting the Preferences window's Destinations section and choosing a new location for your encoded assets. To learn more, see "Setting the encoding location."

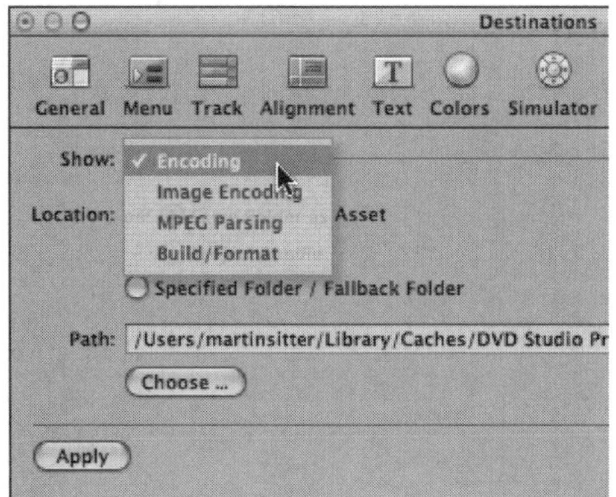

Figure 10.19 To specify where encoded MPEG files are stored, open the Show menu and choose Encoding.

Project Bundle. This setting saves the files within the project file itself. (If you have not saved your project yet, the files are saved at your specified folder or fallback folder location.) This is a great setting to use if you want to keep your projects self-contained, which in turn makes them very easy to transport from computer to computer—just grab the project file and go! But keep in mind that this setting may result in very large project files.

Specified Folder/Fallback Folder. This setting saves the files to a disk and folder of your choosing. By default, it is also used when DVD Studio Pro is unable to write to the folder that the asset is stored in or to the project bundle location (for example, if your hard disk becomes full). The default path leads to your home folder at /Library/Caches/DVD Studio Pro Files, but you can easily change this default path if desired.

To set the encoding location:

1. Choose DVD Studio Pro > Preferences.

   The Preferences window opens.

2. At the top of the Preferences window, click the Destinations icon (refer to Figure 10.18)

   The Destinations section of the Preferences window is displayed.

3. From the Show menu, choose Encoding (**Figure 10.19**).

4. From the Destinations section's Location setting, select Same Folder as the Asset, Project Bundle, or Specified Folder/Fallback Folder (refer to Figure 10.18).

   All files encoded by DVD Studio Pro will now be placed in the specified location.

5. Click OK to close the Preferences window.

To set the fallback folder's location:

1. In the Location area of the Preferences window's Destinations section, choose Specified Folder/Fallback Folder.
2. *Do one of the following:*
   - ▲ Type a new path directly in the Path text box (**Figure 10.20**).
   - ▲ Click the Choose button (**Figure 10.21**).

   The Encoding Folder dialog opens (**Figure 10.22**).
3. In the Encoding Folder dialog, choose the folder in which you want DVD Studio Pro to place the encoded files.
4. At the bottom right of the Encoding Folder dialog, click the Choose button.

   The Encoding Folder dialog closes. DVD Studio Pro will now place all encoded files in the selected folder.

✔ Tip

- If you type a location directly in the Path text box, you should make sure there's already a folder in that location ready to accept your encoded files. However, if there is no folder matching the one you've typed into the Path text box, DVD Studio Pro will automatically create a new folder with the name you've entered.

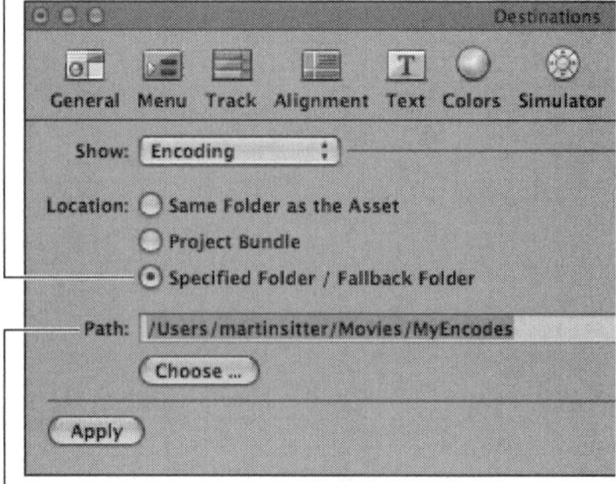

Figure 10.20 With Specified Folder/Fallback Folder selected in the Preferences window's Destinations section, you can either type a new path for your encoded files directly in the Path text box, or...

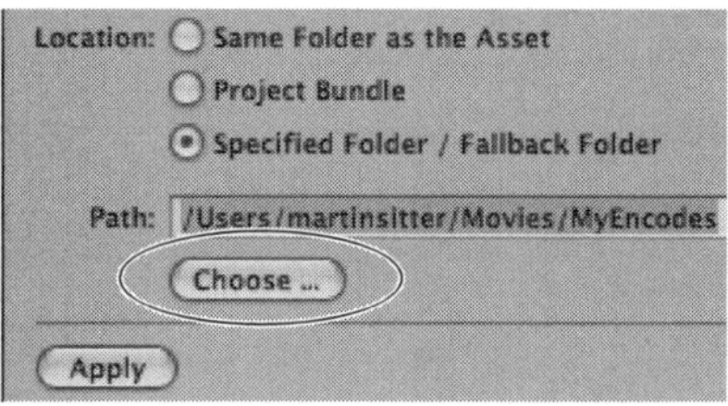

Figure 10.21 ...click the Choose button to select a folder on your hard disks.

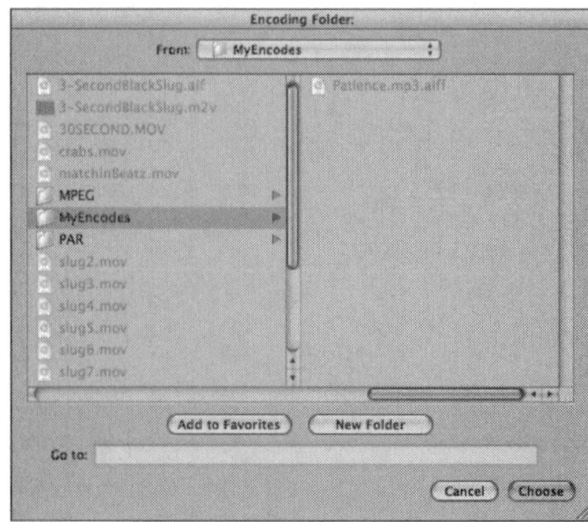

Figure 10.22 If you click the Choose button, the Encoding Folder dialog opens. Use this dialog to select the folder in which you want DVD Studio Pro to place the encoded files.

Exploring the Project Bundle

A DVD Studio Pro 3 project file is much more than meets the eye. In fact, it is no longer even called a "project file"; now it's a *project bundle*. With DVD Studio Pro 3, you can save various parts of your project right inside the project bundle itself. In the section "Setting the encoding location," for example, you saw that files encoded by DVD Studio Pro can be stored directly inside the project bundle. Project templates, styles, and shapes can also be stored there, as can audio assets and menu files.

The biggest advantage to storing media files directly in the project bundle is that you always know exactly where to find your media files when you need them. But, obviously, storing assets inside the project bundle will lead to project bundles with large file sizes, so it's a good idea to make sure you have enough space on the hard disk that contains the project bundle before you tell DVD Studio Pro to place encoded assets there.

If you want to open a project bundle and take a look around, just Control-click the project bundle and choose Show Package Contents (**Figure 10.23**). The project bundle will open, and inside the Contents/Resources folder you'll find several preconfigured subfolders that are ready to receive assets (**Figure 10.24**).

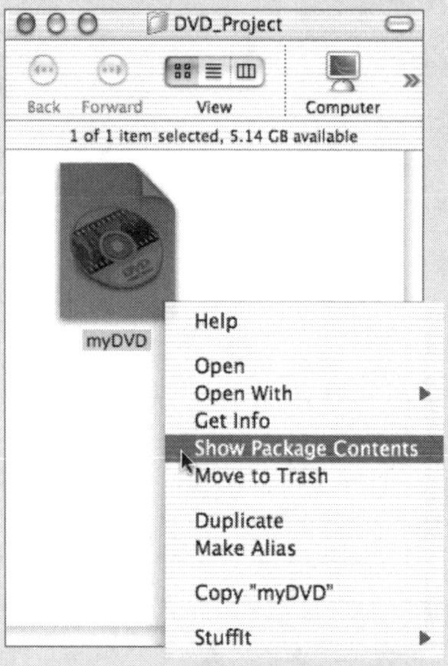

Figure 10.23 To open a project bundle, Control-click it and choose Show Package Contents.

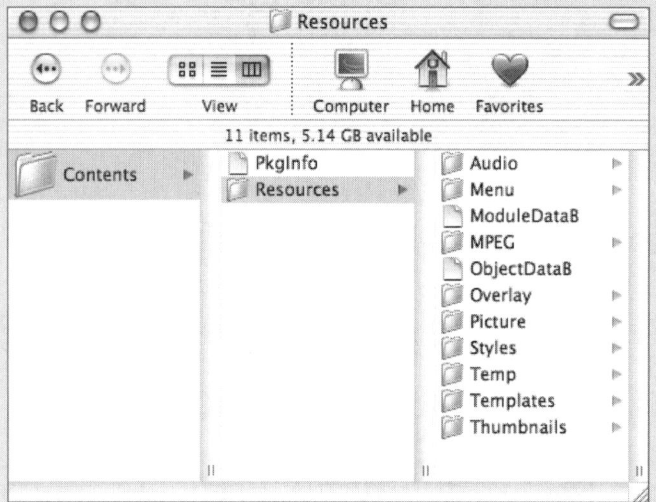

Figure 10.24 Inside the project bundle, the Contents/Resources folder holds several subfolders used to store project assets.

Using Tracks

Tracks are DVD Studio Pro's version of the ultimate storage container. Pretty much everything, from video and audio to subtitle streams, gets tucked away in a track. And unlike your cramped Victorian one-bedroom San Francisco apartment, DVD Studio Pro affords you ample storage space, allowing you to have up to 99 separate tracks per project. Each track can hold:

- 9 video streams (8 alternate angles and 1 main video stream)
- 8 audio streams
- 32 subtitle streams
- 99 chapter markers
- Up to 98 user-created stories

With all of those tracks, streams, markers, and stories crammed into one track, managing your media can get complex. Fortunately, with the introduction of DVD Studio Pro's timeline-based Track editor, it's now easier than ever to turn tracks into complex media displays that will keep your viewer interested and add extra value to your DVD-Videos.

About the Track Editor

Before getting into the nitty-gritty of how to create tracks, let's take a moment to look at DVD Studio Pro 3's timeline-based Track editor (**Figure 11.1**). The Track editor looks very similar to the timeline in Final Cut Pro or Final Cut Express, and indeed, it functions in much the same way. Media in the Track editor is organized in *streams*, with video streams located at the top of the editor, audio streams in the middle, and subtitle streams at the bottom. The streams themselves are used to organize individual video, audio, and subtitle assets—called *clips*—into a single unit called a *track*.

Across the bottom of the Track editor, you'll find the Stream Height presets, zoom slider, and scroll bar. The Stream Height presets enable you to increase or decrease the height of the Track editor's streams, so you can see more or fewer streams in the editor, depending on your authoring needs. The zoom slider controls the streams' horizontal display so you can see more or fewer clips in each Track editor stream, and the scroll bar lets you move back and forth across the Track editor when you're zoomed in on its clips.

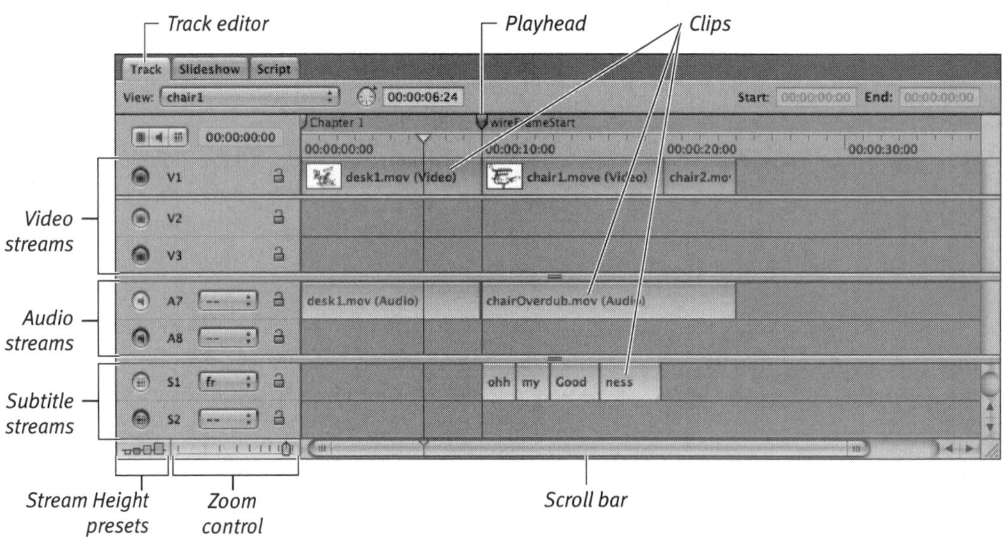

Figure 11.1 DVD Studio Pro 3's Track editor.

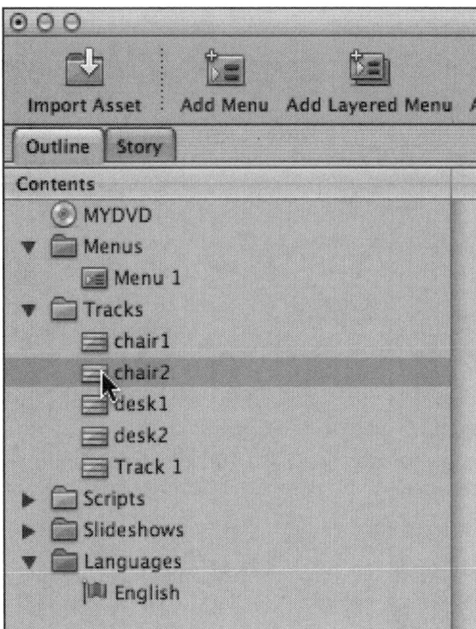

Figure 11.2 To open a track in the Track editor, select it in the Outline view, or...

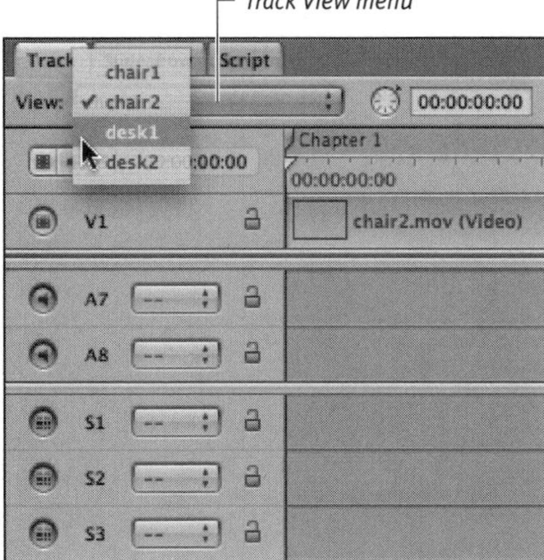

Figure 11.3 ...in the Track editor itself, choose the track from the View pop-up menu.

To open a track in the Track editor:

◆ *Do one of the following:*

▲ In the Outline or Graphical view, select a track (**Figure 11.2**).

▲ In the Track editor's View menu, choose a track (**Figure 11.3**).

The track is displayed in the Track editor.

Creating Tracks

Each new project is created with a single, empty track ready and waiting for clips to be added to it (**Figure 11.4**). That's a good start, but most projects need more than one track. Fortunately, DVD Studio Pro provides several ways to create them. You can create an empty track, for example, and then add video to it later. Or if you have some video streams already imported into the Assets container, you can simply drag the video streams into DVD Studio Pro's Outline or Graphical view to quickly create a new track that's automatically populated with the video. This section covers all of the different ways in which you can create new tracks in DVD Studio Pro.

✔ Tip

- According to the DVD specification, all DVD-Videos must have at least one track. DVD Studio Pro acknowledges this fact by automatically adding at least one track to each new project. If you try to build a project that does not have at least one track, you are stopped by a dialog (**Figure 11.5**).

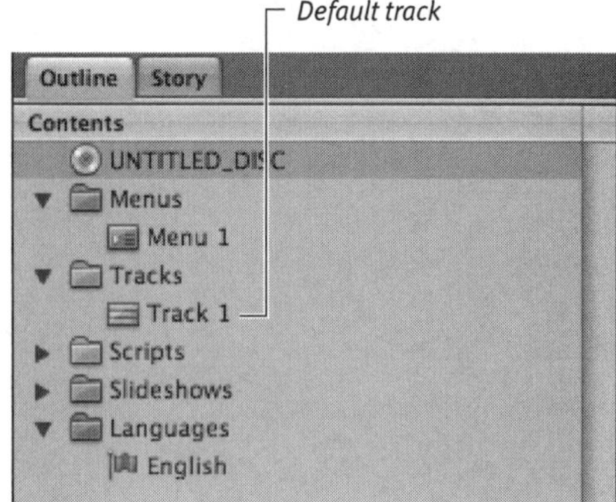

Figure 11.4 By default, each new project has one empty track. You can fill this track with video and then create up to 98 additional tracks for your project.

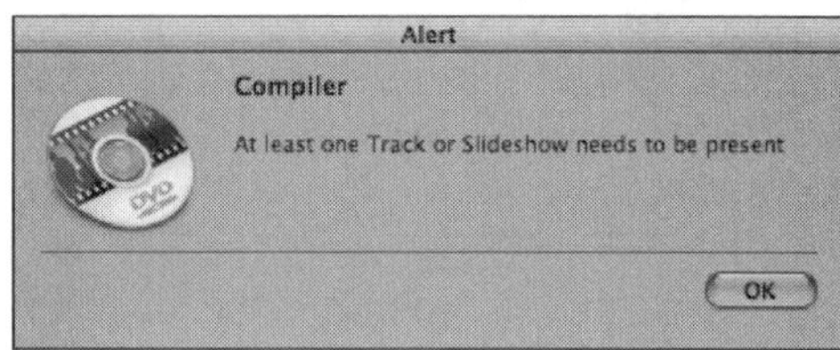

Figure 11.5 Every project must have at least one track.

Figure 11.6 To create a new, empty track in the Outline view, Control-click the Outline view and choose Add > Track, or...

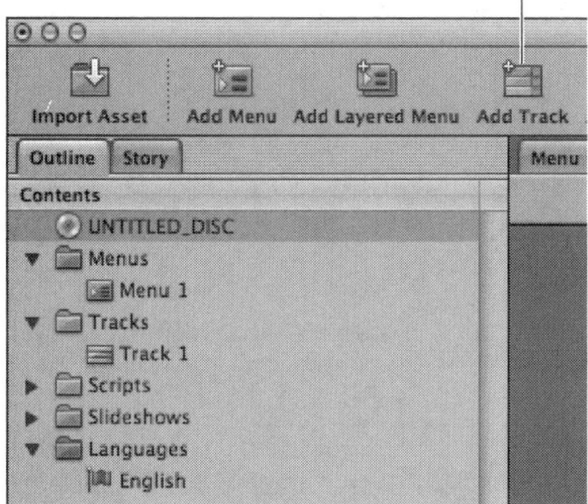

Figure 11.7 ...click the Add Track tool, or...

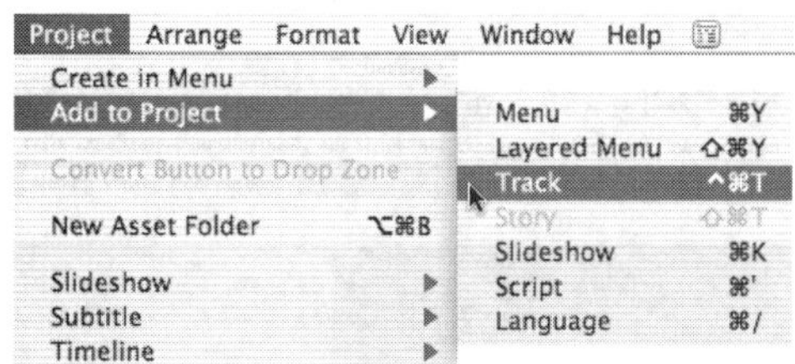

Figure 11.8 ...choose Project > Add to Project > Track.

To create an empty track:

◆ *Do one of the following:*

▲ In the Outline or Graphical view, Control-click anywhere to call up a shortcut menu and then choose Add > Track (**Figure 11.6**).

▲ In the toolbar, click the Add Track tool (**Figure 11.7**).

▲ Choose Project > Add to Project > Track (Control-Command-T) (**Figure 11.8**).

A new, empty track is added to the Outline or Graphical view (**Figure 11.9**).

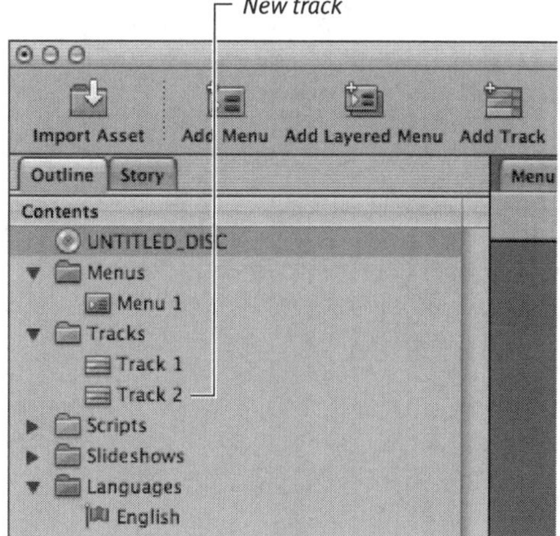

Figure 11.9 A new track is added to the Outline view.

To create a track and automatically assign a video or audio stream:

- In the Assets container, select a video or audio asset and drag it into the Outline or Graphical view (**Figure 11.10**).

  A new track is created, which is given the same name as the asset (**Figure 11.11**). The asset is automatically added to the track (**Figure 11.12**).

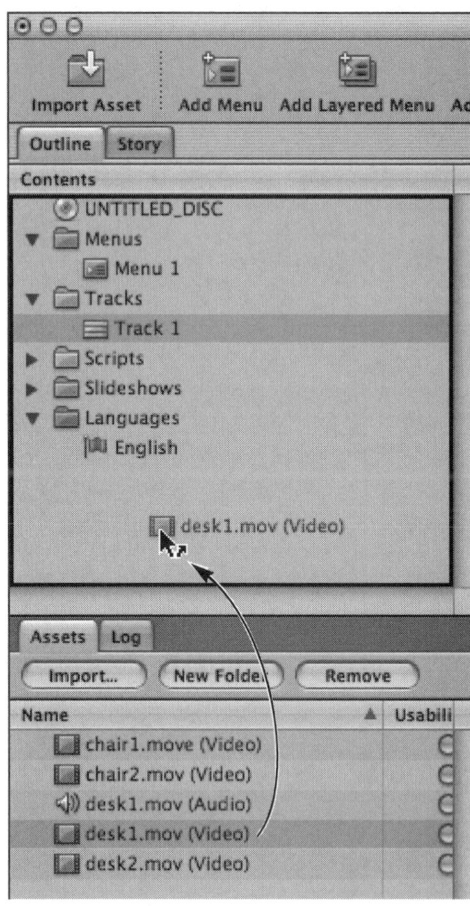

Figure 11.10 To create a track and assign a video asset to it, drag the video asset directly into the Outline view.

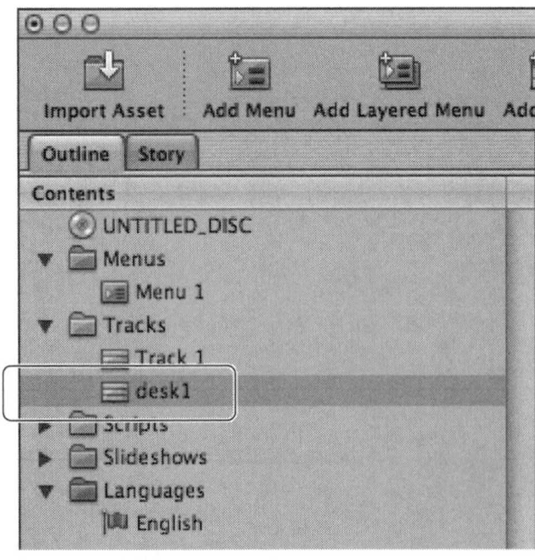

Figure 11.11 When you drag a video or audio asset into the Outline view, the newly created track is automatically given the same name as the asset, and...

Figure 11.12 ...the asset is added to the new track.

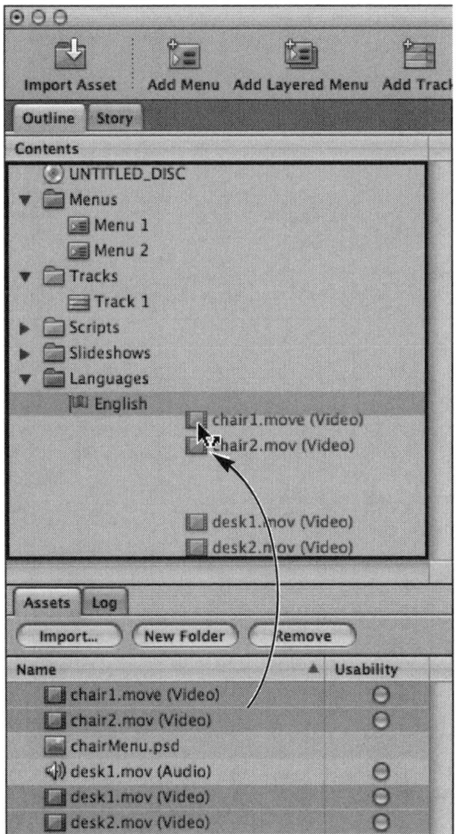

Figure 11.13 To create several tracks at once, drag and drop multiple assets from the Assets container into the Outline view at the same time.

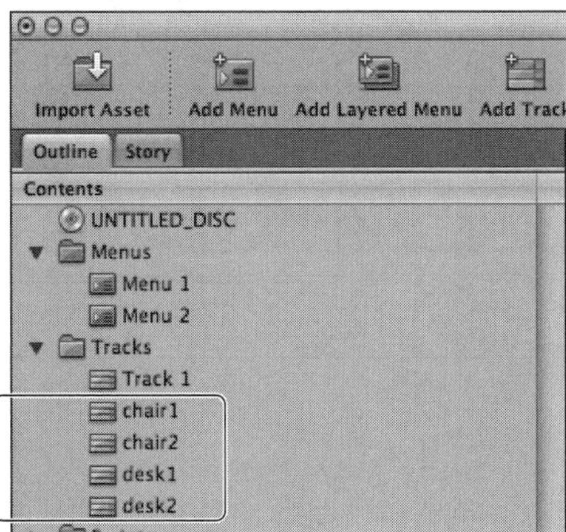

Figure 11.14 Several tracks are created, and each new track is named after its asset.

✔ Tips

- If you drag an asset into the Outline view, you don't have to drop the asset onto the track heading—you can just drop it anywhere in the Outline view.
- To create multiple tracks at once, select several assets of the same type in the Assets container and drag them all into the Outline or Graphical view at the same time (**Figure 11.13**). DVD Studio Pro will create a separate track for each asset (**Figure 11.14**). Be sure that the assets are all the same type; if they're not, this trick won't work.
- You can also drag an audio/video file directly from DVD Studio Pro's Palette—or even a Finder window—and drop it into the Outline or Graphical view to quickly import an asset and create a new track with it (**Figure 11.15**).

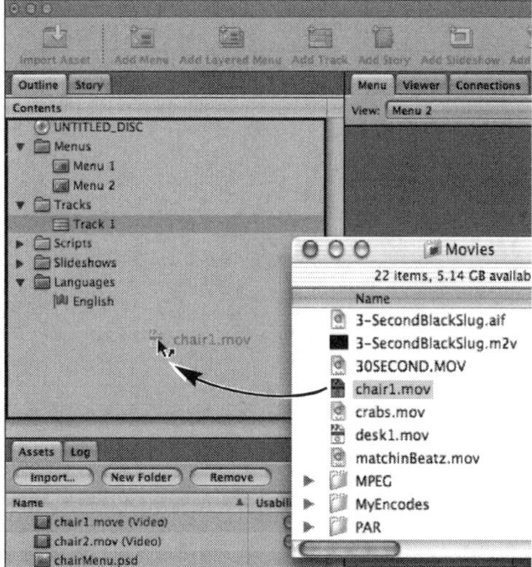

Figure 11.15 You can also drag audio or video files from a Finder window and drop them into the Outline view to import an asset and create a track, all in one fell swoop.

To create a track and assign it as a menu button's target:

1. In the Assets container, select a video or audio asset.
2. Drag the asset over a button in the Menu editor, but don't drop it (**Figure 11.16**).

   The menu button is momentarily outlined in yellow, and then a drop palette appears.

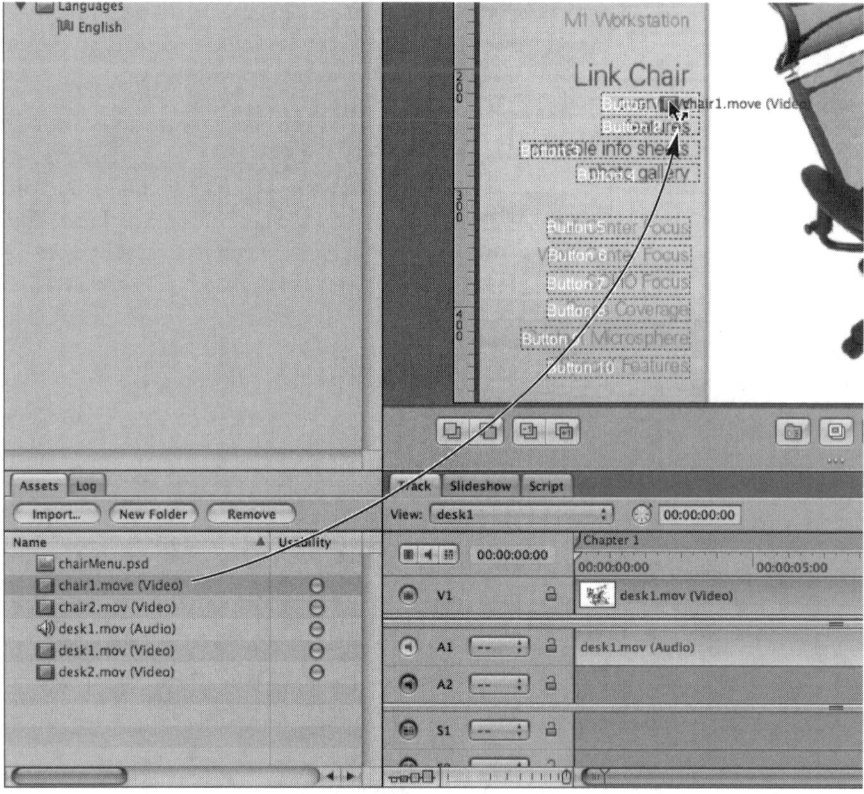

Figure 11.16 To create a track and automatically assign it to a menu button, drag an asset from the Assets container and hold it over a button in the Menu editor.

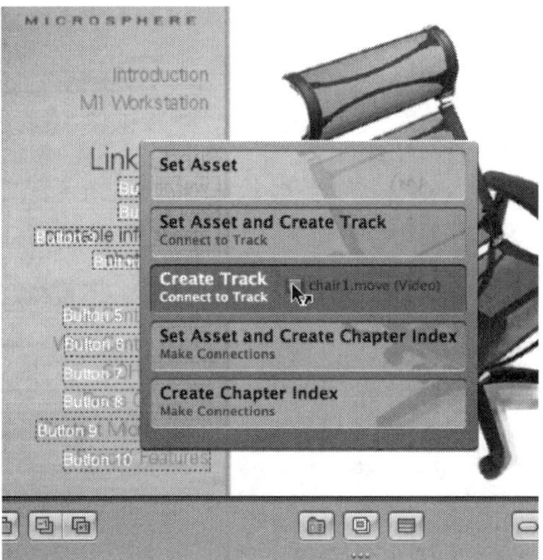

Figure 11.17 When the drop palette appears, drop the asset on the Create Track: Connect to Track option.

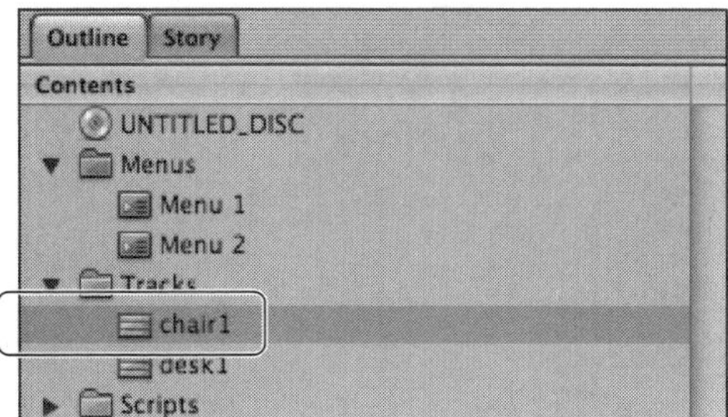

Figure 11.18 A new track is created and automatically assigned as the menu button's target.

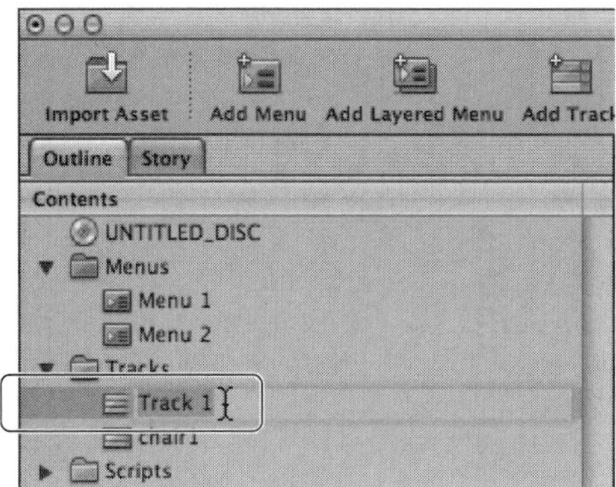

Figure 11.19 To name a track in the Outline view, click it once to select it, press Return to open a text box, and then type a new name for the track.

3. On the drop palette, drop the asset on the Create Track: Connect to Track option (**Figure 11.17**).

   A new track is created and named after the asset (**Figure 11.18**). In addition, the track is populated by the asset and automatically assigned as the menu button's target. As a final bonus, the video track's end jump is automatically assigned to target the menu button—four jobs in one! (To learn more about menu button targets, see Chapter 13, "The Menu Editor.")

✔ Tip

- You can also drag audio and video files directly from DVD Studio Pro's Palette—or even from a Finder window—and drop them onto menu buttons to create new tracks and assign them as the button's target.

To change a track's name in the Outline or Graphical view:

1. In the Outline or Graphical view, click a track once to select it.
2. *Do one of the following:*
   - ▲ Press the Return key.
   - ▲ Click the track a second time.

   A text box appears (**Figure 11.19**).
3. Type a name in the text box and press Return.

✔ Tip

- If you want to rename a track, don't double-click it in the Outline view. This opens the track in DVD Studio Pro's Viewer, but does not allow you to rename the track.

Creating Tracks

To change a track's name in the Inspector:

1. In the Outline or Graphical view, click a track once to select it.

   The Inspector updates to show you the track's properties. At the top of the Inspector is a Name field (**Figure 11.20**).

2. In the Inspector's Name field, enter a new name for the track and press Return.

To delete a track:

1. In the Outline or Graphical view, click a track once to select it.

2. *Do one of the following:*

   ▲ Press the Delete key.

   ▲ Control-click the track and choose Delete from the shortcut menu that appears (**Figure 11.21**).

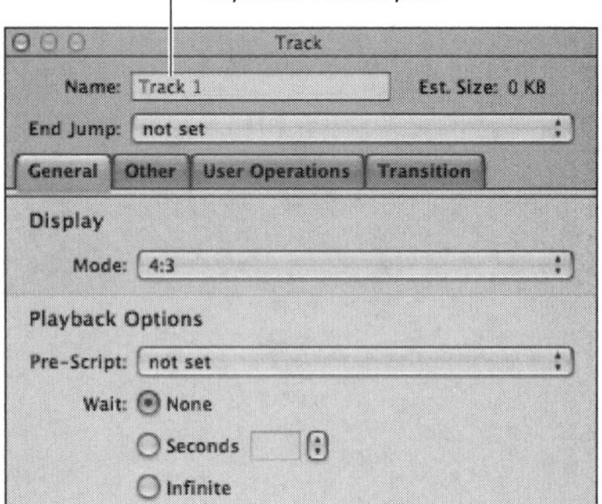

Figure 11.20 If you select a track in the Outline view, the Inspector updates to show you the track's properties. You can type a new track name in the Inspector's Name field.

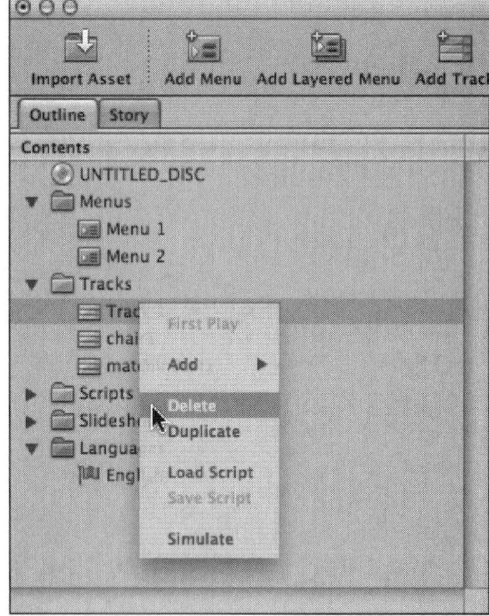

Figure 11.21 To delete a track from the Outline view, Control-click the track and choose Delete from the shortcut menu.

Changing Track Order in the Outline View

Track order in the Outline view is important for one reason only: *tracks are built to the DVD disc in exactly the same order that they appear in the Outline view.*

Most DVD-Video players will let you skip through your DVD-Video's tracks by pressing the Next and Previous keys on the remote control (however, the Apple DVD Player, for example, does not work this way). Thus, it stands to reason that you'll want your project's tracks to follow the logical order of your presentation. To do this, make sure that the tracks in the Outline view are listed from top to bottom in the order that you want them to record to disc.

✔ **Tip**

- If you forget to set a startup action for your disc, most DVD-Video players will begin playback at track 1, or the track at the top of the Outline view's track list. To learn more about startup actions, see Chapter 19, "Finishing the DVD."

Using the Remote Control's Next and Previous Keys

The remote control's Next and Previous keys are not guaranteed to jump from track to track in your DVD-Video. In fact, the proper names for these keys are the Next Program and Previous Program keys. In a DVD-Video, a *program* is a chapter (for more information, see Chapter 2, "DVD 101"). Consequently, the Next and Previous keys are really meant to jump between chapters—or programs—in a track, not between tracks. Many DVD-Video players will automatically jump from track to track when you press these keys; many others, including the Apple DVD Player, will not.

To force the Next and Previous keys to jump to the next or previous track regardless of the DVD-Video player used, use the Connections tab's Advanced view to manually assign the keys' actions on a track-by-track basis (**Figure 11.22**).

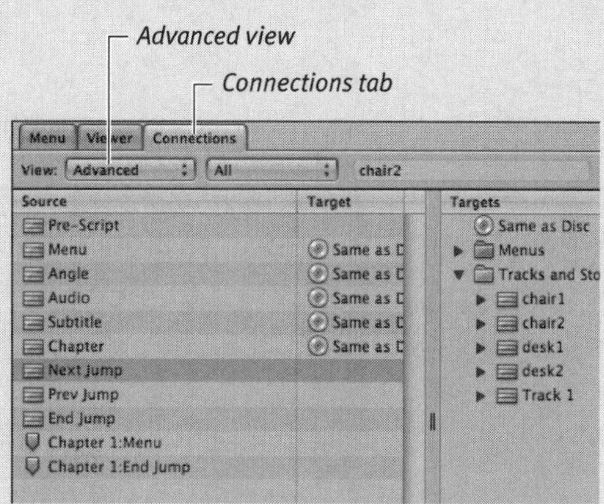

Figure 11.22 The Connections tab's Advanced view allows you to manually assign the actions of the remote control's Next and Previous keys on a track-by-track basis.

To change track order in the Outline view:

1. In the Outline view, select the track that you want to reorder.
2. Drag the track up or down the track list (**Figure 11.23**).

   As you drag, a black indicator line shows you where the track will drop when you release the mouse button.
3. When the black indicator line is where you want the track to be positioned, release the mouse and drop the track into place.

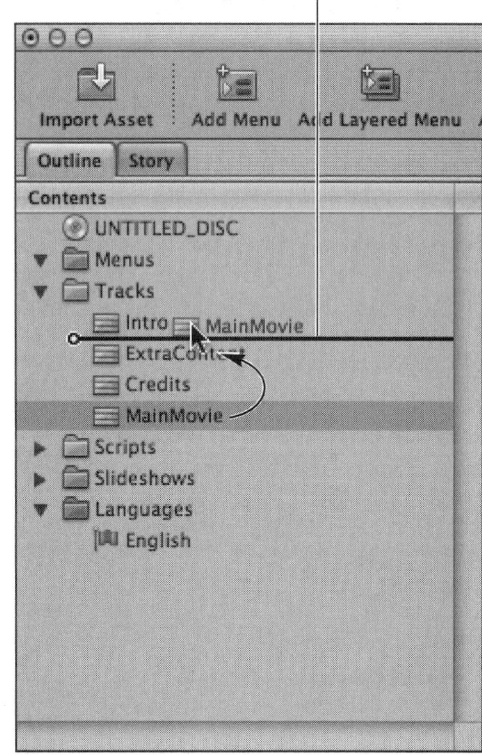

Figure 11.23 When you build your DVD-Video, tracks are recorded to the disc in exactly the same order as they appear in the Outline view. Consequently, you should always arrange the tracks so they are listed in the correct order.

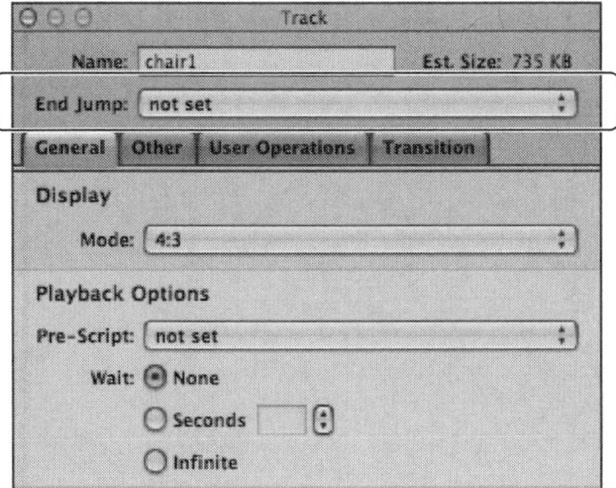

Figure 11.24 The track's End Jump setting tells your DVD-Video what to do once the track finishes playing.

Figure 11.25 The End Jump menu lists all project elements by category.

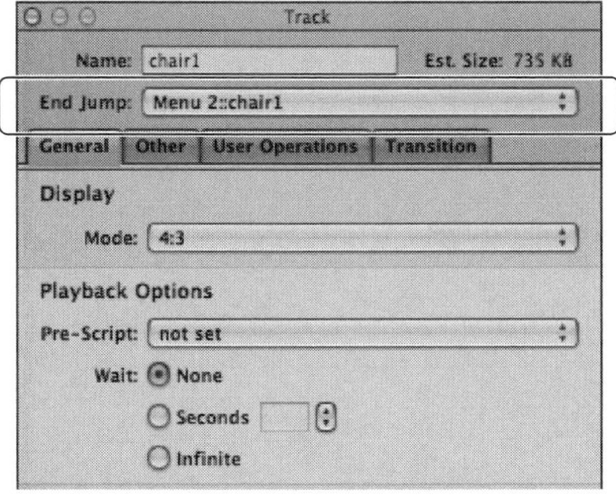

Figure 11.26 The end jump action you select is displayed in the End Jump menu.

Setting Jump Actions

The DVD-Video needs to know what to do with itself once it has finished playing a track. As the DVD author, you tell it what to do by setting each track's end jump action. If you don't set the end jump action, your DVD-Video will pause indefinitely on the track's last frame, which will more than likely confuse the viewer, who is expecting the DVD to do something. As a result, setting the end jump action should be one of the first things you do after creating a track.

You can set a track to jump to any other project element—including the menu that jumped you to the track, other tracks, chapter markers and stories, slideshows, and even scripts—once it finishes playing.

To set a track's jump action:

1. In the Outline or Graphical view, select a track.

   The Inspector updates to display the track's properties. In the top section of the Inspector is a property called End Jump (**Figure 11.24**).

2. From the End Jump menu, choose the project element that you want to play immediately after the track is finished (**Figure 11.25**).

✔ Tip

- The element you select as the track's end jump target appears in the End Jump menu (**Figure 11.26**).

Choosing a wait time

The track's wait time tells the track how long to wait before executing its end jump. The values are:

- **None.** The track does not wait; it immediately jumps to the project element selected as its end jump.
- **Seconds.** The track pauses for the specified number of seconds. You can choose any number of seconds from 1 to 254.
- **Infinite.** The track pauses until the viewer presses the remote control's Menu or Title key or until the viewer stops playback. (To learn more about the remote control's Menu and Title keys, see Chapter 19.)

To set a wait time for a track's end jump:

1. In the Outline or Graphical view, select a track.

   The Inspector updates to show the track's properties.
2. In the Inspector, make sure that the General tab is selected (**Figure 11.27**).
3. In the Wait area, select None, Seconds, or Infinite.
4. If you selected Seconds, enter a number in the Seconds text box to indicate how many seconds the track should wait before jumping to the next project element.

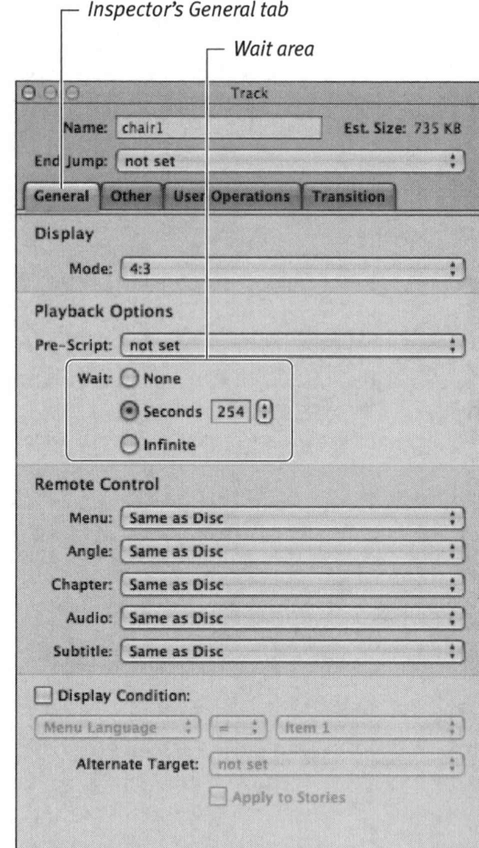

Figure 11.27 The Inspector's General tab has a Wait area used to specify how long the DVD-Video should wait before executing the track's end jump.

Adding Clips to Streams

Creating a track is only the beginning; next you must add assets to it. As you've seen, you use the Track editor to organize individual video, audio, and subtitle assets (clips) for playback.

There are a few considerations you must keep in mind when adding assets to the Track editor. First, all video assets added to the same video stream must have the exact same dimensions and resolution. This means that you can't combine MPEG-1 and MPEG-2 assets in the same stream, nor can you mix 4:3 and 16:9 clips.

On the audio side, all assets added to the same audio stream must be of the same type and format and also must use the exact same channel configuration, bit depth, and sampling rate. This means that you can't combine an AC-3 asset with an AIFF asset in the same stream, nor can you combine a two-channel AC-3 asset with a 5.1 AC-3 asset. Similarly, combining a 24-bit AIFF file with a 16-bit AIFF file is also a no-no.

But this limitation operates only on a per-stream basis—you *can* add a 5.1 AC-3 file to the first audio stream in the Track editor and then add a two-channel AC-3 asset to the second stream without incident.

To add a clip to the Track editor:

- *Do one of the following:*
  - ▲ From the Assets container, Palette, or Finder, drag an asset into the Track editor and drop it on an appropriate stream (**Figure 11.28**).

  The asset is added to the stream and becomes a clip.

continues on next page

Figure 11.28 To add an asset to the Track editor, drag it from the Assets container, Palette, or Finder to an appropriate stream in the Track editor, or...

- From the Assets container, Palette, or Finder, drag an asset into the Outline or Graphical view and drop it on a track (**Figure 11.29**).

DVD Studio Pro adds the clip to the first stream of the appropriate type. For example, if you drag a video asset onto a track in the Outline view, the asset is added to the V1 stream. If there are already clips in the V1 stream, the asset is appended to the end of the V1 stream.

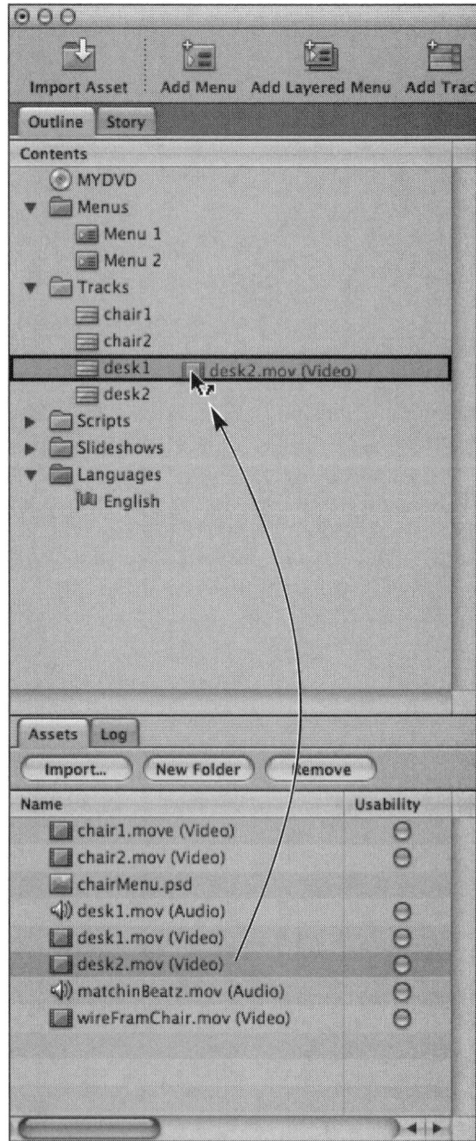

Figure 11.29 ...drag an asset to a track in the Outline view.

Working in Pairs

As you drag video assets into the Track editor (from the Assets container, Palette, or Finder), DVD Studio Pro checks to see if there's an audio asset with the same file name in the same folder on your hard disk as the video asset. If there is, DVD Studio Pro automatically adds the audio asset to the Track editor. (Note that this feature depends on the asset's source media file name, not the name in the Assets container). To override this feature, open the Preferences window's Track section and deselect the Find Matching Audio When Dragging check box (**Figure 11.30**) or hold down the Command key as you drag assets into the Track editor.

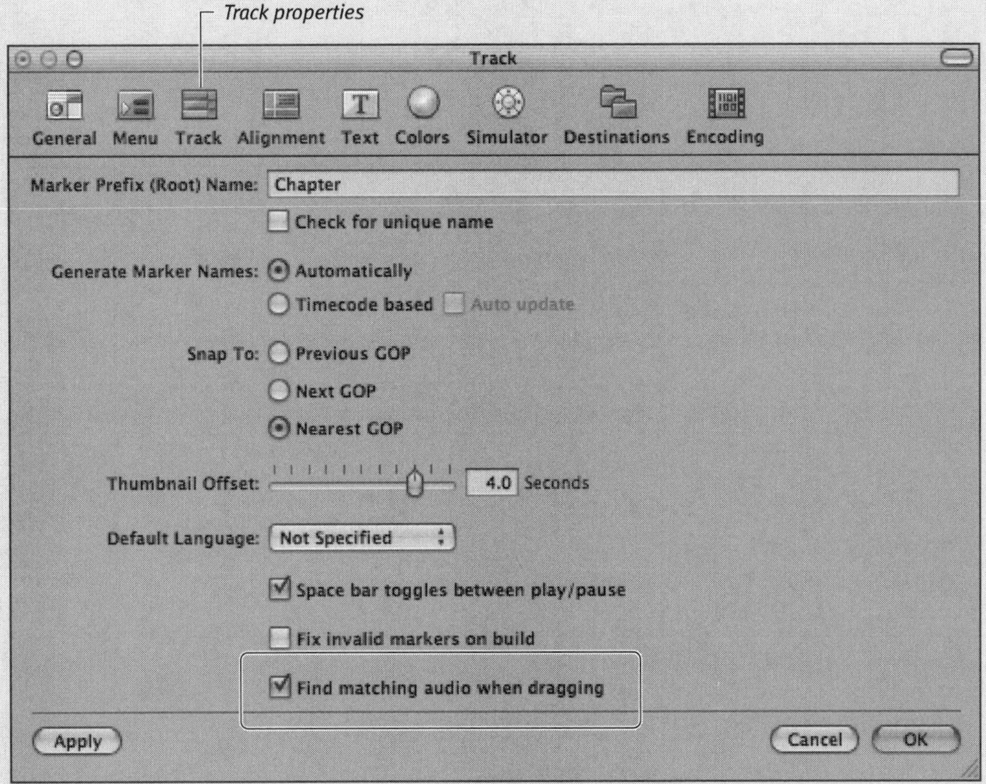

Figure 11.30 When you drag a video asset into the Track editor, the Find Matching Audio When Dragging property tells DVD Studio Pro to also add any audio asset with a name that matches the dragged video asset.

To browse a video clip:

1. In the Track editor, select a video clip.

   The Inspector updates to display the clip's properties. At the bottom of the Inspector is the Browse Clip area, which has a slider along the bottom (**Figure 11.31**).

2. Drag the slider to browse the clip.

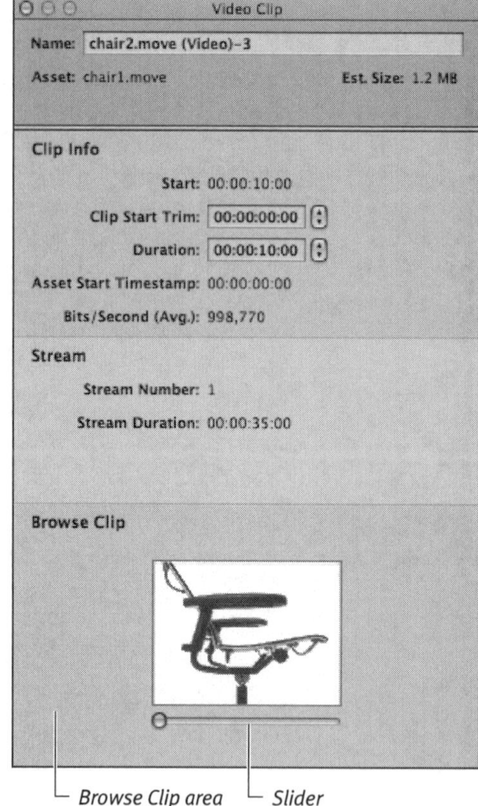

Figure 11.31 With a video clip selected in the Track editor, you can use the Inspector's Browse Clip area to see what the clip contains.

Using Timecode in the Track Editor

The Track editor has four different timecode displays. From left to right, they show the timecode value representing the pointer's position in the timeline, the playhead's position in the timeline, the start time of a selected clip, and the end time of a selected clip (**Figure 11.32**).

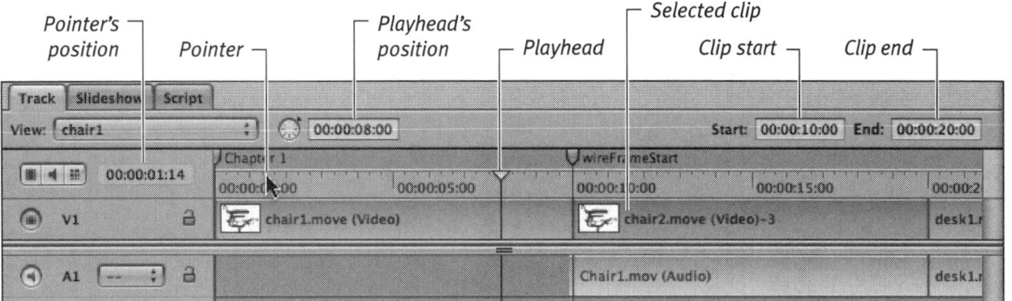

Figure 11.32 The Track editor has four different timecode displays.

Entering Timecode

Values in the timecode displays are listed using Society of Motion Picture and Television Engineers (SMPTE) timecode, which follows this format: *Hours:Minutes: Seconds:Frames*. When typing a timecode value, you don't need to enter every single colon—or even every single number—because DVD Studio Pro provides a few shortcuts to help speed along your data entry. For example, you can substitute a period for the colon, and DVD Studio Pro will understand exactly what you mean (this is a common feature in all video programs, including Final Cut Pro).

Nor must you enter every number. If you enter 1.25.25 in a timecode display, DVD Studio Pro automatically interprets it as 00:01:25:25. Similarly, typing 5.05 is interpreted as 00:00:05:05.

Drop- versus non-drop-frame timecode

As you saw in Chapter 4, "The QuickTime MPEG-2 Exporter," NTSC video can be either drop frame or non-drop frame. Drop-frame timecode is differentiated from non-drop-frame timecode by the use of a semicolon between the seconds and frames values, while non-drop-frame timecode uses a colon.

Each track in your project can also use drop- or non-drop-frame timecode, and you can have a mixture of both types of tracks in your project. The type of timecode used in the first video asset added to the track's V1 stream determines the type of timecode used for each track. If the first video asset added to the track is drop frame, all timecode displays will display drop-frame timecode (**Figure 11.33**). If the first asset added to the track is non-drop frame, all timecode displays for that track will display non-drop-frame timecode (**Figure 11.34**).

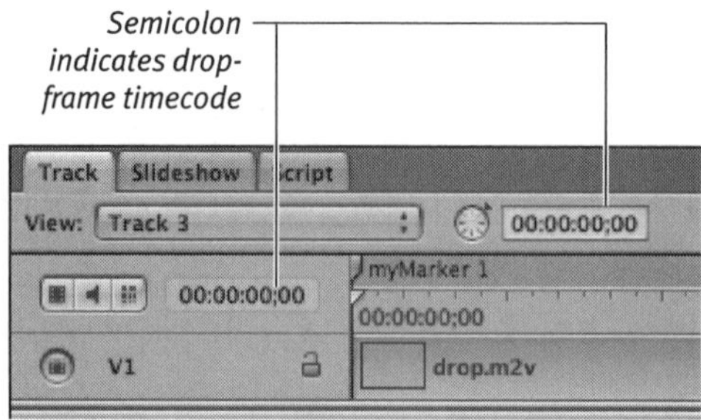

Figure 11.33 If the first video asset added to a track uses drop-frame timecode, the track will automatically use drop-frame timecode.

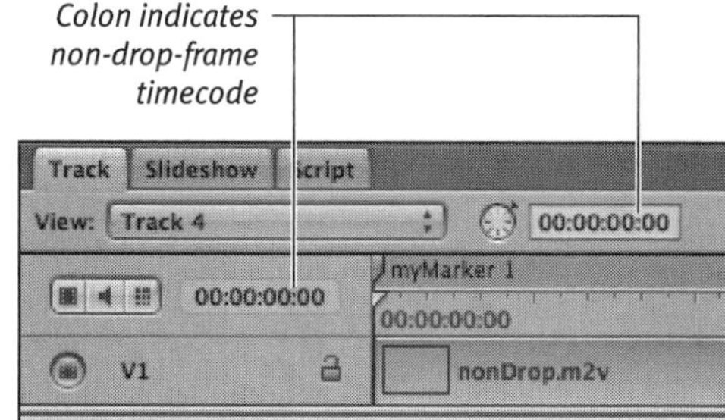

Figure 11.34 If the first video asset added to a track uses non-drop-frame timecode, the track will use non-drop-frame timecode (this is the DVD Studio Pro default timecode for tracks).

Drop- or Non-Drop-Frame Timecode?

If possible, *always use non-drop-frame timecode.* This is the Track editor's default timecode value, and it's the default for a reason.

Drop-frame timecode is necessary only for video that is headed for broadcast. It works by dropping two frames every minute in the timecode's numbering scheme, except for every tenth minute where the first two frames are maintained. It's important to note, however, that no frames of video are actually dropped—only the numbering of the frames changes over time.

The QuickTime MPEG-2 Exporter encodes I-frames every 15 frames and never varies. This means that I-frames always fall on frame 0 and frame 15. But if you use drop-frame timecode, after the first minute of the video stream the I-frames will no longer fall on frames 0 and 15 but rather on frames 2 and 17. After the second minute, they'll fall on frames 4 and 19. In fact, they'll jump forward by two frames every minute (except for minutes 10, 20, and so on), which makes it hard to keep track of where those I-frames are as you edit in DVD Studio Pro.

Using zero-based versus asset-based timecode

DVD Studio Pro allows you to configure a track's timecode as either zero based or asset based. Under normal authoring conditions, each track is set to zero-based timecode, and the timecode values used in the Track editor start at 00:00:00:00.

Under certain circumstances, however, you may want to change the timecode so that it begins at a different value. For example, Final Cut Pro sequences typically begin with a timecode value of 01:00:00:00. If you've created an event list based on Final Cut Pro's timecode values, you may want to set the track offset in DVD Studio Pro so that the Track editor's timecodes match the ones on your event list. DVD Studio Pro lets you adjust the tracks' timecode offset, but to do so, you must use asset-based timecode.

✔ Tip

- The ability to adjust a track's timecode offset also comes in handy when you are importing a marker list or subtitle file that begins with a timecode value that is not 00:00:00:00.

To choose asset-based timecode:

- ◆ Control-click the timeline and choose Asset-Based Timecode from the shortcut menu that appears (**Figure 11.35**).

  The track's timecode is now asset based. This allows you to set a track offset, as demonstrated in the next task.

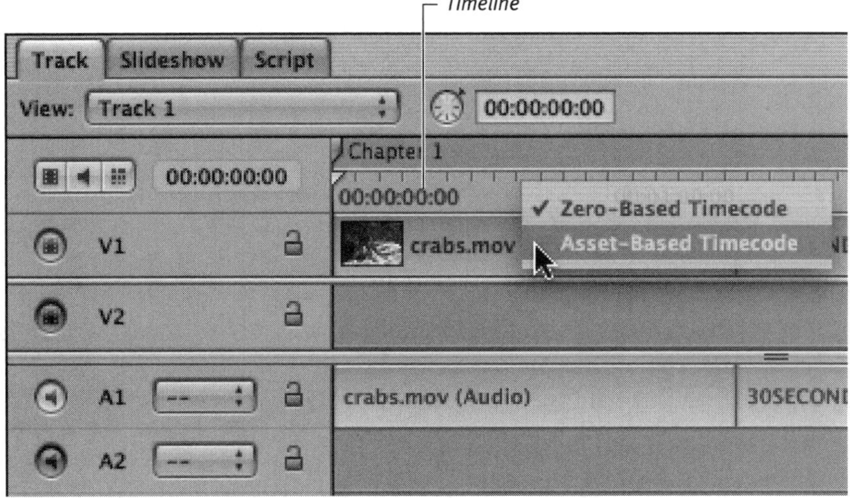

Figure 11.35 To ensure that your track offset is displayed in the Track editor, Control-click the timeline and choose Asset-Based Timecode from the shortcut menu that appears.

To set a track offset:

1. Control-click the timeline and choose Asset-Based Timecode from the shortcut menu that appears.
2. In the Outline or Graphical view, select the track for which you want to adjust the timecode offset.

   The Inspector updates to display the selected track's properties.
3. In the Inspector, choose the Other tab (**Figure 11.36**).

   Toward the middle of the Other tab is the Timestamps area. This area displays two timecode values: First Asset Start and Track Offset. The First Asset Start timecode can't be changed—it shows the timecode value of the first frame of the first clip in the V1 stream. In most situations, this value is 00:00:00:00. But if you trim the front of the first clip, the value displayed here changes to show the value of the clip's first frame in relation to the timecode of the clip's source asset. With the Track Offset box set to 00:00:00:00 and the track set to use asset-based timecode, the track will begin counting timecode at the value displayed at the top of the Inspector's Timestamps area (refer to Figure 11.36).
4. In the Track Offset text box, enter a new timecode value (**Figure 11.37**).

   All timecode values in the track will now start at the specified timecode offset (**Figure 11.38**).

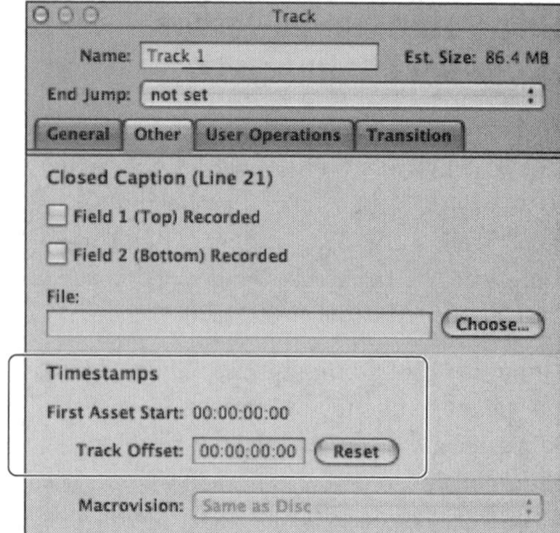

Figure 11.36 The Track Inspector's Other tab has a Timestamps area that you can use to adjust the offset of the timecode values displayed in the Track editor.

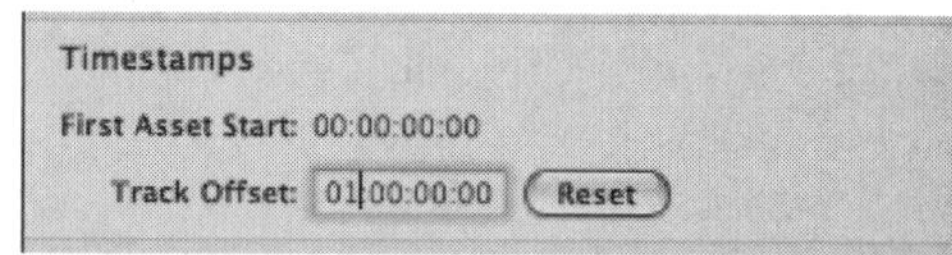

Figure 11.37 Enter a value in the Timecode Offset text box. In this example, the timecode value 01:00:00:00 has been entered to ensure that the track's timecode matches an event list compiled from a sequence in Final Cut Pro.

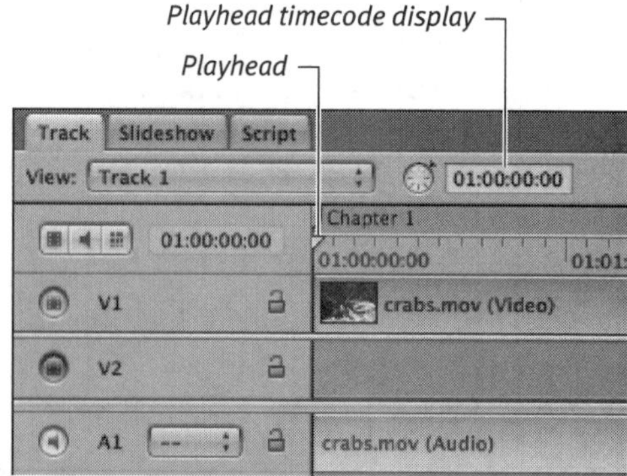

Figure 11.38 In the Track editor, the track now begins at 01:00:00:00. With the playhead parked on the very first frame of the track, notice how the playhead's timecode display box now says 01:00:00:00.

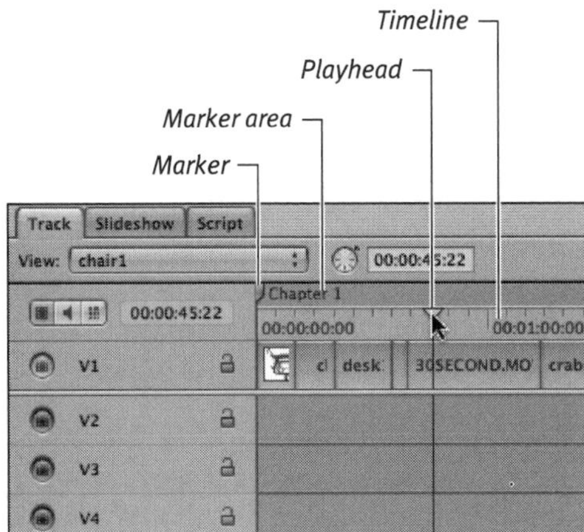

Figure 11.39 When moving the playhead, make sure you click and drag the playhead within the Timeline. If you click the Marker area above the timeline, instead of moving the playhead, you'll create a new marker.

Positioning the Playhead

The playhead works in tandem with DVD Studio Pro's Viewer to show you the video you're editing in the Track editor. As you move the playhead back and forth across the Track editor's timeline, the Viewer updates to display the frame directly under the playhead's current position. This provides a quick way for you to view tracks as you make edits, set markers, create subtitles, and position alternate video and audio streams.

To position the playhead by dragging:

- In the timeline, select the playhead and drag it back and forth.

  The playhead moves back and forth along the timeline, and the Viewer updates to show you the frame directly under the playhead.

✔ Tip

- When moving the playhead, make sure you click in the timeline and don't accidentally click the Marker area (**Figure 11.39**). Doing so creates a new marker and doesn't move the playhead. To learn more about markers, see Chapter 12, "Enhancing Tracks."

Positioning the playhead using timecode

If you need to move the playhead to an exact timecode value (for example, to place a marker), the Playhead Timecode box provides just the ticket.

To position the playhead using timecode:

1. In the Track editor, triple-click the Playhead Timecode text box (**Figure 11.40**).

   If you triple-click the Playhead Timecode text box (or any timecode text box in DVD Studio Pro), all of the timecode in the box is selected. Double-clicking selects only the section immediately under the pointer (the hours, or the minutes, or the seconds, or the frames).

2. Enter a new timecode value and press Return.

   The playhead jumps to the specified timecode.

Positioning the playhead using keyboard shortcuts

A true DVD Studio Pro professional finds a hand on the keyboard just as useful as a hand on the mouse. Using keyboard shortcuts (key commands) speeds up your workflow significantly. Here are a few keyboard shortcuts that you'll find helpful for quickly positioning the playhead:

- **Left arrow and right arrow.** Move the playhead one frame at a time.
- **Shift-left arrow and Shift-right arrow.** Move the playhead one second at a time.
- **Option-left arrow and Option-right arrow.** Move the playhead one group of pictures (GOP) at a time.
- **Control-left arrow and Control-right arrow.** Move the playhead to the next marker.
- **Command-left arrow and Command-right arrow.** Move the playhead to the start or end of the selected clip.
- **Up arrow and down arrow.** Move the playhead to the next clip edge (includes all clips in all streams) or marker.
- **Home and End.** Move the playhead to the start or end of the timeline.

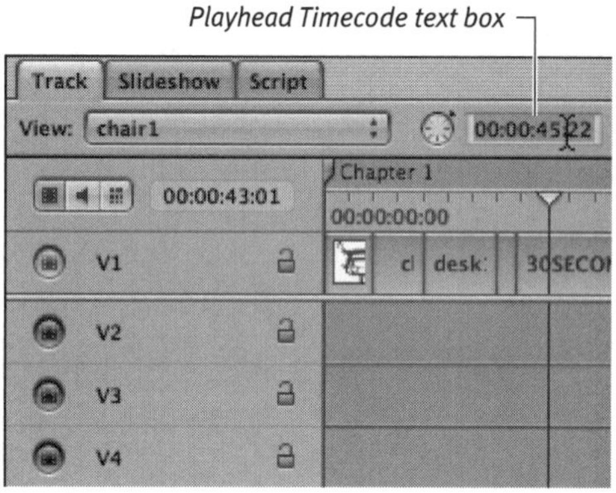

Playhead Timecode text box

Figure 11.40 The Playhead Timecode text box lets you move the playhead to a specific timecode value.

Zooming in the Timeline

As you edit tracks in the timeline, often you must balance the need to see the entire track and all of its clips at once (for example, when arranging clips and alternate audio streams) against the need to see clips in close detail (for example, when adding chapter markers or subtitles). To help you achieve this balance, use the Track editor's Zoom control and/or Zoom Scroller (**Figure 11.41**).

✔ Tip

- Just as in Final Cut Pro, you can press Shift-Z to instantly zoom the Track editor so it displays all of a track's clips.

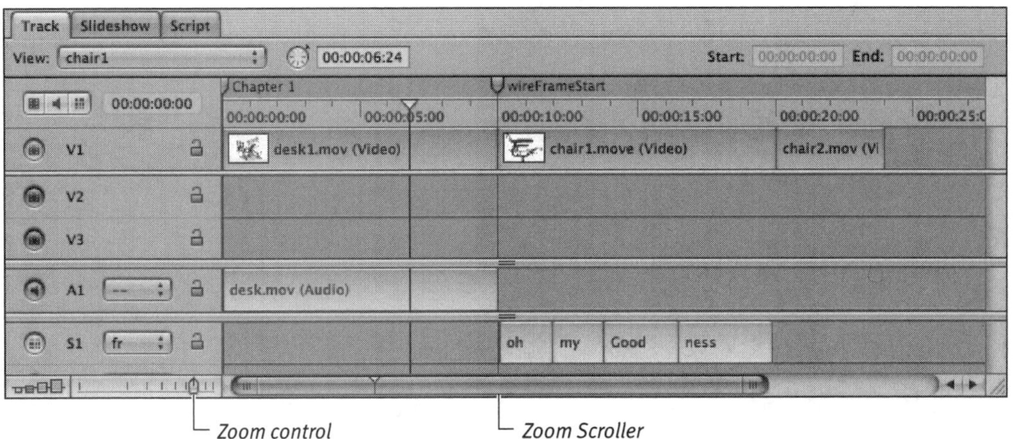

Figure 11.41 The Zoom control and Zoom Scroller work together to let you see more or fewer clips in each stream.

Using the Zoom control

The Zoom control allows you to horizontally expand or contract the timeline, which lets you see either more or fewer clips in each stream. The Zoom control is fairly intuitive, but it does have one little quirk: when you zoom in or out on the timeline, if the playhead is not currently visible, the Zoom control automatically becomes centered in the Track editor, and the clips are zoomed in or out around it. This behavior can be confusing if, for example, the playhead is at the beginning of the track and you are trying to zoom in on clips at the end of the track. In this case, the Track editor will automatically jump back to the beginning of the track, where the playhead is currently sitting.

To zoom in on the timeline:

- Move the Zoom control to the left (or press Command-+) to zoom in on the timeline.

  The timeline's clips appear bigger and show greater detail (**Figure 11.42**).

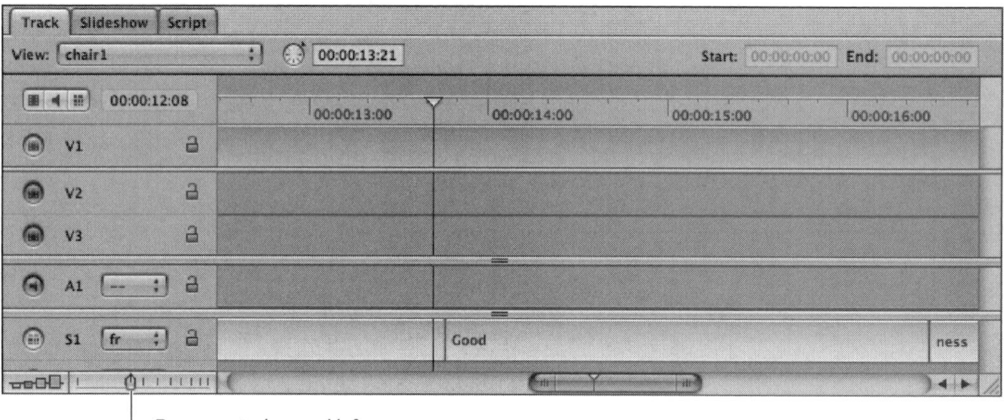

Figure 11.42 Move the Zoom control to the left to see the timeline's clips in greater detail.

To zoom out on the timeline:

- ◆ Move the Zoom control toward the right, or press Command- – (hyphen), to zoom out on the timeline.

  The timeline's clips appear smaller, and more clips are visible in each stream (**Figure 11.43**).

✔ Tips

- To zoom in or out without centering the playhead in the timeline, hold down the Shift key as you move the Zoom control, or press Shift-Command-– (hyphen) or Shift-Command-+.
- As in Final Cut Pro, you can press Shift-Z to fit the entire timeline into the Track editor.
- Press Shift-Option-Z to make the currently selected clip fill the timeline.

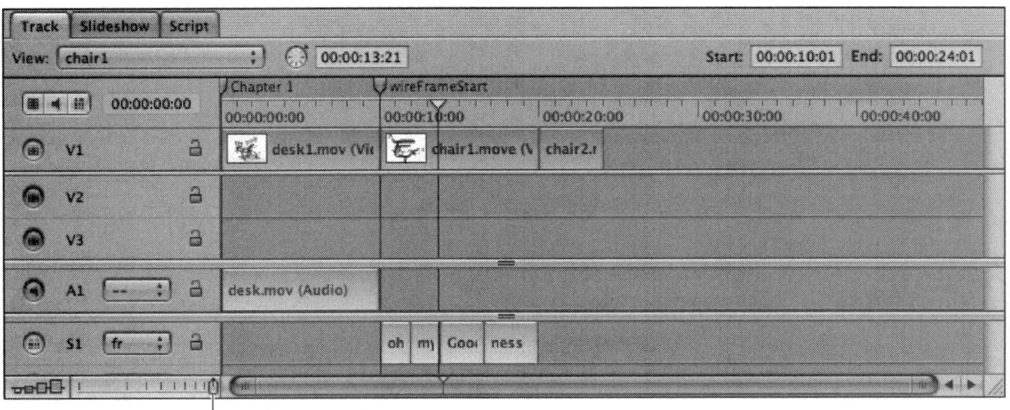

Figure 11.43 Move the Zoom control to the right to see more clips at once in the timeline.

Using the Zoom Scroller

The Track editor's Zoom Scroller lets you zip back and forth across the timeline; it's particularly handy when editing long tracks or when zoomed in closely on individual clips. DVD Studio Pro's Zoom Scroller is remarkably similar to the Zoom Scroller at the bottom of the timeline in Final Cut Pro. In fact, just as in Final Cut Pro, you can drag the edges of the Zoom Scroller to quickly zoom in or out on the timeline (**Figure 11.44**). When you drag the edge of the Zoom Scroller, the timeline is zoomed around the center of the currently visible area. If you hold down the Shift key while dragging the edge of the Zoom Scroller, only the edge you are dragging will move, which lets you scroll linearly left or right.

To help you orient yourself in the track, the length of the Zoom Scroller area always reflects the length of the track, while the length of the Zoom Scroller itself reflects the visible area of the Track editor. As you zoom in on the track, the Zoom Scroller becomes smaller, reflecting the fact that less of the track is currently visible. Zooming out causes the Zoom Scroller to become bigger. If you look carefully at the Zoom Scroller area, you'll also see a small playhead icon that shows you the playhead's current position in the track in relation to the visible area. If the playhead is to the left of the Zoom Scroller, for example, you can tell at a glance that the playhead is to the left, or outside of, the visible area in the Track editor.

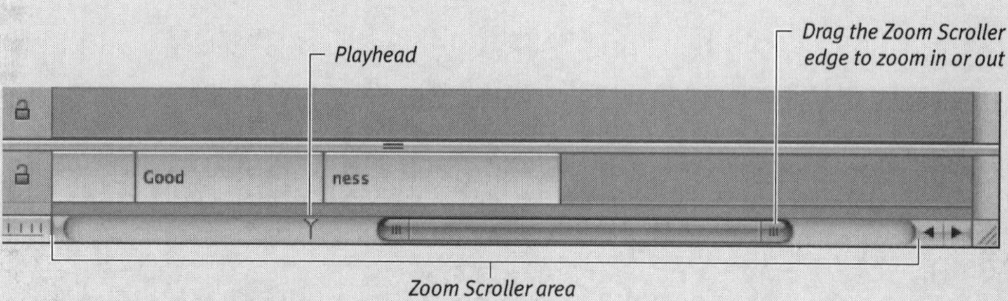

Figure 11.44 The Zoom Scroller's size reflects the visible area of the Track editor, while the Zoom Scroller area reflects the length of the track itself.

Working with Streams in the Track Editor

At its heart, the Track editor is a tool for organizing separate video, audio, and subtitle streams into a finished track that plays as a unit. Streams are listed horizontally across the Track editor. Working down, in addition to the main video stream, or the V1 stream, at the top of the Track editor, there are 8 alternate video streams, 8 audio streams, and 32 subtitle streams. In total, you have access to 49 different streams per track. That's a lot to keep organized, but the Track editor provides a few cool features to help you. For example, you can filter the Track editor's stream display by using the stream configuration buttons to show or hide certain types of streams. You can also take advantage of the Stream Height presets to decrease or increase stream height so that more or fewer streams are visible in the Track editor (**Figure 11.45**).

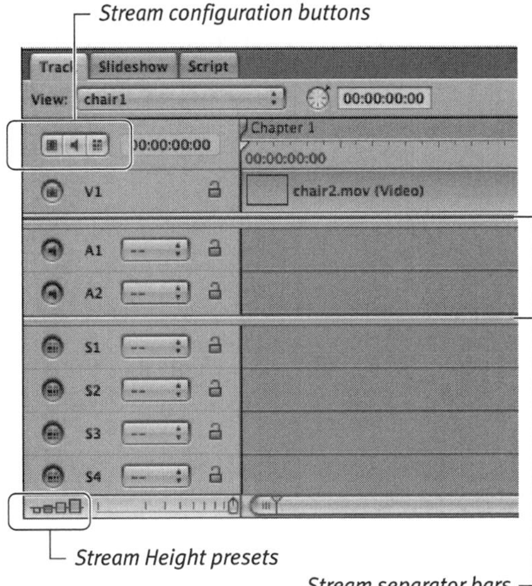

Figure 11.45 The Track editor has several controls that let you determine how streams are displayed.

Filtering stream display

Every track must have a V1 stream. This is the most important stream in the track—all other video, audio, and subtitle streams are synchronized to it. The V1 stream is the king of any track, and as a sign of its importance, the V1 stream is always displayed across the top of the Track editor—you can't hide it.

You can display or hide the other streams as needed using the stream configuration buttons (**Figure 11.46**). Clicking the stream configuration button on the left shows video streams only, clicking the middle button shows audio streams only, and clicking the right button shows subtitle streams only. If you click a combination of stream configuration buttons, you will see a combination of different streams. Clicking both the video and subtitle stream configuration buttons, for example, causes the Track editor to display video and subtitle streams but not audio streams.

To filter the Track editor's stream display:

- At the top left of the Track editor, click a stream configuration button (refer to Figure 11.46).

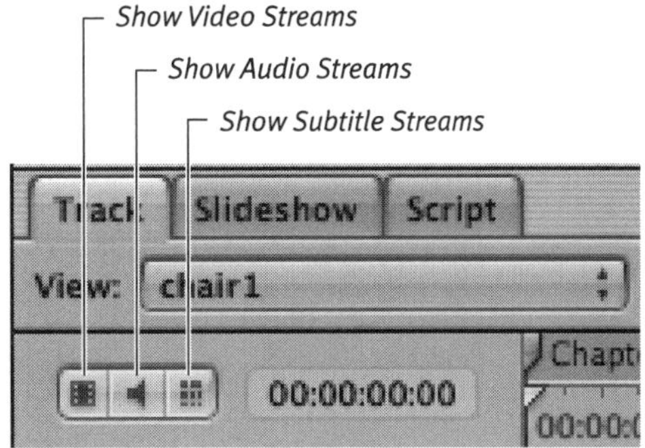

Figure 11.46 The stream configuration buttons determine the types of streams displayed in the Track editor.

Adjusting stream separator bars

The stream separator bars let you manually adjust the number of each type of stream displayed in the Track editor.

To adjust the stream separator bars:

- In the Track editor, select a stream separator bar and drag it up or down (**Figure 11.47**).

  Depending on whether you drag the stream separator bar up or down, more or fewer streams are displayed.

Changing stream height

At the bottom left of the Track editor, you'll find four Stream Height presets, which you can use to make streams either taller or shorter (**Figure 11.48**). The preset at the left creates short tracks and lets you see as many streams as possible in the Track editor (**Figure 11.49**). The preset at the right makes tracks very tall, but to the detriment of your ability to see many streams at once (**Figure 11.50**). While tall streams are easier to edit, it's often convenient to see many streams at once. Consequently, selecting the correct stream height can be a bit of a balancing act.

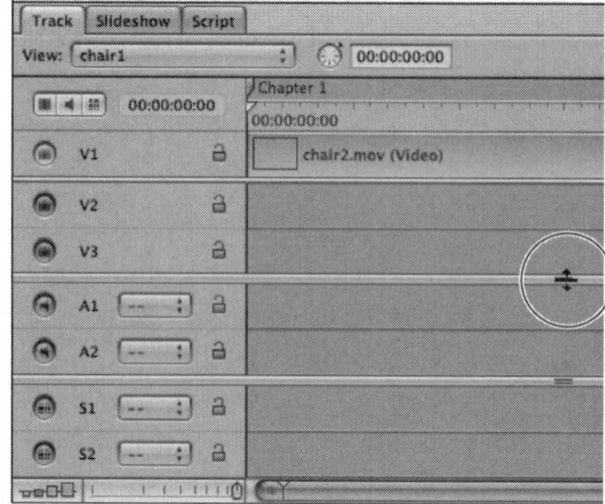

Figure 11.47 Drag the stream separator bar up or down to manually adjust the type and number of streams displayed in the Track editor.

Figure 11.48 The Stream Height presets allow you to make the Track editor's streams either taller or shorter, letting you see more or fewer streams at once in the Track editor.

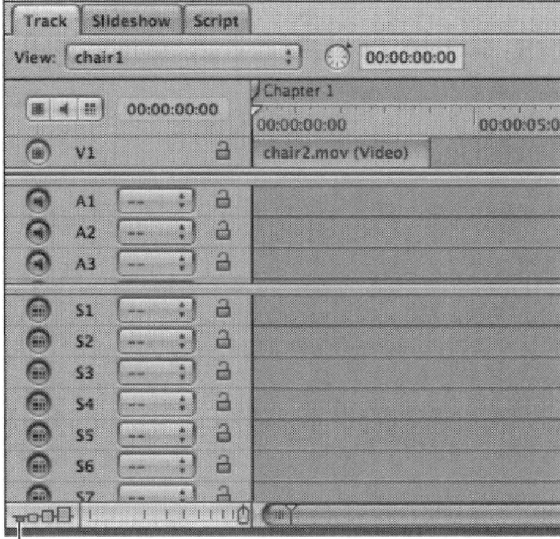

Figure 11.49 The Stream Height preset on the left makes the Track editor's streams very short, letting you see as many streams as possible at once.

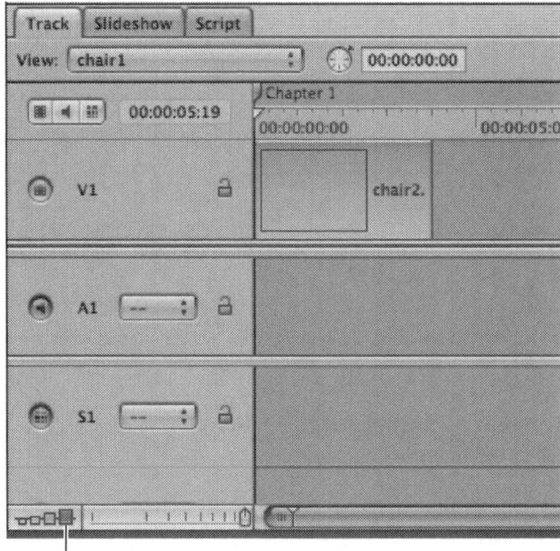

Figure 11.50 The Stream Height preset on the right makes the Track editor's streams very tall, causing fewer streams to be displayed in the Track editor.

To change stream height:

- At the bottom left of the Track editor, select a Stream Height preset (refer to Figures 11.49 and 11.50).

✔ Tip

- Stream Height presets are assigned on a track-by-track basis. Consequently, changing the stream height of one track does not automatically change the stream height of your project's other tracks.

Locking streams

It's easy to accidentally move clips in streams. This can be a real problem if you've synchronized audio or subtitle clips with video in the track's V1 stream. To guard against this, DVD Studio Pro lets you lock streams.

To lock a stream:

- In the Track editor, click the Stream Lock icon for each stream that you want to lock (**Figure 11.51**).

  The Stream Lock icon snaps shut, and the track is textured with diagonal lines to visually indicate that it's locked (**Figure 11.52**).

To unlock a stream:

- In the Track editor, click the Stream Lock icon for each locked stream that you want to unlock.

To lock all streams in a track:

- Choose Project > Timeline > Lock All Streams (**Figure 11.53**), or press Shift-F4.

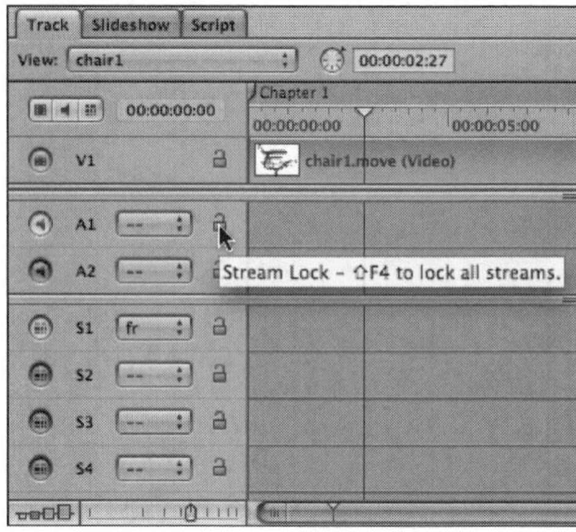

Figure 11.51 Click the Stream Lock icon to lock a stream so that it can't be edited.

Figure 11.52 Locked tracks are textured with diagonal lines.

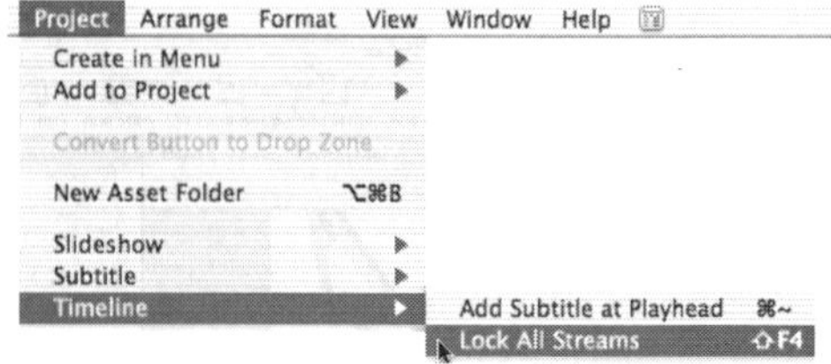

Figure 11.53 To lock all of the streams in a track, choose Project > Timeline > Lock All Streams.

Editing Video and Audio Clips

The Track editor lets you make quick edits to the length and position of clips in the timeline. This provides a great way to trim excess or unneeded video off an MPEG stream. If your MPEG stream has unnecessary or unwanted footage—such as a leader, countdown, or calibration colorbars—at the front, you can trim it off right in DVD Studio Pro, which saves you from having to open the clip's source video in a video-editing program to make the edit. Only the part of the clip that's visible in the Track editor's timeline will be used in the final DVD-Video, so trimming clips in the Track editor provides the perfect way for you to use a small part of a longer video stream.

Moving clips

Not all clips are treated equally in DVD Studio Pro. If you're moving a video clip in the V1 stream, for example, the other clips will jump either forward or backward to make room for the moved clip (**Figure 11.54**). But for all other clips—including alternate video, audio, and subtitle clips—the other clips in the stream don't budge an inch. On top of that, if you move a clip into a space that isn't big enough, the end of the clip will be mercilessly truncated (**Figure 11.55**).

continues on next page

About the V1 Stream

The V1 stream is the most important stream in the track; consequently, it demands special treatment when it comes to editing. Here are a few rules to keep in mind:

- The first clip in the V1 track must sit at the very beginning of the timeline. All other streams can have their first clip start later in the timeline.
- There can be no spaces or gaps between clips in the V1 stream.
- When DVD Studio Pro builds your project, the track always ends at the last frame of the V1 stream. If other streams have clips that extend beyond the last frame of the V1 stream, those clips will be truncated.

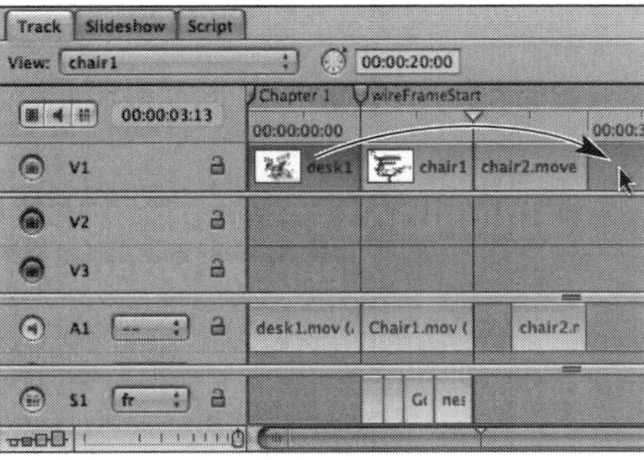

Figure 11.54 To move a clip in the timeline, grab it and drag it to a new position.

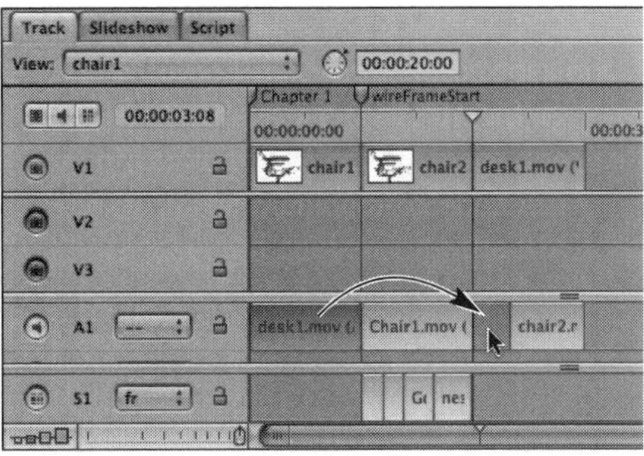

Figure 11.55 If you drag an audio, subtitle, or alternate video clip to a space that's not quite big enough to accept the clip's full length, the clip will be truncated.

There's one more thing to keep in mind when moving clips. Earlier in this chapter, you learned that dragging a video asset into the timeline causes any audio asset with a matching file name to also be added to the track. This synchronization between audio and video assets does not continue after the assets have been added to the timeline. If you move a video clip within the V1 stream, the matching audio clip does not automatically move with it. To keep video and audio clips synchronized, you'll have to do some rearranging by hand.

To move a clip in the same stream:

- In the Track editor, select a clip and drag it to the left or right.

✔ Tip

- You cannot move multiple clips at the same time. You can select multiple clips in the timeline and delete them all together, but if you try to move multiple clips, DVD Studio Pro will move only the clip that you click and drag.

To copy a clip:

- In the timeline, select and drag a clip while pressing the Option key.

  The original clip stays in its current position in the timeline, and a copy appears at the new position in the timeline.

To duplicate a clip:

- In the timeline, Control-click a clip and choose Duplicate Media Clip from the resulting shortcut menu (**Figure 11.56**).

  In the timeline, a duplicate is created immediately following the clip. If there's already a clip following the duplicated clip, the duplicate is placed in the next available space in the stream.

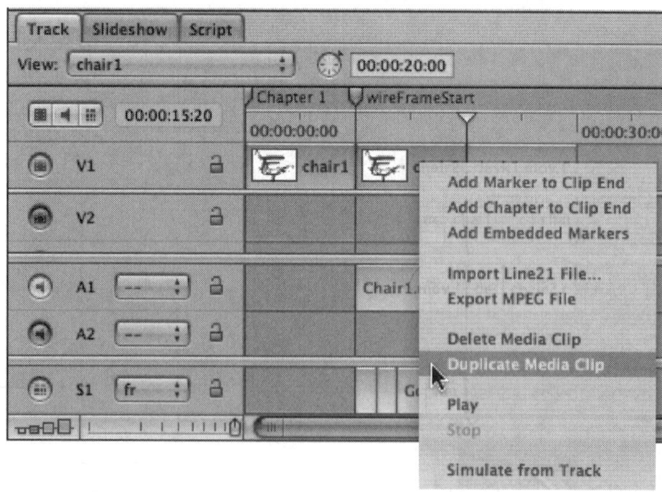

Figure 11.56 To duplicate a clip, Control-click it and choose Duplicate Media Clip from the resulting shortcut menu.

To delete a clip:

- *Do one of the following:*
  - ▲ In the timeline, select the clip that you want to delete and press the Delete key.
  - ▲ In the timeline, Control-click the clip that you want to delete and choose Delete Media Clip from the shortcut menu (**Figure 11.57**).

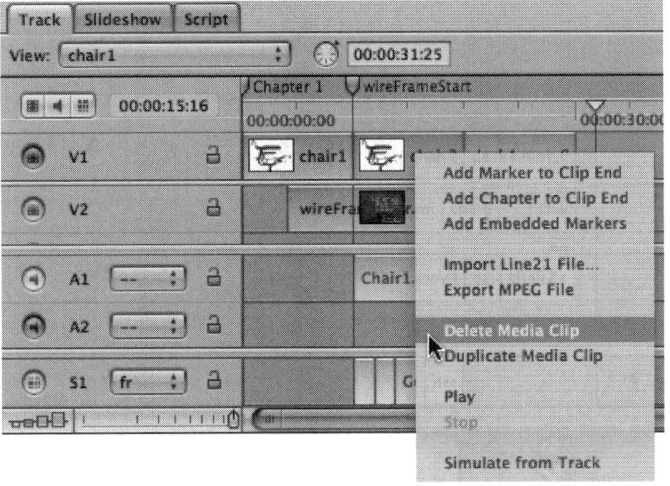

Figure 11.57 To remove a clip from a track, Control-click it and choose Delete Media Clip.

Adjusting clip duration

Video clips in DVD Studio Pro are trimmed based on GOP boundaries, so you can't make frame-accurate edits in the timeline. For example, NTSC MPEG streams typically use a GOP size of 15 frames. As a result, all edits to video clips in an NTSC project will typically be accurate only to within 15 frames. This is good enough for rough edits, but if you need to make frame-accurate edits, you'll have to open the clip in an external video editor such as Final Cut Pro. Audio, on the other hand, does not suffer from this limitation; you can make frame-accurate edits to audio streams right in the timeline.

DVD Studio Pro provides several ways to trim video and audio clips. The easiest—but least exact—way is to select the edge of a clip and drag it to the left or right. But for some situations—such as lining up an audio edit with the edge of a video clip—dragging a clip's edge may not be accurate enough. In this situation, you can turn to the Clip Timecode boxes in either the Track editor or the Clip Inspector.

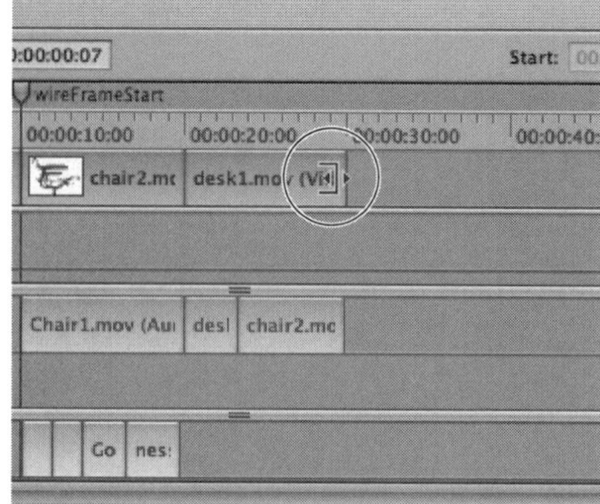

Figure 11.58 To trim a clip directly in the Track editor, move the pointer over the edge of the clip. The pointer turns into a bracket with arrows.

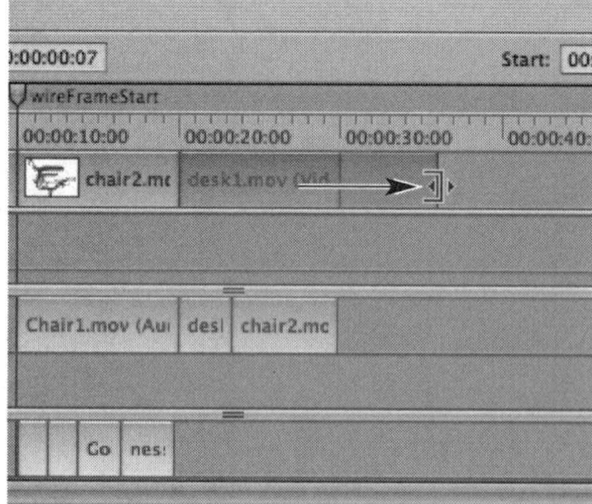

Figure 11.59 Drag the clip's edge to resize it.

To trim or lengthen a clip using the pointer:

1. In the timeline, position the pointer over the left or right edge of a clip.

   The pointer turns into a bracket with arrows, indicating that you can drag the clip edge to the left or right (**Figure 11.58**).

2. Drag the clip's edge to resize the clip (**Figure 11.59**).

✔ Tip

- You cannot adjust a clip so that it is longer than the clip's source media.

Figure 11.60 To adjust the size of a clip to an exact timecode value, first select the clip in the Track editor.

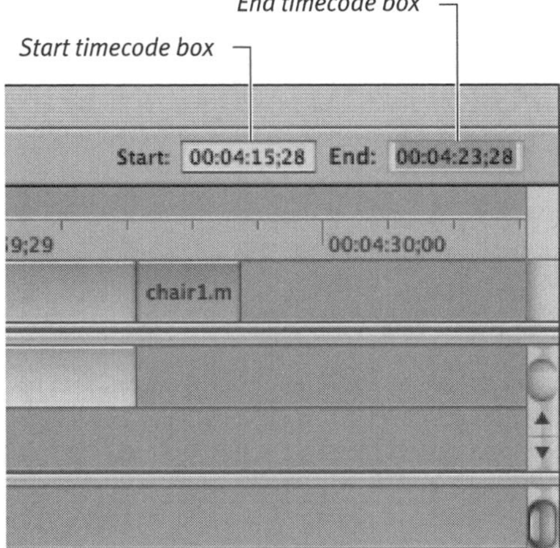

Figure 11.61 Then enter a new timecode value in the Start and/or End timecode boxes.

To trim or lengthen a clip using timecode:

1. In the Track editor, select the clip that you want to either trim or lengthen (**Figure 11.60**).
2. In the Start and End timecode boxes, enter a new start and/or end timecode for the clip (**Figure 11.61**).

   The clip is adjusted to match the length specified by the start and end timecode.

✔ Tip

- Video clips can be resized only to GOP boundaries. If you enter a timecode value that does not represent an exact GOP boundary, DVD Studio Pro will automatically snap the clip's edge to the nearest GOP boundary.

To trim or lengthen a clip using the Clip Inspector:

1. In the Track editor, select a clip.

   The Clip Inspector updates to show the clip's properties (**Figure 11.62**).

2. In the Clip Inspector's Clip Start Trim text box, enter a timecode value.

   This Clip Start Trim setting adjusts the clip so it begins at the specified timecode, but it does not move the start of the clip in the timeline. The Clip Start Trim setting has an effect similar to a slide edit in Final Cut Pro: it maintains the clip's duration in the timeline but shuffles the asset forward or backward underneath.

3. In the Clip Inspector's Duration text box, enter the length you want the clip to be.

   The result of this edit is visible in the timeline as the clip actually becomes longer or shorter.

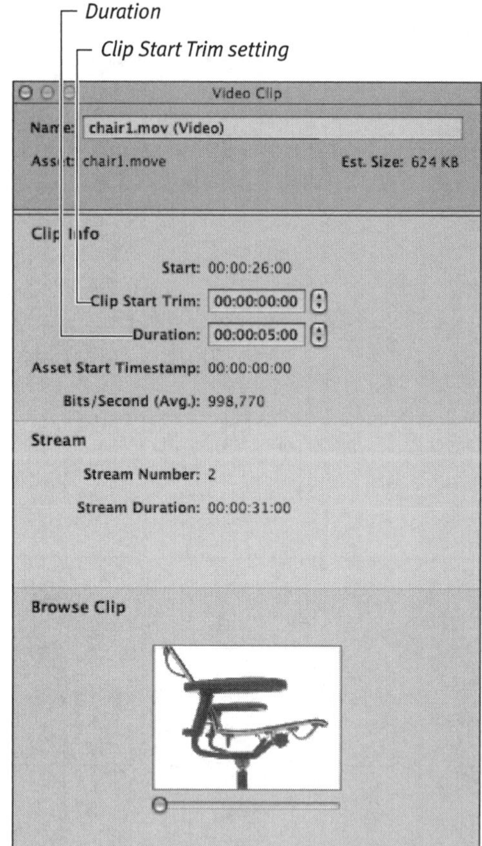

Figure 11.62 The Clip Inspector has Clip Start Trim and Duration settings that you can use to change the length of any clip selected in the timeline.

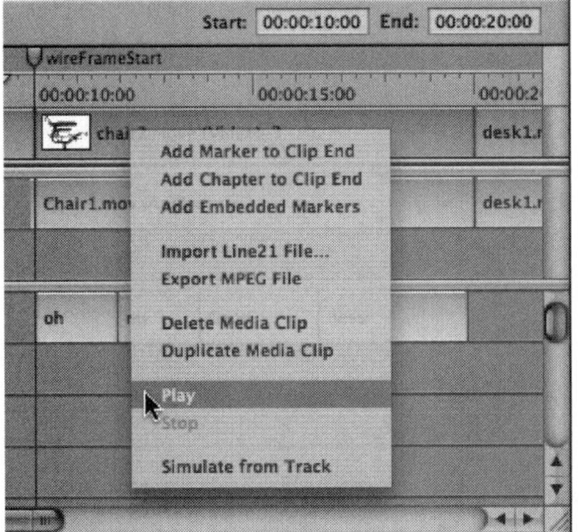

Figure 11.63 To preview a clip, Control-click it and choose Play from the shortcut menu.

Viewing Tracks

Now that you understand how to arrange and delete clips, it's time to check out how your tracks will look in the finished DVD. DVD Studio Pro provides the Viewer for just this purpose. (You can also use DVD Studio Pro's built-in Simulator to preview the track as if you were watching the finished DVD-Video on a TV. See Chapter 19 for information on how to do this.)

To view a clip:

- In the Track editor, Control-click the clip that you want to view and choose Play from the resulting shortcut menu (**Figure 11.63**).

  The clip plays in the Viewer. If the Viewer isn't already visible, it opens automatically.

✔ Tip

- With the Viewer playing the video, you can press the spacebar to stop or start playback.

Changing a Clip's Thumbnail Icon

Most video clips in the timeline have a thumbnail area that provides a visual hint of the clip's content. By default, this is set to show the first frame of the clip. The majority of clips, however, fade in from black, and a black thumbnail doesn't tell you much about the clip. You can change the default thumbnail offset to show a thumbnail frame from anywhere within the first five seconds of a clip by making changes in the Preferences window's Track section (**Figure 11.64**). Note that this setting also affects the offset of video thumbnails displayed in the Palette.

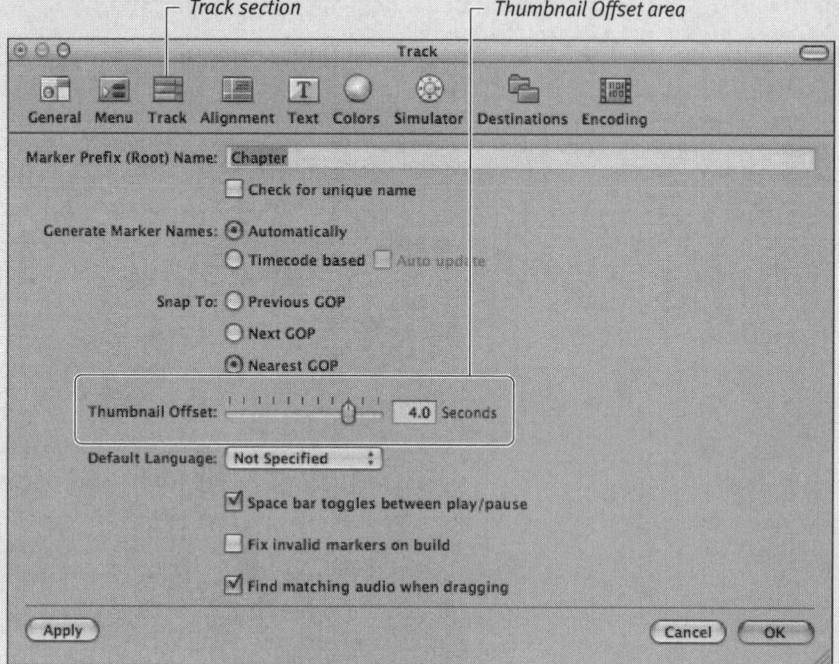

Figure 11.64 In the Track section of the Preferences window, the Thumbnail Offset area lets you choose any frame within the first five seconds of a clip to use as the clip's thumbnail icon in the Track editor.

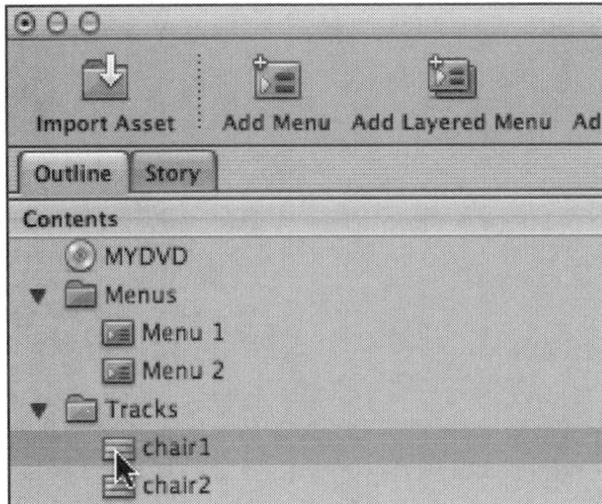

Figure 11.65 To view a track, begin by double-clicking it in the Outline view, or...

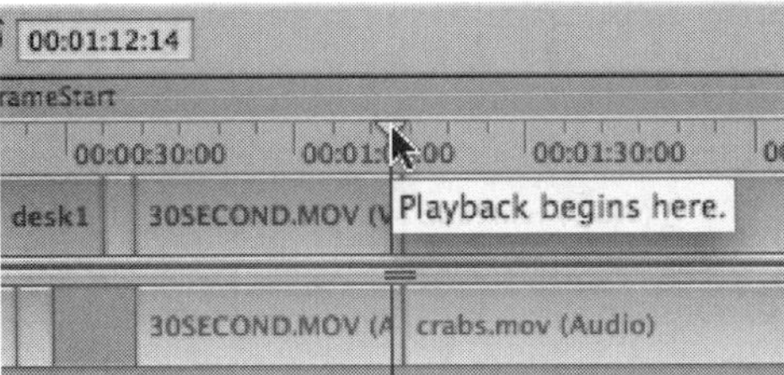

Figure 11.66 ...click the Track editor's timeline ruler to move the playhead to the position from which you want to start viewing.

To view a track:

1. *Do one of the following:*
   - ▲ In the Outline view, double-click the track that you want to preview (**Figure 11.65**).
   - ▲ In the Track editor, click the timeline ruler to move the playhead to the place from which you want to start viewing (**Figure 11.66**).

   The Viewer opens to show the frame of the track that's located at the playhead's current position in the timeline.
2. In the Viewer, click the Play button to play the track (**Figure 11.67**).

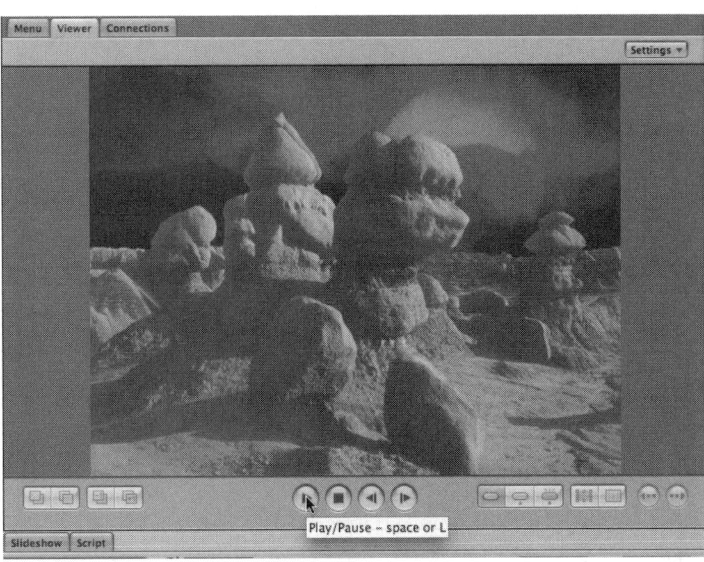

Figure 11.67 Click the Viewer's Play button to view the track.

To view alternate streams in the track:

- In the Viewer, click the stream selection button for the stream that you want to view (**Figure 11.68**).

  The Viewer displays the selected stream. This procedure works for video, audio, and subtitle streams alike.

✔ Tip

- You can click the stream selection buttons while playing a track, and the Viewer will instantly update to show the selected stream.

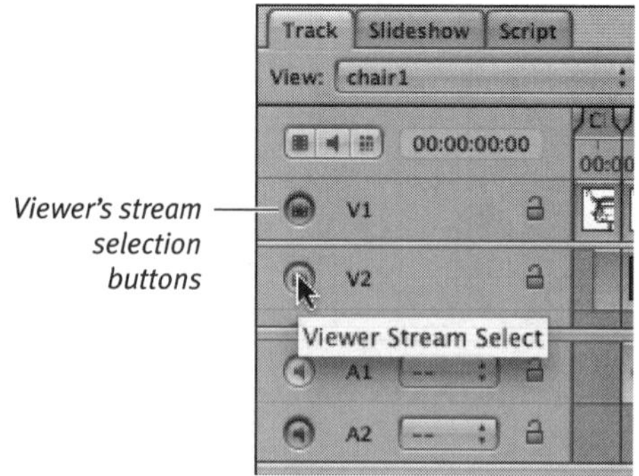

Figure 11.68 The Viewer's stream selection buttons let you choose the streams that the Viewer will display.

The Viewer's Playback Controls

Along the bottom of the Viewer, you'll find four playback controls. From left to right, they are the Play, Stop, Reverse, and Advance buttons (**Figure 11.69**).

The Play (keyboard shortcut L) and Stop (keyboard shortcut K) buttons work as expected, and you can also toggle between playing and stopping by pressing the spacebar. The Reverse and Advance buttons move the playhead one frame at a time, or one second at a time if you also hold down the Shift key while clicking them. You can also reverse and advance by pressing the keyboard's left and right arrow keys. Holding down the Shift key while pressing the left or right arrow key also jumps the playhead one second at a time.

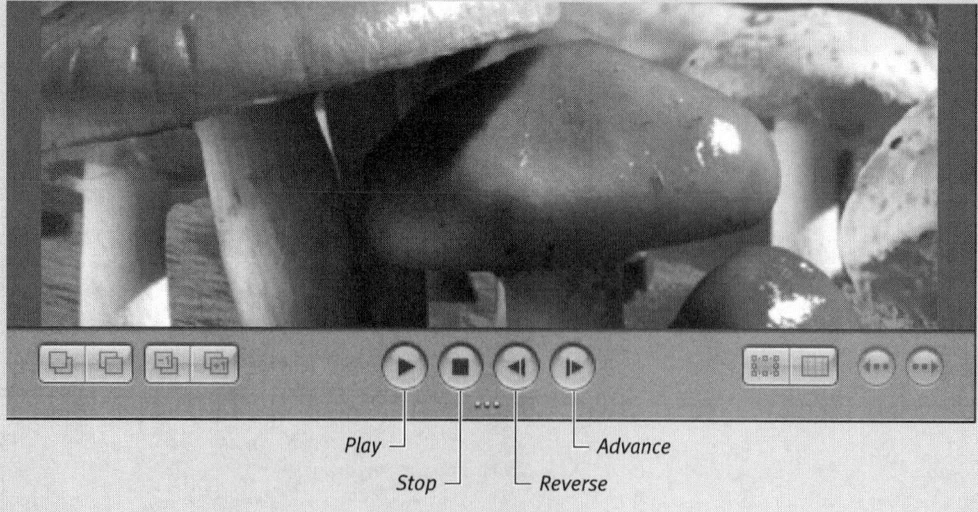

Figure 11.69 The buttons at the bottom of the Viewer control playback.

12

Enhancing Tracks

In the last chapter, you explored the Track editor and learned how to use it to assemble and edit clips. You also learned how to add audio to a track and preview the track in DVD Studio Pro's Viewer. Basically, you learned how to create a track that plays linearly from beginning to end in much the same fashion as a VHS video. That's all fine, but you can do so much more!

In this chapter, you will pick up some serious DVD authoring skills as you learn how to dress up your tracks with chapters, stories, and alternate video angles, which allow you to provide different ways for viewers to navigate through a track's content (chapters and stories) or even alternate content to keep your viewers entertained (alternate angles). Chapters, stories, and alternate angles add real value to any DVD-Video by making the DVD-Video fun for the viewer to explore. Pushing the limits of the DVD-Video specification should also be fun for you, the DVD author, so let's get started.

About Markers

Markers, which are marked points in a track (**Figure 12.1**), serve many useful purposes, which you'll learn about in this chapter. For example, you can use markers to align video clips in mixed-angle tracks. Another good use of markers is to specify random access points in a track, which viewers can jump to by pressing the remote control's Next Program (Next) and Previous Program (Previous) keys.

Each track in your project can hold up to 256 markers. While this plentitude of markers provides many possibilities to DVD authors, there is one limitation: you can add only 99 chapter markers to each track. (Chapter markers are discussed in "Specifying the Marker Type" later in this chapter.)

✔ Tip

- Here's something for you number geeks out there: The first marker in each track is locked onto the first frame of the track and cannot be moved. DVD Studio Pro lets you add up to 255 additional markers to the track, for a total of 256 markers—an 8-bit number!

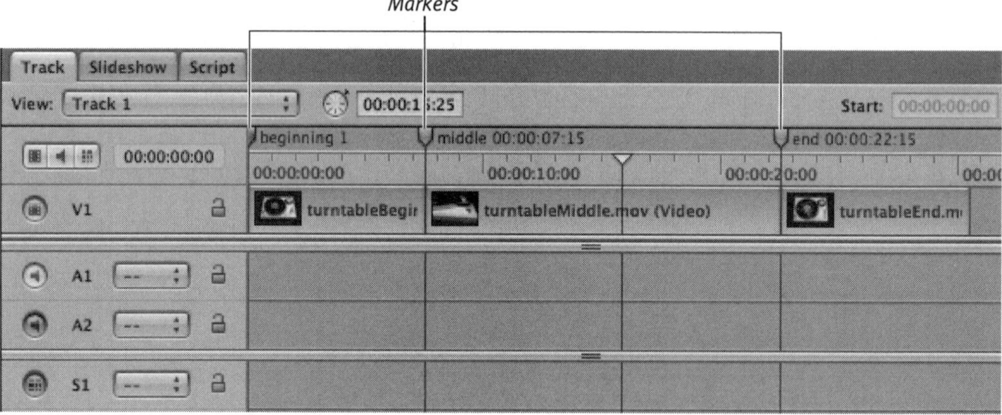

Figure 12.1 Markers indicate specific points in the track.

Figure 12.2 To create a new marker, position the pointer over the Marker area...

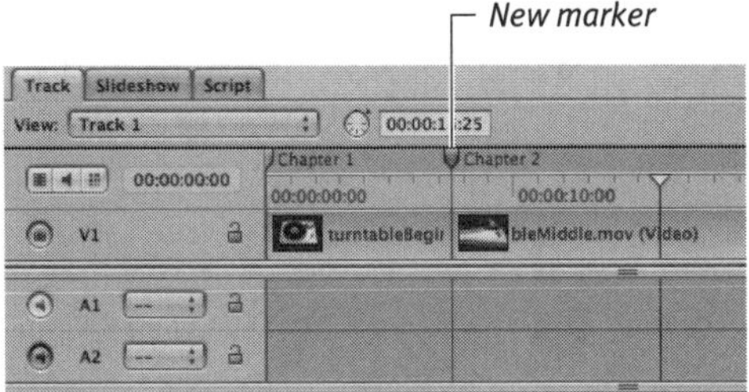

Figure 12.3 ...and then click to create a new marker.

Using Markers and I-frames

When it comes to using markers, I-frames are essential. The reason? *Markers can be attached only to I-frames in the MPEG stream.* Consequently, for a typical MPEG-2 stream, you can set a marker only once every 15 frames (12 for PAL). If your video has a hard cut between scenes, for example, and you want to place a marker directly on that cut, you have only a 1 in 15 chance of succeeding. Typically, you'll have to place the marker a few frames before the hard cut, or a few frames after, and this can wreak havoc on your presentation.

However, you can encode markers directly into the MPEG stream using Final Cut Pro, Final Cut Express, iMovie, or Compressor, which all let you place markers exactly where you need them, right down to the frame. The use of Final Cut Pro to encode markers into your MPEG streams is covered later in this chapter, in the section "Adding Markers with Final Cut Pro." For now, let's look at the procedure for adding markers within DVD Studio Pro.

To create a marker in the Track editor:

1. In the Track editor, place the pointer over the Marker area at the position where you want to create the new maker (**Figure 12.2**).
2. Click the Marker area to create a new marker.

   A marker is added to the Marker area (**Figure 12.3**).

✔ Tip

- Just as in Final Cut Pro, you can also press the M key on your keyboard to create a marker at the playhead's current position in the timeline.

To create a marker at the end of a clip:

1. In the timeline, Control-click a clip.

   A shortcut menu appears (**Figure 12.4**).

2. From the shortcut menu, choose Add Marker to Clip End or Add Chapter to Clip End. (The distinction between markers and chapter markers is discussed in "Specifying the Marker Type" later in this chapter.)

   A new marker is added at the end of the clip (**Figure 12.5**).

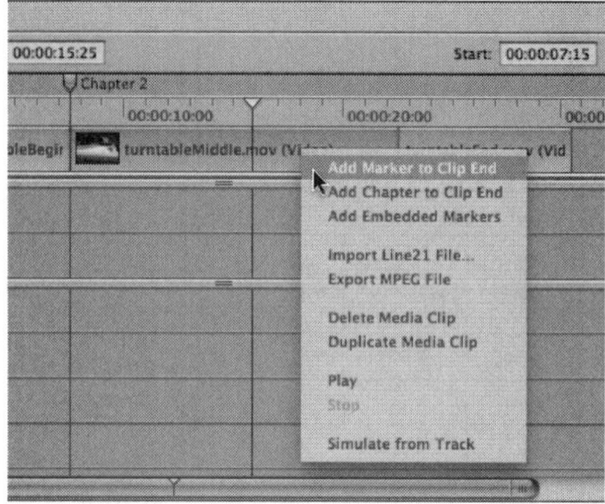

Figure 12.4 To add a marker to the end of a clip, Control-click the clip and choose Add Marker to Clip End.

✔ Tip

- If the stream contains only one clip, or if you Control-click a clip that extends to the end of the track, the options for adding markers to the clip's end are dimmed. This is DVD Studio Pro's way of telling you it's illegal to add a marker at the end of a stream.

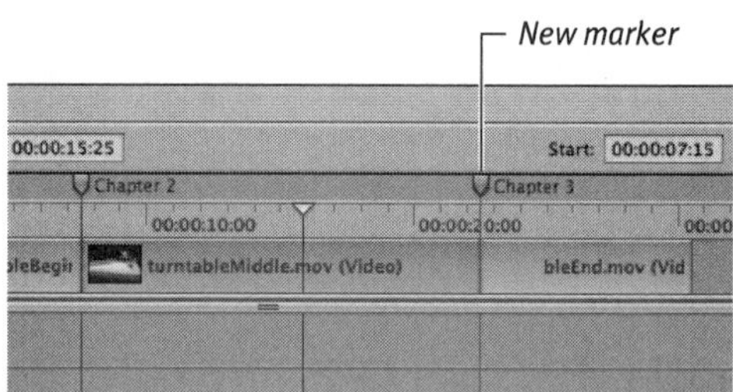

Figure 12.5 A new marker is added at the end of the clip.

To delete a marker:

- In the timeline, *do one of the following:*
  - Click a marker to select it; then press the Delete key.
  - Control-click the marker; then choose Delete Marker from the shortcut menu that appears (**Figure 12.6**).

  The marker is deleted.

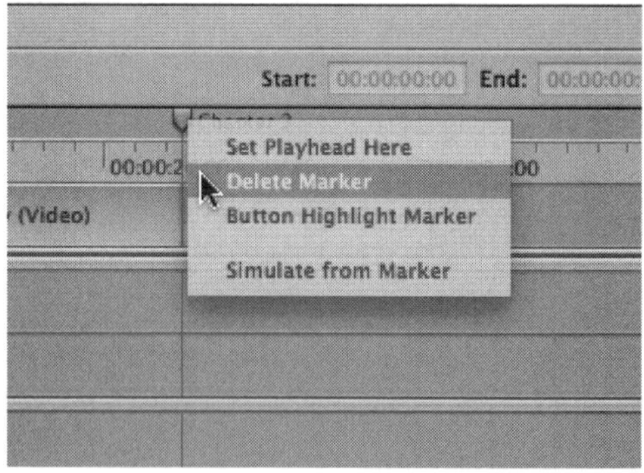

Figure 12.6 To delete a marker, Control-click it and choose Delete Marker from the shortcut menu.

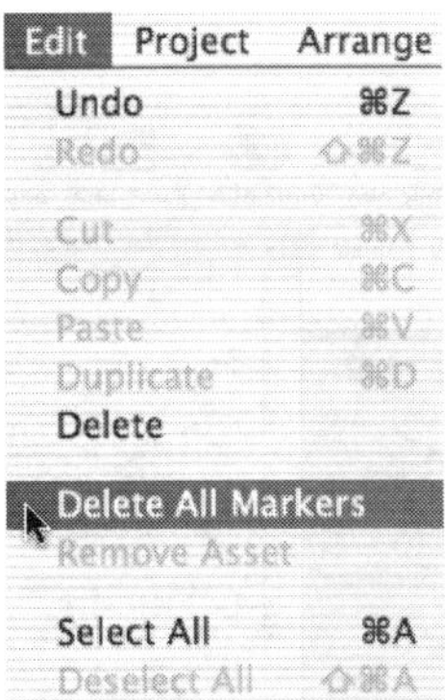

Figure 12.7 To delete all of a track's markers, choose Edit > Delete All Markers, or...

Figure 12.8 ...Control-click an empty part of the Track editor's Marker area and choose Delete All Markers from the resulting shortcut menu.

To delete all markers in a track:

- *Do one of the following:*
  - ▲ From the Edit menu, choose Delete All Markers (**Figure 12.7**).
  - ▲ In the timeline, Control-click an empty part of the Marker area and choose Delete All Markers from the shortcut menu that appears (**Figure 12.8**).

All of the track's markers are deleted.

Using Marker Snapping

As discussed earlier, markers must be placed on I-frames, which means that for a typical NTSC MPEG stream, markers can be placed only once every 15 frames. If you attempt to create a marker on a frame that is not an I-frame, DVD Studio Pro must decide whether to snap the marker to the next I-frame or the preceding I-frame in the MPEG stream. This behavior is controlled by a DVD Studio Pro preference.

✔ Tip

- You can't place two markers on the same I-frame. If you try, DVD Studio Pro will move the second marker to the nearest I-frame that does not have a marker.

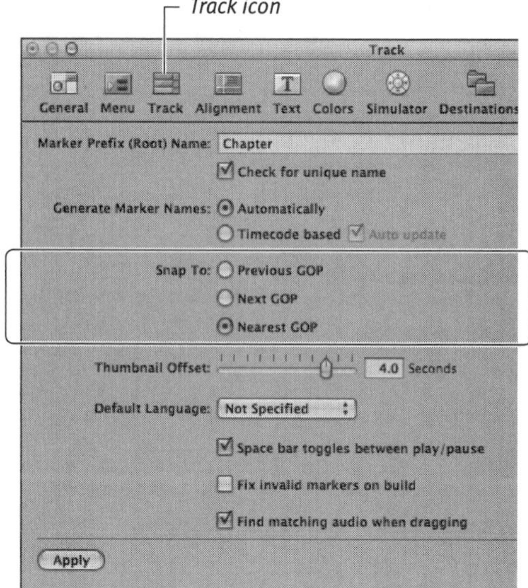

Figure 12.9 The Track section of DVD Studio Pro's Preferences window has a Snap To setting that determines how markers are moved to the nearest I-frame.

To specify how markers snap to I-frames:

1. Choose DVD Studio Pro > Preferences, or press Command-, (comma).

   The Preferences window opens.
2. At the top of the Preferences window, click the Track icon (**Figure 12.9**).

   In the middle of the Track pane is a Snap To area, which contains three radio buttons: Previous GOP, Next GOP, and Nearest GOP. (Don't get confused by the fact that the setting says Nearest *GOP* or Next *GOP*—DVD Studio Pro actually moves the marker to an I-frame in the GOP.)
3. In the Track pane's Snap To area, choose an option.

✔ Tips

- To prevent markers from becoming detached from I-frames, add markers only after you've finished arranging clips to create the track.
- DVD Studio Pro will not build a project if any tracks have a marker on the last frame of video. If you select the Fix Invalid Markers on Build check box, DVD Studio Pro will move the offensive marker forward in the stream by exactly one GOP when it builds your project.
- When using the Slideshow editor's Convert to Track function, make sure Fix Invalid Markers on Build is selected, or you may experience an Illegal Angle error when building your project. To learn more about slideshows, see Chapter 18, "Slideshows."

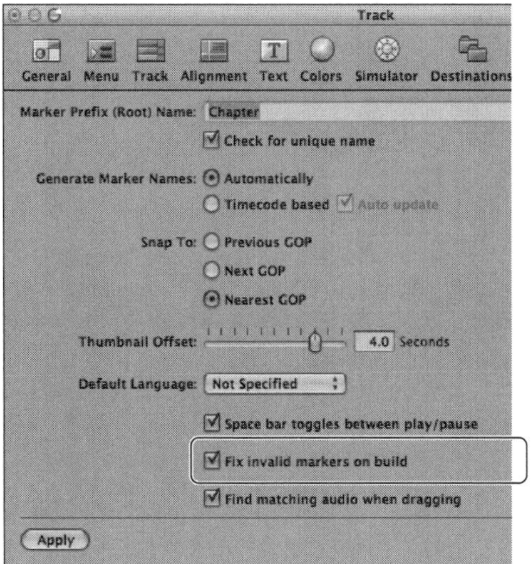

Figure 12.10 Select the Fix Invalid Markers on Build check box to avoid problems when you later build your project. This option ensures that every marker is locked onto the nearest I-frame.

Placing Markers Where There Is No Video

In preparation for adding a video clip later, you may decide to place a few markers beyond the right edge of a track, or even in a track that doesn't currently have a video asset. In this situation, the track's groups of pictures (GOP) structure hasn't been set up yet. As a result, when you eventually add the video asset, DVD Studio Pro must reconcile the difference between the markers' current position in the timeline and the position of the video stream's GOPs. To do so, DVD Studio Pro relies on the setting you made in the Snap To area of the Preferences window's Track section.

Fixing Invalid Markers

If you add markers to a track but then rearrange the video streams in the track, the markers do not automatically shift to lock onto the nearest I-frame. Regardless of the Track section's Snap To setting in the Preferences window, the markers stay steadfastly in their current positions in the timeline. This will cause problems when it comes time to build your project, because DVD Studio Pro needs all markers to be locked onto I-frames before it can compile the finished DVD-Video. To keep DVD Studio Pro from aborting the build process due to invalid marker positions, enable the Fix Invalid Markers on Build preference (**Figure 12.10**).

To fix invalid markers:

1. Choose DVD Studio Pro > Preferences, or press Command-, (comma).

   The Preferences window opens.

2. At the top of the Preferences window, click the Track icon.

   The Track pane opens. At the bottom of the Track pane is the Fix Invalid Markers on Build preference (refer to Figure 12.10).

3. Click the Fix Invalid Markers on Build check box so that it is selected.

Viewing Markers

If you need a reminder of what the video looks like at a certain marker, you must move the playhead to that marker. The Viewer will then update to show you the frame that's located just under the playhead. As you saw in Chapter 11, "Using Tracks," you can move the playhead to the next or previous marker by pressing Control-right arrow or Control-left arrow, but that isn't efficient if a track contains dozens of markers. Instead, try the following trick to jump the playhead right to the marker you need to view.

To move the playhead to a marker:

- In the timeline, Control-click a marker that you want to view and choose Set Playhead Here from the resulting shortcut menu (**Figure 12.11**).

  The playhead jumps to the marker's position, and the Viewer updates to show you the frame of video directly under the playhead, which now also happens to be the frame of video at the marker's position in the track.

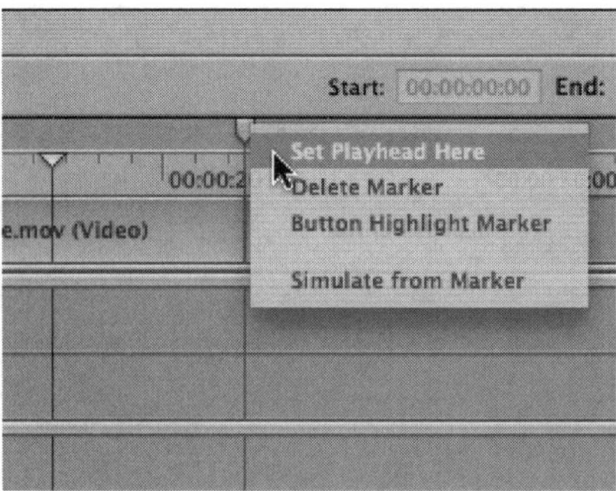

Figure 12.11 To view the video under a marker, Control-click the marker and choose Set Playhead Here from the shortcut menu that appears. The playhead will jump to the marker, and DVD Studio Pro's Viewer will update to show you the frame at the playhead's position.

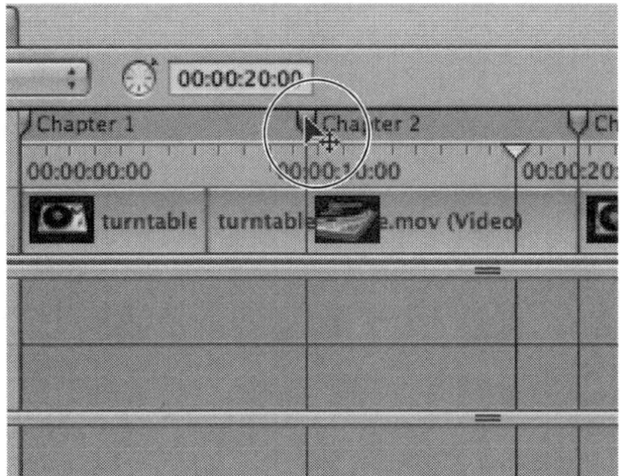

Figure 12.12 To name a marker, select it in the timeline.

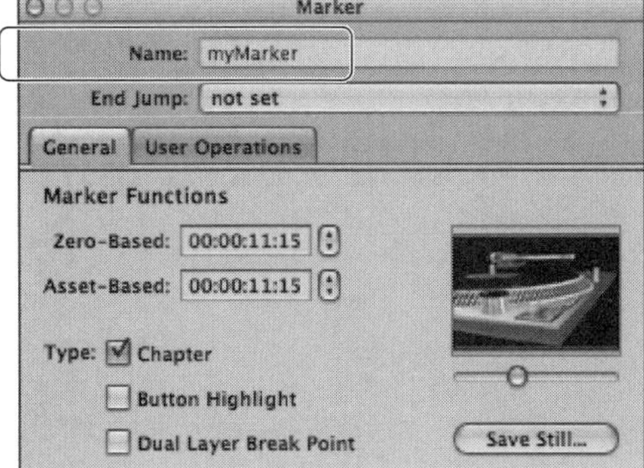

Figure 12.13 The Inspector updates to show the marker's properties. Type a new name in the Name text box.

Naming Markers

DVD Studio Pro automatically supplies every new marker with a name. By default, each newly created marker is a chapter marker and is given the name Chapter *x*, where *x* is a number that increases by one for each new marker created. To make markers easier to recognize, supply each one with a custom name instead.

To name a marker:

1. In the timeline, select a marker (**Figure 12.12**).

   The Inspector updates to display the marker's properties. At the top of the Inspector is a name setting.

2. Type a new name in the Inspector's Name text box (**Figure 12.13**).

✔ Tip

- To enter a new name for a marker, you must use the Inspector. Don't try to double-click the marker's name in the Track editor—doing so just creates a new marker.

Changing the default marker name

As you just learned, when you create a new marker, DVD Studio Pro automatically names it Chapter *x*, where *x* is a number that increases by one for each new marker created. As you'll learn a bit later in this chapter, DVD Studio Pro can create four different types of markers. Consequently, Chapter *x* may not be the best default marker name. You can change the default name in the Track section of the Preferences window.

To change the default marker name:

1. Choose DVD Studio Pro > Preferences, or press Command-, (comma).

   The Preferences window opens.

2. At the top of the Preferences window, click the Track icon.

   At the top of the Track pane is a Marker Prefix (Root) Name setting (**Figure 12.14**). This setting defines the name given to new markers created in the timeline.

3. In the Marker Prefix (Root) Name text box, enter a new default name for your markers.

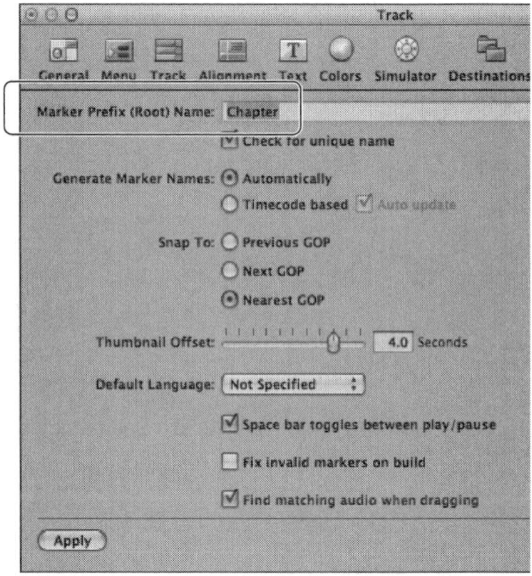

Figure 12.14 Use the Marker Prefix (Root) Name setting in the Track section of the Preferences window to supply the default name given to markers in the Track editor.

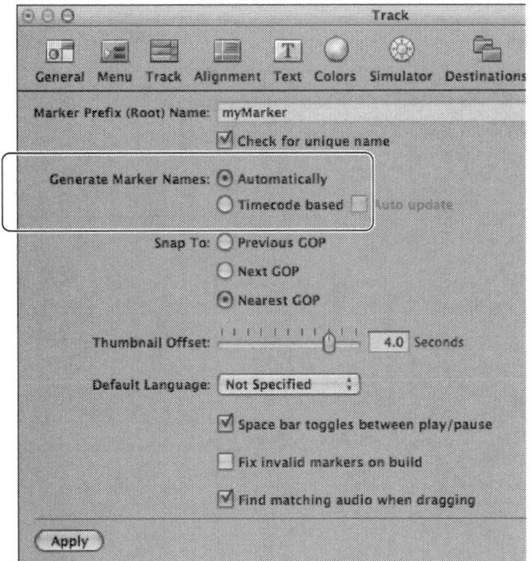

Figure 12.15 The Generate Marker Names settings in the Track section of the Preferences window determine whether new marker names are incremented by one or supplied with a timecode value.

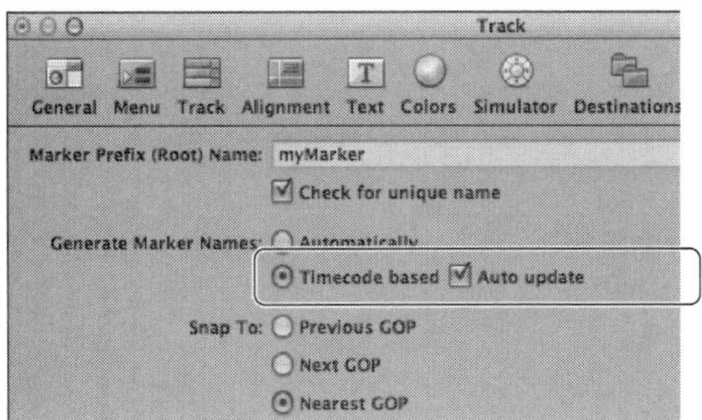

Figure 12.16 Select the Timecode Based radio button and the Auto Update check box to ensure that new markers always maintain their correct timecode values.

Using timecode to name markers

Instead of having each default marker name increase by a value of one, you can tell DVD Studio Pro to name the marker with its timecode value. The timecode value will be displayed to the right of the marker's name in the Track editor and all of DVD Studio Pro's target menus.

To name markers with timecode:

1. Choose DVD Studio Pro > Preferences, or press Command-, (comma).

   The Preferences window opens.

2. From the top of the Preferences window, click the Track icon.

   Close to the top of the Track pane is a Generate Marker Names setting (**Figure 12.15**). By default, Automatically is selected, which causes marker names to increment by one for each new marker added to a track. If you select Timecode Based, new markers will be supplied with a timecode value instead of an incrementing number.

3. In the Generate Marker Names area, select the Timecode Based radio button.

   To the right of the Timecode Based setting is the Auto Update check box. If you select this check box, each time you move a marker along the timeline, the marker's name updates to reflect its new timecode value.

4. Select the Auto Update check box (**Figure 12.16**).

Moving Markers

Sometimes you'll add a marker to the wrong place in a track. Oh, yes, it happens. If you're dealing with a long track and you're zoomed w-a-a-a-y out (so you can see the entire track), for example, you don't have precise control over exactly where the marker is being placed. In this situation, you'll more than likely need to shift the marker a little to the left or right.

To move a marker in the timeline:

- In the timeline, select the marker that you want to move and drag it to the left or right.

✔ Tip

- As you drag the marker to its new location, the Viewer updates to show you the video under the marker's current position. This lets you visually verify the marker's new position.

To move a marker using the marker slider:

1. In the timeline, select a marker.

   The Inspector updates to show the marker's properties. At the top right of the Marker Inspector's General tab is a thumbnail image that shows the frame of video directly under the marker. Under this thumbnail sits a slider (**Figure 12.17**). You can drag this slider to reposition the marker.

2. On the Marker Inspector's General tab, drag the marker slider to the left or right.

   In the timeline, the marker moves to the left or right, following the marker slider's movement.

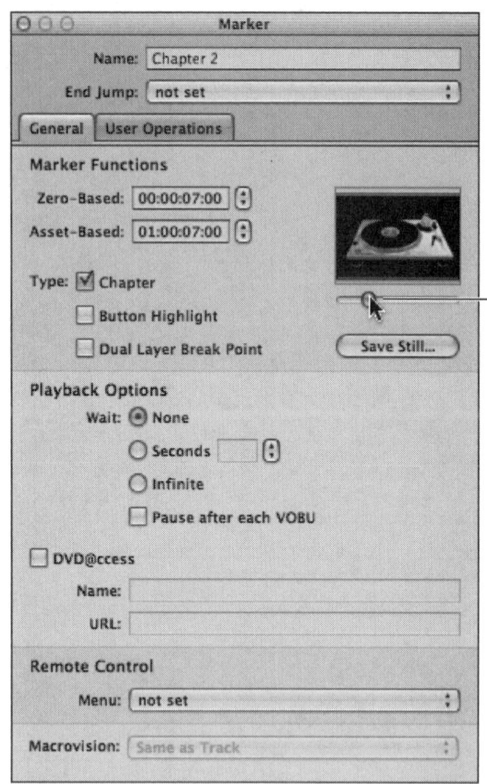

Figure 12.17 The marker slider lets you quickly move a marker along the timeline.

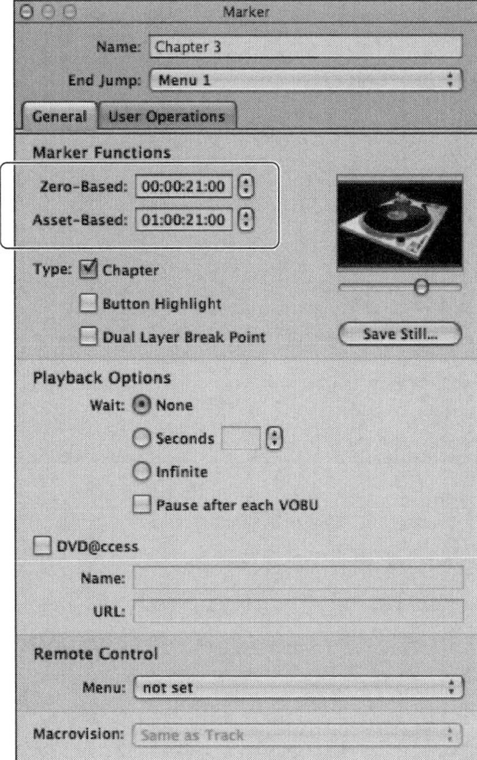

Figure 12.18 The Marker Inspector's timecode boxes allow you to enter exact timecode values as you position markers in a track.

✔ Tips

- The marker slider is very useful if you need to move a marker when the Viewer is not currently open, because you can see the marker's new position without opening the Viewer.
- Under the marker slider is a Save Still button. This button enables you to save a still image (TIFF) of the video frame that's directly under the marker. This still image makes a perfect template for designing motion menus or overlay images for button highlight markers. To learn more, see Chapter 15, "Overlay Menus."

To move a marker using timecode:

1. In the timeline, select the marker that you want to move.

   The Inspector updates to show the marker's properties. In the Marker Functions section near the top of the Marker Inspector's General tab are two timecode boxes: Zero-Based and Asset-Based (**Figure 12.18**). The Zero-Based timecode box always displays the marker's position from the beginning of the track, based on a timescale that begins at 00:00:00:00. The Asset-Based timecode box displays a timescale based on the track offset you entered in the Track Inspector's Track Offset box, as described in Chapter 11.
2. In the Marker Functions section near the top of the Marker Inspector's General tab, enter a new timecode value in either the Zero-Based or Asset-Based timecode box.
3. On your keyboard, press Enter.

   The marker jumps to the new timecode position.

To shift a marker one GOP at a time:

1. In the timeline, select a marker.

   The Inspector updates to show the marker's properties. To the right of the Marker Inspector's Zero-Based and Asset-Based timecode boxes (located on the General tab) are two sets of up and down arrows.

2. Click the up or down arrow beside either the Zero-Based or Asset-Based timecode box (it doesn't matter which) to shift the marker one GOP to the right or one GOP to the left (**Figure 12.19**).

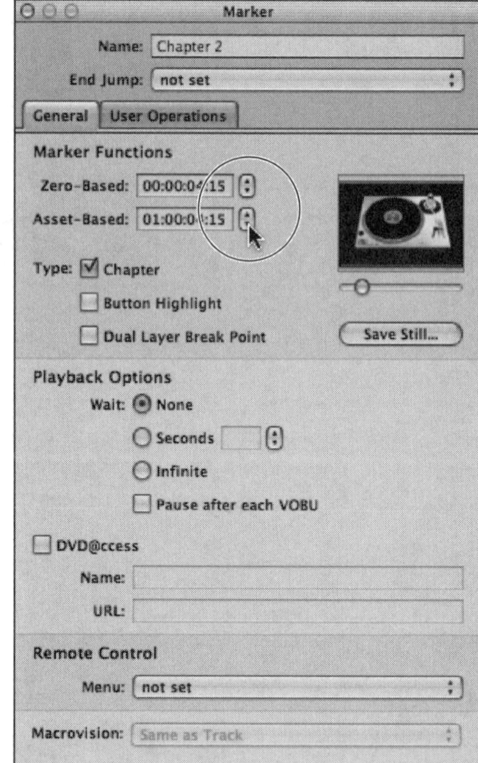

Figure 12.19 Click the up and down arrows beside the Marker Inspector's timecode boxes to shift a selected marker one GOP at a time.

Specifying the Marker Type

While it's common to refer to markers simply as chapters, or chapter markers, they actually come in four varieties (and colors): chapter (purple), button highlight (orange), dual-layer break-point (black dot), and cell (green) markers. Of the four types, chapter markers are the most common, because *only chapter markers can be linked to menu buttons, scripts, and end jumps from other project elements.* However, all four marker types have their special uses, as outlined in this section.

✔ Tip

- A single marker can be any combination of chapter, button highlight, and dual-layer break-point types. For example, a chapter marker may need to have button highlights and also indicate a dual-layer break. If you assign multiple types to a marker, the marker splits to display all relevant colors.

Creating chapter markers

Chapter markers are created by default whenever you add a marker to the timeline. Chapter markers are usually the type you need, as they are the only ones that other project elements can link to. Additionally, the Previous Program and Next Program keys on the remote control skip between chapters, and they are also the only markers that show up in the DVD-Video player's displays.

As mentioned earlier, while you can add up to 255 markers to a track, only 99 of those markers can be chapter markers.

✔ Tips

- Subtitles cannot cross chapter markers. For more information, see Chapter 24, "Subtitles."
- If you watch the Log window while simulating a track and then click the Next or Previous key on the Simulator, the Log window actually says "Next Chapter" or "Previous Chapter."
- If your track needs more than 99 chapters, you must divide the track into two (or more) different tracks.

To create a chapter marker:

1. In the timeline, select a marker.

   The Inspector updates to display the marker's properties.

2. On the Marker Inspector's General tab, select the Chapter check box (**Figure 12.20**).

   In the timeline, the marker turns purple and becomes a chapter marker.

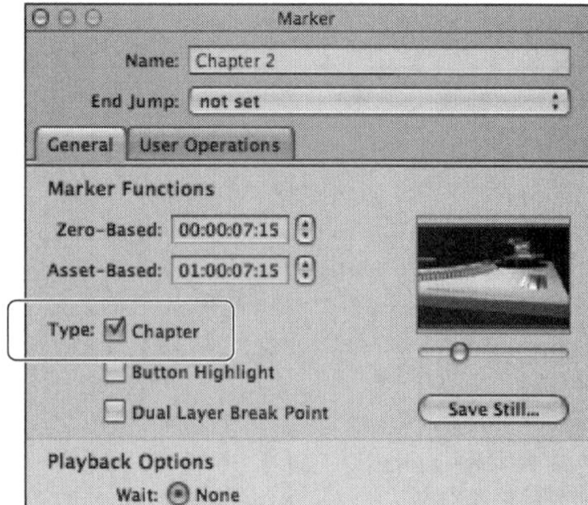

Figure 12.20 To turn a marker into a chapter marker, select the Marker Inspector's Chapter check box.

Creating button highlight markers

Button highlight markers are often called *interactive markers* because they allow you to place buttons over the top of a track, making the track interactive. (Did you think menus were the only project elements that could have buttons?) A button highlight marker essentially allows you to turn a track into a motion menu. As the DVD-Video plays, the buttons turn on when the track reaches the button highlight marker and turn off when the marker finishes playing. Button highlight markers are discussed in Chapter 15.

✔ Tip

- The advantage of using a button highlight marker to create a motion menu is that you can place the marker several seconds or even several minutes down the track's timeline, which lets you add dramatic and seamless transitions to the menu buttons. However, you can't apply a prescript to a marker. If you need to program the menu to make its own decisions (such as choosing the proper button to highlight based on the last project element played), a button highlight marker won't help you.

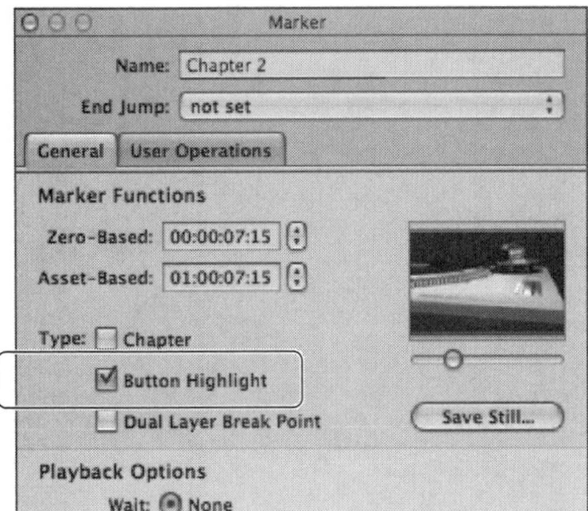

Figure 12.21 To turn a marker into a button highlight marker, select the Marker Inspector's Button Highlight check box.

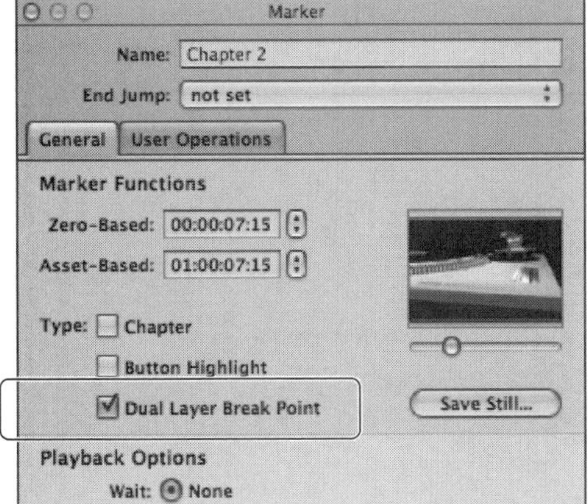

Figure 12.22 To turn a marker into a dual-layer break-point marker, select the Marker Inspector's Dual Layer Break Point check box.

To create a button highlight marker:

1. In the timeline, select a marker.

   The Inspector updates to display the marker's properties.

2. On the Marker Inspector's General tab, select the Button Highlight check box (**Figure 12.21**).

   In the timeline, the marker turns orange and becomes a button highlight marker.

Creating dual-layer break-point markers

In a DVD-9 project, the disc's data is written on two layers of the disc. At a certain point in time, the disc must jump from one layer to the next. You choose that point in time by using a dual-layer break-point marker.

✔ Tip

- When a DVD-Video switches layers, the player's laser must temporarily stop reading one layer and switch to the next layer. Often, this causes a small pause in playback as the laser refocuses. If you've ever watched a Hollywood DVD-Video and noticed a small glitch in playback at around the 45-minute mark, this glitch is the result of the refocusing of the laser as it switches layers.

To create a dual-layer break-point marker:

1. In the timeline, select a marker.

   The Inspector updates to display the marker's properties.

2. On the Marker Inspector's General tab, select the Dual Layer Break Point check box (**Figure 12.22**).

   In the timeline, the marker has a dot placed in it and becomes a dual-layer break-point marker.

Creating cell markers

Use cell markers whenever you need a marker that the remote control's Next Program or Previous Program key will ignore. For example, cell markers are often used to cue DVD@ccess links, turn off buttons in a button highlight marker, or define the in and out points for mixed angles in alternate-angle tracks.

To create a cell marker:

1. In the timeline, select a marker.

   The Inspector updates to display the marker's properties.

2. On the Marker Inspector's General tab, deselect all of the Type check boxes (**Figure 12.23**).

   In the timeline, the marker turns green and becomes a cell marker.

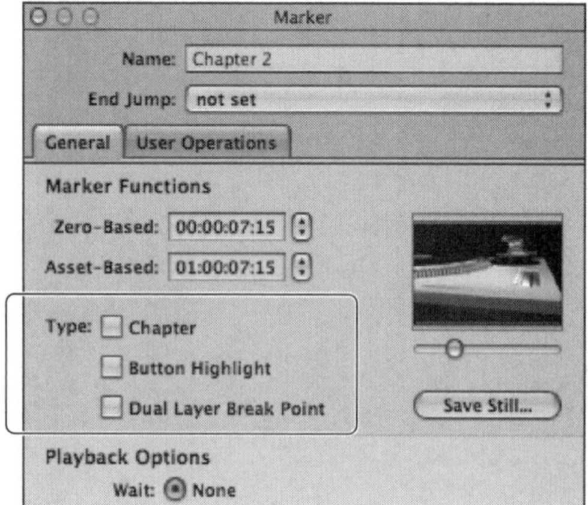

Figure 12.23 To turn a marker into a cell marker, deselect all of the Type check boxes.

Setting a Marker's End Jump

A marker defines a specific section of the track. Each marker's duration is defined by the distance between it and the next marker to its right in the track. If there is no marker to the right, the end of the track determines the duration.

Under normal playback circumstances, once a marker finishes playing, the track moves seamlessly to the next marker. In some situations, however, it's useful to have the DVD-Video jump to a different project element after a marker finishes playing. For example, if you've combined several small videos (such as several music videos) into a single track, you might want to use chapter markers to define each video as a section in the track and then have the DVD-Video jump back to a selection menu after each chapter plays. This is extremely easy to set up using the marker End Jump property.

✔ Tips

- Marker end jumps do not carry over to stories. As a result, you can set end jumps for markers in a track and then add the markers to a story (such as a Play All story) without fear that the DVD-Video will execute the marker end jumps while playing the story.
- You can use the End Jump property to select buttons on menus. In this situation, when the DVD-Video jumps back to the menu, the chosen button is automatically selected and highlighted.

To set a marker's end jump:

1. In the timeline, select a marker.

   The Inspector updates to show the marker's properties. Near the top of the Marker Inspector is an End Jump menu.
2. From the End Jump menu, choose the project element to which you want the marker to jump (**Figure 12.24**).

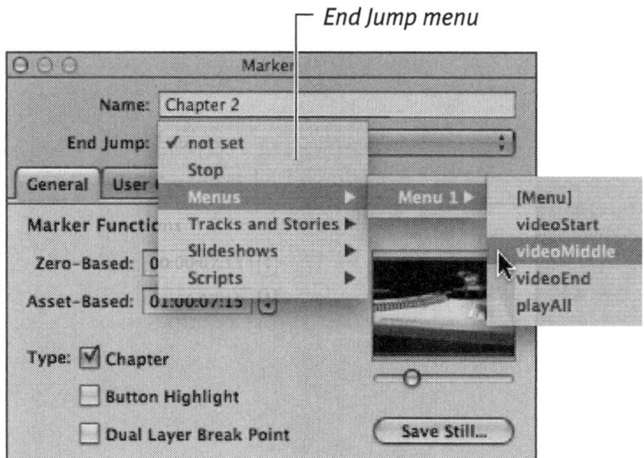

Figure 12.24 The End Jump property tells the DVD-Video to jump to a different project element after playing a marker.

Setting a Marker's End Jump

Using Marker Playback Settings

Marker playback settings are used to pause a track after, or even as, a marker plays. You have two settings at your disposal: Wait, which pauses the DVD-Video at a marker after it finishes playing, and Pause after Each VOBU (video object unit), which continuously pauses at a marker during playback.

Pausing after playback

A marker can be set to pause after playback finishes, before the DVD-Video moves on to the next marker. If the marker has an end jump assigned, the DVD-Video will pause before executing the end jump. This Wait setting is located on the Marker Inspector's General tab (**Figure 12.25**). The choices are:

- **None.** There is no wait, and the DVD-Video immediately jumps to the project item selected as the marker's end jump.
- **Seconds.** The DVD-Video pauses for the specified number of seconds before executing the marker's end jump. You can choose any amount of seconds from 1 to 254.
- **Infinite.** The DVD-Video pauses until the viewer presses the remote control's Menu or Title key, or until the viewer stops playback. (To learn more about the remote control's Menu and Title keys, see Chapter 19. "Finishing the DVD.")

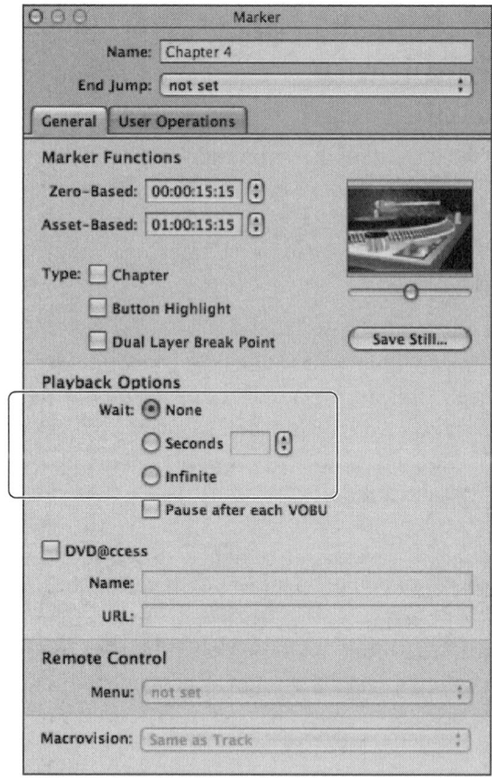

Figure 12.25 The marker's Wait property determines how long the marker should pause before executing a jump action.

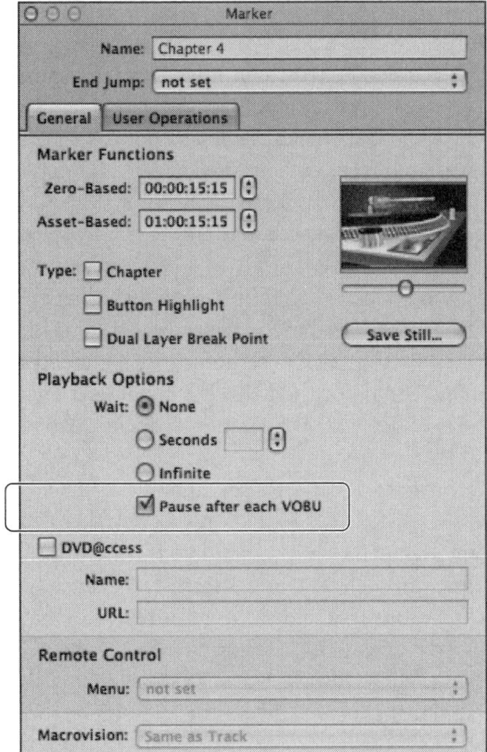

Figure 12.26 The Pause after Each VOBU setting causes the track to pause often as a marker plays. To continue playback, the viewer must press the remote control's Play key.

To set a marker to pause after playback:

1. In the Track editor, select a marker.

   The Inspector updates to show the marker's properties.

2. In the Marker Inspector, make sure the General tab is selected.

   In the middle of the General tab is a section listing the Wait properties (refer to Figure 12.25).

3. In the Wait area, select the None, Seconds, or Infinite radio button.

4. If you clicked the Seconds radio button, enter a number in the Seconds text box to specify the number of seconds the track should wait before the track continues to play.

Pausing after each VOBU

The Marker Inspector has a Pause after Each VOBU setting. This setting causes playback to pause until the viewer presses the remote control's Play key, at which point playback continues until the DVD-Video reaches the next VOBU, and then it pauses again.

For MPEG streams, a VOBU is between 0.4 and 1 second in length. (To learn more about VOBUs, see Chapter 2, "DVD 101.") That's a lot of pausing! On the other hand, for still images added to a track, a VOBU lasts for the entire duration of the still clip. Consequently, the Pause after Each VOBU setting is usually used only on still images in tracks to mimic the effect of a slideshow that pauses until the viewer presses the Play key.

To pause after each VOBU:

1. In the timeline, select a marker.

   The Inspector updates to show the marker's properties.

2. In the Marker Inspector's Playback Options area, select the Pause after Each VOBU check box (**Figure 12.26**).

Adding Markers with Final Cut Pro

Final Cut Pro 3.0.2 introduced the ability to set DVD Studio Pro chapter and compression markers right in Final Cut Pro's timeline, and Final Cut Pro HD continues this excellent tradition. When you encode your Final Cut Pro sequence into MPEG-2 video, either from Final Cut Pro or using Compressor, these markers are encoded directly into the stream.

Final Cut Pro lets you add *named chapter markers* to a video sequence. When you encode the sequence into an MPEG-2 video, the chapter markers and their names are included in the video stream. After you import the stream into DVD Studio Pro, these named markers appear in the Track editor. The big advantage to using Final Cut Pro for embedding chapter markers into your video is that you can place the chapter markers on the exact frame that you need—a level of precision that isn't possible in DVD Studio Pro.

Compression markers force an MPEG I-frame on an exact frame of your video stream. They are designed to improve compression for parts of your video that contain areas of abrupt visual change, such as zooms, fast pans, and hard cuts. In the case of a hard cut, for example, where the video instantly changes from one scene to the next, encoding quality is greatly improved by forcing an I-frame on the first frame of the new scene. Otherwise, that hard cut may occur somewhere within a GOP structure, which creates a nightmare for the MPEG encoder as it tries to use P- and B-frames to encode the sudden switch in visual content. (For more information on GOPs, see Chapter 4, "The QuickTime MPEG-2 Exporter.") This, in turn, leads to compression artifacts as the video momentarily breaks up at the scene transition. To avoid these compression artifacts, place a compression marker on the scene transition as you edit the scene in Final Cut Pro.

✔ Tip

- You can also place compression markers before and/or after transitions to improve their encoding quality. If judicious placement of compression markers does not improve the transition's encoded quality, you can also snip the transition out of the sequence, encode it at a higher bit rate than the rest of the stream, and reassemble the sequence in DVD Studio Pro's Track editor.

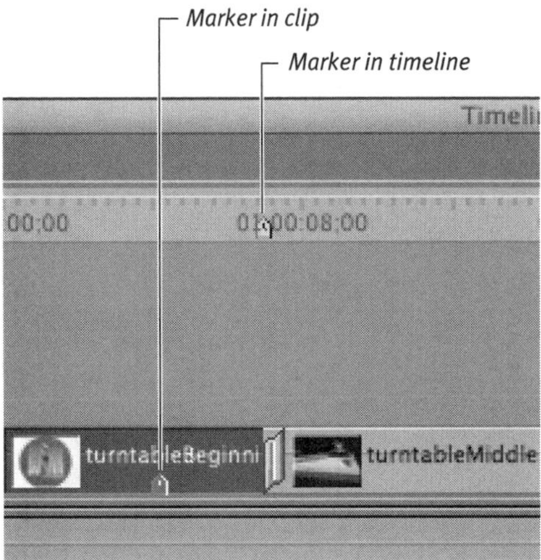

Figure 12.27 Markers added to clips will not be exported into the final MPEG-2 video stream.

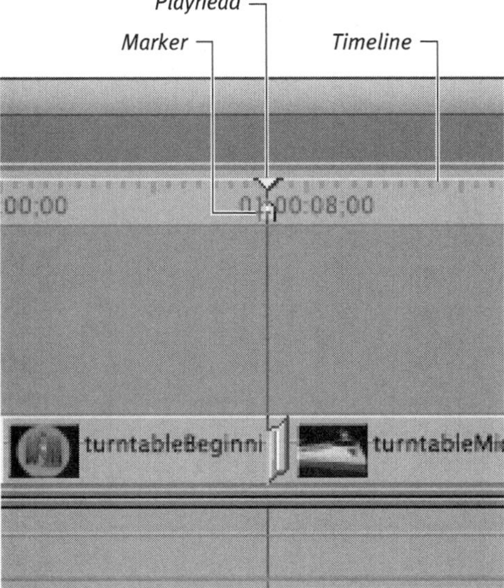

Figure 12.28 To create a marker, move the playhead to the frame where you want to place the marker and press M on your keyboard.

To set markers in Final Cut Pro:

1. In the Final Cut Pro timeline, make sure that no clips are selected.

   This is an important step, because if clips are selected, you may end up adding markers to the clips and not to the sequence timeline itself (**Figure 12.27**). Markers in clips will not be encoded into the MPEG stream!

2. Position the playhead on the frame where you want to place a marker.

3. On your keyboard, press M.

   A new marker is created in the timeline, directly under the playhead's position (**Figure 12.28**).

continues on next page

4. Without moving the playhead, press M a second time.

   The Edit Marker window opens (**Figure 12.29**).

5. In the Edit Marker window's Name text box, enter a name for the marker.

6. *Do one of the following:*

   ▲ To create a compression marker, click the Add Compression Marker button.

   ▲ To create a chapter marker, click the Add Chapter Marker button.

   The Comment field updates to display the type of markers you've just created (**Figure 12.30**).

7. Export an MPEG-2 video stream as described in Chapter 4.

Figure 12.29 Press M a second time to open the Edit Marker window.

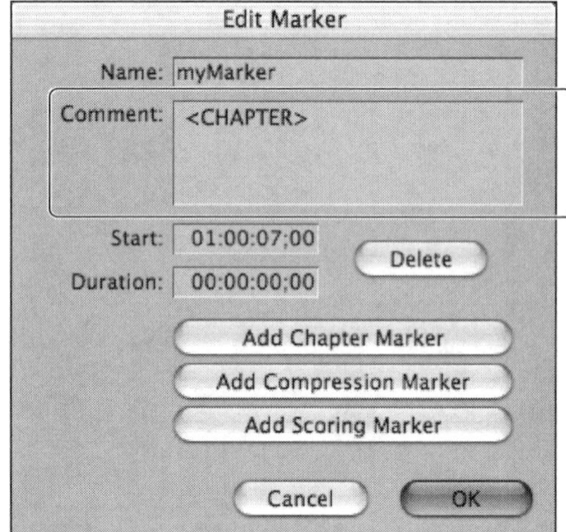

Figure 12.30 The Comment field lists the marker that you've added to this frame.

✔ Tips

- When MPEG streams are exported from Final Cut Pro, there must be at least one second between chapter and compression markers; otherwise, the second marker will be ignored.
- If you accidentally create the wrong type of marker, highlight it in the Marker editor's Comment field and press the Delete key.
- All video streams in multi-angle tracks must have I-frames in exactly the same places (see "Encoding alternate-angle MPEG-2 streams" later in this chapter). Setting chapter or compression markers in Final Cut Pro greatly increases the chance that your video streams will not have corresponding I-frames. Consequently, you should not use Final Cut Pro to set markers in a video stream that you plan to use in a multi-angle or mixed-angle track.

Using Overlays in Final Cut Pro

In Final Cut Pro, it's surprisingly easy to forget to click the Edit Marker window's Add Chapter Marker button when you create chapter markers. To provide yourself with a visual reminder, click the Canvas window and choose View > Show Overlays (**Figure 12.31**). If you now park the playhead over a marker, the Canvas window will show you what type of marker it is (**Figure 12.32**).

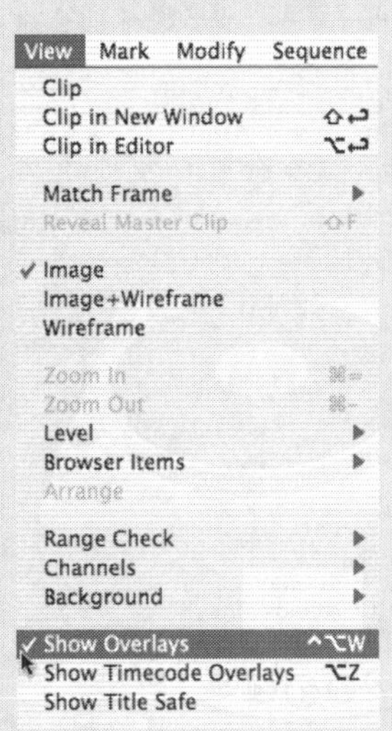

Figure 12.31 In Final Cut Pro, click the Canvas window to make it active; then choose View > Show Overlays.

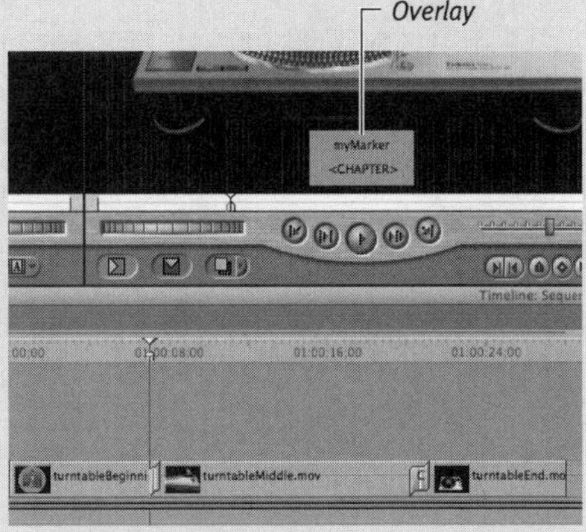

Figure 12.32 The Canvas window shows you the name and type of any marker that the timeline's playhead is parked over. Use this overlay to verify that your markers are the correct type.

Importing Markers into DVD Studio Pro

When you drag an asset with embedded markers into the DVD Studio Pro timeline, one of two things will happen:

- If the track to which you're adding the stream has no markers or other video clips in the V1 stream, the asset's markers are automatically added to the timeline (the marker at the front of the stream does not count). All of the markers maintain the names supplied in Final Cut Pro, iMovie, or Compressor.
- If the track to which you're adding the stream has one or more markers or clips in the V1 stream, the asset's embedded markers are not added.

If the markers are not added, you can use the following trick to force DVD Studio Pro to recognize and add them to the timeline.

To add markers embedded in an MPEG stream to a track's timeline:

1. Add a clip with embedded markers to the V1 stream.
2. In the timeline, Control-click the new clip and choose Add Embedded Markers from the shortcut menu that appears (**Figure 12.33**).

   The clip's embedded markers are added to the timeline.

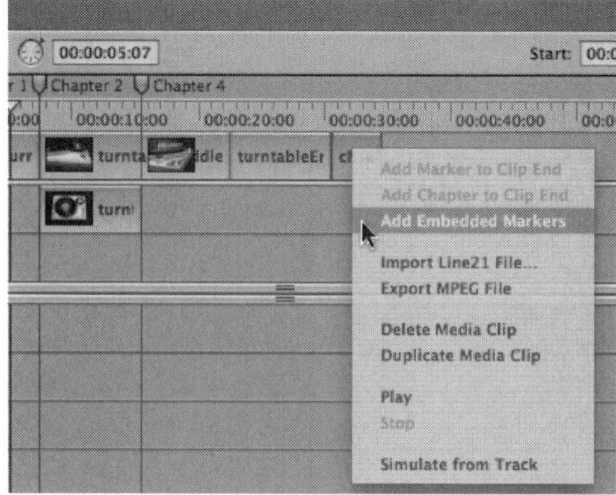

Figure 12.33 To add markers embedded in a clip that you've added to the V1 stream, Control-click the clip and choose Add Embedded Markers from the shortcut menu.

✔ Tips

- You can add only markers embedded in video clips that you've added to the V1 stream. Markers embedded in video clips added to other video streams will not be added to the timeline.
- If there aren't I-frames at the marker list's timecode values, DVD Studio Pro uses the Snap To setting in the Track section of the Preferences window to determine how to shift markers to the nearest I-frame. To learn more, see "Using Marker Snapping" earlier in this chapter.
- If you import markers to a track that already has markers, the new markers are added to the existing ones in the timeline.

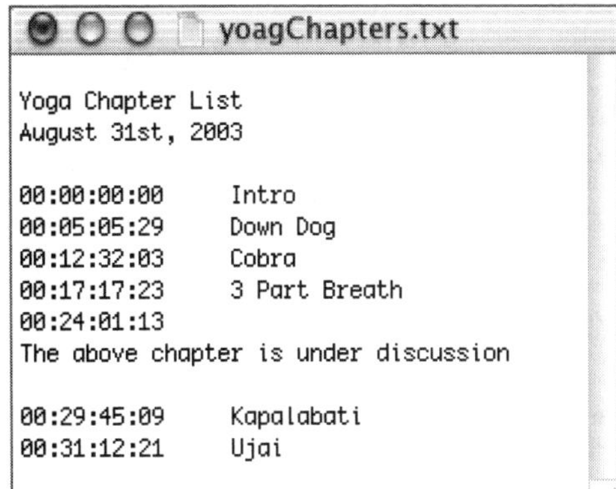
yoagChapters.txt

Yoga Chapter List
August 31st, 2003

00:00:00:00 Intro
00:05:05:29 Down Dog
00:12:32:03 Cobra
00:17:17:23 3 Part Breath
00:24:01:13
The above chapter is under discussion

00:29:45:09 Kapalabati
00:31:12:21 Ujai

Figure 12.34 A marker list saved as a plain-text file can be imported into DVD Studio Pro. Text lists are easy to make, and they save you from having to add chapters to a track by hand.

Importing a marker list

Okay; you've almost finished a DVD-Video project when your client phones and says, "We need to add chapters at X, Y, and Z times in Track A."

"No problem," you reply. "Just e-mail me a list of the chapter timecodes and names" (**Figure 12.34**).

And, indeed, it is no problem, because DVD Studio Pro allows you to import plain-text files directly into the program. This saves you from having to enter each marker by hand. Just follow these rules:

- Only plain-text files with the extension .txt are supported. You can use TextEdit or other word processing programs such as Microsoft Word to create these files. Just make sure that you save the file as plain ASCII text with no formatting; otherwise, DVD Studio Pro may not recognize the file.
- Each marker must be on its own line and must start with a timecode value (either non-drop or drop frame). Timecode values do not have to be listed in chronological order.
- Each marker's name must directly follow the timecode value. Separate the marker name from the timecode value with a comma, space, or tab. If you do not supply a name, DVD Studio Pro automatically names the marker Chapter *x*, where the number *x* is incremented by one for each unnamed marker.
- DVD Studio Pro ignores lines that do not begin with a timecode value. This is not a bug but a feature, because it lets you easily add comments to the marker list.

To import a text marker list:

1. In DVD Studio Pro, in the Track editor, open the track to which you want to add markers.
2. In the Track editor, *do one of the following:*
   - ▲ Control-click the Marker area and choose Import Marker List from the shortcut menu that appears (**Figure 12.35**).
   - ▲ Choose File > Import > Marker List (**Figure 12.36**).

   The Choose Marker File dialog appears (**Figure 12.37**).

Figure 12.35 To import a marker list, Control-click the Marker area and choose Import Marker List from the shortcut menu, or...

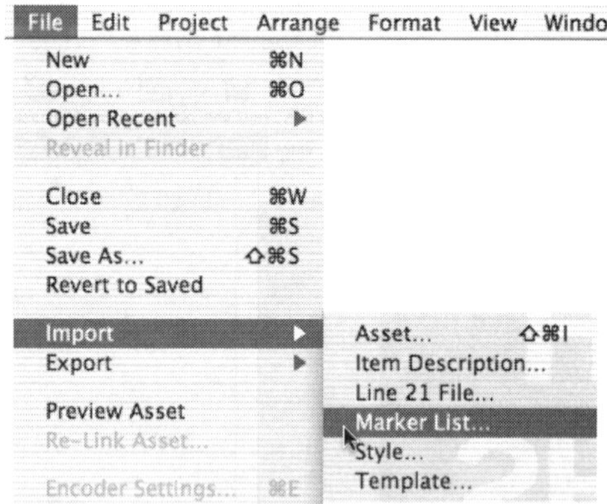

Figure 12.36 ...choose File > Import > Marker List.

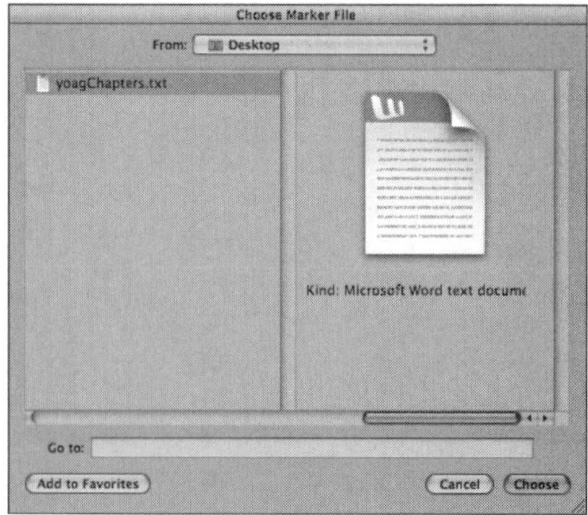

Figure 12.37 The Choose Marker File dialog lets you select the text file containing your marker list.

Figure 12.38 As DVD Studio Pro imports markers from the marker list, this window keeps track of the progress.

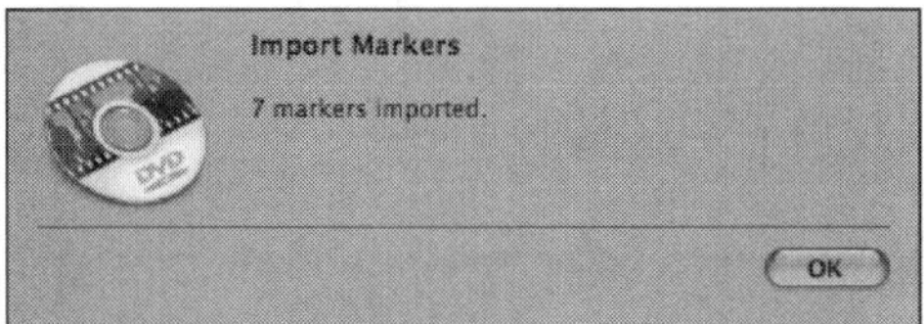

Figure 12.39 When DVD Studio Pro finishes importing the marker list, it tells you how many markers were added to the timeline.

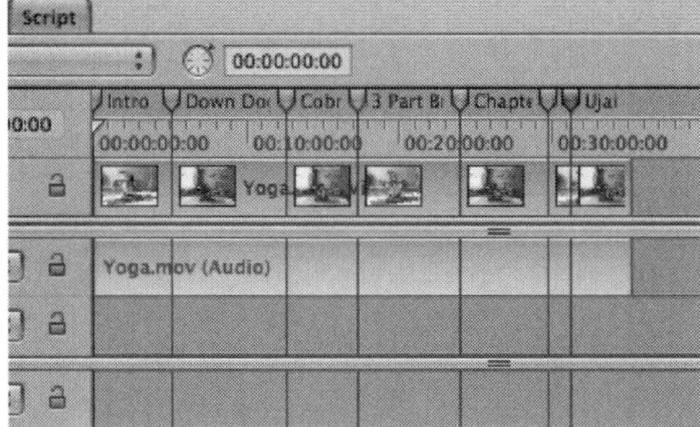

Figure 12.40 The markers imported into the timeline maintain the names supplied in the marker list.

3. Use the Choose Maker File dialog to select the text marker list and then click OK.

   DVD Studio Pro begins importing your markers, and a window opens to let you keep track of the progress (**Figure 12.38**). When DVD Studio Pro is finished, an alert appears telling you how many markers were imported (**Figure 12.39**).

4. In the Import Markers alert dialog, click OK.

   Your imported markers appear in the timeline (**Figure 12.40**).

✔ Tip

- If the video clips in the track's V1 stream are shorter than the timecodes supplied by the marker list, markers will be placed beyond the right edge of the track's clips. You'll need to delete these markers before building the project (or enable the Fix Invalid Markers on Build preference).

About Stories

A *story* is a collection of chapter markers from a single track. As the DVD-Video's author, you get to choose the order of the chapters that make up each story. You can add a single chapter to a story many times, have chapters from later in the track play before chapters from earlier in the track, leave certain chapters out of the story—it's entirely up to you. There are, however, a few limitations on working with stories:

- Stories can contain chapters only from the track to which the story belongs.
- Each project can have only 99 tracks and/or stories combined. This is a big difference from DVD Studio Pro 1.*x*, where you could have 99 tracks, each with up to 99 stories, per project. If you've made the switch from earlier versions of the product, keep this in mind!
- Only chapter markers can be added to stories. (Cell, button highlight, and dual-layer break-point markers are not available for use in stories.)

✔ Tips

- Adding stories does not take up extra room on the DVD disc. The DVD-Video simply references the chapters in the track, skipping back and forth across the track to play the chapters in the same order as they are listed in the story.
- If a story contains chapters that are not sequentially organized in the track, the laser must move and refocus as it jumps from one chapter to the next. Consequently, you may notice a slight pause as the DVD-Video switches from one chapter to the next in the story (only sequential chapters will play seamlessly).

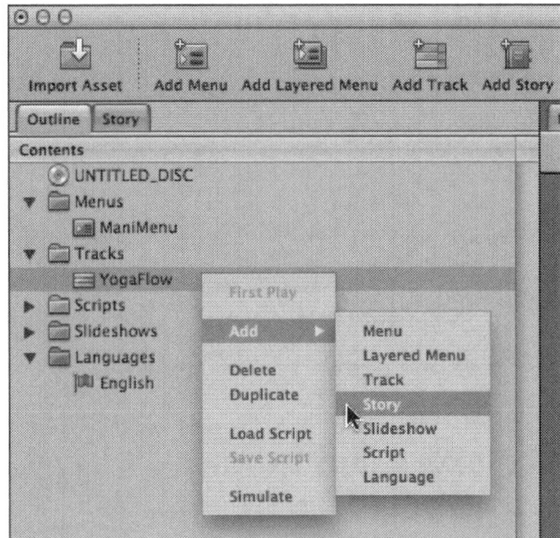

Figure 12.41 To add a story to a track, first select the track in the Outline view; then Control-click anywhere in the Outline view and choose Add > Story, or...

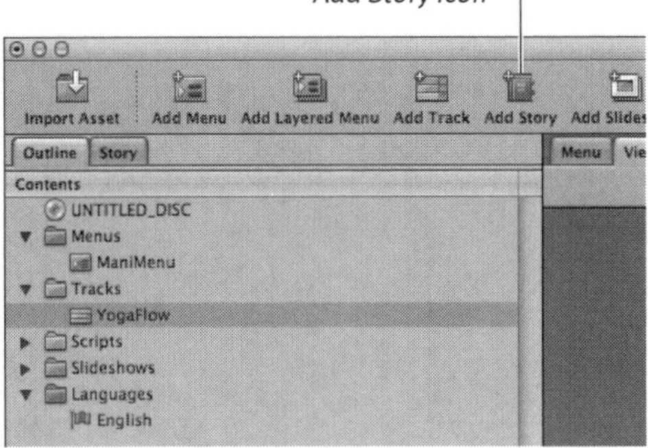

Figure 12.42 ...in the toolbar, click the Add Story icon, or...

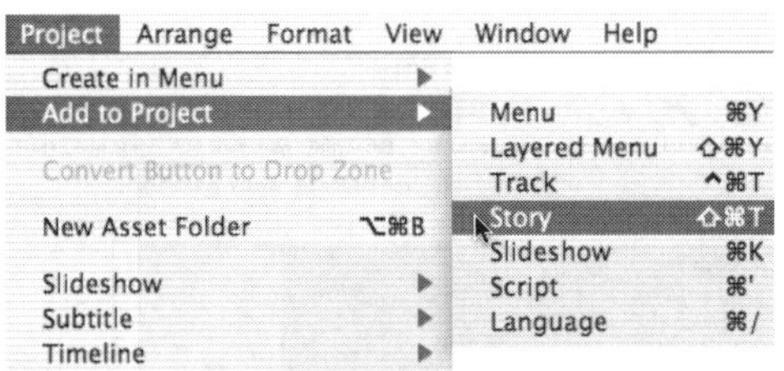

Figure 12.43 ...choose Project > Add to Project > Story.

To create a story:

1. In the Outline view, select the track to which you want to add a story.
2. *Do one of the following:*
   - ▲ Control-click anywhere in the Outline view and choose Add > Story from the shortcut menus that appear (**Figure 12.41**).
   - ▲ In the toolbar, click the Add Story icon (**Figure 12.42**).
   - ▲ Choose Project > Add to Project > Story (**Figure 12.43**).
   - ▲ Press Shift-Command-T.

   A new story is added to the track and appears under the track in the Outline view (**Figure 12.44**).

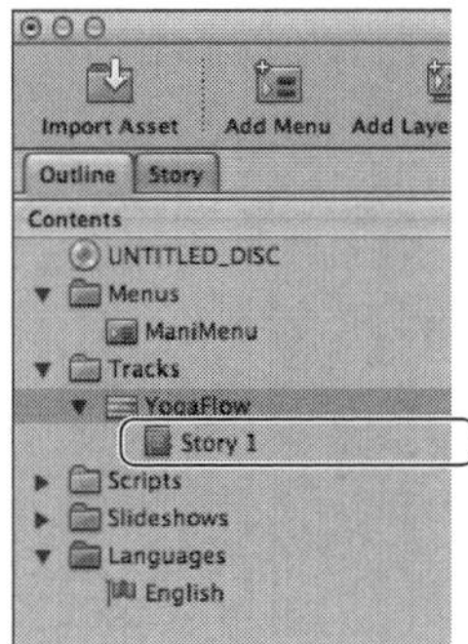

Figure 12.44 A new story is added to the selected track.

Using the Story editor

You use the Story editor to create stories by adding and arranging markers in a finished presentation that plays from the first chapter in the story to the last. The Story editor is divided into halves: the left half is the Source list, and the right half is the Entry list (**Figure 12.45**). The Source list displays a list of all of the markers in the track to which the story belongs, while the Entry list is used to organize the markers that you add to the story.

To open the Story editor:

- *Do one of the following:*
  - ▲ In the Outline view, double-click a story.
  - ▲ Choose Windows > Story Editor, or press Command-8.
  - ▲ Click the Story tab.

  The Story editor opens (refer to Figure 12.45).

To choose a story to edit in the Story editor:

- From the View menu, select the story that you want to edit (**Figure 12.46**).

  The Story editor updates to display the selected story.

View menu
Source list
Entry list

Track | Slideshow | Script | Story

View: Story 1 | YogaFlow

No.	Track Markers	Duration
1	Intro	00:05:06:00
2	Down Dog	00:07:26:00
3	Cobra	00:04:46:00
4	3 Part Breath	00:06:43:15
5	Chapter 5	00:05:44:00
6	Kapalabati	00:01:27:00
7	Ujai	00:04:01:19

No.	Story Markers	Running Time
1	Kapalabati Entry	00:01:27:00
2	Cobra Entry	00:06:13:00
3	Down Dog Entry	00:13:39:00
4	Ujai Entry	00:17:40:19

Figure 12.45 The Story editor

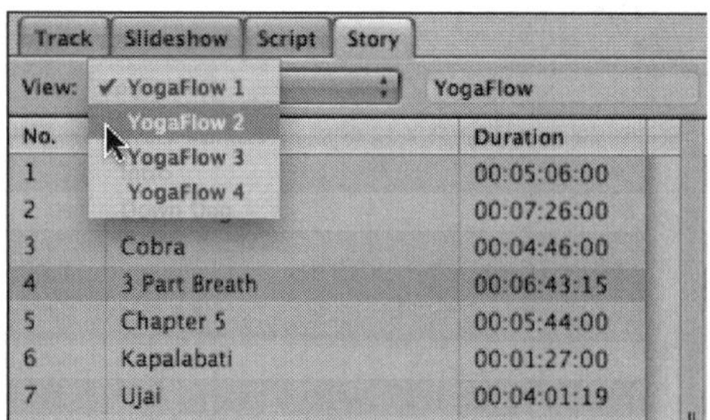

Figure 12.46 The View menu at the top left of the Story editor provides quick access to a track's stories without requiring you to move the pointer out of the Story editor.

To add a marker to the Entry list:

- In the Story editor's Source list, select a marker and drag it into the Entry list (**Figure 12.47**).

✔ Tip

- To see how many markers a story contains without opening the story in the Story editor, hover the pointer over the story for a few seconds in the Outline or Graphical view. A tool tip will pop up, telling you how many markers the story contains (**Figure 12.48**).

To delete a marker from the Entry list:

- In the Story editor's Entry list, select the marker that you want to delete; then press the Delete key.

  The marker is removed from the Entry list.

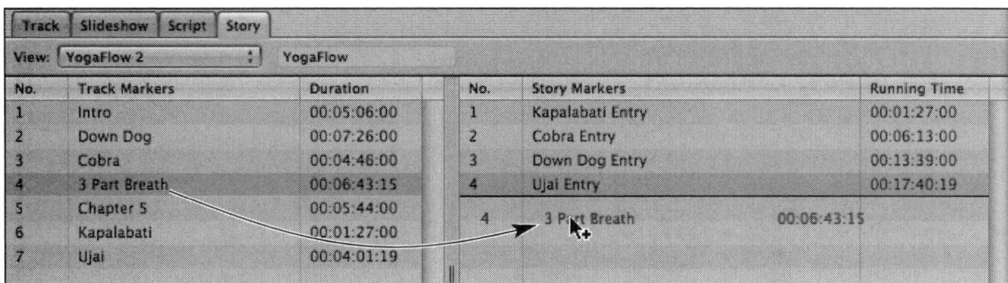

Figure 12.47 To add a marker to a story, drag it from the Source list to the Entry list.

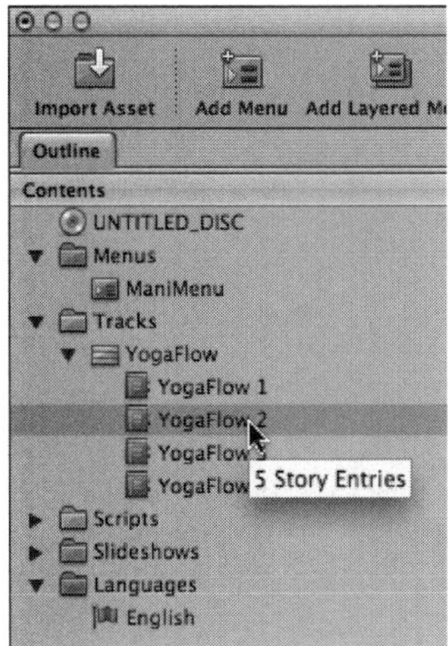

Figure 12.48 In the Outline view, hover the pointer over a story to reveal a tool tip that tells you how many markers (entries) the story contains.

To rearrange markers in the Entry list:

- In the Story editor's Entry list, select the marker that you want to move and drag it up or down the list (**Figure 12.49**).

To replace a marker in the Entry list:

1. In the Story editor's Entry list, Control-click the marker that you want to replace (**Figure 12.50**).

   A shortcut menu opens under the pointer.

2. From the shortcut menu, choose Change Chapter > *Chapter Name*.

   The selected marker replaces the old marker in the Entry list.

✔ Tip

- You can also replace a marker in the Entry list by using the Story Marker Inspector's Track Marker menu (**Figure 12.51**).

Track | Slideshow | Script | Story

View: YogaFlow 2 | YogaFlow

No.	Track Markers	Duration
1	Intro	00:05:06:00
2	Down Dog	00:07:26:00
3	Cobra	00:04:46:00
4	3 Part Breath	00:06:43:15
5	Chapter 5	00:05:44:00
6	Kapalabati	00:01:27:00
7	Ujai	00:04:01:19

No.	Story Markers	Running Time
1	Kapalabati Entry	00:01:27:00
2	Cobra Entry 3 Part Breath Entry	00:06:13:00 00:24:2
3	Down Dog Entry	00:13:39:00
4	Ujai Entry	00:17:40:19
5	3 Part Breath Entry	00:24:24:04

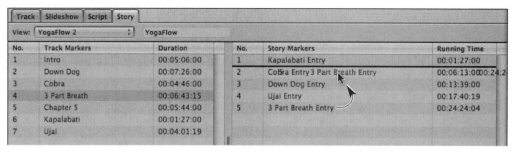

Figure 12.49 To move a marker in the Entry list, drag the marker up or down the list.

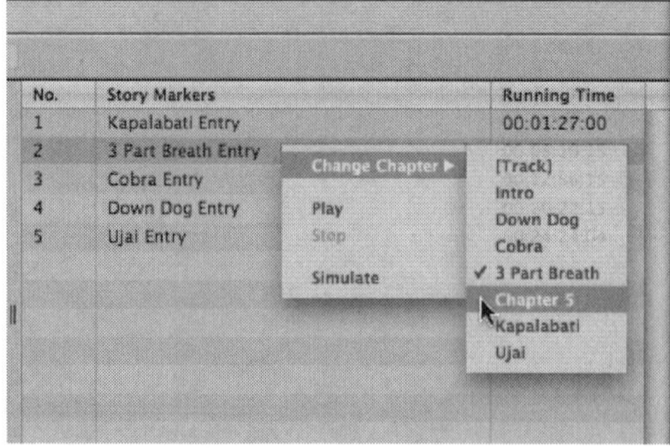

Figure 12.50 To switch a chapter marker in the Story editor's Entry list, Control-click the marker and choose Change Chapter > *Chapter Name*.

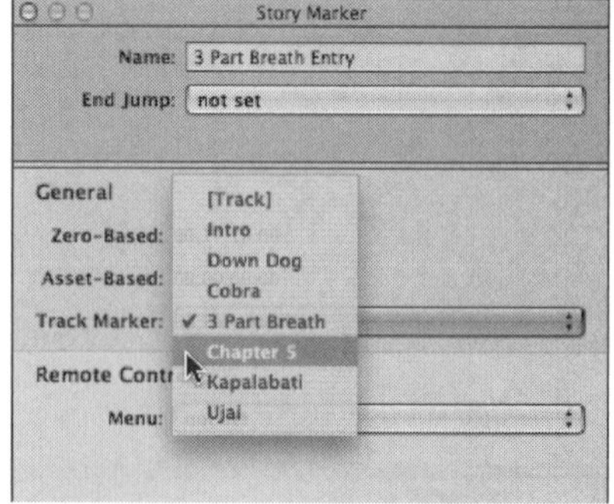

Figure 12.51 You can also use the Story Marker Inspector's Track Marker menu to choose a new marker.

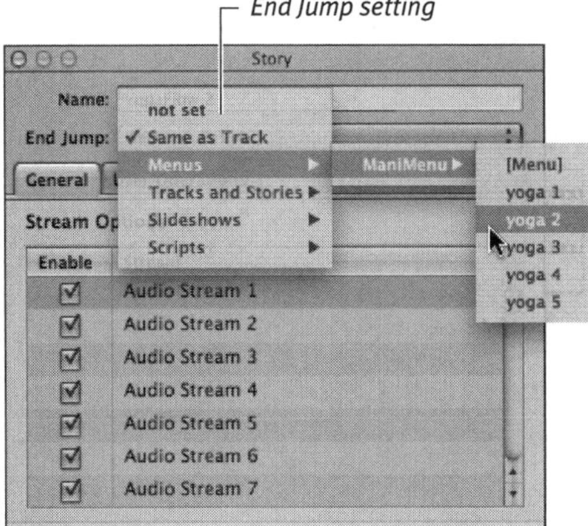

Figure 12.52 The story's End Jump setting tells the story which project element to jump to after it has finished playing.

Setting a story's end jump

A story is really just an alternate presentation of the track's content, and just like the track itself, the story needs to be told what to do after it has finished playing. And just like the track itself, you tell the story what to do by setting its end jump.

To set a story's end jump:

1. In the Outline view, select a story.

   The Inspector updates to show the story's properties. Near the top of the Inspector is the End Jump menu.

2. From the End Jump menu, choose the project element that you want the story to jump to once it has finished playing (**Figure 12.52**).

Using Stories to Create a Play All Button

A common feature of DVD-Video is a Play All button that plays several smaller video clips in sequence. As a video artist, for example, you may want to include several small motion graphics clips in a DVD-Video portfolio. Your project would probably have a menu that allows viewers to select the motion graphics clip that they want to watch. Your project would also likely have a Play All button that allows the viewer to watch all of the clips, back to back. With DVD Studio Pro 3, this type of Play All button is very easy to create. Here are the steps to follow:

1. Use the Track editor to append all of your video clips end to end, one after the other, in a single track.
2. Add chapter markers to the track to define where each clip begins.
3. Set each marker's end jump and Menu key to target the menu. (To learn more about programming the Menu key, see Chapter 19.)
4. Make sure the menu's buttons navigate, or link, to the proper chapter markers in the track.
5. Create a single Play All story that contains all of the chapter markers.
6. Link the menu's Play All button to the Play All story.
7. Set the Play All story's end jump and Menu key to target the menu.

That's all there is to it!

Setting stream options

By default, a story has access to all audio and subtitle streams in a track, and the viewer can flip through these streams using the Audio and/or Subtitle buttons on the remote control. DVD Studio Pro 3, however, gives you the option of excluding certain audio and/or subtitle streams from a story, enabling you to filter out some of the story's content.

For example, you could include a tamer audio stream in a track that normally has objectionable verbal content. Viewers watching the title with children could then choose to watch the story with the family-friendly audio stream instead of the original audio stream. If the parents were to get up and leave the room, the kids couldn't simply switch on the objectionable stream by pressing the Audio button on the remote control. Similarly, you could create a story that plays only a Spanish sound track, or only French, and so on.

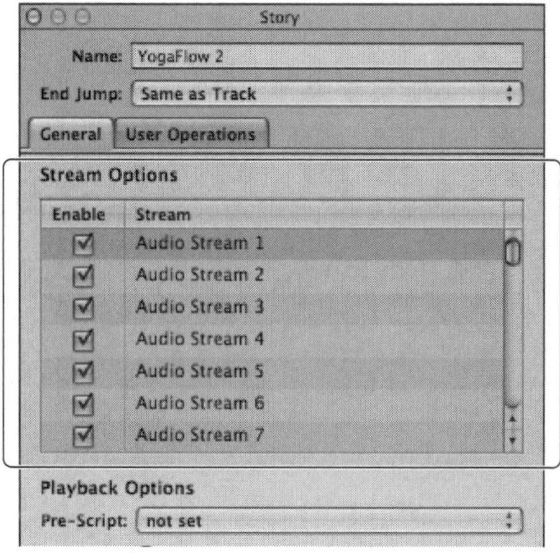

Figure 12.53 The Story Inspector's Stream Options area lets you turn off audio and subtitle streams that you don't want viewers to access as they watch the story.

To set a story's stream options:

1. In the Outline view, select a story.

   The Inspector updates to display the story's properties (**Figure 12.53**). At the top of the General tab is an area labeled Stream Options. All of the track's audio and subtitle streams are listed here.

2. From the Stream Options area, deselect the audio and subtitle streams that you do not want the viewers to access as they play the story.

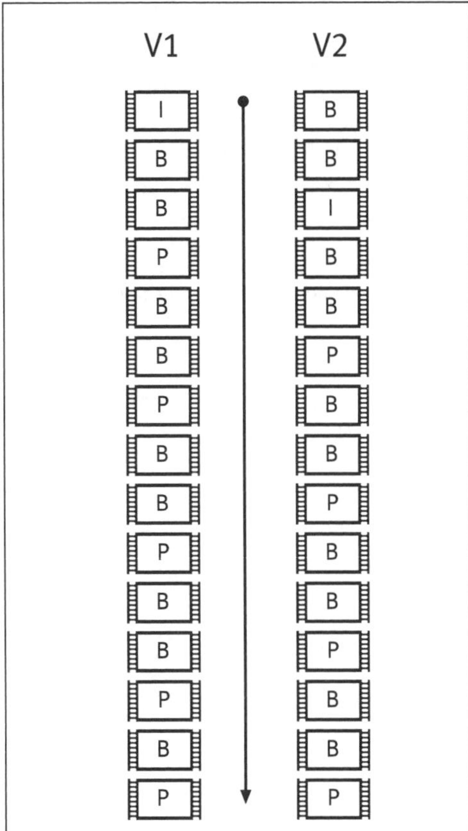

Figure 12.54 An example of GOP structures that are not perfectly aligned. This is an illegal GOP structure for alternate angles in DVD Studio Pro.

About Alternate Angles

One great feature of the DVD-Video specification is the ability to create alternate video streams. These can be used to deliver extra information—such as a wireframe animation that lets you get under the skin of a 3D render, alternate camera streams that show you a yoga instructor from many different sides, or maybe several different "chill-out" video streams that synchronize to a single soundtrack. When it comes to uses for alternate angles, the only limitation is your imagination—and a few DVD-Video specification issues, which you're going to learn about right now.

Encoding alternate-angle MPEG-2 streams

Viewers can switch between alternate angles by pressing the Angle key on the remote control. When a viewer presses the Angle key, however, the DVD player continues playing until it reaches the next I-frame in the video stream; then it switches to the next angle. This explains why a few frames often pass between the time that the viewer presses the button and the moment that the video switches angles.

The DVD-Video player uses the I-frame as a bridge between roads, so to speak, jumping from the I-frame in the first video stream to the I-frame in the second, or alternate, video stream. To complete this exchange, both I-frames must align perfectly. This is the first rule of encoding alternate-angle streams.

Rule #1: To create an alternate video angle, the GOP structure of all alternate-angle streams must be perfectly aligned (**Figure 12.54**)!

continues on next page

If you encode your video streams using the QuickTime MPEG-2 Exporter, all GOPs will be exactly 15 frames, which means that the I-frames from each GOP will align properly in DVD Studio Pro's Track editor. Of course, this assumes that you do not specify predefined chapter or compression markers using a program such as Final Cut Pro or iMovie, which would throw off the GOP structure.

Rule #2: Don't encode chapter or compression markers into alternate-angle MPEG-2 streams (**Figure 12.55**).

On the same note, if you encode your video streams using open GOPs, the I-frame doesn't fall at the exact beginning of each GOP. Even if you use a GOP size of 15 frames, you still can't control whether or not the I-frames line up between streams in DVD Studio Pro. This brings us to the third rule:

Rule #3: Don't use open GOPs for alternate-angle MPEG-2 streams.

✔ Tip

- When it comes to creating alternate-angle tracks, DVD Studio Pro's built-in QuickTime MPEG-2 Exporter really shines. If you set DVD Studio Pro to Encode on Build, you can be sure that your GOP structures will line up perfectly because all GOPs will be exactly 15 frames.

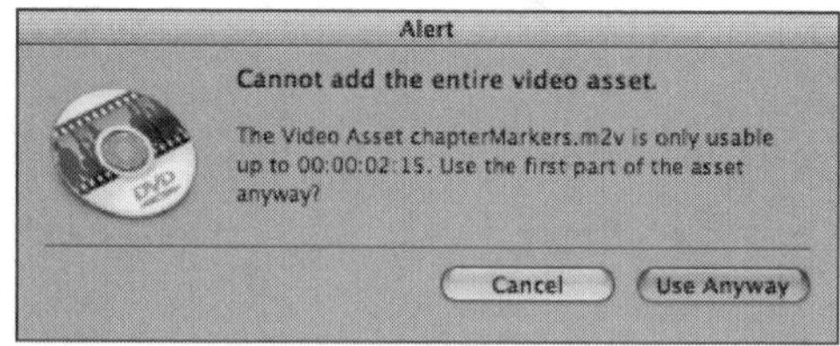

Figure 12.55 If you use Final Cut Pro or iMovie to add chapter markers to your MPEG streams, GOPs in alternate angles won't line up with GOPs in the V1 stream. Trying to add an MPEG-2 stream with embedded chapter markers results in the alert pictured here.

Warning: Exporting to Compressor from Final Cut

Final Cut Pro 4 allows you to export your sequences using Compressor, and in most situations this is a great option. However, when it comes to creating multi-angle or mixed-angle tracks, using Final Cut Pro's Export > Using Compressor function can lead to serious problems if you don't take the correct precautions.

When you export using Compressor, all cuts or edits between clips in the Final Cut Pro timeline are encoded as I-frames in the final MPEG stream. This can lead to better encoding, because Compressor essentially places compression markers at all hard cuts between scenes. The MPEG files it produces will look great in everyday DVD authoring, but if you're attempting to create multi-angle or mixed-angle tracks, these extra I-frames will cause problems. To get around this, you must visit the Compressor preset's Encoding tab, go to the Extras section, and select the Include Chapter Markers Only option (**Figure 12.56**).

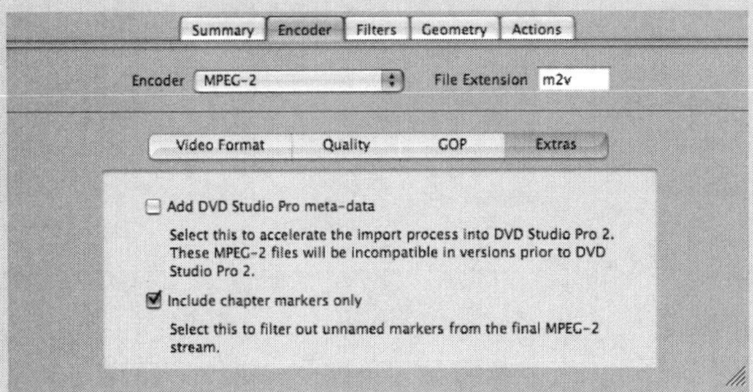

Figure 12.56 If you use Final Cut Pro's Export > Using Compressor option, all edits in the Final Cut Pro timeline are encoded as I-frames in the final MPEG stream. To get around this, select the your Compressor preset's Include Chapter Markers Only option.

Multi-Angle versus Mixed-Angle Tracks

Alternate-angle tracks come in two varieties: multi-angle and mixed-angle. A multi-angle track has two or more angles that stretch the entire length of the track (**Figure 12.57**). A mixed-angle track has alternate angles that do not stretch the entire length of the track (**Figure 12.58**).

In a mixed-angle track, there can be spaces between video clips in the same alternate video stream. Mixed-angle streams are useful for conserving disc space in projects where you don't need an alternate angle to run the entire length of the track, which can sometimes make the difference between fitting your project on a DVD-5 or a DVD-9.

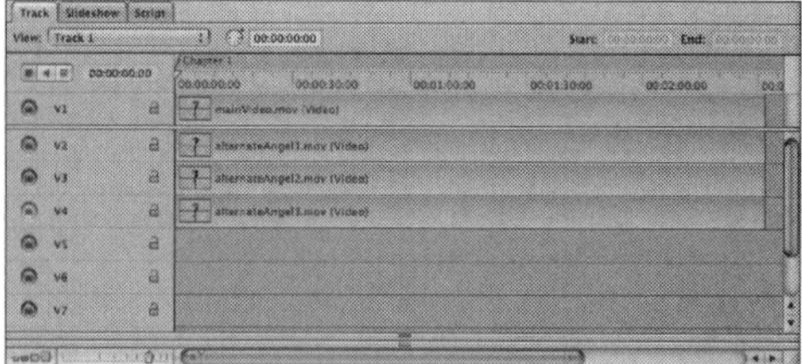

Figure 12.57 In a multi-angle track, all alternate video angles are exactly the same length as the V1 stream.

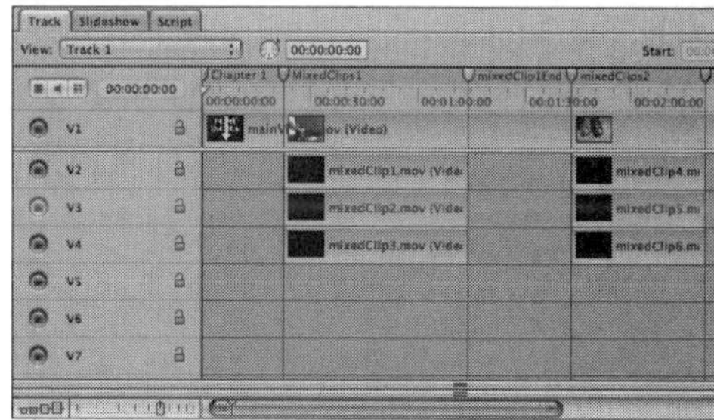

Figure 12.58 In a mixed-angle track, there can be gaps between clips in the alternate-angle streams.

Creating multi-angle tracks

As long as you encode your assets correctly, multi-angle tracks are very easy to create. There's really only one rule to follow: *For multi-angle streams, all alternate angles must use the same GOP structure and must also be exactly the same length as the V1 stream.*

To create a multi-angle track:

1. In the Track editor, click the video stream configuration button so that only video streams are displayed (**Figure 12.59**).
2. From the Assets container, Palette, or Finder, drag the main video asset into the V1 stream.
3. From the Assets container, Palette, or Finder, drag an alternate video asset into the V2 stream.
4. Continue adding assets to alternate video streams until you've added all of the angles you need (**Figure 12.60**).

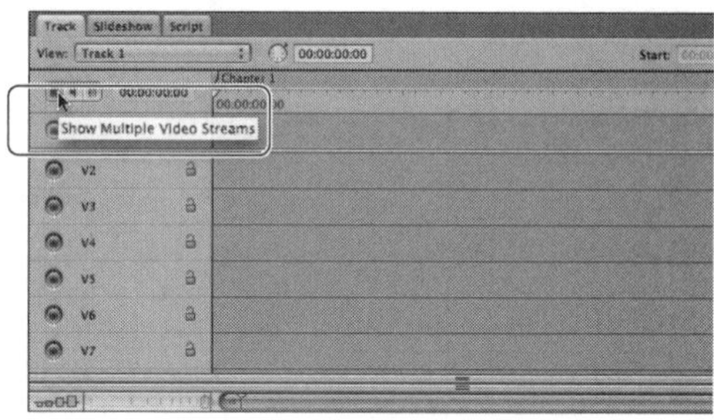

Figure 12.59 When working on multi-angle tracks, it helps to configure the Track editor so that only video streams are showing. To do so, click the appropriate video stream configuration button.

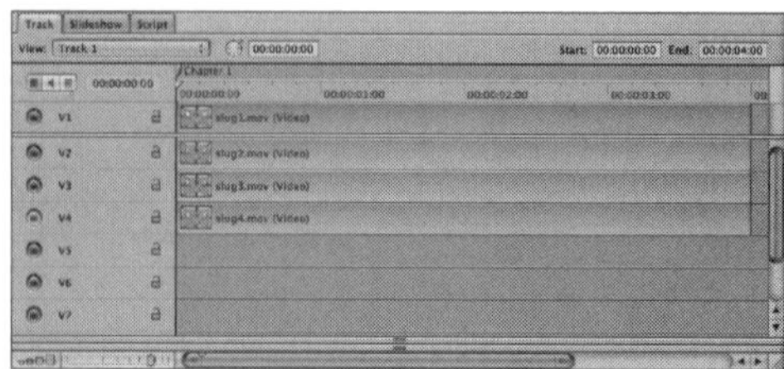

Figure 12.60 A multi-angle track. Notice that all alternate angles begin and end at exactly the same time as the angle in the V1 stream.

Creating mixed-angle tracks

Because of the gaps between clips in the mixed-angle streams, mixed-angle tracks are a little harder to create than simple multi-angle tracks. Here are some rules to keep in mind:

- For mixed-angle streams, all clips arranged vertically across alternate-angle streams must be exactly the same length, which means that they must start and end at exactly the same time—to the frame (**Figure 12.61**).
- There must be a marker at the front *and* end of all clips, as shown in Figure 12.61—or rather, at the front and end of *almost* all clips, because you cannot have a marker at the end of the last clip in a track. When mixed angles stretch right to the very end of a track, you don't need to close them off with a marker. If you *do* add a marker to the end of the last clip in a track, DVD Studio Pro may abort the build process when you compile the project. To learn more, see "Fixing Invalid Markers" earlier in this chapter.

continues on next page

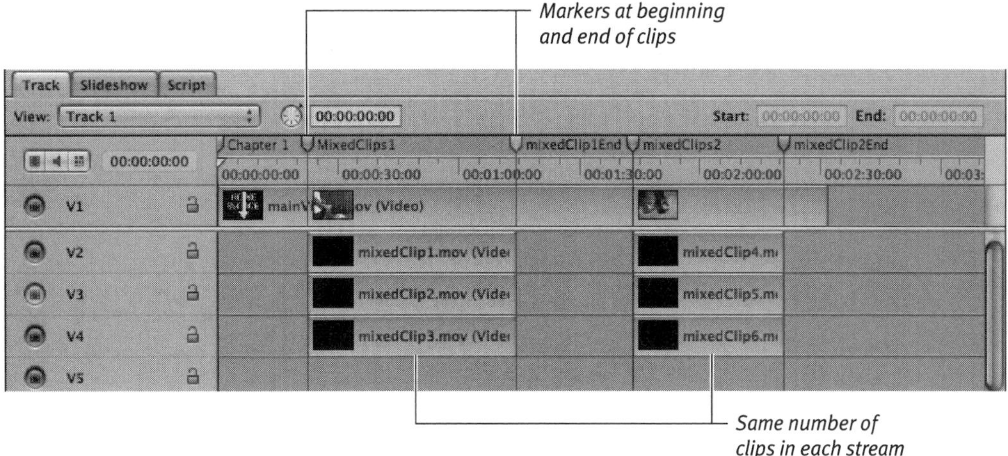

Figure 12.61 Mixed-angle tracks must have clips that align perfectly across all of the alternate-angle streams. Additionally, you must put markers at both the beginning and end of the alternate stream clips.

- Each alternate-angle stream must have the exact same number of clips, in the exact same position in the timeline. If one stream has two alternate-angle clips, for example, every stream that contains alternate angles must have two alternate-angle clips. DVD Studio Pro will let you add different numbers of clips to the alternate streams (**Figure 12.62**), but when you attempt to build the project, the alert shown in **Figure 12.63** will appear, and the build process will stop.

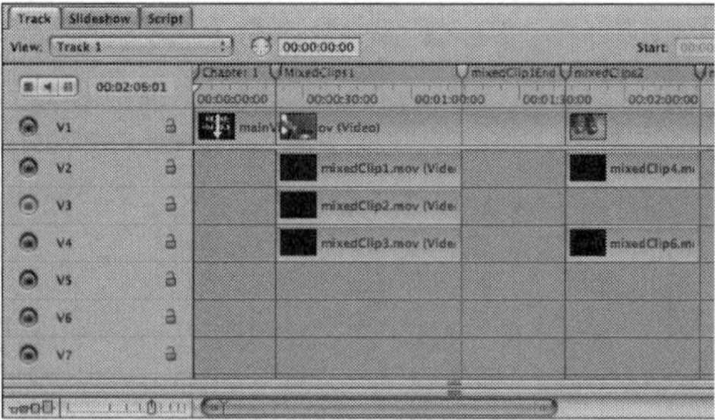

Figure 12.62 This figure shows a mixed-angle track that is illegal in the DVD-Video specification, because the V3 stream does not have the same number of clips in the same position as the V2 and V4 streams.

✔ Tip

- While you're viewing a mixed-angle alternate stream, gaps in the stream revert to the video in the V1 stream. When the gap finishes, the DVD-Video player goes back to displaying the alternate angle.

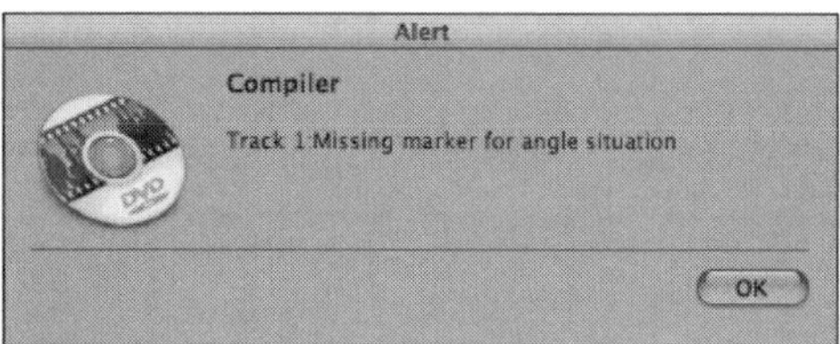

Figure 12.63 Attempting to build an illegal mixed-angle track results in this alert dialog, and the build process stops.

To create a mixed-angle stream:

1. In the Track editor, click the video stream configuration button so that only video streams are displayed.
2. From the Assets container, Palette, or Finder, drag the main video asset into the V1 stream.
3. In the Track editor, double-click the Marker area to add a marker at the spot on the timeline where you want your first mixed-angle clips to begin playing (**Figure 12.64**).

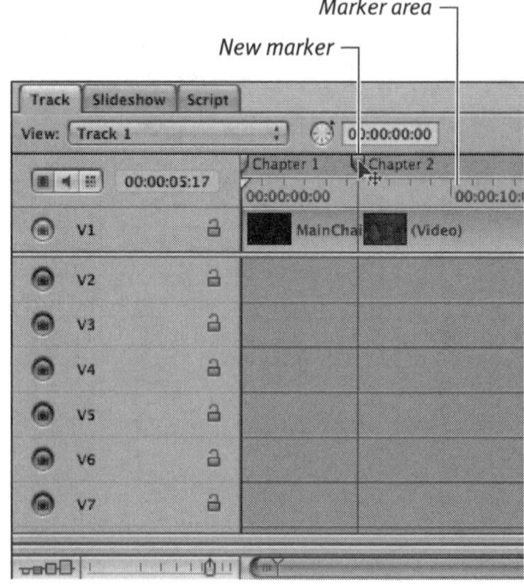

Figure 12.64 Before adding mixed-angle clips to the Track editor, you must create a marker by double-clicking the Marker area.

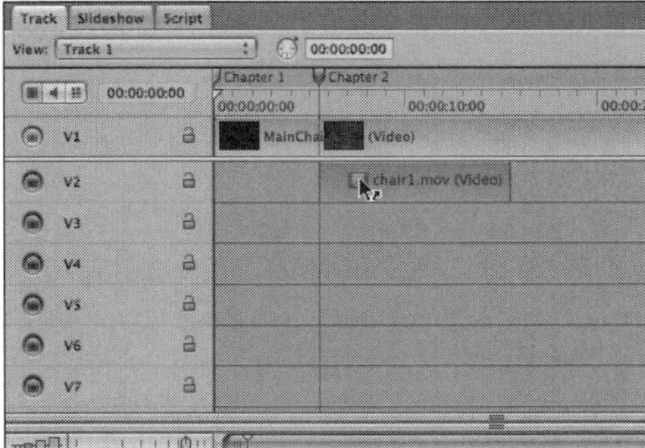

Figure 12.65 Add the first mixed-angle clip to the V2 stream and take care that it begins exactly at the marker.

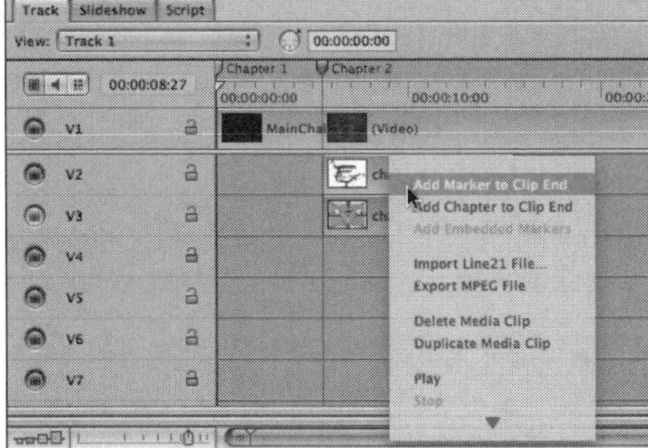

Figure 12.66 Control-click the shortest clip in the alternate video streams; then choose Add Marker to Clip End from the shortcut menu that appears.

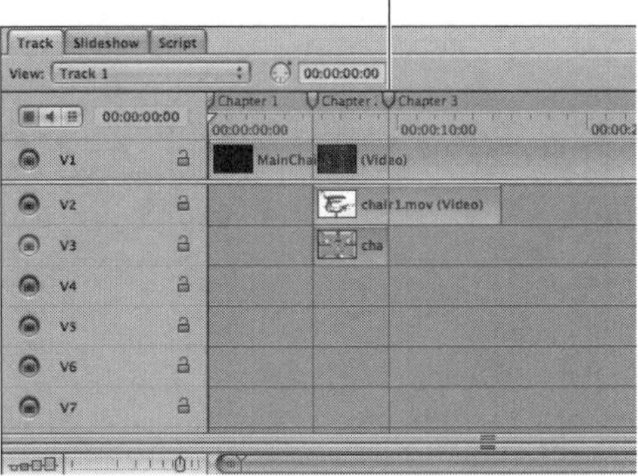

Figure 12.67 A new marker is added to the end of the shortest of the mixed-angle clips.

4. From the Assets container, Palette, or Finder, select the asset that will form the first mixed-angle clip and drag it into the V2 stream, placing it so that it begins at the marker (**Figure 12.65**).

5. Continue adding assets to alternate video streams—taking care to place them so that they begin exactly at the marker—until you've added all of the angles you need.

6. In the timeline, Control-click the shortest mixed-angle clip in your alternate-angle video streams and choose Add Marker to Clip End from the shortcut menu that appears (**Figure 12.66**).

   All mixed-angle clips must be the same length. You can't lengthen clips beyond their source asset's duration, so you must add the second marker at the end of the shortest mixed-angle clip (**Figure 12.67**). You can then trim the other mixed-angle clips to make them the same length as the shortest clip.

continues on next page

7. Trim or lengthen the alternate-angle clips so that they end exactly at the second marker.
8. Repeat steps 3 through 7 until you've added as many alternate-angle clips as you need (**Figure 12.68**).

✔ Tip

- If you build a mixed-angle track but DVD Studio Pro stops and displays a Data Rate Too High alert, the problem is with the encoding of your video streams, not with the placement of markers inside DVD Studio Pro.

To move a clip between streams:

- In the Track editor, select the clip that you want to move and drag it up or down to another stream.

  The clip moves from its current stream to the new stream. If the clip is moved from the V1 stream, all following clips will snap forward in the timeline to close the gap left by the clip. If the clip is in any other stream, the gap will not be closed.

✔ Tip

- When dragging clips between streams, hold down the Shift key to constrain the clip's movement vertically (the clip will move only up or down and not to the left or the right).

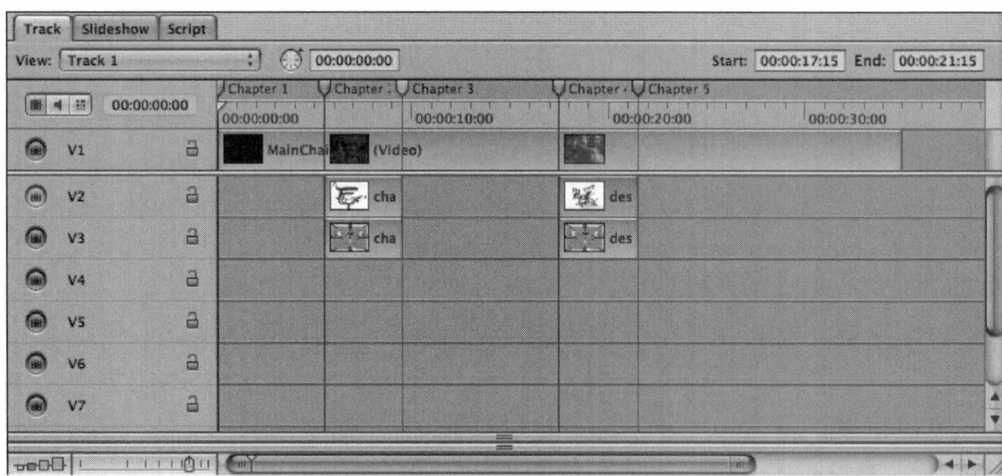

Figure 12.68 A mixed-angle track that's ready to burn!

The Menu Editor

A DVD-Video is only as good as its menus. Not only can menus make or break the DVD-Video's overall look and feel, but they provide the interactivity that sets DVD-Video apart from VHS-Video and gives viewers the control that they crave.

Creating menus is the most important and also the most complex part of the DVD authoring process. Before starting this chapter, be sure to read Chapter 3, "Preparing Graphics," to gain a solid understanding of how to properly design the graphics and video that you'll use for your project's menus.

After you've prepared your materials, you must decide whether your project needs layered menus, highlight menus, motion menus, 16:9 (widescreen) menus, or a combination of the lot. You'll learn how to make and use all of these menus by the time you've finished reading this book—each type is covered in later chapters.

However, this chapter ignores the particulars of these different types of menus and instead focuses on how to use the Menu editor effectively. Creating buttons, aligning menu graphics, using guides, and assigning button targets—these are basic skills you'll need to master to create any menu in DVD Studio Pro.

Creating Menus

All menus fall into one of two categories: layered or overlay. When you create a menu in DVD Studio Pro, you must know which type you want to create.

About layered menus

Layered menus have many more cons than pros, which is why you won't find them in most professional DVD-Videos unless they're serving a specific purpose.

Layered menus—which use separate layers in a Photoshop document to determine a button's normal, selected, and activated states—give you full control over the color, shape, and placement of the menu's graphics. Another advantage of using layered menus is that you can configure their buttons to "turn on" graphics elsewhere on the menu, similar to the way rolling over a button on a Web page can update information elsewhere on the page.

However, layered menus are slow to respond to user input and can't be used to create motion menus. You can't attach audio to them either. Further, none of DVD Studio Pro 3's menu compositing features is available to layered menus, so you can't add text or create drop zones inside the Menu editor if you're working on a layered menu.

To learn how to create layered menus, see Chapter 14, "Layered Menus."

✔ Tip

- DVD Studio Pro 3 has some great menu compositing features that let you add text and graphics to menus right in the Menu editor. These compositing features are covered in Chapter 15, "Overlay Menus," and Chapter 17, "Templates, Styles, and Shapes."

About overlay menus

You'll use overlay menus more than any other type of menu in your DVD-Video projects. In fact, they're so common that they're often called *standard* menus.

Unlike layered menus, overlay menus react instantly to user input and can contain both video backgrounds and audio. The overlay menu's chief disadvantage, however, is that its buttons are generated by the DVD-Video player at runtime, based on a 2-bit (four-color) template image called an *overlay image*. This overlay image limits the buttons to only four colors, which does not allow the graphic complexity afforded by layered menus. Also, you cannot use the buttons to "turn on" graphics elsewhere on the menu, so if you're trying to cross-develop a DVD-Video that mimics the functionality of a Web site, you're probably out of luck with overlay menus.

To learn how to create overlay menus, see Chapter 15.

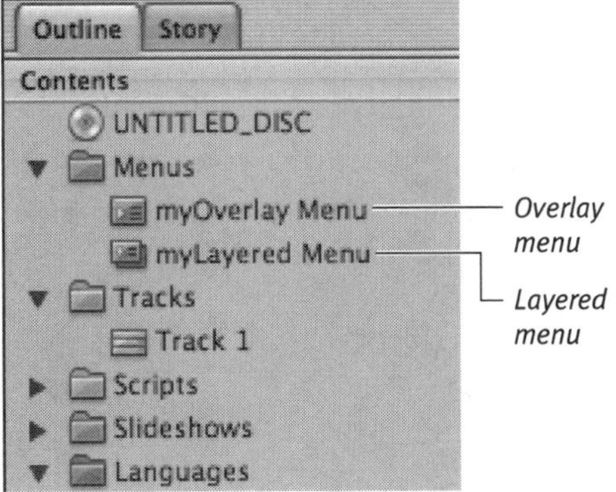

Figure 13.1 If you look closely, you can see that the overlay menu icon has three lines on it, while the layered menu icon has only two. Additionally, the layered menu icon has a small shadowed layer.

✔ Tip

- It's very difficult to tell overlay and layered menus apart in the Outline and Graphical views; consequently, it's easy to accidentally try to create a layered menu in a standard menu, and vice versa. If you look at the menu icons in the Outline view, you'll immediately notice that both are blue (**Figure 13.1**). But upon closer inspection, you'll see that standard menus have three little lines on them, while layered menus have just two. Additionally, layered menus have a second, or shadowed, layer under the first one. It's not much, but at least these minute differences do help you tell the different types of menus apart. In the Graphical view, it's much harder, because both menu tiles just look blue (well, okay, layered menu tiles are a slightly deeper shade of blue, but the difference isn't enough to create a useful visual cue).

To create an overlay menu:

◆ *Do one of the following:*

▲ In the toolbar, click the Add Menu button (**Figure 13.2**).

▲ In the Outline or Graphical view, Control-click anywhere and choose Add > Menu from the shortcut menu that appears (**Figure 13.3**).

▲ Choose Project > Add to Project > Menu (**Figure 13.4**).

▲ Press Command-Y.

A new menu is created and added to the Outline or Graphical view (**Figure 13.5**).

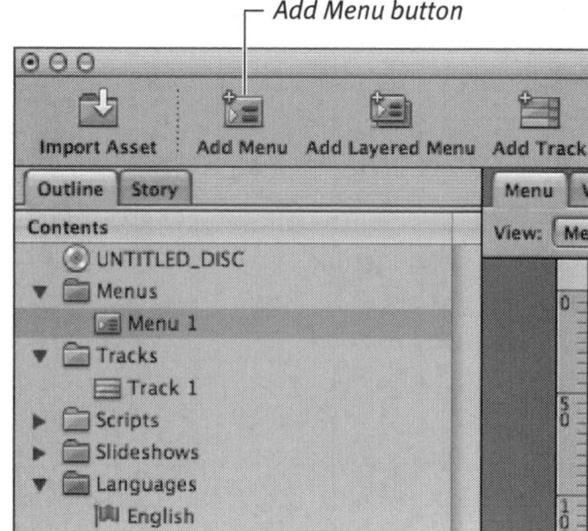

Figure 13.2 To create an overlay menu, in the toolbar, click the Add Menu button to create an overlay menu, or...

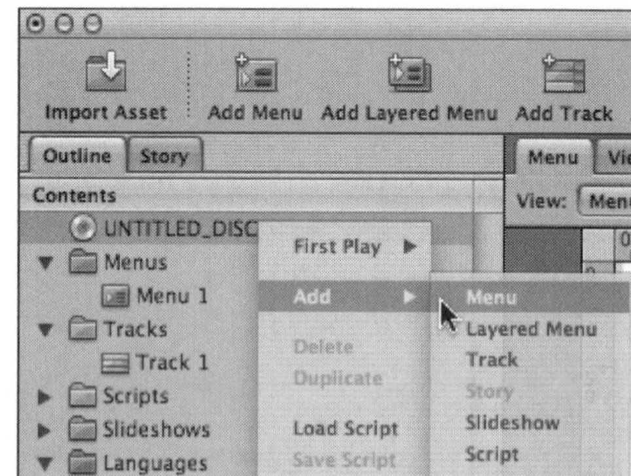

Figure 13.3 ...Control-click the Outline view and choose Add > Menu from the shortcut menu that appears, or...

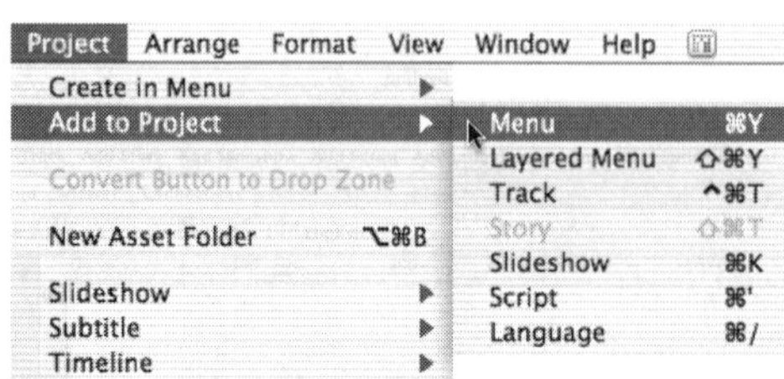

Figure 13.4 ...choose Project > Add to Project > Menu.

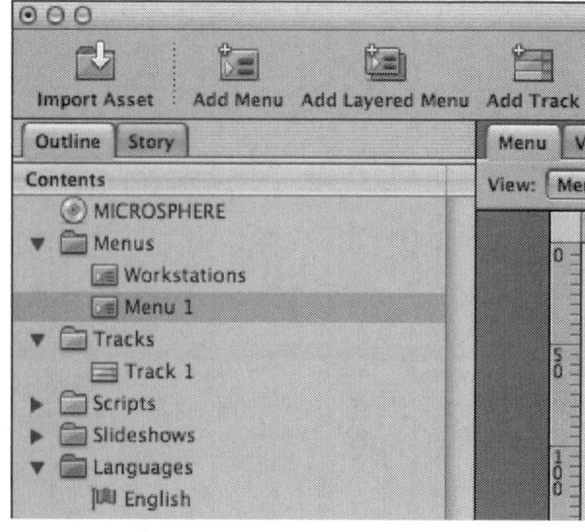

Figure 13.5 A new menu in the Outline view.

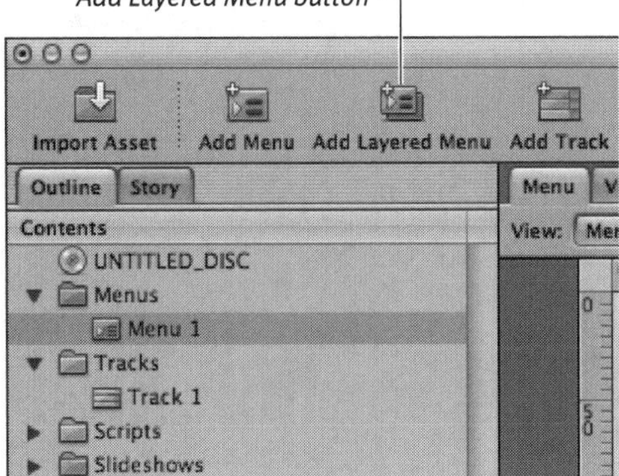

Figure 13.6 To create a layered menu, in the toolbar, click the Add Layered Menu button, or...

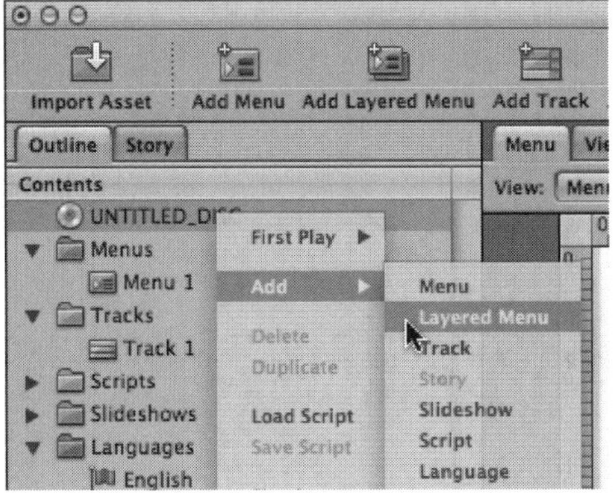

Figure 13.7 ...Control-click anywhere in the Outline view and choose Add > Layered Menu from the shortcut menu that appears, or...

To create a layered menu:

- *Do one of the following:*
  - ▲ In the toolbar, click the Add Layered Menu button (**Figure 13.6**).
  - ▲ In the Outline or Graphical view, Control-click anywhere and choose Add > Layered Menu from the shortcut menu that appears (**Figure 13.7**).
  - ▲ Choose Project > Add to Project > Layered Menu (**Figure 13.8**).
  - ▲ Press Shift-Command-Y.

  A new layered menu is created and added to the Outline view.

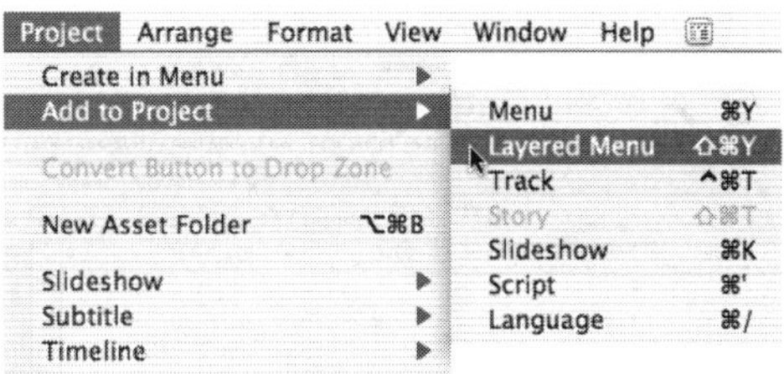

Figure 13.8 ...choose Project > Add to Project > Layered Menu.

Creating Submenus

Menu buttons can link to any other item in the project, including submenus. A submenu, which occupies a lower level in the DVD-Video's hierarchy, is often used to provide extra information, such as a chapter selection menu or an options menu that allows viewers to select the audio or subtitle stream they want to listen to or view.

You can create a submenu just like you do any other menu, or you can create a submenu that automatically links to the next menu up in the DVD-Video's navigational hierarchy. This type of submenu is created by either clicking the Create Submenu button along the bottom of the Menu editor or choosing Project > Add to Menu > Submenu (or pressing Option-Command-Y).

DVD Studio Pro then creates a new submenu and adds a button to the first menu that's currently open in the Menu editor. This new button automatically targets the submenu.

To name a menu in the Outline view:

1. In the Outline view, select the menu that you want to name.

   The menu is highlighted in the Outline view.

2. *Do one of the following:*
   - ▲ Press Return.
   - ▲ Click the menu a second time.

   A text box opens (**Figure 13.9**).

3. In the text box that opens, type a name and press Return.

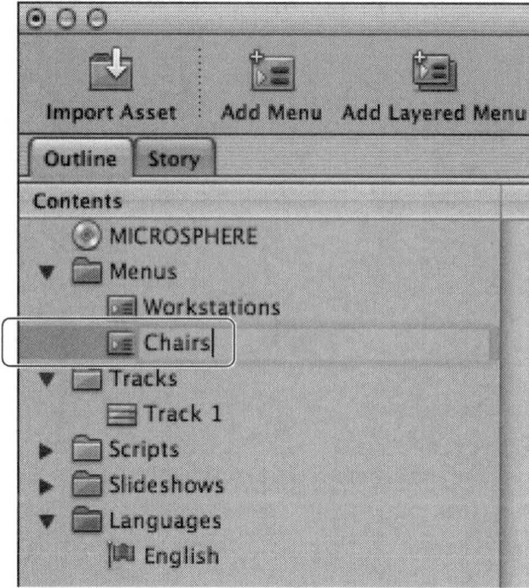

Figure 13.9 To name or rename a menu in the Outline view, click it once to select it; then click it a second time to open a text box in which you can type a name.

✔ Tip

- Double-clicking a menu in the Outline view does not open a text box that lets you rename the menu, but rather opens the menu in the Menu editor. To rename the menu, you must click the menu once, wait a moment, and then click a second time.

To name a menu in the Inspector:

1. In the Outline or Graphical view, select the menu that you want to name.

   The menu is highlighted, and the Inspector updates to display the menu's properties. At the top of the Inspector is the Name text box (**Figure 13.10**).

2. In the Inspector's Name text box, enter a new name for the menu and press Return.

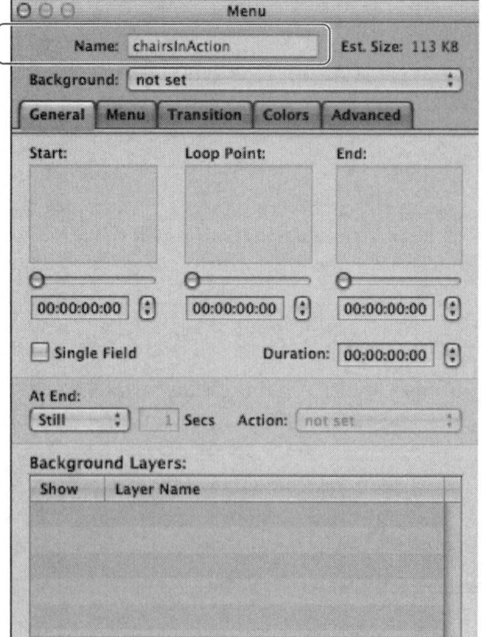

Figure 13.10 With a menu selected in the Outline view, you can type a new menu name in the Inspector's Name text box.

Exploring the Menu Editor

The Menu editor (**Figure 13.11**), which you can access by clicking the Menu tab, is where you'll get your hands dirty making menus. You use the Menu editor to do just about everything, including setting the menu background, adding buttons, linking buttons so that the DVD-Video player's remote control navigates properly, and targeting the buttons to different elements in your project. When it comes to menu creation, this is where all the heavy lifting is done.

To open a menu in the Menu editor:

- In the Outline view, click a menu to select it.

  The menu opens in the Menu editor (refer to Figure 13.11).

To select a new menu to edit in the Menu editor:

- At the top left of the Menu editor, choose a new menu from the View menu (**Figure 13.12**).

  The Menu editor updates to display the new menu.

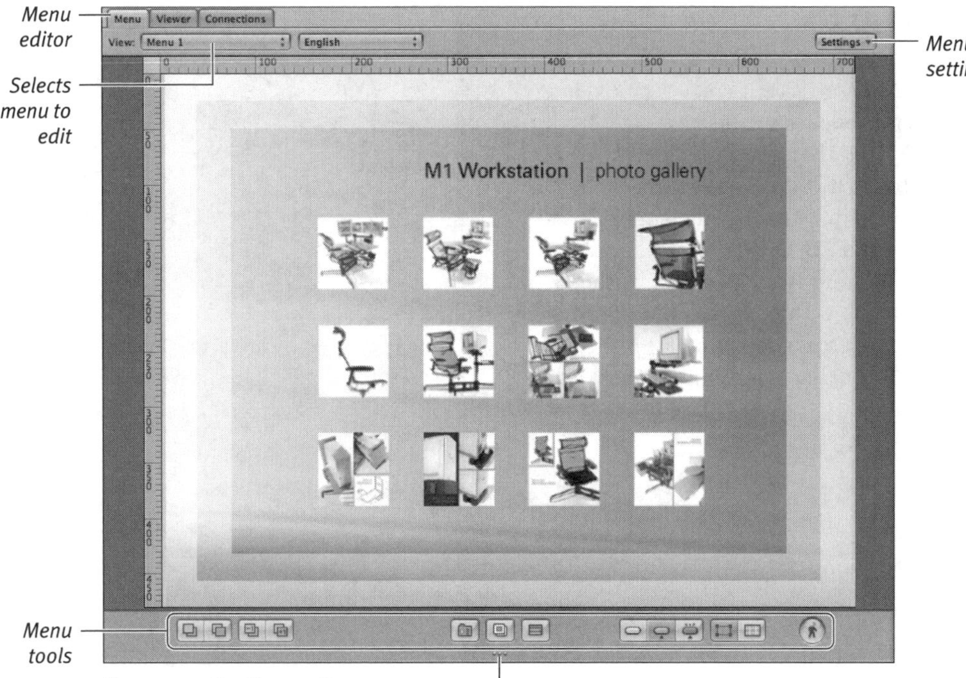

Figure 13.11 The Menu editor

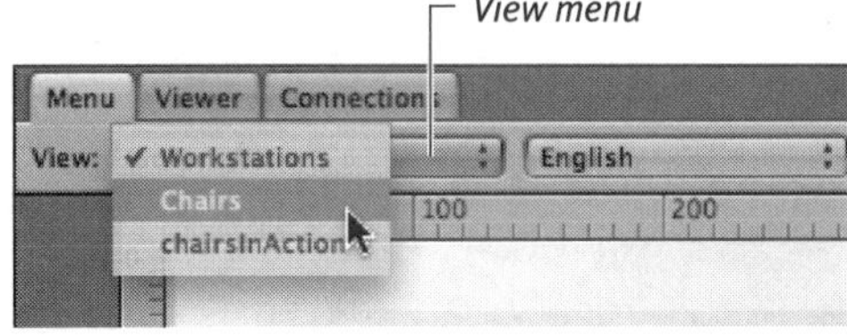

Figure 13.12 While working in the Menu editor, you can quickly choose a new menu to edit by selecting it in the View menu.

Adding Backgrounds

The background is the part of the menu that does not change in response to viewer input. It can be a still image (still menu) or even a video segment that provides motion (motion menu).

To set a background from the Inspector:

1. In the Outline view, select a menu.

   The Inspector updates to display the menu's properties.

2. From the Menu Inspector's Background menu, choose the asset that you want to use as the menu's background (**Figure 13.13**).

   You can select any image or video on the project's Assets tab. If you select a video asset, the video is set as the menu's background, and there's nothing further you need to do. If you choose an image, however, one of two things will happen. If the image is a JPEG, GIF, or Photoshop document with only one layer, or any other graphics file with no layers, DVD Studio Pro automatically sets it as the background, and there's nothing further you need to do.

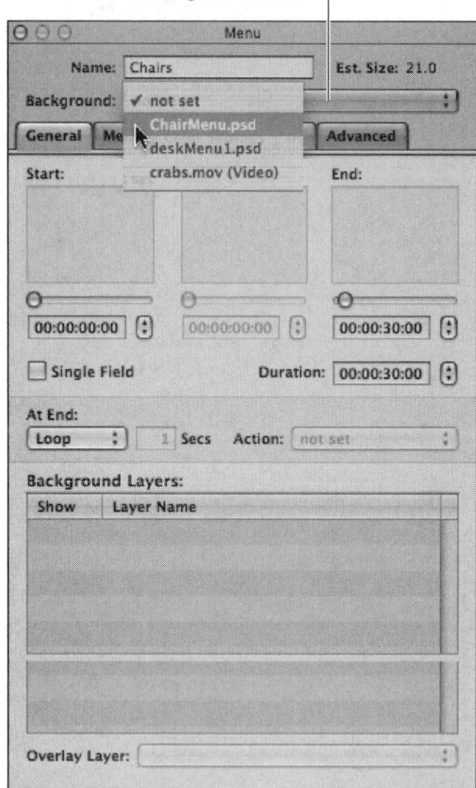

Figure 13.13 Select a menu in the Outline view and then use the Inspector's Background menu to assign an asset as the menu's background.

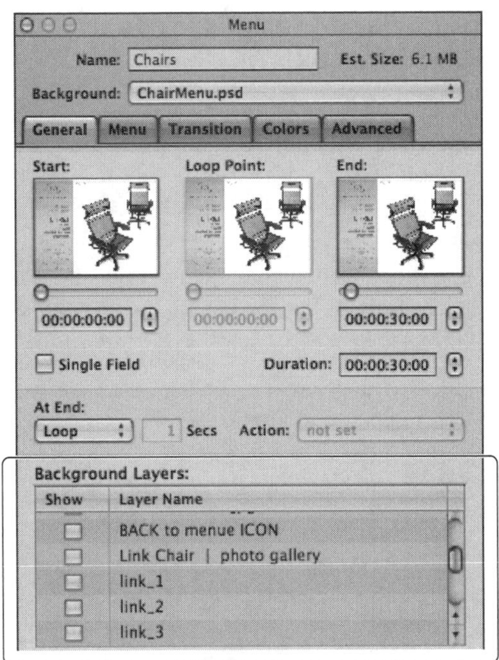

Figure 13.14 The Inspector's Background Layers area allows you to decide which layers from a multilayered image file are used for the menu's background.

If the image has multiple layers, however, you'll need to tell DVD Studio Pro which layers to display for the background. All of the image's layers are displayed in the Inspector's Background Layers area (**Figure 13.14**).

3. In the Inspector's Background Layers area, click the check boxes to the left of the layers that you want to use for the menu's background (refer to Figure 13.14).

   In the Menu editor, the selected layers are made visible.

Should I Flatten My Background?

Many DVD authors find it convenient to create the background as a single layer in a Photoshop document and include the menu buttons' normal states along with it. This makes it easier to create your menus in DVD Studio Pro because you don't have as many layers to juggle.

DVD Studio Pro 3, however, makes working with layered graphics files incredibly easy, so you may want to leave all of your menu's background images on their separate layers in the source file. A flattened image can't be edited, but if you maintain the file's layers as you work with a menu in DVD Studio Pro, you can easily open the menu in Photoshop again and make changes, if needed. When you resave the document, DVD Studio Pro will refresh the asset, and the changes will ripple into your project.

With this in mind, it's often best to leave your menu's layer structure intact!

Using drop palettes

Drop palettes offer a fast way to add assets to menus, particularly when it comes to adding backgrounds. However, the drop palette functions differently depending on whether you're adding a video or a still asset as the menu background. So you can see the differences, this section describes the techniques for doing both.

To use the drop palette to add a video asset as the background:

1. From the Assets tab or the Palette, select a video asset and drag it over the background of the Menu editor (not over a button), but don't release the mouse button.

   A drop palette appears under the pointer's position. At the top of the drop palette is the Set Background option (**Figure 13.15**).

2. Drop the video asset on the drop palette's Set Background option.

   The video asset is set as the menu's background.

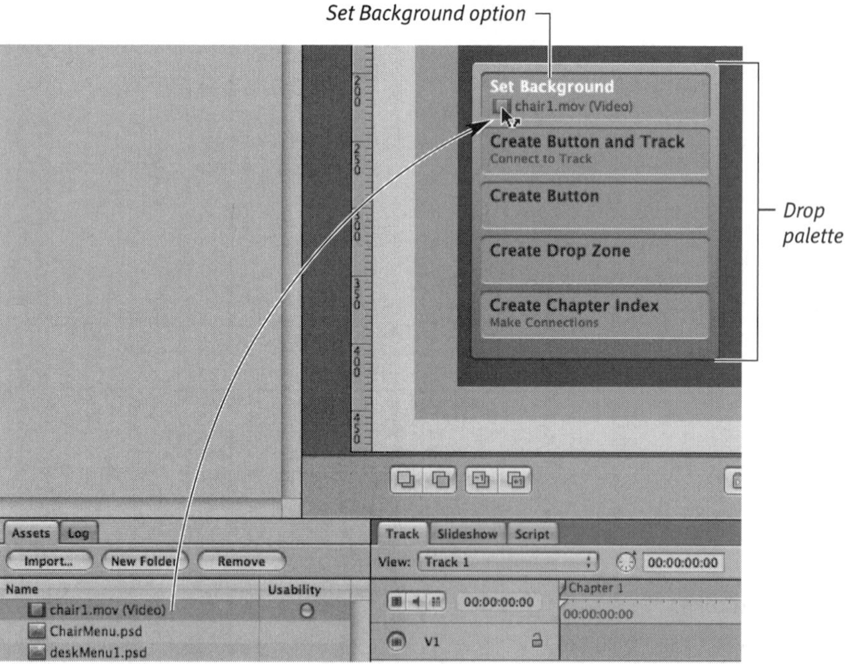

Figure 13.15 To set a video asset as a menu's background, drag it from the Assets tab to the Menu editor and hold it over the menu's background area. A drop palette will appear under the pointer. Use the drop palette's Set Background option to set the video asset as the menu's background.

To use the drop palette to add an image as the background:

1. From the Assets tab, select an image asset and drag it over the Menu editor's background (not over a button), but don't release the mouse button.

   A drop palette appears under the pointer's position. At the top of the drop palette are two options (**Figure 13.16**):

   - **Set Background: All Layers Visible.** If the image document contains nothing but the menu background, choose this option.
   - **Set Background: No Layers Visible.** If the image document contains other layers beside the background, choose this option. Layered menus, for example, may include a single layer as the background as well as other layers to indicate the button's normal, selected, and activated states. In this situation, it's quicker to start with no layers visible and then use the Inspector's Background Layers section to enable only the layers needed for the menu's background.

continues on next page

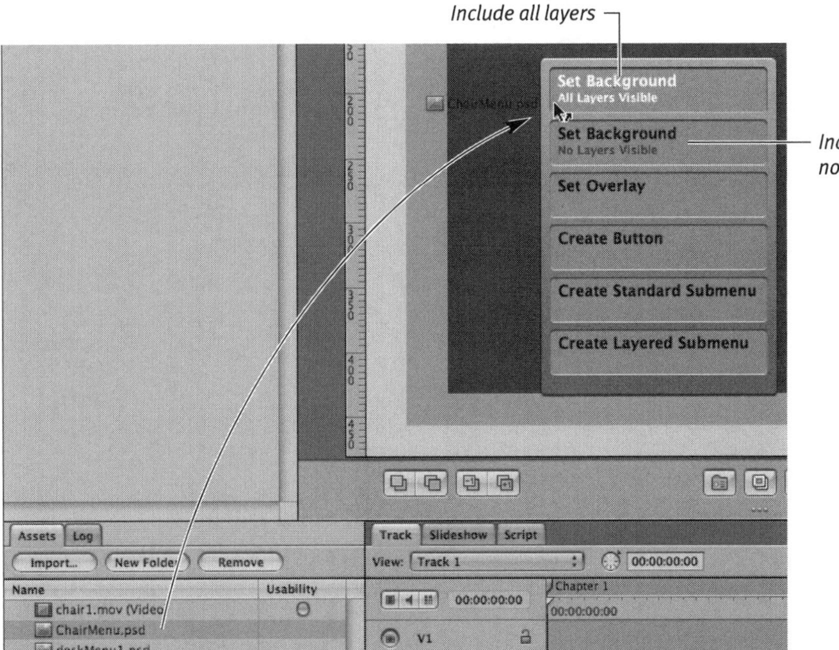

Figure 13.16 If your image document contains only the layers needed to create the menu's background, choose Set Background: All Layers Visible. If the image document contains layers other than the ones needed for the menu background, choose Set Background: No Layers Visible.

2. Drop the image asset on the drop palette choice that is applicable to your image.

   The image asset is set as the menu's background.

3. In the Outline view, select the menu.

   The Inspector updates to display the menu's properties. At the bottom of the Inspector is the Background Layers area (**Figure 13.17**).

4. In the Inspector's Background Layers area, enable the check boxes to the left of the layers needed for your menu's background.

   The layers turn on and are displayed as the menu's background.

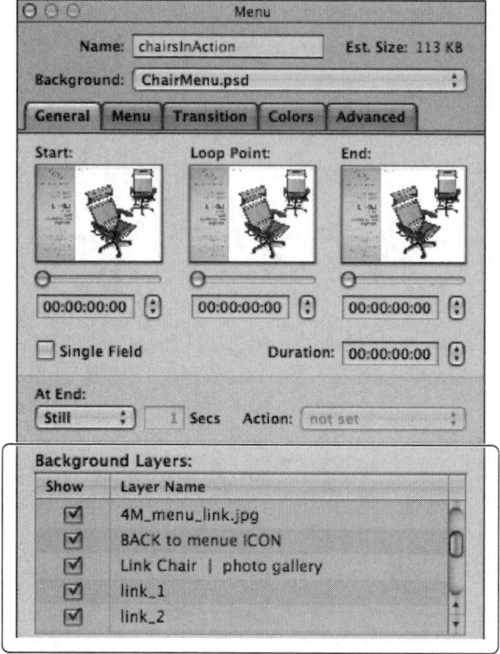

Figure 13.17 From the Inspector's Background Layers area, enable only the layers needed for your menu's background.

Adding Menu Buttons

Viewers click a menu's buttons to navigate the DVD-Video by jumping to tracks, slideshows, other menus, or scripts that allow the DVD-Video to make its own decisions. Each menu in DVD Studio Pro can have up to 36 buttons—except 16:9 menus, which can have only 18 buttons—and the buttons themselves can have three states: normal, selected, and activated.

- **Normal.** The button's state when the viewer is not interacting with it (when it's neither selected nor activated).
- **Selected.** The button's state when the viewer rolls the mouse over it (on a computer) or navigates to it with the remote control's arrow keys or number pad (on a set-top player). The selected state is displayed on the screen until the viewer activates the button or navigates to a new menu button.
- **Activated.** The button's state when the viewer clicks it with the mouse (on a computer) or presses the Enter key (on a set-top player) after selecting it. The activated state is displayed for only a brief period as the DVD-Video player refocuses the laser to jump to the next project item.

✔ Tips

- Pressing W on the keyboard cycles a selected menu button through its normal, selected, and activated states.
- As you press the W key to cycle through button states, be careful you don't accidentally press the Q key! The Q key cycles through the menu's display state (also available by choosing View > Display State), or its Background, Overlay, and Composite (background and overlay) display.

About button hotspots

When you add a menu button to the Menu editor, you are actually defining a *button hotspot,* or an activation area on the menu that is used to determine the button's footprint.

According to the DVD-Video specification, button hotspots must be rectangular. They cannot be round, they cannot be oval, and they cannot be trapezoids. Button hotspots must be rectangles.

Also, button hotspots should not overlap; otherwise, the DVD-Video player may get confused and target the wrong project asset as buttons are activated on the menu. When designing your menus, you should ensure that the menu buttons are positioned so that the hotspots surrounding them don't accidentally overlap. (This is especially a problem in menus that use circular button graphics, particularly if these circles are placed close together on the menu.)

To add a button hotspot to a menu:

1. In the Menu editor, position the pointer at the top left of the button graphic.
2. Click and drag a button hotspot around the button graphic (**Figure 13.18**).

   A rectangular button hotspot is created around the button graphic. Don't worry about being too exact; this is just the button hotspot, and if it's a bit bigger than the button graphic itself, that's fine.

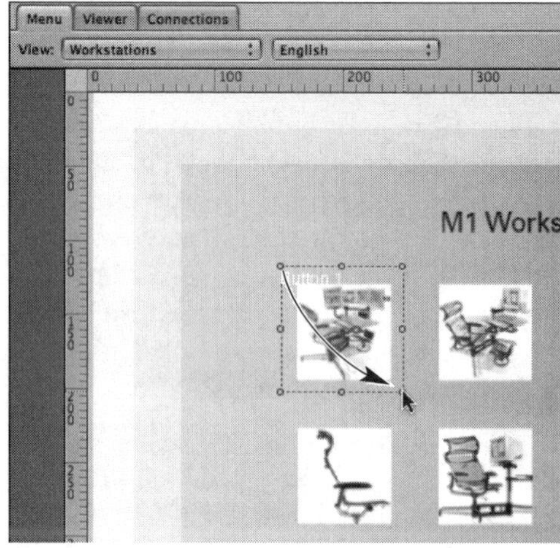

Figure 13.18 To add a button hotspot to a menu, click the Menu editor and drag out the button hotspot around the button's graphic.

✔ Tip

- You can also use DVD Studio Pro's drop palette to drag images and video directly onto a menu to create buttons (**Figure 13.19**). You can drag one asset at a time to create a single button, or multiple assets to create several buttons at once. This feature works only with overlay—not layered—menus.

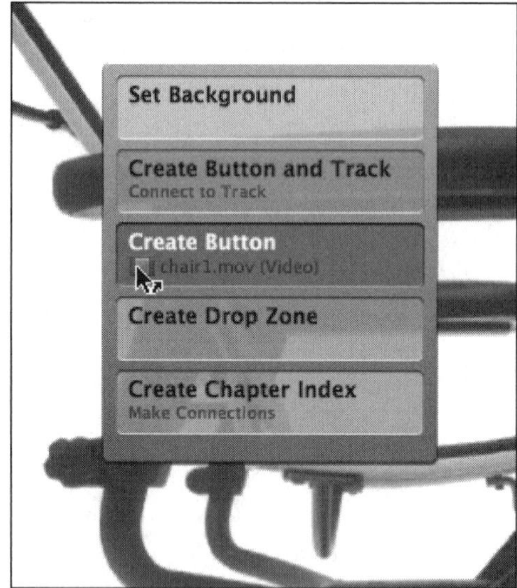

Figure 13.19 To quickly create a button or buttons, drag one or more still or video assets over the Menu editor and choose Create Button (or Create Buttons).

To move a button:

- *Do one of the following:*
  - In the Menu editor, select a button and drag it to a new position on the menu.
  - In the Menu editor, select a button and use the arrow keys on your keyboard to move the button one pixel at a time, or hold down Shift-Option as you press the arrow keys to move buttons 20 pixels at a time.

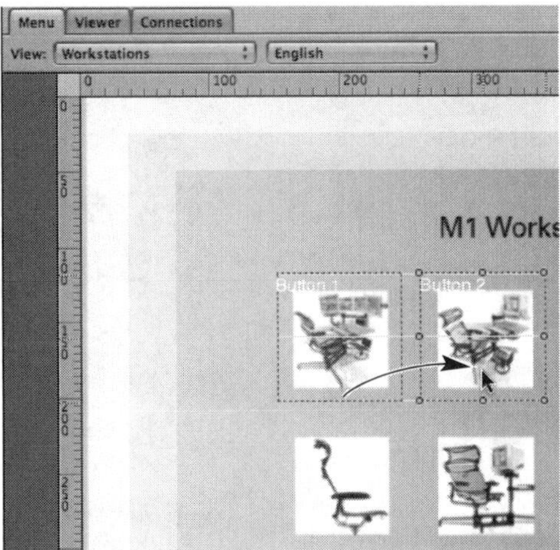

Figure 13.20 To copy a button, hold down the Option key as you drag the button to a new position on the menu.

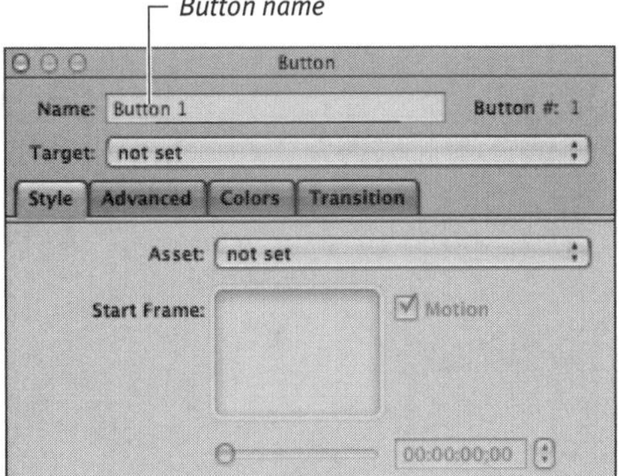

Figure 13.21 To name a button, select it in the Menu editor and then type a new name in the Inspector's Name text box.

To copy a button:

1. In the Menu editor, select the button that you want to copy.
2. Press the Option key while dragging the selected button to a new place on the menu (**Figure 13.20**).

   A copy of the button is created and placed on the menu.

To delete a button:

- In the Menu editor, select the button and press the Delete key.

To name a button:

1. In the Menu editor, select the button that you want to name.

   The Inspector updates to display the button's properties. At the top of the Inspector is a Name text box (**Figure 13.21**).
2. In the Inspector's Name text box, enter a name for your button and press Return.

Selecting multiple buttons

If you want to move or delete several buttons at the same time, you need to select those buttons first. While it may seem natural to just drag a selection range around the buttons to select them, the procedure is actually not that easy because dragging in the Menu editor creates a new button! To override this default action, you can either hold down the Shift key while clicking each button to add it to a selection range or press the Command key as you drag a selection range around multiple buttons.

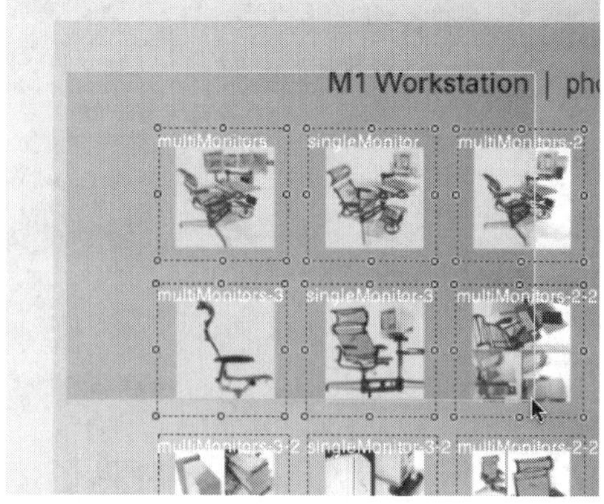

Figure 13.22 To select multiple buttons in the Menu editor, press the Command key while you drag a selection range around them.

To select multiple buttons:

- *Do one of the following:*
  - ▲ Press the Shift key while clicking multiple buttons in the Menu editor to select them.
  - ▲ Press the Command key while dragging a selection range around multiple buttons in the Menu editor (**Figure 13.22**).

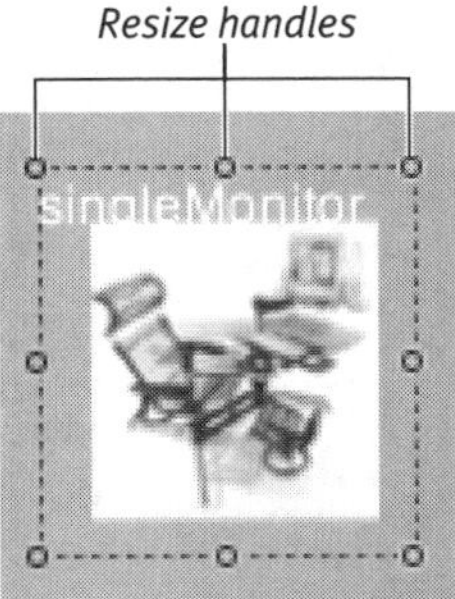

Figure 13.23 Drag the handles around a selected button's edges to resize the button.

Button Inspector's Advanced tab

Coordinates & Size area

Figure 13.24 With a button selected in the Menu editor, the Inspector's Advanced tab displays a Coordinates & Size area that gives you exact control over a button's dimensions.

Adjusting button dimensions

If you drag out a button and it's the wrong size, you can resize it in either the Menu editor or the Button Inspector. In the Menu editor, a selected button displays eight handles that you can drag to quickly change a button's dimensions. For some presentations, however, you may need more precise control over button size. Fortunately, with a button selected in the Menu editor, the Inspector's Advanced tab displays a Coordinates & Size area that lets you adjust the size of your menu's buttons right down to the pixel.

To resize a button in the Menu editor:

1. In the Menu editor, select a button.

   Eight handles appear around the selected button's edges (**Figure 13.23**). The handles on the corners allow you to resize a button both vertically and horizontally at the same time. The handles on the sides allow you to resize a button only vertically or horizontally (depending on the side the handle is on), but not both.

2. Drag one of the button's handles until the button is the correct size.

To resize a button in the Menu Inspector:

1. In the Menu editor, select a button.

   The Inspector updates to display the button's properties.

2. In the Inspector, select the Advanced tab.

   At the bottom of the Advanced tab is the Coordinates & Size area (**Figure 13.24**).

3. Use the Coordinates & Size area's settings to adjust the button's size.

Hiding button outlines in the Menu editor

If you have a lot of buttons on your menu, their outlines can get in the way as you examine the menu's layout to make sure everything looks as it should. To make life easier, you can hide button outlines—and button names—by using the following trick.

To hide button outlines:

- *Do one of the following:*
  - ▲ At the bottom right of the Menu editor, click the Show/Hide Button Outlines button (**Figure 13.25**).
  - ▲ Choose View > Show Button Outline and Name (**Figure 13.26**).

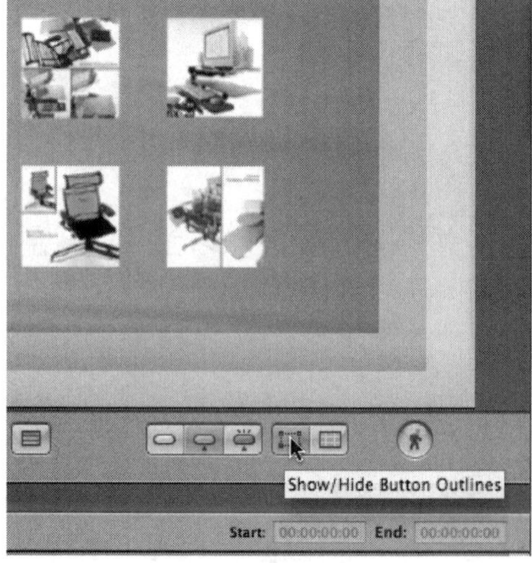

Figure 13.25 To hide (or show) button outlines and names, click the Show/Hide Button Outlines button, or...

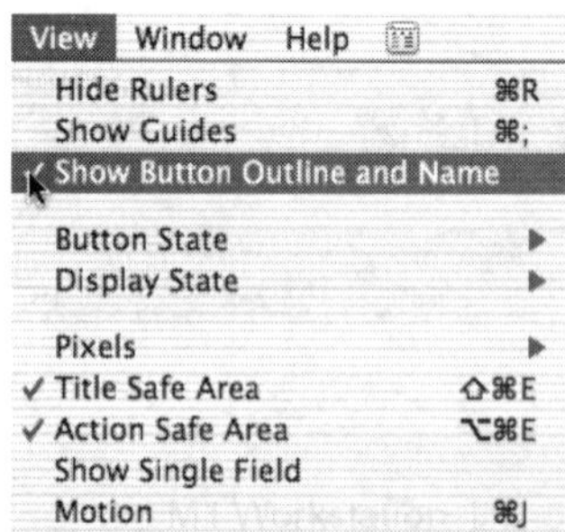

Figure 13.26 ...choose View > Show Button Outline and Name.

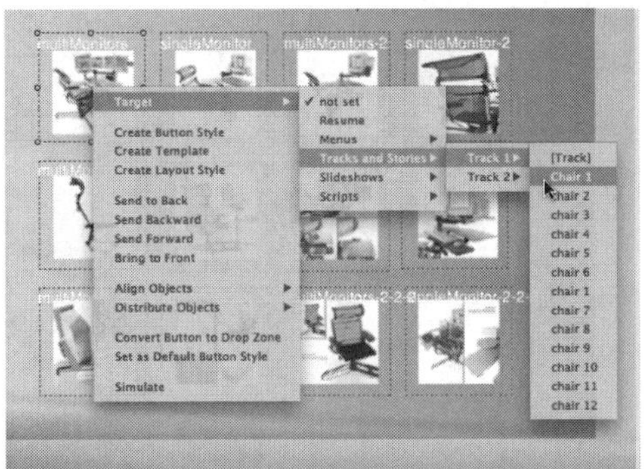

Figure 13.27 To quickly set a button's target, Control-click it in the Menu editor, choose Target from the shortcut menu, and then choose a project item from the hierarchical target menu that appears.

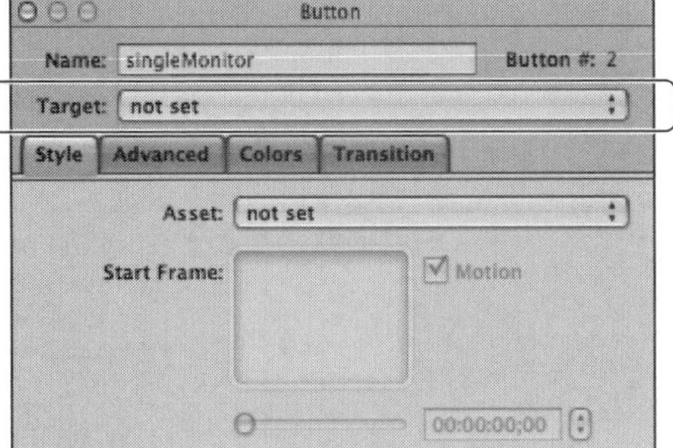

Figure 13.28 With a button selected in the Menu editor, the Inspector updates to show the button's properties. At the top of the Inspector is the Target menu.

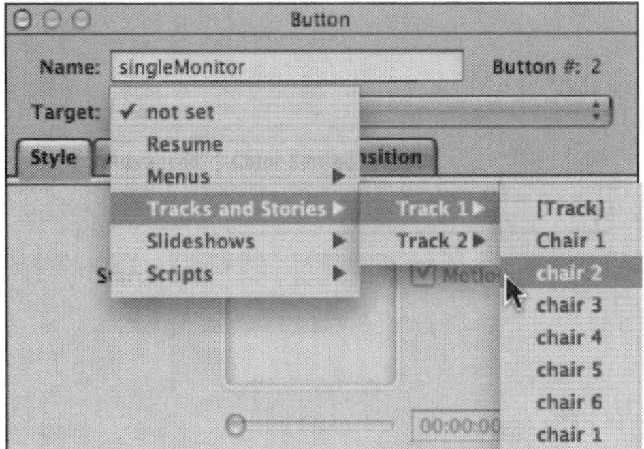

Figure 13.29 Use the Target menu to choose the project item that you want the selected button to target.

Setting Button Targets

When viewers click a button, they don't expect the DVD-Video to just sit there doing nothing—they want action! In other words, the DVD-Video should jump to and play a different project item. The project item that the button plays is called the button's *target,* which you can set in either the Menu editor or the Menu Inspector.

To set a button's target in the Menu editor:

1. In the Menu editor, Control-click the button.

   A shortcut menu appears.

2. From the shortcut menu that appears, choose Target and then choose the project item that the button should target from the hierarchical target menu (**Figure 13.27**).

   When the button is activated, the DVD-Video will jump to and play the targeted project item.

To set a button's target in the Inspector:

1. In the Menu editor, select a button.

   The Inspector updates to display the button's properties. At the top of the Inspector is the Target menu (**Figure 13.28**).

2. From the Inspector's Target menu, choose a target for the button (**Figure 13.29**).

   When the button is activated, the DVD-Video will jump to and play the targeted project item.

Verifying button targets

Let's face it: DVD-Video projects can get complex, making it easy to accidentally set a button to target the wrong project element. To guard against this, the first step in quality assurance (QA) testing is to verify your button targets in the Menu editor. Verifying button targets is as simple as double-clicking the buttons in the Menu editor. The targeted item then opens in DVD Studio Pro's Viewer or Menu editor, depending on the type of project item it is.

✔ Tip

- To see a button's target quickly, hover the pointer over the button for a moment. A tooltip will appear that tells you the name of the button and its target (**Figure 13.30**).

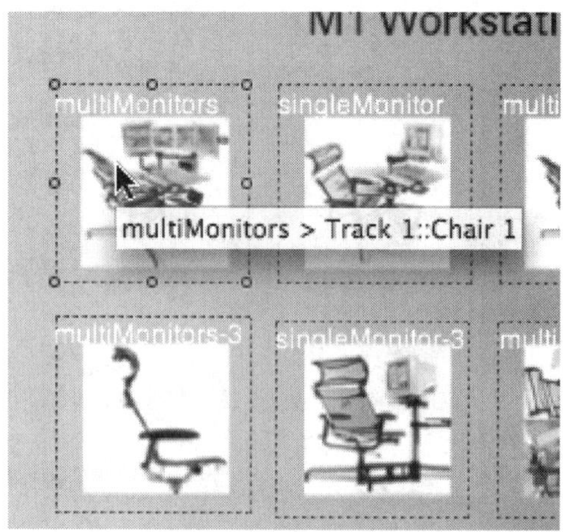

Figure 13.30 Hover the pointer over a button to reveal a tooltip that tells you the button's name and target.

To verify button targets:

- ◆ In the Menu editor, double-click a button.

  If the button targets a track, chapter, or story, the Viewer opens to display the targeted track, chapter, or story. If the button targets another menu, the menu opens in the Menu editor.

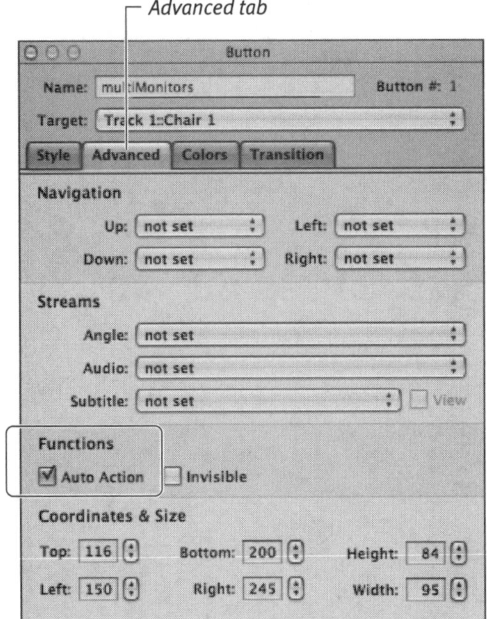

Figure 13.31 With a button selected in the Menu editor, the Inspector's Advanced tab allows you to set the button to activate automatically when it's selected.

Using auto actions

Under normal playback circumstances, activating a button is a two-part process. First you must select the button; then you activate the button to jump to the button's targeted project element. However, you can force your DVD-Video to automatically activate a button as soon as it's selected, using *auto actions.*

Auto actions are great if you want to automatically update menu graphics as buttons are selected. If, for example, a menu has an Info section that provides information about the button's targeted project element, you can use auto actions to ensure that the menu jumps to a new menu containing that information.

However, you should use auto actions sparingly. Each time the viewer selects a button, the DVD-Video is forced to jump to a new project element; if the viewer accidentally selects the wrong button, he or she may become irritated by having to jump back to the menu to select the correct button.

To set a button to activate automatically when selected:

1. In the Menu editor, select a button.
   The Inspector updates to display the button's properties.
2. In the Inspector, choose the Advanced tab.
   Near the bottom of the Advanced tab is the Auto Action check box (**Figure 13.31**).
3. Select the Auto Action check box.
   The menu button will now activate as soon as it's selected.

Setting a Menu Timeout Action

A DVD-Video can go on forever—it never has to stop playing. Usually, you will program tracks to jump back to a menu after they've finished playing, and the menu forms the only natural break in the action. By default, a menu stays on the screen until the viewer activates a button to jump out of it. However, you can program a *timeout action* into the menu so that the menu automatically jumps to a different program element after a set period of time. With timeout actions set, your DVD-Video will continue to play until the next rolling blackout.

✔ Tip

- DVDs destined for playback in a retail environment and "visuals" DVDs used in nightclubs and parties benefit greatly from timeout actions. The reason is simple: the staff can put the DVD on at the beginning of the business day, and that DVD will automatically play through menus and tracks until the staff turns the power off at the end of the business day. Make it easy for them, and your content will always end up on the displays.

To program a timeout action:

1. In the Outline view, select the menu to which you want to assign a timeout action. (If the menu is open in the Menu editor, you can also click the Menu editor's background to select the menu.)

   The Inspector updates to display the menu's properties. Toward the bottom of the Inspector's General tab is an area labeled At End (**Figure 13.32**). Currently, the At End menu is set to Still, which means that the DVD-Video will pause on

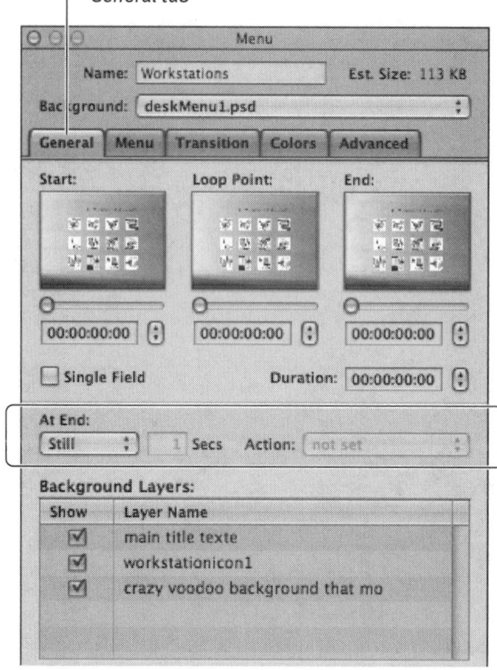

Figure 13.32 You use the Menu Inspector's General tab to determine what a menu does after it is done being displayed.

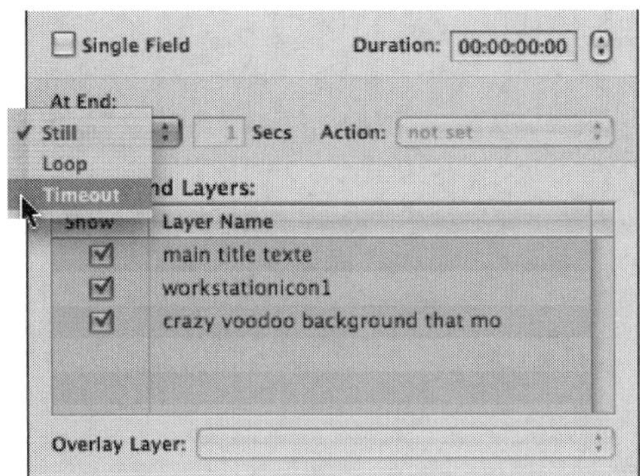

Figure 13.33 To force the menu to jump to a different project element after a set period of time, from the At End menu, choose Timeout.

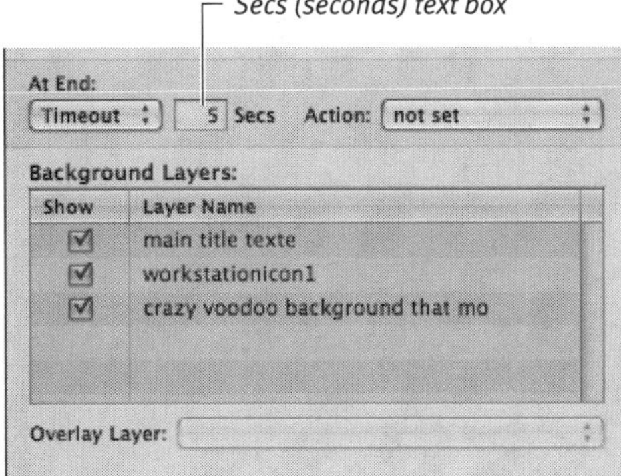

Figure 13.34 Enter a timeout value, in seconds, in the Secs text box.

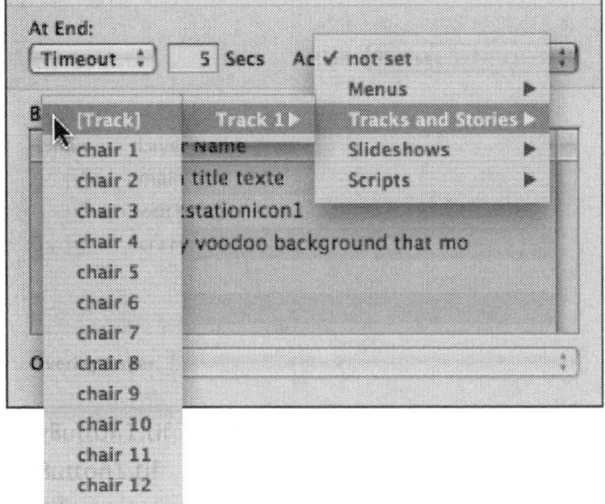

Figure 13.35 Then choose a project element for the menu to jump to after the timeout action's wait period has passed.

the menu and not continue to another project element. (If the menu is a motion menu, it will play to the end and then pause on the last frame of the menu.)

2. From the Inspector's At End menu, choose Timeout (**Figure 13.33**).

   The Secs (seconds) text box and Action menu beside the At End menu become active.

3. In the Secs text box, enter a value between 1 and 254 (**Figure 13.34**).

4. From the Action menu, choose the project element that you want the menu to jump to after the timeout period has passed (**Figure 13.35**).

About Menus and the Remote Control

On a computer, viewers can use the mouse to select and activate buttons on the screen as they watch your project. On a set-top DVD-Video player, however, users must use the remote control to navigate your menu's buttons. This leads to some important considerations as you design your menus. The first is button navigation, or the way the remote control's arrow keys navigate through the buttons on your menu. The second is the way the remote control's number keys are configured to select menu buttons. This section walks you through these important considerations.

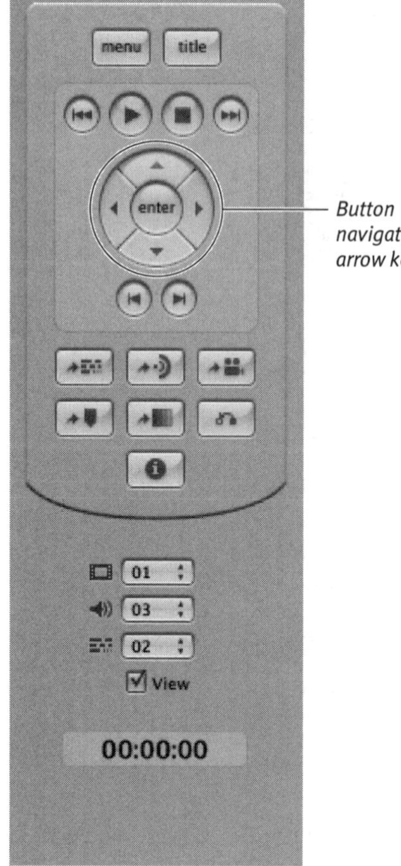

Figure 13.36 The arrow keys on DVD Studio Pro's Simulator remote control provide a good example of the arrow keys that a typical remote control uses to navigate menu buttons.

About button navigation

Button navigation is a key aspect of menu design. While you may be tempted to place your buttons in all sorts of interesting configurations and places on your menu, remember that the majority of viewers will be using the up, down, left, and right arrow keys on their remote controls to select and activate menu buttons (**Figure 13.36**). Consequently, you should always try to place buttons in either a row or a grid that is easy for viewers to navigate and understand. Remember: viewers can navigate only vertically and horizontally with the remote control's arrow keys; navigating diagonally is not an option.

Automatically, DVD Studio Pro will attempt to link buttons in a way that makes logical sense. As a result, if your buttons are in a row or grid, you'll rarely need to manually adjust button navigation because DVD Studio Pro will do most of the work for you. But if your buttons use a more, er, custom layout, you'll probably have to assign button navigation by hand. This section shows you how to use both methods to ensure that your buttons navigate correctly.

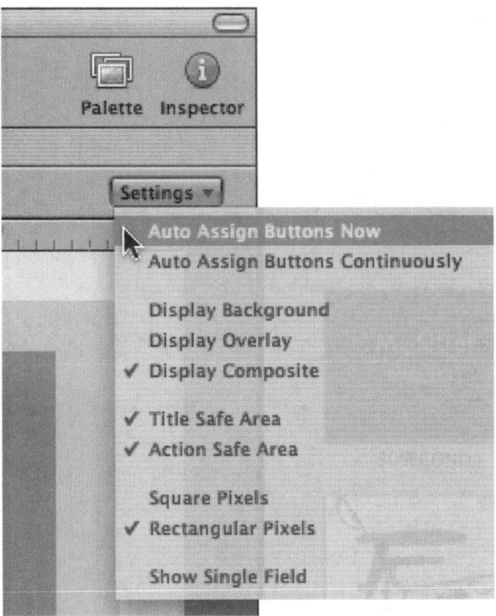

Figure 13.37 To auto assign button navigation to the correct arrow keys on a DVD-Video player's remote control, from the Menu editor choose Settings > Auto Assign Buttons Now.

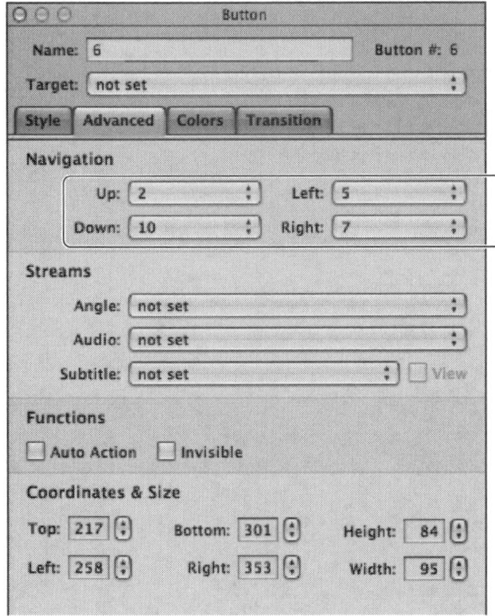

Figure 13.38 The Button Inspector's Navigation section lets you determine the way that the remote control's arrow keys navigate the buttons on your menu.

To auto assign button navigation:

- From the Menu editor's Settings menu, choose Auto Assign Buttons Now (**Figure 13.37**).

  DVD Studio Pro automatically assigns menu button navigation. To do so, it looks at each button and then it looks up, down, left, and right for the nearest button to which it makes logical sense to link.

✔ Tip

- The Settings menu's Auto Assign Buttons Continuously option will automatically relink button navigation every time a button is moved or added to the Menu editor. If you're new to DVD Studio Pro, it's best to leave Auto Assign Buttons Continuously enabled.

To manually set button navigation in the Inspector:

1. In the Menu editor, select a button.

   The Inspector updates to display the button's properties.

2. For overlay menus, click the Button Inspector's Advanced tab; for layered menus, click the Button Inspector's Button tab.

   At the top of the tab is the Navigation section (**Figure 13.38**). This section has Up, Down, Left, and Right menus that you can use to specify the action of the up, down, left, and right arrow keys on the remote control.

continues on next page

3. From the Navigation section's Up, Down, Left, and Right menus, choose the correct button for each of the remote control's arrow keys (**Figure 13.39**).

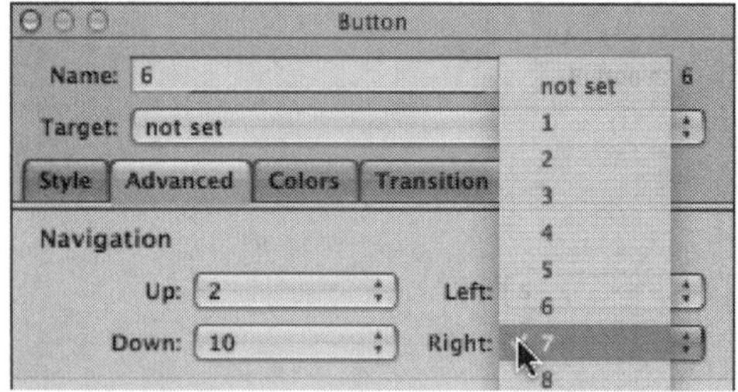

Figure 13.39 Choose buttons from the Navigation area's menus to determine how the remote control's arrow keys navigate through the menu's buttons.

✔ Tip

- To disable button navigation for particular arrow keys, choose Not Set from the Navigation menus.

To use the Button Link tool:

1. In the Menu editor, select a button.
2. Press Option-Command and move the pointer over the left, right, up, or down handle on the selected button.

   The pointer turns into a small triangular arrow (**Figure 13.40**).

Figure 13.40 To use the Button Link tool, press Option-Command while moving the pointer over an edge handle (not the corner handle) of a selected button. The pointer turns into a triangular arrow.

3. While holding down both the Option and Command keys, drag the button handle to reveal a gray link line, and continue dragging until the pointer is over the button you want to link to.

   When the pointer is over the new button, the link line turns green to show you it's ready to link (**Figure 13.41**).
4. Release the mouse when the pointer is over the button to which you want to link.

   The remote control's arrow key is set for that button.
5. Continue around all four edges of the button, following steps 2 through 4 to set the remote control's up, down, left, and right menu keys for that button.

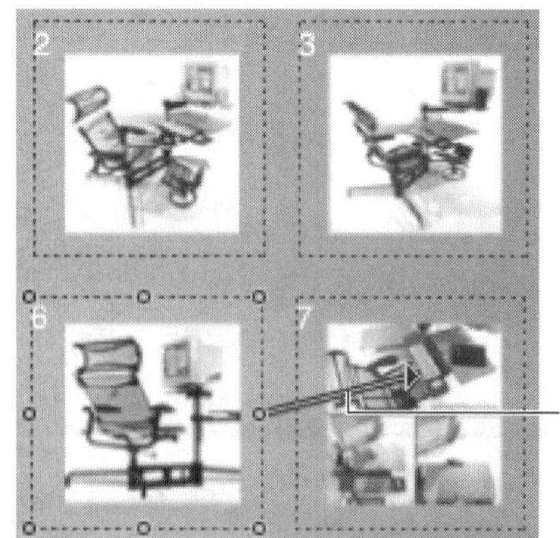

Figure 13.41 As you drag with the Button Link tool, a line follows the pointer to show you the button you are linking to.

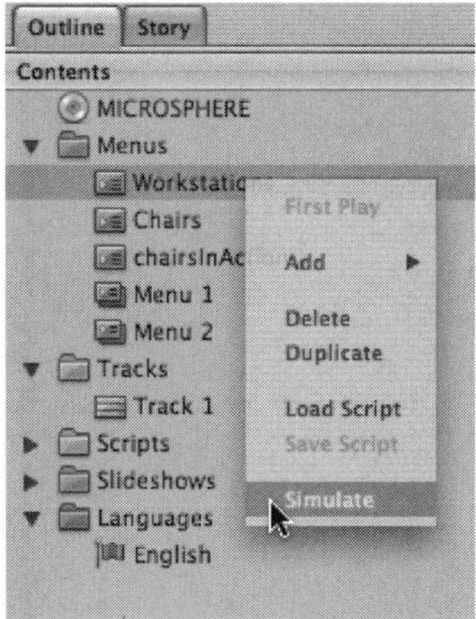

Figure 13.42 To simulate your menu, Control-click the menu in the Outline view and choose Simulate from the shortcut menu.

Previewing button navigation

Once you've wired up your buttons, it's a good idea to open the menu in DVD Studio Pro's Simulator and give those buttons a test drive by navigating through them using the keyboard's arrow keys. These four keys mimic the arrow keys on the remote control, letting you test your buttons to ensure that they link correctly.

To preview button navigation:

1. In the Outline or Graphical view, Control-click the menu you want to preview and choose Simulate from the shortcut menu (**Figure 13.42**).

   The Simulator opens.

2. Use your keyboard's arrow keys to navigate through the menu's buttons.

   Pay close attention to ensure that each button links to the next button as expected.

✔ Tip

- You can also use the up, down, left, and right arrow keys on the Simulator's virtual remote control to simulate the corresponding keys on a real DVD-Video player's remote control.

Using Rulers and Guides

Rulers and guides help ensure that your button hotspots end up exactly where you need them. *Rulers* appear at the top and left edges of the menu in the Menu editor. They can display pixels, percentages, centimeters, or inches—the choice is yours. *Guides* are lines that you can use to align your menu's various buttons (and other elements). To configure rulers and guides, you need to visit the Preferences window.

To enable or disable rulers:

◆ Choose View > Show/Hide Rulers (**Figure 13.43**), or press Command-R.
The Menu editor's rulers appear or disappear, respectively (**Figure 13.44**).

✔ Tip

■ You can also enable or disable rulers using the Rulers area of the Preferences window's Alignment section (**Figure 13.45**).

Figure 13.43 To show or hide the Menu editor's rulers, choose View > Show/Hide Rulers.

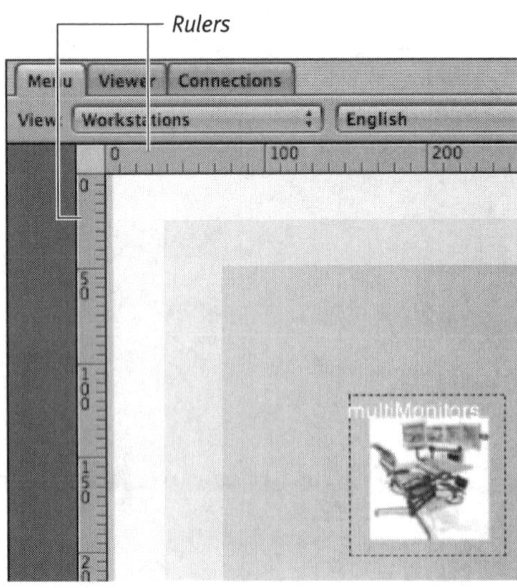

Figure 13.44 The Menu editor's rulers.

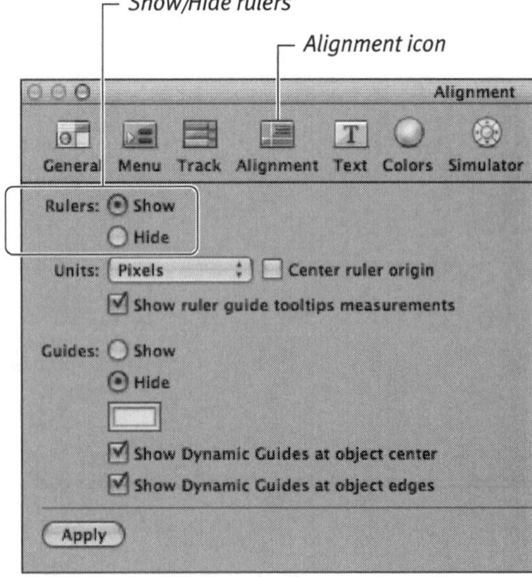

Figure 13.45 The Alignment section of the Preferences window also enables you to show or hide the Menu editor's rulers.

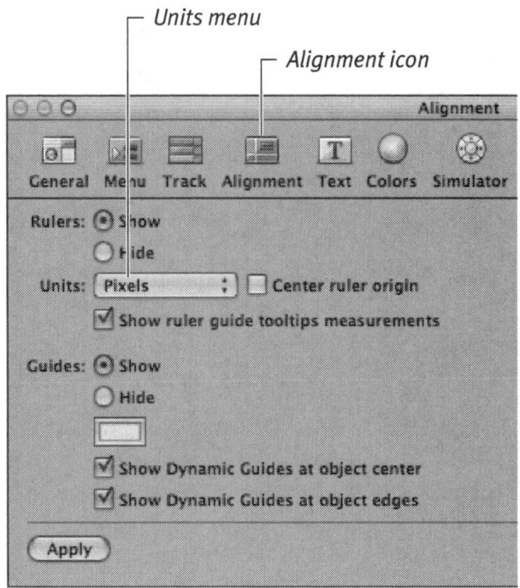

Figure 13.46 The Alignment section of the Preferences window allows you to adjust the units used in the Menu editor's rulers.

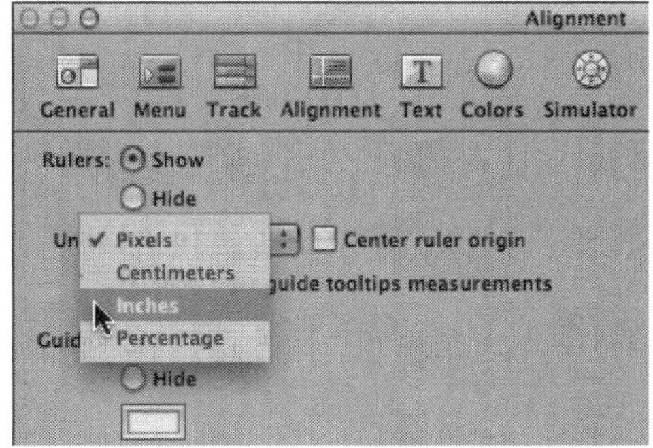

Figure 13.47 From the Units menu, choose Pixels, Centimeters, Inches, or Percentage.

To change ruler units:

1. Choose DVD Studio Pro > Preferences, or press Command-, (comma).

   The Preferences window opens.

2. Click the Preferences window's Alignment icon to open the Alignment section (**Figure 13.46**).

   Near the top of the Alignment section is the Units menu.

3. From the Units menu, choose the units that you want the Menu editor's rulers to use (**Figure 13.47**).

To add guides to the Menu editor:

1. In the Menu editor, enable rulers.

2. Position the pointer over one of the Menu editor's rulers (**Figure 13.48**).

   The pointer turns into a double-pointed arrow, indicating that you can now drag a guide out of the ruler.

3. From the ruler, drag a guide into the Menu editor (**Figure 13.49**).

   A guide drags out to follow the pointer. Notice that a tooltip appears, showing you the pointer's coordinate position in the Menu editor.

continues on next page

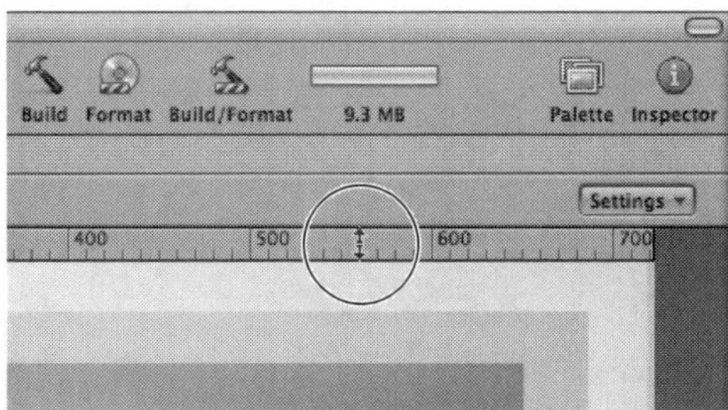

Figure 13.48 When the pointer is over a ruler, it turns into a double-pointed arrow, indicating that you can drag a guide out of the ruler.

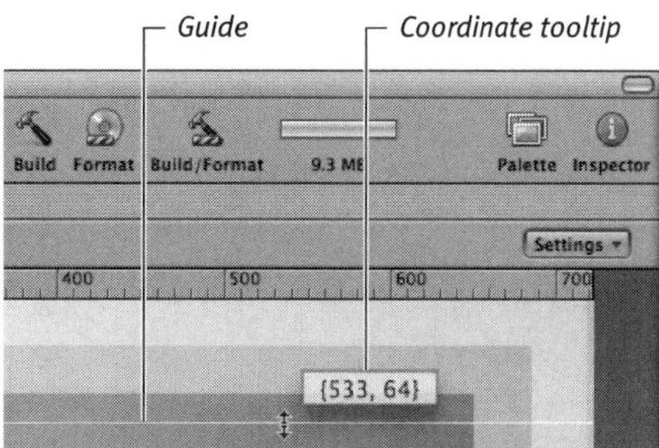

Figure 13.49 As you drag the pointer from the ruler into the Menu editor, a guide follows the pointer, and a tooltip appears, showing you the pointer's coordinates.

4. With an eye on the coordinate tooltip, drop the guide once it's in the correct position in the Menu editor.

✔ Tip

- If the tooltip coordinate measurements do not appear as you drag guides into the Menu editor, open the Alignment section of the Preferences window and click the Show Ruler Guide Tooltips Measurements check box (**Figure 13.50**).

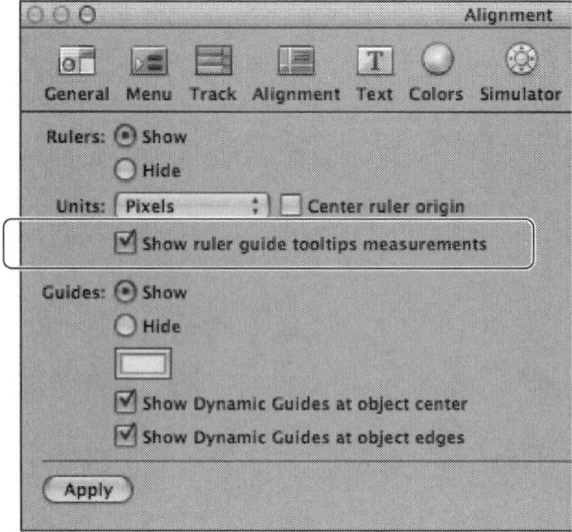

Figure 13.50 To show or hide tooltip coordinate measurements, open the Alignment section of the Preferences window and select the Show Ruler Guide Tooltips Measurements check box.

To show or hide guides:

- Do one of the following:
  - ▲ In the Menu editor, click the Show/Hide Guides button (**Figure 13.51**).
  - ▲ Choose View > Show/Hide Guides (**Figure 13.52**).
  - ▲ Press Command-; (semicolon).

Figure 13.51 To show or hide guides in the Menu editor, click the Show/Hide Guides button, or...

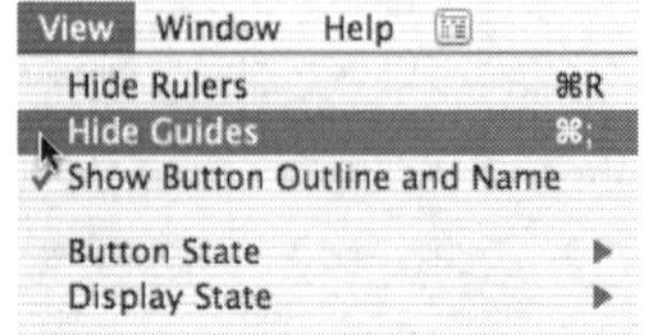

Figure 13.52 ...choose View > Show/Hide Guides.

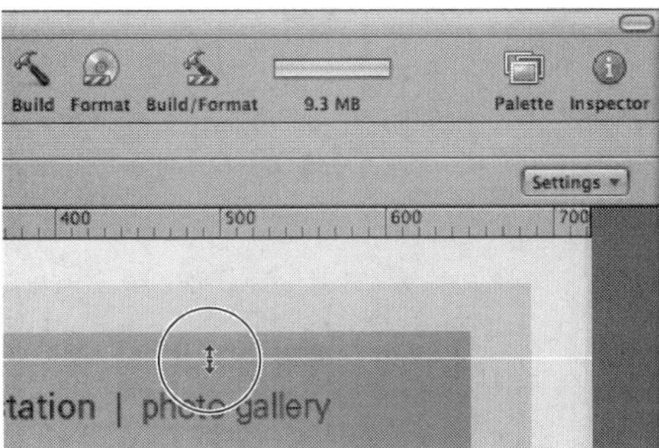

Figure 13.53 To remove a guide, drag it from the Menu editor back over the ruler.

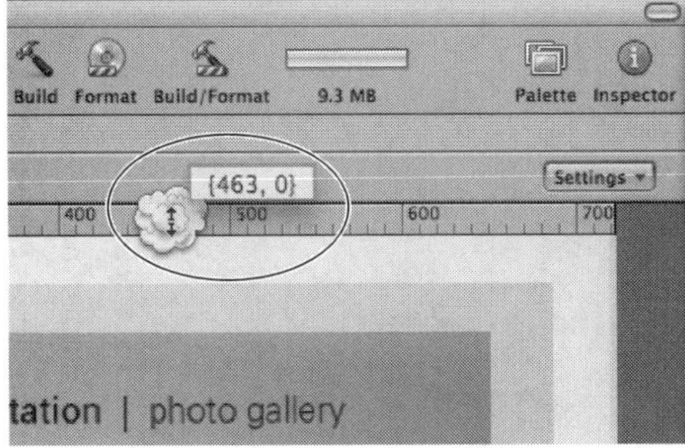

Figure 13.54 When you drop the guide back on the ruler, it blows up and disappears!

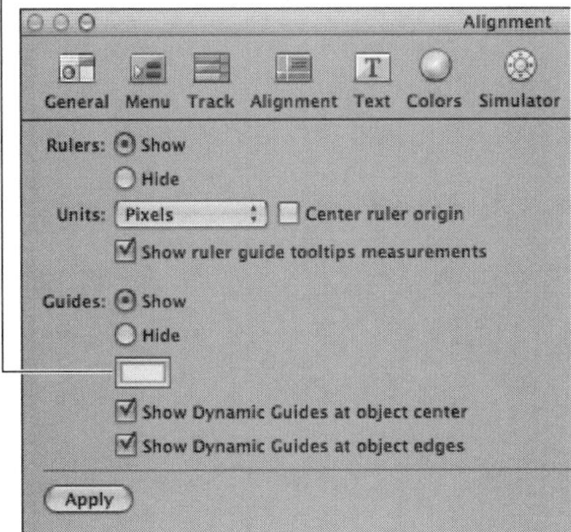

Figure 13.55 To change the color of your guides, open the Alignment section of the Preferences window and click the Guides color swatch.

To delete a guide:

1. In the Menu editor, position the pointer over the guide that you want to delete.

   The pointer turns into a double-pointed arrow (**Figure 13.53**).

2. Drag the guide back over the ruler and release the mouse.

   The guide blows up and disappears (**Figure 13.54**).

To change the guides' color:

1. Choose DVD Studio Pro > Preferences to open the Preferences window.

2. At the top of the Preferences window, click the Alignment icon.

   In the Alignment section's Guides area is a color swatch that you can use to change the color of the Menu editor's guides (**Figure 13.55**).

continues on next page

3. In the Alignment section's Guides area, click the color swatch.

   A Colors dialog opens (**Figure 13.56**).

4. In the Colors dialog, choose a new color for your guides.

5. At the top left of the Colors dialog's, click the close button to close the dialog.

6. In the Preferences window, click OK.

   Your guides will now use the selected color.

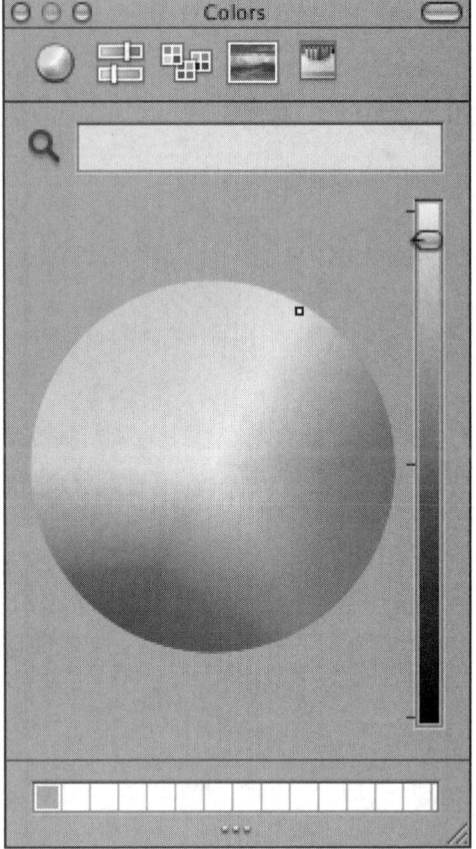

Figure 13.56 Use the Colors dialog to choose a new color for your guides.

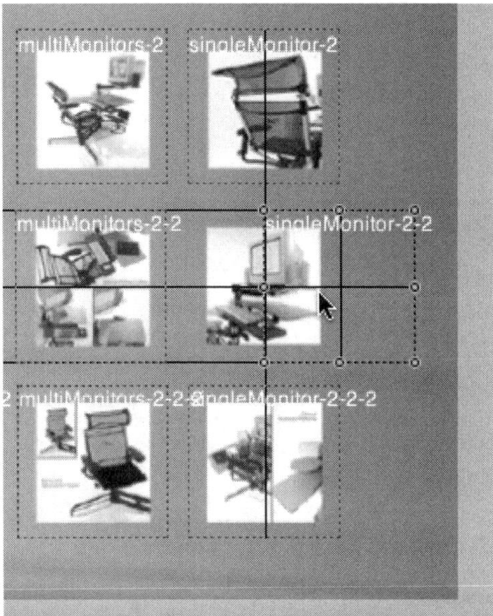

Figure 13.57 When you drag a button around the Menu editor, dynamic guides automatically appear to help you align the button with other elements on the menu.

Using Dynamic Guides

Dynamic guides make it easy to align menu elements. For example, as you drag a button around the Menu editor to reposition it, dynamic guides appear automatically and help you align the button with other menu elements, such as the edges or centers of other buttons or the center of the menu itself.

To use dynamic guides:

- In the Menu editor, select a button and drag it around.

  Dynamic guides automatically appear whenever the button is aligned with the edge or center of other menu elements (**Figure 13.57**). The guides disappear as soon as the button is no longer aligned with the edge or center of the other menu elements.

✔ Tips

- Dynamic guides appear regardless of whether you've instructed DVD Studio Pro to hide guides in the Menu editor. To temporarily ensure that dynamic guides do not appear, hold down the Command key as you drag a button around the Menu editor.

- Dynamic guides are particularly useful when you're copying buttons by pressing the Option key and dragging, because they help to ensure that the copied buttons are properly aligned.

Using Alignment Modes

The Menu editor's alignment modes allow you to align a group of selected objects by either their edges or centers. This is a great time saver when you're creating rows of buttons, because you can just drag your buttons out in any place in the Menu editor and then use the alignment buttons to make them all fall into order.

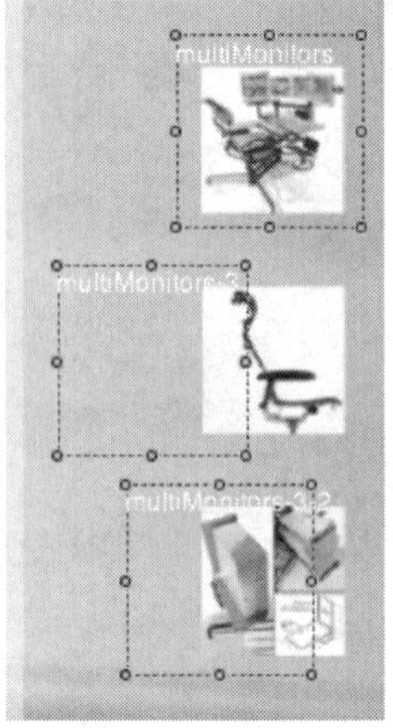

Figure 13.58 To align objects in the Menu editor, begin by selecting the objects.

✔ Tip

- All selected objects align on the last object you select.

To align a group of menu objects:

1. In the Menu editor, select several menu objects.

   As mentioned earlier, you can Shift-click multiple objects to select them all at the same time or press the Command key as you drag a selection range around the objects (**Figure 13.58**).

2. *Do one of the following:*

   ▲ Control-click one of the selected objects and, from the shortcut menu that appears, choose Align Objects and an alignment mode (**Figure 13.59**).

   ▲ Choose Arrange > Align Objects and choose an alignment mode (**Figure 13.60**).

   The objects align on the last object selected.

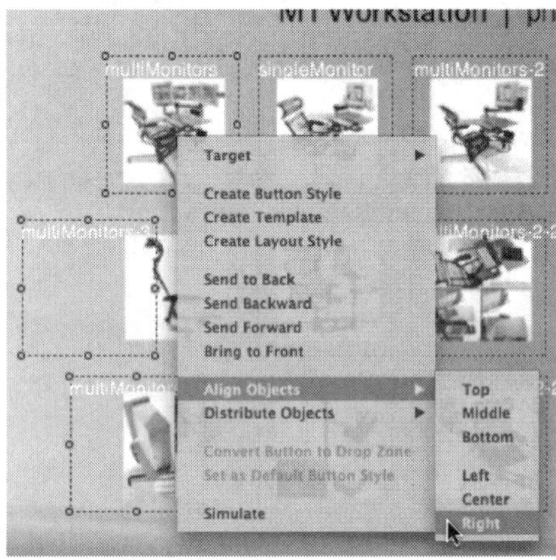

Figure 13.59 Next, Control-click one of the selected objects and choose Align Objects and choose an alignment mode, or...

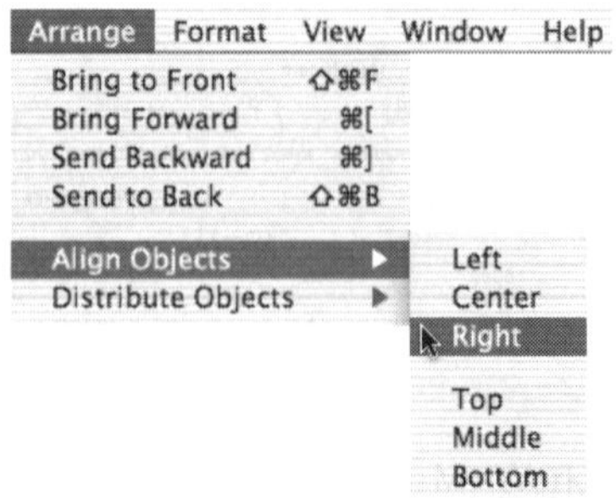

Figure 13.60 ...choose Arrange > Align Objects and an alignment mode.

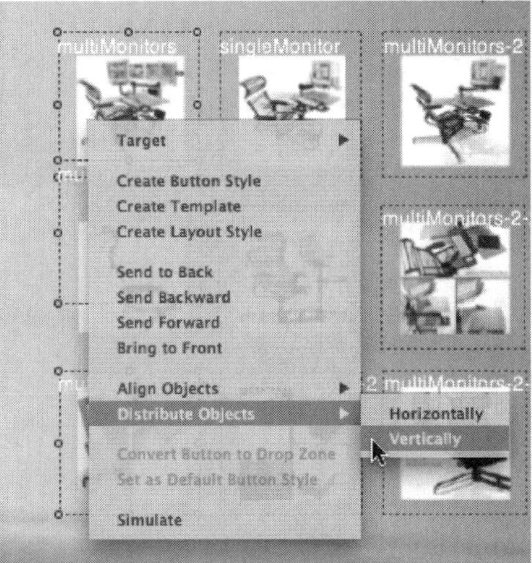

Figure 13.61 To distribute objects in the Menu editor, select the objects, Control-click one of the objects, and choose Distribute Objects and a distribution mode, or...

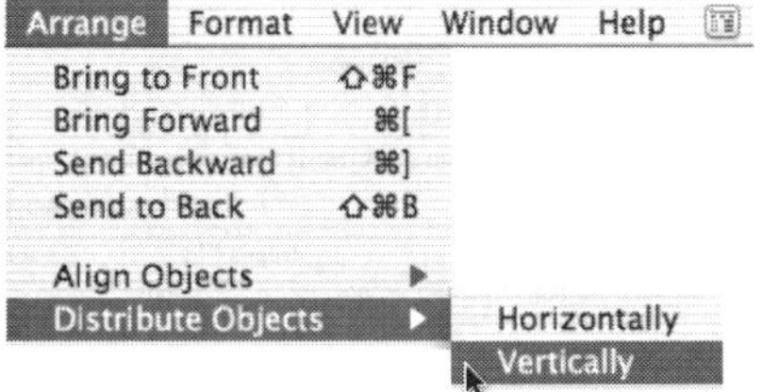

Figure 13.62 ...choose Arrange > Distribute Objects and a distribution mode.

Using Distribution Modes

The Menu editor's distribution modes allow you to distribute a group of selected objects by their edges or centers. Similar to alignment modes, which cause buttons to line up by their edges or centers, distribution modes are used to evenly space buttons in the Menu editor. Using a combination of alignment and distribution modes, often you can lay out your menu's buttons with just a few quick clicks.

To distribute objects:

1. In the Menu editor, select several menu objects.
2. *Do one of the following:*
   - ▲ Control-click one of the selected objects and, from the shortcut menu that appears, choose Distribute Objects and a distribution mode (**Figure 13.61**).
   - ▲ Choose Arrange > Distribute Objects and a distribution mode (**Figure 13.62**).

   The objects snap to the chosen distribution mode.

14

Layered Menus

Layered menus are fast becoming a rare breed. While they give the DVD author unparalleled control over how buttons look—the menu's normal, selected, and activated states are created as separate layers in an image document—layered menus are saddled with enough limitations to make them far less preferred than overlay menus. For example, layered menus are slow to respond to user interaction, and they can't use audio, video backgrounds, or any of DVD Studio Pro's compositing features that let you add text or graphics to menus right in the Menu editor.

But layered menus aren't totally extinct, and that's because they can do a few things that overlay menus can't. For example, you can use a layered menu to create a Web site–type display in which rolling the mouse over a button causes another image elsewhere in the menu to be updated. This trick can be used to create an information panel of sorts that provides additional information about the button's targeted item or maybe even calls up a related photo. This is an especially valuable feature for DVD-Videos that serve as electronic product brochures, as well as for the cross-deployment of Internet content to DVD-Video.

At any rate, knowledge of how to create layered menus is a good arrow to keep in your DVD-Video quiver, so this chapter covers everything you need to know about these visually appealing yet functionally limited menus.

Designing Layered Menus

Although Adobe Photoshop is the software tool of choice for designing layered menus, any graphics application that can export layered image documents will work. This chapter focuses on Photoshop, but you should have no problem translating what you learn here to other graphics applications, such as CorelDRAW or Macromedia Fireworks.

Before going any further, however, it's imperative that you read Chapter 3, "Preparing Graphics." This chapter contains important information on creating graphics for use in DVD Studio Pro, including how to ensure that your still images conform to the NTSC colorspace and pixel aspect ratio.

About layered menus

You don't have to be a Photoshop expert to create layered menus, but you must understand a few key concepts—including, first and foremost, how Photoshop's Layers palette works. For example, you must know how to use the Layers palette to create new layers and how to turn layer visibility on and off, which allows you to preview your button states before you add your menu to your project.

Why So Slow?

In Photoshop, you can preview each menu by turning layers on and off to see how buttons look when selected and activated. Your DVD-Video does more or less the same thing, except the viewer turns the layers on and off by selecting and activating buttons.

Well, actually, nothing gets turned on or off. In fact, layered menus work in a rather deceptive way. In the final DVD-Video, DVD Studio Pro turns each button state into an I-frame—multiplexing the project transforms the menu from a series of layers into a series of I-frames. When a viewer selects a button, the DVD-Video jumps to the I-frame that represents that button's selected state. When the viewer activates a button, the DVD-Video jumps to the activated I-frame, and so on.

Consequently, a layered menu constantly jumps back and forth between different MPEG-2 stills as the viewer selects and activates buttons on the menu. Whenever the DVD-Video player's laser is forced to refocus on another part of the disc, playback pauses for a slight amount of time. Because of all this jumping around, layered menus seem sluggish, or slow to respond.

In an overlay menu, on the other hand, the DVD-Video player generates the overlay graphic at runtime. The DVD-Video player's laser is not forced to jump back and forth across the disc as the menu plays, which means that overlay menus respond to viewer input much more quickly than layered menus do.

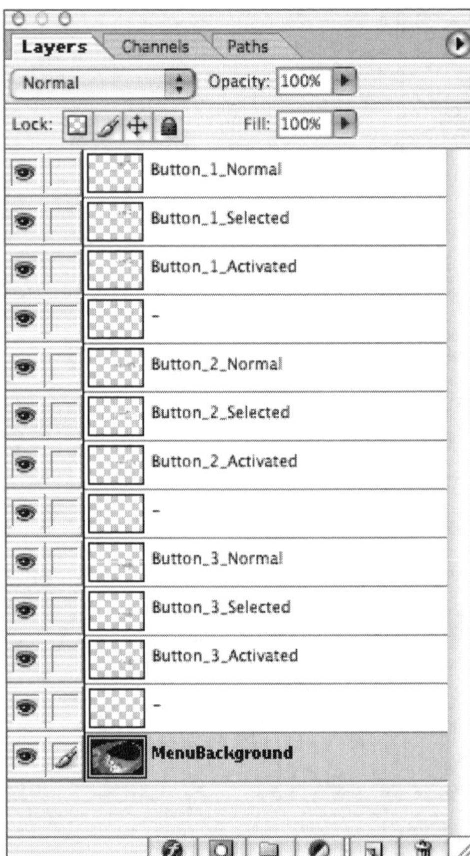

Figure 14.1 Photoshop's Layers palette, displaying well-named and organized layers. This layer naming and organization makes it easy to find and classify each layer after the Photoshop document has been brought into DVD Studio Pro.

Working with Layers in Photoshop

To keep layers clearly organized and easy to work with in DVD Studio Pro, it is common to create layered menus that have all background graphics flattened into a single "menu background" layer. Then each button's normal, selected, and activated graphics are placed on individual layers (one layer per button state for each and every button). At the end of the design process, Photoshop's Layers palette should look similar to **Figure 14.1**.

Note that the graphic in Figure 14.1 has a layer named with a hyphen (-) that separates each group of buttons. This layer is empty and holds no graphics at all. This layer is simply a divider that helps you group your buttons together, making them easier to find in DVD Studio Pro (**Figure 14.2**).

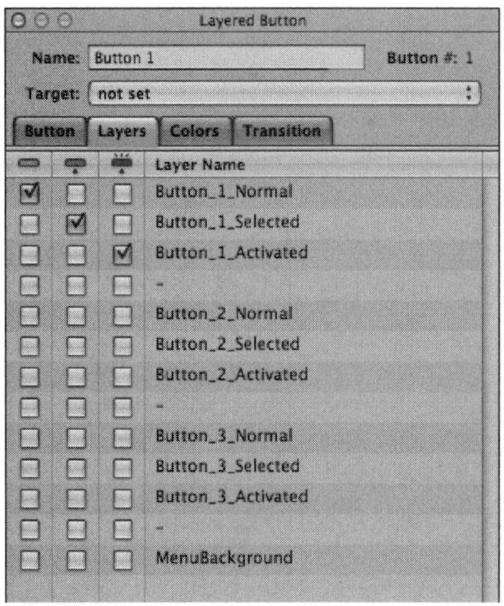

Figure 14.2 This is DVD Studio Pro's Button Inspector, with the Layers tab displayed. Notice how well organized it is!

To create a new Photoshop layer:

- At the bottom right of the Layers palette, click the Create a New Layer button (**Figure 14.3**).

  A new layer appears above the layer currently selected in the Layers palette (**Figure 14.4**).

To name a Photoshop layer:

1. In Photoshop's Layers palette, double-click the layer that you want to rename.

   A text box appears (**Figure 14.5**).

2. Type a new name for the layer and press Return.

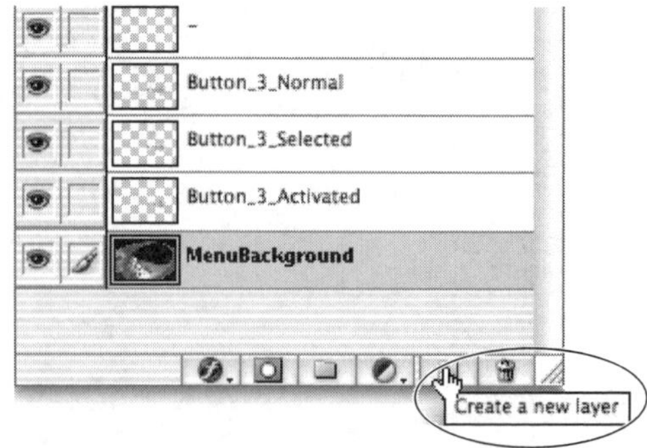

Figure 14.3 To create a new layer in Photoshop, click the Layers palette's Create a New Layer button.

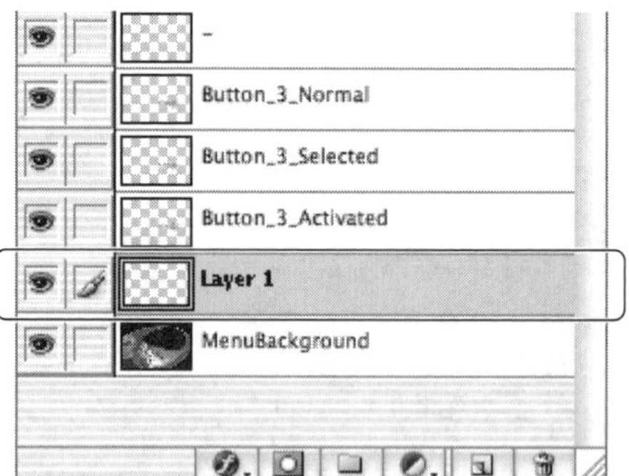

Figure 14.4 The new layer.

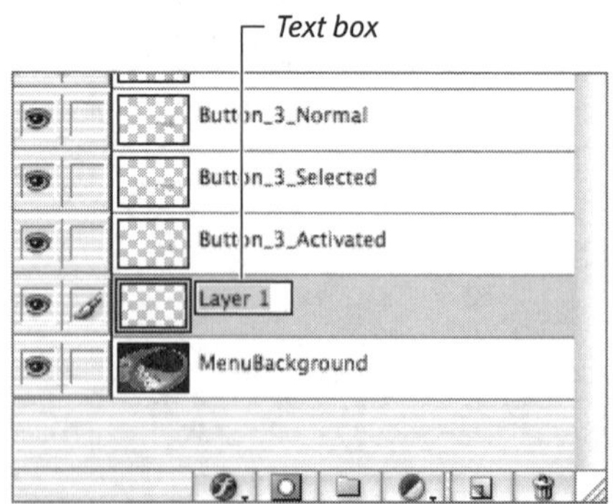

Figure 14.5 To name a Photoshop layer, in the Layers palette, double-click the layer and type a new name in the text box.

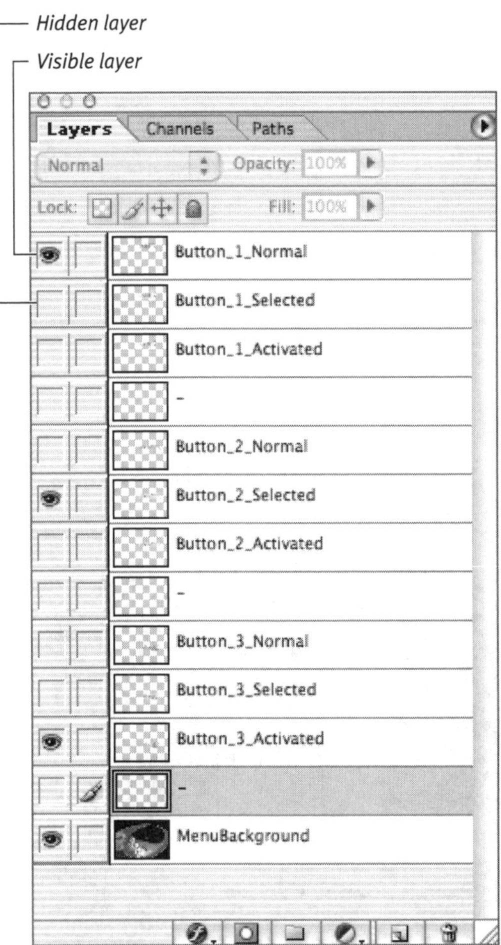

Figure 14.6 On the left side of each layer in Photoshop's Layers palette is an eye icon that controls the layer's visibility in Photoshop.

Enabling and disabling layers

Each layer in the Layers palette has a small eye icon to its left side that's responsible for enabling or disabling the layer's visibility in Photoshop (**Figure 14.6**). This eye icon controls layer visibility in Photoshop only; in DVD Studio Pro's Menu editor, you enable and disable each layer by hand once you start building the layered menu. (Note that the eye icon *does* control which layers are visible in DVD Studio Pro's Slideshow editor; to learn more, see Chapter 18, "Slideshows.")

Photoshop's eye icon has one extremely useful function: it lets you preview the way your menu will look once built by DVD Studio Pro. For example, you can enable and disable layers to preview the appearance of the menu's buttons in the final menu, which in turn lets you ensure that your menus look exactly as you want them to before you bring the menu file into DVD Studio Pro.

To enable or disable a layer:

- In Photoshop's Layers palette, click the eye icon (refer to Figure 14.6).

  If the layer was visible, the eye icon disappears, and the layer is no longer displayed in Photoshop's document window (**Figure 14.7**). If the layer was not visible, the eye icon appears, as does the layer.

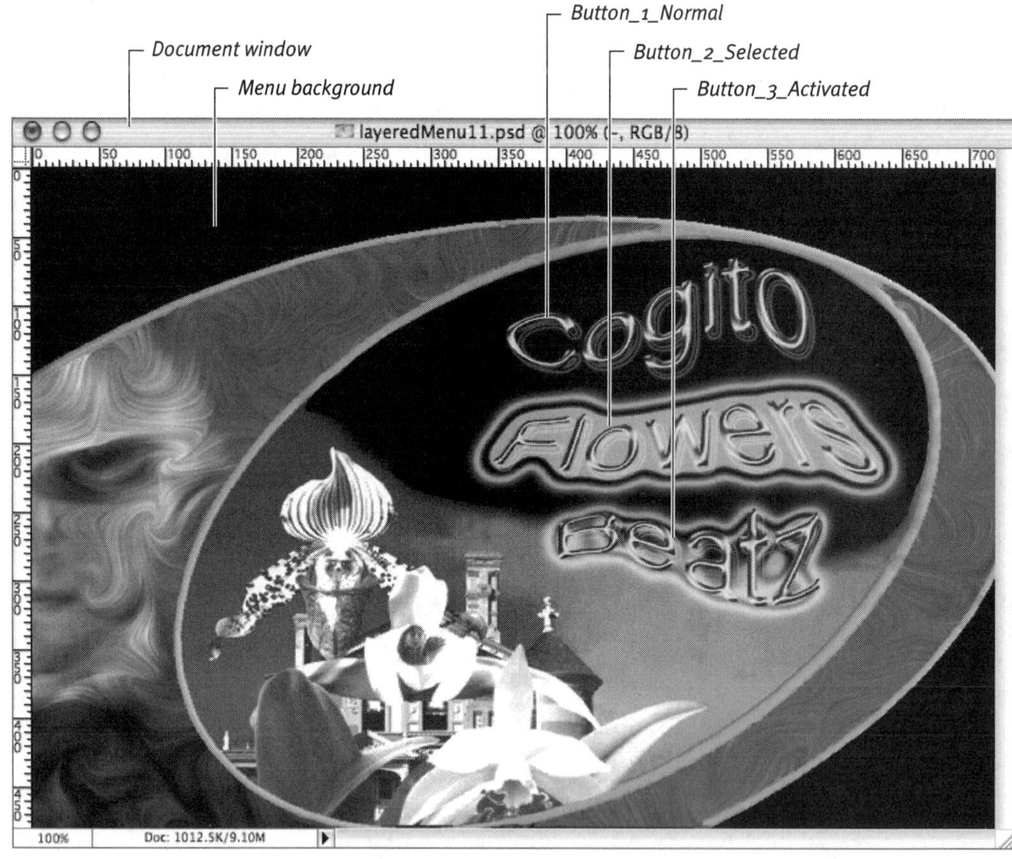

Figure 14.7 In Photoshop's document window, only the layers with the eye icon enabled are visible.

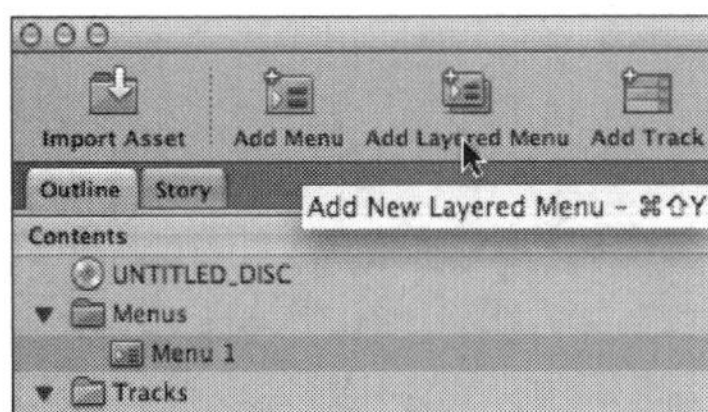

Figure 14.8 To add an empty layered menu to DVD Studio Pro, click the toolbar's Add New Layered Menu icon, or...

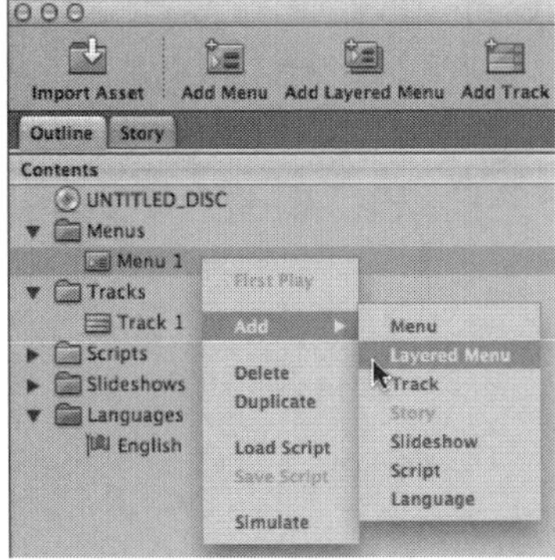

Figure 14.9 ...Control-click the Outline view and choose Add > Layered Menu.

Layer assigned to the menu's background

Asset assigned to the menu

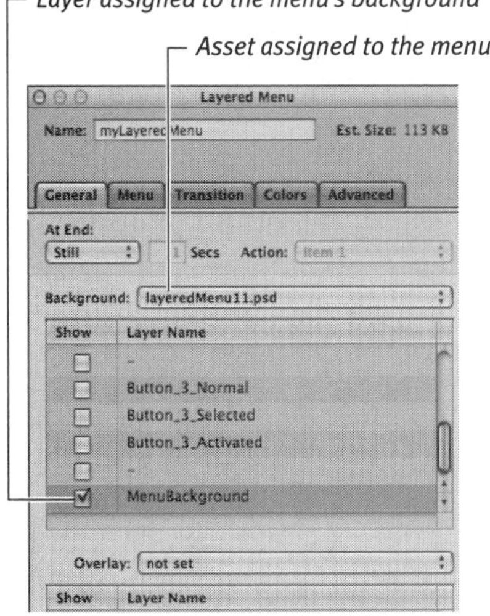

Figure 14.10 Assigning an asset to a layered menu is a two-part process. First, you must assign the asset; then you select the layers that will be used for the menu's background.

Using Layered Menus in DVD Studio Pro

In Chapter 13, "The Menu Editor," you learned a few different ways to create menus, including by clicking the Add New Layered Menu icon in DVD Studio Pro's toolbar (**Figure 14.8**) and by Control-clicking the Outline or Graphical view and then choosing Add > Layered Menu (**Figure 14.9**).

Once you've added a layered menu to your project's Outline view, the next step is to assign a layered asset to the menu. This is a two-part process: add the Photoshop document to the layered menu and then tell DVD Studio Pro which layers to display for the menu's background (**Figure 14.10**). This section walks you through these two steps by first showing you how to assign a layered Photoshop document to a menu and then explaining how to assign its background layers.

Assigning image documents to layered menus

After creating a layered menu, you need to tell the menu which asset to use. As with most things in DVD Studio Pro, there are several ways to do this, and each is covered in this section.

✔ Tip

- DVD Studio Pro's Menu editor does not work with grayscale Photoshop documents. If your Photoshop image does not appear in the Menu editor, open it in Photoshop and convert it to the RBG colorspace (in Photoshop, choose Image > Mode > RGB Color).

To add a Photoshop document to a layered menu with the drop palette:

1. In the DVD Studio Pro toolbar, click the Add Layered Menu icon to create a new, empty layered menu in the Outline view.
2. In the Outline view, double-click the new layered menu to open it in the Menu editor.
3. From the Assets tab, drag a layered Photoshop asset over the Menu editor, but don't release the mouse.

   The Menu editor's drop palette appears. Near the top of the drop palette are two options: Set Background: All Layers Visible and Set Background: No Layers Visible (**Figure 14.11**).
4. *Do one of the following:*
   - ▲ To add the Photoshop document to the menu and assign all layers to the background, drop the asset on the Set Background: All Layers Visible option.
   - ▲ To add the Photoshop document to the menu with no layers assigned to the background, drop the asset on the Set Background: No Layers Visible option.

   If you choose the Set Background: No Layers Visible option, the Menu editor does not update to display menu graphics, but you still need to assign the background layers to the menu.

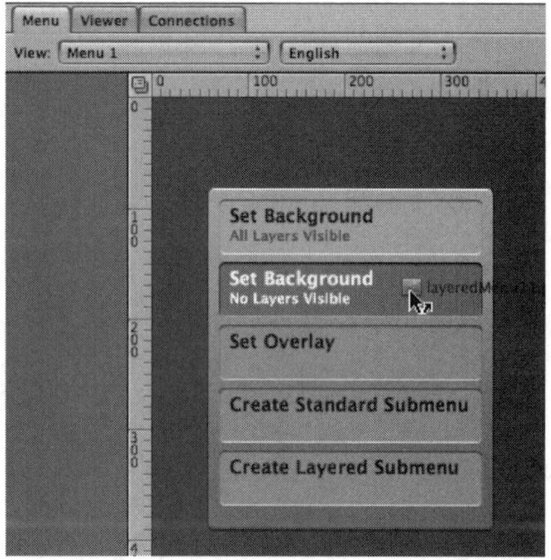

Figure 14.11 When you drag a layered Photoshop file over a layered menu in the Menu editor, the drop palette appears and displays the options shown in this figure. For layered menus, you'll use the Set Background: No Layers Visible option.

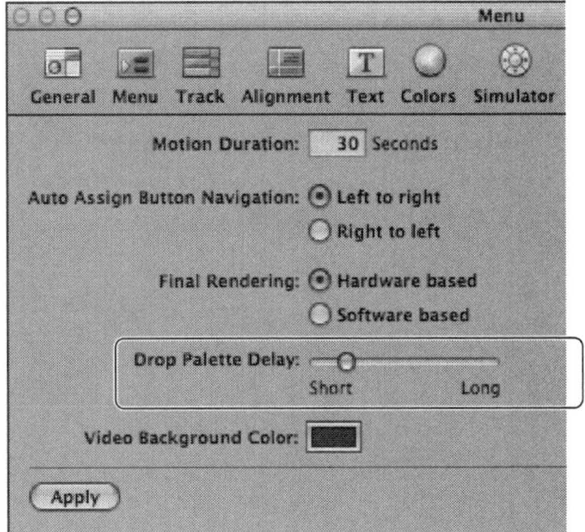

Figure 14.12 The Drop Palette Delay preference slows down (or speeds up) the rate at which the drop palette appears.

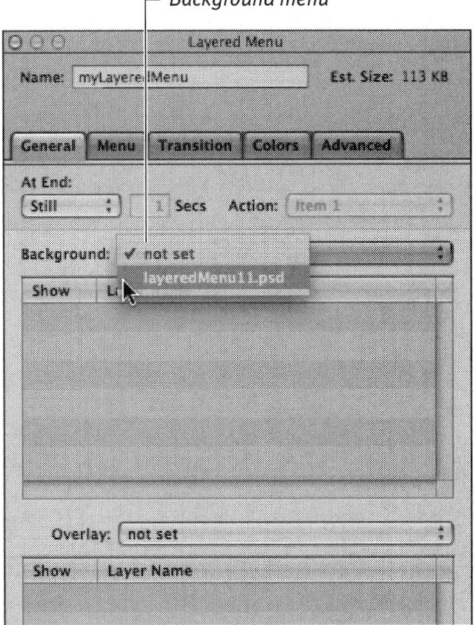

Figure 14.13 To add a Photoshop document to a layered menu, choose it from the Menu Inspector's Background drop-down menu.

✔ Tips

- Typically you'll want to use the second option—Set Background: No Layers Visible—because it's much easier to simply turn on the one or two layers that make up your background than it is to go through and disable all of the different layers that make up your button states.
- If the drop palette opens too quickly (or too slowly) for you as you drag assets over the Menu editor, you can slow it down or speed it up in the Menu section of the Preferences window. Here, you'll find an option that controls the drop palette's delay time (**Figure 14.12**).

To add a Photoshop document to a layered menu with the Inspector:

1. In the DVD Studio Pro toolbar, click the Add New Layered Menu icon to create a new, empty layered menu in the Outline view.
2. In the Outline view, select the new layered menu.

   The Inspector updates to display the menu's properties. Near the top of the Inspector's General tab is the Background drop-down menu (**Figure 14.13**).
3. From the Inspector's Background drop-down menu, choose the Photoshop asset that you want to use for your layered menu.

   The asset is added to the menu, but no layers are visible in the Menu editor. There's a reason for this: you need to tell DVD Studio Pro which layers to use for the layered menu's background (see the next section).

Adding layers to the menu's background

Directly under the Layered Menu Inspector's Background setting is the Background Layers area. You'll use this section to define which of the Photoshop document's layers will make up the layered menu's background (**Figure 14.14**). When you add a layered Photoshop document to the menu, this area updates to display all of the document's layers. You can enable or disable any of them. All enabled layers will be assigned to the background and will always be visible whenever the menu is on the screen.

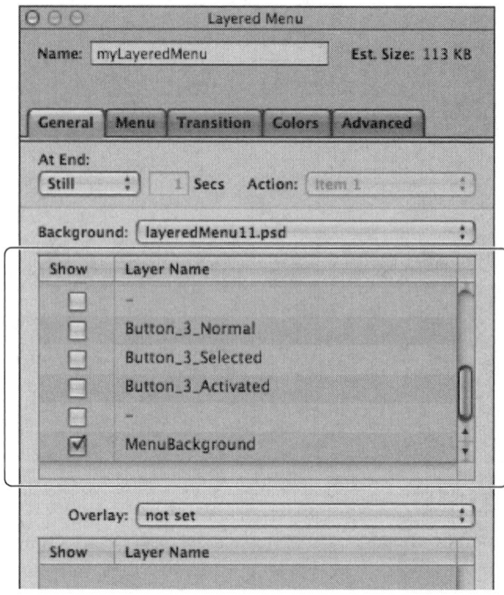

Figure 14.14 Use the Background Layers area of the Menu Inspector's General tab to tell DVD Studio Pro which layers it should use for the menu's background.

✔ Tip

- You can also add a Photoshop document to a layered menu by selecting a layered Photoshop document on the Assets tab and dragging it onto a layered menu in the Outline view (**Figure 14.15**).

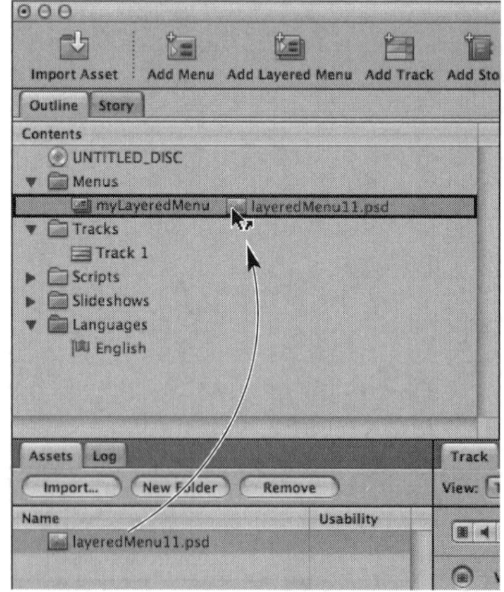

Figure 14.15 A quick way to add a Photoshop document to a layered menu—and assign all of its layers to the background—is to drag it directly onto the layered menu in the Outline view.

To add layers to the background:

◆ From the Inspector's Background Layers area, enable the check boxes to the left of the layers that DVD Studio Pro will use for the menu's background (refer to Figure 14.14).

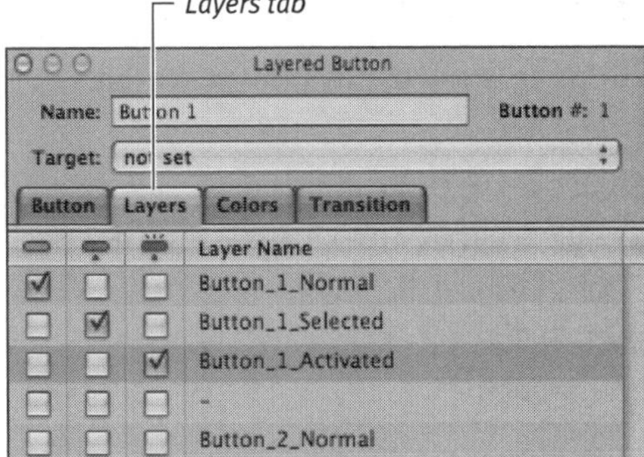

Figure 14.16 Use the Inspector's Layers tab to assign layers from a Photoshop document to a button's normal, selected, and activated states.

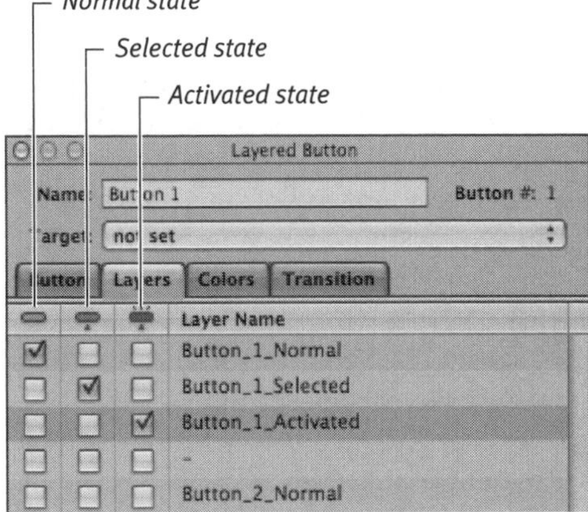

Figure 14.17 The Layers tab has three check boxes for each layer of the Photoshop document.

Assigning button states

Before you can assign a layered menu's button states, you need to create some button hotspots. If you're a bit rusty on that technique, refer to Chapter 13 for a quick refresher course. If creating button hotspots is old hat, then continue reading, because this section shows you how to assign Photoshop layers to each button's normal, selected, and activated states.

When you select a button hotspot on a layered menu, the Inspector updates to display four tabs: Buttons, Layers, Color Settings, and Transitions (transitions are covered in Chapter 16, "Using Transitions"). Use the Buttons tab to set the button size and position and navigational links (which are all covered in Chapter 13). Use the Color Settings tab to assign an overlay image to the layered menu (which you'll learn more about in Chapter 15, "Overlay Menus"). But when it comes to actually making layered menu buttons, it's all up to the Layers tab (**Figure 14.16**).

The Layers tab lists all of the Photoshop document's layers. To the left of each layer are three check boxes, which are used to enable or disable each layer's normal, selected, and activated states (**Figure 14.17**). Assigning a layer to a button is as simple as selecting the button in the Menu editor and then clicking the check box for the layers that correspond to the chosen button's normal, selected, and activated states.

continues on next page

✔ Tips

- Depending on how you've designed your Photoshop document, you may need to enable more than one layer for each button state, and that's fine—DVD Studio Pro lets you do that. But if you're new to layered menus, to stay organized and keep your project manageable it often helps to flatten all of the graphics for each button state into one layer. This will make it easier to locate and enable the layers when you need them, although it will make it more difficult to make changes to the menu's graphics in the source file.
- It is important to note that the Layers tab is available only when a button is selected on a layered menu—this tab is not available to overlay menus. If you have selected a button in the Menu editor but you don't see the Layers tab in the Inspector, you are definitely working in an overlay menu, not a layered menu.

To assign button states:

1. In the Menu editor, create a button hotspot.
2. Select the button hotspot.

   The Inspector updates to show the button's properties.
3. In the Button Inspector, select the Layers tab.
4. On the Layers tab, enable the check boxes to the left of the layers that correspond to the button's normal, selected, and activated button states (refer to Figure 14.17).

✔ Tip

- DVD Studio Pro 2 had a problem compiling layered menus where the selected and activated states are assigned to the same layer in the Photoshop document. In this situation, your button links will not work in the final, multiplexed project (though they will work fine in DVD Studio Pro's internal Simulator). If you are setting your selected and activated states to the same layer, make sure you build your project and test it thoroughly before burning that final DVD disc!

Figure 14.18 To preview a button's normal, selected, and activated states, select the button in the Menu editor.

Previewing Button States

DVD Studio Pro enables you to view the normal, selected, and activated states of each button directly in the Menu editor. You don't have to leave DVD Studio Pro to use this handy QA technique, which should save you time when testing layered menus. After all, it's easy to assign the wrong layer to a button state—so don't feel bad if you do.

To preview button states in the Menu editor:

1. In the Menu editor, select a button (**Figure 14.18**).

continues on next page

Outside the Hotspot

If you take a close look at Figure 14.19, on the next page, you'll notice that some of the button's selected-state graphics extend beyond the button's hotspot. This demonstrates one of the few benefits of layered menus: a layered menu button can be used to turn on images anywhere on the menu, not just under the hotspot itself.

In a layered menu, when you select a button, you turn on an entire layer in the graphic file. If that layer contains a graphic somewhere that is not directly part of the button itself, that graphic turns on anyway. As you'll see in Chapter 15, overlay menus do not allow you to display an image outside of the button's hotspot. This is one of the few advantages that layered menus enjoy over overlay menus. For example, you can use a layered menu to update an information panel on a menu that shows viewers what will happen when they activate a button.

2. *Do one of the following:*
   - ▲ At the bottom of the Menu Inspector, click the Normal, Selected, or Activated State button (**Figure 14.19**).
   - ▲ Choose View > Button State and then choose Selected, Activated, or Normal (**Figure 14.20**).
   - ▲ Press W to step through the button states.

   The selected menu state is displayed in the Menu editor.

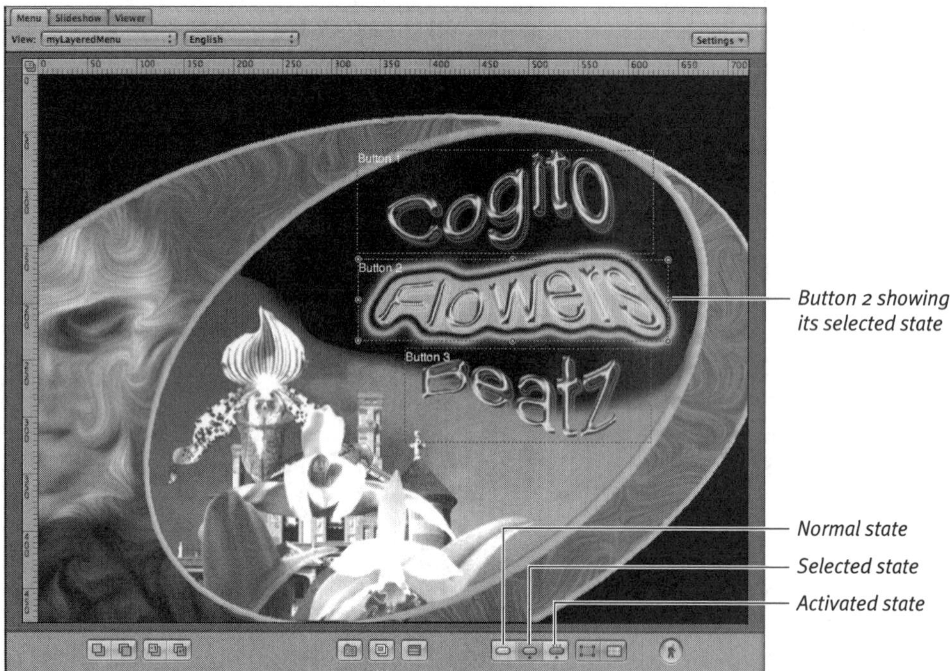

Figure 14.19 Then click the Normal, Selected, or Activated State button at the bottom of the Menu editor.

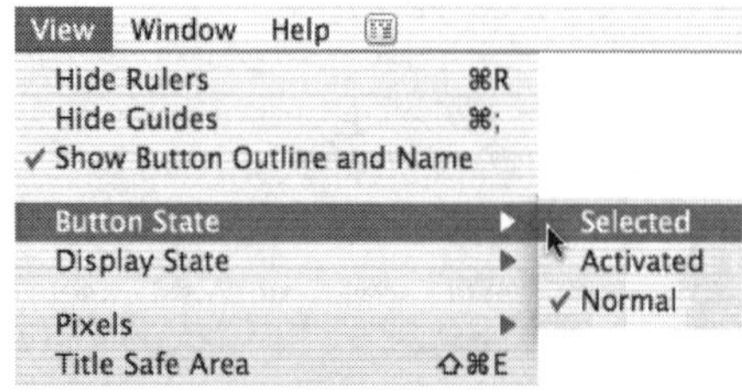

Figure 14.20 To preview your button states in the Menu editor, you can also choose View > Button State and choose a button state.

15

Overlay Menus

Rent a DVD from Blockbuster, and 99.99 percent of the time it's going to have overlay menus. Similar to the way a highlight pen marks text in a book, an overlay menu uses a strip of color (or colors) to indicate button states. The chief benefit? Speed. Although overlay menus don't offer the graphical depth of layer menus, they are quick to react to viewer input and don't feel as sluggish as Photoshop layer menus. When a viewer navigates menu buttons on a computer, for example, overlays "turn on"—or display their selected state—as soon as the viewer places the pointer over button hotspots, whereas a Photoshop layer menu makes the viewer wait up to a second or more (if they turn on at all). But the chief benefit of overlay menus is they can use both sound and video, while layered menus must be silent and still.

Initially, the process of creating overlay menus can be daunting, but after a bit of practice, you'll find overlay menus much easier to create than their layered counterparts. This chapter shows you how to use an overlay image to give your overlays distinct shapes, create simple (single-color) and advanced (multicolor) overlays, attach sound to a menu, and create motion menus that give any Hollywood DVD-Video a run for its money. However, this chapter does *not* cover menu basics such as how to design still images so they look good on a television or how to use DVD Studio Pro's Menu editor. If you're new to menus, before continuing, you should backtrack to Chapter 3, "Preparing Graphics," and Chapter 13, "The Menu Editor," to solidify your menu-making skills.

Creating Overlay Menus

DVD Studio Pro uses two different overlay modes: *simple overlay* and *advanced overlay*. Simple overlay mode provides a fast way to produce single-color highlights (to learn more, see "Creating a Simple Overlay Menu" later in this chapter). For most circumstances, simple overlay mode works well. But there will be times when you need more colors in your button highlights. Using the advanced overlay mode, you can create button highlights with up to four different colors (to learn more, see "Creating an Advanced Overlay Menu" later in this chapter).

But first things first: you can't create an overlay menu until you've added a menu to DVD Studio Pro's Outline view. This section begins by showing you how to add a new overlay menu to your project and then moves on to discuss backgrounds and overlay images, the two main components to any overlay menu.

To create an overlay menu:

◆ *Do one of the following:*

▲ In the toolbar, click the Add Menu icon (**Figure 15.1**).

▲ In the Outline or Graphical view, Control-click anywhere and choose Add > Menu from the shortcut menu that appears (**Figure 15.2**).

▲ Choose Project > Add to Project > Menu (**Figure 15.3**).

▲ Press Command-Y.

A new menu is created and added to the Outline and Graphical views (**Figure 15.4**).

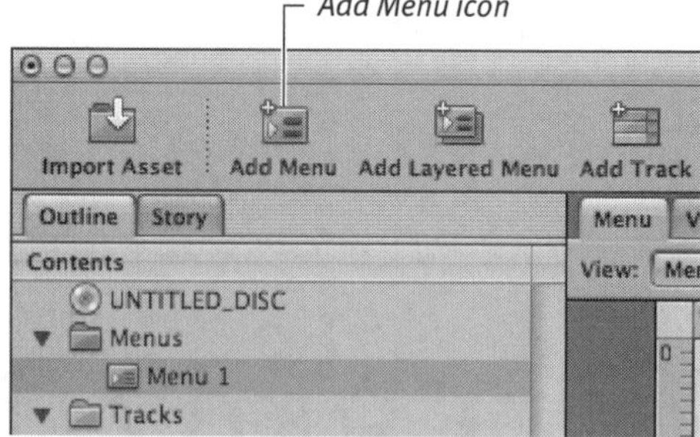

Figure 15.1 To create an overlay menu, in the toolbar, click the Add Menu icon, or...

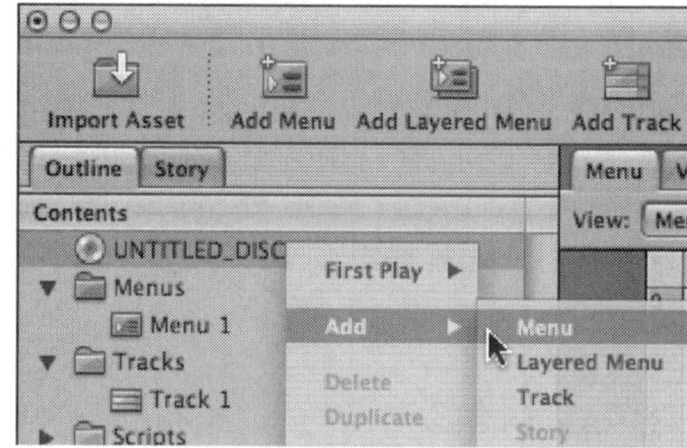

Figure 15.2 ...Control-click the Outline view and choose Add > Menu from the shortcut menu that appears, or...

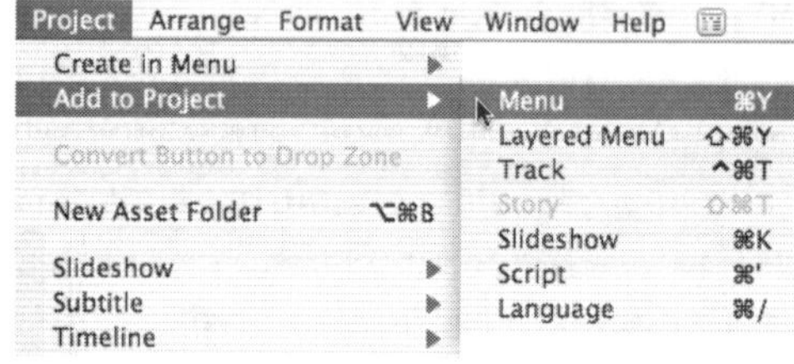

Figure 15.3 ...choose Project > Add to Project > Menu.

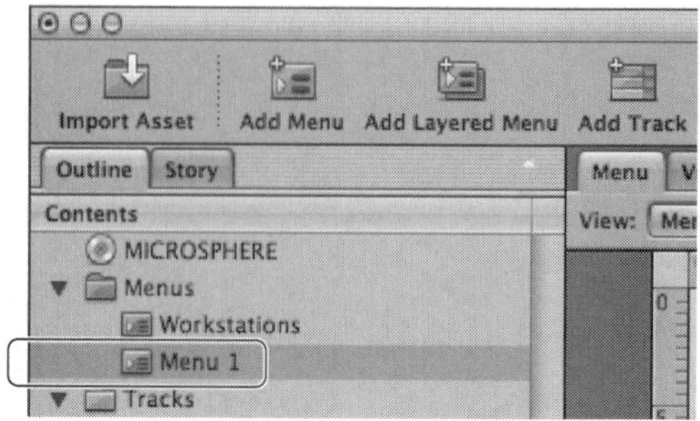

Figure 15.4 A new menu in the Outline view.

How overlay menus work

An overlay menu has two parts: a menu background and an overlay image.

- **Menu background.** The menu background contains the menu's background graphics, plus all images or graphics that make up the menu's buttons (**Figure 15.5**).

continues on next page

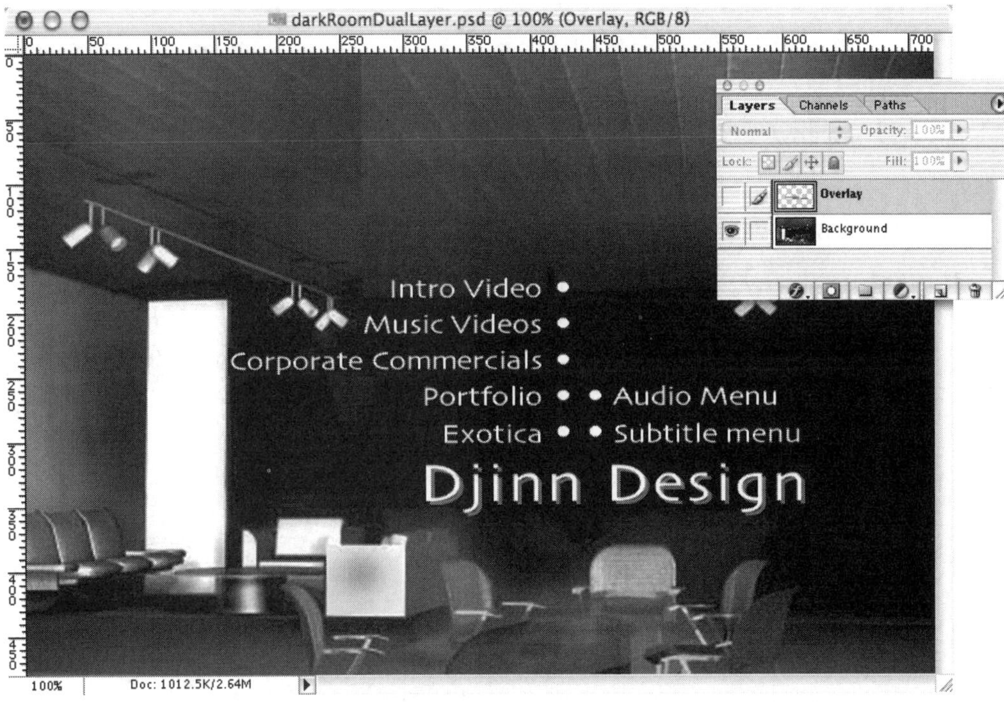

Figure 15.5 A typical overlay menu consists of two parts: a background and...

- **Overlay image.** The overlay image is a single layer that contains a single shape for *each* menu button's normal, selected, and activated states. The important thing to understand about an overlay image is that unlike in a layer menu, where each button state is on its own layer, in an overlay image all button shapes are on the same layer (**Figure 15.6**). These shapes act as guides that tell DVD Studio Pro how to color map highlights on the menu. In other words, DVD Studio Pro looks at the shapes in the overlay image and then supplies colors to the shapes. At run time, the DVD player displays these color-mapped shapes as the normal, selected, and activated button states (**Figure 15.7**).

The process for creating an overlay menu is fairly simple and intuitive; it just takes a bit of practice to design your background and overlay image. Once you've designed your menu background and overlay image, it's a simple matter to create the overlay menu inside DVD Studio Pro.

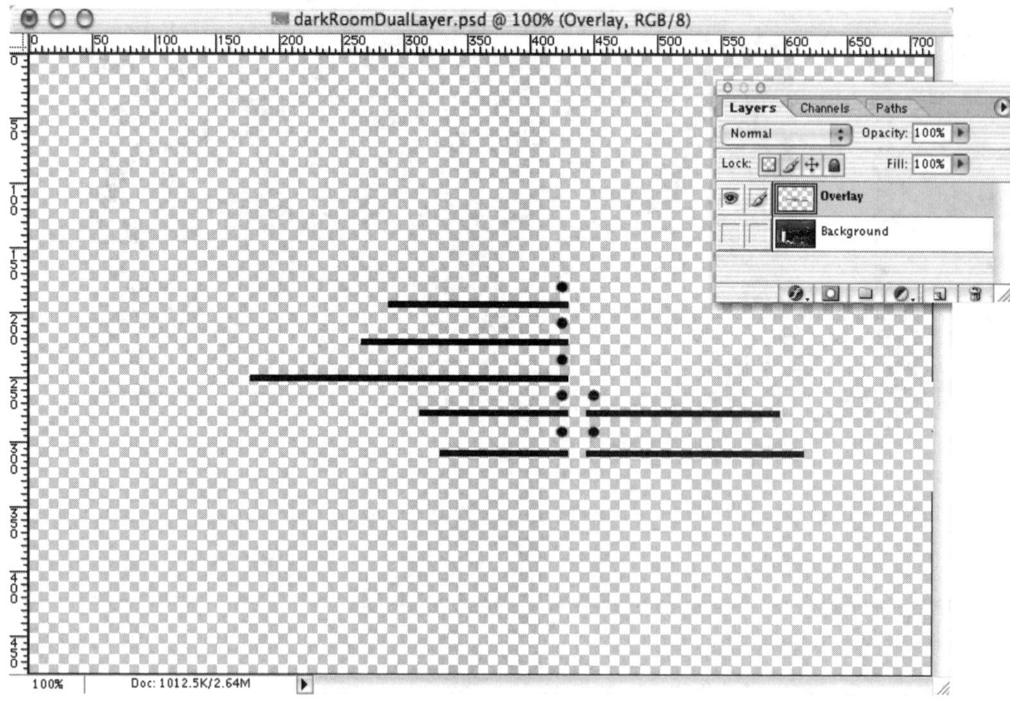

Figure 15.6 ...an overlay layer. Notice that this figure shows only the overlay layer enabled in Photoshop's Layers palette, while Figure 15.5 shows only the background layer enabled.

✔ Tip

- For an overlay menu to work properly, the shapes on the overlay image must align exactly with the button graphics on the background. For this reason, it's common to design the overlay image in the same Photoshop document as the background image, placing the background on one layer and the overlay shapes on a second layer above. This makes it easy to line up the overlay shapes with the button graphics underneath.

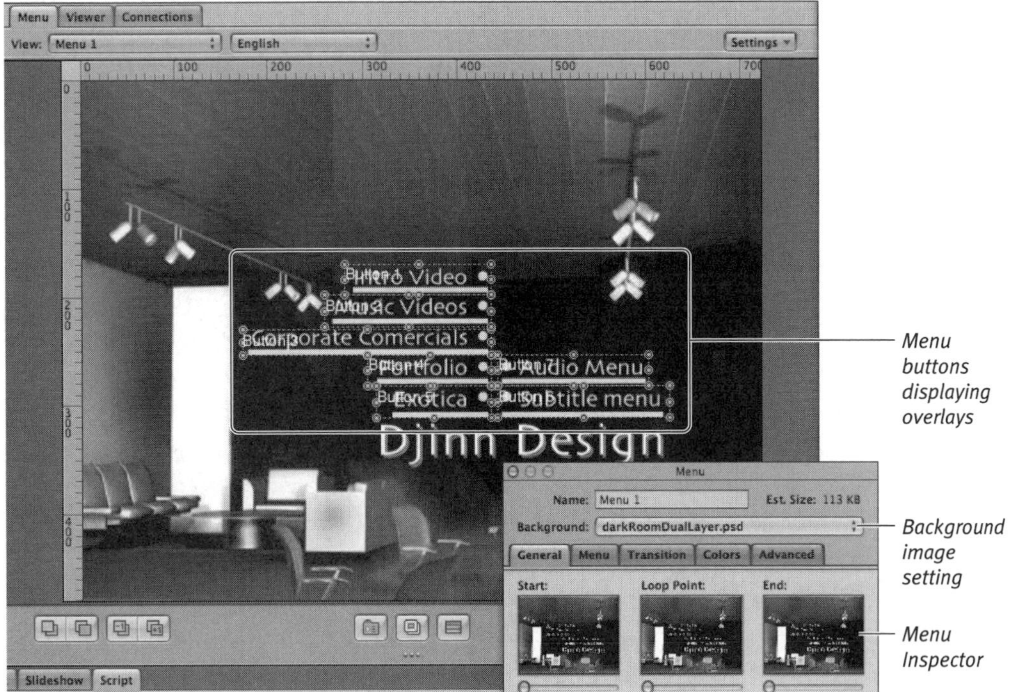

Figure 15.7 In DVD Studio Pro, the menu background and overlay layer are assembled into a complete overlay menu.

To assign an overlay menu's background:

1. In the Outline or Graphical view, select the overlay menu (**Figure 15.8**).

   The Inspector updates to display the menu's properties.

2. From the Inspector's Background menu (**Figure 15.9**), choose an asset for the menu's background (**Figure 15.10**).

   The asset you choose can be either a still image (to create a still menu) or a video (to create a motion menu). If you choose a layered still-image file, you need to complete a few more steps before the background is properly assigned.

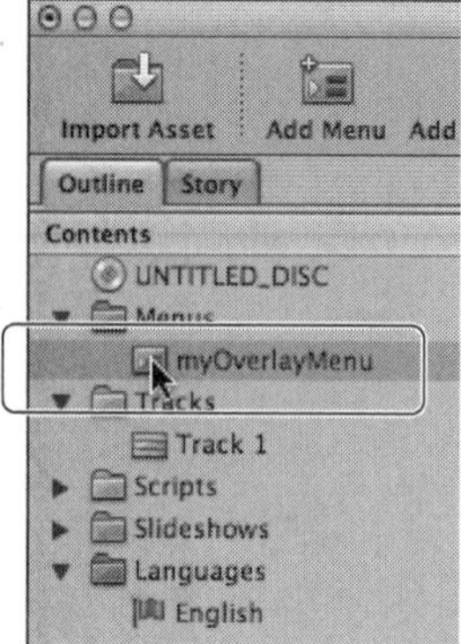

Figure 15.8 To create an overlay menu, you must first select the menu in the Outline view so that the Inspector updates to display the overlay menu's properties.

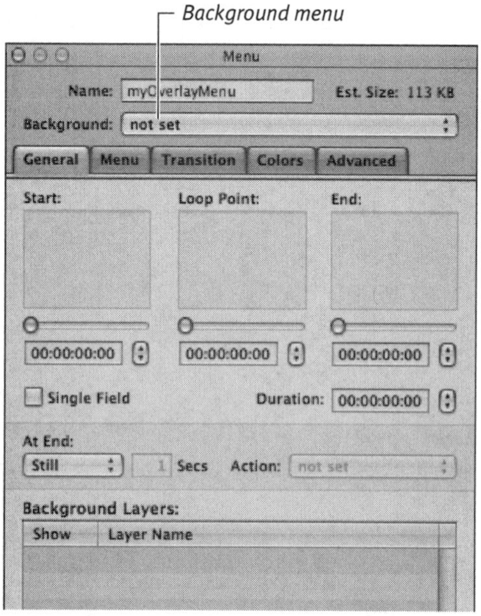

Background menu

Figure 15.9 The Overlay Menu Inspector's Background menu.

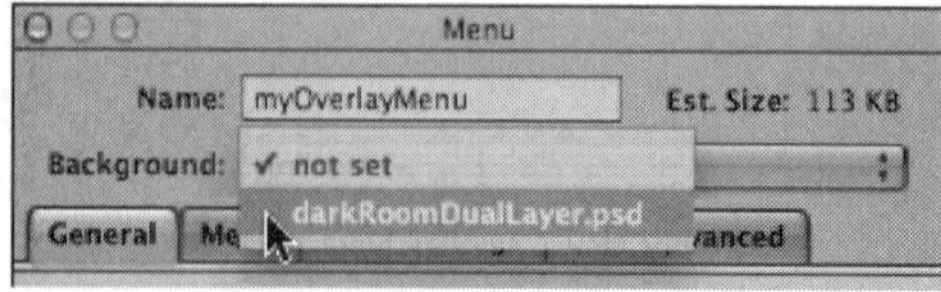

Figure 15.10 From the Inspector's Background menu, choose the image (or video) that you want to use as the menu's background.

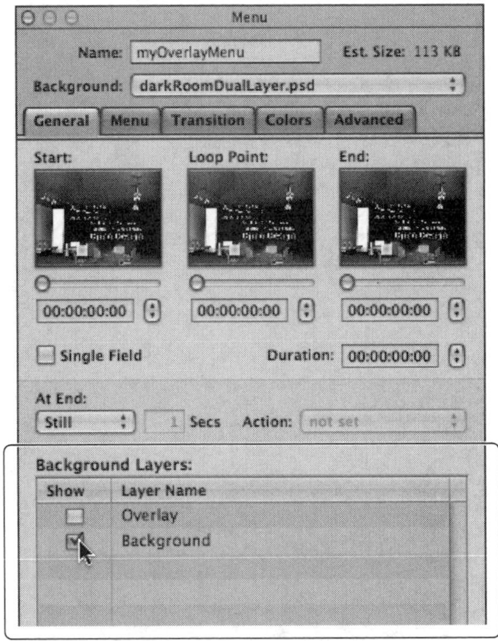

Figure 15.11 If the image containing the background has more than one layer, you must use the Inspector's Background Layers area to tell DVD Studio Pro which layers to use for the menu's background.

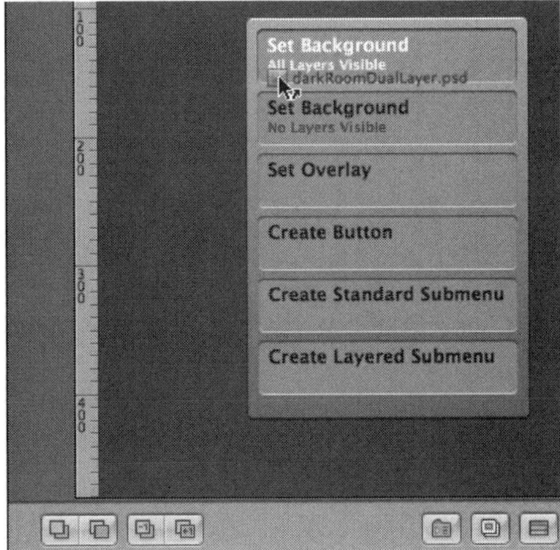

Figure 15.12 The Menu editor's drop palette lets you set a menu's background quickly.

3. If you are using a layered image file, use the Inspector's Background Layers area to select only the layers you want to see in the menu's background (**Figure 15.11**).

✔ Tip

- Don't forget about the drop palette. If you drag an image over the Menu editor, the drop palette appears, and its first two settings let you quickly set the menu's background (**Figure 15.12**).

To assign an overlay image:

1. In the Outline or Graphical view, select the overlay menu.

   The Inspector updates to display the menu's properties.

2. From the Overlay menu on the Inspector's General tab (**Figure 15.13**), choose an asset to use for the menu's overlay image (**Figure 15.14**).

   If the overlay image has only one single layer, you're done. However, if the overlay image has several layers (for example, if the overlay layer is in the same document as the background images), you must tell DVD Studio Pro which layer to use as the overlay layer. To do so, select a layer from the Overlay Layer menu at the very bottom of the Inspector's General tab.

3. From the Overlay Layer menu, select the image layer that holds the overlay graphics (**Figure 15.15**).

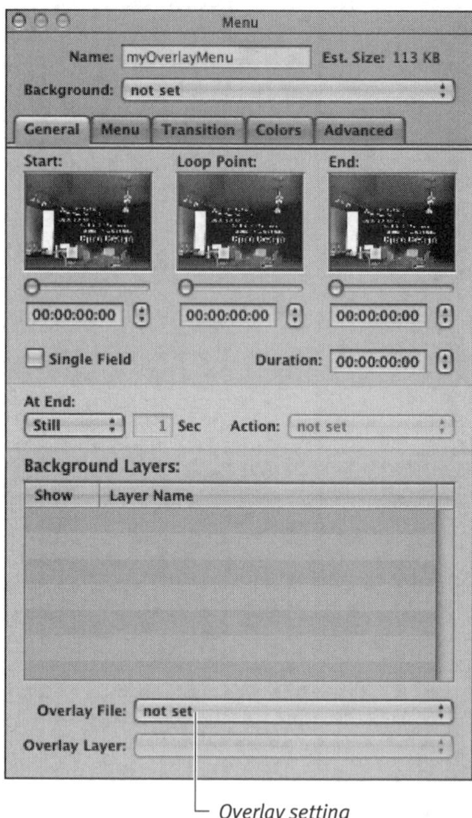

Figure 15.13 The Overlay menu Inspector's Overlay setting.

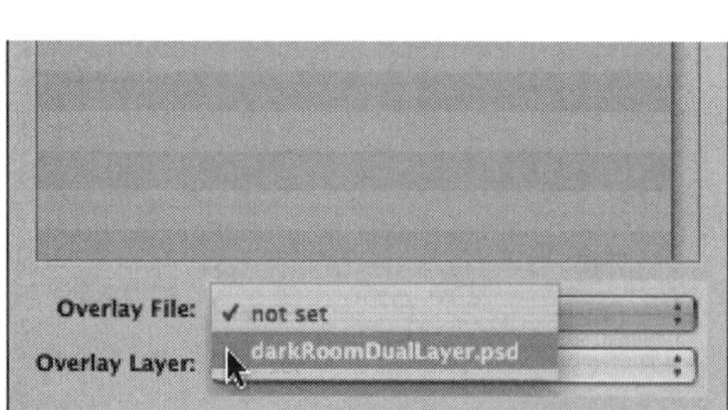

Figure 15.14 From the Inspector's Overlay menu, choose the image that you want to use as the menu's overlay.

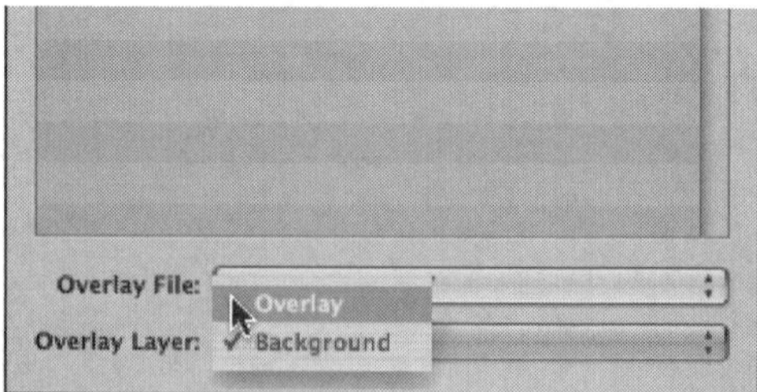

Figure 15.15 If the image containing the overlay has more than one layer, use the Inspector's Overlay Layer menu to tell DVD Studio Pro which layer to use for the menu's overlay.

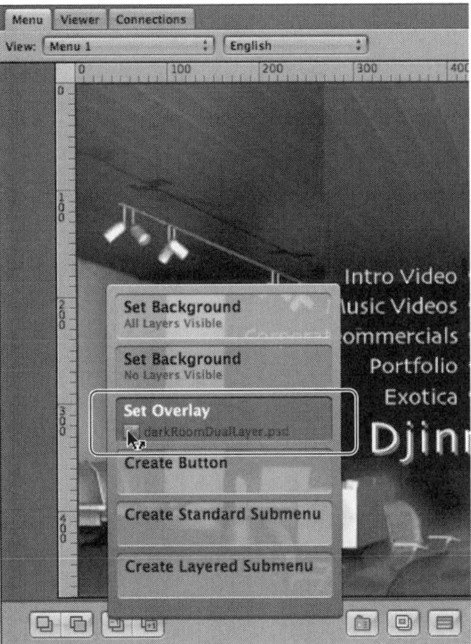

Figure 15.16 The Menu editor's drop palette lets you quickly set a menu's overlay image.

✔ Tips

- You can use the Menu editor's drop palette to quickly assign an overlay image (**Figure 15.16**).
- Overlay highlights are not anti-aliased, which can lead to jagged-looking edges on complex shapes and small, rounded corners. To guard against this, use simple, nonround shapes wherever possible.
- If your overlay image uses squares, circles, or any other shape that must remain proportionally correct in the final DVD-Video, don't forget to design the overlay at 720 × 534 (NTSC) and then resize it to 720 × 480. However, keep in mind that resizing an image can cause the edges to be resampled, which causes solid black edges to become gray. This in turn will cause problems with the way that colors are mapped to your overlay image inside DVD Studio Pro. If at all possible, create your overlay image at 720 × 480 so that resizing or resampling doesn't occur.

Creating a Simple Overlay Menu

A simple overlay menu uses single-colored buttons. In the overlay image itself, all button shapes are colored black, and only black. DVD Studio Pro then uses these black shapes to color map a color of your choice onto the menu. You can use DVD Studio Pro to change the color that's mapped to the overlay as well as the color's opacity, so you actually have a fair degree of control over how your buttons will look in the final DVD-Video.

To create a simple overlay menu:

1. Assign a background and an overlay image to the menu.
2. Create the menu's buttons.

   The menu must have button hotspots defined before you can see the overlay shapes, so this is an important step. For a refresher on how to create menu buttons, see Chapter 13.
3. In the Inspector, select the Colors tab (**Figure 15.17**).

   Use the Colors tab to map colors to the overlay image's shapes.

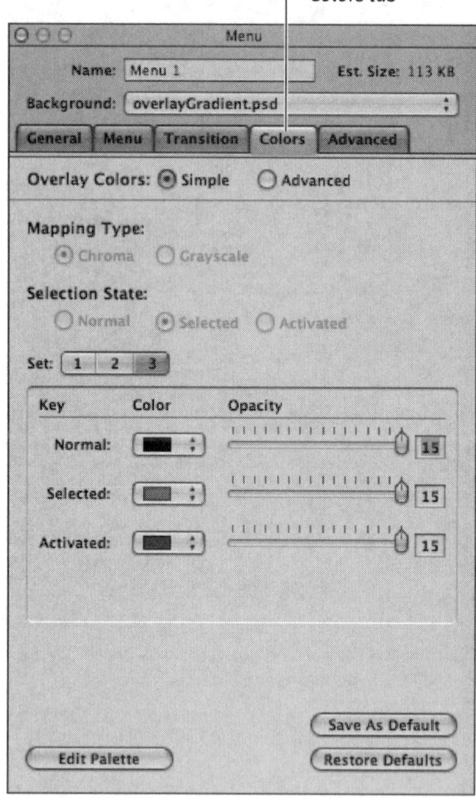

Figure 15.17 The Inspector's Colors tab is used to map colors to button states.

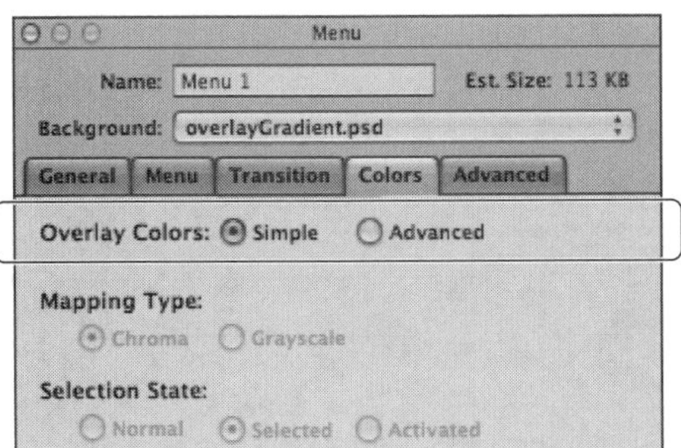

Figure 15.18 Use the Colors tab's Overlay Colors setting to specify whether your menu will use simple or advanced overlays.

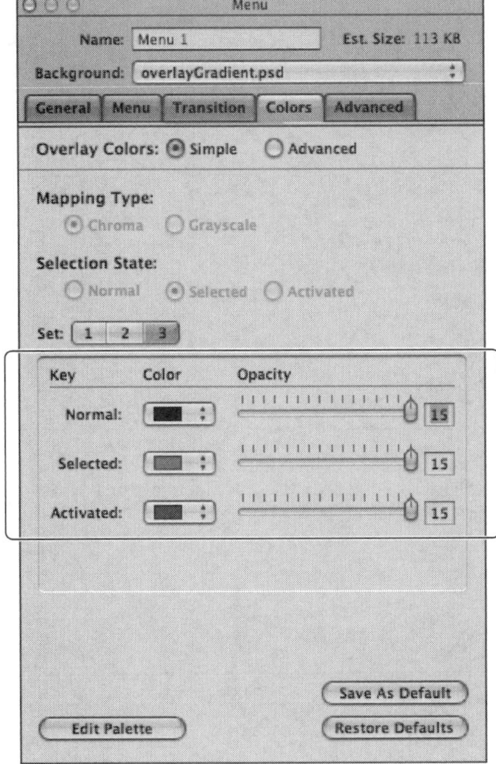

Figure 15.19 Use the Colors tab's Key area to determine the colors mapped to each button state.

4. In the Overlay Colors area, select the Simple radio button (**Figure 15.18**).

   Simple overlay mode is now enabled. In the middle of the Colors tab is the Key area, which displays three states: Normal, Selected, and Activated (**Figure 15.19**). These three states indicate the three states of your menu's buttons, and the color chip to the right of each state determines which color will be mapped to each state.

   Next, you must change the color of each button state, as described in the following section.

Changing button state colors

DVD Studio Pro provides a palette of 16 pre-set colors you can use for your button states. You select a color for each button state by clicking the color chip to the right of each button state in the Inspector and using the Opacity slider to adjust the button state's transparency (**Figure 15.20**). If none of those 16 colors is exactly the color you're after, you can also change the palette colors to something more suitable.

✔ Tip

- Each menu can use a different overlay color palette, so you are not stuck with the same selection of colors in all of your project's menus.

To change the color of a button state:

1. To the right of a button state in the Inspector, click the color chip (refer to Figure 15.20).

   The color palette menu opens (**Figure 15.21**).

2. Click a color icon to select a new color for the button state.

   The color chip changes to display the selected color.

3. To the right of the color chip, use the Opacity slider to choose a transparency value for the button state (**Figure 15.22**).

   If you choose 0, which is fully transparent, you won't see the button state at all, and if you choose 15, which is fully opaque, you won't see the menu graphic under the button whenever the button state is displayed. Values between 0 and 15 provide varying degrees of transparency.

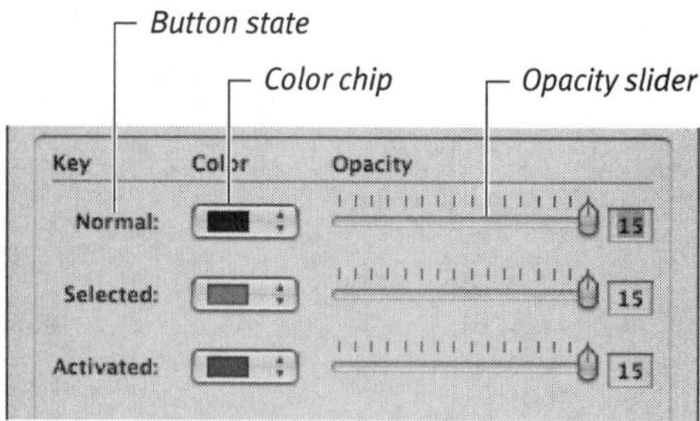

Figure 15.20 Use the Key area's color chip and Opacity slider to set the color of the highlights assigned to the normal, selected, and activated states of each menu button.

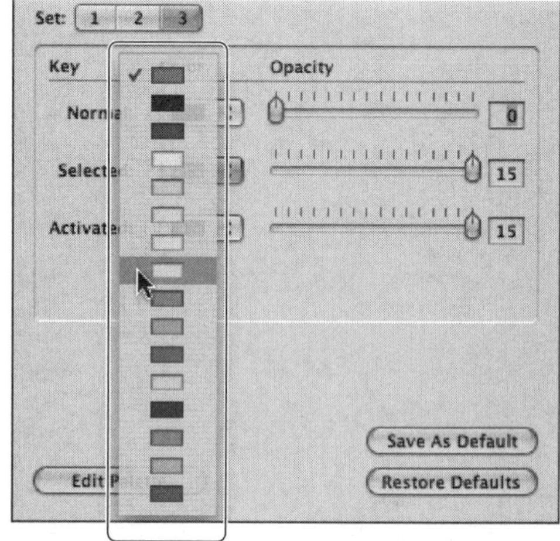

Figure 15.21 The color palette menu appears when you click a color chip. Use this menu to select a color for the button state.

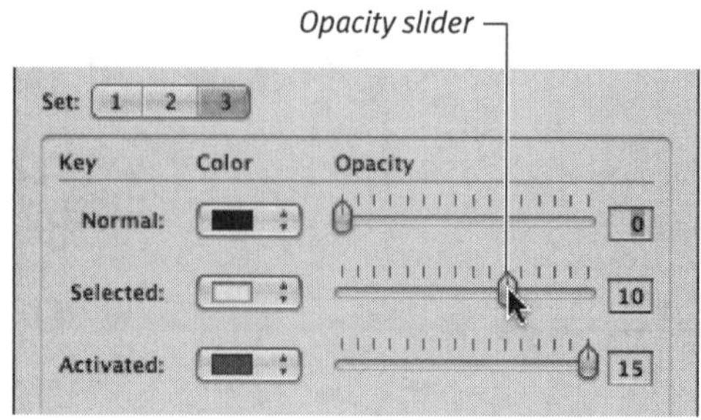

Figure 15.22 The Opacity slider controls the transparency of each menu state.

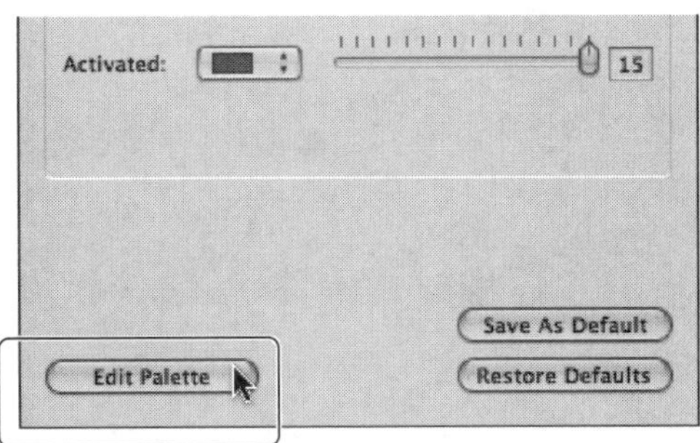

Figure 15.23 To edit the overlay menu's color palette, click the Inspector's Edit Palette button.

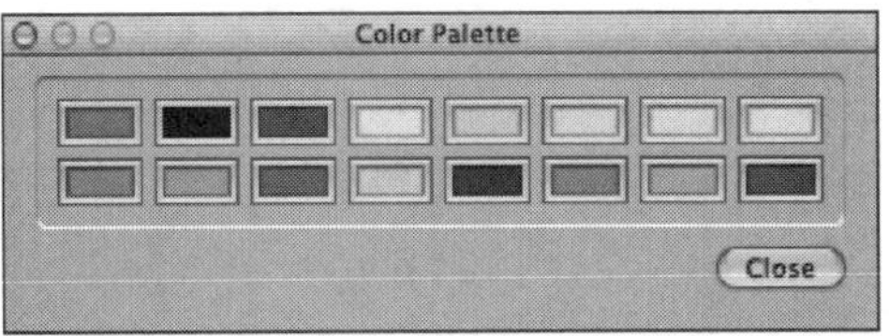

Figure 15.24 The Color Palette window displays a single color chip for every color in the menu's palette. To change the color of a chip, click it to open the color picker.

Figure 15.25 The color picker lets you modify the color palette's colors.

To change the color palette presets:

1. At the bottom of the Inspector's Colors tab, click the Edit Palette button (**Figure 15.23**).

   The Color Palette window opens, containing one color chip for every color in the palette (**Figure 15.24**).

2. Click the color chip for the color you want to edit.

   The color picker opens (**Figure 15.25**).

3. Use the color picker to choose a new color for the palette.

   The selected color is available from the color palette, and you can now use this new color for your button states.

continues on next page

✔ Tip

- To sample colors from anywhere on the screen, use the color picker's magnifying glass (**Figure 15.26**). This lets you sample colors elsewhere on your menu, for example, which in turn allows you to match the colors of your button highlights to colors that already exist on the menu.

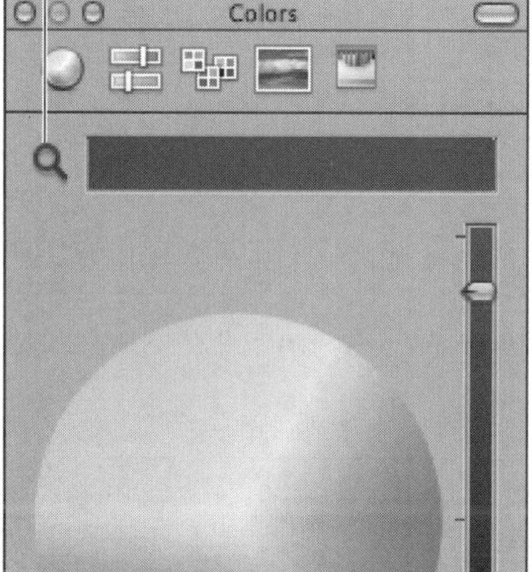

Figure 15.26 Use the color picker's magnifying glass to sample colors from anywhere on your screen.

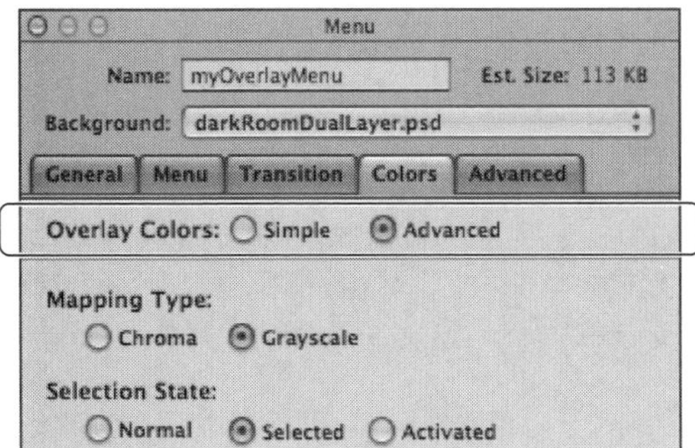

Figure 15.27 To enable advanced overlay mode, select the Advanced button in the Inspector's Overlay Colors area.

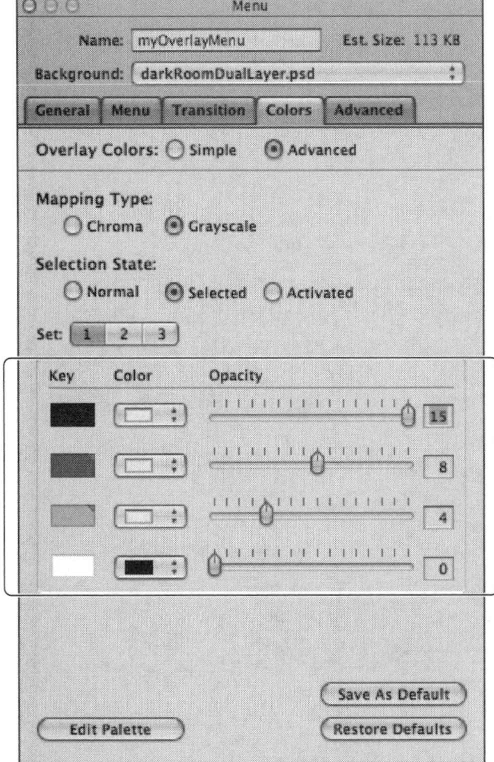

Figure 15.28 In advanced overlay mode, the Inspector's Colors tab updates to display several settings not available to simple overlays. These additional settings are used to create overlays that have up to four different colors.

Creating an Advanced Overlay Menu

Simple overlay highlights are, well, simple. Graphically, they don't offer much, but they're easy to create. The majority of the commercial DVDs on the market use simple highlights—but not for long, because with DVD Studio Pro you can create advanced, or multicolored, overlay menus almost as easily as simple overlay menus.

To choose advanced overlay mode:

1. In the Overlay Menu Inspector, choose the Colors tab.
2. In the Overlay Colors area, select the Advanced radio button (**Figure 15.27**).

   Advanced overlay mode is enabled, and the Colors tab's Mapping Type and Selection State areas are available. Note that the Key area at the bottom of the Colors tab (**Figure 15.28**) has updated to display several settings, which are discussed next, that did not appear in the simple overlay mode.

About advanced overlays

An advanced overlay menu maps up to four different colors to the shapes in the overlay image, using either grayscale or chroma color mapping:

- **Grayscale color mapping.** Grayscale color mapping uses 100 percent black, 66 percent black, 33 percent black, and 0 percent black (white and/or transparent in a Photoshop layer) as *key colors* (**Figure 15.29**). Back in DVD Studio Pro, you can map any color you want to these four key colors in the Key area of the Inspector's Colors tab (**Figure 15.30**). **Table 15.1** lists the four grayscale colors and their corresponding RGB values.

Table 15.1

Grayscale Overlay Color Values

COLOR	RGB VALUE
100% black	0,0,0
66% black	84,84,84
33% black	168,168,168
0% black	255,255,255

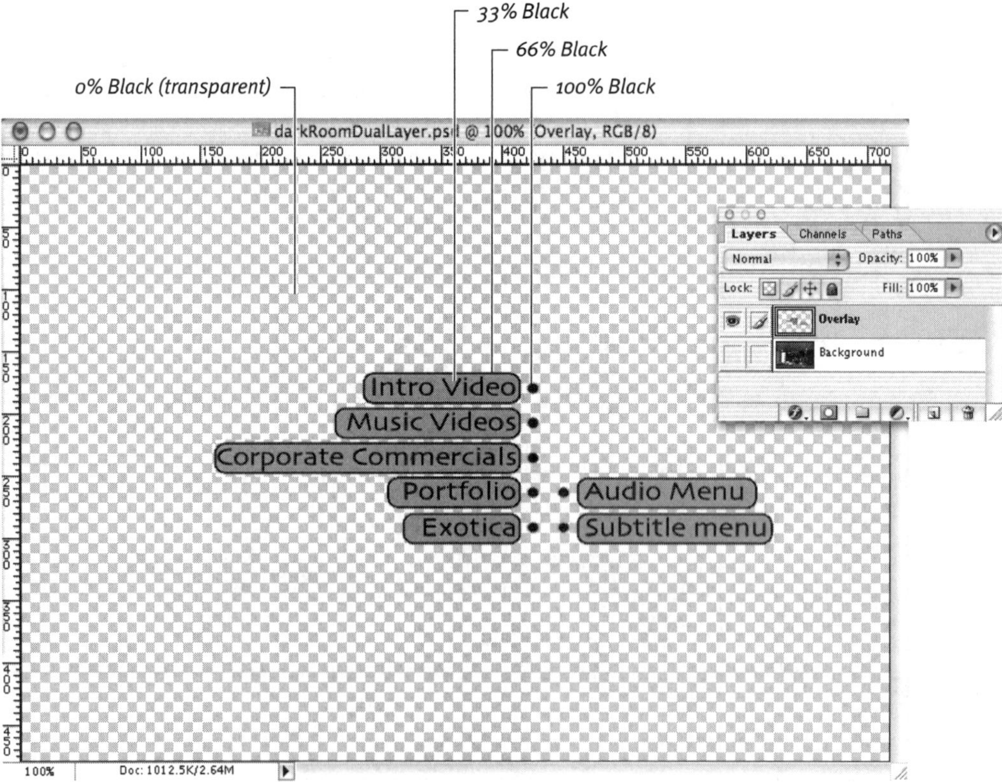

Figure 15.29 An advanced overlay uses four grayscale values as the map for up to four different colors in your overlay menus.

Table 15.2

Chroma Overlay Color Values	
COLOR	RGB VALUE
100% black	0,0,0
100% red	255,0,0
100% blue	0,0,255
100% white	255,255,255

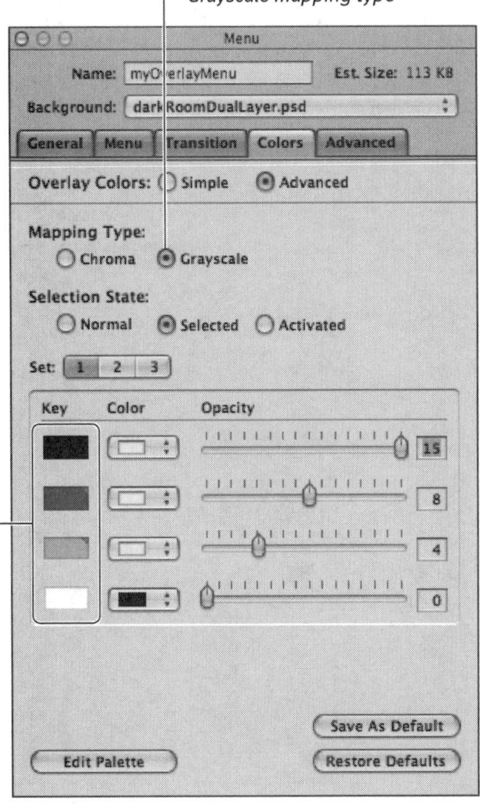

Figure 15.30 The left edge of the Colors tab's Key area shows all four of the grayscale values you can use in an advanced overlay.

- **Chroma color mapping.** If you are using an inexpensive monitor with poor contrast, there might not be a discernable difference between 100 percent black and 66 percent black. In this situation, chroma color mapping comes to the rescue. Chroma color mapping works exactly the same way as grayscale color mapping, except the four colors used in the overlay image are 100 percent black, 100 percent red, 100 percent blue, and 100 percent white. **Table 15.2** lists the four chroma colors and their corresponding RGB values.

✔ Tips

- No part of the overlay image outside a button's hotspot will appear when the button is selected or activated.
- DVD Studio Pro moves the color value of all overlay images to the closest color listed in Tables 15.1 and 15.2. If your overlay contains other colors, they will be shifted to the nearest acceptable color before the button highlight is displayed.

To select a mapping type:

1. Follow the steps in the previous task, "To choose advanced overlay mode," to enable the advanced overlay mode.

   Color mapping is available only in advanced overlay mode, so this is an important step.

2. On the Inspector's Colors tab, in the Mapping Type area, choose either Chroma or Grayscale (**Figure 15.31**).

   Along the left edge of the Colors tab's Key area, the four colors for the selected mapping type are displayed (**Figure 15.32**). If you chose Grayscale, the four colors will be 100 percent black, 66 percent black, 33 percent black, and 0 percent black. If you chose Chroma, the four colors will be 100 percent black, 100 percent red, 100 percent blue, and 100 percent white.

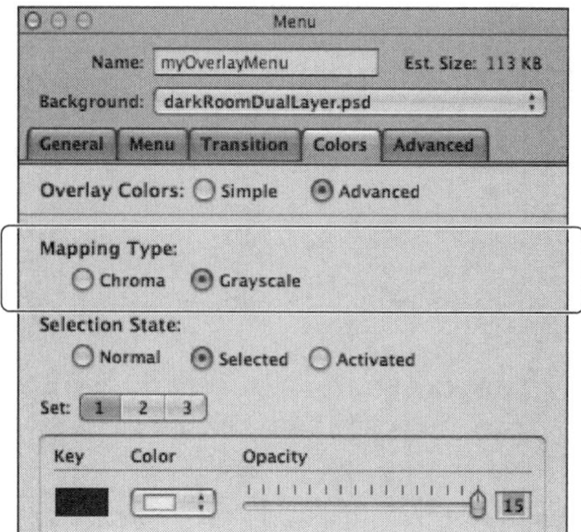

Figure 15.31 In the Colors tab's Mapping Type section, select either chroma or grayscale color mapping.

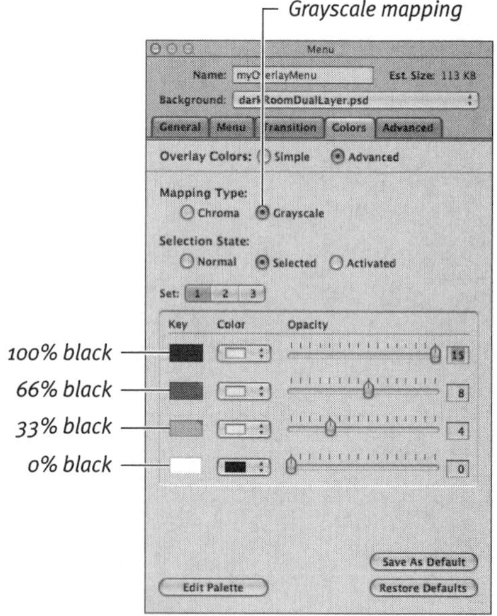

Figure 15.32 With grayscale color mapping enabled, the Colors tab's Key area reflects the four grayscale values you can use in your overlay shapes.

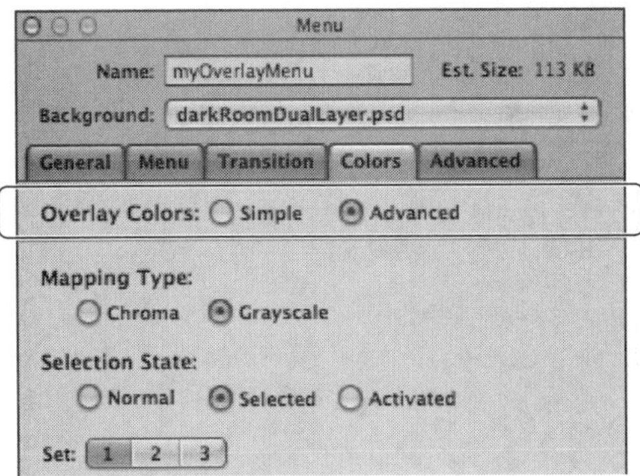

Figure 15.33 The first step in creating an advanced overlay menu is selecting Advanced from the Colors tab's Overlay Colors area.

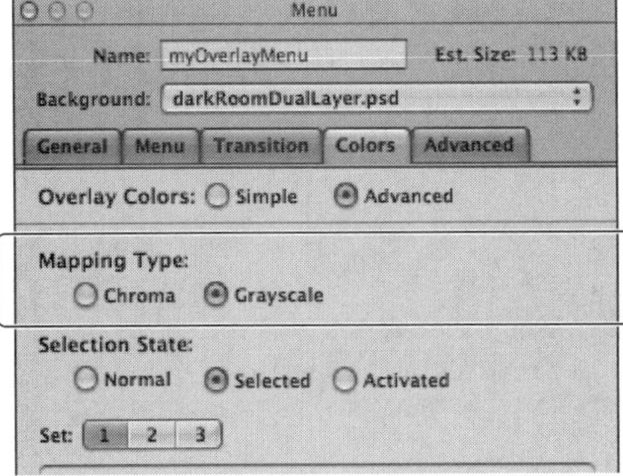

Figure 15.34 Next, choose a mapping type.

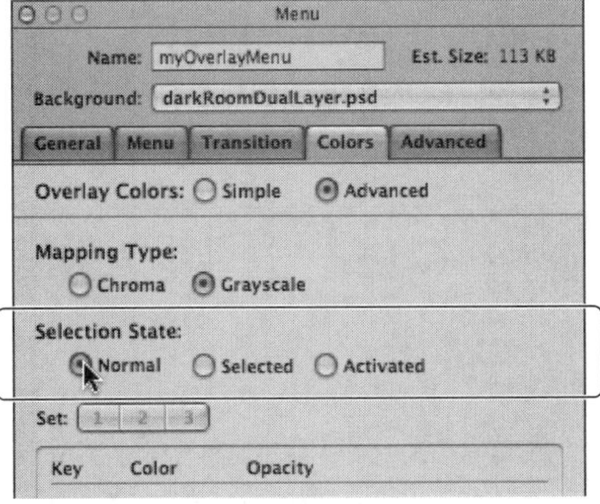

Figure 15.35 Then set overlay colors for each button state, beginning with the normal state.

To create an advanced overlay menu:

1. Assign a background and an overlay image to the menu.
2. Create the menu's buttons.

   The menu must have button hotspots defined before you'll see the overlay shapes in the Menu editor, so this is an important step. For a refresher on how to create menu buttons, see Chapter 13.
3. In the Overlay Colors area of the Inspector's Colors tab, choose Advanced (**Figure 15.33**).
4. In the Mapping Type area of the Inspector's Colors tab, choose either Chroma or Grayscale (**Figure 15.34**).
5. In the Selection State area of the Inspector's Colors tab, select the Normal radio button (**Figure 15.35**).

continues on next page

6. In the Key area of the Inspector's Colors tab, choose a color and opacity value for each key color in the overlay image (**Figure 15.36**).

   These colors will represent the button's normal state. If you don't want the overlay to obstruct the button graphics on the background, set the Opacity sliders for each key color to 0.

7. In the Selection State area of the Inspector's Colors tab, choose the Selected radio button (**Figure 15.37**).

8. In the Key area of the Inspector's Colors tab, choose a color and opacity value for each key color in the overlay image.

   These colors will represent the button's selected state.

9. In the Selection State area of the Inspector's Colors tab, select the Activated radio button (**Figure 15.38**).

10. In the Key area of the Inspector's Colors tab, choose a color and opacity value for each key color in the overlay image.

    These colors will represent the button's activated state.

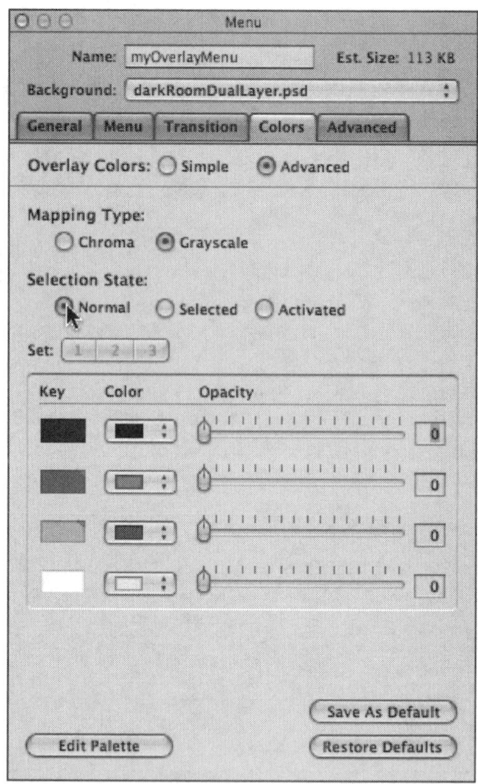

Figure 15.36 With the normal state selected, set the color and opacity value for each key color in the overlay.

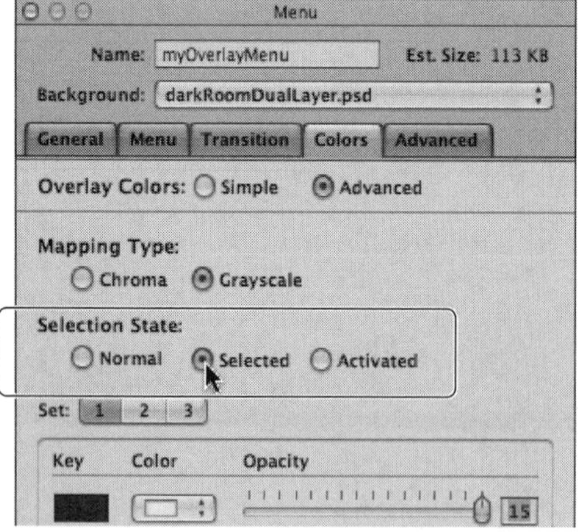

Figure 15.37 Next, choose the Selected radio button and repeat the process to set colors for the button's selected state.

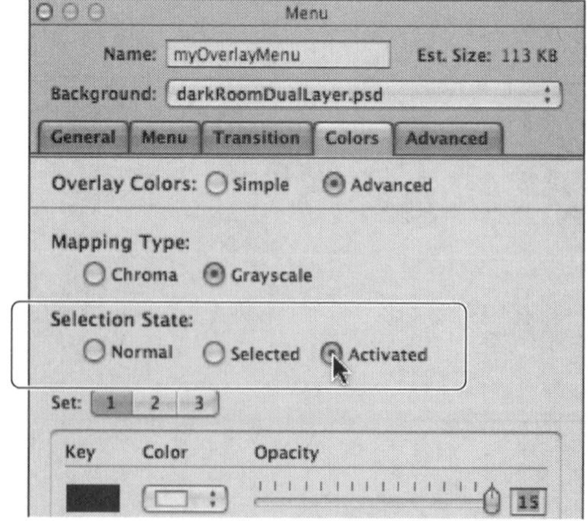

Figure 15.38 Finish by selecting the Activated radio button and setting the colors and opacity values for the menu's activated state.

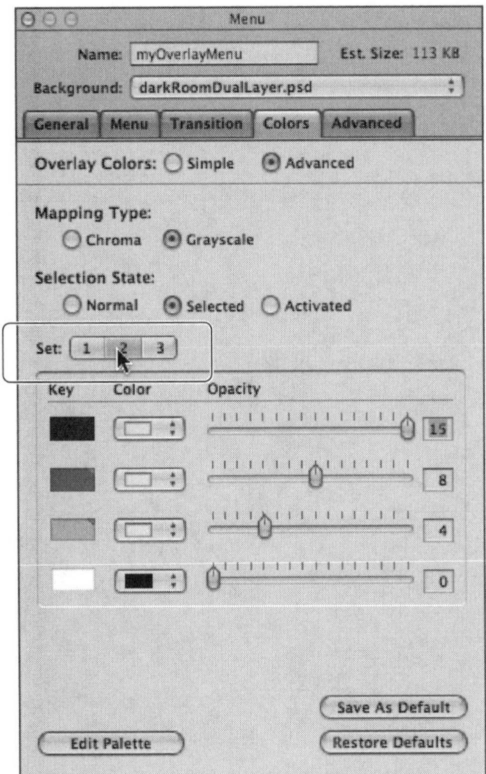

Figure 15.39 Use the Colors tab's Set area to configure up to three different highlight sets for each menu.

Choosing Highlight Sets

If four colors don't provide enough visual bang for your buttons, DVD Studio Pro allows you to use up to three different highlight sets per menu. A *highlight set* is a set of colors used for a button's normal, selected, and activated states, and each of the three available highlight sets can use different colors. This provides you with up to 12 different colors for your button states (four colors for each button state in each highlight set), providing plenty of flexibility when it comes time to create those overlay buttons.

You create highlight sets for each menu and then assign a highlight set to each button individually. This section shows you how.

To configure a highlight set:

1. On the Inspector's Colors tab, choose the highlight set you want to configure (**Figure 15.39**).
2. In the Colors tab's Key area, configure a color and opacity value for each key color in the overlay image (to learn more, see "Creating an Advanced Overlay" earlier in this chapter).

   With the highlight sets configured, all that remains is assigning the highlight sets to individual buttons.

To assign a highlight set to a menu button:

1. In the Menu editor, select a button.

   The Inspector updates to display the button's properties.

2. On the Button Inspector's Style tab, from the Highlight Set area, choose a highlight set to use for the button (**Figure 15.40**).

   The button will now use the overlay colors from the selected highlight set. Note that only the selected button will use this highlight set. If you want other buttons to also use this highlight set, you must select the buttons and assign them to the highlight set.

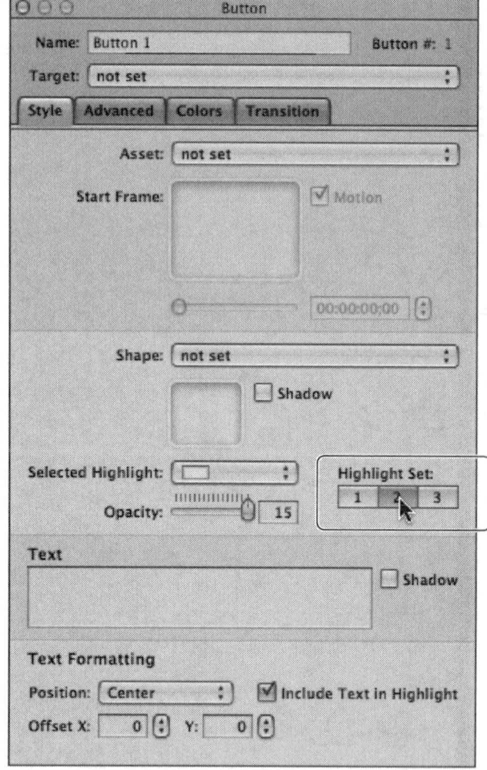

Figure 15.40 To assign a highlight set to a button, first select the button in the Menu editor; then use the Inspector's Style tab to assign a highlight set to the button.

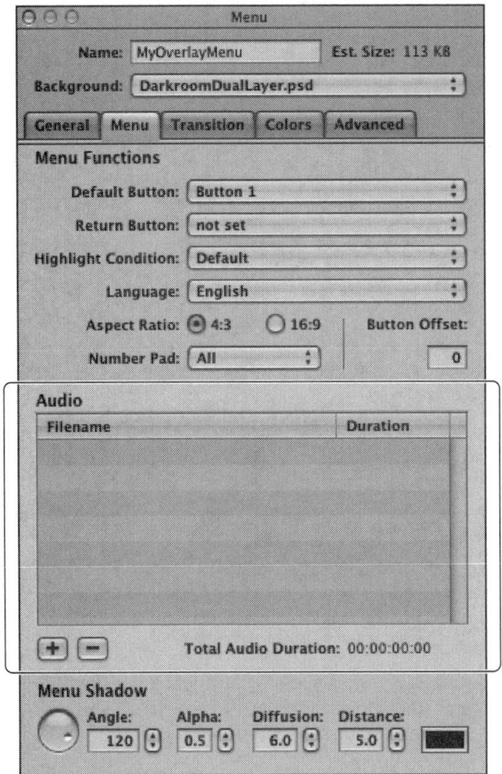

Figure 15.41 For overlay menus, the Inspector's menu tab has an Audio area. This area is not available for layered menus.

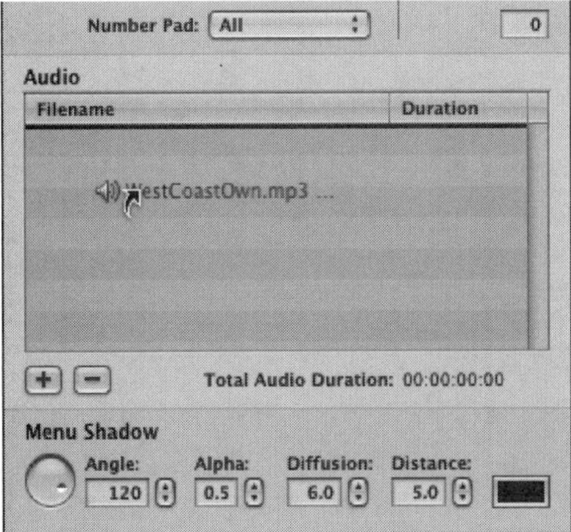

Figure 15.42 To assign audio to an overlay menu, drag the audio file into the Menu tab's Audio area.

Adding Audio to Menus

Unlike Photoshop layer menus, highlight menus can contain audio. It's simple to assign audio to an overlay menu, but you must keep one important point in mind: all menus in your project must use exactly the same type of audio; you can't mix and match. If one menu uses a 5.1 AC-3 file, all menus must use 5.1 AC-3 files; if one menu uses a 48 kHz, 16-bit AIFF file, all menus must use 48 kHz, 16-bit AIFF files.

To add audio to an overlay menu:

1. In the Outline or Graphical view, select the menu to which you want to add audio.

   The Inspector updates to display the menu's properties.

2. On the Inspector's Menu tab (**Figure 15.41**), drag an audio file into the Audio area (**Figure 15.42**).

continues on next page

✔ Tips

- You can use the Menu editor's drop palette to quickly assign an audio asset to a menu (**Figure 15.43**).
- Sound can add ambiance to menus, but it should not distract. To give the main audio more emphasis, make the menu audio slightly quieter.
- Beware of the loop point! Menus do not loop seamlessly; there will always be a slight pause when the menu loops from its end back to the beginning. If you are looping a menu with audio attached, place a fade-in at the front of the audio stream and a fade-out at the end. This makes the loop less jarring to the viewer's ears.

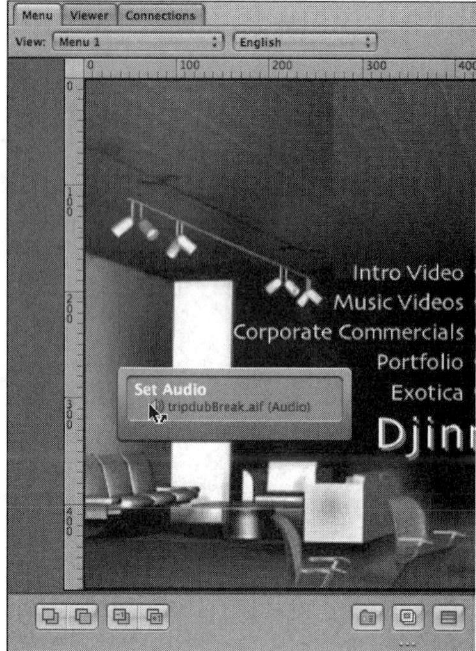

Figure 15.43 When you drag an audio asset over the Menu editor, the drop palette appears. Use it to assign the audio asset to the menu.

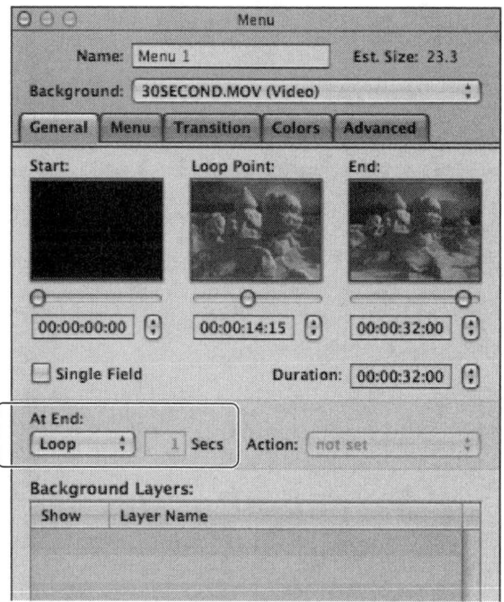

Figure 15.44 A menu's At End setting controls the way that the menu behaves once it plays to its end.

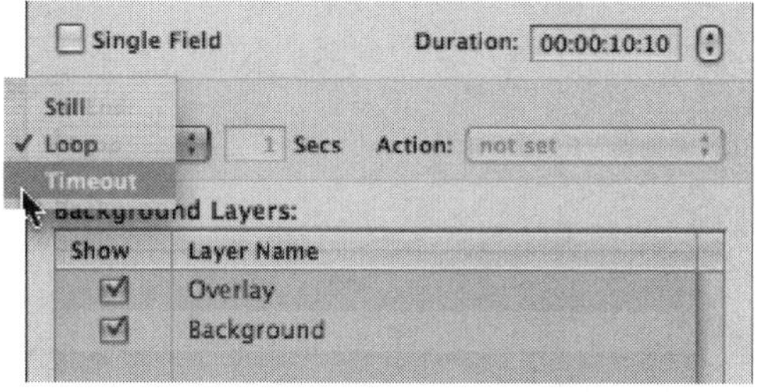

Figure 15.45 To set a timeout action, begin by choosing Timeout from the Menu Inspector's At End setting.

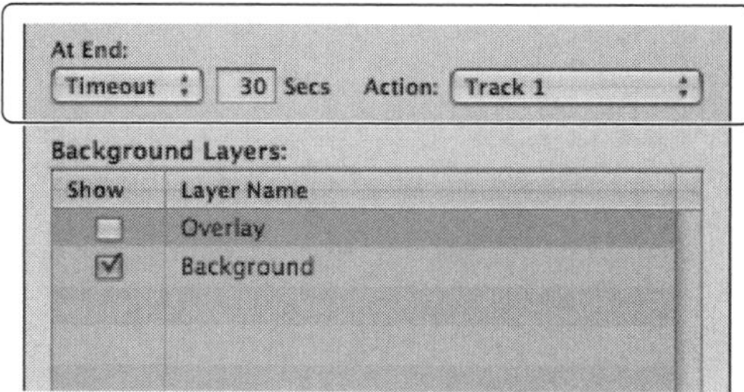

Figure 15.46 Choosing Timeout from the At End setting enables the Secs and Action areas.

Using the At End Setting

By default, the At End feature is set to Still, which means that your menu will play to the last frame (or to the end of the audio loop if there's no video component) and then pause until the viewer activates one of the menu's buttons. The other options for the At End setting are Loop and Timeout.

- **Loop.** Causes a menu to repeat indefinitely, or until the viewer activates a button.
- **Timeout.** Tells the menu to pause at the end for a set amount of time before jumping to another project element. This setting is particularly useful for projects that need to play continuously, such as kiosk installations, because the timeout action ensures that a menu does not remain on the screen indefinitely.

To set a timeout action:

1. In the Outline or Graphical view, select the menu for which you want to set a timeout action.

   The Inspector updates to display the menu's properties.

2. On the Inspector's General tab, from the At End menu (**Figure 15.44**), choose Timeout (**Figure 15.45**).

   Immediately to the right of the At End menu, the Secs (seconds) and Action areas become available (**Figure 15.46**).

continues on next page

3. In the Secs text box, enter a number between 1 and 254.

   This number indicates the *timeout delay*, or the number of seconds the menu pauses before initiating the timeout action.

4. From the Action menu, choose the project element to which you want to jump after the timeout delay has passed (**Figure 15.47**).

   When the timeout delay has passed, the DVD-Video will jump to the selected project element.

Figure 15.47 When the timeout delay has passed, the DVD-Video will jump to the project element that you select from the Action setting.

To loop a menu:

1. In the Outline or Graphical view, select the menu you want to loop.

   The Inspector updates to display the menu's properties.

2. From the At End menu (refer to Figure 15.44), choose Loop (**Figure 15.48**).

   The menu will now loop until the viewer activates a menu button.

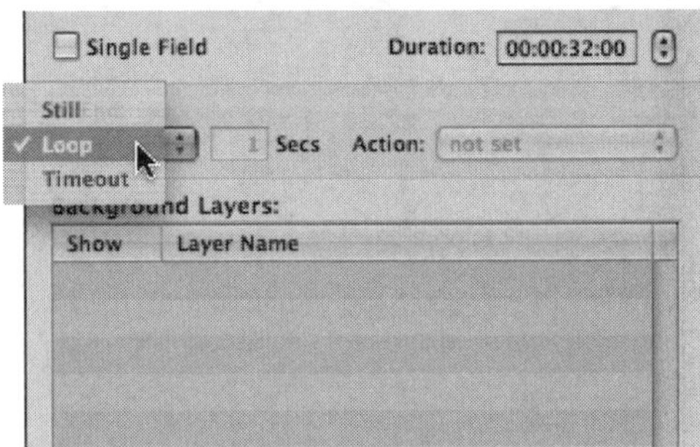

Figure 15.48 To cause a menu to loop, select Loop from the At End setting.

✔ Tips

- When a menu loops, its highlights unavoidably flicker off and on. Unfortunately, there's nothing you can do to fix this, but rest assured that it's not your fault.
- If you want a menu to loop only a certain number of times, you must write a script (for more information on scripting, see Chapter 25, "Scripting").

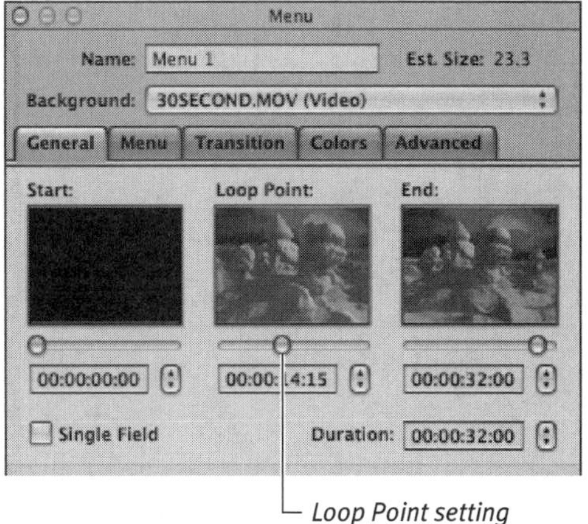

Figure 15.49 When you set a loop point, the menu plays to the end and then loops back to the loop point instead of to the beginning of the menu.

Setting a loop point

The ability to set a loop point is a great DVD Studio Pro feature, because it allows you to include an introduction, such as a fade-in, with a motion menu before the menu buttons appear on the screen (**Figure 15.49**). When you set a loop point, the overlay is not enabled and thus will not show up until after the loop point has been reached. This behavior is called "delaying the subpicture," and it allows you to create a smooth, seamless shift from a menu introduction or transition, for example, to the menu itself. When the menu reaches its end, it will loop back only to the loop point, not to the beginning of the menu's video stream—which means that the menu introduction or transition will not play again.

However, there is one very important point to keep in mind when considering the use of a loop point: the loop point will be disabled if you use any of DVD studio Pro 3's new compositing features. Adding text to the menu or even to the menu's buttons causes the loop point to turn off. Similarly, using drop zones or adding graphics to button hotspots also disables the menu's loop point.

✔ Tip

- You can use the Menu Inspector's Start setting to trim the beginning off of a motion menu. Only the section of the menu between the Start and End settings will be included in the final DVD-Video.

To set a loop point:

1. Set a menu to loop.
2. Use the End slider to specify the point for the menu to play to before looping (**Figure 15.50**).

   It takes a bit of planning, but try to make the frame used in the End setting the same frame used in the Loop Point setting that you specify in the next step. If you don't, your menu loop will seem jarring and disjointed.
3. Use the Loop Point slider to specify the point to which the menu will loop back.

   Now the menu plays to the End setting you specified in step 2, then loops back to the loop point before playing to the end again, then loops back, and so on.

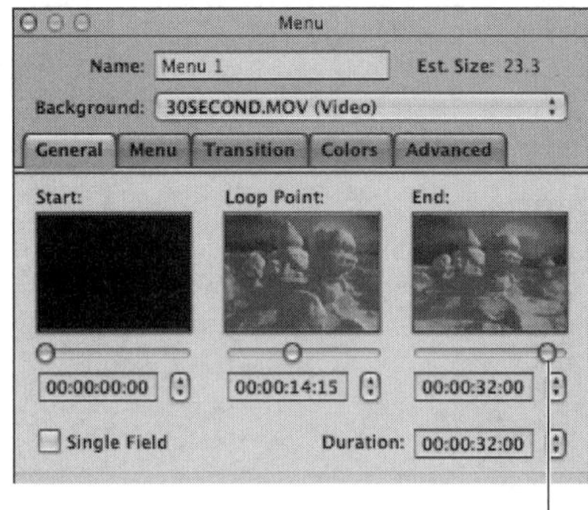

Figure 15.50 Use the End slider to control the end point of the menu loop, or the place in the menu where the menu jumps back to the loop point.

Figure 15.51 To create buttons over a video track, you must first create a button highlight marker.

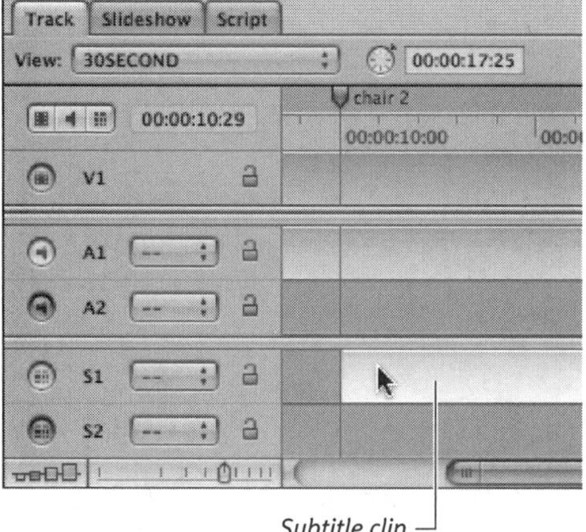

Figure 15.52 Buttons over video are created in subtitle clips.

Using Button Highlight Markers

If you think menus are the only DVD-Video element that contains interactivity, you're in for a pleasant surprise—you can put buttons right over video tracks!

You create buttons on top of video tracks exactly the same way as you create an overlay menu, except the buttons are attached to a button highlight marker in a track. Once you know how to create an overlay menu (review the beginning of this chapter if you don't), creating buttons over video is extremely easy.

To create buttons over video:

1. In the Track editor, create a marker at the point in the track where you want the buttons to turn on.

   For more information on creating buttons, see Chapter 13.

2. Control-click the marker and choose Button Highlight Marker from the shortcut menu (**Figure 15.51**).

   The marker turns orange and is now a button highlight marker.

3. In the first subtitle stream, double-click directly behind the button highlight marker to create an empty subtitle clip (**Figure 15.52**).

   Yes, that's correct: buttons over video are created in subtitle clips. They actually use the subtitle stream to generate the highlights, so you can't have subtitles and buttons over video displayed at the same time. For more information on using subtitles, see Chapter 24, "Subtitles."

continues on next page

4. Select the new subtitle clip.

   The Inspector updates to show the subtitle clip's properties. In the middle of the Subtitle Inspector's General tab is a Graphic area (**Figure 15.53**), which you use to assign the overlay image to the subtitle clip.

5. In the Graphic area, click the Choose button.

   The Choose Subtitle Graphic File dialog opens (**Figure 15.54**).

6. Use the Choose Subtitle Graphic File dialog to navigate to the overlay image you want to use and click the Choose button.

   The graphic file is set in the subtitle clip.

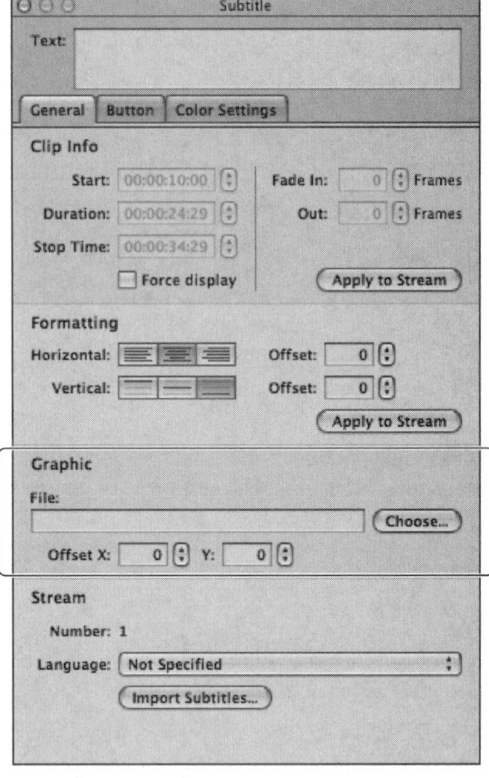

Figure 15.53 The Subtitle Inspector's General tab has a Graphic area, which you use to assign the overlay image to the subtitle clip.

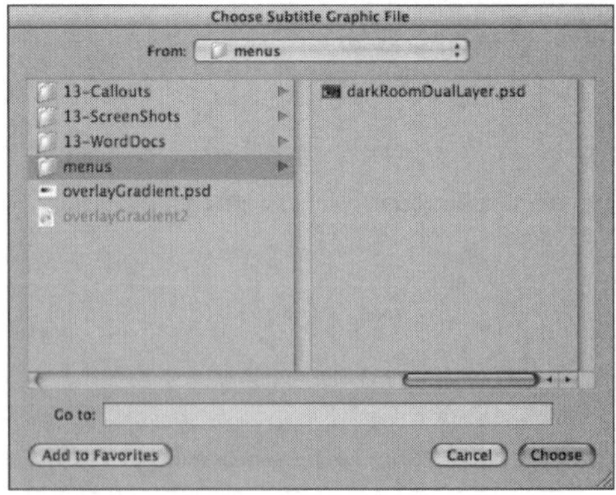

Figure 15.54 The Choose Subtitle File dialog lets you select an image file to use for your button highlights over video.

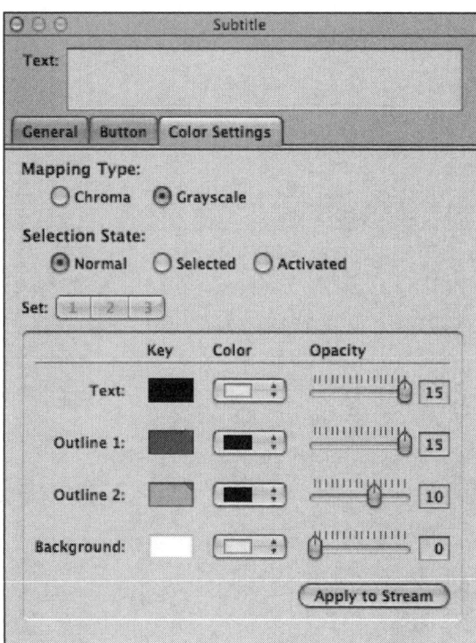

Figure 15.55 The Subtitle Inspector's Color Settings tab works exactly the same way as the Colors tab in the Menu Inspector

7. Use the Subtitle Inspector's Colors tab to set the colors for your highlights in exactly the same way you set the colors for highlights in an overlay menu—there's no difference in the technique (**Figure 15.55**).

8. In the Viewer, drag buttons out over the video, just as you would for a normal menu.

   If you can't drag out the buttons, you have not created a button highlight marker, because only button highlight markers let you drag buttons into the Viewer.

✔ Tips

- The buttons will stay on the screen only as long as the button highlight marker is playing. Consequently, you can turn off the buttons by creating a new marker (of any type) at the point in the track where you want the buttons to be disabled.
- You can also assign an image asset to a subtitle clip by simply dragging the image asset from the Assets container, Palette, or Finder and dropping it directly on the subtitle clip in the Track editor.

Creating a Template Image from a Video Stream

The shapes in an overlay image must align exactly with the button graphics underneath. To create an overlay image for buttons in a video stream, you must first output a single frame of the video stream to use as a template for positioning the overlay shapes. With DVD Studio Pro 3, this is extremely easy to do. Just select the button highlight marker in the Track editor and look at the Inspector. On the Marker Inspector's General tab, click the Save Still button (**Figure 15.56**) to save a still image (TIFF) of the frame directly under the button highlight marker. This makes a perfect template for designing the overlay image!

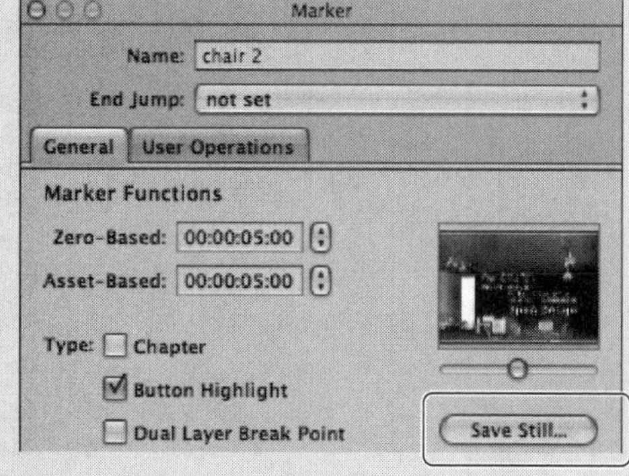

Figure 15.56 The Marker Inspector's Save Still button lets you save a still-image file (TIFF file) of the frame directly under the marker. This image makes a perfect template for designing a button highlight marker's overlay image.

Creating Text Buttons over Video

Believe it or not, you can actually turn text in a subtitle clip into a button, using a button highlight marker, which means that you can create simple buttons over video without having to create an overlay image (**Figure 15.57**). When you turn a marker into a button highlight marker, you can still type text in the subtitle's text field. (For more information on creating text in subtitles, see Chapter 24.) DVD Studio Pro treats this text just like any other image in the subtitle stream, so if the text is part of a subtitle clip in a button highlight marker, you can drag a hotspot around the text to turn it into a button. This trick comes in handy when you need to create an Info button, for example, or a button that switches the viewer to the next video stream.

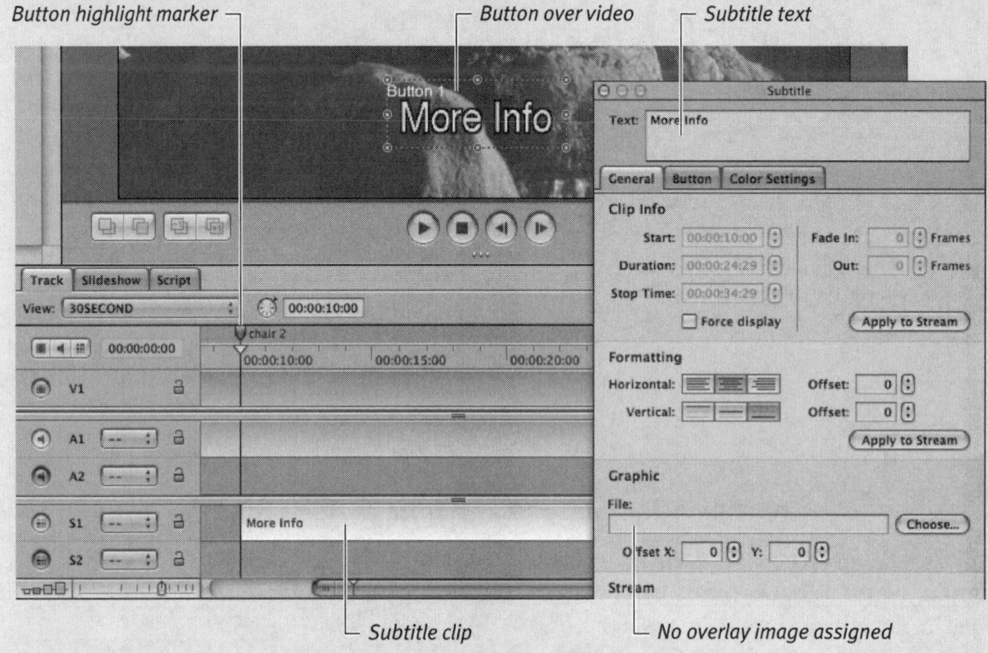

Figure 15.57 Using a combination of a button highlight marker and subtitle text, you can create simple text buttons over a video track without creating an overlay image.

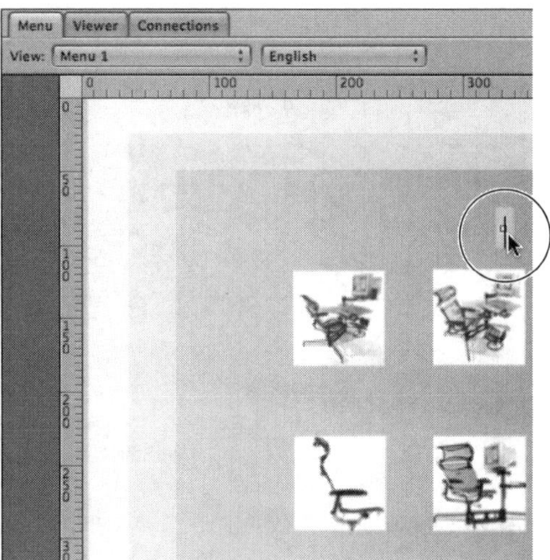

Figure 15.58 Double-click the menu background to create a text insertion point.

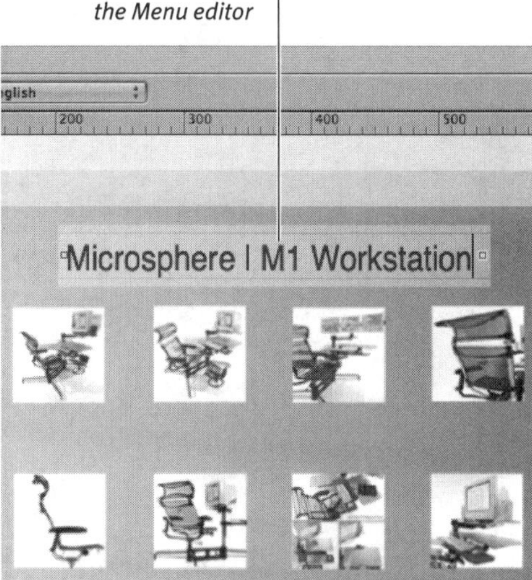

Figure 15.59 Then type some text.

Working with Text

DVD Studio Pro's Menu editor comes fully equipped with some very cool compositing features. For example, you can now add still images, video, and even text to the Menu editor to create menus from scratch, right inside DVD Studio Pro. While these features don't take the place of an actual video compositing program such as Final Cut Pro, Shake, or Photoshop, you can create visually engaging menus without ever having to open another graphics editing program.

There's one point to note when adding text to menu buttons: you can add text only to overlay menus; layered menus do not allow text of any type.

✔ Tip

- Also note when adding text to overlay menus that if you add text, you cannot assign a loop point.

Creating text objects

DVD Studio Pro's text composition capabilities are surprisingly well developed. You can add text to the menu background to create titles, add information about the menu options, create a contact page that uses DVD@ccess to link to a Web page or launch a PDF file, and so on. When you add text to a menu, you create a *text object,* and DVD Studio Pro lets you justify the text or even rotate it on the menu, so you're not just stuck with horizontal lines.

To add a text object to a menu:

1. Double-click the menu background.

   A text insertion point appears (**Figure 15.58**).

2. Type your text directly in the Menu editor (**Figure 15.59**).

To justify text:

1. In the Menu editor, select a text object.

   The Inspector updates to display the text object's properties.

2. From the Inspector's Formatting area, choose a justification option: left, center, or right (**Figure 15.60**).

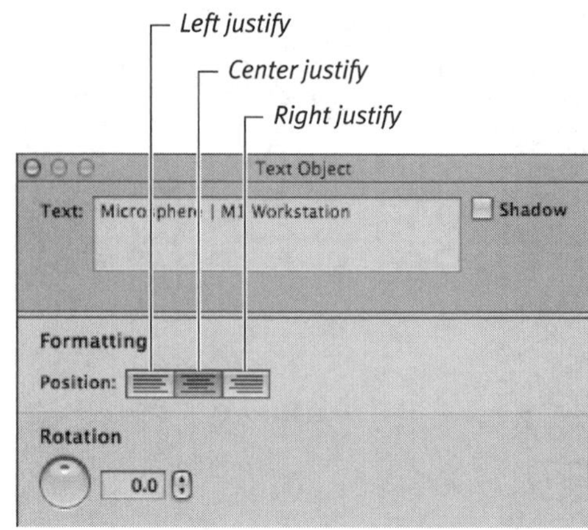

Figure 15.60 The Text Object Inspector has a Formatting area for justifying your text.

To rotate text:

1. In the Menu editor, select a text object.

   The Inspector updates to display the text object's properties.

2. *Do one of the following:*

   ▲ Drag the Rotation area's dial to spin the selected text object (**Figure 15.61**).

   ▲ Enter a rotation value in the Rotation area's text box and press Return.

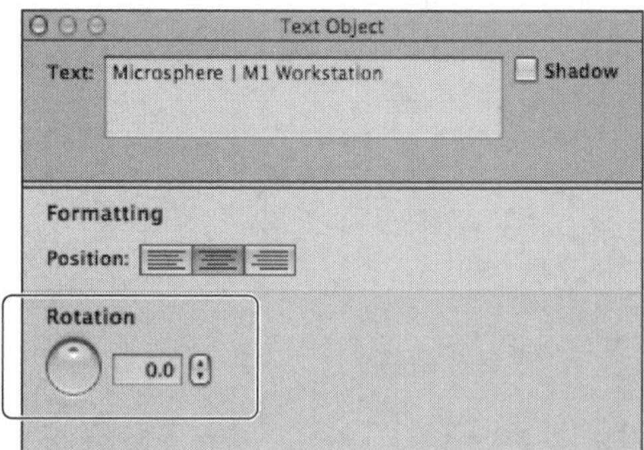

Figure 15.61 The Text Inspector's Rotation area lets you rotate text objects on your menu.

✔ Tip

- You can rotate text objects on the menu only. You cannot rotate text in buttons.

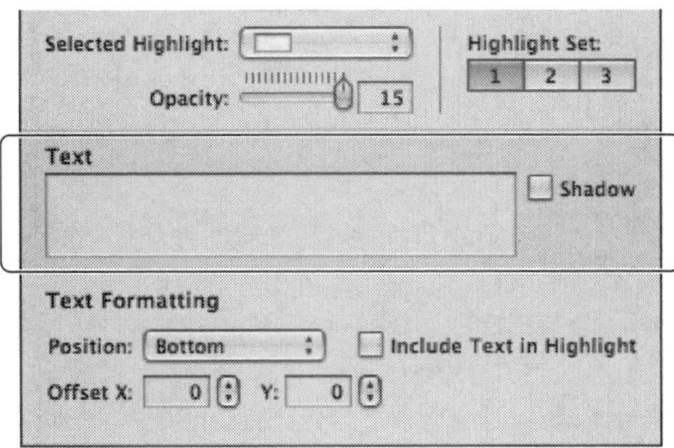

Figure 15.62 When a button is selected in the Menu editor, the Inspector's Style tab displays a Text area.

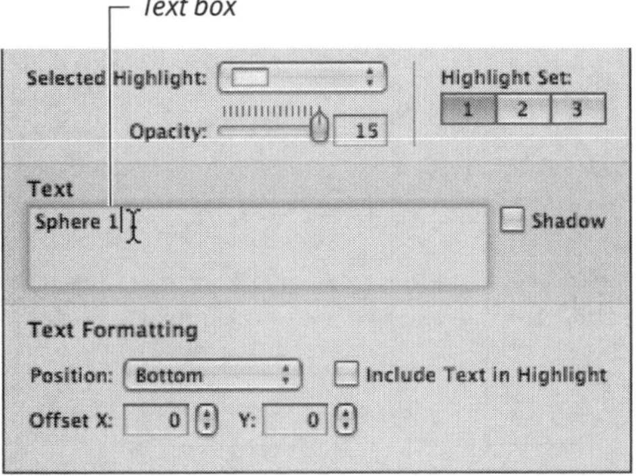

Figure 15.63 Type text directly in the Text area's text box.

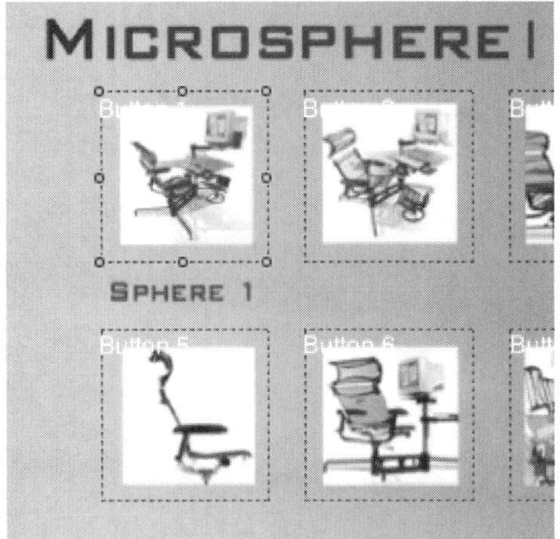

Figure 15.64 By default, text is added below a button.

Adding text to a button

In the preceding section, you learned a few tricks for adding text to menus, including how to justify text and even rotate text to add a bit of pizzazz to menus without opening a graphics application like Photoshop. If Photoshop isn't your cup of tea, you will be pleased to know you can even add text to menu buttons right in DVD Studio Pro's Menu editor.

✔ Tip

- Remember: you can add text to overlay menus only; layered menus do not allow text objects or text added to buttons.

To add text to a button:

1. In the Menu editor, select the button to which you want to add text.

   The Inspector updates to display the button's properties.

2. In the Text area of the Inspector's Style tab, in the large text box (**Figure 15.62**), type some text (**Figure 15.63**).

   Back in the Menu editor, your text appears under the button (**Figure 15.64**). By default, all text appears under the button, though you can change this behavior by justifying your button text, as described in the next section.

continues on next page

✔ Tips

- With a button selected in the Menu editor, pressing the Enter key (that's Enter, not Return) takes you in and out of text mode. Just remember to press the Enter key; pressing the Return key creates a new line and does not toggle in and out of text mode.
- Once you've added text to a button, you can change it quickly by double-clicking the text. The text will be highlighted, and you can then type new text for the button. However, this procedure works only with text already added to a button, and you must be sure to double-click directly on the text (otherwise DVD Studio Pro will jump to the button's target).

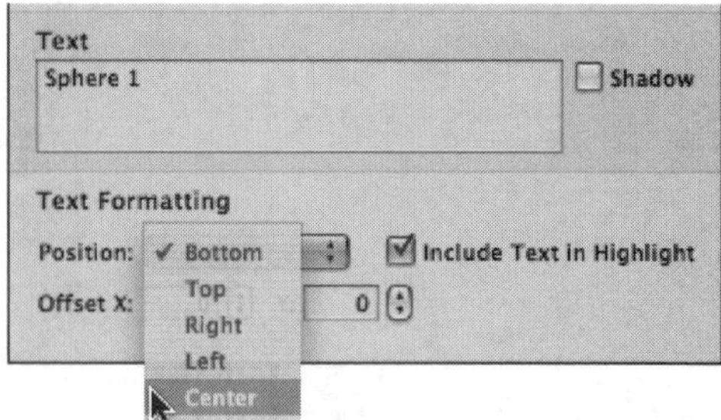

Figure 15.65 Use the Text Formatting area's Position menu to position text around a button.

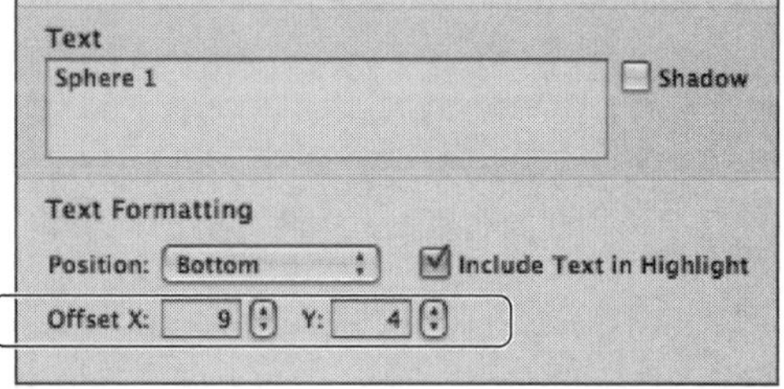

Figure 15.66 Use the Text Formatting area's Offset settings to shift text in one-pixel increments, which allows you to position button text exactly where you need it.

Positioning button text

As mentioned earlier, all button text is created at the bottom of a button by default. However, you can move the text to the middle of the button, to the top, or to the left or right edge of the button. In fact, using the Button Inspector's Offset settings, you can shift the text around inside the button until it's exactly where you want it.

To change button text position:

1. In the Menu editor, select the button.
   The Inspector updates to display the button's properties.
2. In the General tab's Text Formatting area, select a position for the button text from the Position menu (**Figure 15.65**).
3. Use the Offset settings, directly below the Text Formatting area's Position menu, to fine-tune the text position and shift text one pixel at a time (**Figure 15.66**).

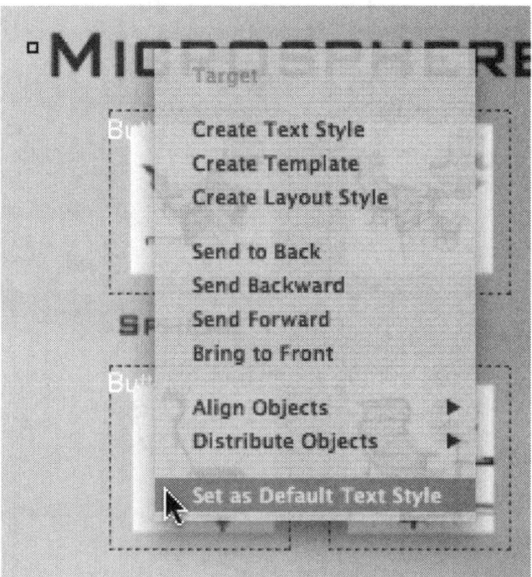

Figure 15.67 Control-click a text object and choose Set as Default Text Style to ensure that all new text objects use the same style as the clicked text object.

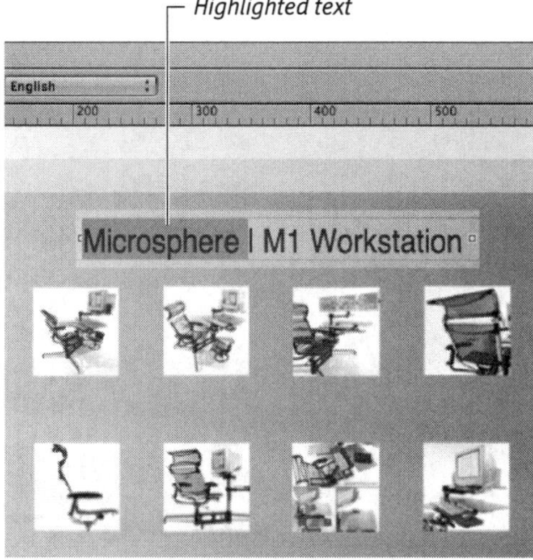

Figure 15.68 To change your text's font, begin by highlighting the text you want to change.

Styling Text

You can style all text you add in the Menu editor. You can apply underlining or italics, change the color, and use any font currently installed on your computer. DVD Studio Pro also lets you spell check text right in the Menu editor, which can help you avoid those embarrassing mistakes that can occur when you're back from a coffee break but your brain isn't.

✔ Tip

- After you've styled a text object in a menu, Control-click the text object and choose Set as Default Text Style from the shortcut menu (**Figure 15.67**). Now, each new text object you create in the menu will use this new default text style.

To change text font:

1. In the Menu editor, select a text object.
2. Within the text object, highlight the text for which you want to change the font (**Figure 15.68**).

   Only highlighted text is affected, so if you want to change the font of only certain words in a sentence, select only those words.

continues on next page

3. *Do one of the following:*
   - ▲ Control-click the highlighted text and choose Font > Show Fonts (**Figure 15.69**).
   - ▲ Choose Format > Font > Show Fonts (**Figure 15.70**).
   - ▲ Press Command-T.

   The Fonts dialog opens (**Figure 15.71**).
4. In the Fonts dialog, select a font for your text.

   As you select new fonts, the highlighted text automatically changes to show you what the new font will look like.
5. Click the close button in the top-left corner of the Fonts dialog to close the dialog.

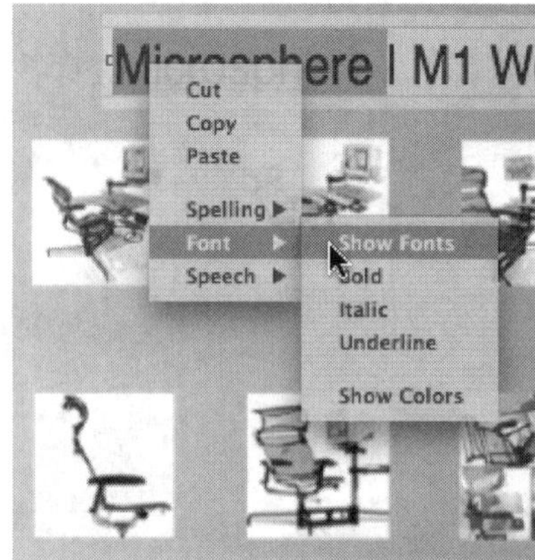

Figure 15.69 Next, Control-Click the highlighted text and choose Font > Show Fonts from the shortcut menu, or...

Figure 15.70 ...choose Format > Font > Show Fonts.

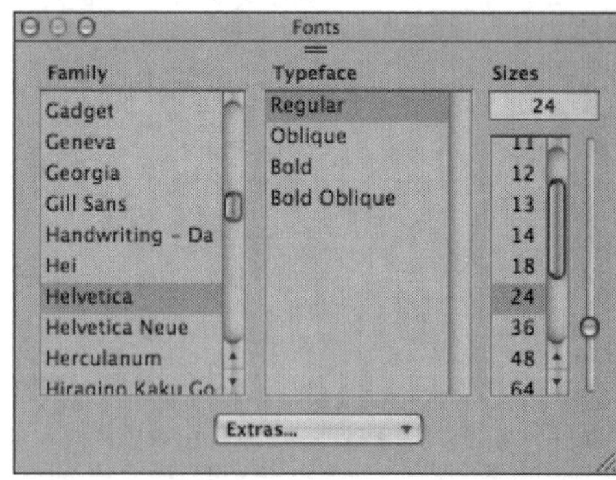

Figure 15.71 The Fonts dialog lets you change the font of your highlighted text.

Styling Text

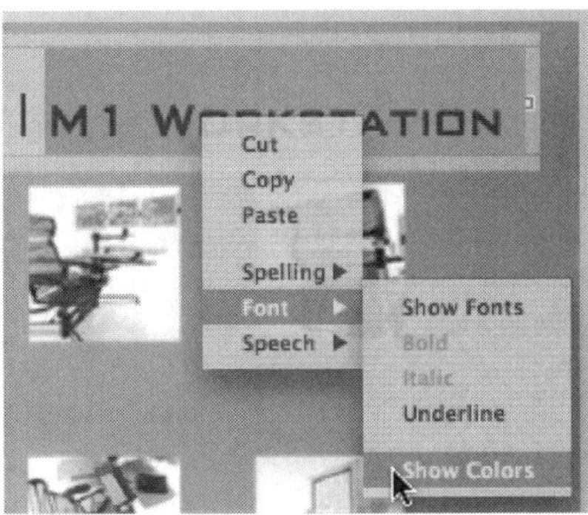

Figure 15.72 To change the color of highlighted text, Control-click the text and choose Font > Show Colors, or...

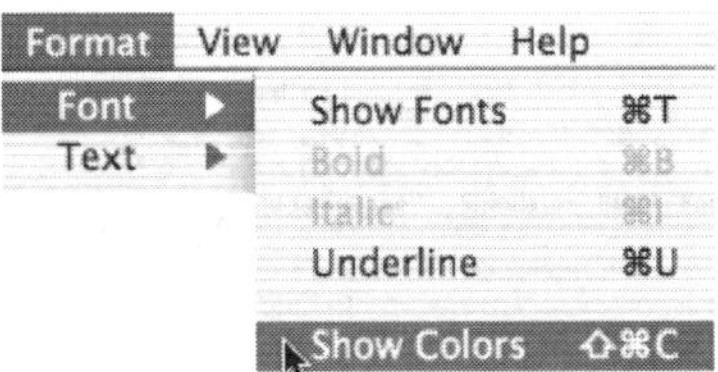

Figure 15.73 ...choose Format > Font > Show Colors.

Figure 15.74 The Colors dialog opens to let you change the color of the highlighted text.

To change text color:

1. In the Menu editor, select a text object.
2. Within the text object, highlight the text that you want to change to a different color.
3. *Do one of the following:*
   - ▲ Control-click the highlighted text and choose Font > Show Colors (**Figure 15.72**).
   - ▲ Choose Format > Font > Show Colors (**Figure 15.73**).
   - ▲ Press Shift-Command-C.

   The Colors dialog opens (**Figure 15.74**).
4. Use the Colors dialog to select a color for your text.
5. Click the close button in the top-left corner of the Colors dialog to close the dialog.

The DVDSP Spelling Bee

In DVD Studio Pro, you can Control-click any text and choose Spelling > Spelling from the shortcut menu (**Figure 15.75**). The Spelling dialog opens and checks the spelling of any selected text (**Figure 15.76**). Two other useful options are the shortcut menu's Spelling > Check Spelling and Spelling > Check Spelling as You Type options, which underline any misspelled words in red, letting you see at a glance if something is spelled incorrectly.

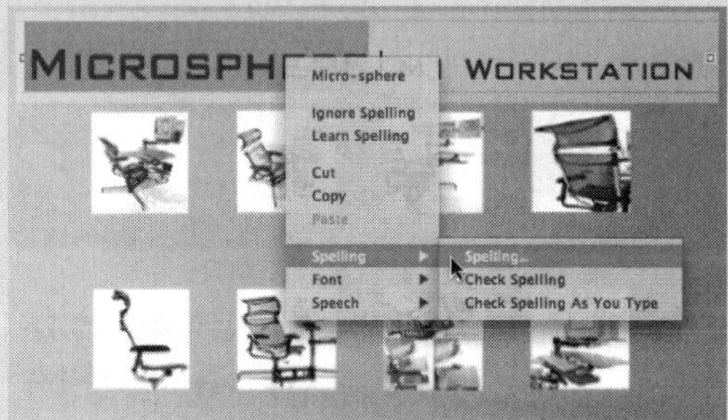

Figure 15.75 If you Control-click some highlighted text, the shortcut menu gives you access to several spelling functions.

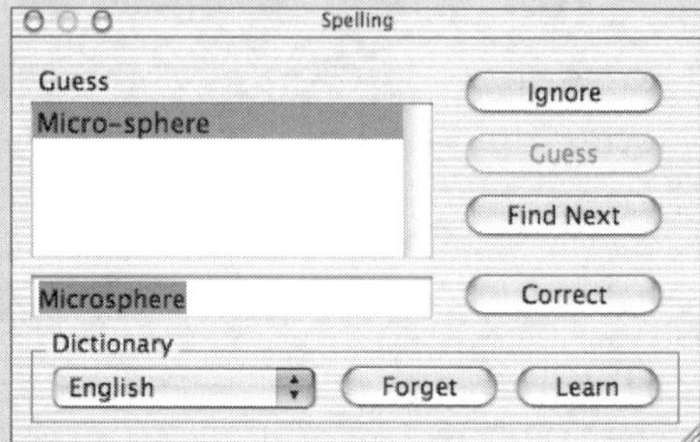

Figure 15.76 The Spelling dialog checks the spelling of words you're not quite sure of.

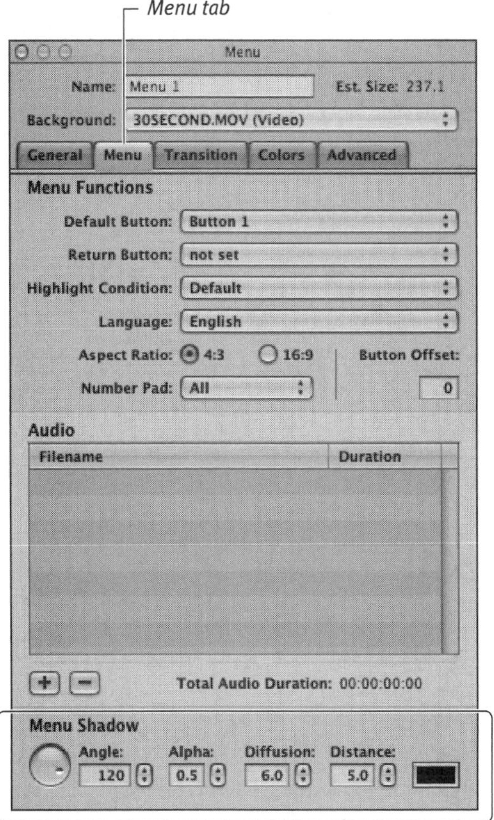

Figure 15.77 Use the Menu tab's Menu Shadow area to configure the menu's drop shadow.

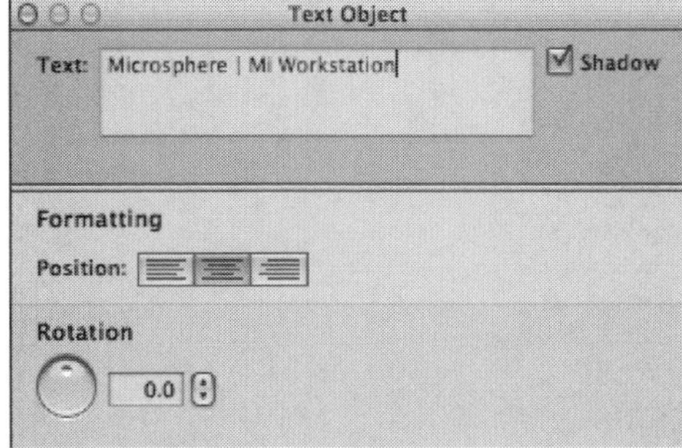

Figure 15.78 Click the Text Object Inspector's Shadow check box to enable its drop shadow.

Creating Drop Shadows

Drop shadows add depth to a menu by making the text seem to hover above the background graphics. You set drop shadows globally for the entire menu, including all text objects and text added to buttons. To use drop shadows on a menu, you must first configure the drop shadow itself and then enable the drop shadow only for the menu elements to which you want the drop shadow applied.

To configure a menu's drop shadow:

1. In the Outline view, select the menu.

   The Inspector updates to display the menu's properties.

2. In the Menu Inspector, select the Menu tab.

3. Use the settings in the Menu tab's Menu Shadow area (**Figure 15.77**) to configure the menu's drop shadow.

To enable a text object's drop shadow:

1. In the Menu editor, select the text object to which you want to apply a drop shadow.

   The Inspector updates to display the text object's properties.

2. At the top right of the Text Object Inspector, select the Shadow check box (**Figure 15.78**).

To enable a drop shadow for button text:

1. In the Menu editor, select the button that contains the text to which you want to apply a drop shadow.

   The Inspector updates to display the button's properties.

2. In the Style tab's Text area, select the Shadow check box (**Figure 15.79**).

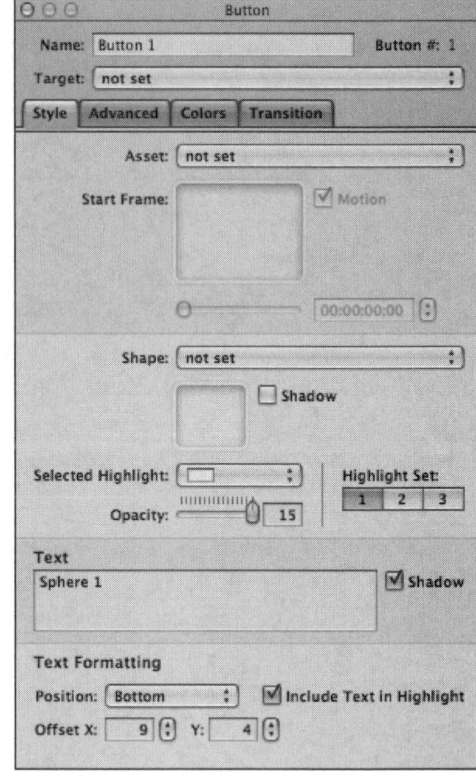

Figure 15.79 On the Button Inspector's Style tab, click the Text area's Shadow check box to enable a drop shadow for a button's text.

16

Using Transitions

Transitions are a perfect way to add a professional touch to your DVD-Video presentations. A transition is a segue from one project element to another. For example, when you click a menu button, a common DVD-Video trick is to have the menu fade out before the next item begins playing. In the old days of DVD-Video authoring, you had to create your transitions by hand in a nonlinear editor like Final Cut Pro, import those transitions into DVD Studio Pro, create a new track (or menu) to hold the transition, and then link the menu button to the transition track, before linking that track to the target element. Phew! That was a lot to go through—particularly if your transition simply fades from the menu to black. Thankfully, DVD Studio Pro 3's new transition features let you create this advanced DVD-Video navigation right inside DVD Studio Pro, with little more than a few button clicks.

Using Transitions

DVD Studio Pro 3 comes with 30 built-in transitions, ranging from basic fades and wipes to some complex video transitions (**Figure 16.1**). You can assign these transitions to individual slides in slideshows, to still image clips in tracks, to menus, and even to individual menu buttons. Furthermore, you can assign a different transition to each button on a menu, which really helps to customize your presentation.

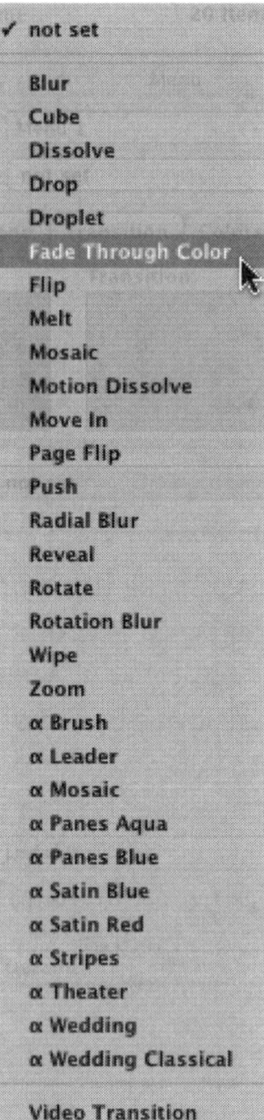

Figure 16.1 DVD Studio Pro 3's built-in transitions.

How transitions work

A transition is a smooth change from one project element to another. To create the transition, two separate parts are blended together: the last frame of the source item and the first frame of the target item.

The source item is the project item the transition is applied to; the target item is the project item that the source item links to. For example, if a menu button targets a video track, then the source item is the menu button, and the target item is the video track. Consequently, the transition is always applied to the tail of the source element, and not the front; in other words, you can use a transition to create a fade-out, but not a fade-in.

DVD Studio Pro creates transitions in much the same way that Logic creates fade files or Final Cut Pro renders dissolves. In all of these examples, the host program renders a new piece of media that it plays to create the effect of one thing blending into another. In the case of DVD Studio Pro, this transition file is not only rendered, but also encoded to MPEG-2 video for inclusion in the finished project. To learn more about how transitions are made, see the sidebar "Where's the Transition?"

Where's the Transition?

DVD Studio Pro renders transitions as strips of video. When the project is built, these new strips of video are added to the end of the transition's source element. For example, a transition assigned to a track will be added to the end of the track, while a transition assigned to a slide will be added to the end of the slide. The only exception is menus—all menu transitions, for every menu in your project, are added to the end of the menu domain on the final DVD disc (for reference, the menu domain is VTS_01_0.VOB).

To truly understand how DVD Studio Pro creates transitions, you need to build a project and then de-mux (demultiplex), or break apart, the project's VOB files and watch the resultant video streams (to learn more about VOB files and DVD-Video disc architecture, see Chapter 2, "DVD 101"). De-muxing VOB files is a fairly simple process using a tool like bbDEMUX, available on Version Tracker:

`www.versiontracker.com`

When you de-mux a VOB file, you break it into its elementary streams. Using bbDEMUX, for example, de-muxing creates an .m2v file and one or more AC3 files. If you open the .m2v file in QuickTime Player, you can watch the video stream to see how DVD Studio Pro has created the transitions and where in the stream it has placed them.

Adding Track Transitions

Track transitions are a bit confusing at first, because any transition applied to a track affects only still-image clips arranged in the track's video streams. All video clips remain unaffected by your transition settings.

✔ Tip

- You can use track transitions to create a quick and dirty fade-in for tracks by using the following trick. In Photoshop, create a document that is only a black frame at the same resolution as the video format you are working in. Next, insert this still image at the very front of the track's video stream. Now apply a transition to this still image, and it will fade into the video stream behind. Voila! Instant fade-in.

To assign a transition to a track:

1. In the Outline view, select the track you want to apply a transition to.
   The Inspector updates to display the track's properties.
2. Click the Inspector's Transition tab (**Figure 16.2**).
3. From the Transition tab's Transition menu, select a transition (**Figure 16.3**).

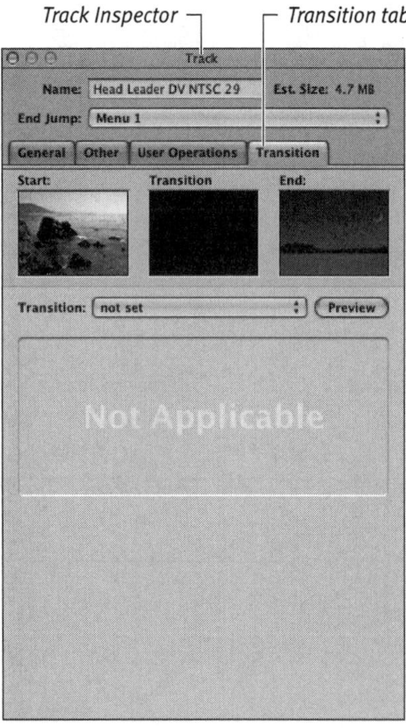

Figure 16.2 The Track Inspector's Transition tab lets you create fades from the track into the target project element (the one defined for the track's end jump).

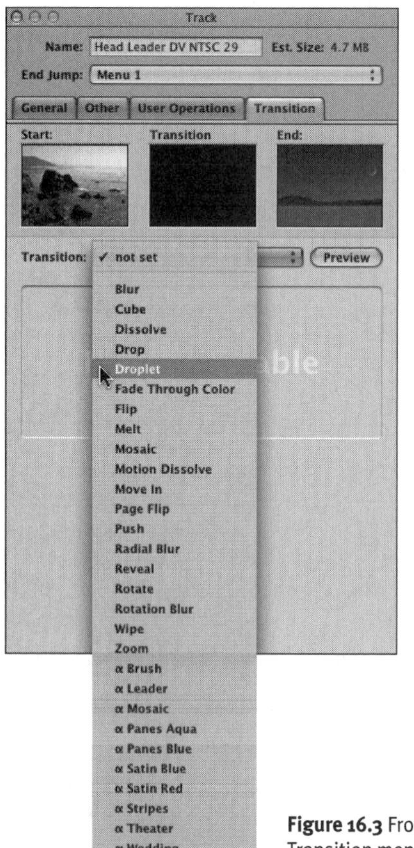

Figure 16.3 From the Transition menu, choose a transition.

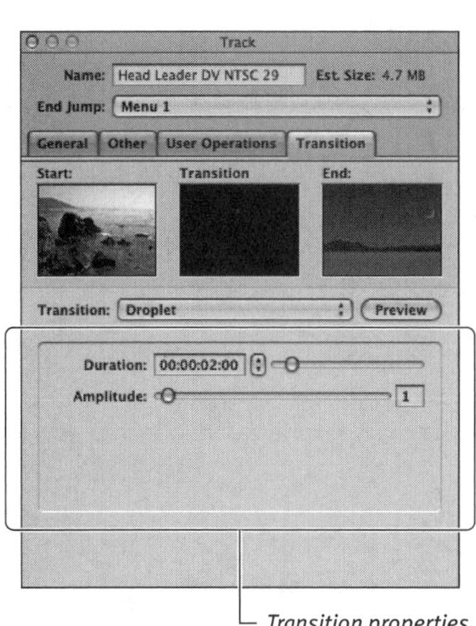

Figure 16.4 Each transition has unique properties that you can adjust, including duration.

Once you've selected a transition, properties unique to that transition appear in the Inspector (**Figure 16.4**).

4. Adjust the transition properties (to learn more about transition properties, see the sidebar "Modifying Transitions").

Modifying Transitions

Each transition has it's own unique set of parameters that you can modify to customize the transition's appearance (**Figure 16.5**). For example, duration (the total time of the transition) and rotation are parameters you may want to adjust. By carefully tweaking a transition's parameters, you can customize DVD Studio Pro's stock transitions to suit your particular needs. Thanks Apple!

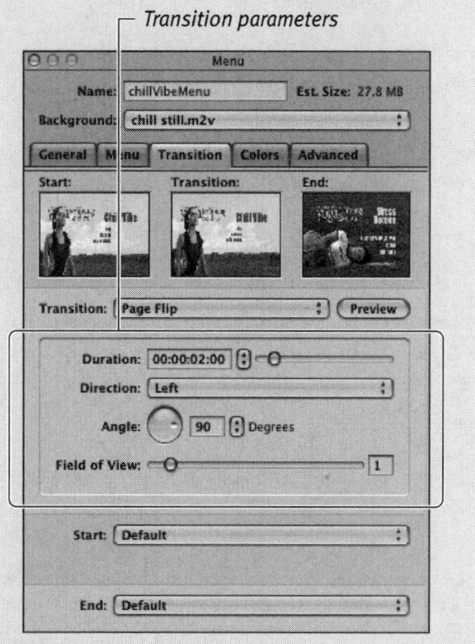

Figure 16.5 From the Transition tab, you can customize the look of DVD Studio Pro's built-in transitions.

Adding Slideshow Transitions

Slideshow transitions seem a natural fit. Here's an example of why: the Palette's link to your iPhoto library offers a quick way to create a slideshow of photos, but by default the photos hard-cut from one to the next, rather than each fading, or transitioning, smoothly into the following one. Transitions to the rescue!

DVD Studio Pro 3 allows you to assign a default transition to each slideshow. Alternatively, you can assign transitions to individual slides.

To assign a default slideshow transition:

1. In the Outline or Graphical View, select the slideshow.

   The Inspector updates to display the Slideshow's properties.

2. Click the Inspector's Transition tab (**Figure 16.6**).

3. *Do one of the following:*

   ▲ From the Transition tab's Transition menu, select a transition (**Figure 16.7**).

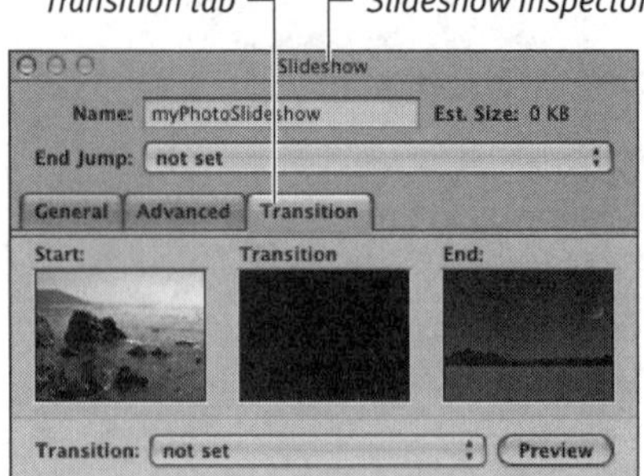

Figure 16.6 The Slideshow Inspector's Transition tab lets you create fades between slides.

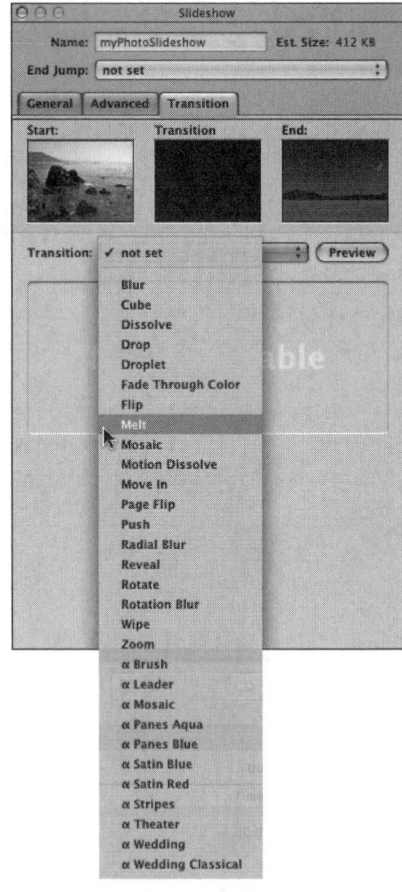

Figure 16.7 From the Inspector's Transition menu, choose a transition, or ...

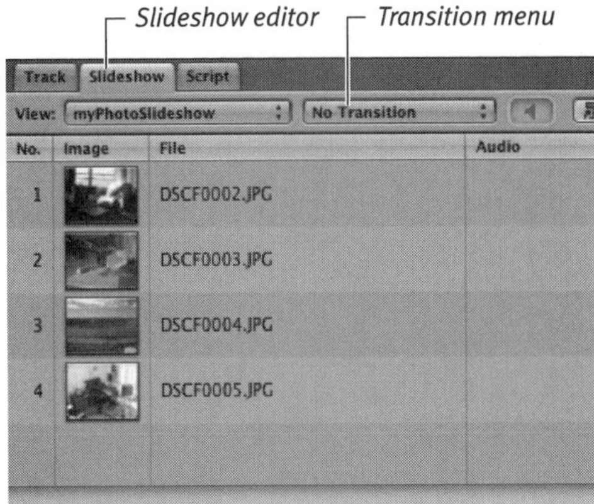

Figure 16.8 ... from the Slideshow editor's Transition menu, choose a transition.

- ▲ At the top of the Slideshow editor, choose a transition from the Transition menu (**Figure 16.8**).

  Once you've selected a transition, properties unique to that transition appear in the Inspector (**Figure 16.9**).

4. Adjust the transition properties (to learn more about transition properties, see the sidebar "Modifying Transitions" earlier in this chapter).

   Each slide in the slideshow will now use this default transition. To override the default transition, you can set transitions for individual slides, as shown in the next task.

To assign a transition to a single slide:

1. In the Slideshow editor, select the slide.

   The Inspector updates to display the slide's properties.

2. Click the Inspector's Transition tab (**Figure 16.10**).

continues on next page

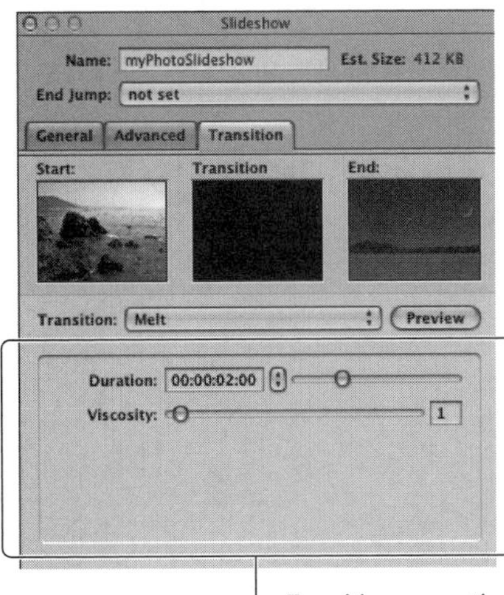

Figure 16.9 Each transition has unique properties that you can adjust.

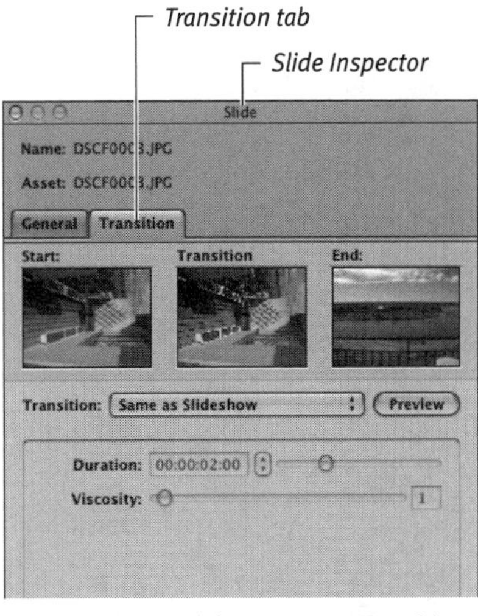

Figure 16.10 The Slide Inspector's Transition tab lets you create fades between slides.

3. From the Transition tab's Transition menu, select a transition (**Figure 16.11**).

   Once you've selected a transition, properties unique to that transition appear in the Inspector.

4. Adjust the transition properties (to learn more about transition properties, see the sidebar titled "Modifying Transitions" earlier in this chapter).

✔ Tip

- To quickly change a slide's transition, in the Slideshow editor Control-click a slide and choose Transition from the shortcut menu. (**Figure 16.12**).

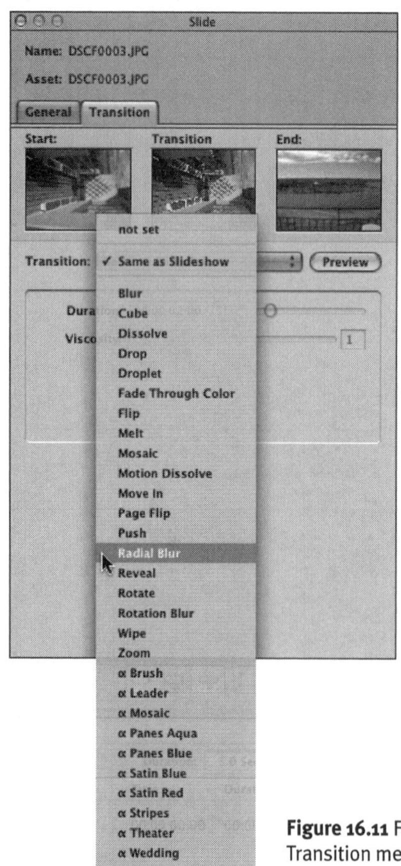

Figure 16.11 From the Transition menu, choose a transition.

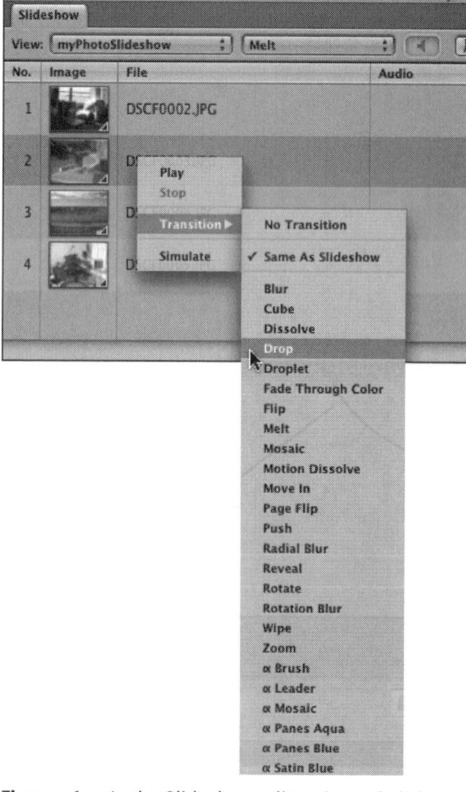

Figure 16.12 In the Slideshow editor, Control-click a slide and choose Transition to quickly change or set a slide transition.

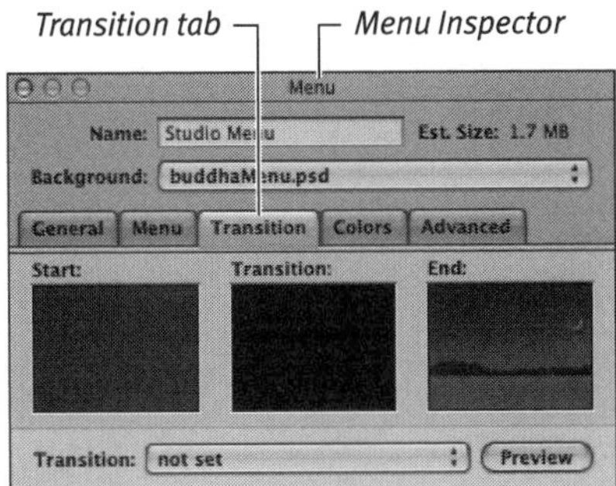

Figure 16.13 The Menu Inspector's Transition tab lets you create fades between buttons.

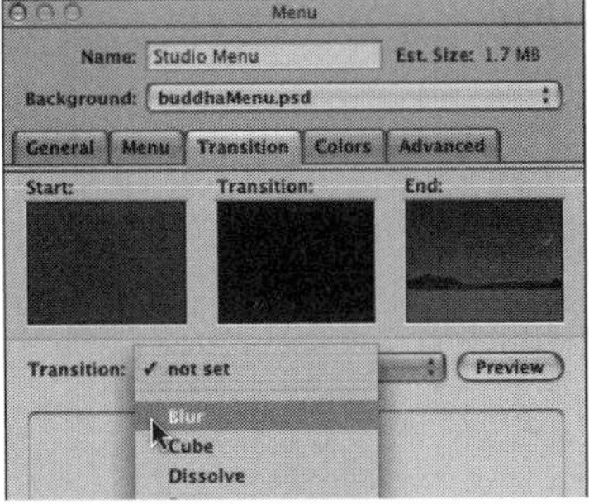

Figure 16.14 From the Inspector's Transition menu, choose a transition.

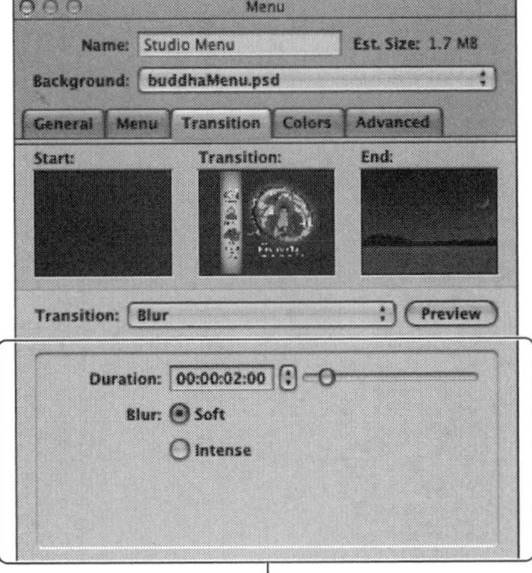

Figure 16.15 Each transition has unique properties that you can adjust.

Adding Menu Transitions

Menus are the place where DVD Studio Pro's transitions features shine. As with tracks and slideshows, you can assign a default transition to an entire menu or even assign different transitions to each individual button on the menu.

As of this writing, DVD Studio Pro 3 creates menu transitions by blending the first frame of the menu with the first frame of the targeted item. This works fine for all menus that do not have a loop point, but not at all well if you have used a loop point to create a menu introduction transition (for more information, see Chapter 15, "Overlay Menus"). However, there's a strong possibility that future versions of DVD Studio Pro will use the frame of video under the loop point as the first frame of the transition. Let's see what the future holds.

To assign a default menu transition:

1. In the Outline or Graphical view, select the menu.

   The Inspector updates to display the menu's properties.

2. Click the Inspector's Transition tab (**Figure 16.13**).

3. From the Transition tab's Transition menu, select a transition (**Figure 16.14**)

   Once you've selected a transition, properties unique to that transition appear in the Inspector (**Figure 16.15**).

4. Adjust the transition properties (to learn more about transition properties, see "Modifying Transitions" earlier in this chapter).

   Each button in the menu will now use this default transition. To override the default transition, you can set transitions for individual buttons, as shown in the next task.

To assign a transition to a single button:

1. In the menu editor, select the button.

   The Inspector updates to display the button's properties.

2. Click the Inspector's Transition tab (**Figure 16.16**).

3. From the Transition tab's Transition menu, select a transition (**Figure 16.17**).

   Once you've selected a transition, properties unique to that transition appear in the Inspector.

4. Adjust the transition properties (to learn more about transition properties, see "Modifying Transitions" earlier in this chapter).

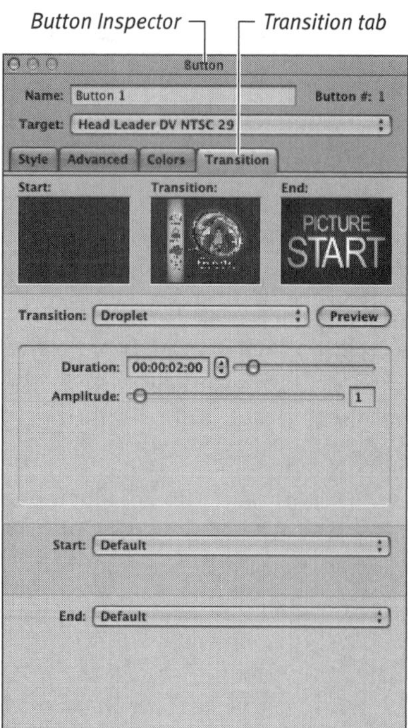

Figure 16.16 The Button Inspector's Transition tab lets you create fades between buttons.

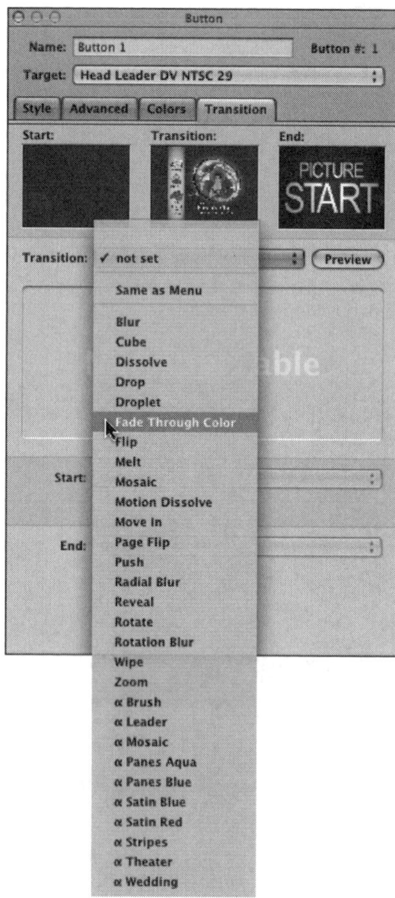

Figure 16.17 From the Transition menu, choose a transition.

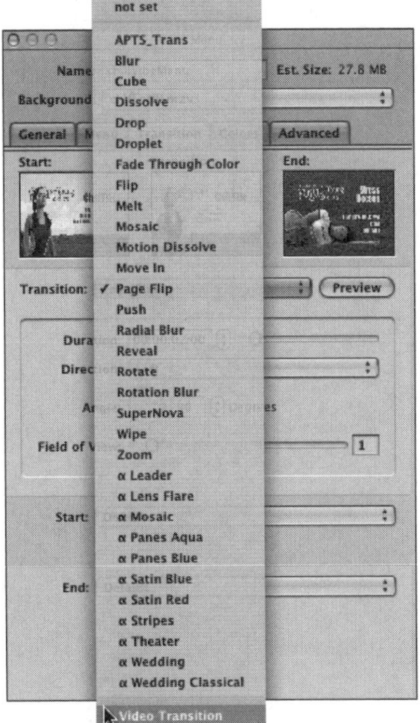

Figure 16.18 Video clips made in Final Cut Pro or Motion can be used as transitions between menu's and other project items.

Using a Video Clip as a Transition

Once upon a time, DVD-Video authors had to create transitions manually, spending hours in programs like Final Cut Pro or Shake animating the perfect transition for the project at hand. And indeed, if it should happen that DVD Studio Pro's built-in transitions don't supply the effect you're after, feel free to work the old-fashioned way and create your own.

If you create your own transitions, keep these two points in mind:

- Video transitions created outside of DVD Studio Pro can be assigned only to menus and menu buttons.
- Don't mix codecs or you'll notice a "color-pop" when the transition starts playing. If your menu's video uses the DV codec, ensure that the transition clip also uses the DV codec. Similarly, if you encode your project's video using Compressor, encode the transition using Compressor (at the exact same settings used for the menu's video).

To use a video clip as a transition:

1. From the Transition tab's Transition menu, select Video Transition (**Figure 16.18**).

   The Transition parameters area updates to display an Asset menu.

continues on next page

2. From the Asset menu, select the video clip you want to use for the video transition (**Figure 16.19**).

   The selected video clip will play as the transition between the exiting menu and the incoming project item.

✔ Tip

- Only video assets can be used as video transitions for menus. Consequently, the Video Transition Asset menu doesn't list any still-image assets.

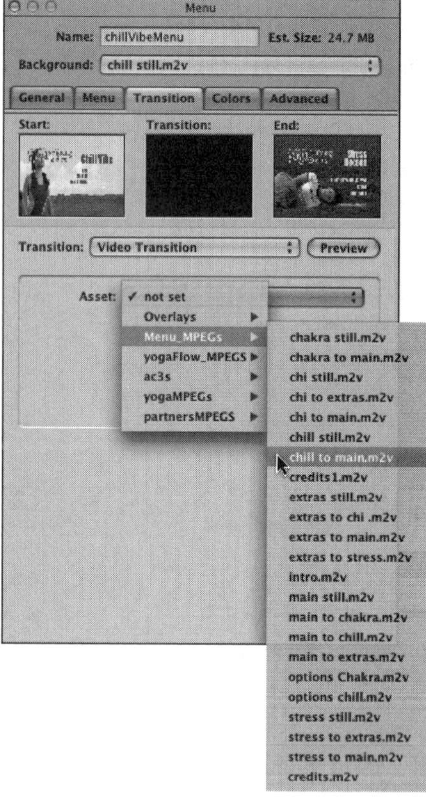

Figure 16.19 You can use any video asset in your project as a video transition.

17 Templates, Styles, and Shapes

If you're looking for an easy way out of creating menus, DVD Studio Pro 3 provides you with plenty of options. These options come in the form of professionally designed templates, which contain the background picture and overlay, buttons, drop zones, text, and all of the preset color and font attributes you need to create a near-finished menu.

You can customize DVD Studio Pro's stock templates to fit your needs or create your own templates for later use. Templates are easy to create and can easily be moved from computer to computer. This chapter shows you how to create your own custom templates and also how to share them with others.

For a series of DVD projects that need to have the same look and feel with minor alterations for each menu, templates can save you both time and money. You can create an entire template, or you can save text, button, and other settings as a custom *style*, or favorite, for easy access in future projects.

Another cool feature in DVD Studio Pro 3 is the ability to use the Menu editor to create *shapes*—four-layer Photoshop documents that you can use to give irregular edges to your buttons and drop zones.

There is only one drawback to using templates, styles, and shapes: they can be used only with standard menus; you still have to create Photoshop layer menus the hard way.

About Templates

A template is a compilation of the background picture, buttons, text, and all colors, fonts, and highlight settings that a menu uses. Templates also contain the menu's button navigation and any shapes that will be applied to your buttons. You can use the templates supplied with DVD Studio Pro or create your own.

Templates are located in DVD Studio Pro's Palette, where they are tucked away under the Templates tab and then further separated into three additional tabs: Apple, Custom, and Project (**Figure 17.1**):

- **Apple.** Apple stock templates are shipped with DVD Studio Pro and stored inside the DVD Studio Pro application package. (See "To open the application package," next, for directions on how to locate these templates.)

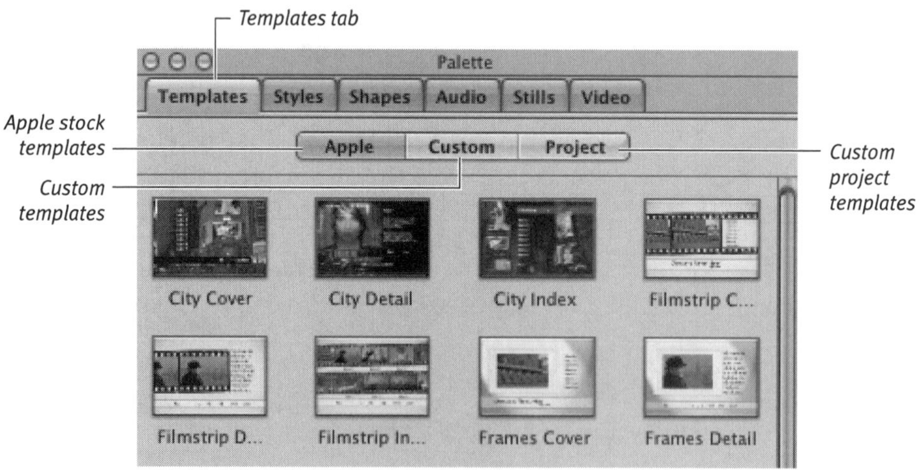

Figure 17.1 All templates are stored on the Palette's Templates tab by category. Stock templates are stored on the Apple tab, templates that you've created are on the Custom tab, and custom templates that you save to the project file are on the Project tab.

Figure 17.2 Templates that you create are saved to your hard disk in *root*/Library/Application Support/DVD Studio Pro/Templates.

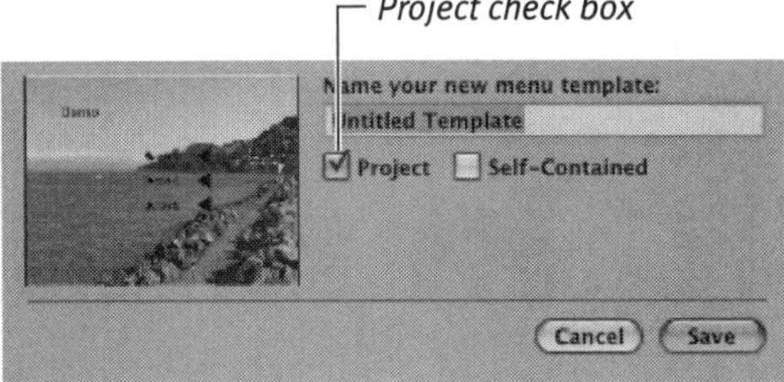

Figure 17.3 When you create a template, DVD Studio Pro displays this dialog. Select the Project check box to save your template to the project file. Leave the Project check box deselected to make your templates available for use in all future projects.

Figure 17.4 Saving templates to the project file can make it easier to move entire projects that use templates to another computer.

- **Custom.** Templates that you create are saved to your hard disk in *root*/Library/Application Support/DVD Studio Pro/Templates (**Figure 17.2**). Steps for creating custom templates are detailed later in this chapter.
- **Project.** When you create a custom template, you can save the template for use with the current project only or store the template for use with all projects (**Figure 17.3**). Selecting the Project check box will save your template to the project file (**Figure 17.4**), and the template will not be available for use with other projects. (For information on the Self-Contained check box, see "To create a custom template" later in this chapter.)

  If you pass project files from one computer to another, or if you want to save hard disk space and store the project file on another hard disk, select the Project check box. Be careful, though: this may cause your project files to balloon into the gigabytes.

To open the application package:

1. On your computer's hard disk, open your Applications folder and Control-click the DVD Studio Pro icon.

   A shortcut menu appears (**Figure 17.5**).

2. Choose Show Package Contents (refer to Figure 17.5).

   DVD Studio Pro's Contents folder opens in a separate window (**Figure 17.6**).

3. From the Contents folder, choose Resources/Templates (**Figure 17.7**).

   DVD Studio Pro's stock templates are located inside the Templates folder.

Figure 17.5 Control-click the DVD Studio Pro icon and choose Show Package Contents from the shortcut menu to see what's inside the application package.

Figure 17.6 When you open the Contents folder, you can navigate to all of the application package's applications.

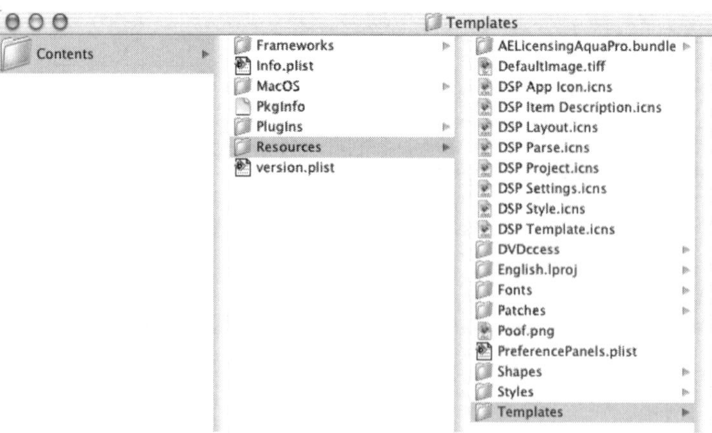

Figure 17.7 DVD Studio Pro's stock templates are located inside the application package in the Contents/Resources/Templates folder.

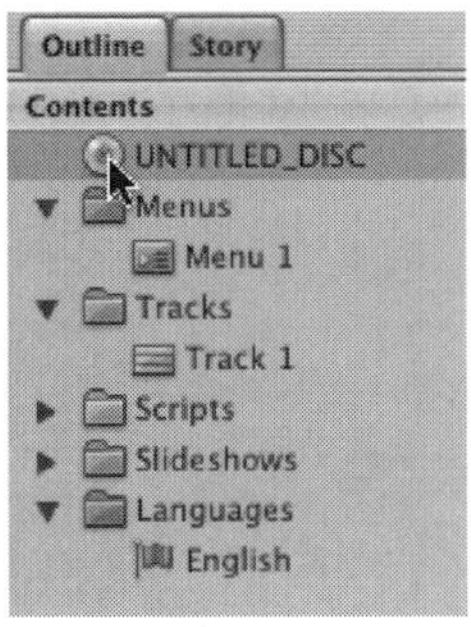

Figure 17.8 Click the disc in the Outline view to display its properties in the Inspector.

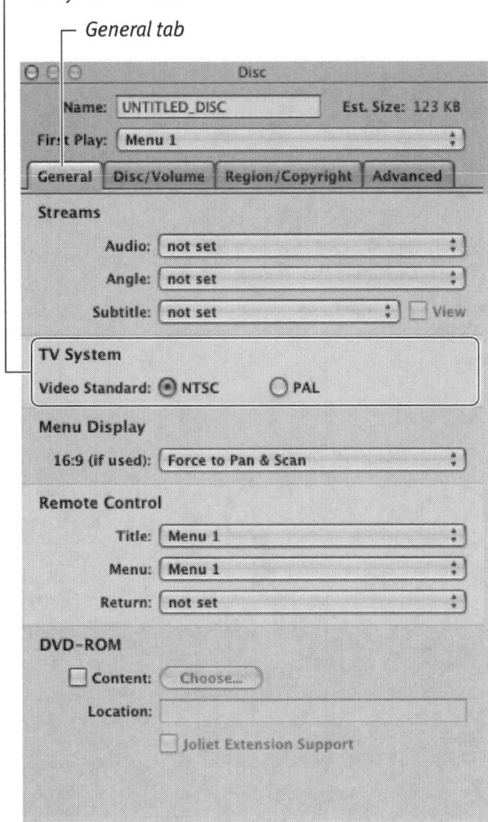

Figure 17.9 The Disc Inspector displays the TV System settings for your project on the General tab.

Using Templates

DVD Studio Pro comes with templates for both NTSC and PAL, but when you set the video standard for your project, you'll see in the Palette only templates that correspond to your video standard. The Palette, for example, automatically updates to display PAL templates when you change your video standard to PAL. (To learn about video standards, see Chapter 2, "DVD 101.")

Applying a template to your menu sets the background picture, audio stream, number of buttons on the menu, button style or shape, button location, menu navigation between buttons, and menu text (styles and shapes are discussed later in this chapter). Applying a template results in a near-complete menu—all you need to do is link the button's target to a track or other project element or modify parts of the menu as desired.

To set the project's video standard:

1. In the Outline view, click the disc to select it (**Figure 17.8**).

   The Inspector updates to display the disc's properties (**Figure 17.9**).

2. In the Disc Inspector, click the General tab to display the Disc's General properties.

3. In the General tab's TV System section, click the NTSC or PAL radio button (refer to Figure 17.9).

   The video standard is set for the project; all templates that correspond to the selected video standard are displayed in the Palette.

To apply a template to a menu:

1. In the Outline or Graphical view, double-click an empty, standard menu (**Figure 17.10**).

   The menu opens in the Menu editor (**Figure 17.11**).

2. Choose View > Show Palette (**Figure 17.12**), or press Option-Command-P, to open the Palette.

   The Palette opens displaying the last tab you selected (**Figure 17.13**).

3. In the Palette, click the Templates tab (refer to Figure 17.13).

   On the Templates tab, the Apple tab is selected by default.

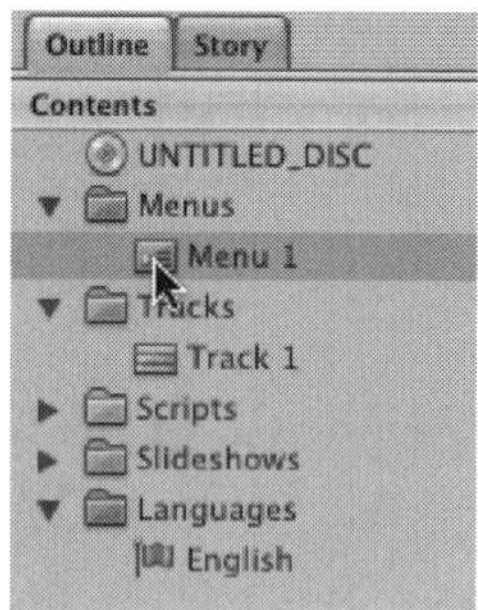

Figure 17.10 Double-click an empty menu to open it in the Menu editor.

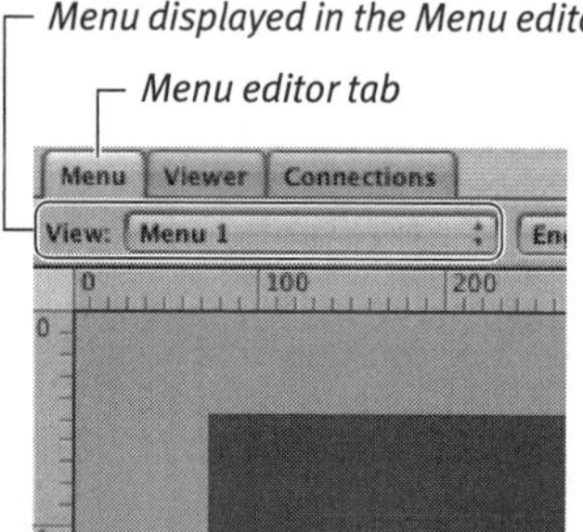

Figure 17.11 The menu opens in the Menu editor.

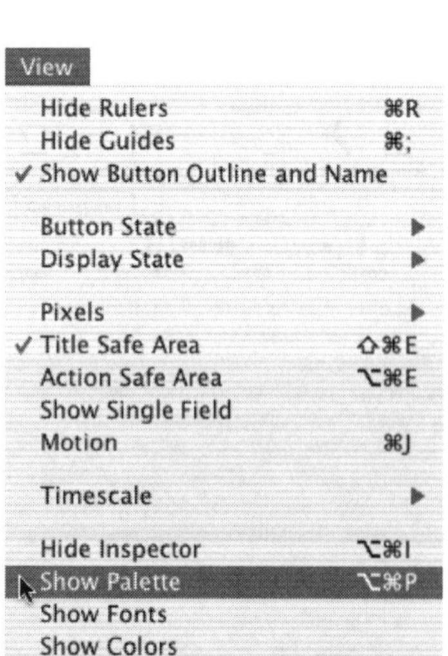

Figure 17.12 Choose View > Show Palette to open the Palette.

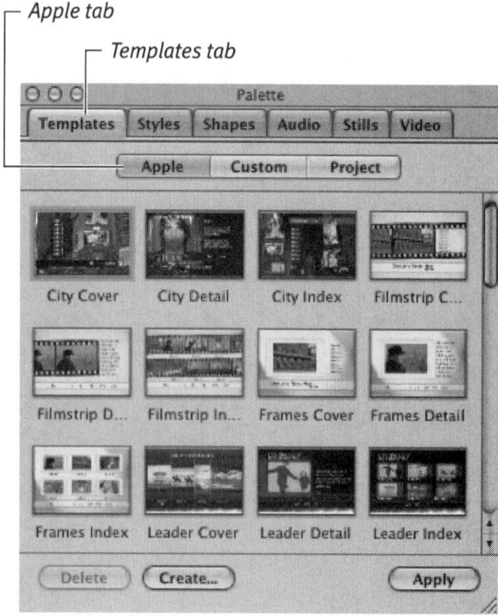

Figure 17.13 The Apple tab is selected by default when you click the Templates tab in the Palette.

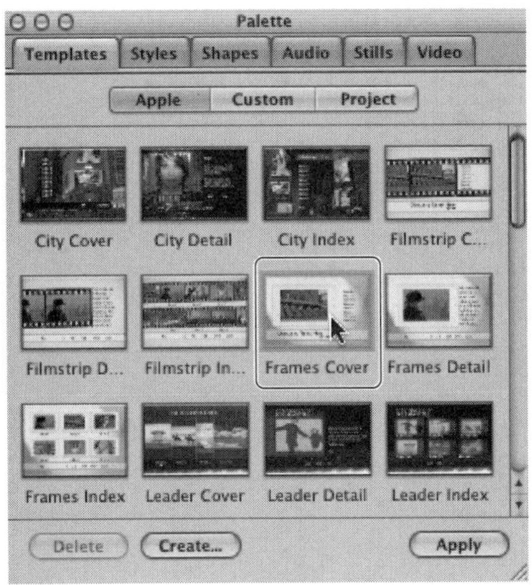

Figure 17.14 Select a template on the Apple tab.

Figure 17.15 Select a template in the Palette and click Apply to apply the template to your menu.

4. On the Apple tab, click a template to select it (**Figure 17.14**).

5. *Do one of the following:*

   ▲ In the Palette, double-click the template.

   ▲ Drag the selected template to the Menu editor.

   ▲ At the bottom right of the Templates tab, click the Apply button (**Figure 17.15**).

continues on next page

DVD Studio Pro displays a message letting you know that the template is being applied (**Figure 17.16**). Once DVD Studio Pro has finished gathering information for the template, the template is applied to your menu (**Figure 17.17**).

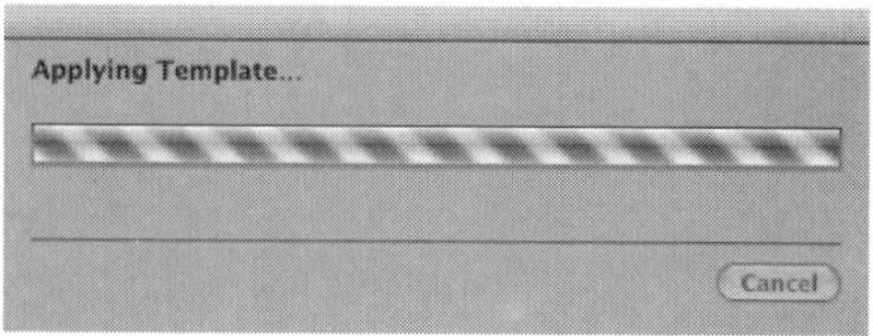

Figure 17.16 DVD Studio Pro lets you know that the template is being applied.

✔ Tip

- Because of the way templates, styles, and shapes are processed when your project is compiled, you can't use them with layered menus. (For an explanation of the differences between standard and Photoshop layer menus, see Chapter 13, "The Menu Editor.")

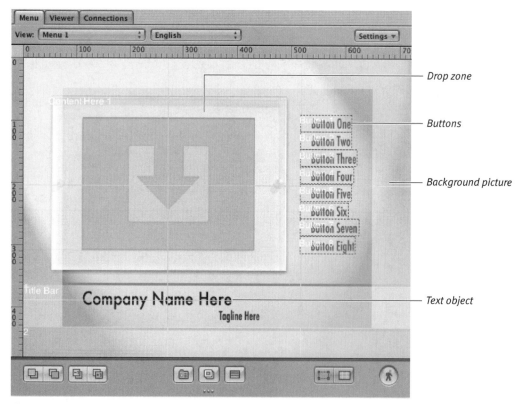

Figure 17.17 The template is applied to your menu. The applied template shown in this figure has set the background picture, eight buttons, one drop zone, and two text objects. Button navigation, highlight colors, and the text font were also set when the template was applied.

Chapter Index Menus

When you drag a video track into the Menu editor, a shortcut menu appears asking how you want the Menu editor to handle your track (**Figure 17.18**). You can choose either to create a new button and connect the button to the track or to create a button that will link to a chapter index menu designed specifically for that track.

Figure 17.18 When you drag a track into the Menu editor, this shortcut menu appears asking you what you want the Menu editor to do with your track.

If you choose to have the Menu editor generate a chapter index menu for you, a scene selection button will be created for each marker in the track, and all button navigation and connections will be made for you automatically.

If the current menu into which you dragged your track is empty (does not have buttons, text, a background picture, or anything else in it), the current menu will be used as the chapter index menu. If the current menu contains buttons or anything else, a new menu will be created for the start of your chapter index menu, and a button will be created and linked to the new chapter index menu.

When you choose to have the Menu editor generate a chapter index menu for you, the Choose Template or Layout Style dialog appears (**Figure 17.19**). Use this dialog to select a template or layout style for the Menu editor to use when creating the menus for your chapter index menus. (Layout styles are discussed later in this chapter in the section "About Styles.")

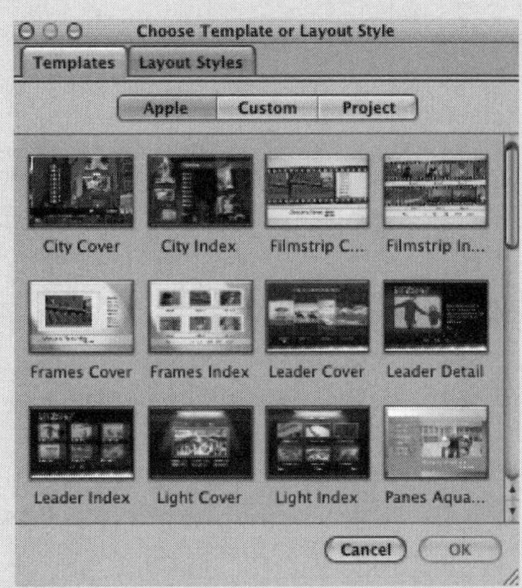

Figure 17.19 Using the Choose Template or Layout Style dialog, select a template or layout style for use with your chapter index menu.

The template or layout style you choose for your chapter index menu determines the number of buttons on each menu, the button layout, the shape of the buttons, the navigation among buttons, whether the marker's first frame is used as the button's picture asset, the background picture, and all color and text attributes. That's a lot for the Menu editor to automatically generate for you—just think of all the time you'll be saving!

Creating Custom Templates

Any menu that you create in the Menu editor can be saved as a template. (See Chapter 13 for information on how to create menus in the Menu editor.) Templates can be self-contained (all assets are copied to a separate template file), or they can reference all pictures, video clips, and other assets used in the project where they are currently residing on your hard disk. As long as you don't move the assets from their location on your hard disk, templates that reference those assets will be available for future use with any project you create.

You can also save templates to the project file, which makes them easily transferable from one computer to another. Templates that are saved to the project file are available for use only with the current project, which makes the project easier to store if you need to archive it.

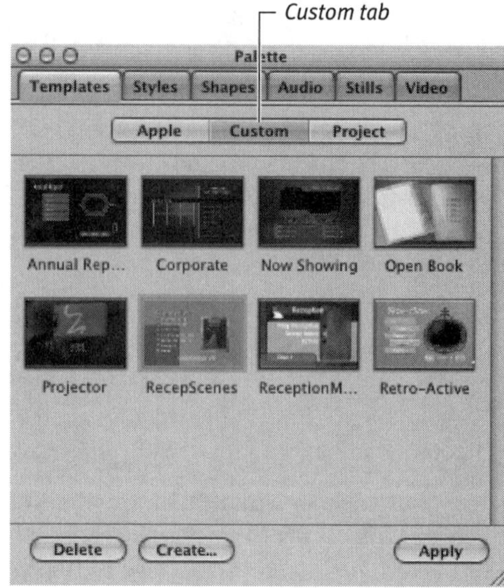

Figure 17.20 Click the Custom tab to view custom templates.

To create a custom template:

1. In the Menu editor, create a menu and set the button navigation, highlight colors, and all other properties as desired. (See Chapter 13 for instructions on how to create menus in the Menu editor.)
2. Choose View > Show Palette, or press Option-Command-P, to open the Palette.

   The Palette displays the last tab you had selected.
3. In the Palette, click the Templates tab to reveal the project's Apple, Custom, and Project template tabs.
4. Click the Custom tab to view custom templates (**Figure 17.20**).

   Your custom templates are displayed on the Custom tab. If you haven't created any templates yet, the Custom tab's list of templates will be empty.

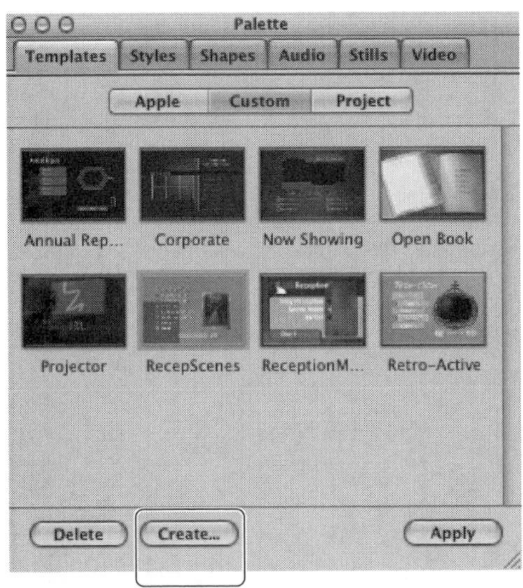

Figure 17.21 Click Create to save your menu and all of its properties as a template.

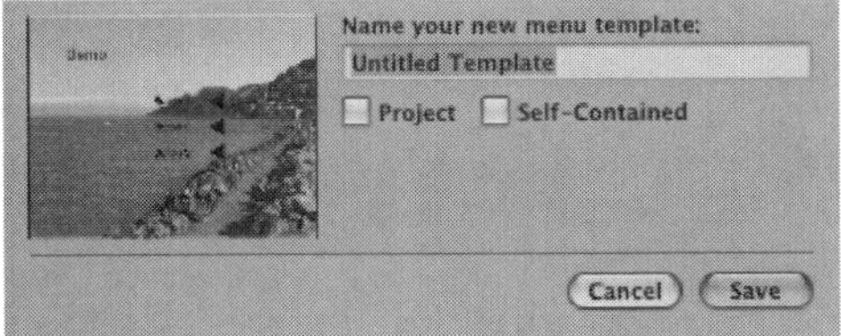

Figure 17.22 Type a name for your template in this Save dialog.

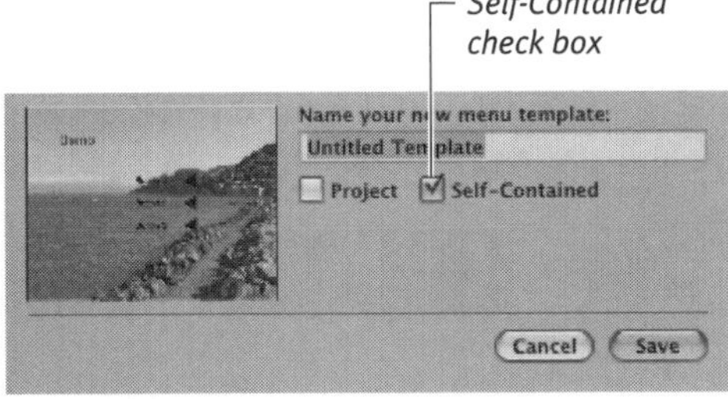

Figure 17.23 Select the Self-Contained check box to have DVD Studio Pro save a copy of each picture, button shape, and audio stream used for the menu in one template file. DVD Studio Pro will simply reference these items from your hard disk if you leave the check box unselected.

5. At the bottom of the Custom tab, click Create (**Figure 17.21**).

   A Save dialog appears, asking you to name the template (**Figure 17.22**).

6. In the Save dialog, type a new name for your template (refer to Figure 17.22).

7. Select the Self-Contained check box (**Figure 17.23**).

   DVD Studio Pro makes a copy of each picture, button shape, and audio stream used in the menu and saves the copies to the template file.

8. In the Save dialog, click Save.

   DVD Studio Pro saves your template, and your new template appears in the Palette on the Custom tab (**Figure 17.24**).

continues on next page

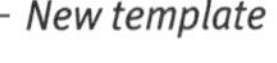

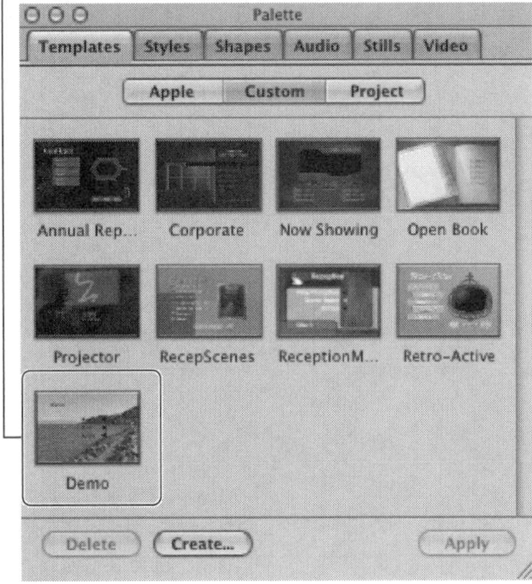

Figure 17.24 Your new template is displayed on the Palette's Custom tab.

✔ Tips

- If your project hasn't been saved, you won't be able to save the template to the project file. Instead, DVD Studio Pro will display an alert dialog asking you to save your project (**Figure 17.25**).
- If you save your template to the project file, your new template will appear only on the Palette's Project tab. The template will not be available for use in other projects.
- A quick way to save your menu as a template is to Control-click the background image in the Menu editor and choose Create Template from the shortcut menu that appears (**Figure 17.26**).

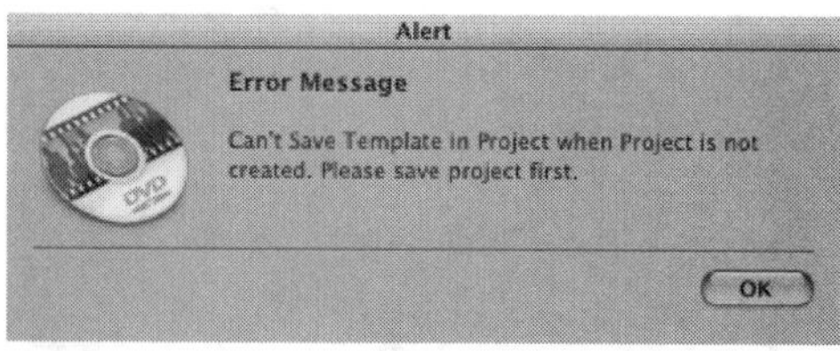

Figure 17.25 DVD Studio Pro can't save your template to your project file if you haven't yet saved the project. Click OK to close the dialog and save your project first.

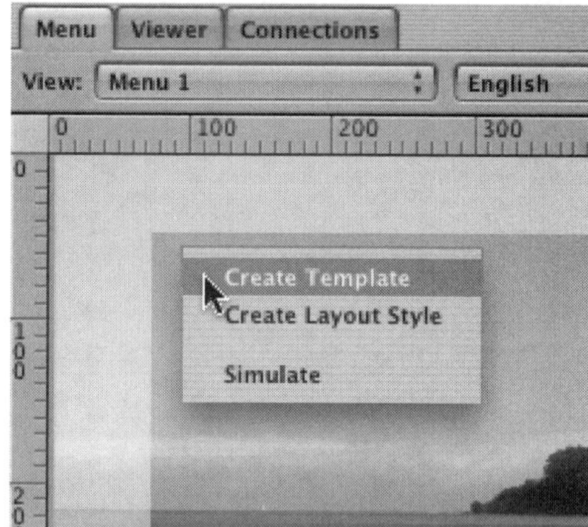

Figure 17.26 To save your menu as a template, Control-click the background picture in the Menu editor and choose Create Template from the shortcut menu.

Sharing Custom Templates

Custom templates are saved to your computer's hard disk in the *root*/Library/Application Support/DVD Studio Pro/Templates folder (**Figure 17.27**).

You can easily share your custom templates with friends and colleagues if you save them as self-contained.

Selecting the Self-Contained check box in the Save dialog causes DVD Studio Pro to make a copy of each picture, button shape, and audio file used in the template and to store those copies on your hard disk. To then share the template with your friends, simply open the Templates folder on your hard disk and e-mail your friends the self-contained file; just keep in mind that some templates may be larger than others due to the size of the pictures or video clips used.

To import a custom template that's already been created, choose File > Import > Template (**Figure 17.28**).

Figure 17.27 The templates you create are saved to your hard disk's *root*/Library/Application Support/DVD Studio Pro/Templates folder. Make copies of the templates to send them to friends.

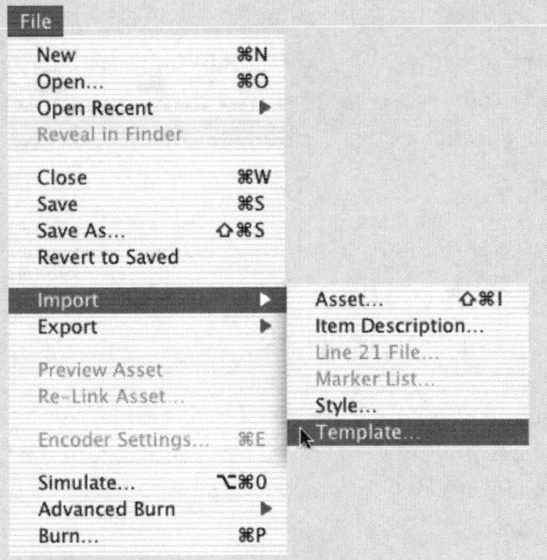

Figure 17.28 You can import shared templates by choosing File > Import > Template.

To delete a custom template:

1. In the Palette, click the Templates tab.
2. On the Templates tab, click the Custom tab to view your custom templates.
3. On the Custom tab, select the template to be removed (**Figure 17.29**).
4. At the bottom left of the Custom tab, click the Delete button, or press the Delete key (refer to Figure 17.29).

   DVD Studio Pro gives you the option of canceling or continuing to delete the template (**Figure 17.30**). Note that once deleted, a template is gone forever, and there's nothing you can do to bring it back.
5. In the Delete dialog that appears, click OK to delete your custom template.

   The template is removed from your hard disk and disappears from the Palette.

✔ Tips

- Apple templates cannot be deleted from the Palette.
- You can delete templates saved to your project file in the same way that you delete other custom templates: simply select the Project tab, select the template that you want to remove, and press the Delete key.

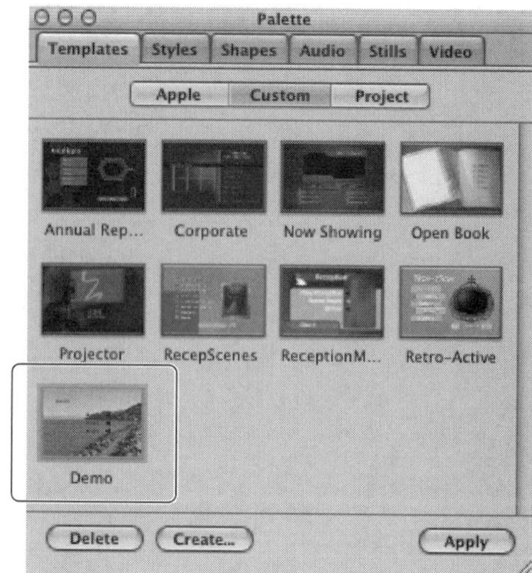

Figure 17.29 Select the custom template to be removed and click Delete.

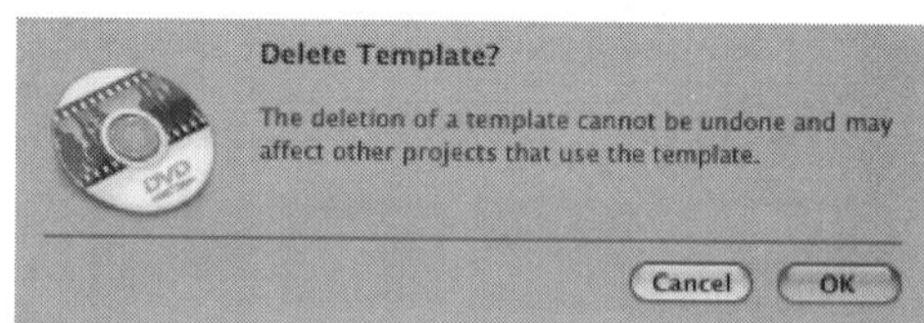

Figure 17.30 Click OK to delete the selected template, or click Cancel if you've changed your mind.

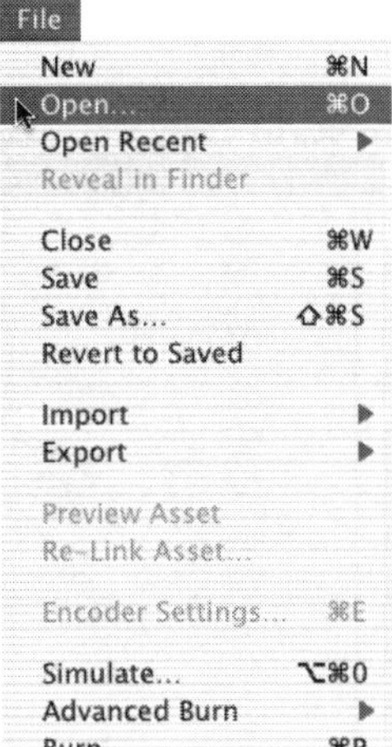

Figure 17.31 Choose File > Open to open a project.

Figure 17.32 Navigate to where your iDVD project is located and click Open in the Open dialog.

Importing iDVD Themes

You can't directly import an iDVD theme for use in DVD Studio Pro—the menu size used for iDVD projects is different than the menu size required by DVD Studio Pro, among other inconsistencies. To get around this problem, Apple created a set of DVD Studio Pro templates that mimic the themes in iDVD 2 and 3. These templates are installed when you install DVD Studio Pro 3; therefore, you don't necessarily need to have iDVD installed on your computer to import an iDVD project.

Third-party iDVD themes, however, are another story. Unless third-party iDVD themes have matching DVD Studio Pro templates, they can't be imported into DVD Studio Pro 3.

To import an iDVD theme, you first need to create a project in iDVD using the theme that you want to use in DVD Studio Pro. Then you need to save the iDVD project and import it into DVD Studio Pro, where the theme is converted into a menu using the iDVD button shapes, drop zones, background picture, text title, and audio. (Button shapes are described later in this chapter in the section "About Shapes.") Once the iDVD project has been imported into DVD Studio Pro, simply save the menu as a template.

To import an iDVD project:

1. Create a project in iDVD using the theme that you want to use as a template for your project.
2. In DVD Studio Pro, choose File > Open (**Figure 17.31**), or press Command-O.
   The Open dialog appears (**Figure 17.32**).

continues on next page

3. Using the Open dialog, navigate to where your iDVD project file is located on your hard disk.
4. Select your iDVD project and click Open at the bottom right of the Open dialog (refer to Figure 17.32).

   DVD Studio Pro displays a progress bar letting you know that the iDVD project is being imported (**Figure 17.33**). The iDVD project opens in DVD Studio Pro, and its themes are converted into menus (**Figure 17.34**).
5. Save the menus as custom templates following the instructions outlined earlier in this chapter in the section "To create a custom template."

Figure 17.33 DVD Studio Pro displays a progress indicator to let you know that the iDVD project is being imported.

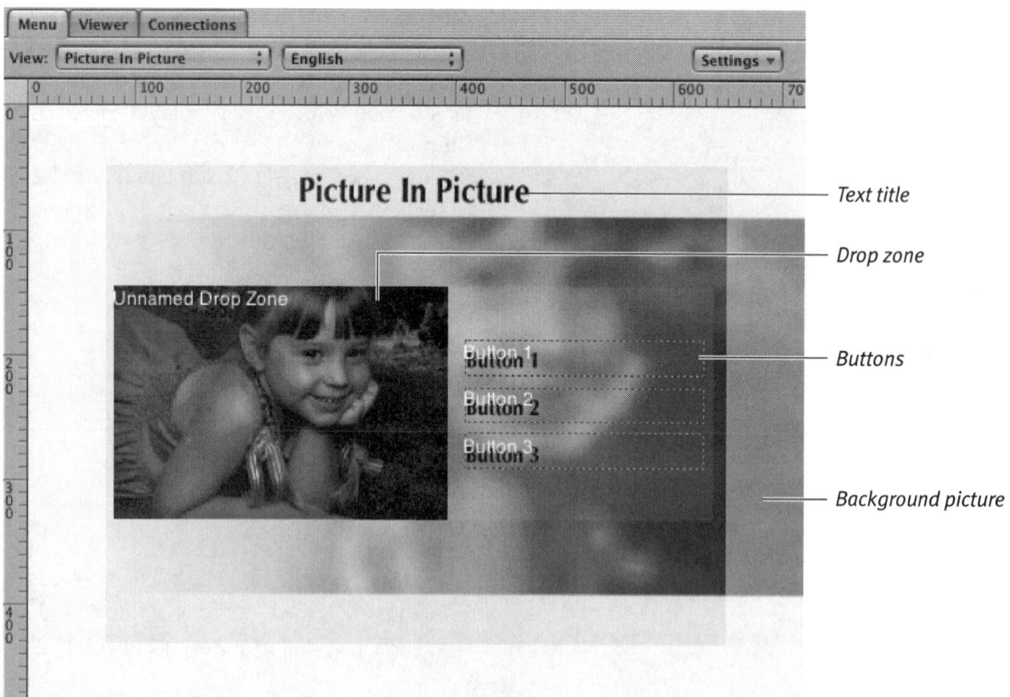

Figure 17.34 The iDVD theme is converted into a menu when imported into DVD Studio Pro. You can modify any text, drop zones, or buttons or even the background picture and then save the menu as a custom template.

About Styles

Styles, which are stored on the Styles tab of the Palette, contain color, font, and other attributes for menu *objects* (**Figure 17.35**). Menu objects include buttons, text, drop zones, and even the layout for the alignment of the other objects on the menu. Not only can styles help you maintain a consistent image for the projects you create, it can save you quite a lot of time as well.

You can apply Apple stock styles as is, modify the stock styles, or create your own styles, much as you can with templates. And as with templates, you can create styles for use in future projects or save them to your project file. You must save your project, however, before you can save a style to the project's file.

Styles are also video standard–specific. You'll need to create different styles for NTSC and for PAL projects.

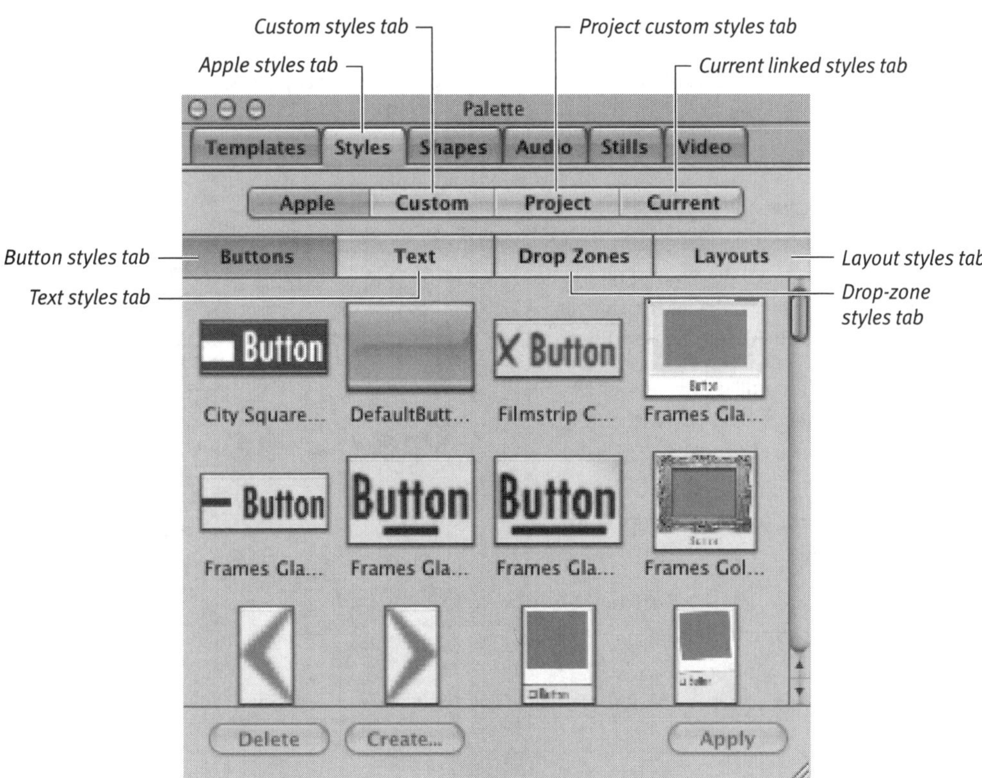

Figure 17.35 The Palette separates styles based on their type and origin. For example, you can view Apple styles, which come with DVD Studio Pro, or you can view styles you've created. (Current linked styles are discussed later in this chapter in the section "Linking Styles to Templates.")

Using Styles

You can assign a style to an existing menu object, or you can drag a style from the Palette to the Menu editor to create a new button, text object, or drop zone that uses the selected style.

The steps for using button, text, drop-zone, and layout styles are similar. The steps outlined in this section show you how to apply a button style to a menu, but you can apply any other style using the same steps.

To apply a style to a button:

1. In the Menu editor, create a standard menu containing at least one button.
2. Choose View > Show Palette, or press Option-Command-P, to open the Palette.
3. In the Palette, click the Styles tab (**Figure 17.36**).

   The Styles tab opens, displaying all of the styles that you can use in your project; the Apple tab is displayed by default.
4. If the Apple tab is not displayed, click it to view the styles that come with DVD Studio Pro (refer to Figure 17.36).

   Apple's styles are displayed. You can choose among button, text, drop-zone, and layout styles.
5. On the Apple tab, click the Buttons tab to view the stock button styles.

   The button styles that come with DVD Studio Pro are displayed in the Palette (**Figure 17.37**).

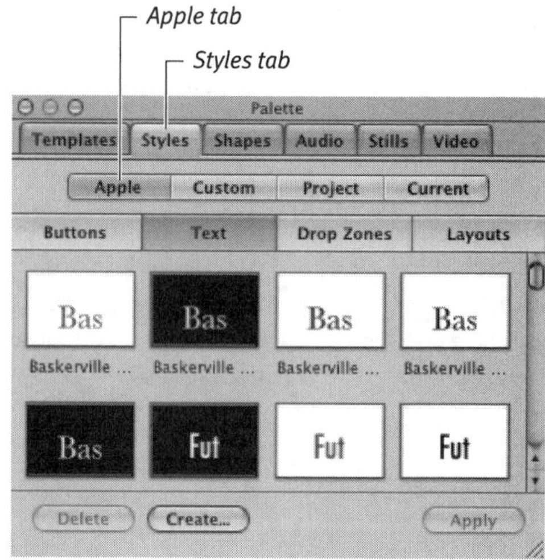

Figure 17.36 Click the Styles tab in the Palette to view all styles.

Figure 17.37 Click the Styles tab, Apple tab, and then Buttons tab in the Palette to display the button styles that come with DVD Studio Pro.

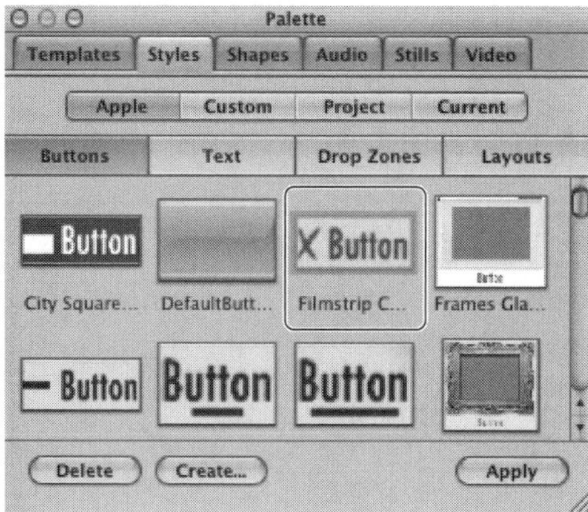

Figure 17.38 Select a button style in the Palette to apply it to a button on your menu.

6. On the Buttons tab, select a button style (**Figure 17.38**).
7. In the Menu editor, select the button to which you want to apply the style.
8. *Do one of the following:*
   - ▲ In the Palette, double-click the button style.
   - ▲ At the bottom right of the Palette, click the Apply button.
   - ▲ From the Palette, drag the button style into the Menu editor and drop it on top of your button (**Figure 17.39**).

   The button style is applied, and the button resizes to fit the style. The size, shape, highlight colors, text, font, and button shadow attributes are assigned for the button. You can, however, modify the button as desired.

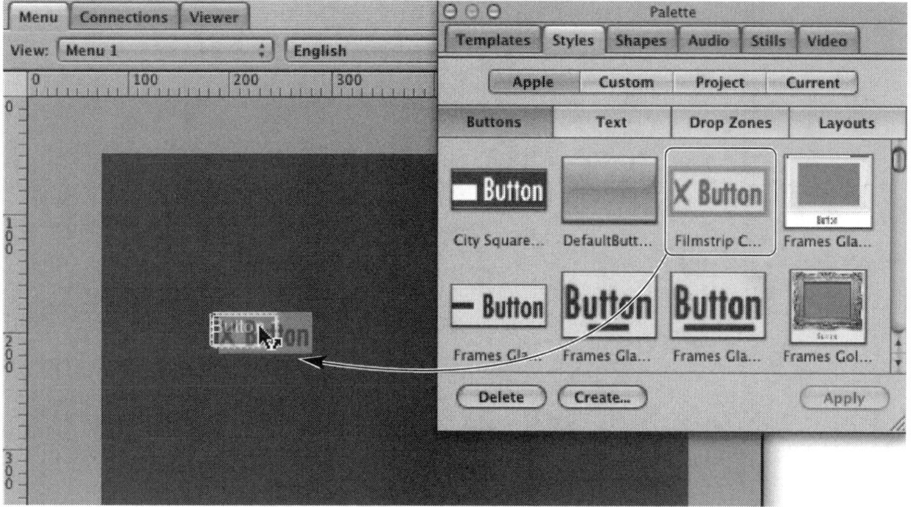

Figure 17.39 You can drag a button style directly to the button in the Menu editor.

To create a new button using a style:

1. In the Outline or Graphical view, create a new standard menu.
2. Double-click the new menu.
   The menu opens in the Menu editor.
3. If the Palette is closed, choose View > Show Palette, or press Option-Command-P, to open it.
4. In the Palette, click the Styles tab, Apple tab, and then Buttons tab to display the styles that come with DVD Studio Pro.
5. Select a button style from the list in the Palette (**Figure 17.40**).
6. Drag the selected button style to any empty area in the Menu editor (**Figure 17.41**) and hold down your mouse button for about 2 seconds.
   A shortcut menu appears in the Menu editor (refer to Figure 17.41).

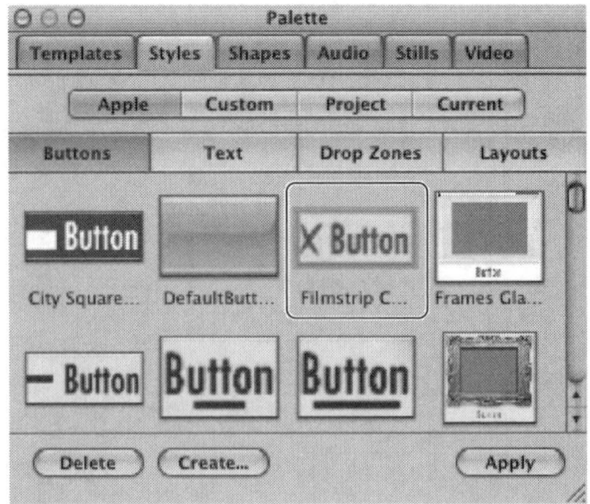

Figure 17.40 Select a button style in the Palette to use when creating your new button.

Figure 17.41 Drag a button style from the Palette to any empty area in the Menu editor. If you wait about 2 seconds before releasing the mouse button, this shortcut menu will appear.

7. From the shortcut menu that appears, *choose one of the following options:*
   - **Create Button: Set Style.** A button is created, and the style is set for that button only. You will need to assign the button style to any new button you create if you want to use the same style.
   - **Create Button: Set Default Button Style in Menu.** A button is created, and the style is set for the selected menu. Any new buttons you create will use the same style automatically.
   - **Set Default Button Style.** A button is not created, but the button style is set for the selected menu. Any new buttons you create on the selected menu will use the set style (existing buttons are not affected).

✔ Tips

- You cannot remove a button style from a menu once it has been set unless you undo the action. However, you can replace the menu's set button style by setting a new button style for the menu.
- The default action when you drag and drop a style on any empty area in the Menu editor is to create a new button and set the style. You don't have to wait for the shortcut menu unless you want to set the default button style for the entire menu.
- If you've already added buttons to your menu and want to change the style for all buttons, hold down the Shift key to select all of the buttons on your menu. Select a style in the Palette and click Apply to apply the style to all selected buttons.

Creating Custom Styles

You can save a button, text object, drop-zone, or menu layout—and all of its attributes—as a single style for future use. If you use similar settings for multiple menus or projects, creating styles will save you valuable time.

The steps for creating different style types are similar. To create a button style, start by creating a button and setting its attributes; to create a menu layout style, create your menu in the Menu editor and save the layout as a layout style.

To create a text style:

1. Double-click the Menu editor.

   A text insertion cursor appears (**Figure 17.42**).
2. Type your text in the Menu editor.
3. Set text color, font, size, drop shadow, and other text attributes as desired.
4. Choose View > Show Palette, or press Option-Command-P, to open the Palette.

   The Palette opens, displaying the tab you selected last.
5. In the Palette, click the Styles tab (**Figure 17.43**).

   The styles are separated into four groups, Apple (stock), Custom (which you create), Project (custom styles saved to the project file), and Current (discussed later in this chapter in the section "Linking Styles to Templates").

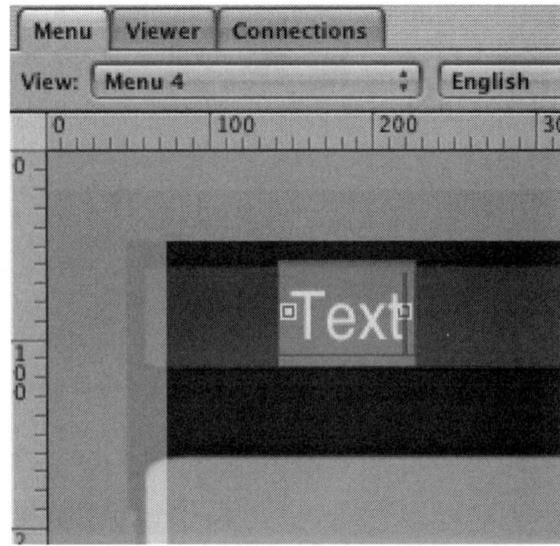

Figure 17.42 Double-click anywhere in the Menu editor and type your text directly on the menu.

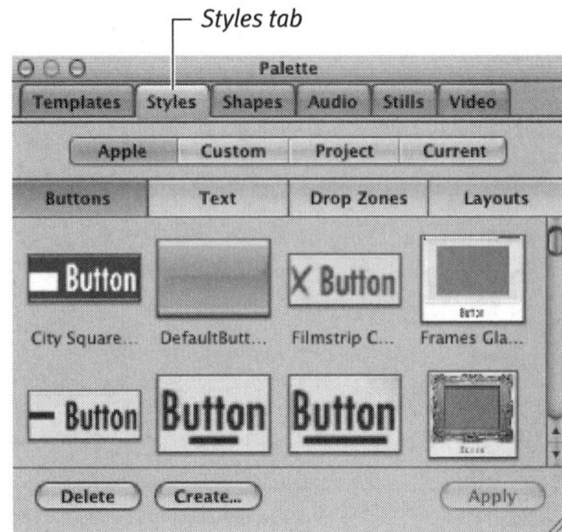

Figure 17.43 Click the Styles tab in the Palette to display the styles that are available for use in your project.

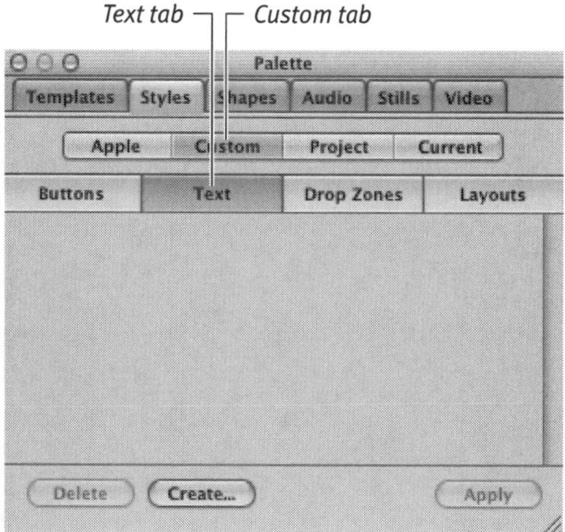

Figure 17.44 Click the Custom tab to display your custom styles; then click the Text tab to display your custom text styles.

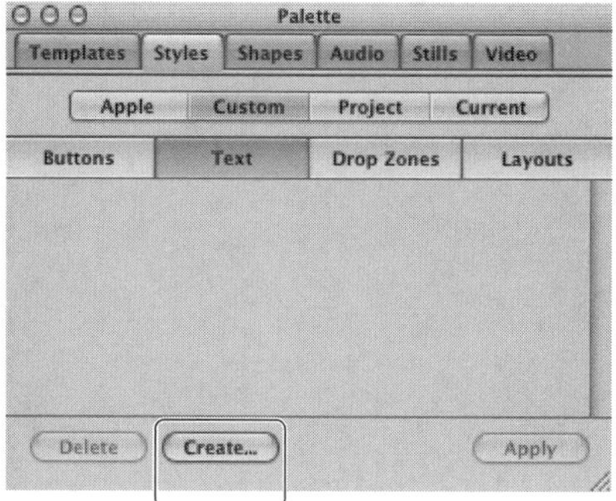

Figure 17.45 Click the Text tab's Create button to create a new text style.

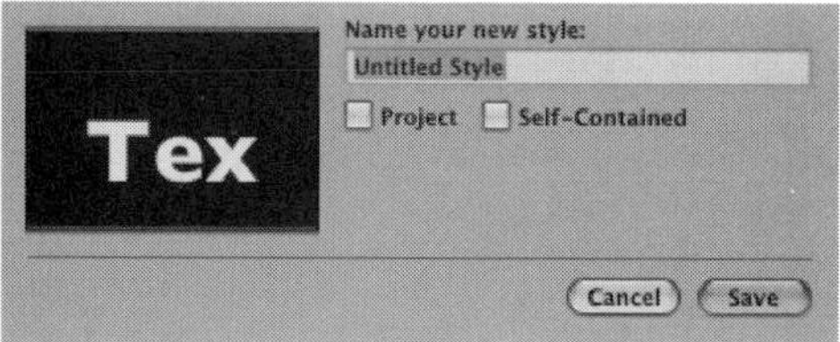

Figure 17.46 Type a name for your text style in the Save dialog.

6. On the Styles tab, click the Custom tab (**Figure 17.44**).

   Custom styles—which are divided into button styles, text styles, drop-zone styles, and layout styles—are displayed.

7. On the Custom tab, click the Text tab (refer to Figure 17.44).

   The text styles that you've created are displayed on the Text tab. If you haven't created any text styles, the list will be empty.

8. At the bottom of the Text tab, click Create (**Figure 17.45**).

   A Save dialog appears asking you to name the new text style (**Figure 17.46**).

continues on next page

9. In the Save dialog, type a name for your text style and click Save (refer to Figure 17.46).

   Your text style is saved and appears on the Palette's Custom Text tab (**Figure 17.47**).

✔ Tips

- Follow the same steps to create button styles, drop-zone styles, and layout styles.
- You can also Control-click your text in the Menu editor and choose Create Text Style from the shortcut menu that appears to quickly save your text as a style (**Figure 17.48**).

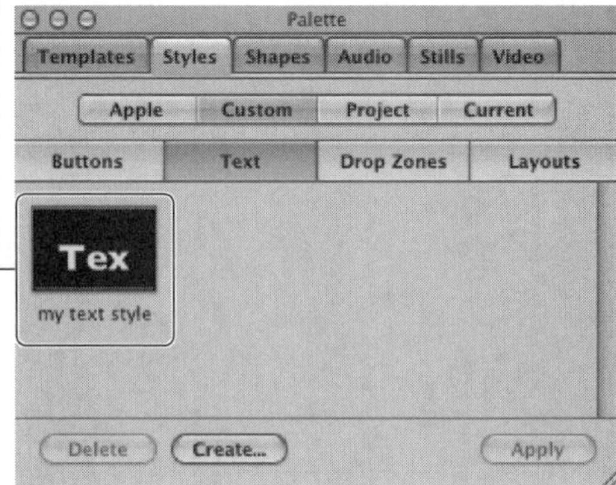

Figure 17.47 Your new text style appears on the Palette's Custom Text tab.

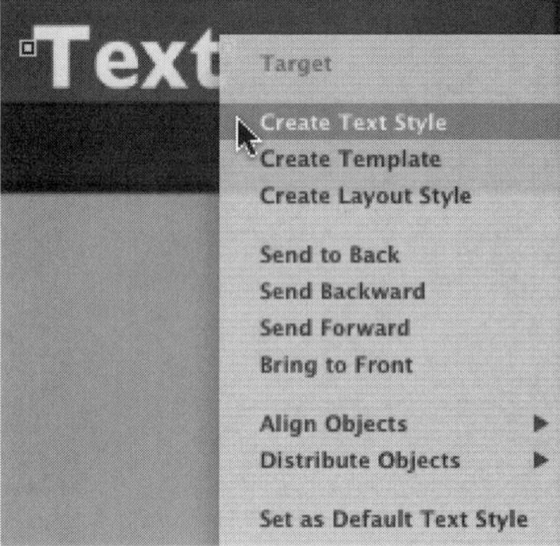

Figure 17.48 Control-click the text you created in the Menu editor and choose Create Text Style from the shortcut menu to save the text as a style.

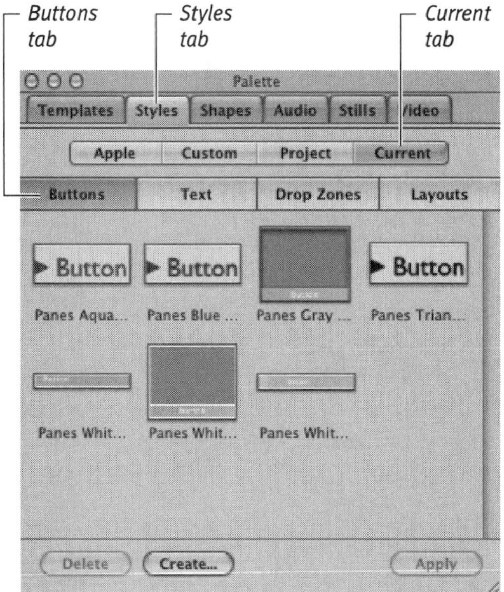

Figure 17.49 Button styles that are linked to a template are displayed on the Styles tab, on the Buttons tab of the Current tab.

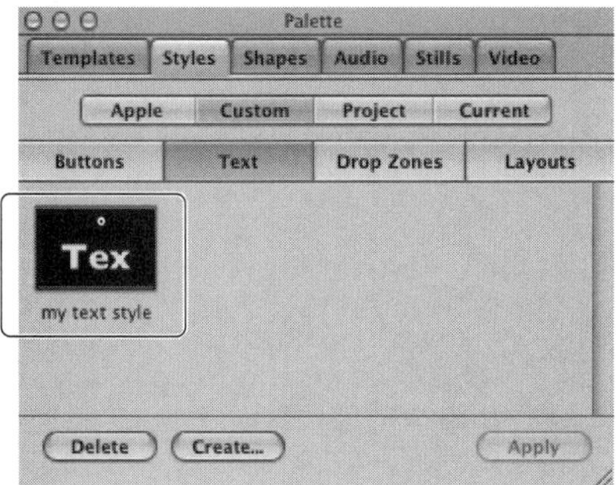

Figure 17.50 Open the Palette and click Styles and then Custom and then Text to view your custom text styles.

Linking Styles to Templates

Linking styles to templates is like creating a favorites playlist of similar styles for each template. You can link any of your custom styles to any template so that when you use the template, you can quickly see the styles used to create it. Linking styles helps you see what styles were used, or are associated with, a particular template. This is useful when, for example, you want to quickly find the button size, font, and drop shadow placement used in one template so you can use the button style in another menu.

Apple stock templates are linked to the styles that they use. As a result, when you apply an Apple template to your menu, you can see the associated button, text, drop-zone, and layout styles (if any) on the Current tab (**Figure 17.49**).

You can't link the styles that come with DVD Studio Pro to your custom templates, but you can link your custom styles to Apple's stock templates. You can also link your custom styles to your own custom templates.

To link a style to a template:

1. Choose View > Show Palette, or press Option-Command-P, to open the Palette.
2. In the Palette, click Styles and then Custom and then Text to view your custom text styles (**Figure 17.50**).

continues on next page

3. On the Text tab, Control-click your custom text.

   A shortcut menu appears (**Figure 17.51**).

4. From the shortcut menu, choose Link to Templates (refer to Figure 17.51).

   A dialog appears, asking you to select all templates to which you want to link your text style (**Figure 17.52**). The list contains all templates: stock and custom.

5. Select the check boxes of the templates that you want to link to your text style (**Figure 17.53**).

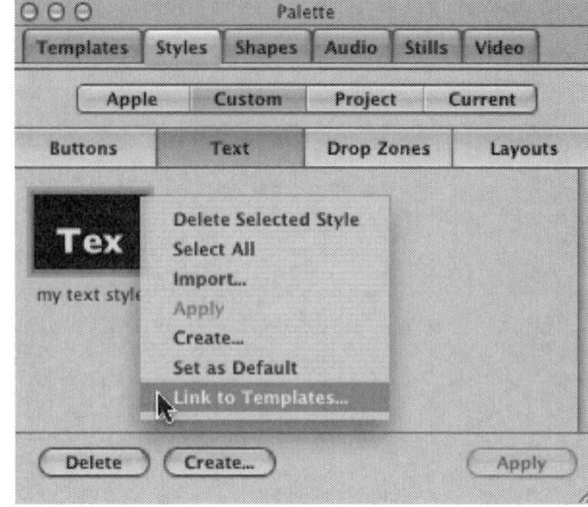

Figure 17.51 Control-click your text style on the Palette's Text tab and choose Link to Templates from the shortcut menu that appears.

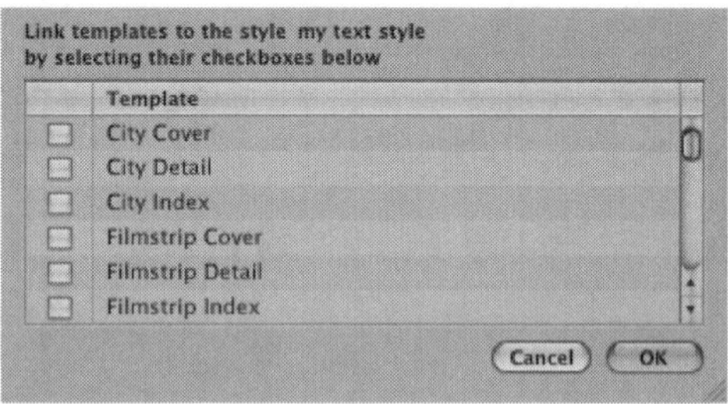

Figure 17.52 The dialog lists all templates, both stock and custom.

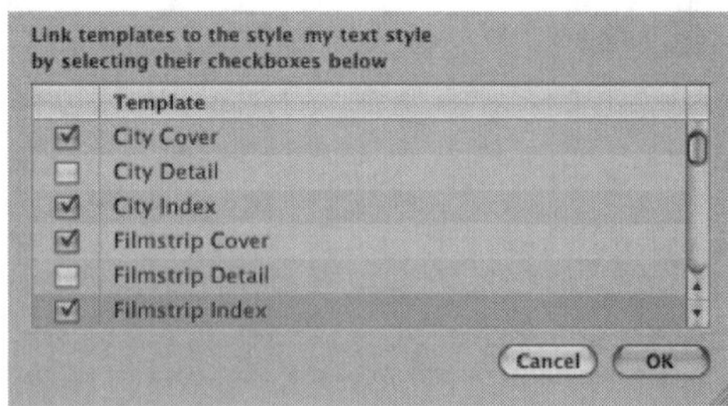

Figure 17.53 Select all of the templates to which you want to link your style and click OK.

Linking Styles to Templates

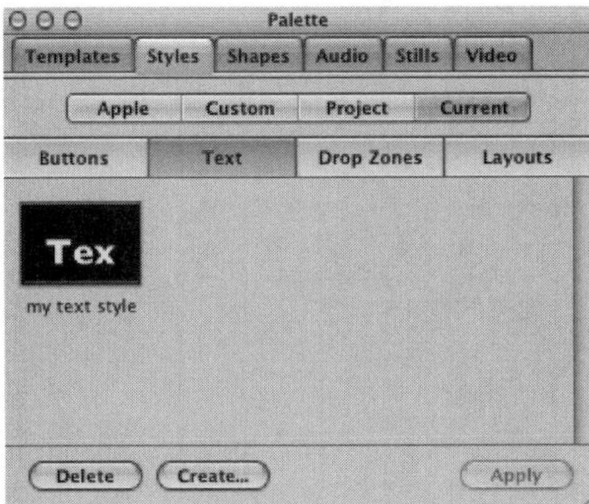

Figure 17.54 When a template that has been linked to your text style is applied to a menu, the text style appears on the Palette's Current Text Styles tab.

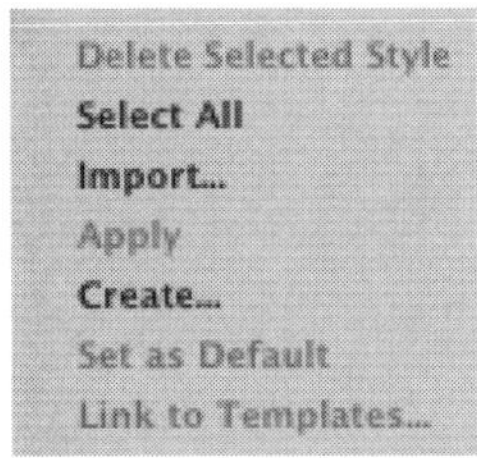

Figure 17.55 Apple styles cannot be linked to templates. They are, however, linked to the Apple templates.

6. Click OK to close the dialog.

   The dialog closes, and all links are created. When you apply a template to your menu in the Menu editor to which the text style has been linked, the text style appears on the Palette's Current Text Styles tab (**Figure 17.54**).

✔ Tips

- If Link to Templates is dimmed in the Text tab's shortcut menu (**Figure 17.55**), check to make sure that you have Control-clicked a custom template. Apple styles cannot be linked.
- You can link your style to as many templates as you like by selecting multiple check boxes.

About Shapes

Normal buttons and drop zones are square; applying a shape allows you to make them look round, triangular, octagonal—or any other shape that strikes your fancy. You create button or drop-zone shapes using Photoshop layers, which provide a *mask* with irregular edges for your video or picture to show through. Thanks to shapes, you're no longer limited to a square. You can customize the appearance of your picture and its active elements by controlling its borders with a shape.

Unlike styles—which contain attributes for buttons, text, drop zones, and layouts—shapes are four-layer Photoshop documents that can be used only for buttons and drop zones. Shapes do not contain the settings for these buttons and drop zones; they merely contain the graphics used for their edges and highlight overlays.

✔ Tips

- Shapes aren't video standard–specific. You can easily create one shape and apply it to drop zones and buttons on both your NTSC and PAL DVD-Video projects.
- DVD Studio Pro provides a few prefab shapes, but you may find it easier to create your own and reuse the ones that suit the types of projects you create.

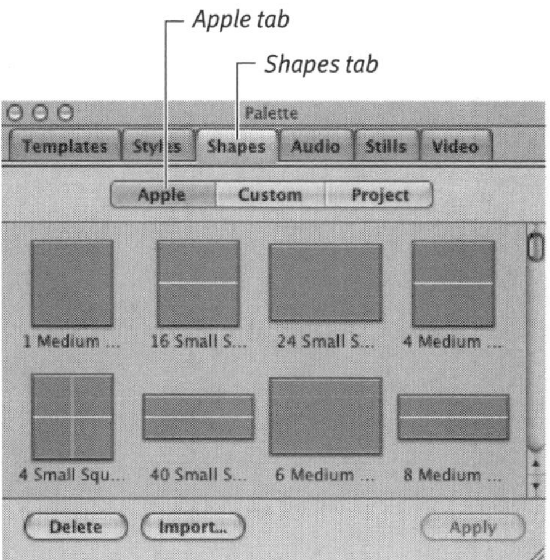

Figure 17.56 The Apple tab is selected by default when you click the Shapes tab.

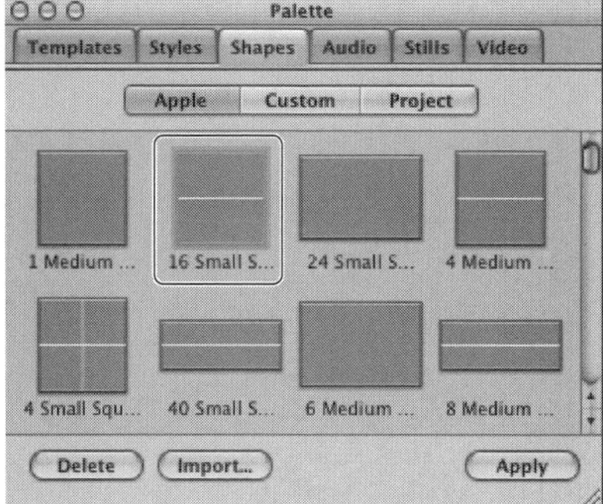

Figure 17.57 Select one of DVD Studio Pro's prefab shapes from the Apple tab.

Using Shapes

You can dress up your buttons and drop zones with irregular edges by applying shapes to them in the Menu editor. Although the button hotspot will still be square, the button itself will appear round or irregularly shaped.

The best thing about shapes is that once they're applied to a menu, you can set assets inside them. The shape itself acts like a frame that displays the asset over the menu. Consequently, shapes are a good way to quickly customized menus.

To apply a shape to a button:

1. In the Menu editor, open a standard menu and create at least one button.
2. If the Palette is closed, choose View > Show Palette, or press Option-Command-P, to open it.
3. In the Palette, click the Shapes tab (**Figure 17.56**).

   The Shapes tab is separated into three categories: Apple's stock shapes, custom shapes that you create, and custom project shapes that you've saved to your project file. The Apple tab is selected by default, displaying the shapes that came with DVD Studio Pro. If the Apple tab is not selected, click it to display the Apple shapes.
4. On the Apple tab, select a shape (**Figure 17.57**).

continues on next page

5. In the Menu editor, select a button and *do one of the following:*
   - ▲ At the bottom right of the Apple tab, click Apply (**Figure 17.58**).
   - ▲ On the Apple tab, double-click the selected shape.

   The shape is applied to the button that you selected in the Menu editor.

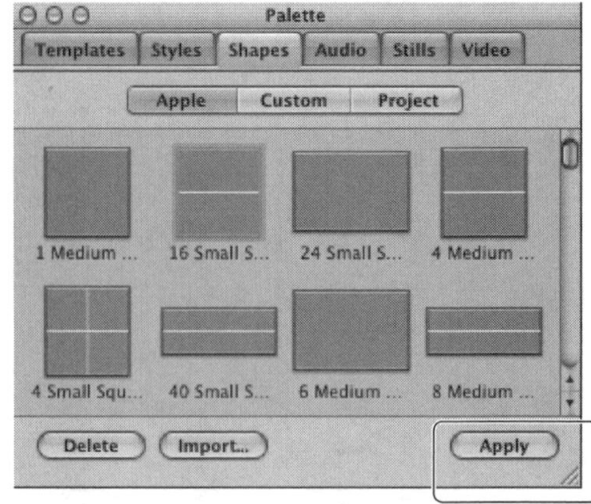

Figure 17.58 Click Apply at the bottom right of the Palette, or double-click the selected shape, to apply the shape to a menu.

✔ Tips

- You can apply shapes to drop zones the same way that you apply them to buttons.
- Drop zones ignore button highlights.
- You can also drag a shape from the Palette to the Menu editor to create a new button or drop zone that automatically uses the shape (**Figure 17.59**). When you drag the shape into the Menu editor, hold down the mouse button for about 2 seconds to display a shortcut menu. The shortcut menu lets you choose whether to create a button or a drop zone and set the shape.
- Some stock Apple shapes are intended for drop zones only. These shapes do not contain button highlights.

Figure 17.59 Drag a shape from the Palette to the Menu editor and hold down the mouse button for about 2 seconds to see this shortcut menu.

Creating Custom Shapes

Making your own shapes involves creating a four-layer image in Photoshop and adding graphics to each layer. This chapter assumes that you have a basic understanding of how to use Photoshop. If you need a Photoshop primer, see Chapter 3. "Preparing Graphics."

The Photoshop document used to create a DVD Studio Pro shape is made up of these four layers:

- **Icon layer.** When you import your shape into DVD Studio Pro, it's displayed in the Palette. The Palette uses thumbnail images to display a fair representation of the shapes that you can use in your projects. The fourth layer at the top of your layer stack, the Icon layer contains a picture of your shape that acts as a thumbnail in the Palette.
- **Highlight layer.** The Highlight layer is the third layer in the Photoshop document. For shapes that are intended for use with buttons, you can include a button highlight overlay right in the same Photoshop document. (For information on how to create button highlights, see Chapter 15, "Overlay Menus.") Later you can set the highlight colors used in the Menu editor.
- **Shape layer.** The Shape layer, the second layer from the bottom of the Photoshop document, uses RGB colors to display the edges of the shape. This is the layer that the viewer will see and is the normal state for buttons. Transparent areas of the Shape layer allow you to see through to the menu background and/or the asset set into the shape. Graduated transparency is allowed.
- **Mask layer.** The first layer (bottom layer) is the mask, which determines the viewable area of assets set into the shape. The Mask layer uses grayscale colors to tell the Menu editor what part of the set asset should be opaque (100 percent white) and what part of the shape should be transparent (100 percent black).

continues on next page

What Are Patches?

A *patch* is a special type of Apple shape that ships with DVD Studio Pro 3—you cannot create your own patches. What makes them so special? They contain animated or still graphic overlays, which apply effects such as wipes, fades, and color hues.

DVD Studio Pro comes with several patch shapes for you to use in your projects. You can apply Apple's patches to any drop zone or button that you create in the Menu editor. When you place a picture or video clip inside a drop zone, the patch overlay changes its look. When you apply a patch shape to a drop zone and drop a video clip into the drop zone, the video clip shows film scratches over the video frame when it's played instead of the plain video without the special effect, for example.

Normal shapes use the Photoshop document extension (.psd). Patches use the .pox extension, which is associated with the tool that Apple uses to create the unique effects overlays.

Using Photoshop, you must create all four layers of the shape. Layer names are unimportant, but you must ensure that each layer contains only the correct type of graphics and is in the right place in the layer order. If you don't, DVD Studio Pro will not parse the shape correctly.

✔ Tips

- When shapes are used in the Menu editor, they are automatically scaled to the Photoshop document's proportions.
- You can resize shapes in the Menu editor, but as with all bitmapped images, if you increase the size of a shape, the shape will start to look pixilated. Because of this, it's a good idea to create the shape at the largest size for which you intend to use it and then reduce the size in the Menu editor.
- Keep square pixels in mind—especially when creating circles—and resize your graphics accordingly. (For more information on square pixels, see Chapter 3.)

To create a new Photoshop document for use with shapes:

1. Open Photoshop.
2. Choose File > New (**Figure 17.60**), or press Command-N, to create a new document.

   The New dialog appears (**Figure 17.61**).
3. In the New dialog, type a name for your shape (**Figure 17.62**).

   This name appears in DVD Studio Pro's Palette when you import the shape.
4. From the Width and Height pop-up menus, choose Pixels to display your document size in pixels (**Figure 17.63**).

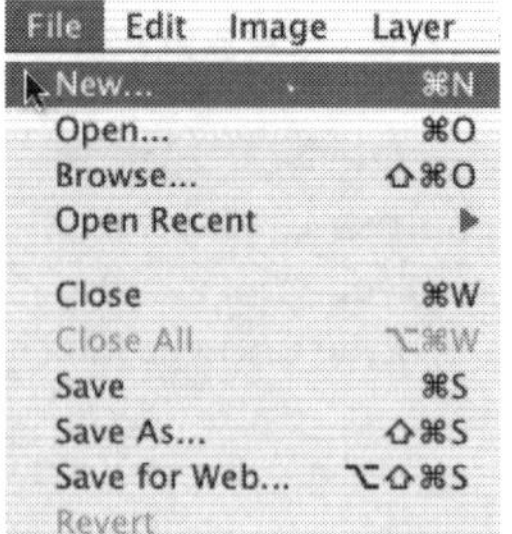

Figure 17.60 Choose File > New to create a new Photoshop document.

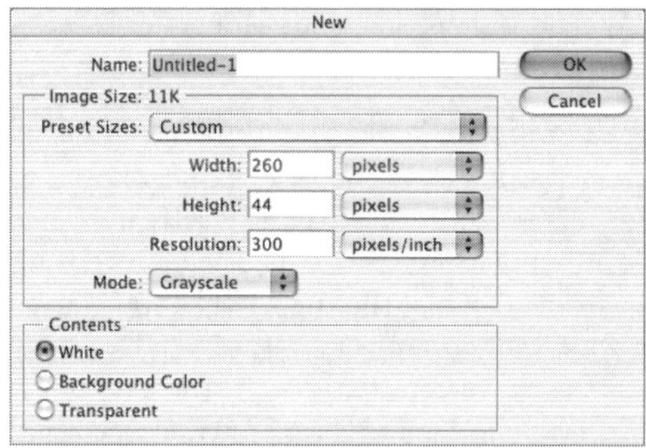

Figure 17.61 Configure the New dialog's settings to prepare the Photoshop document for use with shapes.

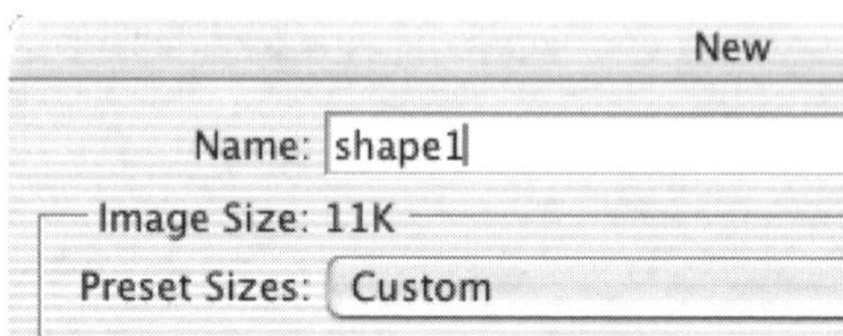

Figure 17.62 Type a new name for your shape.

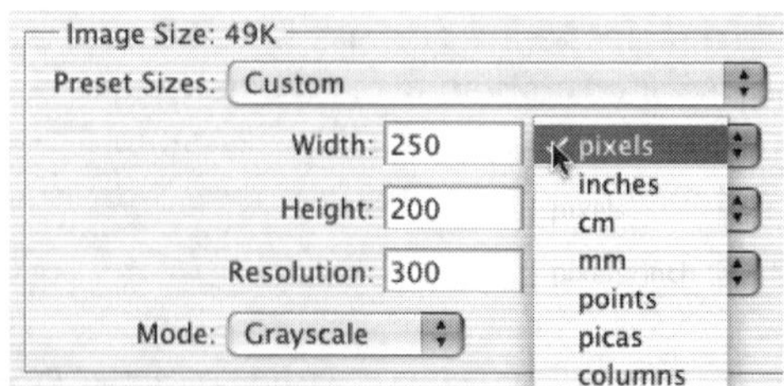

Figure 17.63 Select Pixels from the Width and Height pop-up menus to display your document size measurements in pixels.

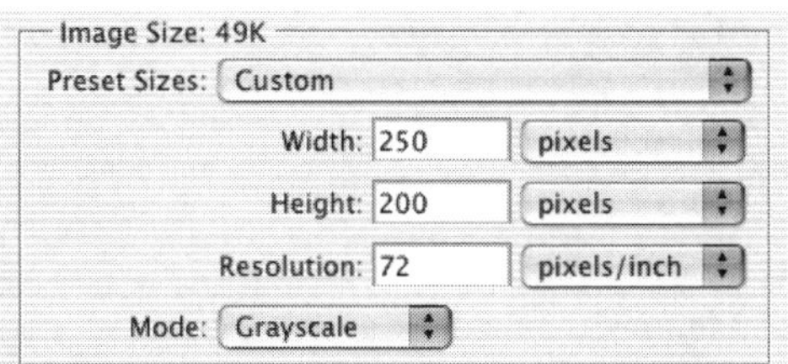

Figure 17.64 In the Width and Height text boxes, enter your shape's measurements (in pixels). Type 72 in the Resolution field to set the document's resolution.

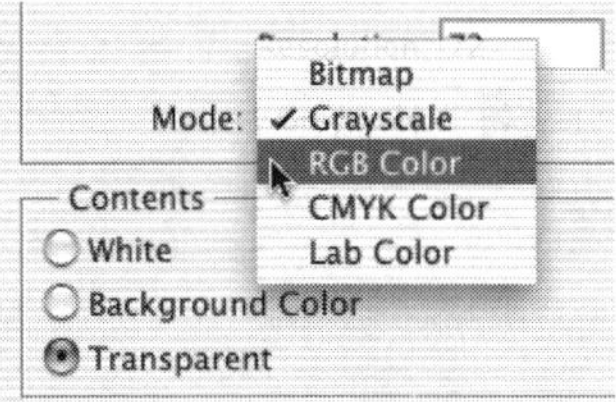

Figure 17.65 Shapes are created using RGB colors and a transparent background.

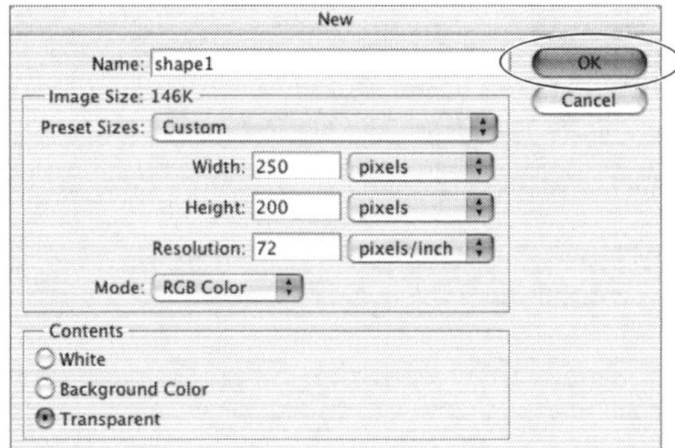

Figure 17.66 Click OK to create a new document with the settings you've specified.

5. In the Width and Height text boxes, type your desired measurements (in pixels). The measurements you choose depend on the shape's intended use (**Figure 17.64**).
6. In the Resolution text box, type 72 (refer to Figure 17.64).
7. From the Mode pop-up menu, choose RGB Color (**Figure 17.65**).
8. In the New dialog's Contents section, select the Transparent radio button (refer to Figure 17.65).

   All shapes, whether intended for buttons or drop zones, should be transparent documents.
9. At the top right of the New dialog, click OK (**Figure 17.66**).

   A new Photoshop document is created with the settings that you entered.

To create a shape:

1. Create a new Photoshop document with the same width and height as the shape you want to create.
2. In Photoshop, choose Window > Layers to open the Layers palette (**Figure 17.67**).

   The Layers palette appears (**Figure 17.68**).
3. At the bottom of the Layers palette, click the New Layer icon to create a new layer (refer to Figure 17.68).

   A new layer, Layer 2, is created in your Photoshop document and displayed in the Layers palette (**Figure 17.69**).

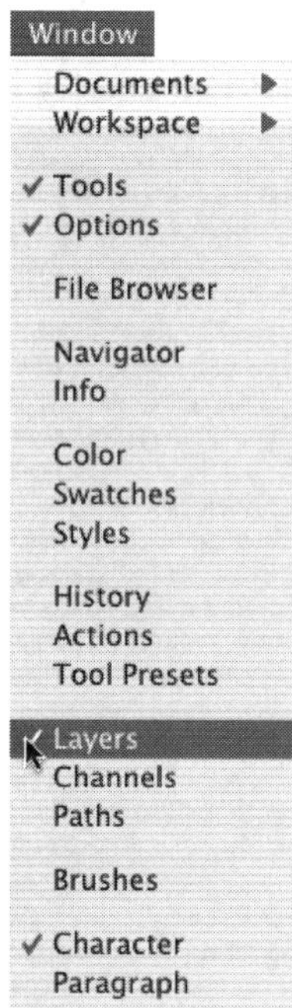

Figure 17.67 Choose Window > Layers to open the Layers palette.

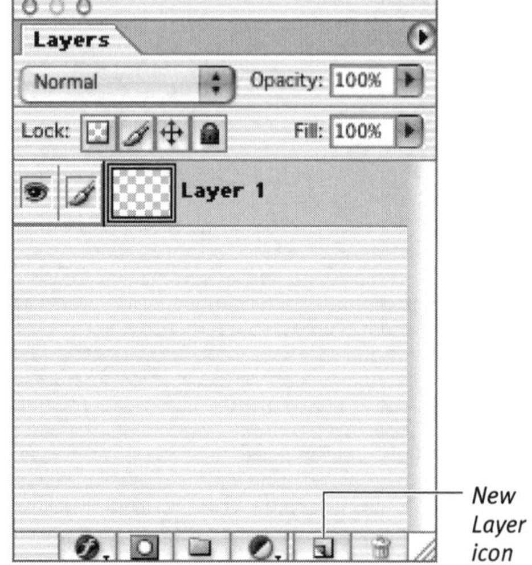

Figure 17.68 Click the New Layer icon to create a new layer in your Photoshop document.

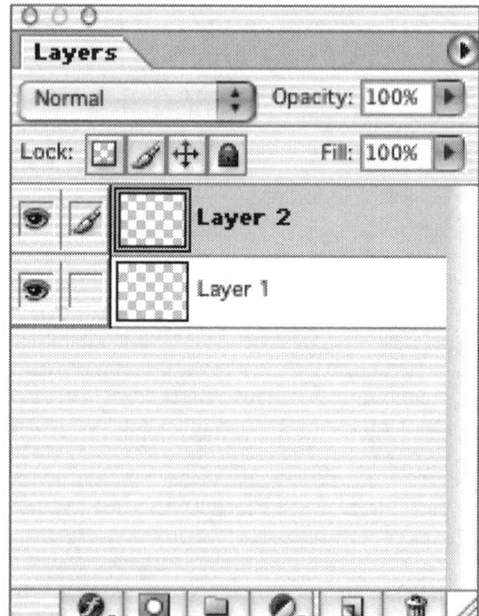

Figure 17.69 When you click the New Layer icon, a new layer is created in the Layers palette.

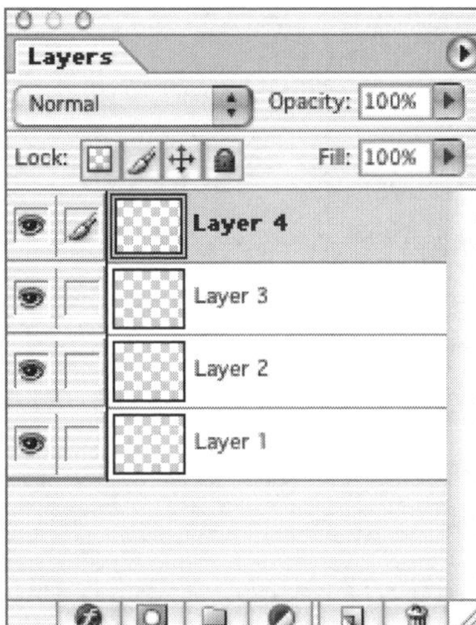

Figure 17.70 Create a total of four layers in your Photoshop document. DVD Studio Pro will not import a shape unless it has four layers.

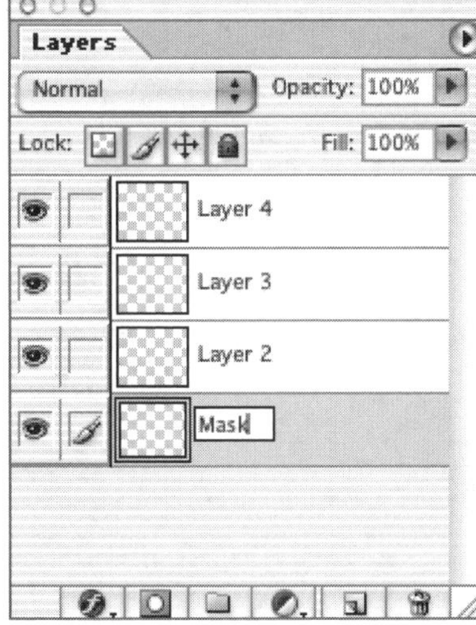

Figure 17.71 Rename Layer 1 as Mask.

4. Repeat step 3 until you have a total of four layers in your Photoshop document (**Figure 17.70**).
5. In the Layers palette, double-click Layer 1 and type the word `Mask`.

   Layer 1's name changes to Mask (**Figure 17.71**).
6. With the Mask layer (Layer 1) still selected in the Layers palette, draw an image on the canvas using grayscale (shades of white and black) colors only (**Figure 17.72**).

continues on next page

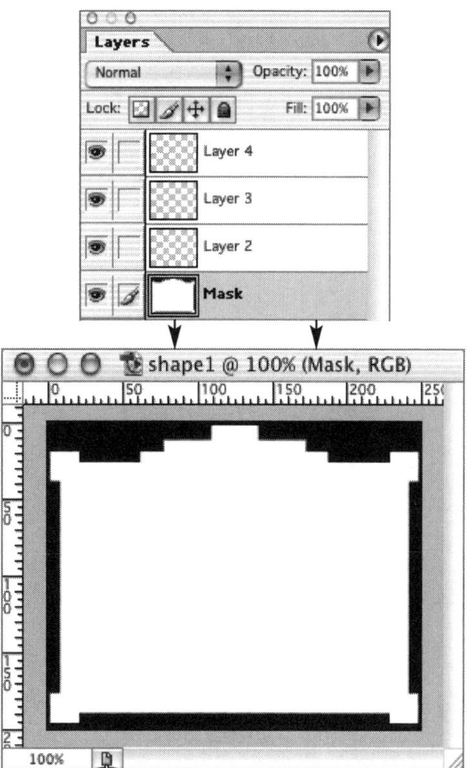

Figure 17.72 Select the Mask layer in the Layers palette (top) and create a grayscale image on the canvas (bottom).

The Mask layer determines the viewable area of any asset set into the shape.

White areas on your Mask layer will display set assets at 100 percent opaque; black areas on the Mask layer will display pictures at 100 percent transparent.

7. In the Layers palette, double-click Layer 2 and type Shape.

   Layer 2's name changes to Shape (**Figure 17.73**).

8. With the Shape layer still selected in the Layers palette, add the graphics to the shape (**Figure 17.74**).

   This is the graphic that viewers will see when you use this shape with buttons or drop zones—in essence, this graphic forms the frame that appears around assets set in the shape. The Shape layer also constitutes the Normal state for buttons that use this shape.

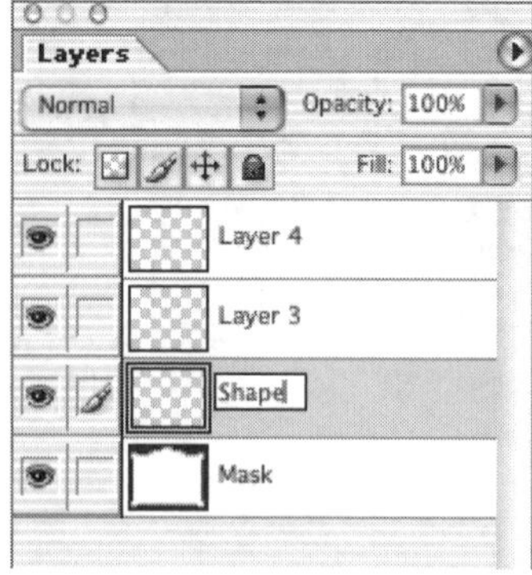

Figure 17.73 Rename Layer 2 as Shape.

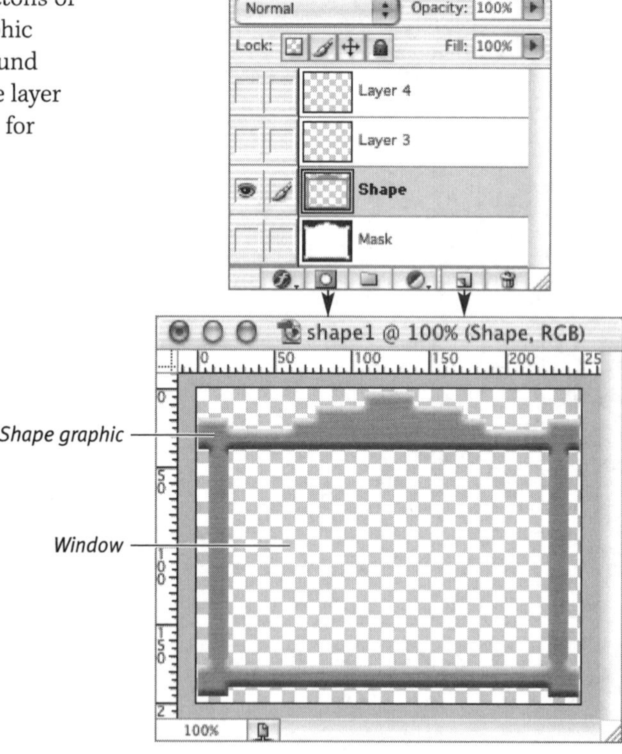

Figure 17.74 The Shape layer is the graphic that viewers will see when this shape is used on buttons or drop zones. To allow pictures to show through, you need to leave a transparent window inside the graphic.

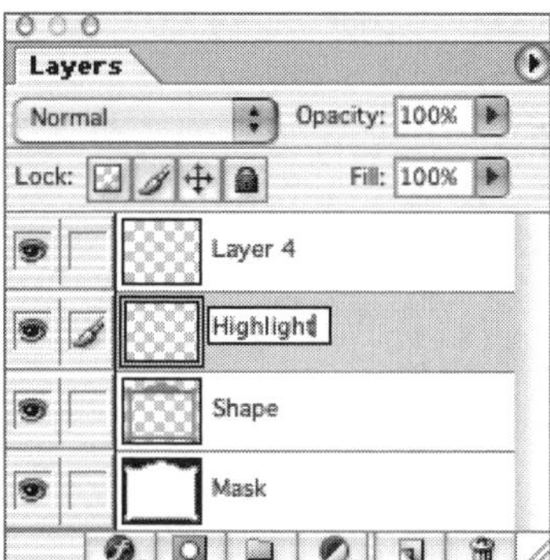

Figure 17.75 Double-click Layer 3 and rename it as Highlight.

9. In the Layers palette, double-click Layer 3 and type `Highlight`.

   Layer 3's name changes to Highlight (**Figure 17.75**).

10. With the Highlight layer still selected in the Layers palette, paint the desired button highlight area (**Figure 17.76**).

    The highlight area will be used as the button-color mapping key in DVD Studio Pro's Menu editor.

11. In the Layers palette, double-click Layer 4 and type `Icon`. (This layer can also be called Thumbnail; either name will work.)

    Layer 4's name changes to Icon (**Figure 17.77**).

continues on next page

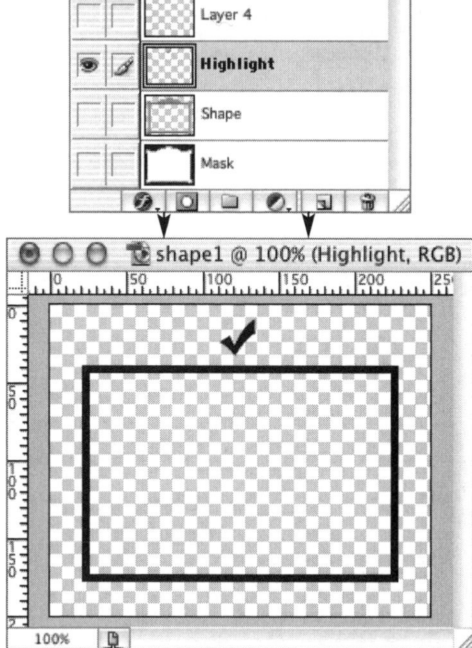

Figure 17.76 Select the Highlight layer in the Layers palette (top) and create a grayscale button highlight image on the canvas (bottom). The Highlight layer is used by buttons to display the highlight overlay. Drop zones ignore this layer.

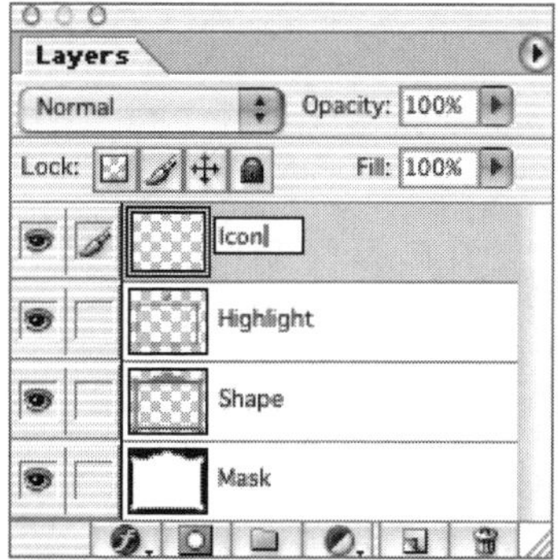

Figure 17.77 Double-click Layer 4 and rename it as Icon. This layer is used to display the thumbnail on DVD Studio Pro's Custom Shapes tab on the Palette.

12. With the Icon layer still selected in the Layers palette, create an RGB graphic to use as the thumbnail in DVD Studio Pro's Palette (**Figure 17.78**).

13. Choose File > Save (**Figure 17.79**), or press Command-S, to save the four-layered Photoshop document.

    The Save As dialog appears (**Figure 17.80**).

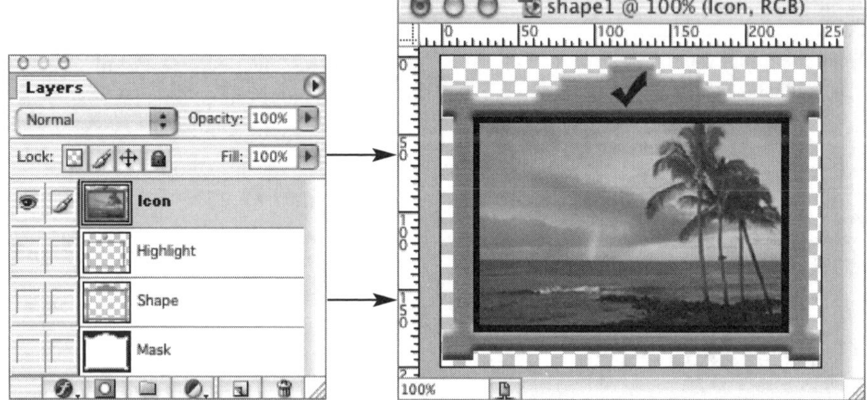

Figure 17.78 Select the Icon layer in the Layers palette (left) and create an RGB thumbnail image on the canvas (right). The Icon layer should be representative of your shape so that it's easily recognizable in the Palette. This picture will be displayed as a thumbnail in DVD Studio Pro's Palette.

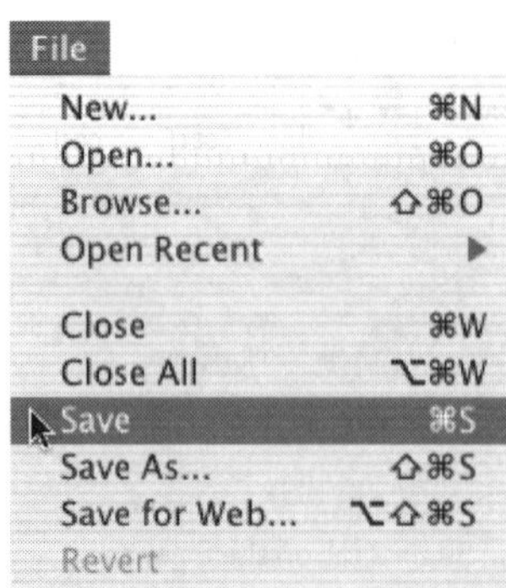

Figure 17.79 Choose File > Save to save the Photoshop document.

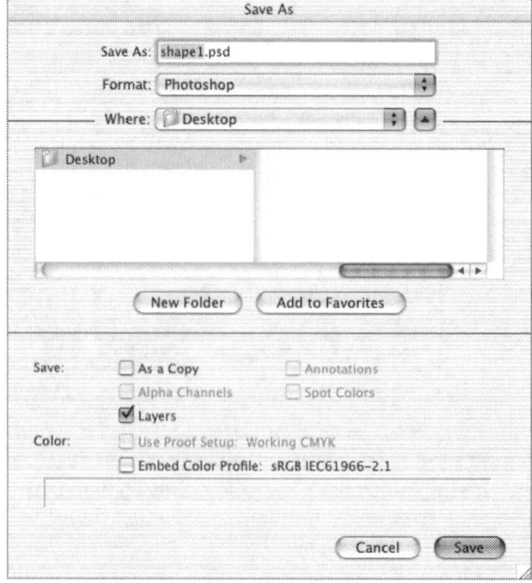

Figure 17.80 The Save As dialog appears when you save your Photoshop document.

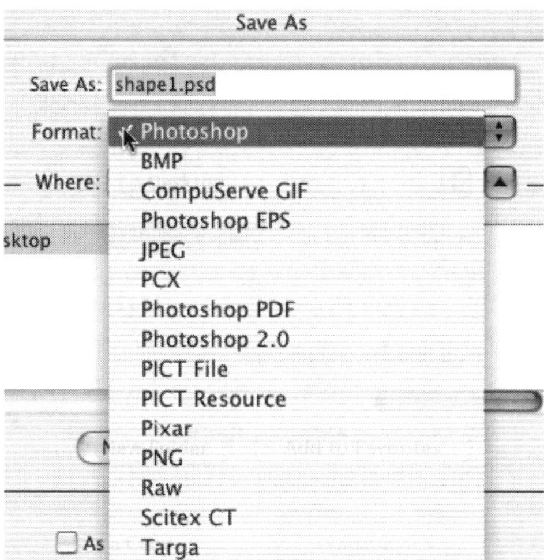

Figure 17.81 Save your shape as a Photoshop document by choosing Photoshop from the Format pop-up menu.

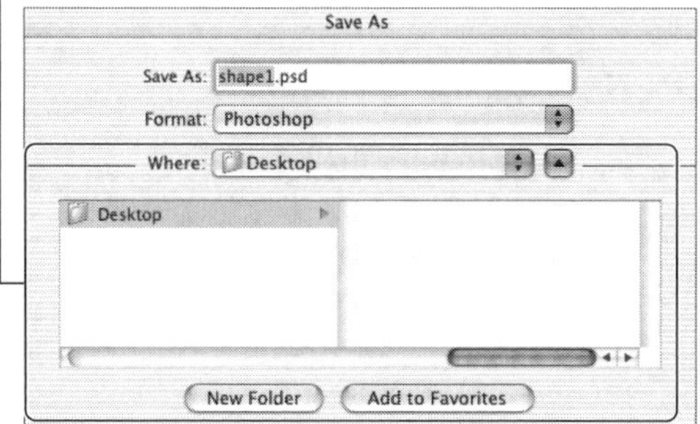

Figure 17.82 Navigate to the location where you want to save your Photoshop document.

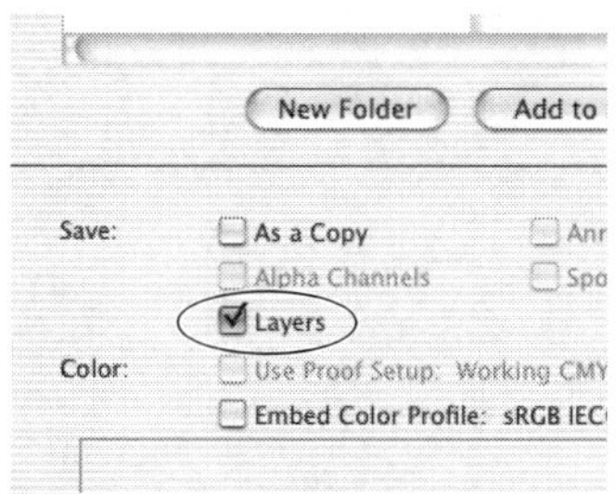

Figure 17.83 Select the Layers check box to save all layers with your Photoshop document.

14. From the Save As dialog's Format pop-up menu, choose Photoshop (**Figure 17.81**).

The document is saved as a PSD file.

15. In the Save As dialog's Where section, navigate to the location on your hard disk where you want to save the shape (**Figure 17.82**).

Choose a location that's easy to find because you'll need to import that shape into DVD Studio Pro later.

16. At the bottom left of the Save As dialog, click the Layers check box if it is not already selected (**Figure 17.83**).

17. At the bottom right of the Save As dialog, click Save (**Figure 17.84**).

Your four-layered shape is saved in the location you specified.

continues on next page

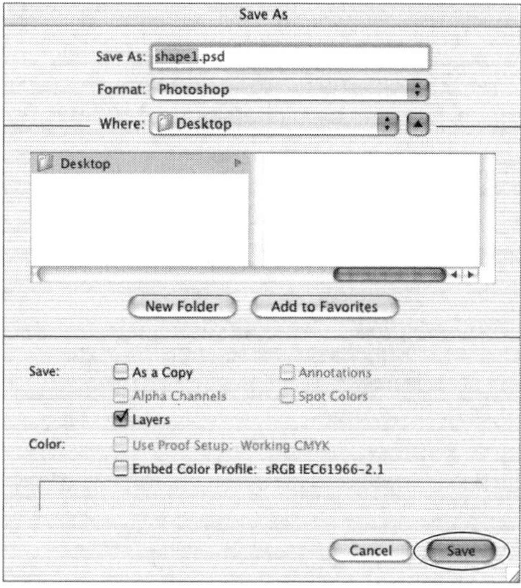

Figure 17.84 Click Save to save your four-layered shape.

✔ Tips

- The Mask layer should not be empty. If this layer doesn't contain anything, DVD Studio Pro cannot import the shape. If you don't want a viewable surface area for your shape, paint the layer black.
- There's a catch to creating multicolored highlights in shapes: DVD Studio Pro reads the transparency value of the highlight layer, not the grayscale value. For reference, 100 percent opaque maps to 100 percent black, 75 percent opaque maps to 66 percent black, 50 percent opaque maps to 33 percent black, and 0 percent opaque maps to 0 percent black.
- You don't need to add a highlight to a shape. If you intend to use the shape only for drop zones, you can leave the Highlight layer empty—but don't delete the layer!
- The Icon layer (Layer 4) cannot be left empty! If you don't provide a graphic on this layer, no graphic will appear in the Palette, and there will be no way to select or drag the shape into your project.
- Do not change the order of any layers in this Photoshop document.

Flattening Effects

All effects used when creating layers in a Photoshop shape document must be *flattened* before they can be imported into DVD Studio Pro. Flattening a layer stamps all effects into one layer. Transparency (or opacity) is an effect, but it isn't listed below the layer heading with the other effects (**Figure 17.85**). You can set the opacity for the Shape layer (**Figure 17.86**), but remember to create a new layer and merge the two layers together to stamp the opacity onto the layer. To merge the two layers, link them and press Command-E.

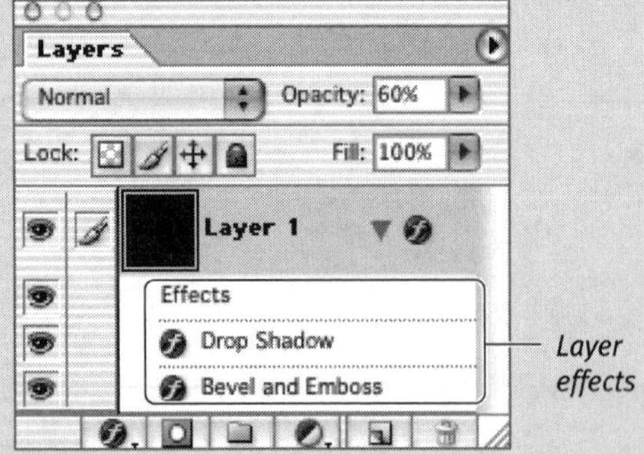

Figure 17.85 The layer effects displayed in this picture must be flattened before this shape document can be imported into DVD Studio Pro.

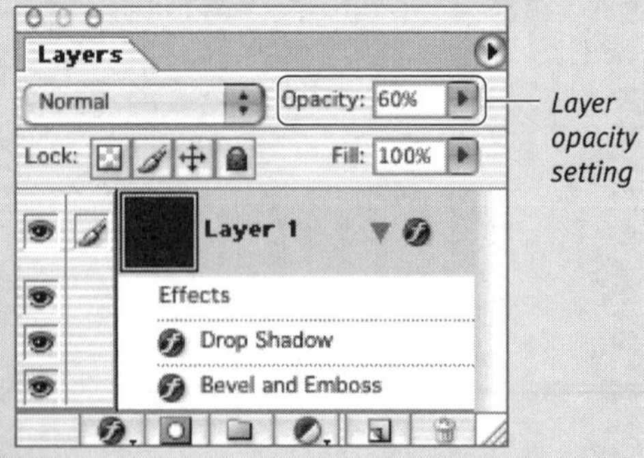

Figure 17.86 You can set an individual layer's opacity, but make sure to merge the opacity into the layer. The selected layer is 60 percent opaque.

Cropping Corners

If you've created your original Photoshop document so that it's much larger than it actually needs to be for your shape's mask area, you can crop the document down to the appropriate size.

Once you've finish creating all of the layers, use Photoshop's Rectangular Marquee tool (**Figure 17.87**) to draw a box around the area that you want to include in the document (**Figure 17.88**).

With the marquee in place, choose Image > Crop, and the document will be resized (**Figure 17.89**).

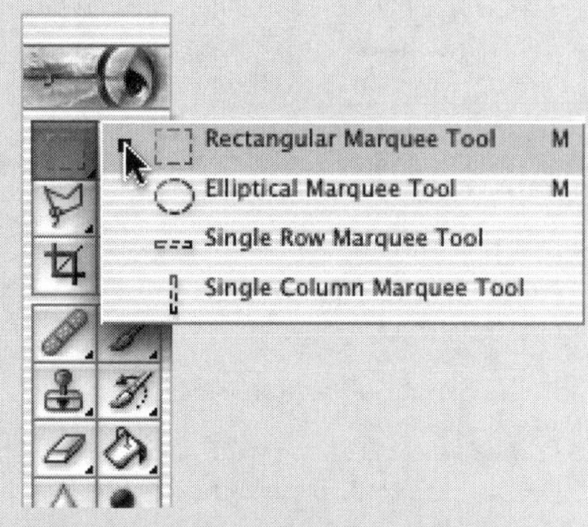

Figure 17.87 The Rectangular Marquee tool is located at the top left of the tool palette.

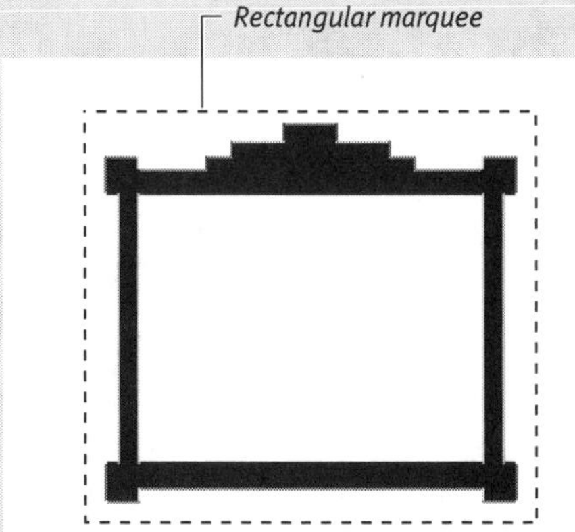

Figure 17.88 Use the Rectangular Marquee tool to draw a dotted-line box around the area that you want to include in the Photoshop document.

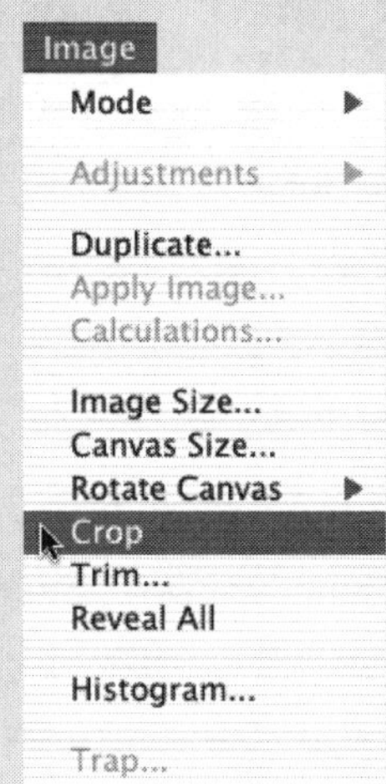

Figure 17.89 Choose Image > Crop to crop your document down to the area that you selected with your rectangular marquee.

Importing Custom Shapes

You can import the custom shapes that you create in Photoshop for use with all future projects, or you can save shapes in the project file.

To import a custom shape:

1. In DVD Studio Pro, choose View > Show Palette, or press Option-Command-P, to open the Palette.
2. In the Palette, click the Shapes tab.
3. On the Palette's Shapes tab, click the Custom tab to display your custom shapes (**Figure 17.90**).
4. At the bottom of the Custom tab, click Import (refer to Figure 17.90).

   The Import dialog appears (**Figure 17.91**).
5. Using the Import dialog, navigate to where your shape is located.

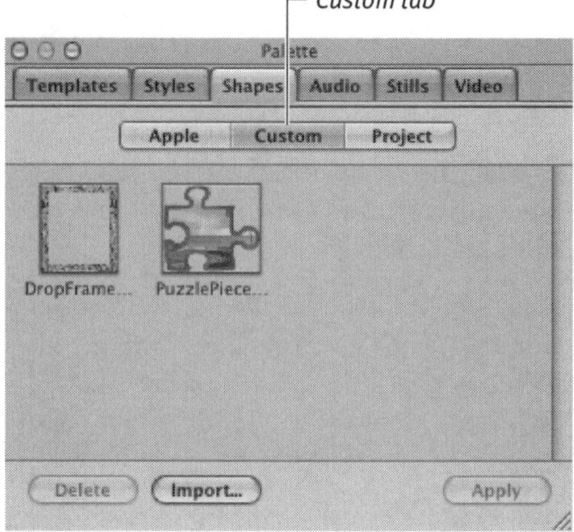

Figure 17.90 Select the Shapes tab and then the Custom tab; then click Import to import your custom shape.

Figure 17.91 Navigate to where your shape is located and click Import.

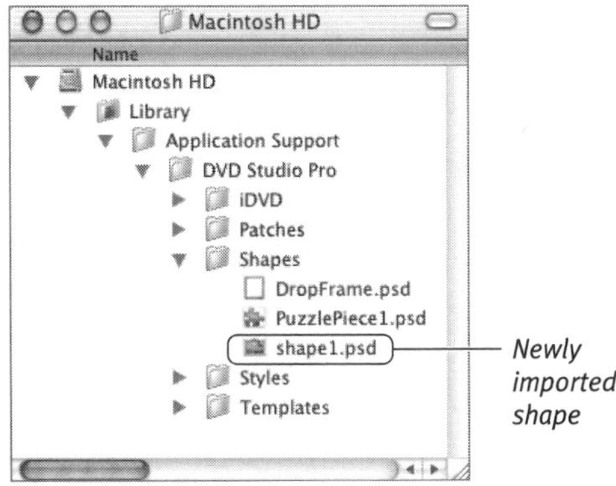

Figure 17.92 When you import a shape, DVD Studio Pro creates a copy of it and places the copy at the end of the path displayed in this figure.

6. At the bottom right of the Import dialog, click the Import button to import your shape (refer to Figure 17.91).

   DVD Studio Pro creates a copy of your shape and places it in your *root*/Library/Application Support/DVD Studio Pro/Shapes folder (**Figure 17.92**), and the imported shape is displayed in the Palette (**Figure 17.93**).

✔ Tip

- To import your shape for use with the current project only, click the Import dialog's Project check box (**Figure 17.94**). DVD Studio Pro will create a copy of the shape and place it in the project file.

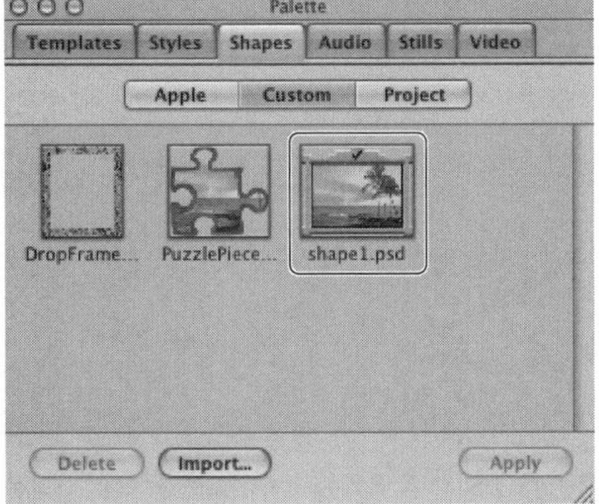

Figure 17.93 The imported shape appears on the Custom shapes tab, displaying the thumbnail that you set for it in the Icon layer of the Photoshop document.

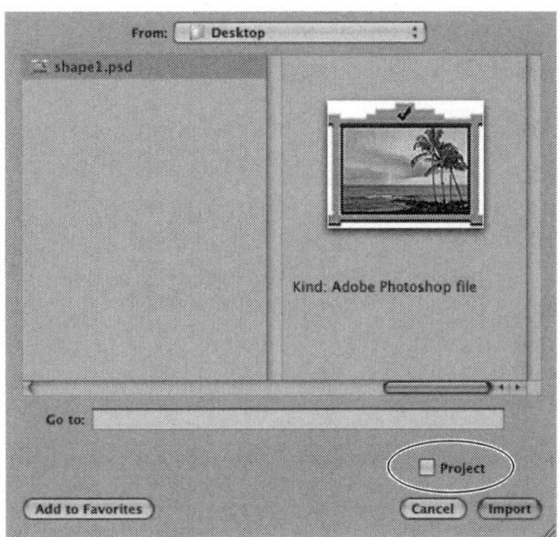

Figure 17.94 You can save shapes in the project file if you want to keep shapes for one project together. If you select the Project check box, however, the shape won't be available for use in other projects unless you reimport it.

To delete a custom shape:

1. On the Palette's Shapes tab, select the shape that you want to delete (**Figure 17.95**).
2. *Do one of the following:*
   - ▲ Press the Delete key.
   - ▲ At the bottom of the Palette's Shapes tab, click the Delete button.

   DVD Studio Pro gives you a chance to back out by asking if you're sure you want to delete the shape (**Figure 17.96**).
3. Click OK to delete the selected shape.

   The shape is deleted from your hard disk and removed from the Shapes tab.

✔ Tips

- You can delete Apple's stock shapes, but if you do you'll need to run the DVD Studio Pro installer to get them back.
- You cannot delete a shape that is in use. If you try, DVD Studio Pro will display an error dialog, letting you know that the shape is in use on one of your menus (**Figure 17.97**). Click OK to close the dialog.

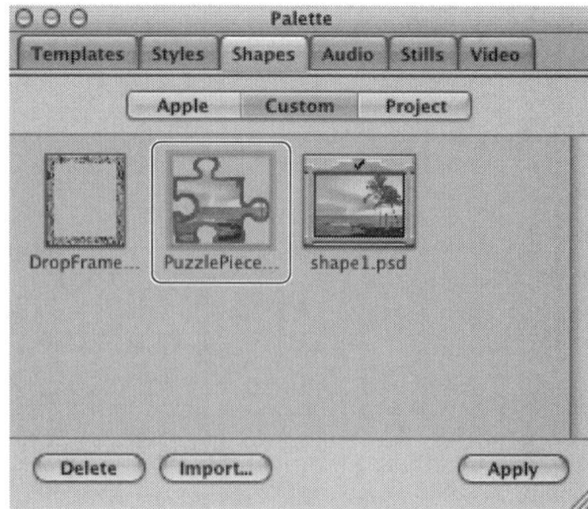

Figure 17.95 In the Palette, select the shape to be deleted.

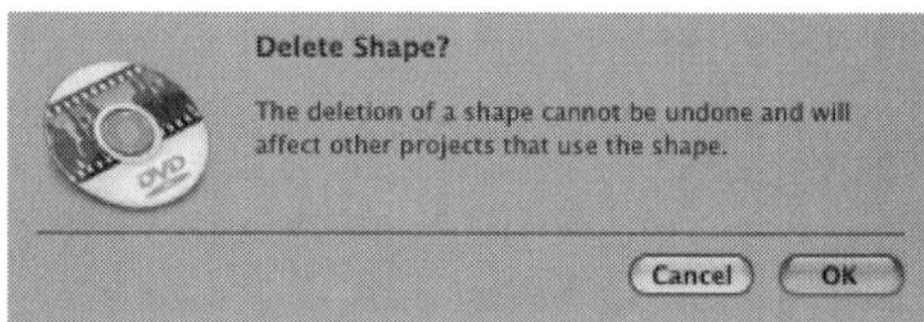

Figure 17.96 Click OK to confirm that you want to delete the selected shape. The shape is removed from your hard disk, and the deletion can't be undone.

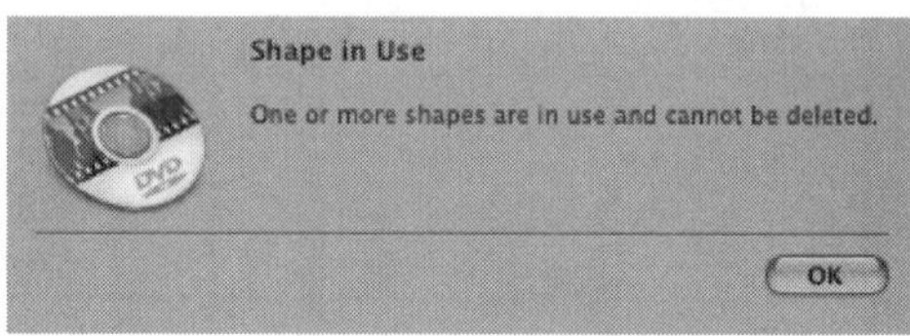

Figure 17.97 DVD Studio Pro displays this error dialog if you attempt to delete a shape that is in use. Replace the shape in your menus and click Delete again to remove the shape from your hard disk.

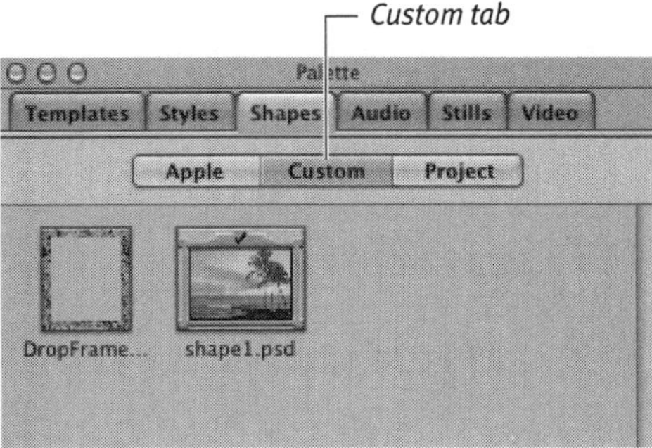

Figure 17.98 Click the Custom tab below the Shapes tab to display your custom shapes.

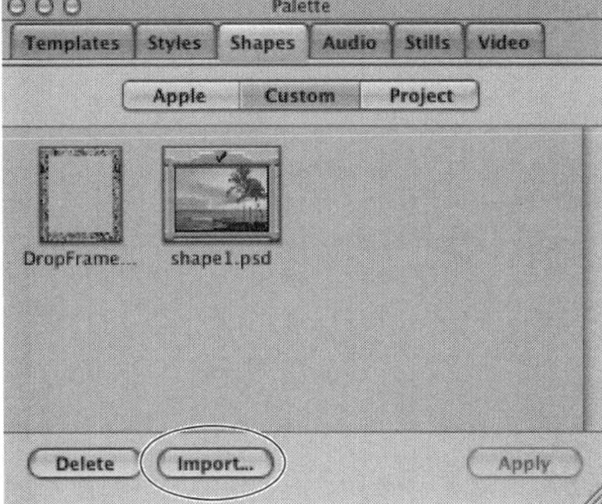

Figure 17.99 Click Import to reimport a custom shape.

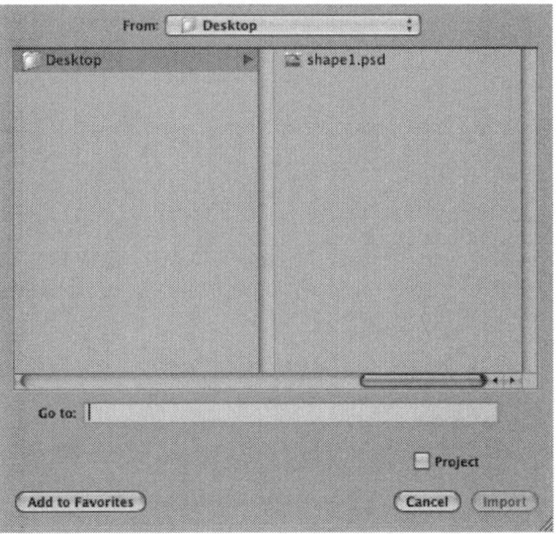

Figure 17.100 Use this dialog to select the file that you want to import.

Updating Custom Shapes

When you make changes to your Photoshop four-layer shape documents, the changes are not automatically applied to the shape that appears in DVD Studio Pro's Palette. To update the shape, you must reimport it. Once the shape is reimported, all buttons and drop zones that use the custom shape will automatically be updated in your menus the next time you open the project in DVD Studio Pro.

To reimport a custom shape:

1. In DVD Studio Pro, choose View > Show Palette, or press Option-Command-P, to open the Palette.

   The Palette opens displaying the last tab that you selected.

2. In the Palette, click the Shapes tab.

   The project's available shapes are displayed.

3. On the Shapes tab, click the Custom tab (**Figure 17.98**).

   Your custom shapes are displayed.

4. At the bottom of the Custom tab, click Import (**Figure 17.99**).

   An Import dialog appears (**Figure 17.100**).

continues on next page

5. Using the Import dialog, navigate to the updated Photoshop document that you want to import and click the Import button at the bottom right (**Figure 17.101**).

   DVD Studio Pro lets you know that a shape with the same name already exists in the Palette and asks if you want to replace it (**Figure 17.102**).

6. Click Replace (refer to Figure 17.102).

   Your shape is replaced, and all menus that currently use the shape are updated to reflect the changes that you made to your shape document in Photoshop. You won't see the changes, however, until you restart DVD Studio Pro and reopen your project.

✔ Tip

- If you change the name of your Photoshop document, the shape you import will be added to your list of available shapes; it will not replace the original shape.

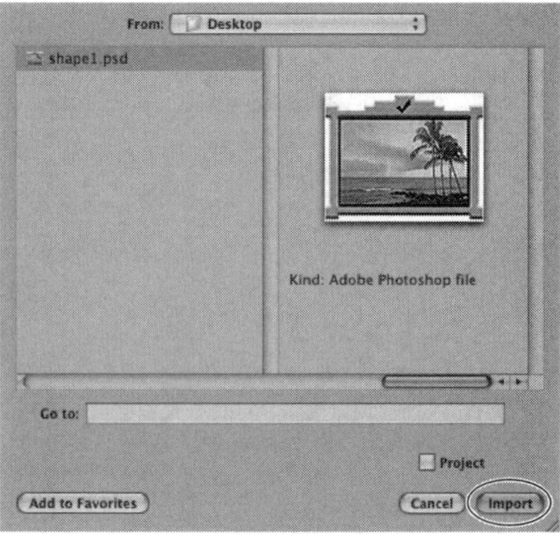

Figure 17.101 Click Import in the Import dialog to reimport your shape.

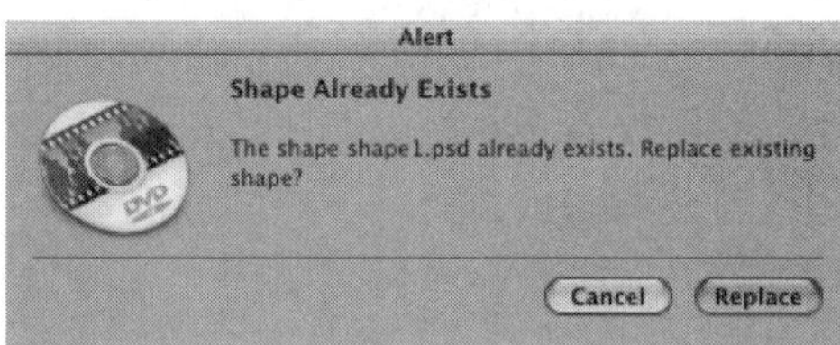

Figure 17.102 If you import a shape that already exists in the Palette, DVD Studio Pro asks if you want to replace the existing shape.

SLIDESHOWS

Slideshows are notoriously boring—but not in DVD Studio Pro! Using the Slideshow editor, you can create presentations and family photos that literally speak for themselves by assigning audio files either to individual slides or to an entire slideshow.

But that's not all you can do.

In DVD Studio Pro, you can set each slide to last for a specific duration, or you can put the viewers in control and let them manually advance each slide. You can also leave it up to DVD Studio Pro, which will happily calculate each slide's duration based on the length of the audio file. And with DVD Studio Pro 3, you can now insert transitions between each slide to create a smooth presentation.

If you find that you need more from your slideshow, just convert it into a track to add video transitions, interactive button highlights, and more!

About Slideshows

A slideshow is a sequence of still images (slides) that play from beginning to end in a linear order. When DVD Studio Pro multiplexes your project, the slideshow is turned into a track, with a chapter marker added to the beginning of each still image, or slide.

Just as a track can have a maximum of 99 chapters, slideshows are limited to 99 slides. And, as with tracks, each slideshow is multiplexed into its own individual video title set, or VTS (see Chapter 2, "DVD 101"). Because each DVD-Video can have a maximum of 99 VTSs, your project is limited to a combined total of 99 tracks *and* slideshows. So remember: when you use slideshows, the number of available tracks is reduced, and vice versa.

Preparing source files

Slideshow still images can use a mix of any DVD Studio Pro–supported image formats (see the sidebar "Supported Slideshow Formats"). When a still image is imported into DVD Studio Pro, it's converted to MPEG format and scaled to fit the frame size of 720 × 480 for NTSC or 720 × 576 for PAL. If any of your still images do not fit the frame size, the image will be scaled to the appropriate dimensions, and DVD Studio Pro will add a background color to fill the gaps. It's not as bad as it sounds—DVD Studio Pro doesn't just pick any color like, say, maraschino red; you can choose the background color that is used for the entire project. (To learn how to change the background color, see "Setting Slideshow Preferences" later in this chapter.)

Other than the considerations mentioned in this section, the procedures for preparing still-image source files for slideshows are exactly the same as those for source files for menus. To learn how to prepare still images, see Chapter 3, "Preparing Graphics."

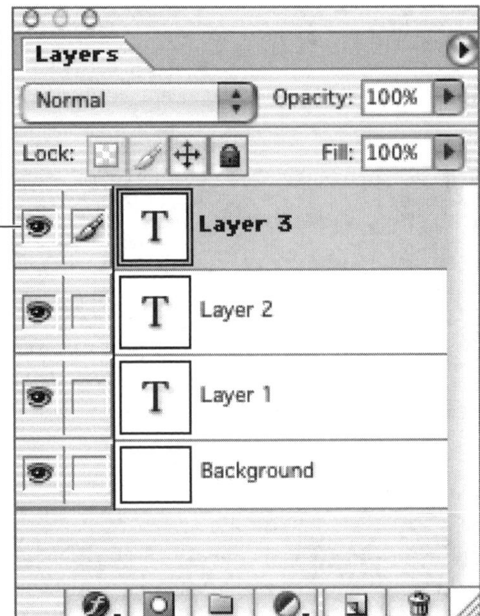

Figure 18.1 All visible layers in Photoshop become the visible slide image.

Supported Slideshow Formats

DVD Studio Pro supports a wide variety of picture formats for use with slideshows. You can mix picture formats as desired, and without consequences, in the Slideshow editor. You can use the following formats:

- PSD (Photoshop document)
- PICT (Apple graphics format)
- BMP (bitmap format)
- JPEG (Joint Photographic Experts Group format)
- QTIF (QuickTime Image format)
- TGA (Targa graphics file format)
- TIFF (tagged image file format)

✔ Tips

- When you use a multilayered Photoshop document, all layers that were visible when the document was last saved in Photoshop become the visible image for the slide, making it look as if you've merged all layers into one single layer (**Figure 18.1**). For information on Photoshop layers, see Chapter 14, "Layered Menus."
- If you're wondering why your slideshows look different when viewed on a TV rather than on your computer, the answer boils down to color. TVs can't display as many colors as computers can. In particular, televisions struggle to display bright red, green, yellow, white, and even deep black. For more information, see Chapter 3.
- If you want to use widescreen slides and have them appear at a 16:9 aspect ratio, you need to convert the slideshow into a track before multiplexing your project. Set the track's aspect ratio to 16:9, and you're ready. (For more information, see Chapter 22, "Widescreen: 16:9.")

Preparing audio files

As noted earlier, you can assign a single audio stream to an entire slideshow or an individual audio file to each slide. If you assign an individual audio file to each slide, each file must have the same format, bit rate, and sample rate.

To keep matters simple, the Slideshow editor supports the same audio formats as the Track editor, including uncompressed stereo PCM (AIFF, WAV, SDII), MPEG-1 Layer 2, and digitally compressed AC-3 audio streams. These audio streams can be mono, stereo, or multichannel surround.

Creating slideshow project elements

When you create a new project, a slideshow project element is not created by default, unlike Menu 1 and Track 1. You must add a new slideshow to include one in your project. You can add a slideshow to your project in several ways.

To create a slideshow project element:

◆ *Do one of the following:*

- ▲ In the toolbar, click the Add Slideshow icon (**Figure 18.2**).
- ▲ Choose Project > Add to Project > Slideshow, or press Command-K (**Figure 18.3**).
- ▲ In Outline or Graphical view, Control-click and select Add > Slideshow from the shortcut menu (**Figure 18.4**).

DVD Studio Pro creates a slideshow element named Slideshow 1 and lists it in the Outline view (**Figure 18.5**).

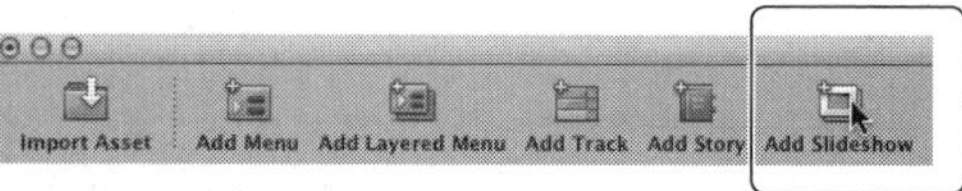

Figure 18.2 To add a slideshow to your project, click the Add Slideshow icon in the toolbar...

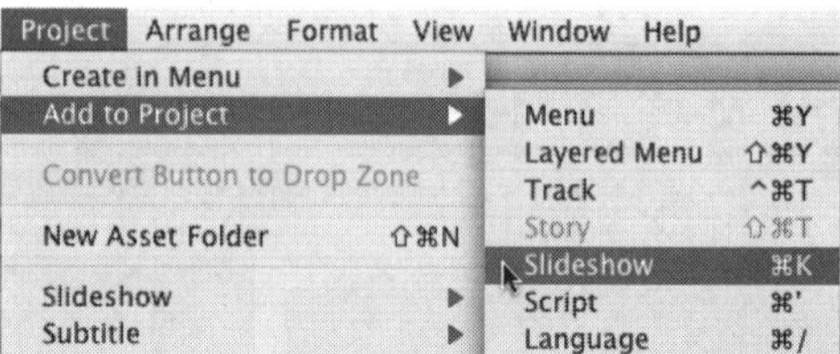

Figure 18.3 ...or choose Project > Add to Project > Slideshow...

Figure 18.4 ...or Control-click in Outline view and select Add > Slideshow from the shortcut menu.

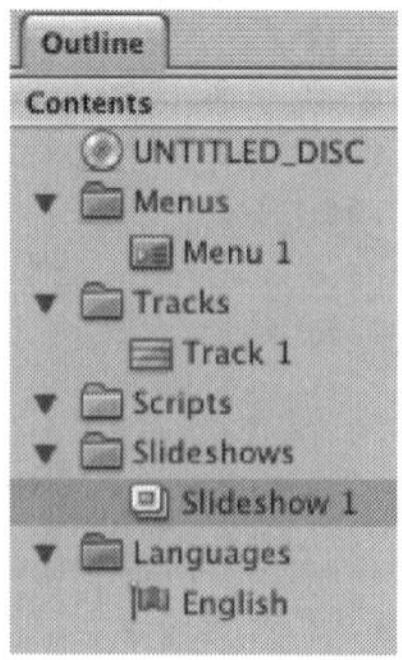

Figure 18.5 When you add a new slideshow to your project, a slideshow element named Slideshow 1 is added to the Outline view.

Figure 18.6 Select DVD Studio Pro > Preferences to open the Preferences window.

Figure 18.7 Click the General icon to open the General Preferences window.

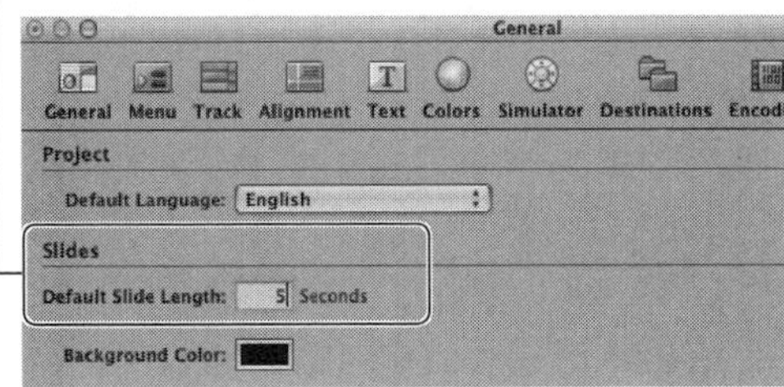

Figure 18.8 Enter a default slide length in seconds.

Setting Slideshow Preferences

Before you begin adding slides to your slideshows, you should set the following slideshow preferences in DVD Studio Pro:

- **Default Slide Length.** Set this value in seconds; it applies to all slides when you create a new slideshow.
- **Slide Background Color.** This color is used to fill the gaps for all slides that do not fit the 720 × 480 (NTSC) or 720 × 576 (PAL) frame.
- **Slide Thumbnail Size.** This preference controls the size of slide image thumbnails. If you want to see more slides on the screen, choose the Small thumbnail size. If you want to see a larger preview of each slide in your slideshow, choose the Large thumbnail size.

To set the default slide duration:

1. Select DVD Studio Pro > Preferences (**Figure 18.6**), or press Command-, (comma), to open the Preferences window.
2. In the Preferences toolbar, click the General icon to open the General Preferences pane (**Figure 18.7**).
3. In the Default Slide Length text box, type a number of seconds (**Figure 18.8**).

   This number is the default slide duration for all of the still images in your slideshows.
4. Click Apply to apply the changes and make additional changes in the Preferences window, or click OK to apply changes and close the window.

✔ Tip

- You can override the default slide length in the Slideshow editor. The number set in the General Preferences window is used when you add slides to the slideshow.

To select a background color:

1. Select DVD Studio Pro > Preferences, or press Command-, (comma), to open the Preferences window.
2. In the Preferences toolbar, click the General icon to open the General Preferences window.
3. In the Slides section, click the Background Color button (**Figure 18.9**).

   The Color palette opens.
4. In the Color palette, click the desired color to select it.

   This color is used as the background color for all slides that do not fit the 720 × 480 (NTSC) or 720 × 576 (PAL) frame.

To set the thumbnail image size:

1. Select DVD Studio Pro > Preferences, or press Command-, (comma), to open the Preferences window.
2. In the Preferences toolbar, click the General icon to open the General Preferences window.
3. In the Thumbnail Size section, select either the Large or Small Slideshow radio button (**Figure 18.10**).

   If you select Small, your slide thumbnails will be 45 × 35 pixels. If you select Large, your slide thumbnails will be 60 × 45 pixels.

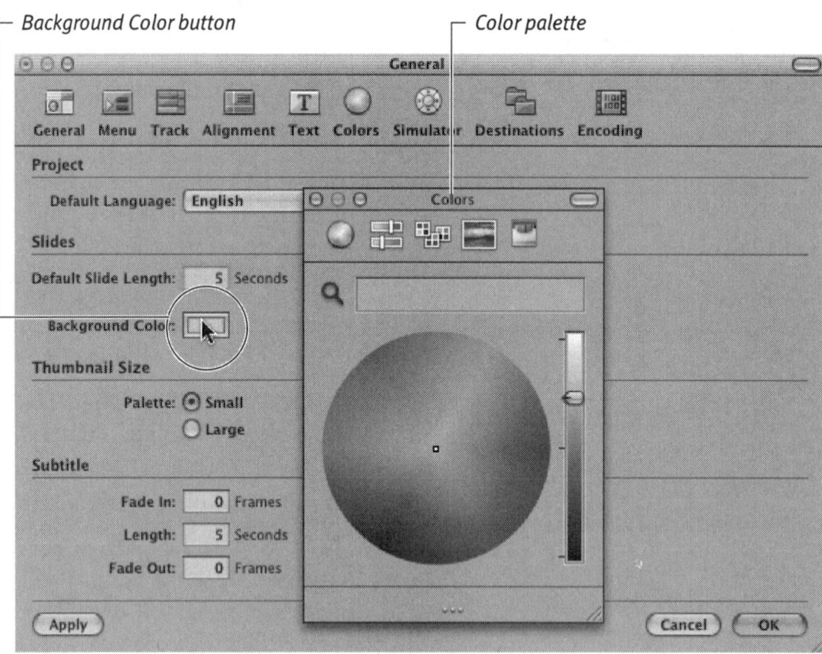

Figure 18.9 Click the Background Color button to open the Color palette.

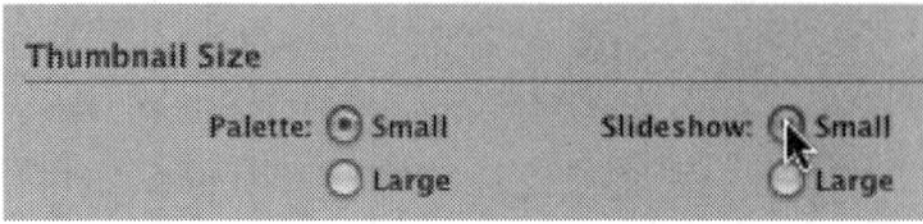

Figure 18.10 Choose a default size for viewing thumbnails in the Slideshow editor.

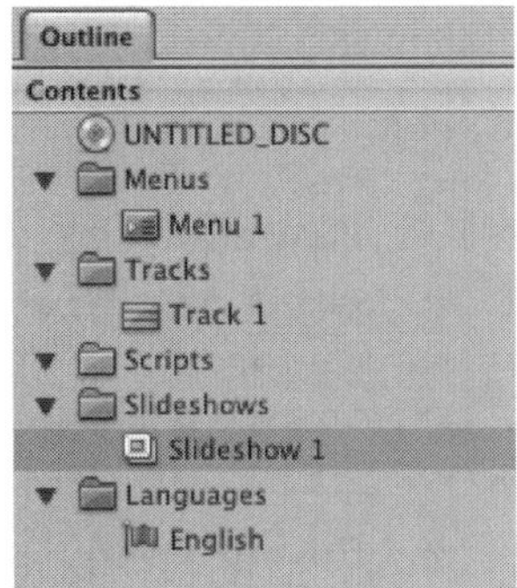

Figure 18.11 Double-click a slideshow element to open it in the Slideshow editor.

Using the Slideshow Editor

Use the Slideshow editor to orchestrate your slideshows. Within the Slideshow editor, you drag slides in, rearrange them, add audio, and set slide duration.

To open the Slideshow editor:

- In the Outline view, double-click your slideshow project element (**Figure 18.11**).

  The Slideshow editor opens (**Figure 18.12**).

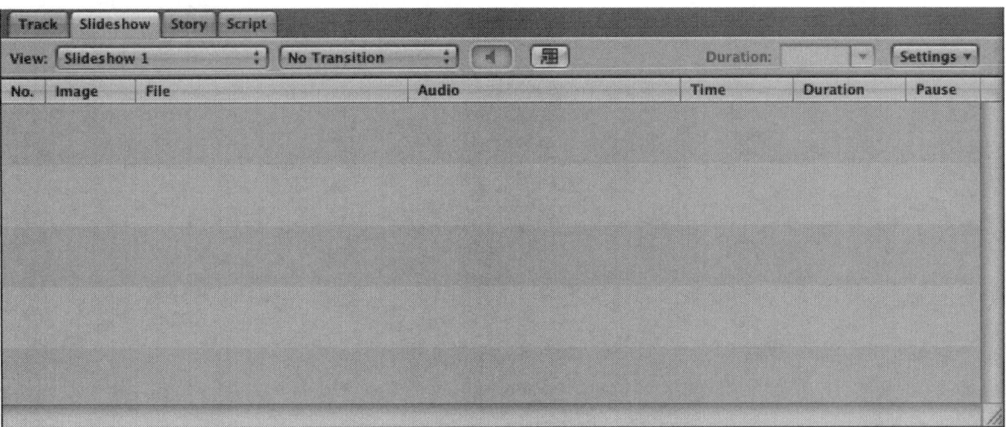

Figure 18.12 The Slideshow editor.

To add pictures to a slideshow:

- On the Assets tab, select (by clicking) an asset and drag and drop it into the Slideshows list (**Figure 18.13**).

✔ Tips

- You can drag an entire folder of still pictures into the Slideshow editor's slide list to add multiple assets at once.
- You can drag entire iPhoto albums into the slide list from the Palette's Stills tab. The Slideshow editor will create a slideshow using all the stills in the iPhoto album.

To reorder pictures in the slide list:

- In the slide list, select an asset and drag it either up or down to move its location within the slideshow (**Figure 18.14**).

  Watch the slide list closely. A thin black bar appears between slides, indicating the slide's new position after you release the mouse button.

To delete a slide from the slide list:

1. In the slide list, click a slide to select it.

   The slide is highlighted (that is, barely highlighted; it changes color only by a shade).
2. Press the Delete key on your keyboard to remove the slide from the slide list.

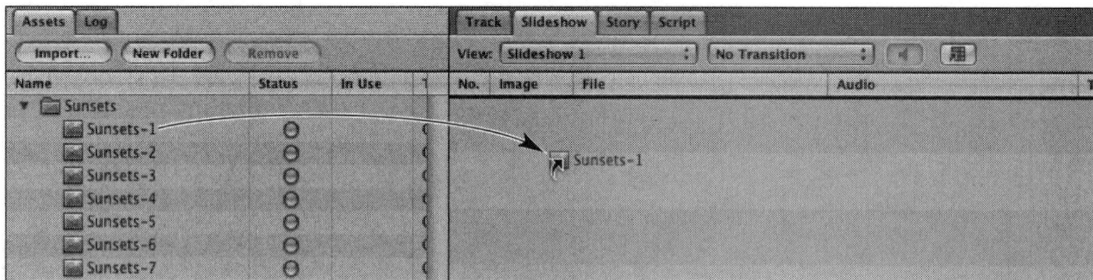

Figure 18.13 Drag one or more still pictures from the Assets tab into the slide list to add slides to your slideshow.

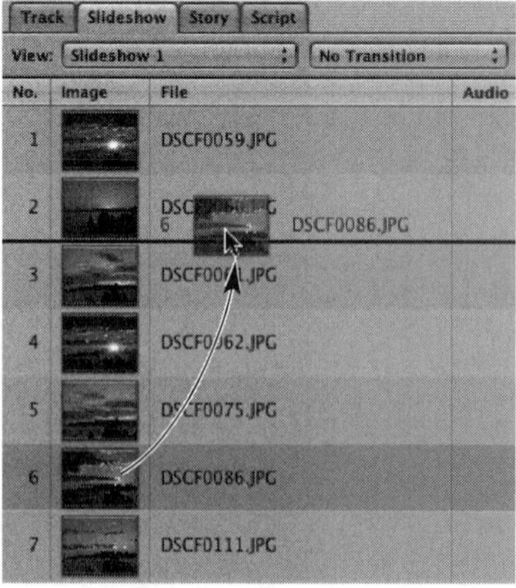

Figure 18.14 To change the slide order, select a slide and drag it up or down within the slide list.

Setting slide duration

Slides play for a certain length of time before the show moves on to the next slide. The default slide length is five seconds, but you can change this setting in your Preferences window. You can either manually change each slide's duration or let the viewer choose when to advance to the next slide by adding an infinite pause at the end of the slide's duration.

To set a slide's duration:

1. In the Slideshow editor, select one or more slides from the slide list.
2. Click the Slide Duration pop-up menu and choose the new duration (in seconds) for your slide (**Figure 18.15**).

   The slide's duration is changed to whatever interval you chose from the pop-up menu (**Figure 18.16**).

✔ Tips

- To choose a slide duration that isn't listed in the Slide Duration pop-up menu, type an interval (in seconds) in the Slide Duration Seconds text box and press Enter.
- If a slide uses audio, the slide duration will adjust itself to play the slide for the entire length of the audio stream. Attaching audio to slides is covered later in this chapter, in the section "Adding Audio Streams."

Figure 18.15 Choose a new duration from the Slide Duration pop-up menu or manually type a duration in seconds; then press Enter to apply the change.

Figure 18.16 The slide's duration is updated to reflect the change.

To pause a slide:

1. In the Slideshow editor, select one or more slides from the slide list.
2. At the bottom right of the Slideshow editor, select the Manual Advance check box (**Figure 18.17**).

   When played, the selected slides pause until the viewer presses the Next button on the remote control.

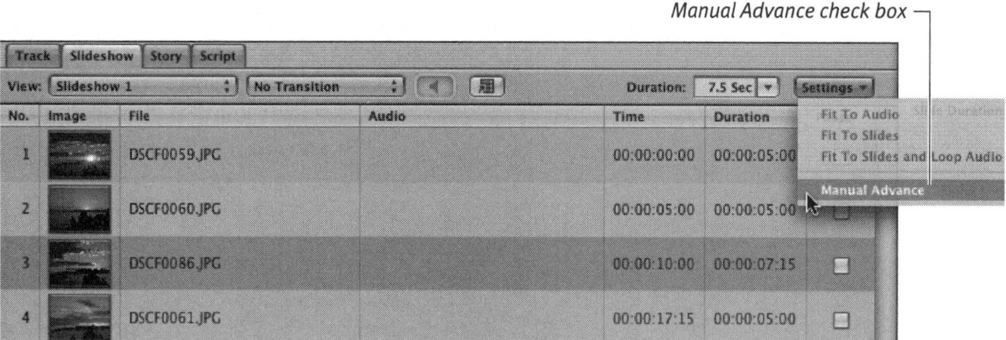

Figure 18.17 Select the Manual Advance check box to have a slide pause during playback until the viewer presses the remote control's Next key.

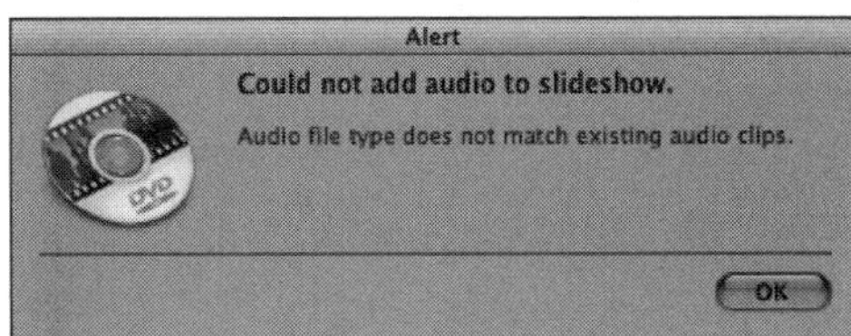

Figure 18.18 DVD Studio Pro displays an Alert dialog if you attempt to mix audio stream types.

Adding Audio Streams

As you read earlier, you can assign an individual audio file to each slide or to the entire slideshow. If you assign one audio stream to the entire slideshow, the following options in the Slideshow editor become active:

- **Fit to Audio.** If you choose to fit the slideshow to the audio stream, DVD Studio Pro will calculate each slide's duration based on the length of the audio file.
- **Fit to Slides.** If you choose this option, the audio will stop when the slideshow is finished, cutting off the end of the audio if the audio stream lasts longer than the slideshow. The slide's duration is not changed when you fit the audio stream to the current length of the slideshow.
- **Loop Audio.** If you choose to fit the audio to the slideshow and the slideshow is longer than the audio stream, you can also choose to loop the audio for as long as the slideshow is playing.

As noted earlier, slideshows do suffer a limitation: *All of the audio assets used in a slideshow must be the exact same file format.* For example, you can't mix AC-3 with PCM or MPEG-1 Layer 2 audio.

The first audio asset you add to any of the slides sets the default audio type for the entire slideshow. If you try to drag a different type of audio into the slideshow, DVD Studio Pro will display an Alert dialog (**Figure 18.18**) and block the second audio file from being added to the slideshow.

To add audio to a slide:

- On the Assets tab, select an audio file and drag it to a slide in the slide list, dropping it in the Audio column (**Figure 18.19**).

  The audio file is assigned, and the slide's duration is changed to fit the length of the audio stream.

To remove audio from a slide:

- In the slide list, select the audio file and press the Delete key (**Figure 18.20**).

  The audio file is removed from the slide list.

To add an audio file to an entire slideshow:

1. From the Assets tab, drag an audio file and drop it on the Slideshow Inspector's Audio area (**Figure 18.21**).

   The audio file is added to the slideshow. Directly above the Slideshow Inspector's Audio area, the Slideshow Duration options become active (**Figure 18.22**).

Figure 18.19 A black box appears around the slide to which the audio asset will be attached.

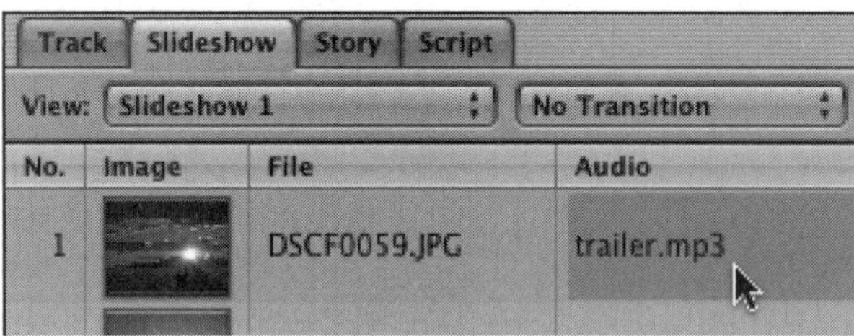

Figure 18.20 Select the audio file to be removed and press Delete.

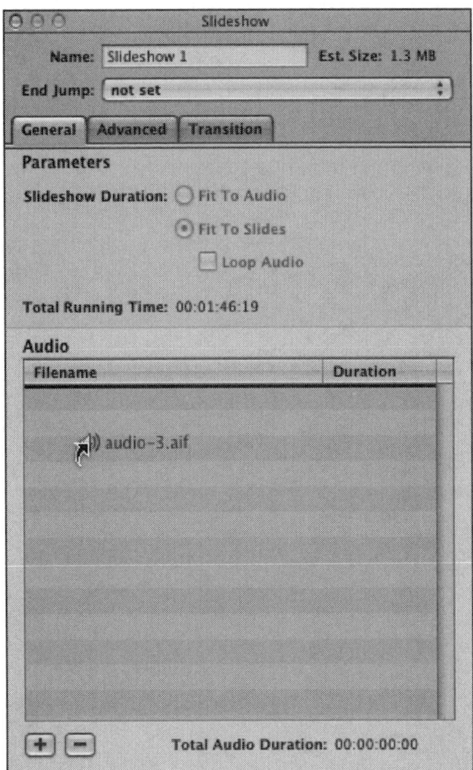

Figure 18.21 Add audio to the slideshow by dragging an audio file and dropping it on the Slideshow Inspector's Audio area.

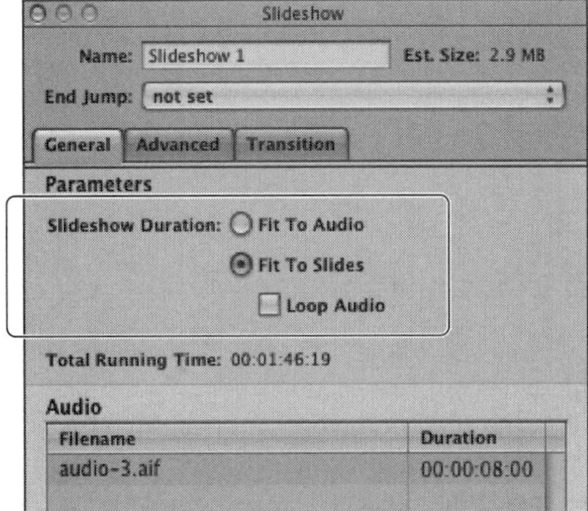

Figure 18.22 The Slideshow Duration options become active, enabling you to choose how you want the Slideshow editor to fit the set audio stream to your slideshow.

2. From the Slideshow Duration options, *select one of the following:*

   ▲ **Fit to Audio.** If you choose to fit the slideshow to the audio stream, DVD Studio Pro calculates each slide's duration based on the length of the audio file.

   ▲ **Fit to Slides.** If you choose this option, the audio will stop when the slideshow finishes, which may cut off the audio stream before it's finished, if the audio stream is longer than the slideshow. However, if your slideshow is longer than the audio stream, you can click the Loop Audio check box to have the audio stream loop until the slideshow has finished playing.

To remove the audio file from a slideshow:

◆ In the Slideshow Inspector, select the slide and click the Delete button (**Figure 18.23**).

The audio file is removed from the slideshow.

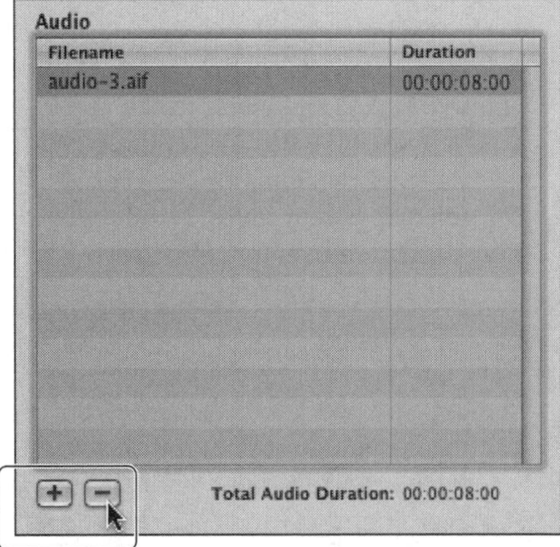

Figure 18.23 To remove an audio file from the slideshow, select it in the Inspector and click the Delete button.

Converting Slideshows to Tracks

Even with all that you can do in the Slideshow editor, you may find yourself wanting more out of your slideshows. If you want to use 16:9 pictures, subtitles, buttons over video, alternate languages, or multiple audio streams, you'll need to convert your slideshow into a track and use the Track editor to finish the job. When you click the Convert to Track button in the Slideshow editor, the slideshow element is removed from the Slideshows list in the Outline view and becomes a track. Chapter markers are placed at the beginning of each slide, allowing you to add interactive markers, video transitions between slides, subtitles, multilanguage audio streams, and DVD@ccess Web links to your slideshows. (For more information on using the Track editor, see Chapter 11, "Using Tracks," and Chapter 12, "Enhancing Tracks.")

Figure 18.24 After you've configured your slideshow, click the Convert to Track button.

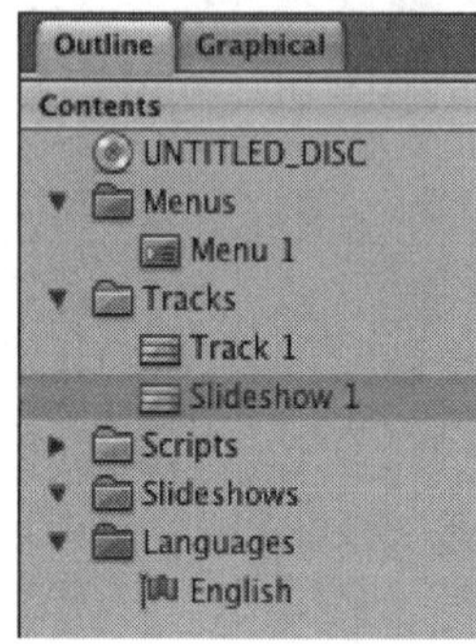

Figure 18.25 The slideshow item is converted into a track item and moved into the Tracks list in the Outline view.

Figure 18.26 The slideshow is converted to a track, and chapter markers are added to the beginning of each slide.

To convert a slideshow to a track:

1. Configure your slideshow as desired in the Slideshow editor.
2. At the top of the Slideshow editor, click the Convert to Track button (**Figure 18.24**).

   In the Outline view, the slideshow is moved from the Slideshows list to the Tracks list (**Figure 18.25**) and opens in the Track editor (**Figure 18.26**). DVD Studio Pro adds chapter markers, which bear the same names as your slides, to the beginning of each slide in the new track.

Creating Interactive Slideshows

Rather than forcing viewers to skim through your DVD-Video slide by slide using the Previous and Next buttons on their remote controls, wouldn't it be nice to put buttons right on top of the slideshow so viewers (especially those at a computer) can click onscreen buttons to progress through slides? Or how about a product catalog with buttons that use DVD@ccess links to send the viewer straight to the ordering section of your company's Web site? Unfortunately, you can't add buttons to slideshows, but you *can* add buttons to your video after you convert the slideshow to a track. See Chapter 12 to learn how to create interactive buttons over video.

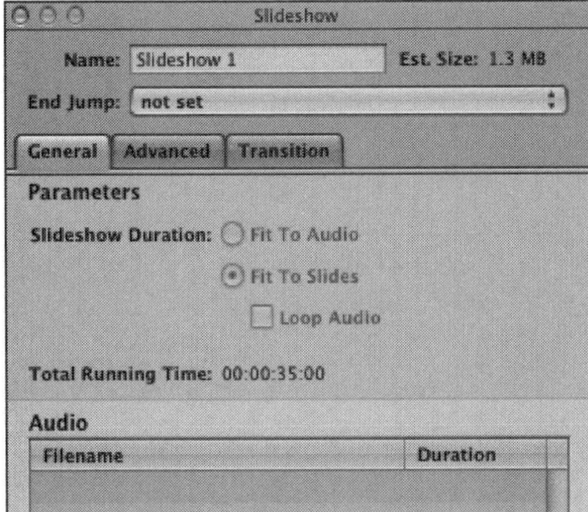

Figure 18.27 Set the slideshow's properties in the Slideshow Inspector.

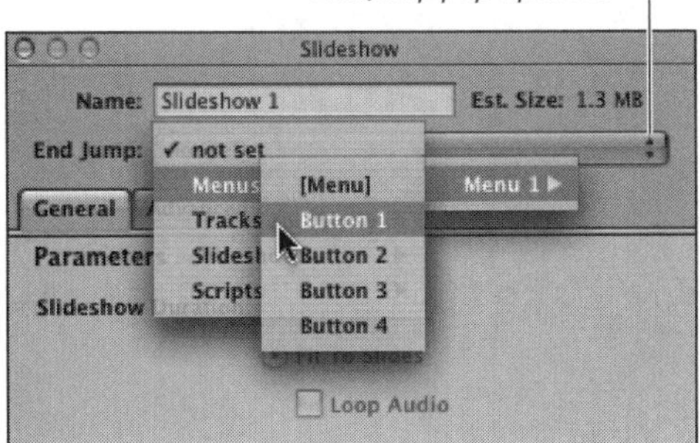

Figure 18.28 Select an end jump from the pop-up menu to tell the DVD player where to go when the slideshow has finished playing.

Setting Slideshow End Jumps

Just like a track, a slideshow must be set to do something once it has finished playing; otherwise, the DVD-Video simply stops. You can tell the slideshow what to do by supplying it with an *end jump*. You can set anything that's listed in the Outline view as the end jump, but most likely you'll want to return viewers to a menu.

To set an end jump:

1. In Outline view, select your Slideshow project element to display its properties in the Inspector (**Figure 18.27**).
2. In the Slideshow Inspector, choose a menu, track, or other item from the End Jump pop-up menu (**Figure 18.28**).

   When the last slide in the slideshow finishes playing, your DVD-Video will jump to the selected item.

✔ Tip

- If you convert your slideshow to a track, you must set the track's end jump in the Track Inspector. The steps are the same; start by selecting the track in the Outline view to view the Track Inspector.

Previewing Slideshows

Previewing slideshows is easy. After all, slideshows are not interactive; all you can do is jump back and forth between slides using the Simulator's Previous and Next buttons (**Figure 18.29**).

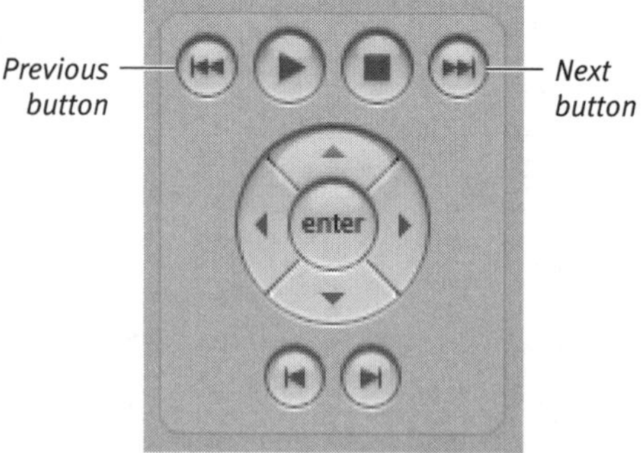

Figure 18.29 The Simulator's Previous and Next buttons allow you to navigate quickly between slides in your slideshow.

Nonetheless, previewing slideshows is important because you must ensure that your pause intervals are long (or short) enough and that the slides play in the correct order. If you've supplied your slides with audio streams, listen to verify that the correct audio stream is attached to each slide and cycle through all alternate audio streams. If everything works in the Simulator, you can build your project confidently and burn it to a DVD disc.

To simulate a slideshow:

1. In the Outline view, Control-click the slideshow project element.

   A shortcut menu appears (**Figure 18.30**).

2. From the shortcut menu, choose Simulate.

   The Simulator launches and plays the slideshow.

3. In the Simulator, use the Previous and Next buttons to move forward or backward through the slides (refer to Figure 18.29).

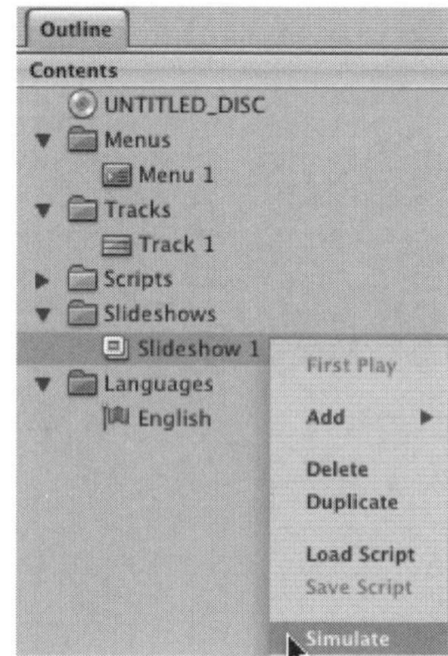

Figure 18.30 Control-click your slideshow element in the Outline view to start simulation from the beginning of the slideshow.

Finishing the DVD

The process of finishing a DVD creates great excitement but also some anxiety. After all those creative hours, it's finally time to output your video to disc! But before you spend time and money building and formatting a DVD-R disc, it's wise to test your project a few more times to ensure that every aspect of your project works as anticipated.

Who wants the embarrassment of delivering a project to a client that doesn't work as it should (even if the client is your mother)? To guard against broken button links, improperly encoded assets, and other DVD-Video traumas, make sure that each project passes rigorous quality assurance (QA) testing before you record it to a DVD-R disc or DLT tape. QA begins in DVD Studio Pro's Simulator. The Simulator is an excellent means for testing your project's interactivity because it plays all button links, jump actions, alternate angles, and alternate audio streams faithfully, just like a set-top DVD-Video player does.

However, the Simulator is not infallible; from time to time it makes mistakes or doesn't perform as it should, and thus the Simulator offers only a first line of defense. The next step in the QA process is building the project, which places a working copy of the DVD-Video on your computer's hard disk. Using Apple's DVD Player, you can open the project and play it just like a DVD-Video on a DVD-Video disc. If everything checks out, you can move forward to formatting the disc or DLT tape with a final version of your project.

To help you get it right from the beginning, this chapter demonstrates how to simulate and test your project before you build it. It also discusses First Play (startup) actions, region codes, copy protection, and a few other settings that help ensure that your DVD-Video plays the way you designed it to, every time.

Setting the First Play Action

The First Play action is the DVD's autorun sequence. It tells the DVD-Video what to do once it's placed in a DVD-Video player. The First Play action may be a script that checks the DVD player's settings, an introductory animation, an FBI warning, a transition that leads from black to a menu, or even a menu itself; in fact, anything listed in your Outline or Graphical view makes an acceptable First Play action.

Not setting the First Play action leads to problems with your finished DVD-Video disc. In the best scenario, the DVD-Video won't autostart, and viewers will have to press Play to get the action rolling. The DVD-Video then starts playback at track 1 by default, which may not be the first thing you want viewers to see. In the worst scenario, the DVD-Video player won't play the disc at all. For example, Apple's DVD-Player won't play a disc if its First Play action isn't set.

DVD Studio Pro sets Menu 1 as the First Play action when you create a new project. If you want a different project element to play first, you must set the First Play action in the Disc Inspector.

✔ Tip

- Items are burned to disc in the same order they appear in the Outline view. For example, the track at the top of the Outline view's track area is recorded first, then the next one down the list, and so on. Consequently, if you forget to set the First Play action, at best your DVD-Video will begin playback with the track at the top of the Outline view's track list; at worst, it won't play at all.

To set the First Play action:

1. In the Outline view, select the disc icon (**Figure 19.1**) to display its properties in the Inspector.

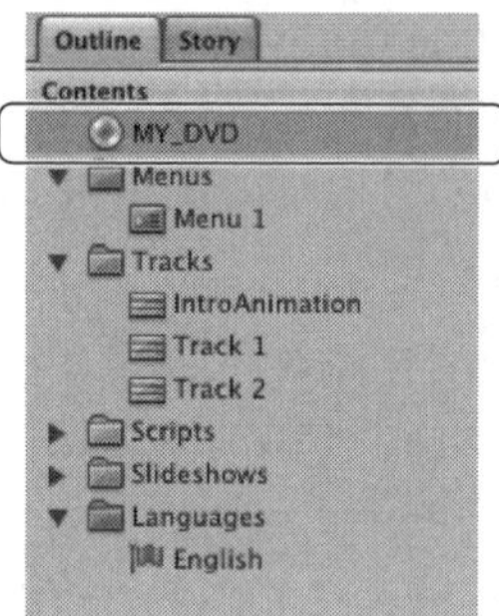

Figure 19.1 Select your disc in the Outline view to see its properties in the Inspector.

First Play pop-up menu

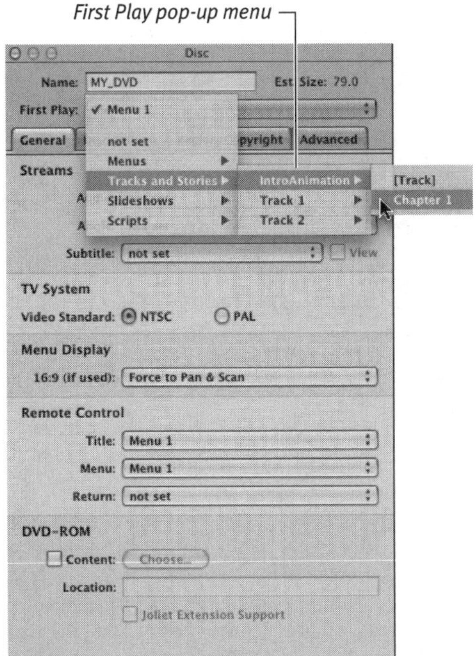

Figure 19.2 The First Play action tells the DVD-Video player which chapter to play first.

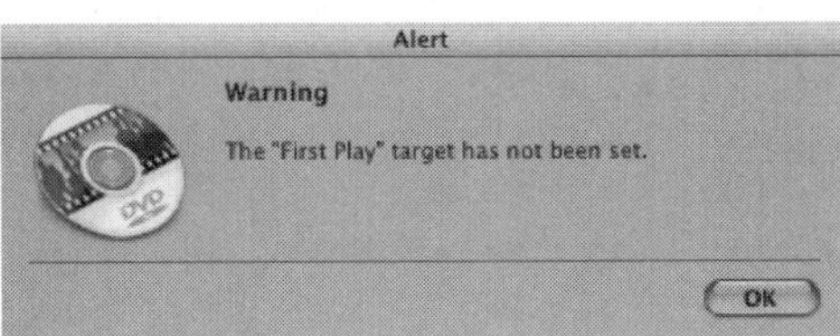

Figure 19.3 The Simulator warns you if you are about to simulate a project that doesn't have a First Play action assigned.

2. Using the Disc Inspector's First Play pop-up menu, select a First Play action (**Figure 19.2**).

   This menu lists all of your menus and tracks as well as buttons, chapters, and slides. There's a lot to choose from, but fortunately the decision is simple: just select the item you want your viewers to see first. If your First Play action is a track, select the first marker in that track. If your First Play action is a slideshow, select the first slide in that slideshow.

   When the DVD-Video disc is inserted into a DVD-Video player, the selected item starts to play automatically.

✔ Tips

- To quickly set the First Play item, in the Graphical view control-click any item and choose First Play. (For more information, see Chapter 8, "Viewing Your Project.")
- If you forget to set a First Play action before testing your project in DVD Studio Pro's Simulator, the Simulator warns you of your mistake (**Figure 19.3**).
- Although increasingly rare, some DVD-Video players have problems displaying discs using a menu or script as a First Play action. To guard against this, place a short (say, four-second) black MPEG-2 video stream in a track that plays just before the menu. Set the First Play action to this black track so that it plays before the menu appears on the screen.

Assigning Remote-Control Buttons

The Remote Control area of the Disc Inspector's General tab allows you to set the functions of several important remote-control buttons, including Title, Menu, and Return (**Figure 19.4**). Additional important DVD-Video player remote-control buttons that you may want to set are located a bit higher on the tab (refer to Figure 19.4). You can set the Streams remote-control buttons if you want viewers to see a specific audio stream, track angle, or subtitle stream when they press the respective remote-control buttons.

You can assign any track, menu, slideshow, or script listed in the Outline view as the target action for the remote-control buttons listed in the Disc Inspector's Remote Control area. Although it's nice to have this level of control, most of the time you should follow simple rules that guarantee navigational uniformity across all DVD-Videos. (To learn more, see the "Navigational Uniformity" sidebar.)

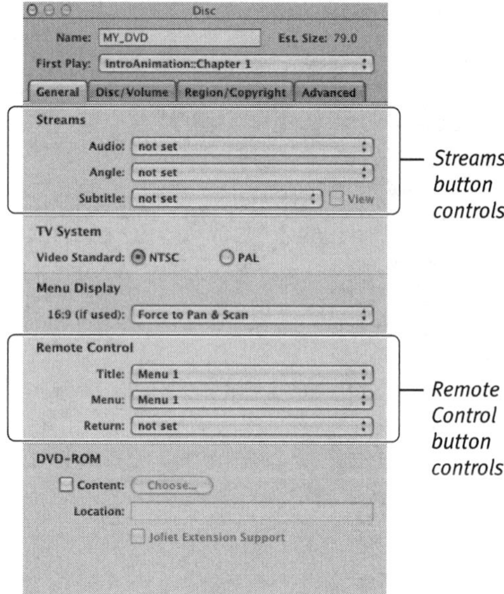

Figure 19.4 The Disc Inspector's Streams and Remote Control areas set the functions of certain buttons on the DVD-Video player's remote control.

Navigational Uniformity

As the DVD-Video's author, you can set several remote control buttons to play whatever project item you want. You can get very creative with the way remote controls play the DVD, but most of the time viewers expect their remote controls to work in a certain, logical way.

Navigational uniformity refers to the use of simple rules to ensure that remote controls always behave as expected, regardless of the DVD-Video that's playing. Pressing the Title button, for example, should always bring the DVD-Video's main menu (or top menu) onscreen, and pressing the Menu button should return viewers to the menu that jumped them to the currently playing track or slideshow. The Return button should help viewers navigate between several linking menus by allowing them to jump back to the previous menu.

The Angle (or Track Angle), Audio, and Subtitle buttons are more of a challenge. By default, all DVD-Video player remote controls use these buttons to cycle through alternate angle, audio, and subtitle streams in tracks. Imagine you have a track with three audio streams: English, French, and Spanish. When the English audio stream is playing, pressing the Audio button swaps in the French stream (which is the next audio stream for that track). Pressing the Audio button again brings in the Spanish stream, and a third press brings back the English audio stream.

But you might not want viewers to be able to cycle through audio streams by clicking the Audio button. Instead, you may want to create an Audio menu that lists all three audio streams and assign that menu to the Audio button. In this case, pressing the Audio button would take viewers straight to an Audio setup menu where they can specifically select the stream they want instead of cycling through each audio stream while viewing the track (on some remotes, the viewer must press the Audio button and then the Menu button for this setup to work).

Like the Audio button, the Angle button may jump to a track-angle selection menu listing all possible angles for the selected track, and the Subtitle button may link to a Subtitle menu listing all available text-based director and cast commentaries. Just remember: If you set the Angle, Audio, or Subtitle buttons, viewers lose the ability to cycle through alternate streams by pressing these buttons. To preserve the ability to cycle through streams, select Not Set from the pop-up settings menus.

DVD players and their remotes work in different ways. You can't count on a consistent experience for all viewers. With some remotes, pressing the Audio button will cycle through available audio streams within a track, while others will display a selection menu on the TV screen. If you assign an audio setup menu to the remote-control button, some DVD players still won't go directly to the menu but will continue to cycle through audio streams; if this happens, the viewer must press the Audio button and then the Menu button to jump to the setup menu that you assigned.

To set the disc's remote-control buttons:

1. In the Outline view, click the disc icon to display the disc's properties in the Inspector.
2. In the Disc Inspector, click the General tab (**Figure 19.5**) to display the disc's general properties.
3. In the General tab's Remote Control area, choose a menu, track, slideshow, or script from the Title pop-up menu (**Figure 19.6**).
4. Choose a menu from the Menu pop-up menu (**Figure 19.7**).
5. Choose an item to return to from the Return pop-up menu or, if you want the return function to work properly, leave it set to Not Set (**Figure 19.8**).

   When viewers press the Return button on their remote controls, they will automatically be returned to the project element they were just viewing.

✔ Tip

- DVD Studio Pro sets the Title and Menu buttons to Menu 1 by default. Unless you want something else to be set, you do not need to assign a new project element.

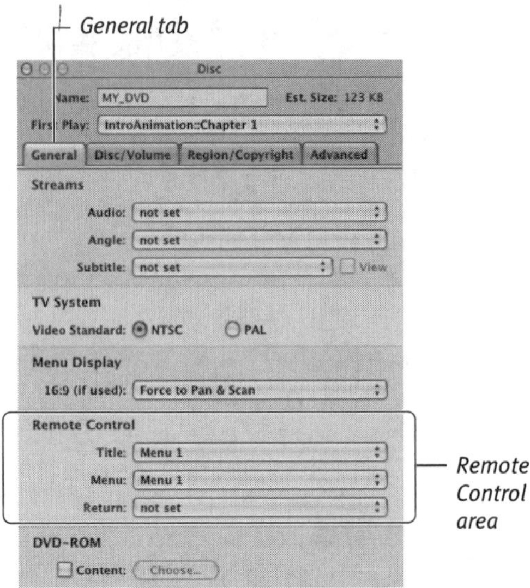

Figure 19.5 Click the General tab in the Disc Inspector to see the remote control settings.

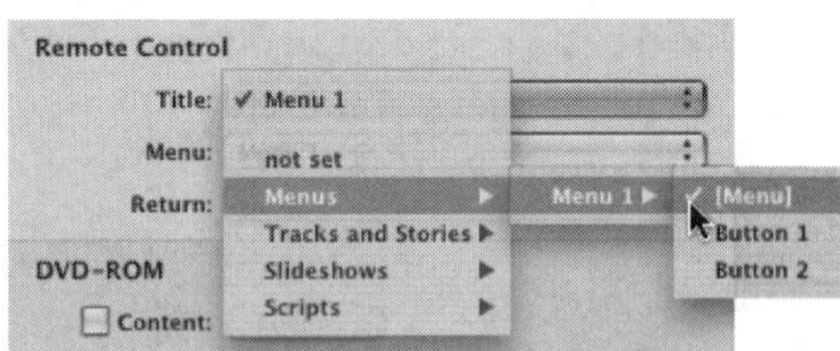

Figure 19.6 The Title button should be set to take the viewer to your DVD-Video's main menu.

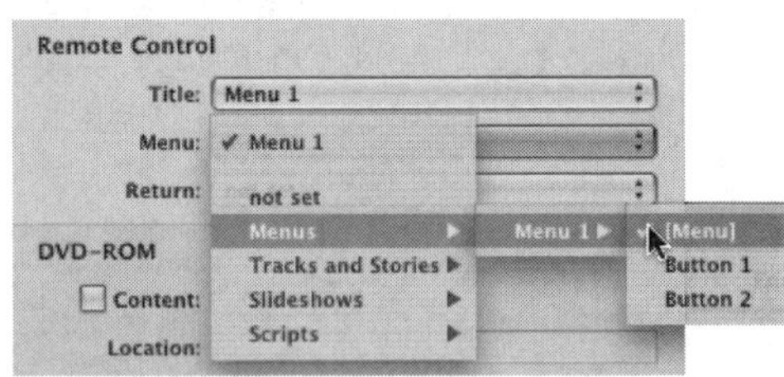

Figure 19.7 The Menu button should be set to take the viewer to your DVD-Video's main menu.

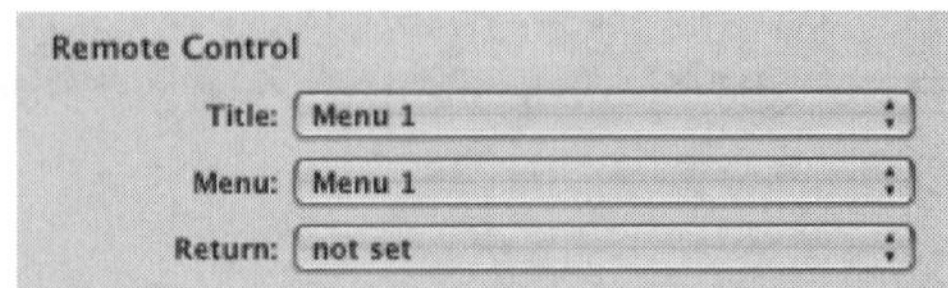

Figure 19.8 Leave the Return button set to Not Set so the Return function will work properly.

To set the disc's Streams remote-control buttons:

1. Open the Disc Inspector and click the General tab to select it.
2. From the Audio pop-up menu in the Streams section, choose an audio stream, or leave the Audio button set to Not Set (**Figure 19.9**) so viewers can cycle through available audio streams on their remotes.
3. Choose a video angle from the Streams Angle pop-up menu to set the remote control's Angle button, or leave the Angle button set to Not Set so viewers can cycle through available video angles using their remotes (refer to Figure 19.9).
4. Choose a subtitle stream within a track from the Streams Subtitle pop-up menu to set the remote control's Subtitle button, or leave the Subtitle button set to Not Set so viewers can cycle through available subtitles using their remotes (refer to Figure 19.9).

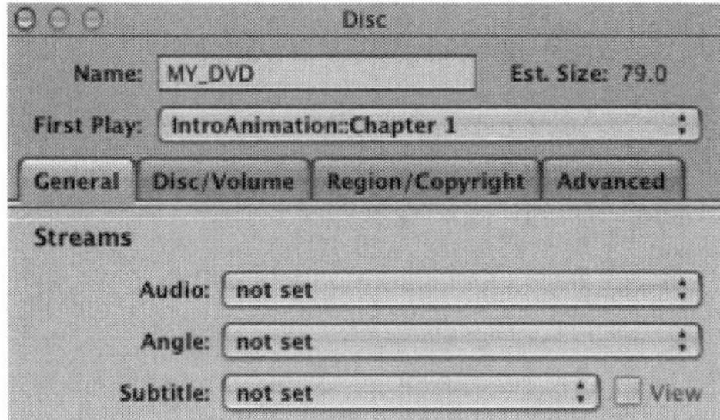

Figure 19.9 Leave the Streams remote control settings set to Not Set if you want viewers to be able to cycle through streams on their remotes.

Track and Slideshow Remote-Control Settings

Each track and slideshow has its own Remote Control area, located at the bottom of the Track or Slideshow Inspector (**Figure 19.10**). By default, these buttons are set to Same as Disc and adopt the settings that you define in the Disc Inspector.

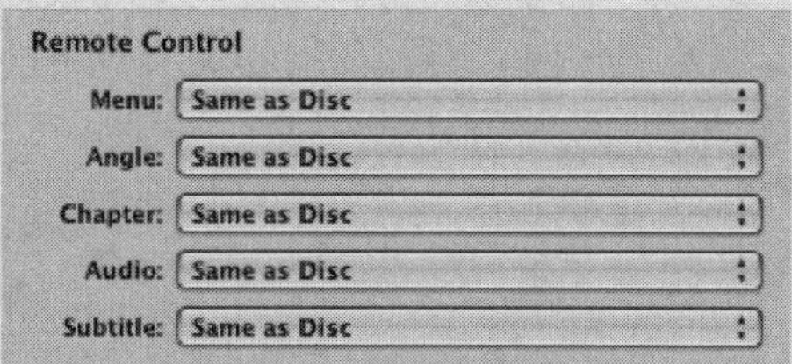

Figure 19.10 Remote-control buttons can behave differently depending on the track or slideshow that the DVD-Video player is playing.

Depending on the complexity of your project, you may want to change these settings. The Menu button, for example, should always return viewers to the menu that jumped them to the currently playing track or slideshow. If your project has multiple menus linking to many different tracks and slideshows, you may need to set the Menu button on a track-by-track basis. Similarly, the Track, Audio, and Subtitle buttons should return viewers to, respectively, the Scene menu, Audio menu, and Subtitle menu for the currently playing track or slideshow.

Track and slideshow remote-control settings override the disc settings.

Disabling the remote control

There will be times when you don't want the remote-control buttons to work. For example, you may have an introductory sequence (such as the FBI warning) that you want to force your viewers to sit through, no matter what. In this situation, you can disable the remote control by denying user operations.

To disable the remote control for an entire track:

1. In the Outline or Graphical view, select a track to display its properties in the Inspector.
2. In the Track Inspector, select the User Operations tab (**Figure 19.11**).
3. On the Track Inspector's User Operations tab, click the check box of each user operation that you want to prevent viewers from selecting on their remote controls (refer to Figure 19.11).

   The viewer is unable to use the disabled remote control settings while that track is playing.

✔ Tips

- By default, all user operations are enabled for tracks. When a check box is selected, the option becomes disabled.
- To clear all selections you've made, click the User Operations tab's Enable All button.
- Chapter markers can have user operation settings independent of the track to which they belong. This setup comes in handy when you've added buttons to one or more chapters in a track. Select the chapter marker in the Track editor and click the User Operations tab to see the marker's settings in the Inspector.

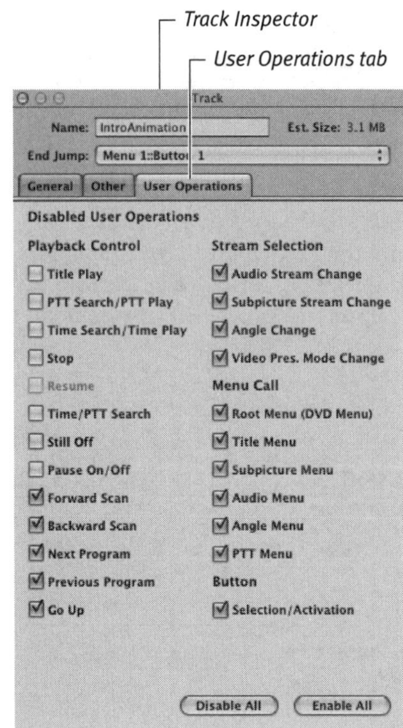

Figure 19.11 Disabling user operations prevents viewers from accessing certain features with their remote controls.

Hiding Easter Eggs

Easter egg is a generic term for anything hidden within your DVD-Video disc that contains bonus content. Viewers are supposed to hunt for Easter eggs by finding hidden buttons, navigating tracks in a certain order, or activating a passcode from an onscreen button pad. Easter eggs should be hard to find, but if you don't plan ahead, on some DVD-Video players, viewers can jump straight to them by pressing the remote control's Next key to skip through tracks and chapters. In this situation, disabling the Next Program user operation saves the day.

Using the Connections Tab

You can set connections, button links, and end actions in a number of places throughout DVD Studio Pro. Although you can make most connections in the Inspector, you may find it easier to see all links and actions for a menu, track, or slideshow all lined up in one place. The Connections tab displays all of the links and possible connections for each asset, making it easy to see broken links without opening each individual track, slideshow, or menu.

The Connections tab is located in the top-right quadrant if you're using an Advanced window configuration that displays all four quadrants. If you're not using an Advanced layout, you can view the Connections tab by choosing Window > Connections.

When you select an item in the Outline view, its links are displayed on the Connection tab. This tab is divided into two panes (**Figure 19.12**):

- The Source pane displays all links and connections of the item selected in the Outline view.
- The Targets pane displays possible connection targets.

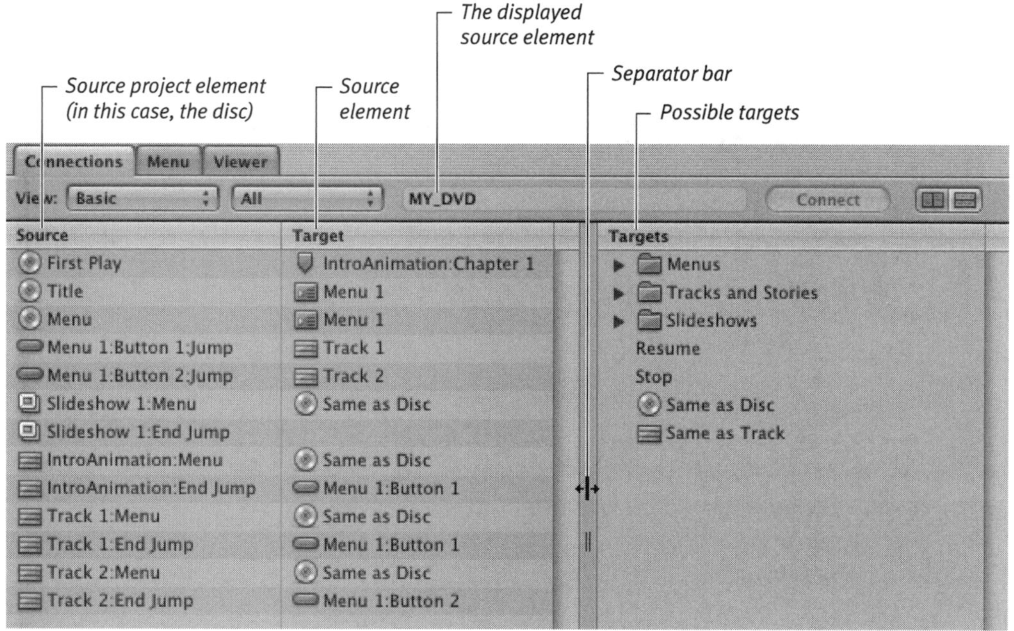

Figure 19.12 The Connections tab consists of the Source pane and the Targets pane, which are separated by a flexible separator bar.

To open the Connections tab:

- Choose Window > Connections (**Figure 19.13**), or press Command-2.

  The Connections tab opens.

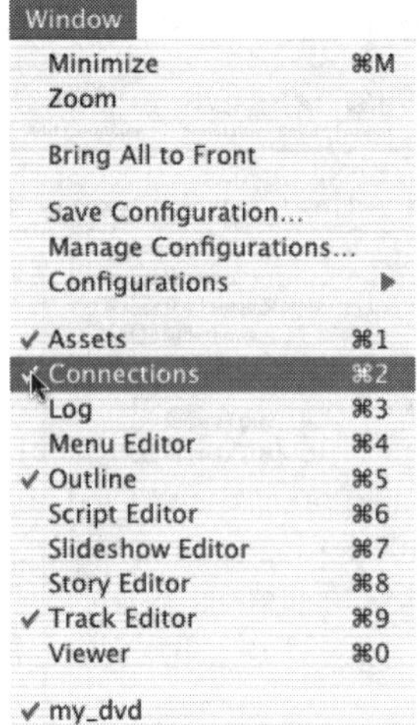

Figure 19.13 Choose Window > Connections to open the Connections tab.

Choosing the level of detail on the Connections tab

You can choose the level of detail—Basic, Standard, or Advanced—displayed on the Connections tab as well as whether the tab shows all connections or only unconnected items.

- **Basic** shows all project connections that *must* be linked for your project to play correctly. For example, an item's end jump is a basic connection.
- **Standard** displays deeper functions of a track or menu that you *should* connect before multiplexing your project. You don't have to make all the connections, such as to optional features like pre-scripts and timeout targets, but you should ensure that all end actions are connected so that your disc doesn't stop playing because the DVD-Video player doesn't know what to do next.
- **Advanced** shows all possible connections, including those that can be made only on the Advanced Connections tab, such as connections to the remote control's Previous and Next buttons (discussed later in this chapter). You don't need to link all connections. For example, by default, at each marker's end, playback will automatically jump to the next marker's start—you don't often need to set marker end actions.

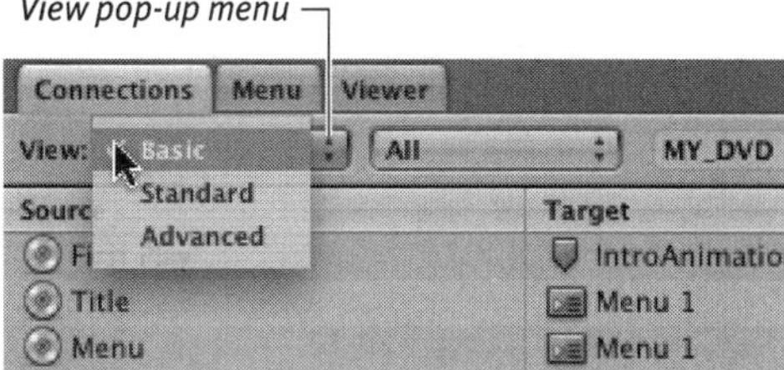

Figure 19.14 You can choose the level of detail displayed in the Connections tab's Source pane by selecting a view type from the View pop-up menu.

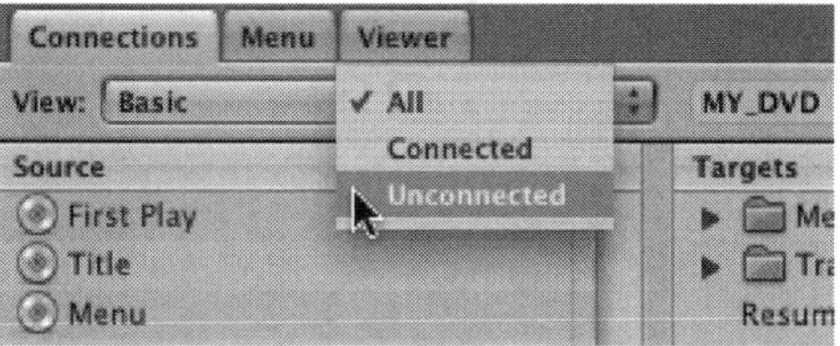

Figure 19.15 Choose Unconnected from the second View pop-up menu to show only the unconnected links on the Connections tab.

To change the level of view detail on the Connections tab:

- At the top left of the Connections tab, choose Basic, Standard, or Advanced from the View pop-up menu (**Figure 19.14**).

To show unconnected links only:

- At the top left of the Connections tab, choose Unconnected from the second View pop-up menu (**Figure 19.15**).

Making connections on the Connections tab

Chapter 13, "The Menu Editor," discussed how to link buttons to their target actions. If a menu contains more than one button, linking targets in the Menu Inspector can be a tedious task; you must select each button, one at a time, in the Menu editor and set the target (jump) action in the Inspector. But there is a better way: select a menu in the Outline view to display it on the Connections tab; all buttons and their targets are displayed in a list, where you can quickly make all button connections at one time.

Making connections on the Connections tab is quick and easy, and you can choose among several ways in which to link connections based on your desired workflow. For example, you can see all buttons on a menu that need to be linked so they can jump *somewhere* when activated, and you can link all menu buttons by dragging a track or slideshow onto each button's target on the Connections tab.

To link a button's target on the Connections tab:

1. Select a menu in the Outline view.

   The menu is displayed on the Connections tab using the Basic view by default (**Figure 19.16**).

2. On the Connections tab, select a button from the Source list.

   The Source list shows all items that can be linked within the menu. The list of possible targets within the Targets pane is updated to display only the links that can be connected to the selected button (**Figure 19.17**).

3. In the Targets pane, select a Jump When Activated item to link to the button (**Figure 19.18**).

   The panes behave separately, so the button that you selected in the first pane stays selected.

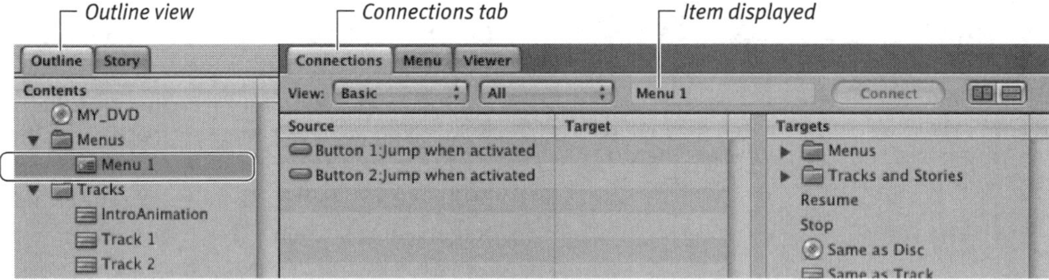

Figure 19.16 When you select a menu in the Outline view, the menu's buttons are listed on the Connections tab. The name of the item you've selected in the Outline view is displayed in the center of the Connections tab.

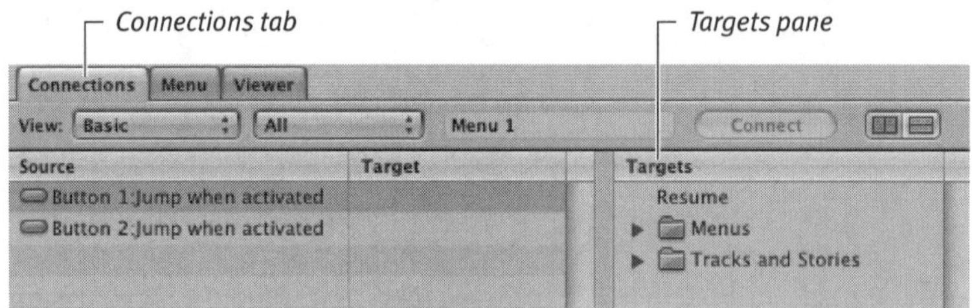

Figure 19.17 When you select a button on the Connections tab, the list of possible targets that can be connected to the button is updated in the Targets pane.

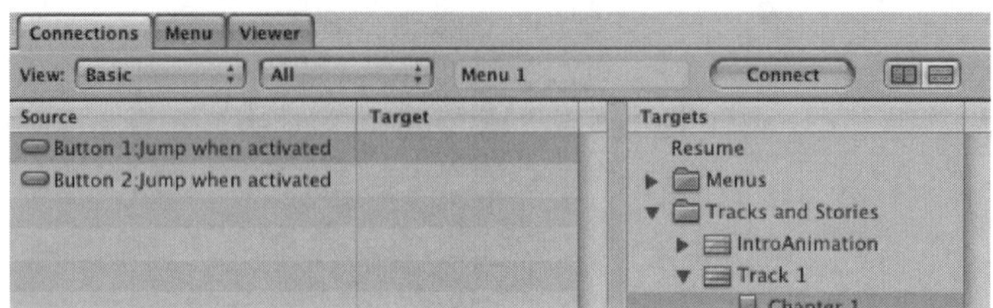

Figure 19.18 Select a Jump When Activated target for the button that you selected.

4. To connect the Jump When Activated target that you selected in step 3 to the button that you selected in step 2, *do one of the following:*

   ▲ Double-click the item that you selected in the Targets pane.

   ▲ Click the Connect button at the top right of the Connections tab.

   ▲ Drag the selected target from the Targets pane to the Target column in the Source pane (**Figure 19.19**).

   The connection is made, and the linked item shows up in the Source pane (**Figure 19.20**).

✔ Tips

- Key commands can save hours when you're working on the Connections tab. Use the up and down arrow keys to move your selection up and down the pane currently in focus on the Connections tab. Use the Control key to switch focus from the Target pane to the Source pane. Use the Return key to connect the currently selected source item to the currently selected target item.
- To connect the same target to multiple buttons, drag the connected target in the Source pane to any other unlinked target in the Source pane. A copy of the connected target will be made, and the button will be linked using the same target.

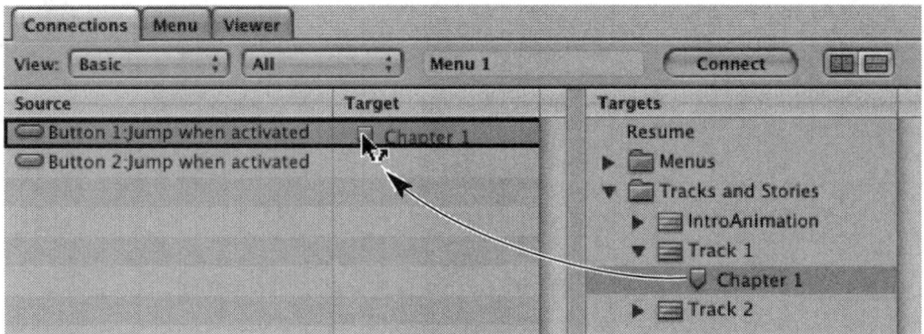

Figure 19.19 Drag the selected button jump target from the Targets pane into the Source pane and drop it on the button's Jump When Activated target to make the connection.

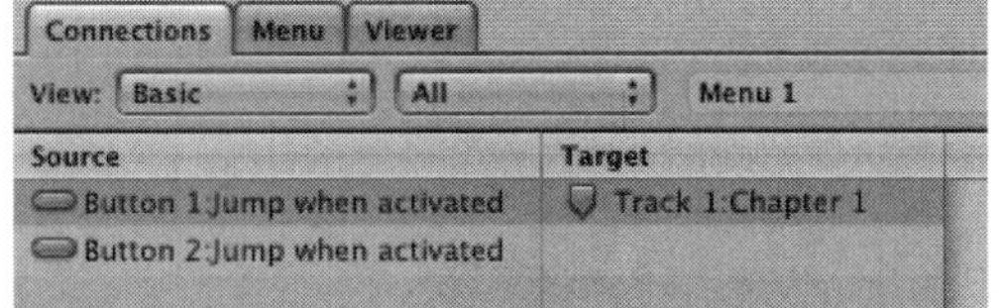

Figure 19.20 The button's Jump When Activated target is displayed in the Connections tab's Source pane to show that the button has been linked. This figure shows that Button 1 will jump to track 1, chapter marker 1, when the viewer activates the button on the menu.

To remove a button's linked connection:

1. Select the button's target in the Source pane.
2. *Do one of the following:*
   - ▲ Press the Delete key on your keyboard.
   - ▲ Click the Disconnect button at the top right of the Connections tab (**Figure 19.21**).

Assigning the Next and Previous buttons

Every DVD-Video player remote control has Previous and Next keys (Previous Program and Next Program keys) that allow you to jump back and forth through chapters in a track (or slides in a slideshow). In DVD Studio Pro, you can manually assign connections for the remote control's Previous and Next buttons, using the Advanced view on the Connections tab. (Earlier in this chapter, in the section "To change the level of view detail on the Connections tab," you learned that you can choose the level of detail displayed on the Connections tab.)

Figure 19.21 To remove a connection, select a button's connected target in the first pane of the Connections tab and click Disconnect.

✔ Tip

- Many DVD-Video players do not allow you to skip to the next track using the remote control's Next Program key. In fact, this key is designed to skip from chapter to chapter (program to program) inside a particular track. However, by manually assigning the Next Program remote-control key using the Connections tab's Advanced view, you can ensure that your Next Program key works exactly as you want it to.

To assign the Next remote-control button:

1. In the Outline view, select a track to display it on the Connections tab.
2. From the Connections tab's View pop-up menu, choose Advanced.

   The track's advanced connections are displayed (**Figure 19.22**).

continues on next page

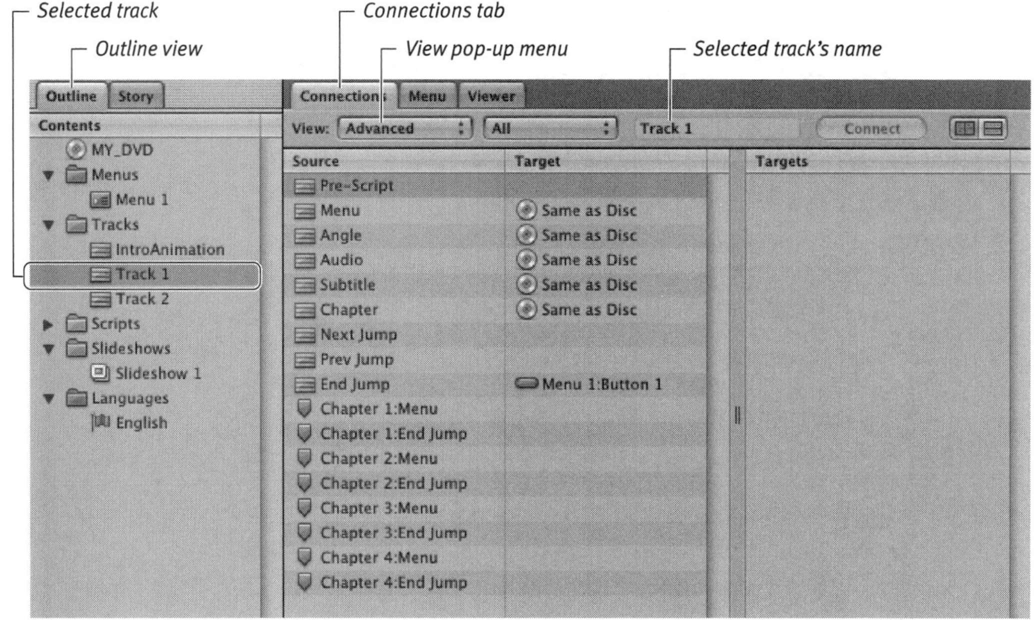

Figure 19.22 Select a track in the Outline view to see its connections on the Connections tab. Choose Advanced from the View pop-up menu to see all of the connections for the track.

3. In the Connections tab's Source pane, select Next Jump to highlight it (**Figure 19.23**).

   Now the Targets pane displays all of the possible links that can be connected to the track's next jump.

4. In the Targets pane, select a Next Jump action item for your track (**Figure 19.24**).

Figure 19.23 Select the track's next jump action in the Source pane. The possible links that can be connected to the next jump action are displayed in the Targets pane.

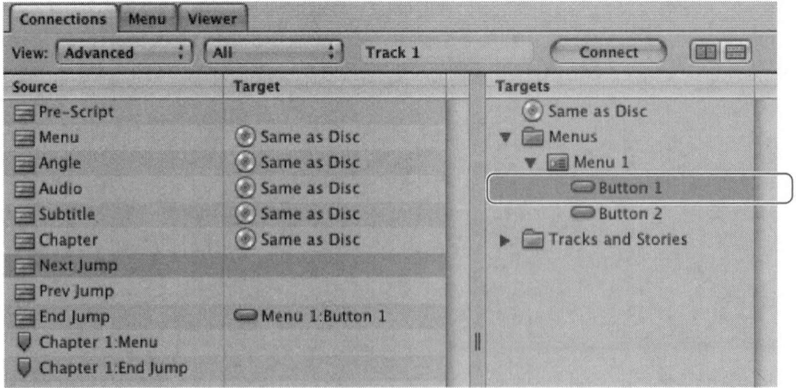

Figure 19.24 Select a Next Jump action item so the viewer can skip past the last chapter marker in the track and jump back to the menu.

5. To connect the Next Jump action target that you selected in the Targets pane to the Next Jump button that you selected in the Source pane, *do one of the following:*

   ▲ Double-click the item that you selected in the Targets pane.

   ▲ Click the Connect button at the top right of the Connections tab.

   ▲ Drag the selected target from the Targets pane to the Target column in the Source pane.

   The connection is made, and the linked item shows up in the first pane (the Source pane; **Figure 19.25**). Now when viewers press the Next button on their remote controls, they will be jumped to the next action instead of having to watch the video of the last chapter marker.

✔ Tip

■ You cannot assign the Next button when working with stories. The Next Jump button isn't available if you select a story in the Outline view to see the story's links on the Connections tab.

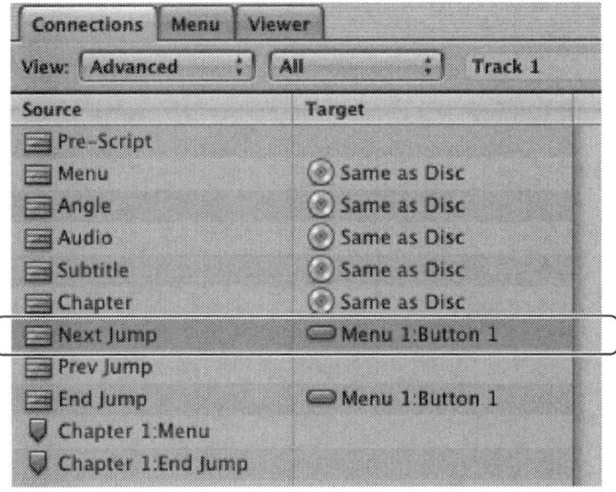

Figure 19.25 You can set the Next Jump button only in the Advanced view of the Connections tab. When viewers press the Next button on their remote controls, they will be jumped to the next action, which is set to Menu 1, Button 1, in this figure.

Using the Resume function

The remote control's Resume key performs the opposite function of the Menu key. For example, if a viewer is watching a track and then presses the remote control's Menu key to jump to a menu, the viewer can then press the Resume key to jump from the menu back to the last track he or she was watching, and playback will commence from exactly where the viewer left off.

You can also use the Resume function more creatively. Are you familiar with those choose-your-own-adventure books? Well, you can offer the same sort of experience with a DVD-Video. For example, when a video segment reaches a specified marker, viewers could be jumped to a menu with several buttons providing links to other video tracks as well as a button that returns the viewers to the original marker and continued playback where they left off. The choose-your-own-adventure video is just one use you can make of the Resume function, returning playback to the marker that the viewer jumps out of.

Best of all, viewers don't need a remote-control to access the Resume feature because DVD Studio Pro has a Return function available for use with any menu button. Using the Inspector, you can assign the Return function to any button, on any menu. When the menu button is activated, the viewer will be jumped back to the last-played project element.

To link the Resume command to a button:

1. In the Outline view, select a menu that contains the button to which you want to link the Resume command.

   The Connections tab updates to display the menu's links.

2. From the View pop-up menu, choose Advanced (**Figure 19.26**).

3. In the Source pane of the Connections tab, select the button that will return viewers to the track from which they jumped (**Figure 19.27**).

   When activated, this button will jump the viewer back to the last-viewed chapter marker in a track or slide in a slideshow.

4. In the Targets pane, select Resume.

   The panes on the Connections tab are independent of each other, so the button selected in step 3 remains selected.

5. Double-click Resume in the second pane to link it to the button that you selected in step 3.

   Resume is linked to the button (**Figure 19.28**) and, when activated, will jump the viewer back to the last item played on the DVD-Video disc.

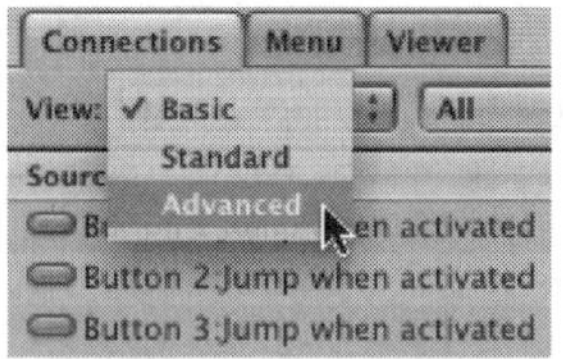

Figure 19.26 Choose Advanced to view all of the menu connections that you can make.

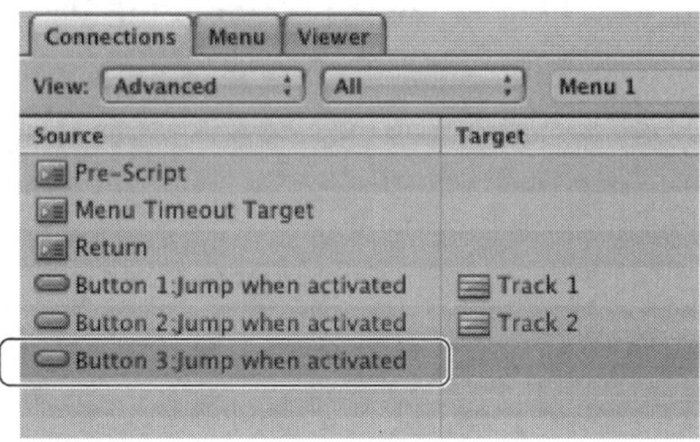

Figure 19.27 Select the button in the Connections tab's Source pane that you want to use as the Resume button. When activated on the menu, this button will jump the viewer back to the last-viewed item.

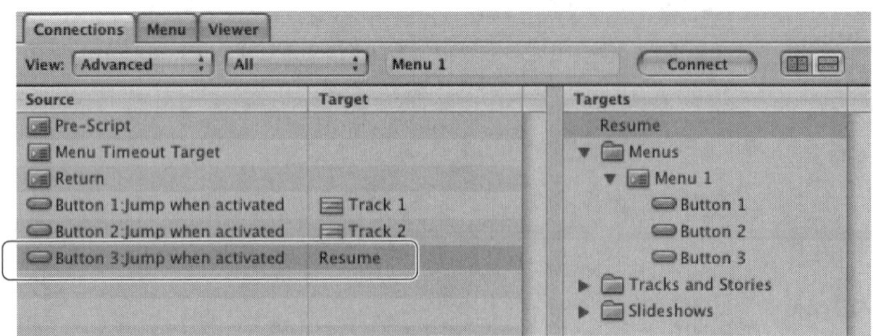

Figure 19.28 This figure shows that Resume is connected to Button 3 of this menu.

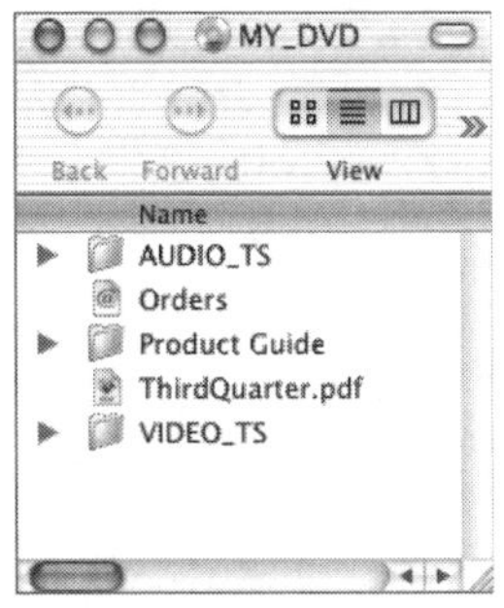

Figure 19.29 On a hybrid DVD, ROM data is recorded at the root level of the DVD disc beside the VIDEO_TS and AUDIO_TS folders.

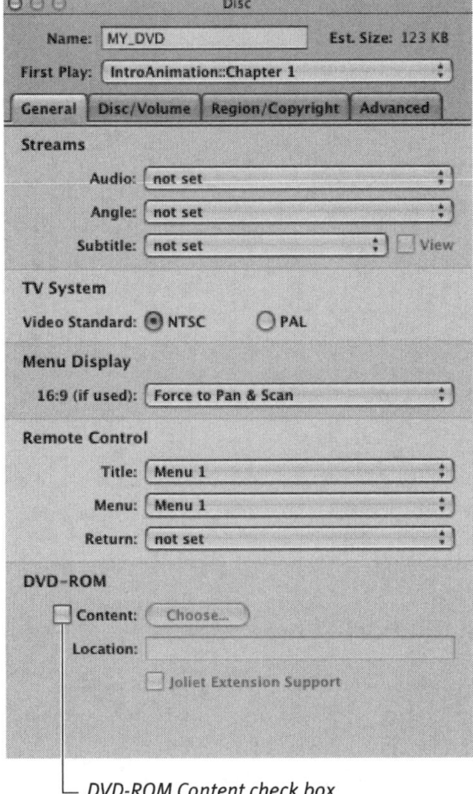

Figure 19.30 Select the DVD-ROM Content check box and choose a folder to add extra content to your disc.

Creating Hybrid DVDs

Hybrid DVDs are DVDs that contain computer data—anything from PDF files and QuickTime movies to PowerPoint presentations—alongside the VIDEO_TS and AUDIO_TS folders at the disc's root level. To create a hybrid DVD, you must specify a ROM folder that contains computer files. The ROM folder's *contents* will then be included at the DVD disc's *root* level beside the VIDEO_TS and AUDIO_TS folders (**Figure 19.29**).

When hybrid DVDs are played on a set-top DVD-Video player, the extra files are ignored. The viewer can access the data files only when the hybrid disc is played on a computer.

To select a ROM folder:

1. In the Outline view, click the disc icon, or in the Graphical view, click the background.

   The Inspector updates to display the disc's properties. The General tab should be selected by default; if it isn't, select it.

2. In the Disc Inspector's DVD-ROM section at the bottom of the General tab, select the Content check box (**Figure 19.30**).

   The Choose button becomes active.

continues on next page

3. Click the Choose button (**Figure 19.31**).

   The DVD-ROM Contents dialog appears (**Figure 19.32**).

4. In the DVD-ROM Contents dialog, navigate to the location of your DVD-ROM folder and click the Choose button (refer to Figure 19.32).

   When you later build and format your disc, the contents of the selected folder will be recorded at the root level of the final DVD disc. (To learn more about recording DVD discs, see Chapter 20, "Outputting the Project.")

✔ Tips

- To remove a specified DVD-ROM folder, deselect the DVD-ROM Content check box.
- The DVD-ROM content you choose must be contained within a folder; you cannot select a specific file. The selected folder does not appear on the final disc, though any folders nested inside it will.
- The DVD-ROM folder's content contributes to the size of your DVD-Video project. Be careful not to exceed your target DVD disc's capacity.
- DVD@ccess links can open data files stored in ROM folders on a hybrid DVD. To learn more, see Chapter 21, "DVD@ccess."

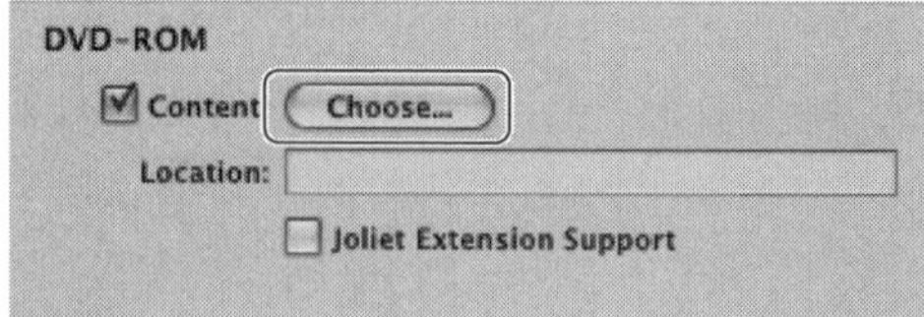

Figure 19.31 Click the Choose button to select a DVD-ROM folder for your disc.

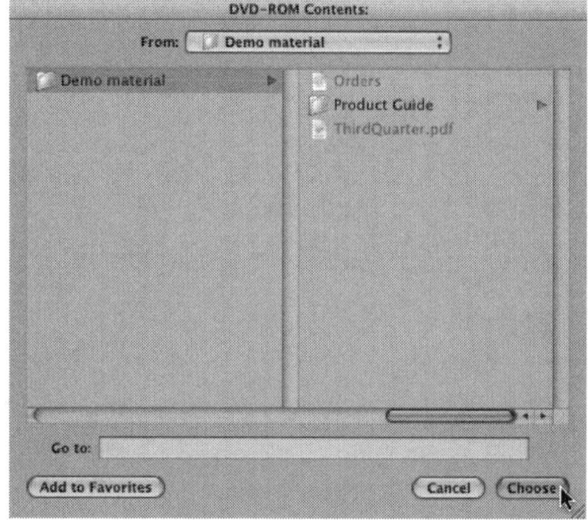

Figure 19.32 Navigate to the folder that contains your DVD-ROM content and click Choose.

Joliet Extension Support

DVD discs are restricted to the 8.3 file-naming convention (eight characters, a period, and a three-letter extension), which supports uppercase letters, numbers, and underscores only—no other characters can be used. To get around this restriction, you can select the Disc Inspector's Joliet Extension Support check box, which is found on the General tab in the DVD-ROM section (**Figure 19.33**), to enable disc support for file names up to 26 characters plus the three-letter extension.

Select the Joliet Extension Support check box only if you need support for extra characters, as the Joliet extension may cause playback problems on some DVD-Video players.

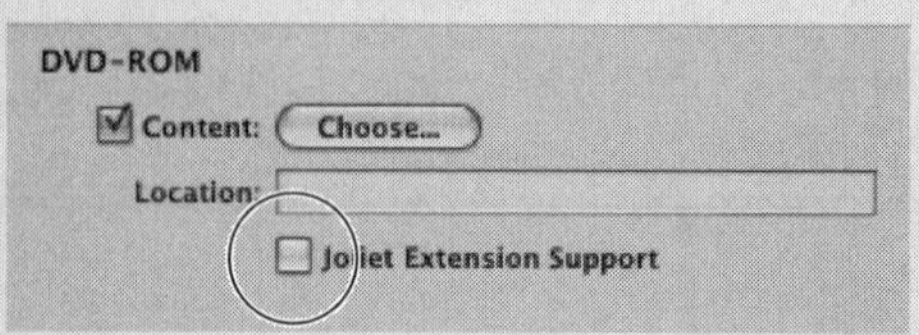

Figure 19.33 To include support for file names of up to 26 characters, select the Joliet Extension Support check box.

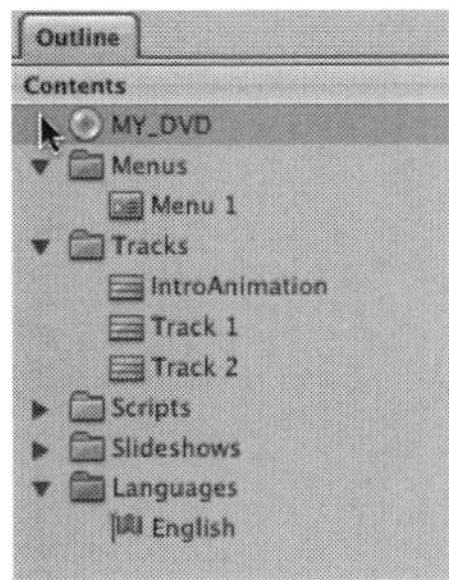

Figure 19.34 Click the disc in the Outline view to view its properties in the Inspector.

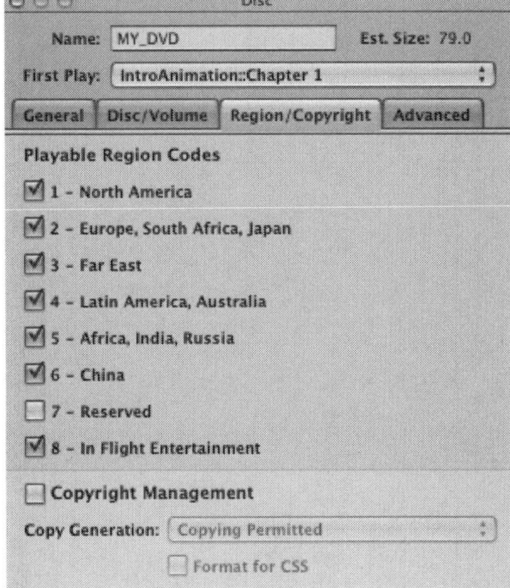

Figure 19.35 Select the check boxes of all regions that you want to include on your disc.

✔ Tip

- Projects recorded to DVD-R cannot be region-protected. If you need to protect your content with region codes, you must click the check boxes of the regions you want to include on your disc to set the region code flags, or warnings, in DVD Studio Pro and then give a DLT tape to your replicator to add region coding (see the sidebar "CSS and Sector Sizes" later in this chapter).

Protecting Your Content

DVD discs hold digital data, which is easy to copy. To keep your DVD-Video on the disc and out of the grip of those who might want to reproduce it, DVD Studio Pro offers three forms of content protection: region codes, the Content Scrambling System (CSS), and the Macrovision Analog Protection System (APS).

About region codes

All DVD-Video players are hardwired with a certain region code when they are manufactured. Using DVD Studio Pro's Region Code property, you can set exactly where in the world your DVD-Video can play (see Chapter 2, "DVD 101," for a list of regions and their codes).

Region coding does not encrypt any of the files on the DVD; it simply tells the DVD-Video player to accept or reject the disc.

To set the disc's region code:

1. In the Outline view, click the disc (**Figure 19.34**) to display its properties in the Inspector.
2. Click the Region/Copyright tab in the Disc Inspector to display the disc's region code settings.
3. Click a region code check box to select or deselect that region (**Figure 19.35**).

   By default, all regions (except Region 7) are selected, which means that your DVD-Video disc will play on any DVD-Video player, anywhere in the world (that is, any player that understands your DVD-Video's broadcast standard—most NTSC DVD-Video players won't play PAL DVD-Videos regardless of region code).

About CSS copy protection

CSS is a data-encryption system that prevents viewers from dragging your DVD-Video off of the DVD disc and onto their computers. CSS encrypts the DVD-Video's data by scrambling the audio and video in certain sectors on the disc (see the sidebar "CSS and Sector Sizes"). The keys used to put this data back together are stored in two places right on the DVD-Video disc. The first key, called the Title key, is stored in the *header* of each scrambled sector. The second key, the Disc key, is locked away in the disc's control area.

Computer DVD-ROM drives cannot harvest information from either sector headers or the disc's control area. Consequently, when someone drags your DVD-Video off of the disc and onto his or her computer, the person gets only the scrambled data—the key to unscramble that data is left behind on the DVD disc.

CSS encryption can be applied by qualified replicators only—you can't CSS-protect your disc with DVD Studio Pro alone. However, you do need to turn on CSS to set a flag that tells the replicator to apply CSS copy protection. Setting this flag doesn't automatically give you CSS encryption; you must pay for it. If you intend to use CSS copy protection, make sure you discuss costs with the replicator before you send your DLT tapes.

CSS and Sector Sizes

Data on DVD discs is stored in sectors. CSS copy-protected discs (including most Hollywood DVD-Videos) use a sector size of 2,054 bytes, whereas DVD-R discs use a sector size of 2,048 bytes. The replicator places encryption keys in the extra few bytes that DVD-R discs don't have, which makes it physically impossible for a DVD-R to hold a CSS-protected DVD-Video. DLT tapes, however, can record a sector size of 2,054 bytes, making them suitable for transporting your CSS-protected DVD-Video to the replicator.

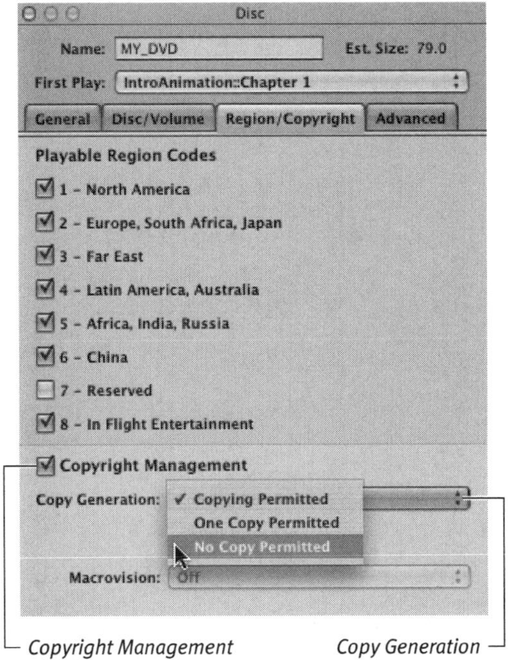

Figure 19.36 Select the Copyright Management check box on the Region/Copyright tab and select a copy generation type from the pop-up menu.

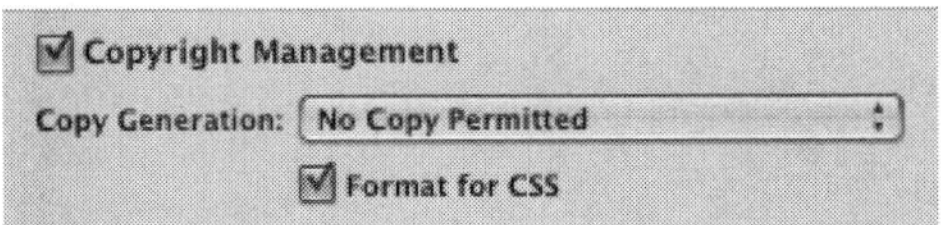

Figure 19.37 Selecting the Format for CSS check box tells your replicator to add CSS keys to your DVD-Video disc.

To enable CSS copy protection:

1. In the Outline view, select the disc to display its properties in the Inspector.
2. Click the Region/Copyright tab in the Disc Inspector.
3. Select the Copyright Management check box at the bottom of the Region/Copyright tab (**Figure 19.36**).

   The Copy Generation pop-up menu becomes active.
4. Select No Copy Permitted from the Copy Generation pop-up menu (refer to Figure 19.36).

   The Format for CSS check box becomes active.
5. Select the Format for CSS check box (**Figure 19.37**).

   When formatted to DLT, DVD Studio Pro will add flags to let the replicator know to add CSS copy-protection keys to your DVD disc.

About Macrovision protection

The Macrovision Analog Protection System (APS) keeps people from recording your DVD-Videos onto VHS tapes. The system works by tricking the VHS recorder's automatic gain control (AGC) circuit into thinking that the video stream is either brighter or darker than it actually is. To fix the problem, the VHS player's AGC circuit jumps in and increases or reduces the video's brightness. The result is a video stream that alternates between too bright and too dark, making it unpleasant to watch. Some forms of Macrovision also *colorstripe* the video, adding colored horizontal stripes across the video (see the sidebar "What's Colorstripe?").

To use Macrovision copy protection, you must enter into a license agreement with Macrovision Corporation and have a Macrovision-licensed replicator professionally replicate your project. In return for giving you access to its APS, Macrovision charges you a per-disc fee (usually around a few cents per disc; the higher the number of units, the lower the per-unit price). You then activate Macrovision copy protection for certain tracks or chapters as you create the disc. After you deliver the disc to the replication facility, the replicator checks the disc using a software verifier, such as Eclipse—made by Eclipse Data Technologies (`www.eclipsedata.com`)—to see which parts you want protected and then reports this information to the folks at Macrovision, who complete the process by sending you a bill.

Before using Macrovision, contact the company to find out the cost for protecting your discs. For more information, either visit Macrovision's company Web site at `www.macrovision.com` or send an e-mail directly to `acp-na@macrovision.com`.

What's Colorstripe?

Colorstripe modifies the colorburst signal, which is a reference contained within the analog video signal. TVs and video monitors use this colorburst reference to decode and properly display color information. Although this modification is transparent to display devices, it dramatically upsets the VCR's color playback circuitry if it is recorded and played back.

So Many Types

Macrovision-protected discs contain *trigger bits* that tell the DVD-Video player whether or not to enable the Macrovision APS. Macrovision copy protection comes in three types:

- Type 1: AGC protection only
- Type 2: AGC plus two-line colorstripe protection
- Type 3: AGC plus four-line colorstripe protection

While Type 3 is the default, or standard, configuration, the two other types are available as alternatives in the event that DVD playback problems occur on certain televisions. (According to Macrovision, no problems have ever been reported.)

Type 3 protection is recommended for NTSC video, and Type 2 for PAL video—with a caveat. Current PAL DVD-Video players use AGC copy protection *only* and do not have colorstripe enabled. If you're working on a PAL project, you should hedge your bets by choosing Type 2 protection; if you decide to enable colorstripe for PAL in the future, the discs will already be set to use it.

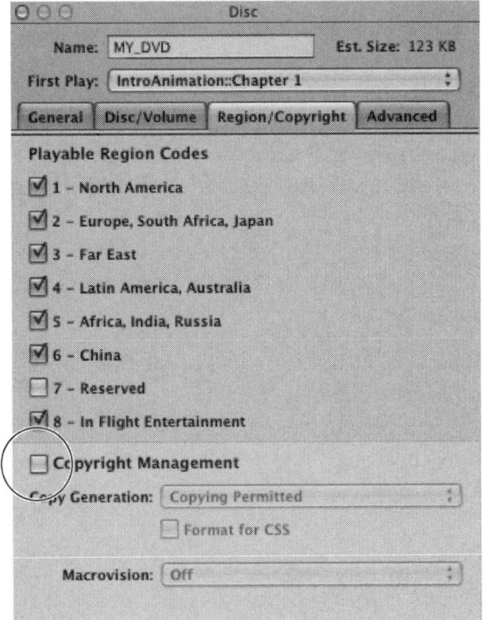

Figure 19.38 Select the Copyright Management check box to activate the Copy Generation property and turn on Macrovision copy protection.

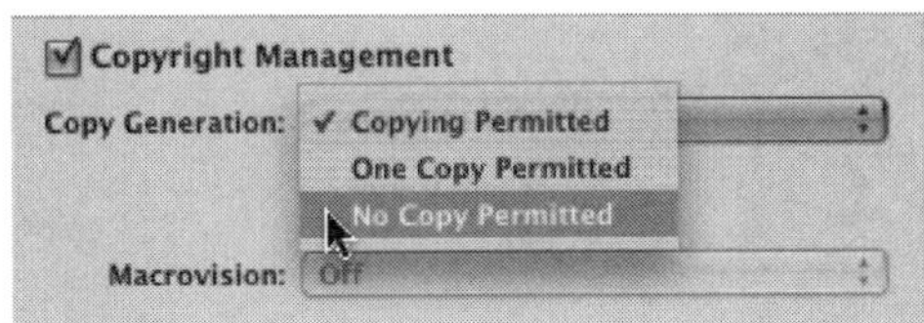

Figure 19.39 Choose No Copy Permitted to enable the Macrovision copy protection pop-up menu and choose a Macrovision type.

Figure 19.40 Select a Macrovision type from the pop-up menu.

To enable Macrovision copy protection:

1. In DVD Studio Pro's Outline view, select the disc to display its properties in the Inspector.
2. In the Disc Inspector, click the Region/Copyright tab.

   The disc's Copyright Management settings are displayed at the bottom of the Region/Copyright tab (**Figure 19.38**). All settings are dimmed.
3. Click the Copyright Management check box in the Disc Inspector.

   The Copy Generation pop-up menu becomes active.
4. From the Copy Generation pop-up menu, choose No Copy Permitted (**Figure 19.39**).

   The Macrovision pop-up menu becomes active.
5. From the Macrovision pop-up menu, choose a Macrovision APS type (**Figure 19.40**).

   Macrovision copy protection is enabled for the disc.

Simulating the Project

DVD Studio Pro's Simulator mimics a set-top DVD Player, but you don't have to build your project to see it in action. The Simulator allows you to test your project's connections to verify that all links work as expected while you're still creating the project. You can start simulating from any point in the project or start playback from the beginning of the disc.

Playback controls

The Simulator's remote control is split into three sections: playback controls, menu call controls, and video stream controls.

The playback controls in the Simulator are similar to those found on a DVD player's remote control (**Figure 19.41**). Use them to navigate the project's menus, tracks, and slideshows.

The Simulator's menu call controls are used to test your project's remote-control button assignments (**Figure 19.42**). See "To set the disc's remote-control buttons" earlier in this chapter for information on how to assign these buttons. DVD players and their remotes behave differently. Some remotes include these buttons, though most require the user to press Audio and then Menu to access the audio setup menu, for example.

The Info button is unique to the Simulator. This button opens the Simulator's Information panel, which is discussed later in this chapter.

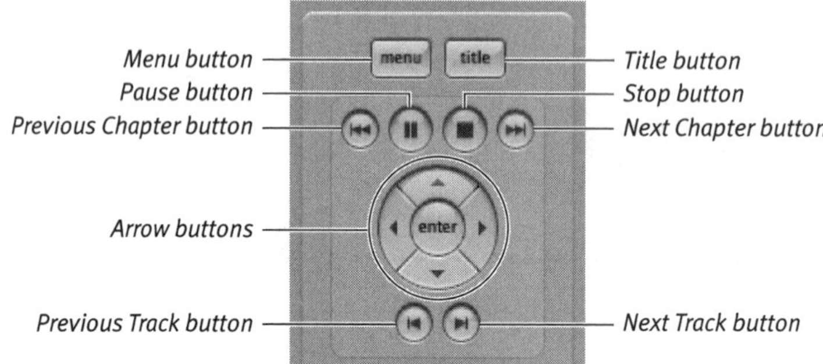

Figure 19.41 The buttons along the side of the Simulator window mimic the buttons on a DVD-Video player's remote control.

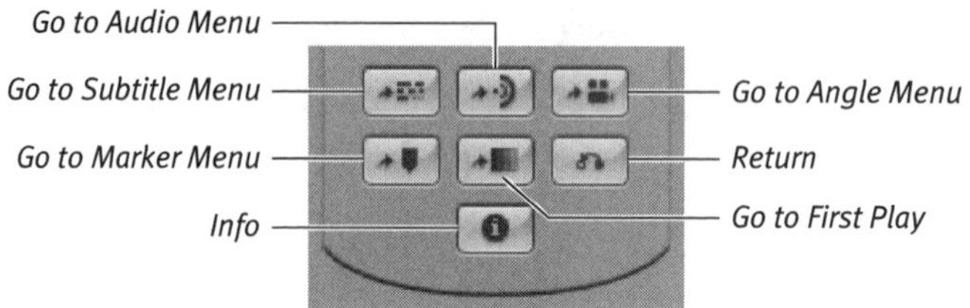

Figure 19.42 The menu call buttons are used to jump to a menu you've set.

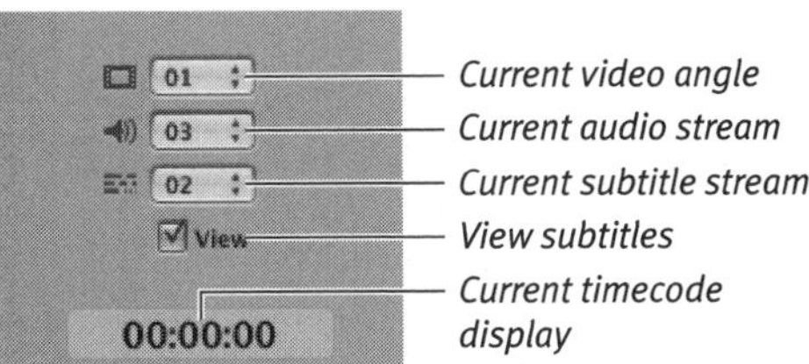

Figure 19.43 The stream selection section of the Simulator's remote-control buttons allows you to quickly change the displayed video track's angle, audio, or subtitle stream.

Figure 19.44 There are several ways to begin simulation from the start of the disc. One option is to choose File > Simulate from the application menu.

The Simulator's video stream selection controls are also unique to the Simulator and provide a quick way to test all streams within a track (**Figure 19.43**). Each pop-up menu lists all streams available in the track that is currently playing in the Simulator. You can select any of the streams from the pop-up menu at any time. The Simulator window will update to show the currently selected video angle, audio stream, or subtitle stream. Use the View check box to turn subtitles on (select the check box) or off (deselect the check box).

Using the Simulator

Before building the final project, open the Simulator one last time and use it to test the disc itself, checking that all menus, tracks, and slideshows play as expected.

To open the Simulator:

1. To open the Simulator window and start playback at the First Play item on your disc, *do one of the following:*
   - ▲ Choose File > Simulate (**Figure 19.44**).
   - ▲ Control-click the disc in the Outline view and choose Simulate from the shortcut menu.
   - ▲ Click the Simulator icon in the DVD Studio Pro toolbar.
   - ▲ Press Option-Command-0 (zero).
2. Play all menus, tracks, and slideshows in turn, using the simulation buttons to make sure that each item plays as expected.

Debugging your project

While you're testing your project in the Simulator, DVD Studio Pro generates a simulation log for you (**Figure 19.45**).

The simulation log lists all items played, all jumps made, all buttons selected, and the SPRM value of each item previewed. (To learn more about SPRM values, see Chapter 25, "Scripting").

To open the Log tab:

◆ Choose Window > Log (**Figure 19.46**), or press Command-3.

✔ Tip

■ You can copy text from the log and paste the text into TextEdit to print your simulation report.

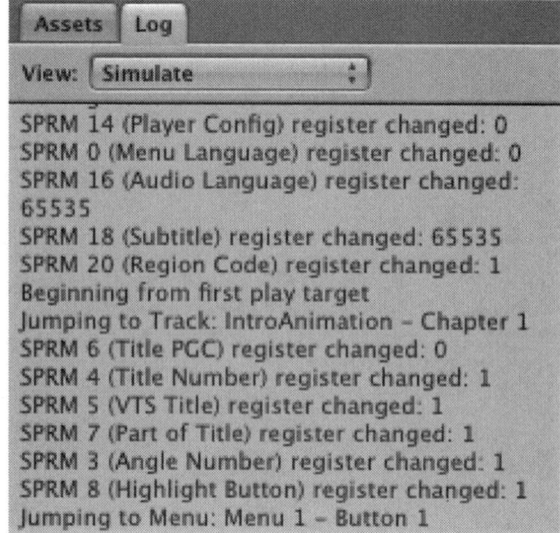

Figure 19.45 On the Log tab, the Simulator generates a text description of your actions when you select items and activate buttons in the project's menus.

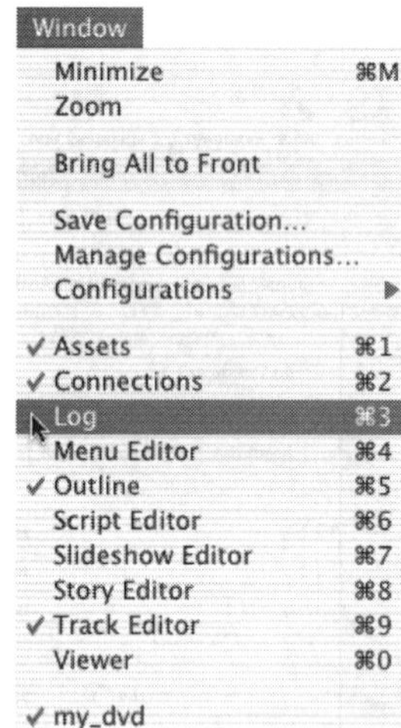

Figure 19.46 Choose Window > Log to display the Log tab.

Displaying Simulator's Information panel

The Log tab is a bit complicated to understand unless you're familiar with scripting terminology. Fortunately, there is another way to view simulation information while still using the Simulator: the Simulator's Information panel. This panel shows all of the currently displayed items and their properties, so you can look for any values that aren't set and buttons that are set to the wrong jump actions. For advanced users, the Information panel also lets you keep track of SPRM and GPRM values as your project simulates (to learn more about SPRM and GPRM values, see Chapter 25).

To open the Information panel:

- Click the Info button on the left side of the Simulator window (**Figure 19.47**).

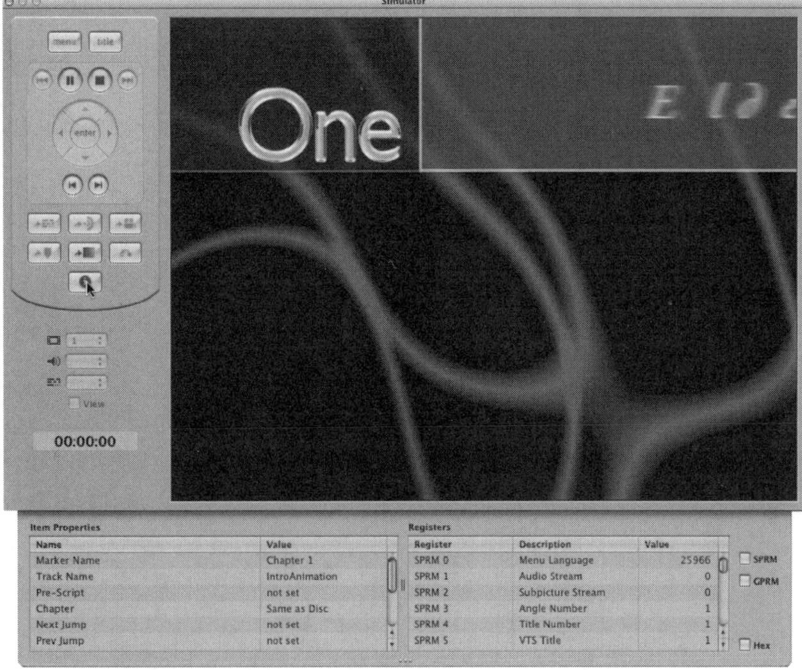

Figure 19.47 The Simulator's Information panel displays all of the properties for the currently playing project element.

Quality Assured

QA is the process of testing a finished project to make sure it plays as expected. There are three levels of QA testing:

- **Use the Simulator—often.** As you author your project, you should constantly use the Simulator to discover and correct mistakes. By the time you're ready to record the project to disc, most problems will already be fixed.
- **Play the project in Apple's DVD Player.** When you build a project, you create a finished copy of the DVD-Video on your computer's hard disk. Using the Apple DVD Player, you can open the DVD-Video from your hard disk and watch it just like you would watch a DVD-Video placed in a set-top DVD-Video player. If your project plays correctly in the Apple DVD Player, most likely it will play correctly on a television. Once you've tested all of your menus, watched the tracks, and cycled through all of the alternate angles and audio streams in the Apple DVD Player, you can record a DVD-ROM.
- **Create a test DVD-R disc.** Recording your project onto a DVD-R disc lets you test it on a TV. If you're not replicating your project, this DVD-R is more than just a test disc—it's the final DVD-Video. If you're sending your project to a replication facility, this DVD-R allows you to watch the project the way most other viewers will: on a television set. If the DVD-R plays properly, you can confidently send off your DLT tapes.

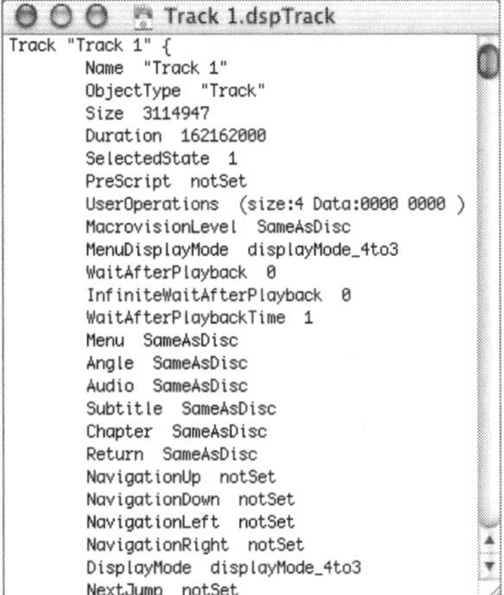

```
Track 1.dspTrack
Track "Track 1" {
        Name  "Track 1"
        ObjectType  "Track"
        Size  3114947
        Duration  162162000
        SelectedState  1
        PreScript  notSet
        UserOperations  (size:4 Data:0000 0000 )
        MacrovisionLevel  SameAsDisc
        MenuDisplayMode  displayMode_4to3
        WaitAfterPlayback  0
        InfiniteWaitAfterPlayback  0
        WaitAfterPlaybackTime  1
        Menu  SameAsDisc
        Angle  SameAsDisc
        Audio  SameAsDisc
        Subtitle  SameAsDisc
        Chapter  SameAsDisc
        Return  SameAsDisc
        NavigationUp  notSet
        NavigationDown  notSet
        NavigationLeft  notSet
        NavigationRight  notSet
        DisplayMode  displayMode_4to3
        NextJump  notSet
```

Figure 19.48 This figure shows a track description file opened in TextEdit. All settings and properties for the selected track are listed.

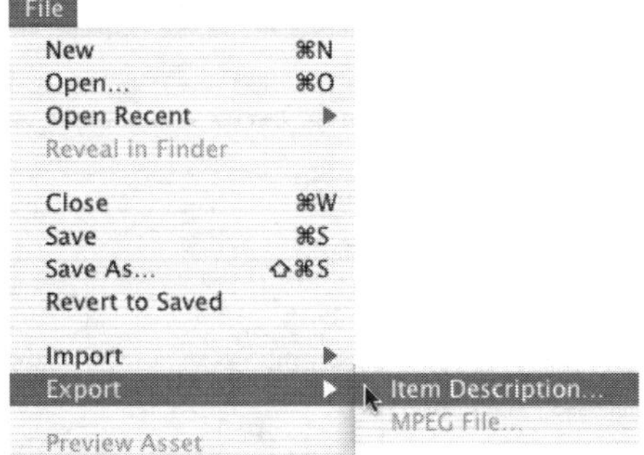

Figure 19.49 Choose File > Export > Item Description to save a description of the selected project element.

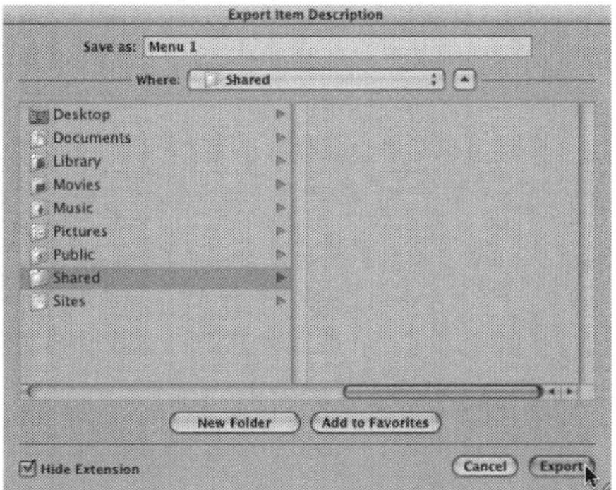

Figure 19.50 Use the Export Item Description dialog to navigate to the location where you want your description file saved.

About Item Description Files

An item description file is a text-based file that contains a complete description of any specific item in your project (a track, menu, script, or anything else listed in the Outline view). Every setting that can be made for the selected item, from the size to the playback settings, is listed in the description file.

You can export any selected item in the Outline or Graphical view to create a description file that you can later import into another DVD Studio Pro project. If you have multiple projects with similar track settings, or an FBI warning track that is used in all of your projects, you may want to consider exporting the track as a description file and importing the description file containing all settings for the track into each of your projects.

When you import a description file for a track, a new track is created, the video and audio assets used are imported, and all settings are implemented.

You can also open description files in TextEdit (**Figure 19.48**) or Bare Bones Software's BBEdit to view an item's settings.

To export an item description file:

1. Select anything listed in the Outline view (a menu, a track, a slideshow, a script, or even the disc itself).
2. Choose File > Export > Item Description (**Figure 19.49**).

   The Export Item Description dialog opens (**Figure 19.50**).

continues on next page

3. At the top of the Export Item Description dialog box, in the Save As text box, type a name for your description file.
4. Navigate to the location where you want to save the file and click the Export button.

   The item description file is saved in the specified location.

To import an item description file:

1. Choose File > Import > Item Description (**Figure 19.51**).

   The Import Item Description file dialog appears (**Figure 19.52**).
2. Navigate to where the description file is located on your hard disk and click Import (refer to Figure 19.52).

   The imported description file is loaded into DVD Studio Pro, and a new item is created in the Outline view. The new project element (menu, track, slideshow, or script) is fully configured based on the item's description, and all referenced assets are imported into the current DVD Studio Pro project.

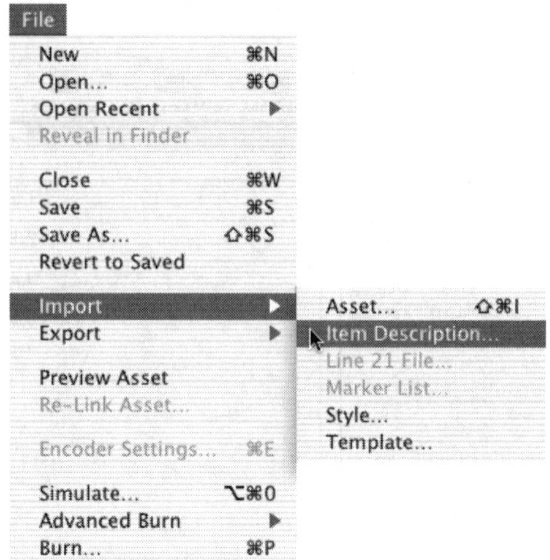

Figure 19.51 To import a description file, choose File > Import > Item Description.

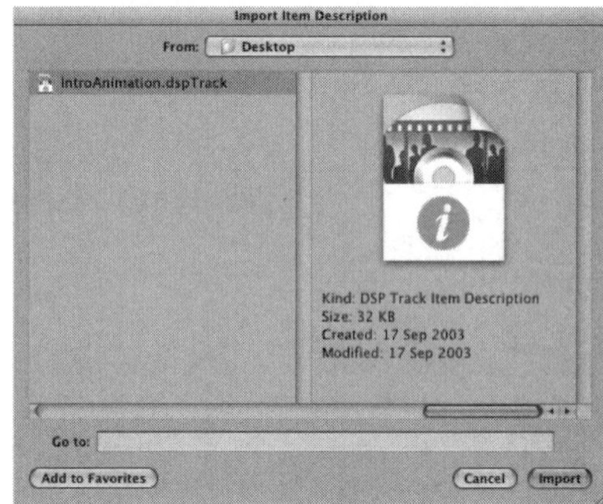

Figure 19.52 Locate the item description file and click Import.

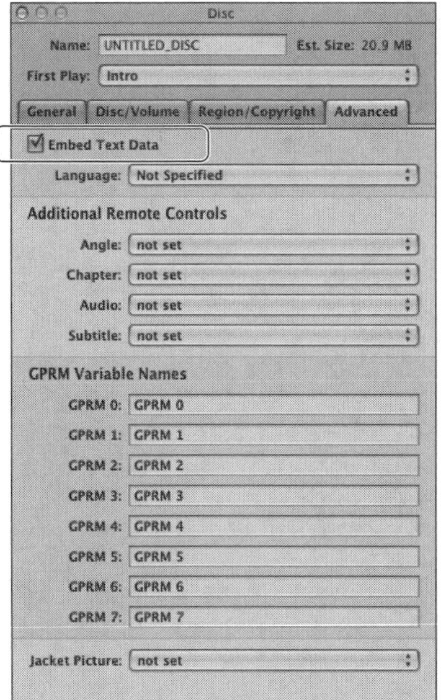

Figure 19.53 To embed the names of tracks and other text information in your title, select the Disc Inspector's Embed Text Data check box.

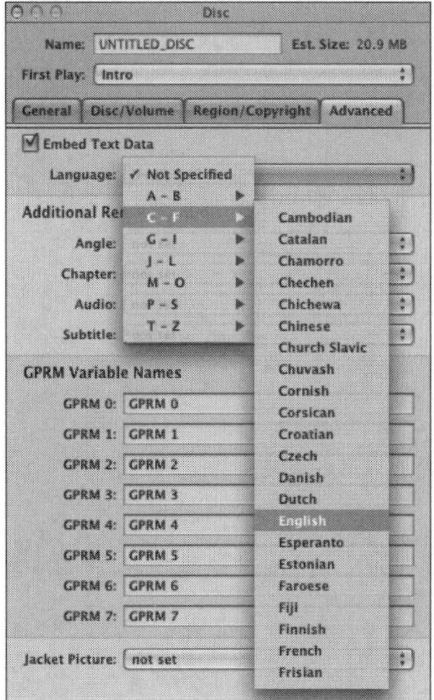

Figure 19.54 Then select a language for the embedded text data.

Embedding Text

Embedded text is extra information included with the DVD-Video; some DVD-Video players recognize embedded text, and others do not. For example, DVD@ccess links are sent as text data embedded with the title. Also, you can include the name of your tracks as embedded text; if the DVD-Video player supports this feature, the name of the track will appear on the player as the track plays.

To embed text:

1. In the Graphical view, click the background to select the disc itself.

   The Inspector updates to display the disc's properties.

2. In the Disc Inspector, select the Advanced tab.

3. At the top of the Advanced tab, select the Embed Text Data check box (**Figure 19.53**).

   Directly below the Embed Text Data check box is a Language menu.

4. From the Language menu, select the language of your embedded text (**Figure 19.54**).

✔ Tip

- If the DVD-Video player is set to a different language, your embedded text may not be displayed. Leave the language setting at Not Specified if you want the embedded text to appear regardless of the DVD-Video player's language setting.

Using Jacket Pictures

Jacket pictures are definitely an underutilized feature of the DVD-Video specification. A jacket picture appears on the screen when users stop DVD-Video playback. For example, you could maintain your product branding by using your brand's image from the DVD-Video's cover (or jacket) as the jacket picture.

However, be forewarned; many manufacturers disable jacket picture display, instead displaying a proprietary sleep screen that shows the DVD-Video player's brand name. Consequently, you can't be certain that your jacket picture, if you include one, will appear.

To include a jacket picture:

1. Import a still image to use as a jacket picture.
2. In the Graphical view, click the background to select the disc itself.
   The Inspector updates to display the disc's properties.
3. In the Disc Inspector, select the Advanced tab.
4. At the bottom of the Advanced tab, use the Jacket Picture menu to choose the asset you want to use as your disc's jacket picture (**Figure 19.55**).
   If the DVD-Video player supports jacket picture display, the jacket picture will appear whenever playback is stopped while the DVD-Video player is still on.

✔ Tip

- To test your jacket picture display, open the file in the Simulator and stop playback. Your jacket picture will appear just as it will upon normal playback.

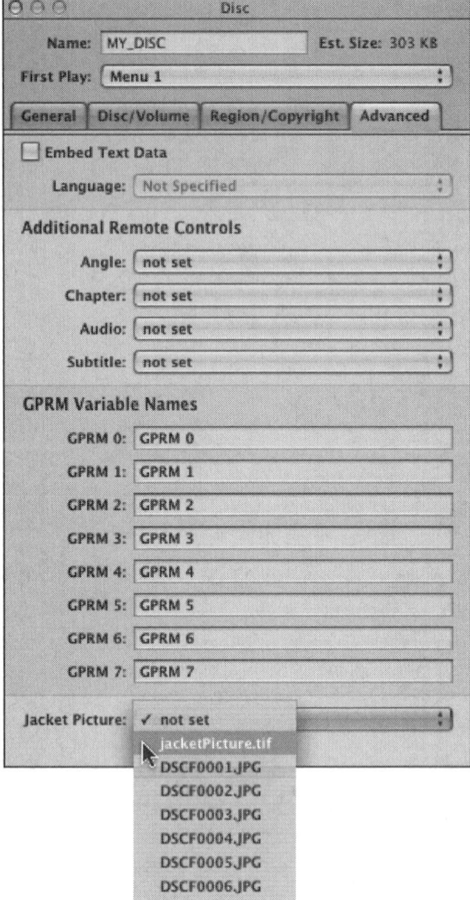

Figure 19.55 Jacket pictures appear whenever the DVD-Video player is stopped, if the player supports this feature.

OUTPUTTING THE PROJECT

Outputting your project is an exciting process; after all, you finally get to see what it looks like on a TV! But DVD-R discs are expensive, so you want to make sure that the project records correctly the first time, every time.

As a first line of defense, always test your project using DVD Studio Pro's Simulator before outputting it. This is especially important if you intend to replicate the project in large quantities; if you fail to notice a mistake in the DVD-Video, that mistake will be replicated hundreds or even thousands of times.

Multiplexing is the process of taking separate media streams and combining them into one unified stream. In DVD Studio Pro, this process is called *building the project*. After testing the project with Simulator, you can test your project one last time by building the DVD-Video directly to your hard disk and then opening it in Apple's DVD Player. If the project looks good and navigates correctly, it's time to burn that final DVD disc and watch it in a set-top player. You'll go through all of these steps in this chapter.

DVD Studio Pro can also output to digital linear tape (DLT; discussed later in this chapter), which is a standard delivery format for projects going to a replication facility. Replicated discs can be copy-protected and are supported in every DVD player (some DVD players can't play DVD-R media, as you'll learn in this chapter).

If you take just a few simple precautions, DVD Studio Pro will successfully record your DVD-R every time. To help you make sure you get it right the first time, this chapter shows you—step by step—how to record your project to disc.

Exporting the Project

DVD Studio Pro offers you four ways to export your project: Burn, Build, Build and Format, and Format. Choose the method that best meets your needs. Each situation is different, so read the options carefully before exporting your project.

- **Burn.** Burning is a simple, one-step process that builds all items in your project and writes them to DVD-R. Insert a blank DVD-R when prompted, and your part is done. DVD Studio Pro builds your project, burns it, and removes the built files from your hard disk when it's finished. The Burn option cannot be used for more complex processes such as writing a DLT or formatting a disk image.
- **Build.** Before a DVD can be written, it must be built. Both the Burn and the Build and Format options build and write a DVD all in one step. The main reason for choosing just the Build option, however, is to create a VIDEO_TS folder on your hard disk without actually burning the DVD. Why would you want to do this? Quality assurance testing! The Apple DVD-Video player can open a VIDEO_TS folder on your hard disk, so you can open and test a built version of the project before burning that final DVD disc.
- **Build and Format.** DVD Studio Pro can build and format your project, all in one step. Depending on the type of output devices you have connected to your computer, you can choose to format your project to DVD-R, to DLT, or to a disk image.
- **Format.** Formatting usually comes into play after you've had a chance to test your project using Apple's DVD Player. You can choose to format a VIDEO_TS folder that is already on your hard disk to DVD-R, to DLT, or to a disk image. Formatting is a good option to choose when you've already built a project and you need to make copies.

Building versus Formatting

In DVD Studio Pro–speak, *building* a project is synonymous with *multiplexing* or *compiling* a project; they mean the exact same thing. In this case, the metaphor of *building* is well chosen, as multiplexing takes a lot of little parts (such as the video and audio streams) and snaps them together, building a solid stream of data.

Formatting is the process of taking the build files and recording them to an output media such as a DVD-R disc or DLT tape.

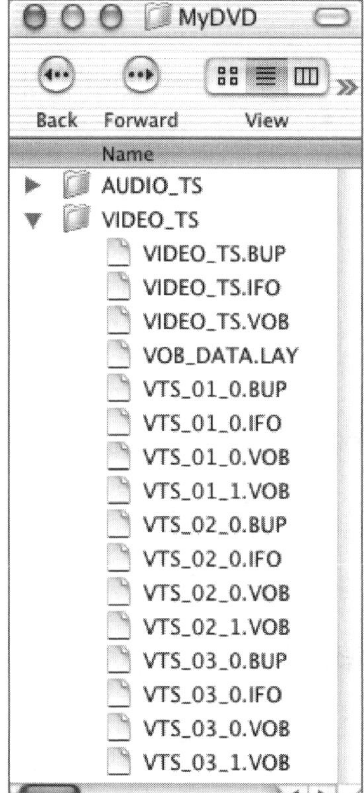

Figure 20.1 Multiplexing a project creates an AUDIO_TS folder and a VIDEO_TS folder. The AUDIO_TS folder is empty, and the VIDEO_TS folder contains all the navigation and video files for a DVD-Video.

Building the Project

Multiplexing combines all project items into a VIDEO_TS folder, which contains the information that a DVD-Video player can read and display (**Figure 20.1**). The VIDEO_TS folder holds files with three types of file extensions: VOB, IFO, and BUP files. VOB files contain the video, audio, subtitles, and other media that comprise your DVD-Video. IFO files contain button definitions, jumps, Wait After Playback values, and other navigation information that the DVD-Video player needs to assemble and play the media in the VOB files.

Usually, IFO files are less than 20 kilobytes. In DVD terms, this is microscopic, and indeed, every byte of that information is important to the correct display of your project. Should an IFO file become corrupted by a scratch or some other trauma to the disc's surface, the BUP file serves as a backup copy that provides the exact same information as the IFO file. To minimize the chance that a scratch might corrupt both files, the IFO file is written on the inside edge of the disc, while the BUP file is written on the outside.

Multiplexing a project also creates an empty AUDIO_TS folder (refer to Figure 20.1). AUDIO_TS folders hold information that is used for DVD-Audio discs, which DVD-Audio players understand but which have no significance to your DVD-Video projects. Although rarely a problem in today's DVD-Video players, vintage playback devices sometimes become confused if the DVD disc doesn't contain both a VIDEO_TS folder and an AUDIO_TS folder. Including an AUDIO_TS folder doesn't hurt anything, so DVD Studio Pro obligingly creates both folders when it multiplexes, or *builds*, the project.

Building projects to disk

Building the disc is a fairly simple process that occurs after your project is finished and tested. When you select Build from the File menu in DVD Studio Pro, the DVD disc does not get burned. Build only multiplexes your project and produces the VIDEO_TS and AUDIO_TS folders on your hard disk. The VIDEO_TS folder can be opened in Apple's DVD Player for further tests or can be used to later format a disc (formatting is discussed later in this chapter, in the section "Making Multiple Copies").

To build a project to disk:

1. *Do one of the following:*
   - ▲ Choose File > Advanced Burn > Build (**Figure 20.2**).
   - ▲ Click the toolbar's Build button.
   - ▲ Press Option-Command-C.

   The Choose Build Folder dialog opens (**Figure 20.3**).
2. In the Choose Build Folder dialog, navigate to the folder on your hard disk where you want the build files to be placed and click Choose.

   DVD Studio Pro immediately begins multiplexing your project. The Compiler—also called the *Multiplexer*—progress dialog opens (**Figure 20.4**).

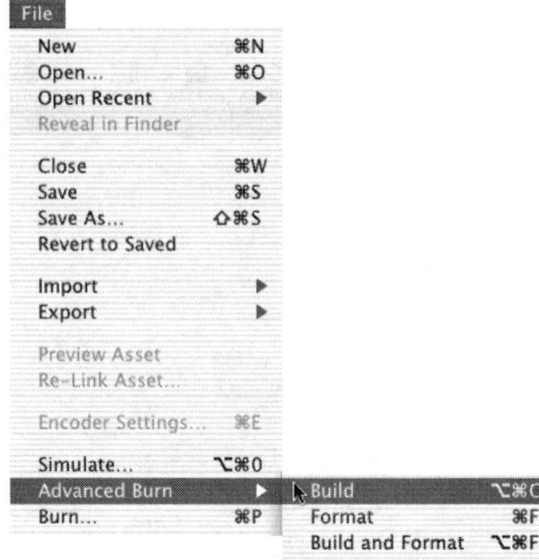

Figure 20.2 The File > Advanced Burn > Build option multiplexes your project to your hard disk.

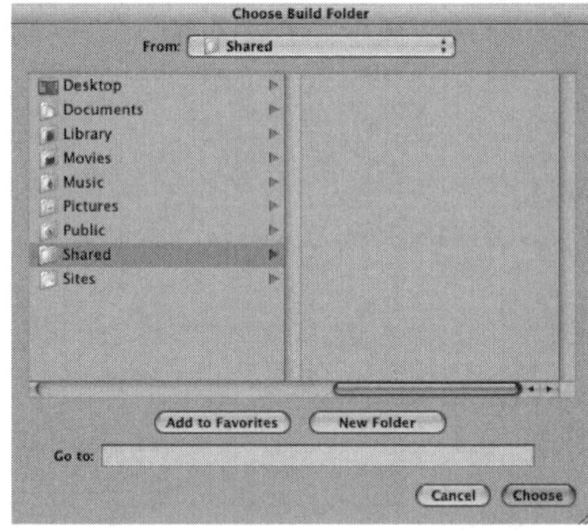

Figure 20.3 Choose a folder on your hard disk for storing your VIDEO_TS and AUDIO_TS folders when they are built.

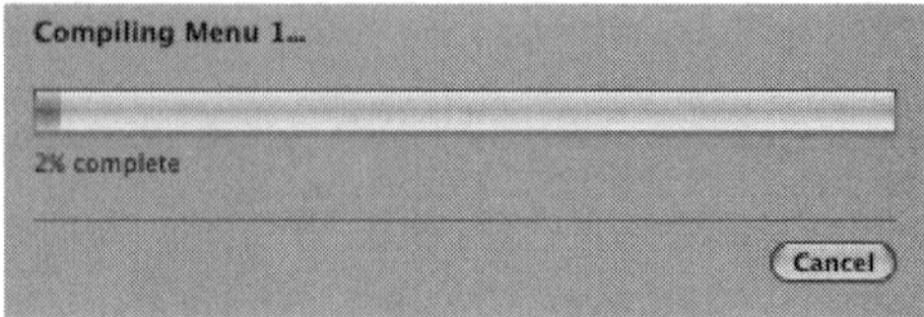

Figure 20.4 The progress window displays the Compiler's activity (the Compiler is also known as the Multiplexer).

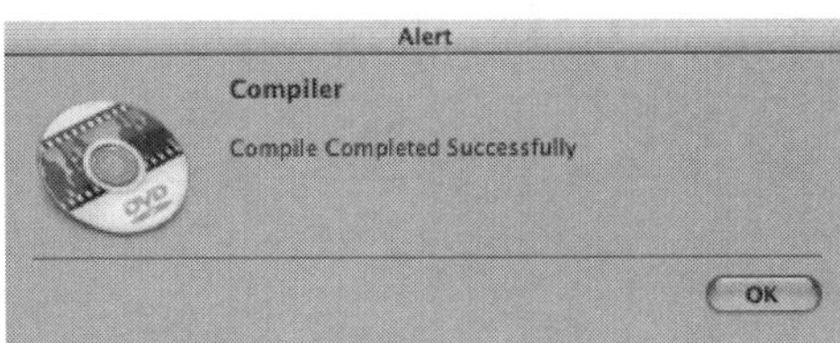

Figure 20.5 When the Compiler finishes creating the VIDEO_TS folder, an alert appears.

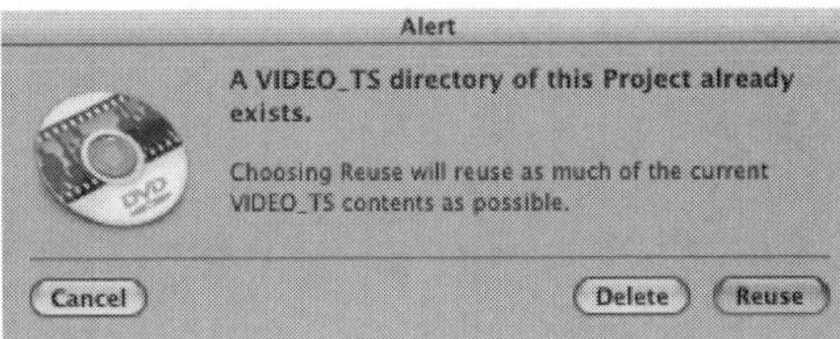

Figure 20.6 DVD Studio Pro allows you to incrementally build and reuse matching, already-built IFO and VOB files to save time when you're building a project that has not changed significantly between builds.

3. When it finishes multiplexing, DVD Studio Pro displays a completion dialog (**Figure 20.5**). Click OK to close it.

   DVD Studio Pro creates the multiplexed VIDEO-TS and empty AUDIO_TS folders and creates a small layout file when you build the project. See the sidebar "Layout Files" for more information on the layout file that is created.

✔ Tips

- Your computer's speed combined with your project's size and built-in encode settings determine how long it takes to build a project. Relax—the process may take hours.
- If the folder you choose as the target for your multiplexed project contains an old VIDEO_TS folder, an alert dialog appears (**Figure 20.6**). If your project hasn't changed much from the last time you built it, select Reuse to speed up the process.

Layout Files

In addition to the VIDEO-TS and AUDIO_TS folders, DVD Studio Pro creates a small layout file when you build the project. The file is called *MY_DVD*.layout (**Figure 20.7**), where *MY_DVD* is the name of your project. The layout file contains project layout details, dual-layer break points, and other information that DVD Studio Pro's Formatter uses to ensure that your project formats smoothly. This file is *not* included on the final DVD disc or DLT when you use DVD Studio Pro to format your project. Although the file is fairly benign, you may not want to copy it if you use Toast Titanium to format your disc.

Figure 20.7 DVD Studio Pro creates a layout file when you build your project. DVD Studio Pro's Formatter uses the file, which is not included on the final DVD disc.

Building the Project

About the Log tab

The Log tab opens automatically while DVD Studio Pro multiplexes your project and lists each multiplexed item along with any errors (**Figure 20.8**). Minor errors, such as unassigned buttons, are listed in yellow as warnings. Errors in yellow may cause navigation issues that confuse the viewer, but they won't have much impact on the DVD-Video disc itself. It's your choice to either go back and fix the errors or leave them as they are.

Some minor errors are unavoidable and appear in the log simply to alert you to what's going on with your project. For example, subtitle clips cannot cross chapter marker boundaries. DVD Studio Pro corrects this for you automatically and writes a yellow warning in the log to let you know that your subtitles have been modified (refer to Figure 20.8).

Significant errors immediately stop the multiplexing process and cause an alert dialog to appear (**Figure 20.9**). The item that caused the error is listed in red at the bottom of the Log tab (**Figure 20.10**). You must fix the error to build your project.

The Log tab should open automatically when you build your project, but you may want to open it *before* you build your project so that you can resize the tab to see more of the log.

If you're working with an Advanced window configuration, the Log tab defaults to the bottom-left quadrant, next to the Assets tab (also called the Assets container). If the Log tab is closed, or if you're working with a Basic or Extended window configuration, you'll need to open the Log tab to resize it before building your project.

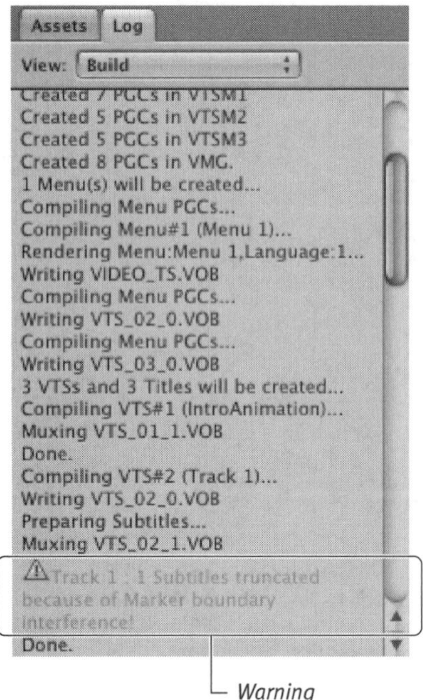

Figure 20.8 The Log tab lists all project items that are built. Minor errors and alerts appear in yellow with a yield symbol.

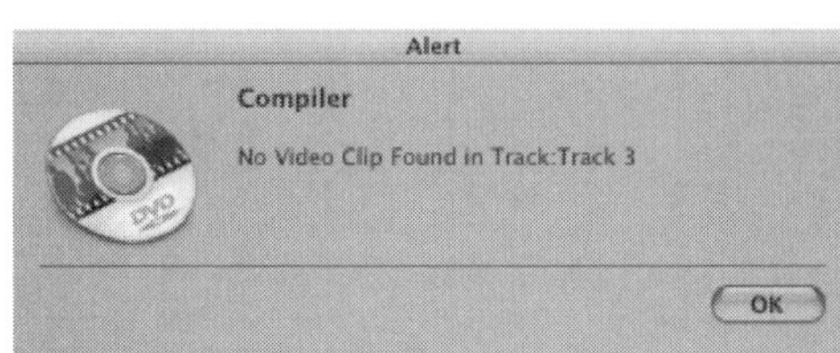

Figure 20.9 An alert dialog appears when your build cannot be completed.

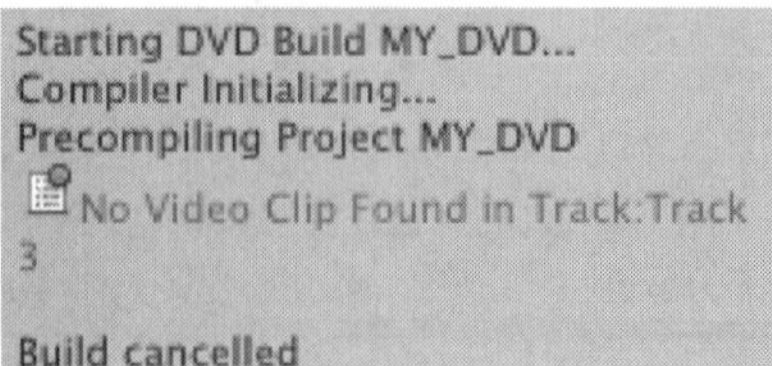

Figure 20.10 The reason the build was canceled is listed in the log.

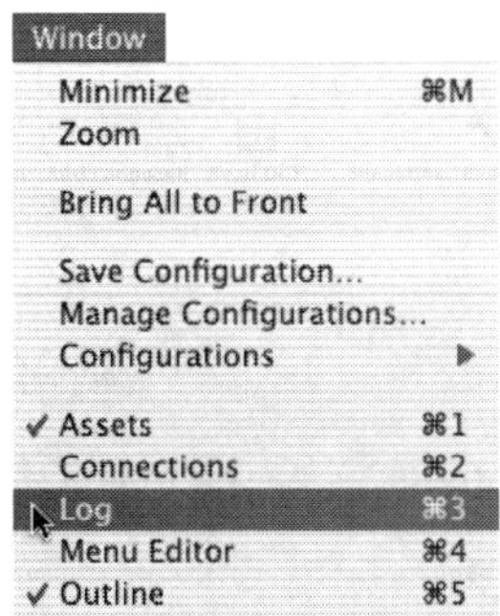

Figure 20.11 To open the Log tab, choose Window > Log.

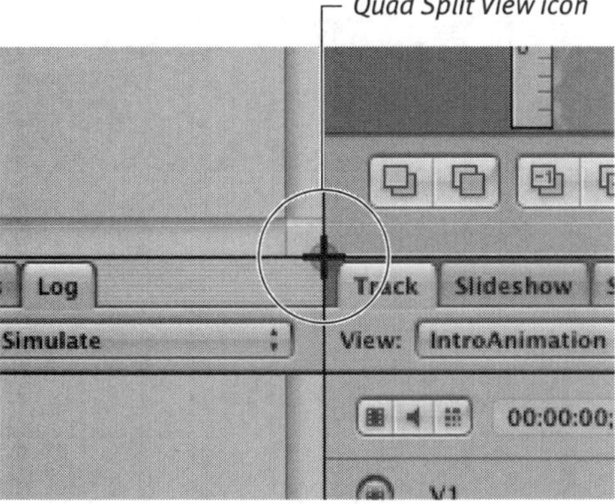

Figure 20.12 Click and drag the center of the quadrants to resize them. The Quad Split View cursor icon will appear to let you know that the quadrants can be resized.

Figure 20.13 Drag the bottom-right corner to resize the window.

To open the Log tab:

- Choose Window > Log (**Figure 20.11**), or press Command-3.

  The Log tab opens.

To resize the Log tab:

- *Do one of the following:*
  - If the Log tab opens within one of the quadrants, click in the center of the quadrants to display the Quad Split View cursor icon; then drag the mouse to resize the quadrants (**Figure 20.12**).
  - If the Log tab opens in a new window, click the bottom-right corner of the window and drag down and to the right to enlarge the window (**Figure 20.13**).

Using Apple's DVD Player

Apple's DVD Player plays your DVD-Video just as a set-top DVD-Video player would. DVD Player has two main parts: the Viewer and the Controller (**Figure 20.14**). The Viewer is the screen that displays your DVD-Video. The Controller mimics a DVD-Video player's remote control by allowing you to select menu buttons, start and stop playback, and choose alternate angles.

Earlier in this chapter, you learned that multiplexing a project writes VIDEO_TS and AUDIO_TS folders to your computer's hard disk. The VIDEO_TS folder is an exact copy of the final DVD-Video. By opening this folder in DVD Player, you can check your DVD-Video to ensure that it plays correctly before you record it to a DVD-R disc. Remember: DVD-R discs are expensive, so you should fully test your project in DVD Player before wasting a DVD-R disc on a malfunctioning project.

Figure 20.14 DVD Player's Controller (top) is used to control the DVD-Video displayed in the Viewer (bottom).

To open a VIDEO_TS folder in DVD Player:

1. Open DVD Player.
2. From DVD Player's File menu, choose Open VIDEO_TS Folder (**Figure 20.15**), or press Command-0.

   The Choose a Folder dialog opens (**Figure 20.16**).
3. Use the Choose a Folder dialog to navigate to the VIDEO_TS folder and click Choose.

   DVD Player plays the DVD-Video that's in the VIDEO_TS folder.
4. On the DVD Player remote control, click Play.

Figure 20.15 To open a VIDEO_TS folder stored on your computer's hard disk, choose File > Open VIDEO_TS Folder.

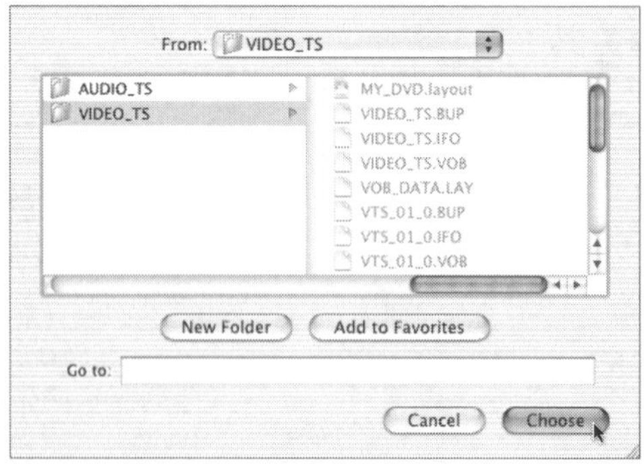

Figure 20.16 Choose a VIDEO_TS folder in the dialog that appears.

Building and Formatting

This shot is for all the marbles. Formatting the final DVD disc can be a nerve-wracking process; DVD-R discs are expensive, and wasting them on bad burns means you're losing money as well as time. If you've read Chapter 19, "Finishing the DVD," you've learned that you can minimize problems by carefully previewing every part of your project before you burn it. If everything plays correctly, you're ready to record a DVD disc.

Building and formatting a DVD disc is a two-part process. The first part, the build, multiplexes your project into VIDEO_TS and AUDIO_TS folders on your computer's hard disk. Once multiplexing is complete, DVD Studio Pro formats and records a DVD-R disc or DLT tape, using the multiplexed files.

Rock-Solid Burns

DVD Studio Pro rarely makes mistakes as it burns DVD discs, but you can take a few precautionary steps to ensure a smooth recording process. Start by closing all other applications so that nothing unexpectedly jumps to life and interrupts DVD Studio Pro as it records the disc. Also, set your hard disk so that it doesn't unexpectedly go to sleep (**Figure 20.17**). For that extra level of security, also turn off AppleTalk, File Sharing, and Web Sharing. The only application left running should be DVD Studio Pro, which can safely record the DVD disc, free from any interruption.

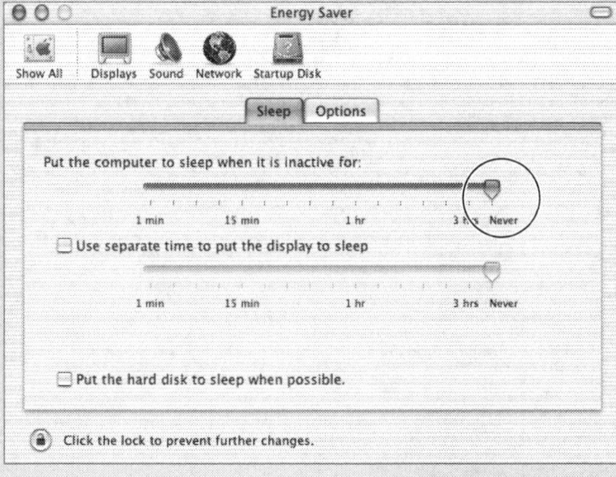

Figure 20.17 To keep your computer from going to sleep as it multiplexes and records your project, set all of the Sleep tab's Energy Saver preferences to Never.

To build and format a DVD-R disc:

1. Choose File > Advanced Burn > Build and Format (**Figure 20.18**), or press Option-Command-F.

   The Formatting window opens with the General tab displayed.

2. In the General tab's Source section, click the Current Build Choose button (**Figure 20.19**).

   The Choose Source dialog opens (**Figure 20.20**).

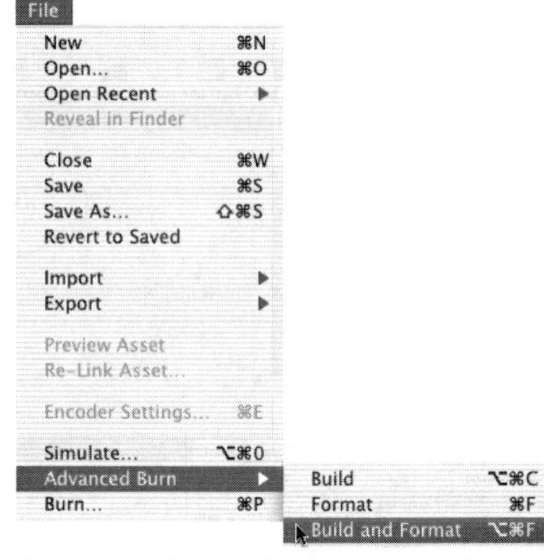

Figure 20.18 To build and format your project all in one step, choose File > Advanced Burn > Build and Format.

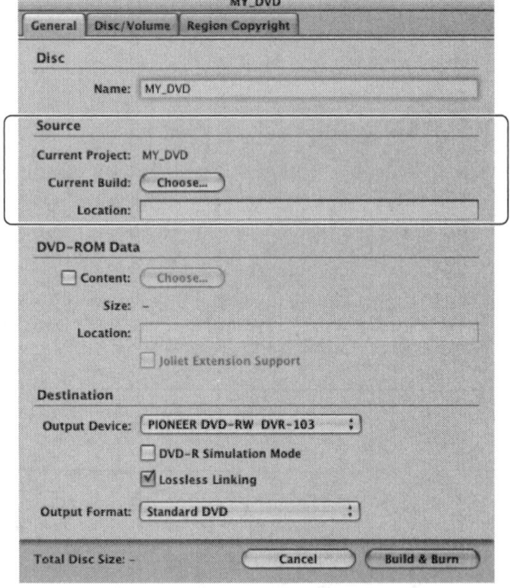

Figure 20.19 In the Formatting window's Source section, click the Current Build Choose button to choose a folder for your multiplexed files.

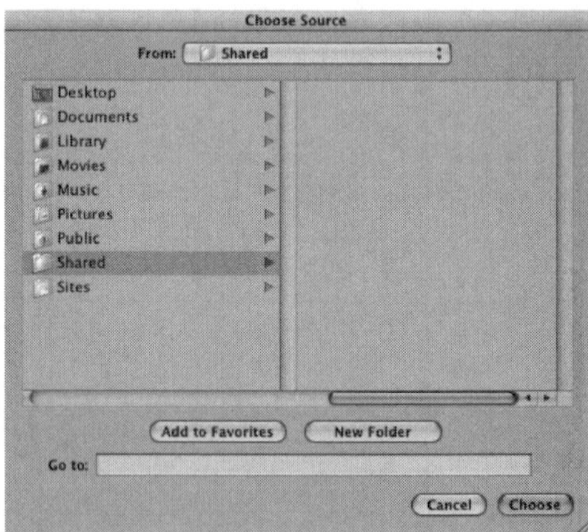

Figure 20.20 Use the Choose Source dialog to navigate to the folder where you want the built files placed.

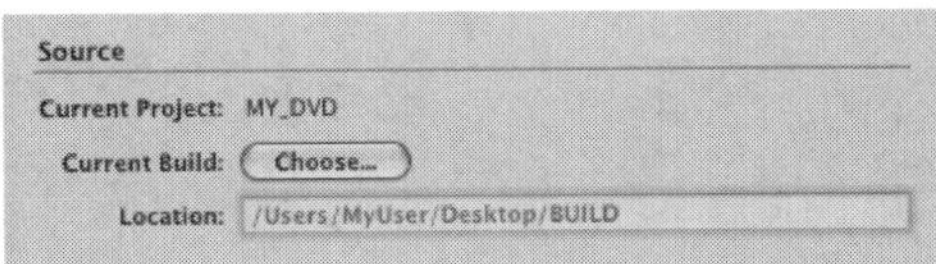

Figure 20.21 When you choose a source folder, the location path appears in the Location text box.

Figure 20.22 Type a name for the DVD disc.

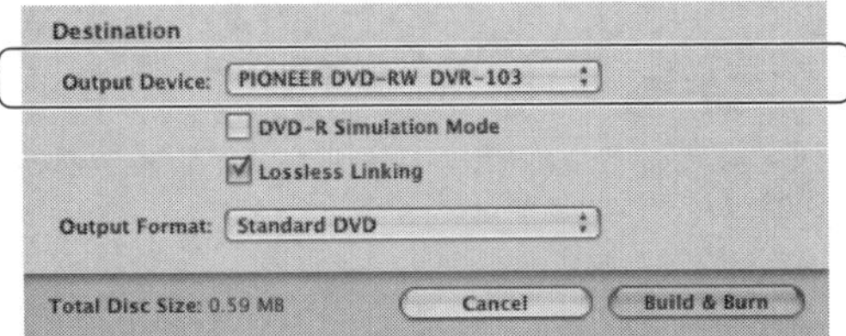

Figure 20.23 Choose the output device that you'll use to record your project. An internal SuperDrive is selected here.

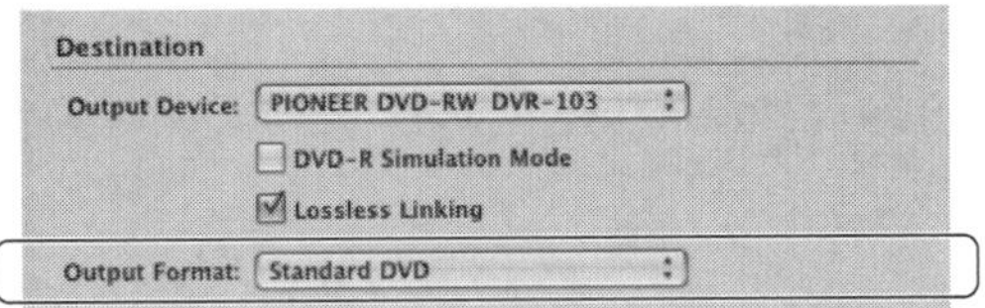

Figure 20.24 Choose Standard DVD as the output format type when you want to output to DVD-R media.

3. In the Choose Source dialog, navigate to the location where you want DVD Studio Pro to place the VIDEO_TS and AUDIO_TS folders when it builds your project; then click Choose.

   The folder is selected, and the Choose Source dialog closes. The location path of the folder you selected is displayed in the Formatting window's Location text box (**Figure 20.21**).

4. On the Formatting window's General tab, type a name for the disc in the Name text box (**Figure 20.22**).

   The name you typed will appear when the viewer inserts the DVD-Video disc into a computer.

5. In the General tab's Destination section, choose your DVD-R output device from the Output Device pop-up menu (**Figure 20.23**).

   All connected DVD burners, your hard disk, and DLT drives appear in the menu. Choosing an output device tells DVD Studio Pro to which hard disk, DLT tape drive, or DVD burner you want to write your project.

6. From the Output Format pop-up menu, choose Standard DVD (**Figure 20.24**).

   The outputting formats vary depending on the output device you selected in step 5. Choosing Standard DVD tells DVD Studio Pro that you'll be burning the project to a DVD-R disc.

continues on next page

7. At the bottom of the General tab, click Build & Burn (**Figure 20.25**).

   DVD Studio Pro asks you to insert a blank DVD-R Disc (**Figure 20.26**).

8. Insert a blank DVD-R disc.

   DVD Studio Pro builds your project and records your VIDEO_TS folder and an empty AUDIO_TS folder to the DVD-R disc. When DVD Studio Pro finishes writing the DVD-Video disc, it displays an alert, telling you that the formatting was successful (**Figure 20.27**).

✔ Tip

- Do not insert a blank DVD disc until DVD Studio Pro asks for it. If you place a blank DVD disc in your computer before DVD Studio Pro needs it, a dialog opens telling you that the disc must be prepared for burning (**Figure 20.28**). Click the dialog's Eject button and wait until DVD Studio Pro asks before reinserting the disc.

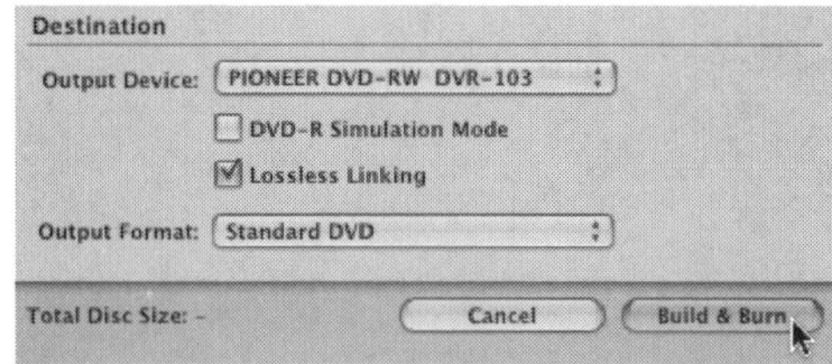

Figure 20.25 When you're finished configuring your output device and output format, click Build & Burn to begin the two-step process of building and burning your DVD.

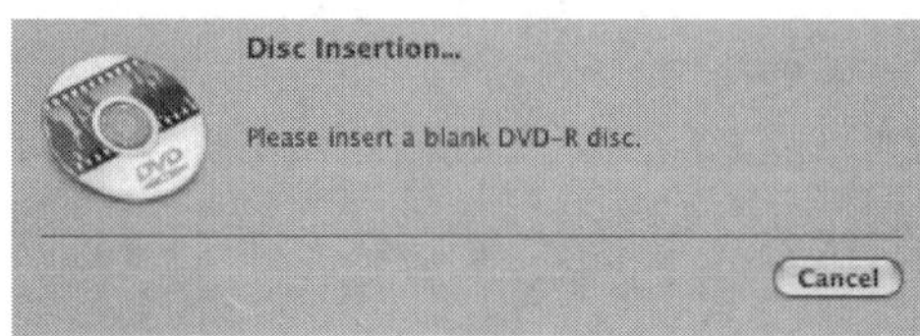

Figure 20.26 Do not insert a blank DVD-R disc until DVD Studio Pro asks for one.

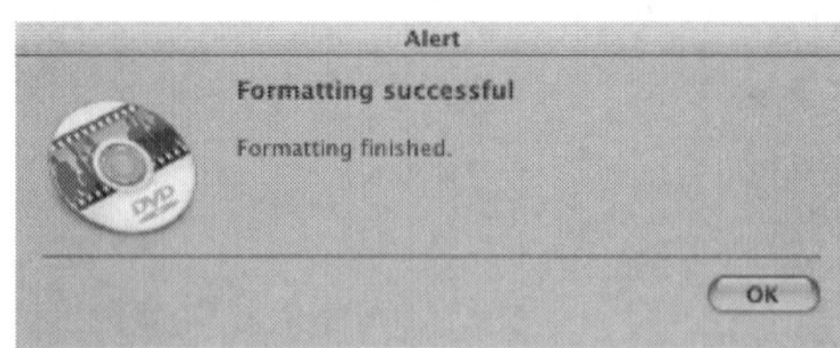

Figure 20.27 After DVD Studio Pro finishes writing all data to the DVD-R disc, this alert dialog appears.

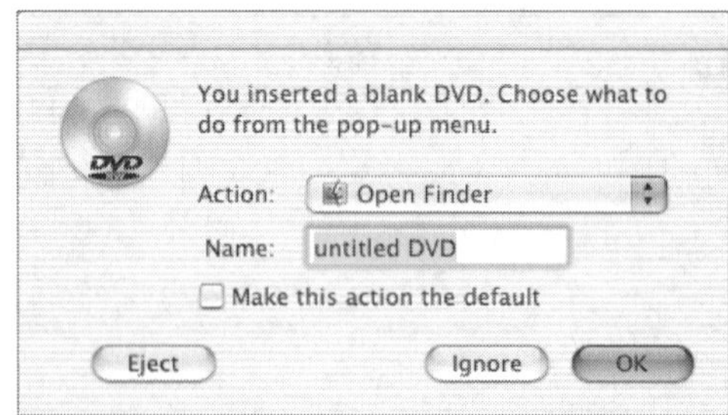

Figure 20.28 If you insert a blank DVD-R disc before DVD Studio Pro asks for it, this dialog opens. Eject the disc and reinsert it when DVD Studio Pro tells you to.

Buffer Underruns

During disc recording, an interrupted data stream from the hard disk to the DVD drive causes buffer underrun errors. Some DVD drives have internal memory buffers to guard against errors, but even that may not always be enough to prevent faulty burns. Any time your computer's hard disk is interrupted, the flow of data to the DVD drive is halted. There are a few measures you can take to prevent wasted DVD-R discs caused by buffer underrun errors:

1. Quit all other applications before burning the DVD disc. Although Mac OS X is a multitasking OS, your hard disk may not be.
2. Do not format data that is on a networked drive or server. Move all files to a local drive before you build and format. The Internet cannot prepare files quickly enough to send a constant stream of data to the DVD writer.
3. If you're using Toast Titanium to burn your DVD disc, set the burn speed to 1*x*. Burn speeds of 2*x* or higher require your hard disk to send data at a faster rate to keep the buffer full. DVD Studio Pro burns discs at the fastest speed your drive supports, which is usually 2*x* (or 4*x* with newer drives).

After following these steps, you can test for buffer underrun errors by simulating a burn. Select the DVD-R Simulation Mode check box in DVD Studio Pro's Formatting window to send DVD Studio Pro through the motions of writing a DVD-R disc.

If you're still having trouble with buffer underrun errors, select the Lossless Linking check box in the Formatting window (**Figure 20.29**) to allow the DVD drive to pause as needed and pick up where it left off when the data is available. This allows discs to record successfully even if the data flow to the recorder is interrupted. Some DVD-Video players won't play discs recorded using lossless linking, or they may have playback problems such as stuttering, so you should enable this option only if you're still experiencing problems burning to disc.

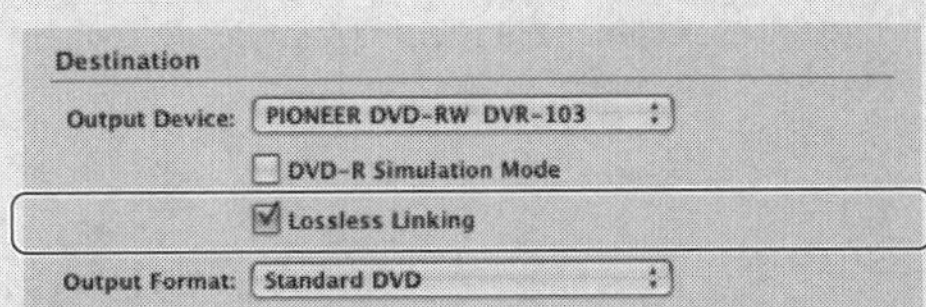

Figure 20.29 Select the Lossless Linking check box only if you are having trouble burning a DVD due to buffer underrun errors.

Output Devices and Formats

DVD Studio Pro supports four types of output devices. Depending on the one you select for burning your project, the Output Format pop-up menu displays different formatting options (**Figure 20.30**). If you plan to send your project to a replication facility, check with your replicator to see which format he or she prefers.

DVD Studio Pro supports the following output devices:

- **DVD-R General drive.** Uses standard DVD-R general media and can output only to a standard DVD format. (Apple SuperDrives are DVD-R General drives.)
- **DVD-R Authoring drive.** Uses specialized DVD-R Authoring media and can output using Cutting Master Format (CMF) version 1.0, or the standard DVD format. Replication facilities use CMF in the same way DLT tapes are used (see "Outputting to DLT" later in this chapter). Before sending your disc to a replication facility, make sure to check to see if it supports CMF-formatted media.
- **DLT drive.** Uses DLT tapes and can be formatted as either Data Description Protocol (DDP) version 2.0 or CMF version 1.0.
- **Hard disk.** Allows formatting the AUDIO_TS and VIDEO_TS folders as a disk image (.img), in DDP 2.0 format, or in CMF version 1.0.

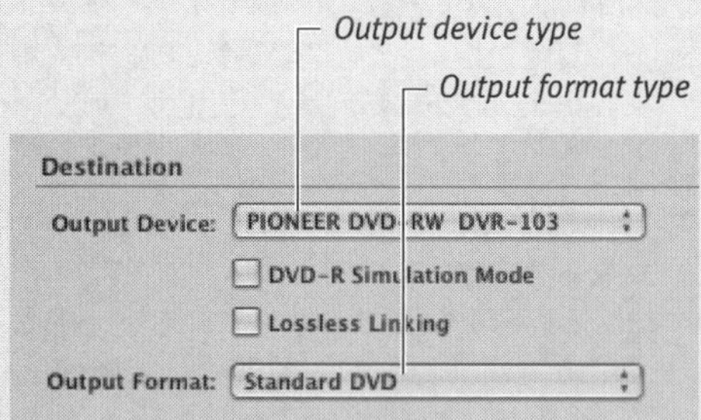

Figure 20.30 Different output format types will appear in the pop-up menu depending on the output device you choose.

DVD Studio Pro and DVD-RW

With DVD Studio Pro 3, the program now officially supports DVD-RW recording. Even better, if you insert an already formatted DVD-RW disc, DVD Studio Pro will ask if you want to erase it (**Figure 20.31**). If you say yes, the disc is erased and formatted with the new project, all in one simple step!

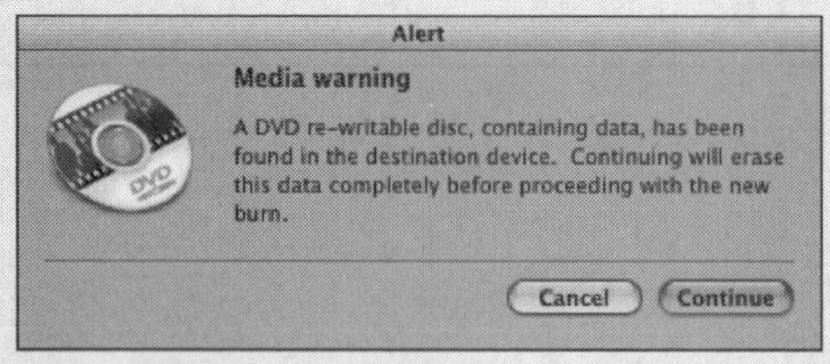

Figure 20.31 DVD Studio Pro 3 automatically erases and re-records DVD-RW discs.

Figure 20.32 Choose File > Advanced Burn > Build and Format to multiplex your project and format it as a disk image.

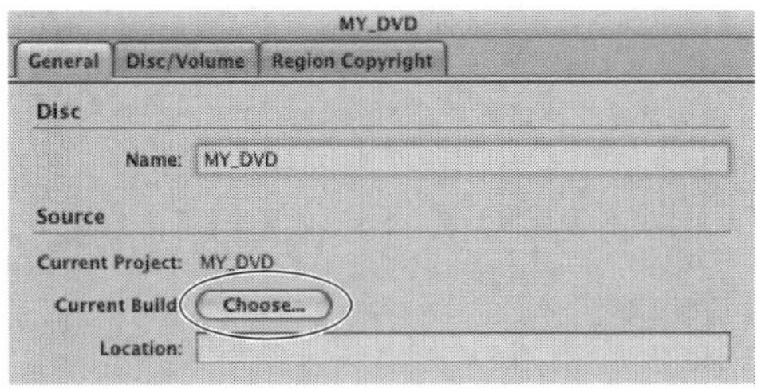

Figure 20.33 Click Choose to select a destination folder for the multiplexed files.

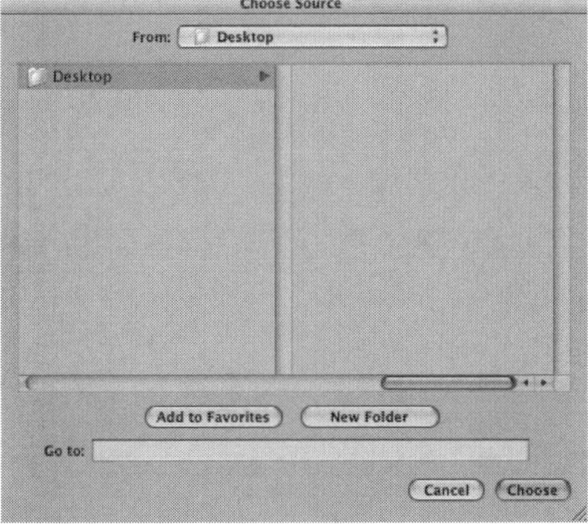

Figure 20.34 Use the Choose Source dialog to navigate to the location where you want your multiplexed files placed.

Building disk images

Building a disk image multiplexes the DVD-Video and then creates a complete image of the final DVD disc on your computer. Building a disk image does not record a DVD-R disc, but rather it creates a virtual DVD-Video disc on your computer, including all ROM information and DVD@ccess installers for projects that include DVD-ROM folders or DVD@ccess links.

Building a disk image is useful for archiving projects that you are not quite ready to record to DVD disc, or for creating a disk image that you'll later open and record using an application such as Apple Disk Utility (located in your Applications/Utilities folder).

✔ Tip

- If you are creating a master DVD-R disc for a client, it pays in spades to build a disc image first and then build the image using Apple Disc Utility or Roxio Toast Titanium. Why? Because these applications let you set your burn speed to 1*x*, and this slow speed allows well-defined pits to be burned into the disc. Additionally, these applications verify the disc once burning is complete, ensuring that every bit is exactly where it should be, and that the disc contains no errors.

To build and format a disk image:

1. Choose File > Advanced Burn > Build and Format (**Figure 20.32**), or press Option-Command-F.

   The Formatting window opens with the General tab displayed.

2. In the Formatting window's Source section, click the Choose button to select a location for the multiplexed files (**Figure 20.33**).

   The Choose Source dialog opens (**Figure 20.34**).

continues on next page

3. In the Choose Source dialog, navigate to the folder on your hard disk where you want DVD Studio Pro to place the multiplexed VIDEO_TS and AUDIO_TS folders; then click Choose.

   The folder is selected, and the Choose Source dialog closes.

4. In the Formatting window's Destination section, from the Output Device pop-up menu, choose Hard Drive (**Figure 20.35**).

   The Output Format pop-up menu updates to show formatting options that are compatible with the hard drive as an output device.

5. From the Output Format pop-up menu, choose .img to format your project as a disc image on your hard disk (**Figure 20.36**).

6. At the bottom right of the Formatting window, click the Build & Format button (**Figure 20.37**) to start the two-part process of building and formatting your project.

   DVD Studio Pro builds the VIDEO_TS folder containing the DVD navigation information and multiplexed video streams along with the empty AUDIO_TS folder and then formats the folder's contents as a disk image on your hard disk.

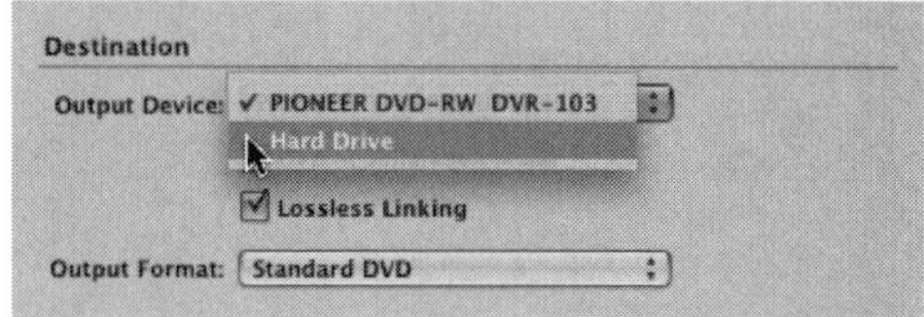

Figure 20.35 Choose Hard Drive from the Output Device pop-up menu to format your project for your hard disk instead of your DVD drive.

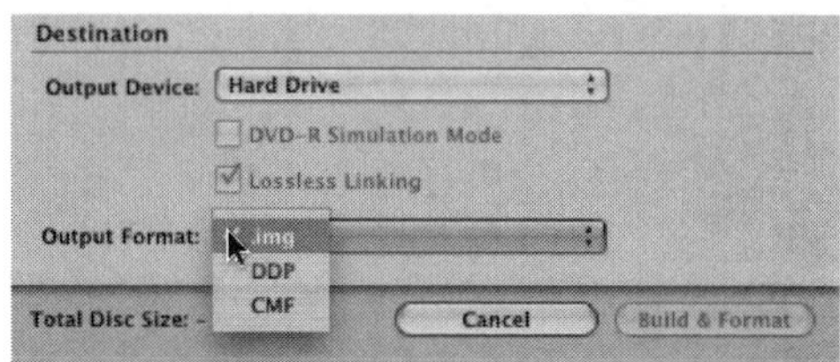

Figure 20.36 Choose .img to format your project as a disk image on your hard disk.

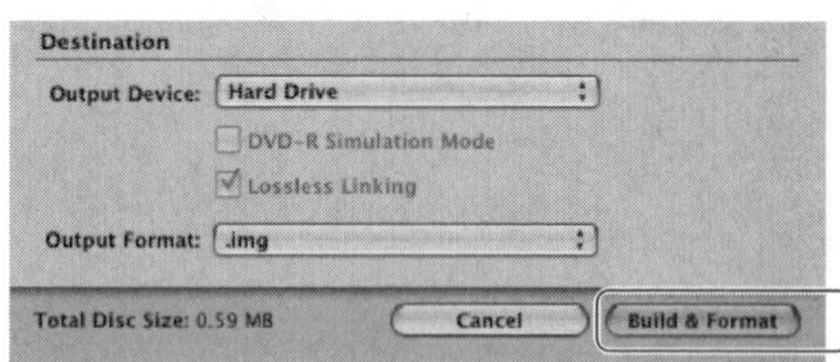

Figure 20.37 Click Build & Format to begin the two-part process of building your project and formatting it as a disk image.

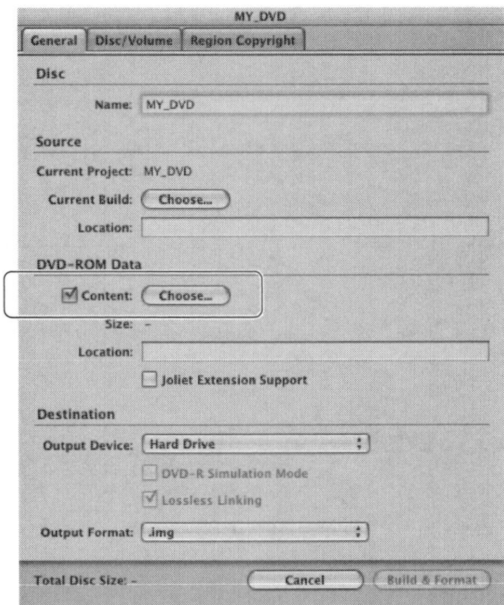

Figure 20.38 You can add DVD-ROM content to your disk image by selecting the Content check box and choosing a folder.

Figure 20.39 Locate the DVD disk image on your hard disk and double-click it to open it.

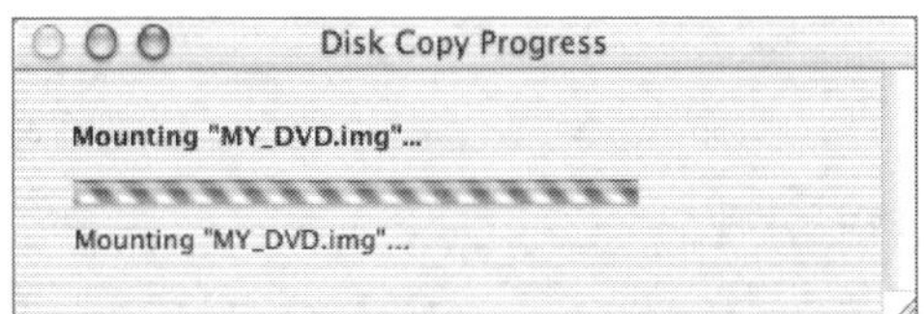

Figure 20.40 Double-clicking a disk image causes Apple's Disk Copy utility to mount the disk image to your desktop.

✔ Tips

- To add DVD-ROM data to your disk image, in the Formatting window's DVD-ROM Data section, select the Content check box (**Figure 20.38**) and choose a folder to archive in the DVD-Video disk image before you click the Build & Format button.
- If your project contains DVD@ccess links, the Windows DVD@ccess installer is automatically included in the disk image.

To open a disk image:

- Locate the project image on your hard disk and double-click it (**Figure 20.39**).

  The Disc Copy utility opens (**Figure 20.40**) and mounts the disc image on your computer's desktop. Once the project has been successfully mounted, you can use Apple's DVD Player to open the VIDEO_TS folder (for steps, see "Using Apple's DVD Player" earlier in this chapter).

Making Multiple Copies

Once you've burned one copy of your DVD-Video project, there's nothing to stop you from making multiple copies of it using just your computer, the appropriate media, and a DVD writer. If your project has already been built to your hard disk, use the Format option in DVD Studio Pro to format your VIDEO_TS and AUDIO_TS folders on a DVD-Video disc.

You can also use Toast Titanium to format and burn the VIDEO_TS folder, as discussed later in this chapter in "Using Toast 6 Titanium."

Using the Format option

If you've already built the project to your hard disk, you do not need to select the Build and Format option in DVD Studio Pro. Instead, choose File > Advanced Burn > Format to format the VIDEO_TS and AUDIO_TS folders on a DVD-Video disc. You can format as many copies as you need using the build files you've already created.

To format a DVD-Video disc:

1. Choose File > Advanced Burn > Format (**Figure 20.41**), or press Command-F.

   The Formatting window opens with the General tab displayed (**Figure 20.42**).

2. In the General tab's Source section, click the Choose button.

   The Choose Source dialog opens, allowing you to navigate to the VIDEO_TS and AUDIO_TS folders that you've already built on your hard disk (**Figure 20.43**).

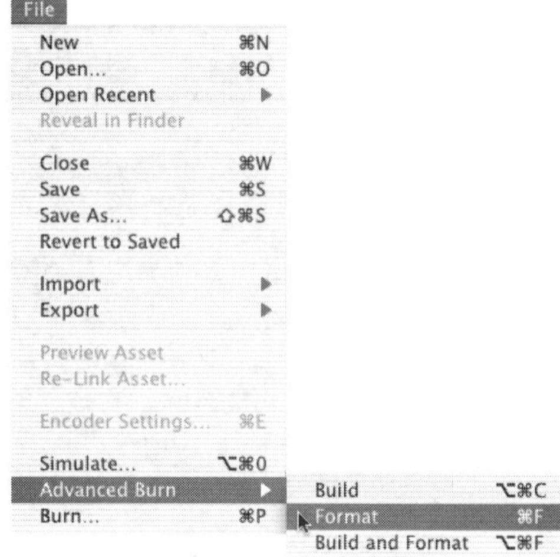

Figure 20.41 To format the VIDEO_TS and AUDIO_TS folders that you've already built, choose File > Advanced Burn > Format.

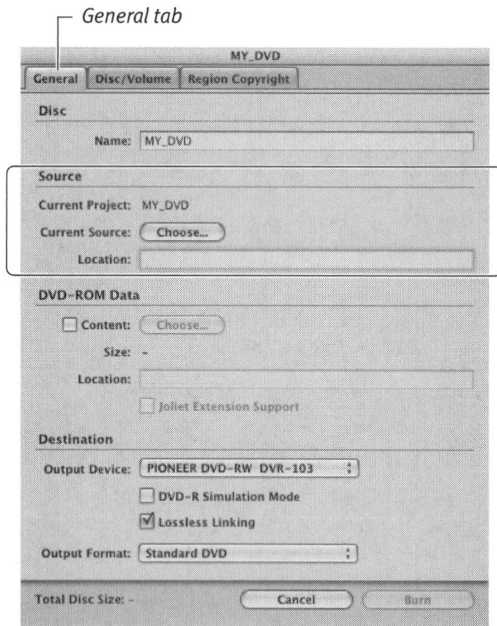

Figure 20.42 In the Formatting window, click the Source section's Choose button to choose the project you've already built.

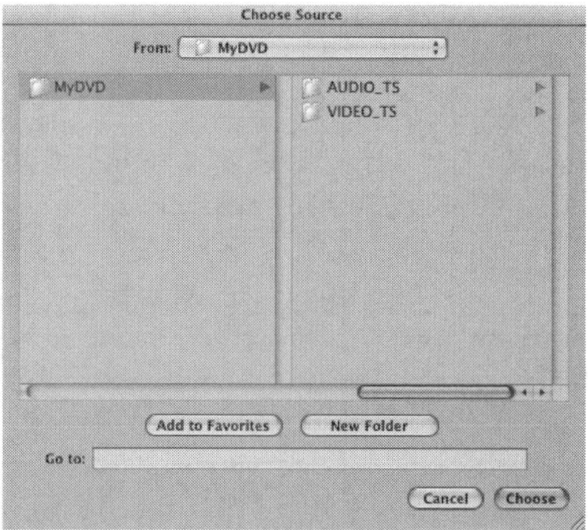

Figure 20.43 Select the folder that contains your prebuilt VIDEO_TS and AUDIO_TS folders; then click Choose.

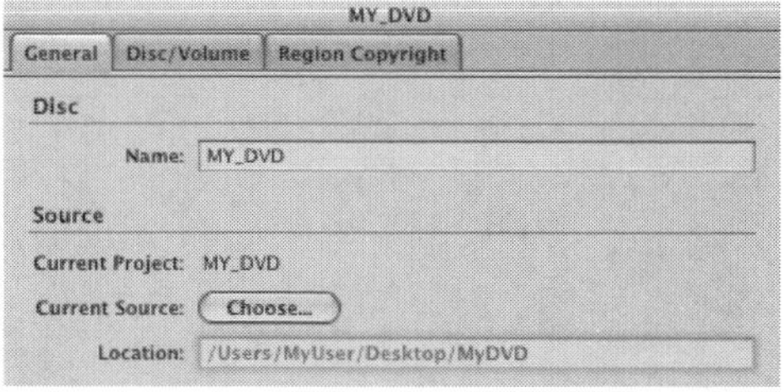

Figure 20.44 When you choose the folder containing your VIDEO_TS and AUDIO_TS source folders, the location path appears in the Source section's Location text box.

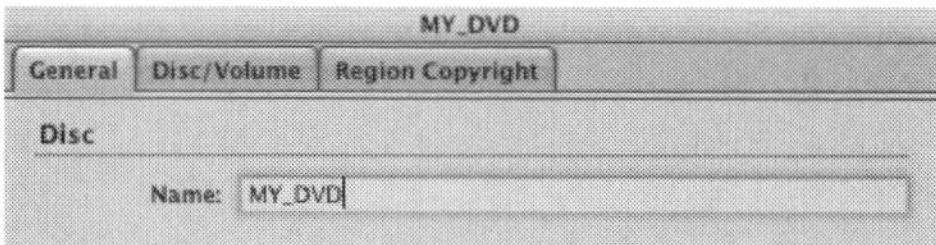

Figure 20.45 The name you type will appear when the DVD disc is inserted into a computer.

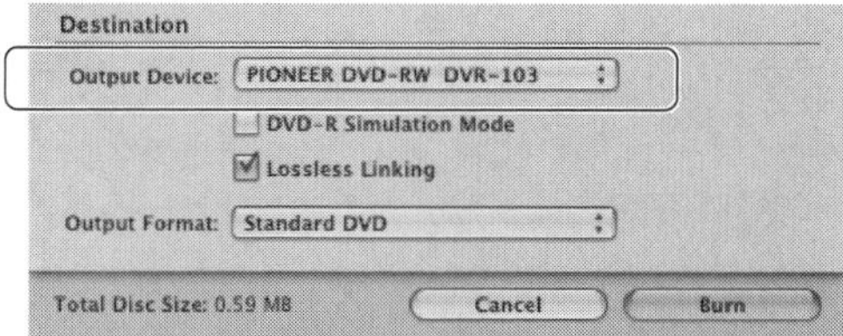

Figure 20.46 Choose the output device that you'll use to record your VIDEO_TS folder. In this figure, an internal SuperDrive is selected.

3. Using the Choose Source dialog that appears, navigate to the folder that contains your AUDIO_TS and VIDEO_TS folders and click Choose.

   The folder is selected, and the Choose Source dialog closes. In the Formatting window, the location of the folder you selected is displayed in the Location text box (**Figure 20.44**).

4. In the Formatting window, type a disc name (**Figure 20.45**).

   The name you type will appear on the DVD-Video disc when the viewer inserts it into a computer.

5. In the Destination section, from the Output Device pop-up menu choose the drive that you will use to burn your project to disc (**Figure 20.46**).

   The Output Format pop-up menu updates to show formatting options that are compatible with the drive that you've just chosen.

6. From the Output Format pop-up menu, choose an appropriate format.

continues on next page

7. Click the Burn button (**Figure 20.47**).

   DVD Studio Pro asks you to insert a blank DVD-R disc (**Figure 20.48**).

8. Insert a blank DVD-R disc.

   DVD Studio Pro records your VIDEO_TS folder and an empty AUDIO_TS folder to the DVD-R disc. When DVD Studio Pro has finished writing the DVD-Video disc, it displays a Formatting Successful alert (**Figure 20.49**).

9. Click OK to close the Formatting Successful alert.

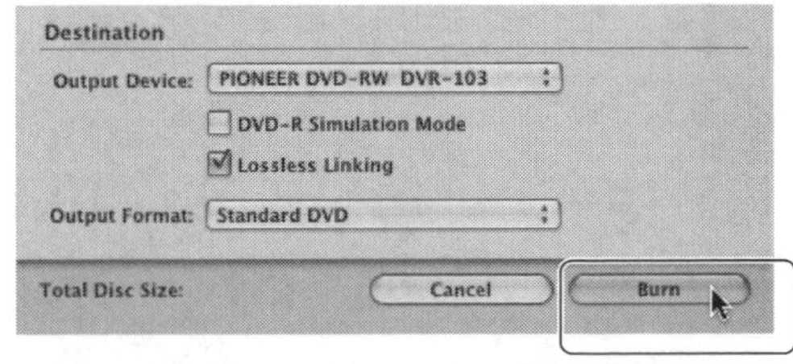

Figure 20.47 When you've finished configuring your output device and output format, click Burn to begin burning your DVD.

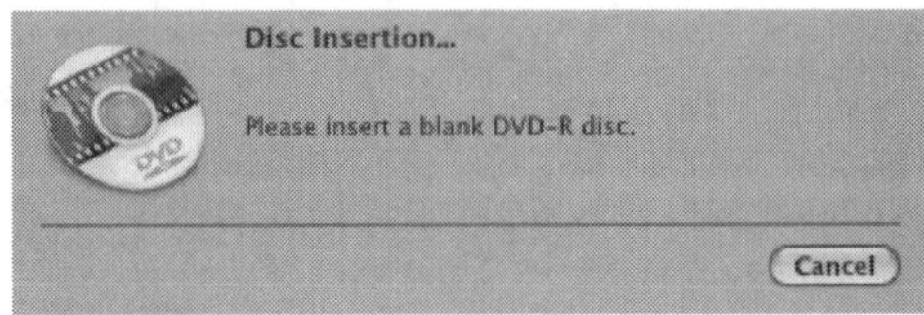

Figure 20.48 Do not insert a blank DVD-R disc until DVD Studio Pro asks for one.

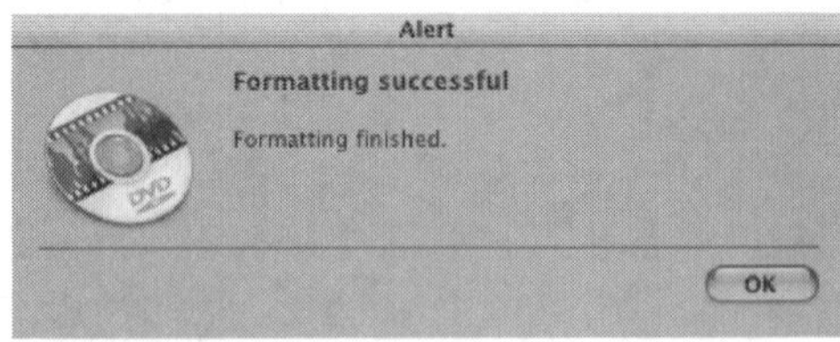

Figure 20.49 After DVD Studio Pro has finished writing all data to the DVD-R, this alert appears.

Replication versus Duplication

Discs that you *duplicate* on your computer may have compatibility problems with set-top DVD players. This is not the fault of DVD Studio Pro or your authoring, as some DVD players simply do not support all brands of DVD-R media for playback. If full compatibility is important to you, consider having your disc professionally *replicated* at a disc replication facility.

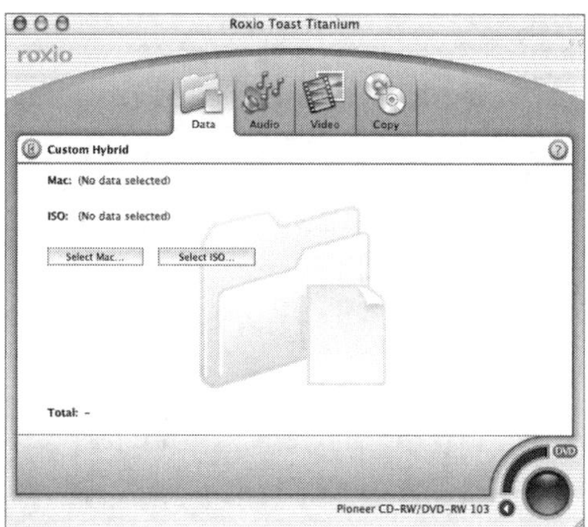

Figure 20.50 The Roxio Toast Titanium window opens, displaying the settings from the last disc that you burned.

Show Disc Options button

roxio

Data

Custom Hybrid

Mac: (No data selected)

ISO: (No data selected)

Figure 20.51 To record a DVD-Video disc using the VIDEO_TS and AUDIO_TS folders created using DVD Studio Pro, click the Data tab and open the Disc Options panel.

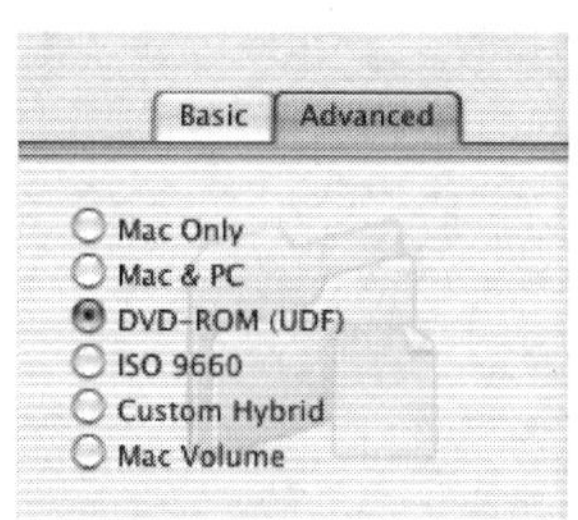

Figure 20.52 A panel of optical disc formats opens on the Advanced tab of the Disc Options panel. Choose DVD-ROM (UDF).

Using Toast 6 Titanium

Roxio's Toast 6 Titanium burns optical discs, allowing you to record data DVD-ROMs, DVD-Video discs, or hybrid DVDs (a DVD-Video and DVD-ROM combo) by simply dragging files into the Toast window and clicking the Record button. Toast's advantages over DVD Studio Pro include the following:

- Toast burns disc images at 1x, and it also allows you to verify your projects to ensure that every bit is exactly where it should be. When creating a master DVD-R for a client, this is a big advantage.
- If you need to make several copies of the same disc, Toast turns your computer into a virtual assembly line; when one disc finishes burning, remove it, put in a new disc, and click the Record button again.

To burn your VIDEO_TS and AUDIO_TS folders to a DVD disc using Toast, you will need to create a DVD-ROM (UDF) formatted DVD. And before burning the DVD, you must remove from the VIDEO_TS folder a few files—layout files, for example—that DVD Studio Pro's Formatter uses.

To burn a DVD-Video disc using Toast:

1. Open Toast.

   The Roxio Toast Titanium window opens (**Figure 20.50**).
2. At the top of the Roxio Toast Titanium window, click the Data tab (refer to Figure 20.50).

   The Data tab opens.
3. At the top left of the Data tab, click the Show Disc Options button (**Figure 20.51**).

   The Disc Options panel opens (**Figure 20.52**). The Advanced tab is displayed by default.

continues on next page

4. On the Disc Options panel's Advanced tab, select the DVD-ROM (UDF) radio button.

   The Roxio Toast Titanium window updates to display DVD-ROM (UDF) (**Figure 20.53**).

5. At the bottom left of the Roxio Toast Titanium window, click the New Disc button (**Figure 20.54**).

   A new DVD disc named My Disc is created in the Roxio Toast Titanium window.

6. Click My Disc to select it and then type a new name (**Figure 20.55**).

   This name identifies the DVD and appears when the disc is placed in a computer DVD-ROM drive, so make sure you choose your name carefully.

7. From the Finder, drag a VIDEO_TS folder and an AUDIO_TS folder into the Roxio Toast Titanium window (**Figure 20.56**).

   To record a hybrid DVD, drag other data files into the Roxio Toast Titanium window along with your VIDEO_TS and AUDIO_TS folders.

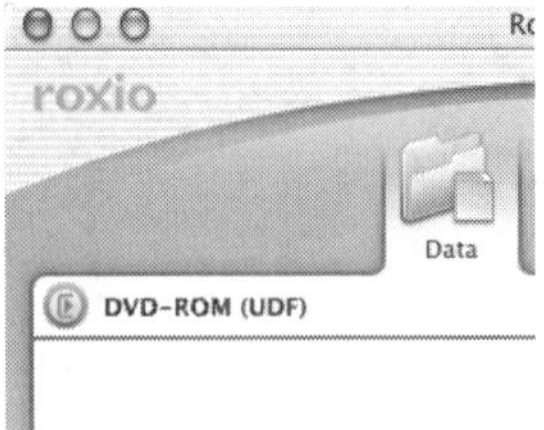

Figure 20.53 The Roxio Toast Titanium window tells you that it's ready to record a DVD.

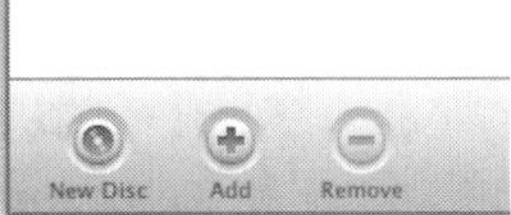

Figure 20.54 Click the New Disc button to start a new DVD disc.

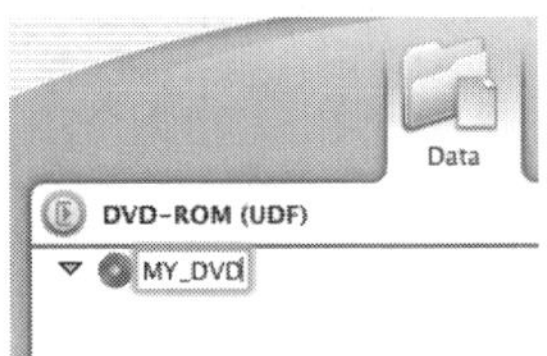

Figure 20.55 To name your DVD, click My Disc once and then type a new name.

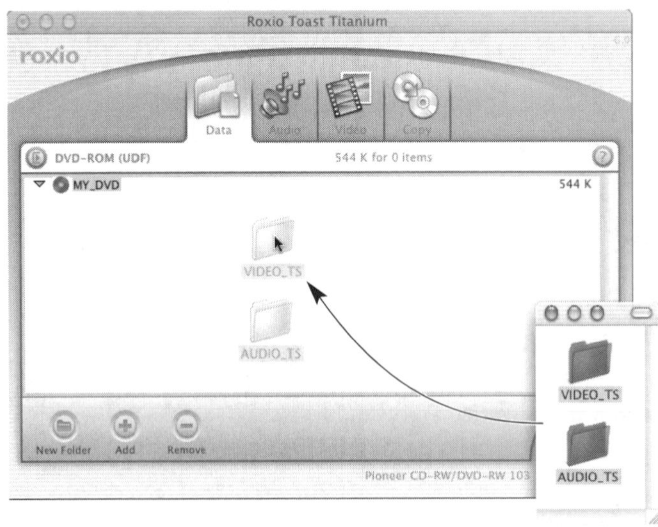

Figure 20.56 Drag a VIDEO_TS folder and an AUDIO_TS folder into the Roxio Toast Titanium window.

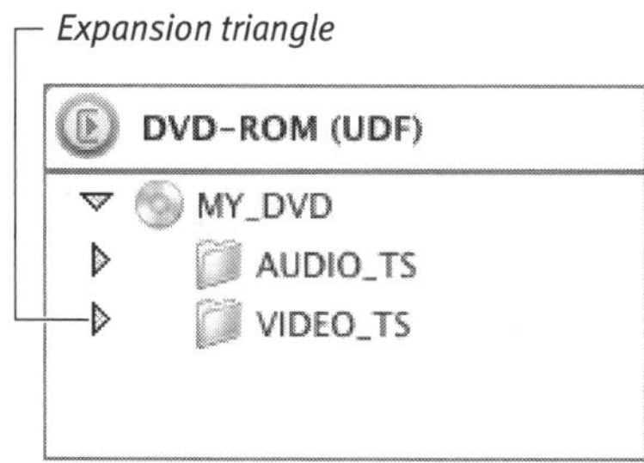

Figure 20.57 Click the expansion triangle to view all of the VIDEO_TS folder's contents.

8. In the Roxio Toast Titanium window, click the VIDEO_TS folder's expansion triangle to view all of the folder's contents (**Figure 20.57**).

9. Select DS_Store, *MY_DVD*.layout (where *MY_DVD* is the name of your DVD), and all VOB_DATA.LAY files. If the VIDEO_TS folder contains a Render Data and/or Transition Data folder, select these folders, too (**Figure 20.58**).

   If you perform incremental builds in DVD Studio Pro, you may have several layout files inside the VIDEO_TS folder; if so, you should delete all layout files from the Toast window.

continues on next page

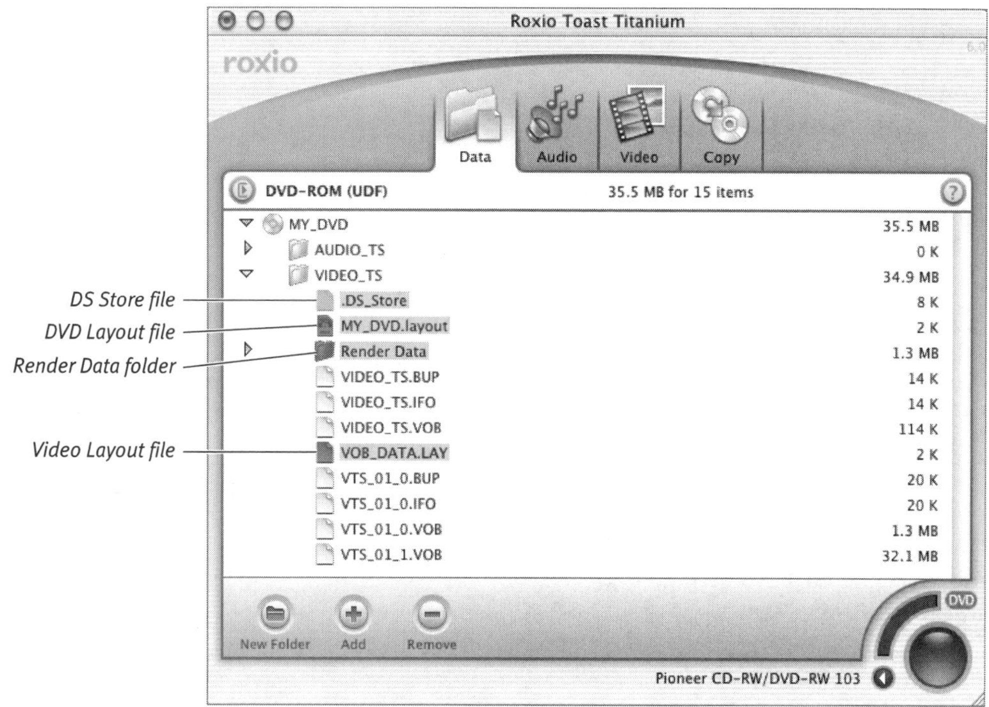

Figure 20.58 DS_Store is a file used by Mac OS X for indexing; DVD Studio Pro's Formatter uses the two layout files. These files may cause playback issues on your final DVD disc and should be deleted from the Toast window. If a Render Data folder sneaks into your VIDEO_TS folder, delete that, too.

10. Delete the selected folders.

11. At the bottom right of the Toast window, click the big, red Record button (**Figure 20.59**).

    The Record dialog opens, allowing you to select a burn speed (**Figure 20.60**).

12. In the middle of the Record dialog's Basic tab, from the Write Speed pop-up menu, choose a burn speed (refer to Figure 20.60).

13. Click Record.

    Your DVD drive's tray opens, and Toast asks you to insert a blank disc (**Figure 20.61**).

Record button

Figure 20.59 When you're ready to record the DVD, click the big, red Record button at the bottom of the Toast window.

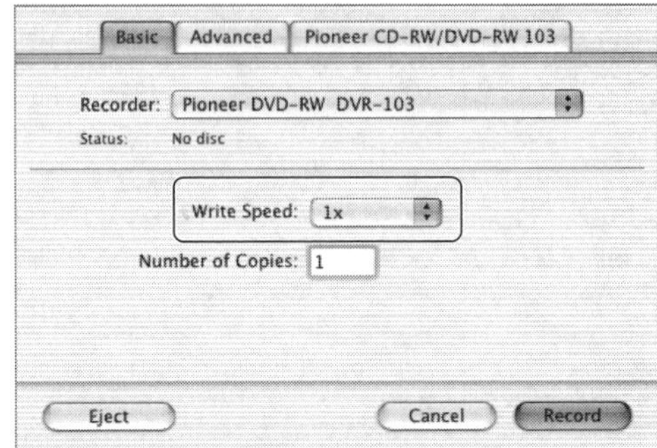

Figure 20.60 From the Write Speed pop-up menu, select a speed; 1x is recommended, especially if you experience buffer underrun errors.

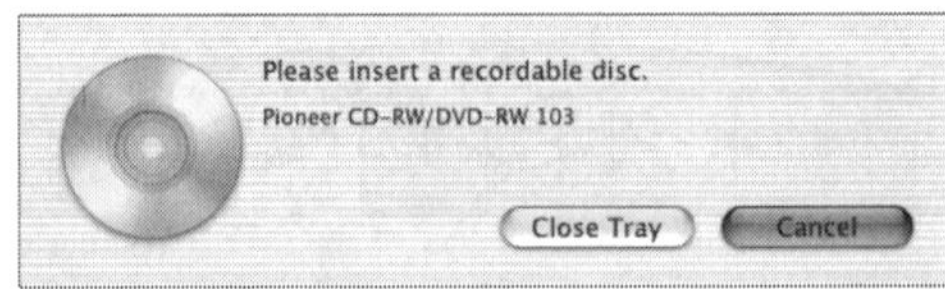

Figure 20.61 When Toasts asks, insert a recordable disc.

Key Files to Delete

As mentioned earlier, Mac OS X uses the DS_Store file for indexing; it is not needed on the DVD-Video disc and should be removed when burning a disc with Toast.

MY_DVD.layout and VOB_DATA.LAY are used by DVD Studio Pro's Formatter and should not be placed on the final DVD-Video disc. (DVD Studio Pro removes these files automatically when formatting.) Some DVD-Video players will ignore these files, but in rare cases they may cause playback issues. To be safe, delete them from the Toast window before burning your DVD.

If you use uncompressed QuickTime files and have your DVD Studio Pro preferences set to encode on build, a Render Data folder may end up inside the VIDEO_TS folder. If you find a Render Data folder, delete this folder from the Toast window before using Toast to burn your DVD-Video disc.

Additionally, if you've used DVD Studio Pro's built-in transition features, a Transition Data folder will be included in your VIDEO_TS folder. Remove this folder before burning the final DVD-Video disc.

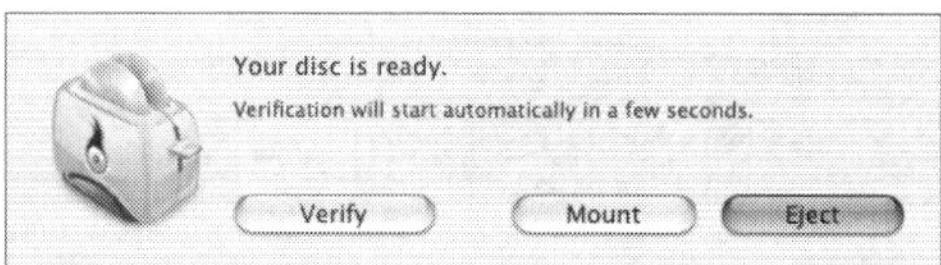

Figure 20.62 When Toast has finished writing data to your disc, it will ask you to verify, mount, or eject the disc.

DVD-Video on CD-ROM

If your multiplexed project is small (less than 700 MB), you don't have to record it on a DVD-R disc. Using Toast, you can instead record the DVD-Video on a CD-R disc. Apple's DVD Player reads DVD-Videos recorded on CD-R discs just as well as it reads DVD-Videos recorded on DVD-R discs.

However, not all DVD players support DVD-Video on CD-R. Although several Windows-based DVD-Video players also read DVD-Videos on CDs, set-top DVD-Video players rarely support this approach. If your project might be played on anything other than a Macintosh, ensure its playback success by burning it on a DVD-R disc.

To record a DVD-Video on a CD, you must use Toast 5 Titanium or higher; simply record the project as if you were writing a DVD-R, but when prompted for a blank DVD-R, insert a CD-R disc instead.

14. Insert a blank DVD-R disc.

Toast begins writing the disc as soon as you insert a blank DVD-R disc. When Toast has finished recording, it asks if you want to verify, mount, or eject the disc (**Figure 20.62**).

15. Choose to verify, mount, or eject the disc.

Verifying the disc takes a while, but it ensures that all of the data has been properly recorded to the disc. If you have time, verify the disc. If you choose Mount, the disc is mounted to your desktop and opens automatically in DVD Player.

✔ Tips

- Finishing the disc takes a long, long time. Don't jump the gun and abort the finishing process, or you'll just have to re-record the disc and sit through the process a second time. Even short projects need to write the lead out, which can take up to 10 minutes! But don't worry; Toast is not hung, and everything is working fine. Patience is not only a virtue; in this case, it will also save you time and money. (By the way, shorter projects take longer to write the lead out than larger projects do).
- When recording DVD-RW discs, do not abort the process as Toast is recording the disc's lead-in—doing so permanently destroys the DVD-RW disc.

To erase a DVD-RW disc:

1. Open Toast.
2. Insert an already recorded DVD-RW disc into your Rewritable DVD drive.
3. Choose Recorder > Erase (**Figure 20.63**), or press Command-B.

   A dialog opens asking if you are sure that you want to erase the disc (**Figure 20.64**). At the bottom of the dialog are three buttons: Cancel, Quick Erase, and Erase. Quick Erase is much faster than the Erase option, but if you choose Quick Erase, you should use only Toast or Jam (another Roxio application for burning discs) to record the DVD-RW the next time you use the disc.
4. Click Quick Erase or Erase.

   The Progress window opens, alerting you that Toast is erasing the disc (**Figure 20.65**). When Toast has finished erasing the disc, an alert appears (**Figure 20.66**).
5. In the alert dialog, click OK to close the window.

   Your disc is ejected.

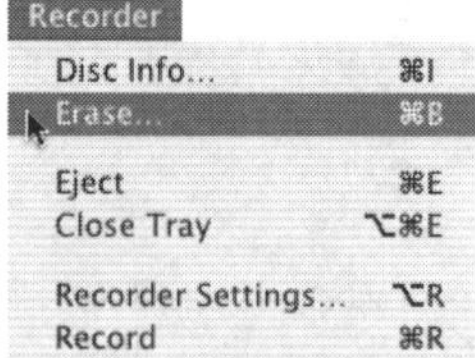

Figure 20.63 To erase a DVD-RW disc, insert a DVD-RW disc and choose Recorder > Erase from the application menu.

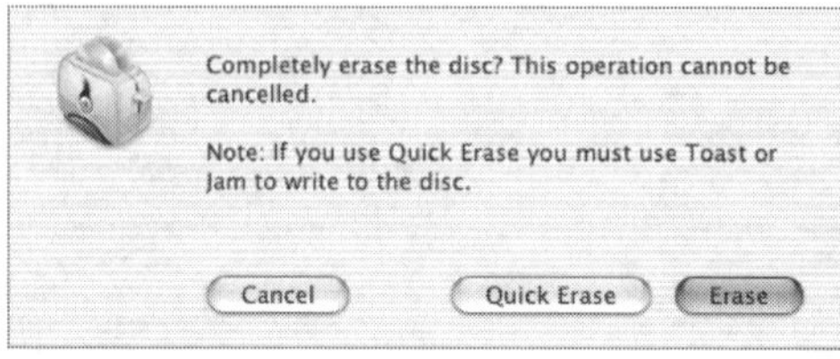

Figure 20.64 Toast gives you one last chance to back out of erasing the disc. Click Erase to completely erase the disc.

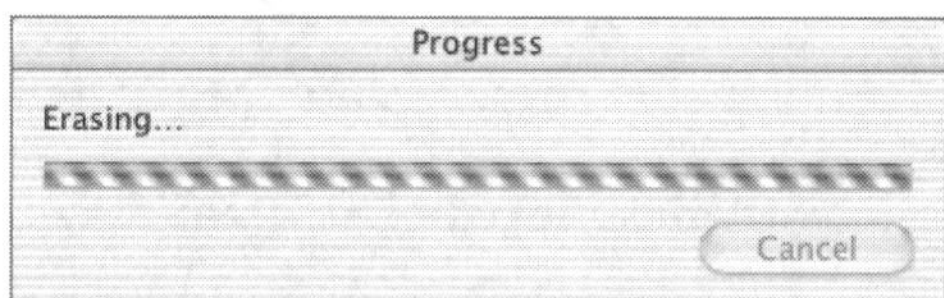

Figure 20.65 The progress meter spins to let you know that Toast is actively erasing the disc.

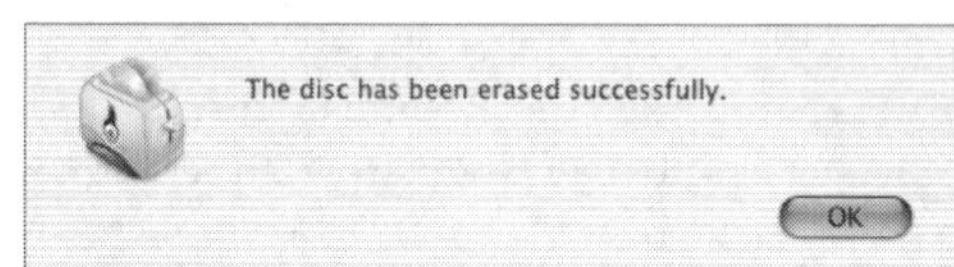

Figure 20.66 When Toast has finished erasing the disc, this alert is displayed.

Figure 20.67 Type a name for your DVD in the Name text box.

Finding a Replication Service

If you need to make a thousand or more DVD disc copies, apply copy protection or region coding, or have a dual-layer DVD-9 project, you must send your project to a professional replication facility (replicator).

The best way to find a reputable replicator is to ask for recommendations at DVD user forums, such as Apple's discussion forum. There is also a list of respected replication facilities, separated by location, on the Web at `www.dvdmadeeasy.com/business/`.

Get in touch with a replicator at least a month in advance—several months, if possible—to set up arrangements for your project delivery date.

Before you output your project, you should ask your replicator what delivery formats he or she accepts. Most replicators accept DDP-formatted DLT Type III tapes and/or DVD-R discs, but you should still check with your individual replicator to see which format he or she prefers.

Outputting to DLT

DLT is an older, tape format that in today's high-tech world seems ancient, slow, and expensive. The drives are clunky, and DLT tapes are both costly and hard to find. However, DLT tapes are reliable, offer massive storage capacity, and serve as the standard delivery format for DVD mastering (all replication facilities accept DLT tapes). Also, if you're going to use any form of copy protection—whether it's region coding, CSS, or Macrovision—DLT is one of your only options.

To record to a DLT tape:

1. Choose File > Advanced Burn > Build and Format, or press Option-Command-F.

   The Formatting window opens. The General tab is selected by default.

2. In the General tab's Disc section, type a name for your disc in the Name text box (**Figure 20.67**).

   The name you type here is the disc name that viewers will see when they insert the manufactured disc into their computers.

continues on next page

3. In the Source section, click the Choose button to choose a destination for the multiplexed files (**Figure 20.68**).

   The Choose Source dialog opens (**Figure 20.69**).

4. Use the Choose Source dialog to select a destination folder on your hard disk for your multiplexed files and then click Choose (refer to Figure 20.69).

   The folder is selected, and the Choose Source dialog closes.

5. In the Formatting window's Destination section, choose your connected DLT drive from the Output Device pop-up menu (**Figure 20.70**).

   The Output Format menu updates to reflect the formatting options compatible with a DLT drive.

6. From the Output Format pop-up menu, choose either DDP or CMF (refer to Figure 20.70).

7. At the bottom of the Formatting window, click the Build & Format button to start the two-part process of building and formatting your project to the DLT tape.

   DVD Studio Pro asks you to insert a DLT tape (**Figure 20.71**).

8. Insert a DLT tape.

   The DLT drive rewinds the DLT tape. When the tape is ready, DVD Studio Pro multiplexes your project and records it to the DLT tape. If you are formatting a DVD-9 project, you'll need to switch tapes midway through the writing process when DVD Studio Pro asks for the second tape.

Figure 20.68 Click Choose to select a folder for the multiplexed files.

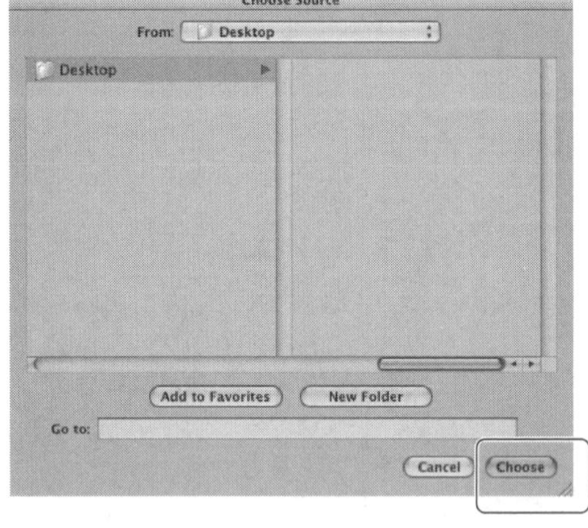

Figure 20.69 Click Choose to set the selected folder.

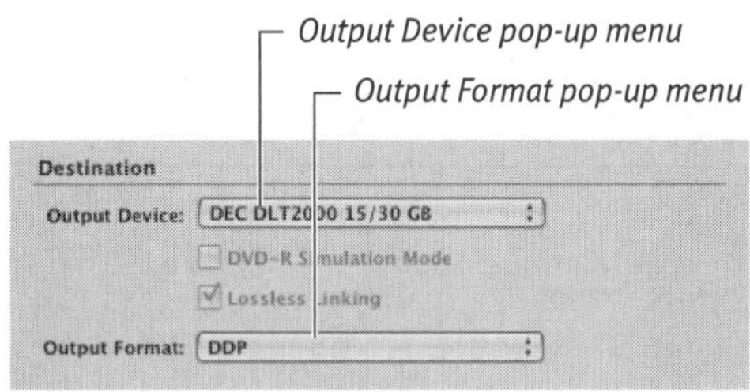

Figure 20.70 Select your DLT drive from the Output Device pop-up menu; then select the output format from the Output Format pop-up menu.

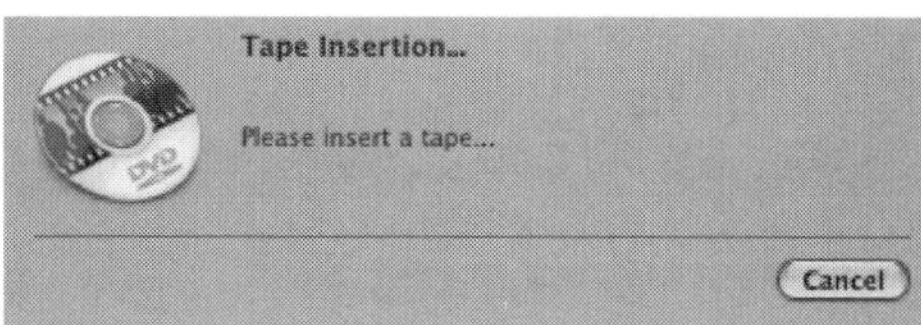

Figure 20.71 When DVD Studio Pro asks, insert a DLT tape.

✔ Tips

- DLT drives are plug and play. Don't be surprised if that DLT drive you bought from eBay arrives without any software, because it doesn't need any. If the DLT drive doesn't show up in the Disc Format window, shut down your computer, power up the DLT drive, and restart the computer. If you're still experiencing problems, reinstall your SCSI card's drivers.
- Generally, both DLT Type III and Type IV tapes can be used to deliver DVD disc images to replicators. At about $30 per unit, Type III tapes are half the price of Type IV tapes and provide more than enough storage space to hold a DVD-Video project. Some DLT drives will read only Type III tapes, so stick with DLT Type III tapes and save your money.

DLT Formats

DVD Studio Pro writes DLT tapes in two formats: Disc Description Protocol (DDP) and Cutting Master Format (CMF). CMF is the format of choice in Japan, whereas DDP is more common in the United States. CMF's main advantage is that it's designed to work with DVD-R (Authoring) discs to create a master disc for replication. Consequently, if you have a Pioneer DVR-201 DVD recorder, you'll be able to send a DVD-R Authoring disc to the replicator instead of a DLT tape.

Both formats tell the replicator how to create a master disc that's used as the basis for each replicated copy. If you're in North America, it's pretty safe to assume that your replicator will accept a DDP-formatted DLT tape, although CMF-formatted tapes are also widely accepted. DVD Studio Pro doesn't care which format you use, so contact the replicator and see which one the replicator requires or prefers before you record DLT tapes.

Creating DVD-9 Projects

DVD-9 projects use dual-layer DVD discs. At some point in the disc's playback, the reading laser must switch from the first layer to the second. This point is called the *layer break.*

To record a DVD-9 project, you need two DLT tapes: one for each layer of the DVD disc. DVD Studio Pro automatically decides where the project's layer break should be and tells you when it's time to insert the second DLT tape. DVD Studio Pro usually places the layer break between tracks. Failing that, it places the layer break on a marker. You can, however, manually designate a specific marker to be the layer break marker within a track.

If you have one large track, such as a feature movie, you'll see a slight glitch or pause in playback when the DVD-Video player switches layers. This glitch happens on every DVD-9 project, so don't worry if you notice this when you play back your replicated project. (Rent a Hollywood title and you'll see this same glitch, usually somewhere around the 45-minute mark.)

Finally, the DVD specification allows dual-layer DVD-Videos to play back using one of two methods: OTP (opposite track path) or PTP (parallel track path). Regardless of the method, the laser starts reading from the inside of the disc and moves toward the outer edge on layer zero (the first layer). When it's time to switch layers, the laser refocuses and either begins reading the second layer from the outside of the disc back toward the middle (OTP) or skips back to the middle of the disc and once again reads out toward the edge (PTP).

DVD Studio Pro allows you to choose which method you prefer. The default setting is OTP, which saves the laser from having to move all the way back to the center of the disc and creates a shorter glitch as the laser switches layers. As the DVD's author, it's your choice to set OTP or PTP.

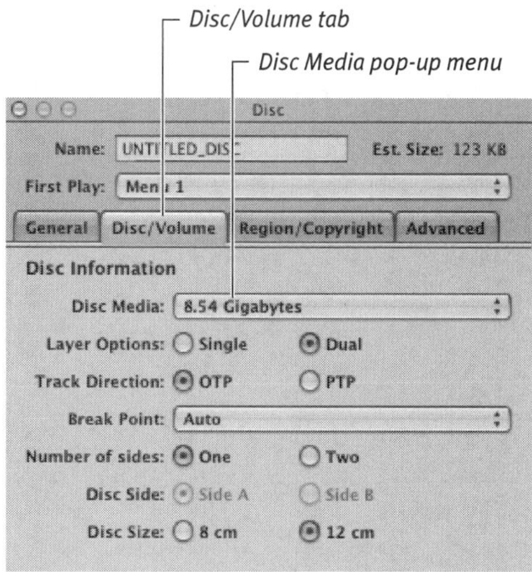

Figure 20.72 Set disc options in the Disc Inspector.

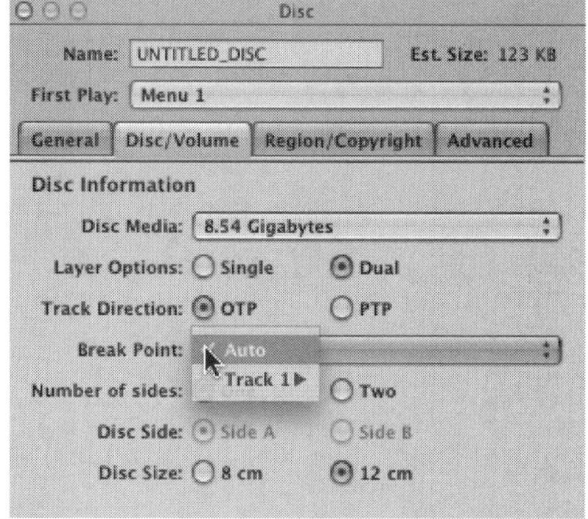

Figure 20.73 Choose a layer break marker from the Break Point pop-up menu, or choose Auto to let DVD Studio Pro choose the layer break marker for you.

✔ Tips

- As this book was being written, DVD-9 DVD-R recorders had been announced, but DVD Studio Pro 3 did not support DVD-9 DVD-R recording.
- Do not use seamless dual-layer break points. Only DVD-Video players that can successfully buffer playback information will be able to play seamless layer breaks. All other DVD-Video players will hang and stop playing.

To create a DVD-9 project:

1. Click the disc in the Outline view to display its properties in the Inspector.
2. In the Disc Inspector, click the Disc/Volume tab (**Figure 20.72**).
3. On the Disc/Volume tab, choose 8.54 Gigabytes from the Disc Media pop-up menu (refer to 20.72).

   The Layer Option automatically changes to Dual, letting you know that you've chosen a dual-layer disc option.
4. Select either the OTP or the PTP Track Direction radio button.

   Depending on the radio button you select, DVD Studio Pro will write the second DLT tape for the second layer to read from the outer circle of the DVD disc back in (OTP) or from the inner circle of the DVD disc back out (PTP) when the disc has been replicated.
5. Choose a break point from the pop-up menu, or leave the setting at Auto to let DVD Studio Pro choose a layer break automatically (**Figure 20.73**).

   When DVD Studio Pro multiplexes your project, the layer break will automatically be set or will be set on the chapter marker you've chosen.

Is That a DVD in Your Pocket?

DVD Studio Pro supports 80 mm (8 cm) pocket-sized DVD-Video discs. An 8 cm disc can either hold 1.46 GB of data or be turned into a dual-layer project, which holds 2.66 GB.

To create an 8 cm disc, you'll need to send a DLT tape out for professional replication. Although DVD Studio Pro can't output an 8 cm DVD-R disc, you can use DVD Studio Pro to set the disc size flags for the replicator by selecting the 8 cm radio button on the Disc Inspector's Disc/Volume tab before recording the project to a DLT tape (**Figure 20.74**). The replication facility will apply the correct lead-in so DVD players will know how to play the disc.

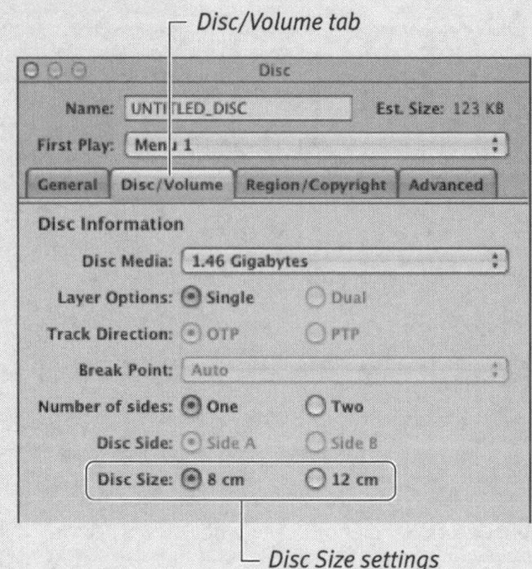

Figure 20.74 Set the DVD disc size on the Disc/Volume tab of the Formatter window. Standard 12 cm DVD discs are set by default.

Testing DVD-9 Projects

Before replicating a project, you always should test it in a set-top DVD-Video player to make sure that buttons link to the right track, that alternate angles are in the right order, and that the project generally works as expected when seen on a television. Unfortunately, testing DVD-9 projects is a bit of a hassle, as the media won't fit onto a DVD-5 DVD-R disc.

To get around this problem, encode a second set of MPEG streams using extremely low bit rates (a little less than half the normal bit rate should work fine). Save a copy of your DVD Studio Pro project. In the project copy, use the Assets tab to replace the high-data-rate MPEG streams with the low-data-rate imposters. Now you can record the project on a DVD-R disc and test it on a television. The video quality will look terrible, but if everything navigates correctly, you can confidently open the original DVD Studio Pro project and record your DLT tapes.

Figure 20.75 Choose View > Customize Toolbar to customize your toolbar.

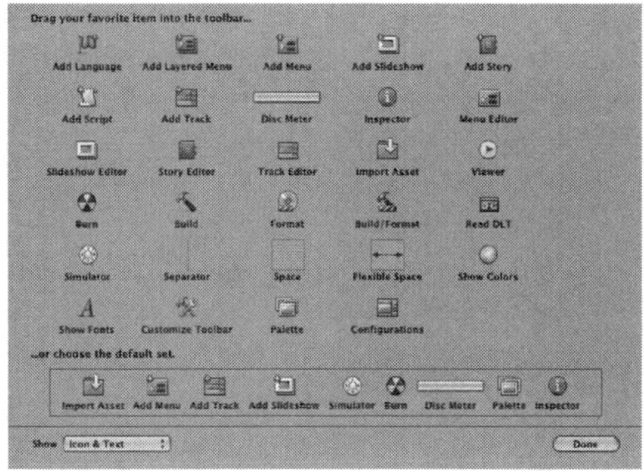

Figure 20.76 The Toolbar Customization panel.

Reading a DLT Tape

DLT tapes have large storage capacities, and they are great for backing up your projects. With DVD Studio Pro, you can read projects from DLT tapes just as easily as you recorded them onto DLT tape in the first place. There's just one point to keep in mind: DVD Studio Pro doesn't offer a menu option for reading DLT tapes; you'll need to customize your toolbar.

To customize the toolbar:

1. Choose View > Customize Toolbar (**Figure 20.75**).

   The Toolbar customization panel opens (**Figure 20.76**).

2. In the Toolbar Customization panel, select the Read DLT icon and drag it onto your toolbar (**Figure 20.77**).

   The Read DLT icon is added to your toolbar.

3. At the bottom right of the Toolbar Customization panel, click the Done button.

   The Toolbar Customization panel closes.

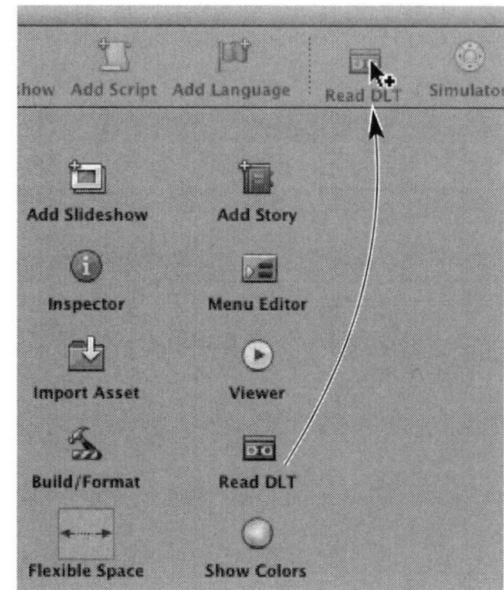

Figure 20.77 Drag the Read DLT icon onto your toolbar.

To save DLT data to your hard disk:

1. In your toolbar, click the Read DLT icon.
   The Save Disc Image dialog appears (**Figure 20.78**).
2. In the Save Disc Image dialog, navigate to the location on your hard disk where you want to save the data from the DLT drive.
3. In the Save As text box, type a name for your disk image (**Figure 20.79**).
4. Click Save.
   DVD Studio Pro asks you to insert the tape to be read (**Figure 20.80**).
5. Insert a tape.
   DVD Studio Pro rewinds your tape and saves the data as a disk image in the folder you selected.

✔ Tip

- DVD Studio Pro can read only DLT tapes that are DDP or CMF formatted. If you insert a tape using a different format, DVD Studio Pro will display an alert message letting you know that the tape can't be read (**Figure 20.81**).

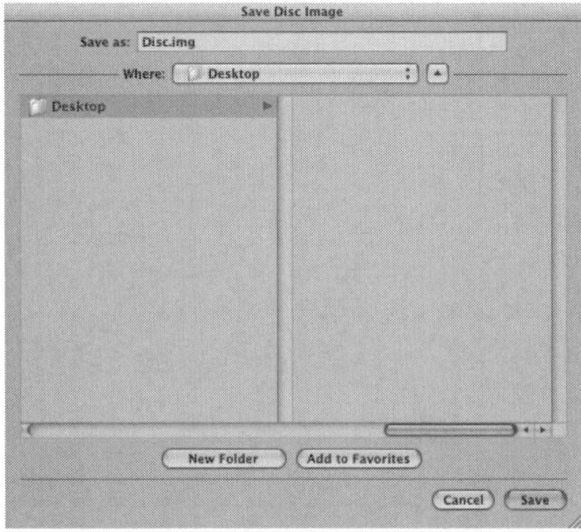

Figure 20.78 In the Save Disc Image dialog, navigate to the location where you want the DLT disk image saved and click Save.

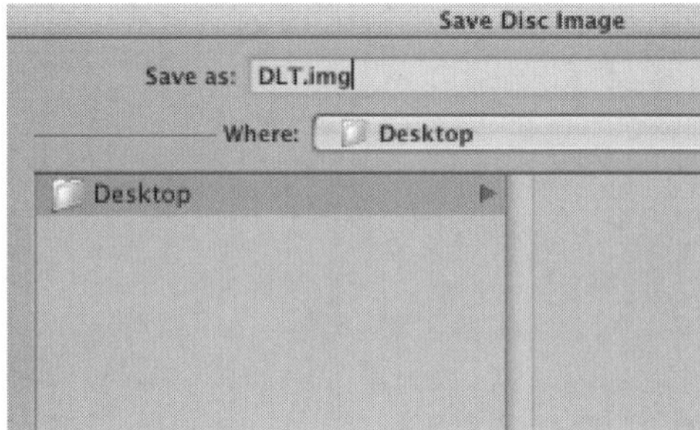

Figure 20.79 Type a name for your disk image.

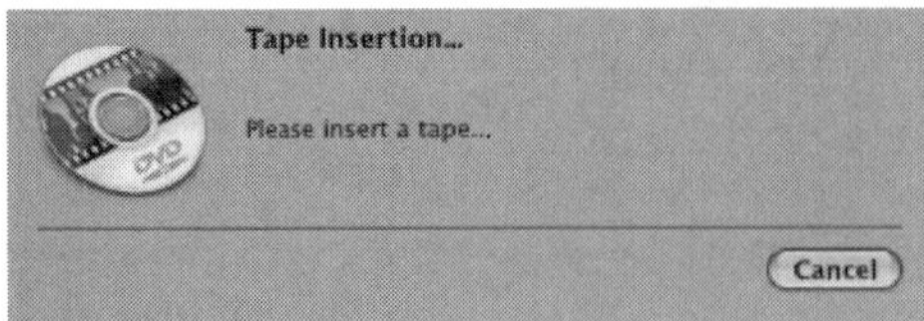

Figure 20.80 Insert your DLT tape when prompted.

Figure 20.81 DVD Studio Pro displays this alert message if you try to read a tape with an unsupported DLT format.

Part III: Advanced DVD Authoring

Chapter 21 DVD@ccess 531

Chapter 22 Widescreen: 16:9 551

Chapter 23 Working with Languages................569

Chapter 24 Subtitles...587

Chapter 25 Scripting...627

Part III: Advanced DVD Authoring

21. DVD@ccess
About DVD@ccess
Installing DVD@ccess on Windows PCs
Enabling DVD@ccess on the Macintosh
Using DVD@ccess
Linking to Buttons
Linking to the Disc
Simulating DVD@ccess

22. Widescreen: 16:9
About Widescreen Video
Using DVD Studio Pro's Embedded Encoder
Using the QuickTime MPEG-2 Exporter
About Anamorphic Video
Playing Widescreen Tracks on 4:3 TVs
Creating 16:9 Menus
Simulating 16:9 Projects

23. Working with Languages
About Multilingual DVDs
Working with Multiple-Language Menus
Working with Multilingual Tracks
Previewing Multiple-Language Projects

24. Subtitles
About the Subtitle Editor
Setting Subtitle Text Preferences
Creating Subtitles
Editing Subtitles
Formatting Subtitle Text
Positioning Subtitles
Changing Subtitle Duration
Using Fades
Using Color
Forcing Subtitle Display
Simulating Subtitles
Creating Text Subtitles
Importing Text Subtitles
Using Subtitle Graphics
About Closed Captions

25. Scripting
Creating a Script
Using the Script Editor
Using Prescripts
Programming Commands
Using Parameter Registers
Using a Compare Command
Troubleshooting Scripts

DVD@ccess

DVD Studio Pro uses a proprietary system called DVD@ccess to launch URLs and provide specialized interactivity as your DVD-Video plays. URLs (also called DVD@ccess links) can launch Web pages, send e-mail, and even open files stored in a ROM folder on a hybrid DVD disc. But there is one catch: DVD@ccess interactivity is available only when the DVD-Video is played on a computer. When the disc is played on a television, the links are ignored. In fact, DVD@ccess is guaranteed to work only on a Macintosh computer. Windows PC users will need to install the DVD@ccess application on their hard drives before the DVD@ccess links will work.

DVD@ccess does not bring any content into the DVD-Video, but instead it opens separate applications to display the files that the URLs point to. If you provide a DVD@ccess link to a Web site, for example, the computer's default browser will automatically launch and display the Web page. Similarly, if you add a DVD@ccess link to a PDF file on a hybrid DVD disc, Adobe Acrobat launches, and the PDF file appears onscreen.

Both Macs and PCs equipped with a DVD player can launch DVD@ccess links. The playback functionality is built into recent versions (version 2.4 or higher) of Apple's DVD Player on the Macintosh, but Windows users must install DVD@ccess for DVD@ccess links to work.

About DVD@ccess

You can use DVD@ccess links throughout your DVD-Video to open:

- **A Web link.** If the computer is connected to the Internet, the computer's default Web browser launches and loads the specified Web page when the viewer activates the link on the DVD-Video disc.
- **An e-mail link.** The computer's default e-mail application launches and addresses a new e-mail message to the defined recipient when the link is activated on the DVD.
- **A file.** If the computer has a suitable application installed in which the file can open, the application is launched and the file is opened.

How DVD@ccess works

DVD@ccess intercepts a DVD-Video's call for a URL or a file path and then opens the URL in a Web browser or some other application. DVD@ccess itself is not part of the DVD-Video; it is a separate application that runs quietly in the background whenever a DVD-Video disc is placed in the computer's DVD drive. Because the URLs are encoded into the DVD-Video stream as embedded text messages that only DVD@ccess understands, the viewer never sees the URLs but only witnesses the results (for more information on embedded text, see Chapter 19, "Finishing the DVD"). Consequently, Web links in DVD Studio Pro projects work only on computers that have DVD@ccess installed.

While DVD@ccess comes with the Apple DVD Player and is pre-installed on all Macintosh computers, your Windows PC users must be proactive and install the program before your project's DVD@ccess links will work. They need to know this fact, so be sure to include text instructions on a DVD menu or on the outside of your DVD's case.

Fortunately, when you add DVD@ccess links to your DVD-Video, Windows PC DVD@ccess installers are automatically included in a folder named DVDccess on the final DVD-Video disc (**Figure 21.1**), which makes tracking down the installers a breeze for viewers who need to install them.

Figure 21.1 When you add Web links to your project, DVD Studio Pro includes the Windows DVD@ccess installer on the final DVD disc in a folder named DVDccess.

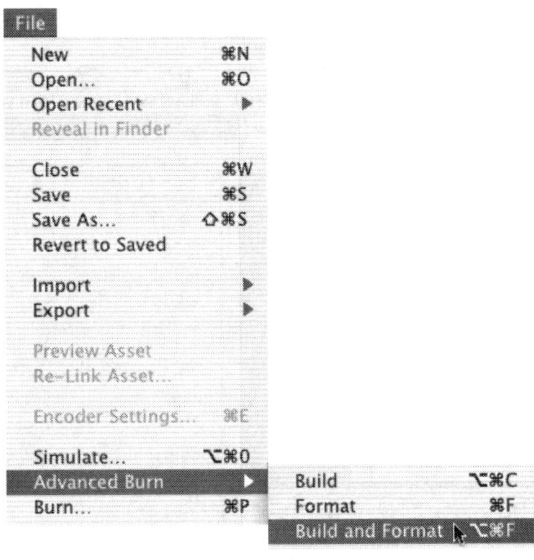

Figure 21.2 If you want the DVD@ccess installer on your finished DVD, make sure you choose Build and Format to compile the project.

Figure 21.3 A shortcut menu appears when you Control-click the application icon.

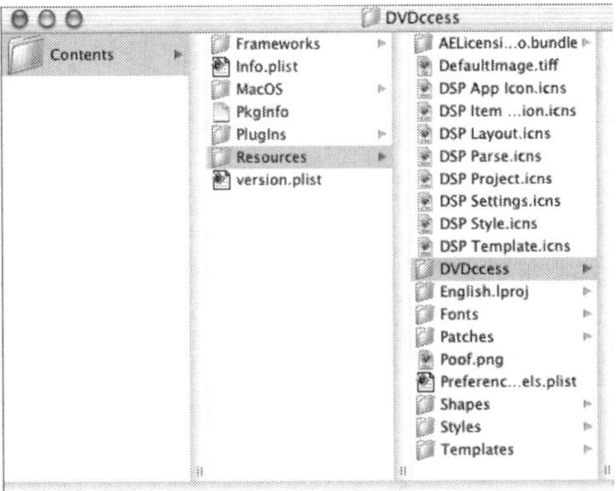

Figure 21.4 Inside the DVD Studio Pro application package, navigate to Contents/Resources/DVDccess to locate the Windows DVD@ccess installer.

✔ Tip

- DVD Studio Pro does not include the DVD@ccess installers with projects that you built directly to your hard disk using File > Build Disc. The DVD@ccess installers are included only with projects that you build using File > Advanced Burn > Build and Format (**Figure 21.2**). However, you can build and format a disk image to your hard drive that includes the Windows DVD@ccess installer.

To locate the Windows installer:

1. The Windows DVD@ccess installer is located in the DVD Studio Pro application package in a subfolder named Resources. In the Finder, locate the DVD Studio Pro application (Hard Disk/ Applications/DVD Studio Pro).
2. Control-click the DVD Studio Pro application icon.
3. Select Show Package Contents from the shortcut menu that appears (**Figure 21.3**).

   A new Finder window opens displaying the Contents folder.
4. Open the Contents folder and navigate to Contents/Resources/DVDccess (**Figure 21.4**).

   The DVDccess folder contains the Windows DVD@ccess installer.

✔ Tips

- Do not remove the DVDccess folder from the application package. If you alter the DVDccess folder in any way, you will need to reinstall DVD Studio Pro to build and format a disc that uses DVD@ccess links.
- If you are using Roxio Toast Titanium to burn your final DVD-Video, include a copy of the installer with your DVD-Video.

Installing DVD@ccess on Windows PCs

For your Web links to work on a Windows PC, the viewer must first install DVD@ccess. Most Windows users won't instinctively know this, so you'll need to tell them. A common way to do this is to include a text warning on the menu with the Web links, but you can also add an Info button that links to a menu with text instructions (or a video segment) that walk viewers through the installation process. Whatever method you choose, make sure it's obvious enough that Windows users understand that they must install DVD@ccess and restart their computers before the DVD-Video's Web links will work.

✔ Tips

- Even with proper warning, it's hard to convince some viewers to install new software on their computers. As a result, count on the fact that some people won't see your Web links. In addition to the automatic DVD@ccess links, you may want to include a text Web link on your menu that viewers can manually enter into their Web browsers.
- You should take some satisfaction in getting Windows users to install DVD@ccess, because you're paving the way for all your kindred DVD Studio Pro authors. As long as the program remains installed on the Windows PC, DVD Studio Pro DVD-Videos that use DVD@ccess will play without a hitch.

DVD@ccess on Windows PCs

In DVD Studio Pro 1.*x*, DVD@ccess links didn't always work as expected on Windows PCs. Most of those issues have been addressed, but some may remain. Here are a few points to be aware of when playing DVD@ccess links on Windows-based computers:

- The DVD@ccess Web link utility may not start automatically on all Windows XP computers.

  After installing DVD@ccess and restarting the machine, you may get an error message saying that Windows could not locate the necessary files. To get around this, double-click the DVD@ccess utility located in the Program Files/Apple Computer/DVD@ccess folder to manually start the DVD@ccess utility. Your Web links on the disc should then work.

- DVD@ccess doesn't work automatically with certain FireWire and USB external DVD drives on some Windows computers.

  Web links on DVDs that are played on an external drive work on Windows 2000 and Windows XP but not on Windows 98, Windows 98SE, or Windows Me. To have Web links work when your movie is played back on any external DVD drive on any Windows computer, quit and relaunch the DVD@ccess utility manually.

- DVD@ccess links do not work with WinDVD 2.*x* DVD Players on Windows 2000, Windows XP, or Windows NT computers.

- To enhance the compatibility of DVDs using DVD@ccess Web links that will be played on Windows XP PCs using the Media Player and on any Windows PC using Power DVD, use motion menus in place of still DVD@ccess menus.

- Links that access files on the DVD disc itself need to conform to the 8.3 file-naming convention for the links to work on Windows NT computers.

  The 8.3 file-naming convention restricts file names to a maximum of eight characters, followed by a period and a three-letter extension. Letters, numbers, and underscores are supported, but other characters are not.

- Copying a .vob file from the DVD onto a PC's hard disk causes the default Web browser to open and connect to all URLs embedded in the DVD.

Enabling DVD@ccess on the Macintosh

Most Macintosh users won't need to install DVD@ccess; it's included with Apple DVD Player version 2.4 and later. If your Web links don't work in Apple DVD Player, it's probably because DVD@ccess isn't turned on. A quick visit to DVD Player's Preferences dialog provides an easy fix.

To enable DVD@ccess on the Macintosh:

1. Locate the Apple DVD Player application in the Applications folder and open the program (**Figure 21.5**).
2. Choose DVD Player > Preferences (**Figure 21.6**) to open the DVD Player Preferences dialog.
3. Click the Disc tab (**Figure 21.7**).

   The Disc tab tells DVD Player how to display the disc and includes settings for the disc's default languages and a check box at the bottom that turns on DVD@ccess.
4. Select the Enable DVD@ccess Web Links check box.
5. Click OK.

   The Preferences dialog closes. Now whenever DVD Player encounters a DVD@ccess Web link, DVD@ccess opens the corresponding Web page.

Figure 21.5 Apple's DVD Player works in tandem with DVD@ccess to show Web links, but only if the DVD@ccess preference is enabled.

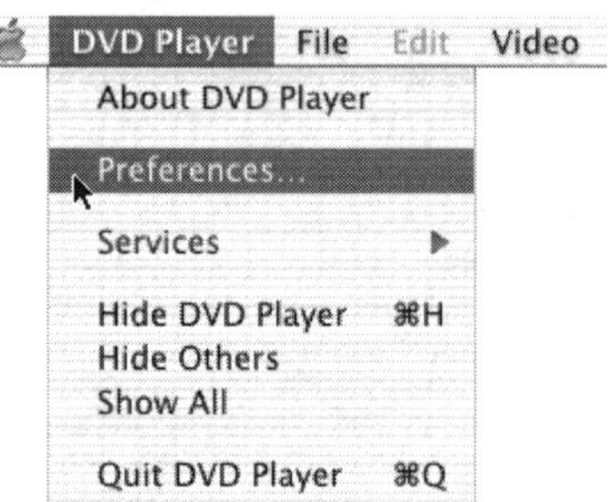

Figure 21.6 To open DVD Player's preferences, choose DVD Player > Preferences.

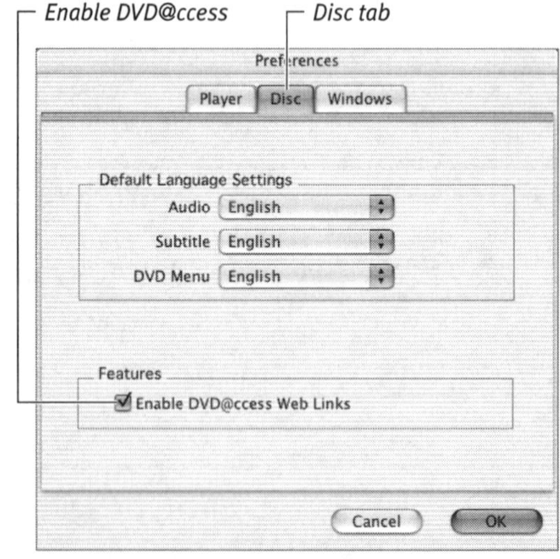

Figure 21.7 At the bottom of the DVD Player's Disc tab is a check box that turns DVD@ccess on or off.

Using DVD@ccess

DVD@ccess links can be attached to several types of project items, including chapter markers, menus, and slides. If a project item has a DVD@ccess link, the link's URL opens as soon as the project item appears onscreen.

The only slight difficulty with DVD@ccess lies in using the correct syntax. All links, for example, use full path names only. For links to the Internet, this means that you must include the `http://` prefix—for example:

`http://www.apple.com/dvdstudiopro`

Without the `http://` prefix, DVD@ccess won't understand how to follow the link's path to the Internet. Links must be typed exactly as they appear in a Web browser.

DVD@ccess links can also launch the viewer's e-mail application, link to an FTP server, or open files off the DVD disc using path names similar to the following:

- `mailto:`*`myEmailAddress@myDomain`*`.com`
- `ftp://`*`myDomain`*`.com/`*`myMovie`*`.mov`
- *`file:///DiscName/Folder/FileName.extension`*

DVD@ccess Rules

You must follow three simple rules when using DVD@ccess links in your project; not following these rules results in links that don't work.

- Use full path names only. Notice the extra forward slash in the file path. There are a total of three forward slashes, followed by the disc name.
- The entry cannot contain any spaces.
- File paths are case-sensitive. If you place a PDF file in the DVD-ROM folder, for example, you need to include all capital letters within the path name.

To set a DVD@ccess Web link for a chapter marker:

1. In the Outline view, double-click a track to open it in the Track editor.
2. In the Track editor, select one of the markers on the timeline (**Figure 21.8**).
   The Inspector updates to display the marker's properties (**Figure 21.9**).
3. Click the DVD@ccess check box to select it.
4. Type a name for the link in the DVD@ccess Name text box.
   This name serves only as a personal reminder about where the link points. It does not appear in the final DVD-Video, so you can enter whatever you want.
5. In the DVD@ccess URL text box, type a URL (**Figure 21.10**).

✔ Tips

- DVD@ccess marker links are ignored by any stories you create using this marker. Stories cannot have DVD@ccess links.
- DVD@ccess causes the Web browser to open directly on top of your DVD-Video. For specialized presentations that synchronize Web content to the video on the DVD disc, you may want to pause the video so the viewer has time to reposition the Web browser before continuing.

Figure 21.8 Click a marker in the timeline to select it and display the marker's properties in the Inspector.

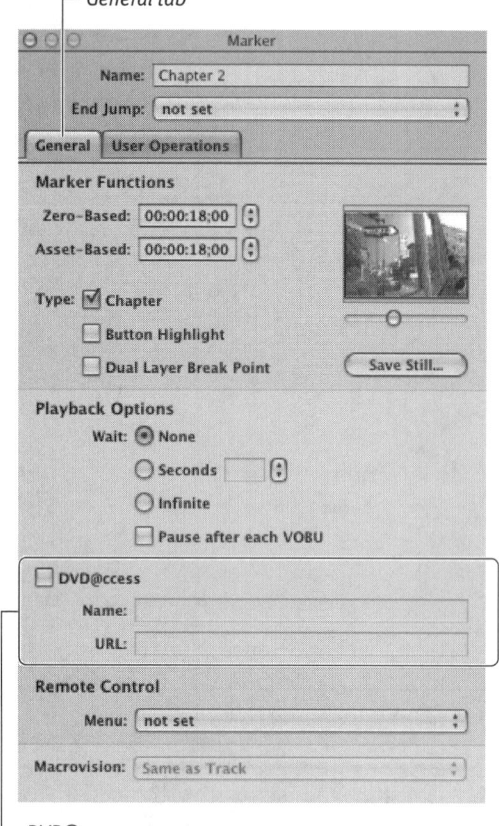

Figure 21.9 When you select a marker in the timeline, the Inspector updates to display the marker's properties.

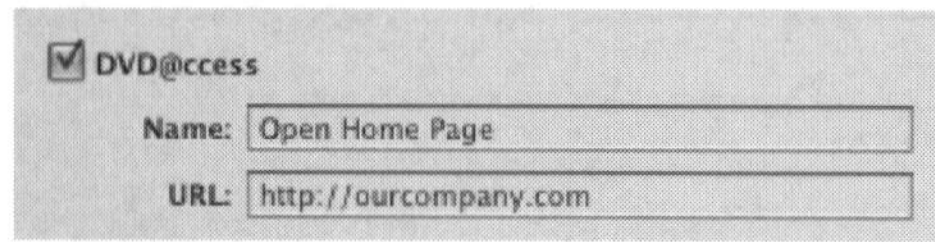

Figure 21.10 Enter the DVD@ccess link's full URL in the URL text box.

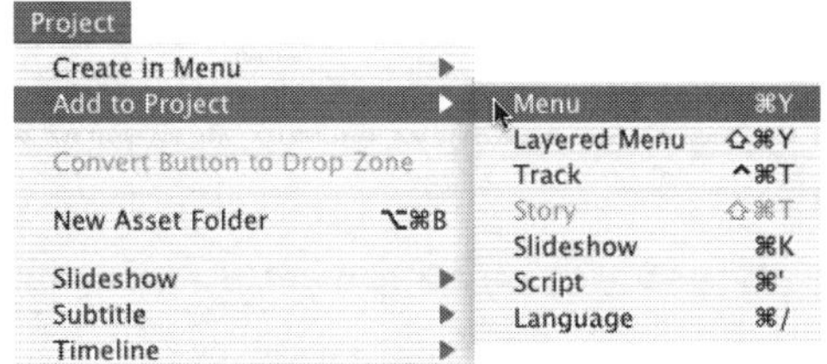

Figure 21.11 To add a new standard menu to your project, choose Project > Add to Project > Menu.

To set a DVD@ccess e-mail link for a menu:

1. From DVD Studio Pro's main menu, choose Project > Add to Project > Menu (**Figure 21.11**), or press Command-Y.
   A new menu is created.
2. In the Outline view, double-click the new menu to bring it into focus in the Menu editor and in the Inspector (**Figure 21.12**).

continues on next page

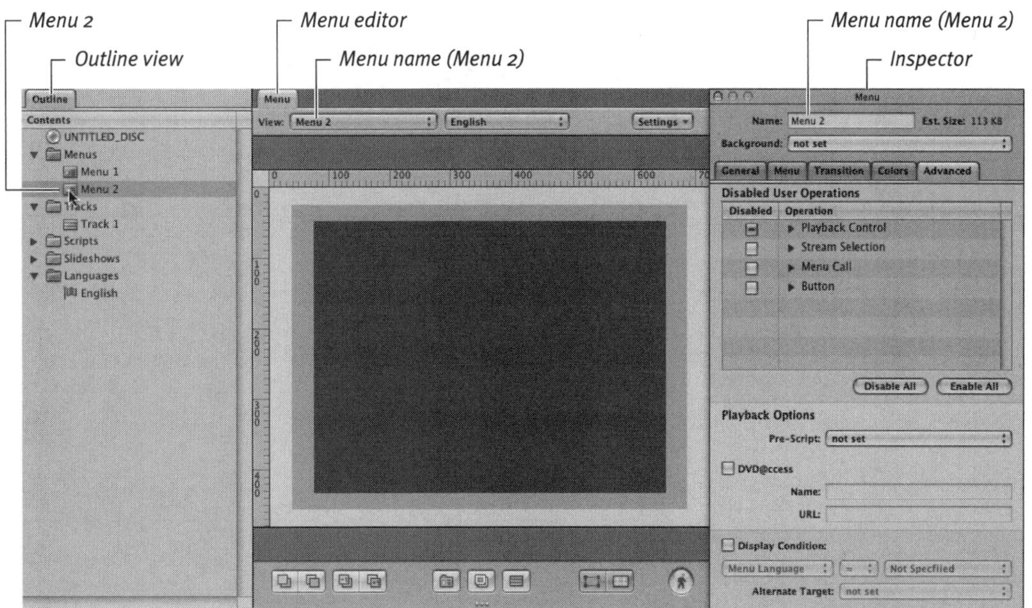

Figure 21.12 Double-click the new menu in the Outline view to bring it into focus in the Menu editor and the Inspector.

3. In the Inspector, select the Advanced tab (**Figure 21.13**).
4. In the Playback Options section, click the DVD@ccess check box to select it.
5. In the DVD@ccess Name text box, type a name for the e-mail link.

   This name serves only as a personal reminder about where the link points. It does not appear in the final DVD-Video, so you can enter whatever you want.
6. Type an e-mail address in the DVD@ccess URL text box (**Figure 21.14**).

   DVD Studio Pro embeds the text URL in the menu when you multiplex the project. As soon as the menu appears, the link will open the viewer's default e-mail program. If you want the viewer to activate a button to launch a URL, you must link that button to a second menu that contains the DVD@ccess link. This process is described in the next section.

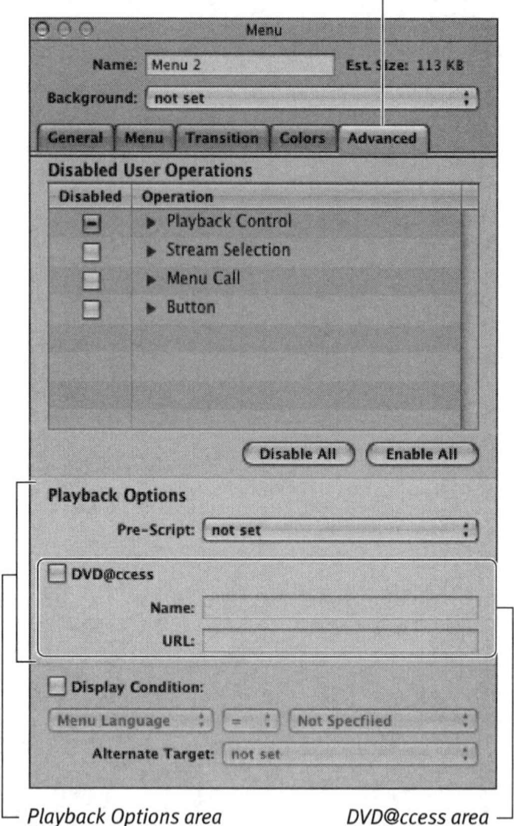

Figure 21.13 To create a DVD@ccess link that is activated when a menu is played, click the DVD@ccess check box, enter a name in the Name text box, and enter a URL in the URL text box.

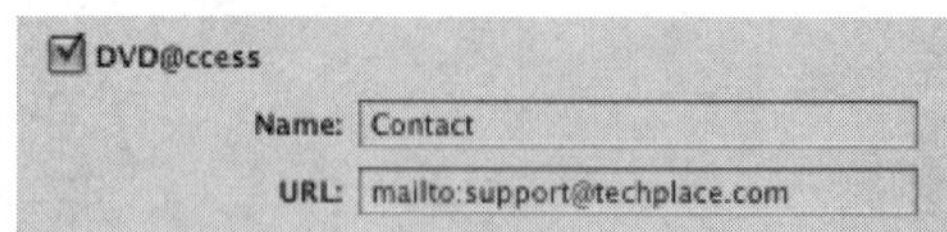

Figure 21.14 When the menu appears onscreen, the computer's default e-mail application will open and automatically fill in the recipient's e-mail address.

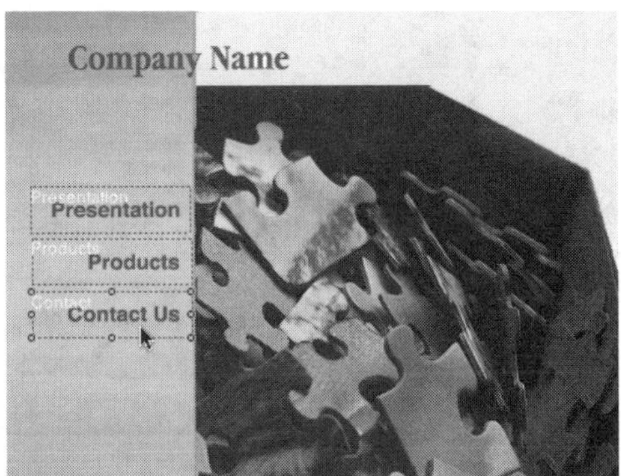

Figure 21.15 A menu that includes a DVD@ccess link button.

Linking to Buttons

You'll probably find yourself frequently using DVD@ccess to create menu buttons that open Web pages or send e-mails. You've seen, for example, the Contact button found on most Web pages—using DVD@ccess, you can add a similar Contact button to your DVD-Video. Viewers watching the disc on a computer can click the Contact button, and their default e-mail program will open with your e-mail address in the Send To field.

But here's the catch: You can't create buttons with direct DVD@ccess links. Instead, you must use a workaround that jumps the button to a second menu with a DVD@ccess link attached to it. The second menu looks exactly like the first menu, but it has a very short timeout action that jumps the video back to the first menu after the second menu launches the URL. With all of the action that accompanies the opening of the browser, viewers won't even notice that they're jumping back and forth between menus.

To open a URL from a button:

1. Create a menu that includes a DVD@ccess link button (**Figure 21.15**). Finish the menu by naming each button and assigning them selected and activated states. (For more information on creating menus, see Chapter 13, "The Menu Editor.")
2. In the Outline view, click the menu to select it.

continues on next page

3. Duplicate the menu by *doing one of the following:*

   ▲ Choose Edit > Duplicate.

   ▲ Press Command-D.

   ▲ Control-click the menu and choose Duplicate from the shortcut menu that appears.

   A copy of the menu is added to your list of menus in the Outline view. The new menu is an exact copy of the first menu, so both menus look identical.

4. In the Outline view, double-click Menu 1 to open it in the Menu editor (**Figure 21.16**).

5. In the Menu editor, select the Contact button on the menu.

   The Inspector updates to display the Contact button's properties (**Figure 21.17**).

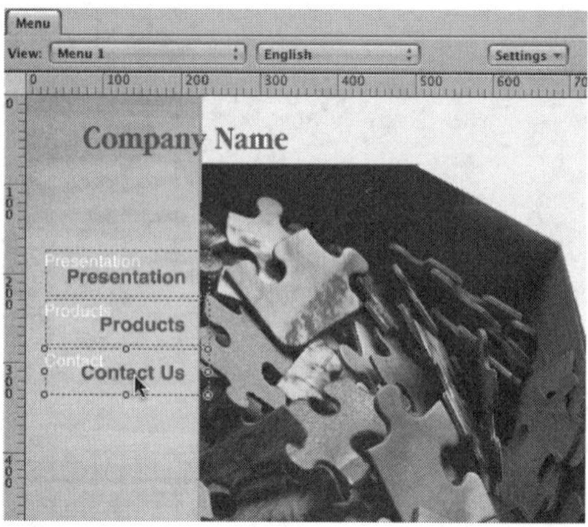

Figure 21.16 Menu 1 opens in the Menu editor.

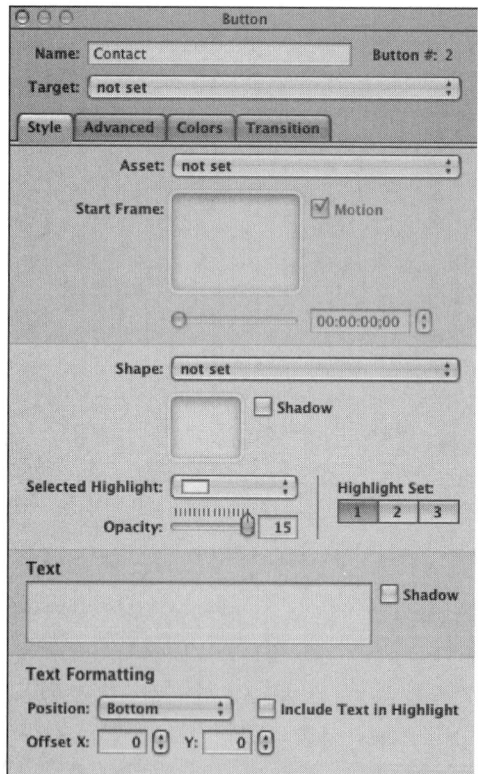

Figure 21.17 All button settings can be configured in the Button Inspector. (For information on other button settings, see Chapter 13.)

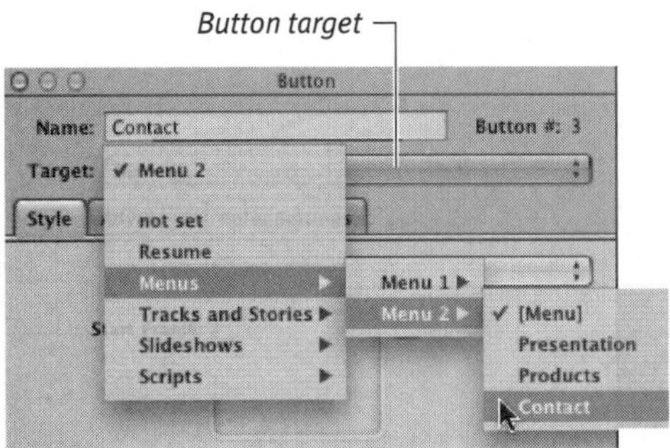

Figure 21.18 Set the button target in the Button Inspector.

6. Set the button's target. In the Button Inspector, choose Menus > Menu 2 > Contact from the Target pop-up menu (**Figure 21.18**).

   This is the button's jump action when activated.

7. In the Outline view, double-click Menu 2 to open it in the Menu editor (**Figure 21.19**).

   The Inspector updates to display Menu 2's properties (**Figure 21.20**).

continues on next page

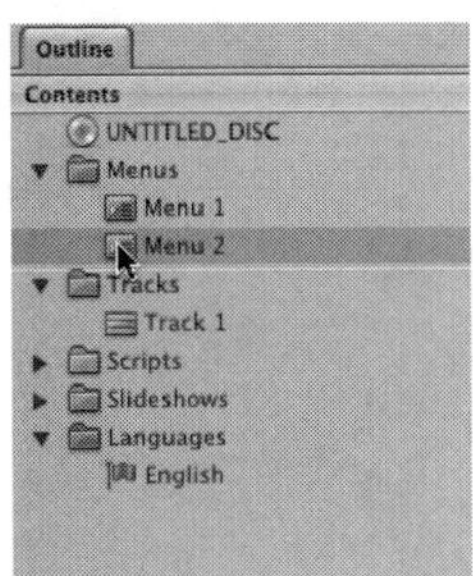

Figure 21.19 Double-click Menu 2 to open it in the Menu editor.

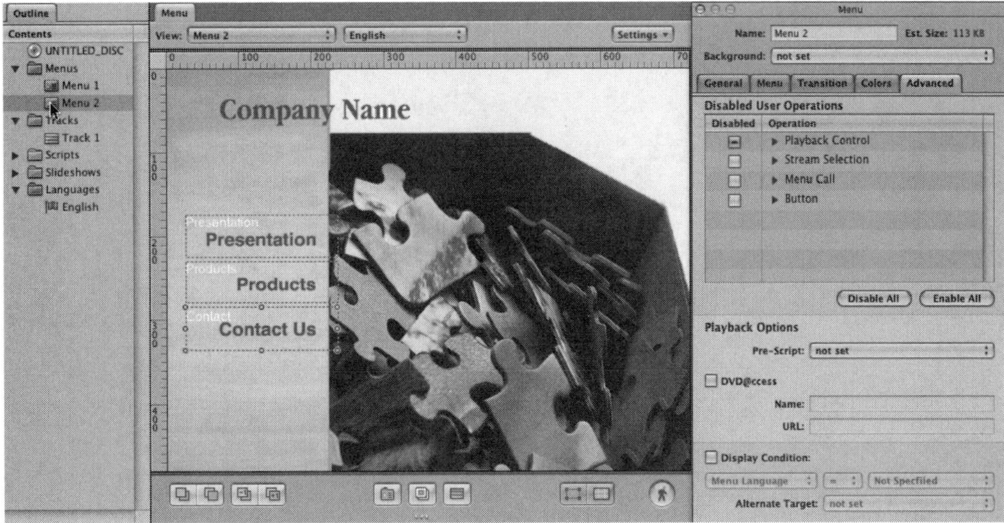

Figure 21.20 Menu 2 opens in the Menu editor, and the Inspector updates to display Menu 2's properties.

8. In the Inspector, select the Advanced tab (**Figure 21.21**).
9. On the Advanced tab in the Menu Inspector, click the DVD@ccess check box to select it.
10. In the DVD@ccess Name text field, type a name for your link (**Figure 21.22**).
11. In the DVD@ccess URL text field, type a URL.

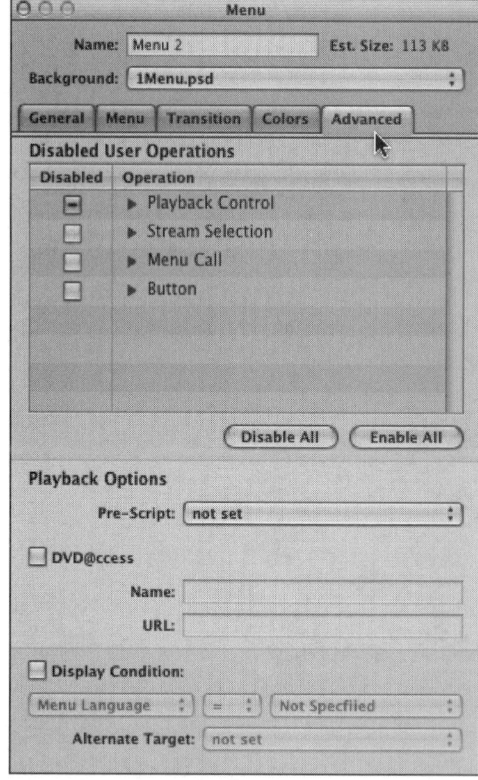

Figure 21.21 The Menu Inspector Advanced tab.

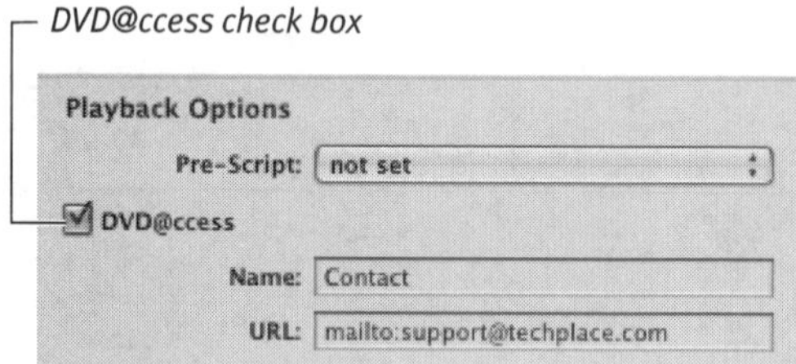

Figure 21.22 Select the DVD@ccess check box; then type a name and URL.

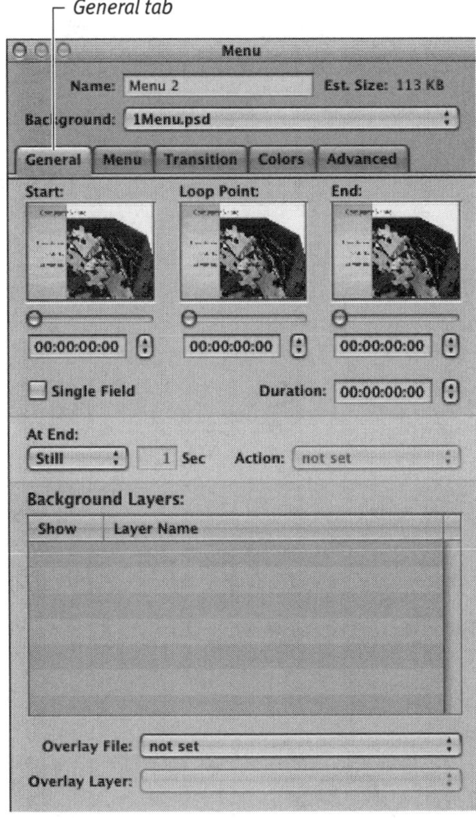

Figure 21.23 Select the General tab in the Menu Inspector.

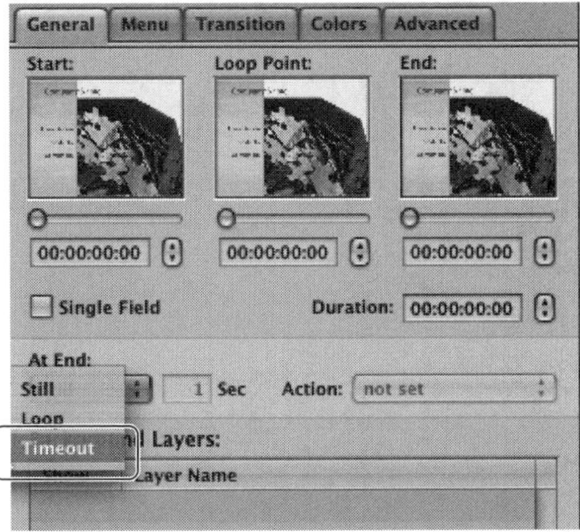

Figure 21.24 Select Timeout from the At End pop-up menu on the General tab.

12. In Menu 2's Inspector, select the General tab (**Figure 21.23**).

13. Select Timeout from the At End pop-up menu (**Figure 21.24**) to activate the Secs (Seconds) and Action settings.

    This allows you to configure the menu so it counts down the specified number of seconds and then jumps to the specified location.

    If a viewer does not select a button for several seconds, you can determine what the viewer sees next by having the menu time out and jump to another asset.

    The minimum timeout duration you can set is 1 second; the maximum is 254 seconds.

    The countdown will not begin until the video or audio finishes playing. If the audio and video on a menu is set to loop, you cannot set the timeout countdown duration in the Menu Inspector. However, you can script a timeout action for menus that loop. (For more information on scripting, see Chapter 25, "Scripting."

continues on next page

14. On the Menu Inspector's General tab for Menu 2, type the duration (in seconds) for the timeout (**Figure 21.25**).

    This short timeout causes Menu 2 to quickly jump back to Menu 1 without the viewer's ever being the wiser.

15. Set the jump action for Menu 2. Choose Menus > Menu 1 > Contact from the Action pop-up menu (**Figure 21.26**).

    The DVD-Video will jump to Menu 1 after the timeout countdown is complete.

✔ Tip

- If you set the menu default button for your DVD@ccess menus, the viewer may not notice the slight flicker that occurs when Menu 2 times out and jumps back to Menu 1.

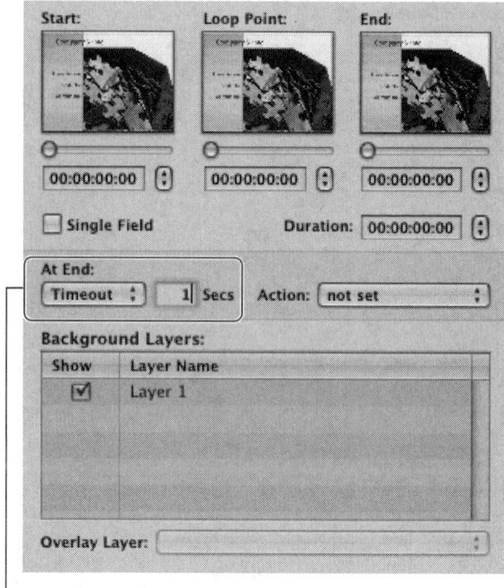

Figure 21.25 Set the Timeout duration to 1 second by typing 1 in the Secs field.

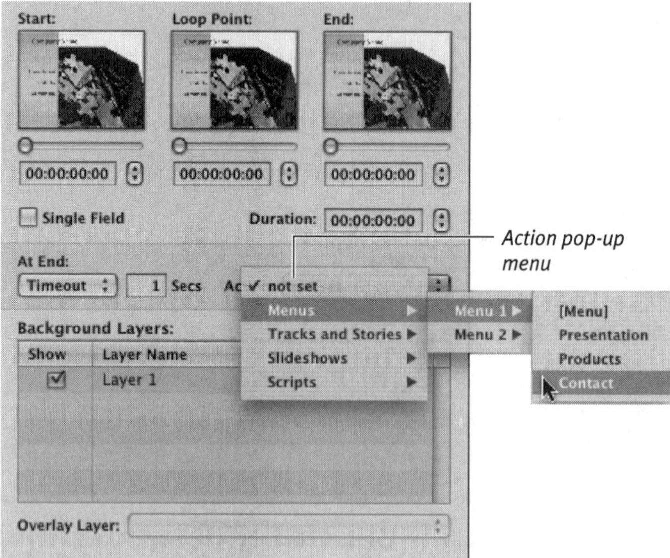

Figure 21.26 Select Menus > Menu 1 > Contact from the Action pop-up menu to set the jump action.

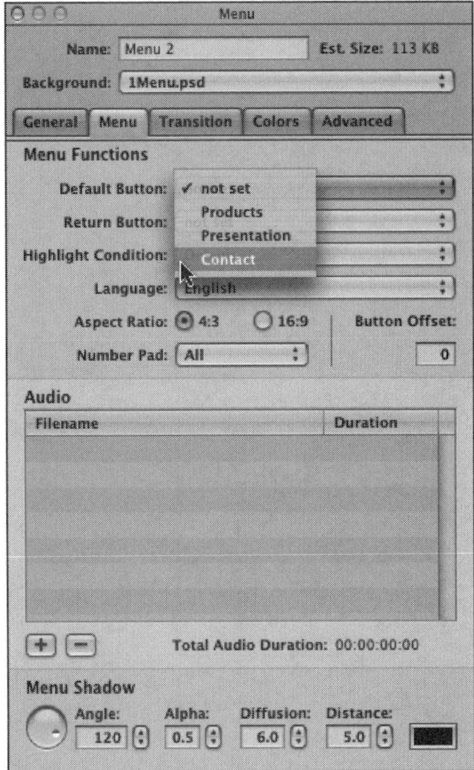

Figure 21.27 Select the DVD@ccess link button from the Default Button pop-up menu.

To set the default button for DVD@ccess menus:

1. Open Menu 2's Inspector on the Menu tab.
2. From the Default Button pop-up menu, select the DVD@ccess link button that you want to set as the default button for the menu (**Figure 21.27**).

✔ Tips

- Although Menu 2 flashes onscreen only briefly, it still has time to display the default button. Setting the Contact button as the default button ensures that Contact is the button that is automatically highlighted.
- For additional sleight-of-hand, change the button's selected state to match the activated state of the button on Menu 1. Now when Menu 2 appears onscreen, it looks the same as Menu 1 looked when it left the screen, making the transition between the two menus appear seamless.
- If your menu uses audio or video streams, playback will be interrupted when the DVD-Video jumps between menus. To make the interruption less jarring, make sure that the second menu has no audio.

Linking to the Disc

DVD@ccess can open files located on the finished DVD disc, which means that you can create hybrid discs that include PDFs, HTML pages, high-resolution slides, or even Flash vector animations that launch as the DVD-Video plays. (To learn more about hybrid DVDs, see Chapter 19.)

To link to files on the DVD disc, use the following path as the URL:

file:///DiscName/Folder/FileName.extension

Note that the *file:///* path prefix has three forward slashes (///), which is one more than the `http://` or `ftp://` path prefixes. Additionally, think carefully about how data folders will be written on your final DVD disc, because if you don't use exactly the same path in your URLs, DVD@ccess won't be able to locate the files.

✔ Tips

- If you create a hybrid DVD with a DVD-ROM folder, DVD Studio Pro takes all the files out of the ROM folder and writes them alongside the VIDEO_TS and AUDIO_TS folders at the root level of the final DVD disc (**Figure 21.28**). The ROM folder itself is not included on the disc, so be careful that you don't include its name in the DVD@ccess link's path name.
- When creating DVD@ccess files, keep in mind that your file names are restricted by the DVD-ROM character limitations. File names can have only eight characters (letters, numbers, and the underscore only) plus a three-character extension.

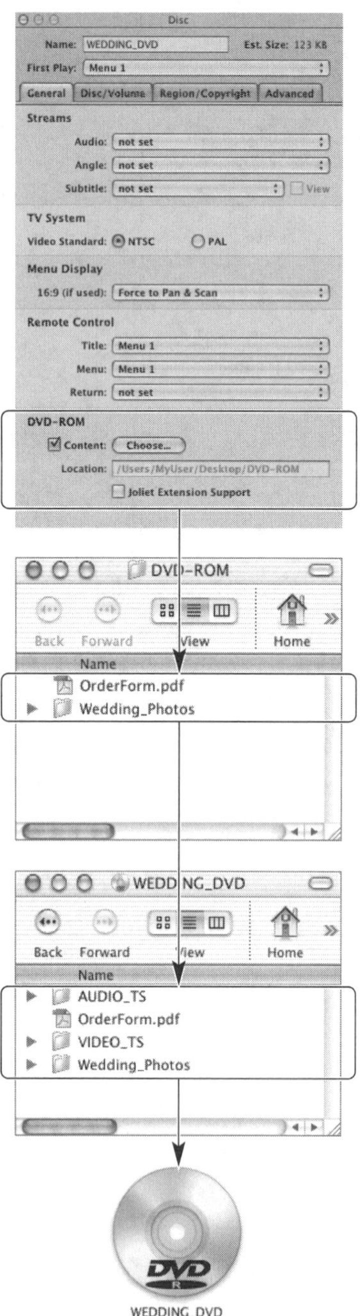

Figure 21.28 This figure traces the contents of the ROM folder as it moves from your computer's hard disk to the hybrid DVD disc. Note that the ROM folder selected in DVD Studio Pro does not actually end up on the DVD disc.

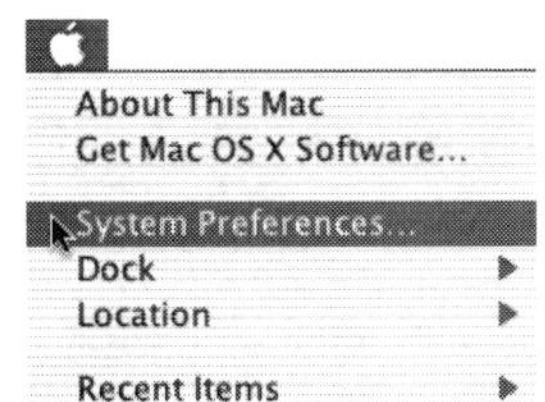

Figure 21.29 In Mac OS X, open the System Preferences window by choosing the Apple menu and then System Preferences.

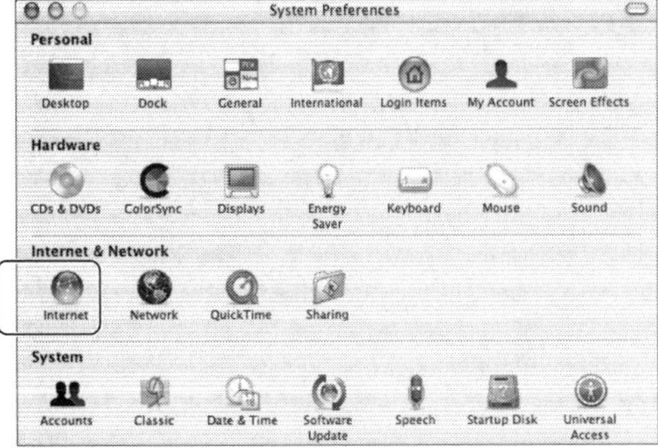

Figure 21.30 In the System Preferences window, click the Internet icon to open the Internet preferences window.

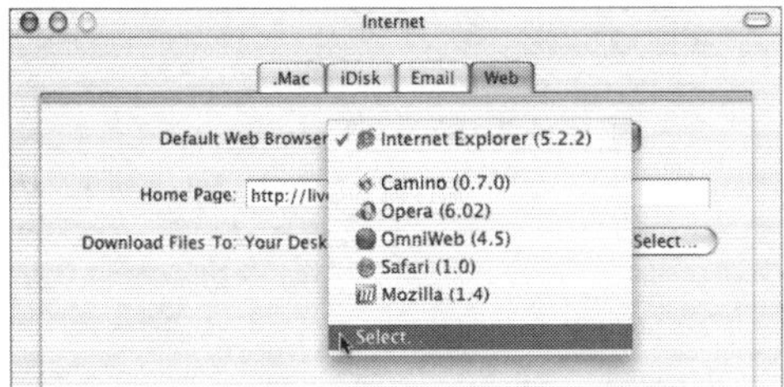

Figure 21.31 Set the default browser on the Web tab of the Internet preferences window.

Simulating DVD@ccess

The Simulator launches DVD@ccess links, which lets you verify that your links point where you want them to point. If the Simulator doesn't launch the links, it's because the DVD@ccess preference has been disabled or the links are invalid. Enable DVD@ccess previewing, and your links should work as expected (for steps to enable DVD@ccess previewing, see "Enabling DVD@ccess on the Macintosh" earlier in this chapter).

Setting the default browser

By default, all Web links open in Safari. To use a different browser, such as The Omni Group's OmniWeb browser or Netscape Navigator, you will have to change your computer's default browser.

To set the default browser:

1. In the Finder, choose the Apple menu and then System Preferences (**Figure 21.29**).
2. Click the Internet icon (**Figure 21.30**) to open the Internet preferences window.
3. Select the Web tab in the Internet preferences window.
4. Select the Web browser that you want to set as the default browser (**Figure 21.31**).

   When DVD@ccess encounters a Web link, it will open the link in the selected browser.

Testing ROM File Links

DVD@ccess file links that have DVD-ROM paths can be simulated in DVD Studio Pro only if you've already selected the ROM folder in the Disc Inspector.

If a ROM folder has been selected, DVD Studio Pro will assume that the files will be placed on the finished DVD-Video disc and will obligingly follow your DVD@ccess link to the correct file.

22

WIDESCREEN: 16:9

Our eyes are designed to view the world in a landscape orientation, through a frame that is much wider than it is tall. That's why it is so much more exciting to see a movie in the theater than it is to watch one on TV: the wide screen conforms to our field of vision. Film directors know this. They stimulate our sense of sight by showing us intensely vivid, panoramic scenes at the theater. So how do we take that same breathtaking picture home with us while preserving the experience that the director intended for us to have? The short answer: buy the widescreen version of the DVD and show it on a widescreen TV.

Widescreen televisions are, well, wider than normal TVs. The standard television has a 4:3 aspect ratio (four units across for every three units high), while a widescreen TV uses a 16:9 aspect ratio (in this chapter, the terms *widescreen* and *16:9* are used interchangeably). When represented as pixels on a computer screen, the 16:9 video frame is 864 × 480 pixels for NTSC (1,024 × 576 pixels for PAL). While the height is the same as a standard 4:3 (720 × 480) television, the difference in width means that widescreen video does not fit on a standard TV without help. Fortunately, DVD-Video players can resize 16:9 video so that it looks good on a 4:3 television. With just a bit of extra work you can create widescreen DVDs that will play on any television, regardless of its aspect ratio.

Is widescreen the future of television? Definitely. In a few short years, widescreen TVs will replace their low-definition counterparts to become the centerpiece of many North American living rooms. While full-scale market penetration is still a way down the road, you don't have to wait to jump on the widescreen bandwagon—DVD Studio Pro lets you author widescreen DVD-Video content today.

As with all things DVD, the best way to understand how widescreen works is to actually create a project—in this case, a 16:9 movie. This chapter covers all of the necessary steps, including encoding 16:9 MPEG-2 video streams and preparing widescreen menus.

About Widescreen Video

The big challenge in porting movies to DVD is fitting the rectangular, 16:9 image within the narrower 4:3 television frame. To display the best-quality image on 4:3 televisions, the video must be either cropped or condensed, which is not easy to do while still preserving the director's original vision.

Note that widescreen DVD is not HDTV. Let's clear that up right now to avoid any misconceptions. The DVD-Video specification does not currently support HDTV. It supports frame sizes of 720 × 480 pixels for NTSC and 720 × 576 pixels for PAL only. HDTV's average frame size is 1,920 × 1,080 pixels. Widescreen simply offers a way to stretch a 720 × 480 (or 720 × 576 pixel, for PAL) image across a wide television screen to display more of the movie's original content. This is called *anamorphic* playback. (For more information, see the sidebar "Rubberized Video" later in this chapter.)

Preparing Video

If you've read Chapter 4, "The QuickTime MPEG-2 Exporter," you should already know how to prepare MPEG-2 streams that are suitable for viewing on standard-issue TVs (4:3). The only difference in encoding widescreen video streams is that instead of setting the encoder's aspect ratio to 4:3, you set it to 16:9 (**Figure 22.1**).

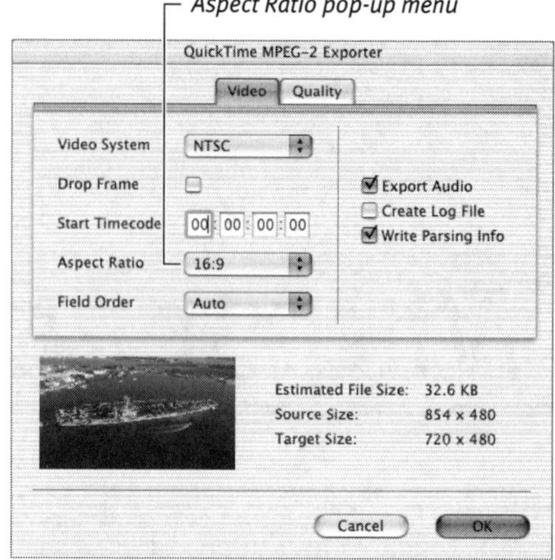

Figure 22.1 The QuickTime MPEG-2 Exporter's 16:9 Aspect Ratio setting is key to encoding widescreen MPEG-2 streams.

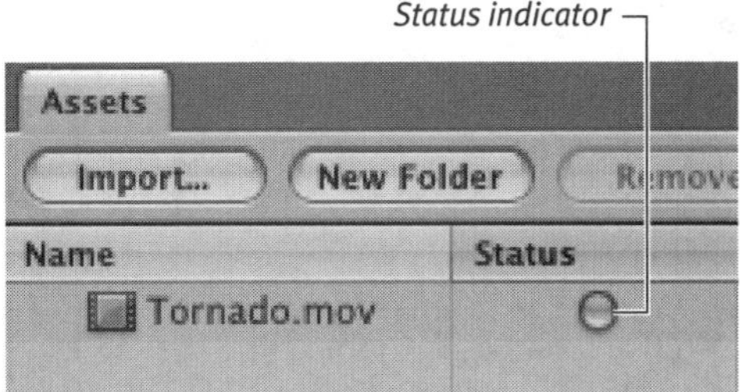

Figure 22.2 When DVD Studio Pro has finished encoding your video files, the Status indicator turns green.

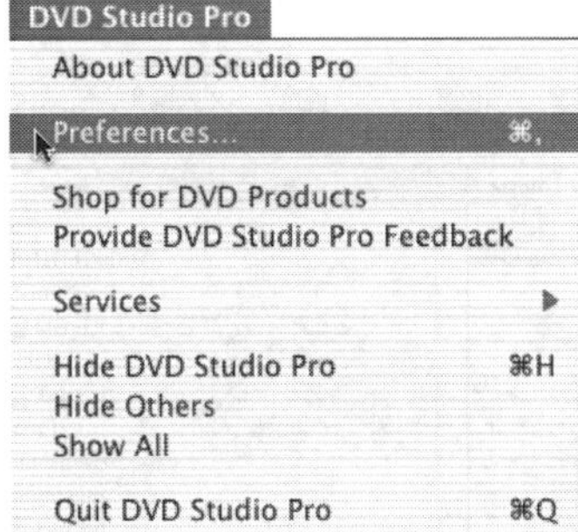

Figure 22.3 Choose DVD Studio Pro > Preferences to open the Preferences window.

Using DVD Studio Pro's Embedded Encoder

The embedded MPEG-2 encoder can encode only one aspect ratio at a time. If you need to encode both 4:3 and 16:9 source media files, you must set your preferences to encode files upon import. Import your 4:3 source video files and wait for them to finish encoding. The Status indicator will turn green (**Figure 22.2**). When DVD Studio Pro finishes encoding the 4:3 files, change the aspect ratio preferences and import your 16:9 source files.

As with most encoders, the default aspect ratio flag is set to 4:3. Before you import any uncompressed widescreen QuickTime movies, you must change DVD Studio Pro's embedded encoding preferences.

To encode 16:9 video using DVD Studio Pro's embedded encoder:

1. Choose DVD Studio Pro > Preferences, or press Command-, (comma) (**Figure 22.3**).

   The Preferences window opens, displaying the last preference you selected.

continues on next page

2. In the Preferences window toolbar, click the Encoding icon (**Figure 22.4**) to open the Encoding section of the Preferences window (**Figure 22.5**).
3. In the Encoding section of the Preferences window, select the 16:9 Aspect Ratio radio button (**Figure 22.6**).
4. Set the rest of the encoding preferences as desired.
5. At the bottom right of the Encoding section of the Preferences window, click OK to apply changes and close the window.

✔ Tip

- You should not import uncompressed 4:3 and 16:9 video streams into the same project if your preferences are set to encode files at build time. All video streams will be encoded using the encoder's preference settings. If you need to encode 4:3 and 16:9 video streams, you should use the QuickTime MPEG-2 encoder to encode your video streams separately. Once the streams are encoded, you can safely import both aspect ratios into DVD Studio Pro.

Figure 22.4 Click the Encoding icon to open the Encoding section of the Preferences window.

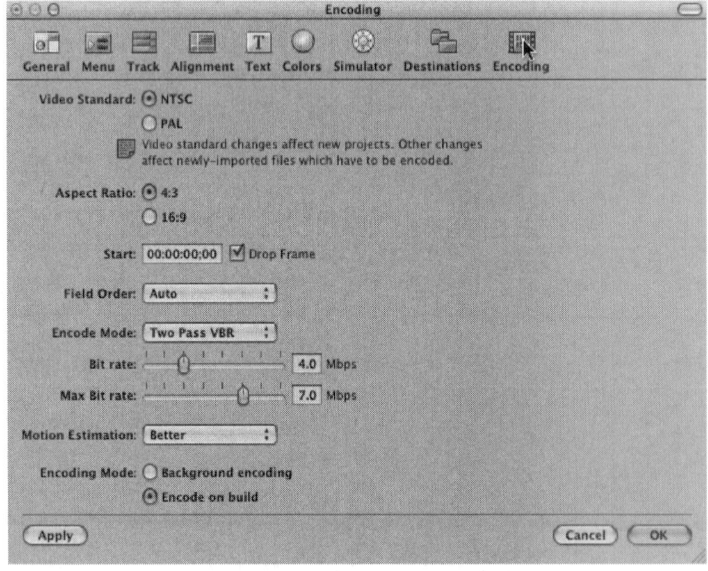

Figure 22.5 The Encoding section of the Preferences window.

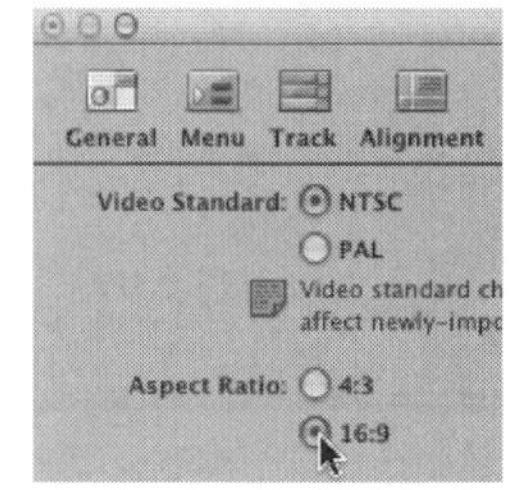

Figure 22.6 Select the 16:9 Aspect Ratio radio button.

Using the QuickTime MPEG-2 Exporter

Although background encoding within DVD Studio Pro is nice, you may find it easier to encode your video outside of DVD Studio Pro.

To encode 16:9 video using the QuickTime MPEG-2 Exporter:

1. Choose File > Open Movie in New Player, or press Command-O (**Figure 22.7**), to open the Open dialog (**Figure 22.8**).
2. Navigate to your widescreen video and click Open to open the video in the QuickTime Pro player.
3. In the QuickTime Pro menu, choose File > Export (**Figure 22.9**), or press Command-E, to open the Save Exported File As dialog (**Figure 22.10**).

continues on next page

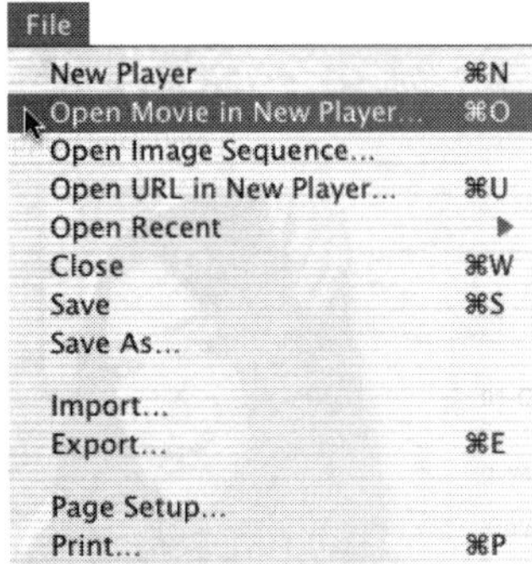

Figure 22.7 Choose File > Open Movie in New Player to open a video stream in the QuickTime Pro player.

Figure 22.8 The Open dialog.

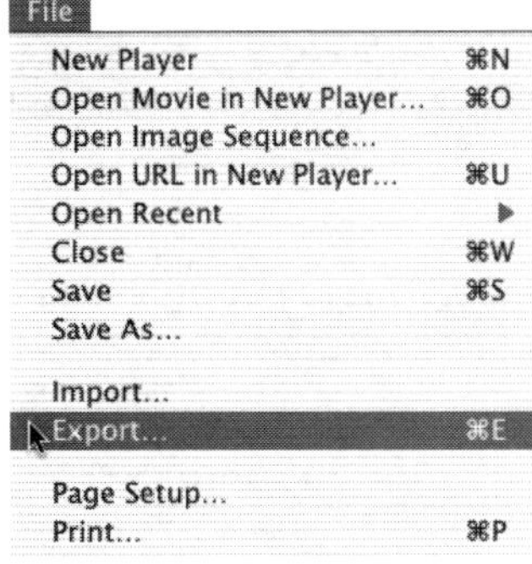

Figure 22.9 Choose File > Export to open the Save Exported File As dialog.

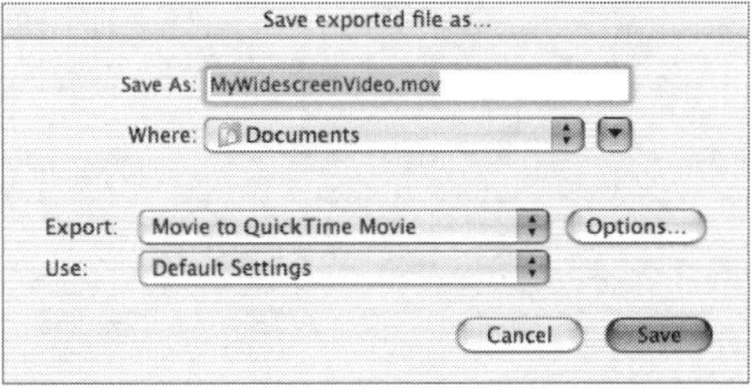

Figure 22.10 The Save Exported File As dialog.

4. In the Save As text box at the top of the window, type a file name.
5. Click the disclosure triangle to the right of the Where drop-down menu (**Figure 22.11**).

   This expands the Navigation window, allowing you to navigate to the folder where you want the encoded file to be placed.
6. Navigate to the directory where you want your MPEG-2 file to be saved (refer to Figure 22.11).

   The exported file's Where location updates to reflect your directory selection (**Figure 22.12**). You do not need to click anything other than the folder in which you want to save the MPEG-2 file.
7. In the Save Exported File As dialog, choose Movie to MPEG2 as the export type (**Figure 22.13**).

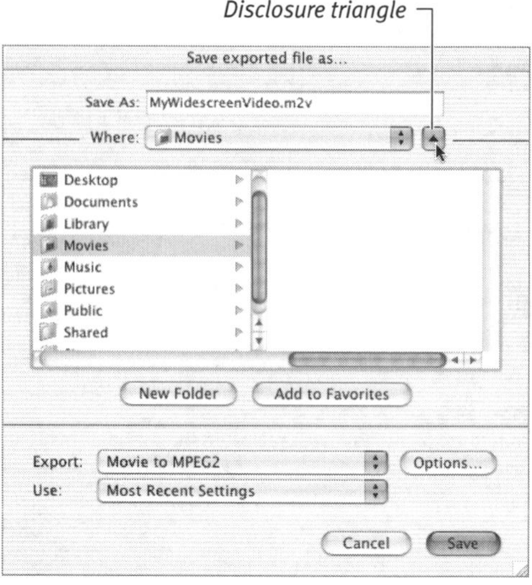

Figure 22.11 Click the disclosure triangle to expand the navigation window.

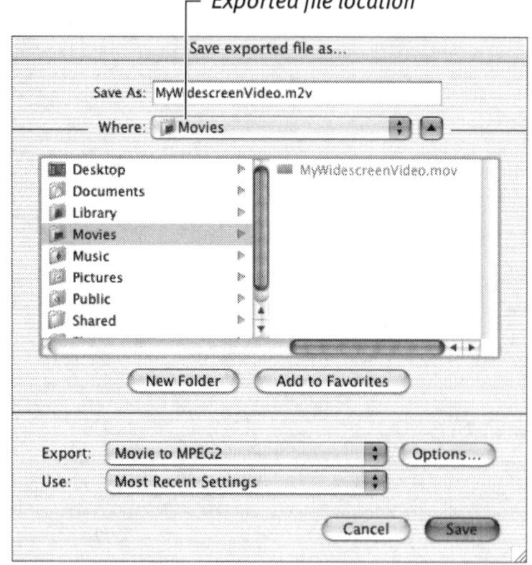

Figure 22.12 The Where location updates to display the folder you select.

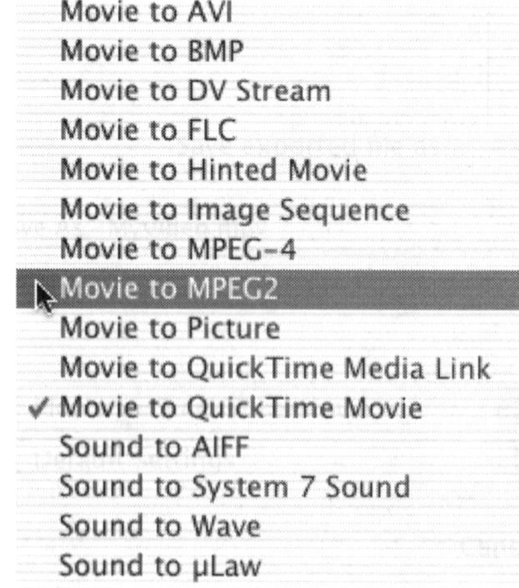

Figure 22.13 Choose Movie to MPEG2 from the Export pop-up menu.

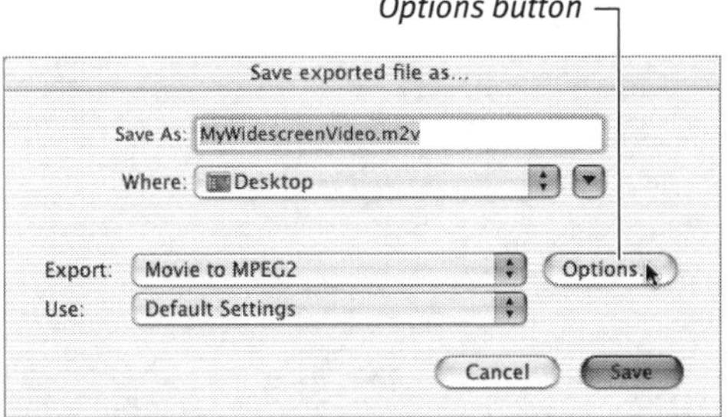

Figure 22.14 Click the Options button to open the QuickTime MPEG-2 Exporter window.

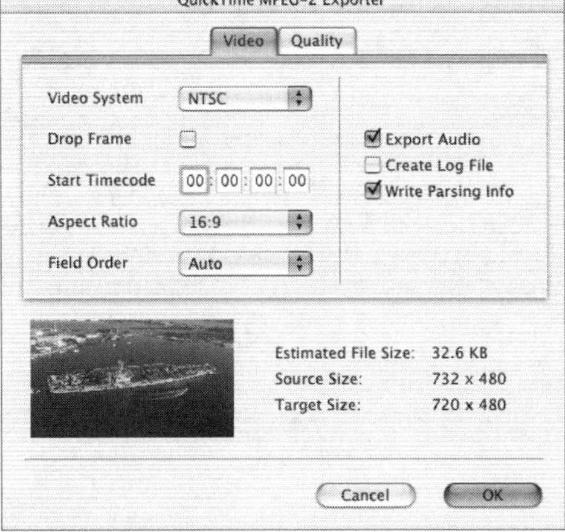

Figure 22.15 The QuickTime MPEG-2 Exporter window.

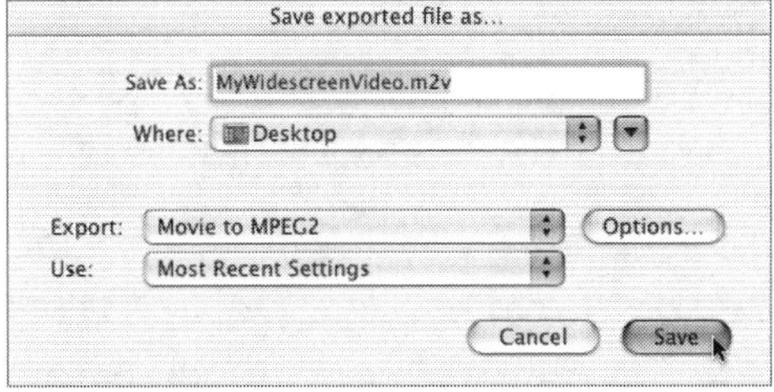

Figure 22.16 Click the Save button to begin encoding.

8. In the Save Exported File As dialog, click the Options button (**Figure 22.14**) to open the QuickTime MPEG-2 Exporter window (**Figure 22.15**).
9. In the QuickTime MPEG-2 Exporter window, choose 16:9 from the Aspect Ratio pop-up menu (refer to Figure 22.15).
10. Set the rest of the QuickTime MPEG-2 options as desired.

    The QuickTime MPEG-2 Exporter and the rest of the settings in this window are discussed in detail in Chapter 4.
11. Click OK to close the QuickTime MPEG-2 Exporter window.

    The Save Exported File As window remains open on your screen.
12. Back in the Save Exported File As window, click Save to begin encoding the 16:9 MPEG-2 stream (**Figure 22.16**).

    The QuickTime MPEG-2 Exporter's Progress window opens, allowing you to keep an eye on the encoder's progress.

About Anamorphic Video

When faced with a 16:9 video stream, the QuickTime MPEG-2 Exporter's Info area displays a curious detail (**Figure 22.17**): while the source movie is sized at 864 × 480 pixels (NTSC), the target movie is only 720 × 480 pixels. What's up?

This apparent contradiction arises from the fact that all DVD-Video must use a frame dimension of 720 × 480 pixels (NTSC). There's no provision in the DVD-Video specification for larger frame sizes. Consequently, to squeeze that extra girth into the tight 4:3 frame, encoders strap a digital girdle around the 16:9 image and compress it horizontally. When the DVD-Video is played on a 16:9 widescreen television, the DVD player stretches the frame back to its proper size using a process known as *anamorphic transfer* (see the sidebar "Squeezing and Stretching").

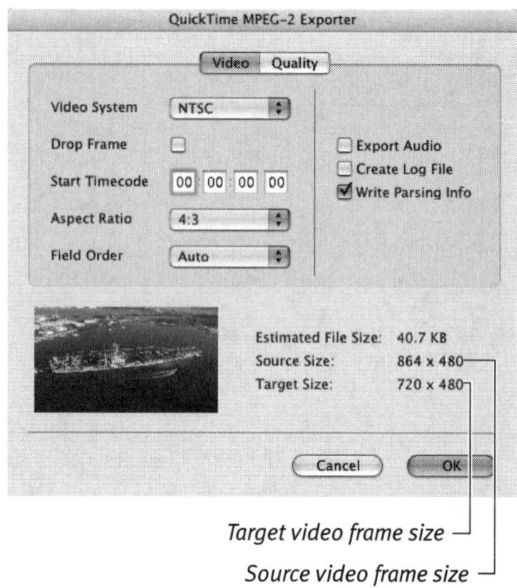

Figure 22.17 The QuickTime MPEG-2 Exporter squeezes widescreen video into the standard 4:3 frame dimensions of 720 × 480 pixels. At playback, the DVD-Video player stretches the video back to the correct size.

Squeezing and Stretching

When an image that uses either the 4:3 or 16:9 aspect ratio is broadcast, television signals stretch the image horizontally and then vertically to fit the screen. This technique of stretching the image horizontally and then vertically sometimes results in a degraded final image, especially on widescreen TVs. Vertical lines of resolution (the maximum number of visible pixels per square inch) are sometimes lost during the vertical stretch step.

When the DVD specification was being drawn up, it was calculated that if the video could be prestretched vertically, widescreen televisions would then have to stretch the image only horizontally to fill the screen. A video image that is prestretched vertically is called *anamorphic widescreen video.* When such an image is displayed on a 4:3 standard TV, the DVD player automatically removes extra horizontal lines and may add black bars to the top and bottom of the frame to preserve the aspect ratio. On a widescreen TV, the DVD player simply stretches the image horizontally.

Figure 22.18 The 864-pixel-wide 16:9 video (top) is reduced to a 720-pixel-wide MPEG-2 frame (bottom) before it's stored on the DVD disc.

The QuickTime MPEG-2 Exporter creates *anamorphic video streams.* By definition, an anamorphic video stream is precompressed horizontally. While the source video may be 864 × 480, the final stream is encoded at 720 × 480. Were you to look at that video stream without enlarging it to its proper size, everything would appear extremely tall and thin (**Figure 22.18**). The DVD-Video player stretches it all back out, however, so upon playback the video looks proportionally correct.

Rubberized Video

Imagine that you've been asked to print a picture on a flat piece of rubber. When you compare the picture to the rubber, you notice that the picture is too wide to fit on the rubber's surface. But the rubber is pliable, so you devise a clever plan: Why not stretch out the rubber before you print the picture?

Once printed, the picture looks great—as long as the rubber remains stretched. As soon as you let go of the edges, however, the rubber snaps back to its normal shape, and the picture looks pinched. But hey, that's no problem, because to see the picture in its full glory, all you need to do is stretch out the rubber again. In the anamorphic process, the video frame is the piece of rubber, and the DVD-Video player is the stretching device. Get it?

Playing Widescreen Tracks on 4:3 TVs

When a widescreen track is played on a widescreen television, the whole image is visible at all times, covering the entire screen. When the same track is displayed on a 4:3 television, the DVD player is forced to do some work. The player must either selectively display part of the picture using a process called *pan and scan* or add black bars to the top and bottom of the picture, which is called *letterboxing*.

Pan and scan involves picking and choosing the part of the widescreen image that is displayed within the 4:3 frame at any given moment. The frame normally follows the action in a scene, panning from left to right—hence the name, pan and scan.

To effectively add pan and scan *vector information*, the video editor must watch the whole movie and set the position of the 4:3 frame to match the action from one shot to the next. The problem is that some widescreen scenes may feature action on opposite edges of the image. Then the editor has to choose what's most important without taking away from the movie's tone. Needless to say, when treated by an inexperienced hand, a lot can be lost in the process (**Figure 22.19**).

You must have a pan and scan vector present when encoding the video stream for true pan and scan to work. *The QuickTime-based encoder supplied with DVD Studio Pro does not currently support true pan and scan.* You must use a different encoder to embed the pan and scan vectors *before* bringing the MPEG-2 stream into DVD Studio Pro. (For more information, see the sidebar "Pan and Scan Vectors.") Very few high-end encoders actually support true pan and scan.

Figure 22.19 Pan and scan cuts off the edges of 16:9 video streams.

Pan and Scan Vectors

In the pan and scan process, you move a 4:3 frame from one place to another within a widescreen image. The direction and distance of that frame's movement is called a *vector*. The video editor builds the list of vectors, and the encoder adds them to the MPEG-2 stream. Well, in theory, anyway.

At the time of this writing, DVD Studio Pro just places the 4:3 frame right in the middle of the widescreen video stream and leaves it there. As a result, DVD Studio Pro's pan and scan function is more like "crop and chop."

Figure 22.20 Letterboxing 16:9 video reduces the frame size so that the movie's full width fits within a 4:3 television screen. Black mattes are added to the top and bottom of the screen to maintain the aspect ratio.

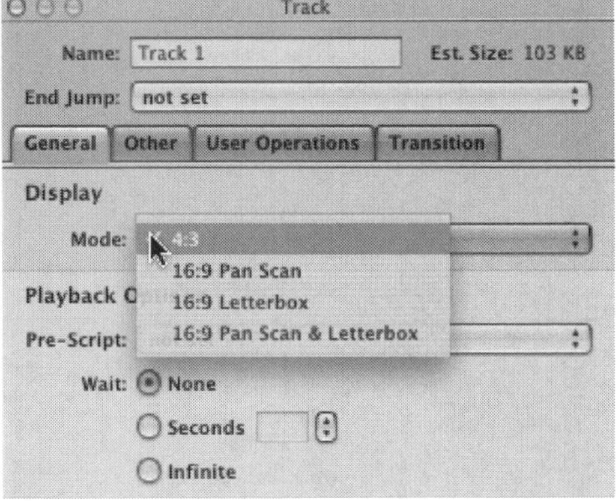

Figure 22.21 The track's Display Mode setting sets a flag that tells the DVD-Video player how to display your 16:9 track on a 4:3 television.

Letterboxing displays the entire widescreen image on a 4:3 television's screen by adding black bars, known as *mattes,* to the top and bottom of the picture (**Figure 22.20**). Letterboxing reframes the original widescreen aspect ratio so that the film can be seen in its entirety, without chopping off the edges of the frame. The problem with letterboxing is that it shrinks the vertical viewing area on the television screen. When viewing the movie on a 4:3 standard television, the mattes (black bars) are visibly present to compensate for the TV's smaller width.

As the DVD's author, the decision to use letterboxing or pan and scan is yours, unless a video editor delivers pan and scan–encoded video streams for you to use when authoring. If this is the case, the editor will let you know.

Each track in your project has a Display Mode property with three 16:9 video content playback settings (**Figure 22.21**). Choosing one of these settings adds a flag to your video track. The flag tells the DVD player exactly what to do when a 16:9 anamorphic video is displayed on a 4:3 television.

FCP Letterbox Matting

One of the most common mistakes DVD-Video authors make is to letterbox their videos before encoding them. Do not letterbox your video in Final Cut Pro or in any other editing application unless you are aiming for a letterboxed look for video content that is not widescreen. If the DVD player encounters a 16:9 letterbox video stream flag, the player will letterbox your video automatically when it is played back on a 4:3 television.

If you want to see what your video will look like in letterbox mode before you encode the stream, try adding a widescreen image mask filter in Final Cut Pro (**Figure 22.22**). The widescreen filter adds a letterbox matte to the top and bottom of your screen. To simulate the appearance of the widescreen movie on a 4:3 TV, use the Motion Scale tool to resize the video frame so that it fits within the image mask.

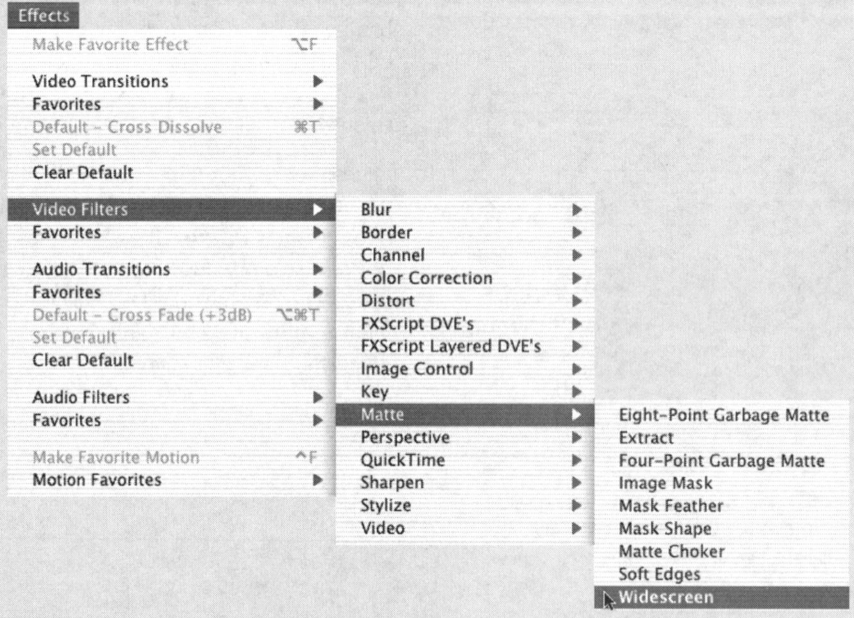

Figure 22.22 To see how your video will look in letterbox mode, choose Effects > Video Filters > Matte > Widescreen.

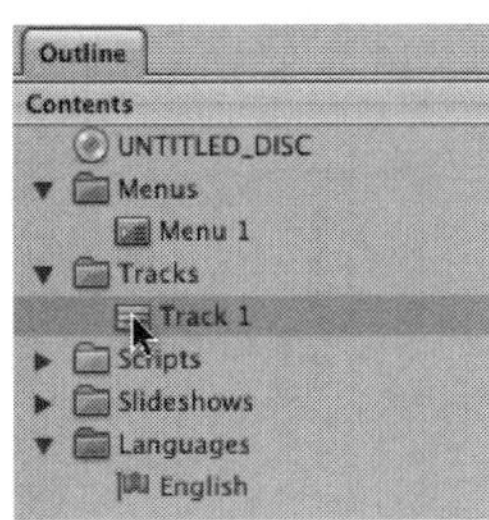

Figure 22.23 Select a track project element in the Outline view to see its properties in the Inspector.

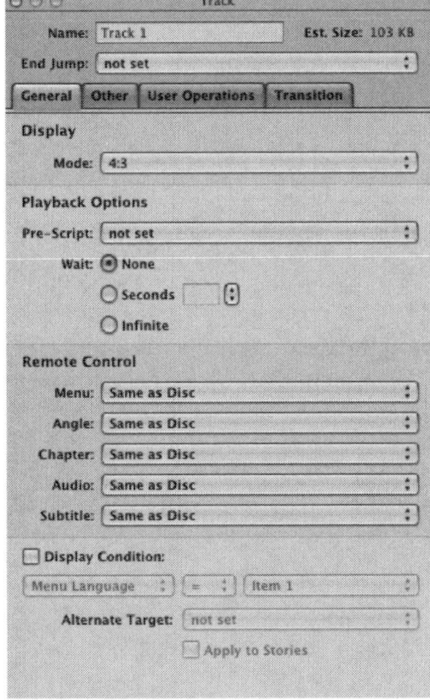

Figure 22.24 The Track Inspector displays the track's properties.

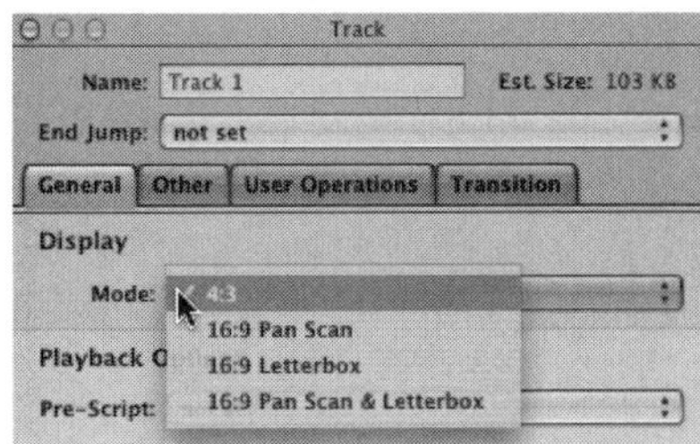

Figure 22.25 All tracks' display modes are 4:3 by default. To flag a track as widescreen, choose a 16:9 display mode.

To set a 16:9 track's display mode:

1. In DVD Studio Pro's Outline view, select a track project element that contains a 16:9 video asset (**Figure 22.23**).

   The Inspector updates to display the track's properties (**Figure 22.24**).

2. Click the Track Inspector's General tab to display the track's General settings.

3. On the Track Inspector's General tab, choose one of the widescreen track display modes (**Figure22.25**):

   - ▲ **16:9 Pan Scan.** Choose this mode if you want the DVD-Video player to fill a 4:3 television screen by cropping off the video's edges, or if the video stream uses embedded pan and scan vector data.

   - ▲ **16:9 Letterbox.** Choose this mode if you want the DVD-Video player to display the entire picture frame on any TV by letterboxing your video and applying black mattes to the top and bottom of the frame.

   - ▲ **16:9 Pan Scan & Letterbox.** Choose this mode to use the DVD player's widescreen playback settings (which are set by the viewer). Some viewers prefer to see full-screen movies, not caring that the action can sometimes go off of the screen.

Using 16:9 Subtitles

Creating 16:9 subtitles is a lot like creating 4:3 subtitles. You can import graphic files or subtitle streams created outside of DVD Studio Pro, or you can use DVD Studio Pro's Subtitle editor to add subtitle streams to a video track. To learn more about subtitles, see Chapter 24, "Subtitles."

Whether your video is 4:3 or 16:9, subtitle graphics need to be created at 720 × 480 for NTSC and 720 × 576 for PAL. You need to consider a few points when creating subtitles for use with a widescreen video track:

- All subtitle text must be within the title safe area. Any text outside of the title safe area will be cut off on a 4:3 television.
- When playing widescreen video on a widescreen TV, the DVD player stretches the video frame horizontally and then vertically. While the subtitle text may look good on a 4:3 television, it may look overly stretched (horizontally) on a 16:9 TV.
- You can add a total of 32 subtitle streams per video track, so why not make a second subtitle stream that uses a thinner font? When the subtitle stream with the thinner font size is stretched horizontally, it will look just fine. With a little scripting handiwork, you can have the appropriate subtitle track appear automatically according to the TV's aspect ratio. (To learn more about scripting, see Chapter 25, "Scripting.")
- Overlay graphics for subtitles that use buttons over video need to be vertically compressed for the highlights to line up with the buttons on a 16:9 TV. You should create the graphic file in Photoshop using widescreen dimensions (864 × 480 pixels for NTSC), add the button highlight text or graphic, and then resize the image to 720 × 480 pixels. When the graphic is horizontally stretched, the graphic overlay will appear proportionally correct on a 16:9 television. However, the same graphic overlay will appear squashed on a 4:3 TV, so you should create a second subtitle stream using a 720 × 480 uncompressed graphic overlay. To learn more about placing buttons over video, see Chapter 24.
- As discussed in Chapter 13, "The Menu Editor," you are limited to 18 menu buttons. The same applies to widescreen tracks that use buttons over video. When a track is set to 16:9 Pan Scan or Letterbox mode, you can create only 18 buttons over video. Since the DVD player needs to do some extra calculations, you are limited even further, to only 12 buttons, when you use the 16:9 Pan Scan & Letterbox mode (a reason to avoid this option).

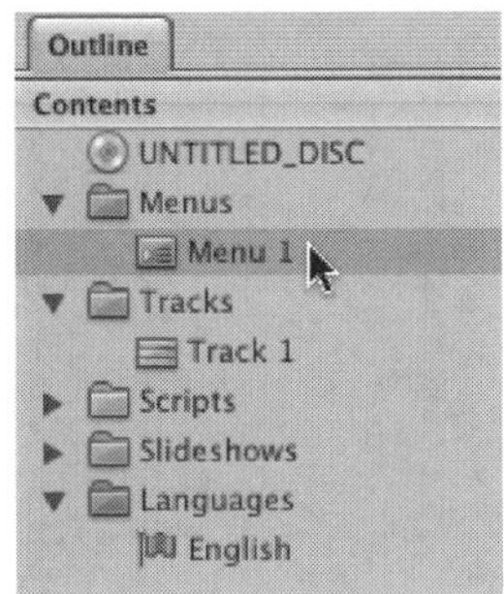

Figure 22.26 Click a menu in the Outline view to see its properties in the Inspector.

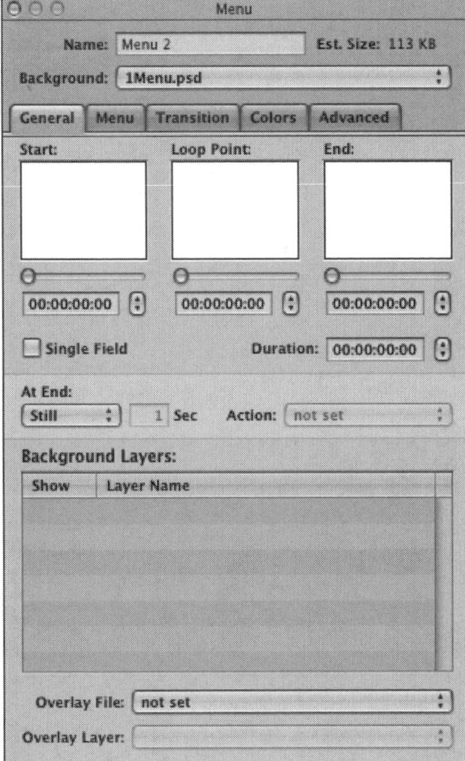

Figure 22.27 The Inspector updates to display the menu's properties.

Creating 16:9 Menus

In earlier chapters, you learned how to create menus using the Menu editor, the highlight overlay method, and the Photoshop layered menu method. You can use any of these methods to create 16:9 widescreen menus. You can also safely mix 4:3 menus with 16:9 tracks in the same project—and indeed, this is what most widescreen projects do.

The only limitation to 16:9 menus is they can have only half the buttons of a 4:3 menu, or 18 instead of 36 buttons.

To use 16:9 menus in your project:

1. In the Outline or Graphical view, select your widescreen menu project element (**Figure 22.26**).

   The Inspector updates to display the menu's properties (**Figure 22.27**).

2. Click the Menu tab in the Inspector to display the menu's functions and playback options.

continues on next page

3. In the Menu Functions section, select the 16:9 Aspect Ratio radio button (**Figure 22.28**).

   DVD Studio Pro flags this menu as a widescreen menu. At playback, this flag tells the DVD-Video player to stretch out the menus to the widescreen dimensions.

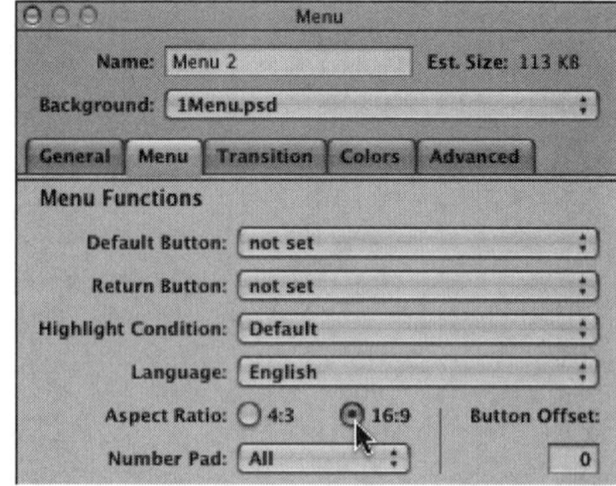

Figure 22.28 Choose 16:9 on the Menu Inspector's Menu tab to flag the menu playback as widescreen.

✔ Tip

- The default aspect ratio for all menus is 4:3, so you need to change this option only when using widescreen menus.

Menu display types

So the DVD player will know how to display a widescreen menu if it encounters a 16:9 flag in your DVD-Video, you must set the disc's menu display to either letterbox or pan and scan by choosing a Menu Display 16:9 (If Used) option in the Disc Inspector:

- **Force to Letterbox.** Choose this option to apply black mattes to the top and bottom of the menu to correct the aspect ratio on 4:3 televisions.
- **Force to Pan & Scan.** Choose this option to chop off the left and right edges of the menu, sometimes cutting off button art or important text, to correct the aspect ratio on a 4:3 television.

If your video content is flagged to be letterboxed, you should stay consistent by flagging the widescreen menus to be letterboxed as well.

Creating 16:9 Menus in Photoshop

When you create standard menus that use highlight overlays or layered menus, design the source documents for your Photoshop menus at the following dimensions:

- **NTSC:** 864 × 480
- **PAL:** 1,024 × 576

When the document is finished, resize it to 720 × 480 (NTSC) or 720 × 576 (PAL). This creates an anamorphic menu that, upon playback, the DVD-Video player stretches to normal widescreen dimensions.

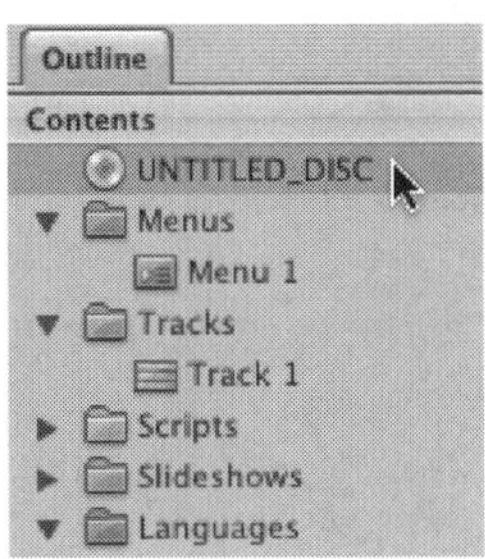

Figure 22.29 Select the disc item in the Outline view to see the DVD disc's properties in the Inspector.

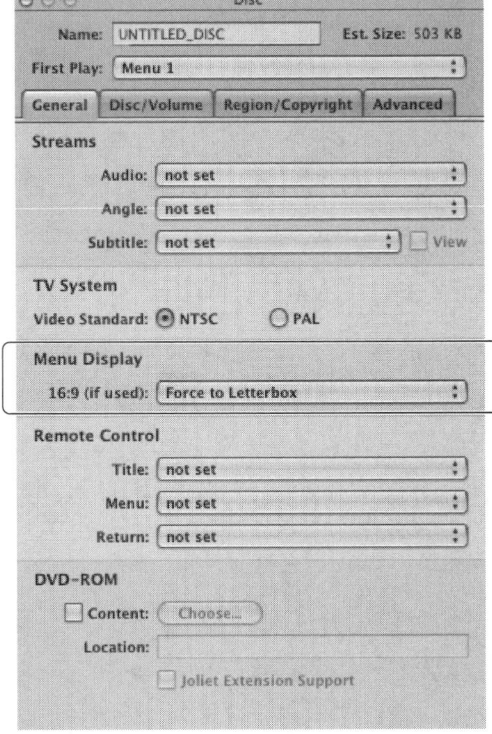

Figure 22.30 Set 16:9 menu display types in the Disc Inspector.

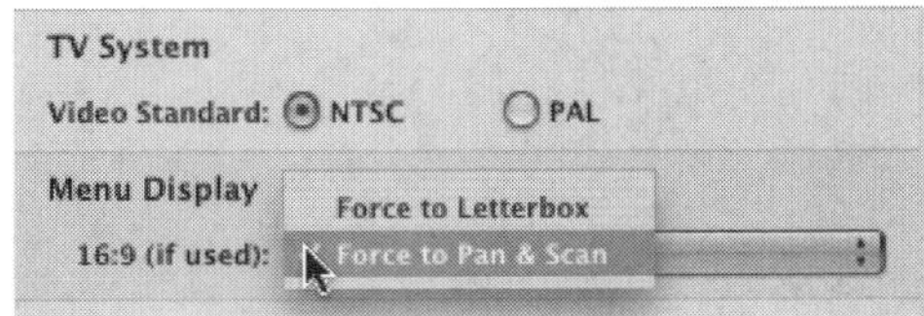

Figure 22.31 Choose Force to Pan & Scan.

To set the menu display type for your project:

1. Click the disc in the Outline view (**Figure 22.29**).

   The Inspector updates to show the disc's properties (**Figure 22.30**).

2. Choose Force to Pan & Scan from the pop-up menu (**Figure 22.31**).

   Menus flagged as 16:9 will now be forced into pan and scan mode on a 4:3 television and will stretch to fill the screen on widescreen TVs.

✔ Tip

- The default setting for Menu Display 16:9 (If Used) is Force to Letterbox. You don't need to change the menu display mode unless you want to set the widescreen menu's display mode to pan and scan.

About 16:9 Slideshows

In Chapter 18, "Slideshows," you learned that the Slideshow editor doesn't display assets that aren't 720 × 480 pixels for NTSC or 720 × 576 pixels for PAL. As a result, your widescreen 864 × 480 stills will be resized to 720 × 480 slides when DVD Studio Pro multiplexes your slideshow.

You can get around this limitation by creating a slideshow using your widescreen stills and converting the slideshow into a track. (For information on creating a slideshow and converting a slideshow into a track, see Chapter 18.)

Simulating 16:9 Projects

You might want to test out your widescreen project before building it to disc, especially if you don't have a widescreen TV handy. DVD Studio Pro lets you set the display mode so you can see how your project will look on any TV.

To simulate the appearance of your project on 4:3 and 16:9 televisions, you must change the Simulator's preferences to play back in a 16:9 mode.

To simulate 16:9 widescreen projects:

1. Choose DVD Studio Pro > Preferences, or press Command-, (comma) (**Figure 22.32**).

   The Preferences window opens displaying the last pane that you selected.
2. Click the Simulator icon to open the Simulator section of the Preferences window (**Figure 22.33**).
3. From the Aspect area's Ratio settings (**Figure 22.34**), *select one of the following:*
   - ▲ **4:3 Letterbox.** Choose this option to add black mattes to the top and bottom of the screen to maintain the aspect ratio of the content as would be the case on a 4:3 TV.
   - ▲ **4:3 Pan & Scan.** Choose this option to cut off the far left and far right edges of the content as would happen when the video is played back in pan and scan mode on a 4:3 TV.
   - ▲ **16:9.** Choose this option to stretch the menu horizontally and display the final picture as it would look on a widescreen TV.
4. Click OK to apply changes and close the Preferences window.

   When the simulator encounters a track or menu flagged as 16:9, it emulates the stretching and squeezing action of a DVD player..

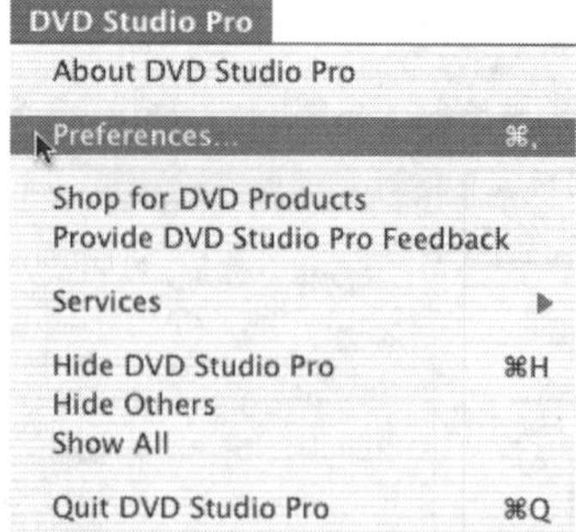

Figure 22.32 To change DVD Studio Pro's preferences, choose DVD Studio Pro > Preferences.

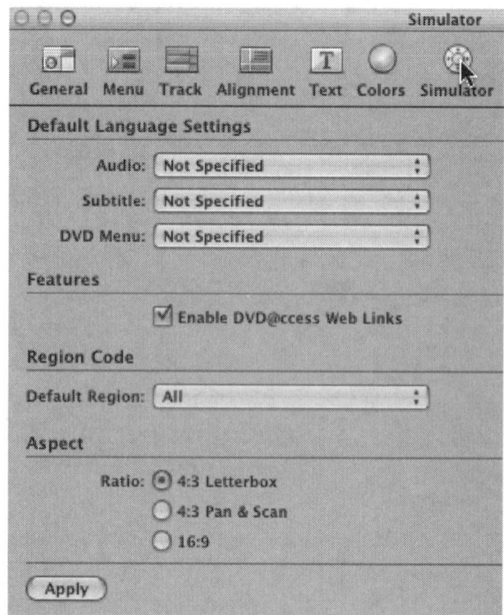

Figure 22.33 The Simulator section of the Preferences window holds settings that change the mode of the Simulator, allowing you to fully test your project before burning a DVD disc.

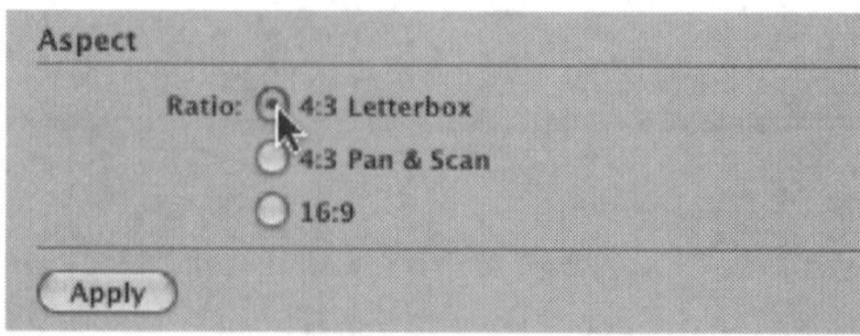

Figure 22.34 Choose the aspect ratio playback type to simulate your widescreen project

23 Working with Languages

As globalization brings the world's markets closer together, the need to provide content in alternate languages is imperative. In North America alone, there are many widely spoken languages, so why limit your DVD's reach by excluding viewers who don't speak English?

DVD Studio Pro allows you to easily create multilingual DVDs in two ways: using multilanguage menus, and using the video tracks' language settings for audio and subtitle streams. You can choose to translate the menus only, the audio or subtitles only, or a combination of menus, audio, and subtitles.

This chapter shows you how to create a menu language in the Outline view. You'll also learn how to set the audio or subtitle stream's language in the Track editor so that when viewers insert the finished DVD disc into a DVD player, they automatically see and hear only the language that they want.

About Multilingual DVDs

All DVD-Video players have a series of setup menus that allow users to specify the language used automatically when a DVD-Video is inserted. On a properly configured DVD-Video player, the language selection process is transparent because the correct language is used automatically.

A French speaker watching a DVD, for example, probably wants to hear it in French. Most likely, the person has already set up the DVD player to play the French content automatically. However, it's up to *you* to create the language-specific audio tracks, subtitles, and menus so that your DVD can provide the seamless experience that every viewer expects.

Setting the project's default language

DVD Studio Pro automatically detects and sets your project's default language for menus and tracks based on the Mac OS version you have installed. For example, if your Mac OS version uses English, DVD Studio Pro's project language is English by default. If the default language is incorrect, or you want to change the default project language, simply select a different default language in DVD Studio Pro's Preferences window. Set the default menu language in the General section of the Preferences window and set the default language for subtitle and audio streams in tracks in the Track section of the Preferences window.

To change a project's default menu language:

1. Choose DVD Studio Pro > Preferences (**Figure 23.1**), or press Command-, (comma), to open the Preferences window.
2. In the Preferences window, click the General icon in the toolbar to view the General preferences (**Figure 23.2**).

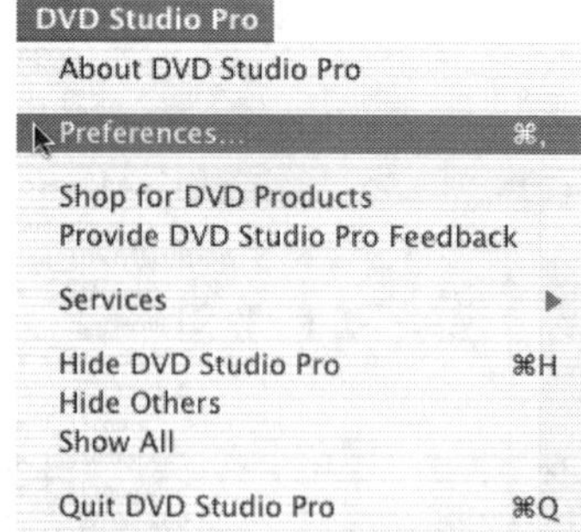

Figure 23.1 Choose DVD Studio Pro > Preferences to open the Preferences window.

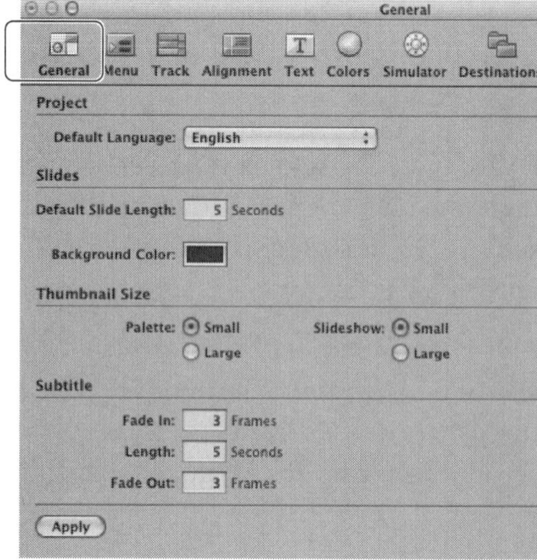

Figure 23.2 Click the General icon at the top left of the toolbar to open the General section of the Preferences window.

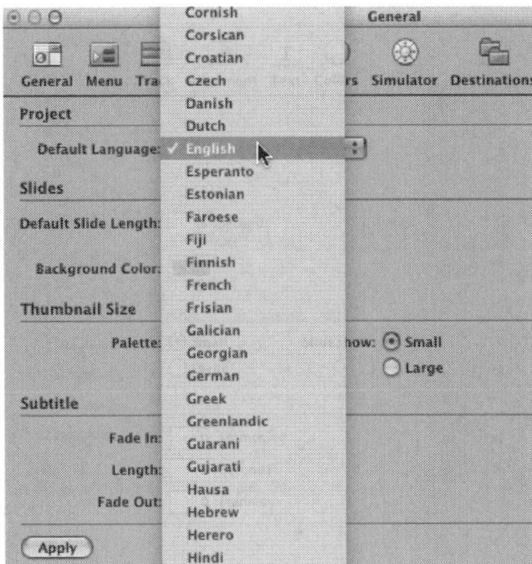

Figure 23.3 Select a default project language to be used by your project's menus.

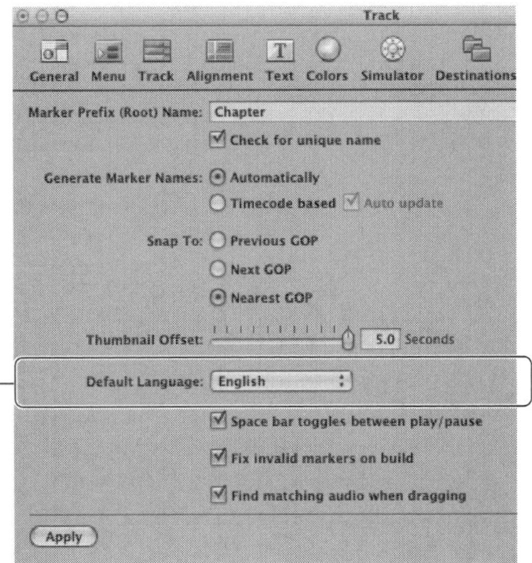

Figure 23.4 Click the Track icon at the upper left of the Preferences window's toolbar to display the Track preferences; then select a default subtitle and audio stream language from the Default Language pop-up menu.

3. In the General section of the Preferences window, choose a language from the Default Language pop-up menu (**Figure 23.3**).
4. Click Apply at the bottom left of the General section of the Preferences window to apply the changes, or click OK to apply changes and close the Preferences window.

   The new default menu project language is applied to newly created projects. The current project is unaffected. To use the new language setting, you must create a new project in DVD Studio Pro.

To change a project's default track language:

1. Open the Preferences window.
2. In the Preferences window's toolbar, click the Track icon to view the Track preferences (**Figure 23.4**).
3. In the Track section of the Preferences window, choose a language from the Default Language pop-up menu (refer to Figure 23.4).
4. At the bottom right of the Track section of the Preferences window, click Apply to apply changes and close the window.

   The language you select is set for all audio and subtitle streams within your project. Changes take effect when you create a new project.

Working with Multiple-Language Menus

Language is all about words, and words are printed on all of your project's menus. If the viewer can't read a menu, choosing which track to play becomes an exercise in random selection. To prevent this, DVD Studio Pro lets you create menus using up to 16 different languages.

Menu languages are created in the Outline view. By default, the main project default language appears in the Outline view. You can create a maximum of 16 different menu languages.

When you multiplex your project, DVD Studio Pro creates a separate menu for each language that your menus use. Each language menu is tied to a unique language ID that the DVD player understands. When viewers insert the DVD disc into their players, they will see only the menus that their DVD players are set to show.

Sixteen Menu Languages

When a viewer watches a DVD, menus designed in the viewer's native language are displayed automatically. However, with only 16 languages available for menus, chances are good that some people's languages will be excluded from your DVD.

If a viewer's menu language isn't available on the DVD disc, the DVD player displays the DVD disc's default menu language instead of the viewer's language (to set the disc's default language, see "Setting the project's default language" earlier in this chapter).

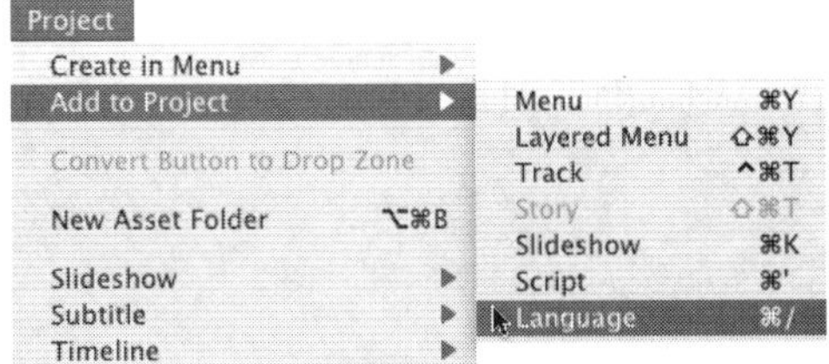

Figure 23.5 Choose Project > Add to Project > Language to add a menu language to your project.

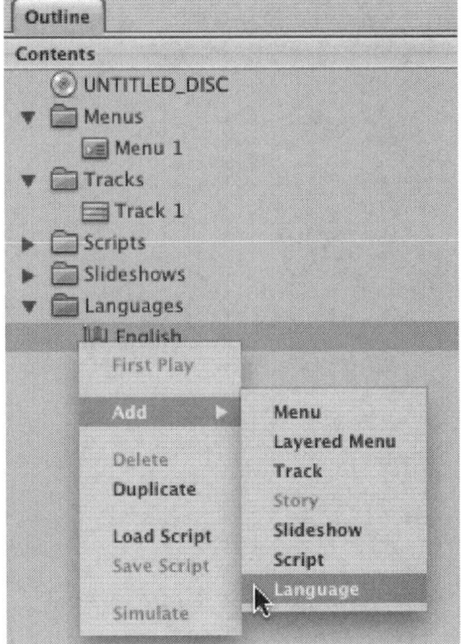

Figure 23.6 Control-click anywhere in the Outline view to display the Add Language shortcut menu.

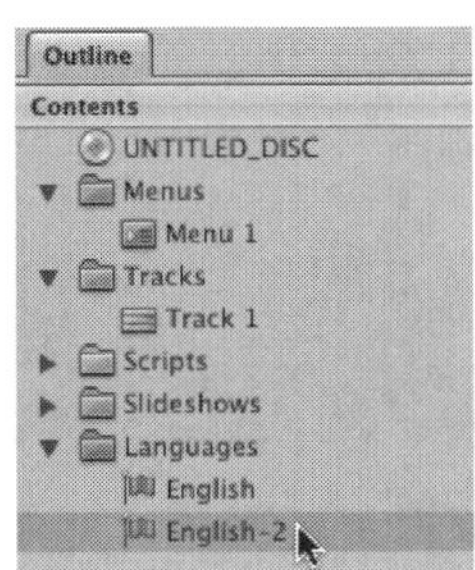

Figure 23.7 This figure shows that a new language named English-2 was created in the Outline view.

Creating alternate languages for use with menus

Menu languages all begin in the Outline view. To use alternate language menus, you must create a language in the Outline view and configure it in the Language Inspector.

To create a new language:

1. To add a language to your project, *do one of the following:*
   - ▲ Choose Project > Add to Project > Language (**Figure 23.5**), or press Command-/ (slash).
   - ▲ Control-click anywhere in the Outline view and choose Add > Language from the shortcut menu (**Figure 23.6**).

   A new language named *X*-2 is created in the Outline view (**Figure 23.7**), where *X* is your project's default language. If English is set as your default language, for instance, the new language element you create is called English-2.

continues on next page

2. Click the language in the Outline view to select it (refer to Figure 23.7).

   The Inspector updates to display the language's properties (**Figure 23.8**).

3. In the Language Inspector, choose a language from the Language Code pop-up menu (**Figure 23.9**).

   In the Language Inspector, the Language Name text box automatically updates to reflect your Language Code selection (**Figure 23.10**). If desired, you can type a new name in the Language Name text box. The name you enter is visible only to you, the DVD's author; the viewer never sees the name you enter.

✔ Tip

- To delete a language from your project, click the language element in the Outline view and press the Delete key.

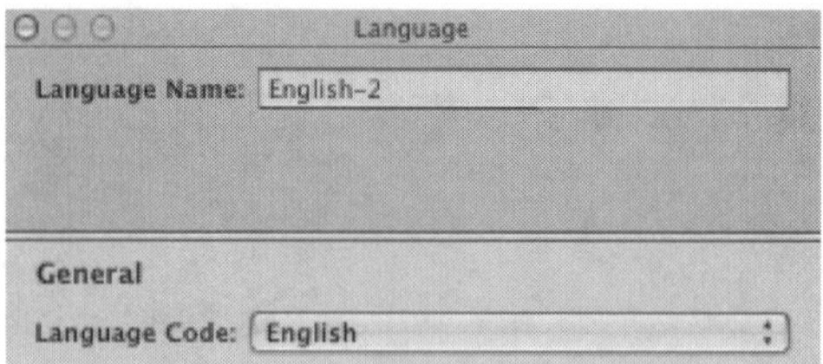

Figure 23.8 The Language Inspector displays the language's settings.

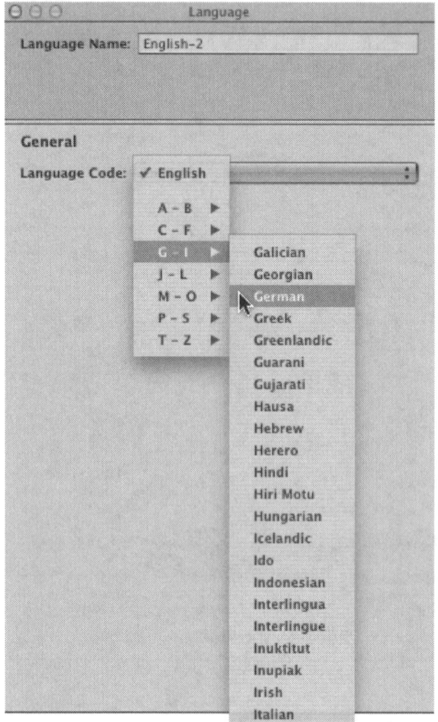

Figure 23.9 Choose a new language setting in the Language Inspector.

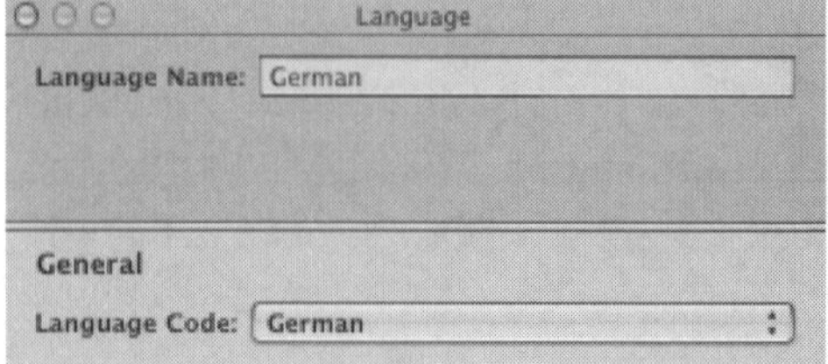

Figure 23.10 The Language Name text box automatically updates to reflect your Language Code selection.

Using multiple-language menus

In most cases, menus use only a single asset to set the background picture. When you add languages to a project, however, you need to add a background picture for each language. If you create 16 languages, you need to assign 16 background pictures, button highlight overlays, and audio files—one per language—to an individual menu, for example. That may seem like a lot of work, but when you configure a menu for the main language, DVD Studio Pro carries over the buttons, button highlight colors, and button links to all localized versions of the menu. All you need to do is select a language from a pop-up menu in the Menu Inspector and set the corresponding background picture. If you use button highlight overlays, you can reuse the overlay graphic for each language, but you do need to set the overlay for each language selected.

Alternate language menus can use different audio streams, but each stream must use the same audio file format. If the default menu language uses an AC-3 stream, for example, the other menus must also use AC-3 streams. The duration of the audio streams can differ, but the format must be the same.

Designing Multilingual Menu Graphics in Photoshop

To use each of the languages you've created, you must translate the text from each of your project's menus and design a separate set of menu graphics for each language. For example, if your project contains English, German, and Spanish, you should create three separate sets of menu graphics—one in English, one in German, and one in Spanish. Back in DVD Studio Pro, you'll assign each translated menu background picture to its corresponding language.

When you create buttons in DVD Studio Pro's Menu editor for the default language's menu, the buttons are carried over to all other languages for that menu. If you move a button in one of the menu languages, the button is moved for all menu languages. You need to keep this in mind when creating menus in Photoshop. The best way to make sure that your menu buttons all line up correctly for multilingual menus is to create one background picture in Photoshop and make copies of the document for each language used before translating the background pictures.

If you use Photoshop layer menus, each menu language must use the same number of Photoshop layers, and each Photoshop layer must be named the same and be in the same order. For information on creating Photoshop layer menus, see Chapter 14, "Layered Menus."

To assign a menu's background picture for each language:

1. In the Outline view, select a menu (**Figure 23.11**) to display its properties in the Inspector.
2. In the Menu Inspector, select the Menu tab (**Figure 23.12**).

   On the Menu Inspector's Menu tab, the project's default language is selected. All of the project's additional menu languages can be accessed from the Language pop-up menu (refer to Figure 23.12).
3. In the Menu Inspector, use the Background pop-up menu to select a background picture for the project's default language (**Figure 23.13**).
4. In the Menu editor, create buttons on your menu.
5. To select a different language to configure for the menu, *do one of the following:*
   - ▲ On the Menu Inspector's Menu tab, select a different language from the Language pop-up menu (refer to Figure 23.12).
   - ▲ In the Menu editor, select a different language from the Language pop-up menu (**Figure 23.14**)

   The button links and all other menu settings implemented for the default language remain set for all language versions of your menu, but you will need to assign a new background picture.

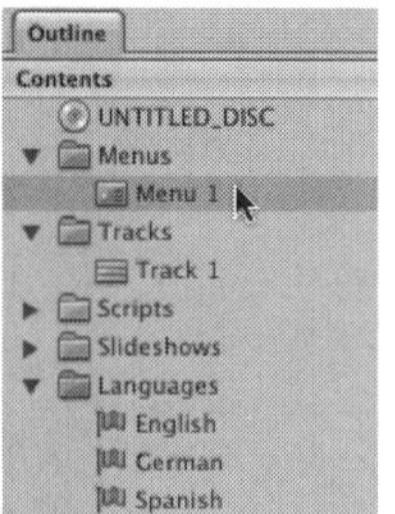

Figure 23.11 Select a menu in the Outline view to see its properties in the Inspector.

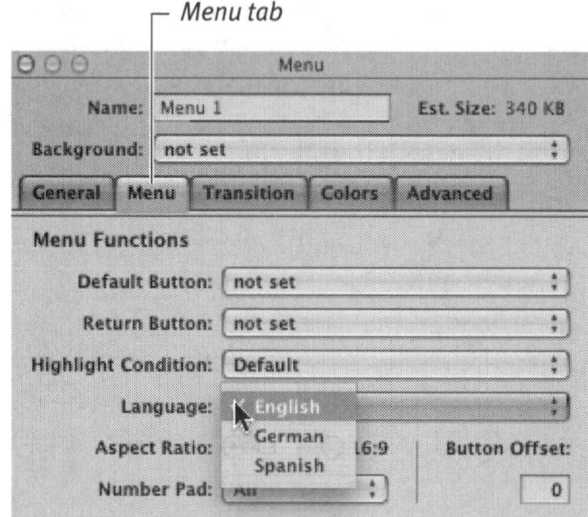

Figure 23.12 All of the languages you create in the Outline view are listed in the Menu Inspector's Language pop-up menu.

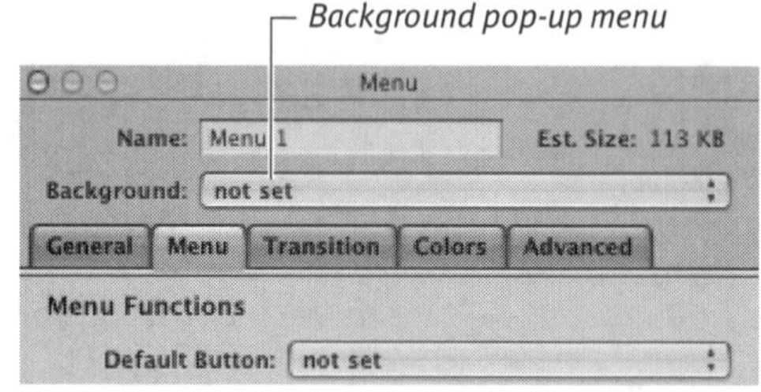

Figure 23.13 Choose a background picture using the Background pop-up menu.

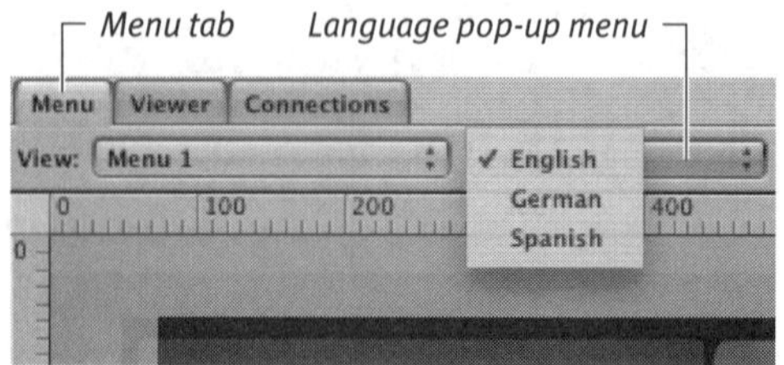

Figure 23.14 Select a different language from the Menu tab's Language pop-up menu to choose a version of the menu to configure.

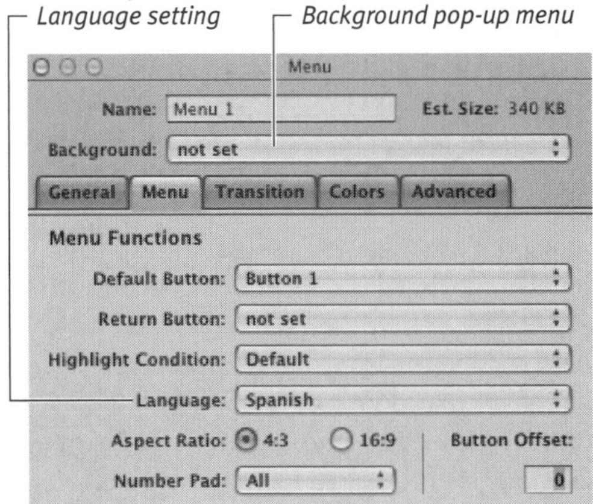

Figure 23.15 Every language version of your menu needs to have a background picture assigned.

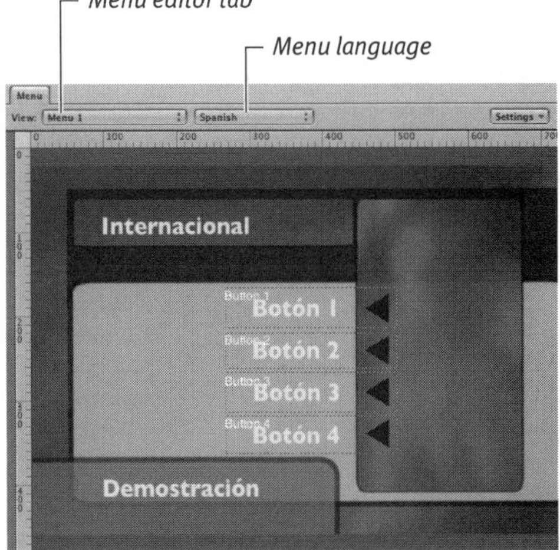

Figure 23.16 In this figure, the Menu editor shows that the selected language is Spanish, and the Spanish localized version of the background picture is assigned. Buttons created in the English version of the menu are automatically set in the Spanish version of the menu.

6. With a different language selected, select a background picture from the Menu Inspector's Background pop-up menu (**Figure 23.15**).

   The background picture you select will be set for the selected language (**Figure 23.16**).

7. Repeat steps 5 and 6 until all menu languages have a background picture assigned.

   When DVD Studio Pro multiplexes your project, it builds a separate menu for each alternate language. When the DVD disc is placed in a DVD-Video player, the player determines which menu to play based on its language setting. The corresponding language menu is the only menu that appears on the screen.

✔ Tip

- The DVD specification limits every DVD-Video to 1 GB of menus per aspect ratio—2 GB total if you use 4:3 and 16:9 menus. If you are using MPEG-2 video to create motion menus, you could easily surpass this 1 GB limit when assigning a different motion background for each language.

Working with Multilingual Tracks

Tracks use languages differently than menus do. You don't need to create a language in the Outline view to use a language in a track; you can use *any* language for any individual audio and subtitle streams within a track.

You might, for example, assign one audio stream to English, one to German, and one to Spanish. Although you have three different audio streams, only the one that matches the DVD-Video player's language setting plays. To viewers, the language selection process is transparent because they hear only the language that they understand.

Defining multiple language audio and subtitle streams

Each track can hold up to 8 audio streams and up to 32 subtitle streams. These streams either can be set to use different languages or can all use the same language to achieve different goals. For example, you could create subtitles for an English movie transcript, director's commentary, cast commentary, and scene anecdotes, and then translate each of the four subtitle streams into a different language. All you need to do to set the language is choose the language that corresponds to your audio and subtitle streams from the Language pop-up menu just to the left of each stream in the Track editor.

What's a Language Code?

Like all machines, DVD players can understand only numbers and codes. When the DVD specification was drawn up, each spoken language was assigned a two-letter, lowercase code. For example, English is represented as *en*. Each two-letter, lowercase language code is also represented by a decimal value that the DVD player can understand.

When a multilanguage DVD-Video is played in a DVD player, the player tells the disc which language code it uses. The DVD-Video disc then responds by playing only the content that is flagged with that particular language code.

By adding a language options menu to your project, you can allow the viewer to switch on subtitles or even change the language in which the audio and subtitles are played. For more information, see "Linking menu buttons to alternate audio streams in a track" later in this chapter.

To define the language for an audio stream:

1. Open the Track editor (**Figure 23.17**) and assign a video clip to it (for steps, see Chapter 11, "Using Tracks").

   Note that the audio and subtitle streams are set to the project's default language. When you create a new project in DVD Studio Pro, all project language defaults are set using your Mac OS system language. (For steps on how to change the track's default language, see "Setting the project's default language" earlier in this chapter).

2. Drag an audio stream from the Assets tab into audio stream 1 in the Track editor to assign the first audio stream (**Figure 23.18**).

   The audio stream is set for stream 1.

continues on next page

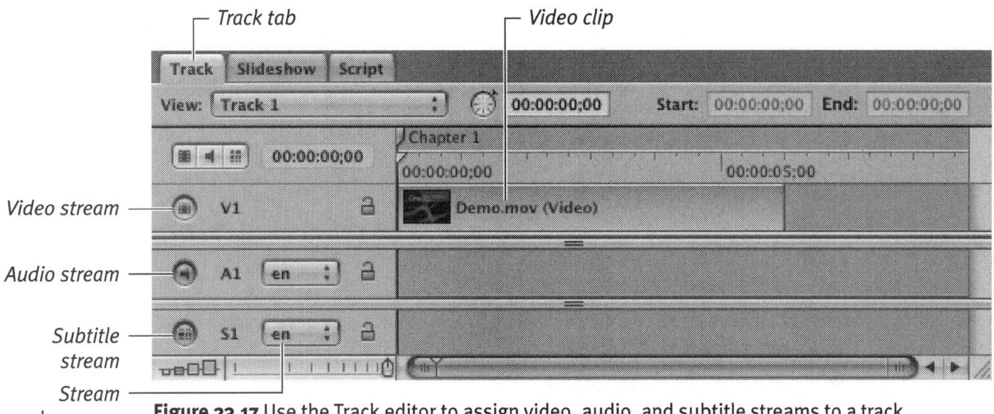

Figure 23.17 Use the Track editor to assign video, audio, and subtitle streams to a track.

Figure 23.18 Drag an audio stream from the Assets tab to the Track editor to assign an audio clip for audio stream 1.

3. Set the audio stream language for audio stream 1 by selecting a language from the stream language pop-up menu, just to the left of the audio stream in the Track editor (**Figure 23.19**).

   If your track's default language is English and you assign an English audio stream for stream 1, you don't need to change the audio language.

4. Repeat steps 2 and 3 until you've assigned all audio streams (**Figure 23.20**).

   Provided that their DVD-Video players are properly configured, when viewers insert the DVD disc, they will automatically hear the language that they understand.

✔ Tips

- With 8 audio streams per track, you can provide 8 different audio translations for each track; if you need more than 8 languages, you can use a combination of audio and subtitles. As mentioned earlier, you have access to a total of 32 subtitle streams.
- DVD Studio Pro displays the two-letter language code in the Track editor for each audio or subtitle stream you use (refer to Figure 23.20). The DVD player uses the language code to display the correct content for the viewer. See the sidebar "What's a Language Code?" earlier in this chapter for more information on language codes.

Figure 23.19 Choose a language from the language pop-up menu that corresponds to the language of the audio stream you assigned for stream 1.

Figure 23.20 Select up to eight audio languages in the Track editor and assign an audio stream for each language you choose.

Creating Multilingual Slideshows

Slideshows cannot have multiple audio streams or subtitles assigned to them. If you want to create a multilingual slideshow, you must convert it to a track and use the Track editor to add multiple audio streams to your slideshow.

If you import a project from DVD Studio Pro 1.*x* that uses multilanguage audio streams with slideshows, the slideshows are converted into a multilingual track.

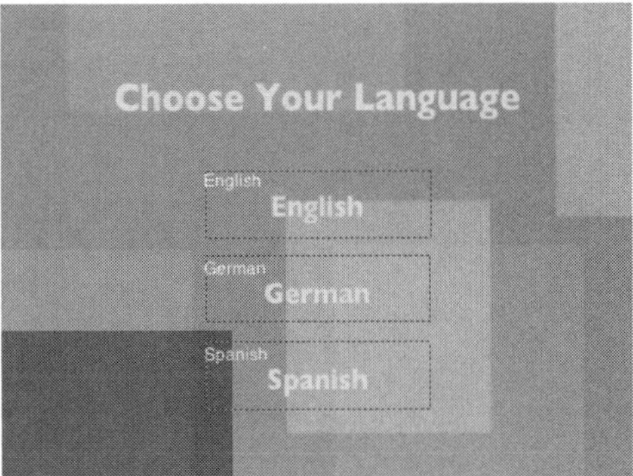

Figure 23.21 Create a language selection menu and add buttons that link to each corresponding audio stream in a track.

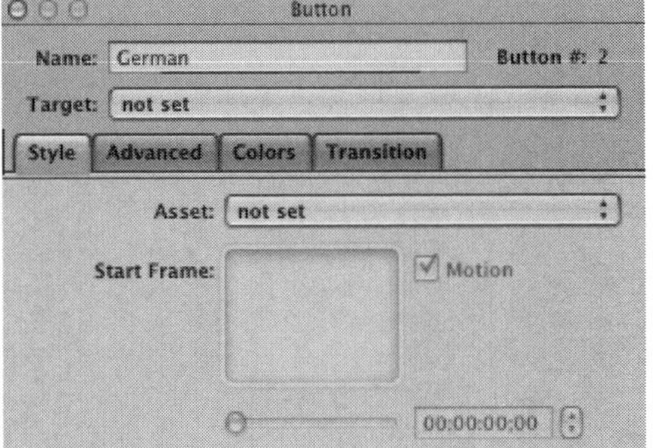

Figure 23.22 The Button Inspector displays the selected button's properties.

Figure 23.23 Choose the first chapter marker of your multilanguage track as the button's target.

Linking menu buttons to alternate audio streams in a track

Earlier in this chapter, you learned how to set audio streams so that the correct language plays automatically when viewers insert the DVD disc into their players. That's convenient, but it doesn't help viewers whose DVD-Video players' audio language settings are configured incorrectly. To guard against this possibility, supply your project with a language (or audio) setup menu that viewers can use to select the language in which they want to hear the project.

A language selection menu has a button for each language in the project (**Figure 23.21**). By tweaking a few settings in the Button Inspector, you can link each of those buttons to its corresponding language track, so that the selected audio language plays when a viewer activates the button.

To link a menu button to an alternate language audio stream:

1. In the Track editor, create a multilingual track that has multiple language audio streams assigned to it.
2. In the Menu editor, create a menu with buttons that will be used as your language selection menu (one button for each audio language for the track).
3. In the Menu editor, click a button to select it.

   The Button Inspector updates to display the button's properties (**Figure 23.22**).
4. From the Button Inspector's Target pop-up menu, choose Tracks and Stories > Track 1 > Chapter 1 (**Figure 23.23**) to set the button target menu to your multilingual track.

   This is the track that plays when the viewer selects this button from the menu.

continues on next page

5. In the Button Inspector, click the Advanced tab to select it (**Figure 23.24**).
6. In the Advanced tab's Streams section in the Button Inspector, choose an audio stream from the Audio pop-up menu (**Figure 23.25**).

   The audio stream number corresponds to the order in which you assigned audio streams in the Track editor. For example, Audio Stream 1 in the Button Inspector's pop-up menu is labeled A1 in the Track editor (**Figure 23.26**).

   When the viewer activates the button, the DVD-Video jumps to the multilingual track and automatically plays the audio stream that the viewer wants to hear.
7. Repeat steps 3 through 6 until you've linked all buttons on the menu to their corresponding audio streams on the track.

✔ Tip

- The Button Inspector's Advanced tab also hosts a Subtitle pop-up menu that you can use to link buttons to specific subtitle streams. This comes in handy if you need to create a subtitle selection menu.

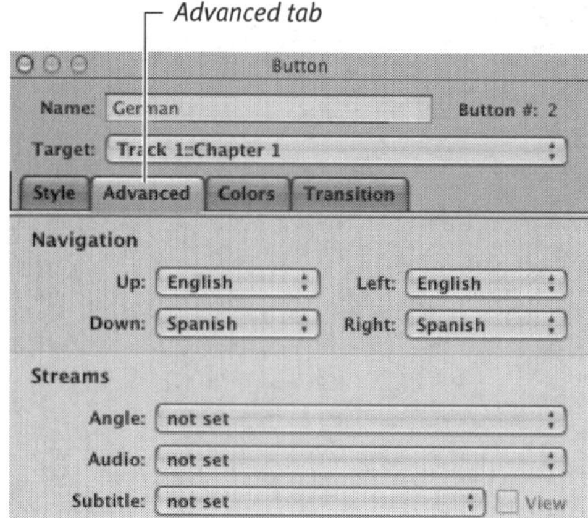

Figure 23.24 Click the Advanced tab in the Button Inspector to select an audio stream.

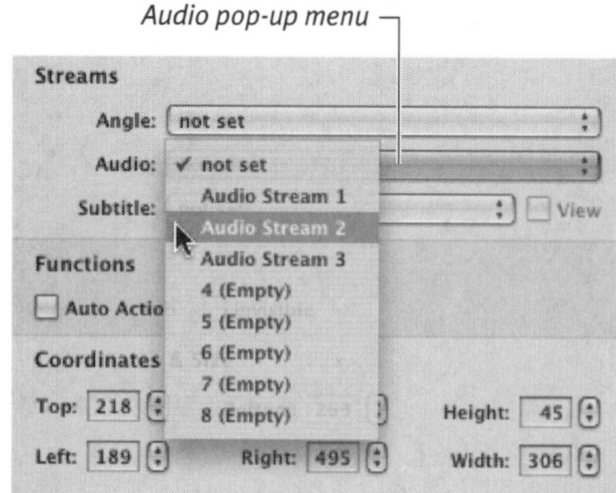

Figure 23.25 From the Audio pop-up menu, select an audio stream that corresponds to the audio stream number on your multilingual track.

Figure 23.26 When you select an audio stream for a button in the Button Inspector, the Audio pop-up menu lists all audio streams in your track.

Default Language Settings area

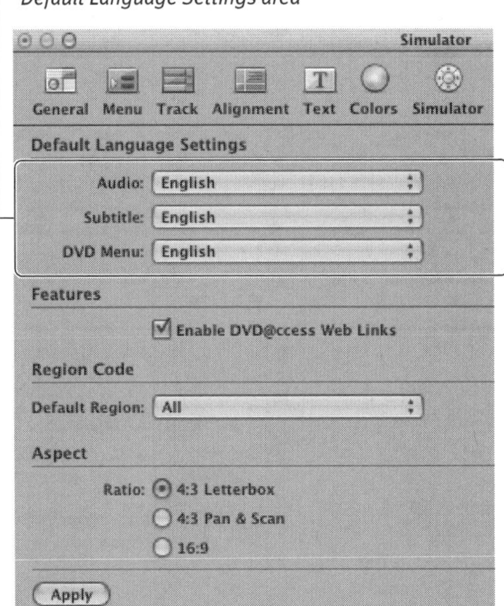

Figure 23.27 The Simulator section of the Preferences window houses settings that change the Simulator's default language settings, allowing you to fully test your project before burning it to disc.

Previewing Multiple-Language Projects

Multilingual projects use a lot of assets (including background pictures, audio streams, and subtitle clips). With so much going on in the project, it's easy to mistakenly assign the wrong language to an audio stream, for example. If a German viewer clicks a menu button and a Spanish audio track starts playing, the German viewer is going to be left wondering what's up. Consequently, with alternate-language projects, it is important to check that all menus navigate as expected and that audio streams all play in the proper tongue.

To see how your multilingual project will behave in the real world, test it in the Simulator or in Apple's DVD Player. In either application, you can set the playback preferences to choose a default audio, subtitle, and menu language.

To test multilingual projects using the Simulator:

1. Choose DVD Studio Pro > Preferences, or press Command-, (comma), to open DVD Studio Pro's Preferences window.
2. In the Preferences window, click the Simulator icon to view the Simulator section of the Preferences window (**Figure 23.27**).
3. Select a language from the Audio pop-up menu in the Default Language Settings area of the Simulator preferences (refer to Figure 23.27).
4. Select a language from the Subtitle pop-up menu.

continues on next page

5. Select a language from the DVD Menu pop-up menu.

   The language you select is the language that the Simulator emulates.

6. Click Apply at the bottom right of the Simulator section of the Preferences window to close the window and save your changes.

   When you simulate your project, DVD Studio Pro will imitate a set-top DVD-Video player's language settings.

To test multilingual projects using Apple's DVD Player:

1. In DVD Studio Pro, choose File > Advanced Burn > Build (**Figure 23.28**), or press Option-Command-C, to build a copy of your project on your computer's hard disk.

   Building a project creates a VIDEO_TS and an AUDIO_TS folder on your computer's hard disk. To learn more, see Chapter 19, "Finishing the DVD."

   The Choose Build Folder dialog appears (**Figure 23.29**).

2. Using the Choose Build Folder dialog, navigate to where you want DVD Studio Pro to place the VIDEO_TS and AUDIO_TS folders that are created when it builds your project.

3. When you've selected a folder, click Choose in the Choose Build Folder dialog.

   DVD Studio Pro builds your project in the selected folder and displays a completion dialog when it is finished (**Figure 23.30**).

4. Open Apple's DVD Player.

Figure 23.28 Choose File > Advanced Burn > Build to build your project on your hard disk.

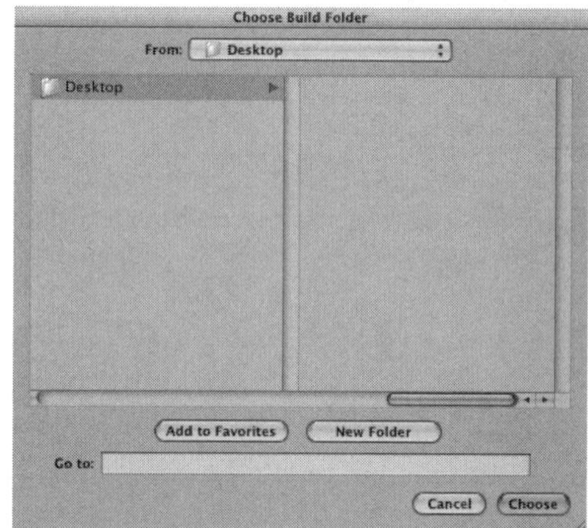

Figure 23.29 Choose the folder in which DVD Studio Pro will place the VIDEO_TS and AUDIO_TS folders that it creates when it builds your project.

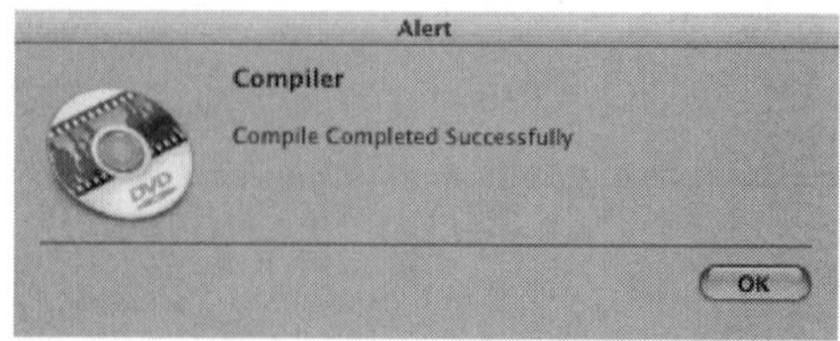

Figure 23.30 When it is finished building your project, DVD Studio Pro displays this dialog.

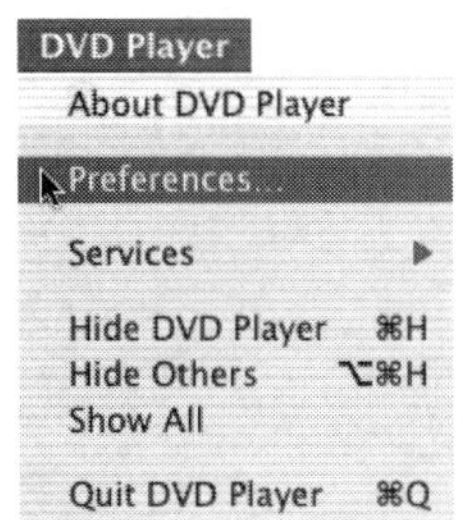

Figure 23.31 Choose DVD Player > Preferences to open DVD Player's Preferences dialog.

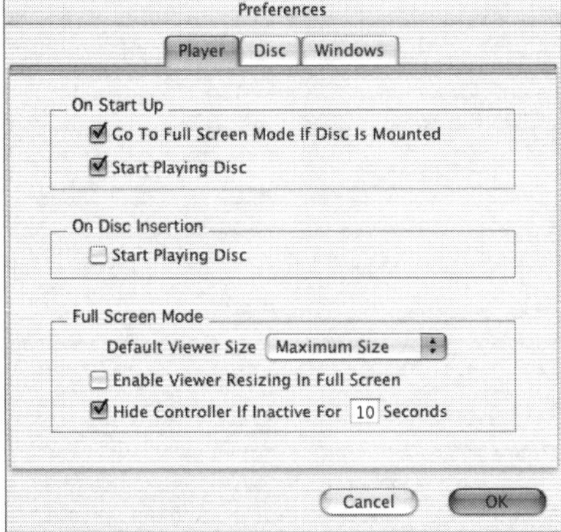

Figure 23.32 DVD Player's Preferences dialog displays settings for Apple's DVD Player.

5. Choose DVD Player > Preferences (**Figure 23.31**).

   DVD Player's Preferences dialog opens (**Figure 23.32**).

6. In the Preferences dialog, select the Disc tab (**Figure 23.33**).

   In the center of the Disc tab is a Default Language Settings area that hosts the Audio, Subtitle, and DVD Menu pop-up menus.

7. In the Default Language Settings section, choose a default audio language from the Audio pop-up menu (**Figure 23.34**).

8. Choose a default subtitle language from the Subtitle pop-up menu.

9. Choose a default DVD menu language from the DVD Menu pop-up menu.

continues on next page

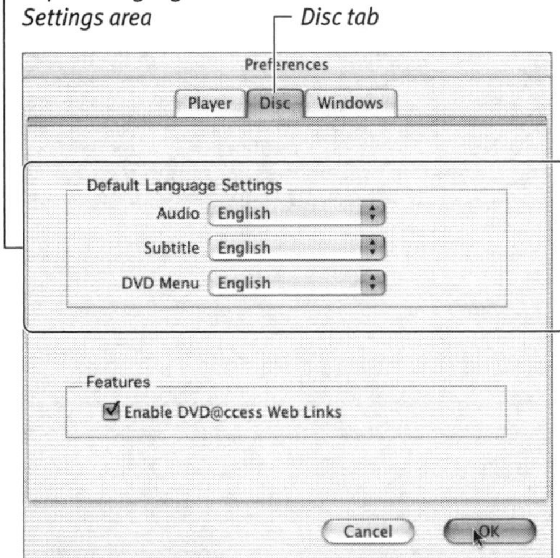

Figure 23.33 Select the Disc tab in the Preferences window to display DVD Player's default language settings.

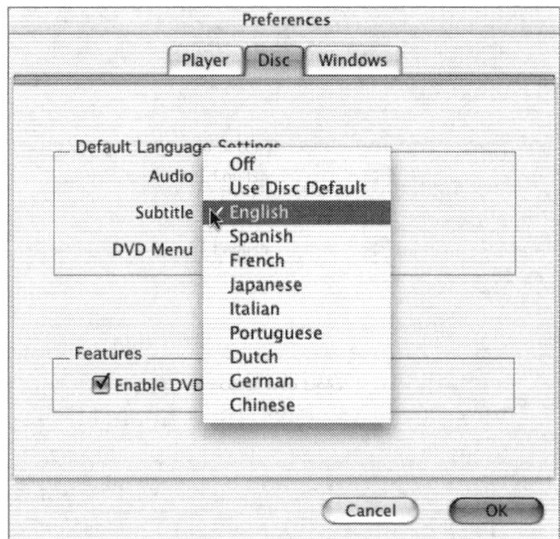

Figure 23.34 Choose a DVD player's default audio, subtitle, and DVD menu languages from the respective pop-up menus.

10. Click OK to save your changes and close the Preferences dialog.

    Apple's DVD Player imitates a set-top DVD-Video player's language settings using the default language settings you've selected.

11. In Apple DVD Player, choose File > Open VIDEO_TS Folder (**Figure 23.35**), or press Command-0.

    The VIDEO_TS folder selection sheet drops down from within the DVD Player Viewer (**Figure 23.36**).

12. Navigate to the VIDEO_TS folder that you built in step 1 and click the Choose button in the DVD Player Viewer selection sheet.

    The VIDEO_TS folder that you chose opens in DVD Player.

13. Click the Play button on the DVD Player remote (**Figure 23.37**).

    Your project won't autostart in DVD Player until it has been formatted to a DVD disc or a disk image; you must click the Play button.

    The built project opens in DVD Player. All menus as well as track audio and subtitle streams are played in the language you set as DVD Player's default language.

14. Repeat steps 5 through 13 until you've tested each language that your project uses.

✔ Tip

- DVD Player works with languages in exactly the same way as a set-top DVD-Video player. By switching Apple's DVD Player's language preferences, you can preview all of the languages used by your DVD-Video.

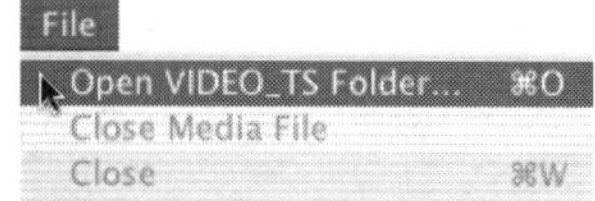

Figure 23.35 Choose File > Open VIDEO_TS Folder to open a VIDEO_TS folder on your hard disk or any other mounted drive or DVD.

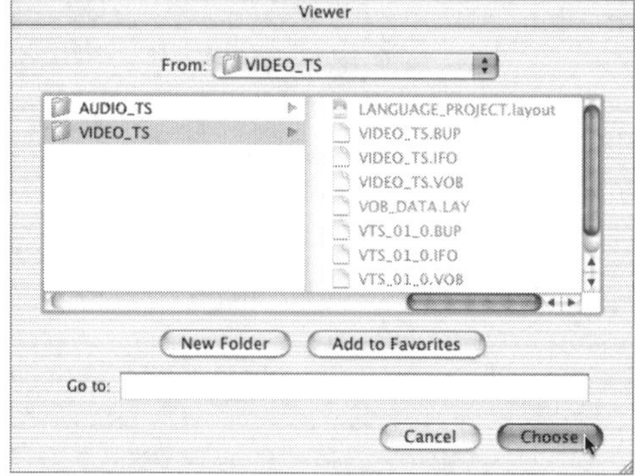

Figure 23.36 The VIDEO_TS folder selection sheet drops down from within the DVD Player Viewer, allowing you to choose a VIDEO_TS folder on your hard disk.

Figure 23.37 Click the Play button on DVD Player's remote control to play your project.

24

SUBTITLES

If you've ever rented a foreign film, you're probably already familiar with subtitles. Subtitles—text displayed on top of video—are most often used to supply alternate-language translations of the video's main dialogue. But there's no need to stop there, as subtitles are equally effective at displaying button highlights and company logos. After all, subtitles are merely overlay highlights, just like the ones used on menus.

Subtitles are extremely easy to create, thanks to DVD Studio Pro's internal Subtitle editor. With it, you can use any font on your computer to create text-based subtitles. You can also format the text, change the color, and even use special Unicode characters such as those found in Japanese or Hebrew.

You create subtitle streams in the Subtitle editor in much the same way that you create menus in the Menu editor. You can add text by either typing directly on top of a video stream in the Track editor or importing subtitles created with a third-party subtitling program. DVD Studio Pro supports a wide variety of subtitle formats, which means that you can use virtually any PC or Mac subtitling program at your disposal.

You can also use graphic overlay files for your video stream. Graphic files can come in the form of still text images or still picture overlays—and they can even be made to appear animated. Did you ever wonder how to add a bouncing ball that the viewer can toggle on or off over karaoke text? (Really, who *hasn't* wondered that at one point or another?) By importing a series of graphics that play for 10 or 15 frames each, you can make a subtitle stream that looks as if it's animated when played back. Pretty cool, don't you think?

About the Subtitle Editor

There isn't actually a separate editor for subtitles. Instead, you to use three tools together: the Track editor, to create your subtitle clips; the Subtitle Inspector, to configure the clips; and the Viewer tab, to type your text.

The Viewer tab actually plays two roles: it allows you to preview your work frame by frame as well as edit subtitles by typing directly on the video (**Figure 24.1**). On the Viewer tab, you can skip between subtitles using the Go to Previous and Go to Next buttons, which helps you move quickly through each subtitle clip you create.

The Track editor always has 9 video streams, 8 audio streams, and 32 subtitle streams available for you to use. You don't have to use every stream with every project, but remember that they're there when you need them. You can create a subtitle clip in any of the subtitle streams within the Track editor.

When you double-click a subtitle clip in the Track editor, all subtitle editing tools become active on the Viewer tab, including the Go to Previous and Go to Next subtitle buttons.

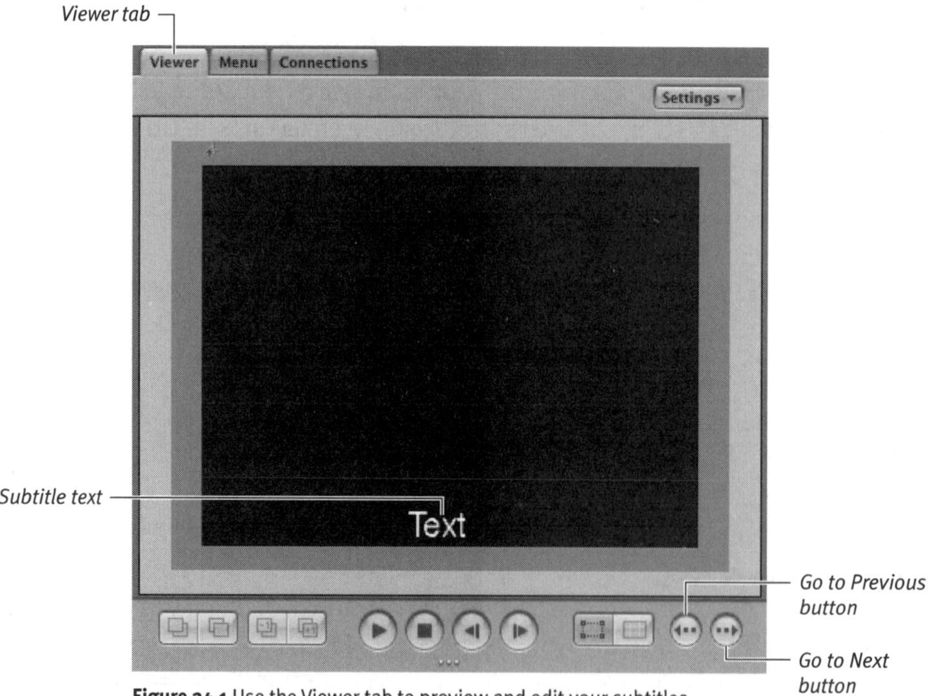

Figure 24.1 Use the Viewer tab to preview and edit your subtitles.

Figure 24.2 Choose DVD Studio Pro > Preferences to open the Preferences window.

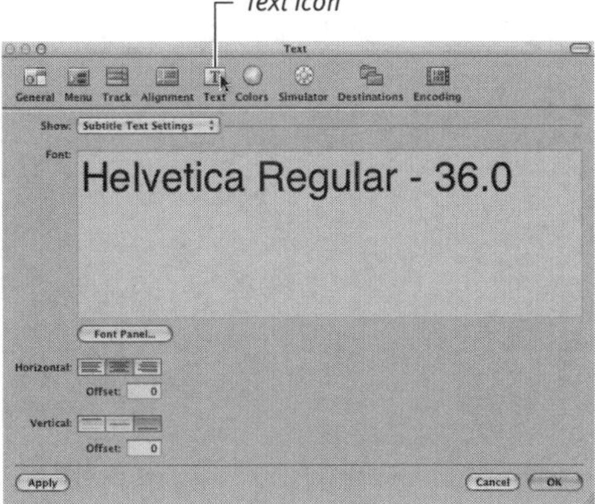

Figure 24.3 Use the Text Preferences window to set the default font for your subtitles.

Figure 24.4 Select Subtitle Text Settings from the Show pop-up menu to display the default subtitle text preferences.

Setting Subtitle Text Preferences

No two projects are alike. Whether you import your subtitles from another application or create them directly in DVD Studio Pro, you may want to first change the default subtitle text preferences before adding text-based subtitles to your project. Setting the default subtitle font will save you time when you create subtitle clips.

To set a default font:

1. Choose DVD Studio Pro > Preferences (**Figure 24.2**), or press Command-, (comma), to open the Preferences window.
2. In the Preferences toolbar, click the Text icon (**Figure 24.3**).

   The Text Preferences window opens.
3. From the Text Preferences window's Show pop-up menu, choose Subtitle Text Settings (**Figure 24.4**).

   The default subtitle text preferences are displayed.

continues on next page

4. Near the middle of the Text Preferences window, click the Font Panel button (**Figure 24.5**).

   DVD Studio Pro's Fonts panel opens in a separate window (**Figure 24.6**).

5. In the Fonts panel, select your preferred default font, typeface (style), and text size.

   The Font preview area in the Text Preferences window updates to display your default subtitle font selection (**Figure 24.7**).

Figure 24.5 Click the Font Panel button to open DVD Studio Pro's Fonts panel.

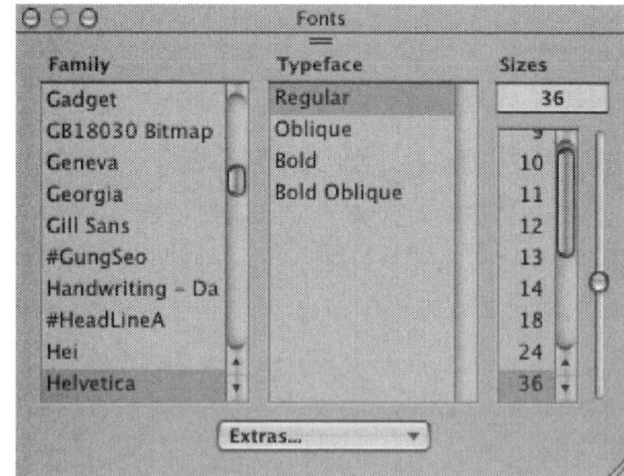

Figure 24.6 The system's Fonts panel lists all of the available fonts found on your Mac OS X partition.

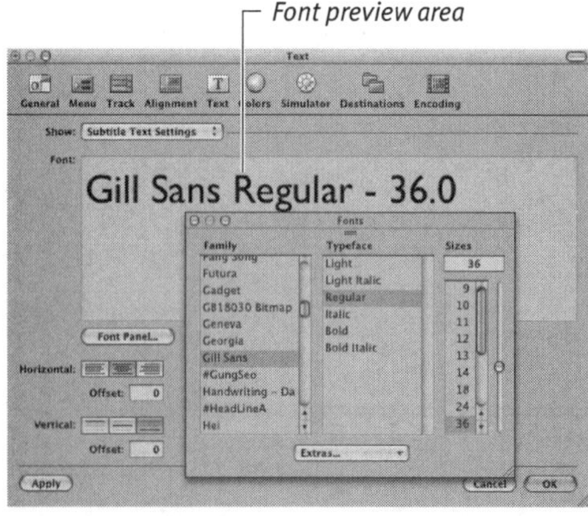

Figure 24.7 The Font preview area updates to display the font you selected.

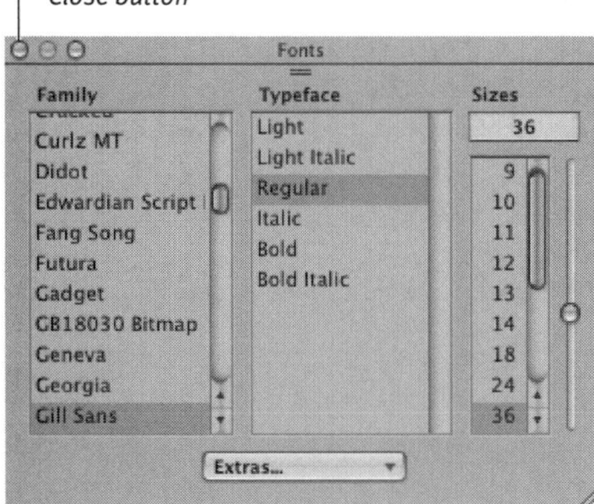

Figure 24.8 Click the Close button to close the Fonts panel.

Figure 24.9 Click OK to apply changes and close the Preferences window.

6. When you're happy with the default font you've chosen, click the Close button in the top-left corner of DVD Studio Pro's Fonts panel to close the window (**Figure 24.8**).
7. In the Text Preferences window, click OK to apply the changes and close the window (**Figure 24.9**).

   The default subtitle font that you selected will now be used when you create new subtitles.

✔ Tips

- DVD Studio Pro's Fonts panel lists all available fonts found on your Mac OS X startup disk. Fonts placed on a Mac OS 9 partition or other partitions will not appear in the Fonts panel list.
- When creating subtitles, you can override the default font you set in the Preferences window.
- Your project's preexisting subtitles are not affected by the changed font preference. The default subtitle font you selected affects only newly created subtitles.

Creating Subtitles

Before learning more about how to use subtitles, you should know exactly what you're dealing with. Subtitles can be either text or graphic highlight overlays, which are displayed on top of video. To learn more about creating overlays, see Chapter 15, "Overlay Menus."

Each subtitle clip can be as short as one second or as long as your video stream. You can add an infinite number of subtitle clips to each stream or use a single subtitle clip to span the entire length of the video stream.

In the same way that a video track can have alternate angles and multiple audio streams, it can also have multiple subtitle streams—up to 32, in fact. Each subtitle stream can be assigned a language so that viewers automatically see subtitles in their native tongue, but alternate subtitles don't have to be in different languages. You can use alternate subtitles to provide a text transcript of the movie, a director's commentary, or even a display of your company logo and contact information on top of the video.

No matter how many alternate subtitles you use and no matter whether they're text or graphic overlays, you always need to do two things:

- ◆ Create a subtitle clip.
- ◆ Set the clip's language in the Track editor.

✔ Tip

- ■ When working with multiple subtitle streams, you can change the stream that appears in the Viewer by clicking the orange Viewer Stream Selection button on the subtitle stream that you want to view (**Figure 24.10**).

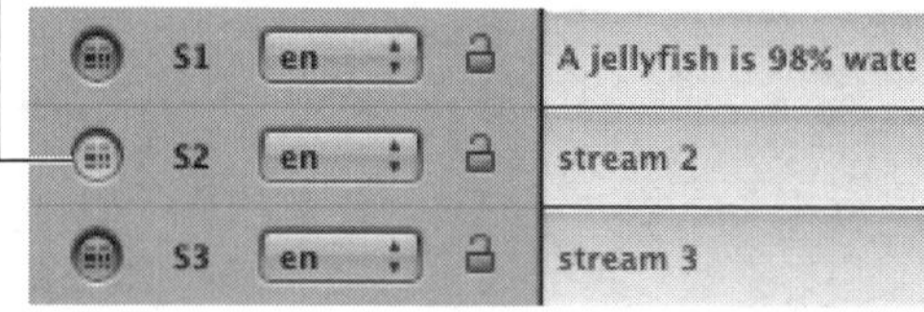

Figure 24.10 Click the orange Viewer Stream Selection button to preview the selected stream in the Viewer.

Figure 24.11 Control-click the empty gray area of any subtitle stream to see the shortcut menu.

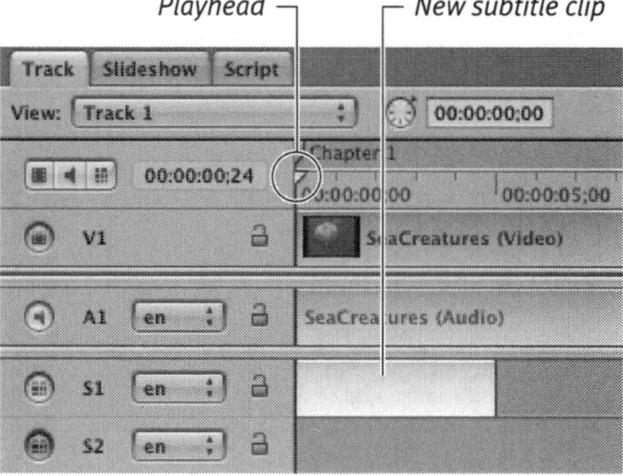

Figure 24.12 The new subtitle clip is added to the track starting at the playhead.

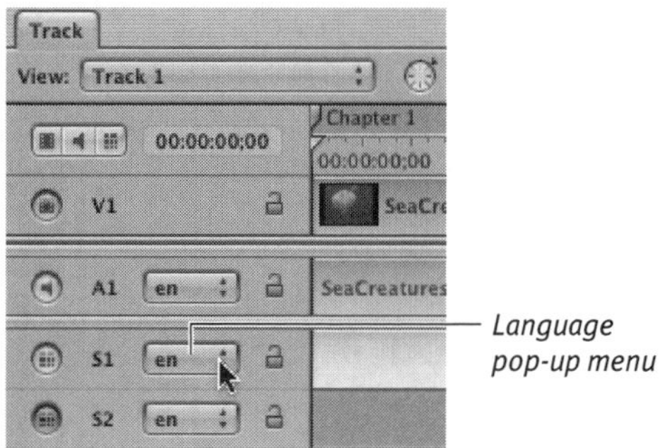

Figure 24.13 Select a language for the subtitle stream from the Language pop-up menu.

To create a subtitle clip:

1. On the Track tab, Control-click the empty, gray area of the first subtitle stream.

   A shortcut menu appears (**Figure 24.11**).

2. From the shortcut menu, choose Add Subtitle at Playhead.

   A subtitle clip is created in the track at the location of the playhead (**Figure 24.12**).

✔ Tips

- Select Add Subtitle from the shortcut menu, and a subtitle will be created where your pointer is in the subtitle stream.
- You can drag subtitles along the stream to a new location, if desired.
- You can duplicate subtitles easily by holding down the Option key and dragging a copy of the subtitle out from the original.
- The default subtitle length is five seconds. For steps to change this default length, see "Changing Subtitle Duration" later in this chapter.

To set a subtitle stream's language:

◆ In the Track editor's Language pop-up menu to the left of the subtitle stream, choose a language (**Figure 24.13**).

  The language used for the subtitle stream is set. (To learn more, see Chapter 23, "Working with Languages.")

Editing Subtitles

When you double-click a subtitle clip in the Track editor, a text insertion cursor appears in the Viewer. You can type directly on top of your video or use the Subtitle Inspector to type your subtitle text.

To enter text:

1. In the Track editor, create a subtitle clip. (To learn more about how to create a subtitle clip, see "Creating Subtitles" earlier in this chapter.)
2. In the Track editor, double-click the subtitle clip.

   The subtitle clip opens in the Viewer displaying a text insertion cursor (**Figure 24.14**), and the Inspector updates to display the subtitle clip's properties (**Figure 24.15**).

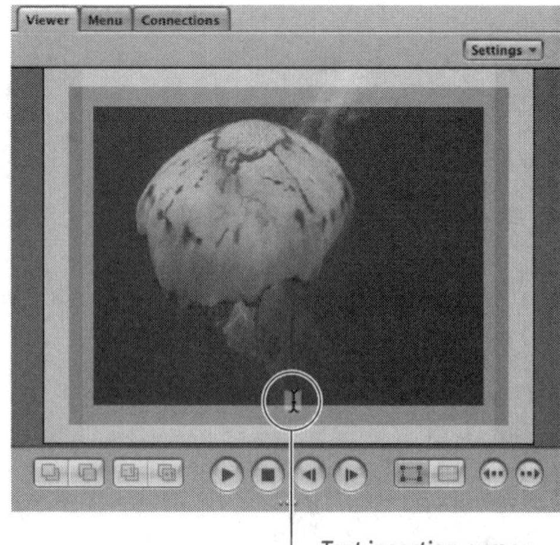

Figure 24.14 When you double-click a subtitle, the Viewer opens with a text insertion cursor ready for you to begin typing.

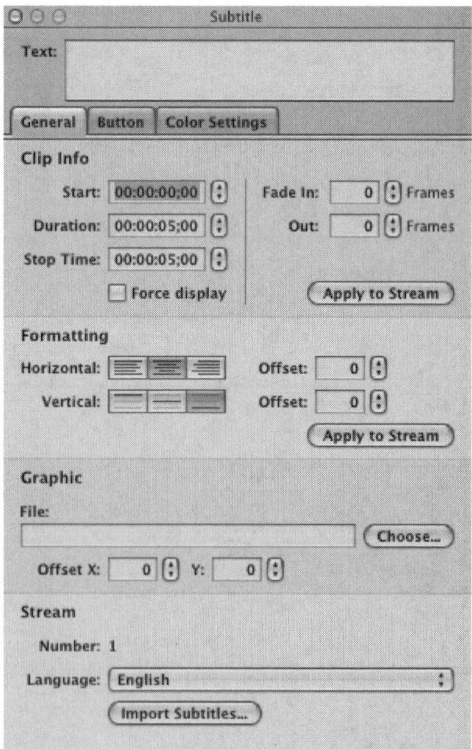

Figure 24.15 When you select a subtitle clip in the Track editor, the Inspector updates to display its properties.

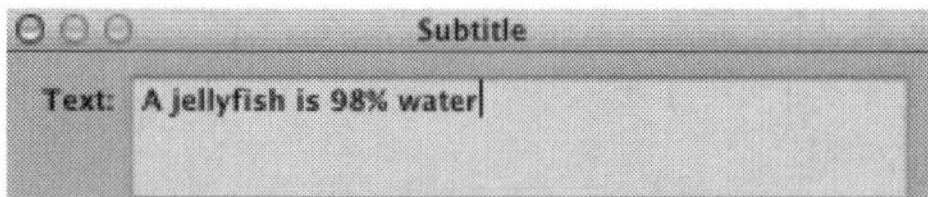

Figure 24.16 Type your text in the Subtitle Inspector, as shown here, or directly on top of your video in the Viewer.

Figure 24.17 Control-click your text and choose Spelling > Check Spelling as You Type from the shortcut menu that appears.

3. To add text to your subtitle clip, *do one of the following:*

   ▲ Type your text directly in the Viewer, using the text insertion cursor.

   ▲ In the Subtitle Inspector, type your text in the Text box located above the General tab (**Figure 24.16**).

   Your text is displayed in both the Viewer and the Subtitle Inspector. There isn't an advantage or disadvantage to typing in either location; use the method you prefer.

✔ Tips

- DVD Studio Pro has a built-in spell checker. To check spelling as you type, Control-click the text you've added and choose Spelling > Check Spelling as You Type from the shortcut menu (**Figure 24.17**). All misspelled words will be underlined in red once you've turned on this option.
- It's sometimes tedious to enter subtitles one by one. To learn how you can create and import batches of subtitles, see "Creating Text Subtitles" and "Importing Text Subtitles" later in this chapter.

Formatting Subtitle Text

DVD Studio Pro works with any font on your Mac OS X hard disk or partition. You can format the text or font size and even use special Unicode characters to customize your subtitles.

Newly created subtitles use the default font that you set in your preferences. However, you can override this default font at any time.

✔ Tip

- If you use two different machines, one to create subtitles and one to build the VIDEO_TS folder, be sure that all fonts used in your subtitles are installed on both machines. If the font you used is not available on the build machine, DVD Studio Pro will use Helvetica by default.

To override the default font type:

1. In the Track editor, create a subtitle clip. For steps to create a subtitle clip, see "Creating Subtitles" earlier in this chapter.
2. In the Subtitle Inspector, select all of the text in the subtitle clip (**Figure 24.18**). You can select all text quickly by triple-clicking the Subtitle Inspector's Text box.
3. From DVD Studio Pro's Format menu, choose Font > Show Fonts (**Figure 24.19**), or press Command-T.

   The Fonts panel opens in a separate window (**Figure 24.20**).
4. In the Fonts panel, select a new font, typeface, and size for the selected subtitle clip's text.

   The new font is applied to your selected text automatically.
5. When you're finished, click the Close button in the Fonts panel's top-left corner.

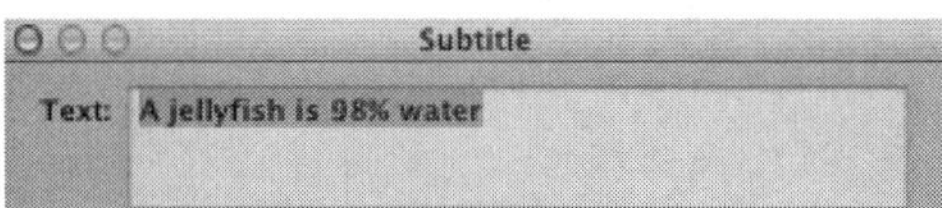

Figure 24.18 You can select all text quickly by triple-clicking the Subtitle Inspector's Text box.

Figure 24.19 Choose Format > Font > Show Fonts to open the Fonts panel.

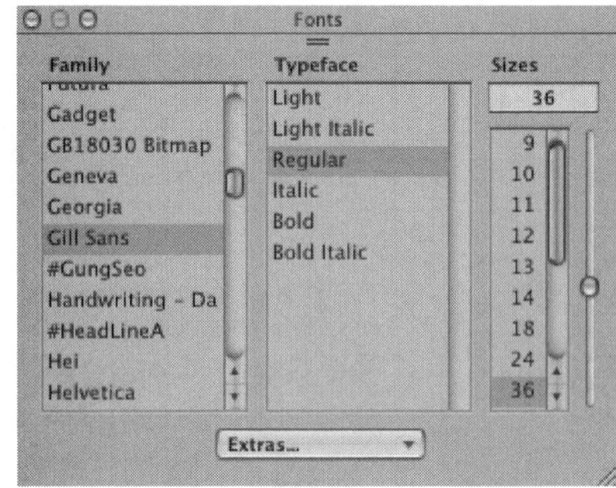

Figure 24.20 Select a new font in the Fonts panel.

Positioning Subtitles

Like any other text or graphics in your project, subtitles must sit inside the video frame's title safe area, a border set 10 percent in from the edge of the video frame. (To learn more about the title safe area, see Chapter 3, "Preparing Graphics.") For subtitles on NTSC video tracks, the left and right margins should be no less than 72 pixels, and the top and bottom margins should be at least 48 pixels. For PAL video, the margins must be 72 pixels from the left and right edges and 58 pixels from the top and bottom. Setting text inside the title safe area is easier than it sounds—just turn on the title safe filter in the Viewer's Settings menu and move your text around as desired.

Keep a careful eye on the edges of your subtitles to make sure that they don't get cropped off. Any text that falls outside the title safe area may not be viewable on cathode-ray tube (CRT) TVs.

To turn on the Viewer's title safe filter:

◆ From the Viewer's Settings menu, choose Title Safe Area (**Figure 24.21**).

  A check mark appears next to the Title Safe Area setting, and the transparent gray title safe box appears in the Viewer.

✔ Tip

■ You can toggle the Title Safe setting on or off as desired. In the Settings menu, a check mark to the left of the Title Safe Area setting tells you that the filter is on.

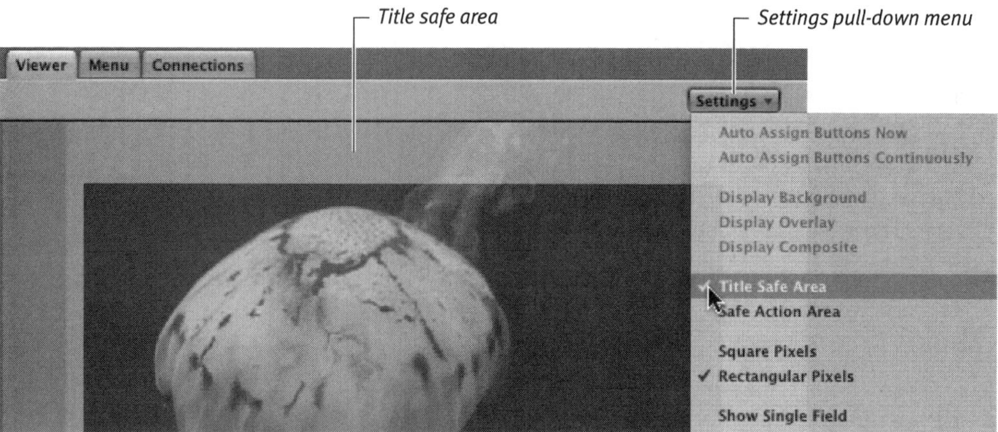

Figure 24.21 Choose Title Safe Area from the Viewer's Settings menu to display the transparent gray title safe area.

To position a subtitle:

1. In the Track editor, double-click a subtitle clip.

   The subtitle opens in the Viewer.

2. In the Viewer, drag the text to the desired location (**Figure 24.22**).

Figure 24.22 Drag the text anywhere within the Viewer window to relocate it.

To shift text horizontally:

- In the Subtitle Inspector, click one of the Horizontal text alignment buttons (**Figure 24.23**):
  - **Left.** All text is positioned at the left of the screen, just inside the title safe area.
  - **Center.** All text is centered within the title safe area.
  - **Right.** All text is positioned at the right of the screen, just inside the title safe area.

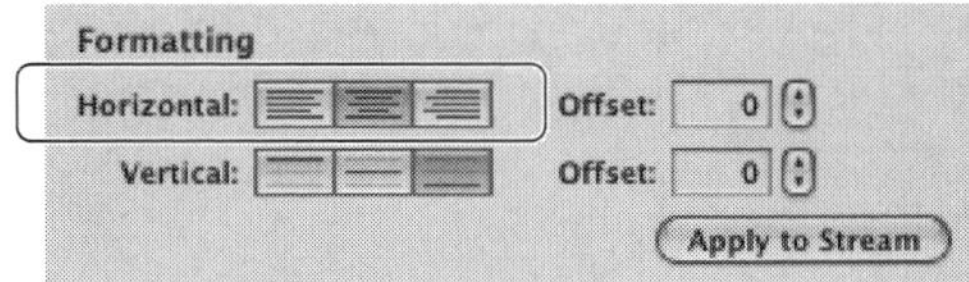

Figure 24.23 Click one of the Horizontal alignment buttons to position text horizontally.

✔ Tips

- To have your text line up to the right, but not against the right edge, of the title safe area, you can offset the text by clicking the up and down Horizontal Offset arrows or by entering a numerical value.
- If your text goes offscreen and out of sight, you can enter the default offset values of zero to bring your text back into the Viewer.
- You can apply the new text justification to the entire subtitle stream, and to every subtitle in it, by clicking the Subtitle Inspector's Apply to Stream button (**Figure 24.24**).

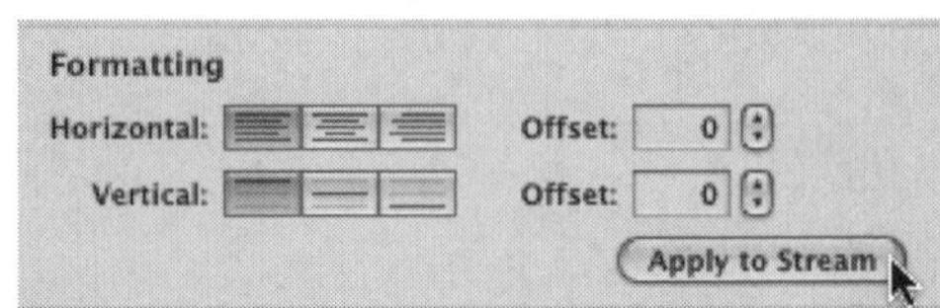

Figure 24.24 You can apply your changes to the entire subtitle stream by clicking the Apply to Stream button.

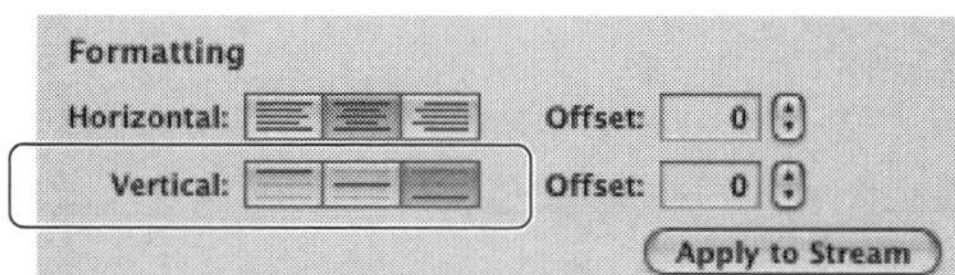

Figure 24.25 Click one of the Vertical text alignment buttons to position text vertically.

To shift text vertically:

- In the Subtitle Inspector, click one of the Vertical text alignment buttons (**Figure 24.25**):
  - **Top.** All text is positioned at the top of the screen, just inside the title safe area.
  - **Center.** All text is centered within the title safe area.
  - **Bottom.** All text is positioned at the bottom of the screen, just inside the title safe area.

Changing Subtitle Duration

As mentioned earlier, subtitles can last as long as your video track, or they can be as short as one second. DVD Studio Pro's default subtitle duration is five seconds. If the majority of your subtitle clips are longer or shorter than five seconds, you can change the default duration in the Preferences window to save yourself time later. You can also override the default duration in the Subtitle Inspector for each individual subtitle clip as necessary.

To change the default subtitle duration:

1. Choose DVD Studio Pro > Preferences (**Figure 24.26**), or press Command-, (comma), to open the Preferences window.
2. In the Preferences window toolbar, click the General icon.

   The General preferences are displayed (**Figure 24.27**).
3. In the Subtitle section's Length text box, type a new default subtitle length (in seconds; **Figure 24.28**).

   (Fades are discussed in the section "Using Fades" later in this chapter.)
4. In the Preferences window, click OK to save changes and close the window.

   All new subtitle clips will automatically use the new duration you entered. Preexisting subtitles are not affected.

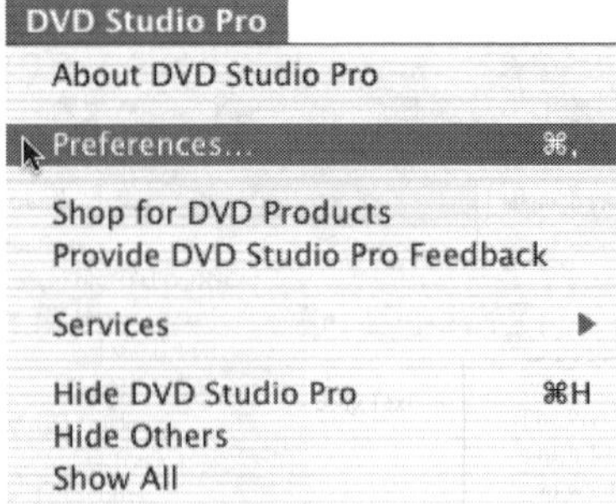

Figure 24.26 Choose DVD Studio Pro > Preferences to open the Preferences window.

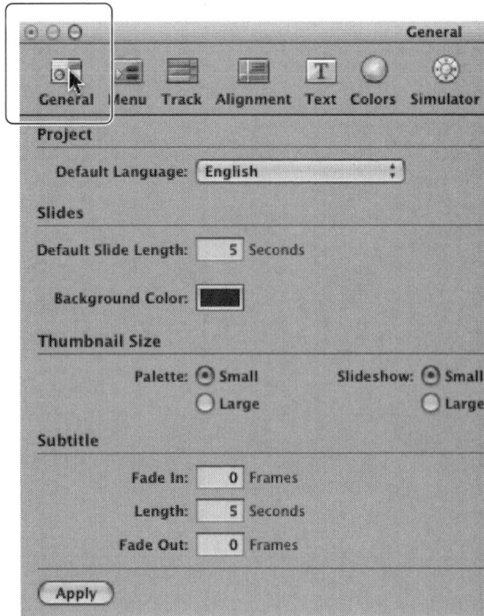

Figure 24.27 Click the General icon in the Preferences toolbar to display the General preferences.

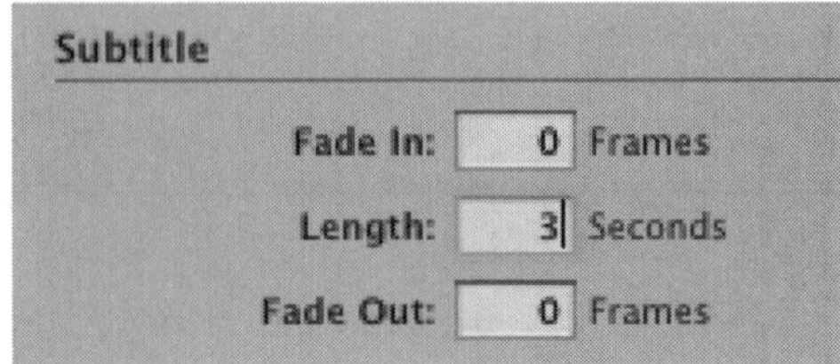

Figure 24.28 In the Length text box, type a new default subtitle length.

Figure 24.29 Click a subtitle clip to display its properties in the Inspector.

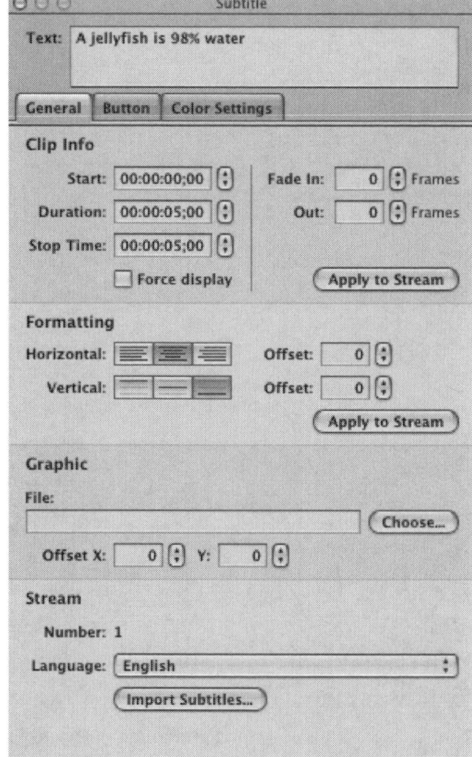

Figure 24.30 The Subtitle Inspector displays the subtitle's properties.

To change the default duration for an individual subtitle clip:

1. In the Track editor, select a subtitle clip (**Figure 24.29**).

   The Inspector updates to display the subtitle's properties (**Figure 24.30**). The General tab in the Inspector is open by default.

2. In the Clip Info section's Duration text box, type a new duration, or click the duration arrows up or down to change the duration one frame at a time (**Figure 24.31**).

continues on next page

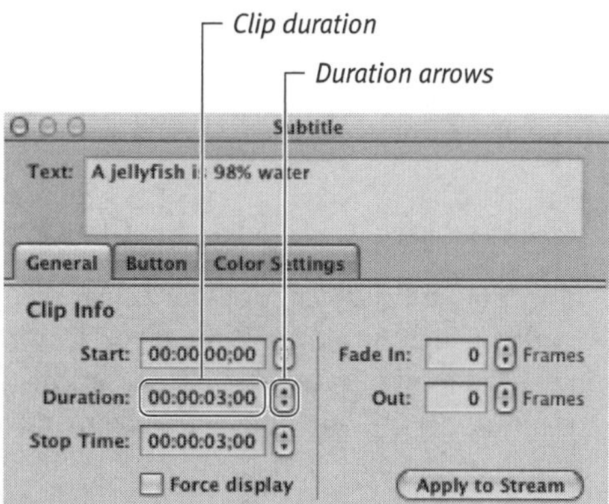

Figure 24.31 To change the subtitle clip's duration, type a new duration in the Subtitle Inspector's Duration text box, or click the arrows to the right of the text box.

✔ Tip

- You can lengthen or trim a subtitle clip by dragging the end of the clip in the Track editor. Move the pointer over the end of the clip until the cursor icon changes to the resizing icon; then drag the clip left or right to trim or lengthen the duration (**Figure 24.32**).

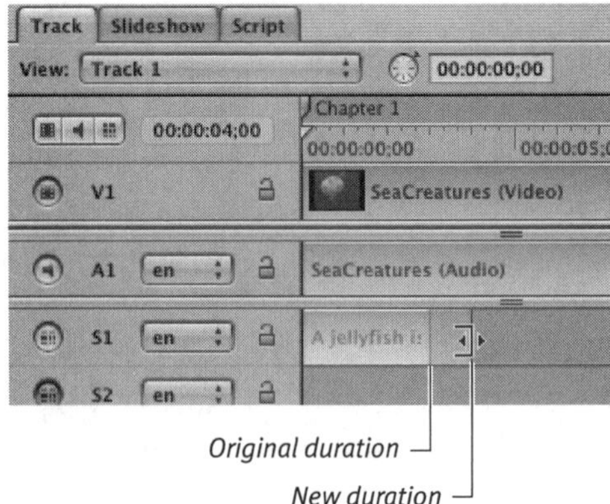

Figure 20.32 Drag the end of a subtitle clip on the timeline to change its duration.

Crossing Boundaries

Individual subtitles cannot cross chapter markers. In DVD Studio Pro 1.*x*, you may have had to duplicate the subtitle, setting one portion of the subtitle before the marker and the other part after the marker. This approach caused problems—for instance, the subtitle flickered off and on again when a chapter marker was reached, and users had to waste considerable time tweaking the subtitles' start and end times.

Now we can thank the excellent DVD Studio Pro engineering team for doing the tedious work for us. Now, when you build your project in DVD Studio Pro 3, you may see a yellow warning in the log that reads something like:

```
Track 1 : 2 Subtitles truncated because of marker boundary interference!
```

This is DVD Studio Pro telling you that it has automatically fixed your subtitles so they meet DVD spec requirements; the warning lets you know that your subtitles have been modified.

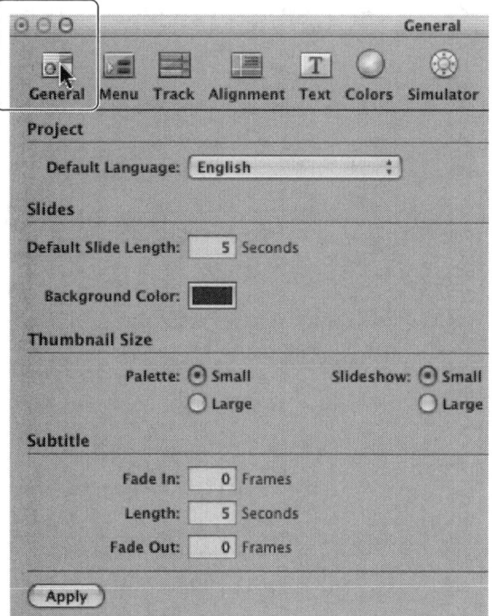

Figure 24.33 Click the General icon in the Preferences toolbar to display the General preferences.

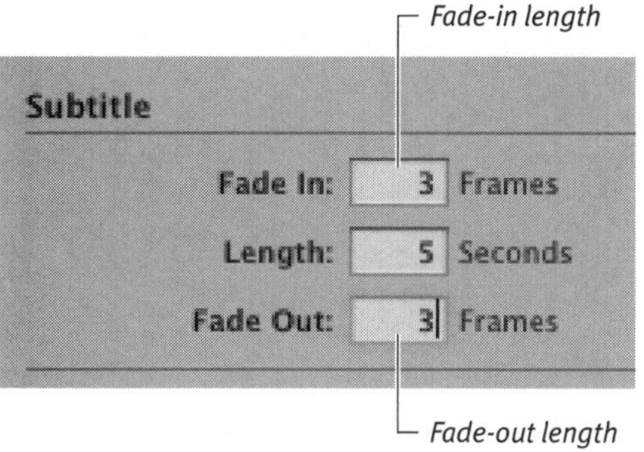

Figure 24.34 Subtitle fades are entered in frames, not seconds.

Using Fades

By default, subtitles pop in and out with a jarring effect. To provide a better viewing experience, you may want to consider having your subtitles fade in and out.

You can set the default fade-in and fade-out durations in the Preferences window, and as with all subtitle preferences, you can override the default in the Subtitle Inspector.

To apply a default fade-in and fade-out duration for all new subtitles:

1. Choose DVD Studio Pro > Preferences, or press Command-, (Command-comma), to open the Preferences window.
2. In the Preferences window, click the General icon on the toolbar.

   The General preferences are displayed (**Figure 24.33**).
3. In the Subtitle section's Fade In and Fade Out text boxes, type new default durations (in frames; **Figure 24.34**).
4. Click OK in the Preferences window to save your changes and close the window.

   All new subtitles now fade in and fade out based on these settings. Preexisting subtitles are not affected.

✔ Tip

- For the best results with fading subtitles, use an average fade of three to six frames.

To apply fade-in and fade-out durations for an individual subtitle clip:

1. In the Track editor, select a subtitle clip (**Figure 24.35**) to display its properties in the Inspector.
2. In the Subtitle Inspector, click the General tab.
3. In the Clip Info section's Fade In and Out text boxes, type new durations (in frames), or use the duration arrows to the right of the text boxes to change the durations (**Figure 24.36**).

   The subtitle clip now fades in and out based on your settings.

Figure 24.35 Select a subtitle clip in the Track editor.

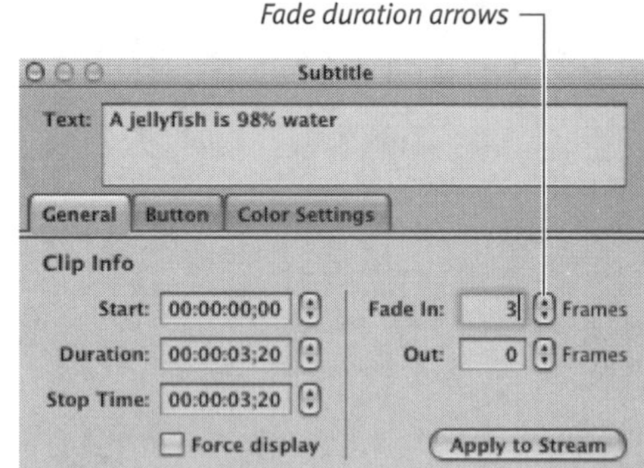

Figure 24.36 Use the fade duration arrows to set the subtitle fade duration.

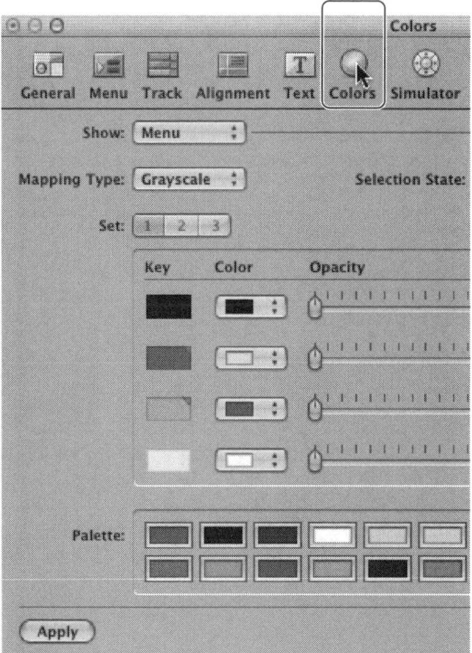

Figure 24.37 Click the Colors icon in the Preferences toolbar to display the Colors preferences.

Figure 24.38 Select Subtitle from the Show pop-up menu to display the Subtitle's default color preferences.

Using Color

The Subtitle Inspector provides you with a preset palette of 16 default colors to use for your subtitles. Just as with the color palette used to create menu overlays and button highlights, you can choose four colors—the main text color (Text), Outline 1, Outline 2, and the background color (Background)—from the palette to use as your subtitle text colors. You can also change the transparency (opacity) of each color used. For more information on using overlay colors, see Chapter 15.

Subtitle color applies to all of the characters in the selected subtitle clip, which means that you can't change the color of certain text characters within a clip without changing the color of all the others. However, you can change your subtitle colors between clips in the same subtitle stream.

Changing default colors

If the subtitle color that you want to use is not offered in the palette of 16 default colors at your disposal, open the Subtitle Color Preferences window and change them.

Before changing the colors, however, keep in mind that all colors used in your project must be TV safe. For more information on TV safe colors, see Chapter 3.

To set a subtitle's default color:

1. Open the Preferences window.
2. In the Preferences toolbar, click the Colors icon (**Figure 24.37**).

   The Colors preferences are displayed.
3. From the Show pop-up menu, select Subtitle (**Figure 24.38**).

   The Subtitle default colors are displayed.

continues on next page

4. Click any of the color palettes at the bottom of the Color Preferences window (**Figure 24.39**).

   The DVD Studio Pro Colors palette opens (**Figure 20.40**).

5. Click a new color from DVD Studio Pro's Colors palette to select it.

   The new color is applied automatically when selected.

6. When you're finished, click the red Close button in the top-left corner of the palette to close the Colors palette.

   The new color is available in your default color palette for use with all subtitles (**Figure 24.41**).

✔ Tip

- With the Colors palette open, you can click the Magnifying Glass tool to sample colors from anywhere on your screen (**Figure 24.42**). When you click the Magnifying Glass tool, your pointer will change into a magnifying glass, enlarging all colors on your screen. Roll the mouse over the color you want to use and click to select that color.

Figure 24.39 Click any of the color palettes found at the bottom of the Preferences window to change the color setting.

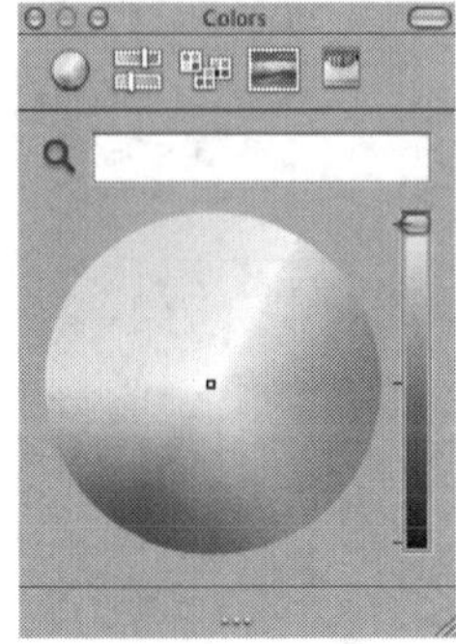

Figure 20.40 Click any color in DVD Studio Pro's Colors palette to select it.

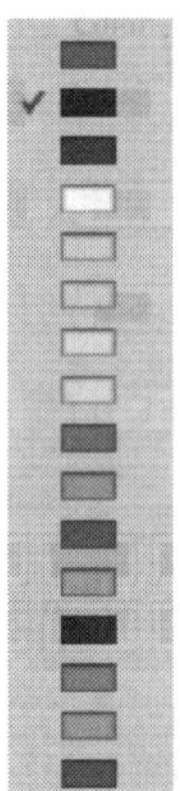

Figure 24.41 The new color you selected is available in your default color palette.

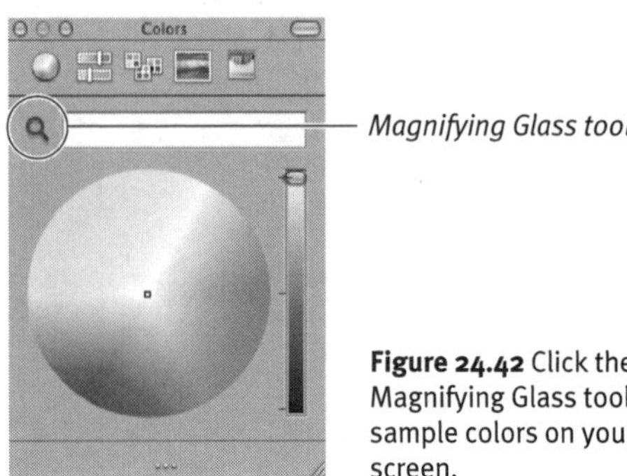

Figure 24.42 Click the Magnifying Glass tool to sample colors on your screen.

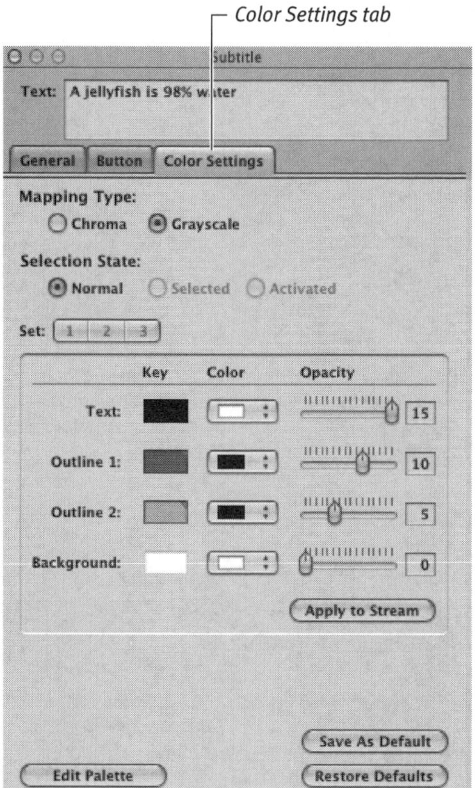

Figure 24.43 Click the Color Settings tab to see the color settings for your subtitle.

Setting subtitle colors within a stream

All newly created subtitles will use the colors set in your preferences by default. Since subtitles lay on top of the video, you may want to change the default color within a subtitle stream depending on the video's background color. For example, yellow subtitles won't show up very well on top of a washed-out video background. DVD Studio Pro allows you to change the subtitle color used for the entire stream or for an individual subtitle clip within the stream.

Subtitles are highlight overlays, just like the ones you use for button highlights on your menus. They can use chroma or grayscale color mapping, depending on your preference. See Chapter 15 for more information on chroma and grayscale color mapping.

To set the color for an individual subtitle clip:

1. In the Track editor, select a subtitle clip to display its properties in the Inspector.
2. At the top of the Subtitle Inspector, click the Color Settings tab (**Figure 24.43**).
   The subtitle's color settings are displayed.

continues on next page

3. At the top of the Subtitle Inspector, click the Chroma or Grayscale Mapping Type radio button that corresponds to your subtitle clip's overlay (**Figure 24.44**):

   ▲ **Chroma.** Maps to black, red, blue, and white highlight colors on your overlay.

   ▲ **Grayscale.** Maps to black, dark gray, light gray, and white highlight colors on your overlay.

   Unless you have added a graphic overlay to your subtitle clip that uses chroma color mapping (black, red, blue, and white), you can leave the mapping type set to Grayscale.

4. At the top of the Subtitle editor, for Selection State, click the Normal radio button, if it is not already selected (refer to Figure 24.44).

   The Normal selection state causes the subtitle's normal colors to be displayed when the subtitle appears onscreen.

   The Selected and Activated Selection State radio buttons refer to buttons on video that uses subtitle overlays to display the selected and activated button states. These options will be dimmed unless you are working with an interactive marker. For more information, see Chapter 12, "Enhancing Tracks."

5. In the Subtitle Inspector's Text Color pop-up menu, choose the color to be used for the text in your subtitle clip (**Figure 24.45**).

6. Drag the Opacity slider left or right as desired to set the chosen color's opacity (refer to Figure 24.45).

   The subtitle text is less opaque when you drag the Opacity slider to the left and more opaque when you drag it to the right.

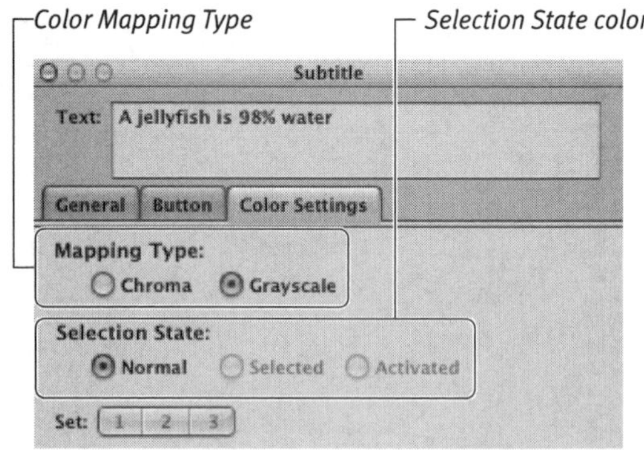

Figure 24.44 Click a Mapping Type radio button to select your color mapping type. The mapping type you select is used for your subtitle overlay color mapping.

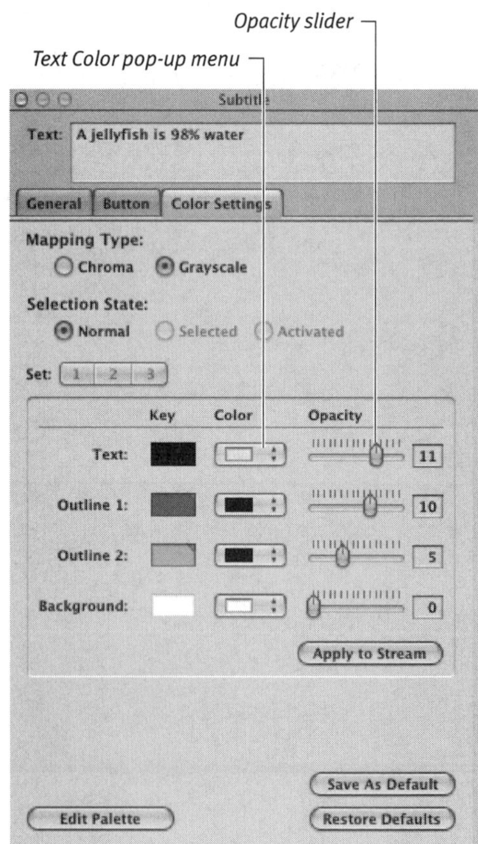

Figure 24.45 Select the text color from the Text Color pop-up menu.

Text outline color settings

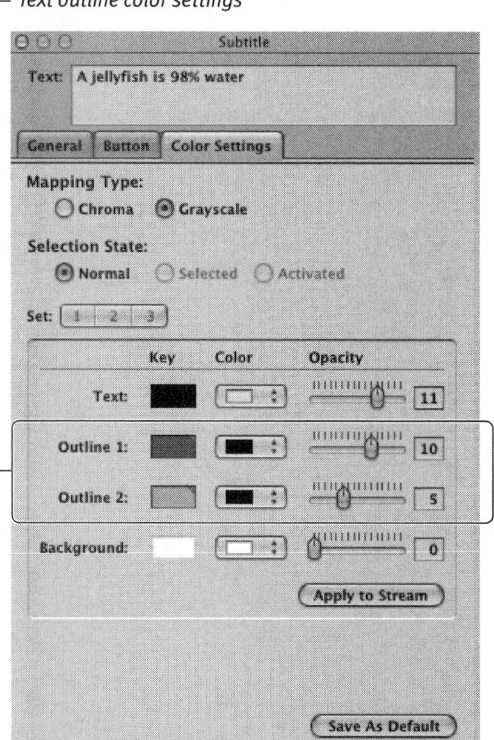

Figure 24.46 Choose your text outline colors from the Color pop-up menu and set the opacity.

The text highlight in the selected subtitle clip uses the color you selected.

You can also set the text's opacity level by typing a number in the Opacity text box. Zero equals 100 percent translucent, and 15 equals 100 percent opaque.

7. In the Subtitle Inspector's Outline 1 Color pop-up menu, choose the color to be used for the first outline of your subtitle clip (**Figure 24.46**).

   This can be the same color you chose for your text color, or you can choose a different color.

   The outline color is set for the selected subtitle clip.

8. Drag the Opacity slider left or right as desired to set the chosen Outline 1 color's opacity, or enter a numerical opacity value between 0 and 15.

9. In the Subtitle Inspector's Outline 2 Color pop-up menu, choose the color to be used for the second outline of your subtitle clip (refer to Figure 24.46).

   This can be the same color you chose for your text color, a black outline for the outer edge, or any other color you desire.

   The Outline 2 color is set for the selected subtitle clip.

✔ Tips

- To get rid of the "jaggies" that appear around your subtitle text, set the Outline 2 opacity so that it's less than the Outline 1 opacity.
- You don't need to set the subtitle's background color attributes unless you want a partially translucent color overlay on top of your video. If you want to fade out a section of your video so your subtitle text or graphic becomes the main focus of the video clip, you can choose a background color from the Color pop-up menu in the Inspector, for example.

To apply a color set to the entire stream:

1. Set your subtitle clip's colors. (See the previous task for step-by-step instructions on how to do this.)
2. In the Subtitle Inspector, click the Apply to Stream button (**Figure 24.47**).

   The subtitle clip's individual color settings are applied to all current subtitle clips in your stream. All newly created subtitle clips in this stream will use these applied color settings instead of the project's default color settings.

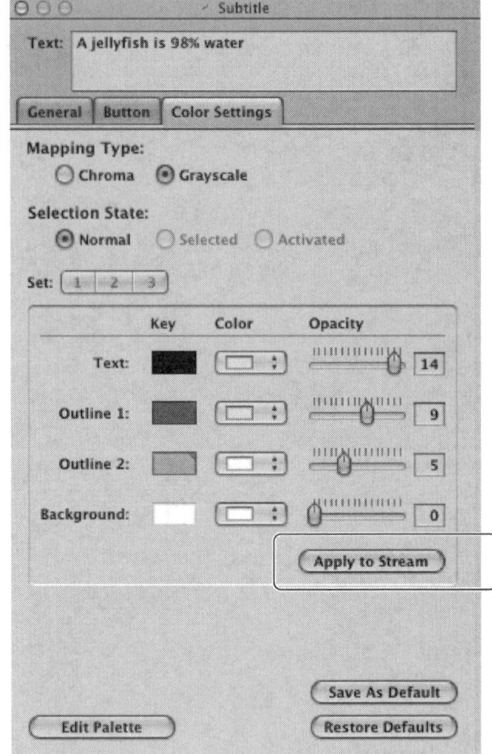

Figure 24.47 Click the Subtitle Inspector's Apply to Stream button to apply your color setting changes to all subtitle clips in the same stream.

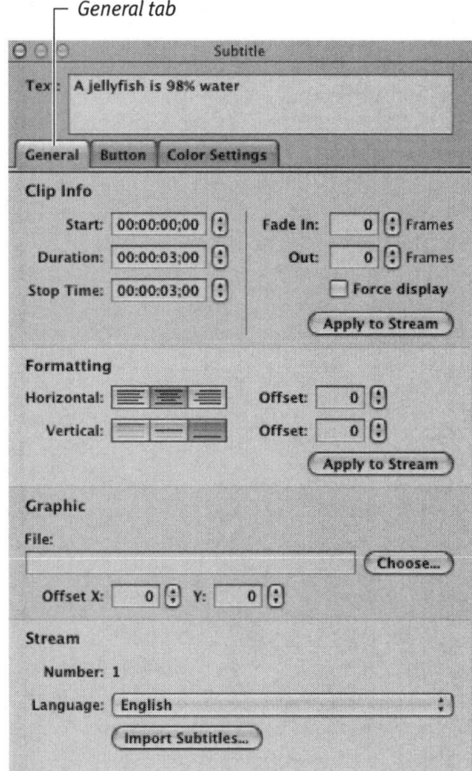

Figure 24.48 Select the General tab in the Subtitle Inspector to view the subtitle's general properties.

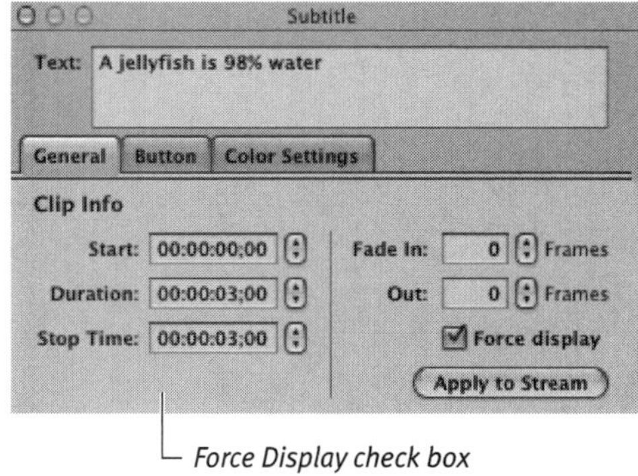

Figure 24.49 Select the Force Display check box to force a subtitle clip to be displayed.

Forcing Subtitle Display

When you force a subtitle to be displayed, the subtitle will be visible even if the viewer has subtitles turned off. For example, you can force some subtitles to appear even if the viewer hasn't turned on subtitles. You might want to do this if, for example, you want your company logo constantly visible onscreen, or you want your contact number displayed over a video stream.

If you have multiple subtitle streams that are set to force their display, Stream 1 will be displayed by default, and the viewer will need to press the Subtitle button on his or her remote control to switch to the other streams.

To force subtitle display:

1. In the Track editor, click a subtitle to select it.

   The Inspector updates to display the subtitle's properties.

2. In the Subtitle Inspector, click the General tab to display the subtitle's general properties (**Figure 24.48**).

3. On the General tab, select the Force Display check box (**Figure 24.49**).

   The selected subtitle clip is visible, even if the viewer has subtitles turned off.

✔ Tip

- The Apply to Stream setting will not apply the forced display setting to the entire stream. Only the selected subtitle clip will be set.

Simulating Subtitles

Once you've finished creating your subtitles, it's a good idea to open the Simulator window and test them to ensure that all the durations and colors of your subtitles perform according to your expectations.

If you have more than one subtitle stream per track, you can view each stream one at a time by selecting a different subtitle stream number from the Simulator's Subtitle Stream pop-up menu (**Figure 24.50**). But take careful note of this fact: *unless you have set each subtitle clip to force display, you'll need to click the Simulator's View check box to see them* (for more information on setting subtitle clips to force display, see "Forcing Subtitle Display" earlier in this chapter).

✔ Tip

- You can use the Simulator to verify subtitle languages if you set the subtitle language preference in the Simulator pane of DVD Studio Pro's Preferences window. For more information on using multiple languages with subtitles, see Chapter 23.

Figure 24.50 All subtitle streams appear in the Simulator's Subtitle Stream pop-up menu.

Figure 24.51 In the Outline view, Control-click the track that contains subtitle streams and select Simulate from the shortcut menu.

To test subtitles in the Simulator:

1. In DVD Studio Pro's Outline or Graphical view, Control-click the track with subtitles that you want to test.

   A shortcut menu appears (**Figure 24.51**).
2. From the shortcut menu, choose Simulate (refer to Figure 24.51).

   The Simulator opens and starts playing the track you've selected.
3. On the left side of the Simulator, click the View check box to see your subtitles (**Figure 24.52**).

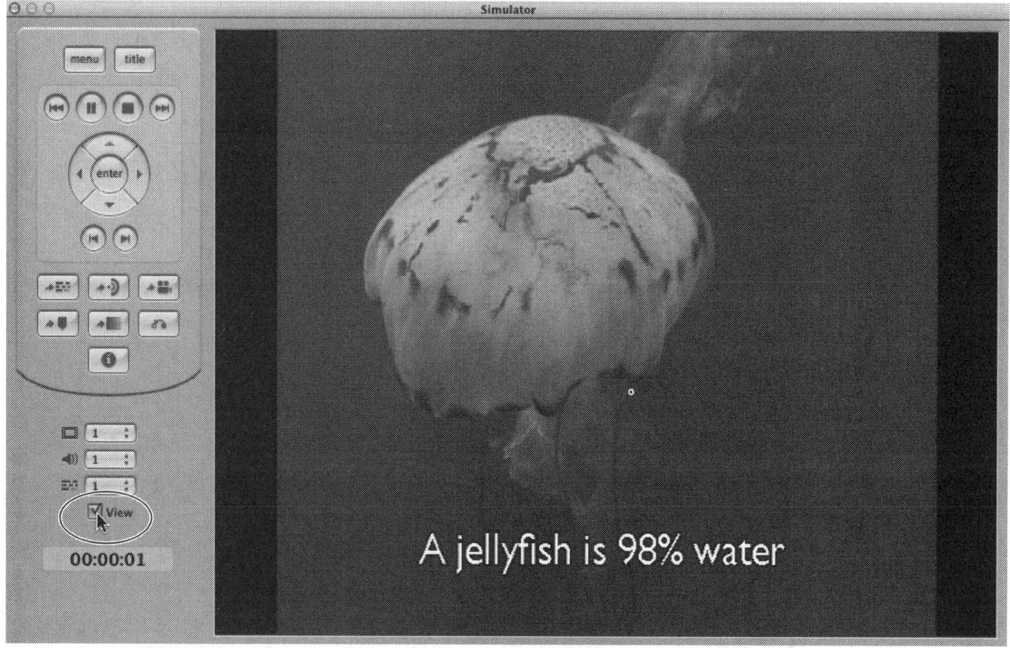

Figure 24.52 Select the Simulator's View check box to see your subtitles.

To change the subtitle stream in the Simulator:

1. Simulate a track with multiple subtitle streams. (For more information on how to simulate a track, see the steps in the previous task.)
2. In the Simulator, select a subtitle stream number from the Subtitle Stream pop-up menu (**Figure 24.53**).

   In the Simulator, the subtitle stream changes to reflect your selection (**Figure 24.54**).
3. Repeat step 2 until you have tested all of the track's subtitle streams.

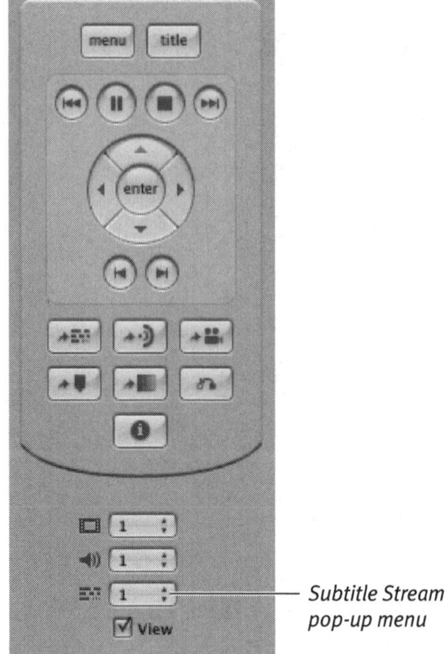

Figure 24.53 Choose the subtitle stream you want to view in the Simulator.

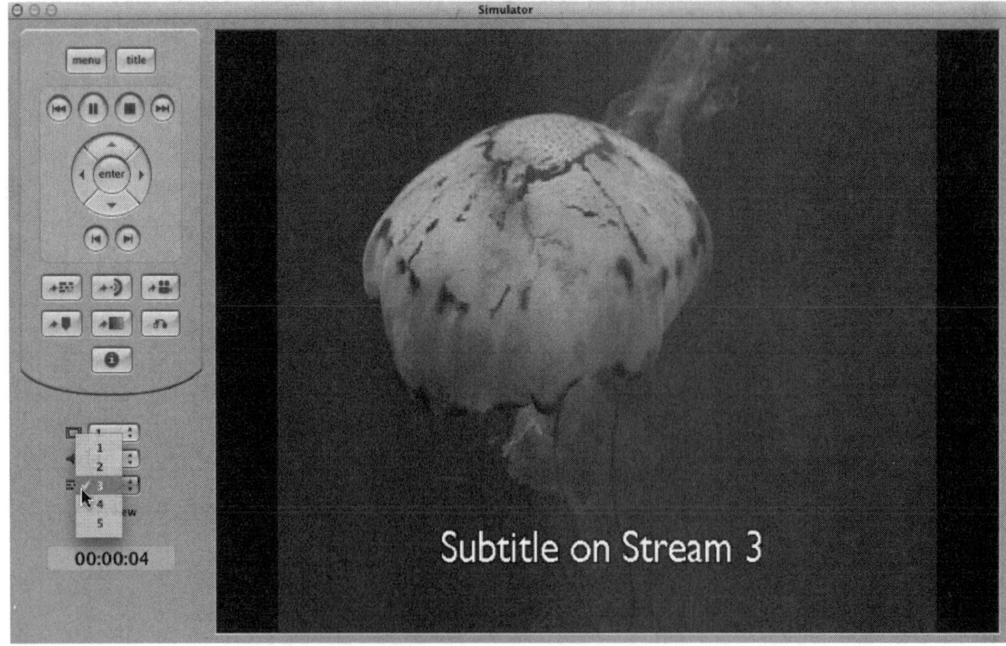

Figure 24.54 The Simulator window displays the subtitle stream you selected.

Creating Text Subtitles

Entering subtitles can be a time-consuming task. Moving the playhead along the video track and typing subtitle text is tedious at the best of times. There is an easier way: you can create subtitles by listing them in a plain-text document along with their corresponding timecode values and then import that text file straight into DVD Studio Pro's Track editor.

The only downside to using a text file to import a subtitle list is that it must be in *plain-text* format. Unicode and rich-text files—which use types of text encoding that allow you to display any special language characters—are not supported. This means that you cannot easily create alternate-language subtitles that require special characters, such as those used in Japanese, Greek, or Hebrew.

You have three options for creating subtitles that use special characters: create subtitles directly in DVD Studio Pro, create a series of graphic files, or create a bitmap-based subtitle stream using a third-party subtitling application. DVD Studio Pro supports the following subtitle formats:

- STL (Spruce Technologies format)
- SON (Sonic bitmap-based format)
- TXT (plain text)
- SCR (Daiken-Comtec Laboratories Scenarist bitmap-based format)

Creating subtitles in a text file does have several advantages; not only is the process quick, but you can also use your word processing program to spell check your subtitles. The greatest benefit, however, comes when you need to translate the subtitles into other languages (other than those that use special characters). Rather than struggle through the translation yourself, you can simply send the text file to a translator. When the translated text file is returned, you just import the file into the Track editor.

SPU Not Supported?

You cannot directly import files with the .spu extension that were created in DVD Studio Pro 1.*x*'s Subtitle editor. You can, however, create a project in DVD Studio Pro 1.*x* that uses the Subtitle editor's SPU subtitle streams and import that entire project into DVD Studio Pro 3. Note, though, that SPU files are imported as TIFF overlay graphic subtitles, which cannot be edited.

Formatting the text file

The text file contains a list of all of your subtitles with their corresponding timecodes.

There is one important point to keep in mind: *the timecode that you type in your text subtitle files corresponds to the source video timecode,* not the timecode displayed in DVD Studio Pro's Track editor. The source video timecode is the video's exact timecode when output from Final Cut Pro. You need to write down a list of timecodes when you are working in your video-editing software before you encode all of your video to the MPEG-2 format.

If you didn't write down a list of source video timecode values before encoding the video to MPEG-2, you can still view the source timecode in DVD Studio Pro. Simply Control-click anywhere on the timeline (time scale) and select Asset-Based Timecode from the shortcut menu (**Figure 24.55**).

Each subtitle in the text list must have these three values, all separated by a comma followed by a single space (**Figure 24.56**):

- **Start timecode.** The beginning of the subtitle clip.
- **End timecode.** The end of the subtitle clip.
- **Subtitle text.** The text for the subtitle clip.

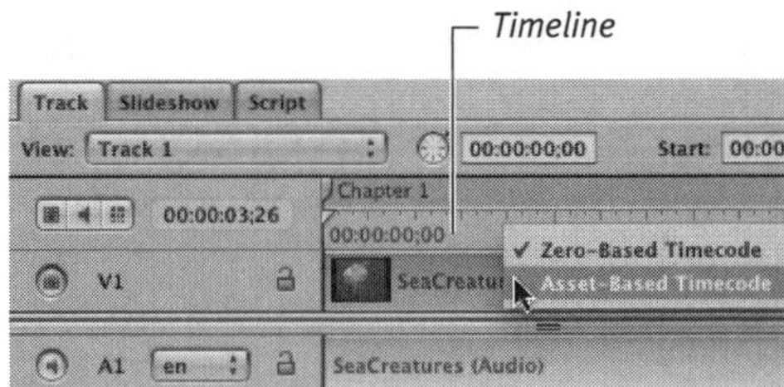

Figure 24.55 Control-click anywhere on the timeline to display this shortcut menu.

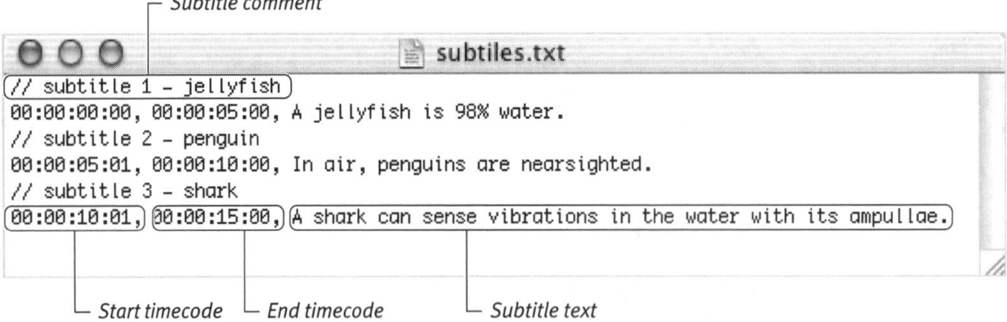

Figure 24.56 The plain-text file must have at least three values: the start timecode, the end timecode, and the subtitle text. Comments are optional.

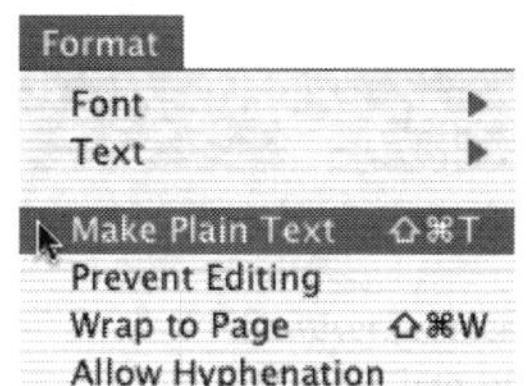

Figure 24.57 To convert a rich-text document to plain text in TextEdit, choose Format > Make Plain Text.

Figure 24.58 Save your plain-text file as Western (Mac OS Roman).

You can add comments for yourself or for the person to whom you are passing off the subtitle text file by typing two forward slashes (//) at the beginning of the text (refer to Figure 24.56). The comment will appear only in the text file; it will not be imported into DVD Studio Pro.

The subtitle text file must be plain text. If you've created your text in Apple's TextEdit program, the default document type is rich text, which must be converted to plain text.

To convert a rich-text document to plain text in TextEdit:

1. Choose Format > Make Plain Text (**Figure 24.57**), or press Shift-Command-T.
2. Choose Western (Mac OS Roman) from the Plain Text Encoding pop-up menu (**Figure 24.58**).

   When you save your plain-text file in TextEdit, make sure your file is saved as Western (Mac OS Roman). DVD Studio Pro doesn't support other formats.

Importing Text Subtitles

Before you import your text subtitles, make sure that your subtitle text and color default preferences are set and that the video asset used in your subtitle track has been assigned to the track.

Text lists cannot be imported into the Track editor if a video asset hasn't been assigned. When you import your text list of subtitles, DVD Studio Pro will create individual subtitle clips in the specified subtitle stream. Once the list is imported, you can edit the individual subtitle clips as if you had manually created them in the Track editor.

✔ Tip

- Imported text subtitles use your default subtitle text font and color preferences.

To import subtitles from a text file:

1. In DVD Studio Pro's Outline or Graphical view, double-click a track that has video assigned to it (**Figure 24.59**).

   The track opens in the Track editor.

2. In the Track editor, Control-click the gray area of the first subtitle stream.

   The subtitle shortcut menu appears (**Figure 24.60**).

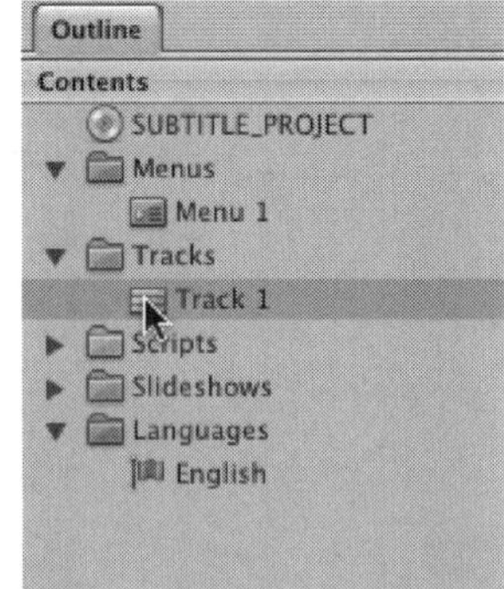

Figure 24.59 Double-click a track project item in the Outline view (top), and it opens in the Track editor (bottom).

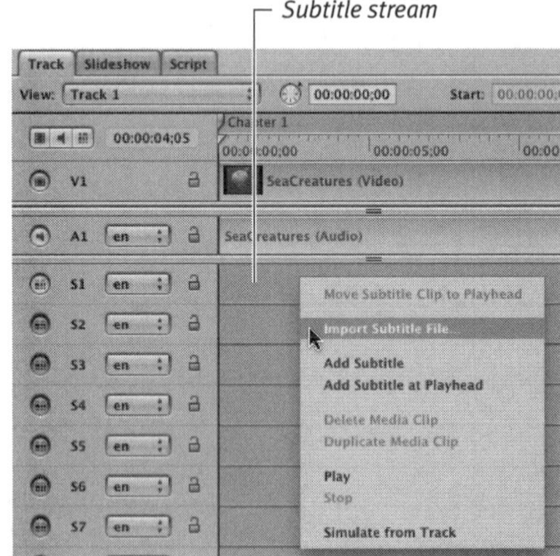

Figure 24.60 Control-click the first subtitle stream to open the shortcut menu.

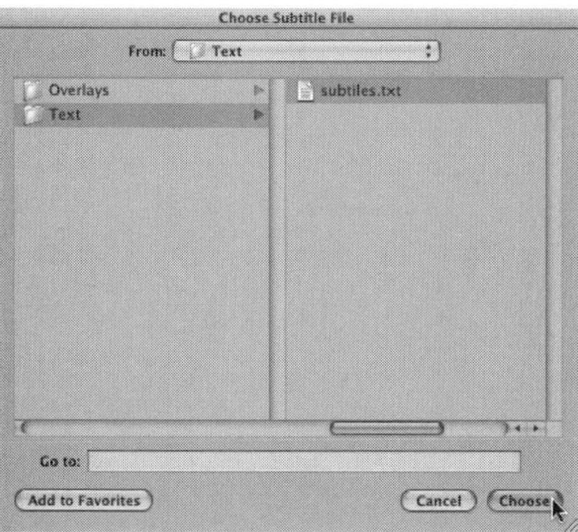

Figure 24.61 In the Choose Subtitle File dialog, navigate to your plain-text file.

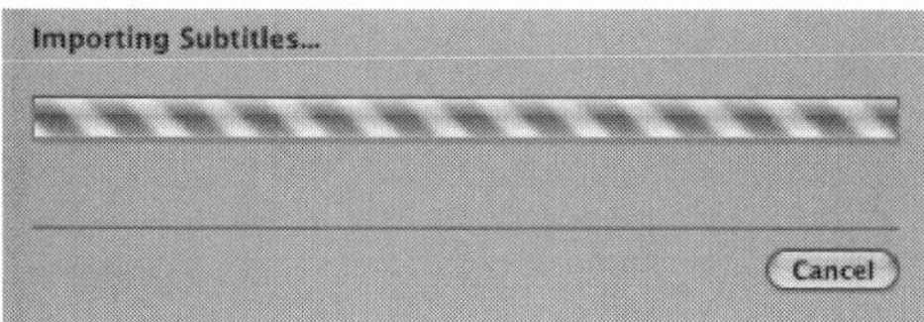

Figure 24.62 DVD Studio Pro displays a progress bar while it reads the text subtitle file.

Figure 24.63 The Subtitle Importer displays an alert to let you know how many subtitle files have been imported. Click OK to close the dialog.

Figure 24.64 Individual subtitle clips are created when the plain-text file is imported.

3. From the shortcut menu, select Import Subtitle File (refer to Figure 24.60).

   The Choose Subtitle File dialog opens (**Figure 24.61**).

4. Navigate to your plain-text subtitle file and click it to select it.

5. Click the Choose button to import the selected text file.

   DVD Studio Pro begins importing the text file, and a progress bar appears (**Figure 24.62**).

6. After the text-based subtitle file has been imported, the Subtitle Importer displays an Alert dialog telling you how many subtitle files have been imported (**Figure 24.63**). To close the Alert dialog, click the OK button.

   Individual subtitle clips are created in the specified subtitle stream, allowing you to modify each clip's settings as if you had created the subtitle clip directly in the Track editor (**Figure 24.64**).

Using Subtitle Graphics

To preserve text positioning, fonts, or special Unicode characters for use in DVD Studio Pro, you can embed your text and any fonts used in a graphic file. But that's not all subtitle graphics are good for. You can create a subtitle graphic overlay for button highlights over video, your company logo, or a video watermark. Graphic overlays can be used in conjunction with DVD Studio Pro's internal subtitle text features or on their own.

If you've read Chapter 15, you learned how to create overlay graphics for use with menus. Subtitle graphics use the same types of files. For more information on how to create overlay graphics in Photoshop and for details on supported graphics formats, see that chapter.

You can add a graphic file from the Finder to the Track editor's subtitle stream in two ways:

- Drag a file directly onto the subtitle stream.
- Import a file from within the Subtitle Inspector.

Either way, DVD Studio Pro will link the graphic on your hard disk to the subtitle clip. The graphic file never actually gets imported into DVD Studio Pro's Assets container, but rather, DVD Studio Pro links the graphic file to the subtitle clip and uses it when multiplexing the video stream (see Chapter 20, "Outputting the Project," for information on multiplexing).

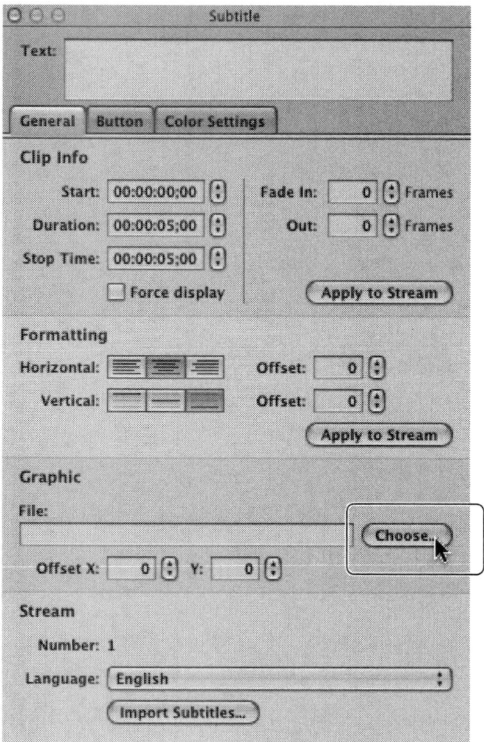

Figure 24.65 Click the Choose button to choose a graphic file.

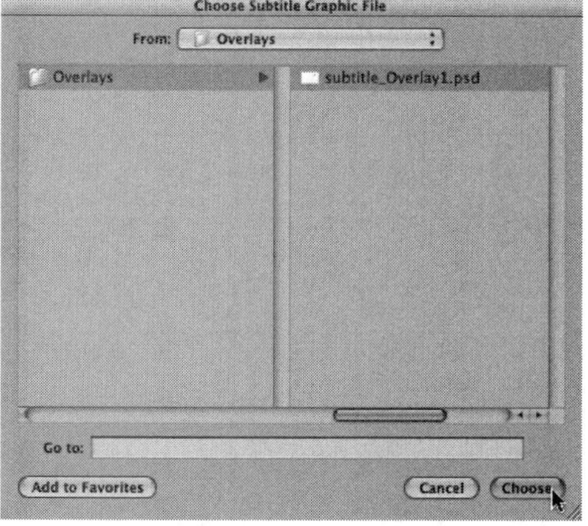

Figure 24.66 Navigate to the graphic file that you want to import, select it, and click Choose.

To import a graphic file using the Subtitle Inspector:

1. In the Track editor, create a subtitle clip.
2. Click the subtitle clip to select it.

   The Inspector updates to display the subtitle's properties. The General tab opens by default.
3. In the Subtitle Inspector's Graphic section, click the Choose button (**Figure 24.65**).

   The Choose Subtitle Graphic File dialog opens (**Figure 24.66**).
4. In the Choose Subtitle Graphic File dialog, navigate to the graphic file on your hard disk that you want to import and click it to select it.

continues on next page

5. Click Choose.

   The graphic's file path to the hard disk is listed in the Subtitle Inspector's File text box, and the graphic is set for the selected subtitle clip (**Figure 24.67**).

✔ Tip

- The graphic appears over the video on the Viewer tab. If the graphic file isn't lined up exactly where you want it, you can offset the overlay to move it to the desired location. To offset your graphic overlay, in the Subtitle Inspector's Graphic section, click the up and down arrows next to the Offset X and Y text boxes, or type location values in the X- and Y-axis text boxes (**Figure 24.68**).

To remove a graphic file:

◆ On the Subtitle Inspector's General tab, in the Graphic section, triple-click the File text box to select all text and then press the Delete key (**Figure 24.69**).

The graphics file is no longer attached to the subtitle clip.

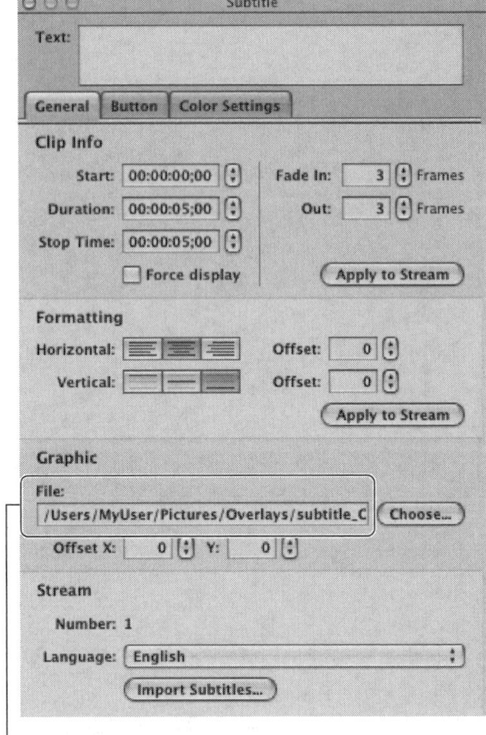

Figure 24.67 The Inspector displays the graphic file's path.

Figure 24.68 Move an overlay graphic to the desired location by offsetting it.

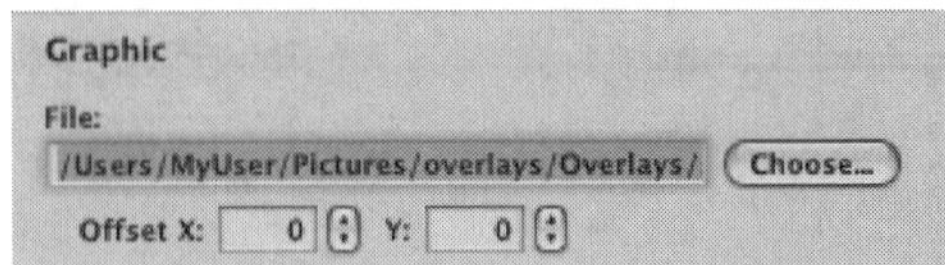

Figure 24.69 Select all of the text in the File text box and press Delete to remove the graphic file.

Adding Closed Captions

Generally, subtitles are intended to provide a text translation of the movie for hearing audiences. Although closed captions are similar to subtitles in that they display text on top of video, they are designed for the hearing impaired. Closed captions provide extra text to also translate all of the video's audio, including sound effects, such as a door slamming or the wind howling.

Subtitles can be viewed by pressing the Subtitle button on a DVD player's remote control. Closed captions, however, are disguised within the video signal in what's called the vertical blanking area (VBA). The VBA requires special decoders to view the closed-caption signal. You can purchase an external decoder to see closed captions (also known as Line 21, because that's the line they're stored on in the VBA), but most TVs have built-in decoders. (Note that computers do not have built-in decoders to view closed captions; you can't preview them on any computer.)

The method used to disguise closed captions within a video stream was developed in the United States, which uses an NTSC video stream. Closed captions can store two characters in each video frame. NTSC video displays 30 frames per second (29.97 actually), so roughly 60 characters can be displayed every second. Because of the way Line 21 is added to video, only NTSC video streams can have closed captions. PAL actually has its own methods for providing captioning for the hearing impaired, but DVD Studio Pro currently doesn't support PAL captioning.

You cannot create closed captions directly in DVD Studio Pro. You need to use specialized equipment or closed-captioning software like CPC's MacCaption (`www.ccaption.com`). Special service providers can provide closed-caption files that sync with your video. Closed-captioning specialists will transcribe all audible spoken word and sound effects and then produce Line 21–compatible caption files for you. Most captioning specialists will test the files and timing for you before passing off the file. If you do have someone else prepare the files for you, let the person know that DVD Studio Pro supports both .cc and .scc closed-captioning file types.

There are two fields that can be used on Line 21 to store the captions: Field 1 (top recorded) and Field 2 (bottom recorded). You can use the two fields to provide two closed-caption versions of your movie in two different languages; usually Field 1 is used for English captions, and Field 2 is used for Spanish. In DVD Studio Pro, you can either set Field 1 to be displayed or set both fields to be displayed; you cannot set Field 2 to play by itself.

Factoring in the Subpicture Stream

When your project is multiplexed, subtitles are stored in a special graphics layer called the *subpicture stream*. The subpicture stream uses a maximum of four colors to display text (Text, Outline 1, Outline 2, and Background). Subpicture streams take up little space when compared to MPEG-2 video, but you still must account for them when determining your project's bit rate.

All subpictures are multiplexed right along with the video and audio streams to create the finished DVD-Video, so if your project uses several subtitle streams, you should prepare for an increase in your DVD-Video's overall bit rate. (For more information on creating a bit budget, see Appendix A, "Surviving on a Bit Budget.")

Assigning closed-caption files to tracks

Once your closed-captioning file has been generated, you need to assign the file to your track in the Track Inspector. DVD Studio Pro will link the closed-caption file on your hard disk and later multiplex the file along with your video stream when you build the project.

To assign a closed-caption file to a track:

1. In DVD Studio Pro's Outline view, select a track with video assigned to it (**Figure 24.70**).

   The Inspector updates to display the track's properties.
2. In the Track Inspector, click the Other tab (**Figure 24.71**).

   The closed-caption settings are displayed.
3. In the Closed Caption (Line 21) section, click the Choose button to choose a .cc or .scc closed-caption file.

   The Choose Line21 File dialog opens (**Figure 24.72**).

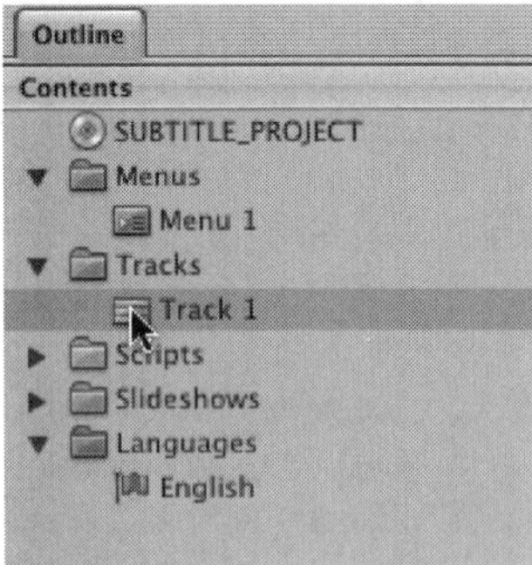

Figure 24.70 Select a track in the Outline view to view its properties in the Inspector.

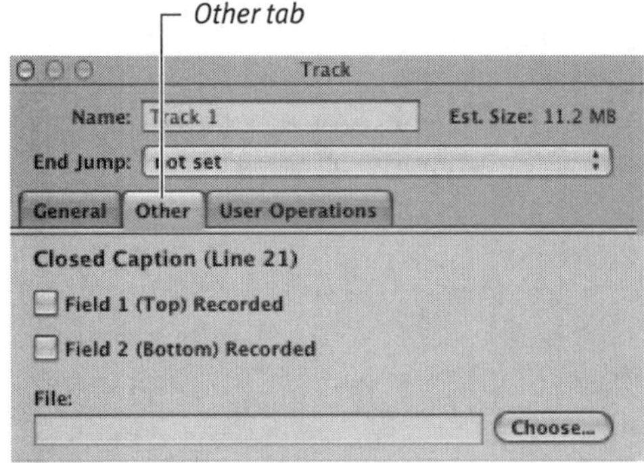

Figure 24.71 The Other tab hosts the closed-caption settings.

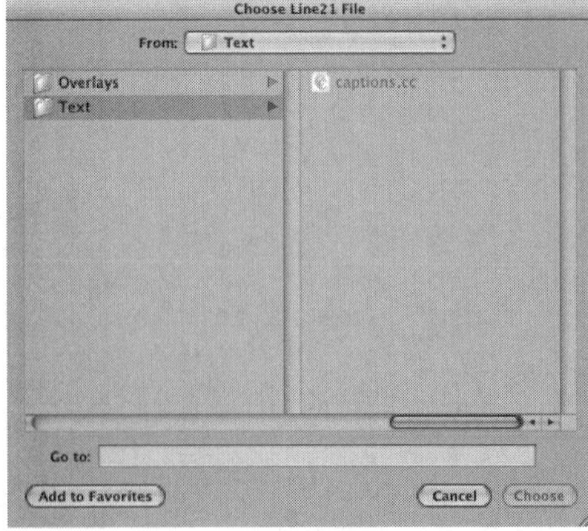

Figure 24.72 Navigate to your closed caption file, select it, and click the Choose button to open the Choose Line21 File dialog.

Field 1 check box

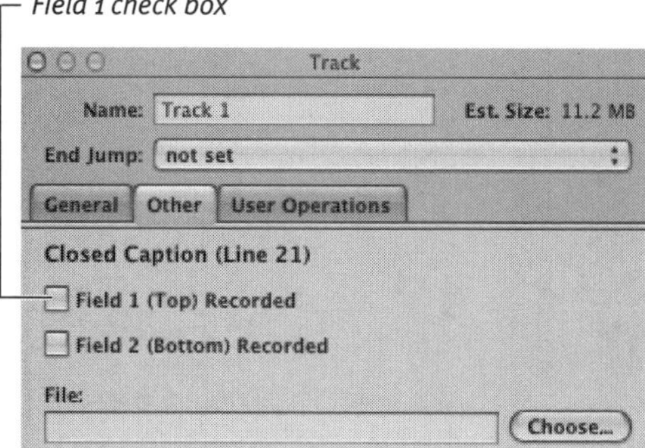

Figure 24.73 Select the Field 1 check box to assign a closed-caption file to a track.

4. In the Choose Line21 File dialog, navigate to your closed-caption file on your hard disk and click it to select it.
5. Click Choose to set the file.

   The file is set, and the Choose Line21 File dialog closes.
6. Back in the Track Inspector, select the Field 1 (Top) Recorded check box. If your closed-caption file also contains Field 2 data, select the Field 2 (Bottom) Recorded check box as well (**Figure 24.73**).

   The closed-caption file is assigned to your track.

✔ Tip

- You cannot test closed captioning on a computer. To verify that captions work as expected, you'll need to build your project to a DVD-R disc and play the DVD-Video disc in a set-top DVD-Video player.

Using Animated Subtitles

Graphic overlays can be made to appear animated by setting each subtitle clip on the stream to play for several frames before the next subtitle clip plays. When played back in real time, the subtitle stream looks like it's moving. However, DVD-Video players often can't display subtitles at the full frame rate of your video format, so to maximize the effect of your animated subtitle stream, make sure that each subtitle clip spans at least 5 to 10 frames.

25

SCRIPTING

Scripting lets you program your DVD-Video to make its own decisions. Using scripting, you can program advanced levels of interactivity into your DVD-Video—levels of interactivity not available by just linking project items together using end jumps and target actions. For example, using scripting you can program a menu to loop only a certain number of times, play your project's tracks in random order, check the aspect ratio of the viewer's DVD-Video player to ensure that your project displays either a 4:3 or 16:9 menu, and so on.

Scripting is at once rewarding and intimidating. DVD Studio Pro 3 has a scripting environment that is both powerful and easy to learn. Indeed, putting in a little effort pays huge dividends, because to really explore the potential of DVD-Video, you need to know how to script—there are things you can do with scripting that just can't be done in any other way.

When you script a DVD-Video, you are actually programming machine code. You are telling your DVD disc how to interact with the DVD-Video player, and that player (particularly if it's a set-top player) is not a very smart machine. It needs perfect code, written in a logical fashion to achieve an exact goal. There's no room for error.

But before we jump into scripting, one quick disclaimer: There is no possible way to teach every script you may need in one chapter, because there's no one perfect way to write a script. Different situations will require different scripts. Consequently, scripting takes practice, and it also takes a logical train of thought. This chapter focuses on introducing you to scripting by providing an overview of scripting in DVD Studio Pro 3. The rest is up to you.

Creating a Script

Before you can write a script, you first must add a script to your project (**Figure 25.1**). The script itself acts as a container that holds lines of commands, which you write using DVD Studio Pro's Script editor (**Figure 25.2**).

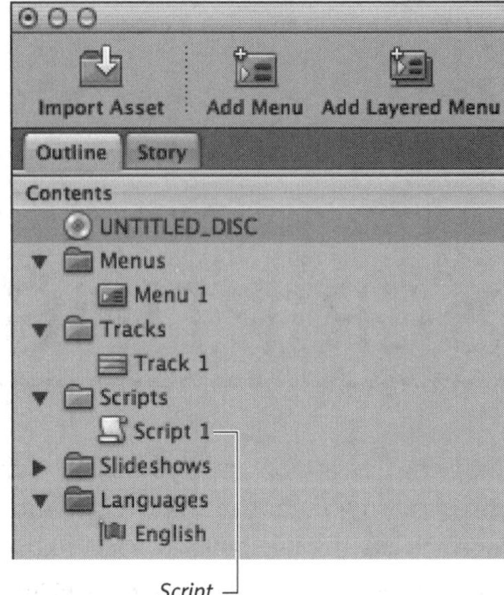

Figure 25.1 A script in the Outline view.

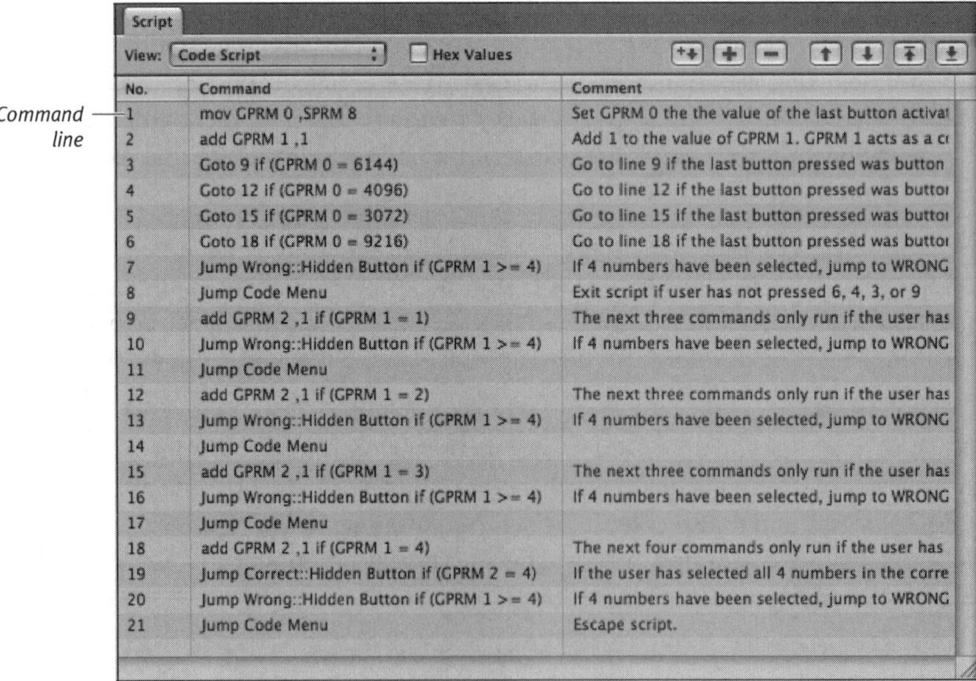

Figure 25.2 This figure shows the Script editor with 21 command lines.

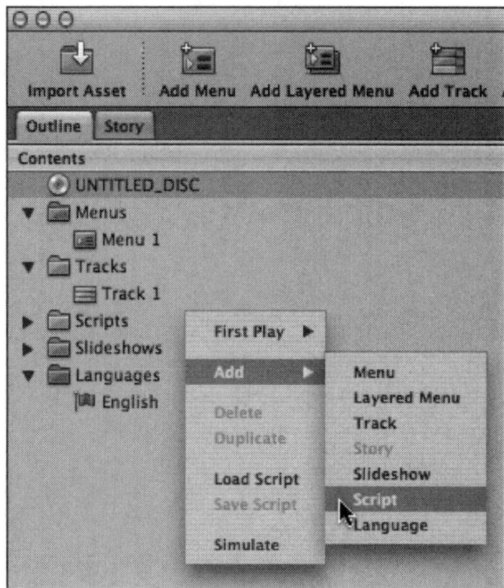

Figure 25.3 To add a script to your project, Control-click the Outline view and select Add > Script, or...

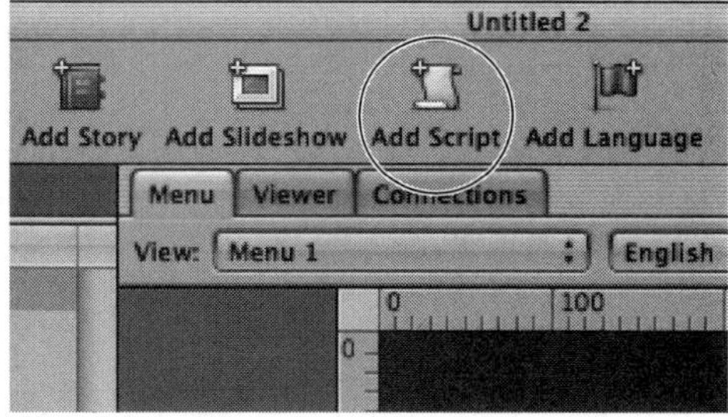

Figure 25.4 ...in the toolbar, click Add Script, or...

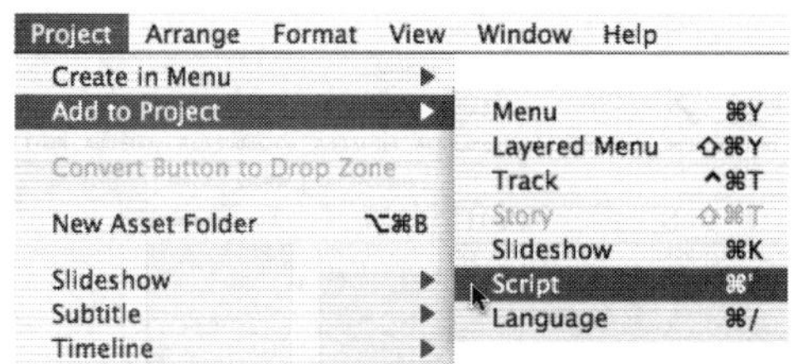

Figure 25.5 ...choose Project > Add to Project > Script.

To create a script:

- *Do one of the following:*
  - Control-click the Outline or Graphical view and choose Add > Script from the shortcut menu (**Figure 25.3**).
  - In the toolbar, click Add Script (**Figure 25.4**).
  - Choose Project > Add to Project > Script (**Figure 25.5**).
  - Press Command-' (apostrophe).

  A new script is created (refer to Figure 25.1).

Using the Script Editor

As you saw earlier, scripts are a series of commands, and these commands are programmed in DVD Studio Pro's Script editor. By default, every script is provided with a single Nop, or "no operation" command (**Figure 25.6**). The Nop command does exactly what it says—nothing! In other words, when a DVD-Video player encounters the Nop command, it literally stops and does nothing. Black screen.

Step 1 of programming a script is to change this command to something a bit more useful, and you'll learn all about that in "Programming Commands" later in this chapter. For now, let's take a quick look at how to add and delete command lines and also how to move command lines around in the Script editor.

✔ Tip

- In a prescript, the Nop command acts as an exit command. For more information, see "Using Prescripts" later in this chapter.

To open a script in the Script editor:

- ◆ In the Outline view, double-click the script.

  The Script editor opens to display the script's commands.

Creating and deleting commands

The Script editor contains three buttons for creating and deleting commands. The first button inserts a command line under the currently selected command in the Script editor, the second adds a new command line at the bottom of the command lines currently in the Script editor, and the third deletes the currently selected command line (**Figure 25.7**).

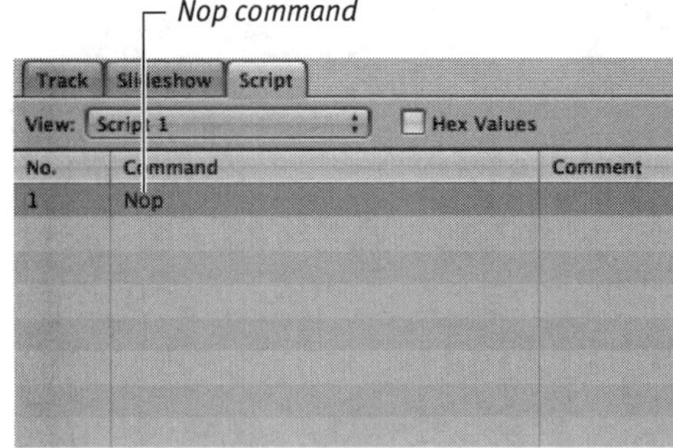

Figure 25.6 By default, the Script editor is provided with a single command: the Nop command.

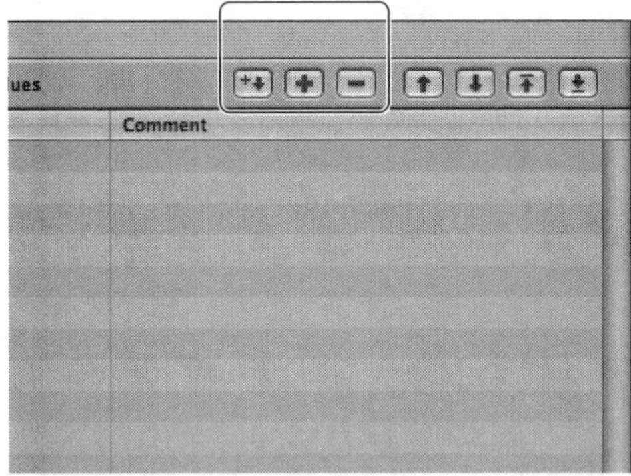

Figure 25.7 These three buttons are used to create and delete command lines.

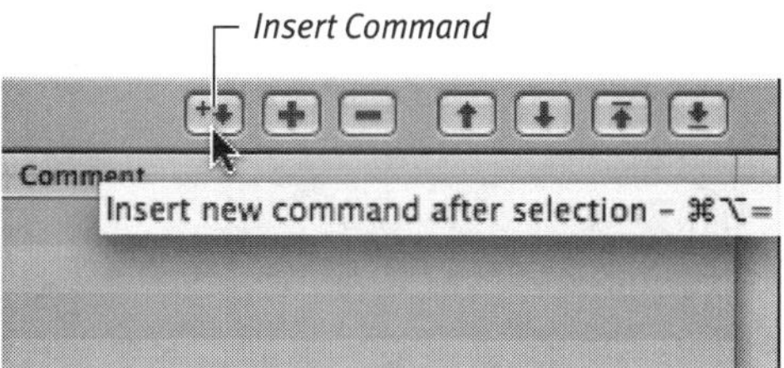

Figure 25.8 Click the Insert Command button to insert a new command line under the currently selected command line in the Script editor.

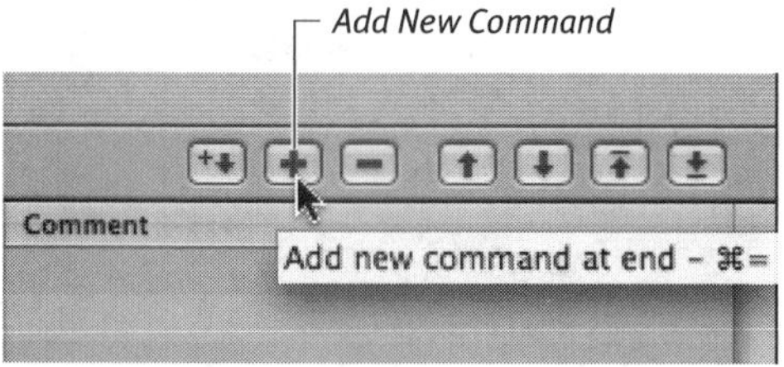

Figure 25.9 Click the Add New Command button to add a new command line at the bottom of the Script editor.

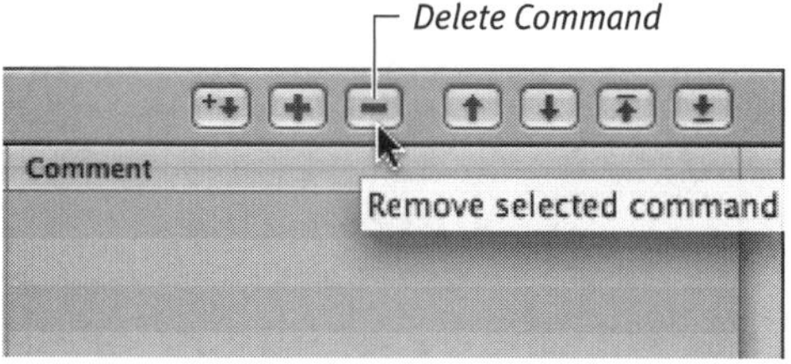

Figure 25.10 Click the Delete Command button to delete the currently selected command line.

To insert a command line:

- Click the Script editor's Insert Command button (**Figure 25.8**).

  A new command line is inserted under the currently selected command line.

To create a new command line:

- Click the Script editor's Add New Command button (**Figure 25.9**).

  A new command line is added at the bottom of the Script editor.

To delete a command line:

- Do one of the following:
  - Click the Script editor's Delete Command button (**Figure 25.10**).
  - Press the Delete key.

  The currently selected command line is deleted.

To copy and paste a command line:

1. In the Script editor, select the command line.
2. Press Command-C to copy the command line to the clipboard.
3. Press Command-V to past the copied command line back into the Script editor.

Reordering command lines

When a DVD-Video player executes a script, it progresses line by line, from the top down. Consequently, as you work through the logic of your scripts, you will often need to shuffle command lines up and down in the Script editor to ensure that they are all in the correct order. You can either grab the command line and drag it up or down the Script editor or use the four buttons at the top right of the Script editor (**Figure 25.11**).

To reorder command lines:

- *Do any of the following:*
  - Grab a command line and drag it to a new position in the Script editor.
  - Use the Move Command Up One Line button to move the selected command up one line (refer to Figure 25.11).
  - Use the Move Command Down One Line button to move the selected command down one line (refer to Figure 25.11).
  - Use the Move Command to Top of Script Editor button to move the selected command to the top of the Script editor (refer to Figure 25.11).
  - Use the Move Command to Bottom of Script Editor button to move the selected command to the bottom of the Script editor (refer to Figure 25.11).

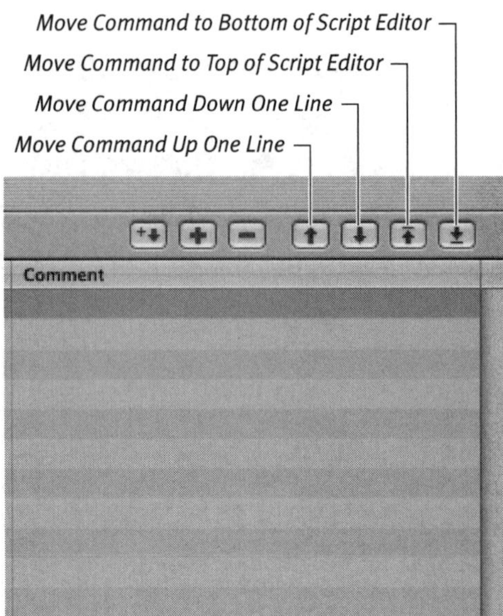

Figure 25.11 These four buttons are used to reorder command lines in the Script editor.

Using Prescripts

Prescripts are attached to menus, tracks, and slideshows. As the name implies, prescripts run *before* the item they are attached to is displayed, instead of afterward. Other than that, you create prescripts exactly the same way as normal scripts.

Prescripts are useful whenever you need your DVD-Video to make a decision before a project item is displayed. For example, if a track has several audio streams, you can use a prescript to determine which audio stream to play. Prescripts are often attached to menus to look at the last project item played to determine which button should be selected when the menu appears on the screen.

When it comes to prescripts, you need to keep one thing in mind: *a prescript is executed only when you jump to the root of the item that the prescript is attached to* (**Figure 25.12**). Note the word *root* in the last sentence, because this is important. The root of an item is the item itself. For example, the root of a menu is the menu, and not the menu's buttons, while the root of a track is the track, and not the track's chapters. Consequently, *if you jump directly to a button or to a track chapter, a prescript attached to the menu or track will not run.*

✔ Tip

- Unlike a prescript, a selection condition will run whenever you jump to any part of a project item, including a button or chapter.

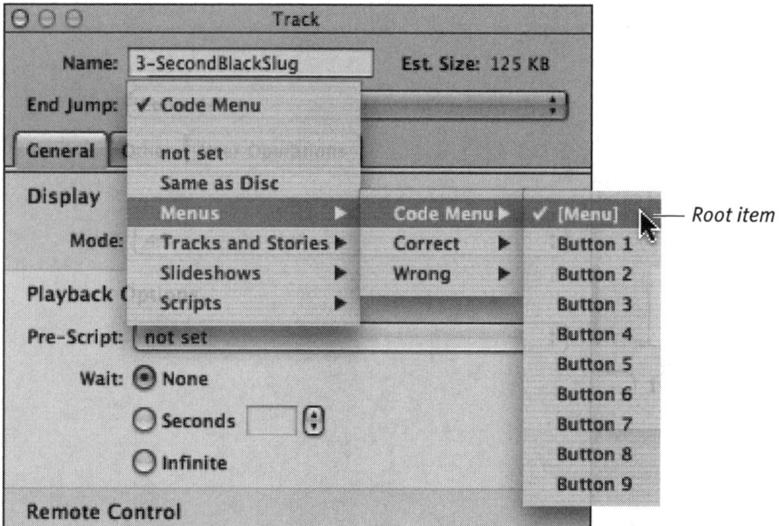

Figure 25.12 In DVD Studio Pro's target menus, the root of an item is always enclosed in square brackets.

To assign a prescript to a menu, track, or slideshow:

1. In the Outline view, select the menu, track, or slideshow.

   The Inspector updates to display the selected item's properties.

2. On the General tab of the Track or Slideshow Inspector (**Figure 25.13**) or the Advanced tab of the Menu Inspector (**Figure 25.14**), locate the Prescript setting.

3. From the Prescript setting, choose a script.

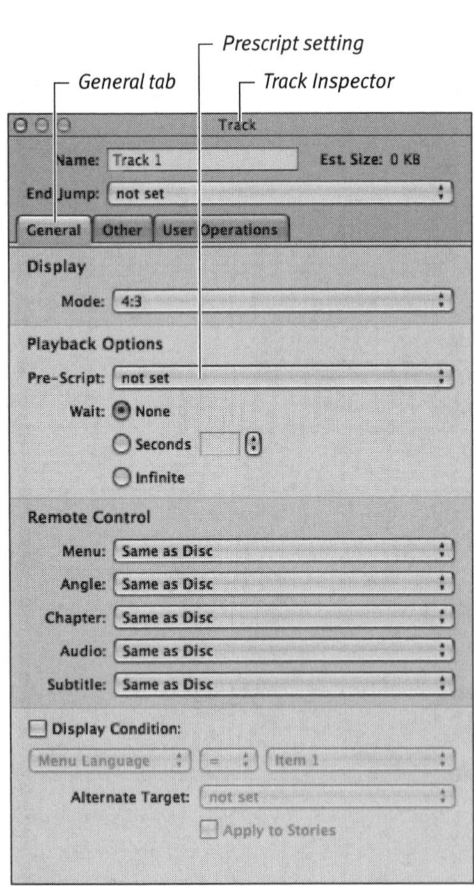

Figure 25.13 In the Track and Slideshow Inspectors, the Prescript setting is on the General tab.

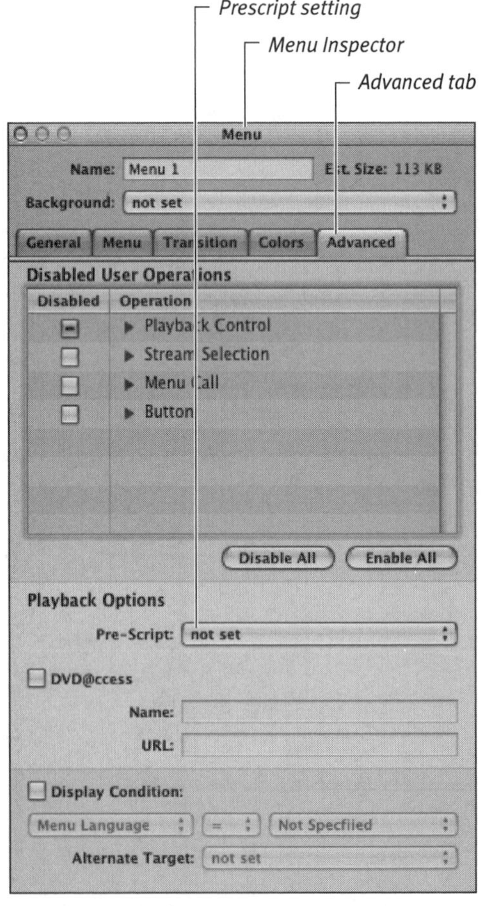

Figure 25.14 In the Menu Inspector, the Prescript setting is on the Advanced tab.

Programming Commands

Unlike DVD Studio Pro 1.5, where you could simply type your script directly into the Script editor, in DVD Studio Pro 3 all script commands are configured using the Inspector. When you select a command line in the Script editor, the Inspector updates to show you the command's properties, and it's here that all the heavy lifting takes place (**Figure 25.15**).

When a DVD-Video player executes a script, it starts at the first command and then progresses sequentially through the script, line after line. If a command line can be executed, it is. If a command line cannot be executed, the DVD-Video player doesn't stop; it simply moves on to the next command line. (See the sidebar "Using Escape Commands.")

continues on next page

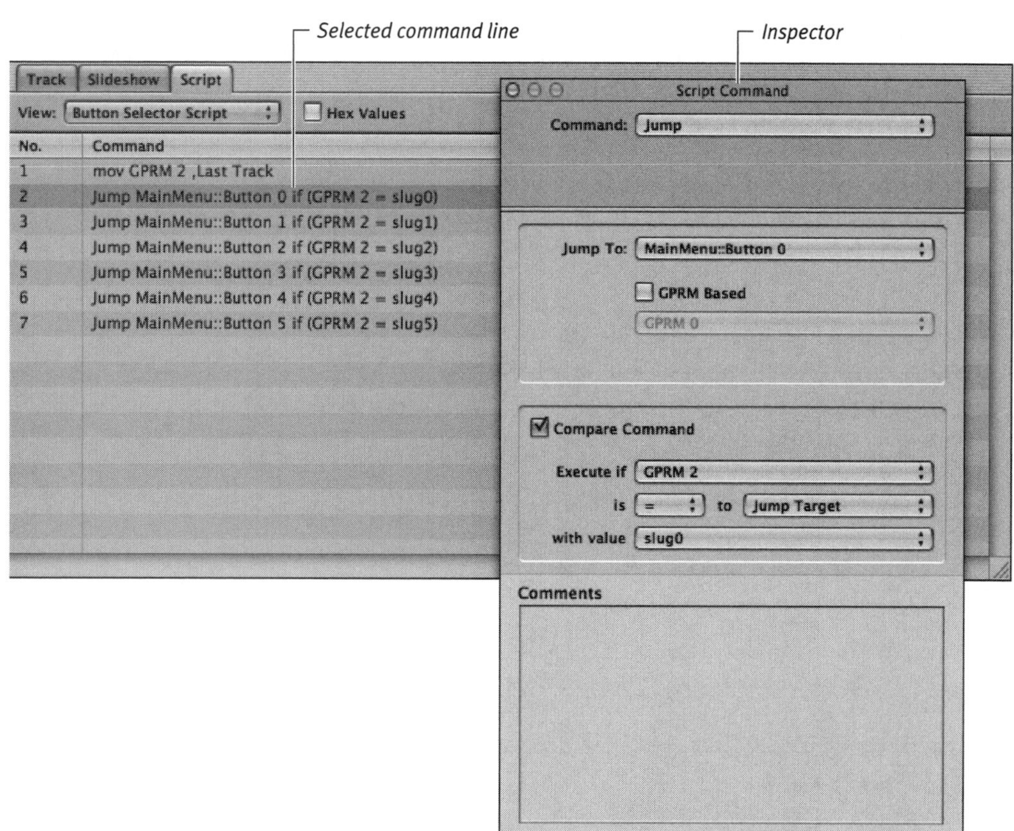

Figure 25.15 When you select a command line in the Script editor, the Inspector updates to display the command's properties. It's here, in the Inspector, that you actually write the script.

DVD Studio Pro 3 offers exactly 10 different commands (**Figure 25.16**). While this may seem restrictive, you can program pretty much anything you want with these commands. It just takes a bit of practice and a little planning. In fact, you can do so much with these commands that this chapter can't show you how to use each and every one. Instead, we will focus on a few of the most popular commands. Once you have a bit of experience using the commands in this chapter, the others will fall into place. For a description of what the other commands do, see the DVD Studio Pro manual, page 449.

✔ Tips

- Each script can contain a maximum of 128 different commands.
- Because command lines are executed in a linear progression, you must take care to ensure that the logic of your scripts makes sense. For example, if you are loading a GPRM with a value (see "About GPRMs" later in this chapter), you must not place that command line after a Jump command. If you do so, the DVD-Video player will execute the Jump command before loading the value into the GPRM.

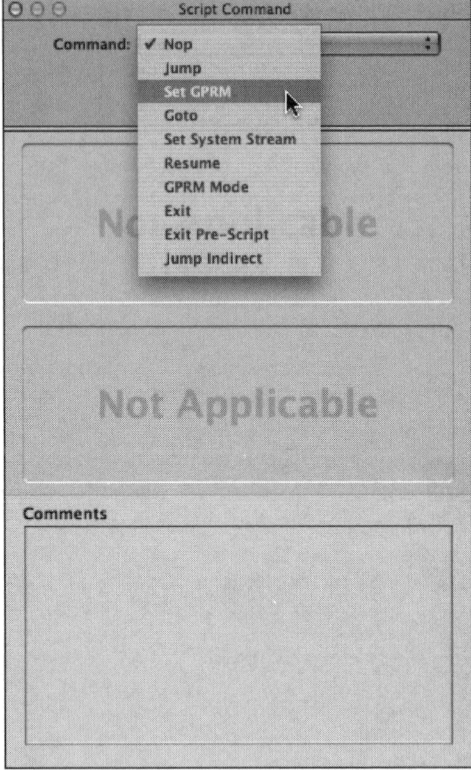

Figure 25.16 The Script Inspector's Command menu displays all 10 commands available to scripts in DVD Studio Pro 3.

Using Escape Commands

An escape command is a command at the end of a script that jumps to a "safe" target, such as the DVD-Video's main menu (**Figure 25.17**). An escape command is an important part of any script, as it guards against potential logical errors that can unexpectedly stop playback of your DVD. As you've seen earlier, DVD-Video players execute command lines from the top down, until a command line is found that jumps to a different program item. If the DVD-Video player gets to the last line of the script and has still not found a suitable jump action, the script will stop—and so will your project. (Note, in the case of a prescript, that if no Jump command is executed, the DVD-Video player jumps to the root of the item that the prescript is attached to.)

To guard against this situation, it's always a good idea to place a Jump command at the end of each script. Target that Jump command at an appropriate project item and rest safe in the knowledge that your project will continue to play even if there's an error in your script's logic.

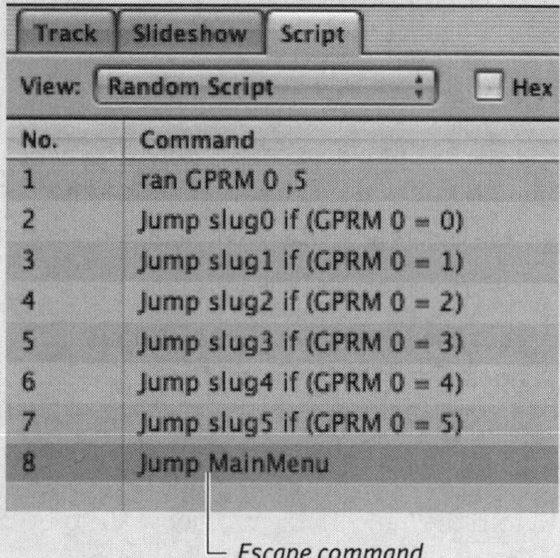

Figure 25.17 An escape command is a jump action at the end of the script that tells the DVD-Video player what to do if it finds no executable command lines in the script.

Using the Jump command

You use the Jump command to script a jump to a different project item. It accomplishes exactly the same thing as a button target or track end jump. The Jump command is easy to use, so let's whet our scripting appetite by taking a look at this command.

To program a Jump command:

1. In the Script editor, create a new command line and make sure it is selected.

   The Inspector updates to display the command's properties.

2. From the Inspector's Command menu, choose Jump (**Figure 25.18**).

   Directly below the Inspector's Command menu, a Jump To menu appears.

3. From the Jump To menu, choose the project item that you want the command line to jump to (**Figure 25.19**).

   Notice that the Jump To menu looks exactly the same as the menu that appears when you set a button target or track end jump—and it does exactly the same thing.

   In the Script editor, your Jump command is displayed (**Figure 25.20**).

4. Assign the script that contains this Jump command to a track end jump or button target.

   And there you have it—you've just scripted a Jump action.

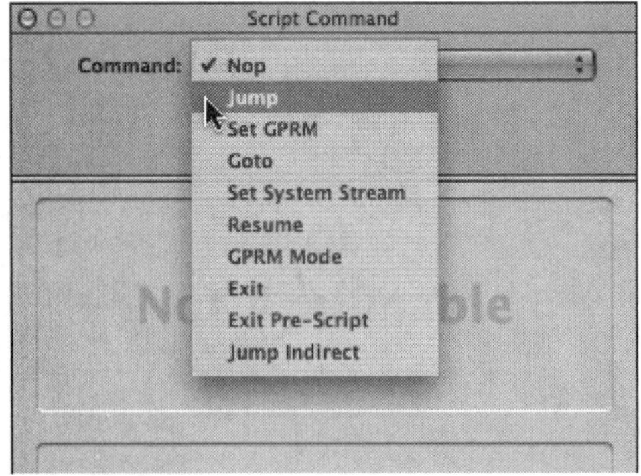

Figure 25.18 Choose Jump from the Inspector's Command menu.

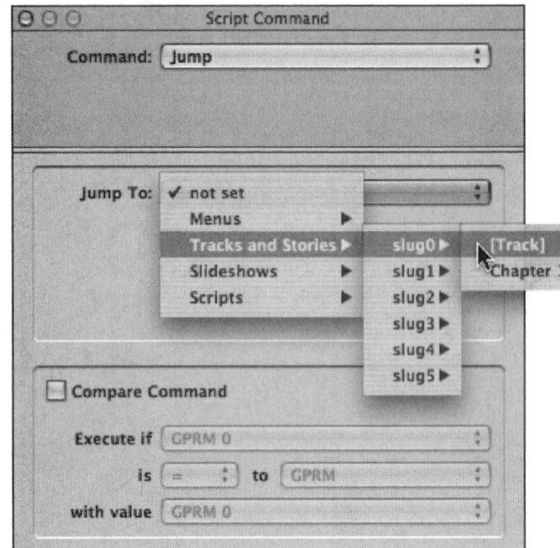

Figure 25.19 Use the Inspector's Jump To menu to select the project item that you want the Jump command to target.

Figure 25.20 In the Script editor, your Jump command is displayed.

Programming Commands

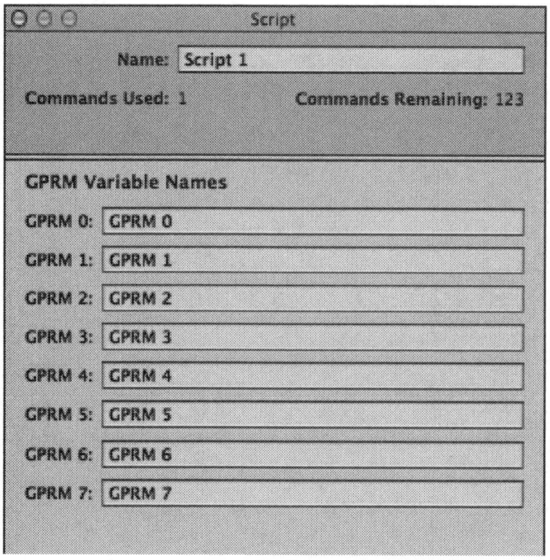

Figure 25.21 There are eight GPRMs available to your projects.

Using Parameter Registers

DVD-Video players have two types of parameter registers that hold information that controls how the DVD-Video plays. These registers are called GPRMs (general parameter registers, or general parameter register memory) and SPRMs (system parameter registers, or system parameter register memory).

About GPRMs

GPRMs are central to any script you write in DVD Studio Pro. In fact, 99 percent of the time your scripts will begin with a Set GPRM command. The reason? GPRMs are the DVD-Video equivalent of a variable. Because they are variables, you can both read and write to GPRMs.

You can load a GPRM with almost any value you want, including numbers, project items, and even the value contained in an SPRM. A typical script involves loading a GPRM with a value and then using successive command lines to check that value and execute a different command. For example, you can use a special DVD-Video function called Last Track to load a GPRM with the last track played in your project. Depending on the value in the GPRM (the last track played), the script could then jump to the correct button on a menu.

✔ Tip

- There are eight GPRMs available to your projects (**Figure 25.21**).

About SPRMs

SPRMs hold information about your DVD-Video as it plays, including information about the last button selected or last track played and about the way the DVD-Video player is set up, including its language and aspect ratio. Unlike with GPRMs, you cannot write to SPRMs, but you can read them with your scripts, which allows you to program your DVD-Video with complex decision-making capabilities. For example, you can check SPRM 8 to see which button was last selected, or SPRM 7 to determine which chapter was just playing.

DVD-Video players use 24 different SPRMs. To see a list of these SPRMs and their possible values, refer to page 457 of the DVD Studio Pro manual (the full manual is available from DVD Studio Pro's Help menu).

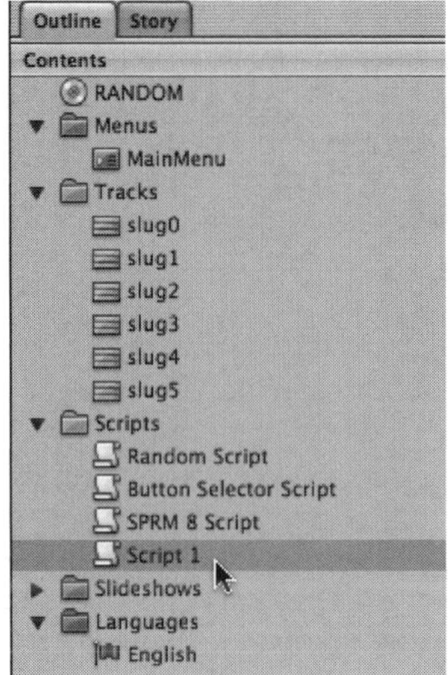

Figure 25.22 To customize the names of your project's GPRMs, begin by selecting any script in the Outline view.

Naming GPRMs

By default, GPRMs are named GPRM 0 through GPRM 7. To make your scripts more readable, you can customize GPRM names to anything you like.

To customize GPRM names:

1. In the Outline view, select a script (**Figure 25.22**).

   The Inspector updates to show a list of your Project's eight GPRMs (**Figure 25.23**).

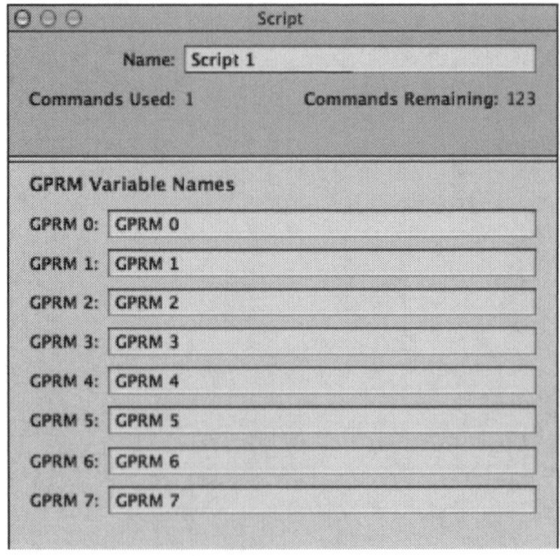

Figure 25.23 The Inspector updates to display a list of the project's GPRMs.

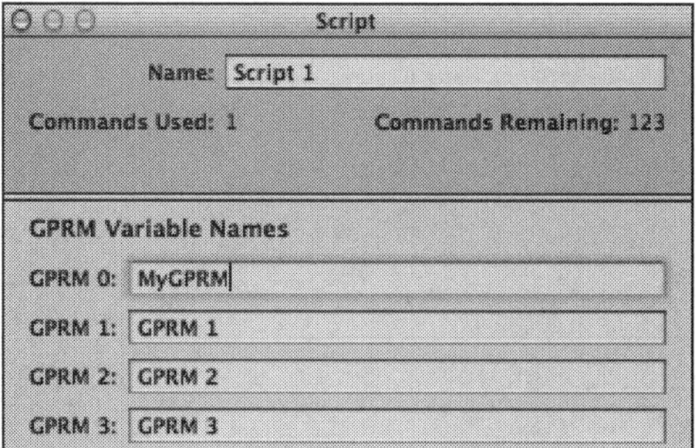

Figure 25.24 Type a name in the text box beside each GPRM you want to rename.

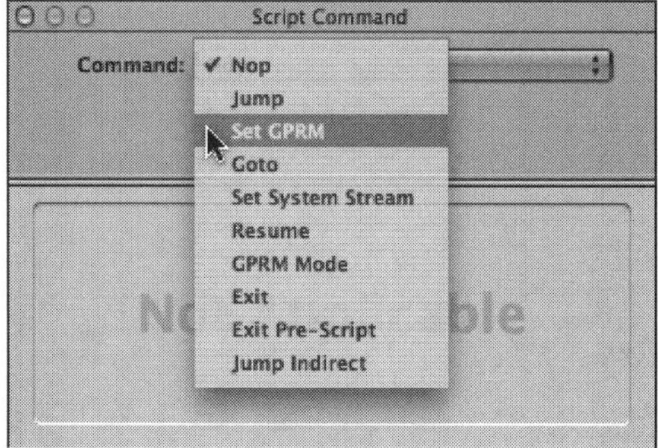

Figure 25.25 Use the Set GPRM command to provide a GPRM with a value.

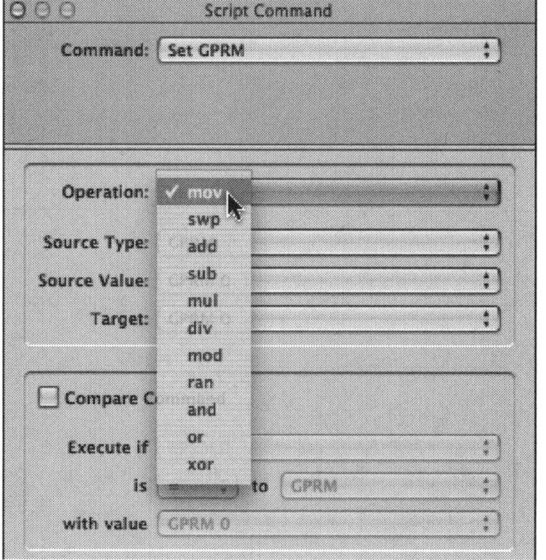

Figure 25.26 The Operation setting determines how a value is written to the GPRM.

2. In the text box beside the GPRMs, enter your new names (**Figure 25.24**).

   In your scripts, the new GPRM names will be used instead of the default GPRM names.

✔ Tip

- You can also name GPRMs by selecting the disc in the Outline view and then switching to the Inspector's Advanced tab.

Setting GPRMs

Setting a GPRM is the process of filling a GPRM with a value. By default, all GPRMs are automatically set to the value 0 whenever a disc is inserted into the DVD-Video player. However, you can easily change a GPRM's value using the Set GPRM command (**Figure 25.25**). Once you initiate a Set GPRM command, the Inspector updates to display an Operation area, which you use to define the value given to the GPRM (**Figure 25.26**). This is where your work becomes complex, because you have 11 operations to choose from. For a detailed description of each operation, refer to page 449 of the DVD Studio Pro manual.

continues on next page

If you are new to scripting, the operations that are most important are Mov, Add, and Ran. In DVD Studio Pro, Mov (move) is the same thing as the equal sign (=) in other scripting languages, Add adds a value to the value currently stored in a GPRM, and Ran tells the DVD-Video player to generate a random number.

Once you've selected an operation type, you have to configure the operation by choosing a source type, source value, and target (**Figure 25.27**).

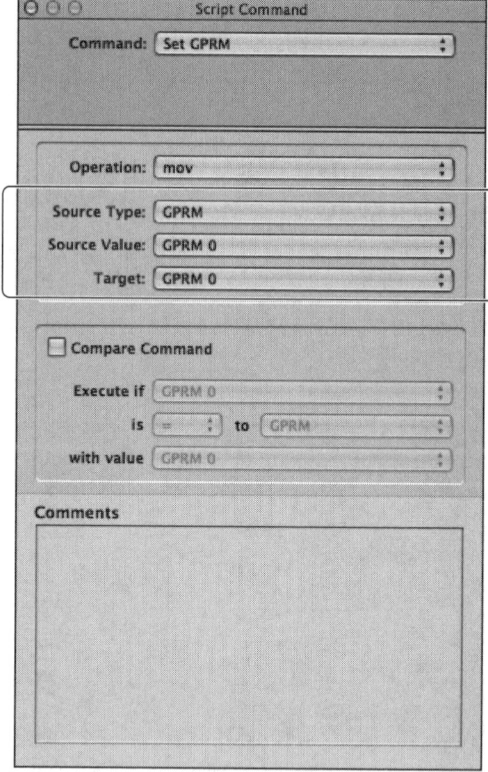

Figure 25.27 After you select a type of operation, you configure the operation using the Source Type, Source Value, and Target settings.

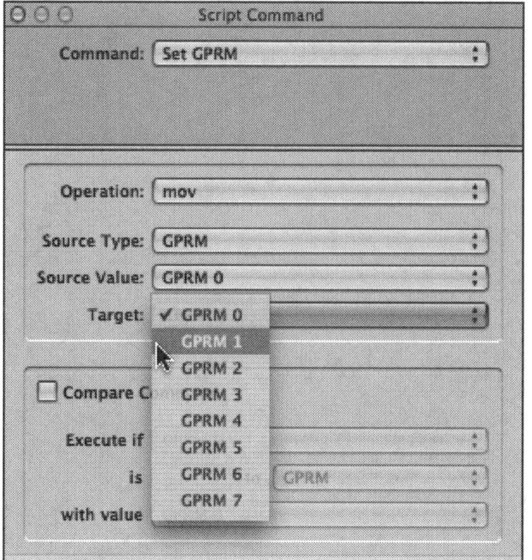

Figure 25.28 The Target setting defines the GPRM that you set. Consequently, the Target menu lists only GPRMs as potential settings.

Selecting a source type, source value, and target

The Source Type and Source Value settings work together to provide a value that is written to the GPRM specified in the Target setting (**Figure 25.28**). The Source Type setting itself contains up to five choices (**Figure 25.29**):

- **GPRM.** The GPRM Source Type setting allows you to transfer values from one GPRM to another GPRM. When you select the GPRM source type, the Source Value setting displays only GPRMs (**Figure 25.30**).

continues on next page

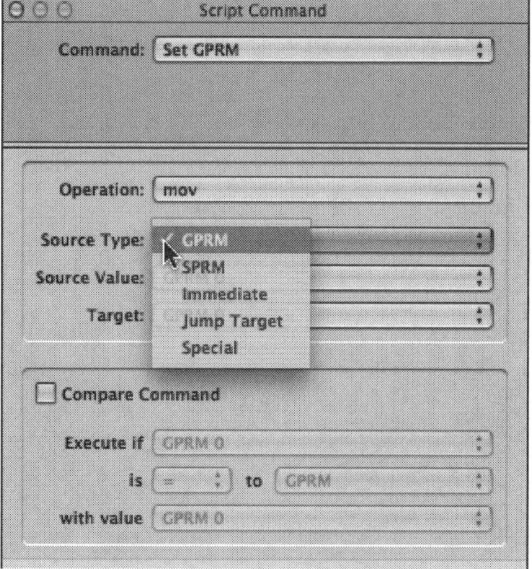

Figure 25.29 The Source Type setting provides up to five options (the number of options available depends upon the type of operation specified in the Operation setting).

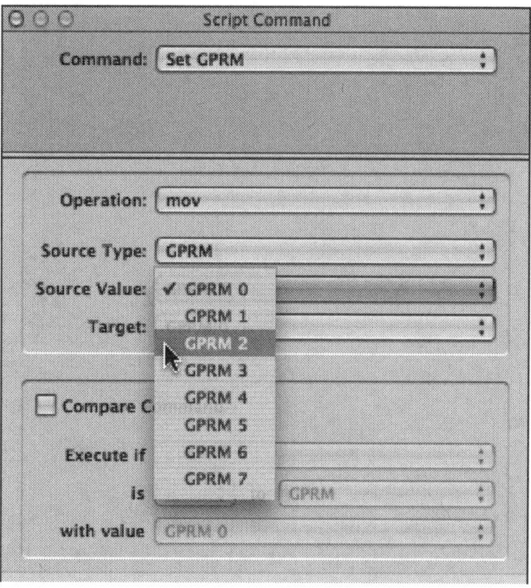

Figure 25.30 The GPRM Source Type setting lets you move the value of the GPRM selected in the Source Value setting to the GPRM specified in the Target setting.

◆ **SPRM.** The SPRM Source Type setting allows you to set the target GPRM to the value of any of the 24 available SPRMs. When you select the SPRM source type, the Source Value setting displays only SPRMs (**Figure 25.31**).

◆ **Immediate.** The Immediate Source Type setting lets you write a specific integer value to the target GPRM (**Figure 25.32**). Use this source type to set a GPRM to a specific number (for example, GPRM 0 = *x*, where *x* is a number). You can also enter letters in the Source Value text box.

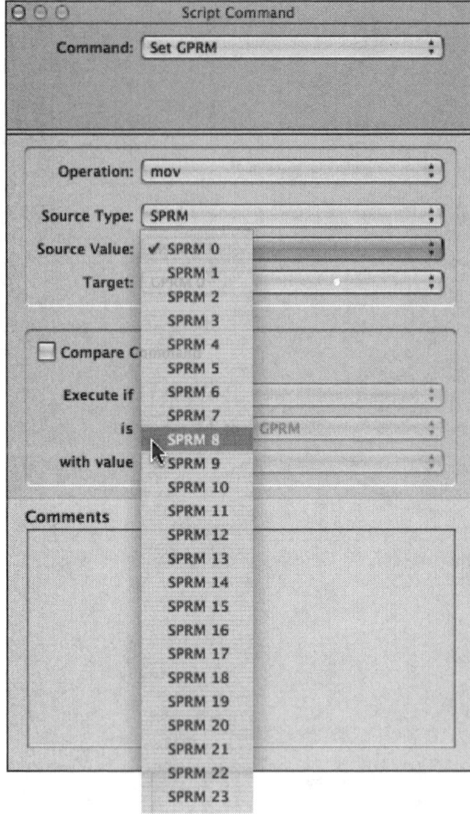

Figure 25.31 The SPRM Source Type setting lets you move the value of any of the 24 SPRMs available in the Source Value setting to the GPRM specified in the Target setting.

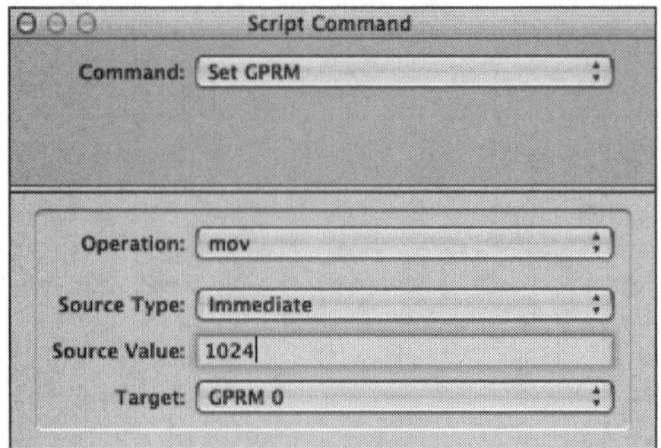

Figure 25.32 The Immediate Source Value setting lets you move any number (or combination of numbers and letters) into the target GPRM.

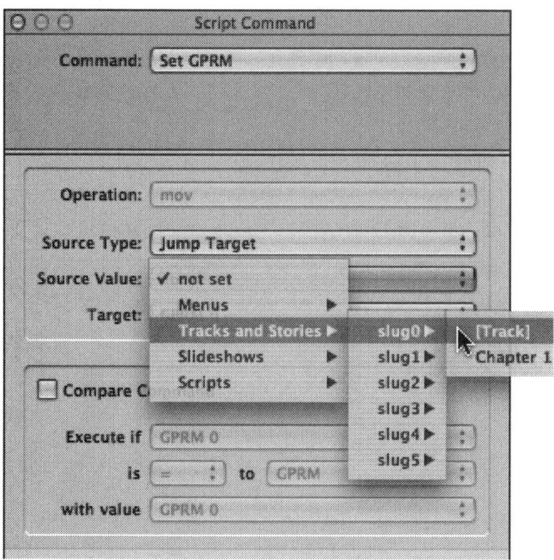

Figure 25.33 The Jump Target Source Type setting lets you select any project item as the value that is moved into the target GPRM.

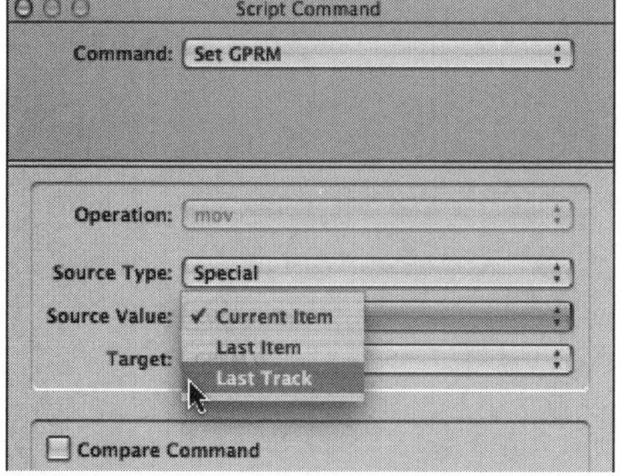

Figure 25.34 The Special Source Type setting provides access to three functions that set the target GPRM to the current item, last item, or last track played.

- **Jump Target**. The Jump Target Source Type setting is used to set the target GPRM to any project item available in the Source Value menu (**Figure 25.33**).
- **Special.** The Special Source Type setting is used to set the target GPRM to the current item, last item, or last track played in the project (**Figure 25.34**). This source type is particularly useful for creating scripts that highlight certain menu buttons depending on the last track, chapter, or menu played in the project.

Using a Compare Command

To program decision-making skills into your DVD-Video, you must use conditional statements. In most scripting languages, conditional statements take the form of an if-then statement: for example, "if A, then B." This type of script literally performs the action B *on the condition that* A is true. In DVD Studio Pro, you program conditional statements using Compare commands.

Figure 25.35 shows a script for a random-number generator. In this figure, a command line is selected, and the Inspector displays its corresponding Compare command. Note how, in DVD Studio Pro, a conditional statement is written in reverse. For example, the selected command line says "Jump to slug0 *if* GPRM 0 is equal to 0." In the Inspector, you also configure the conditional statement in reverse. First you select the Jump command target and then you create the Compare command that the DVD-Video player must check before executing the Jump command.

✔ Tip

- If a Compare command is not true, the DVD-Video player simply skips it and moves on to the next command line.

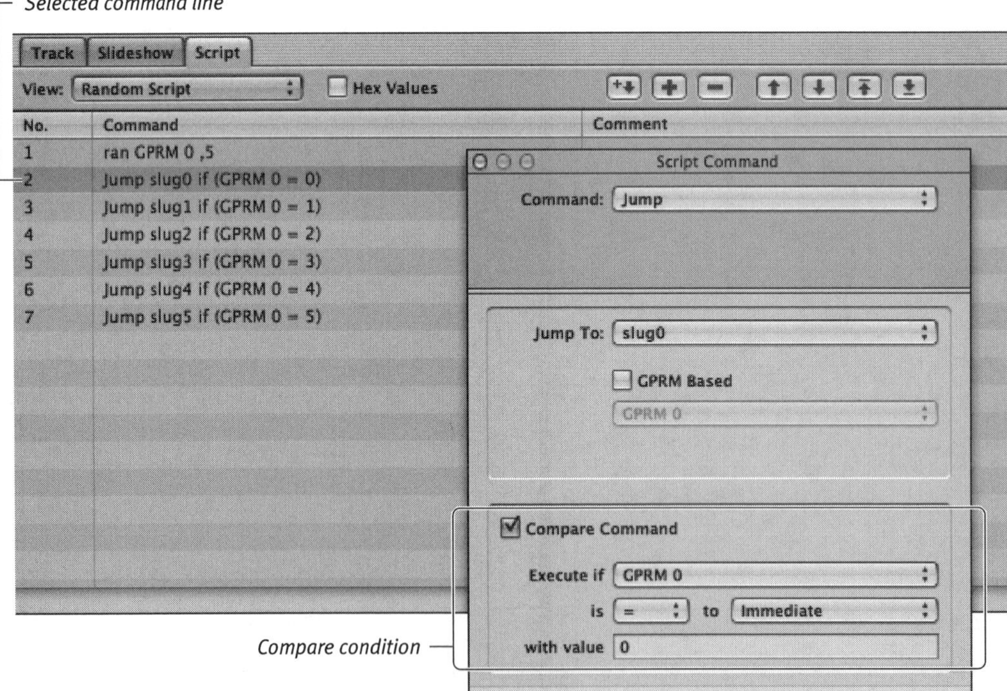

Figure 25.35 In DVD Studio Pro, you write conditional statements using Compare commands.

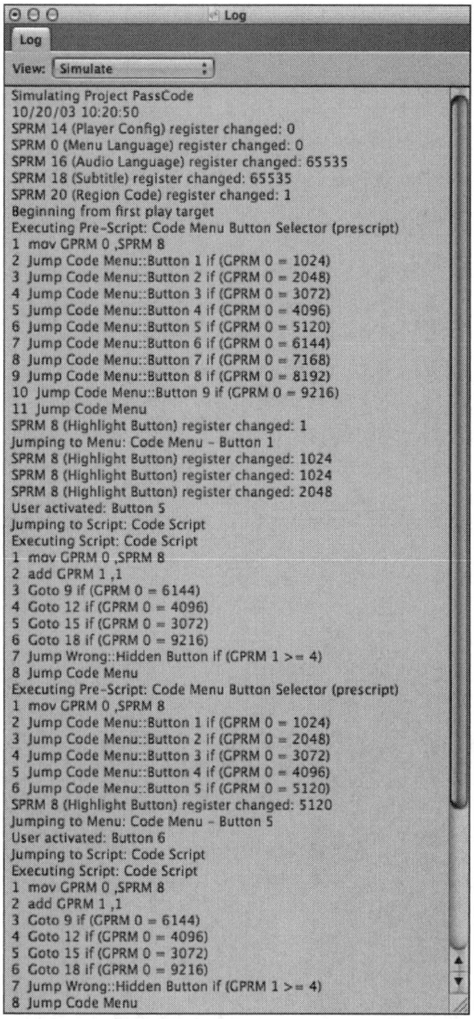

```
Log
Log
View: Simulate
Simulating Project PassCode
10/20/03 10:20:50
SPRM 14 (Player Config) register changed: 0
SPRM 0 (Menu Language) register changed: 0
SPRM 16 (Audio Language) register changed: 65535
SPRM 18 (Subtitle) register changed: 65535
SPRM 20 (Region Code) register changed: 1
Beginning from first play target
Executing Pre-Script: Code Menu Button Selector (prescript)
1 mov GPRM 0 ,SPRM 8
2 Jump Code Menu::Button 1 if (GPRM 0 = 1024)
3 Jump Code Menu::Button 2 if (GPRM 0 = 2048)
4 Jump Code Menu::Button 3 if (GPRM 0 = 3072)
5 Jump Code Menu::Button 4 if (GPRM 0 = 4096)
6 Jump Code Menu::Button 5 if (GPRM 0 = 5120)
7 Jump Code Menu::Button 6 if (GPRM 0 = 6144)
8 Jump Code Menu::Button 7 if (GPRM 0 = 7168)
9 Jump Code Menu::Button 8 if (GPRM 0 = 8192)
10 Jump Code Menu::Button 9 if (GPRM 0 = 9216)
11 Jump Code Menu
SPRM 8 (Highlight Button) register changed: 1
Jumping to Menu: Code Menu - Button 1
SPRM 8 (Highlight Button) register changed: 1024
SPRM 8 (Highlight Button) register changed: 1024
SPRM 8 (Highlight Button) register changed: 2048
User activated: Button 5
Jumping to Script: Code Script
Executing Script: Code Script
1 mov GPRM 0 ,SPRM 8
2 add GPRM 1 ,1
3 Goto 9 if (GPRM 0 = 6144)
4 Goto 12 if (GPRM 0 = 4096)
5 Goto 15 if (GPRM 0 = 3072)
6 Goto 18 if (GPRM 0 = 9216)
7 Jump Wrong::Hidden Button if (GPRM 1 >= 4)
8 Jump Code Menu
Executing Pre-Script: Code Menu Button Selector (prescript)
1 mov GPRM 0 ,SPRM 8
2 Jump Code Menu::Button 1 if (GPRM 0 = 1024)
3 Jump Code Menu::Button 2 if (GPRM 0 = 2048)
4 Jump Code Menu::Button 3 if (GPRM 0 = 3072)
5 Jump Code Menu::Button 4 if (GPRM 0 = 4096)
6 Jump Code Menu::Button 5 if (GPRM 0 = 5120)
SPRM 8 (Highlight Button) register changed: 5120
Jumping to Menu: Code Menu - Button 5
User activated: Button 6
Jumping to Script: Code Script
Executing Script: Code Script
1 mov GPRM 0 ,SPRM 8
2 add GPRM 1 ,1
3 Goto 9 if (GPRM 0 = 6144)
4 Goto 12 if (GPRM 0 = 4096)
5 Goto 15 if (GPRM 0 = 3072)
6 Goto 18 if (GPRM 0 = 9216)
7 Jump Wrong::Hidden Button if (GPRM 1 >= 4)
8 Jump Code Menu
```

Figure 25.36 The Log tab keeps a running tally of everything that's happening behind the scenes as your project runs in the Simulator, including the values of SPRMs and the command lines of scripts as they execute.

Troubleshooting Scripts

DVD Studio Pro provides two separate tools for troubleshooting your scripts: the Log tab and the Simulator's Information panel.

Using the Log tab

Whenever you simulate a project, the Log tab keeps a running tally of everything that is happening behind the scenes (**Figure 25.36**). For example, the Log window shows all SPRM values as they are set or changed while the project runs and also shows the script command lines as they execute. This information is an invaluable asset when it comes to debugging your scripts.

✔ Tip

- When simulating projects that use scripts, tear the Log tab out into its own window and make it nice and big. The Log tab will now jump to the surface of the screen whenever you launch the Simulator so you can easily follow along as scripts are executed while the Simulator runs.

Using the Simulator's Information panel

Another great feature of DVD Studio Pro is the Simulator's Information panel (**Figure 25.37**). You open the Information panel by clicking the Simulator control's Show Information Panel button. You can use the Information panel to follow along as SPRMs and (most important) GPRMs are set and changed as your project is simulated.

Furthermore, the SPRM and GPRM fields in the Simulator's Information panel are editable. You can check scripts and complex projects by editing values in the Simulator to emulate different DVD player configurations, or you can set values as if the disc has already played a particular portion of the disc so you don't have to start from the beginning of a disc to check scripting after the main movie has played, for example.

✔ Tip

- The bottom-left corner of the Simulator's Information panel contains two check boxes used to hide and show SPRMs and GPRMs (refer to Figure 25.37). Use these check boxes to keep the panel uncluttered when, for example, you are interested in following along only as GPRMs are set and changed while the Simulator runs.

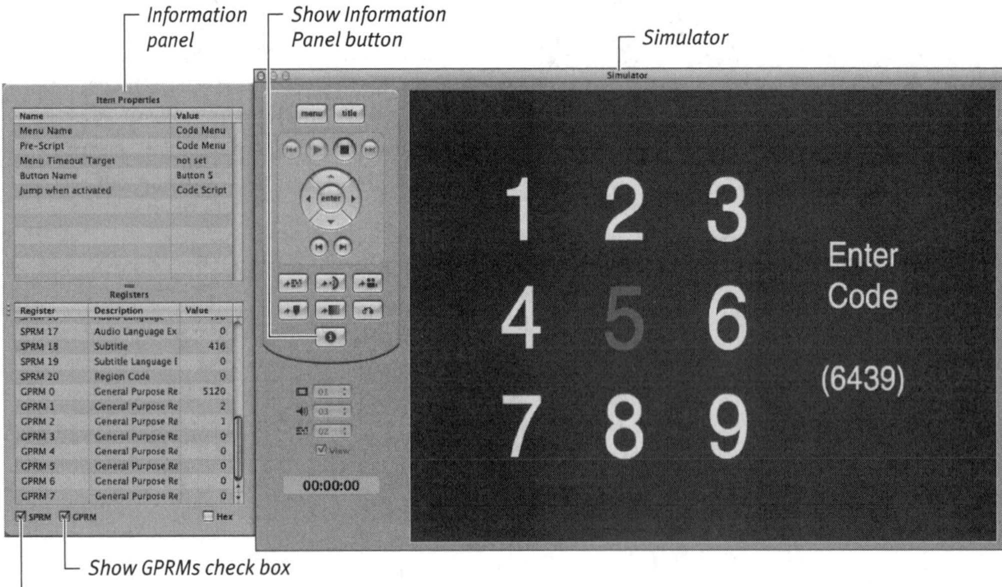

Figure 25.37 The Simulator's Information panel provides essential Information about the values of your project's SPRMs and GPRMs, letting you watch as these registers are set and changed while the project runs.

A

Surviving on a Bit Budget

A bit budget helps you determine the data rate to use when encoding your MPEG-2 streams. If your project uses less than an hour of video, a bit budget isn't terribly important because an hour of MPEG-2 video, encoded at a bit rate of 9.8 Mbps, will easily fit on a DVD-5. But once you get above an hour of video, you'll need a bit budget to calculate the highest-quality MPEG-2 video that you can include on a DVD disc, given its available storage capacity.

Making a Bit Budget

To make things easy, bit budgets are calculated in bytes rather than kilobytes, megabytes, or gigabytes. This takes a lot of confusion out of the process, because you don't have to convert between kilobytes and megabytes or compensate for the differences between computer and DVD storage conventions. Whether on a computer or on a DVD disc, a byte is always 8 bits, which makes the calculations easier to handle (to learn more about the differences in how computers and DVD discs store data, see Chapter 2, "DVD 101").

You can't control the size of subtitle streams or menu images, and audio streams need to be encoded at very particular settings to maintain quality. Of all of your project's assets, video is the only one that can handle large shifts in encoding quality. For example, there's not a terribly noticeable difference between video encoded at 6.5 Mbps and video encoded at 7.5 Mbps. A practiced eye can see the difference, but not as easily as any untrained ear can hear the difference between an AC-3 stream encoded at 96 kbps and one encoded at 192 kbps. You can't scrimp on the sound, but video can vary.

A bit budget subtracts the storage space needed for all of the assets over which you have no control and fills the rest of the disc with video. The following is an overview of how to make a bit budget. Each step is explained later in this appendix.

To make a bit budget:

1. Determine the storage capacity of your target DVD.
2. Reserve 5 percent of the target DVD disc as overhead for assets that may be added at a later point in the authoring process. Subtract this 5 percent reserve from the total capacity of the target DVD disc.
3. Calculate the storage space needed for your project's audio streams. Subtract this figure from the target DVD disc's total storage capacity.
4. Calculate the storage space needed for all subtitle streams. Subtract this figure from the target DVD disc's total storage capacity.
5. Calculate the storage space needed for highlight and Photoshop layer menus. Subtract this figure from the target DVD disc's total storage capacity.
6. Calculate the storage space needed for any DVD-ROM content (on a hybrid DVD). Subtract this figure from the target DVD disc's total storage capacity.
7. Use all remaining storage capacity for the project's video streams (including motion menus).

Table A.1

DVD Storage Capacity

Media Type	Disc Capacity (in bytes)
DVD-5 (DVD-R)	4,700,000,000
DVD-9	8,540,000,000
DVD-10	9,400,000,000
DVD-18	17,080,000,000

Table A.2

Five Percent Reserve Values

Media Type	Reserve (in bytes)
DVD-5 (DVD-R)	235,000,000
DVD-9	427,000,000
DVD-10	470,000,000
DVD-18	854,000,000

Determining disc capacity

Usually, you decide on a target DVD disc size before authoring a project. If you intend to use your computer's SuperDrive to record a DVD-R, for example, you know that you'll be working with a DVD-5. If you're authoring a disc containing a feature-length movie, you'll need to move up to a DVD-9. This makes the first step of creating a bit budget easy: think of the type of DVD disc on which you'll be distributing your project and then use **Table A.1** to determine its available storage capacity.

Determining the reserve

Multiplexing the project creates control data (.ifo) files and backup (.bup) files that you will not be able to account for in advance, so leaving a bit of extra room on the disc is always a good idea. There will also be times when you unexpectedly need to add assets that you didn't account for in the bit budget. Leaving a reserve gives you a margin of error that often makes the difference between a project that fits on a disc and a project in which you must go back and re-encode video assets at a lower rate.

For most situations, a reserve of 5 percent is more than adequate. **Table A.2** lists the reserve values to use with several types of DVD discs.

Calculating audio storage

The total storage space needed for audio streams depends upon the length and bit rate of each stream. **Table A.3** lists common audio stream bit rates.

To calculate how much of the target DVD disc your audio streams will consume, use the following formula:

```
audio data storage (bytes) = (total
audio minutes x 60 x bit rate) / 8
```

If your project uses audio streams encoded using several different bit rates, you'll need to do some extra math. First, you must calculate the size of each individual stream. Then add the totals together to determine the storage space needed for all audio streams combined.

Calculating subtitle storage

Each individual subtitle within a subtitle stream uses around 4,000 bytes—that's 4,000 bytes for each group of letters that flicks across the screen. To calculate the storage space for subtitle streams, you must count each separate subtitle in every project subtitle stream and then multiply that number by 4,000, as shown here:

```
subtitle storage (bytes) = number of
subtitles x 4,000
```

✔ Tip

- If you used the Subtitle editor to create the subtitle streams, open the original subtitle project and count the subtitle cells to quickly figure out the number of subtitles in the stream. Either that or watch the video while adding ticks to a pad of paper!

Table A.3

Audio Stream Bit Rates

Stream Type	Bit Rate (in bits/second)
Stereo AC-3	192,000
5.1 AC-3	448,000
16-bit stereo PCM	1,500,000

Calculating still-menu storage

Just as with a JPEG still image, the amount of space needed to store a still menu varies with the menu's visual complexity. Despite this fact, it's rare for a still menu, no matter how visually complex, to take up more than 100,000 bytes on the final DVD disc.

Highlight menus turn a subpicture stream on and off over a single background image, so each highlight menu uses approximately 100,000 bytes. Use the following formula to calculate the storage space needed for a project's highlight menus:

```
highlight menus (bytes) = number of
highlight menus x 100,000
```

Photoshop layer menus work differently. When DVD Studio Pro compiles your project, it creates a new I-frame for each button state of every button on the menu. When buttons are selected or activated, the DVD-Video player actually jumps between these separate I-frames to create a rollover effect. Use this formula for budgeting Photoshop layer menus:

```
Photoshop layer menus = (total number
of buttons on all Photoshop layer menus x
number of button states + 1) x 100,000
```

Button states can be selected and activated. If your Photoshop layer menu uses selected and activated states, the *number of button states* value equals 2. If only selected states are used, then the *number of button states* value equals 1.

✔ Tip

- If your project uses a mix of highlight and Photoshop layer menus, calculate each group of menus separately and add the totals to find the combined storage capacity needed for all of the project's menus.

Calculating DVD-ROM storage

To calculate the size of your project's DVD-ROM content, in the Finder select the folder containing the DVD-ROM content and press Command-I. An Info window will open telling you how big the folder is. You must convert the size of the folder into bytes using this formula:

```
DVD-ROM storage = size of folder in
megabytes x 1,024 x 1,024
```

Calculating video bit rates

In bit budget terms, this is the end game! This two-step process determines the bit rate to use when encoding MPEG-2 video streams for your project's tracks and motion menus. In the first step, you calculate the amount of space left on the disc after all of your audio, subtitle, menu, and DVD-ROM content is accounted for. This leftover space will be filled with video streams. Use the following formula to determine how much space is available for your project's video assets:

```
space available for video assets = DVD
disc capacity - reserve - audio data -
subpicture data - still-menu data -
DVD-ROM data
```

A DVD disc is like an orange cut in half: the fuller the disc is with video content, the sweeter the images are when the DVD-Video player squeezes the disc. You want to fill the disc to the brim with video, which means that you must figure out the compression *sweet spot* (the bit rate that creates the highest-quality video that fits in the leftover space on the target DVD disc) for your video streams. After figuring out how much space is left on the disc, use this formula to determine the maximum bit rate to use when encoding video streams:

```
video data rate = (space available for
video / video minutes / 60) x 8
```

✔ Tip

- Don't forget that the total combined data rate for all assets in a single, multiplexed DVD-Video stream is 10.08 Mbps. If your bit budget says that you can use a high bit rate, take a moment to add up the bandwidth needed for each track in your project (add the video stream's data rate with the combined sum of the track's audio and subtitle stream data rates).

Real-World Bit Budgeting

Here's a real-world example of a bit budget for a project with two menus and four tracks. Each track has three alternate audio streams.

Project Assets:

Track 1: 4 minutes, three AC-3 stereo audio streams

Main Menu

Track 2: 30 minutes, three AC-3 stereo audio streams

Track 3: 45 minutes, three AC-3 stereo audio streams

Track 4: 60 minutes, three AC-3 stereo audio streams

Audio Setup Menu

DVD Capacity: One DVD-9 = 8,540,000,000 bytes

Reserve = 427,000,000 bytes

Total length in minutes of all audio streams: (4 + 30 + 45 + 60) x 3 audio streams per track = 417

Audio data storage (bytes) = (*total audio minutes* x 60 x *bit rate*) / 8

= 417 x 60 x (192,000/8)

= 600,480,000 bytes

Still menu data storage = *number of menus* x 100,000

= 2 x 100,000

= 200,000 bytes

Space available for video = *DVD disc capacity – reserve – audio data – subpicture data – still menu data – DVD-ROM data*

= 8,540,000,000 – 427,000,000 – 600,480,000 – 0 – 200,000 – 0

= 7,512,320,000 bytes

Total length (minutes) of all video streams: 4 + 30 + 45 + 60 = 139

Video data rate = (*space available for video / video minutes* / 60) x 8

= (7,512,320,000 / 139 / 60) x 8

= 7,206,062 bps, or 7.2 Mbps!

Online Resources

DVD-Video Training

macProVideo.com

`http://www.macprovideo.com`

The macProVideo.com site delivers streaming video training for several of Apple's pro video and audio applications. This site lets you see and hear how video is edited, in real time. It provides a great way to supplement your education!

DVD-Video

The Apple DVD Studio Pro Discussion

`http://discussions.info.apple.com`

The Apple DVD Studio Pro discussion forum is devoted to all questions concerning DVD Studio Pro. Ask questions and get answers from people who not only love the product, but also know everything about it. As with all discussion forums, you should check the archives first to see if your question has been answered before. It's also advisable to learn about list etiquette by *lurking* for a while before posting—in other words, spend some time watching and learning, because nobody likes a newbie who charges in and asks without thinking first!

DVD Demystified

`www.dvddemystified.com/dvdfaq.html`

Got a general question about DVD-Video? This FAQ—maintained and updated by Jim Taylor, a community-recognized guru in all things DVD-Video—will have the answer.

dvdsp.com

`www.dvdsp.com`

Learn inside tips and other secrets about DVD Studio Pro.

Macrovision

`www.macrovision.com`

If you intend to use Macrovision AGC copy protection in your project, you must purchase a license from Macrovision. Visit the company's Web site to learn more.

Audio

Emagic

www.emagic.de

When it comes to audio production on the Macintosh platform, Emagic's Logic Pro is the natural choice. A cost-effective surround mixing solution, Logic Pro provides everything the DVD-Video author needs to make great sound for motion menus and video streams alike.

Dolby

www.dolby.com/digital

To get into the nitty-gritty of AC-3 encoding, visit Dolby's Web site. Dolby created the format, and the company's site contains PDF documents that explain everything about AC-3 encoding.

Hit Squad

www.hitsquad.com

If you're looking for a shareware audio editor, the Shareware Music Machine offers over 4,000.

Propellerheads Software

www.propellerheads.se

Propellerheads Reason is a full software audio recording studio. This software sampler/synthesizer/sequencer is all you need to make copyright-free music, and it's fun to use! A demo version is available at the Propellerheads Web site.

INDEX

Symbols and numbers

- (hyphen), 333
= (equal sign), 642
// (two forward slashes), 617
/// (three forward slashes), 548
3dB attenuation, 130
4:3 aspect ratio, 42, 69, 551, 568
4:3 TV screens, 552, 560–561
  anamorphic transfer, 558
  playing widescreen tracks, 560–564
  subtitle graphics, 564
5.1 surround sound
  AC-3 files, 116
  bit rates, 119
8 cm discs, 526
8.3 file-naming convention, 480
16:9 aspect ratio, 69, 551, 568
16:9 Letterbox mode, 563
16:9 Pan Scan mode, 563
16:9 Pan Scan & Letterbox mode, 563
16:9 video, 69, 551–568
  anamorphic, 558–559
  encoding, 553–557
  letterboxing, 561, 562
  menus, 565–567
  pan and scan mode, 560
  simulating, 568
  slideshows as, 447, 567
  subtitles, 564
  track display modes, 563
  See also widescreen video
16-bit audio files, 103
24-bit audio files, 103
48 kHz audio files, 102, 103, 104–105
90° phase-shift option, 130
96 kHz audio files, 102
640 × 480 graphics, 42

A

AC-3 audio, 101, 107, 127–130
  audio coding modes, 114–116
  auditioning, 131–132
  bit rate settings, 112, 119
  decoding, 132
  dialog normalization, 120, 121–122
  dynamic range controls, 112, 123
  encoding process, 111–113
  input channel assignments, 117–118
  miscellaneous settings, 127–130
  surround downmixing, 112, 116, 125–126
  testing, 135
  See also A.Pack utility
AC-3 Monitor, 109, 131–132
action safe overlay, 37
action safe zone, 36
actions
  auto, 315
  jump, 221–222
  timeout, 316–317
activated state, 307
Activity Monitor, 202
Add operation, 642
Add Slideshow icon, 448
Adobe Photoshop. *See* Photoshop
advanced overlay menus, 346, 359–364
  choosing the mode for, 359
  color mappings for, 360–362
  creating, 363–364
advanced overlay mode, 346
Advanced window configuration, 143, 144, 148
AIFF files, 71, 105
aligning
  menu objects, 328
  tiles, 177
alternate-angle streams, 287–288

INDEX

Analog Protection System (APS), 29, 484–485
anamorphic transfer, 558
anamorphic video, 552, 558–559
Angle button, 465
animated subtitles, 625
A.Pack utility, 15, 101–135
  3 dB attenuation, 130
  AC-3 encoding process, 111–113
  audio coding modes, 111, 114–116
  audio interface setting, 133
  auditioning AC-3 files, 131–132
  batch lists, 134–135
  bit rate settings, 112, 119
  bit-stream modes, 128
  compression profiles, 124
  copyright/content options, 128
  DC offset, 130
  decoding AC-3 files, 132
  dialog normalization, 120, 121–122
  dynamic range controls, 112, 123
  faking surround sound, 118
  input channel assignments, 117–118
  launching, 110
  low-pass filter, 129
  overview of, 108–109
  phase-shift option, 130
  quick settings, 113
  RF overmodulation protection, 129
  surround downmixing, 112, 116, 125–126
  target system settings, 127
  testing AC-3 settings, 135
Apple stock items
  shapes, 427
  styles, 415, 420
  templates, 400, 402, 423
Apple SuperDrive, 7–8
Apple System Profiler, 8
Apple Web site, 6
application package, 402
aspect ratios, 69, 551, 568
asset-based timecode, 229, 263, 264
assets, 179–192
  adding to streams, 223–224
  assigning to layered menus, 337–339
  explained, 181
  importing, 193–207
  managing, 183–185, 197
  menu backgrounds as, 304
  nondestructive editing of, 181
  previewing, 190–192
  relinking, 189
  removing, 185
  renaming, 184
  reordering, 184
  revealing in Finder, 182
  sorting, 185
Assets tab, 180
  adjusting columns in, 186–188
  dragging assets onto, 197
  importing assets to, 194–197
  managing assets in, 183–185
  Status column, 203
  widening, 186
At End setting, 369–372
  loop option, 369, 370–371
  timeout option, 369–370
ATA device tree, 8
attenuation
  applying 3dB, 130
  dialog normalization and, 122
  surround downmixing and, 125, 126
Audio button, 465
audio clips
  copying, 242
  deleting, 243
  duration settings, 244–245
  editing, 241–246
  moving, 241–242
audio coding modes, 111, 114–116
audio files
  auditioning, 131–132
  importing, 204
  input channel assignments, 117–118
  overlay menus and, 367–368
  slide shows and, 448, 455–457
  Track editor option, 225
audio formats, 101
  A.Pack utility and, 102
  converting, 104–105
  language menus and, 575
audio interface, 133
audio resources, 658
audio streams, 27
  A.Pack utility and, 102
  adding clips to, 223–224
  bit rates for, 652
  determining DNVs for, 121–122
  encoding AC-3 audio, 111–113
  filtering the display of, 237
  height adjustment, 238–239
  language definition for, 579–580
  locking/unlocking, 240
  looping, 368, 455, 457
  remote-control buttons for, 467
  saving in QuickTime MPEG-2 Exporter, 71
  slide shows and, 455–457

INDEX

storage calculations for, 652
track creation and, 214–215
viewing alternate, 250
AUDIO_TS folder, 26
building process and, 497, 498, 499
hybrid DVDs and, 479
auditioning AC-3 files, 131–132
auto actions, 315
Auto Assign Buttons options, 319
Auto Layout option, 177
automatic gain control (AGC), 484

B

B-frames, 56
background encoding, 60, 202
backgrounds, 302–306
colors for, 450
flattening, 303
images used as, 305–306
layered menu, 340
multiple-language, 575, 576–577
overlay menu, 347, 350–351
video assets as, 304
Basic window configuration, 143, 148, 149
Batch Encoder, 108, 109
batch lists, 82, 134–135
Batch Monitor, 91, 99
batch rendering, 134
Batch window, 81, 82–91
importing files into, 82–84
presets in, 84–86, 92–93
previewing compression in, 96–97
setting destinations in, 87–90
submitting files for encoding in, 91
bit budgets, 76, 649–655
audio storage, 652
disc storage capacity, 651
DVD-ROM storage, 654
real-world example, 655
reserve values, 651
steps in making, 650
still-menu storage, 653
subtitle storage, 652
video bit rates, 654
bit depth
checking, 106
explained, 103
bit rates, 75–76
AC-3 file, 112, 119
calculating, 654
choosing, 75–76
guidelines, 119
limiting, 76
testing, 75
video, 654
bit-stream modes, 128
BitVice MPEG-2 encoder, 18, 59
Broadcast Safe filter, 39
Browse Asset area, 190–191
browser, default, 549
buffer underrun errors, 507
Build & Format button, 510
building and formatting projects, 496, 503–511
disk images, 509–511
DVD-R discs, 504–506
explained, 503
building (multiplexing) projects, 495, 497–501
explained, 497
formatting and, 496, 503–511
layout files and, 499
Log tab and, 500–501
process of, 498–499
BUP files, 497
burning process, 496
deleting files for, 518
DVD-Video discs, 515–519
preparations for, 503
button highlight markers, 266
creating, 267
overlay menus and, 373–376
subtitle text and, 376
button hotspots
adding to menus, 308
explained, 307
layered menus and, 341, 343
Button Link tool, 320
button navigation, 318–320
auto assigning, 319
manually setting, 319–320
previewing, 321
button states, 307, 341–344
assigning, 341–342
changing colors of, 356
previewing, 343–344
button targets
setting, 313
verifying, 314
button text
creating, 379–380
drop shadows for, 386
positioning, 380
buttons, 27, 307–315
auto actions for, 315
command, 630–632
copying, 309
creating, 308

buttons, *continued*
deleting, 309
disconnecting, 474
DVD@ccess menu, 547
hiding outlines to, 312
highlight sets for, 366
language selection, 581–582
linking to targets, 472–473
moving, 308
naming, 309
navigation settings, 318–321
opening URLs from, 541–546
placing over video, 373–376
previewing, 321
remote-control, 464–468
resizing, 311
selecting multiple, 310
shapes applied to, 427–428
states of, 307, 341–344
styles applied to, 416–419
targets for, 216–217, 313–314, 472–473
text, 376, 379–380, 386
transitions for, 396

C

camera angles, 27
Canvas window, 275
captions
closed, 623–625
See also subtitles
CBR encoding, 74
CDs
DVDs compared to, 20–23
labeling process for, 21
recording DVD-Video on, 519
storage capacity of, 22
cell markers, 268
cells, 31
chapter index menus, 407
chapter markers, 265
creating, 266
named markers, 272
subtitles and, 602
Web links for, 538
Choose Application Configuration dialog, 142–143, 144
Choose Build Folder dialog, 498, 584
Choose Line21 File dialog, 624–625
Choose Marker File dialog, 278–279
Choose Source dialog, 504–505, 509–510, 513, 522
Choose Subtitle Graphic File dialog, 374, 621
chroma color mapping, 361, 608
circles, drawing, 46
Clip Inspector, 246
clips, 210
adding, 223–224
copying, 242
deleting, 243
duplicating, 242
duration settings for, 244–246
editing, 241–246
markers at end of, 254
moving, 241–242, 294
thumbnail display, 248
viewing, 247
closed captions, 623–625
closed GOPs, 58
codecs, 397
color depth, 39
color mapping
chroma, 361
grayscale, 360
selecting, 362
Color Palette window, 357
color picker, 357–358
colors
broadcast safe, 39
chroma, 361
grayscale, 360
guide, 325–326
subtitle, 605–610
text, 383
video safe, 51–52
Colors dialog, 326, 383
Colors palette, 606
colorstripe, 484
columns, Asset tab, 186–188
changing width of, 188
displaying hidden, 187
reordering, 187
tips on working with, 188
commands
Compare, 646
copying and pasting, 631
creating and deleting, 630, 631
escape, 637
inserting, 630, 631
Jump, 637, 638
programming, 635–638
reordering, 632
See also scripts
comments, subtitle, 617
Compare commands, 646
Compiler, 498–499
compiling projects, 496
compression

previewing, 96–97
source video and, 59
compression markers, 272
compression profiles, 124
Compressor, 16, 81–99
Batch window, 81, 82–91, 92, 96
droplet creation, 98–99
encoding files in, 60, 82–91
exporting from Final Cut Pro using, 289
GOP creation, 58
importing files into, 82–84
MPEG-2 export, 80
presets used in, 84–86, 92–95
previewing compression in, 96–97
setting destinations in, 87–90
submitting files for encoding in, 91
Connections tab, 469–478
level of detail displayed on, 470–471
linking buttons to targets on, 472–473
making connections on, 471–474
Next/Previous button assignments, 219
opening, 470
panes available in, 469
Resume function and, 477–478
unconnected links displayed on, 471
Contact button, 541
content protection, 481–485
See also copy protection
Content Scrambling System (CSS), 25, 29, 482–483
Contents folder, 402
control parameters, 107
Controller, 502
copy protection, 29, 481–485
CSS, 482–483
Macrovision, 484–485
region codes, 481
copying
buttons, 309
clips, 242
DVD discs, 521
Copyright Management options, 483, 485
CPU load, 202
cropping shapes, 439
CSS copy protection, 25, 29, 482–483
custom configurations, 155
custom shapes, 429–439
creating, 432–438
cropping, 439
deleting, 442
importing, 440–441, 443–444
layers used in, 429–430, 438
Photoshop documents and, 429–438
updating, 443–444
custom styles, 420–422
custom templates, 401, 408–412
creating, 408–410
deleting, 412
saving, 409, 410
sharing, 411
Cutting Master Format (CMF), 25, 523

D

D1 NTSC video, 41, 42
DC offset, 130
debugging projects, 488
decoding AC-3 files, 132
default browser, 549
default language settings, 570–571
default transitions
menus, 395
slideshows, 392–393
deleting/removing
assets, 185
audio from slideshows, 456, 457
buttons, 309
clips, 243
encode jobs, 135
files before recording, 518
folders from the Palette, 163
guides, 325
languages, 574
linked connections, 474
markers, 254–255
shapes, 442
slides from slideshows, 452
subtitle graphics, 622
templates, 412
tools from the toolbar, 158
tracks, 218
de-muxing files, 389
destinations, 87–90
custom templates for, 89–90
setting for encoded files, 87–88, 204–206
Destinations window
Compressor, 89–90
Preferences window, 204
dialog normalization, 112, 120, 121–122
dialog normalization values (DNVs), 120
determining for audio streams, 121–122
reference tone level and, 121
Digigami Mpressionist.X, 18
digital linear tape (DLT), 495, 521–528
drives for, 11, 508
DVD-9 projects and, 524–526
formats for, 523

INDEX

digital linear tape (DLT), *continued*
  reading, 527
  recording to, 521–523
  saving DLT data, 528
Digital Video Noise Canceling (DVNC) filter, 59
disabling. *See* enabling/disabling
Disc Description Protocol (DDP), 523
Disc Options panel, 515–516
Disconnect button, 474
discs vs. disks, 24
disk images
  building, 509–511
  opening, 511
  uses for, 509
Disk Utility, 13
Display Mode setting, 561
displaying
  Asset tab columns, 187
  subtitles, 611
  widescreen video, 566–567
  See also showing/hiding; viewing
distributing
  menu objects, 329
  tiles, 177
DLT. *See* digital linear tape
DNVs. *See* dialog normalization values
Dolby Web site, 658
downmixing surround sound, 112, 116, 125–126
  attenuating the downmix, 125, 126
  tips related to, 126
drop palettes
  layered menu assets and, 338–339
  menu backgrounds and, 304–306
drop shadows, 385–386
drop zones
  patches applied to, 429
  shapes applied to, 428
drop-frame timecode, 66–67, 228
Droplet window, 99
droplets
  creating, 98–99
  encoding files using, 99
DS_Store file, 517, 518
dual-layer break-point markers, 267
dual-layer DVD discs, 524
duplicating
  clips, 242
  replicating vs., 514
  subtitles, 593
DV NTSC video, 41, 42
DVD-9 projects, 524–526
  creating, 525
  explained, 524
  testing, 526
DVD Demystified Web site, 657
DVD discs, 20–26
  burning, 503
  CDs compared to, 20–23
  copy protecting, 29, 481–485
  dual-layer, 23
  finishing, 461
  formatting, 503
  hybrid, 26, 479–480
  labeling process for, 21
  linking to files on, 548
  logical formats for, 26
  next generation of, 20
  physical formats for, 24–25
  region coding for, 28
  size settings for, 526
  storage capacity of, 22–23, 651
DVD Player
  enabling DVD@ccess, 536
  multilingual project testing, 584–586
  opening VIDEO_TS folders, 502
  Preferences dialog, 536, 585
  quality assurance testing, 490
DVD Studio Pro
  configuring, 144
  DVD-RW recording, 508
  editing features, 27–29
  installing, 14
  launching, 142
  online resources, 657
  output device support, 508
  pixel display, 46
  registering, 14
  safe zone overlays, 37
  still image formats, 40
  video standards, 35
  workflow process, 30
  workspace, 145–147
DVD@ccess, 531–549
  button links, 541–547
  disk images and, 511
  e-mail links, 532, 539–540
  enabling on the Macintosh, 536
  file links, 532, 548, 549
  how it works, 532–533
  locating Windows installer for, 533
  menu default button, 547
  rules for using, 537
  simulating, 549
  Web links, 532, 538
  Windows PCs and, 534–535
DVD-Audio discs, 26
DVD-compliant assets, 193
DVD+R discs, 25

DVD+RW discs, 25
DVD-R Authoring drives, 508
DVD-R discs, 24
  buffer underruns and, 507
  building and formatting, 504–506
  burning projects to, 496
  finishing process for, 461
  general vs. authoring, 21, 25
  playing on DVD-Video players, 9
  quality testing with, 490
  region coding and, 481
DVD-R General drives, 508
DVD-RAM discs, 24
DVD-ROM Contents dialog, 480
DVD-ROM discs, 24, 26
DVD-ROM folders, 479–480
DVD-ROM storage, 654
DVD-RW discs, 24
  erasing, 520
  recording to, 508
DVD-Video
  CD-ROM discs and, 519
  data structure, 31–32
  DVD@ccess links, 532
  editing features, 27–29
  online training site, 657
  programs, 219
  recording, 515–519
DVD-Video authoring
  hard disk setup for, 12–13
  overview of possibilities for, 27–29
DVD-Video discs, 26
  formatting, 512–514
  virtual, 509
DVD-Video players, 9
dynamic guides, 327
dynamic range controls, 112, 123

E

Easter eggs, 468
Eclipse software verifier, 484
Edit Marker window, 274
editing
  clips, 241–246
  nondestructive, 181
  properties, 170
  subtitles, 594–595
effects, flattening, 438
elementary files, 71
Elliptical Marquee tool, 46
eMac G4 platform, 5
Emagic Web site, 17, 658
e-mail links, 532, 539–540
embedded encoder, 553–554
embedded markers, 276
embedded text, 493
empty tracks, 213
enabling/disabling
  CSS copy protection, 483
  DVD@ccess on Macs, 536
  layers, 335
  remote control, 468
  rulers, 322
Encode on Build option, 202–203
Encoder Settings window, 200–201
encoding, 60, 82–91
  AC-3 audio, 111–113
  alternate-angle streams, 287–288
  background, 60, 202
  batch lists, 135
  bit rates, 75–76
  destinations for, 87–90
  droplets for, 98–99
  importing files for, 82–84
  internal options for, 198–199
  location settings for, 204–206
  mode preferences for, 202–203
  presets for, 84–86, 92–95
  previewing, 96–97
  Progress window for, 78
  quality settings for, 74–76
  QuickTime movies, 200–201
  submitting files for, 91
  testing settings for, 135
  video previews while, 78
  widescreen video, 553–557
Encoding Folder dialog, 206
encoding jobs, 111, 134–135
encryption, CSS, 482
End Jump action, 221–222
  marker setting for, 269
  slide show setting for, 459
  story setting for, 285
  track setting for, 221
  wait time for, 222
End Jump menu, 221
End slider, 372
Energy Saver preferences, 503
Entry list, Story editor, 283–284
erasing DVD-RW discs, 520
errors
  buffer underrun, 507
  Log tab list of, 500
escape commands, 637
Export dialog, 63
Export Item Description dialog, 491–492

exporting
item description files, 491–492
MPEG streams from Final Cut Pro, 79–80, 289
projects, 496
Expose feature, 155
Extended window configuration, 143, 148, 149
external hard disks, 10
eye icon, 335

F

fade-in/out effect
audio streams and, 368
subtitles and, 603–604
fallback folder, 206
field order, 70
fields, 70
file:/// path prefix, 548
files
encoding, 60, 82–91
layout, 499
links to, 532, 548, 549
managing, 197
naming, 480
filtering stream display, 237
Final Cut Pro 4, 16
Broadcast Safe filter, 39
determining DNVs in, 121
DVD Studio Pro compared to, 79
exporting MPEG streams from, 79–80, 289
overlays used in, 275
safe zone overlays in, 38
setting markers in, 272–275
Find Matching Audio When Dragging option, 225
Finder window, 182
finishing DVDs, 461–494
Connections tab options, 469–478
embedding text, 493
First Play action setting, 462–463
hybrid DVD creation, 479–480
item description files, 491–492
jacket pictures, 494
protecting disc content, 481–485
remote-control assignments, 464–468, 474–478
simulating projects, 486–490
FireWire DVD recorders, 7
FireWire hard disks, 10, 12
First Play setting, 178, 462–463
fixing invalid markers, 257
flagging tiles, 174
flattening
backgrounds, 303
effects, 438
layers, 48–49, 438
flicker, 50
folders
adding to the Palette, 162
choosing for encoded files, 88
deleting from Folder list, 163
encoding location, 204–206
importing, 196
renaming, 184
reordering, 163, 184
ROM, 479–480
fonts, 50
changing, 381–382, 596
subtitle, 589–591, 596
Fonts dialog, 382
Fonts panel, 590–591
Force to Letterbox display option, 566, 567
Force to Pan & Scan display option, 566, 567
formatting, 496
building and, 496, 503–511
DVD-R discs, 504–506
DVD-Video discs, 512–514
subtitle text, 596
Formatting window, 504–506, 509–511, 512, 521
frames, 55
frequency masking, 107
function keys
for Expose feature, 155
for window configurations, 154–155

G

gain pumping, 123
GOPs (groups of pictures), 31, 55, 56–58
alignment of, 287–288
explained, 56–57
markers and, 257, 264
open vs. closed, 58
GPRMs (general parameter registers), 638, 640–645
explained, 639
naming, 640–641
setting, 641–642
Simulator information, 648
Source Type settings, 643, 644–645
Graphical view, 168, 171–178
exploring, 171
flagging tiles in, 174
laying out tiles in, 177
locking/unlocking, 171
Macro view in, 175–176
renaming tracks in, 217
setting First Play item in, 178

track creation and, 214–215
zooming, 172–173, 176
graphics, 33–52
still, 40–52
subtitle, 620–622
video, 34–39
grayscale color mapping, 360, 608
Grayspace color scheme, 79
groups of pictures. *See* GOPs
guides, 322
adding to Menu editor, 323–324
changing color of, 325–326
deleting, 325
dynamic, 327
showing/hiding, 324

H

hard disks, 10, 508
building to, 498–499
external, 10
optimizing, 12–13
partitioning, 13
hardware components
digital linear tape drives, 11
DVD-Video player, 9
hard disks, 10
SuperDrive, 7–8
hiding. *See* showing/hiding
Highlight layer, 429, 435
highlight sets, 365–366
assigning to menu buttons, 366
configuring, 365
Hit Squad Web site, 658
horizontal text alignment, 598
hotspots. *See* button hotspots
http:// prefix, 537
hybrid DVDs, 26, 479–480, 548

I

I-frames, 56, 57
alignment of, 287, 288
markers and, 253, 256
iBook G4 platform, 5
Icon layer, 429, 435–436, 438
iDVD themes, 413–414
IFO files, 497
iMac G4 platform, 5
Image Size dialog, 43
images
layered menu, 337–339
menu backgrounds as, 305, 347, 350–351, 575, 576–577
overlay menu, 348–349, 352–353
resolution of, 47
See also pictures; still graphics
Immediate Source Type setting, 644
Import Assets dialog, 195
Import dialog, 440–441, 443–444
Import Item Description dialog, 492
importing, 193–207
assets to Assets tab, 194–197
audio assets, 204
custom shapes, 440–441, 443–444
files into Compressor, 82–84
folders into DVD Studio Pro, 196
iDVD themes, 413–414
item description files, 492
markers into DVD Studio Pro, 276–279
QuickTime movies, 198–206
subtitle graphics, 621–622
text subtitles, 618–619
Information panel, Simulator, 489, 648
inkjet-printable DVD-Rs, 21
input channels, 117–118
Input Channels matrix, 111, 115
Inspector, 147, 159
button navigation settings, 319–320
button target settings, 313
editing item properties in, 170
layered menu assets and, 339
menu background settings, 302–303
naming menus in, 300
previewing assets in, 190–191
renaming tracks in, 218
showing or hiding, 159
installing
DVD Studio Pro, 14
DVD@ccess on Windows PCs, 534
Instant Encoder, 108, 109
interactive markers, 266
interactive slideshows, 458
interlacing, 70
Internet resources, 657–658
item description files, 491–492
exporting, 491–492
importing, 492
items
creating, 169, 171
editing properties of, 170, 171
naming/renaming, 169, 171
reordering, 170

J

jacket pictures, 494
Joliet Extension Support, 480

INDEX

jump actions, 221–222
  marker setting for, 269
  scripting, 638
  slide show setting for, 459
  story setting for, 285
  track setting for, 221
  wait time for, 222
Jump command, 637, 638
Jump Target Source Type setting, 645
Jump To menu, 638
Jump When Activated target, 472–473
justifying text, 378

K

key colors, 360
key commands, 473
keyboard shortcuts, 232

L

language code, 578, 580
languages, 569–586
  adding to projects, 573–574
  audio stream settings for, 579–580
  buttons for selecting, 581–582
  default settings for, 570–571
  deleting from projects, 574
  embedded text, 493
  menu options for, 570–571, 572–577
  previewing projects using, 583–586
  track options for, 571, 578–582
layer breaks, 524, 525
layer styles, 48–49
layered menus, 296, 299, 331–344
  background layers, 340
  button hotspots, 341, 343
  button states, 341–344
  creating, 299, 332, 333–336
  explained, 296, 332
  images assigned to, 337–339
  Photoshop documents and, 338–339
  slowness of, 332
layers, 333–336
  background, 340
  creating, 334
  enabling/disabling, 335
  flattening, 48–49, 438
  naming, 334
  shape, 429–430
Layers palette, 48–49, 333–336, 432
layout files, 499
lengthening clips, 244–246
letterboxing process, 561, 562
Levels dialog, 52
Licensing dialog, 14
Line 21 caption files, 623
linking
  buttons to targets, 472–473
  styles to templates, 423–425
  URLs to buttons, 541–546
links, 531, 532
  button, 541–547
  e-mail, 532, 539–540
  file, 532, 548, 549
  rules for, 537
  simulating, 549
  testing, 549
  Web, 532, 538
LiveType application, 16
locking/unlocking
  Graphical view, 171
  streams, 240
log files
  QuickTime, 72
  Simulator, 488, 647
Log tab, 500–501
  opening, 488, 501
  resizing, 501
  simulation log, 488, 647
Logic Pro audio editor, 17, 658
logical formats, 26
loop points, 371–372
  audio, 368
  explained, 371
  menu transitions and, 395
  setting, 372
looping
  audio streams, 368, 455, 457
  overlay menus, 370–372
Lossless Linking check box, 507
low-frequency effects (LFE) channel, 126
low-pass filter, 129

M

MacCaption software, 623
Macintosh computers
  enabling DVD@ccess on, 536
  optical drive determination for, 8
macProVideo.com Web site, 657
Macro view, 175–176
macroblocks, 56
Macrovision copy protection, 29, 484–485, 657
Magnifying Glass tool, 606
Manage Configurations dialog, 155
managing assets, 183–185, 197
marker links, 538
marker lists, 277–279

marker slider, 262–263
markers, 252–279
  button highlight, 266–267
  cell, 268
  chapter, 265–266, 272
  compression, 272
  creating, 253–254
  default name of, 260
  deleting, 254–255
  dual-layer break-point, 267
  DVD@ccess links to, 538
  embedded, 276
  end jump setting for, 269
  Entry list options, 283–284
  explained, 252
  fixing invalid, 257
  I-frames and, 253, 256
  importing, 276–279
  interactive, 266
  moving, 262–264
  naming, 259–261
  placing without video, 257
  playback settings for, 270–271
  setting in Final Cut Pro, 272–275
  shifting by GOP, 264
  snapping, 256
  stories and, 280–286
  subtitles and, 602
  types of, 265–268
  viewing, 258
Mask layer, 429, 433–434, 438
masking, 107
mattes, letterbox, 561, 562
Max Bitrate slider, 75
media files
  assigning presets to, 85–86
  opening in external editors, 161
  previewing in the Palette, 164
menu buttons. *See* buttons
Menu editor, 295, 301
  alignment modes in, 328
  buttons created in, 307–312
  chapter index menus and, 407
  distribution modes in, 329
  guides added to, 323–324
  navigation settings in, 319
  opening menus in, 301
  previewing button states in, 343
  selecting new menus in, 301
  setting button targets in, 313–314
  track creation in, 216–217
menu flicker, 50
menu objects, 328–329, 415
menus, 27, 295–329
  16:9 video, 565–567
  aligning objects in, 328
  backgrounds for, 302–306, 575, 576–577
  buttons for, 307–314
  chapter index, 407
  creating, 298–299
  default language for, 570–571
  display types for, 566–567
  distributing objects in, 329
  drop palettes and, 304–306
  DVD@ccess, 547
  dynamic guides for, 327
  e-mail links for, 539–540
  guides for, 322, 323–327
  layered, 296, 299, 331–344
  multiple-language, 572–577, 581–582
  naming, 300
  navigation settings, 318–321
  opening, 301
  overlay, 297–298, 345–386
  prescripts assigned to, 634
  previewing, 321
  remote control and, 318
  rulers for, 322–323
  selecting, 301
  space limitations on, 577
  storage calculations for, 653
  submenus and, 299
  templates applied to, 404–406
  text added to, 377–384
  timeout actions for, 316–317
  transitions for, 395–396
  widescreen video, 565–567
mixed-angle streams, 292–294
mixed-angle tracks, 290, 291–294
  Compressor options and, 289
  creating, 291–292
  mixed-angle streams and, 292–294
  moving clips between streams in, 294
  presets for, 94–95
mono bit rates, 119
motion estimation, 77
Motion Scale tool, 562
motion vectors, 55, 56
Mov (move) operation, 642
Movie Properties window, 61
moving
  buttons, 308
  clips, 241–242, 294
  markers, 262–264
MPEG video, 54–59
  encoding, 60
  explained, 54–55
  exporting, 79–80

INDEX

MPEG video, *continued*
formats, 54–59
source video tips, 59
See also QuickTime MPEG-2 Exporter
MPEG-1 video format, 54
MPEG-2 video format, 55–59
encoding quality, 74
GOPs, 56–58
internal encoding options, 199
motion vectors, 56
noise filters, 59
stream exporting, 79–80, 289
Mpressionist.X program, 18
multi-angle tracks, 290
Compressor options and, 289
creating, 290
presets for, 94–95
multilingual DVDs, 569, 570–571
default language settings, 570–571
menu graphics for, 575, 576–577
multilingual tracks and, 578–582
multiple-language menus and, 572–577
previewing, 583–586
multilingual project previews, 583
using DVD Player, 584–586
using the Simulator, 583–584
multilingual slideshows, 580
multilingual tracks, 578–582
audio stream language setting, 579–580
language code and, 578, 580
selection menu buttons for, 581–582
multiple DVD copies, 512–514, 521
multiple-language menus, 572–577
adding languages to, 573–574
background pictures for, 575, 576–577
default language settings, 570–571
deleting languages from, 574
language selection buttons, 581–582
Multiplexer, 498
multiplexing, 495, 496, 497, 498–499
See also building (multiplexing) projects
MY_DVD.layout file, 499, 518

N

named chapter markers, 272
naming/renaming
buttons, 309
destination templates, 90
files, 480
folders, 184
GPRMs, 640–641
layers, 334
markers, 259–261
menus, 300
project items, 169
tracks, 217–218
navigation
button, 318–321
uniformity of, 465
Next Jump action, 476–477
Next/Previous keys, 219, 474–477
noise filter, 59
nondestructive editing, 181
non-drop-frame timecode, 66–67, 228
non-DVD-compliant assets, 193
Nop command, 630
normal state, 307
normalization, 120
NTSC Colors filter, 51
NTSC video standard, 34–35
16:9 menus, 566
setting, 34
two forms of, 41
video safe colors and, 51–52

O

objects
menu, 328–329, 415
text, 377
one-pass VBR encoding, 74
online resources, 657–658
Opacity slider, 356, 608–609
Opacity text box, 609
open GOPs, 58
operations, scripting, 642
optical disc drives, 8
optimizing hard disks, 12–13
ordering/reordering
Asset tab columns, 187
assets, 184
folders, 163
pictures in slideshows, 452
project items, 170
tabs, 153
tracks, 219–220
OTP playback method, 524, 525
Outline view, 168, 169–170
naming menus in, 300
renaming tracks in, 217
reordering tracks in, 219–220
track creation and, 214–215
output color range, 52
output devices, 508
Output Format pop-up menu, 510, 513
outputting projects, 495–528
Apple DVD Player and, 502
building and formatting process, 503–511
building (multiplexing) process, 497–501

INDEX

burning DVD-Video discs, 515–519
disk image creation, 509–511
DLT tape recording, 521–523
duplicating discs, 512–514
DVD-9 project creation, 524–526
overview of methods for, 496
replicating discs, 514, 521
Toast Titanium and, 515–520
overlay images, 297, 348–349
assigning, 352–353
subtitles as, 564, 620–622
template for designing, 375
tips for using, 353
overlay menus, 345–386
advanced, 346, 359–364
At End setting, 369–372
audio added to, 367–368
background of, 347, 350–351
benefits of, 345
buttons over video in, 373–376
creating, 298, 346
drop shadows in, 385–386
explained, 297
highlight sets for, 365–366
how they work, 347–349
images for, 348–349, 352–353
looping, 370–372
simple, 346, 354–358
text added to, 377–384
timeout action, 369–370
overlays
action and title safe, 37–38
using in Final Cut Pro, 275
overmodulation protection, 129
overscanning, 36

P

P-frames, 56
PAL video standard, 34–35, 566
Palette, 147, 160–165
adding folders to, 162
deleting folders from, 163
opening media files from, 161
previewing media files in, 164
reordering folders in, 163
showing or hiding, 161
thumbnail display, 165
pan and scan process, 560
parameter registers, 639–645
GPRMs, 638, 640–645
SPRMs, 639, 640
parsing information, 73
partitioning hard disks, 13
patch shapes, 429
pausing
after each VOBU, 271
after playback, 270–271
slides in slideshows, 454
PCM audio format, 102
phase-shift option, 130
Photoshop, 15
16:9 menu creation, 566
creating layers in, 334
cropping shapes in, 439
drawing circles in, 46
layer styles, 48–49
layered menu assets, 338–339
Levels dialog, 52
multilingual menu creation, 575
new document creation, 44–45
NTSC Colors filter, 51–52
pixel aspect ratios, 43, 44–45
resizing files in, 43
resolution settings, 47
shape creation in, 429–438
working with layers in, 333–336
physical formats, 24–25
pictures
jacket, 494
slideshow, 452
See also images; still graphics
pixel aspect ratios, 41–46
DVD Studio Pro and, 46
explanation of, 41–42
image resizing and, 43
Photoshop and, 43, 44–45
test graphics for, 46
pixels, 55
plain-text files, 277, 615, 617
platforms, 4–6
iMac and eMac, 5
Power Mac G5, 4
PowerBook G4 and iBook G4, 5
system requirements, 6
Play All button, 285
playback
anamorphic, 552, 558–559
marker settings for, 270–271
pausing after, 270–271
Simulator controls, 486–487
playhead positioning, 231–232
pointer, 244
positioning
playhead, 231–232
subtitles, 597–599
text, 380
Power Mac G5 platform, 4
PowerBook G4 platform, 5

Preferences window
  Alignment section, 322, 323, 324, 325
  Destinations section, 204
  Encoding section, 199, 554
  Subtitle section, 600
  Track section, 256
prescripts, 633–634
presets, 84, 92–95
  assigning to media files, 85–86
  changing for color palette, 357–358
  multi-angle or mixed-angle, 94–95
  steps for creating, 92–93
Presets window, 92–93, 95, 98
Preview window, 97
previewing
  assets, 190–192
  button navigation, 321
  button states, 343–344
  compression, 96–97
  media files in the Palette, 164
  multilingual projects, 583–586
  slideshows, 460
  video encoding and, 78
Previous/Next keys, 219, 474–477
printers, CD/DVD, 21
program chains, 32
program streams, 71
programming commands, 635–638
programs, 32, 219
Progress window, QuickTime MPEG-2
    Exporter, 78
project bundle, 205, 207
project elements, 448
project templates, 401, 410
projects
  building, 496, 497–511
  burning, 496, 515–519
  debugging, 488
  exporting, 496
  formatting, 496, 503–511
  multiple copies of, 512–514
  simulating, 486–490
  viewing, 167–178
  workflow, 30
Propellerheads Web site, 658
properties, editing, 170
Properties window, 106
protecting disc content, 481–485
  CSS copy protection, 482–483
  Macrovision protection, 484–485
  region codes, 481
PTP playback method, 524, 525

Q

Quad Split View cursor icon, 501
quadrants, 146
  moving tabs between, 152–153
  resizing, 151
quality
  encoding process settings for, 74–76
  testing projects for, 461, 490
quality assurance (QA) testing, 461, 490
Quick Erase option, 520
QuickTime
  exporting MPEG files from, 63–64
  high-quality playback in, 61
QuickTime movies
  importing, 198–206
  setting encoding options for, 200–201
QuickTime MPEG-2 Exporter, 53, 60, 62–80
  alternate-angle tracks, 288
  anamorphic video and, 558–559
  aspect ratio settings, 69, 552
  audio streams saved in, 71
  encoding quality settings, 74–76
  field order selection, 70
  GOP size limits, 57
  log file creation, 72
  motion estimation settings, 77
  opening, 62–64
  parse file creation, 73
  Progress window, 78
  timecode options, 66–68
  video system settings, 65
  widescreen video encoding, 555–557
QuickTime MPEG Encoder, 60

R

Ran operation, 642
Read DLT tape icon, 527
Record dialog, 518
recordable discs, 20
recording
  DLT tapes, 521–523
  DVD-RW discs, 508
  DVD-Video discs, 515–519
Rectangular Marquee tool, 439
reference frames, 56
region coding, 28, 481
registering DVD Studio Pro, 14
reimporting shapes, 443–444
relinking assets, 189
Relinking File dialog, 189
remote control
  button assignments, 464–468, 474–478
  disabling, 468

menus and, 318
Next/Previous keys, 219, 474–477
Resume key, 477–478
Simulator, 486–487
slideshows and, 467
tracks and, 219, 467
removing. *See* deleting/removing
renaming. *See* naming/renaming
reordering. *See* ordering/reordering
replicating discs, 514, 521
replicators, 521
reserve values, 651
resizing. *See* sizing/resizing
resolution, still-image, 47
Resume function, 477–478
Reveal in Finder function, 182
RF overmodulation protection, 129
rich-text documents, 617
ROM discs, 20
ROM folders, 479–480, 548, 549
rotating text, 378
Roxio Toast Titanium. *See* Toast Titanium
rubberized video, 559
rulers, 322
changing units on, 323
enabling/disabling, 322

S

safe zones, 36–38
action and title, 36
overlays for, 37–38
sampling rate
checking, 106
explained, 103
Save dialog, 98
Save Disc Image dialog, 528
Save Exported File As dialog, 104, 105, 555–557
Save Still button, 263
saving
DLT data, 528
shapes, 436–437
styles, 421–422
templates, 409, 410
window configurations, 154
SCR files, 615
Script editor, 630–632
command line options, 630–632
opening scripts in, 630
scripts, 28, 627–648
command buttons, 630–632
Compare commands, 646
creating, 628–629
escape commands, 637
Jump command, 637, 638
operation types in, 642
parameter registers and, 639–645
prescripts and, 633–634
programming, 635–638
Simulator info on, 648
troubleshooting, 647–648
scroll bars, 172
sector size, 482
selected state, 307
serif fonts, 50
Set GPRM command, 641
set-top DVD-Video players, 9
shadows, drop, 385–386
Shape layer, 429, 434
shapes, 426–444
button, 427–428
creating, 432–438
cropping, 439
custom, 429–444
deleting, 442
drop zone, 428
explained, 426
importing, 440–441, 443–444
layers used in, 429–430, 438
patch, 429
Photoshop documents and, 429–439
resizing, 430
saving, 436–437
updating, 443–444
sharing
custom templates, 411
window configurations, 155
shortcut menus, 153
showing/hiding
button outlines, 312
guides, 324
Inspector, 159
Macro View, 175
Palette, 161
toolbar, 156
See also displaying
simple overlay menus, 346, 354–358
button state colors, 356
color palette presets, 357–358
creating, 354–355
simple overlay mode, 346
simulation log, 488, 647
Simulator, 461, 486–490
DVD@ccess links, 549
First Play warning, 463
Information panel, 489, 648
multilingual project test, 583–584
opening, 487

INDEX

Simulator, *continued*
- playback controls, 486–487
- quality assurance testing, 490
- simulation log, 488, 647
- slideshow previews, 460
- subtitle simulation, 612–614
- widescreen video simulation, 568

sizing/resizing
- buttons, 311
- Log tab, 501
- Macro View, 175
- Photoshop files, 43
- shapes, 430
- window quadrants, 151

Slideshow editor, 451–454
- opening, 451
- slide list options, 452
- transition settings, 393–394

slideshows, 27, 445–460
- 16:9 format, 447, 567
- adding pictures to, 452
- audio files for, 448, 455–457
- background colors for, 450
- converting to tracks, 458
- deleting slides from, 452
- duration settings, 449, 453, 457
- end jump settings, 459
- explained, 446
- formats supported for, 447
- interactive, 458
- multilingual, 580
- pausing slides in, 454
- Photoshop files and, 40
- preparing source files for, 446
- prescripts assigned to, 634
- previewing, 460
- project elements for, 448
- remote-control settings for, 467
- reordering pictures in, 452
- setting preferences for, 449–450
- simulating, 460
- thumbnail size for, 450
- transitions for, 392–394
- widescreen, 447, 567

SMPTE timecode, 227

snapping, marker, 256

sorting assets, 185

Sound Settings dialog, 104–105

Soundtrack application, 16

source media files
- audio streams, 102
- locating, 181–182
- preparing, 446

Source pane, Connection tab, 469

Source Type settings, 643–645

Source Value settings, 643, 644

Special Source Type setting, 645

spelling checker, 384, 595

SPRMs (system parameter registers), 639, 640
- Simulator information, 648
- Source Type setting, 644

SPU files, 615

standard menus, 297

starting DVD Studio Pro, 142

stereo bit rates, 119

still graphics, 40–52
- formats, 40
- layer styles, 48–49
- menu flicker prevention, 50
- pixel aspect ratios, 41–46
- preparing for slide shows, 446
- resizing, 43
- resolution, 47
- saving video frames as, 263
- subtitles as, 620–622
- video safe colors, 51–52
- *See also* images; pictures

still-menu storage, 653

STL files, 615

stories, 280–286
- creating, 281
- DVD@ccess links and, 538
- editing, 282–284
- end jump for, 285
- explained, 280
- Play All button and, 285
- stream options for, 286

Story editor, 282–284
- choosing stories in, 282
- Entry list options, 283–284
- opening, 282

streams, 210
- adding clips to, 223–224
- alternate-angle, 287–288, 292–294
- filtering the display of, 237
- height adjustment, 238–239
- locking/unlocking, 240
- mixed-angle, 292–294
- moving clips between, 294
- remote-control buttons for, 467
- separator bar adjustment, 238
- story options for, 286
- subtitle color for, 607–610
- viewing alternate, 250

styles, 415–425
- button, 416–419
- custom, 420–422
- explained, 415

INDEX

layer, 48–49
linking to templates, 423–425
saving, 421–422
text, 381–383, 420–422
video standards and, 415
submenus, creating, 299
subpicture stream, 623
Subtitle button, 465
subtitle clips
adding text to, 595
buttons over video using, 373–376
changing duration of, 601–602
color settings for, 607–609
creating, 593
fade in/out durations, 603–604
removing graphics from, 622
Subtitle editor, 588
Subtitle File dialog, 619
Subtitle Importer, 619
Subtitle Inspector, 621–622
subtitle streams
color settings for, 610
multiple language, 578, 580
remote-control buttons for, 467
setting the language for, 593
Simulator changes to, 614
widescreen video and, 564
subtitles, 27, 587–625
animated, 625
closed-caption, 623–625
colors for, 605–610
comments added to, 617
creating, 592–593, 615–617
duplicating, 593
duration of, 600–602
editing, 594–595
entering text for, 594–595
fade in/out durations for, 603–604
font selection for, 589–591, 596
forcing the display of, 611
formatting text for, 596, 616–617
graphics used as, 620–622
horizontal alignment of, 598
importing, 618–619
marker boundaries and, 602
positioning, 597–599
simulating, 612–614
storage calculations for, 652
testing, 613
text formats for, 615
timecode settings for, 616
vertical alignment of, 599
widescreen video, 564
SuperDrive, 7–8
superwhite, 39
surround sound
AC-3 audio and, 116
downmixing, 112, 116, 125–126
faking, 118
System Preferences window, 549
system requirements, 6

T

tabbed editors, 145
tabs, 145
moving, 152–153
reordering, 153
Target Bitrate slider, 75
Target setting, 643
Targets pane, Connection tab, 469, 472
templates, 400–412
Apple stock, 400, 402, 423
applying to menus, 404–406
categories of, 400–401
chapter index menu, 407
creating, 408–410
custom, 401, 408–412
deleting, 412
destination, 89–90
iDVD themes and, 413–414
linking styles to, 423–425
overlay image, 375
project, 401, 410
saving, 409, 410
sharing, 411
video standards and, 403
Templates tab, 400, 404
testing
AC-3 settings, 135
bit rates, 75
DVD-9 projects, 526
multilingual projects, 583–586
quality assurance, 461, 490
ROM file links, 549
subtitles, 613
text, 377–384
button, 379–380, 386
colors, 383
creating text objects, 377
drop shadows for, 385–386
embedding, 493
fonts, 381–382
formatting, 596
horizontal alignment of, 598
justifying, 378
positioning, 380
rotating, 378
spelling checker, 384, 595

text, *continued*
  styling, 381–383, 420–422
  subtitle, 589–591, 594–595
  vertical alignment of, 599
text buttons over video, 376
Text Formatting area, 380
text marker lists, 277–279
text objects, 377
Text Preferences window, 589
text styles, 381–383, 420–422
TextEdit program, 617
thumbnails
  changing for clips, 248
  Palette display of, 165
  size for slideshows, 450
tiles
  flagging, 174
  laying out, 177
  zooming, 173
timecode, 66–68
  drop-frame vs. non-drop-frame, 66–67, 228
  format for entering, 227
  moving markers using, 263
  naming markers using, 261
  offset setting, 230
  playhead positioning using, 232
  start value setting, 68
  subtitle settings, 616
  Track editor displays, 227–230
  trimming/lengthening clips using, 245
  zero-based vs. asset-based, 229
timeline
  moving markers in, 262
  playhead positioning on, 231
  zooming in/out on, 233–236
timeout action, 316
  overlay menu, 369–370
  programming, 316–317
timeout delay, 370
title area, 32
Title button, 465
title safe filter, 597
title safe overlay, 37, 38
title safe zone, 36, 564
Toast Titanium, 515–520
  burning DVD-Video discs in, 515–519
  CD-R disc support in, 519
  erasing DVD-RW discs in, 520
  setting burn speed in, 507
toolbar, 156–158
  adding tools to, 157–158
  display options for, 156
  Read DLT tape icon, 527
  removing tools from, 158
  showing or hiding, 156
Toolbar Customization panel, 527
Toolbar palette, 157–158
Track editor, 210–211
  adding clips to, 223–224
  browsing video clips in, 226
  creating markers in, 253
  editing clips in, 241–246
  Find Matching Audio option, 225
  importing marker lists in, 278
  opening tracks in, 211
  timecode displays, 227–230
  viewing tracks in, 247–250
  working with streams in, 237–240
  Zoom options, 233–236
tracks, 27, 209–250
  adding assets to, 223–225
  alternate-angle, 290–294
  browsing clips in, 226
  buttons created over, 373–376
  closed-caption files in, 624–625
  converting slideshows to, 458
  creating, 212–217
  deleting, 218
  display modes, 563
  empty, 213
  jump actions for, 221–222
  language settings for, 571
  locking streams in, 240
  markers in, 252–279
  menu button targets as, 216–217
  mixed-angle, 94–95, 291–294
  multi-angle, 94–95, 290
  multilingual, 578–582
  multiple creation of, 215
  Next/Previous keys and, 219
  offset setting for, 230
  opening in Track editor, 211
  playhead positioning for, 231–232
  prescripts assigned to, 634
  remote-control settings for, 219, 467
  renaming, 217–218
  storage capacity of, 209
  stories in, 280–286
  timecode settings for, 227–230
  transitions for, 390–391
  viewing, 247–250
  zooming in/out on, 233–236
transient distortion, 124
transitions, 387–398
  built-in, 388
  codecs and, 397
  how they work, 388–389
  menu, 395–396
  modifying, 391

slideshow, 392–394
track, 390–391
video clips as, 397–398
trigger bits, 484
trimming clips, 244–246
troubleshooting scripts, 647–648
two-pass VBR encoding, 74

U

unlocking. *See* locking/unlocking
updating shapes, 443–444
URLs, 531
opening from buttons, 541–546
rules for using, 537
See also links

V

V1 stream, 241
VBR encoding, 74, 76
vector information, 560
Version Tracker Web site, 389
vertical blanking area (VBA), 623
vertical text alignment, 599
video
anamorphic, 552, 558–559
bit rates, 654
buttons over, 373–376
color depth, 39
encoding, 60
NTSC vs. PAL, 34–35
safe zones, 36–38
text buttons over, 376
widescreen, 551–568
video assets
menu backgrounds as, 304
nondestructive editing of, 181
video clips
browsing, 226
copying, 242
deleting, 243
duration settings, 244–245
editing, 241–246
moving, 241–242
transitions using, 397–398
video object units. *See* VOBUs
video safe colors, 51–52
video standards, 34–35
16:9 menus and, 566
choosing, 65, 142
styles and, 415
templates and, 403
video streams
adding clips to, 223–224
alternate-angle, 287–288, 292–294
anamorphic, 559
encoding, 554
filtering the display of, 237
height adjustment, 238–239
locking/unlocking, 240
mixed-angle, 292–294
moving clips between, 294
remote-control buttons for, 467
template images from, 375
track creation and, 210
viewing alternate, 250
video title sets (VTSs), 32
video transitions, 397–398
VIDEO_TS folder, 26
building process and, 497, 498, 499
hybrid DVDs and, 479
opening in DVD Player, 502, 586
Viewer, 502
playback controls in, 250
previewing assets in, 191–192
title safe filter in, 597
viewing tracks in, 249–250
Viewer tab, 588
viewing
clips, 247
markers, 258
projects, 167–178
tracks, 247–250
See also displaying; previewing
views, 167–178
explained, 168
Graphical, 168, 171–178
Macro, 175–176
Outline, 168, 169–170
VOB files, 497, 518
VOB_DATA.LAY file, 518
VOBUs (video object units), 31
pausing after, 271

W

wait time, 222, 270, 271
Web links, 532, 538
Web resources, 657–658
widescreen video, 69, 551–568
anamorphic, 558–559
embedded encoder and, 553–554
encoding process for, 553–557
explained, 551, 552
letterboxing, 561, 562
menu display types, 566–567
pan and scan process, 560
playing on 4:3 TV screens, 560–564
preparing MPEG-2 streams for, 552

INDEX

widescreen video, *continued*
  QuickTime MPEG-2 Exporter and, 555–557
  simulating, 568
  slideshows as, 447, 567
  subtitles and, 564
  track display modes, 563
window configurations, 142–143, 148–155
  choosing, 150
  function keys for, 154–155
  saving, 154
  sharing, 155
  types of, 143, 148–149
Windows DVD@ccess installer, 533
Windows PCs, DVD@ccess on, 534–535
workflow process, 30
workspace, 141, 145–147
  customizing, 151–155
  Inspector, 147, 159
  Palette, 147, 160–165
  quadrants, 146
  tabbed editors, 145
  toolbar, 156–158
  window configurations, 148–155

Z

zero-based timecode, 229, 263, 264
Zoom control, 233, 234–235
Zoom Scroller, 233, 236
Zoom to Fit button, 173
Zoom tool, 172, 173
zooming
  the Graphical view, 172–173, 176
  the timeline, 233–236